CONSTITUTIONAL TORTS
Fourth Edition

CONSTITUTIONAL TORTS

Fourth Edition

Sheldon H. Nahmod
Distinguished Professor of Law
Chicago-Kent College of Law

Michael L. Wells
Marion and W. Colquitt Carter Chair in Tort and Insurance Law
University of Georgia School of Law

Thomas A. Eaton
J. Alton Hosch Professor of Law
University of Georgia School of Law

Fred Smith
Assistant Professor of Law
University of California Berkeley School of Law

ISBN: 978-1-6328-1550-7
Looseleaf ISBN: 978-1-6328-1600-9
eBook ISBN: 978-1-6328-1551-4

Library of Congress Cataloging-in-Publication Data

Nahmod, Sheldon H., 1940- author.

Constitutional torts / Sheldon H. Nahmod, Distinguished Professor of Law, Chicago-Kent College of Law; Michael L. Wells, Marion and W. Colquitt Carter, Chair in Tort and Insurance Law, University of Georgia School of Law; Thomas A. Eaton, J. Alton Hosch Professor of Law, University of Georgia School of Law; Fred Smith, Assistant Professor of Law, University of California Berkeley School of Law. — Fourth Edition.

pages cm

Includes index.

ISBN 978-1-63281-550-7 (hardbound)

1. Constitutional torts — United States. 2. State action (Civil rights) — United States. I. Wells, Michael L. II. Eaton, Thomas A., 1950- III. Smith, Fred (Assistant professor of law) IV. Title.

KF1306.C64N34 2015

342.7308'8—dc23

2015004681

NOTE TO USERS

To ensure that you are using the latest materials available in this area, please be sure to periodically check the LexisNexis Law School web site for downloadable updates and supplements at www.lexisnexis.com/lawschool.

Editorial Offices

630 Central Ave., New Providence, NJ 07974 (908) 464-6800

201 Mission St., San Francisco, CA 94105-1831 (415) 908-3200

www.lexisnexis.com

MATTHEW◆BENDER

Dedication

This edition is dedicated to the memory of J. Ralph Beaird (1925–2014) and Anne P. Dupre (1952–2011).

Preface to the Fourth Edition

This edition covers Supreme Court decisions from the past several years, including *Minneci v. Pollard* (chapter 1), *Lane v. Franks* and *Plumhoff v. Rickard* (chapter 3), *Connick v. Thompson* (chapter 5), *Rehberg v. Paulk* (chapter 7), *Carroll v. Carman*, *Reichle v. Howards*, *Ashcroft v. Al-Kidd*, *Camreta v. Greene*, *Tolan v. Cotton*, *Ortiz v. Johnson* and *Filarsky v. Delia* (chapter 8), *Lefemine v. Wideman* and *Perdue v. Kenny A.* (chapter 12). The circuit courts have been active over the past few years. We have extensively revised the notes to take account of the recent developments. With this edition we also welcome Fred Smith as a coauthor.

Sheldon Nahmod
Distinguished Professor of Law
Chicago-Kent College of Law
snahmod@kentlaw.edu
312-906-5261

Michael L. Wells
Marion and W. Colquitt Carter Chair in Tort and Insurance Law
University of Georgia School of Law
mwells@uga.edu
706-542-5142

Thomas A. Eaton
J. Alton Hosch Professor of Law
University of Georgia School of Law
teaton@uga.edu
706-542-5177

Fred Smith
Assistant Professor of Law
University of California Berkeley School of Law
fredosmithjr@gmail.com
510-642-3943

Preface to the Third Edition

Since publication of the second edition, the Supreme Court has handed down decisions bearing on nearly every area of constitutional tort litigation. This edition covers *Ashcroft v. Iqbal* (2009) (chapters 1, 5, and 8); *Brosseau v. Haugen* (2004) (chapter 8); *Castle Rock v. Gonzales* (2005) (chapter 3); *Engquist v. Oregon Dep't of Agriculture* (2008) (chapter 3); *Fitzgerald v. Barnstable School Committee* (2009) (chapters 1 and 4); *Garcetti v. Ceballos* (2006) (chapter 3); *Groh v. Ramirez* (2004) (chapter 8); *Haywood v. Drown* (2009) (chapter 11); *Hartman v. Moore* (2006) (chapter 6); *Pearson v. Callahan* (2009) (chapter 8); *Scott v. Harris* (2007) (chapter 3); *Sole v. Wyner* (2007) (chapter 12); *Van de Camp v. Goldstein* (2009) (chapter 7); *Wallace v. Kato* (2007) (chapter 10); and *Wilkinson v. Austin* (2005) (chapter 3). We have also updated the notes with recent lower court rulings.

The membership of the Supreme Court has changed since publication of the second edition. John Roberts has replaced William Rehnquist as Chief Justice, Samuel Alito has replaced Sandra Day O'Connor as Associate Justice, and Sonia Sotomayor has replaced David Souter as Associate Justice.

Sheldon Nahmod
Distinguished Professor of Law
Chicago-Kent College of Law
snahmod@kentlaw.edu
312-906-5261

Michael L. Wells
Marion and W. Colquitt Carter Chair in Tort and Insurance Law
University of Georgia School of Law
mwells@uga.edu
706-542-5142

Thomas A. Eaton
J. Alton Hosch Professor of Law
University of Georgia School of Law
teaton@uga.edu
706-542-5177

Preface to the Second Edition

Since we prepared the First Edition of *Constitutional Torts* some years ago, there have been extensive developments in the Supreme Court, the circuits (and, to a lesser extent, the states) and the literature. As a result, every Chapter of this Second Edition has been changed and expanded, several significantly. For example, Chapter 3, dealing with constitutional violations that are actionable under section 1983, has been considerably revised to take account of developments in substantive due process. So, too, has Chapter 4, particularly in light of the Supreme Court's revisionist *Gonzaga University* "laws" decision. In addition, Chapter 5, dealing with local government liability, has been expanded dramatically, as has Chapter 8, addressing qualified immunity, because of the many important Supreme Court decisions on these topics since the First Edition.

In addition to taking account of relevant Supreme Court decisions, we have also continued to be sensitive to developments in the circuits, a much-praised feature of the First Edition that enables students to see how principles set out by the Supreme Court are applied by lower courts. We have consequently updated our notes, comments and questions to make maximum pedagogical use of circuit case law. As before, we have also included current academic commentary because an important function of *Constitutional Torts* is to explicate the relationship between theory and doctrine. Further, we have made changes throughout this Second Edition as a result of our own experiences teaching *Constitutional Torts* and your feedback.

We were pleased with the reception to the First Edition and hope that we have made *Constitutional Torts* even better with this new edition. As always, we invite you to contact us personally by email or phone with any questions or comments you may have.

May, 2004

Sheldon Nahmod
Distinguished Professor of Law
Chicago-Kent College of Law
snahmod@kentlaw.edu
312-906-5261

Michael L. Wells
Marion and W. Colquitt Carter Chair in Tort and Insurance Law
University of Georgia School of Law
mwells@uga.edu
706-542-5142

Thomas A. Eaton
J. Alton Hosch Professor of Law
University of Georgia School of Law
teaton@uga.edu
706-542-5177

Preface to the First Edition

Constitutional Torts is the first casebook to focus exclusively on constitutional tort damages actions brought against governments and their officials under 42 U.S.C. section 1983 and the United States Constitution (*Bivens* actions). A course in constitutional torts allows students to integrate their knowledge of torts, constitutional law, federal courts and civil procedure and apply it to a dynamic field of litigation. We also include materials addressing strategic and ethical decisions facing those who litigate those issues. Our primary objective is to offer materials that teach the underlying theories of constitutional tort liability while at the same time providing a solid foundation for practicing in the field.

This casebook is unique in several other respects. Unlike other casebooks dealing with related topics, *Constitutional Torts* emphasizes important circuit court decisions together with relevant Supreme Court case law. This enables students to see how principles articulated in Supreme Court decisions are implemented by lower courts. The casebook also addresses affirmative duties, constitutional tort actions in state courts and attorney's fees, topics that are frequently slighted in civil rights and federal courts casebooks and courses. Further, *Constitutional Torts* is organized around the statutory language of section 1983, thereby driving home the crucial distinction between prima facie case and constitutional tort immunities and defenses.

The notes, comments and questions that precede and follow the cases are vital components of this casebook. These materials are carefully designed to lead students to understand the cases they read, to consider the implications of those cases, to perceive the questions left unanswered and to force students to connect what they have just finished reading to issues they previously encountered. These materials often raise difficult theoretical questions that must be confronted if constitutional torts are to be understood. As a result, insightful ideas and perspectives contained in treatises and law review articles play a prominent role in *Constitutional Torts*.

Constitutional Torts can be used in both introductory and advanced courses meeting either two hours or three hours weekly. What is covered obviously depends on the number of hours allotted. Our experience is that each chapter requires at least two hours of classroom time for adequate coverage. However, some difficult chapters will profit from twice that, while others can be covered in somewhat less time with selective deletions.

Each of the authors carefully read and is jointly responsible for the entire manuscript. However, we individually assumed primary responsiblity for the following chapters: Nahmod, chapters 1, 5, 7, and 8; Wells, chapters 2, 3, part of 4, 9 and 11; and Eaton, part of 4, 6, 10 and 12.

We wish to express our appreciation to our law schools for their support of this project. We thank Professors Kathryn Urbonya and Dan Coenen for their helpful comments on an earlier draft of these materials. We also want to thank Ashley Sexton, Derick Gilbert Jay Nohr for their valuable research assistance.

Please feel free to contact any of us by phone or by email via the Internet.

Preface to the First Edition

Sheldon Nahmod
Distinguished Professor of Law
Chicago-Kent College of Law
Illinois Institute of Technology
snahmod@kentlaw.edu
312-906-5261

Michael L. Wells
Marion and W. Colquitt Carter Chair in Tort and Insurance Law
University of Georgia School of Law
mwells@uga.edu
706-542-5142

Thomas A. Eaton
J. Alton Hosch Professor of Law
University of Georgia School of Law
teaton@uga.edu
706-542-5177

Table of Contents

Chapter 1   **CONSTITUTIONAL TORTS: A FIRST LOOK** 1

I.   THE TEXT OF SECTION 1983 AND ITS JURISDICTIONAL
COUNTERPART 2

II.   HISTORY AND PURPOSES OF SECTION 1983 2

III.   *MONROE v. PAPE*, THE SEMINAL DECISION 3

       Monroe v. Pape 4

       Notes 16

IV.   CONSTITUTIONAL TORTS AND EXHAUSTION OF JUDICIAL
REMEDIES 18

V.   CONSTITUTIONAL TORTS AND EXHAUSTION OF
ADMINISTRATIVE REMEDIES 20

VI.   CONSTITUTIONAL TORTS OF FEDERAL OFFICIALS: *BIVENS*
ACTIONS 22

       Bivens v. Six Unknown Named Agents 22

       Notes 29

VII.   THE CURRENT STATUS OF *BIVENS* ACTIONS 30

       Minneci v. Pollard 31

       Notes 35

Chapter 2   **"UNDER COLOR OF" STATE LAW** 43

I.   THE MEANING OF "UNDER COLOR OF" 43

  A.   *Monroe* and "Under Color Of" 43

  B.   The Boundaries of "Under Color Of" 43

II.   "UNDER COLOR OF" AND STATE ACTION 47

       Lugar v. Edmondson Oil Co. 47

       Notes 53

III.   SUING PRIVATE ACTORS UNDER SECTION 1983 56

  A.   Self-Help Remedies 57

       Flagg Bros., Inc. v. Brooks 57

       Notes 63

  B.   Contracting Out and Other Symbiotic Relationships 64

       Burton v. Wilmington Parking Authority 64

       Note 68

       Rendell-Baker v. Kohn 69

       Notes 75

  C.   "Entwinement" Between Public Officers and Private Actors 80

       *Brentwood Academy v. Tennessee Secondary School Athletic
Association, Et Al.* 80

Table of Contents

Notes on Entwinement 89

Notes on Conspiracy 90

Chapter 3 "SECURED BY THE CONSTITUTION AND LAWS" . . . 97

MAJOR SUBSTANTIVE THEMES IN CONSTITUTIONAL
TORTS 97

I. THE DUE PROCESS CLAUSE IN CONSTITUTIONAL TORT LAW . . 98
  A. "Property" 98
    Town of Castle Rock v. Gonzales 98
    Notes on *Castle Rock* and State-Created Property 109
  B. "Liberty" 114
    Sandin v. Conner 114
    Notes 121
  C. Procedural Due Process 125
    Gilbert v. Homar 126
    Notes 130
  D. Substantive Due Process 134
    Daniels v. Williams 135
    Notes 137
    County of Sacramento v. Lewis 139
    Notes 145
  E. Constitutional Rights of Persons in Custody 151
    Farmer v. Brennan 152
    Notes 157
  F. The Relevance of State Remedies to Due Process Litigation 164
    Zinermon v. Burch 167
    Notes 172

II. OTHER CONSTITUTIONAL CLAIMS 176
  A. Fourth Amendment Rights 177
    Graham v. Connor 177
    Notes 182
    Scott v. Harris 190
    Notes on Excessive Force Claims After *Scott* 198
  B. Equal Protection 201
    Village of Willowbrook v. Olech 201
    Notes 202
  C. Public Employee Speech 205
    Connick v. Myers 206
    Notes 210
    Garcetti v. Ceballos 214
    Notes on *Garcetti* 215

Table of Contents

Chapter 4 **"SECURED BY THE CONSTITUTION AND LAWS"**
AFFIRMATIVE CONSTITUTIONAL DUTIES AND
RIGHTS SECURED BY FEDERAL LAWS **219**

I. AFFIRMATIVE DUTIES 219
  A. The Supreme Court's Framework 220
    Deshaney v. Winnebago County Department of Social Services 220
    Notes 229
  B. Affirmative Duties, State Created Dangers, and Special Relationships . 233
    Kneipp v. Tedder 233
    Notes 238
II. SECTION 1983 AND FEDERAL "LAWS" 247
  A. Enforceable Rights 248
    Gonzaga University v. Doe 248
    Notes 256
  B. Congressional Preclusion 260
    Lisa Fitzgerald v. Barnstable School Committee 260
    Note 266

Chapter 5 **"EVERY PERSON": GOVERNMENTAL LIABILITY** . . **267**

I. WHAT GOVERNMENTAL BODIES ARE PERSONS? 267
  A. The Prior Law Under *Monroe* 269
  B. The Change in *Monell* 270
    Monell v. Department of Social Services 270
    Notes 278
II. MUNICIPAL GOVERNMENTS HAVE NO IMMUNITY FROM
    SUIT 282
    Owen v. City of Independence, Missouri 282
    Notes 288
III. FOUR ROUTES TO GOVERNMENTAL LIABILITY 289
  A. Formal Official Policy 290
  B. Custom 292
  C. Final Policy Makers 294
    Pembaur v. City of Cincinnati 294
    Note 300
    City of St. Louis v. Praprotnik 300
    Notes 309
    McMillian: Policymaker for Which Entity, The Local Government
    or the State? 314
    McMillian v. Monroe County, Alabama 314
    Notes 320
  D. Failure to Adequately Hire, Train, and Supervise 322

Table of Contents

1.   Failure to Train 323

       City of Canton, Ohio v. Harris 323

       Notes 328

2.   *Bryan County* and Single Hiring Decisions by Policymakers 331

       Board of County Commissioners of Bryan County, Oklahoma

       v. Brown 331

       Notes 343

3.   Supervisory Liability 345

IV.   ETHICAL CONSIDERATIONS 348

       Dunton v. County of Suffolk, State of New York 349

       Notes 353

Chapter 6   "[S]UBJECTS OR CAUSES: TO BE SUBJECTED . . .":
**   CAUSATION 357**

I.   CAUSE IN FACT 357

  A.   Mixed Motives 358

       Mt. Healthy City School District Board of Education v. Doyle 358

       Notes 362

       Texas v. Lesage 368

       Notes 370

  B.   Governmental and Supervisory Liability 372

       Allen v. Muskogee 373

       Notes 380

II.   PROXIMATE OR LEGAL CAUSE 386

  A.   Remote Consequences 386

       Martinez v. California 386

       Notes 387

  B.   Intervening Acts 390

       Townes v. City of New York 390

       Notes 395

Chapter 7   "EVERY PERSON": ABSOLUTE IMMUNITY 401

I.   ABSOLUTE LEGISLATIVE IMMUNITY 402

  A.   *Tenney*: The Seminal Case on Absolute Legislative Immunity 402

       Tenney v. Brandhove 402

       Notes 407

  B.   The Functional Approach of *Lake Country Estates*: Local and

     Regional Legislators 407

  C.   *Bogan v. Scott-Harris*: The Broad Scope of Local Legislator

     Immunity 410

       Bogan v. Scott-Harris 410

Table of Contents

	Notes	414
D.	A Note on Prospective Relief	415
II.	ABSOLUTE JUDICIAL IMMUNITY	418
A.	The Common Law Immunity Background in 1871: *Bradley*	418
B.	*Pierson*: The Seminal Case on Section 1983 Absolute Judicial Immunity	419
C.	The Broad Scope of Absolute Judicial Immunity: *Stump*	420
	Stump v. Sparkman	420
	Notes	425
D.	The Functional Approach to Judicial Immunity as a Double-Edged Sword: Judges, Court Reporters and Prison Disciplinary Hearing Officers	427
E.	*Pulliam* and Prospective Relief	430
F.	A Note on Witness Immunity and Its Connection to Judicial Immunity: *Briscoe*	431
III.	ABSOLUTE PROSECUTORIAL IMMUNITY	433
A.	*Imbler*: The Seminal Absolute Prosecutorial Immunity Case	433
	Imbler v. Pachtman	433
	Notes	438
B.	*Burns*: The Prosecutor as Legal Advisor	439
	Burns v. Reed	439
	Notes	444
C.	*Kalina*: The Prosecutor as Applicant for an Arrest Warrant	446
	Kalina v. Fletcher	446
	Notes	451
D.	Circuit Court Cases	451
E.	A Note on Prospective Relief	454
IV.	PROCEDURAL ASPECTS OF ABSOLUTE IMMUNITY	454
A.	The Burden of Pleading	454
B.	A Note on Appeal from Denial of an Absolute Immunity Motion to Dismiss or for Summary Judgment	455
Chapter 8	**"EVERY PERSON": QUALIFIED IMMUNITY**	**457**
I.	THE EVOLUTION OF QUALIFIED IMMUNITY	457
	Pierson v. Ray	457
	Notes	460
	Harlow v. Fitzgerald	462
	Notes	467
	Anderson v. Creighton	470
	Notes	474
II.	WHEN IS LAW "CLEARLY ESTABLISHED"?	475

Table of Contents

		Hope v. Pelzer	475
		Notes	485
		Wilson v. Layne	487
		Notes	494
III.		THE "ORDER OF BATTLE"	496
		Pearson v. Callahan	496
		Notes	503
IV.		PROCEDURAL ASPECTS OF QUALIFIED IMMUNITY	504
	A.	Motions to Dismiss	504
	B.	Motions for Summary Judgment	507
		Tolan v. Cotton	507
		Notes	513
	C.	Interlocutory Appeals	514
		Mitchell v. Forsyth	515
		Notes	518
		Johnson v. Jones	519
		Notes	525
	D.	Qualified Immunity at Trial	526
V.		WHO IS PROTECTED BY QUALIFIED IMMUNITY?	527
		Wyatt v. Cole	528
		Notes	535
		Richardson V. McKnight	535
		Notes	542

| **Chapter 9** | **"SHALL BE LIABLE TO THE PARTY INJURED IN AN ACTION AT LAW, SUIT IN EQUITY OR OTHER PROPER PROCEEDING FOR REDRESS": CONSTITUTIONAL TORT REMEDIES** | **545** |

I.		DAMAGES	545
	A.	Compensatory Damages	545
		Carey v. Piphus	545
		Notes	551
		Memphis Community Schooldistrict v. Stachura	562
		Notes	567
	B.	Punitive Damages	569
		Smith v. Wade	569
		Notes	578
	C.	Survival, Wrongful Death, and Other Damages Issues Ordinarily Addressed by Statutes	584
		Robertson v. Wegmann	585
		Notes	591

Table of Contents

II.   PROSPECTIVE RELIEF 595

 City of Los Angeles v. Lyons 595

 Notes 603

 Rule 23.   Class Actions 610

Chapter 10   **PROCEDURAL DEFENSES** **613**

I.   STATUTES OF LIMITATIONS 613

 Wilson v. Garcia 614

 Notes 619

II.   RELEASE-DISMISSAL AGREEMENTS 622

 Town of Newton v. Rumery 623

 Notes 631

III.   ISSUE AND CLAIM PRECLUSION 634

 Migra v. Warren City School District Board of Education 635

 Notes 639

 University of Tennessee v. Elliot 642

 Notes 646

IV.   EXHAUSTION OF REMEDIES 648

 Porter v. Nussle 648

 Notes 654

 Heck v. Humphrey 658

 Notes 665

 Other Situations that Present Exhaustion-Like Issues 670

Chapter 11   **LITIGATING SECTION 1983 CLAIMS IN STATE
      COURTS** **675**

I.   MUST STATE COURTS HEAR SECTION 1983 CLAIMS? 675

 Haywood v. Drown 675

 Notes 684

II.   THE CHOICE BETWEEN STATE AND FEDERAL LAW 688

 Felder v. Casey 688

 Notes 692

 Johnson v. Fankell 696

 Note 700

Chapter 12   **ATTORNEY'S FEES** **701**

I.   LEGISLATIVE HISTORY 702

 The Civil Rights Attorney's Fees Award Act of 1976 702

 Notes 705

Table of Contents

II.   WHEN IS A PARTY ENTITLED TO ATTORNEY'S FEES UNDER
        42 U.S.C. § 1988? 705
        Farrar v. Hobby 705
        Notes 712
        *Buckhannon Board and Care Home, Inc. v. West Virginia Department
        of Health and Human Resources* 717
        Notes 728

III.   WHAT IS A "REASONABLE" FEE? 731
        Hensley v. Eckerhart 731
        Notes 737
        Jane L. v. Bangerter 742
        Notes 754

IV.   STRATEGIC AND ETHICAL ASPECTS OF ATTORNEY'S FEE
        AWARDS 764
        Evans v. Jeff D. 764
        Notes 772

Table of Cases **TC-1**

Index **I-1**

Chapter 1

CONSTITUTIONAL TORTS: A FIRST LOOK

Constitutional torts are actions brought against governments and their officials and employees seeking damages for the violation of federal constitutional rights, particularly those arising under the Fourteenth Amendment and the Bill of Rights. Tens of thousands of such actions are filed annually in the federal courts, with some in the state courts as well. *See generally* Eisenberg and Schwab, *The Reality of Constitutional Tort Litigation*, 72 CORNELL L. REV. 641 (1987). In addition, hardly a term of the United States Supreme Court goes by without at least a half-dozen important constitutional tort-related decisions handed down. The overwhelming majority of these actions are brought against state and local governments and their officials and employees under 42 U.S.C. § 1983, probably the most resorted-to federal civil rights statute. A minority are brought against federal officials pursuant to *Bivens v. Six Unknown Named Agents*, 403 U.S. 388 (1971).

Constitutional torts are of considerable practical significance. They represent attempts to render governments and their officials and employees accountable in damages for the constitutional harm they cause. Large sums of money are frequently at stake, a factor that is accentuated by the availability of attorney's fees to prevailing plaintiffs under the Civil Rights Attorney's Fees Awards Act of 1976, 42 U.S.C. § 1988, as discussed in Chapter 12. Constitutional tort actions are thus often bitterly contested.

Constitutional torts raise fascinating and difficult theoretical issues of constitutional and statutory interpretation. Indeed, some of these issues are captured by the term "constitutional torts" itself. For example, what is the connection between tort concepts of accountability and the proper interpretation of section 1983? To what extent does the possibility of damages liability for constitutional torts affect judicial decisions on constitutional issues? Constitutional torts raise different questions as well. For example, federalism concerns are deeply implicated in many constitutional tort cases because in such cases federal courts interpret and apply federal law to the conduct of state and local governments and their officials and employees. Government efficiency is also implicated in constitutional tort litigation because the specter of liability may over deter government officials and employees in the performance of their government duties. Moreover, there is the often-stated position (especially by some federal judges) that federal courts are being overburdened by constitutional tort cases of questionable merit.

It will prove helpful as you go through these materials to envision the structure (as distinct from the substance) of constitutional torts in tort-like terms. From this structural perspective, the doctrine of constitutional torts can be divided into two parts: the elements of the prima facie case — including duty, basis of liability and causation — on the one hand, and various immunities and defenses on the other.

1

These are extensively considered in this casebook. There are subsidiary doctrines relating to federal court jurisdiction, procedural defenses such as statutes of limitations and preclusion and state court constitutional tort actions that also are addressed. These doctrines, interesting in their own right, often have a good deal of practical significance in the real world of constitutional torts and, together with attorney's fees issues, must therefore be mastered.

I. THE TEXT OF SECTION 1983 AND ITS JURISDICTIONAL COUNTERPART

42 U.S.C. § 1983 reads as follows:

> Every person who, under color of any statute, ordinance, regulation, custom, or usage, of any State or Territory or the District of Columbia, subjects, or causes to be subjected, any citizen of the United States or other person within the jurisdiction thereof to the deprivation of any rights, privileges, or immunities secured by the Constitution and laws, shall be liable to the party injured in an action at law, suit in equity, or other proper proceeding for redress, except that in any action brought against a judicial officer for an act or omission taken in such officer's judicial capacity, injunctive relief shall not be granted unless a declaratory decree was violated or declaratory relief was unavailable. For the purposes of this section, any Act of Congress applicable exclusively to the District of Columbia shall be considered to be a statute of the District of Columbia.

28 U.S.C. § 1343(3) reads in relevant part as follows:

> (a) The district courts shall have original jurisdiction of any civil action authorized by law to be commenced by any person:

> . . .

> (3) To redress the deprivation, under color of any State law, statute, ordinance, regulation, custom or usage, of any right, privilege or immunity secured by the Constitution of the United States or by any Act of Congress providing for equal rights of citizens or of all persons within the jurisdiction of the United States; . . .

> (b) For purposes of this section —

> (1) the District of Columbia shall be considered to be a State; and

> (2) any Act of Congress applicable exclusively to the District of Columbia shall be considered to be a statute of the District of Columbia.

II. HISTORY AND PURPOSES OF SECTION 1983

Section 1983 is modeled on section 2 of the Civil Rights Act of 1866, which made criminal certain acts committed by persons "under color of any law, statute, ordinance, regulation, or custom." Section 2 of the 1866 Act is the predecessor of 18 U.S.C. § 242, the criminal counterpart of section 1983 used as the basis for the federal criminal prosecutions of various Los Angeles police officers involved in the Rodney King controversy in the mid-1990s. *See Adickes v. Kress*, 398 U.S. 144, 162–63 (1970). Section 1983 and its jurisdictional counterpart, 28 U.S.C. § 1343(3), specifically began as section 1 of the Ku Klux Klan Act of April 20, 1871, which was enacted by Congress pursuant to section 5 of the Fourteenth Amendment in order to enforce that amendment. *See Monroe v. Pape*, 365 U.S. 167, 171 (1961). This purpose is clear from the title of section 1, "An Act to enforce the Provisions of the Fourteenth Amendment to the Constitution of the United States, and for other Purposes." 17 Stat. 13 (1871).

In 1874 Congress codified existing law and, as a result, the substantive portion of section 1 of the 1871 Act became a separate section identical to the present section 1983. The section's coverage also was expanded beyond constitutionally secured rights, privileges, and immunities to include those secured by federal laws as well. Ultimately, the jurisdictional counterpart became 28 U.S.C. § 1343(3). *See Lynch v. Household Finance Corp.*, 405 U.S. 538, 543 n.7 (1972).

The Supreme Court has broadly described the primary purpose of section 1983 in the following terms:

> As a result of the new structure of law that emerged in the post-Civil War era — and especially of the Fourteenth Amendment, which was its centerpiece — the role of the Federal Government as a guarantor of basic federal rights against state power was clearly established. Section 1983 opened the federal courts to private citizens, offering a uniquely federal remedy against incursions under the claimed authority of state law upon rights secured by the Constitution and laws of the Nation. . . .
>
> The very purpose of section 1983 was to interpose the federal courts between the States and the people, as guardians of the people's federal rights — to protect the people from unconstitutional action under color of state law, "whether that action be executive, legislative, or judicial."

Mitchum v. Foster, 407 U.S. 225, 238–39, 242 (1972). The Court has also indicated that section 1983 was designed both to prevent the states from violating the Fourteenth Amendment and certain federal statutes and to compensate injured plaintiffs for deprivations of their federal rights. *Carey v. Piphus*, 435 U.S. 247 (1978).

Section 1983 is directed not only at unconstitutional laws, but also at affording protection of "a federal right in federal courts because, by reason of prejudice, passion, neglect, intolerance or otherwise, state laws might not be enforced and the claims of citizens to the enjoyment of rights, privileges and immunities guaranteed by the Fourteenth Amendment might be denied by the state agencies." *Monroe v. Pape*, 365 U.S. 167, 180 (1961).

III.   *MONROE v. PAPE*, THE SEMINAL DECISION

Although section 1983 was enacted in 1871, it was largely dormant for ninety years for various reasons. One was the restrictive application of the state action doctrine as exemplified in the *Civil Rights Cases*, 109 U.S. 3 (1883). A second was the narrow reading of the Fourteenth Amendment's privileges and immunities clause and section 1983's jurisdictional counterpart. *See Slaughter-House Cases*, 83 U.S. 36 (1873) and *Hague v. CIO*, 307 U.S. 496, 531 (1939) (concurring opinion of Justice Stone). Still another was the Supreme Court's initial refusal to incorporate completely the provisions of the Bill of Rights, *e.g., Adamson v. California*, 332 U.S. 46 (1947), although the Supreme Court has since selectively incorporated most of those provisions. See, on the importance of this last factor, Weinberg, *The* Monroe *Mystery Solved: Beyond the "Unhappy History" Theory of Civil Rights Litigation*, 1991 B.Y.U. L. REV. 737. However, in 1961 a sea change occurred in the status of section 1983 with the seminal decision in *Monroe v. Pape*. In that year, there were approximately 150 nonprisoner section 1983 cases filed, while twenty-five years later, in 1986, there were approximately 10,000. *See id.* at 738, n.9.

MONROE v. PAPE
365 U.S. 167 (1961)

MR. JUSTICE DOUGLAS delivered the opinion of the Court.

This case presents important questions concerning the construction of R.S. § 1979, 42 U.S.C. § 1983, which reads as follows:

> "Every person who, under color of any statute, ordinance, regulation, custom, or usage, of any State or Territory, subjects, or causes to be subjected, any citizen of the United States or other person within the jurisdiction thereof to the deprivation of any rights, privileges, or immunities secured by the Constitution and laws, shall be liable to the party injured in an action at law, suit in equity, or other proper proceeding for redress."

The complaint alleges that 13 Chicago police officers broke into petitioners' home in the early morning, routed them from bed, made them stand naked in the living room, and ransacked every room, emptying drawers and ripping mattress covers. It further alleges that Mr. Monroe was then taken to the police station and detained on "open" charges for 10 hours, while he was interrogated about a two-day-old murder, that he was not taken before a magistrate, though one was accessible, that he was not permitted to call his family or attorney, that he was subsequently released without criminal charges being preferred against him. It is alleged that the officers had no search warrant and no arrest warrant and that they acted "under color of the statutes, ordinances, regulations, customs and usages" of Illinois and of the City of Chicago. Federal jurisdiction was asserted under R.S. § 1979, which we have set out above, and 28 U.S.C. § 1343 and 28 U.S.C. § 1331.

The City of Chicago moved to dismiss the complaint on the ground that it is not liable under the Civil Rights Acts or for acts committed in performance of its governmental functions. All defendants moved to dismiss, alleging that the complaint alleged no cause of action under those Acts or under the Federal Constitution. The District Court dismissed the complaint. The Court of Appeals affirmed, relying on its earlier decision, *Stift v. Lynch*. The case is here on a writ of certiorari which we granted because of a seeming conflict of that ruling with our prior cases.

I

Petitioners claim that the invasion of their home and the subsequent search without a warrant and the arrest and detention of Mr. Monroe without a warrant and without arraignment constituted a deprivation of their "rights, privileges, or immunities secured by the Constitution" within the meaning of R.S. § 1979. It has been said that when 18 U.S.C. § 241 made criminal a conspiracy "to injure, oppress, threaten, or intimidate any citizen in the free exercise or enjoyment of any right or privilege secured to him by the Constitution," it embraced only rights that an individual has by reason of his relation to the central government, not to state governments. But the history of the section of the Civil Rights Act presently involved does not permit such a narrow interpretation.

Section 1979 came onto the books as § 1 of the Ku Klux Act of April 20, 1871. It was one of the means whereby Congress exercised the power vested in it by § 5 of the Fourteenth Amendment to enforce the provisions of that Amendment. Senator Edmunds, Chairman of the Senate Committee on the Judiciary, said concerning this section:

> "The first section is one that I believe nobody objects to, as defining the rights secured by the Constitution of the United States when they are assailed by any State law or under color of any State law, and it is merely carrying out the principles of the civil rights bill, which has since become a part of the Constitution," the Fourteenth Amendment.

Its purpose is plain from the title of the legislation, "An Act to enforce the Provisions of the Fourteenth Amendment to the Constitution of the United States, and for other Purposes." Allegation of facts constituting a deprivation under color of state authority of a right guaranteed by the Fourteenth Amendment satisfies to that extent the requirement of R.S. § 1979. So far petitioners are on solid ground. For the guarantee against unreasonable searches and seizures contained in the Fourth Amendment has been made applicable to the States by reason of the Due Process Clause of the Fourteenth Amendment.

II

There can be no doubt at least since *Ex parte Virginia*, that Congress has the power to enforce provisions of the Fourteenth Amendment against those who carry a badge of authority of a State and represent it in some capacity, whether they act in accordance with their authority or misuse it. The question with which we now deal is the narrower one of whether Congress, in enacting § 1979, meant to give a remedy to parties deprived of constitutional rights, privileges and immunities by an official's abuse of his position. We conclude that it did so intend.

It is argued that "under color of" enumerated state authority excludes acts of an official or policeman who can show no authority under state law, state custom, or state usage to do what he did. In this case it is said that these policemen, in breaking into petitioners' apartment, violated the Constitution and laws of Illinois. It is pointed out that under Illinois law a simple remedy is offered for that violation and that, so far as it appears, the courts of Illinois are available to give petitioners that full redress which the common law affords for violence done to a person; and it is earnestly argued that no "statute, ordinance, regulation, custom or usage" of Illinois bars that redress.

The Ku Klux Act grew out of a message sent to Congress by President Grant on March 23, 1871, reading:

> "A condition of affairs now exists in some States of the Union rendering life and property insecure and the carrying of the mails and the collection of the revenue dangerous. The proof that such a condition of affairs exists in some localities is now before the Senate. That the power to correct these evils is beyond the control of State authorities I do not doubt; that the power of the Executive of the United States, acting within the limits of existing laws, is sufficient for present emergencies is not clear. Therefore, I urgently recommend such legislation as in the judgment of Congress shall effectually secure life, liberty, and property, and the enforcement of law in all parts of the United States. . . ."

The legislation — in particular the section with which we are now concerned — had several purposes. There are threads of many thoughts running through the debates. One who reads them in their entirety sees that the present section had three main aims.

First, it might, of course, override certain kinds of state laws. Mr. Sloss of Alabama, in opposition, spoke of that object and emphasized that it was irrelevant because there were no such laws:

> "The first section of this bill prohibits any invidious legislation by States against the rights or privileges of citizens of the United States. The object of this section is not very clear, as it is not pretended by its advocates on this floor that any State has passed any laws endangering the rights or privileges of the colored people."

Second, it provided a remedy where state law was inadequate. That aspect of the legislation was summed up as follows by Senator Sherman of Ohio:

> " . . . it is said the reason is that any offense may be committed upon a negro by a white man, and a negro cannot testify in any case against a white man, so that the only way by which any conviction can be had in Kentucky in those cases is in the United States courts, because the United States courts enforce the United States laws by which negroes may testify."

> But the purposes were much broader. The third aim was to provide a federal remedy where the state remedy, though adequate in theory, was not available in practice. The opposition to the measure complained that "It overrides the reserved powers of the States," just as they argued that the second section of the bill "absorb[ed] the entire jurisdiction of the States over their local and domestic affairs."

It was precisely that breadth of the remedy which the opposition emphasized. Mr. Kerr of Indiana referring to the section involved in the present litigation said:

> "This section gives to any person who may have been injured in any of his rights, privileges, or immunities of person or property, a civil action for

damages against the wrongdoer in the Federal courts. The offenses committed against him may be the common violations of the municipal law of his State. It may give rise to numerous vexations and outrageous prosecutions, inspired by mere mercenary considerations, prosecuted in a spirit of plunder, aided by the crimes of perjury and subornation of perjury, more reckless and dangerous to society than the alleged offenses out of which the cause of action may have arisen. It is a covert attempt to transfer another large portion of jurisdiction from the State tribunals, to which it of right belongs, to those of the United States. It is neither authorized nor expedient, and is not calculated to bring peace, or order, or domestic content and prosperity to the disturbed society of the South. The contrary will certainly be its effect."

Mr. Voorhees of Indiana, also speaking in opposition, gave it the same construction:

"And now for a few moments let us inspect the provisions of this bill, inspired as it is by the waning and decaying fortunes of the party in power, and called for, as I have shown, by no public necessity whatever. The first and second sections are designed to transfer all criminal jurisdiction from the courts of the States to the courts of the United States. This is to be done upon the assumption that the courts of the southern States fail and refuse to do their duty in the punishment of offenders against the law."

Senator Thurman of Ohio spoke in the same vein about the section we are now considering:

"It authorizes any person who is deprived of any right, privilege, or immunity secured to him by the Constitution of the United States, to bring an action against the wrong-doer in the Federal courts, and that without any limit whatsoever as to the amount in controversy. The deprivation may be of the slightest conceivable character, the damages in the estimation of any sensible man may not be five dollars or even five cents; they may be what lawyers call merely nominal damages; and yet by this section jurisdiction of that civil action is given to the Federal courts instead of its being prosecuted as now in the courts of the States."

The debates were long and extensive. It is abundantly clear that one reason the legislation was passed was to afford a federal right in federal courts because, by reason of prejudice, passion, neglect, intolerance or otherwise, state laws might not be enforced and the claims of citizens to the enjoyment of rights, privileges, and immunities guaranteed by the Fourteenth Amendment might be denied by the state agencies.

Although the legislation was enacted because of the conditions that existed in the South at that time, it is cast in general language and is as applicable to Illinois as it is to the States whose names were mentioned over and again in the debates. It is no answer that the State has a law which if enforced would give relief. The federal remedy is supplementary to the state remedy, and the latter need not be first sought and refused before the federal one is invoked. Hence the fact that Illinois by its constitution and laws outlaws unreasonable searches and seizures is no barrier to the present suit in the federal court.

We had before us in *United States v. Classic*, § 20 of the Criminal Code, which provides a criminal punishment for anyone who "under color of any law, statute, ordinance, regulation, or custom" subjects any inhabitant of a State to the deprivation of "any rights, privileges, or immunities secured or protected by the Constitution or laws of the United States." Section 242 first came into the law as § 2 of the Civil Rights Act, 1866. After passage of the Fourteenth Amendment, this provision was re-enacted and amended by §§ 17, 18, Act of May 31, 1870. The right involved in the *Classic* case was the right of voters in a primary to have their votes counted. The laws of Louisiana required the defendants "to count the ballots, to record the result of the count, and to certify the result of the election." But according to the indictment they did not perform their duty. In an opinion written by Mr. Justice (later Chief Justice) Stone, in which Mr. Justice Roberts, Mr. Justice Reed, and Mr. Justice Frankfurter joined, the Court ruled, "Misuse of power, possessed by virtue of state law and made possible only because the wrongdoer is clothed with the authority of state law, is action taken 'under color of' state law." There was a dissenting opinion; but the ruling as to the meaning of "under color of" state law was not questioned.

That view of the meaning of the words "under color of" state law, was reaffirmed in *Screws v. United States*. The acts there complained of were committed by state officers in performance of their duties, making an arrest effective. It was urged there, as it is here, that "under color of" state law should not be construed to duplicate in federal law what was an offense under state law. It was said there, as it is here, that the ruling in the Classic case as to the meaning of "under color of" state law was not in focus and was ill-advised. It was argued there, as it is here, that "under color of" state law included only action taken by officials pursuant to state law. We rejected that view.

Mr. Shellabarger, reporting out the bill which became the Ku Klux Act, said of the provision with which we now deal:

> "The model for it will be found in the second section of the act of April 9, 1866, known as the 'civil rights act.'. . . . This section of this bill, on the same state of facts, not only provides a civil remedy for persons whose former condition may have been that of slaves, but also to all people where, under color of State law, they or any of them may be deprived of rights. . . ."

Thus, it is beyond doubt that this phrase should be accorded the same construction in both statutes — in § 1979 and in 18 U.S.C. § 242.

We conclude that the meaning given "under color of" law in the *Classic* case and in the *Screws* and *Williams* cases was the correct one; and we adhere to it.

In the *Screws* case we dealt with a statute that imposed criminal penalties for acts "wilfully" done. We construed that word in its setting to mean the doing of an act with "a specific intent to deprive a person of a federal right." We do not think that gloss should be placed on § 1979 which we have here. The word "wilfully" does not appear in § 1979. Moreover, § 1979 provides a civil remedy, while in the *Screws* case we dealt with a criminal law challenged on the ground of vagueness. Section

1979 should be read against the background of tort liability that makes a man responsible for the natural consequences of his actions.

So far, then, the complaint states a cause of action. There remains to consider only a defense peculiar to the City of Chicago.

III

The City of Chicago asserts that it is not liable under § 1979. We do not stop to explore the whole range of questions tendered us on this issue at oral argument and in the briefs. For we are of the opinion that Congress did not undertake to bring municipal corporations within the ambit of § 1979.

When the bill that became the Act of April 20, 1871, was being debated in the Senate, Senator Sherman of Ohio proposed an amendment which would have made "the inhabitants of the county, city, or parish" in which certain acts of violence occurred liable "to pay full compensation" to the person damaged or his widow or legal representative. The amendment was adopted by the Senate. The House, however, rejected it. The Conference Committee reported another version. The House rejected the Conference report. In a second conference the Sherman amendment was dropped and in its place § 6 of the Act of April 20, 1871, was substituted. This new section, which is now R.S. § 1981, dropped out all provision for municipal liability and extended liability in damages to "any person or persons, having knowledge that any" of the specified wrongs are being committed. Mr. Poland, speaking for the House Conferees about the Sherman proposal to make municipalities liable, said:

> "We informed the conferees on the part of he Senate that the House had taken a stand on that subject and would not recede from it; that that section imposing liability upon towns and counties must go out or we should fail to agree."

The objection to the Sherman amendment stated by Mr. Poland was that "the House had solemnly decided that in their judgment Congress had no constitutional power to impose any obligation upon county and town organizations, the mere instrumentality for the administration of state law." The question of constitutional power of Congress to impose civil liability on municipalities was vigorously debated with powerful arguments advanced in the affirmative.

Much reliance is placed on the Act of February 25, 1871, entitled "An Act prescribing the Form of the enacting and resolving Clauses of Acts and Resolutions of Congress, and Rules for the Construction thereof." Section 2 of this Act provides that "the word 'person' may extend and be applied to bodies politic and corporate." It should be noted, however, that this definition is merely an allowable, not a mandatory, one. It is said that doubts should be resolved in favor of municipal liability because private remedies against officers for illegal searches and seizures are conspicuously ineffective, and because municipal liability will not only afford plaintiffs responsible defendants but cause those defendants to eradicate abuses that exist at the police level. We do not reach those policy considerations. Nor do we reach the constitutional question whether Congress has the power to make municipalities liable for acts of its officers that violate the civil rights of individuals.

The response of the Congress to the proposal to make municipalities liable for certain actions being brought within federal purview by the Act of April 20, 1871, was so antagonistic that we cannot believe that the word "person" was used in this particular Act to include them.

Accordingly we hold that the motion to dismiss the complaint against the City of Chicago was properly granted. But since the complaint should not have been dismissed against the officials the judgment must be and is

Reversed.

MR. JUSTICE FRANKFURTER, dissenting except insofar as the Court holds that this action cannot be maintained against the City of Chicago.

Abstractly stated, this case concerns a matter of statutory construction. So stated, the problem before the Court is denuded of illuminating concreteness and thereby of its far-reaching significance for our federal system. Again abstractly stated, this matter of statutory construction is one upon which the Court has already passed. But it has done so under circumstances and in settings that negative those considerations of social policy upon which the doctrine of stare decisis, calling for the controlling application of prior statutory construction, rests.

* * *

Of course, if Congress by appropriate statutory language attempted to reach every act which could be attributed to the States under the Fourteenth Amendment's prohibition: "No State shall . . . ," the reach of the statute would be the reach of the Amendment itself. Relevant to the enforcement of such a statute would be not only the concept of state action as this Court has developed it, but also considerations of the power of Congress, under the Amendment's Enforcement Clause, to determine what is "appropriate legislation" to protect the rights which the Fourteenth Amendment secures. In this supposed case we would arrive at the question of what Congress could do only after we had determined what it was that Congress had done. So, in the case before us now, we must ask what Congress did in 1871. We must determine what Congress meant by "under color" of enumerated state authority.

Congress used that phrase not only in R.S. § 1979, but also in the criminal provisions of § 2 of the First Civil Rights Act of April 9, 1866, from which is derived the present 18 U.S.C. § 242, and in both cases used it with the same purpose. During the seventy years which followed these enactments, cases in this Court in which the "under color" provisions were invoked uniformly involved action taken either in strict pursuance of some specific command of state law or within the scope of executive discretion in the administration of state laws. The same is true, with two exceptions, in the lower federal courts. In the first of these two cases it was held that § 1979 was not directed to instances of lawless police brutality, although the ruling was not put on "under color" grounds. In the second, an indictment charging a county tax collector with depriving one Ah Koo of a federally secured right under color of a designated California law, set forth in the indictment, was held insufficient against a demurrer. The court wrote:

"The indictment contains no averment that Ah Koo was a foreign miner, and within the provisions of the state law. If this averment be unnecessary . . . the act of congress would then be held to apply to a case of illegal extortion by a tax collector from any person, though such exaction might be wholly unauthorized by the law under which the officer pretended to act.

"We are satisfied that it was not the design of congress to prevent or to punish such abuse of authority by state officers. The object of the act was, not to prevent illegal exactions, but to forbid the execution of state laws, which, by the act itself, are made void. . . .

"It would seem, necessarily, to follow, that the person from whom the tax was exacted must have been a person from whom, under the provisions of the state law, the officer was authorized to exact it. The statute requires that a party shall be subjected to a deprivation of right secured by the statute under color of some law, statute, order or custom; but if this exaction, although made by a tax collector, has been levied upon a person not within the provisions of the state law, the exaction cannot be said to have been made 'under color of law,' any more than a similar exaction from a Chinese miner, made by a person wholly unauthorized, and under the pretense of being a tax collector."

Throughout this period, the only indicator of this Court's views on the proper interpretation of the "under color" language is a dictum in the *Civil Rights Cases*. There, in striking down other Civil Rights Act provisions which as the Court regarded them, attempted to reach private conduct not attributable to state authority, Mr. Justice Bradley contrasted those provisions with § 2 of the Act of 1866 "This [latter] law is clearly corrective in its character, intended to counteract and furnish redress against State laws and proceedings and customs having the force of law, which sanction the wrongful acts specified."

A sharp change from this uniform application of seventy years was made in 1941, but without acknowledgment or indication of awareness of the revolutionary turnabout from what had been established practice. The opinion in *United States v. Classic*, accomplished this. The case presented an indictment under § 242 charging certain local Commissioners of Elections with altering ballots cast in a primary held to nominate candidates for Congress. Sustaining the sufficiency of the indictment in an extensive opinion concerned principally with the question whether the right to vote in such a primary was a right secured by the Constitution, Mr. Justice Stone wrote that the alteration of the ballots was "under color" of state law. This holding was summarily announced without exposition; it had been only passingly argued. Of the three authorities cited to support it, two did not involve the "under color" statutes, and the third, *Hague v. C.I.O.*, was a case in which high-ranking municipal officials claimed authorization for their actions under municipal ordinances (here held unconstitutional) and under the general police powers of the State. All three of these cases had dealt with "State action" problems, and it is "State action," not the very different question of the "under color" clause, that Mr. Justice Stone appears to have considered. (I joined in this opinion without having made an independent examination of the legislative history of the relevant legislation or of the authorities drawn upon for the *Classic* construction. Acquiescence so founded does not preclude the responsible recognition of error disclosed by subsequent study.) When, however, four years later the Court was called on to review the conviction under § 242 of a Georgia County Sheriff who had beaten a Negro prisoner to death, the opinion of four of he six Justices who believed that the statute applied merely invoked *Classic* and stare decisis and did not reconsider the meaning which that case had uncritically assumed was to be attached to the language, "under color" of state authority. The briefs in the *Screws* case did not examine critically the legislative history of the Civil Rights Acts. The only reference to this history in the plurality opinion, insofar as it bears on the interpretation of the clause "under color of . . . law," is contained in a pair of sentences discounting two statements by Senators Trumbull and Sherman regarding the Civil Rights Acts of 1866 and 1870, cited by the minority. The bulk of the plurality opinion's treatment of the issue consists of the argument that "under color" had been construed in Classic and that the construction there put on the words should not be abandoned or revised. The case of *Williams v. United States*, reaffirmed *Screws* and applied it to circumstances of third-degree brutality practiced by a private detective who held a special police officer's card and was accompanied by a regular policeman.

"The rule of stare decisis, though one ending to consistency and uniformity of decision, is not inflexible." It is true, of course, that the reason for the rule is more compelling in cases involving inferior law, law capable of change by Congress, than in constitutional cases, where this Court — although even in such cases a wise consciousness of the limitations of individual vision has impelled it always to give great weight to prior decisions — nevertheless bears the ultimate obligation for the development of the law as institutions develop. But the Court has not always declined to re-examine cases whose outcome Congress might have changed.

And with regard to the Civil Rights Acts there are reasons of particular urgency which authorize the Court — indeed, which make it the Court's responsibility — to reappraise in the hitherto skimpily considered context of R.S. § 1979 what was decided in *Classic, Screws* and *Williams*. This is not an area of commercial law in which, presumably, individuals may have arranged their affairs in reliance on the expected stability of decision. Nor is it merely a minerun statutory question involving a narrow compass of individual rights and duties. The issue in the present case concerns directly a basic problem of American federalism: the relation of the Nation to the States in the critically important sphere of municipal law adminis-tration. In this aspect, it has significance approximating constitutional dimension. Necessarily, the construction of the Civil Rights Acts raises issues fundamental to our institutions. This imposes on this Court a corresponding obligation to exercise its power within the fair limits of its judicial discretion. "We recognize that stare decisis embodies an important social policy. It represents an element of continuity in law, and is rooted in the psychologic need to satisfy reasonable expectations. But stare decisis is a principle of policy and not a mechanical formula of adherence to the latest decision, however recent and questionable. . . ."

Now, while invoking the prior decisions which have given "under color of [law]" a content that ignores the meaning fairly comported by the words of the text and confirmed by the legislative history, the Court undertakes a fresh examination of that legislative history. The decision in this case, therefore, does not rest on stare decisis, and the true construction of the statute may be thought to be as free from the restraints of that doctrine as though the matter were before us for the first time. Certainly, none of the implications which the Court seeks to draw from silences in the minority reports of congressional committees in 1956, 1957, and 1960, or from the use of "under color" language in the very different context of the Act of May 6, 1960, — concerned, in relevant part, with the preservation of election records and with the implementation of the franchise — serves as an impressive bar to re-examination of the true scope of R.S. § 1979 itself in its pertinent legislative setting.

This case squarely presents the question whether the intrusion of a city policeman for which that policeman can show no such authority at state law as could be successfully interposed in defense to a state-law action against him, is nonetheless to be regarded as "under color" of state authority within the meaning of R.S. § 1979. Respondents, in breaking into the Monroe apartment, violated the laws of the State of Illinois. Illinois law appears to offer a civil remedy for unlawful searches; petitioners do not claim that none is available. Rather they assert that they have been deprived of due process of law and of equal protection of the laws under color of state law, although from all that appears the courts of Illinois are available to give them the fullest redress which the common law affords for the violence done them, nor does any "statute, ordinance, regulation, custom, or usage" of the State of Illinois bar that redress. Did the enactment by Congress of § 1 of the Ku Klux Act of 1871 encompass such a situation?

The general understanding of the legislators unquestionably was that, as amended, the Ku Klux Act did "not undertake to furnish redress for wrongs done by one person upon another in any of the States . . . in violation of their laws, unless he also violated some law of the United States, nor to punish one person for an ordinary assault and battery. . . ." Even those who — opposing the constitutional objectors — found sufficient congressional power in the Enforcement Clause of the Fourteenth Amendment to give this kind of redress, deemed inexpedient the exercise of any such power: "Convenience and courtesy to the States suggest a sparing use, and never so far as to supplant the State authorities except in cases of extreme necessity, and when the State governments criminally refuse or neglect those duties which are imposed upon them." Extreme Radicals, those who believed that the remedy for the oppressed Unionists in the South was a general expansion of federal judicial jurisdiction so that "loyal men could have the privilege of having their causes, civil and criminal, tried in the Federal courts," were disappointed with the Act as passed.

Finally, it is significant that the opponents of the Act, exhausting ingenuity to discover constitutional objections to every provision of it, also construed § 1 as addressed only to conduct authorized by state law, and therefore within the admitted permissible reach of Fourteenth Amendment federal power. "The first section of this bill prohibits any invidious legislation by States against the rights or privileges of citizens of the United States," one such opponent paraphrased the provision. And Senator Thurman, who insisted vociferously on the absence of federal power to penalize a conspiracy of individuals to violate state law ("that is a case of mere individual violence, having no color whatsoever of authority of law, either Federal or State; and to say that you can punish men for that mere conspiracy, which is their individual act, and which is a crime against the State laws themselves, punishable by the State laws, is simply to wipe out all the State jurisdiction over crimes and transfer it bodily to the Congress"), admitted without question the constitutionality of § 1 ("It refers to a deprivation under color of law, either statute law or 'custom or usage' which has become common law").

The Court now says, however, that "It was not the unavailability of state remedies but the failure of certain States to enforce the laws with an equal hand that furnished the powerful momentum behind this 'force bill.'" Of course, if the notion of "unavailability" of remedy is limited to mean an absence of statutory, paper right, this is in large part true Insofar as the Court undertakes to demonstrate — as the bulk of its opinion seems to do — that § 1979 was meant to reach some instances of action not specifically authorized by the avowed, apparent, written law inscribed in the statute books of the States, the argument knocks at an open door. No one would or could deny this, for by its express terms the statute comprehends deprivations of federal rights under color of any "statute, ordinance, regulation, custom, or usage" of a State. The question is, what class of cases other than those involving state statute law were meant to be reached. And, with respect to this question, the Court's conclusion is undermined by the very portions of the legislative debates which it cites. For surely the misconduct of individual municipal police officers, subject to the effective oversight of appropriate state administrative and judicial authorities, presents a situation which differs toto coelo from one in which "Immunity is given to crime, and the records of the public tribunals are searched in vain for any evidence of effective redress," or in which murder rages while a State makes "no successful effort to bring the guilty to punishment or afford protection or redress," or in which the "State courts . . . [are] unable to enforce the criminal laws . . . or to suppress the disorders existing," or in which, in a State's "judicial tribunals one class is unable to secure that enforcement of their rights and punishment for their infraction which is accorded to another," or "of . . . hundreds of outrages . . . not one [is] punished," or "the courts of the . . . States fail and refuse to do their duty in the punishment of offenders against the law," or in which a "class of officers charged under the laws with their administration permanently and as a rule refuse to extend [their] protection." These statements indicate that Congress — made keenly aware by the post-bellum conditions in the South that States through their authorities could sanction offenses against the individual by settled practice which established state law as truly as written codes — designed § 1979 to reach, as well, official conduct which, because engaged in "permanently and as a rule," or "systematically," came through acceptance by law-administering officers to constitute "custom, or usage" having the cast of law. They do not indicate an attempt to reach, nor does the statute by its terms include, instances of acts in defiance of state law and which no settled state practice, no systematic pattern of official action or inaction, no "custom, or usage, of any State," insulates from effective and adequate reparation by the State's authorities.

Rather, all the evidence converges to the conclusion that Congress by § 1979 created a civil liability enforceable in the federal courts only in instances of injury for which redress was barred in the state courts because some "statute, ordinance, regulation, custom, or usage" sanctioned the grievance complained of. This purpose, manifested even by the so-called "Radical" Reconstruction Congress in 1871, accords with the presuppositions of our federal system. The jurisdiction which

Article III of the Constitution conferred on the national judiciary reflected the assumption that the state courts, not the federal courts, would remain the primary guardians of that fundamental security of person and property which the long evolution of the common law had secured to one individual as against other individuals. The Fourteenth Amendment did not alter this basic aspect of our federalism.

Its commands were addressed to the States. Only when the States, through their responsible organs for the formulation and administration of local policy, sought to deny or impede access by the individual to the central government in connection with those enumerated functions assigned to it, or to deprive the individual of a certain minimal fairness in the exercise of the coercive forces of the State, or without reasonable justification to treat him differently than other persons subject to their jurisdiction, was an overriding federal sanction imposed. As between individuals, no corpus of substantive rights was guaranteed by the Fourteenth Amendment, but only "due process of law" in the ascertainment and enforcement of rights and equality in the enjoyment of rights and safeguards that the States afford. This was the base of the distinction between federal citizenship and state citizenship drawn by the Slaughter-House Cases. This conception begot the "State action" principle on which, from the time of the Civil Rights Cases, this Court has relied in its application of Fourteenth Amendment guarantees. As between individuals, that body of mutual rights and duties which constitute the civil personality of a man remains essentially the creature of the legal institutions of the States.

But, of course, in the present case petitioners argue that the wrongs done them were committed not by individuals but by the police as state officials. There are two senses in which this might be true. It might be true if petitioners alleged that the redress which state courts offer them against the respondents is different than that which those courts would offer against other individuals, guilty of the same conduct, who were not the police. This is not alleged. It might also be true merely because the respondents are the police — because they are clothed with an appearance of official authority which is in itself a factor of significance in dealings between individuals. Certainly the nighttime intrusion of the man with a star and a police revolver is a different phenomenon than the night-time intrusion of a burglar. The aura of power which a show of authority carries with it has been created by state government. For this reason the national legislature, exercising its power to implement the Fourteenth Amendment, might well attribute responsibility for the intrusion to the State and legislate to protect against such intrusion. The pretense of authority alone might seem to Congress sufficient basis for creating an exception to the ordinary rule that it is to the state tribunals that individuals within a State must look for redress against other individuals within that State. The same pretense of authority might suffice to sustain congressional legislation creating the exception. But until Congress has declared its purpose to shift the ordinary distribution of judicial power for the determination of causes between cocitizens of a State, this Court should not make the shift. Congress has not in § 1979 manifested that intention.

[The concurring opinion of JUSTICES HARLAN and STEWART is omitted.]

NOTES

1. What constitutional violations are the defendants accused of? Are these Fourteenth Amendment violations, Bill of Rights violations or both? What difference does it make? Why did the plaintiff seek damages and not prospective relief, such as an injunction against future unwarranted intrusions?

2. What is the defendants' argument regarding "color of law?" Is their argument one of statutory interpretation or is it based on Congressional power under section 5 of the Fourteenth Amendment?

3. In *Monroe*, what is the connection between section 1983's "color of law" language and the Fourteenth Amendment's state action requirement? According to the Court, are they coextensive? According to Justice Frankfurter? *Monroe* indicates that color of law is for the most part coextensive with state action under the Fourteenth Amendment. Color of law and state action are discussed in detail in Chapter 2.

4. Who is more persuasive on the color of law argument, the Court or Justice Frankfurter? For extensive discussions, contrast Zagrans, *"Under Color Of" What Law: A Reconstructed Model of Section 1983 Liability*, 71 VA. L. REV. 499 (1985), arguing that Justice Frankfurter was correct and Winter, *The Meaning of "Under Color of" Law*, 91 MICH. L. REV. 323 (1992), maintaining that the Court was correct and that "color" means "pretense." Suppose Justice Frankfurter had prevailed? What would that have done to the scope of section 1983? What would the relation between state law and section 1983 have been? What would the *Monroe* plaintiff's remedy have been?

5. *Monroe* rejects a specific intent requirement and declares that section 1983 is to be interpreted against a "background of tort liability" that makes a person responsible for the consequences of his or her conduct. What could this mean: Does it refer to duty? To causation in fact? To proximate cause? Whatever it means, is *Monroe* itself an easy or hard case in which to hold the defendants accountable in damages?

6. What intentional torts did the *Monroe* defendants allegedly commit? If intent in the tort sense is present, does it automatically follow that the defendants should be liable in damages for constitutional harm caused? *Restatement (Second) of Torts* § 8A (1965) defines intent " . . . to denote that the actor desires to cause the consequences of his act, or that he believes that the consequences are substantially certain to result from it." Is this what the Court means by the "background of tort liability"?

7. The "background of tort liability" language in *Monroe* proved troublesome for a time. Some federal courts began to talk in terms of section 1983 "negligence" actions and section 1983 "recklessness" actions, on the assumption that *Monroe* articulated some kind of state of mind requirement for the section 1983 prima facie case as a *matter of statutory interpretation*. This position is described and rebutted in Nahmod, *Section 1983 and the "Background" of Tort Liability*, 50 IND. L.J. 5

(1974). Thereafter, the Supreme Court rejected this position in *Parratt v. Taylor*, 451 U.S. 527 (1981), where it held that section 1983 does not contain a state of mind requirement for the prima facie case.

Parratt, a very important case in several respects, is analyzed in a due process context in Chapter 3. For present purposes, you should keep in mind that while section 1983 in fact does not have its own state of mind requirement for the prima facie case, certain constitutional provisions do have particular state of mind requirements *as a matter of constitutional interpretation*. For example, at least deliberate indifference is necessary to make out an Eighth Amendment violation, *Estelle v. Gamble*, 429 U.S. 97 (1976); purposeful discrimination is necessary for an equal protection violation, *Washington v. Davis*, 426 U.S. 229 (1976); and negligence is not enough for a due process violation, *Daniels v. Williams*, 474 U.S. 327 (1986); *County of Sacramento v. Lewis*, 523 U.S. 833 (1998) (conscience-shocking conduct required for substantive due process violation in high speed police pursuit cases). Thus, a section 1983 plaintiff claiming an equal protection violation must allege and prove purposeful discrimination; one claiming an Eighth Amendment violation must allege and prove at least deliberate indifference; and so on.

8.　　The "background of tort liability" is important in another respect: To what extent, if at all, is section 1983 doctrine to be determined by tort law? Should tort concepts of responsibility, including, for example, causation in fact, proximate cause, joint and several liability and damages, govern section 1983 liability? Should these tort concepts govern constitutional interpretation in a section 1983 setting? *See* Abernathy, *Section 1983 and Constitutional Torts*, 77 Geo. L.J. 1441 (1989) and Wells, *Constitutional Remedies, Section 1983 and the Common Law*, 68 Miss. L.J. 157 (1998). What is the role, if any, of fault? See Jeffries, *Compensation for Constitutional Torts: Reflections of the Significance of Fault*, 88 Mich. L. Rev. 82 (1989), arguing that the section 1983 damages remedy is predominantly based on fault. See also Dauenhauer and Wells, *Corrective Justice and Constitutional Tort*, 35 Ga. L. Rev. 903 (2001), which criticizes the position that there is no "persuasive non-deterrence rationale for forcing government to pay compensation to the victims of constitutional torts" taken in Levinson, *Making Government Pay: Markets, Politics and the Allocation of Constitutional Costs*, 67 U. Chi. L. Rev. 345, 402 (2000), and argues instead that corrective justice is applicable to harm-causing constitutional violations). Compare Professor Armacost's view that section 1983 damages liability has a "moral blaming function" analogous to criminal prosecution. Armacost, *Qualified Immunity: Ignorance Excused*, 51 Vand. L. Rev. 583, 591 (1998).

Notice that the characterization "constitutional tort" appears to give prominence to the noun "tort" and to make the adjective "constitutional" secondary. For the argument that the use of tort rhetoric in section 1983 cases does in fact tend improperly to encourage tort-like approaches to section 1983 liability while minimizing the significance of section 1983's constitutional dimension, see Nahmod, *Section 1983 Discourse: The Move from Constitution to Tort*, 77 Geo. L.J. 1719 (1989).

Whether this argument is correct or not, the nature of the relationship among constitutional interpretation, section 1983 interpretation and tort law pervades all of section 1983 doctrine. See, by way of example, Chapter 6 on causation, Chapter 7 on absolute immunity, Chapter 8 on qualified immunity and Chapter 9 on remedies.

9. What is the scope of section 1983 damages actions after *Monroe*? Does it include *all* Fourteenth Amendment violations, whether due process, equal protection or incorporated provisions of the Bill of Rights, and however "trivial"? Consider Shapo, *Constitutional Tort:* Monroe v. Pape *and the Frontiers Beyond,* 60 Nw. U. L. Rev. 277 (1965), which argues that the proper standard of section 1983 liability should be "outrageous conduct" going beyond the garden variety tort action.

10. Section 1983 is intended to promote compliance with the Fourteenth Amendment as well as to compensate for harm caused by Fourteenth Amendment violations. Does Monroe's remedial scheme, in which government officials and correct spacing are personally liable while local governments are not, effectively promote compliance with the Fourteenth Amendment? Does it effectively promote the compensation function of section 1983? Or might this scheme sometimes overdeter state and local government officials and correct spacing by discouraging them from exercising independent judgment because of the fear of liability?

The concern with overdeterrence is especially implicated in section 1983 case law dealing with immunities, as discussed extensively in Chapters 7 and 8. In this connection, notice that the language of section 1983 does not on its face refer to the availability of affirmative defenses to individual liability. Yet it turns out that the Supreme Court, relying on the "background of tort liability," has found absolute and qualified immunity applicable to certain persons sued under section 1983. The first such immunity case, *Tenney v. Brandhove,* 341 U.S. 367 (1951), analyzed in Chapter 7, applied absolute legislative immunity ten years before *Monroe* was decided.

11. Can you imagine situations in which the regulation of conduct function and the compensation function of section 1983 are in conflict? Consider that the portion of *Monroe* holding that local governments are not suable persons under section 1983 was overruled by the Supreme Court in 1978 in *Monell v. Department of Social Services,* 436 U.S. 658 (1978). Did that change render section 1983 more effective by providing a deep pocket defendant so that constitutionally damaged persons would have a greater incentive to sue? *Monell* and local government liability in general are considered at length in Chapter 5.

12. For discussion of the civil rights context in which *Monroe* arose as well as the roles played by Justices Douglas and Frankfurter, see Nahmod, *Section 1983 Is Born: The Interlocking Supreme Court Stories of Tenney and Monroe,* 17 Lewis & Clark L. Rev. 1019 (2013).

IV. CONSTITUTIONAL TORTS AND EXHAUSTION OF JUDICIAL REMEDIES

Monroe makes clear that a plaintiff who has a section 1983 cause of action for damages need not exhaust or pursue state judicial remedies before filing in a federal forum. (Why should this be?) The Court rejected the arguments of the defendants in *Monroe* that the plaintiff should proceed in state court. It asserted: "It is no answer that the State has a law which if enforced would give relief. The federal remedy is supplementary to the state remedy, and the latter need not first be sought and refused before the federal one is invoked." Significantly, *Monroe*'s choice of judicial forum rule applies irrespective of the adequacy of the state judicial remedy. There are, however, several important qualifications of this no-exhaustion rule that you should be aware of.

Habeas Corpus. A prisoner, like other section 1983 plaintiffs, need not exhaust state judicial remedies as, for example, in challenging prison procedures or conditions, or the acts of prison authorities generally. However, the Supreme Court held in *Preiser v Rodriguez*, 411 U.S. 475 (1973), that a prisoner's section 1983 challenge to the *fact or duration of his or her confinement* is in substance a petition for habeas corpus and must be treated as such by the federal courts. Because the federal habeas corpus statute requires exhaustion of state judicial remedies, 28 U.S.C. § 2254, the effect of treating the section 1983 claim as federal habeas corpus is the dismissal of that claim from the federal forum altogether in situations where state judicial remedies have not yet been pursued. As a practical matter, if a prisoner challenges both the conditions of confinement and its length or fact, the latter challenge, being in the nature of habeas corpus, will be dismissed and the prisoner sent to the state courts. However, the former claim can still be pursued in federal court while state judicial proceedings are being conducted.

In an important section 1983 habeas corpus-related decision, the Supreme Court held in *Heck v. Humphrey*, 512 U.S. 477 (1994) that "in order to recover damages for allegedly unconstitutional conviction or imprisonment, or for other harm caused by actions whose unlawfulness would render a conviction or sentence invalid, a section 1983 plaintiff must prove that the conviction or sentence has been reversed on direct appeal, expunged by executive order, declared invalid by a state tribunal authorized to make such a determination, or called into question by a federal court's issuance of a writ of habeas corpus." See Chapter 10 for a fuller discussion of Heck.

Due Process. In certain cases a decision adverse to a plaintiff's due process challenge amounts to a *de facto* requirement that state judicial remedies be exclusively pursued. For example, in *Paul v. Davis*, 424 U.S. 693 (1976) the Supreme Court held that a section 1983 claim based on the due process clause was not stated where the plaintiff sought relief from being listed as an active shoplifter by police authorities. The Court held that no liberty or property interest was implicated; plaintiff's sole legal remedy was an action for defamation in the state courts. Similarly, in *Ingraham v. Wright*, 430 U.S. 651 (1977), the Court held that procedural due process was not violated when school authorities imposed corporal punishment on students because students against whom excessive force was used would have a tort cause of action in the state courts. Finally, in *Hudson v. Palmer*, 468 U.S. 517 (1984), the Court held that, in certain circumstances, intentional deprivations of property do not violate procedural due process where adequate postdeprivation remedies are available.

Indeed, these cases go well beyond a *de facto* exhaustion of judicial remedies requirement in holding that no section 1983 cause of action is stated at all; the federal forum is rendered totally unavailable at any time. This rule is broader than an exhaustion of judicial remedies requirement which would only *postpone* access to the federal forum. Procedural due process is addressed in Chapter 3.

Prospective Relief and the Younger *Rule*. Mention should be made of yet another qualification of this rule of no exhaustion of judicial remedies: where a section 1983 plaintiff seeks not damages but prospective relief. When state criminal judicial proceedings are already pending, a federal plaintiff seeking declaratory or injunctive relief against their continuation will typically be barred from the federal forum by reason of the Supreme Court's decision in *Younger v. Harris*, 401 U.S. 37 (1971). Barring the federal plaintiff amounts to a de facto exhaustion of judicial remedies requirement. Furthermore, the *Younger* rule has since been extended by the Supreme Court to include suitable relief against state judicial proceedings between private litigants where important state interests are implicated, *e.g., Pennzoil Co. v Texaco, Inc.*, 481 U.S. 1 (1987), as well as pending state administrative proceedings, *e.g., Ohio Civil Rights Commission v. Dayton Christian Schools*, 477 U.S. 619 (1986), where important state interests are involved and there is a full and fair opportunity to litigate any constitutional claims upon state judicial review of that proceeding. The *Younger* rule and its progeny are extensively treated in most federal courts courses. *See* Chapter 10.

Do these qualifications of the no-exhaustion rule tend to undermine the effectiveness of Section 1983 in enforcing the Fourteenth Amendment? Or do they promote federalism and other important values? For an answer from the bench, see Blackmun, *Section 1983 and Federal Protection of Individual Rights — Will the Statute Remain Alive or Fade Away?*, 60 N.Y.U. L. REV. 1 (1985).

V. CONSTITUTIONAL TORTS AND EXHAUSTION OF ADMINISTRATIVE REMEDIES

Suppose that a state provides an administrative proceeding, which a prospective section 1983 plaintiff can use in an attempt to be made whole. Is the plaintiff required to exhaust that administrative remedy as a condition precedent to filing a section 1983 action in federal (or state) court? Might it not make sense to submit the plaintiff's claim first to an administrative tribunal which possesses expertise and experience in such matters? Although *Monroe* does not specifically address that question, consider the suggestion that it would have been anomalous to hold that exhaustion of judicial remedies *not* required while at the same time ruling that exhaustion of administrative remedies *is* required. It would appear that a state administrative tribunal should be entitled to no more deference than that accorded a state judicial tribunal. In fact, the Supreme Court repeatedly asserted, beginning with *McNeese v. Board of Education*, 373 U.S. 668 (1963), that state administrative remedies, like judicial remedies, need not be exhausted before maintaining a section 1983 action in federal court. In addition, the Court never in fact required exhaustion of state administrative remedies in a section 1983 case.

However, it was not until 1982, when the Court decided *Patsy v. Florida Board of Regents*, 457 U.S. 496 (1982), that the Supreme Court definitively ruled that exhaustion of administrative remedies is not a condition precedent to filing a section 1983 action. *Patsy* involved a section 1983 race and sex discrimination action brought by a secretary against a state university. Taking what it called a "flexible" approach, the Fifth Circuit had emphasized that exhaustion of administrative remedies should be required in section 1983 cases where an orderly system of review is provided; the agency is able to grant the relief requested; relief is available promptly; agency procedures are fair, not unduly burdensome, and not used to harass; and interim relief is available to preserve the litigant's section 1983 rights until the administrative process is concluded.

The Supreme Court reversed in an opinion by Justice Marshall. At the outset the Court asserted that the no-exhaustion requirement was not an issue of first impression but rather had not been deviated from for 19 years. Next, the Court rejected the argument that an exhaustion requirement should be adopted. It emphasized that section 1983's legislative history shows that "Congress assigned to the federal courts a paramount role in protecting constitutional rights"; that the "1871 Congress would not have wanted to impose an exhaustion requirement"; and that many legislators interpreted section 1983 as "enabling the plaintiff to choose the forum in which to seek relief." The Court then went on to reject the defendants' contention that various policy considerations, including federal court burdens, comity, and improved federal-state relations, warranted an exhaustion requirement. According to the Court, the policy considerations respecting the existence of such a requirement, besides being complex, did not all cut in the same direction. Furthermore, the design and scope of an exhaustion requirement were equally difficult, and included categories of section 1983 claims, standards for evaluating administrative procedures, tolling and limitations problems, res judicata and collateral estoppel issues, and the like.

State Prisoners and Exhaustion of Administrative Remedies. As mentioned above, a prisoner's section 1983 claim is sometimes treated as federal habeas corpus and thereby becomes subject to an exhaustion of state judicial remedies requirement. In contrast, a section 1983 claim attacking prison conditions and events unrelated to the fact and duration of confinement is not, as a matter of section 1983 interpretation, subject to an exhaustion of administrative remedies requirement. However, Congress in 1980 legislated an exhaustion of administrative remedies requirement in certain circumstances for persons institutionalized in state or local government correctional facilities. The statute, the Civil Rights of Institutionalized Persons Act was codified as 42 U.S.C. § 1997e. Among other things, the Act specifically provided that an inmate who sued under section 1983 shall, if appropriate and the interests of justice warrant, have his or her case continued by the court for 90 days so that the inmate may exhaust "such plain, speedy, and effective administrative remedies as are available."

Exhaustion under the Act was only ordered, however, where the applicable administrative procedures were either certified by the Attorney General or were determined by the court to comply substantially with certain minimum acceptable standards. These standards, promulgated by the Attorney General and published in the Code of Federal Regulations, 28 C.F.R. §§ 4.01–.22 (pt. 40), included an advisory role for the inmates; time limits for written replies to inmate grievances; priority processing of emergency grievances; safeguards to avoid reprisals; and independent review of the disposition of grievances.

However, in section 803 of the Prison Litigation Reform Act of 1995, effective April 26, 1996, Congress significantly amended the Civil Rights of Institutionalized Persons Act to broaden the scope of its exhaustion of administrative remedies requirement to cover even those administrative remedies not certified by the Attorney General, at least with respect to prison conditions litigation. In relevant part, section 803 provides: "No action shall be brought with respect to prison conditions under [section 1983] by a prisoner confined in any jail, prison, or other correctional facility until such administrative procedures as are available are exhausted." Pub L. No. 104-134, 1996 HR 3019.

Why, as a matter of policy, should prisoners alone be subject to an exhaustion of administrative remedies requirement? *See* Chapter 10.

Note that in *Jones v. Bock*, 549 U.S. 199 (2007), the Supreme Court answered both the of the following questions dealing with exhaustion and the Prison Litigation Reform Act (PLRA) in the negative: (1) Must the plaintiff inmate allege and prove exhaustion of administrative remedies, or is non-exhaustion an affirmative defense that must be pleaded and proved by the defendant? (2) Does the PLRA require "total exhaustion" so that where there is a single unexhausted claim, the plaintiff inmate's complaint must be dismissed even though there are also exhausted claims set out in the complaint?

VI. CONSTITUTIONAL TORTS OF FEDERAL OFFICIALS: *BIVENS* ACTIONS

Suppose *federal* law enforcement officers violate a person's Fourth Amendment rights. Is a section 1983 damages remedy available? The clear answer is that it is *not* because section 1983 governs only conduct under color of state law, *not* federal law. Does it therefore follow that there is no damages remedy available? Consider carefully the following very important and influential Supreme Court decision.

BIVENS v. SIX UNKNOWN NAMED AGENTS
403 U.S. 388 (1971)

MR. JUSTICE BRENNAN delivered the opinion of the Court.

The Fourth Amendment provides that:

> "The right of the people to be secure in their persons, houses, papers, and effects, against unreasonable searches and seizures shall not be violated. . . ."

In *Bell v. Hood*, we reserved the question whether violation of that command by federal agent acting under color of his authority gives rise to a cause of action for damages consequent upon his unconstitutional conduct. Today we hold that it does.

This case has its origin in an arrest and search carried out on the morning of November 26, 1965. Petitioner's complaint allege that on that day respondents, agents of the Federal Bureau of Narcotics acting under claim of federal authority, entered his apartment and arrested him for alleged narcotic violations. The agents manacled petitioner in front of his wife and children, and threatened to arrest the entire family. They searched the apartment from stem to stern. Thereafter petitioner was taken to the federal courthouse in Brooklyn, where he was interrogated, booked, and subjected to a visual strip search.

On July 7, 1967, petitioner brought suit in Federal District Court. In addition to the allegations above, his complaint asserted that the arrest and search were effected without a warrant, and that unreasonable force was employed in making the arrest; fairly read, it alleges as well that the arrest was made without probable cause. Petitioner claimed to have suffered great humiliation, embarrassment, and mental suffering as a result of the agents' unlawful conduct, and sought $15,000 damages from each of them. The District Court, on respondents' motion, dismissed the complaint on the ground, inter alia, that it failed to state a cause of action. The Court of appeals, one judge concurring specially, affirmed on that basis. We granted certiorari.

We reverse.

I

Respondents do not argue that petitioner should be entirely without remedy for an unconstitutional invasion of his rights by federal agents. In respondents' view, however, the rights that petitioner asserts — primarily rights of privacy — are creations of state and not of federal law. Accordingly, they argue, petitioner may obtain money damages to redress invasion of these rights only by an action in tort, under state law, in the state courts. In this scheme the Fourth Amendment would serve merely to limit the extent to which the agents could defend the state law tort suit by asserting that their actions were a valid exercise of federal power: if the agents were shown to have violated the Fourth Amendment, such a defense would be lost to them and they would stand before the state law merely as private individuals. Candidly admitting that it is the policy of the Department of Justice to remove all such suits from the state to the federal courts for decision, respondents nevertheless urge that we uphold dismissal of petitioner's complaint in federal court, and remit him to filing an action in the state courts in order that the case may properly be removed to the federal court for decision on the basis of state law. We think that respondents' thesis rests upon an unduly restrictive view of the Fourth Amendment's protection against unreasonable searches and seizures by federal agents, a view that has consistently been rejected by this Court. Respondents seek to treat the relationship between a citizen and a federal agent unconstitutionally exercising his authority as no different from the relationship between two private citizens. In so doing, they ignore the fact that power, once granted, does not disappear like a magic gift when it is wrongfully used. An agent acting — albeit unconstitutionally — in the name of the United States possesses a far greater capacity for harm than an individual trespasser exercising no authority other than his own. Accordingly, as our cases make clear, the Fourth Amendment operates as a limitation upon the exercise of federal power regardless of whether the State in whose jurisdiction that power is exercised would prohibit or penalize the identical act if engaged in by a private citizen. It guarantees to citizens of the United States the absolute right to be free from unreasonable searches and seizures carried out by virtue of federal authority. And "where federally protected rights have been invaded, it has been the rule from the beginning that courts will be alert to adjust their remedies so as to grant the necessary relief."

First. Our cases have long since rejected the notion that the Fourth Amendment proscribes only such conduct as would, if engaged in by private persons, be condemned by state law. Thus in *Gambino v. United States*, petitioners were convicted of conspiracy to violate the National Prohibition Act on the basis of evidence seized by state police officers incident to petitioners' arrest by those officers solely for the purpose of enforcing federal law. Notwithstanding the lack of probable cause for the arrest, it would have been permissible under state law if effected by private individuals. It appears, moreover, that the officers were under direction from the Governor to aid in the enforcement of federal law. Accordingly, if the Fourth Amendment reached only to conduct impermissible under the law of the State, the Amendment would have had no application to the case. Yet this Court held the Fourth Amendment applicable and reversed petitioners' convictions as having been based upon evidence obtained through an unconstitutional search and seizure. Similarly, in *Byars v. United States*, the petitioner was convicted on the basis of evidence seized under a warrant issued, without probable cause under the Fourth Amendment, by a state court judge for a state law offense. At the invitation of state law enforcement officers, a federal prohibition agent participated in the search. This Court explicitly refused to inquire whether the warrant was "good under the state law . . . since in no event could it constitute the basis for a federal search and seizure." And our recent decisions regarding electronic surveillance have made it clear beyond peradventure that the Fourth Amendment is not tied to the niceties of local trespass laws. In light of these cases, respondents' argument that the Fourth Amendment serves only as a limitation on federal defenses to a state law claim, and not as an independent limitation upon the exercise of federal power, must be rejected.

Second. The interests protected by state laws regulating trespass and the invasion of privacy, and those protected by the Fourth Amendment's guarantee against unreasonable searches and seizures, may be inconsistent or even hostile. Thus, we may bar the door against an unwelcome private intruder, or call the police if he persists in seeking entrance. The availability of such alternative means for the protection of privacy may lead the State to restrict imposition of liability for any consequent trespass. A private citizen, asserting no authority other than his own, will not normally be liable in trespass if he demands, and is granted, admission to another's house. But one who demands admission under a claim of federal authority stands in a far different position. The mere invocation of federal power by a federal law enforcement official will normally render futile any attempt to resist an unlawful entry or arrest by resort to the local police; and a claim of authority to enter is likely to unlock the door as well. 'In such cases there is no safety for the citizen, except in the protection of the judicial tribunals, for rights which have been invaded by the officers of the government, professing to act in its name. There remains to him but the alternative of resistance, which may amount to crime." Nor is it adequate to answer that state law may take into account the different status of one clothed with the authority of the Federal Government. For just as state law may not authorize federal agents to violate the Fourth Amendment, neither may state law undertake to limit the extent to which federal authority can be exercised. The inevitable consequence of this dual limitation on state power is that the federal question becomes not merely a possible defense to the state law action, but an independent claim both necessary and sufficient to make out the plaintiff's cause of action.

Third. That damages may be obtained for injuries consequent upon a violation of the Fourth Amendment by federal officials should hardly seem a surprising proposition. Historically, damages have been regarded as the ordinary remedy for an invasion of personal interests in liberty. Of course, the Fourth Amendment does not in so many words provide for its enforcement by an award of money damages for the consequences of its violation. But "it is . . . well settled that where legal rights have been invaded, and a federal statute provides for a general right to sue for such invasion, federal courts may use any available remedy to make good the wrong done." The present case involves no special factors counselling hesitation in the absence of affirmative action by Congress. We are not dealing with a question of "federal fiscal policy," as in *United States v. Standard Oil Co.* In that case we refused to infer from the Government-soldier relationship that the United States could recover damages from one who negligently injured a soldier and thereby caused the Government to pay his medical expenses and lose his services during the course of his hospitalization. Noting that Congress was normally quite solicitous where the federal purse was involved, we pointed out that "the United States [was] the party plaintiff to the suit. And the United States has power at any time to create the liability." Nor are we asked in this case to impose liability upon a congressional employee for actions contrary to no constitutional prohibition, but merely said to be in excess of the authority delegated to him by the Congress. Finally, we cannot accept respondents' formulation of the question as whether the availability of money damages is necessary to enforce the Fourth Amendment. For we have here no explicit congressional declaration that persons injured by a federal officer's violation of the Fourth Amendment may not recover money damages from the agents, but must instead be remitted to another remedy, equally effective in the view of Congress. The question is merely whether petitioner, if he can demonstrate an injury consequent upon the violation by federal agents of his Fourth Amendment rights, is entitled to redress his injury through a particular remedial mechanism normally available in the federal courts. "The very essence of civil liberty certainly consists in the right of every individual to claim the protection of the laws, whenever he receives an injury." Having concluded that petitioner's complaint states a cause of action under the Fourth Amendment, we hold that petitioner is entitled to recover money damages for any injuries he has suffered as a result of the agents' violation of the Amendment.

II

In addition to holding that petitioner's complaint had failed to state facts making out a cause of action, the District Court ruled that in any event respondents were immune from liability by virtue of their official position. This question was not passed upon by the Court of Appeals, and accordingly we do not consider here. The judgment of the Court of Appeals is reversed and the case is remanded for further proceedings consistent with this opinion.

So ordered.

Mr. Justice **Harlan**, concurring in the judgment.

For the reasons set forth below, I am of the opinion that federal courts do have the power to award damages for violation of "constitutionally protected interests" and I agree with the Court that a traditional judicial remedy such as damages is appropriate to the vindication of the personal interests protected by the Fourth Amendment.

I

I turn first to the contention that the constitutional power of federal courts to accord Bivens damages for his claim depends on the passage of a statute creating a "federal cause of action." Although the point is not entirely free of ambiguity, I do not understand either the Government or my dissenting Brothers to maintain that Bivens' contention that he is entitled to be free from the type of official conduct prohibited by the Fourth Amendment depends on a decision by the State in which he resides to accord him a remedy. Such a position would be incompatible with the presumed availability of federal equitable relief, if a proper showing can be made in terms of the ordinary principles governing equitable remedies. However broad a federal court's discretion concerning equitable remedies, it is absolutely clear — at least after *Erie R. Co. v. Tompkins* — that in a nondiversity suit a federal court's power to grant even equitable relief depends on the presence of a substantive right derived from federal law.

Thus the interest which Bivens claims — to be free from official conduct in contravention of the Fourth Amendment — is a federally protected interest. Therefore, the question of judicial *power* to grant Bivens damages is not a problem of the "source" of the "right"; instead, the question is whether the power to authorize damages as a judicial remedy for the vindication of a federal constitutional right is placed by the Constitution itself exclusively in Congress' hands.

III

The major thrust of the Government's position is that, where Congress has not expressly authorized a particular remedy, a federal court should exercise its power to accord a traditional form of judicial relief at the behest of a litigant, who claims a constitutionally protected interest has been invaded, only where the remedy is "essential," or "indispensable for vindicating constitutional rights." While this "essentiality" test is most clearly articulated with respect to damage remedies, apparently the Government believes the same test explains the exercise of equitable remedial powers. It is argued that historically the Court has rarely exercised the power to accord such relief in the absence of an express congressional authorization and that "[i]f Congress had thought that federal officers should be subject to a law different than state law, it would have had no difficulty in saying so, as it did with respected to state officers * * *." Although conceding that the standard of determining whether a damage remedy should be utilized to effectuate statutory polices is one of "necessity" or "appropriateness," the Government contends that questions concerning congressional discretion to modify judicial remedies relating to constitutionally protected interests warrant a more stringent constraint on the exercise of judicial power with respect to this class of legally protected interests.

These arguments for a more stringent test to govern the grant of damages in constitutional cases seem to be adequately answered by the point that the judiciary has a particular responsibility to assure the vindication of constitutional interests such as those embraced by the Fourth Amendment. To be sure, "it must be remembered that legislatures are ultimate guardians of the liberties and welfare of the people in quite as great a degree as the courts." But it must also be recognized that the Bill of Rights is particularly intended to vindicate the interests of the individual in the face of the popular will as expressed in legislative majorities; at the very least, it strikes me as no more appropriate to await express congressional authorization of traditional judicial relief with regard to these legal interests than with respect to interests protected by federal statutes.

The question then, is, as I see it, whether compensatory relief is "necessary" or "appropriate" to the vindication of the interest asserted. In resolving that question, it seems to me that the range of policy considerations we may take into account is at least as broad as the range of a legislature would consider with respect to an express statutory authorization of a traditional remedy. In this regard I agree with the Court that the appropriateness of according Bivens compensatory relief does not turn simply on the deterrent effect liability will have on federal official conduct. Damages as a traditional form of compensation for invasion of a legally protected interest may be entirely appropriate even if no substantial deterrent effects on future official lawlessness might be thought to result. Bivens, after all, has invoked judicial processes claiming entitlement to compensation for injuries resulting from allegedly lawless official behavior, if those injuries are properly compensable in money damages. I do not think a court of law — vested with the power to accord a remedy — should deny him his relief simply because he cannot show that future lawless conduct will thereby be deterred.

And I think it is clear that Bivens advances a claim of the sort that, if proved, would be properly compensable in damages. The personal interests protected by the fourth Amendment are those we attempt to capture by the notion of "privacy"; while the Court today properly points out that the type of harm which officials can inflict when they invade protected zones of an individual's life are different from the types of harm private citizens inflict on one another, the experience of judges in dealing with private trespass and false imprisonment claims supports the conclusion that courts of law are capable of making the types of judgment concerning causation and magnitude of injury necessary to accord meaningful compensation of invasion of Fourth Amendment rights.

On the other hand, the limitation on state remedies for violation of commonlaw rights by private citizens argue in favor of federal damages remedy. The injuries inflicted by officials action under color of law, while no less compensable in damages than those inflicted by private parties, are substantially different in kind, as the Court's opinion today discusses in detail. *See Monroe v. Pape* (Harlan, J., concurring). It seems to me entirely proper that these injuries be compensable according to uniform rules of federal law, especially in light of the very large element of federal law which must in any event control the scope of official defenses to liability. Certainly, there is very little to be gained from the standpoint of federalism by preserving different rules of liability for federal officers dependent on the State where the injury occurs.

Putting aside the desirability of leaving the problem of federal official liability to the vagaries of common-law actions, it is apparent that some form of damages is the only possible remedy for someone in Bivens' alleged position. It will be a rare case indeed in which an individual in Bivens' position will be able to obviate the harm by securing injunctive relief from any court. However desirable a direct remedy against the Government might be as a substitute for individual official liability, the sovereign still remains immune to suit. Finally, assuming Bivens' innocence of the crime charged, the "exclusionary rule" is simply irrelevant. For the people in Bivens' shoes, it is damages or nothing.

The only substantial policy consideration advanced against recognition of a federal cause of action for violation of Fourth Amendment rights by federal officials is the incremental expenditure of judicial resources that will be necessitated by this class of litigation. There is, however, something ultimately selfdefeating about this argument. For if, as the Government contends, damages will rarely be realized by plaintiffs in these cases because of jury hostility, the limited resources of the official concerned, etc., then I am not ready to assume that there will be a significant increase in the expenditure of judicial resources on these claims. Few responsible lawyers and plaintiffs are likely to choose the course of litigation if the statistical chances of success are truly *de minimis*. And I simply cannot agree with my Brother Black that the possibility of "frivolous" claims — if defined simply as claims with no legal merit — warrants closing the courthouse doors to people in Bivens' situation. There are other ways, short of that, of coping with frivolous lawsuits.

On the other hand, if — as I believe is the case with respect, at least, to the most flagrant abuses of official power — damages to some degree will be available when the option of litigation is chosen, then the question appears to be how Fourth Amendment interests rank on a scale of social values compared with, for example, the interests of stockholders defrauded by misleading proxies. Judicial resources, I am well aware, are increasingly scarce these days. Nonetheless, when we automatically close the courthouse door solely on this basis, we implicitly express a value judgment on the comparative importance of classes of legally protected interests. And current limitations upon the effective functioning of the courts arising from budgetary inadequacies should not be permitted to stand in the way of the recognition of otherwise sound constitutional principles.

Of course, for a variety of reasons, the remedy may not often be sought. And the countervailing interests in efficient law enforcement of course argue for a protective zone with respect to many types of Fourth Amendment violations. But, while I express no view on the immunity defense offered in the instant case, I deem it proper to venture the thought that at the very least such a remedy would be available for the most flagrant and patently unjustified sorts of police conduct. Although litigants may not often choose to seek relief, it is important, in a civilized society, that the judicial branch of the Nation's government stand ready to afford a remedy in these circumstances. It goes without saying that I intimate no view on the merits of petitioner's underlying claim.

[The dissenting opinions of CHIEF JUSTICE BURGER and JUSTICES BLACK and BLACKMUN are omitted.]

NOTES

1.   Why does the plaintiff in *Bivens* seek damages? Was any other remedy available?

2.   What is the purpose of a *Bivens* Fourth Amendment damages remedy? To compensate? To deter? To punish?

3.   Why not a state tort remedy? Is a Fourth Amendment damages remedy more effective? Does it protect different interests? Does it provide surer access to a federal forum? Do the Court and Justice Harlan differ on these matters?

4.   Recall the Court's "background of tort liability" approach to interpreting section 1983 in *Monroe*. Does the Court adopt a similar approach to the nature and scope of Fourth Amendment damages actions in *Bivens*? Does Justice Harlan?

5.   What is the role of Congress, according to the *Bivens* majority? According to Justice Harlan? What if Congress had provided a constitutional damages remedy against federal officials or the United States itself in such cases? Would that have made a difference in the outcome? Should it have? Is the creation of a constitutional damages action against federal officials primarily within the discretion with the Court?

6.   Notice the implicit use in *Bivens* of 28 U.S.C. § 1331, the general federal question jurisdiction statute which at the time had a $10,000 amount in controversy requirement. In contrast, section 1983 has its own jurisdictional counterpart, 28 U.S.C. § 1343(3). Currently, section 1983 plaintiffs can use either section 1343(3) or section 1331, which no longer has an amount in controversy requirement.

7.   Recall that *Monroe v. Pape* made clear that section 1983 creates a damages action against state and local government officials and employees for their Fourteenth Amendment violations. What if there were no section 1983, or if section 1983 were repealed? Is it plausible to maintain, based on *Bivens*, that a Fourteenth Amendment damages action could be implied? Whatever your answer to this question, it appears that currently no such damages action is available apart from section 1983. Indeed, Justice Powell so declared in his concurring opinion in *Monell v. Department of Social Services*, 436 U.S. 658, 713–14 (1978). See, to the same effect, *Thomas v. Shipka*, 818 F.2d 496, 499 (6th Cir. 1987), *vacated on other grounds and remanded*, 488 U.S. 1036 (1989) and *Williams v. Bennett*, 689 F.2d 1370, 1390 (11th Cir. 1982). *Compare Lake Nacimiento Ranch Co. v. San Luis Obispo County*, 841 F.2d 872, 880 (9th Cir. 1988) which left the question undecided after noting that the Supreme Court had not resolved the matter.

VII. THE CURRENT STATUS OF *BIVENS* ACTIONS

Eight years after *Bivens* the Supreme Court confronted a similar issue in *Davis v. Passman*, 442 U.S. 228 (1979), which held, in reliance on *Bivens*, that the plaintiff, a female deputy administrative assistant to a United States congressman, had a Fifth Amendment damages action against the congressman for his alleged violation of her right to be free from gender discrimination. The Court observed that a damages remedy was appropriate in the case before it; there were no "special concerns counselling hesitation"; there was no explicit congressional declaration that money damages should not be available; and there was little likelihood that the federal courts would be deluged with claims. Chief Justice Burger and Justices Powell and Rehnquist dissented, arguing among other things that separation of powers concerns, buttressed by congressional refusal to provide damages remedies to its staff employees, warranted a contrary result. *Davis* was shortly thereafter followed by *Carlson v. Green*, 446 U.S. 14 (1980), which similarly implied an Eighth Amendment damages action against federal prison officials, even though there was a damages remedy against the United States under the Federal Tort Claims Act, 60 Stat. 812, 842 (1946).

The tide began to turn in *Chappell v. Wallace*, 462 U.S. 296 (1983), where the Court unanimously ruled against enlisted personnel who, alleging racial discrimination in job assignments, sought damages from their commanding officers under the Constitution. The Court emphasized the existence of special factors counselling hesitation: control over the military and the command structure. Significantly, even though *Chappell's* refusal to extend *Bivens* could have been limited to the special situation of the military, it quickly became clear that this would not be the case. Thus, in *Bush v. Lucas*, 462 U.S. 367 (1983), the Court ruled that there was no damages remedy for a federal employee who sued his supervisor for disciplining him for the exercise of his First Amendment rights. As in *Chappell*, here, too, there were "special factors counselling hesitation in the absence of affirmative action by Congress," namely, that the federal employment relationship "is governed by comprehensive procedural and substantive provisions giving meaningful remedies against the United States." *Bush v. Lucas*, 462 U.S. at 368. The Court reaffirmed the holding of *Bush* again in *Schweiker v. Chilicky*, 487 U.S. 412 (1988). There, the Court concluded that a *Bivens* remedy was unavailable to a group of plaintiffs who alleged, among other things, that inadequate process caused the wrongful denial of their Social Security benefits. The Court explained that Congress had enacted a comprehensive remedial scheme for addressing the wrongful denial of Social Security benefits.

What principles undergird the Court's reluctance to authorize a *Bivens* remedy when Congress has acted? Is the reluctance sustained by separation-of-powers principles? That is, are courts reluctant to displace a co-equal branch of government's considered legislative judgments? Or in the alternative, are *Bivens* remedies unjustified whenever the goals of deterrence and compensation can be fulfilled without judicial intervention? Consider the following case.

MINNECI v. POLLARD
132 S. Ct. 617 (2012)

JUSTICE BREYER delivered the opinion of the Court.

The question is whether we can imply the existence of an Eighth Amendment-based damages action (a *Bivens* action) against employees of a privately operated federal prison. See generally *Bivens v. Six Unknown Fed. Narcotics Agents*, 403 U.S. 388, 389 (1971). Because we believe that in the circumstances present here state tort law authorizes adequate alternative damages actions — actions that provide both significant deterrence and compensation — we cannot do so.

I

Richard Lee Pollard was a prisoner at a federal facility operated by a private company, the Wackenhut Corrections Corporation. In 2002 he filed a pro se complaint in federal court against several Wackenhut employees, who include a security officer, a food-services supervisor, and several members of the medical staff. Pollard claimed that these employees had deprived him of adequate medical care, had thereby violated the Eighth Amendment's prohibition against "cruel and unusual" punishment, and had caused him injury. He sought damages.

Pollard said that a year earlier he had slipped on a cart left in the doorway of the prison's butcher shop. The prison medical staff took x rays, thought he might have fractured both elbows, brought him to an outside clinic for further orthopedic evaluation, and subsequently arranged for surgery. In particular, Pollard claimed, among other things, that prison officials: (1) deprived him of basic hygienic care to the point where he could not bathe for two weeks; (2) provided him with insufficient medicine, to the point where he was in pain and could not sleep; and (3) forced him to return to work before his injuries had healed.

The District Court [dismissed Pollard's complaint]. But on appeal the Ninth Circuit found that the Eighth Amendment provided Pollard with a *Bivens* action, and it reversed the District Court.

The defendants sought certiorari. And, in light of a split among the Courts of Appeals, we granted the petition.

II

Recently, in *Wilkie v. Robbins*, 551 U.S. 537 (2007), we rejected a claim that the Fifth Amendment impliedly authorized a *Bivens* action that would permit landowners to obtain damages from government officials who unconstitutionally interfere with their exercise of property rights. After reviewing the Court's earlier *Bivens* cases, the Court stated:

"[T]he decision whether to recognize a *Bivens* remedy may require two steps. In the first place, there is the question whether any alternative, existing process for protecting the [constitutionally recognized] interest amounts to a convincing reason for the Judicial Branch to refrain from providing a new and freestanding remedy in damages. . . . But even in the absence of an alternative, a *Bivens* remedy is a subject of judgment: 'the federal courts must make the kind of remedial determination that is appropriate for a common-law tribunal, paying particular heed, however, to any special factors counselling hesitation before authorizing a new kind of federal litigation.' " 551 U.S., at 550 (quoting *Bush v. Lucas*, 462 U.S. 367, 378 (1983)).

These standards seek to reflect and to reconcile the Court's reasoning set forth in earlier cases. In *Bivens* itself the Court held that the Fourth Amendment implicitly authorized a court to order federal agents to pay damages to a person injured by the agents' violation of the Amendment's constitutional strictures. The Court noted that "where federally protected rights have been invaded," courts can "adjust their remedies so as to grant the necessary relief. It pointed out that the Fourth Amendment prohibited, among other things, conduct that state law might permit (such as the conduct at issue in that very case). *Bivens*, 403 U.S., at 392–393. It added that the interests protected on the one hand by state "trespass" and "invasion of privacy" laws and on the other hand by the Fourth Amendment's guarantees "may be inconsistent or even hostile." *Id.*, at 394. It stated that "[h]istorically, damages have been regarded as the ordinary remedy for an invasion of personal interests in liberty." *Id.*, at 395. And it found "no special factors counselling hesitation in the absence of affirmative action by Congress." Id., at 396.

In *Davis v. Passman*, 442 U.S. 228 (1979), the Court considered a former congressional employee's claim for damages suffered as a result of her employer's unconstitutional discrimination based on gender. The Court found a damages action implicit in the Fifth Amendment's Due Process Clause. *Id.*, at 248–249. In doing so, the Court emphasized the unavailability of "other alternative forms of judicial relief." *Id.*, at 245. And the Court noted that there was "no evidence" that Congress (or the Constitution) intended to foreclose such a remedy. *Id.*, at 247.

In *Carlson v. Green*, 446 U.S. 14 (1980), the Court considered a claim for damages brought by the estate of a federal prisoner who (the estate said) had died as the result of government officials' "deliberat[e] indifferen[ce]" to his medical needs — indifference that violated the Eighth Amendment. *Id.*, at 16, n. 1, 17 (citing *Estelle v. Gamble*, 429 U.S. 97 (1976)). The Court implied an action for damages from the Eighth Amendment. 446 U.S., at 17–18. It noted that state law offered the particular plaintiff no meaningful damages remedy. *Id.*, at 17, n. 4. Although the estate might have brought a damages claim under the Federal Tort Claims Act, the defendant in any such lawsuit was the employer, namely the United States, not the individual officers who had committed the violation. *Id.*, at 21. A damages remedy against an individual officer, the Court added, would prove a more effective deterrent. *Ibid.* And, rather than leave compensation to the "vagaries" of state tort law, a federal *Bivens* action would provide "uniform rules." 446 U.S., at 23.

Since *Carlson*, the Court has had to decide in several different instances whether to imply a *Bivens* action. And in each instance it has decided against the existence of such an action. These instances include:

(1) A federal employee's claim that his federal employer dismissed him in violation of the First Amendment, *Bush*, supra, at 386–388;

(2) A claim by military personnel that military superiors violated various constitutional provisions, *Chappell v. Wallace*, 462 U.S. 296, 298–300 (1983);

(3) A claim by recipients of Social Security disability benefits that benefits had been denied in violation of the Fifth Amendment, *Schweiker v. Chilicky*, 487 U.S. 412, 414, 425 (1988);

(4) A former bank employee's suit against a federal banking agency, claiming that he lost his job due to agency action that violated the Fifth Amendment's Due Process Clause, *FDIC v. Meyer*, 510 U.S. 471, 484–486, (1994);

(5) A prisoner's Eighth Amendment-based suit against a private corporation that managed a federal prison, *Correctional Services Corp. v. Malesko*, 534 U.S. 61 (2001).

Although the Court, in reaching its decisions, has not always similarly emphasized the same aspects of the cases, *Wilkie* fairly summarizes the basic considerations that underlie those decisions. 551 U.S., at 550. We consequently apply its approach here. And we conclude that Pollard cannot assert a *Bivens* claim. That is primarily because Pollard's Eighth Amendment claim focuses upon a kind of conduct that typically falls within the scope of traditional state tort law. And in the case of a privately employed defendant, state tort law provides an "alternative, existing process" capable of protecting the constitutional interests at stake. 551 U.S., at 550. The existence of that alternative here constitutes a "convincing reason for the Judicial Branch to refrain from providing a new and freestanding remedy in damages."

III

Pollard asks us to imply a *Bivens* action for four basic reasons — none of which we find convincing. First, Pollard argues that this Court has already decided in *Carlson* that a federal prisoner may bring an Eighth Amendment-based *Bivens* action against prison personnel; and we need do no more than simply apply *Carlson*'s holding here. *Carlson*, however, was a case in which a federal prisoner sought damages from personnel employed by the government, not personnel employed by a private firm. 446 U.S., at 25. And for present purposes that fact — of employment status — makes a critical difference.

The potential existence of an adequate "alternative, existing process" differs dramatically in the two sets of cases. Prisoners ordinarily cannot bring state law tort actions against employees of the Federal Government. See 28 U.S.C. §§ 2671, 2679(b)(1) (Westfall Act) (substituting United States as defendant in tort action against federal employee); *Osborn v. Haley*, 549 U.S. 225, 238 (2007) (Westfall Act immunizes federal employee through removal and substitution of United States as defendant). But prisoners ordinarily can bring state-law tort actions against employees of a private firm.

Second, Pollard argues that, because of the "vagaries" of state tort law, *Carlson*, 446 U.S., at 23, we should consider only whether federal law provides adequate alternative remedies. This argument flounders. State tort law, after all, can help to deter constitutional violations as well as to provide compensation to a violation's victim. And it is consequently unsurprising that several cases have considered the adequacy or inadequacy of state-law remedies when determining whether to imply a *Bivens* remedy.

Third, Pollard argues that state tort law does not provide remedies adequate to protect the constitutional interests at issue here. Pollard's claim, however, is a claim for physical or related emotional harm suffered as a result of aggravated instances of the kind of conduct that state tort law typically forbids. That claim arose in California, where state tort law provides for ordinary negligence actions, for actions based upon "want of ordinary care or skill," for actions for "negligent failure to diagnose or treat," and for actions based upon the failure of one with a custodial duty to care for another to protect that other from " 'unreasonable risk of physical harm.' "California courts have specifically applied this law to jailers, including private operators of prisons.

Moreover, California's tort law basically reflects general principles of tort law present, as far as we can tell, in the law of every State. See Restatement (Second) of Torts §§ 314A(4), 320 (1963–1964). We have found specific authority indicating that state law imposes general tort duties of reasonable care (including medical care) on prison employees in every one of the eight States where privately managed secure federal facilities are currently located: Georgia, California, Mississippi, New Mexico, North Carolina, Ohio, Pennsylvania, and Texas.

We note, as Pollard points out, that state tort law may sometimes prove less generous than would a *Bivens* action, say, by capping damages, see Cal. Civ. Code Ann. § 3333.2(b) (1997), or by forbidding recovery for emotional suffering unconnected with physical harm, or by imposing procedural obstacles, say, initially requiring the use of expert administrative panels in medical malpractice cases. But we cannot find in this fact sufficient basis to determine state law inadequate. State-law remedies and a potential *Bivens* remedy need not be perfectly congruent. Indeed, federal law as well as state law contains limitations. Prisoners bringing federal lawsuits, for example, ordinarily may not seek damages for mental or emotional injury unconnected with physical injury. See 42 U.S.C. § 1997e(e). And *Bivens* actions, even if more generous to plaintiffs in some respects, may be less generous in others. For example, to show an Eighth Amendment violation a prisoner must typically show that a defendant acted, not just negligently, but with "deliberate indifference." *Farmer v. Brennan*, 511 U.S. 825, 834, 114 S. Ct. 1970, 128 L.Ed.2d 811 (1994). And a *Bivens* plaintiff, unlike a state tort law plaintiff, normally could not apply principles of respondeat superior and thereby obtain recovery from a defendant's potentially deep-pocketed employer. See *Ashcroft v. Iqbal*, 556 U.S. 662, 676 (2009).

Fourth, Pollard argues that there "may" be similar kinds of Eighth Amendment claims that state tort law does not cover. But Pollard does not convincingly show that there are such cases. We concede that we cannot prove a negative or be totally certain that the features of state tort law relevant here will universally prove to be, or remain, as we have described them. Nonetheless, we are certain enough about the shape of present law as applied to the kind of case before us to leave different cases and different state laws to another day. That is to say, we can decide whether to imply a *Bivens* action in a case where an Eighth Amendment claim or state law differs significantly from those at issue here when and if such a case arises. The possibility of such a different future case does not provide sufficient grounds for reaching a different conclusion here.

For these reasons, where, as here, a federal prisoner seeks damages from privately employed personnel working at a privately operated federal prison, where the conduct allegedly amounts to a violation of the Eighth Amendment, and where that conduct is of a kind that typically falls within the scope of traditional state tort law (such as the conduct involving improper medical care at issue here), the prisoner must seek a remedy under state tort law. We cannot imply a *Bivens* remedy in such a case. The judgment of the Ninth Circuit is reversed.

JUSTICE SCALIA, with whom JUSTICE THOMAS joins, concurring.

I join the opinion of the Court because I agree that a narrow interpretation of the rationale of *Bivens v. Six Unknown Fed. Narcotics Agents*, 403 U.S. 388, 91 S. Ct. 1999, 29 L. Ed. 2d 619 (1971), would not cause the holding of that case to apply to the circumstances of this case. Even if the narrowest rationale of *Bivens* did apply here, however, I would decline to extend its holding. *Bivens* is "a relic of the heady days in which this Court assumed common-law powers to create causes of action" by constitutional implication. We have abandoned that power in the statutory field, see *Alexander v. Sandoval*, 532 U.S. 275, 287 (2001), and we should do the same in the constitutional field, where (presumably) an imagined "implication" cannot even be repudiated by Congress.

JUSTICE GINSBURG, dissenting.

Were Pollard incarcerated in a federal- or state-operated facility, he would have a federal remedy for the Eighth Amendment violations he alleges. See *Carlson v. Green*, 446 U.S. 14 (1980) (*Bivens* action); *Estelle v. Gamble*, 429 U.S. 97, 97 S. Ct. 285 (1976) (42 U.S.C. § 1983 action). I would not deny the same character of relief to Pollard, a prisoner placed by federal contract in a privately operated prison. Pollard may have suffered "aggravated instances" of conduct state tort law forbids, but that same aggravated conduct, when it is engaged in by official actors, also offends the Federal Constitution. Rather than remitting Pollard to the vagaries of state tort law, I would hold his injuries, sustained while serving a federal sentence, "compensable according to uniform rules of federal law," *Bivens v. Six Unknown Fed. Narcotics Agents*, 403 U.S. 388, 409 (1971) (Harlan, J., concurring in judgment).

NOTES

1. Does the remedy provided by state law adequately compensate individuals like the plaintiff in *Minneci*? Do the majority and the dissenter disagree on the answer to this question? If they do not, what accounts for the different views on the *Bivens* issue?

2. As noted, the Court has sometimes declined to recognize causes of action under *Bivens* in light of comprehensive congressionally authorized remedies. In *Minneci*, the Court extends the rationale of those opinions to adequate state law remedies. Is this analogy convincing? On the one hand, important separation-of-powers concerns are served by deferring to Congressional remedies, concerns that are not as evident in the context of state-law tort remedies. *See* Thomas Frampton, *Bivens Revisions: Constitutional Torts After* Minneci v. Pollard, 100 CAL. REV. 1711 (2012) (arguing that separation-of-powers concerns historically sustained objections to *Bivens*). On the other hand, if the chief goals of *Bivens* are compensation and deterrence, a cause of action under state law will presumably often serve those goals.

3. What does it mean for an alternative remedy to be adequate? In *Engel v. Buchan*, 710 F.3d 698, 699 (7th Cir. 2013), the Seventh Circuit held that neither the writ of habeas corpus, nor statutes providing compensation for wrongful convictions, served as an adequate substitute for a *Bivens* remedy when a federal official wrongfully fabricated evidence against a criminal defendant in violation of due process. Those alternative remedies, the court reasoned, failed to "provide roughly similar incentives for potential defendants to comply with [the constitutional requirements] while also providing roughly similar compensation to victims of violations."

4. In *Minneci*, the underlying constitutional violations had common law tort analogues such as negligence. Do all constitutional rights have analogues in state common law? Would the holding or reasoning of the case have been different if the defendants had violated plaintiffs' First Amendment right to free speech or exercise of religion? In considering that last question, would your answer change if the challenged unconstitutional conduct took place in a locale where the state constitution contained parallel protections for speech or religion?

5. *Minneci* involves private prison employees' alleged violations of the Eighth Amendment, including allegations of deliberate indifference to serious medical needs. What if the officials were employees of the federal government? At least two other legal provisions would bear on one's analysis. First, under the Westfall Act, suits against federal officials acting under the color of federal law for common law torts will generally be removed to federal court, and the federal government will be substituted as the defendant. 28 U.S.C. §§ 2671, 2679(b)(1).

Second, in *Hui v. Castaneda*, 559 U.S. 799, 800 (2010), the Supreme Court held that plaintiffs may not file constitutional claims for personal injuries against employees of the United States Public Health Service (PHS) for alleged inadequate medical care. In reaching this conclusion, the Court relied on the language of 42 U.S.C. § 233(a), a provision of the Federal Tort Claims Act. Section 233(a) permits plaintiffs to initiate suits against the United States for personal injuries arising from medical treatment performed by PHS officials acting within the scope of their employment. The section also provides that suits initiated directly against the United States "shall be exclusive of any other civil action or proceeding by reason of the same subject-matter against the officer or employee." The Court concluded that the existence of a federal remedy against the United States, accompanied by this clear language of exclusivity, precluded petitioner's claims against PHS employees for deliberate indifference to serious medical needs in violation of his Fifth and Eighth Amendment rights.

6.   The Court's holding in *Hui* — that the FTCA precluded *Bivens* remedies — was unanimous. Along parallel lines, can Congress preempt particular section 1983 constitutionally based claims by providing a different damages remedy? Consider *Smith v. Robinson*, 468 U.S. 992 (1984), where the Supreme Court held that Congress, in enacting the Education of the Handicapped Act (EHA), 20 U.S.C. § 1401 *et seq*, intended to exclude from section 1983's coverage independent equal protection claims identical to claims covered by the Act. Thus, according to the Court, the Act was the exclusive avenue for such claims. Congress responded to Smith by amending the EHA to provide explicitly that parallel equal protection and other constitutional claims are not preempted by the EHA and can in fact accompany claims based on the Act. However, such preemption issues continue to be litigated in the circuits. See, for example, *Pfeiffer v. School Board for Marion Center Area*, 917 F.2d 779 (3d Cir. 1990), where the Third Circuit relied on *Smith* in ruling that a former high school student's section 1983 sex discrimination claims were preempted by Title IX of the Education Amendments of 1972, 20 U.S.C. § 1681 et seq. However, the Sixth Circuit ruled to the contrary in *Lillard v. Shelby County Bd. of Educ.*, 76 F.3d 716 (6th Cir. 1996).

The Supreme Court, in *Fitzgerald v. Barnstable School Committee*, 555 U.S. 246 (2009), a unanimous decision written by Justice Alito, resolved the foregoing split in the circuits about Title IX and § 1983 equal protection sex discrimination claims and held that Title IX does not preempt such claims. The plaintiffs alleged that the defendant school committee and its superintendent inadequately responded to their allegations of sexual harassment of their daughter by an older student. This, according to plaintiffs, was actionable under both Title IX and the Equal Protection Clause pursuant to § 1983. The First Circuit dismissed the § 1983 claim on the ground that Title IX's implied private remedy was sufficiently comprehensive to preempt § 1983 equal protection peer-on-peer sexual harassment claims. However, the Supreme Court reversed.

According to the Court, there was no congressional intent to preempt: the absence of a comprehensive remedial scheme under Title IX and the divergent coverage of Title IX and the Equal Protection Clause so demonstrated. Title IX's only enforcement mechanism was an administrative procedure that could result in the withdrawal of federal funds. In addition, Title IX was narrower than the Equal Protection Clause insofar as Title IX did not authorize suits against school officials. But it was also broader insofar as Title IX covered even nonpublic institutions that receive federal funds. Congress thus did not see Title IX as the sole means of remedying sex discrimination in schools. Finally, this conclusion was consistent with Title IX's context and history, including the modeling of Title IX on Title VII, which lower courts regularly interpreted to allow for Title VII and parallel § 1983 claims.

7.   Are issues of Congressional intent and the administration of federal regulatory schemes that are implicated in *Bivens* actions comparable to those implicated in section 1983 "laws" actions, that is, actions based on state and local government violations of certain federal statutes? Should they be? After all, *Bivens* actions are based on the Constitution while "laws" actions are based on federal statutes. See Chapter 4 on "laws" actions.

8. When *Minneci* is read with *Chappell* and *Bush*, does it indicate that the development of *Bivens* actions has come to a halt? If so, is that necessarily a bad thing, given that Congress can create *Bivens*-like remedies for constitutional violations by federal officials similar to those provided by section 1983 for constitutional violations by state and local government officials? Consider that the Federal Tort Claims Act, noted above, provides damages remedies against the United States for certain wrongful conduct of its employees and officials, including "any claim . . . arising out of assault, battery, false imprisonment, false arrest, abuse of process or malicious prosecution [committed through the] acts or omissions of investigative or law enforcement officers of the United States government. . . ." Consider, too, that the Tucker Act and Little Tucker Act provide jurisdiction to specified federal courts to hear claims against the federal government for certain constitutional and contractual claims. All three of these acts, whose study are beyond the scope of this casebook, should be consulted whenever a damages action against federal officials is contemplated.

9. Should a *Bivens* action be available against a federal *agency*? In *F.D.I.C. v. Meyer*, 510 U.S. 471 (1994), the Supreme Court unanimously answered in the negative. The Court observed that *Bivens* itself was premised on the *absence* of a damages remedy against a federal agency. Thus, it would be illogical to extend *Bivens* to federal agencies. The Court also reasoned that such an extension would allow plaintiffs to bypass federal officials with qualified immunity and go directly after the federal agency. This would undermine the deterrent effect of *Bivens* actions, according to the Court. Do you agree with the latter argument? *Compare* local government liability, discussed in Chapter 5.

Consider also *Correctional Services v. Malesko*, 534 U.S. 61 (2001), which suggests that the current Court is especially reluctant to extend the *Bivens* doctrine. The plaintiff, an inmate at a halfway house for federal prisoners run by a private corporation under color of federal law, sought to use *Bivens* to bring an Eighth Amendment cruel and unusual punishment claim against the corporation. The Court rejected the *Bivens* claim, reasoning that the purpose of *Bivens* is to deter individual federal officers from committing constitutional violations and that a *Bivens* remedy would not further that purpose here. In addition, the availability of administrative remedies as well as state tort remedies for negligence adequately served a deterrent function as to the corporation. Thus, the plaintiff here was not a plaintiff in search of a remedy.

The Court's 2007 decision in *Wilkie v. Robbins*, 551 U.S. 537 (2007), similarly reflects its reluctance to expand the *Bivens* doctrine. Here, the plaintiff sued officials of the Federal Bureau of Land Management under *Bivens* alleging that they violated his Fifth Amendment rights in repeatedly trying to extort an easement from him. In an opinion by Justice Souter, the Court ruled that he had no *Bivens* claim. The Court first acknowledged that the forums and defenses available to the plaintiff were such a patchwork that it was difficult to infer from them whether Congress expected that the Court would not imply a *Bivens* remedy. However, the Court went on, over a dissent by Justices Ginsburg which was joined by Justice Stevens, to find that there were special factors counseling hesitation here, specifically "the difficulty of defining limits to legitimate zeal on the public's behalf in situations where hard bargaining is to be expected in the back-and-forth between public and private interests that the Government's employees engage in every day."

. Is *Bivens* effectively frozen? Consider the short concurring opinion by Justice Scalia which was joined by Justice Thomas, where they repeated their view that "*Bivens* is a relic of the heady days in which this Court assumed common-law powers to create causes of action" and that it should never be extended.

10. Keep in mind that in situations where *Bivens* actions are available, many of the legal rules applicable to section 1983 damages actions are similarly applicable to *Bivens* actions. For example, section 1983's absolute and qualified immunity rules govern *Bivens* actions. *See Butz v. Economou*, 438 U.S. 478 (1978), applying immunity rules and the functional approach to *Bivens* actions. *See also Mitchell v. Forsyth*, 472 U.S. 511 (1985), *Harlow v. Fitzgerald*, 457 U.S. 800 (1982) and *Anderson v. Creighton*, 483 U.S. 635 (1987), which developed complicated qualified immunity rules in *Bivens* settings and announced that those rules equally apply to section 1983 actions. Chapters 7 and 8 address absolute and qualified immunity. It is also likely that section 1983 damages rules apply to *Bivens* actions as well. See Chapter 9 on section 1983 remedies.

On the other hand, there is at least one situation in which *Bivens* immunity rules do *not* apply to section 1983. A state governor, a state's highest ranking executive official, is protected only by qualified immunity in section 1983 cases, but the President of the United States, the nation's highest ranking executive official, is protected by absolute immunity. *Compare Scheuer v. Rhodes*, 416 U.S. 232 (1974) (governor), *with Nixon v. Fitzgerald*, 457 U.S. 731 (1982) (President).

11. In *Ashcroft v. Iqbal*, 556 U.S. 662 (2009), the United States Supreme Court reversed a Second Circuit case involving *Bivens* claims against various federal officials (including John Aschroft, the former United States Attorney General, and Robert Mueller, Director of the F.B.I.) in the aftermath of 9/11. The plaintiff, a Muslim Pakastani, alleged that the defendants acted unconstitutionally in connection with his confinement under harsh conditions at a detention center after his separation from the general prison population. Specifically, he alleged that, as supervisors, they adopted and implemented an unconstitutional policy subjecting him to those harsh conditions because of his race, religion or national origin. Extensively discussing the possible effect of *Bell Atlantic v. Twombly*, 550 U.S. 544 (2007), on constitutional tort pleading requirements, the Second Circuit rejected the defendants' assertion of qualified immunity as to the supervisory liability claims against Ashcroft and Mueller and ruled that the plaintiff stated supervisory liability causes of action under *Bivens* against them. Thereafter, the Supreme Court granted certiorari to address the following Questions Presented:

> 1. Whether a conclusory allegation that a cabinet-level officer or other high-ranking official knew of, condoned, or agreed to subject a plaintiff to allegedly unconstitutional acts purportedly committed by subordinate officials is sufficient to state individual-capacity claims against those officials under *Bivens*.

> 2. Whether a cabinet-level officer or other high-ranking official may be held personally liable for the allegedly unconstitutional acts of subordinate

officials on the ground that, as high level supervisors, they had constructive notice of the discrimination allegedly carried out by such subordinate officials.

The Supreme Court reversed in a 5-4 opinion by Justice Kennedy. He observed at the outset that the defendants' motion to dismiss was made in connection with their qualified immunity defense. This defense was in large measure designed to protect them and defendants in general from the costs of defending, including the costs of discovery, and not just from liability — see Chapter 8. Accordingly, the plausibility standard of *Twombly* was fully applicable to *Bivens* and § 1983 claims, and was not limited to antitrust.

Next, the Court went on to declare that because respondeat superior liability was unavailable under *Bivens* and § 1983 — see Chapter 5 — it was not sufficient for supervisory liability purposes that the defendants might have acted with deliberate indifference to known violations by their subordinates of the plaintiff's constitutional rights. Rather, the plaintiff had to allege and ultimately prove that the defendants themselves actually had the impermissible purposes required for these alleged Due Process Clause (and its equal protection component) and Free Exercise Clause violations. Here, the plaintiff's allegations as to these purposes were conclusory and were thus not entitled to the presumption that they were true. As to the plaintiff's factual allegations, they were insufficient to render the plaintiff's allegations of purposeful and unlawful discrimination against these defendants plausible under F.R.C.P. 8(a)(2): they did not show that the defendants adopted and implemented the challenged policies because of race, religion or national origin rather than for neutral, investigative reasons. For all these reasons, the Court reversed the Second Circuit but remanded for that court to consider whether to allow the plaintiff to seek leave to amend the complaint against Ashcroft and Mueller.

Justice Souter, the author of *Twombly*, dissented in an opinion joined by Justices Stevens, Breyer and Ginsburg. He strongly disagreed with what he called the Court's rejection of the concession by the defendants that they could be held liable as supervisors for their deliberate indifference when they had actual knowledge of their subordinates' constitutional violations and criticized the Court for reaching out to declare that such deliberate indifference was insufficient for supervisory liability. Justice Souter contended that the Court had thereby effectively eliminated supervisory liability in *Bivens* (and § 1983) cases. He also accused the Court of misapplying *Twombly* to conclude that the plaintiff failed to state a claim. In his view, the factual allegations in the complaint as to the defendants' impermissible purposes sufficed to state a *Bivens* claim against them because he had alleged that at the very least they were aware of the discriminatory detention policy and condoned it. "*Twombly* does not require a court at the motion-to-dismiss stage to consider whether the factual allegations are *probably* true. We made it clear, on the contrary, that a court must take the allegations as true, no matter how skeptical the court may be." He concluded that there was no principled basis for the Court's disregard of plaintiff's allegations linking the defendants to their subordinates' racial, ethnic and religious discrimination.

As you proceed through the rest of this casebook you might ask yourself whether Congress should do for constitutional tort actions against federal officials (and perhaps the United States as an entity) what it did over one hundred years ago for Fourteenth Amendment violations committed by state and local government officials and employees and local governments themselves. *See* Nichol, *Bivens, Chilicky and Constitutional Damages Claims*, 75 VA. L. REV. 1117 (1989). Recall also, as you study the rest of these materials, the underlying structure of all constitutional tort actions: (1) the elements of the prima facie case, including duty, basis of liability and causation, and (2) available immunities and defenses.

12. In *Iqbal*, the Court assumed without deciding that plaintiffs could rely on *Bivens* to vindicate alleged violations of First Amendment Free Exercise claims. Before doing so, however, the Court reiterated its traditional reluctance toward expanding *Bivens* liability "to any new context." As noted, the Court has been especially reluctant to expand *Bivens* to new contexts when (1) alternative remedies were available, or (2) "special factors" counsel hesitation before finding an implied constitutional cause of action. "That reluctance" the majority wrote in *Iqbal*, "might well have disposed of respondent's First Amendment claim of religious discrimination." Noting that the defendants did not press that particular argument, however, the Court declined to further engage it.

13. An open question after *Iqbal* is whether the Court's reluctance toward expanding *Bivens* to new contexts applies only to new legal contexts, or whether it applies to new factual contexts as well. The Second Circuit recently relied primarily on a plaintiff's factual allegations in concluding that he sought to expand *Bivens* to "a new context." *Arar v. Ashcroft*, 585 F.3d 559, 564 (2d Cir. 2009) (*en banc*).

Maher Arar, a dual Syrian-Canadian citizen who resided in Canada, alleged that he was stopped during a layover at John F. Kennedy Airport in New York, New York in 2002. Based on a tip, federal officials suspected Arar of terrorism and detained him. He alleged that he was then interrogated for six hours, during which his requests for a lawyer went unheeded. He further alleged that in accordance with a practice of the federal government known as "extraordinary rendition," that he was transported to Syria so that officials there could torture him. Arar contended that when federal officials shipped him to a foreign country to be tortured, his conduct violated his Substantive Due Process rights.

While the Second Circuit had previously recognized Substantive Due Process damages claims against federal officials, the Second Circuit concluded 6-4 that "extraordinary rendition" constituted a new context. The majority explained that no other court had yet recognized a *Bivens* claim for the practice of extraordinary rendition. The court then observed that special factors hesitated against extending *Bivens* to Arar's claims. Specifically, Arar's suit implicated national security, an area in which the judiciary often defers to executive branch. In addition, federal courts would have to review classified information to adjudicate Arar's claims. This reality carried one of two risks. On the one hand, public disclosure of classified information could compromise the federal government's relationship with other countries. On the other hand, reviewing key evidence through limited *in camera* review would undermine the United States' commitment to open courts.

The dissenters disagreed that Arar's claims constituted a new context, marshaling prior cases within that circuit that recognized *Bivens* claims for conduct against federal detainees that "shocked the conscience." They also weighed the special factors differently than the majority. "The conduct of foreign policy and the maintenance of national security are surely executive and legislative powers," Judge Barrington Parker wrote in dissent. "Yet those powers are not limitless. The bounds in both wartime and peacetime are fixed by the same Constitution. Where appropriate, deference to the coordinate branches is an essential element of our work. But there is, in my view, an enormous difference between being deferential and being supine in the face of governmental misconduct." Judge Guido Calabresi authored a dissent that used similarly strong language, charging that the majority had engaged in "extraordinary judicial activism," unjustifiably leaving a victim of lawless conduct with no remedy.

How narrowly should courts define "new context" when determining whether to apply *Bivens* liability? Consider that each case comes with unique facts, and the level of generality a court uses to characterize those facts is important. Consider also that unlike constitutional claims against state actors, Congress has not yet created a similar private cause of action for most constitutional violations committed by officials acting under the color of federal law. Which federal branches are best equipped to fashion the scope of remedies for constitutional violations?

14. In the years following *Arar*, the Fourth, Seventh, and D.C. Circuits all similarly held that special factors counseled against recognizing a *Bivens* remedy for alleged torture that had a nexus with the United States' military and national security interests. In *Lebron v. Rumsfeld*, 670 F.3d 540 (4th Cir. 2012), a United States citizen who was detained as an enemy combatant attempted to seek redress both for his designation as an enemy combatant, and torture that he purportedly experienced while in military custody. The Fourth Circuit declined to recognize a *Bivens* remedy, citing the importance of "[p]reserving the constitutionally prescribed balance of powers," and the ways in which the case implicated the military command structure.

Similarly, in *Vance v. Rumsfeld*, 701 F.3d 193 (7th Cir. 2012), the Seventh Circuit held that no *Bivens* remedy was available for an American citizen who alleged that he was wrongfully detained and tortured when serving as a military contractor in Iraq. The court relied in part on the special factors counseling hesitation, observing that "the torture claims [arose] from military custody in the controlled, non-combat environment of military prisons in an overseas war zone."

Cases in the D.C. Circuit have met a similar fate. In *Ali v. Rumsfeld*, 649 F.3d 762 (D.C. Cir. 2011), that court addressed whether Iraqi and Afghan detainees captured and held abroad by the United States military could bring constitutional claims against United States military personnel. In rejecting such claims, the court explained that "allowing a *Bivens* action to be brought against American military officials engaged in war would disrupt and hinder the ability of our armed forces to act decisively and without hesitation in defense of our liberty and national interests." *Ali*, 649 F.3d at 773. That court reaffirmed that holding in *Doe v. Rumsfeld*, 683 F.3d 390 (D.C. Cir. 2012), dismissing similar claims by United States citizens.

Chapter 2

"UNDER COLOR OF" STATE LAW

Section 1983 grants a remedy only for acts taken "under color of any statute, ordinance, regulation, custom, or usage, of any State or Territory or the District of Columbia." The Fourteenth Amendment, which furnishes the substantive law for most section 1983 suits, declares that "[n]o *State* shall . . . deprive any person of life, liberty, or property, without due process of law; nor deny to any person . . . the equal protection of the laws." (emphasis added). This chapter addresses three questions raised by these provisions: (1) Which acts of public officials are covered by the statute, and which are not? (2) What is the relationship between "under color of" and the "state action" requirement for application of the Fourteenth Amendment? (3) When may a plaintiff sue private actors under section 1983?

Part I takes up the first of these questions, Part II the second, and Part III the third. Although the first two inquiries are of great theoretical importance and sometimes present difficult issues, the third is the most complex of the three and receives the most attention here. With the growth of privatization these issues will likely increase in importance. *See* Gillian Metzger, *Privatization as Delegation*, 103 COLUM. L. REV. 1367 (2003).

I. THE MEANING OF "UNDER COLOR OF"

A. *Monroe* and "Under Color Of"

The Supreme Court construed the statutory term "under color of [state law]" in *Monroe v. Pape.* That case is discussed at length in Chapter 1. The Court held that actions by state officers that violate state law may still be "under color of" state law. According to the Court, "it is no answer that the state has a law which if enforced would give relief. The federal remedy is supplementary to the state remedy, and the latter need not be first sought and refused before the federal one is invoked." Quoting an earlier case construing the same phrase in a criminal civil rights statute, the Court said the phrase "under color of" embraces "[m]isuse of power, possessed by virtue of state law and made possible only because the wrongdoer is clothed with the authority of state law." *Monroe v. Pape*, 365 U.S. 167, 184, *quoting United States v. Classic*, 313 U.S. 299, 326 (1941).

B. The Boundaries of "Under Color Of"

Though officers whose conduct is proscribed by state law nonetheless act under color of law, it does not follow that every single action taken by a state officer is actionable under section 1983. A distinction must be drawn between cases where the actor's official status is more or less irrelevant, and those where, however personal the officer's aims, his use of the authority or accoutrements of office contributes significantly to the harm he is able to do. Some cases are easy. A high school principal who shoots his neighbor in the course of an argument over a noisy stereo does not act under color of state law. A policeman who, in the course of an arrest, carries out a personal grudge by beating a helpless suspect does act under color of state law. Consider *Johnson v. Phillips*, 664 F.3d. 232, 240 (8th Cir. 2011), in which the court thought the facts presented an issue for the jury:

> Here, Phillips first effected a traffic stop, arrested Johnson on an outstanding warrant, and searched her car. Then, while wearing a police uniform and operating a police car, he released Johnson from the patrol car and directed her to follow him in her car. A reasonable factfinder believing these facts could conclude that Phillips was purporting to act as a police officer performing official duties when he led Johnson to the empty parking lot and committed the sexual assault.

Here are some cases that present a variety of line-drawing problems:

1. A recurring fact-pattern features the conduct of off-duty officers. Consider *Rossignol v. Voorhaar*, 316 F.3d 516 (4th Cir. 2003): "Several deputies in the Sheriff's Office anticipated that the election day issue of [the local newspaper] would be critical of them and their favored candidates. [Over] the course of a series of meetings and conversations, both on the job at the Sheriff's Office and in the evening at private homes, some of the deputies formulated a plan to deal with this problem. They decided to form two teams on election day, each comprising three sheriff's deputies, and buy out the stock of the [newspaper] at vending locations throughout the county. [Late] on the night before the election, [off-duty,] wearing plainclothes, and driving their personal cars[,] they drove through the county, buying newspapers. [Many] of the clerks who interacted with defendants during the night knew that they were sheriff's deputies." One clerk testified that he felt intimidated by the officers. After establishing that the purchases would violate the First Amendment if carried out by state actors, the court addressed the state action issue. It stressed the job-related motivation behind the purchase:

> The requisite nexus between defendants' public office and their actions during the seizure arose initially out of their censorial motivation. [They] executed a systematic, carefully-organized plan to suppress the distribution of [the newspaper.] And they did so to retaliate against those who questioned their fitness for public office and who challenged many of them in the conduct of their official duties.

What result if there were no evidence of intimidation? Would the officers commit a constitutional violation if they pooled their resources and bought the company that publishes the newspaper?

In the more typical case, the off-duty officer inflicts personal injury. "[W]hile it is clear that 'personal pursuits' of police officers do not give rise to section 1983 liability, there is no bright line test for distinguishing 'personal pursuits' from activities taken under color of law." *Pitchell v. Callan*, 13 F.3d 545, 548 (2d Cir. 1994). If the officer uses police equipment, and is doing police business, courts generally hold that the policeman acts under color of law. *See, e.g., Layne v. Sampley*, 627 F.2d

12 (6th Cir. 1980); *Stengel v. Belcher*, 522 F.2d 438 (6th Cir. 1975). Suppose the off-duty officer violently attacks someone for purely personal reasons? If he uses a weapon that belongs to him and is not doing police business, the act is not under color of law. *See, e.g., Huffman v. County of Los Angeles*, 147 F.3d 1054 (9th Cir. 1998) (ruling that, in such circumstances, using bullets supplied by the county is not sufficient to establish state action).

When the officer abuses his position for the sake of a personal motive, the cases are mixed. *See United States v. Tarpley*, 945 F.2d 806, 809 (5th Cir. 1991) (prosecution under the criminal counterpart of section 1983; defendant assaulted his former wife's lover using his service weapon; then he and another officer ran the victim out of town in a squad car; this amounted to action under color of law). By contrast, *Parrilla-Burgos v. Hernandez-Rivera*, 108 F.3d 445 (1st Cir. 1997), stressed the personal motivation of the police officers in finding no state action where off-duty police officers displayed their badges and used their service revolvers in the course of a bar room brawl.

On duty officers who do harm while pursuing their private ends are often, though not always, deemed to act under color of law. In *Doe v. Smith*, 470 F.3d 331 (7th Cir. 2006), the plaintiff, Doe, was a public school student who had been charged with delinquency. Smith was the Dean of Students at the school. Doe accused Smith of sexual abuse off school property. The court denied Smith's motion for summary judgment, ruling that if Doe could prove his allegations he could meet the "under color of" requirement:

> [T]he juvenile court released Doe to Smith's custody with the express agreement that the dean would take the boy to register for [school.] Doe alleges that he was never taken to register for school that day, but was instead taken to Smith's home for further [sexual abuse.] Smith's opportunity to molest him that day was made possible because Smith used his authority as the dean to persuade the juvenile court judge to release Doe to his custody.

470 F.3d at 340. *Compare Cassady v. Tackett*, 938 F.2d 693, 695 (6th Cir. 1991) (defendant, an elected county jailor, allegedly threatened to kill the plaintiff, the executive director of the jail, on jail premises; defendant "had the authority or power to carry the gun in the jail only because he was the elected jailor of [the county]. That [defendant] acted against a fellow employee is of no matter . . . ";), *with Honaker v. Smith*, 256 F.3d 477 (7th Cir. 2001) (fire chief did not act under color of state law when he set a fire for personal reasons).

2. What result if a police officer who was suspended as mentally unfit for duty, yet was permitted to keep his gun and ammunition, shoots someone with the gun? *Gibson v. City of Chicago*, 910 F.2d 1510, 1517 (7th Cir. 1990) holds that he is not a state actor. "[W]hether Novit acted under color of law turns primarily on the legal effect of the March 3 order that directed Novit not to carry a weapon or exercise any police powers . . . While it is no doubt true that an officer who, motivated by personal animus, misuses his lawfully possessed authority to injure the plaintiff may be found to be acting under 'pretense' of law, we have found no authority for expanding this concept of 'pretense' of law to encompass the actions of an official who possessed *absolutely no authority* to act but nonetheless assumed the position of an imposter in pretending that he did." (emphasis in original). Is this reasoning compatible with *Monroe*? Suppose the officer kept his uniform as well?

Under the reasoning of *Gibson*, would a game warden who has no power generally to enforce state law act under color of law when he calls a deputy sheriff to have the plaintiff arrested? *See Hughes v. Meyer*, 880 F.2d 967, 972 (7th Cir. 1989) (not state action). Would an officer act under color of state law when the terms of his employment provide that he is under no obligation to intervene while off-duty, but he does so anyway? Suppose he is forbidden to intervene while off duty?

3. Police officers sometimes take second jobs as security guards. Are their actions under color of law? *See, e.g., Griffin v. Maryland*, 378 U.S. 130 (1964); *Lusby v. TG&Y Stores, Inc.*, 749 F.2d 1423 (10th Cir. 1984); *Traver v. Meshriy*, 627 F.2d 934 (9th Cir. 1980) (holding that they are). In all three cases the policeman's work as a security guard was related to his official status. *Griffin* found state action when an amusement park security guard had been deputized as a county sheriff and identified himself as a deputy sheriff when arresting the plaintiffs. The officer in *Traver* identified himself as a police officer when he stopped the plaintiff, and had obtained his job through a police department program. In *Lusby*, the officer "flashed his badge and identified himself as a Lawton police officer working as a security guard for T.G.&Y."

Would the result be different if the officer makes no pretense that he is acting under state authority? *See Watkins v. Oaklawn Jockey Club*, 183 F.2d 440, 443 (8th Cir. 1950) (no state action). What if the plaintiff knows that the officer is acting as a private guard, even though he is in police uniform? *Robinson v. Davis*, 447 F.2d 753, 758–59 (4th Cir. 1971) holds that the officer does not act under color of state law. Sound?

In *Chapman v. Higbee Co.*, 256 F.3d 416 (6th Cir. 2001), a Sixth Circuit panel ruled that an off-duty sheriff's deputy, working as a security guard, was not a state actor when he detained and searched the plaintiff, even though he was wearing his uniform, badge, and sidearm at the time. But the en banc court reversed. *See* 319 F.3d 825 (6th Cir. 2003) (*en banc*). Which ruling seems more consistent with the other police-officer-as-security guard cases?

4. Does a county magistrate judge act under color of state law when he participates with local police in the pursuit and arrest of his daughter's former boyfriend, whom he accuses of having stolen the family dog? *See Myers v. Bowman*, 713 F.3d 1319 (11th Cir. 2013) (no, because the police officer "would have made the arrest even if [the judge] had not been present at the scene or directed [the officer] to remove [plaintiff] from the vehicle"). In another Eleventh Circuit case, the complaint asserted that the defendant, a corrections officer in the sheriff's office, returned home from work wearing her uniform, gun belt and pistol, to find the plaintiff (a young man) naked in the bedroom closet of her (also naked) daughter. She punched him, held him at gunpoint, handcuffed him, threatened to shoot him and "made him get down on his knees . . . for a prolonged period." Did she act under color of state law? *See Butler v. Sheriff of Palm Beach County*, 685 F.3d 1261 (11th Cir. 2012) (no, because "any irate mother with an anger management problem could have done what Collier did.") Are state law tort suits available to the plaintiffs in these cases?

II. "UNDER COLOR OF" AND STATE ACTION

The relation between "under color of" law and state action is addressed in the following case. This case is relevant as well to Part III, which discusses the use of section 1983 to sue private actors.

LUGAR v. EDMONDSON OIL CO.
457 U.S. 922 (1982)

JUSTICE WHITE delivered the opinion of the Court.

This case concerns the relationship between the § 1983 requirement of action under color of state law and the Fourteenth Amendment requirement of state action.

I

In 1977, petitioner, a lessee-operator of a truckstop in Virginia, was indebted to his supplier, Edmondson Oil Co., Inc. Edmondson sued on the debt in Virginia state court. Ancillary to that action and pursuant to state law, Edmondson sought prejudgment attachment of certain of petitioner's property. The prejudgment attachment procedure required only that Edmondson allege, in an ex parte petition, a belief that petitioner was disposing of or might dispose of his property in order to defeat his creditors. Acting upon that petition, a Clerk of the state court issued a writ of attachment, which was then executed by the County Sheriff. This effectively sequestered petitioner's property, although it was left in his possession. Pursuant to the statute, a hearing on the propriety of the attachment and levy was later conducted. Thirty-four days after the levy, a state trial judge ordered the attachment dismissed because Edmondson had failed to establish the statutory grounds for attachment alleged in the petition.

Petitioner subsequently brought this action under 42 U.S.C. § 1983 against Edmondson and its president. His complaint alleged that in attaching his property respondents had acted jointly with the State to deprive him of his property without due process of law. The lower courts construed the complaint as alleging a due process violation both from a misuse of the Virginia procedure and from the statutory procedure itself. He sought compensatory and punitive damages for specified financial loss allegedly caused by the improvident attachment . . . .

[The Court of Appeals] distinguished between the acts directly chargeable to respondents and the larger context within which those acts occurred, including the direct levy by state officials on petitioner's property. While the latter no doubt amounted to state action, the former was not so clearly action under color of state law. The court held that a private party acts under color of state law within the meaning of § 1983 only when there is a usurpation or corruption of official power by the private litigant or a surrender of judicial power to the private litigant in such a way that the independence of the enforcing officer has been compromised to a significant degree. Because the court thought none of these elements was present here, the complaint failed to allege conduct under color of state law.

Because this construction of the under-color-of-state-law requirement appears to be inconsistent with prior decisions of this Court, we granted certiorari.

II

Although the Court of Appeals correctly perceived the importance of *Flagg Brothers v. Brooks* to a proper resolution of this case, it misread that case. It also failed to give sufficient weight to that line of cases, beginning with *Sniadach v. Family Finance Corp.*, in which the Court considered constitutional due process requirements in the context of garnishment actions and prejudgment attachments. See *North Georgia Finishing, Inc. v. Di-Chem, Inc., Mitchell v. W.T. Grant Co., Fuentes v. Shevin*. Each of these cases involved a finding of state action as an implicit predicate of the application of due process standards. *Flagg Brothers* distinguished them on the ground that in each there was overt, official involvement in the property deprivation; there was no such overt action by a state officer in *Flagg Brothers*. Although this case falls on the *Sniadach*, and not the *Flagg Brothers*, side of this distinction, the Court of Appeals thought the garnishment and attachment cases to be irrelevant because none but *Fuentes* arose under 42 U.S.C. § 1983 and because *Fuentes* was distinguishable. It determined that it could ignore all of them because the issue in this case was not whether there was state action, but rather whether respondents acted under color of state law.

As we see it, however, the two concepts cannot be so easily disentangled. Whether they are identical or not, the state-action and the under-color-of-state-law requirements are obviously related.[1] Indeed, until recently this Court did not distinguish between the two requirements at all.

In *United States v. Price* we explicitly stated that the requirements were identical: "In cases under § 1983, 'under color' of law has consistently been treated as the same thing as the 'state action' required under the Fourteenth Amendment." In support of this proposition the Court cited *Smith v. Allwright* and *Terry v. Adams*. In both of these cases black voters in Texas challenged their exclusion from party primaries as a violation of the Fifteenth Amendment and sought relief under 8 U.S.C. § 43 (1946 ed.). In each case, the Court understood the problem before it to be whether the discriminatory policy of a private political association could be characterized as "state action within the meaning of the Fifteenth Amendment." *Smith*, supra. Having found state action under the Constitution, there was no further inquiry into whether the action of the political associations also met the statutory requirement of action "under color of state law."

Similarly, it is clear that in a § 1983 action brought against a state official, the statutory requirement of action "under color of state law" and the "state action" requirement of the Fourteenth Amendment are identical. The Court's conclusion in *United States v. Classic* that "[misuse] of power, possessed by virtue of state law

---

[1] [8] The Court of Appeals itself recognized this when it stated that in two of three basic patterns of section 1983 litigation — that in which the defendant is a public official and that in which he is a private party — there is no distinction between state action and action under color of state law. Only when there is joint action by private parties and state officials, the court stated, could a distinction arise between these two requirements.

and made possible only because the wrongdoer is clothed with the authority of state law, is action taken 'under color of' state law," was founded on the rule announced in *Ex parte Virginia* that the actions of a state officer who exceeds the limits of his authority constitute state action for purposes of the Fourteenth Amendment.

[To] read the "under color of any statute" language of the Act in such a way as to impose a limit on those Fourteenth Amendment violations that may be redressed by the § 1983 cause of action would be wholly inconsistent with the purpose of § 1 of the Civil Rights Act of 1871, from which § 1983 is derived. The Act was passed "for the express purpose of [enforcing] the Provisions of the Fourteenth Amendment." *Lynch v. Household Finance Corp.* The history of the Act is replete with statements indicating that Congress thought it was creating a remedy as broad as the protection that the Fourteenth Amendment affords the individual. Perhaps the most direct statement of this was that of Senator Edmunds, the manager of the bill in the Senate: "[Section 1 is] so very simple and really [reenacts] the Constitution." Cong. Globe, 42d Cong., 1st Sess., 569 (1871). Representative Bingham similarly stated that the bill's purpose was "the enforcement . . . of the Constitution on behalf of every individual citizen of the Republic . . . to the extent of the rights guarantied to him by the Constitution."

In sum, the line drawn by the Court of Appeals is inconsistent with our prior cases and would substantially undercut the congressional purpose in providing the § 1983 cause of action. If the challenged conduct of respondents constitutes state action as delimited by our prior decisions, then that conduct was also action under color of state law and will support a suit under § 1983.[2]

---

[2] [18] Our conclusion in this case is not inconsistent with the statement in *Flagg Brothers* that "these two elements [state action and action under color of state law] denote two separate areas of inquiry." First, although we hold that conduct satisfying the state-action requirement of the Fourteenth Amendment satisfies the statutory requirement of action under color of state law, it does not follow from that all conduct that satisfies the under-color-of-state-law requirement would satisfy the Fourteenth Amendment requirement of state action. If action under color of state law means nothing more than that the individual act "with the knowledge of and pursuant to that statute," *Adickes v. S.H. Kress & Co.* then clearly under *Flagg Brothers* that would not, in itself, satisfy the state-action requirement of the Fourteenth Amendment. Second, although we hold in this case that the under-color-of-state-law requirement does not add anything not already included within the state-action requirement of the Fourteenth Amendment, § 1983 is applicable to other constitutional provisions and statutory provisions that contain no state-action requirement. Where such a federal right is at issue, the statutory concept of action under color of state law would be a distinct element of the case not satisfied implicitly by a finding of a violation of the particular federal right.

Nor is our decision today inconsistent with *Polk County v. Dodson*. In *Polk County*, we held that a public defender's actions, when performing a lawyer's traditional functions as counsel in a state criminal proceeding, would not support a § 1983 suit. Although we analyzed the public defender's conduct in light of the requirement of action "under color of state law," we specifically stated that it was not necessary in that case to consider whether that requirement was identical to the "state action" requirement of the Fourteenth Amendment: "Although this Court has sometimes treated the questions as if they were identical, we need not consider their relationship in order to decide this case." We concluded there that a public defender, although a state employee, in the day-to-day defense of his client, acts under canons of professional ethics in a role adversarial to the State. Accordingly, although state employment is generally sufficient to render the defendant a state actor under our analysis, it was "peculiarly difficult" to detect any action of the State in the circumstances of that case. In *Polk County*, we also rejected respondent's claims against governmental agencies because he "failed to allege any policy that arguably violated his rights under the Sixth, Eighth, or Fourteenth Amendments." Because respondent failed to

III

As a matter of substantive constitutional law the state-action requirement reflects judicial recognition of the fact that "most rights secured by the Constitution are protected only against infringement by governments," *Flagg Brothers*. As the Court said in *Jackson v. Metropolitan Edison Co.*:

> "In 1883, this Court in the *Civil Rights Cases* affirmed the essential dichotomy set forth in [the Fourteenth] Amendment between deprivation by the State, subject to scrutiny under its provisions, and private conduct, 'however discriminatory or wrongful,' against which the Fourteenth Amendment offers no shield."

Careful adherence to the "state action" requirement preserves an area of individual freedom by limiting the reach of federal law and federal judicial power. It also avoids imposing on the State, its agencies or officials, responsibility for conduct for which they cannot fairly be blamed. A major consequence is to require the courts to respect the limits of their own power as directed against state governments and private interests. Whether this is good or bad policy, it is a fundamental fact of our political order.

Our cases have accordingly insisted that the conduct allegedly causing the deprivation of a federal right be fairly attributable to the State. These cases reflect a two-part approach to this question of "fair attribution." First, the deprivation must be caused by the exercise of some right or privilege created by the State or by a rule of conduct imposed by the State or by a person for whom the State is responsible. In *Sniadach, Fuentes, W. T. Grant*, and *North Georgia*, for example, a state statute provided the right to garnish or to obtain prejudgment attachment, as well as the procedure by which the rights could be exercised. Second, the party charged with the deprivation must be a person who may fairly be said to be a state actor. This may be because he is a state official, because he has acted together with or has obtained significant aid from state officials, or because his conduct is otherwise chargeable to the State. Without a limit such as this, private parties could face constitutional litigation whenever they seek to rely on some state rule governing their interactions with the community surrounding them.

Although related, these two principles are not the same. They collapse into each other when the claim of a constitutional deprivation is directed against a party whose official character is such as to lend the weight of the State to his decisions. See *Monroe v. Pape*. The two principles diverge when the constitutional claim is directed against a party without such apparent authority, i.e., against a private party. The difference between the two inquiries is well illustrated by comparing *Moose Lodge No. 107 v. Irvis* with *Flagg Brothers*, supra.

In *Moose Lodge*, the Court held that the discriminatory practices of the appellant did not violate the Equal Protection Clause because those practices did not constitute "state action." The Court focused primarily on the question of whether

---

challenge any rule of conduct or decision for which the State was responsible, his allegations would not support a claim of state action under the analysis proposed below. Thus, our decision today does not suggest a different outcome in *Polk County*.

the admittedly discriminatory policy could in any way be ascribed to a governmental decision. The inquiry, therefore, looked to those policies adopted by the State that were applied to appellant. The Court concluded as follows:

> "We therefore hold, that with the exception hereafter noted, the operation of the regulatory scheme enforced by the Pennsylvania Liquor Control Board does not sufficiently implicate the State in the discriminatory guest policies of Moose Lodge to . . . make the latter 'state action' within the ambit of the Equal Protection Clause of the Fourteenth Amendment." In other words, the decision to discriminate could not be ascribed to any governmental decision; those governmental decisions that did affect Moose Lodge were unconnected with its discriminatory policies.[3]

Flagg Brothers focused on the other component of the state-action principle. In that case, the warehouseman proceeded under New York Uniform Commercial Code, § 7-210, and the debtor challenged the constitutionality of that provision on the grounds that it violated the Due Process and Equal Protection Clauses of the Fourteenth Amendment. Undoubtedly the State was responsible for the statute. The response of the Court, however, focused not on the terms of the statute but on the character of the defendant to the § 1983 suit: Action by a private party pursuant to this statute, without something more, was not sufficient to justify a characterization of that party as a "state actor." The Court suggested that "something more" which would convert the private party into a state actor might vary with the circumstances of the case. This was simply a recognition that the Court has articulated a number of different factors or tests in different contexts: *e.g.*, the "public function" test, see *Terry v. Adams*; *Marsh v. Alabama*; the "state compulsion" test, see *Adickes v. S.H. Kress & Co.*; the "nexus" test, see *Jackson v. Metropolitan Edison Co.*; *Burton v. Wilmington Parking Authority*; and, in the case of prejudgment attachments, a "joint action test," *Flagg Brothers*. Whether these different tests are actually different in operation or simply different ways of characterizing the necessarily fact-bound inquiry that confronts the Court in such a situation need not be resolved here. See *Burton*, supra, ("Only by sifting facts and weighing circumstances can the nonobvious involvement of the State in private conduct be attributed its true significance").

IV

Turning to this case, the first question is whether the claimed deprivation has resulted from the exercise of a right or privilege having its source in state authority. The second question is whether, under the facts of this case, respondents, who are private parties, may be appropriately characterized as "state actors."

Both the District Court and the Court of Appeals noted the ambiguous scope of petitioner's contentions: "There has been considerable confusion throughout the

---

[3] [20] The "one exception" further illustrates this point. The Court enjoined enforcement of a state rule requiring Moose Lodge to comply with its own constitution and bylaws insofar as they contained racially discriminatory provisions. State enforcement of this rule, either judicially or administratively, would, under the circumstances, amount to a governmental decision to adopt a racially discriminatory policy.

litigation on the question whether Lugar's ultimate claim of unconstitutional deprivation was directed at the Virginia statute itself or only at its erroneous application to him." Both courts held that resolution of this ambiguity was not necessary to their disposition of the case: both resolved it, in any case, in favor of the view that petitioner was attacking the constitutionality of the statute as well as its misapplication. In our view, resolution of this issue is essential to the proper disposition of the case.

Petitioner presented three counts in his complaint. Count three was a pendent claim based on state tort law; counts one and two claimed violations of the Due Process Clause. Count two alleged that the deprivation of property resulted from respondents' 'malicious, wanton, willful, oppressive [sic], [and] unlawful acts." By "unlawful," petitioner apparently meant "unlawful under state law." To say this, however, is to say that the conduct of which petitioner complained could not be ascribed to any governmental decision; rather, respondents were acting contrary to the relevant policy articulated by the State. Nor did they have the authority of state officials to put the weight of the State behind their private decision, i.e., this case does not fall within the abuse of authority doctrine recognized in *Monroe v. Pape*. That respondents invoked the statute without the grounds to do so could in no way be attributed to a state rule or a state decision. Count two, therefore, does not state a cause of action under § 1983 but challenges only private action.

Count one is a different matter. That count describes the procedures followed by respondents in obtaining the prejudgment attachment as well as the fact that the state court subsequently ordered the attachment dismissed because respondents had not met their burden under state law. Petitioner then summarily states that this sequence of events deprived him of his property without due process. Although it is not clear whether petitioner is referring to the state-created procedure or the misuse of that procedure by respondents, we agree with the lower courts that the better reading of the complaint is that petitioner challenges the state statute as procedurally defective under the Fourteenth Amendment.

While private misuse of a state statute does not describe conduct that can be attributed to the State, the procedural scheme created by the statute obviously is the product of state action. This is subject to constitutional restraints and properly may be addressed in a § 1983 action, if the second element of the state-action requirement is met as well.

As is clear from the discussion in Part II, we have consistently held that a private party's joint participation with state officials in the seizure of disputed property is sufficient to characterize that party as a "state actor" for purposes of the Fourteenth Amendment.

[In] summary, petitioner was deprived of his property through state action; respondents were, therefore, acting under color of state law in participating in that deprivation. Petitioner did present a valid cause of action under § 1983 insofar as he challenged the constitutionality of the Virginia statute; he did not insofar as he alleged only misuse or abuse of the statute.

NOTES

1. Notice that the statutory "under color of" requirement and the constitutional "state action" requirement turn out to be coextensive, or nearly so. Does the convergence stem more from the intentions of the framers of the Fourteenth Amendment and section 1983, or from modern Supreme Court policy-making?

In 1871, at the time section 1983 was enacted, Congress seems to have given little attention to the possibility that a "state action" requirement may significantly limit the reach of the Fourteenth Amendment. That constitutional provision had just been ratified and there was much uncertainty about its proper interpretation. Turning to section 1983, the debates indicate that many members of Congress viewed it as a means by which to regulate the conduct of private citizens. Indeed, the central aim of the Civil Rights Act of 1871 was to provide means by which federal officers and federal courts could fight Ku Klux Klan terrorism against blacks and their white supporters. *See* Michael Wells, *The Past and the Future of Constitutional Torts*, 19 CONN. L. REV. 53, 65–68 (1986).

Similar observations have been made about other Reconstruction-Era statutes. According to Professor Eisenberg, "Congress' enactment and the Court's invalidation of the Civil Rights Act of 1875 . . . and of other nineteenth century civil rights laws suggest that the Reconstruction Congresses did not anticipate the broad outlines of the state action doctrine." Theodore Eisenberg, *Section 1983: Doctrinal Foundations and an Empirical Study*, 67 CORNELL L. REV. 482, 509 n.108 (1982). Professor Eisenberg refers to the Civil Rights Act of 1875, which had prohibited private proprietors of hotels, theaters, railroads, and other public accommodations from discriminating on the basis of race. The Court struck down the statute on the ground that the Fourteenth Amendment reaches only state action and not the acts of private individuals. *Civil Rights Cases*, 109 U.S. 3 (1883).

2. One circumstance in which the "under color of state law" requirement has teeth independent of "state action" arises when someone tries to sue a federal official under section 1983. Only where the federal officials have collaborated with state officers will they be deemed to have acted under color of *state law. See, e.g., Beechwood Restorative Care Ctr. v. Leeds*, 436 F.3d 147, 154 (2d Cir. 2006); *Strickland v. Shalala*, 123 F.3d 863 (6th Cir. 1997). Otherwise, the plaintiff is required to find some other statute authorizing suit against the federal officer, or else to bring a *Bivens* suit. On the latter, see Chapter 1. *See, e.g., Rogers v. Vicuna*, 264 F.3d 1 (1st Cir. 2001).

Cabrera v. Martin, 973 F.2d 735 (9th Cir. 1992), is an illustrative case. Labor organizations and private employers challenged a decision by the governor of California to unilaterally request the United States Secretary of Labor to withdraw approval of California's occupational safety and health plan. Besides the Governor and other state officials, they sued the Secretary of Labor and two other federal Labor Department officials seeking injunctive relief prohibiting the Secretary from accepting the Governor's request.

The court held that the federal officials did not act under color of state law, despite a lower court finding that they had engaged in " 'significant and substantial cooperation' with the Governor in accepting his withdrawal of Cal-OSHA." In particular, the district court "placed special emphasis on the fact that the Secretary changed his policy in mid-stream by deciding in September 1987 to accept Governor Deukmejian's letter of withdrawal and assume exclusive jurisdiction over California's occupational safety matters." The court continued:

> [Even so,] [f]ederal officials do not become state actors unless [t]he State has so far insinuated itself into a position of interdependence with [the federal officials] that it must be recognized as a joint participant in the challenged activity. [To] transform a federal official into a state actor, the appellee must show there is a symbiotic relationship between the [federal defendant] and the state such that the challenged action can fairly be attributed to the state. [The] Secretary actively opposed Governor Deukmejian's attempt to terminate Cal-OSHA as evidenced by the fact that he refused to withdraw approval when the Governor first notified DOL of his plan in February 1987. The Secretary did not finally approve Deukmejian's request and assume exclusive federal jurisdiction in California until after the California legislature adjourned on September 11, 1987, without either providing additional funds for Cal-OSHA or overriding the Governor's line-item veto. The evidence demonstrates, in other words, that the Governor and the federal defendants were involved in an antagonistic relationship, not a "symbiotic" venture. The Governor induced the federal defendants to terminate Cal-OSHA; they did not "act in concert" with him.

> [Even though] the federal defendants met with Governor Deukmejian's agents on several occasions and cooperated with the Governor to fill the gap created by his veto of funding for Cal-OSHA, we do not agree that the federal defendants' contacts and discussions [transformed] them into state actors whose actions could fairly be attributed to the state. This was not a case where federal officials conspired or cooperated with state agents to deprive individuals of their federal rights. The federal defendants only resumed jurisdiction over California's occupational health matters out of a need to fill the gap in coverage left by [the termination] and to ensure that California's workers would be adequately protected by federal safety standards. Far from being a symbiotic participant, whose actions could fairly be attributed to the State, we hold as a matter of law that the federal defendants' decision to resume exclusive federal jurisdiction over the State's occupational health and safety matters was taken under color of federal law and that the state played no significant role in the challenged activity.

The court distinguished *Hampton v. Hanrahan*, 600 F.2d 600, 623 (7th Cir. 1979) (federal officers who collaborated with the Chicago police in a raid on the Black Panther Party acted under color of state law because the action was the "joint product of the exercise of a State power and of a non-State power" and the State and its officials played a "significant role in the result").

The District of Columbia is treated as a state for purposes of § 1983. Yet some officers who work there cannot be sued under that statute, as they derive their authority not from the "local" District of Columbia law, but from national law. *See Johnson v. Government of the District of Columbia*, 734 F.3d 1194 (D.C. Cir. 2013) (holding that the Superior Court Marshal "is not a District official" but rather "qualifies as a federal official" on account of the statute under which he serves; therefore the District cannot be sued under § 1983 for his actions).

3. Conversely, state officials sometimes administer federal programs. They may be deemed to be acting under color of federal law and hence not amenable to suit under section 1983. *See, e.g., Rosas v. Brock,* 826 F.2d 1004, 1007 (11th Cir. 1987) (Florida disaster relief workers acted under color of federal law when they denied a claim of compensation under federal guidelines). Similarly, when state police officers are assigned to work with federal agencies on a full-time basis, courts have held that they act under color of federal law, even though they are paid by the state. *See, e.g., Askew v. Bloemker,* 548 F.2d 673, 677 (7th Cir. 1976). Officers of Indian tribes act under color of tribal law, not state law. *See E. F. W. v. St. Stephen's Indian High School,* 264 F.3d 1297 (10th Cir. 2001).

In *Ellis v. Blum,* 643 F.2d 68, 83 n.17 (2d Cir. 1981), state officials were charged with employing improper termination procedures for Social Security benefits. "[T]he funds are entirely of federal origin and the state agencies function solely as agents of the Secretary [of Health and Human Services] in making determinations of disability, applying federal law and federal regulations in accordance with procedures prescribed by her." Section 1983 was therefore unavailable and the plaintiffs were required to pursue a *Bivens* suit.

4. National Guard activities give rise to similar problems, for the Guards have both state and federal characteristics. According to the Seventh Circuit, "[n]o set formula exists for determining whether the representatives of an agency with both state and federal characteristics act under color of law. Our evaluation of whether particular conduct constitutes action taken under color of state law focuses on the nature of the action and functional capacity of the actor." *Knutson v. Wisconsin Air National Guard,* 995 F.2d 765, 767 (7th Cir. 1993). In *Knutson,* the Adjutant General of the Guard dismissed plaintiff from the Guard on account of bad performance evaluations. This was done "under color of" state law in spite of "the overarching scheme of federal authorization for the Guard [and] the fact that Wisconsin adopts and WIANG opts to utilize federal substantive and procedural rules in the exercise of its authority. [No] one is claiming that the Guard had been called into service by the federal government at the time of the termination. Moreover, WIANG is a part of the Wisconsin militia, with the governor serving as commander-in-chief. The Adjutant General, an appointee of the governor, effected the termination of Knutson." *Id.* at 768. *See also Johnson v. Orr,* 780 F.2d 386 (3d Cir. 1986) (reaching the same result on similar facts).

Suppose two states, with the approval of Congress, create an interstate compact to carry out certain common goals. Do those officials act under color of state or federal law? *See Lake Country Estates, Inc. v. Tahoe Regional Planning Agency,* 440 U.S. 391 (1979) (holding that they act under color of state law).

5. Since *Lugar,* lower courts have treated the statutory "under color of state law" and the constitutional "state action" requirements as equivalent in the typical constitutional tort case where the plaintiff relies on the Fourteenth Amendment (including the 1st, 4th, 5th, 6th, and 8th amendment rights the Supreme Court has incorporated into that amendment) to establish a breach of constitutional duty. Yet the Court does not rule that the two inquiries are *always* identical. *See* footnote 18. Why is the Court reluctant to take that step?

Consider two possibilities:

(a) Almost all constitutional provisions are directed at the state. The Thirteenth Amendment is the sole exception. It outlaws slavery whether or not the state sponsors or condones the practice. Suppose a farm worker kept on the land through intimidation and blackmail by the landowner brought a section 1983 suit to recover damages and obtain injunctive relief, and the court agrees that the landowner's practices amount to slavery. Suppose further that the landowner's practices violate state law. Would the victim still fail on account of his failure to meet the "under color of" requirement?

(b) Section 1983 grants a cause of action not only to enforce constitutional provisions but also to redress violations of federal "laws." The Court's doctrine on whether a given federal statute may be enforced through a section 1983 suit is examined in chapter 4. Suppose that the Court were to hold (as it has not yet done) that a federal statute directed at private conduct (as opposed to one regulating the actions of state and local governments) can be enforced under section 1983. *Cf. Hobbs v. Hawkins*, 968 F.2d 471 (5th Cir. 1992) where the plaintiff unsuccessfully argued that section 1983 should be available for disputes between union organizers and employers in connection with an organizing campaign. If the plaintiff had prevailed on that issue, would he then have to overcome the "under color of" hurdle as well?

6. The limitations on civil rights remedies addressed in this chapter apply only to suits brought under section 1983. Some civil rights statutes do not require a showing of state action. *E.g.*, 42 U.S.C. § 1981 provides that "[a]ll persons within the jurisdiction of the United States shall have the same right in every State and Territory to make and enforce contracts, to sue, be parties, give evidence, and to the full and equal benefit of all laws and proceedings for the security of persons and property as is enjoyed by white citizens . . . ." No showing of state action is required in order to state a cause of action under this provision. *See Runyon v. McCrary*, 427 U.S. 160 (1976).

III. SUING PRIVATE ACTORS UNDER SECTION 1983

Lugar illustrates that in the proper circumstances private persons commit "state action," act "under color of" state law, and thus may be sued under section 1983 for Fourteenth Amendment violations. Persons who employ self-help remedies, like the defendant in *Lugar*, are but one of several groups who may be vulnerable to section 1983 suits. Others include private individuals or firms to whom the state has contracted out some function that would otherwise be performed by state employees and persons who conspire with public officers to deprive the plaintiff of federal rights.

A. Self-Help Remedies

FLAGG BROS., INC. v. BROOKS
436 U.S. 149 (1978)

Mr. Justice Rehnquist delivered the opinion of the Court.

The question presented by this litigation is whether a warehouseman's proposed sale of goods entrusted to him for storage, as permitted by New York Uniform Commercial Code § 7-210 is an action properly attributable to the State of New York. The District Court found that the warehouseman's conduct was not that of the State, and dismissed this suit for want of jurisdiction under 28 U.S.C. § 1343(3). The Court of Appeals for the Second Circuit, in reversing the judgment of the District Court, found sufficient state involvement with the proposed sale to invoke the provisions of the Due Process Clause of the Fourteenth Amendment. We agree with the District Court, and we therefore reverse.

I

According to her complaint, the allegations of which we must accept as true, respondent Shirley Brooks and her family were evicted from their apartment in Mount Vernon, N.Y., on June 13, 1973. The city marshal arranged for Brooks' possessions to be stored by petitioner Flagg Brothers, Inc., in its warehouse. Brooks was informed of the cost of moving and storage, and she instructed the workmen to proceed, although she found the price too high. On August 25, 1973, after a series of disputes over the validity of the charges being claimed by petitioner Flagg Brothers, Brooks received a letter demanding that her account be brought up to date within 10 days "or your furniture will be sold." App. 13a. A series of subsequent letters from respondent and her attorneys produced no satisfaction.

Brooks thereupon initiated this class action in the District Court under 42 U.S.C. § 1983, seeking damages, an injunction against the threatened sale of her belongings, and the declaration that such a sale pursuant to § 7-210 would violate the Due Process and Equal Protection Clauses of the Fourteenth [Amendment.]

II

[It] must be noted that respondents have named no public officials as defendants in this action. The city marshal, who supervised their evictions, was dismissed from the case by the consent of all the parties.[4] This total absence of overt official involvement plainly distinguishes this case from earlier decisions imposing procedural restrictions on creditors' remedies such as *North Georgia Finishing, Inc. v. Di-Chem, Inc.*; *Fuentes v. Shevin*; *Sniadach v. Family Finance Corp.* In those

---

[4] [5] Of course, where the defendant is a public official, the two elements of a § 1983 action merge. 'The involvement of a state official . . . plainly provides the state action essential to show a direct violation of petitioner's Fourteenth Amendment . . . rights, whether or not the actions of the police were officially authorized, or lawful." *Adickes v. S.H. Kress & Co.* (citations omitted).

cases, the Court was careful to point out that the dictates of the Due Process Clause "[attach] only to the deprivation of an interest encompassed within the Fourteenth Amendment's protection." While as a factual matter any person with sufficient physical power may deprive a person of his property, only a State or a private person whose action "may be fairly treated as that of the State itself," may deprive him of "an interest encompassed within the Fourteenth Amendment's protection." Thus, the only issue presented by this case is whether Flagg Brothers' action may fairly be attributed to the State of New York. We conclude that it may not.

III

Respondents' primary contention is that New York has delegated to Flagg Brothers a power "traditionally exclusively reserved to the State." They argue that the resolution of private disputes is a traditional function of civil government, and that the State in § 7-210 has delegated this function to Flagg Brothers. Respondents, however, have read too much into the language of our previous cases. While many functions have been traditionally performed by governments, very few have been "exclusively reserved to the State."

One such area has been elections. While the Constitution protects private rights of association and advocacy with regard to the election of public officials, our cases make it clear that the conduct of the elections themselves is an exclusively public function. This principle was established by a series of cases [including *Terry v. Adams*] challenging the exclusion of blacks from participation in primary elections in Texas . . . . The doctrine does not reach to all forms of private political activity, but encompasses only state-regulated elections or elections conducted by organizations which in practice produce "the uncontested choice of public officials." . . .

A second line of cases under the public-function doctrine originated with *Marsh v. Alabama*, . . . [T]he Gulf Shipbuilding Corp. performed all the necessary municipal functions in the town of Chickasaw, Ala., which it owned. Under those circumstances, the Court concluded it was bound to recognize the right of a group of Jehovah's Witnesses to distribute religious literature on its streets.

These two branches of the public-function doctrine have in common the feature of exclusivity. Although the elections held by the Democratic Party and its affiliates were the only meaningful elections in Texas, and the streets owned by the Gulf Shipbuilding Corp. were the only streets in Chickasaw, the proposed sale by Flagg Brothers under § 7-210 is not the only means of resolving this purely private dispute. Respondent Brooks has never alleged that state law barred her from seeking a waiver of Flagg Brothers' right to sell her goods at the time she authorized their storage. Presumably, respondent Jones, who alleges that she never authorized the storage of her goods, could have sought t o replevy her goods at any time under state law. The challenged statute itself provides a damages remedy against the warehouseman for violations of its provisions. This system of rights and remedies, recognizing the traditional place of private arrangements in ordering relationships in the commercial world, can hardly be said to have delegated to Flagg Brothers an exclusive prerogative of the sovereign.

Whatever the particular remedies available under New York law, we do not consider a more detailed description of them necessary to our conclusion that the settlement of disputes between debtors and creditors is not traditionally an exclusive public function. Creditors and debtors have had available to them historically a far wider number of choices than has one who would be an elected public official, or a member of Jehovah's Witnesses who wished to distribute literature in Chickasaw, Ala., at the time *Marsh* was decided. Our analysis requires no parsing of the difference between various commercial liens and other remedies to support the conclusion that this entire field of activity is outside the scope of *Terry* and *Marsh*. This is true whether these commercial rights and remedies are created by statute or decisional law. To rely upon the historical antecedents of a particular practice would result in the constitutional condemnation in one State of a remedy found perfectly permissible in another.

Thus, even if we were inclined to extend the sovereign-function doctrine outside of its present carefully confined bounds, the field of private commercial transactions would be a particularly inappropriate area into which to expand it. We conclude that our sovereign-function cases do not support a finding of state action here.

[W]e would be remiss if we did not note that there are a number of state and municipal functions not covered by our election cases or governed by the reasoning of *Marsh* which have been administered with a greater degree of exclusivity by States and municipalities than has the function of so-called "dispute resolution." Among these are such functions as education, fire and police protection, and tax collection. We express no view as to the extent, if any, to which a city or State might be free to delegate to private parties the performance of such functions and thereby avoid the strictures of the Fourteenth Amendment. The mere recitation of these possible permutations and combinations of factual situations suffices to caution us that their resolution should abide the necessity of deciding them.

IV

Respondents further urge that Flagg Brothers' proposed action is properly attributable to the State because the State has authorized and encouraged it in enacting § 7-210. Our cases state "that a State is responsible for the . . . act of a private party when the State, by its law, has compelled the act." This Court, however, has never held that a State's mere acquiescence in a private action converts that action into that of the State. The Court rejected a similar argument in *Jackson*:

> "Approval by a state utility commission of such a request from a regulated utility, where the commission has not put its own weight on the side of the proposed practice by ordering it, does not transmute a practice initiated by the utility and approved by the commission into 'state action.'"

[The] clearest demonstration of this distinction appears in *Moose Lodge No. 107 v. Irvis* which held that the Commonwealth of Pennsylvania, although not responsible for racial discrimination voluntarily practiced by a private club, could not by law require the club to comply with its own discriminatory rules. These cases clearly rejected the notion that our prior cases permitted the imposition of Fourteenth Amendment restraints on private action by the simple device of characterizing the State's inaction as "authorization" or "encouragement."

It is quite immaterial that the State has embodied its decision not to act in statutory form. If New York had no commercial statutes at all, its courts would still be faced with the decision whether to prohibit or to permit the sort of sale threatened here the first time an aggrieved bailor came before them for relief. A judicial decision to deny relief would be no less an "authorization" or "encouragement" of that sale than the legislature's decision embodied in this statute. It was recognized in the earliest interpretations of the Fourteenth Amendment "that a State may act through different agencies, — either by its legislative, its executive, or its judicial authorities; and the prohibitions of the amendment extend to all action of the State" infringing rights protected thereby. If the mere denial of judicial relief is considered sufficient encouragement to make the State responsible for those private acts, all private deprivations of property would be converted into public acts whenever the State, for whatever reason, denies relief sought by the putative property owner.

Not only is this notion completely contrary to that "essential dichotomy," between public and private acts, but it has been previously rejected by this Court. In *Evans v. Abney* our Brother Brennan in dissent contended that a Georgia statutory provision authorizing the establishment of trusts for racially restricted parks conferred a "special power" on testators taking advantage of the provision. The Court nevertheless concluded that the State of Georgia was in no way responsible for the purely private choice involved in that case. By the same token, the State of New York is in no way responsible for Flagg Brothers' decision, a decision which the State in § 7-210 permits but does not compel, to threaten to sell these respondents' belongings.

Here, the State of New York has not compelled the sale of a bailor's goods, but has merely announced the circumstances under which its courts will not interfere with a private sale. Indeed, the crux of respondents' complaint is not that the State has acted, but that it has refused to act. This statutory refusal to act is no different in principle from an ordinary statute of limitations whereby the State declines to provide a remedy for private deprivations of property after the passage of a given period of time.

We conclude that the allegations of these complaints do not establish a violation of these respondents' Fourteenth Amendment rights by either petitioner Flagg Brothers or the State of New York. The District Court properly concluded that their complaints failed to state a claim for relief under 42 U.S.C. § 1983. The judgment of the Court of Appeals holding otherwise is:

Reversed.

[JUSTICE **MARSHALL**'s dissent is omitted.]

MR. JUSTICE **STEVENS**, with whom MR. JUSTICE **WHITE** and MR. JUSTICE **MARSHALL** join, [dissenting.]

There is no question in this case but that respondents have a property interest in the possessions that the warehouseman proposes to sell. It is also clear that, whatever power of sale the warehouseman has, it does not derive from the consent of the respondents. The claimed power derives solely from the State, and specifically from § 7-210 of the New York Uniform Commercial Code. The question is whether a state statute which authorizes a private party to deprive a person of his property without his consent must meet the requirements of the Due Process Clause of the Fourteenth Amendment. This question must be answered in the affirmative unless the State has virtually unlimited power to transfer interests in private property without any procedural protections. . . .

The test of what is a state function for purposes of the Due Process Clause has been variously phrased. Most frequently the issue is presented in terms of whether the State has delegated a function traditionally and historically associated with sovereignty. In this Court, petitioners have attempted to argue that the nonconsensual transfer of property rights is not a traditional function of the sovereign. The overwhelming historical evidence is to the contrary, however, and the Court wisely does not adopt this position. Instead, the Court reasons that state action cannot be found because the State has not delegated to the ware-houseman an exclusive sovereign function. This distinction, however, is not consistent with our prior decisions on state action; is not even adhered to by the Court in this case; and, most importantly, is inconsistent with the line of cases beginning with *Sniadach v. Family Finance Corp.*

Since *Sniadach* this Court has scrutinized various state statutes regulating the debtor-creditor relationship for compliance with the Due Process Clause. See also *North Georgia Finishing, Inc. v. Di-Chem, Inc.*; *Mitchell v. W.T. Grant Co.*; *Fuentes v. Shevin*. In each of these cases a finding of state action was a prerequisite to the Court's decision. The Court today seeks to explain these findings on the ground that in each case there was some element of "overt official involvement." Given the facts of those cases, this explanation is baffling. In *North Georgia Finishing*, for instance, the official involvement of the State of Georgia consisted of a court clerk who issued a writ of garnishment based solely on the affidavit of the creditor. The clerk's actions were purely ministerial, and, until today, this Court had never held that purely ministerial acts of "minor governmental functionaries" were sufficient to establish state action. The suggestion that this was the basis for due process review in *Sniadach, Shevin,* and *North Georgia Finishing* marks a major and, in my judgment, unwise expansion of the state-action doctrine. The number of private actions in which a governmental functionary plays some ministerial role is legion; to base due process review on the fortuity of such governmental intervention would demean the majestic purposes of the Due Process Clause.

Instead, cases such as *North Georgia Finishing* must be viewed as reflecting this Court's recognition of the significance of the State's role in defining and controlling the debtor-creditor relationship. The Court's language to this effect in the various debtor-creditor cases has been unequivocal. In *Fuentes v. Shevin* the Court stressed that the statutes in question "[abdicated] effective state control over state power." And it is clear that what was of concern in *Shevin* was the private use of state power to achieve a nonconsensual resolution of a commercial dispute. The state statutes placed the state power to repossess property in the hands of an interested private party, just as the state statute in this case places the state power to conduct judicially binding sales in satisfaction of a lien in the hands of the warehouseman.

"Private parties, serving their own private advantage, may unilaterally invoke state power to replevy goods from another. No state official participates in the decision to seek a writ; no state official reviews the basis for the claim to repossession; and no state official evaluates the need for immediate seizure. There is not even a requirement that the plaintiff provide any information to the court on these matters." . . .

Yet the very defect that made the statutes in *Shevin* and *North Georgia Finishing* unconstitutional — lack of state control — is, under today's decision, the factor that precludes constitutional review of the state statute. The Due Process Clause cannot command such incongruous results. If it is unconstitutional for a State to allow a private party to exercise a traditional state power because the state supervision of that power is purely mechanical, the State surely cannot immunize its actions from constitutional scrutiny by removing even the mechanical supervision.

Not only has the State removed its nominal supervision in this case, it has also authorized a private party to exercise a governmental power that is at least as significant as the power exercised in *Shevin or North Georgia Finishing*. In *Shevin*, the Florida statute allowed the debtor's property to be seized and held pending the outcome of the creditor's action for repossession. The property would not be finally disposed of until there was an adjudication of the underlying claim. Similarly, in *North Georgia Finishing*, the state statute provided for a garnishment procedure which deprived the debtor of the use of property in the garnishee's hands pending the outcome of litigation. The warehouseman's power under § 7-210 is far broader, as the Court of Appeals pointed out: "After giving the bailor specified notice, . . . the warehouseman is entitled to sell the stored goods in satisfaction of whatever he determines the storage charges to be. The warehouseman, unquestionably an interested party, is thus authorized by law to resolve any disputes over storage charges finally and unilaterally."

Whether termed "traditional," "exclusive," or "significant," the state power to order binding, nonconsensual resolution of a conflict between debtor and creditor is exactly the sort of power with which the Due Process Clause is concerned. And the State's delegation of that power to a private party is, accordingly, subject to due process scrutiny. This, at the very least, is the teaching of *Sniadach, Shevin*, and *North Georgia Finishing*.

[This] conclusion does not even remotely suggest that "all private deprivations of property [will] be converted into public acts whenever the State, for whatever reason, denies relief sought by the putative property owner." The focus is not on the private deprivation but on the state [authorization.] My analysis in this case thus assumes that petitioner Flagg Brothers' proposed sale will conform to the procedure specified by the state legislature and that respondents' challenge therefore will be to the constitutionality of that process. It is only what the State itself has enacted that they may ask the federal court to review in a § 1983 case. If there should be a deviation from the state statute — such as a failure to give the notice required by the state law — the defect could be remedied by a state court and there would be no occasion for § 1983 relief.

[It] is obviously true that the overwhelming majority of disputes in our society are resolved in the private sphere. But it is no longer possible, if it ever was, to believe that a sharp line can be drawn between private and public actions. The Court today holds that our examination of state delegations of power should be limited to those rare instances where the State has ceded one of its "exclusive" powers. As indicated, I believe that this limitation is neither logical nor practical. More troubling, this description of what is state action does not even attempt to reflect the concerns of the Due Process Clause, for the state-action doctrine is, after all, merely one aspect of this broad constitutional protection.

In the broadest sense, we expect government "to provide a reasonable and fair framework of rules which facilitate commercial transactions. . . ." This "framework of rules" is premised on the assumption that the State will control non-consensual deprivations of property and that the State's control will, in turn, be subject to the restrictions of the Due Process Clause. The power to order legally binding surrenders of property and the constitutional restrictions on that power are necessary correlatives in our system. In effect, today's decision allows the State to divorce these two elements by the simple expedient of transferring the implementation of its policy to private parties. Because the Fourteenth Amendment does not countenance such a division of power and responsibility, I respectfully dissent.

NOTES

1. In *Lugar*, the Court distinguished *Flagg Brothers* as a case in which there was no state involvement in the property deprivation. State law allowed the warehouseman to exercise his lien without any action by officials. *Flagg Brothers* holds that the warehouseman does not act under color of state law in selling the plaintiff's property and therefore cannot be sued under § 1983. Does it follow that the plaintiff is without a remedy? What result if the plaintiff brings a common law tort suit, perhaps for conversion, and the defendant warehouseman asserts the state self-help remedy as a defense? Can the plaintiff then challenge that defense on the ground that the due process clause overrides it on the facts of this case?

Given *Lugar*'s distinction of *Flagg Brothers*, does it follow that the state action requirement is met whenever a police officer is present at a private repossession? For a negative answer to that question, see *Harvey v. Plains Township Police Department*, 635 F.3d 606, 610 (3d Cir. 2011). The court contrasted two roles the officer may serve: "An officer's presence may be requested to maintain the peace, and the officer appropriately does so by remaining neutral. An officer abandons neutrality once he takes an active role and assists in the repossession." In the case at hand, the judge had instructed the jury that, on the "under color of" issue, "you must answer only one factual question, and that is did the defendant [officer Dombrowski] order the landlady to open the door to the apartment." This was error, the appellate court ruled, because the "state action question must be addressed after considering the totality of the circumstances and cannot be limited to a single factual question." Thus, "Dombrowski went to the scene of the repossession at [the repossessor's] behest, implied the search was legal by telling the landlord it was all right to open the door, entered the apartment to observe [repossessor] remove items," and took other actions to aid the repossessor.

Lower courts routinely cite *Flagg Brothers* for the proposition that "mere legislative authorization of a creditor's private power of sale with respect to a debt

owed [does not] constitute[] a delegation of traditional government function."
Grapentine v. Pawtucket Credit Union, 755 F.3d 29, 32 (1st Cir. 2014) (rejecting a mortgagor's argument that motrgagee's foreclosure sale of the property was state action.)

Keep in mind that the practical question of what kind of official involvement will trigger *Lugar* is not the same as the theoretical question of whether the Court's distinction between the two cases is sound as a matter of constitutional law. For an argument that there is no substantial difference between *Lugar* and *Flagg Brothers*, see Paul Brest, *State Action and Liberal Theory: A Casenote on* Flagg Brothers v. Brooks, 130 U. PA. L. REV. 1296, 1312–15 (1982).

2. In *Jackson v. Metropolitan Edison Co.*, 419 U.S. 345, 357 (1974), the Court held that a private utility's termination of service was not state action subject to due process constraints. The plaintiff pointed out that state regulators had authorized termination without notice and hearing, and argued that this amounted to state action. The Court said that "[a]pproval by a state utility commission of . . . a request by a regulated utility, where the commission has not put its own weight on the side of the proposed practice by ordering it, does not transmute a practice initiated by the utility and approved by the commission into 'state action.' "

The utility in *Jackson* terminated service for lack of payment. Would the result have been different if the electric company had refused to serve blacks? Consider that question in connection with the next case.

B. Contracting Out and Other Symbiotic Relationships

BURTON v. WILMINGTON PARKING AUTHORITY
365 U.S. 715 (1961)

MR. JUSTICE CLARK delivered the opinion of the Court.

In this action for declaratory and injunctive relief it is admitted that the Eagle Coffee Shoppe, Inc., a restaurant located within an off-street automobile parking building in Wilmington, Delaware, has refused to serve appellant food or drink solely because he is a Negro. The parking building is owned and operated by the Wilmington Parking Authority, an agency of the State of Delaware, and the restaurant is the Authority's lessee. Appellant claims that such refusal abridges his rights under the Equal Protection Clause of the Fourteenth Amendment to the United States Constitution. The Supreme Court of Delaware has held that Eagle was acting in "a purely private capacity" under its lease; that its action was not that of the Authority and was not, therefore, state action within the contemplation of the prohibitions contained in that Amendment. It also held that under [Delaware law] Eagle was a restaurant, not an inn, and that as such it "is not required [to] serve any and all persons entering its place of business." [We conclude] that the exclusion of appellant under the circumstances shown to be present here was discriminatory state action in violation of the Equal Protection Clause of the Fourteenth Amendment.

The Authority was created [to] provide adequate parking facilities for the convenience of the public. [To] this end the Authority is granted wide powers including that of constructing or acquiring by lease, purchase or condemnation, lands and facilities, and that of leasing "portions of any of its garage buildings or structures for commercial use by the lessee, where, in the opinion of the Authority, such leasing is necessary and feasible for the financing and operation of such facilities." The Act provides that the rates and charges for its facilities must be reasonable and are to be determined exclusively by the Authority "for the purposes of providing for the payment of the expenses of the Authority, the construction, improvement, repair, maintenance, and operation of its facilities and properties, the payment of the principal of and interest on its obligations, and to fulfill the terms and provisions of any agreements made with the purchasers or holders of any such obligations or with the city." The Authority has no power to pledge the credit of the State of Delaware but may issue its own revenue bonds which are tax exempt. Any and all property owned or used by the Authority is likewise exempt from state taxation.

The first project undertaken by the Authority was the erection of a parking facility on Ninth Street in downtown Wilmington. The tract consisted of four parcels, all of which were acquired by negotiated purchases from private owners. Three were paid for in cash, borrowed from Equitable Security Trust Company, and the fourth, purchased from Diamond Ice and Coal Company, was paid for "partly in Revenue Bonds of the Authority and partly in cash [$934,000] donated by the City of Wilmington, pursuant to 22 Del. C. c. 5. . . . Subsequently, the City of Wilmington gave the Authority $1,822,827.69 which sum the Authority applied to the redemption of the Revenue Bonds delivered to Diamond Ice & Coal Co. and to the repayment of the Equitable Security Trust Company loan."

Before it began actual construction of the facility, the Authority was advised by its retained experts that the anticipated revenue from the parking of cars and proceeds from sale of its bonds would not be sufficient to finance the construction costs of the facility. Moreover, the bonds were not expected to be marketable if payable solely out of parking revenues. To secure additional capital needed for its "debt-service" requirements, and thereby to make bond financing practicable, the Authority decided it was necessary to enter long-term leases with responsible tenants for commercial use of some of the space available in the projected "garage building." The public was invited to bid for these leases.

In April 1957 such a private lease, for 20 years and renewable for another 10 years, was made with Eagle Coffee Shoppe, Inc., for use as a "restaurant, dining room, banquet hall, cocktail lounge and bar and for no other use and purpose." The multi-level space of the building which was let to Eagle, although "within the exterior walls of the structure, has no marked public entrance leading from the parking portion of the facility into the restaurant proper . . . [whose main entrance] is located on Ninth Street." In its lease the Authority covenanted to complete construction expeditiously, including completion of "the decorative finishing of the leased premises and utilities therefor, without cost to Lessee," including necessary utility connections, toilets, hung acoustical tile and plaster ceilings; vinyl asbestos, ceramic tile and concrete floors; connecting stairs and wrought iron railings; and wood-floored show windows. Eagle spent some $220,000 to make the space suitable for its operation and, to the extent such improvements were so attached to realty as to become part thereof, Eagle to the same extent enjoys the Authority's tax exemption.

The Authority further agreed to furnish heat for Eagle's premises, gas service for the boiler room, and to make, at its own expense, all necessary structural repairs, all repairs to exterior surfaces except store fronts and any repairs caused by lessee's own act or neglect. The Authority retained the right to place any directional signs on the exterior of the let space which would not interfere with or obscure Eagle's display signs. Agreeing to pay an annual rental of $28,700, Eagle covenanted to "occupy and use the leased premises in accordance with all applicable laws, statutes, ordinances and rules and regulations of any federal, state or municipal authority." Its lease, however, contains no requirement that its restaurant services be made available to the general public on a nondiscriminatory basis, in spite of the fact that the Authority has power to adopt rules and regulations respecting the use of its facilities except any as would impair the security of its bondholders.

Other portions of the structure were leased to other tenants, including a bookstore, a retail jeweler, and a food store. Upon completion of the building, the Authority located at appropriate places thereon official signs indicating the public character of the building, and flew from mastheads on the roof both the state and national flags.

In August 1958 appellant parked his car in the building and walked around to enter the restaurant by its front door on Ninth Street. Having entered and sought service, he was refused [it.]

The *Civil Rights Cases*, "embedded in our constitutional law" the principle "that the action inhibited by the first section [Equal Protection Clause] of the Fourteenth Amendment is only such action as may fairly be said to be that of the States. That Amendment erects no shield against merely private conduct, however discriminatory or wrongful." . . . Because the virtue of the right to equal protection of the laws could lie only in the breadth of its application, its constitutional assurance was reserved in terms whose imprecision was necessary if the right were to be enjoyed in the variety of individual-state relationships which the Amendment was designed to embrace. For the same reason, to fashion and apply a precise formula for recognition of state responsibility under the Equal Protection Clause is an "impossible task" which "This Court has never attempted." Only by sifting facts and weighing circumstances can the nonobvious involvement of the State in private conduct be attributed its true significance.

[T]he Delaware Supreme Court seems to have placed controlling emphasis on its conclusion, as to the accuracy of which there is doubt, that only some 15% of the total cost of the facility was "advanced" from public funds; that the cost of the entire facility was allocated three-fifths to the space for commercial leasing and two-fifths to parking space; that anticipated revenue from parking was only some 30.5% of the total income, the balance of which was expected to be earned by the leasing; that the Authority had no original intent to place a restaurant in the building, it being only a happenstance resulting from the bidding; that Eagle expended considerable moneys on furnishings; that the restaurant's main and marked public entrance is on Ninth Street without any public entrance direct from the parking area; and that "the only connection Eagle has with the public facility . . . is the furnishing of the sum of $28,700 annually in the form of rent which is used by the Authority to defray a portion of the operating expense of an otherwise unprofitable enterprise." While these factual considerations are indeed validly accountable aspects of the enterprise upon which the State has embarked, we cannot say that they lead inescapably to the conclusion that state action is not present. Their persuasiveness is diminished when evaluated in the context of other factors which must be acknowledged.

The land and building were publicly owned. As an entity, the building was dedicated to "public uses" in performance of the Authority's "essential governmental functions." The costs of land acquisition, construction, and maintenance are defrayed entirely from donations by the City of Wilmington, from loans and revenue bonds and from the proceeds of rentals and parking services out of which the loans and bonds were payable . . . . [T]he commercially leased areas were not surplus state property, but constituted a physically and financially integral and, indeed, indispensable part of the State's plan to operate its project as a self-sustaining unit. Upkeep and maintenance of the building, including necessary repairs, were responsibilities of the Authority and were payable out of public funds. It cannot be doubted that the peculiar relationship of the restaurant to the parking facility in which it is located confers on each an incidental variety of mutual benefits. Guests of the restaurant are afforded a convenient place to park their automobiles, even if they cannot enter the restaurant directly from the parking area. Similarly, its convenience for diners may well provide additional demand for the Authority's parking facilities. Should any improvements effected in the leasehold by Eagle become part of the realty, there is no possibility of increased taxes being passed on to it since the fee is held by a tax-exempt government agency. Neither can it be ignored, especially in view of Eagle's affirmative allegation that for it to serve Negroes would injure its business, that profits earned by discrimination not only contribute to, but also are indispensable elements in, the financial success of a governmental agency.

Addition of all these activities, obligations and responsibilities of the Authority, the benefits mutually conferred, together with the obvious fact that the restaurant is operated as an integral part of a public building devoted to a public parking service, indicates that degree of state participation and involvement in discriminatory action which it was the design of the Fourteenth Amendment to condemn. It is irony amounting to grave injustice that in one part of a single building, erected and maintained with public funds by an agency of the State to serve a public purpose, all persons have equal rights, while in another portion, also serving the public, a Negro is a second-class citizen, offensive because of his race, without rights and unentitled to service, but at the same time fully enjoys equal access to nearby restaurants in wholly privately owned buildings. As the Chancellor pointed out, in its lease with Eagle the Authority could have affirmatively required Eagle to discharge the responsibilities under the Fourteenth Amendment imposed upon the private enterprise as a consequence of state participation. But no State may effectively abdicate its responsibilities by either ignoring them or by merely failing to discharge them whatever the motive may be. It is of no consolation to an individual denied the equal protection of the laws that it was done in good faith. Certainly the conclusions drawn in similar cases by the various Courts of Appeals do not depend upon such a distinction. By its inaction, the Authority, and through it the State, has not only made itself a party to the refusal of service, but has elected to place its power, property and prestige behind the admitted discrimination. The State has so far insinuated itself into a position of interdependence with Eagle that it must be recognized as a joint participant in the challenged activity, which, on that account, cannot be considered to have been so "purely private" as to fall without the scope of the Fourteenth Amendment.

Because readily applicable formulae may not be fashioned, the conclusions drawn from the facts and circumstances of this record are by no means declared as universal truths on the basis of which every state leasing agreement is to be tested. Owing to the very "largeness" of government, a multitude of relationships might appear to some to fall within the Amendment's embrace, but that, it must be remembered, can be determined only in the framework of the peculiar facts or circumstances present. Therefore respondents' prophecy of nigh universal application of a constitutional precept so peculiarly dependent for its invocation upon appropriate facts fails to take into account "Differences in circumstances [which] beget appropriate differences in law." Specifically defining the limits of our inquiry, what we hold today is that when a State leases public property in the manner and for the purpose shown to have been the case here, the proscriptions of the Fourteenth Amendment must be complied with by the lessee as certainly as though they were binding covenants written into the agreement [itself.]

NOTE

Would *Burton* have come out differently if the substantive complaint were that employees of the coffee shop were entitled to the same procedural due process rights as public employees? For a suggestion that it would have, *see* Henry J. Friendly, *The Public-Private Penumbra — Fourteen Years Later*, 130 U. PA. L. REV. 1289, 1291, 1294 (1982). *See also* Robert Glennon & John Nowak, *A Functional Analysis of the Fourteenth Amendment "State Action" Requirement*, 1976 SUP. CT. REV. 221 (disputing the "widespread belief that state action is a unitary concept," *id.* at 224, and maintaining instead that "the Court decides state action cases by balancing the values which are advanced or limited by each of the conflicting private rights.") *Id.* at 226–27. For a more recent addition to the literature taking this view of state action doctrine, see Michael L. Wells, *Identifying State Actors in Constitutional Litigation*, 26 CARDOZO L. REV. 99 (2004) (arguing that "the current approach pays too much attention to a search for various 'indicia of state action' in the events giving rise to the litigation, while excluding consideration of the substantive context in which the case arises").

For the past 40 years the Court has often employed a "nexus" test for resolving cases where the government has contracted with a private party. It is not enough that there be a mutually beneficial relationship between the state and the private party, or that the private party is heavily regulated. "[T]he inquiry must be whether there is a sufficiently close nexus between the State and the challenged action of the regulated entity so that the action of the latter may be fairly treated as that of the State itself." *Jackson v. Metropolitan Edison Co.*, 419 U.S. 345 (1974). This approach is illustrated by the following case.

RENDELL-BAKER v. KOHN
457 U.S. 830 (1982)

CHIEF JUSTICE BURGER delivered the opinion of the Court.

We granted certiorari to decide whether a private school, whose income is derived primarily from public sources and which is regulated by public authorities, acted under color of state law when it discharged certain employees.

I

A

Respondent Kohn is the director of the New Perspectives School, a nonprofit institution located on privately owned property in Brookline, Massachusetts. The school was founded as a private institution and is operated by a board of directors, none of whom are public officials or are chosen by public officials. The school specializes in dealing with students who have experienced difficulty completing public high schools; many have drug, alcohol, or behavioral problems, or other special needs. In recent years, nearly all of the students at the school have been referred to it by the Brookline or Boston School Committees, or by the Drug Rehabilitation Division of the Massachusetts Department of Mental Health. The school issues high school diplomas certified by the Brookline School Committee.

When students are referred to the school by Brookline or Boston under Chapter 766 of the Massachusetts Acts of 1972, the School Committees in those cities pay for the students' education. The school also receives funds from a number of other state and federal agencies. In recent years, public funds have accounted for at least 90%, and in one year 99%, of respondent school's operating budget. There were approximately 50 students at the school in those years and none paid tuition.

To be eligible for tuition funding under Chapter 766, the school must comply with a variety of regulations, many of which are common to all schools. The State has issued detailed regulations concerning matters ranging from record-keeping to student-teacher ratios. Concerning personnel policies, the Chapter 766 regulations require the school to maintain written job descriptions and written statements describing personnel standards and procedures, but they impose few specific requirements.

The school is also regulated by Boston and Brookline as a result of its Chapter 766 funding. By its contract with the Boston School Committee, which refers to the school as a "contractor," the school must agree to carry out the individualized plan developed for each student referred to the school by the Committee. The contract specifies that school employees are not city employees.

The school also has a contract with the State Drug Rehabilitation Division. Like the contract with the Boston School Committee, that agreement refers to the school as a "contractor." It provides for reimbursement for services provided for students referred to the school by the Drug Rehabilitation Division, and includes requirements concerning the services to be provided. Except for general requirements, such as an equal employment opportunity requirement, the agreement does not cover personnel policies.

While five of the six petitioners were teachers at the school, petitioner Rendell-Baker was a vocational counselor hired under a grant from the federal Law Enforcement Assistance Administration, whose funds are distributed in Massachusetts through the State Committee on Criminal Justice. As a condition of the grant, the Committee on Criminal Justice must approve the school's initial hiring decisions. The purpose of this requirement is to insure that the school hires vocational counselors who meet the qualifications described in the school's grant proposal to the Committee; the Committee does not interview applicants for counselor positions.

B

Rendell-Baker was discharged by the school in January 1977, and the five other petitioners were discharged in June 1978. Rendell-Baker's discharge resulted from a dispute over the role of a student-staff council in making hiring decisions. A dispute arose when some students presented a petition to the school's board of directors in December 1976, seeking greater responsibilities for the student-staff council. Director Kohn opposed the proposal, but Rendell-Baker supported it and so advised the board. On December 13, Kohn notified the State Committee on Criminal Justice, which funded Rendell-Baker's position, that she intended to dismiss Rendell-Baker and employ someone else. Kohn notified Rendell-Baker of her dismissal in January 1977 . . . .

In the spring of 1978, students and staff voiced objections to Kohn's policies. The five petitioners other than Rendell-Baker, who were all teachers at the school, wrote a letter to the board of directors urging Kohn's dismissal. When the board affirmed its confidence in Kohn, students from the school picketed the home of the president of the board. The students were threatened with suspension; a local newspaper then ran a story about the controversy at the school. In response to the story, the five petitioners wrote a letter to the editor in which they stated that they thought the prohibition of picketing was unconstitutional. On the day the letter to the editor appeared, the five teachers told the president of the board that they were forming a union. Kohn discharged the teachers the next day. They brought suit against the school and its directors in December 1978. Like Rendell-Baker, they sought relief under § 1983, alleging that their rights under the First, Fifth, and Fourteenth Amendments had been [violated.]

II
A

[I]t is fundamental that the First Amendment prohibits governmental infringement on the right of free speech. Similarly, the Fourteenth Amendment, which prohibits the states from denying federal constitutional rights and which guarantees due process, applies to acts of the states, not to acts of private persons or entities. And § 1983, which was enacted pursuant to the authority of Congress to enforce the Fourteenth Amendment, prohibits interference with federal rights under color of state [law.]

The core issue presented in this case is not whether petitioners were discharged because of their speech or without adequate procedural protections, but whether the school's action in discharging them can fairly be seen as state action. If the action of the respondent school is not state action, our inquiry ends.

B

In *Blum v. Yaretsky* the Court analyzed the state action requirement of the Fourteenth Amendment. The Court considered whether certain nursing homes were state actors for the purpose of determining whether decisions regarding transfers of patients could be fairly attributed to the State, and hence be subjected to Fourteenth Amendment due process requirements. The challenged transfers primarily involved decisions, made by physicians and nursing home administrators, to move patients from "skilled nursing facilities" to less expensive "health-related facilities." Like the New Perspectives School, the nursing homes were privately owned and [operated.] The Court held that, a State normally can be held responsible for a private decision only when it has exercised coercive power or has provided such significant encouragement, either overt or covert, that the choice must in law be deemed to be that of the State." In determining that the transfer decisions were not actions of the State, the Court considered each of the factors alleged by petitioners here to make the discharge decisions of the New Perspectives School fairly attributable to the State.

First, the nursing homes, like the school, depended on the State for funds; the State subsidized the operating and capital costs of the nursing homes, and paid the medical expenses of more than 90% of the patients. Here the Court of Appeals concluded that the fact that virtually all of the school's income was derived from government funding was the strongest factor to support a claim of state action. But in *Blum v. Yaretsky*, we held that the similar dependence of the nursing homes did not make the acts of the physicians and nursing home administrators acts of the State, and we conclude that the school's receipt of public funds does not make the discharge decisions acts of the State.

The school, like the nursing homes, is not fundamentally different from many private corporations whose business depends primarily on contracts to build roads, bridges, dams, ships, or submarines for the government. Acts of such private contractors do not become acts of the government by reason of their significant or even total engagement in performing public contracts.

The school is also analogous to the public defender found not to be a state actor in *Polk County v. Dodson.* There we concluded that, although the State paid the public defender, her relationship with her client was "identical to that existing between any other lawyer and client." Here the relationship between the school and its teachers and counselors is not changed because the State pays the tuition of the students.

A second factor considered in *Blum v. Yaretsky* was the extensive regulation of the nursing homes by the State. There the State was indirectly involved in the transfer decisions challenged in that case because a primary goal of the State in regulating nursing homes was to keep costs down by transferring patients from intensive treatment centers to less expensive facilities when possible. Both state and federal regulations encouraged the nursing homes to transfer patients to less expensive facilities when appropriate. The nursing homes were extensively regulated in many other ways as well . . . . The Court relied on *Jackson* where we held that state regulation, even if "extensive and detailed," did not make a utility's actions state action.

Here the decisions to discharge the petitioners were not compelled or even influenced by any state regulation. Indeed, in contrast to the extensive regulation of the school generally, the various regulators showed relatively little interest in the school's personnel matters. The most intrusive personnel regulation promulgated by the various government agencies was the requirement that the Committee on Criminal Justice had the power to approve persons hired as vocational counselors. Such a regulation is not sufficient to make a decision to discharge, made by private management, state [action.]

The third factor asserted to show that the school is a state actor is that it performs a "public function." However, our holdings have made clear that the relevant question is not simply whether a private group is serving a "public function." We have held that the question is whether the function performed has been "traditionally the *exclusive* prerogative of the State." *Jackson*, supra; quoted in *Blum v. Yaretsky* (emphasis added). There can be no doubt that the education of maladjusted high school students is a public function, but that is only the beginning of the inquiry. Chapter 766 of the Massachusetts Acts of 1972 demonstrates that the State intends to provide services for such students at public expense. That legislative policy choice in no way makes these services the exclusive province of the State. Indeed, the Court of Appeals noted that until recently the State had not undertaken to provide education for students who could not be served by traditional public schools. That a private entity performs a function which serves the public does not make its acts state action.[5]

Fourth, petitioners argue that there is a "symbiotic relationship" between the school and the State similar to the relationship involved in *Burton v. Wilmington Parking Authority*. Such a claim is rejected in *Blum v. Yaretsky*, and we reject it here. In *Burton*, the Court held that the refusal of a restaurant located in a public parking garage to serve Negroes constituted state action. The Court stressed that the restaurant was located on public property and that the rent from the restaurant contributed to the support of the garage. In response to the argument that the restaurant's profits, and hence the State's financial position, would suffer if it did not discriminate, the Court concluded that this showed that the State profited from the restaurant's discriminatory conduct. The Court viewed this as support for the conclusion that the State should be charged with the discriminatory actions. Here the school's fiscal relationship with the State is not different from that of many

---

[5] [7] There is no evidence that the State has attempted to avoid its constitutional duties by a sham arrangement which attempts to disguise provision of public services as acts of private parties. Cf. *Evans v. Newton* (private trustees appointed to manage previously public park for white persons only).

contractors performing services for the government. No symbiotic relationship such as existed in *Burton* exists here.

JUSTICE **WHITE**, concurring in the judgments.

The issue in *Blum v. Yaretsky* is whether a private nursing home's decision to discharge or transfer a Medicaid patient satisfies the state-action requirement of the Fourteenth Amendment. To satisfy this requirement, respondents must show that the transfer or discharge is made on the basis of some rule of decision for which the State is responsible. *Lugar v. Edmondson Oil Co.* It is not enough to show that the State takes certain actions in response to this private decision. The rule of decision implicated in the actions at issue here appears to be nothing more than a medical judgment. This is the clear import of the majority's conclusion that the "decisions ultimately turn on medical judgments made by private parties according to professional standards that are not established by the State," with which I agree.

Similarly, the allegations of the petitioners in *Rendell-Baker v. Kohn*, fail to satisfy the state-action requirement. In this case, the question of state action focuses on an employment decision made by a private school that receives most of its funding from public sources and is subject to state regulation in certain respects. For me, the critical factor is the absence of any allegation that the employment decision was itself based upon some rule of conduct or policy put forth by the State. As the majority states, "in contrast to the extensive regulation of the school generally, the various regulators showed relatively little interest in the school's personnel matters." The employment decision remains, therefore, a private decision not fairly attributable to the State.

Accordingly, I concur in the judgments.

JUSTICE **MARSHALL**, with whom JUSTICE **BRENNAN** joins, [dissenting.]

The decisions of this Court clearly establish that where there is a symbiotic relationship between the State and a privately owned enterprise, so that the State and a privately owned enterprise are participants in a joint venture, the actions of the private enterprise may be attributable to the State. "Conduct that is formally 'private' may become so entwined with governmental policies or so impregnated with a governmental character" that it can be regarded as governmental action . . . . The question whether such a relationship exists "can be determined only in the framework of the peculiar facts or circumstances present." Here, an examination of the facts and circumstances leads inexorably to the conclusion that the actions of the New Perspectives School should be attributed to the State; it is difficult to imagine a closer relationship between a government and a private enterprise.

The New Perspectives School receives virtually all of its funds from state sources. This financial dependence on the State is an important indicium of governmental involvement. The school's very survival depends on the State. If the State chooses, it may exercise complete control over the school's operations simply by threatening to withdraw financial support if the school takes action that it considers objectionable.

The school is heavily regulated and closely supervised by the State. This fact provides further support for the conclusion that its actions should be attributed to the State. The school's freedom of decision making is substantially circumscribed by the Massachusetts Department of Education's guidelines and the various contracts with state agencies. For example, the school is required to develop and comply with written rules for hiring and dismissal of personnel. Almost every decision the school makes is substantially affected in some way by the State's regulations.

The fact that the school is providing a substitute for public education is also an important indicium of state action. The provision of education is one of the most important tasks performed by government: it ranks at the very apex of the function of a State. Of course, as the majority emphasizes, performance of a public function is by itself sufficient to justify treating a private entity as a state actor only where the function has been "traditionally the exclusive prerogative of the State." But the fact that a private entity is performing a vital public function, when coupled with other factors demonstrating a close connection with the State, may justify a finding of state action.

The school's provision of a substitute for public education deserves particular emphasis because of the role of Chapter 766. Under this statute, the State is required to provide a free education to all children, including those with special needs. Clearly, if the State had decided to provide the service itself, its conduct would be measured against constitutional standards. The State should not be permitted to avoid constitutional requirements simply by delegating its statutory duty to a private entity. In my view, such a delegation does not convert the performance of the duty from public to private action when the duty is specific and the private institution's decisionmaking authority is significantly curtailed.

When an entity is not only heavily regulated and funded by the State, but also provides a service that the State is required to provide, there is a very close nexus with the State. Under these circumstances, it is entirely appropriate to treat the entity as an arm of the State. Here, since the New Perspectives School exists solely to fulfill the State's obligations under Chapter 766, I think it fully reasonable to conclude that the school is a state actor.

Indeed, I would conclude that the actions challenged here were under color of state law, even if I believed that the sole basis for state action was the fact that the school was providing Chapter 766 services. Petitioners claim that they were discharged because they supported student demands for increased responsibilities in school affairs, that is, because they criticized the school's educational policies. If petitioners' allegations are true, then the school has adopted a specific view of the sort of education that should be provided under the statute, and refuses to tolerate departures from that view. The State, by refusing to intervene, has effectively endorsed that view of its duties under Chapter 766. In short, because petitioners' criticism was directly addressed to the State's responsibilities under Chapter 766, a finding of state action is justified.

The majority repeatedly compares the school to a private contractor that "depends primarily on contracts to build roads, bridges, dams, ships, or submarines for the government." The New Perspectives School can be readily distinguished, however. Although shipbuilders and dambuilders, like the school, may be dependent on government funds, they are not so closely supervised by the government. And unlike most private contractors, the school is performing a statutory duty of the State.

The majority also focuses on the fact that the actions at issue here are personnel decisions. It would apparently concede that actions directly affecting the students could be treated as under color of state law, since the school is fulfilling the State's obligations to those children under Chapter 766. It suggests, however, that the State has no interest in personnel decisions. As I have suggested, I do not share this narrow view of the school's obligations; the personnel decisions challenged here are related to the provision of Chapter 766 education. In any event, since the school is funded almost entirely by the State, is closely supervised by the State, and exists solely to perform the State's statutory duty to educate children with special needs — since the school is really just an arm of the State — its personnel decisions may appropriately be considered state action.

NOTES

1.   Charles Black once described state action doctrine as "a conceptual disaster area." Charles L. Black, Jr., *The Supreme Court 1966 Term — Foreword: "State Action," Equal Protection, and California's Proposition 14*, 81 HARV. L. REV. 69, 95 (1967). Some have gone so far as to suggest that the doctrine be abandoned. *See* Erwin Chemerinsky, *Rethinking State Action*, 80 Nw. U. L. REV. 503 (1985) (calling for abandonment of the state action doctrine, because "it requires courts to refrain from applying constitutional values to private disputes even though there is no other form of effective redress.") *Id.* at 506. For a response to Chemerinsky, see William P. Marshall, *Diluting Constitutional Rights: Rethinking "Rethinking State Action,"* 80 Nw. U. L. REV. 558 (1985). As his title indicates, Marshall warns that constitutional rights may be devalued if they were routinely enforced against private actors.

One reason it is hard to make sense of state action doctrine is that the Court identifies a number of factors that should figure in the resolution of state action issues, but does not apply the standards consistently from one case to the next. A skeptical observer may suspect that the Court gives a particular factor more or less weight depending on the conclusion it wishes to reach, employing the factors more to rationalize a result it reaches on unstated grounds than to guide its decision making in the first place. For example, suppose one focuses on the question whether a given activity is "traditionally the exclusive province of the state." *Rendell-Baker* and *Blum* hold that schools and hospitals do not meet this test. According to *Flagg Bros. v. Brooks*, the enforcement of security interests in property is not traditionally the exclusive province of the state. Yet *Lugar*, decided the same day as *Rendell-Baker* and *Blum*, finds state action on facts that differ only slightly from those of *Flagg Brothers*. The Court in *Lugar* preferred to focus on the issue of whether there was joint participation between a state actor and a private actor. If "joint participation" is the central factor, then *Rendell-Baker* seems to stand on shaky ground. The school got nearly all of its funding from the state and carried out a function the state was under a statutory obligation to perform.

2. In *Rendell-Baker* the Court cites *Polk County v. Dodson*, 454 U.S. 312 (1981), in support of its decision. *Dodson* held that a public defender did not act under color of state law "when performing a lawyer's traditional functions," even though he was a state employee. Does the *Polk County* rule cover "a public defender's pre-trial decisions involving the interview and subpoenaing of witnesses?" *See Miranda v. Clark County*, 279 F.3d 1102 (9th Cir. 2002) (yes). Is a legal aid society, funded largely by the state, a state actor? For a case holding that it is not, see *Schnabel v. Abramson*, 232 F.3d 83 (2d Cir. 2000).

Compare *West v. Atkins*, 487 U.S. 42 (1988), where the state had contracted with Atkins, an orthopedic surgeon, to spend two days a week seeing patients at a state prison. West, a prisoner, tore an Achilles tendon and received medical care from Atkins. Unsatisfied with the results of the treatment, West sued Atkins under section 1983, alleging that Atkins acted with "deliberate indifference", in violation of the cruel and unusual punishment clause of the Eighth Amendment. The Fourth Circuit held that persons like Atkins, acting "within the bounds of traditional professional discretion and judgment", do not act under color of state law.

The Supreme Court reversed. Although the Fourth Circuit had relied upon *Dodson*, that case was inapposite, in the Court's view. "[I]n contrast to the public defender, Doctor Atkins' professional and ethical obligation to make independent medical judgments did not set him in conflict with the State and other prison authorities. Indeed, his relationship with other prison authorities was cooperative. . . . [The Court of Appeals] appears to have misread *Polk County* as establishing a general principle that professionals do not act under color of state law when they act in their professional capacities. . . . To the extent this Court in *Polk County* relied on the fact that the public defender is a 'professional' in concluding that he was not engaged in state action, the case turned on the particular professional obligation of the criminal defense attorney to be an adversary of the State, not on the independence and integrity generally applicable to professionals as a class."

West states a general rule for situations in which the plaintiff is confined by the state and the defendant is a private physician with whom the state has contracted for care. *See, e.g., Carl v. Muskegon County*, 763 F.3d 592 (6th Cir. 2014) (private psychiatrist hired by the county as an independent contractor to provide mental health care to pretrial detainees). Are all prison contracting out cases governed by *West*? In *Florer v. Congregation Pidyon Shevuyim*, 639 F.3d 916 (9th Cir. 2011), a state prison contracted with the defendant, a private religious organization, to provide Jewish religious services to prisoners. The plaintiff sued Congregation Pidyon under the Religious Land Use and Institutionalized Persons Act (RLUIPA) when it rejected (on account of its determination that he was not Jewish) his requests for services. For purposes of this case, that statute imposes the same "under color of" requirement as § 1983. The court distinguished *West*: "In *West*, state law barred the prisoner from receiving medical care from anyone other than the state's designated physicians. But Florer has not shown that any law or policy restricted him from receiving a Torah, calendar, or rabbi visit from persons or organizations other than Defendants." Unlike the Eighth Amendment obligation to provide medical care, the state's duty here was merely to "provide reasonable opportunities to exercise religious freedom." In addition, "Defendants' professional standards concerning who is a member of their religion are not dictated by the state."

Compare *Norris v. Premier Integrity Solutions, Inc.*, 641 F.3d 695 (6th Cir. 2011) (prisoner sues a private company with which the state has contracted to conduct drug tests, charging that its methods violate his Fourth Amendment rights; the drug testing company is a state actor).

3.   Within the prison medical care context, a variety of factual nuances may affect the resolution of the state action issue. Suppose Dr. Atkins had worked for a private corporation that had contracted with the state to provide medical services for prison inmates. *Calvert v. Sharp*, 748 F.2d 861 (4th Cir. 1984) held that the conduct of the physician was not under color of state law. Is *Calvert* still good law after *West*? In this regard, consider *Harrison v. Ash*, 539 F.3d 510 (6th Cir. 2008). The plaintiff's deceased died of asthma in the Macomb County jail, while serving a sentence for failure to pay child support. Defendants included, among others, nurses employed by Correctional Medical Services (CMS), a private firm the county had hired to provide medical services at the jail. The court denied the nurses' motion for summary judgment, explaining: "Defendant nurses were acting under the color of state law when the alleged constitutional violation occurred because of the contractual relationship between Macomb County and CMS. [*West*.]" Does it matter whether the medical services are provided at the jail, as in *Harrison*, or at the hospital? *See, e.g., Craig v. Floyd County, Ga.*, 643 F.3d 1306, 1310 (11th Cir. 2011) (here the medical care was provided to a pre-trial detainee at the medical center, not the jail; the court ruled that private entities that contract to provide medical care to inmates are state actors). Suppose the issue is not medical care but decisions the medical care provider makes vis-á-vis its employees? *See Sherlock v. Montefiore Medical Center*, 84 F.3d 522, 527 (2d Cir. 1996) (the medical provider is not a state actor "with respect to its employment decisions").

Can a private pharmacy that supplies prescription drugs to a state prison be sued under section 1983 if its products cause harm to inmates? *See Kost v. Kozakiewicz*, 1 F.3d 176, 184 (3d Cir. 1993) (no). Here the pharmacy, Gatti, sold the drugs not to the prison directly, but through private third party, Corrections Medical Systems, Inc. "Had Gatti contracted directly with the [jail] or Allegheny County to provide off-site prescription filling services, . . . a sufficient connection [might have] existed between a state actor and Gatti to . . . [establish state action]. Gatti contracted, however, with a private, intermediary third party; it had no contact whatsoever with a state actor and was not one itself." What result if the prisoners had sued Corrections Medical Systems (which they did not do)?

Suppose the plaintiff is neither a prisoner nor a pre-trial detainee. The police take the plaintiff into custody and deliver her to a private hospital, where a psychiatrist examines her and decides to involuntarily commit her. She is forced to stay overnight. Are the hospital and its personnel state actors? *See S. P. v. City of Takoma Park*, 134 F.3d 260 (4th Cir. 1998) (holding that they are not). Suppose the facts are similar except that plaintiff is confined for six days and is forcibly injected with medications? *See McGugan v. Aldana-Bernier*, 752 F.3d 224 (2d Cir. 2014) (no state action). Are these cases consistent with *West*? The distinction between pre-trial detainees and prisoners, on the one hand, and other confined persons, on the other, also carried the day in *Sybalski v. Independent Group Home Living Program*, 546 F.3d 255 (2d Cir. 2008) (a group home for adults with mental disabilities is not a state actor even though, pursuant to a contract with the state, it carried out a duty the state had undertaken (by statute) to "provide custody, care and habilitative services to its mentally retarded citizens").

Sometimes contracting out takes place on a larger scale than in the foregoing illustrative cases. In recent years the United States and some state governments have contracted with private businesses to administer prisons. Courts generally hold that these prisons are state actors and must comply with the Eighth Amendment and other constitutional constraints. *See, e.g., Street v. Corrections Corporation of America*, 102 F.3d 810 (6th Cir. 1996). *See also* Ira P. Robbins, *The Legal Dimensions of Private Incarceration*, 38 AM. U.L. REV. 531, 577–604 (1989).

4. In *Black v. Indiana Area School District*, 985 F.2d 707 (3d Cir. 1993), the school district had contracted school bus service to a private company. Plaintiffs were school children who charged that they were molested by a school bus driver while being driven to and from school. They sued the driver, the school district, school officials, and the bus company. Relying on *Rendell-Baker*, the court rejected liability against the private defendants for lack of state action. *West*, it said, was different. "Because the State, through incarceration, had deprived the inmates of access to medical care, it had a non-delegable constitutional duty to provide medical care on its own." 985 F.2d at 711. Are the school children less vulnerable than prisoners to abuse by private contractors hired by the state? Is it a sufficient answer that children are not legally *required* to ride the bus?

In *Smith v. Insley's, Inc.*, 499 F.3d 875 (8th Cir. 2007), Smith was arrested in March 2003 on a murder charge. Insley's (a private company) towed and impounded his truck pursuant to a contract with the sheriff's office. Smith was eventually released from jail but Insley's sold the truck before he could retrieve it. Insley's sought dismissal of Smith's § 1983 suit on the ground that it was not a state actor, but the court rejected the argument: "Insley's relied upon governmental benefits in performing the tow — as the sheriff's contracted vendor for this service, it had a monopoly on sheriff towing during March 2003. [The] situation was aggravated in a unique way by the incidents of governmental authority, because Smith's representatives were told by various government officials that they could *not* retrieve Smith's vehicle from Insleys due to the ongoing criminal investigation." *Id.* at 880. Does *Smith v. Insley's* cast doubt on *Black*?

5. Are *Blum* and *Rendell-Baker* consistent with *West*? In each case the state contracted out its governmental responsibilities to private entities. Why is the act of a self-employed doctor at a state prison properly deemed state action while the act of a hospital administrator whose patients are funded by the state or a private school administrator at a school, most of whose students' tuitions are paid by the state, is not?

In *Jackson v. Metropolitan Edison Co.*, 419 U.S. 345, 350 (1974), the Court said that the complaining party must show that "there is a sufficiently close nexus between the State and the challenged action of the regulated entity so that the action of the latter may be fairly treated as that of the State itself." In *Blum* it added that "[t]he purpose of this requirement is to assure that constitutional standards are invoked only when it can be said that the State is *responsible* for the specific conduct of which the plaintiff complains. The importance of this assurance is evident when, as in this case, the complaining party seeks to hold the State liable for the actions of private parties." 457 U.S. at 1004.

Is the difference between *West* and the other cases that the doctor is carrying out the state's constitutional obligation to care for its prisoners, while the acts complained of in *Rendell-Baker* — firing teachers — are not closely related to the state's obligations to the students? In *Blum* the act complained of was transferring Medicaid patients to facilities offering a lower level of care. Is this act any less closely connected to the state's obligations than the doctor's acts in *West*? Is *West* distinguishable from *Blum* on the ground that the provision of medical services for the poor is not a constitutional requirement but is undertaken at the state's discretion? Is it relevant in this regard that the state voluntarily participated in the federal Medicaid program as a means of delivering those services?

6. Rather than sending patients to a private hospital at public expense, the government sometimes maintains a public hospital but contracts with a private business for management services. Under such an arrangement all the hospital employees are employees of the private firm. Are they state actors? *Compare Carnes v. Parker*, 922 F.2d 1506, 1509 (10th Cir. 1991) (yes) *with Sherlock v. Montefiore Medical Center*, 84 F.3d 522 (2d Cir. 1996) (no, for purposes of employment decisions). Is *Carnes* consistent in principle with *Blum*? *See also Chalfant v. Wilmington Inst.*, 574 F.2d 739 (3d Cir. 1978) (discharge of employee from library system was state action where the state is extensively involved in support and operations of the library).

Chalfant and *Carnes* rely on *Burton*. Is *Burton* good law after *Blum* and *Rendell-Baker*? Is the test set forth in *Burton*, "sifting facts and weighing circumstances," the equivalent of the inquiry undertaken in *Blum* and *Rendell-Baker*? Those cases consider four factors in deciding whether a private actor was engaged in state action: (a) the entity's source of funding, (b) how extensively it is regulated by the state, (c) whether there is a symbiotic relationship between the state and the private entity, and (d) whether it performs a traditionally governmental function. Note that in *Rendell-Baker* the Court does not quote *Burton*'s "sifting facts and weighing circumstances" language, but characterizes the case as one in which there was a "symbiotic" relationship between government and the coffee shop. *Blum* and *Rendell-Baker* further illustrate that the plaintiff will often fail even if she can establish some of these factors, as the funding test is met in both those cases, yet the plaintiff loses.

Do *Blum* and *Rendell-Baker* represent an effort to narrow the scope of *Burton*? If so, why didn't the Court say so? In any event, lower courts do continue to rely on *Burton*, typically in cases like *Chalfant* and *Carnes* where they end up finding state action.

7. The preceding notes are addressed primarily to the problem of whether and when someone to whom the state has contracted out a task acts under color of state law. *Blum* also adverts to another theme that sometimes surfaces in the cases: The private defendant may act under color of state law if he performs an "exclusive public function."

Is a volunteer fire department whose building, fire trucks, and equipment are furnished by the state, and that receives some of this financing from the city a state actor? *Yeager v. City of McGregor*, 980 F.2d 337 (5th Cir. 1993), holds that it is not. Firefighting is not an "exclusive public function" because Texas law did not *require* municipalities to provide fire protection," and "only half the population of the United States is served by exclusive government fire protection." 980 F.2d at 341.

By contrast, *Goldstein v. Chestnut Ridge Volunteer Fire Co.*, 218 F.3d 337 (4th Cir. 2000) found that a volunteer fire department was a state actor, at least with regard to personnel decisions. The court reasoned that the fire department carried out a traditionally state function, was substantially funded by the state, and was extensively regulated by the state.

The "exclusive public function" theme also figures in *Fabrikant v. French*, 691 F.3d 193 (2d Cir. 2012). The plaintiff sued the private Society for the Prevention of Cruelty to Animals for seizing and neutering her dogs. Citing *West* and quoting *Jackson*, the court said the state action requirement was satisfied: "The dogs were in the custody of the SPCA, and subject to its decisions about their appropriate care, as a result of a specific delegation of authority from the state." In so doing the SPCA exercised "powers traditionally exclusively reserved to the state."

Is the involuntary commitment of mentally ill persons an exclusive public function? *See Wittner v. Banner Health*, 720 F.3d 770 (10th Cir. 2013) (no).

C.   "Entwinement" Between Public Officers and Private Actors

BRENTWOOD ACADEMY v. TENNESSEE SECONDARY SCHOOL ATHLETIC ASSOCIATION, ET AL.
531 U.S. 288 (2001)

JUSTICE SOUTER delivered the opinion of the Court.

The issue is whether a statewide association incorporated to regulate interscholastic athletic competition among public and private secondary schools may be regarded as engaging in state action when it enforces a rule against a member school. The association in question here includes most public schools located within the State, acts through their representatives, draws its officers from them, is largely funded by their dues and income received in their stead, and has historically been seen to regulate in lieu of the State Board of Education's exercise of its own authority. We hold that the association's regulatory activity may and should be treated as state action owing to the pervasive entwinement of state school officials in the structure of the association, there being no offsetting reason to see the association's acts in any other way.

I

Respondent Tennessee Secondary School Athletic Association (Association) is a not-for-profit membership corporation organized to regulate interscholastic sport among the public and private high schools in Tennessee that belong to it. No school is forced to join, but without any other authority actually regulating interscholastic athletics, it enjoys the memberships of almost all the State's public high schools (some 290 of them or 84% of the Association's voting membership), far outnumbering the 55 private schools that belong. A member school's team may play or scrimmage only against the team of another member, absent a dispensation.

The Association's rulemaking arm is its legislative council, while its board of control tends to administration. The voting membership of each of these nine-person committees is limited under the Association's bylaws to high school principals, assistant principals, and superintendents elected by the member schools, and the public school administrators who so serve typically attend meetings during regular school hours. Although the Association's staff members are not paid by the State, they are eligible to join the State's public retirement system for its employees. Member schools pay dues to the Association, though the bulk of its revenue is gate receipts at member teams' football and basketball tournaments, many of them held in public arenas rented by the Association.

The constitution, bylaws, and rules of the Association set standards of school membership and the eligibility of students to play in interscholastic games. Each school, for example, is regulated in awarding financial aid, most coaches must have a Tennessee state teaching license, and players must meet minimum academic standards and hew to limits on student employment. Under the bylaws," in all matters pertaining to the athletic relations of his school," the principal is responsible to the Association, which has the power "to suspend, to fine, or otherwise penalize any member school for the violation of any of the rules of the Association or for other just cause."

Ever since the Association was incorporated in 1925, Tennessee's State Board of Education (State Board) has (to use its own words) acknowledged the corporation's functions "in providing standards, rules and regulations for interscholastic competition in the public schools of Tennessee." More recently, the State Board cited its statutory authority, *Tenn. Code Ann. § 49-1-302*, when it adopted language expressing the relationship between the Association and the Board. Specifically, in 1972, it went so far as to adopt a rule expressly "designating" the Association as "the organization to supervise and regulate the athletic activities in which the public junior and senior high schools in Tennessee participate on an interscholastic basis." The Rule provided that "the authority granted herein shall remain in effect until revoked" and instructed the State Board's chairman to "designate a person or persons to serve in an ex-officio capacity on the [Association's governing bodies]." That same year, the State Board specifically approved the Association's rules and regulations, while reserving the right to review future changes. Thus, on several occasions over the next 20 years, the State Board reviewed, approved, or reaffirmed its approval of the recruiting Rule at issue in this case. In 1996, however, the State Board dropped the original Rule expressly designating the Association as regulator; it substituted a statement "recognizing the value of participation in interscholastic athletics and the role of [the Association] in coordinating interscholastic athletic competition," while "authorizing the public schools of the state to voluntarily maintain membership in [the Association]."

The action before us responds to a 1997 regulatory enforcement proceeding brought against petitioner, Brentwood Academy, a private parochial high school member of the Association. The Association's board of control found that Brentwood violated a rule prohibiting "undue influence" in recruiting athletes, when it wrote to incoming students and their parents about spring football practice. The Association accordingly placed Brentwood's athletic program on probation for four years, declared its football and boys' basketball teams ineligible to compete in playoffs for two years, and imposed a $ 3,000 fine. When these penalties were imposed, all the voting members of the board of control and legislative council were public school administrators.

Brentwood sued the Association and its executive director in federal court under 42 U.S.C. § 1983, claiming that enforcement of the Rule was state action and a violation of the First and Fourteenth Amendments. The District Court entered summary judgment for Brentwood and enjoined the Association from enforcing the [Rule.] The United States Court of Appeals for the Sixth Circuit [reversed.]

We granted certiorari, [and] now reverse.

II

A

Our cases try to plot a line between state action subject to Fourteenth Amendment scrutiny and private conduct (however exceptionable) that is not. The judicial obligation is not only to ' "preserve an area of individual freedom by limiting the reach of federal law' and avoid the imposition of responsibility on a State for conduct it could not control," but also to assure that constitutional standards are invoked "when it can be said that the State is *responsible* for the specific conduct of which the plaintiff complains." If the Fourteenth Amendment is not to be displaced, therefore, its ambit cannot be a simple line between States and people operating outside formally governmental organizations, and the deed of an ostensibly private organization or individual is to be treated sometimes as if a State had caused it to be performed. Thus, we say that state action may be found if, though only if, there is such a "close nexus between the State and the challenged action" that seemingly private behavior "may be fairly treated as that of the State itself."

What is fairly attributable is a matter of normative judgment, and the criteria lack rigid simplicity. From the range of circumstances that could point toward the State behind an individual face, no one fact can function as a necessary condition across the board for finding state action; nor is any set of circumstances absolutely sufficient, for there may be some countervailing reason against attributing activity to the government.

Our cases have identified a host of facts that can bear on the fairness of such an attribution. We have, for example, held that a challenged activity may be state action when it results from the State's exercise of "coercive power," when the State provides "significant encouragement, either overt or covert," *ibid.* or when a private actor operates as a "willful participant in joint activity with the State or its agents." We have treated a nominally private entity as a state actor when it is controlled by an "agency of the State," when it has been delegated a public function by the State, when it is "entwined with governmental policies" or when government is "entwined in [its] management or control,"

Amidst such variety, examples may be the best teachers, and examples from our cases are unequivocal in showing that the character of a legal entity is determined neither by its expressly private characterization in statutory law, nor by the failure of the law to acknowledge the entity's inseparability from recognized government officials or agencies. *Lebron v. National Railroad Passenger Corporation*, 513 U.S. 374 (1995) held that Amtrak was the Government for constitutional purposes, regardless of its congressional designation as private; it was organized under federal law to attain governmental objectives and was directed and controlled by federal appointees. *Pennsylvania v. Board of Directors of City Trusts of Philadelphia* held the privately endowed Gerard College to be a state actor and enforcement of its private founder's limitation of admission to whites attributable to the State, because, consistent with the terms of the settlor's gift, the college's board of directors was a state agency established by state law. Ostensibly the converse situation occurred in *Evans v. Newton*, which held that private trustees to whom a city had transferred a park were nonetheless state actors barred from enforcing racial segregation, since the park served the public purpose of providing community recreation, and "the municipality remained entwined in [its] management [and] control."

These examples of public entwinement in the management and control of ostensibly separate trusts or corporations foreshadow this case, as this Court itself anticipated in [*National Cellegiate Athletic Association v. Tarkanian*, 488 U.S. 179 (1988).] *Tarkanian* arose when an undoubtedly state actor, the University of Nevada, suspended its basketball coach, Tarkanian, in order to comply with rules and recommendations of the National Collegiate Athletic Association (NCAA). The coach charged the NCAA with state action, arguing that the state university had delegated its own functions to the NCAA, clothing the latter with authority to make and apply the university's rules, the result being joint action making the NCAA a state actor.

To be sure, it is not the strict holding in *Tarkanian* that points to our view of this case, for we found no state action on the part of the NCAA. We could see, on the one hand, that the university had some part in setting the NCAA's rules, and the Supreme Court of Nevada had gone so far as to hold that the NCAA had been delegated the university's traditionally exclusive public authority over personnel. But on the other side, the NCAA's policies were shaped not by the University of Nevada alone, but by several hundred member institutions, most of them having no connection with Nevada, and exhibiting no color of Nevada law. Since it was difficult to see the NCAA, not as a collective membership, but as surrogate for the one State, we held the organization's connection with Nevada too insubstantial to ground a state action claim.

But dictum in *Tarkanian* pointed to a contrary result on facts like ours, with an organization whose member public schools are all within a single State. "The situation would, of course, be different if the [Association's] membership consisted entirely of institutions located within the same State, many of them public institutions created by the same [sovereign.]"

B

Just as we foresaw in *Tarkanian*, the "necessarily fact-bound inquiry" leads to the conclusion of state action here. The nominally private character of the Association is overborne by the pervasive entwinement of public institutions and public officials in its composition and workings, and there is no substantial reason to claim unfairness in applying constitutional standards to it.

The Association is not an organization of natural persons acting on their own, but of schools, and of public schools to the extent of 84% of the total. Under the Association's bylaws, each member school is represented by its principal or a faculty member, who has a vote in selecting members of the governing legislative council and board of control from eligible principals, assistant principals and superintendents.

Although the findings and prior opinions in this case include no express conclusion of law that public school officials act within the scope of their duties when they represent their institutions, no other view would be rational, the official nature of their involvement being shown in any number of ways. Interscholastic athletics obviously play an integral part in the public education of Tennessee, where nearly every public high school spends money on competitions among schools. Since a pickup system of interscholastic games would not do, these public teams need some mechanism to produce rules and regulate competition. The mechanism is an organization overwhelmingly composed of public school officials who select representatives (all of them public officials at the time in question here), who in turn adopt and enforce the rules that make the system work. Thus, by giving these jobs to the Association, the 290 public schools of Tennessee belonging to it can sensibly be seen as exercising their own authority to meet their own responsibilities. Unsurprisingly, then, the record indicates that half the council or board meetings documented here were held during official school hours, and that public schools have largely provided for the Association's financial support. A small portion of the Association's revenue comes from membership dues paid by the schools, and the principal part from gate receipts at tournaments among the member schools. Unlike mere public buyers of contract services, whose payments for services rendered do not convert the service providers into public actors, the schools here obtain membership in the service organization and give up sources of their own income to their collective association. The Association thus exercises the authority of the predominantly public schools to charge for admission to their games; the Association does not receive this money from the schools, but enjoys the schools' moneymaking capacity as its own.

In sum, to the extent of 84% of its membership, the Association is an organization of public schools represented by their officials acting in their official capacity to provide an integral element of secondary public schooling. There would be no recognizable Association, legal or tangible, without the public school officials, who do not merely control but overwhelmingly perform all but the purely ministerial acts by which the Association exists and functions in practical terms. Only the 16% minority of private school memberships prevents this entwinement of the Association and the public school system from being total and their identities totally indistinguishable.

To complement the entwinement of public school officials with the Association from the bottom up, the State of Tennessee has provided for entwinement from top down. State Board members are assigned ex officio to serve as members of the board of control and legislative council, and the Association's ministerial employees are treated as state employees to the extent of being eligible for membership in the state retirement system.

It is, of course, true that the time is long past when the close relationship between the surrogate association and its public members and public officials acting as such was attested frankly. As mentioned, the terms of the State Board's Rule expressly designating the Association as regulator of interscholastic athletics in public schools was deleted in 1996, the year after a Federal District Court held that the Association was a state actor because its rules were "caused, directed and controlled by the Tennessee Board of [Education."]

But the removal of the designation language from Rule 0520-1-2-.08 affected nothing but words. Today the State Board's member-designees continue to sit on the Association's committees as nonvoting members, and the State continues to welcome Association employees in its retirement scheme. The close relationship is confirmed by the Association's enforcement of the same preamendment rules and regulations reviewed and approved by the State Board (including the recruiting Rule challenged by Brentwood), and by the State Board's continued willingness to allow students to satisfy its physical education requirement by taking part in interscholastic athletics sponsored by the Association. The most one can say on the evidence is that the State Board once freely acknowledged the Association's official character but now does it by winks and nods. The amendment to the Rule in 1996 affected candor but not the "momentum" of the Association's prior involvement with the State Board. The District Court spoke to this point in finding that because of "custom and practice," "the conduct of the parties has not materially changed" since 1996, "the connections between TSSAA and the State [being] still pervasive and entwined."

The significance of winks and nods in state-action doctrine seems to be one of the points of the dissenters' departure from the rest of the Court. In drawing the public-private action line, the dissenters would emphasize the formal clarity of the legislative action providing for the appointment of Gerard College's trustees in preference to our reliance on the practical certainty in this case that public officials will control operation of the Association under its bylaws. Similarly, the dissenters stress the express formality of the special statute defining Amtrak's ties to the Government in contrast to the reality in this case that the Association's organizers structured the Association's relationships to the officialdom of public education. But if formalism were the sine qua non of state action, the doctrine would vanish owing to the ease and inevitability of its evasion, and for just that reason formalism has never been controlling. For example, a criterion of state action like symbiosis looks not to form but to an underlying reality.

The entwinement down from the State Board is therefore unmistakable, just as the entwinement up from the member public schools is overwhelming. Entwinement will support a conclusion that an ostensibly private organization ought to be charged with a public character and judged by constitutional standards; entwinement to the degree shown here requires it.

C

Entwinement is also the answer to the Association's several arguments offered to persuade us that the facts would not support a finding of state action under various criteria applied in other cases. These arguments are beside the point, simply because the facts justify a conclusion of state action under the criterion of entwinement, a conclusion in no sense unsettled merely because other criteria of state action may not be satisfied by the same facts.

The Association places great stress, for example, on the application of a public function test, as exemplified in Rendell-Baker v. Kohn, 457 U.S. 830 (1982). There, an apparently private school provided education for students whose special needs made it difficult for them to finish high school. The record, however, failed to show any tradition of providing public special education to students unable to cope with a regular school, who had historically been cared for (or ignored) according to private choice. It was true that various public school districts had adopted the practice of referring students to the school and paying their tuition, and no one disputed that providing the instruction aimed at a proper public objective and conferred a public benefit. But we held that the performance of such a public function did not permit a finding of state action on the part of the school unless the function performed was exclusively and traditionally public, as it was not in that case. The Association argues that application of the public function criterion would produce the same result here, and we will assume, *arguendo*, that it would. But this case does not turn on a public function test, any more than *Rendell-Baker* had anything to do with entwinement of public officials in the special school.

For the same reason, it avails the Association nothing to stress that the State neither coerced nor encouraged the actions complained of. "Coercion" and "encouragement" are like "entwinement" in referring to kinds of facts that can justify characterizing an ostensibly private action as public instead. Facts that address any of these criteria are significant, but no one criterion must necessarily be applied. When, therefore, the relevant facts show pervasive entwinement to the point of largely overlapping identity, the implication of state action is not affected by pointing out that the facts might not loom large under a different test.

D

This is not to say that all of the Association's arguments are rendered beside the point by the public officials' involvement in the Association, for after application of the entwinement criterion, or any other, there is a further potential issue, and the Association raises it. Even facts that suffice to show public action (or, standing alone, would require such a finding) may be outweighed in the name of some value at odds with finding public accountability in the circumstances. In *Polk County*, 454 U.S. at 322, a defense lawyer's actions were deemed private even though she was employed by the county and was acting within the scope of her duty as a public defender. Full-time public employment would be conclusive of state action for some purposes, see West v. Atkins, 487 U.S. at 50, accord, *Lugar*, 457 U.S. at 935, n.18, but not when the employee is doing a defense lawyer's primary job; then, the public defender does "not act on behalf of the State; he is the State's adversary." *Polk County, supra,* at 323, n.13. The state-action doctrine does not convert opponents into virtual agents.

The assertion of such a countervailing value is the nub of each of the Association's two remaining arguments, neither of which, however, persuades us. The Association suggests, first, that reversing the judgment here will somehow trigger an epidemic of unprecedented federal litigation. Even if that might be counted as a good reason for a *Polk County* decision to call the Association's action private, the record raises no reason for alarm here. Save for the Sixth Circuit, every Court of Appeals to consider a statewide athletic association like the one here has found it a state [actor.] A reversal of the judgment here portends nothing more than the harmony of an outlying Circuit with precedent otherwise uniform.

Nor do we think there is anything to be said for the Association's contention that there is no need to treat it as a state actor since any public school applying the Association's rules is itself subject to suit under § 1983 or Title IX of the Education Amendments of 1972. If Brentwood's claim were pushing at the edge of the class of possible defendant state actors, an argument about the social utility of expanding that class would at least be on point, but because we are nowhere near the margin in this case, the Association is really asking for nothing less than a dispensation for itself. Its position boils down to saying that the Association should not be dressed in state clothes because other, concededly public actors are; that Brentwood should be kept out of court because a different plaintiff raising a different claim in a different case may find the courthouse open. Pleas for special treatment are hard to sell, although saying that does not, of course, imply anything about the merits of Brentwood's complaint; the issue here is merely whether Brentwood properly names the Association as a § 1983 defendant, not whether it should win on its claim.

The judgment of the Court of Appeals for the Sixth Circuit is reversed, and the case is remanded for further proceedings consistent with this opinion.

It is so ordered.

Justice **Thomas**, with whom The **Chief Justice**, Justice **Scalia**, and Justice **Kennedy** join, dissenting.

We have never found state action based upon mere "entwinement." Until today, we have found a private organization's acts to constitute state action only when the organization performed a public function; was created, coerced, or encouraged by the government; or acted in a symbiotic relationship with the government. The majority's holding — that the Tennessee Secondary School Athletic Association's (TSSAA) enforcement of its recruiting rule is state action — not only extends state-action doctrine beyond its permissible limits but also encroaches upon the realm of individual freedom that the doctrine was meant to protect. I respectfully dissent.

I

[Common] sense dictates that the TSSAA's actions cannot fairly be attributed to the State, and thus cannot constitute state action. The TSSAA was formed in 1925 as a private corporation to organize interscholastic athletics and to sponsor tournaments among its member schools. Any private or public secondary school may join the TSSAA by signing a contract agreeing to comply with its rules and decisions. Although public schools currently compose 84% of the TSSAA's membership, the TSSAA does not require that public schools constitute a set percentage of its membership, and, indeed, no public school need join the TSSAA. The TSSAA's rules are enforced not by a state agency but by its own board of control, which comprises high school principals, assistant principals, and superintendents, none of whom must work at a public school. Of course, at the time the recruiting rule was enforced in this case, all of the board members happened to be public school officials. However, each board member acts in a representative capacity on behalf of all the private and public schools in his region of Tennessee, and not simply his individual school.

The State of Tennessee did not create the TSSAA. The State does not fund the TSSAA and does not pay its employees. In fact, only 4% of the TSSAA's revenue comes from the dues paid by member schools; the bulk of its operating budget is derived from gate receipts at tournaments it sponsors. The State does not permit the TSSAA to use state-owned facilities for a discounted fee, and it does not exempt the TSSAA from state taxation. No Tennessee law authorizes the State to coordinate interscholastic athletics or empowers another entity to organize interscholastic athletics on behalf of the State. The only state pronouncement acknowledging the TSSAA's existence is a rule providing that the State Board of Education permits public schools to maintain membership in the TSSAA if they so [choose.]

Moreover, the State of Tennessee has never had any involvement in the particular action taken by the TSSAA in this case: the enforcement of the TSSAA's recruiting rule prohibiting members from using "undue influence" on students or their parents or guardians "to secure or to retain a student for athletic purposes." There is no indication that the State has ever had any interest in how schools choose to regulate recruiting. In fact, the TSSAA's authority to enforce its recruiting rule arises solely from the voluntary membership contract that each member school signs, agreeing to conduct its athletics in accordance with the rules and decisions of the [TSSAA.]

II

Although the TSSAA's enforcement activities cannot be considered state action as a matter of common sense or under any of this Court's existing theories of state action, the majority presents a new theory. Under this theory, the majority holds that the combination of factors it identifies evidences "entwinement" of the State with the TSSAA, and that such entwinement converts private action into state action. The majority does not define "entwinement," and the meaning of the term is not altogether [clear.]

Because the majority never defines "entwinement," the scope of its holding is unclear. If we are fortunate, the majority's fact-specific analysis will have little bearing beyond this case. But if the majority's new entwinement test develops in future years, it could affect many organizations that foster activities, enforce rules, and sponsor extracurricular competition among high schools — not just in athletics, but in such diverse areas as agriculture, mathematics, music, marching bands, forensics, and cheerleading. Indeed, this entwinement test may extend to other organizations that are composed of, or controlled by, public officials or public entities, such as firefighters, policemen, teachers, cities, or counties. I am not prepared to say that any private organization that permits public entities and public officials to participate acts as the State in anything or everything it does, and our state-action jurisprudence has never reached that far. The state-action doctrine was developed to reach only those actions that are truly attributable to the State, not to subject private citizens to the control of federal courts hearing § 1983 actions.

I respectfully dissent.

NOTES ON ENTWINEMENT

1. In *Focus on the Family v. Pinellas Suncoast Transit Authority*, 344 F.3d 1263 (11th Cir. 2003), Pinellas, a government transit authority, had contracted with a private company to maintain bus shelters along its routes. Under the contract, the private company was prohibited from selling space for certain kinds of advertising, including "advertising promoting . . . political or socially embarrassing" subjects. A religious organization sought to advertise an anti-homosexuality conference, was refused space, and sued the Authority under section 1983. The Authority defended on the ground that the private company made the decision to deny space. The court responded that "where the state contractually requires the private actor to take particular actions — *e.g.*, to reject proposed advertisements under certain specifically delineated circumstances — then it can be said at the summary judgment stage that in acting in accordance with the governmental directive the private actor is merely a surrogate for the [state.] This conclusion is strengthened when there is record evidence that the state itself unmistakably directed the private actor to take particular actions." *Id.* at 1278–79. Few would argue with this reasoning. Is *Brentwood Academy* an equally easy case? For another fairly straightforward post-*Brentwood* decision, see *Hughes v. Region VII Area Agency on Aging*, 542 F.3d 169 (6th Cir. 2008). Denise Hughes worked for Region VII Area Agency on Aging ("Region VII"), a non-profit corporation funded by the state and federal government. Region VII distributed those funds to elder-care providers in several Michigan counties. When Hughes was fired from her position she sued Region VII under § 1983, claiming that the termination was in retaliation for her exercise of First Amendment rights. On the "under color of" issue, the court ruled for the plaintiff. It pointed out that "government entities are the sole members of Region VII and they appoint eleven members of Region VII's board of directors, with their chosen representatives appointing the final member of the board. Furthermore, virtually every act that Region VII performs must receive approval from a state agency." For these and other reasons, "[t]he entwinement of government in the management and control of Region VII is thus a matter of statutory policy."

2. *Compare Brentwood Academy* with *Rendell-Baker*. In each of these cases, the constitutional claim arose under the First Amendment. *Rendell-Baker* ruled

that the private school was not a state actor, though funded almost entirely by the state. *Brentwood Academy* held that the TSSAA was a state actor because so many of its members were public schools within the state. Suppose we take as our premise that the underlying aim of the state action rule in constitutional adjudication is to identify those cases in which the state threatens constitutional values. Granting that free speech values are implicated in both fact patterns, which presents the more compelling case for judicial intervention? Could it be argued that the public has a greater interest in hearing criticism of the practices of a school to which the state sends children with special needs than in preventing a high school athletic association from regulating the efforts of its members to recruit football players? If so, should this be considered in deciding the "state action" question?

3. Private security guards may be state actors if they are granted the powers of the police, or if they cooperate with the police. *See, e.g., Payton v. Rush-Presbyterian-St. Luke's Medical* Center, 184 F.3d 623 (7th Cir. 1999) (security guards had the full powers of regular police officers); *Woodward & Lothrop v. Hillary* 598 A.2d 1142, 1144–46 (D.C. 1991) (the guards had been specially commissioned as police officers under a code provision designed to grant security guards the power to make arrests on the premises where they work, and they had acted in that role when they arrested the plaintiff); *El Fundi v. Deroche*, 625 F.2d 195, 196 (8th Cir. 1980) (cooperation between private guard and police). By contrast, *Wade v. Byles*, 83 F.3d 902 (7th Cir. 1996) found no state action when the security guards' authority was circumscribed; and *White v. Scrivner Corp.*, 594 F.2d 140, 143–44 (5th Cir. 1979), (found that the guard did not act under color of law where the police department had a policy of independently investigating before making arrests for shoplifting. See also *Lindsey v. Detroit Entertainment, LLC*, 484 F.3d 824, 829–30 (6th Cir. 2007) (distinguishing between security guards licensed by the state to make arrests (who are state actors) and unlicensed guards, such as those in this case (who are not state actors).

4. Are private individuals who accept money from the police in exchange for information government actors? *See Ghandi v. Police Department of the City of Detroit*, 823 F.2d 959, 963–64 (6th Cir. 1987) (refusing to make a general rule that they are state actors; in affirming a dismissal of the case the court relied upon the district courts findings that this informant acted "on his own behalf").

5. Ultimately, the Supreme Court upheld TSSAA's anti-recruiting rule against Brentwood's First Amendment challenge. *Tennessee Secondary School Athletic Association v. Brentwood Academy*, 551 U.S. 291 (2007).

NOTES ON CONSPIRACY

1. *Dennis v. Sparks*, 449 U.S. 24 (1980), concerned the liability of private actors who conspire with state officials to deprive the plaintiffs of constitutional rights. A state judge had enjoined the plaintiffs from producing oil from their leases. Although the order was overturned on appeal, the holders of the leases lost two years of production because of it. They brought a suit under section 1983 against the judge who issued the injunction and the private actors who had obtained the injunction, alleging that the defendants had corruptly conspired to deprive them of property without due process of law. The judge was immune from suit on account of absolute judicial immunity, a doctrine that is discussed in Chapter 7. The private defendants maintained that they, too, must be dismissed, on account of the dismissal of the case against their alleged co-conspirator.

The Court disagreed. Before disposing of the private defendant's immunity claim, it addressed the "under color" issue:

> [T]o act "under color of" state law for section 1983 purposes does not require that the defendant be an officer of the State. It is enough that he is a wilful participant in joint action with the State or its agents. Private persons, jointly engaged with state officials in the challenged action, are acting "under color" of law for purposes of section 1983 actions. Of course, merely resorting to the courts and being on the winning side of a lawsuit does not make a party a co-conspirator or a joint actor with the judge. But here the allegations were that an official act of the defendant judge was the product of a corrupt conspiracy involving bribery of the judge. Under these allegations, the private parties conspiring with the judge were acting under color of state law; and it is of no consequence in this respect that the judge himself is immune from damages liability. Immunity does not change the character of the judge's action or that of his co-conspirators.

449 U.S. at 28.

In *Tower v. Glover*, 467 U.S. 914 (1984), the plaintiff, a prisoner, sued the public defender who had represented him at his robbery trial, claiming that the public defender had conspired with state judges and other state officials to obtain the plaintiff's conviction. Citing *Dennis*, the Court allowed the suit to go forward. Is this holding consistent with *Polk County v. Dodson*?

2. What evidence is needed in order to establish a conspiracy? Courts have demanded that plaintiffs make a strong showing of an agreement between the private actor and a public official to violate the plaintiff's constitutional rights. Showing that the plaintiff "was arrested upon the false accusation of [crime] made against him by a private citizen to the police [is] insufficient to state a plausible claim that [the private citizen] and the arresting officers shared a common goal of violating [plaintiff's] rights." *Betts v. Shearman*, 751 F.3d 78, 86 (2d Cir. 2014). Something more is required.

(a) In *Brokers' Choice of America v. NBC Universal, Inc.*, 757 F.3d 1125, 1145 (10th Cir. 2014), the court formulated the test this way:

> In looking at concerted or joint activity, we use a two-step inquiry to determine whether a search by a private individual constitutes state action. We ask (1) whether the government knew of and acquiesced in the private person's intrusive conduct, and (2) whether the party performing the search intended to assist law enforcement efforts or to further his own ends. Both prongs must be satisfied considering the totality of the circumstances before the seemingly private search may be deemed a government search.

In *Brokers' Choice*, this test was met by evidence that both Alabama officials and NBC investigators (for its "Dateline" program) were interested in investigating

Brokers' Choice's sales methods. Thus:

> A deal was struck. Knowing the producers would use hidden cameras to record the seminar, Alabama officials supplied the *Dateline* producers with false credentials they could not otherwise obtain. *Dateline* agreed to share the information it obtained with the Alabama officials . . . *Dateline* shared the information with officials, as intended, to further Albama's investigation. 757 F.3d at 1145.

Turning to the merits, the court found that the search was consensual, despite NBC's use of deception to gain entrance to the sales event.

(b) When there is no clear agreement, plaintiffs have been less successful in establishing a conspiracy. According to one court:

> To establish a prima facie case of section 1983 conspiracy, a plaintiff must show, among other things, that the defendants reached an understanding to violate [his] rights. The plaintiff does not have to produce a "smoking gun" to establish the "understanding" or "willful participation" required to show a conspiracy, but must show some evidence of agreement between the defendants.

Rowe v. City of Fort Lauderdale, 279 F.3d 1271, 1283–84 (11th Cir. 2002). In *Rowe* the plaintiff charged that his ex-wife, Cynthia Doss, had conspired with a prosecutor and other officers to wrongfully prosecute and convict him for sexually abusing his daughter. But the evidence he produced was insufficient to establish a conspiracy.

> At the most, the evidence suggests that Doss coaxed allegations of abuse out of her daughter which she knew were untrue, stayed quiet even though she knew Rowe was being wrongfully prosecuted, and testified untruthfully herself at Rowe's trial. If true this is reprehensible behavior, but it does not involve a conspiracy between Doss and anyone against Rowe, except between Doss and her daughter, who is not a state actor. Rowe simply fails to point to any evidence that suggests an "understanding" between Doss and the various state actors who took part in the investigation and prosecution of Rowe.

(c) The plaintiff in *Franklin v. Fox*, 312 F.3d 423, 445 (9th Cir. 2002), claimed that his daughter had conspired with the police, including an officer named Murray, to obtain evidence from him in a jailhouse visit, with the aim of using the evidence to convict him of murder. The court said:

> To be liable as co-conspirators, each participant in a conspiracy need not know the exact details of the plan, but each participant must at least share the common objective of the plan. To be liable as a co-conspirator, a private defendant must share with the public entity the goal of violating a plaintiff's constitutional rights. [Our] cases have been careful to require a substantial degree of cooperation before imposing civil liability for actions by private individuals that impinge on civil rights. [Here] there is no evidence of any conspiracy or joint action between [the daughter] and Murray. Franklin offers no evidence that [his daughter] made repeated requests or solicited Murray's input on the types of questions she should ask her father. It is also

undisputed that the jailhouse visit was [the daughter's] idea, and not a state-initiated effort to use her to extract her father's confession. Although the interview and its subsequent use against Franklin at trial violated *Massiah*, the government did not sufficiently insinuate itself into [the daughter's] jailhouse visit to transform her private actions into one fairly attributable to the state.

(d) In *Mershon v. Beasley*, 994 F.2d 449, 451 (8th Cir. 1993), the Mershon brothers had borrowed money from the Missouri Farmers Association. The MFA made a criminal complaint against the Mershons, claiming that they had defrauded a creditor. The state initiated a prosecution but later dropped the charges. The Mershons then brought a section 1983 suit against the MFA and their employees, including William Beasley. Beasley sought dismissal on the ground that he did not act under color of state law and so could not be sued under section 1983. The Eighth Circuit agreed.

In its order denying a JNOV to Mr. Beasley on this issue, the trial court referred to evidence that the county prosecutor was the son of a "substantial client" of the MFA, that the county prosecutor himself was an officer of a corporation that did "considerable business with [the] MFA," that multiple communications had taken place between Mr. Beasley and the county prosecutor, and that a check that had implicated the Mershons at the state probable cause hearing had been altered by another employee at the MFA. The trial court concluded that "the totality of the evidence" established a submissible case on Mr. Beasley's alleged conspiracy with the county prosecutor. We disagree . . . .

[A] plaintiff seeking to hold a private party liable under section 1983 must allege, at the very least, that there was a mutual understanding, or a meeting of the minds, between the private party and the state actor. [Evidence] must be produced from which reasonable jurors could conclude that such an agreement was come to. [Here] the evidence was insufficient as a matter of law on the question of a mutual understanding, or a meeting of the minds, between Mr. Beasley and the county prosecutor. [It] is undisputed that there were multiple contacts between Mr. Beasley and the county prosecutor. [The] MFA was, however, the complaining party in the criminal case. We do not believe that the fact of these contacts, by themselves and without more, allows the inference that Mr. Beasley and the county prosecutor ever reached any mutual understanding that the MFA would use the criminal process for the purpose of collecting its civil debt. The Mershons offered no evidence, for example, that the MFA had sought criminal prosecution of other defaulting debtors in the past or, indeed, that the county prosecutor had filed criminal charges in the past against other debtors who had defaulted on loans from the MFA.

The Mershons' theory as to why the county prosecutor would agree to misuse the power of his office seems to have been that a criminal conviction of the Mershons would have precluded the discharge in bankruptcy of the debt to the MFA that was secured by the crops sold, that the county prosecutor and his father were owed a debt that was secured by the same crops, and that a criminal conviction of the Mershons would therefore generate a similar exception to bankruptcy discharge of the debt owed to the county prosecutor and his father. [We] consider extremely attenuated [any] connection, based on this theory, between the decision to prosecute and the personal benefit the county prosecutor might have realized from pursuing the criminal action against the Mershons. Any inference of a mutual understanding that would be drawn from this tenuous connection between the county prosecutor and Mr. Beasley, in our view, could be the result only of "mere conjecture and speculation."

Id. at 451–52.

In *Rowe, Franklin*, and *Mershon*, the plaintiffs' conspiracy theory failed. Consider (1) the courts' explanations as to why the plaintiff's conspiracy theory fails, and (2), given those explanations, what additional facts the plaintiffs would have to prove in order to establish a conspiracy.

(e) The foregoing cases suggest that plaintiffs face substantial hurdles in establishing an agreement between officials and private actors. Even so, circumstantial evidence may suffice. For an illustration, see *White v. McKinley*, 519 F.3d 806, 816 (8th Cir. 2008). White had been charged (but eventually acquitted) of molesting his adopted daughter. He then sued his ex-wife (Tina) and a police detective (Richard McKinley) who had investigated the molestation charges. Upholding the district court's denial of summary judgment to the defendants, the court said:

> Viewing the facts in a light most favorable to White, a reasonable juror could find that Tina and Richard reached a meeting of the minds to withhold exculpatory evidence from prosecutors and White. White offers evidence that Tina and Richard were romantically involved shortly after White was accused, and there is also evidence that Tina and Richard knew each other before the abuse allegations even surfaced. Some evidence suggests that Richard reviewed and returned the potentially exculpatory diary to Tina and that the diary then disappeared. There is also evidence that Tina stood to gain financially from White's conviction. Because the elements of conspiracy are rarely established through means other than circumstantial evidence, and here there is sufficient evidence to support a reasonable inference of conspiracy, summary judgment was not appropriate.

Is *White* consistent with *Mershon*?

3. May a conspiracy exist where state officers take no harmful action toward the plaintiff, but simply fail to protect him against private violence? *Dwares v. City of New York*, 985 F.2d 94 (2d Cir. 1993), arose when "skinheads" beat the plaintiffs, who were burning an American flag. The plaintiffs alleged that the police had told the skinheads that, should they beat the plaintiffs, the police would not intervene, "unless they got totally out of control." 985 F.2d at 99. According to the second circuit, this allegation stated a constitutional claim against the skinheads and the police.

Is this holding compatible with *DeShaney v. Winnebago Co. Dep't of Social Services*, 489 U.S. 189 (1989)? *See* Chapter 4.

How would *Dwares* come out if the evidence showed that the police never spoke to the skinheads, but the skinheads inferred from the passivity of the officers that the police would not intervene? Recall from *Mershon, supra*, that "a plaintiff seeking to hold a private party liable under section 1983 must allege, at the very least, that there was a mutual understanding, or a meeting of the minds, between the private party and the state actor." Would this standard be met on the hypothesized facts?

4. Do not be misled by our decision to treat *Dennis* in notes, rather than featuring it as a main case. The opinion is terse and elliptical, and not a particularly good teaching vehicle. Yet from a litigator's point of view, *Dennis* provides the main doctrinal vehicle for plaintiffs seeking to sue private actors under section 1983. Unless the case concerns a self-help remedy like the ones at issue in *Lugar* and *Flagg Brothers*, the plaintiff will frequently need to show a conspiracy between private and public actors in order to maintain his section 1983 case against the private party. If he survives a "state action"/"color of law" challenge, his case against the private defendant may be far stronger than his other claims, for many private actors will not be able to escape damages liability by asserting an immunity defense. *See* Chapter 8.

Chapter 3

"SECURED BY THE CONSTITUTION AND LAWS"

MAJOR SUBSTANTIVE THEMES
IN CONSTITUTIONAL TORTS

This chapter examines many of the substantive constitutional issues that arise when litigants sue under section 1983 or *Bivens*. The next chapter discusses the special problems that come up when a plaintiff claims that government owes him an affirmative constitutional duty or sues for deprivation of federal statutory rights.

Many section 1983 suits rely upon the specifics of the Bill of Rights. Prominent themes in section 1983 litigation include actions brought to enforce (a) the free speech clause of the First Amendment, by public employees who have been fired or disciplined on account of something they said; (b) the "unreasonable search and seizure" clause of the Fourth Amendment, by persons who think the police went too far in going through their homes or their belongings or used excessive force in arresting them; and (c) the "cruel and unusual punishment" clause of the Eighth Amendment, by prisoners claiming that prison conditions or disciplinary measures are too harsh.

Dennis v. Higgins, 498 U.S. 439 (1991), illustrates the breadth of section 1983. The plaintiff used section 1983 as the vehicle for raising a claim that state taxation violated the commerce clause. Noting that section 1983 covered all constitutional rights, and citing a well-established principle that commerce clause violations are violations of constitutional rights, the Court allowed the suit to go forward. *See* Note, *Doctrinal Foundations of Section 1983 and the Resurgent Dormant Commerce Clause*, 77 IOWA L. REV. 1249 (1992). In *Florida Transportation Services, Inc. v. Miami-Dade County*, 703 F.3d 1230 (11th Cir. 2012), for example, the court upheld a jury award of $3.55 million in a § 1983 commerce clause case against a county and its officials. The court characterized the case as one in which the county, in its application of its stevedore permitting ordinance, violated the dormant commerce clause "by rubber-stamping and automatically renewing permits for all existing stevedore permit holders at the Port and automatically denying permits to all new applicants."

In each of these kinds of litigation, the starting point for assessing the substantive viability of the plaintiff's claim is the general body of constitutional doctrine that one studies in courses on constitutional law. Casebooks on constitutional law typically devote little attention to the particular aspects of constitutional law that figure prominently in constitutional tort cases. For example, treatments of the first amendment devote many more pages to such topics as pornography and commercial speech than they do to the first amendment rights of public employees. Because public employee speech is a staple of constitutional tort litigation, we discuss it in this chapter. The fourth amendment is generally dealt with in casebooks on criminal procedure, where the focus, understandably, is on such matters as the requirements for obtaining a warrant, the exceptions to the warrant requirement, and searches incident to arrest. Yet the Fourth Amendment also furnishes the constitutional grounding for section 1983 suits seeking damages for police use of excessive force, of which there are many. Similarly, certain areas of equal protection and Eighth Amendment doctrine have far more prominence in section 1983 litigation than they do in constitutional law casebooks. Because of their significance in constitutional tort law, this chapter examines these substantive constitutional themes in some detail.

I.   THE DUE PROCESS CLAUSE IN CONSTITUTIONAL TORT LAW

The Due Process Clause of the Fourteenth Amendment gives rise to an especially important and complex group of substantive issues in constitutional tort law. That clause provides, in relevant part: "[N]or shall any State deprive any person of life, liberty, or property without due process of law." In the basic constitutional law course, students learn that this provision is the vehicle by which most of the bill of rights have been "incorporated" into the Fourteenth Amendment and applied to the states. And they study the long and checkered history of "substantive due process," both as a tool for striking down economic regulation in the early 20th century and, more recently, as a ground for guaranteeing rights of privacy and personal autonomy against state interference. But the constitutional law casebooks give scant attention to the distinctive "due process" issues that typically arise in constitutional tort litigation. One group of issues, taken up in sections A and B, relates to the content of the terms "property" and "liberty." Given that the plaintiff's property or liberty interests are at stake, sections C and D examine the procedural and substantive constitutional protection those interests receive. Section E explores the issue of constitutional rights for persons in custody, and section F addresses the relevance of state remedies to due process litigation.

A.   "Property"

TOWN OF CASTLE ROCK v. GONZALES
545 U.S. 748 (2005)

JUSTICE SCALIA delivered the opinion of the Court.

We decide in this case whether an individual who has obtained a state-law restraining order has a constitutionally protected property interest in having the police enforce the restraining order when they have probable cause to believe it has been violated.

I

The horrible facts of this case are contained in the complaint that respondent Jessica Gonzales filed in Federal District Court. (Because the case comes to us on appeal from a dismissal of the complaint, we assume its allegations are true.) Respondent alleges that petitioner, the town of Castle Rock, Colorado, violated the Due Process Clause of the Fourteenth Amendment to the United States Constitution when its police officers, acting pursuant to official policy or custom, failed to respond properly to her repeated reports her estranged husband was violating the terms of a restraining order. [The complaint alleged that Gonzales' estranged husband took their daughters from her house between 5:00 p.m. and 5:30 p.m.]

At approximately 8:30 p.m., respondent talked to her husband on his cellular telephone. He told her "he had the three children [at an] amusement park in Denver." She called the police again and asked them to "have someone check for" her husband or his vehicle at the amusement park and "put out an [all points bulletin]" for her husband, but the officer with whom she spoke "refused to do so," again telling her to "wait until 10:00 pm. and see if" her husband returned the girls.

At approximately 10:10 p.m., respondent called the police and said her children were still missing, but she was now told to wait until midnight. She called at midnight and told the dispatcher her children were still missing. She went to her husband's apartment and, finding nobody there, called the police at 12:10 a.m.; she was told to wait for an officer to arrive. When none came, she went to the police station at 12:50 a.m. and submitted an incident report. The officer who took the report "made no reasonable effort to enforce the TRO or locate the three children. Instead, he went to dinner."

At approximately 3:20 a.m., respondent's husband arrived at the police station and opened fire with a semiautomatic handgun he had purchased earlier that evening. Police shot back, killing him. Inside the cab of his pickup truck, they found the bodies of all three daughters, whom he had already murdered.

On the basis of the foregoing factual allegations, respondent brought an action under 42 U.S.C. § 1983, claiming that the town violated the Due Process Clause because its police department had "an official policy or custom of failing to respond properly to complaints of restraining order violations" and "tolerate[d] the non-enforcement of restraining orders by its police officers." [Before] answering the complaint the defendants filed a motion to dismiss under Federal Rule of Civil Procedure 12(b)(6). The District Court granted the motion, concluding that, whether construed as making a substantive due process or procedural due process claim, respondent's complaint failed to state a claim upon which relief could be granted.

A panel of the Court of Appeals affirmed the rejection of a substantive due process claim, but found that respondent had alleged a cognizable procedural due process claim. On rehearing en banc, a divided court reached the same disposition, concluding that respondent had a "protected property interest in the enforcement of the terms of her restraining order" and that the town had deprived her of due process because "the police never 'heard' nor seriously entertained her request to enforce and protect her interests in the restraining order."

II

The Fourteenth Amendment to the United States Constitution provides that a State shall not "deprive any person of life, liberty, or property, without due process of law." In 42 U.S.C. § 1983, Congress has created a federal cause of action for "the deprivation of any rights, privileges, or immunities secured by the Constitution and laws." Respondent claims the benefit of this provision on the ground that she had a property interest in police enforcement of the restraining order against her husband; and that the town deprived her of this property without due process by having a policy that tolerated nonenforcement of restraining orders.

As the Court of Appeals recognized, we left a similar question unanswered in *DeShaney v. Winnebago County Dep't of Social Servs.*, 489 U.S. 189 (1989), another case with "undeniably tragic" facts: Local child-protection officials had failed to protect a young boy from beatings by his father that left him severely brain damaged. We held that the so-called "substantive" component of the Due Process Clause does not "requir[e] the State to protect the life, liberty, and property of its citizens against invasion by private actors." We noted, however, that the petitioner had not properly preserved the argument that — and we thus "decline[d] to consider" whether — state "child protection statutes gave [him] an 'entitlement' to receive protective services in accordance with the terms of the statute, an entitlement which would enjoy due process protection."

The procedural component of the Due Process Clause does not protect everything that might be described as a "benefit": "To have a property interest in a benefit, a person clearly must have more than an abstract need or desire" and "more than a unilateral expectation of it. He must, instead, have a legitimate claim of entitlement to it." *Board of Regents of State Colleges v. Roth*, 408 U.S. 564, 577 (1972). Such entitlements are, " 'of course, . . . not created by the Constitution. Rather, they are created and their dimensions are defined by existing rules or understandings that stem from an independent source such as state law.' "

A

Our cases recognize that a benefit is not a protected entitlement if government officials may grant or deny it in their discretion. The Court of Appeals in this case determined that Colorado law created an entitlement to enforcement of the restraining order because the "court-issued restraining order . . . specifically dictated that its terms must be enforced" and a "state statute command[ed]" enforcement of the order when certain objective conditions were met (probable cause to believe that the order had been violated and that the object of the order had received notice of its existence). Respondent contends that we are obliged "to give deference to the Tenth Circuit's analysis of Colorado law on" whether she had an entitlement to enforcement of the restraining order.

We will not, of course, defer to the Tenth Circuit on the ultimate issue: whether what Colorado law has given respondent constitutes a property interest for purposes of the Fourteenth Amendment. That determination, despite its state-law underpinnings, is ultimately one of federal constitutional law. "Although the underlying substantive interest is created by 'an independent source such as state law,' *federal constitutional law* determines whether that interest rises to the level of a 'legitimate claim of entitlement' protected by the Due Process Clause." *Memphis Light, Gas & Water Div. v. Craft*, 436 U.S. 1, 9 (1978) (emphasis added). Resolution of the federal issue begins, however, with a determination of what it is that state law provides. In the context of the present case, the central state-law question is whether Colorado law gave respondent a right to police enforcement of the restraining order. It is on this point that respondent's call for deference to the Tenth Circuit is relevant.

We have said that a "presumption of deference [is] given the views of a federal court as to the law of a State within its jurisdiction." That presumption can be overcome, however, and we think deference inappropriate here. The Tenth Circuit's opinion, which reversed the Colorado District Judge, did not draw upon a deep well of state-specific expertise, but consisted primarily of quoting language from the restraining order, the statutory text, and a state-legislative-hearing transcript. These texts, moreover, say nothing distinctive to Colorado, but use mandatory language that (as we shall discuss) appears in many state and federal statutes. As for case law: The only state-law cases about restraining orders that the Court of Appeals relied upon were decisions of Federal District Courts in Ohio and Pennsylvania and state courts in New Jersey, Oregon, and Tennessee. Moreover, if we were simply to accept the Court of Appeals' conclusion, we would necessarily have to decide conclusively a federal constitutional question (*i.e.*, whether such an entitlement constituted property under the Due Process Clause and, if so, whether petitioner's customs or policies provided too little process to protect it). We proceed, then, to our own analysis of whether Colorado law gave respondent a right to enforcement of the restraining order.

B

The critical language in the restraining order came not from any part of the order itself (which was signed by the state-court trial judge and directed to the restrained party, respondent's husband), but from the preprinted notice to law-enforcement personnel that appeared on the back of the order. That notice effectively restated the statutory provision describing "peace officers' duties" related to the crime of violation of a restraining order. At the time of the conduct at issue in this case, that provision read as follows:

"(a) Whenever a restraining order is issued, the protected person shall be provided with a copy of such order. *A peace officer shall use every reasonable means to enforce a restraining order.*

"(b) *A peace officer shall arrest, or, if an arrest would be impractical under the circumstances, seek a warrant for the arrest of a restrained person* when the peace officer has information amounting to probable cause that:

"(I) The restrained person has violated or attempted to violate any provision of a restraining order; and

"(II) The restrained person has been properly served with a copy of the restraining order or the restrained person has received actual notice of the existence and substance of such order.

"(c) In making the probable cause determination described in paragraph (b) of this subsection (3), a peace officer shall assume that the information received from the registry is accurate. *A peace officer shall enforce a valid restraining order whether or not there is a record of the restraining order in the registry.*" Colo. Rev. Stat. § 18-6-803.5(3) (Lexis 1999) (emphases added).

The Court of Appeals concluded that this statutory provision-especially taken in conjunction with a statement from its legislative history, and with another statute restricting criminal and civil liability for officers making arrests-established the Colorado Legislature's clear intent "to alter the fact that the police were not enforcing domestic abuse restraining orders," and thus its intent "that the recipient of a domestic abuse restraining order have an entitlement to its enforcement." Any other result, it said, "would render domestic abuse restraining orders utterly valueless."

This last statement is sheer hyperbole. Whether or not respondent had a right to enforce the restraining order, it rendered certain otherwise lawful conduct by her husband both criminal and in contempt of court. The creation of grounds on which he could be arrested, criminally prosecuted, and held in contempt was hardly "valueless" — even if the prospect of those sanctions ultimately failed to prevent him from committing three murders and a suicide.

We do not believe that these provisions of Colorado law truly made enforcement of restraining orders *mandatory.* A well established tradition of police discretion has long coexisted with apparently mandatory arrest statutes.

"In each and every state there are long-standing statutes that, by their terms, seem to preclude nonenforcement by the police. . . . However, for a number of reasons, including their legislative history, insufficient resources, and sheer physical impossibility, it has been recognized that such statutes cannot be interpreted literally. . . . [T]hey clearly do not mean that a police officer may not lawfully decline to make an arrest. As to third parties in these states, the full-enforcement statutes simply have no effect, and their significance is further diminished." 1 ABA Standards for Criminal Justice 1-4.5, commentary, pp 1-124 to 1-125 (2d ed. 1980) (footnotes omitted).

The deep-rooted nature of law-enforcement discretion, even in the presence of seemingly mandatory legislative commands, is illustrated by *Chicago v. Morales,* 527 U.S. 41 (1999), which involved an ordinance that said a police officer " 'shall order' " persons to disperse in certain circumstances. This Court rejected out of hand the possibility that "the mandatory language of the ordinance . . . afford[ed] the police *no* discretion." It is, the Court proclaimed, simply "common sense that *all* police officers must use some discretion in deciding when and where to enforce city ordinances."(emphasis added).

Against that backdrop, a true mandate of police action would require some stronger indication from the Colorado Legislature than "shall use every reasonable means to enforce a restraining order" (or even "shall arrest . . . or . . . seek a warrant"), §§ 18-6-803.5(3)(a), (b). That language is not perceptibly more mandatory than the Colorado statute which has long told municipal chiefs of police that they "shall pursue and arrest any person fleeing from justice in any part of the state" and that they "shall apprehend any person in the act of committing any offense . . . and, forthwith and without any warrant, bring such person before a . . . competent authority for examination and trial." Colo. Rev. Stat. § 31-4-112 (Lexis 2004). It is hard to imagine that a Colorado peace officer would not have some discretion to determine that — despite probable cause to believe a restraining order has been violated — the circumstances of the violation or the competing duties of that officer or his agency counsel decisively against enforcement in a particular instance. The practical necessity for discretion is particularly apparent in a case such as this one, where the suspected violator is not actually present and his whereabouts are [unknown.]

Respondent does not specify the precise means of enforcement that the Colorado restraining-order statute assertedly mandated — whether her interest lay in having police arrest her husband, having them seek a warrant for his arrest, or having them "use every reasonable means, up to and including arrest, to enforce the order's terms," Such indeterminacy is not the hallmark of a duty that is mandatory. Nor can someone be safely deemed "entitled" to something when the identity of the alleged entitlement is [vague.]

Even if the statute could be said to have made enforcement of restraining orders "mandatory" because of the domestic-violence context of the underlying statute, that would not necessarily mean that state law gave *respondent* an entitlement to *enforcement* of the mandate. Making the actions of government employees obligatory can serve various legitimate ends other than the conferral of a benefit on a specific class of people. See, *e.g.*, *Sandin v. Conner*, 515 U.S. 472, 482 (1995) (finding no constitutionally protected liberty interest in prison regulations phrased in mandatory terms, in part because "[s]uch guidelines are not set forth solely to benefit the prisoner"). The serving of public rather than private ends is the normal course of the criminal law because criminal acts, "besides the injury [they do] to individuals, . . . strike at the very being of society; which cannot possibly subsist, where actions of this sort are suffered to escape with impunity." 4 W. Blackstone, Commentaries on the Laws of England 5 (1769); see also *Huntington v. Attrill*, 146 U.S. 657, 668 (1892). This principle underlies, for example, a Colorado district attorney's discretion to prosecute a domestic assault, even though the victim withdraws her charge. See *People v. Cunefare*, 102 P. 3d 302, 311–312 (Colo. 2004) (en banc) (Bender, J., concurring in part, dissenting in part, and dissenting in part to the judgment).

Respondent's alleged interest stems only from a State's *statutory* scheme — from a restraining order that was authorized by and tracked precisely the statute on which the Court of Appeals relied. She does not assert that she has any common-law or contractual entitlement to enforcement. If she was given a statutory entitlement, we would expect to see some indication of that in the statute itself. Although Colorado's statute spoke of "protected person[s]" such as respondent, it did so in connection with matters other than a right to enforcement. It said that a "protected person shall be provided with a copy of [a restraining] order" when it is issued, § 18-6-803.5(3)(a); that a law enforcement agency "shall make all reasonable efforts to contact the protected party upon the arrest of the restrained person,"

§ 18-6-803.5(3)(d); and that the agency "shall give [to the protected person] a copy" of the report it submits to the court that issued the order, § 18-6-803.5(3)(e). Perhaps most importantly, the statute spoke directly to the protected person's power to "initiate contempt proceedings against the restrained person if the order [was] issued in a civil action or request the prosecuting attorney to initiate contempt proceedings if the order [was] issued in a criminal action." § 18-6-803.5(7). The protected person's express power to "initiate" civil contempt proceedings contrasts tellingly with the mere ability to "request" initiation of criminal contempt proceedings — and even more dramatically with the complete silence about any power to "request" (much less demand) that an arrest be made.

The creation of a personal entitlement to something as vague and novel as enforcement of restraining orders cannot "simply g[o] without saying." We conclude that Colorado has not created such an entitlement.

C

Even if we were to think otherwise concerning the creation of an entitlement by Colorado, it is by no means clear that an individual entitlement to enforcement of a restraining order could constitute a "property" interest for purposes of the Due Process Clause. Such a right would not, of course, resemble any traditional conception of property. Although that alone does not disqualify it from due process protection, as *Roth* and its progeny show, the right to have a restraining order enforced does not "have some ascertainable monetary value," as even our "*Roth*-type property-as-entitlement" cases have implicitly required. Merrill, The Landscape of Constitutional Property, *86 Va. L. Rev. 885, 964 (2000)*. Perhaps most radically, the alleged property interest here arises *incidentally*, not out of some new species of government benefit or service, but out of a function that government actors have always performed — to wit, arresting people who they have probable cause to believe have committed a criminal offense.

The indirect nature of a benefit was fatal to the due process claim of the nursing-home residents in *O'Bannon v. Town Court Nursing Center*, 447 U.S. 773 (1980). We held that, while the withdrawal of "direct benefits" (financial payments under Medicaid for certain medical services) triggered due process protections, the same was not true for the "indirect benefit[s]" conferred on Medicaid patients when the Government enforced "minimum standards of care" for nursing-home facilities. "[A]n indirect and incidental result of the Government's enforcement action . . . does not amount to a deprivation of any interest in life, liberty, or property." In this case, as in *O'Bannon*, "[t]he simple distinction between government action that directly affects a citizen's legal rights . . . and action that is directed against a third party and affects the citizen only indirectly or incidentally, provides a sufficient answer to" respondent's reliance on cases that found government-provided services to be entitlements. The *O'Bannon* Court expressly noted, *ibid.*, that the distinction between direct and indirect benefits distinguished *Memphis Light, Gas & Water Div. v. Craft*, 436 U.S. 1 (1978), one of the government-services cases on which the dissent relies.

III

We conclude, therefore, that respondent did not, for purposes of the Due Process Clause, have a property interest in police enforcement of the restraining order against her husband. It is accordingly unnecessary to address the Court of Appeals' determination that the town's custom or policy prevented the police from giving her due process when they deprived her of that alleged interest. In light of today's decision and that in *DeShaney*, the benefit that a third party may receive from having someone else arrested for a crime generally does not trigger protections under the Due Process Clause, neither in its procedural nor in its "substantive" manifestations. This result reflects our continuing reluctance to treat the Fourteenth Amendment as " 'a font of tort law,' " but it does not mean States are powerless to provide victims with personally enforceable remedies. Although the framers of the Fourteenth Amendment and the Civil Rights Act of 1871 did not create a system by which police departments are generally held financially accountable for crimes that better policing might have prevented, the people of Colorado are free to craft such a system under state law.

The judgment of the Court of Appeals is reversed.

[JUSTICE SOUTER's concurring opinion, which was joined by JUSTICE BREYER, is omitted.]

JUSTICE STEVENS, with whom JUSTICE GINSBURG joins, dissenting.

The issue presented to us is much narrower than is suggested by the far-ranging arguments of the parties and their *amici*. Neither the tragic facts of the case, nor the importance of according proper deference to law enforcement professionals, should divert our attention from that issue. That issue is whether the restraining order entered by the Colorado trial court on June 4, 1999, created a "property" interest that is protected from arbitrary deprivation by the Due Process Clause of the Fourteenth Amendment.

It is perfectly clear, on the one hand, that neither the Federal Constitution itself, nor any federal statute, granted respondent or her children any individual entitlement to police protection. See *DeShaney v. Winnebago County Dep't of Social Servs.*, 489 U.S. 189 (1989). Nor, I assume, does any Colorado statute create any such entitlement for the ordinary citizen. On the other hand, it is equally clear that federal law imposes no impediment to the creation of such an entitlement by Colorado law. Respondent certainly could have entered into a contract with a private security firm, obligating the firm to provide protection to respondent's family; respondent's interest in such a contract would unquestionably constitute "property" within the meaning of the Due Process Clause. If a Colorado statute enacted for her benefit, or a valid order entered by a Colorado judge, created the functional equivalent of such a private contract by granting respondent an entitlement to mandatory individual protection by the local police force, that state-created right would also qualify as "property" entitled to constitutional protection.

I do not understand the majority to rule out the foregoing propositions, although it does express doubts Moreover, the majority does not contest that if respondent did have a cognizable property interest in this case, the deprivation of that interest violated due process. As the Court notes, respondent has alleged that she presented the police with a copy of the restraining order issued by the Colorado court and requested that it be [enforced.] The central question in this case is therefore whether, as a matter of Colorado law, respondent had a right to police assistance comparable to the right she would have possessed to any other service the government or a private firm might have undertaken to provide. See *Board of Regents of State Colleges v. Roth*, 408 U.S. 564, 577 (1972) ("Property interests, of course, are not created by the Constitution. Rather, they are created and their dimensions are defined by existing rules or understandings that stem from an independent source such as state law — rules or understandings that secure certain benefits and that support claims of entitlement to those benefits").

[In a section of the opinion that we omit, Justice Stevens maintained that the Court should have deferred to the 10th circuit's reading of state law.]

III

Three flaws in the Court's rather superficial analysis of the merits highlight the unwisdom of its decision to answer the state-law question *de novo*. First, the Court places undue weight on the various statutes throughout the country that seemingly mandate police enforcement but are generally understood to preserve police discretion. As a result, the Court gives short shrift to the unique case of "mandatory arrest" statutes in the domestic violence context. States passed a wave of these statutes in the 1980's and 1990's with the unmistakable goal of eliminating police discretion in this area. Second, the Court's formalistic analysis fails to take seriously the fact that the Colorado statute at issue in this case was enacted for the benefit of the narrow class of persons who are beneficiaries of domestic restraining orders, and that the order at issue in this case was specifically intended to provide protection to respondent and her children. Finally, the Court is simply wrong to assert that a citizen's interest in the government's commitment to provide police enforcement in certain defined circumstances does not resemble any "traditional conception of property"; in fact, a citizen's property interest in such a commitment is just as concrete and worthy of protection as her interest in any other important service the government or a private firm has undertaken to [provide.]

[W]hen Colorado passed its statute in 1994, it joined the ranks of 15 States that mandated arrest for domestic violence offenses and 19 States that mandated arrest for domestic restraining order violations. Given the specific purpose of these statutes, there can be no doubt that the Colorado Legislature used the term "shall" advisedly in its domestic restraining order statute. While "shall" is probably best read to mean "may" in other Colorado statutes that seemingly mandate enforcement, cf. Colo. Rev. Stat. § 31-4-112 (Lexis 2004) (police "*shall suppress* all riots, disturbances, and breaches of the peace, *shall apprehend* all disorderly persons in the city . . ." (emphases added)), it is clear that the elimination of police discretion was integral to Colorado and its fellow States' solution to the problem of underenforcement in domestic violence cases. Since the text of Colorado's statute perfectly captures this legislative purpose, it is hard to imagine what the Court has in mind when it insists on "some stronger indication from the Colorado [Legislature."]

Indeed, the Court fails to come to terms with the wave of domestic violence statutes that provides the crucial context for understanding Colorado's law. The Court concedes that, "in the specific context of domestic violence, mandatory-arrest statutes have been found in some States to be more mandatory than traditional mandatory-arrest statutes," but that is a serious understatement. The difference is not a matter of degree, but of kind. Before this wave of statutes, the legal rule was one of discretion; as the Court shows, the "traditional," general mandatory arrest statutes have always been understood to be "mandatory" in name only. The innovation of the domestic violence statutes was to make police enforcement, not "more mandatory," but simply *mandatory*. If, as the Court says, the existence of a protected "entitlement" turns on whether "government officials may grant or deny it in their discretion," the new mandatory statutes undeniably create an entitlement to police enforcement of restraining orders.

Perhaps recognizing this point, the Court glosses over the dispositive question — whether the police enjoyed discretion to deny enforcement — and focuses on a different question — which "precise means of enforcement," were called for in this case. But that question is a red herring. The statute directs that, upon probable cause of a violation, "a peace officer shall arrest, or, if an arrest would be impractical under the circumstances, seek a warrant for the arrest of a restrained person." Colo. Rev. Stat. § 18-6-803.5(3)(b) (Lexis 1999). Regardless of whether the enforcement called for in this case was arrest or the seeking of an arrest warrant (the answer to that question probably changed over the course of the night as the respondent gave the police more information about the husband's whereabouts), the crucial point is that, under the statute, the police were *required* to provide enforcement; *they lacked the discretion to do nothing*. The Court suggests that the fact that "enforcement" may encompass different acts infects any entitlement to enforcement with "indeterminacy." But this objection is also unfounded. Our cases have never required the object of an entitlement to be some mechanistic, unitary thing. Suppose a State entitled every citizen whose income was under a certain level to receive health care at a state clinic. The provision of health care is not a unitary thing — doctors and administrators must decide what tests are called for and what procedures are required, and these decisions often involve difficult applications of judgment. But it could not credibly be said that a citizen lacks an entitlement to health care simply because the content of that entitlement is not the same in every given situation. Similarly, the enforcement of a restraining order is not some amorphous, indeterminate thing. Under the statute, if the police have probable cause that a violation has occurred, enforcement consists of either making an immediate arrest or seeking a warrant and then executing an arrest — traditional, well-defined tasks that law enforcement officers perform every [day.]

Because the statute's guarantee of police enforcement is triggered by, and operates only in reference to, a judge's granting of a restraining order in favor of an identified " 'protected person,' " there is simply no room to suggest that such a person has received merely an " 'incidental' " or " 'indirect' " benefit.

IV

Given that Colorado law has quite clearly eliminated the police's discretion to deny enforcement, respondent is correct that she had much more than a "unilateral expectation" that the restraining order would be enforced; rather, she had a "legitimate claim of entitlement" to enforcement. *Roth*, 408 U.S. at 577. Recognizing respondent's property interest in the enforcement of her restraining order is fully consistent with our precedent. This Court has "made clear that the property interests protected by procedural due process extend well beyond actual ownership of real estate, chattels, or money." The "types of interests protected as 'property' are varied and, as often as not, intangible, relating 'to the whole domain of social and economic fact.'" *Logan v. Zimmerman Brush Co.*, 455 U.S. 422, 430 (1982); see also *Perry v. Sindermann*, 408 U.S. 593, 601 (1972) ("'[P]roperty' interests subject to procedural due process protection are not limited by a few rigid, technical forms. Rather, 'property' denotes a broad range of interests that are secured by 'existing rules or understandings'"). Thus, our cases have found "property" interests in a number of state-conferred benefits and services, including welfare benefits, *Goldberg v. Kelly*, 397 U.S. 254 (1970); disability benefits, *Mathews v. Eldridge*, 424 U.S. 319 (1976); public education, *Goss v. Lopez*, 419 U.S. 565 (1975); utility services, *Memphis Light, Gas & Water Div. v. Craft*, 436 U.S. 1 (1978); government employment, *Cleveland Bd. of Ed. v. Loudermill*, 470 U.S. 532 (1985), as well as in other entitlements that defy easy categorization, see, *e.g.*, *Bell v. Burson*, 402 U.S. 535 (1971) (due process requires fair procedures before a driver's license may be revoked pending the adjudication of an accident claim); *Logan*, 455 U.S., at 431 (due process prohibits the arbitrary denial of a person's interest in adjudicating a claim before a state commission).

Police enforcement of a restraining order is a government service that is no less concrete and no less valuable than other government services, such as education. The relative novelty of recognizing this type of property interest is explained by the relative novelty of the domestic violence statutes creating a mandatory arrest duty; before this innovation, the unfettered discretion that characterized police enforcement defeated any citizen's "legitimate claim of entitlement" to this service. Novel or not, respondent's claim finds strong support in the principles that underlie our due process jurisprudence. In this case, Colorado law *guaranteed* the provision of a certain service, in certain defined circumstances, to a certain class of beneficiaries, and respondent reasonably relied on that guarantee. As we observed in *Roth*, "[i]t is a purpose of the ancient institution of property to protect those claims upon which people rely in their daily lives, reliance that must not be arbitrarily undermined." 408 U.S., at 577. Surely, if respondent had contracted with a private security firm to provide her and her daughters with protection from her husband, it would be apparent that she possessed a property interest in such a contract. Here, Colorado undertook a comparable obligation, and respondent — with restraining order in hand — justifiably relied on that undertaking. Respondent's claim of entitlement to this promised service is no less legitimate than the other claims our cases have upheld, and no less concrete than a hypothetical agreement with a private firm. The fact that it is based on a statutory enactment and a judicial order entered for her special protection, rather than on a formal contract, does not provide a principled basis for refusing to consider it "property" worthy of constitutional protection.

V.

Because respondent had a property interest in the enforcement of the restraining order, state officials could not deprive her of that interest without observing fair procedures. Her description of the police behavior in this case and the department's callous policy of failing to respond properly to reports of restraining order violations clearly alleges a due process violation. At the very least, due process requires that the relevant state decisionmaker *listen* to the claimant and then *apply the relevant criteria* in reaching his decision. The failure to observe these minimal procedural safeguards creates an unacceptable risk of arbitrary and "erroneous deprivation[s]," *Mathews*, 424 U.S., at 335. According to respondent's complaint — which we must construe liberally at this early stage in the litigation, see *Swierkiewicz v. Sorema N. A.*, 534 U.S. 506, 514 (2002) — the process she was afforded by the police constituted nothing more than a " 'sham or a pretense.' " *Joint Anti-Fascist Refugee Comm. v. McGrath*, 341 U.S. 123, 164 (1951) (Frankfurter, J., concurring).

[Accordingly,] I respectfully dissent.

NOTES ON *CASTLE ROCK* AND STATE-CREATED PROPERTY

1.   Can a plaintiff succeed in a case similar to *Castle Rock* where the state law is more explicitly mandatory than it is in *Castle Rock*? See *Burella v. City of Philadelphia*, 501 F.3d 134, 145 (3d Cir. 2007):

> Jill Burella argues that the Supreme Court's decision in *Castle Rock* does not prevent her from succeeding on her procedural due process claim because the Pennsylvania Protection from Abuse Act states that police "*shall arrest* a defendant for violating an order." It does not, as the Colorado statute provides, state that police "*shall use every reasonable means* to enforce" the restraining order (emphasis added.) Therefore, she contends, under the Pennsylvania statute, police officers do not have discretion not to enforce a protection from abuse order. [However,] the Court in *Castle Rock* unambiguously stated that absent a "clear indication" of legislative intent, a statute's mandatory arrest language should not be read to strip law enforcement of the discretion they have traditionally had in deciding whether to make an arrest. Although the Supreme Court did not specify what language would suffice to strip the police of such discretion, it is clear after *Castle Rock* that the phrase "shall arrest" is insufficient.

Another effort to escape *Castle Rock* was rebuffed in *Hudson v. Hudson*, 475 F.3d 741, 745 (6th Cir. 2007) ("[A] protection order does not create a special relationship between police officers and the individual who petitioned for that order. Nor may the plaintiffs establish their claims under the state-created danger theory.") The state-created danger theory of liability is discussed in chapter 4.

2.   There are two kinds of property, and one needs to distinguish between them in order to avoid confusion. On the one hand, persons hold land, chattels, and intangibles. Our right to keep these things free of government expropriation is well-established, though it is not absolute. For example, a person found guilty of a crime or held civilly liable may be obliged to hand over his money, land, or other property in the form of a fine or as damages or restitution. The (properly conducted) civil or criminal proceeding provides the process to which he is due. Even property holders who have committed no violation of law are somewhat vulnerable, as the "takings" or "just compensation" clause of the Fifth Amendment authorizes the state to seize the property for public use, provided that it pays a fair price. In constitutional jargon, this kind of property is often called "old" property, and we will put it aside for now, as it is not the focus of our attention in this section.

We are concerned here with a different kind of property, sometimes called "new" property because the constitutional doctrine bearing on it is of relatively recent vintage. Individuals receive a variety of benefits from the state — employment, contracts, welfare benefits, one-time grants, and so on. Now suppose the state chooses to stop providing the benefit, by cutting off welfare benefits or firing an employee without any notice or hearing. Does he have grounds for complaint that he has been deprived of property without due process of law? In *Board of Regents v. Roth*, 408 U.S. 564 (1972), and *Perry v. Sindermann*, 408 U.S. 593 (1972), the Supreme Court ruled that in certain circumstances the answer is yes. Roth and Perry were college teachers on one year contracts. When told that their contracts would not be renewed, each of them sued, charging that the nonrenewal amounted to a deprivation of property. Since neither had received a hearing in connection with the decision to let them go, they each claimed that the deprivation was effectuated without due process of law in violation of the Fourteenth Amendment. In considering their claims, the Supreme Court began from the premise that "the property interests protected by procedural due process extend well beyond actual ownership of real estate, chattels, or money." Yet it denied Roth's claim while upholding Perry's.

The Court stressed that "the terms of [Roth's] appointment secured absolutely no interest in re-employment for the next year." In addition, there was no "state statute or University rule or policy that secured his interest in re-employment or that created any legitimate claim to it." Sindermann's situation was different. Though he held no formal "tenure right to re-employment," he would have a property interest in his post if he could show, as he had asserted, that "the college had a de facto tenure program, and that he had tenure under that program." Sindermann would have a right to a hearing if he could prove "the existence of rules and understandings [that] may justify his legitimate claim of entitlement to continued employment absent 'sufficient cause.'"

Taken together, these cases stand for the general principle that Fourteenth Amendment "property" exists if state law (including informal practices) create a "legitimate claim of entitlement" to a benefit. The paramount role of state law was again stressed in *Bishop v. Wood*, 426 U.S. 341 (1976), where the Court found that under the city ordinance governing his employment, the plaintiff, a policeman, held his job at the will of the city and therefore had no property interest in it. What matters, then, is not the *importance* of a benefit to the plaintiff, but its *nature*. See Monaghan, *Of "Liberty" and "Property,"* 62 Cornell L. Rev. 405 (1977). Establishing a "property" interest in this way does not assure that the plaintiff will win the case. The significance of a determination that the plaintiff has been deprived of "property" is that the state must provide "due process of law," such as a hearing at which its reasons can be challenged. We address this requirement of "procedural due process" in section C.

In the years since *Roth* and *Sindermann*, the Supreme Court has rarely returned to the issue of whether someone has a "property" interest in a given benefit. The Court held in *Goss v. Lopez*, 419 U.S. 565 (1975), that state laws recognizing a right to public education have the effect of creating a property right, so that public school students are entitled to procedural due process when authorities seek to suspend or expel them. In *Cleveland Board of Education v. Loudermill*, 470 U.S. 532, 538–39 (1985), the Court, with little discussion, approved a lower court finding that a contract that guaranteed employment "during good behavior and efficient service" created a "property" right. *See also Gilbert v. Homar*, 520 U.S. 924, 928–29 (1997) (characterizing the prior cases as establishing the proposition that "public employees who can be discharged only for cause have a constitutionally protected property interest in their tenure and cannot be fired without due process"). Taking *Loudermill* and *Gilbert* as their starting points, lower courts will typically find a property interest in employment if the state or local government has "guaranteed continued employment absent 'just cause' for discharge." *Harhay v. Town of Ellington Board of Education*, 323 F.3d 206, 212 (2d Cir. 2003). This principle applies to other contractual relationships as well. *See Omni Behavioral Health v. Miller*, 285 F.3d 646, 652 (8th Cir. 2002). But the term "cause" in an ordinance does not guarantee that the plaintiff holds "property." *See, e.g., Kvapil v. Chippewa County*, 752 F.3d 708, 713–15 (7th Cir. 2014). The court said that even though the ordinance "contains the magic words 'for just cause'," it did not create a property interest. The ordinance stated that a seasonal employee "may be disciplined for just cause, including but not limited to . . . infractions of [a long list of] work rules." The ordinance "does not set forth explicit mandatory language providing a legitimate claim of entitlement to continued employment — it merely explains how the County may discharge an employee."

A license, such as a license to practice medicine or drive a taxicab, typically creates a "property" interest. *See, e.g., Gonzalez-Droz v. Gonzalez-Colon*, 660 F.3d 1, 13 (1st Cir. 2011) (medical license); *Nnebe v. Daus*, 644 F.3d 147, 158 (2d Cir. 2011) (taxi license). A contract terminable "at will" typically does not create a "property" interest. *See, e.g., Eisenhour v. Weber County*, 744 F.3d 1220, 1232 (10th Cir. 2014) (plaintiff claimed a property interest in continued employment with the County, but "does not identify a source for this interest" and thus "cannot rebut the presumption under Utah law that her employment with the County was at-will"). A harder question came up in *Eddings v. City of Hot Springs*, 323 F.3d 596, 601 (8th Cir. 2003). In *Eddings* the plaintiff, a police officer who had been fired, lost on account of his at will contract, even though the Hot Springs Police Department Policy and Procedures Manual provided for "an absolute right to due process prior to the imposition of a disciplinary action." *Compare Greenwood v. State Office for Mental Health*, 163 F.3d 119 (2d Cir. 1998), where the issue was whether a psychiatrist's clinical staff privileges at the Manhattan Psychiatric Clinic (MPC) were "property." The MPC bylaws and the Policy and Procedure Manual promulgated pursuant to them provided that staff members had a "right to due process . . . where specific clinical privileges have been denied, disallowed, restricted or suspended." Evidently in reliance on this provision, the court concluded that the clinical privileges were "property."

In other cases, especially those that cannot be resolved by the "at will"/"for cause" distinction, lower courts have focused on whether the circumstances of the case at hand justify finding *Sindermann*'s "legitimate claim of entitlement" to the benefit. *See, e.g., Rosu v. City of New York*, 742 F.3d 523, 526 (2d Cir. 2014) (stating a general rule that a state law cause of action "constitutes a cognizable property interest"); *Charleston v. Bd. of Trustees of Illinois University*, 741 F.3d 769 (7th Cir. 2013) (applying Illinois law, student does not have a "property" interest in the proper application of state-mandated procedures for his dismissal from a state university); *Frey Corp. v. City of Peoria*, 735 F.3d 505 (7th Cir. 2013) (site approval for a liquor store does not create a property interest in operating a liquor store, because "it is expressly conditional on the existence of a liquor license for use on the premises" and is thus insufficiently "secure or durable" to constitute a property interest); *Brown v. Eppler*, 725 F.3d 1221, 1227 (10th Cir. 2013) (concluding that the Metropolitan Tulsa Transportation Authority had, by its rules constraining its own discretion, created a property interest in access); *Barnes v. Zaccari*, 669 F.3d 1295, 1304-05 (11th Cir. 2012) (under Georgia law, a student has a property interest in enrollment at Valdosta State University absent "cause" for dismissal); *Mulvenon v. Greenwood*, 643 F.3d 653 (8th Cir. 2011) (reappointment guidelines did not give professor a legitimate claim of entitlement to reappointment as department chair); *Doe v. Florida Bar*, 630 F.3d 1336 (11th Cir. 2011) (under Florida law, an attorney does not have a property interest in certification as a marital and family law specialist); *Lighton v. University of Utah*, 209 F.3d 1213 (10th Cir. 2000) (non-tenured "tenure track" professor had no "property" interest in the post where he could not "point to any contract showing a specific term of employment existed nor identify any Utah statutes or University policy on which his alleged property interest is grounded."); *Jannsen v. Condo*, 101 F.3d 14 (2d Cir. 1996) (probationary employee has no "property" interest even though state law mandated that supervisors employ certain evaluation procedures for probationary employees); *Furlong v. Shalala*, 156 F.3d 384 (2d Cir. 1998) (a "constant, consistent pattern" of decisions by administrative law judges (ALJs) as to appropriate reimbursement rates under Medicare can create a property interest on the part of physicians in the rates the ALJs deem appropriate); *Hulen v. Yates*, 322 F.3d 1229 (10th Cir. 2003) (professor possessed a property interest not only in employment but in his position in the Accounting Department by virtue of provisions in the Faculty Manual guaranteeing his status). Absent support of the kind found in *Hulen*, a "property" interest in employment does not necessarily imply a property interest in the particular post for which the plaintiff seeks protection. *See, e.g., Ulichny v. Merton Community School District*, 249 F.3d 686 (7th Cir. 2001) (no legitimate expectation of continued employment with the duties of school principal). The "legitimate expectation" test is plainly an objective rather than a subjective one. *See, e.g., Nunez v. Simms*, 341 F.3d 385, 391 (5th Cir. 2003) ("regardless of what Nunez's subjective expectation was, it would not have been objectively reasonable for her to believe, at the time of entering into the contract, that her entitlement to teach would extend beyond the point that her certification expired by its own terms").

3.   Suppose the state legislature has created a property interest. Does it have the power to eliminate that interest prospectively by enacting new legislation? *See Price v. Bd. of Education of the City of Chicago*, 755 F.3d 605 (7th Cir. 2014). Price, a tenured teacher, had been laid off for budgetary reasons and claimed a property right to fill an open position for which she was qualified. The court acknowledged that under an earlier version of Illinois law a tenured teacher who had been laid off would have had a property interest in filling an open position for which she was qualified. But "the legislature's decision in 1995 to remove [the relevant language] was a conscious decision to alter the protectable interests vested in tenured teachers . . . By deleting those provisions, the Illinois legislature made a conscious decision to redefine what interests a 'permanent' or tenured teacher has, and that includes abolishing the right Price now seeks to assert." 755 F.3d at 609.

4.   Some of the problems that come up in connection with state-created property interests are illustrated by the complicated facts of *Wojcik v. City of Romulus*, 257 F.3d 600 (6th Cir. 2001). Rose Wojcik owned a bar in Romulus, Michigan. In 1986 she sold it, "including its Class C liquor license, a dance permit and a Sunday sales permit to Gampp Enterprises . . . under an installment contract for a sum of $85,000. [Gampp] later applied to the City of Romulus and the [Michigan Liquor Control Commission] for an entertainment permit." The permit was granted. "Gampp became delinquent on the payments required under its installment contract with Mrs. Wojcik; but Mrs. Wojcik agreed to forbear eviction and acceleration of the outstanding balance in exchange for a security interest in all of Gampp's assets." Gampp soon defaulted and was shut down by the state. Mrs. Wojcik obtained a state court order reassigning to her "all of the assets of the bar, including its liquor licence according to the terms of the reassignment (security) agreement entered into by the parties, which made the reassignment subject to the consent and approval of the MLCC."

When Mrs. Wojcik's grandson contacted MLCC in an attempt to obtain "reassignment of the liquor license and all of the related permits," which included dance, Sunday Sales, and entertainment permits, he was told "that he must first obtain the approval of the city of Romulus as was required under Michigan state law." Wojcik undertook to do this, and, at the same time, "entered into a conditional sales contract with Edgar, Inc., for the sale of the bar. [Enforcement] of this contract was made subject to Wojcik's ability to transfer the liquor license and all of the permits to Edgar." But Romulus declined to transfer the entertainment license because Edgar planned to "provide continuous topless entertainment" in close proximity to a church.

The Wojciks sued Romulus, claiming that they had a state-created property interest in the entertainment permit, so that the city's refusal to transfer it violated their due process rights. The 6th Circuit affirmed the district court's award of summary judgment to Romulus, ruling that the Wojciks had no property interest in the entertainment license. "In the instant case, Mrs. Wojcik claims to have a recognized property interest in the transfer of an entertainment permit which she has never held. [A] liquor license or related permit may be the subject of a security interest — and . . . security interests are generally considered property." But this principle was no help to Wojcik. "[While] Mrs. Wojcik once owned the liquor license, neither she nor any of the other plaintiffs ever owned the entertainment permit;

rather, Gampp alone applied for and obtained the entertainment permit. Thus, Mrs. Wojcik could not have had a reversionary interest in an entertainment permit she never possessed."

Suppose you represented a client like Mrs. Wojcik in the original sale to Gampp. How might you avoid the problem illustrated by this case?

B. "Liberty"

For the sake of clarity it is useful to draw some comparisons and contrasts between the Supreme Court's doctrine on Fourteenth Amendment "liberty" and its treatment of "property." As with property, there is an "old" liberty, composed of common law interests that the due process clause shields against certain intrusions by the state. And there is a field we can call "new" liberty (by analogy to the property cases discussed in section A), which consists of liberty interests created by state law. The comparison between "new" property and "new" liberty is not altogether apt, however, for there are far fewer state-created liberty interests. The doctrine applies mainly to situations in which prisoners claim that state rules grant them privileges of one kind or another and assert that these privileges should receive constitutional protection.

The opinions in the following case touch on several aspects of both "old" and "new" liberty.

SANDIN v. CONNER
515 U.S. 472 (1995)

CHIEF JUSTICE REHNQUIST delivered the opinion of the Court.

[Conner was a state prisoner. He was charged with a disciplinary infraction, tried before an "adjustment committee" at the prison, found guilty, and sentenced to 30 days of disciplinary segregation. He sued prison officials, charging that by not allowing him to call witnesses at the disciplinary hearing they violated his right to procedural due process. He could prevail on this theory only if he had a liberty interest in remaining free from disciplinary segregation. The 9th circuit ruled that he did have such an interest, based on a prison regulation that instructed the adjustment committee to find guilt when a charge of misconduct is supported by substantial evidence.]

[From] the language of the regulation, [the 9th circuit] drew a negative inference that the committee may not impose segregation if it does not find substantial evidence of misconduct. It viewed this as a state-created liberty interest, and therefore held that [Conner] was entitled to call witnesses.

[The Supreme Court reversed.]

[States] may under certain circumstances create liberty interests which are protected by the Due Process Clause. But these interests will be generally limited to freedom from restraint which, while not exceeding the sentence in such an unexpected manner as to give rise to protection by the Due Process Clause of its own force, nonetheless imposes atypical and significant hardship on the inmate in relation to the ordinary incidents of prison life.

Conner asserts, incorrectly, that any state action taken for a punitive reason encroaches upon a liberty interest under the Due Process Clause even in the absence of any state regulation. Neither *Bell v. Wolfish*, 441 U.S. 520 (1979), nor *Ingraham v. Wright*, 430 U.S. 651 (1977), requires such a rule. *Bell* dealt with the interests of pretrial detainees and not convicted prisoners. The Court in *Bell* correctly noted that a detainee "may not be punished prior to an adjudication of guilt in accordance with due process of law." The Court expressed concern that a State would attempt to punish a detainee for the crime for which he was indicted via preconviction holding conditions. Such a course would improperly extend the legitimate reasons for which such persons are detained — to ensure their presence at trial.

The same distinction applies to *Ingraham*, which addressed the rights of schoolchildren to remain free from arbitrary corporal punishment. The Court noted that the Due Process Clause historically encompassed the notion that the state could not "physically punish an individual except in accordance with due process of law" and so found schoolchildren sheltered. Although children sent to public school are lawfully confined to the classroom, arbitrary corporal punishment represents an invasion of personal security to which their parents do not consent when entrusting the educational mission to the State.

The punishment of incarcerated prisoners, on the other hand, serves different aims than those found invalid in *Bell* and *Ingraham*. The process does not impose retribution in lieu of a valid conviction, nor does it maintain physical control over free citizens forced by law to subject themselves to state control over the educational mission. It effectuates prison management and prisoner rehabilitative goals. Admittedly, prisoners do not shed all constitutional rights at the prison gate, but lawful incarceration brings about the necessary withdrawal or limitation of many privileges and rights, a retraction justified by the considerations underlying our penal system. Discipline by prison officials in response to a wide range of misconduct falls within the expected parameters of the sentence imposed by a court of law.

This case, though concededly punitive, does not present a dramatic departure from the basic conditions of Conner's indeterminate sentence. [We] hold that Conner's discipline in segregated confinement did not present the type of atypical, significant deprivation in which a State might conceivably create a liberty interest. The record shows that, at the time of Conner's punishment, disciplinary segregation, with insignificant exceptions, mirrored those conditions imposed upon inmates in administrative segregation and protective custody. We note also that the State expunged Conner's disciplinary record with respect to the "high misconduct" charge nine months after Conner served time in segregation. Thus, Conner's confinement did not exceed similar, but totally discretionary, confinement in either duration or degree of restriction. Indeed, the conditions at [the prison] involve significant amounts of "lockdown time" even for inmates in the general population. Based on a comparison between inmates inside and outside disciplinary segregation, the State's actions in placing him there for 30 days did not work a major disruption in his environment.

Nor does Conner's situation present a case where the State's action will inevitably affect the duration of his sentence. Nothing in Hawaii's code requires the parole board to deny parole in the face of a misconduct record or to grant parole in its absence, even though misconduct is by regulation a relevant consideration. The decision to release a prisoner rests on a myriad of considerations. And, the prisoner is afforded procedural protection at his parole hearing in order to explain the circumstances behind his misconduct record. The chance that a finding of misconduct will alter the balance is simply too attenuated to invoke the procedural guarantees of the Due Process Clause.

We hold, therefore, that neither the Hawaii prison regulation in question, nor the Due Process Clause itself, afforded Conner a protected liberty interest that would entitle him to the procedural protections set forth in *Wolff*. The regime to which he was subjected as a result of the misconduct hearing was within the range of confinement to be normally expected for one serving an indeterminate term of 30 years to life.

JUSTICE GINSBURG, with whom JUSTICE STEVENS joins, dissenting.

[Unlike] the Court, I conclude that Conner had a liberty interest, protected by the Fourteenth Amendment's Due Process Clause, in avoiding the disciplinary confinement he endured. [Conner's] prison punishment effected a severe alteration in the conditions of his incarceration. Disciplinary confinement as punishment for "high misconduct" not only deprives prisoners of privileges for protracted periods; unlike administrative segregation and protective custody, disciplinary confinement also stigmatizes them and diminishes parole prospects. Those immediate and lingering consequences should suffice to qualify such confinement as liberty depriving for purposes of Due Process Clause protection.[1]

I see the Due Process Clause itself, not Hawaii's prison code, as the wellspring of the protection due Conner. Deriving protected liberty interests from mandatory language in local prison codes would make of the fundamental right something more in certain States, something less in others. Liberty that may vary from Ossining, New York, to San Quentin, California, does not resemble the "Liberty" enshrined among "unalienable Rights" with which all persons are "endowed by their Creator." Declaration of Independence.[2]

---

[1] [5] The Court reasons that Conner's disciplinary confinement, "with insignificant exceptions, mirrored the conditions imposed upon inmates in administrative segregation and protective custody," and therefore implicated no constitutional liberty interest. But discipline means punishment for misconduct; it rests on a finding of wrongdoing that can adversely affect an inmate's parole prospects. Disciplinary confinement therefore cannot be bracketed with administrative segregation and protective custody, both measures that carry no long-term consequences. The Court notes, however, that the State eventually expunged Conner's disciplinary record, as a result of his successful administrative appeal. But hindsight cannot tell us whether a liberty interest existed at the outset. One must, of course, know at the start the character of the interest at stake in order to determine *then* what process, if any, is constitutionally due. "All's well that ends well" cannot be the measure here.

[2] [6] The Court describes a category of liberty interest that is something less than the one the Due Process Clause itself shields, something more than anything a prison code provides. The State may create a liberty interest, the Court tells us, when "atypical and significant hardship [would be borne by] the inmate in relation to the ordinary incidents of prison life." What design lies beneath these key words?

Deriving the prisoner's due process right from the code for his prison, more-over, yields this practical anomaly: a State that scarcely attempts to control the behavior of its prison guards may, for that very laxity, escape constitutional accountability; a State that tightly cabins the discretion of its prison workers may, for that attentiveness, become vulnerable to constitutional claims. An incentive for ruleless prison management disserves the State's penological goals and jeopardizes the welfare of prisoners.

To fit the liberty recognized in our fundamental instrument of government, the process due by reason of the Constitution similarly should not depend on the particularities of the local prison's code. Rather, the basic, universal requirements are notice of the acts of misconduct prison officials say the inmate committed, and an opportunity to respond to the charges before a trustworthy decisionmaker.

[JUSTICE **BREYER**, joined by JUSTICE **SOUTER**, also dissented. Here are excerpts from his opinion:]

[This] Court has said that certain changes in conditions may be so severe or so different from ordinary conditions of confinement that, whether or not state law gives state authorities broad discretionary power to impose them, the state authorities may not do so "without complying with minimum requirements of due process." The Court has also said that deprivations that are less severe or more closely related to the original terms of confinement nonetheless will amount to deprivations of procedurally protected liberty, provided that state law (including prison regulations) narrowly cabins the legal power of authorities to impose the deprivation (thereby giving the inmate a kind of right to avoid it).

If we apply these general pre-existing principles to the relevant facts before us, it seems fairly clear, as the Ninth Circuit found, that the prison punishment here at issue deprived Conner of constitutionally protected "liberty." For one thing, the punishment worked a fairly major change in Conner's conditions. In the absence of the punishment, Conner, like other inmates in Halawa's general prison population would have left his cell and worked, taken classes, or mingled with others for eight *hours* each day. As a result of disciplinary segregation, however, Conner, for 30 days, had to spend his entire time alone in his cell (with the exception of 50 *minutes* each day on average for brief exercise and shower periods, during which he nonetheless remained isolated from other inmates and was constrained by leg irons and waist chains).

Moreover, irrespective of whether this punishment amounts to a deprivation of liberty *independent* of state law, here the prison's own disciplinary rules severely cabin the authority of prison officials to impose this kind of punishment. They provide (among other things):

(a)   that certain specified acts shall constitute *"high misconduct,"* Haw. Admin. Rule § 17-201-7a (1983) (emphasis added);

(b)   that misconduct punishable by more than four hours in disciplinary

---

The Court ventures no examples, leaving consumers of the Court's work at sea, unable to fathom what would constitute an "atypical, significant deprivation," and yet not trigger protection under the Due Process Clause directly.

segregation "shall be punished" through a prison "adjustment committee" (composed of three unbiased members), §§ 17-201-12, 13;

(c) that, when an inmate is charged with such misconduct, then (after notice and a hearing) "[a] finding of guilt shall be made" if the charged inmate admits guilt or the "charge is supported by substantial evidence," §§ 17-201-18(b), (b)(2); see §§ 17-201-16, 17; and

(d) that the "sanctions" for high misconduct that "may be imposed as punishment . . . shall include . . . disciplinary segregation up to thirty days," § 17-201-7(b).

The prison rules thus: (1) impose a punishment that is substantial, (2) restrict its imposition as a punishment to instances in which an inmate has committed a defined offense, and (3) prescribe nondiscretionary standards for determining whether or not an inmate committed that offense. Accordingly, under this Court's liberty-defining standards, imposing the punishment would "deprive" Conner of "liberty" within the meaning of the Due Process Clause. Thus, under existing law, the Ninth Circuit correctly decided that the punishment deprived Conner of procedurally protected liberty and that the District Court should go on to decide whether or not the prison's procedures provided Conner with the "process" that is "due."

The majority, while not disagreeing with this summary of pre-existing law, seeks to change, or to clarify, that law's "liberty" defining standards in one important respect. The majority believes that the Court's present "cabining of discretion" standard reads the Constitution as providing procedural protection for trivial "rights," as, for example, where prison rules set forth specific standards for the content of prison meals. It adds that this approach involves courts too deeply in routine matters of prison administration, all without sufficient justification. It therefore imposes a minimum standard, namely that a deprivation falls within the Fourteenth Amendment's definition of "liberty" only if it "imposes atypical and significant hardship on the inmate in relation to the ordinary incidents of prison life."

I am not certain whether or not the Court means this standard to change prior law radically. If so, its generality threatens the law with uncertainty, for some lower courts may read the majority opinion as offering significantly less protection against deprivation of liberty, while others may find in it an extension of protection to certain "atypical" hardships that pre-existing law would not have covered. There is no need, however, for a radical reading of this standard, nor any other significant change in present law, to achieve the majority's basic objective, namely to read the Constitution's Due Process Clause to protect inmates against deprivations of freedom that are important, not comparatively insignificant. Rather, in my view, this concern simply requires elaborating, and explaining, the Court's present standards (without radical revision) in order to make clear that courts must apply them in light of the purposes they were meant to serve. As so read, the standards will not create procedurally protected "liberty" interests where only minor matters are at stake.

Three sets of considerations, taken together, support my conclusion that the Court need not (and today's generally phrased minimum standard therefore does not) significantly revise current doctrine by deciding to remove minor prison matters from federal-court scrutiny. First, although this Court has said, and continues to say, that *some* deprivations of an inmate's freedom are so severe in kind or degree (or so far removed from the original terms of confinement) that they amount to deprivations of liberty, irrespective of whether state law (or prison rules) "cabin discretion," it is not easy to specify just *when,* or *how much* of, a loss triggers this protection. There is a broad middle category of imposed restraints or deprivations that, considered by themselves, are neither obviously so serious as to fall within, nor obviously so insignificant as to fall without, the Clause's protection.

Second, the difficult line-drawing task that this middle category implies helps to explain why this Court developed its additional liberty-defining standard, which looks to local law (examining whether that local law creates a "liberty" by significantly limiting the discretion of local authorities to impose a restraint). Despite its similarity to the way in which the Court determines the existence, or nonexistence, of "property" for Due Process Clause purposes, the justification for looking at local law is not the same in the prisoner liberty context. In protecting property, the Due Process Clause often aims to protect *reliance,* say, reliance upon an "entitlement" that local (*i.e.,* nonconstitutional) law itself has created or helped to define. See *Board of Regents of State Colleges v. Roth,* 408 U.S. 564, 577 (1972) ("It is a purpose of the ancient institution of property to protect those claims upon which people rely in their daily lives, reliance that must not be arbitrarily undermined"). In protecting liberty, however, the Due Process Clause protects, not this kind of reliance upon a government-conferred benefit, but rather an absence of government restraint, the very absence of restraint that we call freedom.

Nevertheless, there are several *other* important reasons, in the prison context, to consider the provisions of state law. The fact that a further deprivation of an inmate's freedom takes place under local rules that cabin the authorities' discretionary power to impose the restraint suggests, *other things being equal,* that the matter is more likely to have played an important role in the life of the inmate. It suggests, other things being equal, that the matter is more likely of a kind to which procedural protections historically have applied, and where they normally prove useful, for such rules often *single out* an inmate and condition a deprivation upon the existence, or nonexistence, of particular facts. It suggests, other things being equal, that the matter will not involve highly judgmental administrative matters that call for the wise exercise of discretion — matters where courts reasonably should hesitate to second-guess prison administrators. It suggests, other things being equal, that the inmate will have thought that he himself, through control of his own behavior, could have avoided the deprivation, and thereby have believed that (in the absence of his misbehavior) the restraint fell outside the "sentence imposed" upon him. Finally, courts can identify the presence or absence of cabined discretion fairly easily and objectively, at least much of the time. These characteristics of "cabined discretion" mean that courts can use it as a kind of touchstone that can help them, when they consider the broad middle category of prisoner restraints, to separate those kinds of restraints that, in general, are more likely to call for constitutionally guaranteed procedural protection, from those that more likely do not. Given these reasons and the precedent, I believe courts will continue to find this touchstone helpful as they seek to apply the majority's middle category standard.

Third, there is, therefore, no need to apply the "discretion-cabining" approach — the basic purpose of which is to provide a somewhat more objective method for identifying deprivations of protected "liberty" within a broad middle range of prisoner restraints — where a deprivation is unimportant enough (or so similar in nature to ordinary imprisonment) that it rather clearly falls *outside* that middle category. Prison, by design, restricts the inmates' freedom. And, one cannot properly view unimportant matters that happen to be the subject of prison regulations as substantially aggravating a loss that has already occurred. Indeed, a regulation about a minor matter, for example, a regulation that seems to cabin the discretionary power of a prison administrator to deprive an inmate of, say, a certain kind of lunch, may amount simply to an instruction to the administrator about how to do his job, rather than a guarantee to the inmate of a "right" to the status quo. Cf. *Colon v. Schneider*, 899 F.2d 660, 668 (CA7 1990) (rules governing use of Mace to subdue inmates "directed toward the prison staff, not the inmates"). Thus, this Court has never held that comparatively unimportant prisoner "deprivations" fall within the scope of the Due Process Clause even if local law limits the authority of prison administrators to impose such minor deprivations. And, in my view, it should now simply specify that they do not.

I recognize that, as a consequence, courts must separate the unimportant from the potentially significant, without the help of the more objective "discretion-cabining" test. Yet, making that judicial judgment seems no more difficult than many other judicial tasks. It seems to me possible to separate less significant matters such as television privileges, "sack" versus "tray" lunches, playing the state lottery, attending an ex-stepfather's funeral, or the limits of travel when on prison furlough, from more significant matters, such as the solitary confinement at issue here. Indeed, prison regulations themselves may help in this respect, such as the regulations here which separate (from more serious matters) "low moderate" and "minor" misconduct. Compare, on the one hand, the maximum punishment for "moderate" misconduct of two weeks of disciplinary segregation, Haw. Admin. Rule § 17-201-8 (1983), with the less severe maximum punishments, on the other hand, for "low moderate" and "minor" misconduct, §§ 17-201-9, 10 (several hours of disciplinary segregation and "loss of privileges" such as "community recreation; commissary; snacks; cigarettes, smoking; personal visits — no longer than fifteen days; personal correspondence; personal phone calls for not longer than fifteen days"; impounding personal property; extra duty; and reprimand).

The upshot is the following: the problems that the majority identifies suggest that this Court should make explicit the lower definitional limit, in the prison context, of "liberty" under the Due Process Clause — a limit that is already implicit in this Court's precedent. Those problems do not require abandoning that precedent.

The Court today reaffirms that the "liberty" protected by the Fourteenth Amendment includes interests that state law may create. It excludes relatively minor matters from that protection. And, it does not question the vast body of case law, including cases from this Court and every Circuit, recognizing that segregation can deprive an inmate of constitutionally protected "liberty." That being so, it is difficult to see why the Court reverses, rather than affirms, the Court of Appeals in this case.

The majority finds that Conner's "discipline in segregated confinement did not present" an "atypical, significant deprivation" because of three special features of his case, taken together. First, the punishment "mirrored" conditions imposed upon inmates in "administrative segregation and protective custody." Second, Hawaii's prison regulations give prison officials broad discretion to impose these other forms of *nonpunitive* segregation. And, third, the State later "expunged Conner's disciplinary record," thereby erasing any stigma and transforming Conner's segregation for violation of a specific disciplinary rule into the sort of "totally discretionary confinement" that would not have implicated a liberty interest.

I agree with the first two of the majority's assertions. [But], I disagree with the majority's assertion about the relevance of the expungement. How can a *later* decision of prison authorities transform Conner's segregation for a violation of a specific disciplinary rule into a term of segregation under the administrative rules? How can a later expungement restore to Conner the liberty that, in fact, he had already lost? Because Conner was found guilty under prison disciplinary rules, and was sentenced to solitary confinement under those rules, the Court should look to *those* rules.

In sum, expungement or no, Conner suffered a deprivation that was significant, not insignificant. And, that deprivation took place under disciplinary rules that, as described in Part II, *supra*, do cabin official discretion sufficiently. I would therefore hold that Conner was deprived of "liberty" within the meaning of the Due Process Clause.

NOTES

1.   *"Old" Liberty*. The main common law interests that receive protection from state interference in section 1983 litigation are: (a) freedom from confinement and other restrictions on personal freedom; (b) security against physical injury; and (c) reputation. There are references in *Sandin* to each of these. Though we will focus on the items on this list, it is not exhaustive. Other aspects of "liberty" arise less frequently in section 1983 litigation, but of course should not be neglected. *See, e.g.,Chaudhry v. City of Los Angeles*, 751 F.3d 1096, 1106 (9th Cir. 2014) ("parents have a liberty interest in the companionship of their adult children and have a cause of action under the Fourteenth Amendment when the police kill an adult child without legal justification"); *Maddox v. Stephens*, 727 F.3d 1109, 1118–19 (11th Cir. 2013) ("parents have a constitutionally protected liberty interest in the care, custody and management of their children"); *Xiong v. Wagner*, 700 F.3d 282, 291 (7th Cir. 2012) (discussing the Fourteenth Amendment " right to familial integrity", which includes "the right to associate with relatives"); *Elwell v. Byers*, 699 F.3d 1208, 1215–16 (10th Cir. 2012) (discussing "the liberty interest in family association" which "may extend to foster parents in certain circumstances").

With respect to (a), it is plain that state authorities may not simply lock people up and keep them there indefinitely without justification and without process. *Baker v. McCollan*, 443 U.S. 137 (1979). Moreover, each deprivation of liberty requires distinct justification and process. Thus, even though someone has been convicted of a crime, once he has served his sentence he is entitled to go free, absent a rationale for continued detention. Suppose he is then targeted for involuntary civil commitment as a sex offender. He is entitled to due process in connection with this additional deprivation of liberty *Bailey v. Pataki*, 708 F.3d 391 (2d Cir. 2013). And "[a] pretrial detainee cannot be placed in segregation as a punishment for a disciplinary infraction without notice and an opportunity to be heard." *Higgs v. Carver*, 286 F.3d 437 (7th Cir. 2002). "Liberty" is denied not only when the state confines a person but also when it excludes a person from public property. *See, e.g., Catron v. City of St. Petersburg*, 658 F.3d 1260, 1266 (11th Cir. 2011) ("plaintiffs have a constitutionally protected liberty interest to be in parks or other city lands of their choosing that are open to the public generally.") But not all restrictions on movement are deprivations of Fourteenth Amendment "liberty." At the other end of the spectrum, a special education student is not deprived of liberty by being required to sit at a wrap around desk that restricts one's movement. *See Ebonie S. v. Pueblo School Dist. 60*, 695 F.3d 1051 (10th Cir. 2012). Harder questions arise in particular contexts. The Court ruled in *O'Connor v. Donaldson*, 422 U.S. 563 (1975) that persons may not be incarcerated against their will on account of untreated mental illnesses unless they are dangerous to themselves or others. In *Sandin* Justice Ginsburg argued that prisoners hold a liberty interest, independent of any liberty interest created by state law, against the imposition of significantly harsher conditions of confinement than those ordinarily incident to incarceration.

The leading case concerning (b) is *Ingraham v. Wright*, 430 U.S. 651 (1977). The plaintiffs in that case were junior high school students who had been paddled for misbehavior. Though the Court rejected their constitutional claims (for other reasons, discussed in section C) it recognized that Fourteenth Amendment liberty includes "personal security" from physical pain or injury. Later cases have broadened this principle, recognizing that "a liberty claim of a right to bodily integrity is . . . within substantive due process." *Wudtke v. Davel*, 128 F.3d 1057 (1997). In *Wudtke*, for example, the plaintiff stated a good constitutional "liberty" claim by alleging that an official had used his state-granted powers to assault her.

As for (c), *Paul v. Davis*, 424 U.S. 693 (1976) is the major case. The Louisville police chief had distributed to local businesses a list of shoplifters, and had included the plaintiff on the list. The Supreme Court dismissed the case, ruling that defamation deprives one of liberty only if it is accompanied by the loss of some substantial benefit or the imposition of a significant burden. In addition, the plaintiff wins only if he disputes the truth of the defamatory statement. *Codd v. Velger*, 429 U.S. 624, 627 (1977). The principle that a plaintiff must show more than mere defamation applies even if the speaker knows the defamatory statements are false and intends to harm the plaintiff by spreading them. *Siegert v. Gilley*, 500 U.S. 226 (1991). *Paul* and *Seigert* have been the targets of much criticism. *See, e.g.,* Barbara Armacost, *The Real Legacy of* Paul v. Davis, 85 VA. L. REV. 569, 618–28 (1999).

As a result of the ruling in *Paul*, a body of "stigma plus" doctrine has developed. The "stigma" is created by false defamatory statements that are communicated to others, and the "plus" usually is the loss of a government job or some other serious disadvantage.

The "stigma" requirement is met only by the kinds of statements that would be defamatory in common law defamation, and perhaps only a narrower category of especially serious charges. *See, e.g., Jones v. McNeese*, 746 F.3d 887, 889 (8th Cir. 2014) (an internal email charging that the plaintiff "may have engaged in ethically questionable conduct" does not create the level of stigma required to implicate a constitutionally protected liberty interest"); *Mann v. Vogel*, 707 F.3d 872 (7th Cir. 2013) (investigating the operator of a day care center for child abuse or neglect meets the "stigma" requirement); *Doe v. The Florida Bar*, 630 F.3d 1336, 1344 (11th Cir. 2011) (the Bar's refusal to certify the plaintiff as a specialist does not deprive the plaintiff of the ability to practice in that area, but "simply means that an attorney is, like the vast majority of attorneys, not certified in the field. The failure to convey a badge of distinction is not stigmatizing."); *Hedrich v. Board of Regents*, 274 F.3d 1174 (7th Cir. 2001) (labeling an employee as incompetent or otherwise unable to meet an employer's expectations does not infringe the employee's liberty); *Doe v. Dept. of Public Safety ex rel. Lee*, 271 F.3d 38 (2d Cir. 2002) (labeling someone as a dangerous sex offender is stigmatizing); *Garcia v. City of Albuquerque*, 232 F.3d 760 (10th Cir. 2000) (statement that plaintiff is "unable to drive a motor coach" does not meet the stigma threshold).

On the question of what kinds of harm meet the "plus" requirement, see, e.g., *Siegert, supra*, (the loss of employment *opportunities* on account of defamatory statements is not sufficient to create a liberty interest); *Smith v. Siegelman*, 322 F.3d 1290 (11th Cir. 2003) (being listed in a registry of sex abusers is stigmatizing, but does not amount to a deprivation of liberty unless some other disability is also placed on the plaintiff); *Doe v. Dept. of Public Safety ex rel. Lee*, 271 F.3d 38 (2d Cir. 2001) (imposing registration requirement on persons deemed sexually dangerous is enough of a burden to meet the "plus" requirement); *Cypress Insurance Co. v. Clark*, 144 F.3d 1435 (11th Cir. 1998) (loss of business reputation is not deprivation of a tangible property interest sufficient to meet the threshold); *Ferencz v. Hairston*, 119 F.3d 1244 (6th Cir. 1997) (unlike employment, remaining on a list of contractors eligible for city contracts is not sufficiently a "tangible" interest to qualify as an aspect of liberty). *See also Valmonte v. Bane*, 18 F.3d 992, 999 (2d Cir. 1994). Here the "plus" requirement was met where Valmonte's name was put on a list of suspected child abusers, prospective employers in the child care field were required by law to consult the list, and "if they do wish to hire her, those employers are required by law to explain the reasons why in writing." The court continued: "This is not just the intangible deleterious effect that flows from a bad reputation. Rather, it is a specific deprivation of her opportunity to seek employment caused by a statutory impediment established by the state."

Note, too, that liability depends on whether the defendant has publicized the charges. *See, e.g., Hughes v. City of Garland*, 204 F.3d 223 (5th Cir. 2000) (no city liability where city officials did not publicize the charges).

We will return to these aspects of "liberty" in sections C and D, where we take up the procedural and substantive protection they receive under the Fourteenth Amendment.

2.   *"New" Liberty.* Before *Sandin*, the Court had examined state law, including prison guidelines, in deciding whether the state had created a liberty interest. *See, e.g., Hewitt v. Helms*, 459 U.S. 460 (1983). Though the state's prison regulations remain relevant to the inquiry, *Sandin* directs courts to focus as well on whether the action taken against the prisoner is an "atypical and significant hardship in relation to the ordinary incidents of prison life."

In *Wilkinson v. Austin*, 545 U.S. 209 (2005), the Court revisited the "state-created liberty" issue, ruling that an inmate was deprived of "liberty" (and thus entitled to the procedural protections of the due process clause) when he was placed in a Supermax prison, the Ohio State Penitentiary (OSP):

> Conditions at OSP are more restrictive than any other form of incarceration in Ohio, including conditions on its death row or in its administrative control units. [In] the OSP almost every aspect of an inmate's life is controlled and monitored. Inmates must remain in their cells, which measure 7 feet by 14 feet, for 23 hours per day. A light remains on in the cell at all times, though it is sometimes dimmed, and an inmate who attempts to shield the light to sleep is subject to further [discipline].

> Incarceration at OSP is synonymous with extreme isolation. In contrast to any other Ohio prison, including any segregation unit, OSP cells have solid metal doors with metal strips along their sides and bottoms which prevent conversation or communication with other inmates. All meals are taken alone in the inmate's cell instead of in a common eating area. Opportunities for visitation are rare and in all events are conducted through glass walls. It is fair to say OSP inmates are deprived of almost any environmental or sensory stimuli and of almost all human contact.

> Aside from the severity of the conditions, placement at OSP is for an indefinite period of time, limited only by an inmate's sentence. For an inmate serving a life sentence, there is no indication how long he may be incarcerated at OSP once assigned there. Inmates otherwise eligible for parole lose their eligibility while incarcerated at [OSP].

> After *Sandin* it is clear that the touchstone of the inquiry into the existence of a protected state-created liberty interest in avoiding restrictive conditions of confinement is not the language of regulations regarding those conditions but the nature of those conditions themselves "in relation to the ordinary incidents of prison [life."]

> The *Sandin* standard requires us to determine if assignment to OSP "imposes atypical and significant hardship on the inmate in relation to the ordinary incidents of prison life." In *Sandin*'s wake the Courts of Appeals have not reached consistent conclusions for identifying the baseline from which to measure what is atypical and significant in any particular prison system. This divergence indicates the difficulty of locating the appropriate baseline, an issue that was not explored in the briefs. We need not resolve the issue here, however, for we are satisfied that assignment to OSP imposes an atypical and significant hardship under any plausible baseline.

> For an inmate placed in OSP, almost all human contact is prohibited, even to the point that communication is not permitted from cell to cell, the light, though it may be dimmed, is on for 24 hours, exercise is for 1 hour per day, but only in a small indoor room. Save perhaps for the especially severe limitations on all human contact, these conditions likely would apply to most solitary confinement facilities, but here there are two added components. First is the duration. Unlike the 30-day placement in *Sandin*,

placement at OSP is indefinite and, after an initial 30-day review, is reviewed just annually. Second is that placement disqualifies an otherwise eligible inmate for parole consideration.

While any of these considerations standing alone might not be sufficient to create a liberty interest, taken together they impose an atypical and significant hardship within the correctional context. It follows that [inmates] have a liberty interest in avoiding assignment to OSP.

For an application of these principles, *see Brown v. Oregon Dept. of Corrections*, 751 F.3d 983, 988 (9th Cir. 2014) ("Brown's twenty-seven month confinement in the IMU [Intensive Management Unit] imposed an atypical and significant hardship under any baseline." It does not necessarily follow that every assignment to a supermax prison involves a deprivation of "liberty." *See, e.g., Rezaq v. Nalley*, 677 F.3d 1001, 1011 (10th Cir. 2011) (holding, despite *Wilkinson*, that the supermax prison confinement at issue in that case did not amount to a deprivation of "liberty", given, *e.g.*, that the prisoners had been convicted of terror-related crimes and the national security considerations presented by the case). Should the national security factor bear on whether there is a deprivation of liberty, as it did for the court in *Rezaq*, or rather on the justification for the deprivation, in which case it would figure in determining what process is due?

C.   Procedural Due Process

The term "procedural due process" seems redundant, for "procedure" and "process" ordinarily serve as synonyms. Yet the term is well-entrenched in Fourteenth Amendment doctrine, and for good reason. It serves the useful function of helping to avoid confusion between the *procedural* safeguards guaranteed by due process, on the one hand, and certain *substantive* restrictions on state power that are also enforced under the authority of the due process clause on the other. Thus, the Supreme Court distinguishes between "procedural due process," the topic of this section, and "substantive due process," which is discussed in section D.

Procedural due process doctrine begins from the premise that the state possesses the authority to deprive the plaintiff of "liberty" or "property," so long as it proceeds in the appropriate way. The general principle of procedural due process is that persons faced with such a deprivation are entitled to "process," which typically means a hearing at which they may challenge the deprivation. The general requirements of a "due process" hearing are notice of the action to be taken and the reasons for taking it, an opportunity to present arguments against the deprivation, and an impartial decision maker. As the following case illustrates, the constitutional requirements as to the content and timing of the hearing vary depending on the circumstances.

GILBERT v. HOMAR
520 U.S. 924 (1997)

JUSTICE SCALIA delivered the opinion of the Court.

This case presents the question whether a State violates the Due Process Clause of the Fourteenth Amendment by failing to provide notice and a hearing before suspending a tenured public employee without pay.

I

Respondent Richard J. Homar was employed as a police officer at East Stroudsburg University (ESU), a branch of Pennsylvania's State System of Higher Education. On August 26, 1992, when respondent was at the home of a family friend, he was arrested by the Pennsylvania State Police in a drug raid. Later that day, the state police filed a criminal complaint charging respondent with possession of marijuana, possession with intent to deliver, and criminal conspiracy to violate the controlled substance law, which is a felony. The state police notified respondent's supervisor, University Police Chief David Marazas, of the arrest and charges. Chief Marazas in turn informed Gerald Levanowitz, ESU's Director of Human Resources, to whom ESU President James Gilbert had delegated authority to discipline ESU employees. Levanowitz suspended respondent without pay effective immediately. Respondent failed to report to work on the day of his arrest, and learned of his suspension the next day, when he called Chief Marazas to inquire whether he had been suspended. That same day, respondent received a letter from Levanowitz confirming that he had been suspended effective August 26 pending an investigation into the criminal charges filed against him. The letter explained that any action taken by ESU would not necessarily coincide with the disposition of the criminal charges.

Although the criminal charges were dismissed on September 1, respondent's suspension remained in effect while ESU continued with its own investigation. On September 18, Levanowitz and Chief Marazas met with respondent in order to give him an opportunity to tell his side of the story. Respondent was informed at the meeting that the state police had given ESU information that was "very serious in nature," but he was not informed that that included a report of an alleged confession he had made on the day of his arrest; he was consequently unable to respond to damaging statements attributed to him in the police report.

In a letter dated September 23, Levanowitz notified respondent that he was being demoted to the position of groundskeeper effective the next day, and that he would receive backpay from the date the suspension took effect at the rate of pay of a groundskeeper. (Respondent eventually received backpay for the period of his suspension at the rate of pay of a university police officer.) The letter maintained that the demotion was being imposed "as a result of admissions made by yourself to the Pennsylvania State Police on August 26, 1992 that you maintained associations with individuals whom you knew were dealing in large quantities of marijuana and that you obtained marijuana from one of those [Homar sued school officials under section 1983, charging that their] failure to provide him with notice and an opportunity to be heard before suspending him without pay violated due process. The District Court entered summary judgment for petitioners. A divided Court of Appeals reversed the District Court's determination that it was permissible for ESU to suspend respondent without pay without first providing a hearing.

II

The protections of the Due Process Clause apply to government deprivation of those perquisites of government employment in which the employee has a constitutionally protected "property" interest. Although we have previously held that public employees who can be discharged only for cause have a constitutionally protected property interest in their tenure and cannot be fired without due process, [Roth, Perry], we have not had occasion to decide whether the protections of the Due Process Clause extend to discipline of tenured public employees short of termination. Petitioners, however, do not contest this preliminary point, and so without deciding it we will, like the District Court, "assum[e] that the suspension infringed a protected property interest," and turn at once to petitioners' contention that respondent received all the process he was due.

A

In *Cleveland Bd. of Ed. v. Loudermill*, 470 U.S. 532 (1985), we concluded that a public employee dismissible only for cause was entitled to a very limited hearing prior to his termination, to be followed by a more comprehensive post-termination hearing. Stressing that the pretermination hearing "should be an initial check against mistaken decisions — essentially, a determination of whether there are reasonable grounds to believe that the charges against the employee are true and support the proposed action," we held that preterminaition process need only include oral or written notice of the charges, an explanation of the employer's evidence, and an opportunity for the employee to tell his side of the story. In the course of our assessment of the governmental interest in immediate termination of a tenured employee, we observed that "in those situations where the employer perceives a significant hazard in keeping the employee on the job, it can avoid the problem by suspending *with pay*." (emphasis added).

Relying on this dictum, which it read as "strongly suggesting that suspension without pay must be preceded by notice and an opportunity to be heard *in all instances*," (emphasis added), and determining on its own that such a rule would be "eminently sensible," the Court of Appeals adopted a categorical prohibition: "[A] governmental employer may not suspend an employee without pay unless that suspension is preceded by some kind of pre-suspension hearing, providing the employee with notice and an opportunity to be heard." [Homar] makes no attempt to defend this absolute rule, which spans all types of government employment and all types of unpaid suspensions. This is eminently wise, since under our precedents such an absolute rule is indefensible.

It is by now well established that " 'due process,' unlike some legal rules, is not a technical conception with a fixed content unrelated to time, place and circumstances." "Due process is flexible and calls for such procedural protections as the particular situation demands." This Court has recognized, on many occasions, that where a State must act quickly, or where it would be impractical to provide predeprivation process, postdeprivation process satisfies the requirements of the Due Process Clause. [In] *FDIC v. Mallen*, 486 U.S. 230 (1988), where we unanimously approved the Federal Deposit Insurance Corporation's suspension, without prior hearing, of an indicted private bank employee, we said: "An important government interest, accompanied by a substantial assurance that the deprivation is not baseless or unwarranted, may in limited cases demanding prompt action justify postponing the opportunity to be heard until after the initial deprivation."

The dictum in *Loudermill* relied upon by the Court of Appeals is of course not inconsistent with these precedents. To say that when the government employer perceives a hazard in leaving the employee on the job it "can avoid the problem by suspending with pay" is not to say that that is the only way of avoiding the problem. Whatever implication the phrase "with pay" might have conveyed is far outweighed by the clarity of our precedents which emphasize the flexibility of due process as contrasted with the sweeping and categorical rule adopted by the Court of Appeals.

B

To determine what process is constitutionally due, we have generally balanced three distinct factors:

> "First, the private interest that will be affected by the official action; second, the risk of an erroneous deprivation of such interest through the procedures used, and the probable value, if any, of additional or substitute procedural safeguards; and finally, the Government's interest." *Mathews v. Eldridge*, 424 U.S. 319, 335 (1976).

Respondent contends that he has a significant private interest in the uninterrupted receipt of his paycheck. But while our opinions have recognized the severity of depriving someone of the means of his livelihood, they have also emphasized that in determining what process is due, account must be taken of the *length* and *finality* of the deprivation. Unlike the employee in *Loudermill*, who faced *termination*, respondent faced only a *temporary suspension* without pay. So long as the suspended employee receives a sufficiently prompt post-suspension hearing, the lost income is relatively insubstantial (compared with termination), and fringe benefits such as health and life insurance are often not affected at all.

On the other side of the balance, the State has a significant interest in immediately suspending, when felony charges are filed against them, employees who occupy positions of great public trust and high public visibility, such as police officers. Respondent contends that this interest in maintaining public confidence could have been accommodated by suspending him *with* pay until he had a hearing.

We think, however, that the government does not have to give an employee charged with a felony a paid leave at taxpayer expense. If his services to the government are no longer useful once the felony charge has been filed, the Constitution does not require the government to bear the added expense of hiring a replacement while still paying him. ESU's interest in preserving public confidence in its police force is at least as significant as the State's interest in preserving the integrity of the sport of horse racing, an interest we "deemed sufficiently important . . . to justify a brief period of suspension prior to affording the suspended trainer a hearing."

The last factor in the *Mathews* balancing, and the factor most important to resolution of this case, is the risk of erroneous deprivation and the likely value of any additional procedures. Petitioners argue that any presuspension hearing would have been worthless because pursuant to an Executive Order of the Governor of Pennsylvania a state employee is automatically to be suspended without pay "as soon as practicable after [being] formally charged with . . . a felony." According to petitioners, supervisors have no discretion under this rule, and the mandatory suspension without pay lasts until the criminal charges are finally resolved. If petitioners' interpretation of this order is correct, there is no need for any presuspension process since there would be nothing to consider at the hearing except the independently verifiable fact of whether an employee had indeed been formally charged with a felony. Respondent, however, challenges petitioners' reading of the Code, and contends that in any event an order of the Governor of Pennsylvania is a "mere directive which does not confer a legally enforceable right." We need not resolve this disputed issue of state law because even assuming the Code is only advisory (or has no application at all), the State had no constitutional obligation to provide respondent with a presuspension hearing. We noted in *Loudermill* that the purpose of a pre-*termination* hearing is to determine "whether there are reasonable grounds to believe the charges against the employee are true and support the proposed action." By parity of reasoning, the purpose of any pre-*suspension* hearing would be to assure that there are reasonable grounds to support the suspension without pay. But here that has already been assured by the arrest and the filing of charges.

In [a prior case, the Court] concluded that an "*ex parte* finding of probable cause" such as a grand jury indictment provides adequate assurance that the suspension is not unjustified. The same is true when an employee is arrested and then formally charged with a felony. First, as with an indictment, the arrest and formal charges imposed upon respondent "by an independent body demonstrate that the suspension is not arbitrary." Second, like an indictment, the imposition of felony charges "itself is an objective fact that will in most cases raise serious public concern." It is true, as respondent argues, that there is more reason to believe an employee has committed a felony when he is indicted rather than merely arrested and formally charged; but for present purposes arrest and charge give reason enough. They serve to assure that the state employer's decision to suspend the employee is not "baseless or unwarranted," in that an independent third party has determined that there is probable cause to believe the employee committed a serious crime.

Respondent further contends that since (as we have agreed to assume) Levanowitz had discretion *not* to suspend despite the arrest and filing of charges, he had to be given an opportunity to persuade Levanowitz of his innocence before the decision was made. We disagree. [Unlike] in the case of a termination, where we have recognized that "the only meaningful opportunity to invoke the discretion of the decisionmaker is likely to be before the termination takes effect," in the case of a suspension there will be ample opportunity to invoke discretion later — and a short delay actually benefits the employee by allowing state officials to obtain more accurate information about the arrest and charges. Respondent "has an interest in seeing that a decision concerning his or her continued suspension is not made with excessive haste." If the State is forced to act too quickly, the decision maker "may give greater weight to the public interest and leave the suspension in place."

C

Much of respondent's argument is dedicated to the proposition that he had a due process right to a presuspension hearing because the suspension was open-ended and he "theoretically may not have had the opportunity to be heard for weeks, months, or even years after his initial suspension without pay." But, as respondent himself asserts in his attempt to downplay the governmental interest, "because the employee is entitled, in any event, to a prompt post-suspension opportunity to be heard, the period of the suspension should be short and the amount of pay during the suspension minimal."

Whether respondent was provided an adequately prompt *post*-suspension hearing in the present case is a separate question. Although the charges against respondent were dropped on September 1 (petitioners apparently learned of this on September 2), he did not receive any sort of hearing until September 18. Once the charges were dropped, the risk of erroneous deprivation increased substantially, and, as petitioners conceded at oral argument, there was likely value in holding a prompt hearing. Because neither the Court of Appeals nor the District Court addressed whether, under the particular facts of this case, petitioners violated due process by failing to provide a sufficiently prompt postsuspension hearing, we will not consider this issue in the first instance, but remand for consideration by the Court of Appeals.

The judgment of the Court of Appeals is reversed, and the case is remanded for further proceedings consistent with this opinion.

NOTES

1. In *Gilbert* the Court ruled that a post-deprivation hearing met the requirements of due process. The argument that the plaintiff should ordinarily get a hearing *before* termination is forcefully made in *Carmody v. Bd. of Trustees of University of Illinois*, 747 F.3d 470, 475 (7th Cir. 2014):

> A pre-termination hearing "is a critical protection" because "[i]t will be harder to convince an employer to reverse a decision to fire someone than to make sure the initial decision is fair and thoughtful; [once] an individual or group has made a decision to take a particular action, it becomes harder and harder to change course, even in the face of powerful conflicting evidence and reasons." [citing, among other authorities, DANIEL KAHNEMAN, THINKING, FAST AND SLOW (2011)]

Does *Gilbert* nonetheless govern all suspensions of police officers? In *Schmidt v. Creedon*, 639 F.3d 587, 596 (3d Cir. 2011) the court held that a police officer was entitled to a pre-suspension hearing where, in contrast to *Gilbert*, he was accused of misconduct by his superiors and not by an independent third party.

2. *The Matthews Calculus. Gilbert* illustrates the Supreme Court's due process calculus, introduced in *Matthews v. Eldridge*, under which the procedural protections required in a given situation depend on a balancing of competing interests. *See also United States v. James Daniel Good Real Property*, 510 U.S. 43 (1993) (the private interests at stake in the seizure of real property weigh heavily in the *Matthews* balance, in addition, "[b]ecause real property cannot abscond, the court's jurisdiction can be preserved without prior seizure"; thus, a pre-seizure hearing is constitutionally required); *Washington v. Harper*, 494 U.S. 210 (1990) (a prisoner has a "liberty" interest in "avoiding the unwarranted administration of "antipsychotic drugs," but procedural due process does not require a full judicial hearing before administration of such drugs; rather, "the inmate's interests are adequately protected, and perhaps better served, by allowing the decision to be made by medical professionals rather than a judge"). Determining what procedural protections are required in order to satisfy "due process" is a recurring issue in the lower courts. *See, e.g., Ralls Corp. v. Committee on Foreign Investment in the United States*, 758 F.3d 296, 319 (D.C. Cir. 2014) (even when the U.S. acts on national security grounds to deprive Chinese nationals of property interests, "due process requires, at the least, that an affected party be informed of the official action, be given access to the unclassified evidence on which the official actor relied and be afforded an opportunity to rebut that evidence"); *Snider International Corp. v. Town of Forest Heights*, 739 F.3d 140 (4th Cir. 2014) (upholding on efficiency grounds the use of first class mail, against a procedural due process challenge, as a means of providing notice to motorists issued traffic citations for speed camera violations); *J.R. v. Hansen*, 736 F.3d 959 (11th Cir. 2013) (an adversarial judicial hearing is not required before involuntarily admitting intellectually disabled persons to residential services; post-admission review satisfies due process); *Clukey v. Town of Camden*, 717 F.3d 52, 60 (1st Cir. 2013) ("Clukey's uncontested allegation that he received no notice either before or after the Town deprived him of a protected property interest in employment is in itself sufficient to state a procedural due process claim under § 1983"); *Heyne v. Metropolitan Nashville Public Schools*, 655 F.3d 556, 565 (6th Cir. 2011) ("The Due Process Clause does not require that hearings in connection with suspensions [from school] of ten days or fewer follow trial-type procedures."); *Kowalski v. Berkeley County Schools*, 652 F.3d 565 (4th Cir. 2011) (student who admitted her conduct was entitled to an opportunity to respond to charges, but not to a hearing, before being suspended from school).

3. Having ruled that inmates have a liberty interest in avoiding assignment to Supermax prisons, the Court in *Wilkinson, supra*, turned to the issue of whether Ohio's procedure for sending inmates to OSP satisfied the due process clause. The state did not provide an adversary hearing before putting inmates in the facility, *e.g.*, it did not permit inmates to call witnesses. Nonetheless, the Court upheld Ohio's "New Policy."

> Applying the three factors set forth in *Mathews* we find Ohio's New Policy provides a sufficient level of process. We first consider the significance of the inmate's interest in avoiding erroneous placement at OSP. Prisoners held in lawful confinement have their liberty curtailed by definition, so the procedural protections to which they are entitled are more limited than in cases where the right at stake is the right to be free from

confinement at all. The private interest at stake here, while more than minimal, must be evaluated, nonetheless, within the context of the prison system and its attendant curtailment of liberties.

The second factor addresses the risk of an erroneous placement under the procedures in place, and the probable value, if any, of additional or alternative procedural safeguards. The New Policy provides that an inmate must receive notice of the factual basis leading to consideration for OSP placement and a fair opportunity for rebuttal. Our procedural due process cases have consistently observed that these are among the most important procedural mechanisms for purposes of avoiding erroneous deprivations. Requiring officials to provide a brief summary of the factual basis for the classification review and allowing the inmate a rebuttal opportunity safeguards against the inmate's being mistaken for another or singled out for insufficient reason. In addition to having the opportunity to be heard at the Classification Committee state, Ohio also invites the inmate to submit objections prior to the final level of review. This second opportunity further reduces the possibility of an erroneous deprivation.

Although a subsequent reviewer may overturn an affirmative recommendation for OSP placement, the reverse is not true; if one reviewer declines to recommend OSP placement, the process terminates. This avoids one of the problems apparently present under the Old Policy, where, even if two levels of reviewers recommended against placement, a later reviewer could overturn their recommendation without explanation.

If the recommendation is OSP placement, Ohio requires that the decision maker provide a short statement of reasons. This requirement guards against arbitrary decisionmaking while also providing the inmate a basis for objection before the next decisionmaker or in a subsequent classification review. The statement also serves as a guide for future behavior. As we have noted, Ohio provides multiple levels of review of any decision recommending OSP placment, with power to overturn the recommendation at each level. In addition to these safeguards, Ohio further reduces the risk of erroneous placement by providing for a placement review within 30 days of an inmate's initial assignment to OSP.

The third *Mathews* factor addresses the State's interest. In the context of prison management, and in the specific circumstances of this case, this interest is a dominant consideration. Ohio has responsibility for imprisoning nearly 44,000 inmates. The State's first obligation must be to ensure the safety of guards and prison personnel, the public, and the prisoners themselves.

Prison security, imperiled by the brutal reality of prison gangs, provides the backdrop of the State's interest. Clandestine, organized, fueled by race based hostility, and committed to fear and violence as a means of disciplining their own members and their rivals, gangs seek nothing less than to control prison life and to extend their power outside prison [walls].

The problem of scarce resources is another component of the State's interest. The cost of keeping a single prisoner in one of Ohio's ordinary maximum security prisons is $34,167 per year, and the cost to maintain each inmate at OSP is $49,007 per year.

We can assume that Ohio, or any other penal system, faced with costs like these will find it difficult to fund more effective education and vocational assistance programs to improve the lives of the prisoners. It follows that courts must give substantial deference to prison management decisions before mandating additional expenditures for elaborate procedural safeguards when correctional officials conclude that a prisoner has engaged in disruptive behavior.

The State's interest must be understood against this background. Were Ohio to allow an inmate to call witnesses or provide other attributes of an adversary hearing before ordering transfer to OSP, both the State's immediate objective of controlling the prisoner and its greater objective of controlling the prison could be [defeated].

4. *The Role of State Law.* States create "new" property and "new" liberty by identifying the circumstances in which it may take them away, such as misconduct on the part of a prisoner or neglect of duties on the part of an employee. The point of the hearing is to determine whether those conditions have been satisfied. Given that the state creates the "property" interest, may the state also limit the scope of that interest by specifying procedures under which it can take the interest away? In other words, does the state's control over whether "property" exists mean that the state also controls the question of what "due process" requires? The answer is no. In *Cleveland Board of Education v. Loudermill*, 470 U.S. 532 (1985), the Supreme Court ruled that the two issues are separate. Once it is determined that state law has created a property interest, the question of what process is due is a matter of federal constitutional law and is not determined by state law. Is there any reason to think this issue would be resolved differently if it came up in the "new" liberty context?

5. *"Old" Property and the Special Problem of Takings.* Most efforts by the state to deprive a person of "old" property — land, chattels, or money — involve criminal, civil, or administrative enforcement proceedings. In any event, these are the kinds of cases that raise *procedural* due process concerns. The process that is due will typically be determined by reference to principles of criminal, civil, or administrative procedure.

Suppose the property owner is not charged with a violation of law. The state simply seeks to take his land for public use. The "takings" clause of the Fifth Amendment permits this, on the condition that the owner be paid just compensation. Issues may arise as to whether or not a taking has occurred (*e.g.*, by "inverse condemnation) through strict land use regulation), whether the property was appropriately taken for "public" use, and whether the amount offered for it is "just compensation." The process that is due the property owner in resolving such issues will generally take place in state court, because the Supreme Court has held that a section 1983 suit challenging the propriety of the taking or the amount to be paid will not be ripe until the state process is completed. *Williamson County Regional*

Planning Commission v. Hamilton Bank, 473 U.S. 172 (1985).

6. *"Old" Liberty and the Special Problem of Stigma-Plus.* As with "old" property, the main point of procedural due process in relation to "old" liberty is to see to it that the state does not deprive us of our substantive "liberty" rights not to be confined or punished without good reason. Once again, in the ordinary case the process that is due will be derived from principles of criminal, civil, or administrative procedure. But not always. In *Ingraham, supra*, the Court ruled that corporal punishment of students implicated the liberty interest in personal security from physical pain. One may think that the appropriate procedural safeguard would be a pre-paddling hearing of some kind. But the Court held that the availability of state tort remedies satisfied the demands of procedural due process.

The stigma-plus doctrine differs from other kinds of liberty and property (both old and new) in the following way: In all of the other categories, the premise of procedural protection is that the plaintiff holds a substantive right: to a job, to certain prison conditions, to his land and chattels, to freedom of movement and bodily integrity. These can be taken only on certain conditions and the point of the due process hearing is to determine whether those conditions are met. By contrast, the stigma-plus plaintiff has no substantive constitutional right to a job. Procedural due process entitles him to a hearing, but the point of the hearing is just to clear his name. *See, e.g., Quinn v. Shirey*, 293 F.3d 315 (6th Cir. 2002) (discussing the Sixth Circuit's rule that even the right to a name clearing hearing is waived unless the plaintiff asks for one). Even if he is vindicated, he has no constitutional right to reinstatement. Whether the stigma-plus plaintiff has a "substantive due process" right to recover damages to his reputation is a separate question. *See* section D.

D. Substantive Due Process

A premise of the cases discussed in section C is that the state has the authority to deprive persons of Fourteenth Amendment "liberty" and "property" in certain circumstances. The main point of procedural due process is to assure accurate determinations of whether those circumstances exist. But the due process clause also has what the Supreme Court calls a "substantive component," which forbids certain official actions altogether, no matter what the circumstances and no matter what process is followed. This usage is a bit confusing, partly because "substantive due process" is "a contradiction in terms — sort of like 'green pastel redness.'" JOHN HART ELY, DEMOCRACY AND DISTRUST 18 (1980). Professor Ely and other critics would do away with the doctrine altogether, because they think it accords judges more power than they ought to have in our system of government. Others believe that substantive due process is compatible with majoritarian rule. *See, e.g.,* RONALD DWORKIN, FREEDOM'S LAW (1997). This book is not concerned with the debate over constitutional theory.

There is a more subtle reason why the term "substantive due process" is misleading. As we pointed out in the last paragraph of section C, *supra*, the "liberty" and "property" that receive procedural protection are *themselves* substantive rights, just because there are limits on the authority of the state to deprive us of them. *See Roberts v. United States*, 741 F.3d 152, 161 (D.C. Cir. 2014) (noting that the point of due process is to protect substantive liberty and property rights.) The distinctive feature of "substantive due process" rights is not that they are substantive but that the limits on state authority go beyond the procedural restraints discussed in section C.

Another important difference between the domains of substantive and procedural due process relates to the range of cases that will trigger liability. While substantive due process places stricter limits on what state officers are allowed to do, it imposes those limits on a narrower range of conduct. Thus, *Daniels v. Williams* holds that a showing of negligence is insufficient for liability. Officers may be found to have committed violations of the procedural safeguards discussed in section C even if they in good faith believed they were acting properly. (But whether they can be held liable for damages on account of these violations is a separate question, which turns on the applicability of the official immunity doctrines discussed in Chapters 7 and 8 *infra*).

DANIELS v. WILLIAMS
474 U.S. 327 (1986)

JUSTICE REHNQUIST delivered the opinion of the Court.

In *Parratt v. Taylor* a state prisoner sued under 42 U.S.C. § 1983, claiming that prison officials had negligently deprived him of his property without due process of law. After deciding that § 1983 contains no independent state-of-mind requirement, we concluded that although petitioner had been "deprived" of property within the meaning of the Due Process Clause of the Fourteenth Amendment, the State's postdeprivation tort remedy provided the process that was due. Petitioner's claim in this case, which also rests on an alleged Fourteenth Amendment "deprivation" caused by the negligent conduct of a prison official, leads us to reconsider our statement in *Parratt* that "the alleged loss, even though negligently caused, amounted to a deprivation." Id., at 536–537. We conclude that the Due Process Clause is simply not implicated by a negligent act of an official causing unintended loss of or injury to life, liberty, or property.

In this § 1983 action, petitioner seeks to recover damages for back and ankle injuries allegedly sustained when he fell on a prison stairway. He claims that, while an inmate at the city jail in Richmond, Virginia, he slipped on a pillow negligently left on the stairs by respondent, a correctional deputy stationed at the jail. Respondent's negligence, the argument runs, "deprived" petitioner of his "liberty" interest in freedom from bodily injury, *see Ingraham v. Wright*.

Because of the inconsistent approaches taken by lower courts in determining when tortious conduct by state officials rises to the level of a constitutional tort, and the apparent lack of adequate guidance from this Court, we granted certiorari.

[The] Due Process Clause of the Fourteenth Amendment provides: "[Nor] shall any State deprive any person of life, liberty, or property, without due process of law." Historically, this guarantee of due process has been applied to deliberate decisions of government officials to deprive a person of life, liberty, or property. *E.g., Davidson v. New Orleans* (assessment of real estate); *Rochin v. California* (stomach pumping); *Bell v. Burson* (suspension of driver's license); *Ingraham v.*

Wright (paddling student); *Hudson v. Palmer* (intentional destruction of inmate's property).

[The] Due Process Clause, like its forebear in the Magna Carta, was " 'intended to secure the individual from the arbitrary exercise of the powers of government,' "*Hurtado v. California.* [See] also *Wolff v. McDonnell* ("The touchstone of due process is protection of the individual against arbitrary action of government.") [By] requiring the government to follow appropriate procedures when its agents decide to "deprive any person of life, liberty, or property," the Due Process Clause promotes fairness in such decisions. And by barring certain government actions regardless of the fairness of the procedures used to implement them, *e.g., Rochin,* supra, it serves to prevent governmental power from being "used for purposes of oppression."

We think that the actions of prison custodians in leaving a pillow on the prison stairs, or mislaying an inmate's property, are quite remote from the concerns just discussed. Far from an abuse of power, lack of due care suggests no more than a failure to measure up to the conduct of a reasonable person. To hold that injury caused by such conduct is a deprivation within the meaning of the Fourteenth Amendment would trivialize the centuries-old principle of due process of law.

The Fourteenth Amendment is a part of a Constitution generally designed to allocate governing authority among the Branches of the Federal Government and between that Government and the States, and to secure certain individual rights against both State and Federal Government. When dealing with a claim that such a document creates a right in prisoners to sue a government official because he negligently created an unsafe condition in the prison, we bear in mind Chief Justice Marshall's admonition that "we must never forget, that it is a *constitution* we are expounding," *McCulloch v. Maryland* (emphasis in original). Our Constitution deals with the large concerns of the governors and the governed, but it does not purport to supplant traditional tort law in laying down rules of conduct to regulate liability for injuries that attend living together in society. We have previously rejected reasoning that " 'would make of the Fourteenth Amendment a font of tort law to be superimposed upon whatever systems may already be administered by the States,' " *Paul v. Davis.*

The only tie between the facts of this case and anything governmental in nature is the fact that respondent was a sheriff's deputy at the Richmond city jail and petitioner was an inmate confined in that jail. But while the Due Process Clause of the Fourteenth Amendment obviously speaks to some facets of this relationship, we do not believe its protections are triggered by lack of due care by prison officials. "Medical malpractice does not become a constitutional violation merely because the victim is a prisoner," *Estelle v. Gamble,* and "false imprisonment does not become a violation of the Fourteenth Amendment merely because the defendant is a state official." *Baker v. McCollan.* Where a government official's act causing injury to life, liberty, or property is merely negligent, "no procedure for compensation is constitutionally required."

That injuries inflicted by governmental negligence are not addressed by the United States Constitution is not to say that they may not raise significant legal concerns and lead to the creation of protectible legal interests. The enactment of tort claim statutes, for example, reflects the view that injuries caused by such negligence should generally be redressed. It is no reflection on either the breadth of the United States Constitution or the importance of traditional tort law to say that they do not address the same concerns.

In support of his claim that negligent conduct can give rise to a due process "deprivation," petitioner makes several arguments, none of which we find persuasive. He states, for example, that "it is almost certain that some negligence claims are within § 1983," and cites as an example the failure of a State to comply with the procedural requirements of *Wolff v. McDonnell* before depriving an inmate of good-time credit. We think the relevant action of the prison officials in that situation is their deliberate decision to deprive the inmate of good-time credit, not their hypothetically negligent failure to accord him the procedural protections of the Due Process Clause. But we need not rule out the possibility that there are other constitutional provisions that would be violated by mere lack of care in order to hold, as we do, that such conduct does not implicate the Due Process Clause of the Fourteenth Amendment.

Petitioner also suggests that artful litigants, undeterred by a requirement that they plead more than mere negligence, will often be able to allege sufficient facts to support a claim of intentional deprivation. In the instant case, for example, petitioner notes that he could have alleged that the pillow was left on the stairs with the intention of harming him. This invitation to "artful" pleading, petitioner contends, would engender sticky (and needless) disputes over what is fairly pleaded. What's more, requiring complainants to allege something more than negligence would raise serious questions about what "more" than negligence — intent, recklessness, or "gross negligence" — is required, and indeed about what these elusive terms mean. But even if accurate, petitioner's observations do not carry the day. In the first place, many branches of the law abound in nice distinctions that may be troublesome but have been thought nonetheless necessary. [More] important, the difference between one end of the spectrum — negligence — and the other — intent — is abundantly clear. See O. Holmes, *The Common Law* 3 (1923). In any event, we decline to trivialize the Due Process Clause in an effort to simplify constitutional litigation.

NOTES

1.   In *Davidson v. Cannon*, 474 U.S. 344 (1986), a companion case to *Daniels*, a prisoner sued prison officials for failing to protect him against assault by McMillian, another inmate. After being threatened by the attacker, the plaintiff had explained the situation to Cannon, the assistant superintendent of the prison, who passed it on to James, a corrections sergeant. Yet nothing was done to ensure his safety. Two days later McMillian attacked him. Applying the standard it had set forth in *Daniels*, the Court held that this failure did not amount to "deliberate indifference."

> Respondents' lack of due care in this case led to serious injury, but that lack of care simply does not approach the sort of abusive government conduct that the Due Process Clause was designed to prevent. Far from abusing governmental power, or employing it as an instrument of oppression,

respondent Cannon mistakenly believed that the situation was not particularly serious, and respondent James simply forgot about the note. The guarantee of due process has never been understood to mean that the State must guarantee due care on the part of its officials . . . Petitioner's claim, based on respondents' negligence, is quite different from one involving injuries caused by an unjustified attack by prison guards themselves or by another prisoner where officials simply stood by and permitted the attack to proceed . . .

In dissent, Justice Blackmun took issue with the Court's sweeping holding that

> negligent activity can *never* implicate the concerns of the Due Process
> [Clause.] In some cases, by any reasonable standard, governmental
> negligence is an abuse of power. This is one of those cases. It seems
> to me that when a State assumes sole responsibility for one's physical
> security and then ignores his call for help, the State cannot claim that
> it did not know a subsequent injury was likely to occur . . . In the
> context of prisons this means that once the State has taken away an
> inmate's means of protecting himself from attack by other inmates, a
> prison official's negligence in providing protection can amount to a
> deprivation of the inmate's liberty . . . In *Daniels*, the negligence was
> only coincidentally connected to an inmate-guard relationship; the
> same incident could have occurred on any staircase . . . In contrast,
> where the State renders a person vulnerable and strips him of his
> ability to defend himself, an injury that results from a state official's
> negligence in performing his duty is peculiarly related to the govern-
> mental function. [The] deliberate decision not to protect Davidson
> from a known threat was directly related to the often violent life of
> prisoners.

2.   Substantive due process acquired a bad reputation, from which it has never fully recovered, in the late nineteenth and early twentieth centuries when the Court used it as its tool for striking down social legislation like minimum wage and maximum hour laws. *See* K. SULLIVAN & N. FELDMAN , CONSTITUTIONAL LAW 480–86 (18th ed. 2013). After going underground in the wake of the constitutional revolution of the 1930s, substantive due process was revived, if not in *Griswold v. Connecticut*, 381 U.S. 479 (1965) (striking down a statute that outlawed contraceptive drugs by relying on "penumbras and emanations" of various constitutional guarantees), then forthrightly in *Roe v. Wade*, 410 U.S. 113 (1973).

However inelegant the term may be, and however checkered its history, substantive due process has managed to survive the efforts to remove it from our constitutional tradition. *See, e.g., Lawrence v. Texas*, 539 U.S. 558 (2003) (striking down a criminal sodomy law on substantive due process grounds). In particular, it is an important element of constitutional torts. Conservative Justices rail against the substantive due process decision in *Roe*. Why did Justice Rehnquist not take the opportunity afforded by *Daniels* to banish it from the constitutional lexicon altogether?

Daniels stands for the proposition that a plaintiff seeking to establish a substantive violation by the defendant must show a more egregious state of mind than negligence. If negligence is not enough, what state of mind will suffice? In *County of Sacramento v. Lewis* the Court addressed that question.

COUNTY OF SACRAMENTO v. LEWIS
523 U.S. 833 (1998)

JUSTICE SOUTER delivered the opinion of the Court.

The issue in this case is whether a police officer violates the Fourteenth Amendment's guarantee of substantive due process by causing death through deliberate or reckless indifference to life in a high-speed automobile chase aimed at apprehending a suspected offender. We answer no, and hold that in such circumstances only a purpose to cause harm unrelated to the legitimate object of arrest will satisfy the element of arbitrary conduct shocking to the conscience, necessary for a due process violation.

[Smith and another officer saw a motorcycle approaching at high speed.] It was operated by 18-year-old Brian Willard and carried Philip Lewis, respondents' 16-year-old decedent, as a passenger.

[Smith and the other officer pursued the motorcycle, but Willard refused to stop in response to warning lights and commands.] Smith began pursuit at high speed. For 75 seconds over a course of 1.3 miles in a residential neighborhood, the motorcycle wove in and out of oncoming traffic, forcing two cars and a bicycle to swerve off of the road. The motorcycle and patrol car reached speeds up to 100 miles an hour, with Smith following at a distance as short as 100 feet; at that speed, his car would have required 650 feet to stop.

The chase ended after the motorcycle tipped over as Willard tried a sharp left turn. By the time Smith slammed on his brakes, Willard was out of the way, but Lewis was not. The patrol car skidded into him at 40 miles an hour, propelling him some 70 feet down the road and inflicting massive injuries. Lewis was pronounced dead at the scene.

[Lewis's parents brought suit under 42 U.S.C. § 1983 against petitioners Sacramento County, the Sacramento County Sheriff's Department and Deputy Smith, alleging a deprivation of Philip Lewis's Fourteenth Amendment substantive due process right to life.]

The Court of Appeals for the Ninth Circuit [held] that "the appropriate degree of fault to be applied to high-speed police pursuits is deliberate indifference to, or reckless disregard for, a person's right to life and personal security." Since Smith apparently disregarded the Sacramento County Sheriff's Department's General Order on police pursuits, the Ninth Circuit found a genuine issue of material fact that might be resolved by a finding that Smith's conduct amounted to deliberate indifference:

The General Order requires an officer to communicate his intention to pursue a vehicle to the sheriff's department dispatch center. But defendants concede that

Smith did not contact the dispatch center. The General Order requires an officer to consider whether the seriousness of the offense warrants a chase at speeds in excess of the posted limit. But here, the only apparent 'offense' was the boys' refusal to stop when another officer told them to do so. The General Order requires an officer to consider whether the need for apprehension justifies the pursuit under existing conditions. Yet Smith apparently only 'needed' to apprehend the boys because they refused to stop. The General Order requires an officer to consider whether the pursuit presents unreasonable hazards to life and property. But taking the facts here in the light most favorable to plaintiffs, there existed an unreasonable hazard to Lewis's and Willard's lives. The General Order also directs an officer to discontinue a pursuit when the hazards of continuing outweigh the benefits of immediate apprehension. But here, there was no apparent danger involved in permitting the boys to escape. There certainly was risk of harm to others in continuing the pursuit.

We granted certiorari to resolve a conflict among the Circuits over the standard of culpability on the part of a law enforcement officer for violating substantive due process in a pursuit case. We now reverse.

II

Our prior cases have held the provision that "no State shall . . . deprive any person of life, liberty, or property, without due process of law," to "guarantee more than fair process," and to cover a substantive sphere as well, "barring certain government actions regardless of the fairness of the procedures used to implement them," *Daniels v. Williams*. The allegation here that Lewis was deprived of his right to life in violation of substantive due process amounts to a such claim, that under the circumstances described earlier, Smith's actions in causing Lewis's death were an abuse of executive power so clearly unjustified by any legitimate objective of law enforcement as to be barred by the Fourteenth Amendment.

Since the time of our early explanations of due process, we have understood the core of the concept to be protection against arbitrary action:

> "The principal and true meaning of the phrase has never been more tersely or accurately stated than by Mr. Justice Johnson, in *Bank of Columbia v. Okely*, 17 U.S. 235 [(1819)]: 'As to the words from Magna Charta, incorporated into the Constitution of Maryland, after volumes spoken and written with a view to their exposition, the good sense of mankind has at last settled down to this: that they were intended to secure the individual from the arbitrary exercise of the powers of government, unrestrained by the established principles of private right and distributive justice.' "

We have emphasized time and again that "the touchstone of due process is protection of the individual against arbitrary action of government," whether the fault lies in a denial of fundamental procedural fairness, or in the exercise of power without any reasonable justification in the service of a legitimate governmental objective.

Our cases dealing with abusive executive action have repeatedly emphasized that only the most egregious official conduct can be said to be "arbitrary in the constitutional sense," thereby recognizing the point made in different circumstances by Chief Justice Marshall, "that it is a constitution we are expounding," [For] half a century now we have spoken of the cognizable level of executive abuse of power as that which shocks the conscience. We first put the test this way in *Rochin v. California*, where we found the forced pumping of a suspect's stomach enough to offend due process as conduct "that shocks the conscience" and violates the "decencies of civilized conduct."

[It] should not be surprising that the constitutional concept of conscience-shocking duplicates no traditional category of common-law fault, but rather points clearly away from liability, or clearly toward it, only at the ends of the tort law's spectrum of culpability. Thus, we have made it clear that the due process guarantee does not entail a body of constitutional law imposing liability whenever someone cloaked with state authority causes harm. [In] *Daniels v. Williams* we reaffirmed the point that "our Constitution deals with the large concerns of the governors and the governed, but it does not purport to supplant traditional tort law in laying down rules of conduct to regulate liability for injuries that attend living together in society." We have accordingly rejected the lowest common denominator of customary tort liability as any mark of sufficiently shocking conduct, and have held that the Constitution does not guarantee due care on the part of state officials; liability for negligently inflicted harm is categorically beneath the threshold of constitutional due process. It is, on the contrary, behavior at the other end of the culpability spectrum that would most probably support a substantive due process claim; conduct intended to injure in some way unjustifiable by any government interest is the sort of official action most likely to rise to the conscience-shocking level. Whether the point of the conscience shocking is reached when injuries are produced with culpability falling within the middle range, following from something more than negligence but "less than intentional conduct, such as recklessness or 'gross negligence,'" is a matter for closer calls. To be sure, we have expressly recognized the possibility that some official acts in this range may be actionable under the Fourteenth Amendment, and our cases have compelled recognition that such conduct is egregious enough to state a substantive due process claim in at least one instance. We held in *City of Revere v. Massachusetts Gen. Hospital* that "the due process rights of a [pretrial detainee] are at least as great as the Eighth Amendment protections available to a convicted prisoner." Since it may suffice for Eighth Amendment liability that prison officials were deliberately indifferent to the medical needs of their prisoners, it follows that such deliberately indifferent conduct must also be enough to satisfy the fault requirement for due process claims based on the medical needs of someone jailed while awaiting trial.

Rules of due process are not, however, subject to mechanical application in unfamiliar territory. Deliberate indifference that shocks in one environment may not be so patently egregious in another, and our concern with preserving the constitutional proportions of substantive due process demands an exact analysis of circumstances before any abuse of power is condemned as conscience-shocking. [Attention] to the markedly different circumstances of normal pretrial custody and high-speed law enforcement chases shows why the deliberate indifference that shocks in the one case is less egregious in the other (even assuming that it makes sense to speak of indifference as deliberate in the case of sudden pursuit). As the very term "deliberate indifference" implies, the standard is sensibly employed only when actual deliberation is practical, and in the custodial situation of a prison, forethought about an inmate's welfare is not only feasible but obligatory under a regime that incapacitates a prisoner to exercise ordinary responsibility for his own welfare.

But just as the description of the custodial prison situation shows how deliberate indifference can rise to a constitutionally shocking level, so too does it suggest why indifference may well not be enough for liability in the different circumstances of a case like this one. We have, indeed, found that deliberate indifference does not suffice for constitutional liability (albeit under the Eighth Amendment) even in prison circumstances when a prisoner's claim arises not from normal custody but from response to a violent disturbance. Our analysis is instructive here:

> "In making and carrying out decisions involving the use of force to restore order in the face of a prison disturbance, prison officials undoubtedly must take into account the very real threats the unrest presents to inmates and prison officials alike, in addition to the possible harms to inmates against whom force might be used. . . . In this setting, a deliberate indifference standard does not adequately capture the importance of such competing obligations, or convey the appropriate hesitancy to critique in hindsight decisions necessarily made in haste, under pressure, and frequently without the luxury of a second chance." *Whitley v. Albers.*

We accordingly held that a much higher standard of fault than deliberate indifference has to be shown for officer liability in a prison riot. In those circumstances, liability should turn on "whether force was applied in a good faith effort to maintain or restore discipline or maliciously and sadistically for the very purpose of causing harm." The analogy to sudden police chases (under the Due Process Clause) would be hard to avoid. Like prison officials facing a riot, the police on an occasion calling for fast action have obligations that tend to tug against each other. Their duty is to restore and maintain lawful order, while not exacerbating disorder more than necessary to do their jobs. They are supposed to act decisively and to show restraint at the same moment, and their decisions have to be made "in haste, under pressure, and frequently without the luxury of a second chance." A police officer deciding whether to give chase must balance on one hand the need to stop a suspect and show that flight from the law is no way to freedom, and, on the other, the high-speed threat to everyone within stopping range, be they suspects, their passengers, other drivers, or bystanders.

To recognize a substantive due process violation in these circumstances when only mid level fault has been shown would be to forget that liability for deliberate indifference to inmate welfare rests upon the luxury enjoyed by prison officials of having time to make unhurried judgments, upon the chance for repeated reflection, largely uncomplicated by the pulls of competing obligations. When such extended opportunities to do better are teamed with protracted failure even to care, indifference is truly shocking. But when unforeseen circumstances demand an officer's instant judgment, even precipitate recklessness fails to inch close enough to harmful purpose to spark the shock that implicates "the large concerns of the governors and the governed." *Daniels v. Williams.* Just as a purpose to cause harm is needed for Eighth Amendment liability in a riot case, so it ought to be needed for Due Process liability in a pursuit case. Accordingly, we hold that high-speed chases with no intent to harm suspects physically or to worsen their legal plight do not give rise to liability under the Fourteenth Amendment.

The fault claimed on Smith's part in this case accordingly fails to meet the shocks-the-conscience test. In the count charging him with liability under § 1983, respondents' complaint alleges a variety of culpable states of mind: "negligently responsible in some manner," "reckless and careless," "recklessness, gross negligence and conscious disregard for [Lewis's] safety", and "oppression, fraud and malice." The subsequent summary judgment proceedings revealed that the height of the fault actually claimed was "conscious disregard," the malice allegation having been made in aid of a request for punitive damages, but unsupported either in allegations of specific conduct or in any affidavit of fact offered on the motions for summary judgment. The Court of Appeals understood the claim to be one of deliberate indifference to Lewis's survival, which it treated as equivalent to one of reckless disregard for life. We agree with this reading of respondents' allegations, but consequently part company from the Court of Appeals, which found them sufficient to state a substantive due process claim.

Smith was faced with a course of lawless behavior for which the police were not to blame. They had done nothing to cause Willard's high-speed driving in the first place, nothing to excuse his flouting of the commonly understood law enforcement authority to control traffic, and nothing (beyond a refusal to call off the chase) to encourage him to race through traffic at breakneck speed forcing other drivers out of their travel lanes. Willard's outrageous behavior was practically instantaneous, and so was Smith's instinctive response. While prudence would have repressed the reaction, the officer's instinct was to do his job as a law enforcement officer, not to induce Willard's lawlessness, or to terrorize, cause harm, or kill. Prudence, that is, was subject to countervailing enforcement considerations, and while Smith exaggerated their demands, there is no reason to believe that they were tainted by an improper or malicious motive on his part.

Regardless whether Smith's behavior offended the reasonableness held up by tort law or the balance struck in law enforcement's own codes of sound practice, it does not shock the conscience, and petitioners are not called upon to answer for it under § 1983.

[Concurring opinions by CHIEF JUSTICE REHNQUIST and JUSTICES KENNEDY and BREYER, as well as JUSTICE STEVENS' opinion concurring in the judgment, are omitted.]

JUSTICE SCALIA, with whom JUSTICE THOMAS joins, concurring in the judgment.

[Our] established method of substantive-due-process analysis has two primary features: First, we have regularly observed that the Due Process Clause specially protects those fundamental rights and liberties which are, objectively, 'deeply rooted in this Nation's history and tradition,' and 'implicit in the concept of ordered liberty.' Second, we have required in substantive-due-process cases a 'careful description' of the asserted fundamental liberty interest. Our Nation's history, legal traditions, and practices thus provide the crucial 'guideposts for responsible decision-making,' that direct and restrain our exposition of the Due Process Clause.

Justice Souter would largely abandon this restrained methodology, and instead ask 'whether [Washington's] statute sets up one of those "arbitrary impositions" or "purposeless restraints" at odds with the Due Process Clause In our view, however, the development of this Court's substantive-due-process jurisprudence has been a process whereby the outlines of the 'liberty' specially protected by the Fourteenth Amendment have at least been carefully refined by concrete examples involving fundamental rights found to be deeply rooted in our legal tradition. This approach tends to rein in the subjective elements that are necessarily present in due-process judicial review.

[Today's] opinion resuscitates the *ne plus ultra*, the Napoleon Brandy, the Mahatma Ghandi, the Celophane of subjectivity, th' ol' "shocks-the-conscience" test. According to today's opinion, this is the measure of arbitrariness when what is at issue is executive rather than legislative action. [Rather] than ask whether the police conduct here at issue shocks my unelected conscience, I would ask whether our Nation has traditionally protected the right respondents assert. The first step of our analysis, of course, must be a "careful description" of the right asserted. Here the complaint alleges that the police officer deprived Lewis "of his Fourteenth Amendment right to life, liberty and property without due process of law when he operated his vehicle with recklessness, gross negligence and conscious disregard for his safety." I agree with the Court's conclusion that this asserts a substantive right to be free from "deliberate or reckless indifference to life in a high-speed automobile chase aimed at apprehending a suspected offender."

Respondents provide no textual or historical support for this alleged due process right, and I would "decline to fashion a new due process right out of thin air." Nor have respondents identified any precedential support. Indeed, precedent is to the contrary: "Historically, the guarantee of due process has been applied to deliberate decisions of government officials to deprive a person of life, liberty, or property."

If the people of the State of California would prefer a system that renders police officers liable for reckless driving during high-speed pursuits, "they may create such a system . . . by changing the tort law of the State in accordance with the regular lawmaking process." For now, they prefer not to hold public employees "liable for civil damages on account of personal injury to or death of any person or damage to property resulting from the operation, in the line of duty, of an authorized emergency vehicle . . . when in the immediate pursuit of an actual or suspected violator of the law." Cal. Veh. Code Ann. § 17004. It is the prerogative of a self-governing people to make that legislative choice. Political society must consider not only the risks to passengers, pedestrians, and other drivers that high-speed chases engender, but also the fact that if police are forbidden to pursue, then many more suspects will flee — and successful flights not only reduce the number of crimes solved but also create their own risks for passengers and bystanders. In allocating such risks, the people of California and their elected representatives may vote their consciences. But for judges to overrule that democratically adopted policy judgment on the ground that it shocks their consciences is not judicial review but judicial governance.

I would reverse the judgment of the Ninth Circuit, not on the ground that petitioners have failed to shock my still, soft voice within, but on the ground that respondents offer no textual or historical support for their alleged due process right. Accordingly, I concur in the judgment of the Court.

NOTES

1.   Does *Sacramento County v. Lewis* apply only to drivers and passengers of the vehicle being pursued, or does it extend to injuries suffered by innocent bystanders? *See Onossian v. Block*, 175 F.3d 1169 (9th Cir. 1999) (taking the latter, broader, view of the case). After *Lewis*, is a police officer ever liable for a substantive due process violation when the officer injures someone in the course of a high-speed chase? *Compare Davis v. Township of Hillside*, 190 F.3d 167 (3d Cir. 1999) (even if the officer deliberately rammed the pursued car at the conclusion of the chase, "*Lewis* does not permit an inference of intent to harm simply because a chase eventuates in deliberate physical contact causing injury;" here, the officers' "intent was to do their job as law enforcement officers, not to cause injury"), with *Petta v. Rivera*, 143 F.3d 895 (5th Cir. 1998) (upholding a complaint that alleged that the officer engaged in a high-speed pursuit of a motorist suspected only of speeding, who had stopped when asked but then sped off after the officer used abusive language and hit the car with a nightstick) and *Fontana v. Haskin*, 262 F.3d 871, 882 n.7 (9th Cir. 2001) (police officer's alleged conduct in fondling and propositioning a handcuffed suspect would shock the conscience).

2.   In *Sacramento County v. Lewis* the Court rules that the defendant's conduct does not rise to the level of a substantive due process violation unless it "shocks the conscience." In that case, the Court states that sometimes conduct that is "deliberately indifferent" to the plaintiff's well-being may meet that standard. Where there is not time to deliberate, however, the "shock the conscience" test is met only by a "purpose to cause harm unrelated to the legitimate object of arrest." 523 U.S. at 836. Should "deliberate indifference" be the standard whenever there is time for deliberation? In *Collins v. City of Harker Heights*, 503 U.S. 115 (1992), the plaintiff was a city employee who was fatally injured in the course of his duties. His widow sued under section 1983, charging he "had a constitutional right to be free from unreasonable risks of harm to his body, mind, and emotions and a constitutional right to be protected from the City of Harker Heights' . . . deliberate indifference toward the safety of its employees." The complaint alleged that the city "violated that right by . . . not training its employees about the dangers of working in sewer lines and manholes, not providing safety equipment at job sites, and not providing safety warnings." After noting that "[a] fair reading of [the] complaint does not charge the city with a wilful violation of Collins' rights," the Court rejected the claim. The Court was "not persuaded that the city's alleged failure to train its employees, or to warn them about known risks of harm, was an omission that can properly be characterized as arbitrary, or conscience-shocking, in a constitutional sense." What result if a city official deliberately aimed to hurt or punish the plaintiff by assigning him hazardous work? *See Upsher v. Grosse Pointe Public School System*, 285 F.3d 448 (6th Cir. 2002) (holding that this would be a substantive due process violation but finding a lack of evidence "which suggests that any of the defendants made a deliberate decision to inflict pain or bodily injury on any of the plaintiffs" nor any evidence "that the defendants engaged in arbitrary conduct intentionally designed to punish the plaintiffs").

3. Suppose plaintiffs can show that the defendant misled them as to safety. In *Lombardi v. Whitman*, 485 F.3d 73 (2d Cir. 2007), workers who had performed search/rescue or cleanup tasks in the aftermath of the September 11 terrorist attacks, sued Environmental Protection Agency officials and other officials. They "alleg[ed] that defendants' affirmative assurances that the air in Lower Manhattan was safe to breathe created a false sense of security that induced site workers to forgo protective measures, thereby creating a danger where otherwise one would not have existed." After noting that the defendants were subjected to "the pull of competing obligations," the court rebuffed the constitutional claim:

> The EPA and other federal agencies often must decide whether to regulate particular conduct by taking into account whether the risk to the potentially affected population will be acceptable. Such decisions require an exercise of the conscience, but such decisions cannot be deemed egregious, conscience-shocking, and arbitrary in the constitutional sense merely because they contemplate some likelihood of bodily harm. [Accepting] as we must the allegation that the defendants made the wrong decision by disclosing information they knew to be inaccurate, and that this had tragic consequences for the plaintiffs, we conclude that a poor choice made by an executive official between or among the harms risked by the available options is not conscience-shocking merely because for some persons it resulted in grave consequences that a correct decision could have avoided. [When] great harm is likely to befall someone no matter what a government official does, the allocation of risk may be a burden on the conscience of the one who must make such decisions, but does not shock the contemporary conscience.

Id. at 85.

4. The Supreme Court has recognized that Fourteenth Amendment "liberty" includes "personal security from bodily injury", *see Ingraham v. Wright*, 430 U.S. 651, 673–74 (1977). Starting from this premise, courts have recognized a broader "liberty" right of "bodily integrity," and have accorded it substantive due process protection in cases where the defendant's invasion is egregious. *See, e.g., Hawkins v. Holloway*, 316 F.3d 777, 785 (8th Cir. 2003), where a female deputy charged the sheriff with sexual assault. The court found that "the sheriff's repeated intentional touching of her breasts to constitute a violation of her bodily integrity sufficient to support a substantive due process claim." As *Lewis* indicates, however, "conscience-shocking" is a rather hard test for the plaintiff to meet in cases where the officer's purpose is legitimate, though his means are reckless. In *Vaughan v. Cox*, 343 F.3d 1323, 1333 (11th Cir. 2003), the issue was whether a police officer would commit a substantive due process violation by recklessly shooting at the plaintiff's car. The court ruled that "even a showing that the officer's recklessness caused the plaintiff's injury is insufficient to support a substantive due process claim" unless "plaintiff can show that the officer had a purpose to cause harm unrelated to the legitimate object of the arrest."

The "shock the conscience" test is applied in a wide range of cases. Showing lack of a legitimate purpose and grossly inadequate performance of official duties are the keys to success for plaintiffs. *See, e.g., Range v. Douglas*, 763 F.3d 573, 591–92 (6th Cir. 2014) (supervisors of a county morgue may have been reckless in failing to discover that an employee had sexually abused the dead bodies of murder victims, yet summary judgment in their favor was appropriate, because a jury could not conclude that their actions shocked the conscience); *Hernandez v. Ridley*, 734 F.3d 1254 (10th Cir. 2013) (officials' failure to provide safe conditions for highway construction workers, leading to their deaths, did not shock the conscience); *Koessel v. Sublette County Sheriff's Department*, 717 F.3d 736, 750 (10th Cir. 2013) (firing a deputy sheriff in violation of the Americans With Disabilities Act, without any complaints against him or any previous discipline, without telling him the real reason for his termination, and without showing that he is incapable of doing the work does not shock the conscience); *A. D. v. California Highway Patrol*, 712 F.3d 446 (9th Cir. 2013) (upholding a jury verdict holding an officer liable under the "shock the conscience" test for killing a suspect without a legitimate law enforcement objective); *Folkerts v. City of Waverly*, 707 F.3d 975 (8th Cir. 2013) (police officer who arrested and questioned a mentally retarded man without an adequate investigation did not act in a way that shocks the conscience); *EJS Properties v. City of Toledo*, 698 F.3d 845, 862 (6th Cir. 2012) ("solicitation of a bribe by a public official" in connection with a zoning decision "does not shock our collective conscience"); *Winslow v. Smith*, 696 F.3d 716, 732 (8th Cir. 2012) (plaintiffs, who had been convicted on murder charges but have now been exonerated, can meet the shock the conscience test if they can establish that the investigating officers "recklessly investigated the Wilson murder and purposefully manufactured false evidence to implicate Plaintiffs"); *Marsh v. County of San Diego*,680 F.3d 1148, 1155 (9th Cir. 2012) (former prosecutor's act in sending the plaintiff's son's autopsy photograph to the press, without any legitimate governmental purpose, shocks the conscience); *Slaughter v. Mayor and City Council of Baltimore*, 682 F.3d 317 (4th Cir. 2012) (inadequate preparation of a fire training exercise, resulting in the death of the plaintiff's son, does not shock the conscience); *Southerland v. City of New York*, 652 F.3d 2011 (2d Cir. 2011) (removal of children from the home into state custody would shock the conscience if done without adequate grounds or opportunity for prompt judicial review); *Jackson v. Indian Prairie School Dist. 204*, 653 F.3d 647 (7th Cir. 2011) (school principal did not shock the conscience when he directed a special education teacher to deal with "W.K.," a violent fourth grade student, who injured her, "even though he knew W.K. was either in the midst of a violent outburst, or had recently de-escalated from one").

5.   *Ingraham* was a corporal punishment case, in which the Court recognized that "personal security" is an aspect of the "liberty" guaranteed by the Fourteenth Amendment, declined to make a per se rule striking down corporal punishment of public school students. The Court held that state tort remedies meet the requirements of *procedural* due process. But *Ingraham* did not address the criteria for determining which instances of corporal punishment violate the substantive component of due process. These cases present a distinctive issue, in that the force is purposely applied, and not for the law enforcement purpose of subduing suspects but for the less compelling purpose of school discipline.

Although corporal punishment is out of favor in most states, it "retains a hold in many public schools," especially in the South. *See "A Trip to These Principals May Mean a Paddling,"* N.Y. TIMES, March 30, 2011 (discussing Texas and Louisiana incidents). Courts generally deal with the issue of whether it violates substantive due process on a case by case basis, considering "such factors as the need for application of force, the relationship between the need and the amount of force that was used, the extent of injury inflicted, and whether force was applied in a good faith effort to maintain or restore discipline or maliciously and sadistically, for the very purpose of causing harm." *Metzger v. Osbeck,* 841 F.2d 518, 520 (3d Cir. 1988). For example, in *Nolan v. Memphis City Schools,* 589 F.3d 257 (6th Cir. 2009), basketball coaches had paddled a student several times for a variety of infractions of team rules and for unsatisfactory conduct grades. Upholding the jury's verdict in favor of the coaches, the court said "there was sufficient evidence presented to support the jury's conclusion that [defendants'] actions did not cause severe, conscience-shocking injury, were not motivated by malice, and, therefore, did not rise to the level of a substantive due process violation.") *See also Golden ex rel. Bach v. Anders,* 324 F.3d 650, 653 (8th Cir. 2003). In both *Nolan* and *Golden* the courts suggested that the *Sacramento v. Lewis* "shock the conscious" test would apply to such cases. Is this consistent with the Supreme Court's reasoning in *Sacramento County.* Recall, in particular, that the Court justified the "shock the conscience" test on the ground that there was little time for deliberation.

As for the level of severity that may trigger liability, the cases suggest that a few whacks with a paddle are constitutionally permissible. *See, e.g., Nolan, supra,* (high school student; three whacks on several occasions); *Saylor v. Board of Education,* 118 F.3d 507 (6th Cir. 1997) (14-year-old; five whacks, no constitutional violation); *Fee v. Herndon,* 900 F.2d 804 (5th Cir. 1990) (6th grade special education student; three whacks, no constitutional violation). How many whacks does it take to make a constitutional violation? Does the answer depend on the offense?

It is clear that the "personal security" guaranteed by the Fourteenth Amendment includes some limit on the physical injury the school authorities may inflict. Is the student also deprived of "personal security" when the punishment is aimed at embarrassing or humiliating him? Suppose the plaintiff, a high school football player, is bent over and paddled on his bare buttocks in front of the team. The misbehavior is unquestioned, the physical injury is minimal, and this type of punishment has proven, over time, to be an effective means of maintaining team discipline. Has the coach nonetheless deprived plaintiff of "personal security"? If so, is the deprivation necessarily a constitutional violation?

Corporal punishment is regulated by state law and local school district regulations. Would the plaintiff make out a constitutional claim in a corporal punishment case if he could show that the school official violated school regulations or other provisions of state law? (The answer to this last question is clearly "no.")

Several cases concern suits against school officials for inflicting injuries other than by paddling. *Wyatt v. Fletcher,* 718 F.3d 496, 504 (5th Cir. 2013) holds that a coach's "verbal abuse does not give rise to a constitutional violation". *Smith v. Half Hollow Hills Central School District,* 298 F.3d 168 (2d Cir. 2002) applied the "shock the conscience" test, and found that a single slap to the face "fell short of that threshold." *Muskrat v. Deer Creek Public Schools*, 715 F.3d 775 (10th Cir. 2013) found that similar slaps did not shock the conscience, even though the student was disabled, nor did placing the student in "time out" shock the conscience. In *Golden ex rel Bach v. Anders*, 324 F.3d 650 (8th Cir. 2003) the use of force to subdue a student who was kicking a vending machine did not shock the conscience). On the other hand, *Neal ex rel. Neal v. Fulton County Board of Education*, 229 F.3d 1069 (11th Cir. 2002) held that striking a student with a metal weight lock, resulting in the loss of an eye, would violate substantive due process. In *Wyatt*, supra, the abuse took place in a private conversation. What if a teacher berates a student in front of the class? *See Costello v. Mitchell Public School District 79*, 266 F.3d 916, 921 (8th Cir. 2001) (no constitutional violation). *See also Doe v. Hawaii Department of Education*, 334 F.3d 906 (9th Cir. 2003) (taping a 2nd grade student's head to a tree for five minutes for disciplinary purposes could, if "objectively unreasonable," violate the child's Fourth Amendment rights).

6.   Are insults or threats of physical harm, directed at the plaintiff by police officers or prison guards, enough to make out a constitutional claim? Most courts say no. *Compare Siglar v. Hightower*, 112 F.3d 191 (5th Cir. 1997) (verbal abuse not sufficient); *Bender v. Brumley*, 1 F.3d 271 (5th Cir. 1993) (threats not sufficient); and *Swoboda v. Dubach*, 992 F.2d 286 (10th Cir. 1993) (even threats to kill plaintiff are not sufficient) *with McDowell v. Jones*, 990 F.2d 433 (8th Cir. 1993) (threats generally not sufficient but terrorizing prisoner with threats of death would be). *Cf. Hopson v. Fredericksen*, 961 F.2d 1374, 1378–79 (8th Cir. 1992) (police officer's threat to knock the plaintiff's teeth out does not come within the Eighth Circuit's rule that terrorizing the plaintiff with threats of death is actionable). *See also Hawkins v. Holloway*, 316 F.3d 777 (8th Cir. 2003) (verbal harassment is insufficient to support a constitutional violation); *King v. Olmsted County*, 117 F.3d 1065 (8th Cir. 1997), 117 F.3d 1065 (threat by social workers to remove children from the home was not a constitutional violation); *Robertson v. Plano City*, 70 F.3d 21 (5th Cir. 1995) (no "right to be free from an erroneous admonishment regarding punishment and prison").

7.   In our discussion of Fourteenth Amendment "liberty," *supra*, we noted that reputation receives constitutional protection in "stigma plus" cases, *i.e.*, when the defamatory statements are coupled with loss of some other tangible benefit. *Paul v. Davis*, 424 U.S. 693 (1976). In our discussion of procedural due process, *supra*, we saw that a plaintiff who meets the "stigma plus" requirement may sue for violation of his procedural right to a name-clearing hearing.

Exactly what remedy a victorious plaintiff is entitled to receive in stigma plus cases is unclear. Some courts seem to take the view that damages should compensate for the substantive harm to the plaintiff's reputation as well as for the violation of his procedural rights. *See Palmer v. City of Monticello*, 31 F.3d 1499 (10th Cir. 1994) (upholding a jury award of over $250,000 to a police officer who had been wrongfully dismissed). For other courts, the remedy seems to be directed more narrowly at making up for the violation of procedural rights. *See Davis v. City of Chicago*, 53 F.3d 801 (7th Cir. 1995) (the due process clause "does curtail the use of falsehoods that deprive a person of employment, but the remedy for that offense lies in back pay and a name-clearing hearing").

What if the plaintiff cannot meet the "plus" requirement of *Paul*, but can show that the defendant officer not only defamed him, but did so maliciously, knowing that the charges were false and intending to destroy the plaintiff's reputation out of malice? Would this be a sufficient abuse of power to justify a constitutional tort suit for violation of the plaintiff's *substantive* due process right to liberty? In *Siegert v. Gilley*, 500 U.S. 226 (1991), the Court held that such allegations fail to state a constitutional tort claim: "Our decision in *Paul v. Davis* did not turn . . . on the state of mind of the defendant, but on the lack of any constitutional protection for the interest in reputation." Is this ruling consistent with the "shock the conscience" principle of *Sacramento County v. Lewis*?

8.   *Sacramento County v. Lewis* reflects a general principle that a sufficiently egregious act by an official may violate substantive due process, even if no more specific constitutional guarantee is applicable to the case. In order to win, the plaintiff needs to show that the conscience-shocking act does not merely upset him, but deprives him of Fourteenth Amendment "liberty" or "property." In *Mullins v. Oregon*, 57 F.3d 789 (9th Cir. 1995), the issue was whether officials had violated the substantive due process rights of plaintiffs who wished to adopt their granddaughter. The court did not need to reach the question of whether the defendants acted egregiously. It disposed of the case by rejecting the premise that "a grandparent, by virtue of a genetic link alone, enjoys a fundamental liberty interest in the adoption of her grandchildren."

Given that a state official has harmed an interest that falls within the domain of "liberty" or "property," litigants have asserted substantive due process claims in a variety of circumstances. Here are illustrations of two recurring themes in the case law:

(a) dismissals from government jobs: Quite apart from the "stigma plus" doctrine, someone fired from a government job may bring the following theory: 1st, that he has a property interest in the job under the "new property" doctrine discussed in section A; 2nd, that this interest is entitled not just to the procedural protection discussed in section C, but to substantive protection as well, providing he can show irrational, arbitrary, or otherwise egregious conduct by the official who fired him; and 3rd, that on the facts the supervisor did act egregiously. *See, e.g., Yates v. District of Columbia*, 324 F.3d 724 (D.C. Cir. 2003) (rejecting the claim on the facts of the case).

(b) land use regulation: Land developers whose plans are thwarted by local officials often include a substantive due process claim in their complaints. Though they rarely win, the theory is not altogether hopeless. In one case, the owners of property obtained approval from the city council to use it a certain way. Officials nonetheless allowed the issue of how the property could be used to be submitted to the voters in a referendum, at which the site plan was rejected. The owners sued, lost on summary judgment in the district court, but obtained a reversal. The court first found that the property owners (in the "old" property sense) had a property interest (in the "new" property sense) in a particular use of the site, once the site plan was approved by the city council. Next, the court held that, in nonetheless holding a referendum, officials arguably acted arbitrarily and capriciously: "Despite being aware that plaintiffs' project was entirely consistent with the zoning code, the defendants allowed a referendum to decide whether plaintiffs' project would go forward. Clearly plaintiffs have presented sufficient evidence to create an issue of material fact as to whether the defendants, by denying plaintiffs the benefit of the lawfully approved site plan, engaged in arbitrary, irrational, and therefore unconstitutional application of the law in violation of plaintiffs' right to due process." *Buckeye Community Hope v. City of Cuyahoga Falls*, 263 F.3d 627 (6th Cir. 2001).

9.   One circuit has squarely rejected the theory of recovery discussed in note 8. *See McKinney v. Pate*, 20 F.3d 1550 (11th Cir. 1994) (*en banc*). *See also DeKalb Stone, Inc., v. DeKalb County*, 106 F.3d 956, 960 (11th Cir. 1997) (describing *McKinney* as a case holding that "a plaintiff [does] not present a substantive due process claim when he allege[s] an executive deprivation of a state-created right." For criticism of *McKinney*, see David H. Armistead, Note, *Substantive Due Process Limits on Public Officials' Power to Terminate State-Created Property Interests*, 29 GA. L. REV. 769 (1995). The issue evidently is an open one in the Supreme Court. *See Butler v. Rio Rancho Public Schools Bd. of Educ.*, 341 F.3d 1197, 1200 n.3 (10th Cir. 2003) "[T]he Supreme Court has not yet decided whether a state created property right like the right to a public education triggers substantive due process guarantees." In *Butler* the court assumed that the "interest in a public education triggers substantive due process guarantees," and ruled that suspending a student from school for a year for deliberately or negligently bringing a weapon onto school grounds "was not arbitrary; nor does it shock the conscience," given the school's "legitimate interest in providing a safe environment for students and staff."

One way to conceive of the *McKinney* rule is that the Due Process Clause guarantees only procedural protection to state-created property (and liberty). Yet the Eleventh Circuit does not categorically reject *all* substantive due process claims involving deprivations of state-created property. It distinguishes between executive deprivation and legislative deprivation, recognizing the latter as a viable claim. *See, e.g., Kentner v. City of Sanibel*, 750 F.3d 1274, 1280 (11th Cir. 2014) ("Because plaintiffs are challenging the Ordinance on its face rather than contesting a specific zoning or permit decision made under the auspices of the Ordinance, we conclude that they are challenging a legislative act.") Yet *Sacramento County v. Lewis* (and many other cases) demonstrate that the Due Process Clause applies to all state action, whether legislative, judicial, or executive. The reason the plaintiff lost in *Sacramento County* is not that the Due Process Clause did not bind the police officer in that case. It is that the officer's conduct was not sufficiently egregious to violate the plaintiff's substantive due process right. What, then, is the basis for the Eleventh Circuit's distinction?

E.   Constitutional Rights of Persons in Custody

In *Sacramento County v. Lewis* the Court indicated that the calculus of interests would be different if the plaintiff were in custody, deprived by the state of the means to care for himself and defend himself. Accordingly, the plaintiff's interest is stronger and the liability rule ought to be more favorable to his side of the case. In order to describe the doctrine on custody, we need to distinguish between three types of cases: (a) persons under arrest by the police, whose claims are governed by a Fourth Amendment standard; (b) persons convicted of crimes, who generally raise Eighth Amendment claims; and (c) a catch-all "substantive due process" category of those not covered under (a) and (b), which includes, among others, pretrial detainees who remain in custody after the arrest is completed, persons confined in mental institutions, and persons kept in custody after the expiration of their criminal sentences. Claims brought by persons in category (a) are governed by a Fourth Amendment standard of "objective reasonableness." We will examine this and other aspects of fourth amendment doctrine in section E. Though category (b) is Eighth Amendment doctrine, while category (c) is substantive due process doctrine, the rules governing the two types of cases are very similar, if not identical, and it is convenient to deal with them together in this section.

FARMER v. BRENNAN
511 U.S. 825 (1994)

JUSTICE SOUTER delivered the opinion of the Court.

A prison official's "deliberate indifference" to a substantial risk of serious harm to an inmate violates the Eighth Amendment. This case requires us to define the term "deliberate indifference," as we do by requiring a showing that the official was subjectively aware of the risk.

I

[Plaintiff, a transexual with a feminine appearance, was beaten and raped shortly after being placed in the general population at a federal prison.] Acting without counsel, petitioner then filed a *Bivens* complaint, alleging a violation of the Eighth Amendment. See *Bivens v. Six Unknown Named Agents*; *Carlson v. Green*. As defendants, petitioner named respondents [several prison officials] . . . . [T]he complaint alleged that respondents either transferred petitioner to USP-Terre Haute or placed petitioner in its general population despite knowledge that the penitentiary had a violent environment and a history of inmate assaults, and despite knowledge that petitioner, as a transsexual who "projects feminine characteristics," would be particularly vulnerable to sexual attack by some USP-Terre Haute inmates. This allegedly amounted to a deliberately indifferent failure to protect petitioner's safety, and thus to a violation of petitioner's Eighth Amendment rights. Petitioner sought compensatory and punitive damages, and an injunction barring future confinement in any penitentiary, including USP-Terre Haute . . .

[T]he District Court . . . granted summary judgment to respondents, concluding that there had been no deliberate indifference to petitioner's safety . . . The failure of prison officials to prevent inmate assaults violates the Eighth Amendment, the court stated, only if prison officials were "reckless in a criminal sense," meaning that they had "actual knowledge" of a potential danger. Respondents, however, lacked the requisite knowledge, the court found. "[Petitioner] never expressed any concern for his safety to any of [respondents]. Since [respondents] had no knowledge of any potential danger to [petitioner], they were not deliberately indifferent to his safety." The . . . Court of Appeals . . . summarily affirmed without opinion. We granted certiorari because Courts of Appeals had adopted inconsistent tests for "deliberate indifference." Compare, for example, *McGill v. Duckworth* (holding that "deliberate indifference" requires a "subjective standard of recklessness"), with *Young v. Quinlan* (CA3 1992) ("[A] prison official is deliberately indifferent when he knows or should have known of a sufficiently serious danger to an inmate").

II

A

. . . In its prohibition of "cruel and unusual punishments," the Eighth Amendment places restraints on prison officials, who may not, for example, use excessive physical force against prisoners. The Amendment also imposes duties on these officials, who must provide humane conditions of confinement; prison officials must ensure that inmates receive adequate food, clothing, shelter and medical care, and must "take reasonable measures to guarantee the safety of the inmates."

In particular, as the lower courts have uniformly held, and as we have assumed, "prison officials have a duty . . . to protect prisoners from violence at the hands of other prisoners." . . .

It is not, however, every injury suffered by one prisoner at the hands of another that translates into constitutional liability for prison officials responsible for the victim's safety . . . To violate the Cruel and Unusual Punishments Clause, a prison official must have a "sufficiently culpable state of mind." In prison-conditions cases that state of mind is one of "deliberate indifference" to inmate health or safety, a standard the parties agree governs the claim in this case. The parties disagree, however, on the proper test for deliberate indifference, which we must therefore undertake to define.

B

1

Although we have never paused to explain the meaning of the term "deliberate indifference," the case law is instructive. The term first appeared in the United States Reports in *Estelle v. Gamble*, and its use there shows that deliberate indifference describes a state of mind more blameworthy than negligence. In considering the inmate's claim in *Estelle* that inadequate prison medical care violated the Cruel and Unusual Punishments Clause, we distinguished "deliberate indifference to serious medical needs of prisoners," from "negligence in diagnosing or treating a medical condition," holding that only the former violates the Clause. We have since read Estelle for the proposition that Eighth Amendment liability requires "more than ordinary lack of due care for the prisoner's interests or safety." *Whitley v. Albers.*

While *Estelle* establishes that deliberate indifference entails something more than mere negligence, the cases are also clear that it is satisfied by something less than acts or omissions for the very purpose of causing harm or with knowledge that harm will result. That point underlies the ruling that "application of the deliberate indifference standard is inappropriate" in one class of prison cases: when "officials stand accused of using excessive physical force." In such situations, where the decisions of prison officials are typically made "in haste, under pressure, and frequently without the luxury of a second chance," an Eighth Amendment claimant must show more than "indifference," deliberate or otherwise. The claimant must show that officials applied force "maliciously and sadistically for the very purpose of causing harm," or, as the Court also put it, that officials used force with "a knowing willingness that [harm] occur". This standard of purposeful or knowing conduct is not, however, necessary to satisfy the mens rea requirement of deliberate indifference for claims challenging conditions of confinement; "the very high state of mind prescribed by *Whitley* does not apply to prison conditions cases."

With deliberate indifference lying somewhere between the poles of negligence at one end and purpose or knowledge at the other, the Courts of Appeals have routinely equated deliberate indifference with recklessness.[3] It is, indeed, fair to say that acting or failing to act with deliberate indifference to a substantial risk of serious harm to a prisoner is the equivalent of recklessly disregarding that risk.

That does not, however, fully answer the pending question about the level of culpability deliberate indifference entails, for the term recklessness is not self-defining. The civil law generally calls a person reckless who acts or (if the person has a duty to act) fails to act in the face of an unjustifiably high risk of harm that is either known or so obvious that it should be known. The criminal law, however, generally permits a finding of recklessness only when a person disregards a risk of harm of which he is aware. The standards proposed by the parties in this case track the two approaches (though the parties do not put it that way): petitioner asks us to define deliberate indifference as what we have called civil-law recklessness, and respondents urge us to adopt an approach consistent with recklessness in the criminal law.

We reject petitioner's invitation to adopt an objective test for deliberate indifference. We hold instead that a prison official cannot be found liable under the Eighth Amendment for denying an inmate humane conditions of confinement unless the official knows of and disregards an excessive risk to inmate health or safety; the official must both be aware of facts from which the inference could be drawn that a substantial risk of serious harm exists, and he must also draw the inference. This approach comports best with the text of the Amendment as our cases have interpreted it. The Eighth Amendment does not outlaw cruel and unusual "conditions"; it outlaws cruel and unusual "punishments." An act or omission unaccompanied by knowledge of a significant risk of harm might well be something society wishes to discourage, and if harm does result society might well wish to assure compensation. The common law reflects such concerns when it imposes tort liability on a purely objective basis. But an official's failure to alleviate a significant risk that he should have perceived but did not, while no cause for commendation, cannot

---

[3] [4] Between the poles lies "gross negligence" too, but the term is a "nebulous" one, in practice typically meaning little different from recklessness as generally understood in the civil law (which we discuss later in the text). See W. Keeton, D. Dobbs, R. Keeton & D. Owen, Prosser and Keeton on Law of Torts 34, p. 212 (5th ed. 1984) (hereinafter Prosser and Keeton:kc).

under our cases be condemned as the infliction of [punishment.]

To be sure, the reasons for focussing on what a defendant's mental attitude actually was (or is), rather than what it should have been (or should be), differ in the Eighth Amendment context from that of the criminal law. Here, a subjective approach isolates those who inflict punishment; there, it isolates those against whom punishment should be inflicted. But the result is the same: to act recklessly in either setting a person must "consciously disregard" a substantial risk of serious harm. Model Penal Code, supra, § 2.02(2)(c). [Subjective] recklessness as used in the criminal law is a familiar and workable standard that is consistent with the Cruel and Unusual Punishments Clause as interpreted in our cases, and we adopt it as the test for "deliberate indifference" under the Eighth Amendment.

2

Our decision that Eighth Amendment liability requires consciousness of a risk is thus based on the Constitution and our cases, not merely on a parsing of the phrase "deliberate indifference." And we do not reject petitioner's arguments for a thoroughly objective approach to deliberate indifference without recognizing that on the crucial point (whether a prison official must know of a risk, or whether it suffices that he should know) the term does not speak with certainty. Use of "deliberate," for example, arguably requires nothing more than an act (or omission) of indifference to a serious risk that is voluntary, not accidental. And even if "deliberate" is better read as implying knowledge of a risk, the concept of constructive knowledge is familiar enough that the term "deliberate indifference" would not, of its own force, preclude a scheme that conclusively presumed awareness from a risk's [obviousness.]

We are [not] persuaded by petitioner's argument that, without an objective test for deliberate indifference, prison officials will be free to ignore obvious dangers to inmates. Under the test we adopt today, an Eighth Amendment claimant need not show that a prison official acted or failed to act believing that harm actually would befall an inmate; it is enough that the official acted or failed to act despite his knowledge of a substantial risk of serious harm. We doubt that a subjective approach will present prison officials with any serious motivation "to take refuge in the zone between 'ignorance of obvious risks' and actual knowledge of risks.'" Whether a prison official had the requisite knowledge of a substantial risk is a question of fact subject to demonstration in the usual ways, including inference from circumstantial evidence . . . and a fact finder may conclude that a prison official knew of a substantial risk from the very fact that the risk was obvious.[For] example, if an Eighth Amendment plaintiff presents evidence showing that a substantial risk of inmate attacks was "longstanding, pervasive, well-documented, or expressly noted by prison officials in the past, and the circumstances suggest that the defendant-official being sued had been exposed to information concerning the risk and thus 'must have known' about it, then such evidence could be sufficient to permit a trier of fact to find that the defendant-official had actual knowledge of the risk."[4]

---

[4] [8] While the obviousness of a risk is not conclusive and a prison official may show that the obvious

Nor may a prison official escape liability for deliberate indifference by showing that, while he was aware of an obvious, substantial risk to inmate safety, he did not know that the complainant was especially likely to be assaulted by the specific prisoner who eventually committed the assault. The question under the Eighth Amendment is whether prison officials, acting with deliberate indifference, exposed a prisoner to a sufficiently substantial "risk of serious damage to his future health," and it does not matter whether the risk comes from a single source or multiple sources, any more than it matters whether a prisoner faces an excessive risk of attack for reasons personal to him or because all prisoners in his situation face such a risk. If, for example, prison officials were aware that inmate "rape was so common and uncontrolled that some potential victims dared not sleep [but] instead . . . would leave their beds and spend the night clinging to the bars nearest the guards' station," it would obviously be irrelevant to liability that the officials could not guess beforehand precisely who would attack [whom.]

Because, however, prison officials who lacked knowledge of a risk cannot be said to have inflicted punishment, it remains open to the officials to prove that they were unaware even of an obvious risk to inmate health or safety. That a trier of fact may infer knowledge from the obvious, in other words, does not mean that it must do so. Prison officials charged with deliberate indifference might show, for example, that they did not know of the underlying facts indicating a sufficiently substantial danger and that they were therefore unaware of a danger, or that they knew the underlying facts but believed (albeit unsoundly) that the risk to which the facts gave rise was insubstantial or non-existent.

In addition, prison officials who actually knew of a substantial risk to inmate health or safety may be found free from liability if they responded reasonably to the risk, even if the harm ultimately was not averted. A prison official's duty under the Eighth Amendment is to ensure "reasonable safety," a standard that incorporates due regard for prison officials' "unenviable task of keeping dangerous men in safe custody under humane conditions." Whether one puts it in terms of duty or deliberate indifference, prison officials who act reasonably cannot be found liable under the Cruel and Unusual Punishments [Clause.]

III

Against this backdrop, we consider whether the District Court's disposition of petitioner's complaint, summarily affirmed without briefing by the Court of Appeals for the Seventh Circuit, comports with Eighth Amendment principles. We conclude that the appropriate course is to remand.

---

escaped him, he would not escape liability if the evidence showed that he merely refused to verify underlying facts that he strongly suspected to be true, or declined to confirm inferences of risk that he strongly suspected to exist (as when a prison official is aware of a high probability of facts indicating that one prisoner has planned an attack on another but resists opportunities to obtain final confirmation; or when a prison official knows that some diseases are communicable and th at a single needle is being used to administer flu shots to prisoners but refuses to listen to a subordinate who he strongly suspects will attempt to explain the associated risk of transmitting disease). When instructing juries in deliberate indifference cases with such issues of proof, courts should be careful to ensure that the requirement of subjective culpability is not lost. It is not enough merely to find that a reasonable person would have known, or that the defendant should have known, and juries should be instructed accordingly.

In granting summary judgment to respondents . . . the District Court may have placed decisive weight on petitioner's failure to notify respondents of a risk of harm. That petitioner "never expressed any concern for his safety to any of [respondents]," was the only evidence the District Court cited for its conclusion that there was no genuine dispute about respondents' assertion that they "had no knowledge of any potential danger to [petitioner]". But [the] failure to give advance notice is not dispositive. Petitioner may establish respondents' awareness by reliance on any relevant evidence.

The summary judgment record does not so clearly establish respondent's entitlement to judgment as a matter of law on the issue of subjective knowledge that we can simply assume the absence of error below. For example, in papers filed in opposition to respondents' summary-judgment motion, petitioner pointed to respondents' admission that petitioner is a "non-violent" transsexual who, because of petitioner's "youth and feminine appearance" is "likely to experience a great deal of sexual pressure" in prison. And petitioner recounted a statement by one of the respondents, then warden of the penitentiary in Lewisburg, Pennsylvania, who told petitioner that there was "a high probability that [petitioner] could not safely function at USP-Lewisburg," an incident confirmed in a published District Court [opinion.]

We cannot, moreover, be certain that additional evidence is unavailable to petitioner because in denying petitioner's Rule 56(f) motion for additional discovery the District Court may have acted on a mistaken belief that petitioner's failure to notify was dispositive. Petitioner asserted in papers accompanying the Rule 56(f) motion that the requested documents would show that "each defendant had knowledge that USP-Terre Haute was and is, a violent institution with a history of sexual assault, stabbings, etc., [and that] each defendant showed reckless disregard for my safety by designating me to said institution knowing that I would be sexually assaulted." But in denying the Rule 56(f) motion, the District Court stated that the requested documents were "not shown by plaintiff to be necessary to oppose defendants' motion for summary judgment," a statement consistent with the erroneous view that failure to notify was fatal to petitioner's complaint.

Because the District Court may have mistakenly thought that advance notification was a necessary element of an Eighth Amendment failure-to-protect claim, we think it proper to remand for reconsideration of petitioner's Rule 56(f) motion and, whether additional discovery is permitted or not, for application of the Eighth Amendment principles explained above.

[JUSTICE BLACKMUN's concurring opinion, JUSTICE STEVENS' concurring opinion, and JUSTICE THOMAS's opinion concurring in the judgment, are omitted.]

NOTES

1.   The term "deliberate indifference" figures in another constitutional tort issue: governmental liability. In a part of the *Farmer* opinion that is omitted here, the Court indicated that the term should be defined differently when the issue is

governmental liability. In that context, the term refers to an objective standard. *See* Chapter 5.

2. Because Farmer was "a transsexual with a feminine appearance," his argument that prison officials had sufficient knowledge of his vulnerability is an especially strong one. The general principle underlying *Farmer* is that conditions of prison confinement are subject to Eighth Amendment scrutiny. But not every unsafe condition crosses the constitutional threshold. Thus, "[a] slippery shower floor, although a potential hazard, is a daily risk faced by members of the public at large," and "represents at most ordinary negligence rather than a condition so threatening as to implicate constitutional standards." *Coleman v. Sweetin*, 745 F.3d 756, 764 (5th Cir. 2014).

In the "failure to protect" fact pattern illustrated by *Farmer*, courts require the plaintiff to show an especially high level of knowledge of risk to the prisoner on the part of prison officials in order to meet the "deliberate indifference" test. *See, e.g.*, *Harrison v. Culliver*, 746 F.3d 1288, 1299–1300 (11th Cir. 2014) (four prior assaults in the back hallway of the prison in the three years before the assault on the plaintiff, and the absence of a guard there, were not sufficient to withstand defendant's motion for summary judgment on failure to protect claim; "Holman [Correctional Facility] housed between 830 and 900 inmates during the relevant time period — and the thirty three incidents involving weapons, only four of which occurred on the back hallway, are hardly sufficient to demonstrate that Holman was a prison 'where violence and terror reigned' " [citation omitted]); *Webb v. Lawrence County*, 144 F.3d 1131 (8th Cir. 1998), in which the plaintiff was attacked by a sexual predator named Wyman, sued officials for not protecting him, and lost. The court said, among other things: "although defendants knew that Wyman was a sexual offender, there was no evidence that Wyman had assaulted any other inmates or caused any problems while incarcerated." *See also Williams v. Nebraska State Penitentiary*, 57 F.3d 667 (8th Cir. 1995) (in upholding the trial judge's decision to allow the jury to hear of the attack victim's criminal and prison record, the court reasoned that his record could "help to show that he could protect himself against a potentially violent cellmate," thus potentially justifying officials "in ignoring his repeated requests for a cell transfer; [in] calculating risk to a prisoner, prison officials can take into account their subjective belief as to the prisoner's ability to protect himself").

In *Farmer* the prisoner was especially vulnerable on account of his sexual identity. Another circumstance that may expose an inmate to greater than normal danger is cooperation with prison authorities. In *Bistrian v. Levi*, 696 F.3d 352 (3d Cir. 2012), a detainee overcame a motion to dismiss based on his allegation that, despite their knowledge of the danger, the defendants placed him in a locked recreation area with members of a gang who knew of his cooperation, had a violent criminal past, and had previously threatened to attack him because of his cooperation.

3. "Failure to protect" cases can also arise when the inmate is a danger to himself, inadequate precautions are taken, and the inmate commits suicide. For an effort to measure deliberate indifference in this context by estimating costs and benefits, see *Belbachir v. County of McHenry*, 726 F.3d 975, 981 (7th Cir. 2013).

Writing for the panel, Judge Posner said:

> [W]hen an adverse consequence is very great, the failure to take a simple, inexpensive, obvious, and indeed prescribed measure to avert it is inexcusable. In economic terms, an expected loss can be expressed as $P \times L$, where P is the probability that the loss will occur and L is the magnitude of the loss if it occurs. Even if the probability is low, if the loss if the probability materializes is very great, as it was here, and the burden (i.e., the cost), B, of preventing the event causing the loss (the suicide) is very low, as it seems to have been here, as well, the failure to take preventive action may be negligent (if B is smaller than $P \times L$ [or] worse than negligent if B is *much* lower than $P \times L$ as appears to have been the case here, too.

The "simple and obvious precautions" identified by Judge Posner were that "[t]he defendants could have placed Belbachir in a mental hospital or at least on suicide watch." 726 F.3d at 982. The court ruled that the facts were not "so one-sided as to justify taking from a jury the issue of defendant Frederick's refusal to act in the face of a significant risk of suicide known to her."

4. Besides rights arising from guards' "failure to protect," prisoners have Eighth Amendment rights to medical care. *Estelle v. Gamble*, 429 U.S. 97 (1976), held that the Eighth Amendment forbids prison officials from ignoring the serious medical needs of inmates. Prisoners may recover damages if they can show "deliberate indifference" to their serious medical needs. Whether the medical needs are "serious" is an objective test, governed by such factors as whether a reasonable doctor or patient would so perceive it, whether it produces chronic pain, and whether it significantly affects daily life. *See, e.g., Brock v. Wright*, 315 F 3d. 158 (2d Cir. 2003). As *Farmer* shows, whether prison officials are "deliberately indifferent" is a subjective test, harder to meet than the ordinary malpractice standard, but less demanding than the "shock the conscience" standard of *Lewis. See, e.g., Faruq v. Vickers*, 743 F.3d 604, 606 (8th Cir. 2013) (Faruq can win by showing that "Vickers deliberately disregarded electronic medical records confirming that Faruq had approval to use the braces"); *LeMarbe v. Wisneski*, 266 F.3d 429 (6th Cir. 2001) (ruling that a prisoner who suffered injuries as a result of gallbladder surgery could withstand a summary judgment motion when he "presented factual evidence, which . . . would prove that [the doctor] was aware of facts that supported an inference of a substantial harm to [the prisoner] and that [the doctor] had both drawn and disregarded that inference when he closed [the prisoner's] surgical incision . . . and then failed to take the action that his training indicated was necessary to stop the bile leak in a timely manner").

5. Is it appropriate to consider the resources available to the doctor in applying the "deliberate indifference" test for prison medical treatment? In *Peralta v. Dillard*, 744 F.3d 1076 (9th Cir. 2014) (*en banc*), the Ninth circuit overruled earlier cases and approved the following jury instruction:

> Whether a dentist or doctor met his duties to Plaintiff Peralta under the Eighth Amendment must be considered in the context of the personnel, financial, and other resources available to him or her or which he or she could reasonably obtain.

The court explained that "prison officials aren't deliberately indifferent to a prisoner's medical needs unless they act wantonly," and "whether an official's conduct can be characterized as 'wanton' depends upon the constraints facing [him]." As for those constraints, the case involved dental care, and "prisons are a particularly difficult place to provide such care" on account of security concerns. The court also noted that "there simply weren't enough dentists at [the prison] to provide every prisoner with dental care on demand. The ratio of dentists to prisoners was less than half what the state said it should be." 744 F.3d at 1082. Bear in mind that the state itself cannot be sued for damages in a § 1983 case. *See* chapter 5.

Does the "lack of resources" argument apply to *prospective* relief? The court said:

> Lack of resources is not a defense to a claim for prospective relief because prison officials may be compelled to expand the pool of existing resources in order to remedy continuing Eighth Amendment violations. [Although] prisoners can't sue states for monetary relief, they *can* sue for injunctions to correct unconstitutional prison conditions. 744 F.3d at 1083.

The suit for prospective relief (an injunction or a declaratory judgment) is brought against state officials, under the principle, established in *Ex parte Young*, 209 U.S. 123 (1908), that state sovereign immunity is not a bar to prospective relief.

Judge Christen and Hurwitz wrote dissenting opinions, each joined by the other and three additional judges. Among other things, Judge Herwitz argued that

> [T]he majority's focus on the personal liability of prison physicians ignores an important reality — the state is in every respect the real party in interest in a damages suit. California indemnifies employees for torts committed in the scope of their employment [and] pays for their legal defense. 744 F.3d at 1100.

Do you agree that the state's indemnification practice is relevant to whether the dentist has committed a constitutional violation?

If *Peralta* is correct, does it follow that lack of resources is a general defense to "deliberate indifference" claims? Consider *Schaub v. VonWald*, 638 F.3d 905 (8th Cir. 2011). The plaintiff was confined at a county's Adult Detention Center. The director of knew of the prisoner's serious medical needs, knew that the facility lacked the resources needed to address them, assured a judge (in response to the inmate's request for a sentence modification) that the ADC could handle the inmate's needs, and then failed to take the necessary steps to obtain those resources. The Eighth Circuit panel upheld a district court's finding of deliberate indifference on these facts, as well as an award of punitive damages against the director.

6. Is there a danger that courts applying the "deliberate indifference" standard will inevitably slide down a slippery slope into negligence? Consider the following comments:

> Lower federal courts [have] managed quite well to apply the deliberate indifference standard so as to avoid the slippery slope. In resolving inmate

complaints concerning the adequacy of medical care, lower courts have been able to distinguish between simple malpractice and deliberate indifference. Through the traditional process of case-by-case determination, general principles have emerged. To establish a constitutional claim an inmate must allege and prove that the defendant deliberately failed to respond to the inmate's serious medical needs of which he was aware. Thus, refusing to provide prescribed treatment or denying the inmate's access to medical personnel qualified to evaluate his condition can be considered deliberate indifference. On the other hand, disagreements as to diagnosis and treatment do not rise to the level of a constitutional claim.

To be sure, the line separating simple negligence from deliberate indifference is fine, and the resolution of particular claims will necessarily turn on the facts of each case. Requiring an inmate to wait two and one-half days to be examined by the regularly scheduled physician does not violate constitutional standards when the inmate does not manifest outward signs of physical injury. By contrast, a defendant who delays a few hours in providing care to an inmate he knows is stabbed or shot may be properly labeled as deliberately indifferent.

To say that the distinction between constitutional and common law claims turns on the facts of particular cases does not mean that every case must be resolved by a jury. Courts have demonstrated ample ability to summarily dispose of eighth amendment claims that fail to allege or substantiate deliberate indifference.

Eaton & Wells, *Governmental Inaction as a Constitutional Tort: DeShaney and Its Aftermath*, 66 WASH. L. REV. 107, 164–65 (1991).

Are you convinced that the "deliberate indifference" standard gives rise to no danger of a slide down the slippery slope? Is Judge Posner's formula in *Belbachir*, above, helpful in drawing the necessary distinctions?

7.   The legal standard governing liability is somewhat different when the inmate is injured by guards in the course of quelling a disturbance. *See Hudson v. McMillian*, 503 U.S. 1, 7 (1992) (the issue is "whether force was applied in a good-faith effort to maintain or restore discipline, or maliciously and sadistically to cause harm"). Plaintiffs may well lose even if guards deliberately harm them, provided the use of force was justified. In *Hudson* the Court identified some relevant factors, including "the need for application of force, the relationship between that need and the amount of force used, the threat reasonably perceived by the responsible officials, and any efforts made to temper the severity of a forceful response," along with the extent of injury suffered by the inmate. *See, e.g., Combs v. Wilkinson*, 315 F.3d 548 (6th Cir. 2002) (use of mace to control a disturbance is acceptable); *Jeffers v. Gomez*, 267 F.3d 895, 916 (9th Cir. 2001) ("use of firearms during a prison riot is not unlawful"). Given the *Hudson* test, can the plaintiff win by showing that the use of force was motivated by a desire to harm the inmate rather than by the need to keep order, even though it took place during the course of a disturbance?

8. Persons may not ordinarily be confined to mental hospitals against their will unless they are dangerous to themselves or others. *O'Connor v. Donaldson*, 422 U.S. 563 (1975). Involuntarily committed mental patients are not covered by the Eighth Amendment, but have substantive due process rights in connection with their treatment and conditions of confinement. *See Youngberg v. Romeo*, 457 U.S. 307, 321–23 (1982). The Court ruled that "persons who have been involuntarily committed are entitled to more considerate treatment and conditions of confinement than criminals whose conditions of confinement are designed to punish." In addition, the patient is entitled to "minimally adequate training." A decision about the treatment of patients, "if made by a professional, is presumptively valid; liability may be imposed only when the decision by the professional is such a substantial departure from accepted professional judgment, practice, or standards as to demonstrate that the person responsible actually did not base the decision on such a judgment." As for the constitutional standard of medical care of these persons, *see Scott v. Benson*, 742 F.3d 335 (8th Cir. 2014) (deliberate indifference test). A different test may be appropriate for other fact patterns. *See Davis v. Rennie*, 264 F.3d 86 (1st Cir. 2001). In this case officers used force to subdue an involuntarily committed mental patient and one issue was the liability rule. Relying on *Youngberg*, the court opted in favor of requiring that the officials act with "objective reasonableness."

9. The rights of pretrial detainees are also governed by substantive due process. They are entitled to "at least as great" a level of protection as convicted inmates. *City of Revere v. Massachusetts General Hospital*, 463 U.S. 239, 244 (1983). *See, e.g., Ledbetter v. City of Topeka*, 318 F.3d 1183 (10th Cir. 2003); *Perkins v. Grimes*, 161 F.3d 1127 (8th Cir. 1998). *Compare Kingsley v. Hendrickson*, 744 F.3d 443, 449 (7th Cir. 2014) ("Our cases also have noted that the protection afforded by the Due Process clause is broader than that afforded under the Eighth Amendment."), *with Pittman v. County of Madison*, 746 F.3d 766, 775 (7th Cir. 2014) ("The Due Process Clause prohibits deliberate indifference to the serious medical needs of pretrial detainees. This provision applies essentially the same deliberate indifference analysis to detainees as the Eighth Amendment does to inmates.")

In practice, it is often hard to discern any significant difference between the Fourteenth Amendment standard and the Eighth Amendment standard. *Kingsley* approved a "recklessness" instruction. In *Ledbetter* and *Perkiins*, courts simply applied Eighth Amendment principles to the pretrial detainees' claims. In *Shreve v. Franklin County*, 743 F.3d 126, 134 (6th Cir. 2014), the court said that

> [w]hen officials respond to a rapidly evolving, fluid and dangerous predicament, the Fourteenth Amendment's excessive force standard is the same as the Eighth Amendment's: The plaintiff must show that the defendant acted maliciously and sadistically for the very purpose of causing harm rather than in a good faith effort to maintain or restore discipline.

Yet (real or apparent) variations sometimes emerge in other cases. In *Benjamin v. Fraser*, 343 F.3d 35, 50 (2d Cir. 2003), the court ruled that pretrial detainees' challenges to their conditions of confinement, including complaints about ventilation, sanitation, lighting, and heating, should be reviewed under a substantive due process test. It distinguished this test from the Eighth Amendment standard applicable to prisoners on the ground that pretrial detainees have not been found guilty of crimes, and thus "may not be punished in any manner, neither cruelly and unusually nor otherwise." The court went on to rule that "although a pretrial inmate mounting a constitutional challenge to environmental conditions must show deliberate indifference, it may generally be presumed from an absence of reasonable care."

Some cases suggest that pretrial detainees may not be punished. *See Edwards v. Byrd*, 750 F.3d 728, 732 n.2 (8th Cir. 2014). Others rule that pretrial detainees may be punished for their behavior while in jail, but only for a "legitimate penological reason." *Blackmon v. Sutton*, 734 F.3d 1237, 1242–43 (10th Cir. 2013) (holding that the right of an 11-year-old pretrial detainee not to be placed in a restraint chair for punishment, and his right not to be sat upon by a corrections officer for punishment, absent such a legitimate penological reason, was clearly established). The court noted that the restraint chair could be used for other purposes, such as preventing the detainee from banging his head against the wall or committing suicide. More generally, the conditions of confinement of a pretrial detainee, unlike those of a convict, may not be justified as "punishment."

10.   *Farmer* and the cases in the preceding notes (apart from *O'Connor, supra*) concern the rights of persons once they are in custody. In another class of cases the issue is whether the plaintiff can recover for the mere fact of being kept locked up. Freedom of movement is, of course, a basic "old" liberty right, but it is a separate question whether and in what circumstances one may recover for the fact of confinement on a substantive due process theory.

One fact pattern in which this issue arises involves mistaken confinements. In *Baker v. McCollan*, 443 U.S. 137 (1979), the plaintiff had been arrested and incarcerated by mistake. Officials discovered the error three days later and released him. He sued for deprivation of liberty without due process of law, but the Supreme Court rejected his claim. The opinion suggests that three days in jail is not long enough to make out a constitutional violation. It said that "mere detention pursuant to a valid warrant but in the face of repeated protests of innocence will after the lapse of a certain amount of time deprive the accused of 'liberty without due process of law.' " Do you agree that three days incarceration is too short a time to warrant constitutional sanction? Would it be better, especially after *Lewis* and *Daniels*, to read the case as one in which the original mistake plus the three day delay amounted to no more than negligence on the part of the jailors? Suppose the jailor knew that he had the wrong man, and kept the plaintiff locked up for three days out of spite? Three hours?

Consider *Armstrong v. Squadrito*, 152 F.3d 564 (7th Cir. 1998). In this case the plaintiff was wrongly held for 57 days because "someone at the warrants division had transposed his case number before providing it to the court," Relying on their computerized records, jail officials told him that complaining was useless. The court ruled that, "where officials have the luxury of forethought," as in the case of a prolonged detention, *Sacramento County v. Lewis*'s "shock the conscience" test could be met by "deliberate indifference." Distinguishing Eighth from Fourteenth Amendment rights, the court said that for purposes of Fourteenth Amendment rights, "we will define deliberate indifference as conscious disregard of known or obvious dangers." *Id. at* 577. Applying this test, the court found that Armstrong's case survived a summary judgment motion. Does it matter whether a judge has ordered that the plaintiff be held in custody? See *Hernandez v. Sheahan*, 455 F.3d 772 (7th Cir. 2006) (yes; finding no constitutional violation where plaintiff was a victim of mistaken identity, and distinguishing *Squadritto* as a case in which "an error caused a sheriff to imprison for almost two months someone who had *never* been to court"). A nine-day detention, in which the plaintiff "had an initial hearing in front of a judicial officer within seventy-two hours of his arrest", did not violate substantive due process, according to *Holloway v. Delaware County Sheriff*, 700 F.3d 1063, 1070 (7th Cir. 2012).

11. The *O'Connor* principle has implications for other contexts besides involuntary civil commitment. Persons convicted of crimes may be confined after the completion of their sentences, if they are deemed to be dangerous and mentally ill. *Kansas v. Hendricks*, 521 U.S. 346 (1997). There are, however, both substantive and procedural due process limits on this kind of confinement. See *Kansas v. Crane*, 534 U.S. 407 (2002) (as a matter of substantive due process, the state may confine someone in these circumstances only upon proof of serious difficulty in controlling behavior); *Bailey v. Pataki*, 708 F.3d 391 (2d Cir. 2013) (the inmate is, as a matter of due process, entitled to notice and an adversarial hearing prior to commitment to a psychiatric facility). *Bailey* relied on *Vitek v. Jones*, 445 U.S. 480 (1980), in which the Court held that a prisoner is entitled to due process protections before being transferred to a psychiatric facility during the course of his sentence.

Persons confined on these terms may, of course, raise constitutional objections to the conditions of their confinement in § 1983 suits. *See, e.g.*, *Lane v. Williams*, 689 F.3d 879 (7th Cir. 2012); *Hydrick v. Hunter*, 500 F.3d 978 (9th Cir. 2007).

F. The Relevance of State Remedies to Due Process Litigation

1. In *Parratt v. Taylor*, 451 U.S. 527 (1981) the plaintiff, a prisoner, sued prison officials for misplacing hobby materials belonging to him, and thereby depriving him of his property in violation of the due process clause. After declaring that a negligent loss of the plaintiff's property could amount to a "deprivation" within the meaning of the Fourteenth Amendment, the Court nonetheless ruled that he had not stated a constitutional claim, because deprivations of property run afoul of the Fourteenth amendment only when they take place "without due process of law." Here a state remedy was available and could provide the due process to which the plaintiff was entitled. The Court relied in part on the principle, discussed in section C, *supra*, that sometimes procedural due process can be satisfied by a *post-deprivation* remedy. It stressed, for example, that a predeprivation remedy is not practicable in the case of "random and unauthorized" acts by state officers. But the Supreme Court's somewhat opaque opinion did not distinguish between procedural and substantive due process. Echoing *Paul v. Davis, supra*, the Court warned against making the Fourteenth Amendment "a font of tort law." Since the facts of *Parratt* suggest that the plaintiff was asserting a substantive due process claim, the holding implied that the availability of post-deprivation state remedies can preclude a substantive due process claim as well.

We must distinguish between substantive and procedural due process in order to understand *Parratt* and later developments. A person may concede that the state is empowered to deprive him of life, liberty or property, and find fault with the procedures used to accomplish the deprivation, on the ground that he did not receive notice or a hearing, for example. But *Sacramento County v. Lewis* illustrates that due process has a substantive component in the constitutional tort context. Even where officials employ a flawless procedure, an injured person may maintain that their actions are constitutionally impermissible, because they shock the conscience.

The Court in *Parratt* frequently used the language (as well as the case law) of procedural due process. As an exercise in applying procedural due process principles, the case is unexceptionable. There are many instances where circumstances require urgent action or a pre-deprivation hearing is impossible, so that a post-deprivation remedy provides the process that is due.

The difficulty with this reading of the case is that Taylor was not really claiming that the mail room workers would have been entitled to lose his hobby materials, provided they followed proper procedures. The more plausible way to understand the claim for lost hobby materials is that the mail room workers' carelessness violates the prisoner's substantive rights. *See* Michael Wells & Thomas A. Eaton, *Substantive Due Process and the Scope of Constitutional Torts*, 18 GA. L. REV. 201, 222–23 (1984); *see also* Fallon, *Some Confusions About Due Process, Judicial Review, and Constitutional Remedies*, 93 COLUM. L. REV. 309, 341–42 (1993). (Whether this is a viable claim is a separate issue. A few years after *Parratt*, *Daniels v. Williams*, *supra*, repudiated *Parratt*'s assertion that negligence can violate substantive due process rights.)

Viewed as a substantive due process ruling, *Parratt* raises some thorny issues:

(a) Paul Bator asserted that *Parratt* and *Monroe v. Pape* "are on an obvious collision course." Bator, *Some Thoughts on Applied Federalism*, 6 HARV. J.L. & PUB. POL'Y 51, 56 (1982). Do you agree? There is a tension between the two cases, in that *Monroe* opens the federal courts even where adequate state remedies are available, yet *Parratt* closes them to (at least) some due process claims if state remedies are adequate. Are the cases reconcilable on the ground that *Monroe* is an interpretation of section 1983, while *Parratt* is a constitutional ruling? Does *Parratt* make sense in terms of the policies underlying *Monroe*?

(b) Is *Parratt* consistent with *Home Telephone & Telegraph Co. v. City of Los Angeles*, 227 U.S. 278 (1913)? That case was a challenge by the telephone company to a city ordinance fixing its rates at levels it judged to be confiscatory, and hence in violation of the due process clause. The city pointed out that state law provided a remedy, in that the state constitution also proscribed confiscatory takings. In the city's view, the existence of state action violating the Fourteenth Amendment would depend on whether the state courts gave the plaintiff's claim the respect it deserved. The Court rejected the city's argument:

"By the proposition [advanced by the city] the prohibitions and guaranties of the [Fourteenth] Amendment are addressed to and control the states only in their complete governmental capacity, and as a result give no authority to exert Federal judicial power until, by the decision of a court of last resort of a state, acts complained of under the 14th Amendment have been held valid, and therefore state acts in the fullest sense. To the contrary, the provisions of the Amendment as conclusively fixed by previous decisions are generic in their terms, are addressed, of course, to the states, but also to every person, whether natural or juridical, who is the repository of state power. By this construction the reach of the Amendment is shown to be coextensive with any exercise by state of power, in whatever form exerted . . . .

To speak broadly, the difference between the proposition insisted upon and the true meaning of the Amendment is this: that the one assumes that the Amendment virtually contemplates alone wrongs authorized by a state, and gives only power accordingly, while in truth the Amendment contemplates the possibility of state officers abusing the powers lawfully conferred upon them by doing wrongs prohibited by the Amendment."

Home Telephone is a prominent case in the law of constitutional remedies, establishing that a constitutional violation may be found even though the state provides remedies for the challenged conduct. Should *Parratt v. Taylor* be read as having partially overruled *Home Telephone*, without ever mentioning the earlier case? *See* Monaghan, *State Law Wrongs, State Law Remedies, and the Fourteenth Amendment*, 86 COLUM. L. REV. 979, 990–91 (1986); Alexander, *Constitutional Torts, The Supreme Court, and the Law of Noncontradiction: An Essay on* Zinermon v. Burch, 87 NW. U.L. REV. 576, 581–83 (1993) (describing the tension between *Parratt* and *Home Telephone*).

(c) Professor Fallon interprets *Parratt* rather differently. He thinks "*Parratt* would best fit into the surrounding doctrinal framework if it were recharacterized as launching a body of federal abstention doctrine, under which federal courts should sometimes decline to exercise jurisdiction in cases that lie within the literal terms of their statutory authority." Fallon, *Some Thoughts About Due Process, Judicial Review, and Constitutional Remedies*, 93 COLUM. L. REV. 309, 345 (1993). Would this reading of *Parratt* avoid a collision with *Home Telephone*? Would it conflict with *Monroe*? *See* Fallon, *supra*, at 354–55.

2. *Parratt* was the last in a quartet of constitutional tort cases, decided between 1976 and 1981, in which the Court invoked federalism as the ground for requiring plaintiffs to pursue state remedies. *Paul v. Davis, supra*, held that someone complaining of defamation by government officials could not sue under section 1983 for a constitutional violation, but must instead resort to state tort remedies. Another pre-*Parratt* case, *Ingraham v. Wright, supra*, emphasizes the availability of state remedies in rejecting Eighth Amendment and procedural due process challenges brought by public school students complaining of severe corporal punishment. *Baker v. McCollan, supra*, denied relief to an innocent man who had been incarcerated for three days on account of mistaken identity, with the observation that he could pursue a state law action for false imprisonment.

Whatever differences there may be among these cases, they have in common a sensitivity to state prerogatives, a desire on the Court's part not to allow the due process clause to intrude too far into the realm of state tort law. To the extent they are based on a judgment that state interests in setting the rules for recovery are more compelling than the plaintiff's interest in having a constitutional trump to play against state law, they are instances of a common theme in constitutional litigation over the scope of individual rights in the Supreme Court over the past two decades. In this regard, note that in remitting plaintiffs to state remedies the Court does not guarantee that state remedies will provide relief. *Paul*, for example, arose in Kentucky, where state defamation law effectively immunized officials and governments from liability.

3. *Parratt* sowed much confusion in the lower federal courts. Among other issues, courts divided over the issue that underlies the preceding notes: whether *Parratt* applied to substantive due process claims or solely to procedural ones. Courts also split over whether *Parratt* only applied to property claims, or to deprivations of liberty as well. In addition, courts puzzled over the meaning of *Parratt*'s category of "random and unauthorized" deprivations for which pre-deprivation process was impracticable.

A few years later, in *Zinermon v. Burch*, the Court declared that *Parratt*'s approval of post-deprivation remedies applied only to procedural due process, so that the *Parratt* principle fits comfortably into the doctrine described in section C. *See* RICHARD FALLON ET AL., HART & WECHSLER'S THE FEDERAL COURTS AND THE FEDERAL SYSTEM 985 (6th ed. 2009).

ZINERMON v. BURCH
494 U.S. 113 (1990)

JUSTICE BLACKMUN delivered the opinion of the Court.

I

[Burch sued officials at Florida State Hospital (FSH) alleging that they deprived him of his liberty, without due process of law, by admitting him to FSH as a "voluntary" mental patient when he was incompetent to give informed consent to his admission. He claimed that the officials should have afforded him procedural safeguards required by the Constitution before involuntary commitment of a mentally ill person, and that petitioners' failure to do so violated his due process rights. Relying on *Parratt*, the defendants argued that Burch's complaint failed to state a claim under § 1983 because it alleged only a random, unauthorized violation of the Florida statutes governing admission of mental patients.]

[The Court characterized *Parratt* as having held] that a deprivation of a constitutionally protected property interest caused by a state employee's random, unauthorized conduct does not give rise to a § 1983 procedural due process claim, unless the State fails to provide an adequate postdeprivation remedy. [In] a situation where the State cannot predict and guard in advance against a deprivation, a postdeprivation tort remedy is all the process the State can be expected to provide, and is constitutionally sufficient.

[The Supreme Court granted certiorari] to resolve the conflict that has arisen in the Courts of Appeals over the proper scope of the *Parratt* rule.

A

[Burch alleged that someone found him wandering along a highway, evidently hurt and disoriented. He was taken to a mental hospital and asked to sign forms giving his consent to admission and treatment. He signed these forms, and later signed other forms agreeing to admission and treatment at another hospital. He remained in state custody for five months without ever getting a hearing regarding his hospitalization and treatment.]

In February 1985, Burch filed a complaint in the United States District Court for the Northern District of Florida. He alleged, among other things, that ACMHS and the 11 individual petitioners, acting under color of Florida law, and "by and through the authority of their respective positions as employees at FSH . . . as part of their regular and official employment at FSH, took part in admitting Plaintiff to FSH as a "voluntary patient." Specifically, he alleged:

> "Defendants, and each of them, knew or should have known that Plaintiff was incapable of voluntary, knowing, understanding and informed consent to admission and treatment at FSH. Nonetheless, Defendants, and each of them, seized Plaintiff and against Plaintiff's will confined and imprisoned him and subjected him to involuntary commitment and treatment for the period from December 10, 1981, to May 7, 1982. For said period of 149 days, Plaintiff was without the benefit of counsel and no hearing of any sort was held at which he could have challenged his in voluntary admission and treatment at FSH.

> ". . . Defendants, and each of them, deprived Plaintiff of his liberty without due process of law in contravention of the Fourteenth Amendment to the United States Constitution. Defendants acted with willful, wanton and reckless disregard of and indifference to Plaintiff's Constitutionally guaranteed right to due process of law."

B

Burch's complaint thus alleges that he was admitted to and detained at FSH for five months under Florida's statutory provisions for "voluntary" admission. These provisions are part of a comprehensive statutory scheme under which a person may be admitted to a mental hospital in several different ways.

First, Florida provides for short-term emergency admission . . . .

Second, under a court order a person may be detained at a mental health facility for up to five days for evaluation . . . .

Third, a person may be detained as an involuntary patient, if he meets the same criteria as for evaluation, and if the facility administrator and two mental health professional recommend involuntary placement. Before involuntary placement, the patient has a right to notice, a judicial hearing, appointed counsel, access to medical records and personnel, and an independent expert examination. If the court determines that the patient meets the criteria for involuntary placement, it then decides whether the patient is competent to consent to treatment. If not, the court appoints a guardian advocate to make treatment decisions. After six months, the facility must either release the patient, or seek a court order for continued placement by stating the reasons therefor, summarizing the patient's treatment to that point, and submitting a plan for future treatment.

Finally, a person may be admitted as a voluntary patient. Mental hospitals may admit for treatment any adult "making application by express and informed consent," if he is "found to show evidence of mental illness and to be suitable for treatment." "Express and informed consent" is defined as "consent voluntarily given in writing after sufficient explanation and disclosure . . . to enable the person . . . to make a knowing and willful decision without any element of force, fraud, deceit, duress, or other form of constraint or coercion." A voluntary patient may request discharge at any time. If he does, the facility administrator must either release him within three days or initiate the involuntary placement process. At the time of his admission and each six months thereafter, a voluntary patient and his legal guardian or representatives must be notified in writing of the right to apply for a discharge.

Burch, in apparent compliance with [Florida law], was admitted by signing forms applying for voluntary admission. He alleges, however, that petitioners violated this statute in admitting him as a voluntary patient, because they knew or should have known that he was incapable of making an informed decision as to his admission. He claims that he was entitled to receive the procedural safeguards provided by Florida's involuntary placement procedure, and that petitioners violated his due process rights by failing to initiate this procedure. The question presented is whether these allegations suffice to state a claim under § 1983, in light of *Parratt.*

III
A

To understand the background against which this question arises, we return to the interpretation of § 1983 articulated in *Monroe v. Pape.* [Under *Monroe*] . . . overlapping state remedies are generally irrelevant to the question of the existence of a cause of action under § 1983. A plaintiff, for example, may bring a § 1983 action for an unlawful search and seizure despite the fact that the search and seizure violated the State's Constitution or statutes, and despite the fact that there are common-law remedies for trespass and conversion. As was noted in *Monroe,* in many cases there is "no quarrel with the state laws on the books,"; instead, the problem is the way those laws are or are not implemented by state officials.

This general rule applies in a straightforward way to two of the three kinds of § 1983 claims that may be brought against the State under the Due Process Clause of the Fourteenth Amendment. First, the Clause incorporates many of the specific protections defined in the Bill of Rights. A plaintiff may bring suit under § 1983 for state officials' violation of his rights to, *e.g.*, freedom of speech or freedom from unreasonable searches and seizures. Second, the Due Process Clause contains a substantive component that bars certain arbitrary, wrongful government actions "regardless of the fairness of the procedures used to implement them." *Daniels v. Williams*. As to these two types of claims, the constitutional violation actionable under § 1983 is complete when the wrongful action is taken. A plaintiff, under *Monroe v. Pape*, may invoke § 1983 regardless of any state-tort remedy that might be available to compensate him for the deprivation of these rights.

The Due Process Clause also encompasses a third type of protection, a guarantee of fair procedure. A § 1983 action may be brought for a violation of procedural due process, but here the existence of state remedies is relevant in a special sense. In procedural due process claims, the deprivation by state action of a constitutionally protected interest in "life, liberty, or property" is not in itself unconstitutional; what is unconstitutional is the deprivation of such an interest without due process of law. The constitutional violation actionable under § 1983 is not complete when the deprivation occurs; it is not complete unless and until the State fails to provide due process. Therefore, to determine whether a constitutional violation has occurred, it is necessary to ask what process the State provided, and whether it was constitutionally adequate. This inquiry would examine the procedural safeguards built into the statutory or administrative procedure of effecting the deprivation, and any remedies for erroneous deprivations provided by statute or tort law.

In this case, Burch does not claim that his confinement at FSH violated any of the specific guarantees of the Bill of Rights. Burch's complaint could be read to include a substantive due process claim, but that issue was not raised in the petition for certiorari, and we express no view on whether the facts Burch alleges could give rise to such a claim. The claim at issue falls within the third, or procedural, category of § 1983 claims based on the Due Process Clause.

B

Due process, as this Court often has said, is a flexible concept that varies with the particular situation. To determine what procedural protections the Constitution requires in a particular case, we weigh [the *Mathews v. Eldridge* factors, see section C, *supra*.]

Applying this test, the Court usually has held that the Constitution requires some kind of a hearing before the State deprives a person of liberty or property.

. . . .

In some circumstances, however, the Court has held that a statutory provision for a postdeprivation hearing, or a common-law tort remedy for erroneous deprivation, satisfies due process. . . .

This is where the *Parratt* rule comes into play. *Parratt* [represents] a special case of the general *Mathews v. Eldridge* analysis, in which postdeprivation tort remedies are all the process that is due, simply because they are the only remedies the State could be expected to provide. In *Parratt*, a state prisoner brought a § 1983 action because prison employees negligently had lost materials he had ordered by mail.[5] The prisoner did not dispute that he had a postdeprivation remedy. Under state law, a tort-claim procedure was available by which he could have recovered the value of the materials. This Court ruled that the tort remedy was all the process the prisoner was due, because any predeprivation procedural safeguards that the State did provide, or could have provided, would not address the risk of this kind of deprivation. The very nature of a negligent loss of property made it impossible for the State to predict such deprivations and provide predeprivation process. The Court explained:

> "The justifications which we have found sufficient to uphold takings of property without any predeprivation process are applicable to a situation such as the present one involving a tortious loss of a prisoner's property as a result of a random and unauthorized act by a state employee. In such a case, the loss is not a result of some established state procedure and the State cannot predict precisely when the loss will occur. It is difficult to conceive of how the State could provide a meaningful hearing before the deprivation takes place."

Given these special circumstances, it was clear that the State, by making available a tort remedy that could adequately redress the loss, had given the prisoner the process he was due. Thus, *Parratt* is not an exception to the *Mathews* balancing test, but rather an application of that test to the unusual case in which one of the variables in the *Mathews* equation — the value of predeprivation safe-guards — is negligible in preventing the kind of deprivation at issue. Therefore, no matter how significant the private interest at stake and the risk of its erroneous deprivation, the State cannot be required constitutionally to do the impossible by providing predeprivation process.

[The Court went on to hold that in this case, unlike *Parratt*, predeprivation process was required, for several reasons. First, "the deprivation of *Burch*'s liberty was [not] unpredictable." Second, "predeprivation process was [not] impossible here." Third, these defendants "cannot characterize their conduct as 'unauthorized' in the sense that term is used in *Parratt*. [The] state delegated to them the power and authority to effect the very deprivation complained of here. Thus, [u]nlike *Parratt*, [this] case does not represent the special instance of the *Mathews* due process analysis where postdeprivation process is all that is due because no predeprivation safeguards would be of use in preventing the kind of deprivation alleged."

JUSTICE O'CONNOR, with whom THE CHIEF JUSTICE, JUSTICE SCALIA, and JUSTICE KENNEDY join, dissenting.

[The dissent took issue with the majority's distinction between this case and *Parratt*, reasoning that the defendants' "actions were unauthorized," "[t]he wanton or reckless nature of the failure indicates it to be random," and that additional

---

[5] [14] *Parratt* was decided before this Court ruled, in *Daniels v. Williams* that a negligent act by a state official does not give rise to § 1983 liability.

pre-deprivation procedures would be "an impracticable means of preventing the deprivation."]

NOTES

1.   *Zinermon* provides straightforward answers to two of the questions raised in the Note before the case: *Parratt* does apply to liberty as well as property claims, and it does not apply to substantive due process claims. Does the dissent take issue with either of these propositions?

As discussed in the first note after *Parratt*, that case itself seems better characterized as a substantive due process claim. One commentator has argued that *Zinermon* is "mistaken" in limiting *Parratt* to procedural due process claims. *Fallon, supra*, at 341 n.184.

In what sense does the Court commit a mistake when it interprets (or modifies) its own decisions? Would it be appropriate to interpret *Zinermon* as having cleared up some of the confusion and incoherence *Parratt* would create if *Parratt* applied to substantive due process cases?

2.   According to the Court, Burch, the plaintiff in *Zinermon*, made a procedural due process claim. He did not assert that the state is forbidden, under the due process clause, to confine persons who consent to confinement or who pose a danger to themselves or others. He challenged the process by which it was decided that he had validly consented to confinement, and in particular the broad discretion afforded administrators to determine whether someone could validly consent, with no procedural safeguards against errors on their part. But the Fourteenth Amendment does not always require pre-deprivation process. Sometimes the circumstances justify state actions taken with no prior procedural safeguards, followed by a postdeprivation procedure for determining the propriety of the state's action. The majority opinion in *Zinermon* listed some examples:

> *See, e.g., Logan v. Zimmerman Brush Co.*, 455 U.S. 422, 436 (1982) ("The necessity of quick action by the State or the impracticality of providing any predeprivation process" may mean that a postdeprivation remedy is constitutionally adequate, quoting *Parratt*, 451 U.S., at 539); *Memphis Light*, 436 U.S., at 19 ("Where the potential length or severity of the deprivation does not indicate a likelihood of serious loss and where the procedures . . . are sufficiently reliable to minimize the risk of erroneous determination," a prior hearing may not be required); *Ingraham v. Wright*, 430 U.S. 651, 682 (1977) (hearing not required before corporal punishment of junior high school students); *Mitchell v. W.T. Grant Co.*, 416 U.S. 600, 619–620 (1974) (hearing not required before issuance of writ to sequester debtor's property).

Zinermon v. Burch, 494 U.S. at 128. See also section C, *supra*, where we use *Gilbert v. Homar* as an illustration.

Recall from *Gilbert* that in determining the process that is due in a given set of circumstances, the leading case is *Mathews v. Eldridge*, 424 U.S. 319 (1976), where the Court said:

[I]dentification of the specific dictates of due process generally requires consideration of three distinct factors: First, the private interest that will be affected by the official action; second, the risk of an erroneous deprivation of such interest through the procedures used, and the probable value, if any, of additional or substitute procedural safeguards; and finally, the Government's interest, including the function involved and the fiscal and administrative burdens that the additional or substitute procedural requirement would entail.

Id. at 335. *See* Jerry Mashaw, *The Supreme Court's Due Process Calculus for Administrative Adjudication in* Matthews v. Eldredge: *Three Factors in Search of a Theory of Value*, 44 U. CHI. L. REV. 28 (1976). *Daily Services, Inc. v. Valentino*, 756 F.3d 893 (6th Cir. 2014), illustrates the rule. Plaintiff, a provider of short-term temporary employment services, sued officials at the state workers' compensation bureau. The case arose out of a dispute between Daily Services and the bureau over unpaid insurance premiums. The bureau filed a series of liens and judgments against Daily Services, without giving Daily Services notice or an opportunity to be heard beforehand. Daily Services sued officers of the bureau under § 1983, charging that the filings violated its right to procedural due process and damaged it by preventing it from securing conventional financing and increasing its costs of doing business. The court ruled that *Parratt* applied, because the officers who filed the liens and judgments were not authorized to do so under state law, and, in the circumstances of the case, were unpredictable. As a result, "predeprivation process was impracticable." 756 F.3d at 908.

Applying *Parratt/Zinermon*, courts have also ruled, that a construction project may be halted immediately, without pre-deprivation process, when an issue arises as to whether some of the land is in the public domain, *San Gerónimo Caribe Project v. Acevedo-Vilá*, 687 F.3d 465 (1st Cir. 2012); and that taxi drivers' licenses may be suspended upon the arrest of the driver, without a pre-deprivation hearing, *Nnebe v. Daus*, 644 F.3d 147 (2d Cir. 2011).

3.   If the circumstances justify waiting until later to afford a remedy, the question arises whether the state's post-deprivation remedies are adequate. In *Flatford v. City of Monroe*, 17 F.3d 162 (6th Cir. 1994) tenants were evacuated from their apartment without a prior hearing due to a fire hazard, and sued for deprivation of property without due process. The landlord, but not the tenants, were informed of administrative remedies. Though the emergency justified the evacuation without a predeprivation hearing, plaintiffs were entitled to a post-deprivation remedy, and "postdeprivation state tort remedies [were] neither timely nor sufficiently remedial for emergency evacuees. Fundamental fairness expects more of a state than mere tort remedies where government dispossesses its citizens from their homes . . . [F]undamental fairness requires notice in short order of the right to an administrative hearing, including the manner designated for obtaining timely review." *Id.* at 169.

See also *King v. Roy*, 319 F.3d 345, 350 (8th Cir. 2003). The police had seized the plaintiffs' property in an investigation into "chop shops" that resell stolen vehicles and vehicle parts. Plaintiffs sued under section 1983, alleging procedural due process violations and other constitutional violations. The court said: "[A] state remedy is inadequate if it requires the owner of the seized property to go to unreasonable lengths to recover his property." Where the plaintiffs were without their vehicles for six to nine months, there was a genuine issue of material fact as to the adequacy of the remedy. In *Brown v. Muhlenberg*, 269 F.3d 205 (3d Cir. 2001), a police officer shot the plaintiffs' dog. They sued for damages under section 1983, raising procedural due process as well as other constitutional claims. The court found state remedies adequate, where state law provided an action for conversion and did not allow public employees to assert immunity from liability for "wilful misconduct." *Id.* at 213–14.

4.   Professor Larry Alexander is not so sure that Burch's complaint was directed at procedural due process:

> Burch's complaint was ambiguous regarding whether the alleged denial of due process was procedural or substantive. If Burch was claiming that (1) his "consent" was involuntary *and* that (2) he was neither a danger to himself nor a danger to others, then he was claiming a deprivation of substantive due process, namely, that Florida and its officials had no sufficient reason *in fact* to commit him to a mental hospital. On the other hand, if Burch was not denying that he was in fact constitutionally committable, either involuntarily or voluntarily, but only that the procedures the defendants employed were neither sufficient to commit him involuntarily . . . nor sufficient, given the evidence that he might not understand what he was doing, to commit him as a voluntary patient, then his complaint sounded in procedural due process.

Alexander, *Constitutional Torts, the Supreme Court, and the Law of Noncontradiction: An Essay on* Zinermon v. Burch, 87 Nw. U. L. REV. 576, 589–90 (1993). Should the district court have required Burch to rewrite his complaint? Should the Supreme Court have so required?

5.   Does *Zinermon* merely apply *Parratt*, as the majority insists, or significantly modify the *Parratt* test for determining whether post-deprivation remedies are adequate, as the dissent claims? Consider Judge Easterbrook's view:

> *Zinermon* [is] inconsistent with the foundations of *Parratt v. Taylor* and *Hudson v. Palmer*. *Zinermon* said that if errors in the implementation of a state's scheme for civil commitment are foreseeable, then process after the fact is inadequate, and it "distinguished" *Parratt* and *Hudson* on the ground that the wrongs committed in those cases were not foreseeable. This is no distinction at all. It is always foreseeable that there will be some errors in the implementation of any administrative system, and it is never foreseeable which occasions will give rise to those errors. It was foreseeable that some prison guards would lose the prisoners' property (*Parratt*), just as it was foreseeable that some persons would be committed without proper authorization (*Zinermon*); in neither case could the state or a court know in advance just when the errors would occur. If foreseeability of the *category* of blunders requires process in advance, then *Parratt* and *Hudson* were wrongly decided; if the inability to foresee the *particular* blunder makes subsequent remedies all the process "due," then *Zinermon* was wrongly decided.

Easter House v. Felder, 910 F.2d 1387, 1408 (7th Cir. 1990) (*en banc*) (concurring opinion).

6.   Despite the tension between the two cases, *Zinermon* did not overrule *Parratt*; indeed, it claimed that the two cases were compatible. As a result, some lower courts sympathetic to postdeprivation state remedies have been able to rationalize their decisions requiring resort to them in circumstances where *Zinermon* suggests a contrary ruling. For example, *Easter House, supra*, was a case the Supreme Court had remanded for reconsideration in light of *Zinermon*. The Seventh Circuit, sitting en banc, found postdeprivation remedies sufficient for due process where the plaintiff alleged a conspiracy between public officers and private actors to deprive it of its state license to operate an adoption agency. This conspiracy was "random and unauthorized" and hence within *Parratt*, rather than "predictable" (and controlled by *Zinermon*) because, among other reasons, "[t]he state had no opportunity to discover that the [defendants] were disregarding the established state procedures for renewing licenses." 910 F.2d at 1399.

As for Judge Easterbrook, he thought that adherence to *Zinermon* would forbid federal dismissal, yet he joined the majority. Since *Zinermon* did not overrule *Parratt*, it seemed to him unlikely that *Zinermon* represented a stable equilibrium. The majority opinion here "offers the best estimate of the course a majority of the Court will take." 910 F.2d at 1409.

A later Seventh Circuit case, *Cushing v. City of Chicago*, 3 F.3d 1156 (7th Cir. 1993), fell on the *Zinermon* side of the ledger. A city fireman disabled by heart disease left his job. The city continued to pay his medical expenses for a few months, then stopped. In Cushing's section 1983 suit he claimed that he had a property interest in continuing medical coverage, and that the decision to deny benefits was made without adequate procedural safeguards, in violation of his Fourteenth Amendment due process rights. Defendants argued that the City had no practicable way to anticipate the deprivation . . . and to provide Cushing with pre-deprivation notice and a hearing. Consequently, the existence of a postdeprivation remedy (presumably in the form of a tort claim against the City officials in state court) supplies Cushing with adequate process and thus precludes section 1983 liability. *See* 3 F.3d at 1164.

But the court held otherwise.

> The defendants' argument that the City could not have anticipated the deprivation . . . and thus could not have provided him with predeprivation process, is unconvincing. As the defendants concede, "[i]f the City paid the expenses in full for some time it did so mistakenly, and discontinued payments when it determined that Cushing's illness was not duty related." This admission belies the claim that any termination of Cushing's medial benefits was the result of random conduct that would have made a postdeprivation hearing impossible, or even unduly burdensome.

3 F.3d at 1165.

Is this reasoning consistent with *Easter House*? The *Cushing* court thought so, because the officials' actions in *Easter House* violated state law, and "the adoption agency could 'point to nothing which would indicate that the state knew or should have known that the [defendants] or other state employees had disregarded, or were likely to disregard the state's established procedure for processing renewal applications.'" In *Cushing*, "[b]y contrast, the City does not disavow knowledge of Tully's and Knorr's actions, and does not suggest either individual contravened the provisions of the collective bargaining agreement, much less municipal or state law. The defendants' contentions that their actions were of a piece and were entirely proper thus take this case out of the ambit of *Easter House*." *Id.*

See also Caine v. Hardy, 943 F.2d 1406 (5th Cir. 1991) (applying *Parratt* to dismiss a claim by a doctor who lost his staff privileges at a public hospital, allegedly in violation of procedural due process; *Zinermon* did not apply because there the plaintiff "was afforded *no* predeprivation process", *id. at* 1413 (emphasis in original) while here the hospital had "precise and detailed regulations", *id.*, and the plaintiff's allegation was that they were not followed).

7.   In *Moore v. Willis Independent School District*, 233 F.3d 871 (5th Cir. 2000), the plaintiff, a 14-year-old middle school student, misbehaved in gym class and was ordered to do 100 "ups and downs" or squat-thrusts, as punishment. His parents brought a section 1983 suit, claiming a substantive due process violation. The court rejected the claim, on the ground that "as long as the state provides an adequate remedy, a public school student cannot state a claim for denial of substantive due process through excessive corporal punishment." *Id. at* 874. The court distinguished other kinds of substantive due process cases, on the ground that "this case involves excessive exercise imposed as punishment to maintain discipline, and discipline is clearly a legitimate state goal. It must be maintained in school classrooms and gymnasiums to create an atmosphere in which students can learn." *Id. at* 875. Is the Fifth Circuit's rule consistent with *Zinermon*? Does the court persuasively justify a special rule for corporal punishment cases?

For a discussion of post-*Zinermon* cases, in which the lower federal courts take divergent views of *Zinermon* and its effect on the *Parratt* doctrine, *see* Oren, *Signing into Heaven:* Zinermon v. Burch, *Federal Rights, and State Remedies Thirty Years After* Monroe v. Pape, 40 EMORY L.J. 1, 55–69 (1991).

8.   In one area the availability of state remedies does, in effect, bar access to federal court for a section 1983 suit. When the plaintiff claims that state regulation of his property is so severe as to amount to an inverse condemnation of his property, he is ordinarily not permitted to sue under section 1983 for a deprivation of property without due process of law. Instead, he is required to pursue available state remedies for a "taking" of property. *Williamson County Regional Planning Commission v. Hamilton Bank*, 473 U.S. 172 (1985). Only after exhausting this remedy is the plaintiff allowed to sue under section 1983. *See, e.g., Macri v. King County*, 110 F.3d 1496, 1500 (9th Cir. 1997).

II. OTHER CONSTITUTIONAL CLAIMS

Due process is hardly the only doctrinal prong upon which to hang a constitutional tort suit. In this part of the chapter, we consider fact patterns that frequently give rise to Fourth Amendment, Equal Protection, and First Amendment constitutional tort suits.

A.   Fourth Amendment Rights

GRAHAM v. CONNOR
490 U.S. 386 (1989)

CHIEF JUSTICE REHNQUIST delivered the opinion of the Court.

This case requires us to decide what constitutional standard governs a free citizen's claim that law enforcement officials used excessive force in the course of making an arrest, investigatory stop, or other "seizure" of his person. We hold that such claims are properly analyzed under the Fourth Amendment's "objective reasonableness" standard, rather than under a substantive due process standard.

In this action under 42 U.S.C. § 1983, petitioner Dethorne Graham seeks to recover damages for injuries allegedly sustained when law enforcement officers used physical force against him during the course of an investigatory stop. Because the case comes to us from a decision of the Court of Appeals affirming the entry of a directed verdict for respondents, we take the evidence hereafter noted in the light most favorable to petitioner. On November 12, 1984, Graham, a diabetic, felt the onset of an insulin reaction. He asked a friend, William Berry, to drive him to a nearby convenience store so he could purchase some orange juice to counteract the reaction. Berry agreed, but when Graham entered the store, he saw a number of people ahead of him in the checkout line. Concerned about the delay, he hurried out of the store and asked Berry to drive him to a friend's house instead.

Respondent Connor, an officer of the Charlotte, North Carolina, Police Department, saw Graham hastily enter and leave the store. The officer became suspicious that something was amiss and followed Berry's car. About one-half mile from the store, he made an investigative stop. Although Berry told Connor that Graham was simply suffering from a "sugar reaction," the officer ordered Berry and Graham to wait while he found out what, if anything, had happened at the convenience store. When Officer Connor returned to his patrol car to call for backup assistance, Graham got out of the car, ran around it twice, and finally sat down on the curb, where he passed out briefly.

In the ensuing confusion, a number of other Charlotte police officers arrived on the scene in response to Officer Connor's request for backup. One of the officers rolled Graham over on the sidewalk and cuffed his hands tightly behind his back, ignoring Berry's pleas to get him some sugar. Another officer said: "I've seen a lot of people with sugar diabetes that never acted like this. Ain't nothing wrong with the M.F. but drunk. Lock the S.B. up." Several officers then lifted Graham up from behind, carried him over to Berry's car, and placed him face down on its hood. Regaining consciousness, Graham asked the officers to check in his wallet for a diabetic decal that he carried. In response, one of the officers told him to "shut up" and shoved his face down against the hood of the car. Four officers grabbed Graham and threw him headfirst into the police car. A friend of Graham's brought some orange juice to the car, but the officers refused to let him have it. Finally, Officer Connor received a report that Graham had done nothing wrong at the convenience store, and the officers drove him home and released him.

At some point during his encounter with the police, Graham sustained a broken foot, cuts on his wrists, a bruised forehead, and an injured shoulder; he also claims to have developed a loud ringing in his right ear that continues to this day. He commenced this action under 42 U.S.C. § 1983 against the individual officers involved in the incident, all of whom are respondents here, alleging that they had used excessive force in making the investigatory stop, in violation of "rights secured to him under the Fourteenth Amendment to the United States Constitution and 42 U.S.C. § 1983." The case was tried before a jury. At the close of petitioner's evidence, respondents moved for a directed verdict. In ruling on that motion, the District Court considered the following four factors, which it identified as "the factors to be considered in determining when the excessive use of force gives rise to a cause of action under § 1983": (1) the need for the application of force; (2) the relationship between that need and the amount of force that was used; (3) the extent of the injury inflicted; and (4) "whether the force was applied in a good faith effort to maintain and restore discipline or maliciously and sadistically for the very purpose of causing harm." Finding that the amount of force used by the officers was "appropriate under the circumstances," that "there was no discernable injury inflicted," and that the force used "was not applied maliciously or sadistically for the very purpose of causing harm," but in "a good faith effort to maintain or restore order in the face of a potentially explosive situation," the District Court granted respondents' motion for a directed verdict.

A divided panel of the Court of Appeals for the Fourth Circuit affirmed. The majority ruled first that the District Court had applied the correct legal standard in assessing petitioner's excessive force claim. Without attempting to identify the specific constitutional provision under which that claim arose, the majority endorsed the four-factor test applied by the District Court as generally applicable to all claims of "constitutionally excessive force" brought against governmental officials. The majority rejected petitioner's argument, based on Circuit precedent, that it was error to require him to prove that the allegedly excessive force used against him was applied "maliciously and sadistically for the very purpose of causing harm." Finally, the majority held that a reasonable jury applying the four-part test it had just endorsed to petitioner's evidence "could not find that the force applied was constitutionally excessive." The dissenting judge argued that this Court's decisions in *Terry v. Ohio* and *Tennessee v. Garner* required that excessive force claims arising out of investigatory stops be analyzed under the Fourth Amendment's "objective reasonableness" standard. We granted certiorari and now reverse.

Fifteen years ago, in *Johnson v. Glick* [the] Second Circuit addressed a § 1983 damages claim filed by a pretrial detainee who claimed that a guard had assaulted him without justification. In evaluating the detainee's claim, Judge Friendly applied neither the Fourth Amendment nor the Eighth, the two most textually obvious sources of constitutional protection against physically abusive governmental conduct. Instead, he looked to "substantive due process," holding that "quite apart from any 'specific' of the Bill of Rights, application of undue force by law enforcement officers deprives a suspect of liberty without due process of law." As support for this proposition, he relied upon our decision in *Rochin v. California* which used the Due Process Clause to void a state criminal conviction based on evidence obtained by pumping the defendant's stomach. If a police officer's use of force which "shocks the conscience" could justify setting aside a criminal conviction, Judge Friendly reasoned, a correctional officer's use of similarly excessive force must give rise to a due process violation actionable under § 1983. Judge Friendly went on to set forth four factors to guide courts in determining "whether the constitutional line has been crossed" by a particular use of force-the same four factors relied upon by the courts below in this case.

In the years following *Johnson v. Glick*, the vast majority of lower federal courts have applied its four-part "substantive due process" test indiscriminately to all excessive force claims lodged against law enforcement and prison officials under § 1983, without considering whether the particular application of force might implicate a more specific constitutional right governed by a different standard. Indeed, many courts have seemed to assume, as did the courts below in this case, that there is a generic "right" to be free from excessive force, grounded not in any particular constitutional provision but rather in "basic principles of § 1983 jurisprudence."

We reject this notion that all excessive force claims brought under § 1983 are governed by a single generic standard. As we have said many times, § 1983 "is not itself a source of substantive rights," but merely provides "a method for vindicating federal rights elsewhere conferred." In addressing an excessive force claim brought under § 1983, analysis begins by identifying the specific constitutional right allegedly infringed by the challenged application of force. In most instances, that will be either the Fourth Amendment's prohibition against unreasonable seizures of the person, or the Eighth Amendment's ban on cruel and unusual punishments, which are the two primary sources of constitutional protection against physically abusive governmental conduct. The validity of the claim must then be judged by reference to the specific constitutional standard which governs that right, rather than to some generalized "excessive force" standard. *See Tennessee v. Garner*, supra, (claim of excessive force to effect arrest analyzed under a Fourth Amendment standard); *Whitley v. Albers* (claim of excessive force to subdue convicted prisoner analyzed under an Eighth Amendment standard).

Where, as here, the excessive force claim arises in the context of an arrest or investigatory stop of a free citizen, it is most properly characterized as one invoking the protections of the Fourth Amendment, which guarantees citizens the right "to be secure in their persons . . . against unreasonable . . . seizures" of the person. This much is clear from our decision in *Tennessee v. Garner*, supra. In *Garner*, we addressed a claim that the use of deadly force to apprehend a fleeing suspect who did not appear to be armed or otherwise dangerous violated the suspect's constitutional rights, notwithstanding the existence of probable cause to arrest. Though the complaint alleged violations of both the Fourth Amendment and the Due Process Clause, we analyzed the constitutionality of the challenged application of force solely by reference to the Fourth Amendment's prohibition against unreasonable seizures of the person, holding that the "reasonableness" of a particular seizure depends not only on when it is made, but also on how it is carried out. Today we make explicit what was implicit in *Garner's* analysis, and hold that all claims that law enforcement officers have used excessive force-deadly or not-in the course of an arrest, investigatory stop, or other "seizure" of a free citizen should be analyzed under the Fourth Amendment and its "reasonableness" standard, rather than under a "substantive due process" approach. Because the Fourth Amendment provides an explicit textual source of constitutional protection against this sort of physically intrusive governmental conduct, that Amendment, not the more generalized notion of "substantive due process," must be the guide for analyzing these claims.

Determining whether the force used to effect a particular seizure is "reasonable" under the Fourth Amendment requires a careful balancing of " 'the nature and quality of the intrusion on the individual's Fourth Amendment interests' " against the countervailing governmental interests at stake. Our Fourth Amendment jurisprudence has long recognized that the right to make an arrest or investigatory stop necessarily carries with it the right to use some degree of physical coercion or threat thereof to effect it. Because "the test of reasonableness under the Fourth Amendment is not capable of precise definition or mechanical application," however, its proper application requires careful attention to the facts and circumstances of each particular case, including the severity of the crime at issue, whether the suspect poses an immediate threat to the safety of the officers or others, and whether he is actively resisting arrest or attempting to evade arrest by flight . . . .

The "reasonableness" of a particular use of force must be judged from the perspective of a reasonable officer on the scene, rather than with the 20/20 vision of hindsight. The Fourth Amendment is not violated by an arrest based on probable cause, even though the wrong person is arrested, nor by the mistaken execution of a valid search warrant on the wrong premises. With respect to a claim of excessive force, the same standard of reasonableness at the moment applies: "Not every push or shove, even if it may later seem unnecessary in the peace of a judge's chambers," *Johnson v. Glick*, violates the Fourth Amendment. The calculus of reasonableness must embody allowance for the fact that police officers are often forced to make split-second judgments-in circumstances that are tense, uncertain, and rapidly evolving-about the amount of force that is necessary in a particular situation.

As in other Fourth Amendment contexts, however, the "reasonableness" inquiry in an excessive force case is an objective one: the question is whether the officers' actions are "objectively reasonable" in light of the facts and circumstances confronting them, without regard to their underlying intent or motivation . . . An officer's evil intentions will not make a Fourth Amendment violation out of an objectively reasonable use of force; nor will an officer's good intentions make an objectively unreasonable use of force constitutional.

Because petitioner's excessive force claim is one arising under the Fourth Amendment, the Court of Appeals erred in analyzing it under the four-part *Johnson v. Glick* test. That test, which requires consideration of whether the individual officers acted in "good faith" or "maliciously and sadistically for the very purpose of causing harm," is incompatible with a proper Fourth Amendment analysis. We do not agree with the Court of Appeals' suggestion, that the "malicious and sadistic" inquiry is merely another way of describing conduct that is objectively unreasonable under the circumstances. Whatever the empirical correlations between "malicious and sadistic" behavior and objective unreasonableness may be, the fact remains that the "malicious and sadistic" factor puts in issue the subjective motivations of the individual officers, which our prior cases make clear has no bearing on whether a particular seizure is "unreasonable" under the Fourth Amendment. Nor do we agree with the Court of Appeals' conclusion, that because the subjective motivations of the individual officers are of central importance in deciding whether force used against a convicted prisoner violates the Eighth Amendment, it cannot be reversible error to inquire into them in deciding whether force used against a suspect or arrestee violates the Fourth Amendment. Differing standards under the Fourth and Eighth Amendments are hardly surprising: the terms "cruel" and "punishment" clearly suggest some inquiry into subjective state of mind, whereas the term "unreasonable" does not. Moreover, the less protective Eighth Amendment standard applies "only after the State has complied with the constitutional guarantees traditionally associated with criminal prosecutions." The Fourth Amendment inquiry is one of "objective reasonableness" under the circumstances, and subjective concepts like "malice" and "sadism" have no proper place in that inquiry.[6]

Because the Court of Appeals reviewed the District Court's ruling on the motion for directed verdict under an erroneous view of the governing substantive law, its judgment must be vacated and the case remanded to that court for reconsideration of that issue under the proper Fourth Amendment standard.

It is so ordered.

JUSTICE **BLACKMUN**, with whom JUSTICE **BRENNAN** and JUSTICE **MARSHALL** join, concurring in part and concurring in the judgment.

I join the Court's opinion insofar as it rules that the Fourth Amendment is the primary tool for analyzing claims of excessive force in the prearrest context. [I] see no reason for the Court to find it necessary further to reach out to decide that prearrest excessive force claims are to be analyzed under the Fourth Amendment rather than under a substantive due process standard. [I] expect that the use of force that is not demonstrably unreasonable under the Fourth Amendment only rarely will raise substantive due process concerns. But until I am faced with a case in which that question is squarely raised, and its merits are subjected to adversary presentation, I do not join in foreclosing the use of substantive due process analysis in prearrest cases.

---

[6] [12] Of course, in assessing the credibility of an officer's account of the circumstances that prompted the use of force, a factfinder may consider, along with other factors, evidence that the officer may have harbored ill-will toward the citizen. Similarly, the officer's objective "good faith" — that is, whether he could reasonably have believed that the force used did not violate the Fourth Amendment — may be relevant to the availability of the qualified immunity defense to monetary liability under section 1983. See *Anderson v. Creighton.* Since no claim of qualified immunity has been raised in this case, however, we express no view on its proper application in excessive force cases that arise under the Fourth Amendment.

NOTES

1.   The general rule for deciding whether a suit seeking to recover for personal harms is governed by the Fourteenth Amendment substantive due process test or by Fourth Amendment reasonableness is whether, in the circumstances, a "seizure" has occurred. In *Sacramento County v. Lewis, supra,* the Court rejected an argument that liability for injuries committed in the course of high speed chases (other than by an officer's deliberate effort to stop the person being chased) should be governed by a Fourth Amendment standard:

> Because we have "always been reluctant to expand the concept of substantive due process," *Collins v. Harker Heights,* we held in *Graham v. Connor* that "where a particular Amendment provides an explicit textual source of constitutional protection against a particular sort of government behavior, that Amendment, not the more generalized notion of substantive due process, must be the guide for analyzing these claims." Given the rule in *Graham,* we were presented at oral argument with the threshold issue whether facts involving a police chase aimed at apprehending suspects can ever support a due process claim. The argument runs that in chasing the motorcycle, Smith was attempting to make a seizure within the meaning of the Fourth Amendment, and, perhaps, even that he succeeded when Lewis was stopped by the fatal collision. Hence, any liability must turn on an application of the reasonableness standard governing searches and seizures, not the due process standard of liability for constitutionally arbitrary executive action.

> The argument is unsound. *Graham* does not hold that all constitutional claims relating to physically abusive government conduct must arise under either the Fourth or Eighth Amendments; rather, *Graham* simply requires that if a constitutional claim is covered by a specific constitutional provision, such as the Fourth or Eighth Amendment, the claim must be analyzed under the standard appropriate to that specific provision, not under the rubric of substantive due process.

> Substantive due process analysis is therefore inappropriate in this case only if respondents' claim is "covered by" the Fourth Amendment. It is not. The Fourth Amendment covers only "searches and seizures," neither of which took place here. No one suggests that there was a search, and our cases foreclose finding a seizure. [A] police pursuit in attempting to seize a person does not amount to a "seizure" within the meaning of the Fourth Amendment. And a Fourth Amendment seizure does not occur whenever there is a governmentally caused termination of an individual's freedom of movement (the innocent passerby), nor even whenever there is a governmentally caused and governmentally desired termination of an individual's freedom of movement (the fleeing felon), but only when there is a governmental termination of freedom of movement through means intentionally applied. [No] Fourth Amendment seizure would take place where a pursuing police car sought to stop the suspect only by the show of authority represented by flashing lights and continuing pursuit, but accidentally stopped the suspect by crashing into him. That is exactly this

case. Graham's more-specific-provision rule is therefore no bar to respondents' suit.

Compare *Brower v. Inyo County*, 489 U.S. 593 (1989), where the Court held that someone injured when he ran into a police roadblock may have a Fourth Amendment claim, because the Fourth Amendment applies when an officer intentionally applies force to the plaintiff, and "it is enough for a seizure that a person be stopped by the very instrumentality set in motion or put in place in order to achieve the result. It was enough here, therefore, that, according to the allegations of the complaint, Brower was meant to be stopped by the physical obstacle of the roadblock-and that he was so stopped." *Id. at* 599. The Court remanded for consideration of whether the seizure was "unreasonable" in the circumstances.

Lower courts have addressed variants on this theme. *See, e.g., Horta v. Sullivan*, 4 F.3d 2, 10 (1st Cir. 1993). The court said

> Officer Menino's pursuit of the motorcycle on which Horta was riding, without more, was not a Fourth Amendment seizure. If the driver speeds off, pursued by the officer, and a crash ensues, this does not necessarily constitute a seizure, either. Hence, if during the chase here Demoranville's motorcycle had accidentally collided with a tree on Mason Road there would plainly have been no seizure, as Menino would not have terminated Horta's freedom of movement through means intentionally applied, (i.e., Menino did not intentionally cause the motorcycle to strike the tree) . . . By the same token, it is not sufficient that Menino pursued and the pursuit resulted in a collision with another police vehicle . . . to establish that Menino seized her, appellant must show that the collision with Officer Sullivan's cruiser was the means *intended by Menino* to end the pursuit.

The court relied on *Brower*, 489 U.S. at 596–97 (1989):

> [A] Fourth Amendment seizure does not occur whenever there is a governmentally caused termination of an individual's freedom of movement (the innocent passerby), nor even whenever there is a governmentally caused and governmentally *desired* termination of an individual's freedom of movement (the fleeing felon), but only when there is a governmental termination of freedom of movement *through means intentionally applied.* (emphasis in original).

Suppose two officers independently respond to an emergency call. One tells the plaintiff to stop and he complies. Then the other accidentally hits the plaintiff with his car. Has the second officer "seized" the plaintiff? *See Eldredge v. Town of Falmouth*, 662 F.3d 100 (1st Cir. 2011) (no).

By contrast, in *Hawkins v. City of Farmington*, 189 F.3d 695 (8th Cir. 1999) the court found *Brower* applicable to a collision between a police car and Hawkins' motorcycle, for "Hawkins' complaint clearly alleged an intentional stop." *Cf. Donovan v. City of Milwaukee*, 17 F.3d 944, 950–51 (7th Cir. 1994) (intentional striking of plaintiff's vehicle may be Fourth Amendment violation). Does the officer "seize" all of the occupants of a vehicle when he shoots the driver in order to stop the car? *Compare Rodriguez v. Passinault*, 637 F.3d 675, 687 (6th Cir. 2011) (yes) *with Troupe v. Sarasota City, Fla.*, 419 F.3d 1160, 1167 (11th Cir. 2005) (no).

Suppose the officer shoots at the plaintiff's car but misses. Is there a "seizure" giving rise to Fourth Amendment protections? If not, does the result change when the bullet touches the car but does not inflict enough damage to stop it? *See Adams v. City of Auburn Hills*, 336 F.3d 515 (6th Cir. 2003), where the court held that since the plaintiff was not actually restrained, no seizure of the plaintiff occurred, hence there was no Fourth Amendment violation. The court explained:

> Officer Backstrom's firing at the automobile did not impair Adams's movement. Adams was not hit by Officer Backstrom's bullets and was able to leave the scene unharmed despite Backstrom's use of his firearm. Even though the tire of the Taurus was hit, it was still operable and Adams reached his destination, his mother's house. Hence, Adams never was seized, and our holding that no seizure occurred makes the discussion of the reasonableness of Backstrom's conduct unnecessary. Because the Fourth Amendment is not implicated, Adams has not alleged a constitutional violation to support a section 1983 claim.

In *McCoy v. Harrison*, 341 F.3d 600 (7th Cir. 2003), the defendant, an animal welfare investigator, struck the plaintiff while investigating dog kennels on the plaintiff's property, knocking her to the ground. The court ruled that no Fourth Amendment "seizure" occurred:

> McCoy's claim focuses on the unreasonable seizure prong of the Fourth Amendment. The Supreme Court applies a two-part test to decide whether a person has been seized so that Fourth Amendment protections are triggered; first, it must be determined if physical force was used along with a show of authority, and second, whether or not the person submitted to the show of authority. *California v. Hodari D.*, 499 U.S. 621, 624–66 (1991). [McCoy] has failed to address the second prong under *Hodari D.*, arguing that a seizure occurs with "the slightest application of physical force." McCoy must not only show that her personal liberty had been restrained, [but] that she "actually yielded to a show of authority." [*Hodari*] *D.* At no time was McCoy's freedom of movement restrained. There is no question there was some type of altercation, but immediately after, McCoy got up and went into her home, and Harrison left the premises. He made no effort to direct or impede her movements.

2. *Graham* was foreshadowed by *Tennessee v. Garner*, 471 U.S. 1 (1985), where the Court spurned substantive due process in favor of a Fourth Amendment "objective reasonableness" standard for evaluating police use of deadly force against suspects who flee or resist arrest. "Where the officer has probable cause to believe that the suspect poses a threat of serious physical harm, either to the officer or to others, it is not constitutionally unreasonable to prevent escape by using deadly force." *Id. at* 11. After *Graham*, courts subsumed deadly force cases under the more general excessive force principle. *See, e.g., Seiner v. Drenon*, 304 F.3d 810 (8th Cir. 2002). In this case, police officers Drenon and Fowler went to Seiner's home to arrest him for a felony.

The officers were informed Seiner was known to be violent and armed with a knife. Seiner's father told the officers Seiner was hiding in the cellar and did not have a weapon. After Seiner did not respond to the officers' requests to come out, the officers went into the dimly lit cellar with guns drawn. The officers saw Seiner hiding between a hot water heater and a brick column. Drenon repeatedly ordered Seiner to show his hands, but Seiner did not respond. Drenon slowly approached Seiner until he was touching him with his handgun. Fowler yelled that Seiner had something in his hands. The officers ordered Seiner to 'drop it,' but Seiner did not do so. Unbeknownst to Drenon, Fowler then decided to use his extendable baton to strike Seiner's hands, which were in the narrow four-inch opening between the brick column and the water heater, to force Seiner to drop whatever he was holding, At the time, Fowler was holding a flashlight in his left hand and his gun in his right hand. As Fowler attempted to shift his equipment and pull the baton from his belt with his right hand, his gun discharged. The bullet from Fowler's weapon struck the brick column and bullet fragments ricocheted into Drenon, striking him in the face. At the time, Drenon was facing Seiner, not Fowler. Assuming Seiner had shot him Drenon immediately fired three shots into Seiner, killing him.

Seiner's mother brought a constitutional claim for excessive force. Relying on *Graham*, the court affirmed a summary judgment ruling that found no constitutional violation: "Drenon had been shot and an objective officer in Drenon's place would reasonably believe Seiner had done it." Note that this ruling means that, as a matter of law, Drenon's conduct was "objectively reasonable." Should the court have left it up to the jury to decide that question? Could a reasonable jury find otherwise? What result if Drenon had not been told Seiner was known to be armed and dangerous, or if Drenon had not been facing Seiner when he was shot, or if Fowler had not told Drenon that Seiner was holding something?

For a somewhat similar fact pattern, with the same outcome, see *Loch v. City of Litchfield*, 689 F.3d 961, 967 (8th Cir. 2012). Rueckert, a police officer, shot Cassidy Loch, who was unarmed. The court ruled that Rueckert's use of deadly force was objectively reasonable, even if he did not see an object resembling a gun or holster:

> Rueckert knew he was dealing with an intoxicated individual, and he had been told that Cassidy had a gun. Although others on the scene later yelled that Cassidy was unarmed, Rueckert was in no position — with Cassidy continuing toward him — to verify which version was true. Rueckert heard Cassidy say "kill" as he continued toward the officer. Cassidy then slipped on the snow, and one of his hands moved toward his side. In these circumstances, a reasonable officer could believe that deadly force was necessary to protect himself from death or serious harm.

3.   Conversely, courts sometimes hold that, as a matter of law, the force used *was* excessive. *See Deorle v. Rutherford*, 272 F.3d 1272 (9th Cir. 2001). In this case the police had entered Deorle's property "not to arrest him, but to investigate his peculiar behavior." When Deorle approached with a can or bottle in his hand, Rutherford (without first warning Deorle) shot him in the face with a lead-filled beanbag ("something akin to a rubber bullet"), which knocked him off his feet and

removed one of his eyes. The officer "had not observed Deorle attack anyone; nor had he received any report that Deorle had engaged in any such conduct. Deorle had roamed about the area, and shouted in an irrational manner, but had not harmed or attempted to harm anyone." In addition, "Rutherford could easily have avoided a confrontation, and awaited the arrival of the negotiating team by retreating to his original position behind the roadblock."

A big difference between *Seiner* and *Deorle* is that the officer had to react quickly in *Seiner* but not in *Deorle*. In cases where officers must make split second decisions, courts often give a "heat of battle" instruction in order to stress the importance of this factor. *See Cox v. Treadway*, 75 F.3d 230, 236 (6th Cir. 1996) ("heat of battle" instruction was proper even though plaintiffs were not resisting arrest).

Care must be taken in crafting jury instructions on justification. Is it proper to instruct the jury that the use of deadly force is justified if the officer is in danger of serious bodily harm or reasonably believes he is in such danger? The problem with such a seemingly straightforward instruction, according to the majority of a divided 2nd circuit panel, is that it does not limit the use of deadly force *solely* to such situations. *See Rasanen v. Doe*, 723 F.3d 325, 336–37 (2d Cir. 2013).

4. *Deorle* and *Rasenen* illustrate that both the lack of justification for the use of force and the severity of the plaintiff's injury are factors that weigh heavily in the plaintiff's favor in excessive force cases. But, according to *Bastien v. Goddard*, 279 F.3d 10 (1st Cir. 2002), severe injury "is not a pre-requisite to recovery." In that case the court allowed plaintiff to sue for pain in his wrists caused by tight handcuffs. *See also Morrison v. Board of Trustees of Green Township*, 583 F.3d 394, 401 (6th Cir. 2009) (The Fourth Amendment prohibits unduly tight or excessively forceful handcuffing during the course of a seizure.") Some courts are more tentative. In *Goff v. Bise*, 173 F.3d 1068, 1074 (8th Cir. 1999) the court found no need to decide the issue of "whether some minimum level of injury is required" where plaintiff suffered a torn rotator cuff and scarring and nerve damage to his hand. And *Glenn v. City of Tyler*, 242 F.3d 307 (5th Cir. 2001), ruled that "handcuffing too tightly, without more, does not amount to excessive force." How would the issue be resolved under common law negligence principles? Is there good reason to answer the question differently in the constitutional tort context?

In resolving the excessive force issue, is it also relevant that the officer had other courses of action available? *See Retz v. Seaton*, 741 F.3d 913, 917 (8th Cir. 2014) (approving, over the defendant's objection, the admission of testimony as to alternatives on the ground that "determination of whether the course chosen by the officer was objectively reasonable may involve consideration of the range of choices available on the scene at the time force was used").

5. The Fourth Amendment limits the authority of the police to enter someone's home without a warrant. Suppose the police violate this prohibition and then use force in the course of an arrest. Does the illegality of the entry necessarily mean that any force used is excessive? *See Bodine v. Warwick*, 72 F.3d 393, 400 (3d Cir. 1995) (no, though the officers could be sued for damages proximately caused by the illegal entry in such a case, whether or not they used excessive force.) The Fourth Amendment also forbids the police to make a warrantless arrest without probable cause. Suppose the police violate this rule, but use only the force necessary to effect the arrest. May the plaintiff nonetheless recover damages for the force used, on the theory that there was no justification for the use of *any* force? *See Williamson v. Mills*, 65 F.3d 155, 158 (11th Cir. 1995) (yes). Can *Williamson* and *Bodine* both be right?

6.   *Graham* removes from the domain of substantive due process a significant number of cases, for encounters with the police produce more complaints of governmental abuse of power than any other aspect of the relationship between citizens and the government. Under *Graham*, will plaintiffs be able to recover from policemen who act maliciously, but whose conduct is objectively reasonable? If not, isn't the holding in *Graham* at odds with the theory of constitutional tort underlying *Lewis*, that a constitutional cause of action should be available for conduct by officers that "shocks the conscience"? Is malicious or otherwise improperly motivated police conduct any less reprehensible just because some other policeman could quite reasonably have done the same thing? One reason why the Court refuses to extend substantive due process to claims that can be handled under more specific provisions of the bill of rights is candidly discussed by Justice Souter in a concurring opinion:

> We are required by [t]he doctrine of judicial self-restraint to exercise the utmost care whenever we are asked to break new ground in [the] field of substantive due process [citing *Collins*]. Just as the concept of due process does not protect against insubstantial impositions on liberty, neither should the 'rational continuum' be reduced to the mere duplication of protections adequately addressed by other constitutional provisions. [W]e are not free to infer that it was meant to be applied without thereby adding a substantial increment to protection otherwise available. The importance of recognizing [this] limitation is underscored by pragmatic concerns about subjecting government actors to two (potentially inconsistent) standards for the same conduct and needlessly imposing on trial courts the unenviable burden of reconciling well-established jurisprudence under the Fourth and Eighth Amendments with the ill-defined contours of some novel due process right.

Albright v. Oliver, 510 U.S. 266 (1994) (Souter, J., concurring in the judgment). *See also* Richard Fallon, *Some Confusions About Due Process, Judicial Review, and Constitutional Remedies*, 93 COLUM. L. REV. 309, 349 n.226 (1993) (suggesting that the Court's discomfort with substantive due process influenced its decision in *Graham*); Peter Rubin, *Square Pegs and Round Holes: Substantive Due Process, Procedural Due Process and the Bill of Rights*, 103 COLUM. L. REV. 833, 858 (2003) (arguing that "[a] broad reading of *Graham* [has] "an unusual, essentialist cast, suggesting that legal claims have some ascertainable 'true' or essential nature, independent of what legal provision the plaintiff alleges has been violated").

7.   The Court suggests that plaintiffs are actually better off under *Graham* than under the Eighth Amendment standard, discussed at Section II. A. *supra.* That test (like the substantive due process test of *Lewis*) emphasizes the defendant's state of mind. Do you agree with the Court's assessment? (An admittedly unscientific sampling of many cases suggests that plaintiffs do indeed have better

prospects under the "objective reasonableness" test.) And there is another factor to consider: Granted that a bad motive will not establish a constitutional violation under *Graham*, is the plaintiff's attorney always precluded from introducing evidence of bad motive? See footnote 12 in the *Graham* opinion.

A further point in *Graham*'s favor is that "objective reasonableness," like the negligence test in common law torts, helps to simplify trials and provides helpful guidance to police departments and the lower courts. In this sense, it is a more "rule-like" test than the "shock the conscience" approach. Like all rules, it has a cost, in that it will not reach every single case that deserves a remedy. Nonetheless, that cost may be worth the benefit of having a predictable rule to apply, rather than engaging in a consideration of all the circumstances in each case. On the costs and benefits of rule-based decision-making in general, see F. SCHAUER, PLAYING BY THE RULES: AN EXAMINATION OF RULE-BASED DECISION-MAKING IN LAW AND IN LIFE (1991).

Is there any good reason not to apply *Graham*'s test more broadly? Why did the Court in *Lewis* choose instead a "shock the conscience" test for claims falling under substantive due process?

8.   One consequence of the proliferation of standards governing use of force by various state officers is that it becomes necessary to determine the plaintiff's status at the time force was used. *Graham* holds that Fourth Amendment law applies during the arrest. At some point, the arrestee becomes a pretrial detainee and substantive due process governs his rights against his jailors (see the notes after *Farmer v. Brennan*, above.) *See* Erica Haber, Note, *Demystifying a Legal Twilight Zone: Resolving the Circuit Court Split on When Seizure Ends and Pretrial Detention Begins in Section 1983 Excessive Force Cases*, 19 N. Y. L. SCH. J. HUMAN RIGHTS 939 (2003). The distinction is important, because the Fourth Amendment test is "objective reasonableness," while the Fourteenth Amendment "shock the conscience" test is subjective and hard to meet. Thus, "[a] plaintiff has a substantially higher hurdle to overcome to make a showing of excessive force under the Fourteenth Amendment as opposed to under the Fourth Amendment." *Burgess v. Fischer*, 735 F.3d 462, 472 (6th Cir. 2013). In *Burgess*, the court said the Fourth Amendment applied through the booking process at the jail. *Compare Riley v. Dorton*, 115 F.3d 1159 (4th Cir. 1997) (rejecting cases that apply Fourth Amendment rules throughout "the period the suspect remains with the arresting officers" in favor of limiting Fourth Amendment coverage to the "initial act of seizing"). Upon conviction, the inmate is covered by the Eighth Amendment. *See Graham, supra*, at 392 n.6.

9.   *Graham*'s theme of supplanting a substantive due process standard by Fourth Amendment analysis is echoed in *Albright v. Oliver*, 510 U.S. 266 (1994). The plaintiff had earlier won dismissal of a state criminal charge against him on the ground that the charge did not state an offense under state law. In his section 1983 suit, he sought to recover under a substantive due process theory that he had a "right to be free of prosecution without probable cause." A fragmented Court held that "it is the Fourth Amendment, and not substantive due process, under which [Albright's] claims must be judged."

Before *Albright*, some lower courts had recognized a constitutional tort suit roughly paralleling the common law tort of malicious prosecution. *See* 510 U.S. at

270 n.4. In the common law tort, the plaintiff must show "that the plaintiff's wrongful prosecution was (1) directly or indirectly instigated or continued by the defendant, (2) without probable cause, (3) with improper purpose ('malice'), and (4) terminated favorably to the plaintiff." DAN B. DOBBS, THE LAW OF TORTS 1215 (2000). After *Albright* malicious prosecution has become an increasingly important category of constitutional tort litigation.

Albright left many questions unanswered. The lower courts have adopted a variety of approaches. *See* Lyle Kossis, Note, *Malicious Prosecution Claims in Section 1983 Lawsuits*, 99 VA. L. REV. 1635 (2013). Thus, "[l]ower courts are unsure whether the common law elements of malicious prosecution should dominate the analysis, or whether the question should be framed exclusively in light of Fourth Amendment jurisprudence," with "the Second, Fifth, Seventh, and Ninth Circuits [opting] for the common law approach, [and] the First, Third, Fourth, Sixth, Tenth, and Eleventh [focusing exclusively] on Fourth Amendment jurisprudence. Kossis, *supra*, at 1646–47. *See, e.g., Robertson v. Lucas*, 753 F.3d 606 (6th Cir. 2014). *Robertson* applied a Fourth Amendment approach, under which plaintiff must prove:

(1)   a criminal prosecution was initiated against the plaintiff and the defendant made, influenced, or participated in the decision to prosecute;

(2)   there was no probble cause for the criminal prosecution:

(3)   As a consequence of the legal proceeding, the plaintiff suffered a deprivation of liberty apart from the initial seizure; and

(4)   The criminal proceeding was resolved in the plaintiff's favor. Id. at 616.

Kossis would probably disapprove of *Robertson*, as he argues that the Supreme Court was unwise to focus on the Fourth Amendment in *Albright* and seems to favor grounding the doctrine in substantive due process instead.

Whatever variations there are among the lower federal courts on malicious prosecution as a constitutional tort, they all agree that the plaintiff can win only if the criminal prosecution failed. But the plaintiff may succeed on a somewhat different theory even if he is convicted. The plaintiff in *Poventud v. City of New York*, 750 F.3d 121 (2d Cir. 2014) (*en banc*) asserted that he was denied access to exculpatory evidence, in violation of his due process rights under *Brady v. Maryland*, 373 U.S. 83 (1963). He was convicted anyway, but later succeeded in having the conviction overturned on account of the *Brady* violation. He was then retried and pleaded guilty to a crime. He then sued under § 1983 to recover for the *Brady* violation. In reversing the district court's summary judgment for the defendants, the court explained:

> The district court treated Poventud's case as though it were a malicious prosecution claim. It measured his admission in the subsequent plea agreement against his claims in his *Brady* submission. Because his 2006 plea was at odds with his alibi defense at his 1998 trial, Judge Batts concluded that his recovery for a *Brady* claim would call his plea into question. That view misunderstands *Brady* and its correlation to § 1983 claims asserting only violations of the right to due process. The district court's view incorrectly presumes that, on the facts of this case, the State

could violate Poventud's *Brady* rights only if Poventud is an innocent man. This last restriction has no basis in the *Brady* case law; materiality does not depend on factual innocence, but on what would have been proven absent the violation. 750 F.3d at 134.

10. In *Chavez v. Martinez*, 538 U.S. 760 (2003), the issue was the scope of Fifth Amendment rights. Chavez, a police officer, interrogated Martinez in a hospital room where Martinez was being treated, without advising him of his rights, under *Miranda v. Arizona*, 384 U.S. 436 (1966), to remain silent and to have a lawyer present. The statements were not used against Martinez in a criminal prosecution. Martinez brought a section 1983 suit, maintaining that Chavez's actions violated his Fifth Amendment right not to be "compelled in any criminal case to be a witness against himself," as well as his Fourteenth Amendment substantive due process right to be free from coercive questioning. A fragmented Court rejected the Fifth Amendment theory of recovery. Justice Thomas, writing for a plurality of four, reasoned that Martinez had no Fifth Amendment claim because he "was never prosecuted for a crime, let alone compelled to be a witness against himself in a criminal case." Several other Justices agreed that, in the circumstances of this case, there was no good Fifth Amendment claim, but left open the possibility that the absence of *Miranda* warnings may be the basis for a section 1983 suit in other circumstances.

With regard to substantive due process, Justice Thomas, joined by two other Justices, applied the "shock the conscience" test of *Sacramento County v. Lewis* and found no substantive due process violation. A majority of the Justices, however, ruled that this issue should be addressed on remand. For a pre-*Chavez* treatment of issues in this area, see Susan R. Klein, Miranda *Deconstitutionalized: When the Self-Incrimination Clause and the Civil Rights Act Collide*, 143 U. Pa. L. Rev. 417 (1994).

In *Scott v. Harris* the Court addressed the Fourth Amendment excessive force issue in the context of high speed police chases.

SCOTT v. HARRIS
550 U.S. 372 (2007)

Justice Scalia delivered the opinion of the Court.

We consider whether a law enforcement official can, consistent with the Fourth Amendment, attempt to stop a fleeing motorist from continuing his public-endangering flight by ramming the motorist's car from behind. Put another way: Can an officer take actions that place a fleeing motorist at risk of serious injury or death in order to stop the motorist's flight from endangering the lives of innocent bystanders?

I

In March 2001, a Georgia county deputy clocked respondent's vehicle traveling at 73 miles per hour on a road with a 55-mile-per-hour speed limit. The deputy activated his blue flashing lights indicating that respondent should pull over. Instead, respondent sped away, initiating a chase down what is in most portions a two-lane road, at speeds exceeding 85 miles per hour. The deputy radioed his dispatch to report that he was pursuing a fleeing vehicle, and broadcast its license plate number. Petitioner, Deputy Timothy Scott, heard the radio communication and joined the pursuit along with other officers. In the midst of the chase, respondent pulled into the parking lot of a shopping center and was nearly boxed in by the various police vehicles. Respondent evaded the trap by making a sharp turn, colliding with Scott's police car, exiting the parking lot, and speeding off once again down a two-lane highway.

Following respondent's shopping center maneuvering, which resulted in slight damage to Scott's police car, Scott took over as the lead pursuit vehicle. Six minutes and nearly 10 miles after the chase had begun, Scott decided to attempt to terminate the episode by employing a "Precision Intervention Technique ('PIT') maneuver, which causes the fleeing vehicle to spin to a stop." Having radioed his supervisor for permission, Scott was told to " 'go ahead and take him out.' " Instead, Scott applied his push bumper to the rear of respondent's vehicle. As a result, respondent lost control of his vehicle, which left the roadway, ran down an embankment, overturned, and crashed. Respondent was badly injured and was rendered a quadriplegic.

Respondent filed suit against Deputy Scott and others under 42 U.S.C. § 1983, alleging, *inter alia*, a violation of his federal constitutional rights, viz. use of excessive force resulting in an unreasonable seizure under the Fourth Amendment. [The District Court denied Scott's motion for summary judgment and the Eleventh circuit affirmed]. We granted certiorari, and now [reverse].

III

A

The first step in assessing the constitutionality of Scott's actions is to determine the relevant facts. As this case was decided on summary judgment, there have not yet been factual findings by a judge or jury, and respondent's version of events (unsurprisingly) differs substantially from Scott's version. When things are in such a posture, courts are required to view the facts and draw reasonable inferences "in the light most favorable to the party opposing the [summary judgment] motion."

There is, however, an added wrinkle in this case: existence in the record of a videotape capturing the events in question. There are no allegations or indications that this videotape was doctored or altered in any way, nor any contention that what it depicts differs from what actually happened. The videotape quite clearly contradicts the version of the story told by respondent and adopted by the Court of Appeals. For example, the Court of Appeals adopted respondent's assertions that, during the chase, "there was little, if any, actual threat to pedestrians or other motorists, as the roads were mostly empty and [respondent] remained in control of his vehicle." Indeed, reading the lower court's opinion, one gets the impression that respondent, rather than fleeing from police, was attempting to pass his driving test:

> "Taking the facts from the non-movant's viewpoint, [respondent] remained in control of his vehicle, slowed for turns and intersections, and typically used his indicators for turns. He did not run any motorists off the road. Nor was he a threat to pedestrians in the shopping center parking lot, which was free from pedestrian and vehicular traffic as the center was closed. Significantly, by the time the parties were back on the highway and Scott rammed [respondent], the motorway had been cleared of motorists and pedestrians allegedly because of police blockades of the nearby intersections."

The videotape tells quite a different story. There we see respondent's vehicle racing down narrow, two-lane roads in the dead of night at speeds that are shockingly fast. We see it swerve around more than a dozen other cars, cross the double-yellow line, and force cars traveling in both directions to their respective shoulders to avoid being hit. We see it run multiple red lights and travel for considerable periods of time in the occasional center left-turn-only lane, chased by numerous police cars forced to engage in the same hazardous maneuvers just to keep up. Far from being the cautious and controlled driver the lower court depicts, what we see on the video more closely resembles a Hollywood-style car chase of the most frightening sort, placing police officers and innocent bystanders alike at great risk of serious injury.

At the summary judgment stage, facts must be viewed in the light most favorable to the nonmoving party only if there is a "genuine" dispute as to those facts. Fed. Rule Civ. Proc. 56(c). As we have emphasized, "when the moving party has carried its burden under Rule 56(c), its opponent must do more than simply show that there is some metaphysical doubt as to the material facts. . . . Where the record taken as a whole could not lead a rational trier of fact to find for the nonmoving party, there is no 'genuine issue for trial.' " "The mere existence of *some* alleged factual dispute between the parties will not defeat an otherwise properly supported motion for summary judgment; the requirement is that there be no *genuine* issue of *material* fact." When opposing parties tell two different stories, one of which is blatantly contradicted by the record, so that no reasonable jury could believe it, a court should not adopt that version of the facts for purposes of ruling on a motion for summary judgment.

That was the case here with regard to the factual issue whether respondent was driving in such fashion as to endanger human life. Respondent's version of events is so utterly discredited by the record that no reasonable jury could have believed him. The Court of Appeals should not have relied on such visible fiction; it should have viewed the facts in the light depicted by the videotape.

B

Judging the matter on that basis, we think it is quite clear that Deputy Scott did not violate the Fourth Amendment. Scott does not contest that his decision to terminate the car chase by ramming his bumper into respondent's vehicle constituted a "seizure." [It] is also conceded, by both sides, that a claim of "excessive force in the course of making [a] . . . 'seizure' of [the] person . . . [is] properly analyzed under the Fourth Amendment's 'objective reasonableness' standard." *Graham v. Connor*, 490 U.S. 386, 388, 109 S. Ct. 1865, 104 L. Ed. 2d 443 (1989). The question we need to answer is whether Scott's actions were objectively reasonable.

1

Respondent urges us to analyze this case as we analyzed *Garner*. We must first decide, he says, whether the actions Scott took constituted "deadly force." (He defines "deadly force" as "any use of force which creates a substantial likelihood of causing death or serious bodily injury.") If so, respondent claims that *Garner* prescribes certain preconditions that must be met before Scott's actions can survive Fourth Amendment scrutiny: (1) The suspect must have posed an immediate threat of serious physical harm to the officer or others; (2) deadly force must have been necessary to prevent escape; and (3) where feasible, the officer must have given the suspect some warning. Since these *Garner* preconditions for using deadly force were not met in this case, Scott's actions were *per se* unreasonable.

Respondent's argument falters at its first step; *Garner* did not establish a magical on/off switch that triggers rigid preconditions whenever an officer's actions constitute "deadly force." *Garner* was simply an application of the Fourth Amendment's "reasonableness" test, *Graham, supra*, to the use of a particular type of force in a particular situation. *Garner* held that it was unreasonable to kill a "young, slight, and unarmed" burglary suspect, by shooting him "in the back of the head" while he was running away on foot, and when the officer "could not reasonably have believed that [the suspect] . . . posed any threat," and "never attempted to justify his actions on any basis other than the need to prevent an escape." Whatever *Garner* said about the factors that *might have* justified shooting the suspect in that case, such "preconditions" have scant applicability to this case, which has vastly different facts. "*Garner* had nothing to do with one car striking another or even with car chases in general. . . . A police car's bumping a fleeing car is, in fact, not much like a policeman's shooting a gun so as to hit a person." Nor is the threat posed by the flight on foot of an unarmed suspect even remotely comparable to the extreme danger to human life posed by respondent in this case. Although respondent's attempt to craft an easy-to-apply legal test in the Fourth Amendment context is admirable, in the end we must still slosh our way through the factbound morass of "reasonableness." Whether or not Scott's actions constituted application of "deadly force," all that matters is whether Scott's actions were reasonable.

In determining the reasonableness of the manner in which a seizure is effected, "we must balance the nature and quality of the intrusion on the individual's Fourth Amendment interests against the importance of the governmental interests alleged to justify the intrusion." Scott defends his actions by pointing to the paramount governmental interest in ensuring public safety, and respondent nowhere suggests this was not the purpose motivating Scott's behavior. Thus, in judging whether Scott's actions were reasonable, we must consider the risk of bodily harm that Scott's actions posed to respondent in light of the threat to the public that Scott was trying to eliminate. Although there is no obvious way to quantify the risks on either side, it is clear from the videotape that respondent posed an actual and imminent threat to the lives of any pedestrians who might have been present, to other civilian motorists, and to the officers involved in the chase. See Part III-A, *supra*. It is equally clear that Scott's actions posed a high likelihood of serious injury or death to respondent — though not the near *certainty* of death posed by, say, shooting a fleeing felon in the back of the head, see *Garner*, or pulling alongside a fleeing motorist's car and shooting the motorist. So how does a court go about weighing the perhaps lesser probability of injuring or killing numerous bystanders against the perhaps larger probability of injuring or killing a single person? We think it appropriate in this process to take into account not only the number of lives at risk, but also their relative culpability. It was respondent, after all, who intentionally placed himself and the public in danger by unlawfully engaging in the reckless, high-speed flight that ultimately produced the choice between two evils that Scott confronted. Multiple police cars, with blue lights flashing and sirens blaring, had been chasing respondent for nearly 10 miles, but he ignored their warning to stop. By contrast, those who might have been harmed had Scott not taken the action he did were entirely innocent. We have little difficulty in concluding it was reasonable for Scott to take the action that he did.

But wait, says respondent: Couldn't the innocent public equally have been protected, and the tragic accident entirely avoided, if the police had simply ceased their pursuit? We think the police need not have taken that chance and hoped for the best. Whereas Scott's action — ramming respondent off the road — was *certain* to eliminate the risk that respondent posed to the public, ceasing pursuit was not. First of all, there would have been no way to convey convincingly to respondent that the chase was off, and that he was free to go. Had respondent looked in his rear-view mirror and seen the police cars deactivate their flashing lights and turn around, he would have had no idea whether they were truly letting him get away, or simply devising a new strategy for capture. Perhaps the police knew a shortcut he didn't know, and would reappear down the road to intercept him; or perhaps they were setting up a roadblock in his path. Cf. *Brower*. Given such uncertainty, respondent might have been just as likely to respond by continuing to drive recklessly as by slowing down and wiping his brow.

Second, we are loath to lay down a rule requiring the police to allow fleeing suspects to get away whenever they drive *so recklessly* that they put other people's lives in danger. It is obvious the perverse incentives such a rule would create: Every fleeing motorist would know that escape is within his grasp, if only he accelerates to 90 miles per hour, crosses the double-yellow line a few times, and runs a few red lights. The Constitution assuredly does not impose this invitation to impunity-earned-by-recklessness. Instead, we lay down a more sensible rule: A police officer's attempt to terminate a dangerous high-speed car chase that threatens the lives of innocent bystanders does not violate the Fourth Amendment, even when it places the fleeing motorist at risk of serious injury or death.

The car chase that respondent initiated in this case posed a substantial and immediate risk of serious physical injury to others; no reasonable jury could conclude otherwise. Scott's attempt to terminate the chase by forcing respondent off the road was reasonable, and Scott is entitled to summary judgment. The Court of Appeals' decision to the contrary is reversed.

It is so ordered.

JUSTICE GINSBURG, concurring.

I join the Court's [opinion]. I do not read today's decision as articulating a mechanical, *per se* rule. The inquiry described by the Court is situation specific. Among relevant considerations: Were the lives and well-being of others (motorists, pedestrians, police officers) at risk? Was there a safer way, given the time, place, and circumstances, to stop the fleeing vehicle? "Admirable" as "[an] attempt to craft an easy-to-apply legal test in the Fourth Amendment context [may be]," the Court explains, "in the end we must still slosh our way through the factbound morass of '[reasonableness].' "

JUSTICE BREYER, concurring.

I join the Court's [opinion]. Because watching the video footage of the car chase made a difference to my own view of the case, I suggest that the interested reader take advantage of the link in the Court's opinion, and watch it. Having done so, I do not believe a reasonable jury could, in this instance, find that Officer Timothy Scott (who joined the chase late in the day and did not know the specific reason why the respondent was being pursued) acted in violation of the Constitution. [The] video makes clear the highly fact-dependent nature of this constitutional [determination].

I disagree with the Court insofar as it articulates a *per se* rule. The majority states: "A police officer's attempt to terminate a dangerous high-speed car chase that threatens the lives of innocent bystanders does not violate the Fourth Amendment, even when it places the fleeing motorist at risk of serious injury or death." This statement is too absolute. As Justice Ginsburg points out, whether a high-speed chase violates the Fourth Amendment may well depend upon more circumstances than the majority's rule reflects. With these qualifications, I join the Court's opinion.

JUSTICE STEVENS, dissenting.

Today, the Court asks whether an officer may "take actions that place a fleeing motorist at risk of serious injury or death in order to stop the motorist's flight from endangering the lives of innocent bystanders." Depending on the circumstances, the answer may be an obvious "yes," an obvious "no," or sufficiently doubtful that the question of the reasonableness of the officer's actions should be decided by a jury, after a review of the degree of danger and the alternatives available to the officer. A high speed chase in a desert in Nevada is, after all, quite different from one that travels through the heart of Las Vegas.

Relying on a *de novo* review of a videotape of a portion of a nighttime chase on a lightly traveled road in Georgia where no pedestrians or other "bystanders" were present, buttressed by uninformed speculation about the possible consequences of discontinuing the chase, eight of the jurors on this Court reach a verdict that differs from the views of the judges on both the District Court and the Court of Appeals who are surely more familiar with the hazards of driving on Georgia roads than we are. The Court's justification for this unprecedented departure from our well-settled standard of review of factual determinations made by a district court and affirmed by a court of appeals is based on its mistaken view that the Court of Appeals' description of the facts was "blatantly contradicted by the record" and that respondent's version of the events was "so utterly discredited by the record that no reasonable jury could have believed him."

Rather than supporting the conclusion that what we see on the video "resembles a Hollywood-style car chase of the most frightening sort," the tape actually confirms, rather than contradicts, the lower courts' appraisal of the factual questions at issue. More important, it surely does not provide a principled basis for depriving the respondent of his right to have a jury evaluate the question whether the police officers' decision to use deadly force to bring the chase to an end was reasonable.

Omitted from the Court's description of the initial speeding violation is the fact that respondent was on a four-lane portion of Highway 34 when the officer clocked his speed at 73 miles per hour and initiated the chase. More significant — and contrary to the Court's assumption that respondent's vehicle "forced cars traveling in both directions to their respective shoulders to avoid being hit" — a fact unmentioned in the text of the opinion explains why those cars pulled over prior to being passed by respondent. The sirens and flashing lights on the police cars following respondent gave the same warning that a speeding ambulance or fire engine would have provided. The 13 cars that respondent passed on his side of the road before entering the shopping center, and both of the cars that he passed on the right after leaving the center, no doubt had already pulled to the side of the road or were driving along the shoulder because they heard the police sirens or saw the flashing lights before respondent or the police cruisers approached. A jury could certainly conclude that those motorists were exposed to no greater risk than persons who take the same action in response to a speeding ambulance, and that their reactions were fully consistent with the evidence that respondent, though speeding, retained full control of his vehicle.

The police sirens also minimized any risk that may have arisen from running "multiple red lights." In fact, respondent and his pursuers went through only two intersections with stop lights and in both cases all other vehicles in sight were stationary, presumably because they had been warned of the approaching speeders. Incidentally, the videos do show that the lights were red when the police cars passed through them but, because the cameras were farther away when respondent did so and it is difficult to discern the color of the signal at that point, it is not entirely clear that he ran either or both of the red lights. In any event, the risk of harm to the stationary vehicles was minimized by the sirens, and there is no reason to believe that respondent would have disobeyed the signals if he were not being pursued.

My colleagues on the jury saw respondent "swerve around more than a dozen other cars," and "force cars traveling in both directions to their respective shoulders," but they apparently discounted the possibility that those cars were already out of the pursuit's path as a result of hearing the sirens. Even if that were not so, passing a slower vehicle on a two-lane road always involves some degree of swerving and is not especially dangerous if there are no cars coming from the opposite direction. At no point during the chase did respondent pull into the opposite lane other than to pass a car in front of him; he did the latter no more than five times and, on most of those occasions, used his turn signal. On none of these occasions was there a car traveling in the opposite direction. In fact, at one point, when respondent found himself behind a car in his own lane and there were cars traveling in the other direction, he slowed and waited for the cars traveling in the other direction to pass before overtaking the car in front of him while using his turn signal to do so. This is hardly the stuff of Hollywood. To the contrary, the video does not reveal any incidents that could even be remotely characterized as "close calls."

In sum, the factual statements by the Court of Appeals quoted by the Court were entirely accurate. That court did not describe respondent as a "cautious" driver as my colleagues imply, but it did correctly conclude that there is no evidence that he ever lost control of his vehicle. That court also correctly pointed out that the incident in the shopping center parking lot did not create any risk to pedestrians or other vehicles because the chase occurred just before 11 p.m. on a weekday night and the center was closed. It is apparent from the record (including the videotape) that local police had blocked off intersections to keep respondent from entering residential neighborhoods and possibly endangering other motorists. I would add that the videos also show that no pedestrians, parked cars, sidewalks, or residences were visible at any time during the chase. The only "innocent bystanders" who were placed "at great risk of serious injury," were the drivers who either pulled off the road in response to the sirens or passed respondent in the opposite direction when he was driving on his side of the road.

I recognize, of course, that even though respondent's original speeding violation on a four-lane highway was rather ordinary, his refusal to stop and subsequent flight was a serious offense that merited severe punishment. It was not, however, a capital offense, or even an offense that justified the use of deadly force rather than an abandonment of the chase. The Court's concern about the "imminent threat to the lives of any pedestrians who might have been present," while surely valid in an appropriate case, should be discounted in a case involving a nighttime chase in an area where no pedestrians were present.

Whether a person's actions have risen to a level warranting deadly force is a question of fact best reserved for a jury. Here, the Court has usurped the jury's factfinding function and, in doing so, implicitly labeled the four other judges to review the case unreasonable. It chastises the Court of Appeals for failing to "view the facts in the light depicted by the videotape" and implies that no reasonable person could view the videotape and come to the conclusion that deadly force was unjustified. However, the three judges on the Court of Appeals panel apparently did view the videotapes entered into evidence and described a very different version of events:

> "At the time of the ramming, apart from speeding and running two red lights, Harris was driving in a non-aggressive fashion (i.e., without trying to ram or run into the officers). Moreover, . . . Scott's path on the open highway was largely clear. The videos introduced into evidence show little to no vehicular (or pedestrian) traffic, allegedly because of the late hour and

the police blockade of the nearby intersections. Finally, Scott issued absolutely no warning (e.g., over the loudspeaker or otherwise) prior to using deadly force."

If two groups of judges can disagree so vehemently about the nature of the pursuit and the circumstances surrounding that pursuit, it seems eminently likely that a reasonable juror could disagree with this Court's characterization of events. Moreover, under the standard set forth in *Garner*, it is certainly possible that "a jury could conclude that Scott unreasonably used deadly force to seize Harris by ramming him off the road under the instant circumstances."

The Court today sets forth a *per se* rule that presumes its own version of the facts: "A police officer's attempt to terminate a dangerous high-speed car chase *that threatens the lives of innocent bystanders* does not violate the Fourth Amendment, even when it places the fleeing motorist at risk of serious injury or death."(emphasis added). Not only does that rule fly in the face of the flexible and case-by-case "reasonableness" approach applied in *Garner* and *Graham v. Connor*, but it is also arguably inapplicable to the case at hand, given that it is not clear that this chase threatened the life of any "innocent bystander." In my view, the risks inherent in justifying unwarranted police conduct on the basis of unfounded assumptions are unacceptable, particularly when less drastic measures — in this case, the use of stop sticks or a simple warning issued from a loudspeaker — could have avoided such a tragic result. In my judgment, jurors in Georgia should be allowed to evaluate the reasonableness of the decision to ram respondent's speeding vehicle in a manner that created an obvious risk of death and has in fact made him a quadriplegic at the age of 19.

I respectfully dissent.

NOTES ON EXCESSIVE FORCE CLAIMS AFTER *SCOTT*

1. In *Plumhoff v. Rickard*, 134 S. Ct. 2012 (2014), police officers shot the plaintiff 15 times at the conclusion of a high speed chase. Ruling on a motion for summary judgment, the Court held, as a matter of law, that on the undisputed facts this was not excessive force:

[T]he chase in this case exceeded 100 miles per hour and lasted over five minutes. During that chase, Rickard passed more than two dozen other vehicles, several of which were forced to alter course. Rickard's outrageously reckless driving posed a grave public safety risk. And while it is true that Rickard's car eventually collided with a police car and came temporarily to a near standstill, that did not end the chase. Less than three seconds later, Rickard resumed maneuvering his car. Just before the shots were fired, when the front bumper of his car was flush with that of one of the police cruisers, Rickard was obviously pushing down on the accelerator because the car's wheels were spinning, and then Rickard threw the car into reverse "in an attempt to escape." Thus, the record conclusively disproves respondent's claim that the chase in the present case was already over when petitioners began shooting. Under the circumstances at the moment when the shots were fired, all that a reasonable police officer could have concluded was that Rickard was intent on resuming his flight and that, if he was allowed to do so, he would once again pose a deadly threat for others on the road. Rickard's conduct even after the shots were fired — as noted, he managed to drive away despite the efforts of the police to block his path — underscores the point. In light of the circumstances we have discussed, it is beyond serious dispute that Rickard's flight posed a grave public safety risk, and here, as in *Scott*, the police acted reasonably in using deadly force to end that risk.

2. Do *Scott* and *Plumhoff* bar all suits arising out of injuries caused by high speed chases? In *Abney v. Coe*, 493 F.3d 412 (4th Cir. 2007), Abney, a motorcyclist, died in a collision with a sheriff deputy's car following an eight-mile pursuit. The officer, Rodney Coe, had "observed a motorcycle driven by Gerald Abney (who was later determined to be driving under the influence of methamphetamine) crossing double yellow lines while passing a vehicle on a curve. Deputy Coe turned around his patrol car and activated his blue flashing lights and siren in an attempt to pull Abney over. Abney did not stop, however." Coe gave chase. Eventually, under the plaintiff's version of the facts, "Coe intentionally rammed the rear of Abney's motorcycle," resulting in Abney's death at the scene. The Fourth Circuit relied on *Scott* in affirming summary judgment for Coe. Possible distinctions between the two cases were unimportant:

> The fact that unlike Scott, Abney did not accelerate to 85 miles per hour is not dispositive; indeed, the narrow, winding, two-lane roads in this case all but prohibited such speeds. The fact that Abney was driving during the day and Harris in the dead of night means only that Abney had the opportunity to scare more motorists to death. Similarly, the fact that Abney was driving a motorcycle, rather than a car, does not require a different result since the probability that a motorist will be harmed by a Precision Intervention Technique is high in either circumstance.

What result if the chase ends in a collision, the driver survives, and the officer then shoots the driver? *See Adams v. Speers*, 473 F.3d 989 (9th Cir. 2007) (holding that on these facts the officer would be liable.) *Adams* was decided shortly before the Supreme Court ruled in *Scott*. Is it still good law after *Plumhoff*?

Suppose the police chase a motorcyclist and run him off the road without touching the vehicle. One recent case holds that no Fourth Amendment suit can be brought because no "seizure" has taken place absent a touching. *See Steen v. Myers*, 486 F.3d 1017 (7th Cir. 2007). Do the Supreme Court's cases support the proposition that no seizure occurs absent a touching?

3. *Long v. Slaton*, 508 F.3d 576 (11th Cir. 2007), presents an interesting variation on the "vehicular" excessive force issue. Brian Long suffered from psychosis. According to the complaint, his father called the sheriff's department and requested assistance:

> Deputy Slaton responded to the call and arrived at the Long residence shortly thereafter. Slaton, who was alone, got out of his marked sheriff's cruiser, leaving the keys in the ignition and the driver's door open, Slaton then spoke to Long's father, who explained his desire that Long be detained

due to Long's psychosis. When Deputy Slaton asked Long's father if Long had been physically violent with him, the father responded, "no."

Deputy Slaton then approached Long, who was at the end of the driveway, close to the house. Slaton pulled out handcuffs and told Long that Slaton would take Long to jail. Long voiced his disagreement and then ran over to and got inside Slaton's cruiser and closed the door. Slaton then ran to the driver's side of the cruiser, pointed his pistol at Long, and ordered Long to get out of the cruiser. Deputy Slaton threatened to shoot Long if Long did not comply. Long then shifted the cruiser into reverse and began backing away and down the driveway toward the road. Slaton stepped into the middle of the driveway and fired three shots at Long as the sheriff's cruiser moved away. One shot went through the windshield and struck Long in the chest. The cruiser stopped as it rolled into an embankment and Long died after about a minute. At the time, backup law enforcement was en route.

The Eleventh Circuit ruled that the complaint should be dismissed because

Deputy Slaton's force was objectively reasonable under the Fourth Amendment. Although Slaton's decision to fire his weapon risked Long's death, that decision was not outside the range of reasonableness in the light of the potential danger posed to officers and to the public if Long was allowed to flee in a stolen police cruiser. [Even] if we accept that the threat posed by Long to Deputy Slaton was not immediate in that the cruiser was not moving toward Slaton when shots were fired, the law does not require officers in a tense and dangerous situation to wait until the moment a suspect used a deadly weapon to used the police cruiser as a deadly weapon, Long's unstable frame of mind energetic evasion of the deputy's physical control, Long's criminal act of stealing a police cruiser, and Long's starting to drive-even after being warned of deadly force-to a public road gave the deputy reason to believe that Long was dangerous.

Does *Long* fall within the rule announced in *Scott*? The Eleventh Circuit panel cited *Scott*, but did not rely heavily on that case. Are there legally significant differences between the two fact patterns? Does it matter that Long was mentally ill and, before his encounter with Slaton, had not committed a crime? Did Slaton's actions (leaving his key in the ignition of an unlocked police cruiser in the vicinity of a person in the midst of a psychotic episode) contribute to the danger? If so, should this have legal significance? Notice that the court ruled that the complaint should be dismissed. Would factual development be useful in resolving this case? Does *Plumhoff* bolster the Eleventh Circuit's reasoning?

B. Equal Protection

VILLAGE OF WILLOWBROOK v. OLECH
528 U.S. 562 (2000)

PER CURIAM. Respondent Grace Olech and her late husband Thaddeus asked petitioner Village of Willowbrook to connect their property to the municipal water supply. The Village at first conditioned the connection on the Olechs granting the Village a 33-foot easement. The Olechs objected, claiming that the Village only required a 15-foot easement from other property owners seeking access to the water supply. After a 3-month delay, the Village relented and agreed to provide water service with only a 15-foot easement.

Olech sued the Village claiming that the Village's demand of an additional 18-foot easement violated the Equal Protection Clause of the Fourteenth Amendment. Olech asserted that the 33-foot easement demand was "irrational and wholly arbitrary"; that the Village's demand was actually motivated by ill will resulting from the Olechs' previous filing of an unrelated, successful lawsuit against the Village; and that the Village acted either with the intent to deprive Olech of her rights or in reckless disregard of her rights.

[We] granted certiorari to determine whether the Equal Protection Clause gives rise to a cause of action on behalf of a "class of one" where the plaintiff did not allege membership in a class or group. Our cases have recognized successful equal protection claims brought by a "class of one," where the plaintiff alleges that she has been intentionally treated differently from others similarly situated and that there is no rational basis for the difference in treatment. In so doing, we have explained that " 'the purpose of the equal protection clause of the Fourteenth Amendment is to secure every person within the State's jurisdiction against intentional and arbitrary discrimination, whether occasioned by express terms of a statute or by its improper execution through duly constituted agents.' "

That reasoning is applicable to this case. Olech's complaint can fairly be construed as alleging that the Village intentionally demanded a 33-foot easement as a condition of connecting her property to the municipal water supply where the Village required only a 15-foot easement from other similarly situated property owners. The complaint also alleged that the Village's demand was "irrational and wholly arbitrary" and that the Village ultimately connected her property after receiving a clearly adequate 15-foot easement. These allegations, quite apart from the Village's subjective motivation, are sufficient to state a claim for relief under traditional equal protection analysis. We therefore affirm the judgment of the Court of Appeals, but do not reach the alternative theory of "subjective ill will" relied on by that court.

JUSTICE BREYER, concurring in the result.

The Solicitor General and the Village of Willowbrook have expressed concern lest we interpret the Equal Protection Clause in this case in a way that would transform many ordinary violations of city or state law into violations of the Constitution. It might be thought that a rule that looks only to an intentional difference in treatment and a lack of a rational basis for that different treatment would work such a transformation. Zoning decisions, for example, will often, perhaps almost always, treat one landowner differently from another, and one might claim that, when a city's zoning authority takes an action that fails to conform to a city zoning regulation, it lacks a "rational basis" for its action (at least if the regulation in question is reasonably clear).

This case, however, does not directly raise the question whether the simple and common instance of a faulty zoning decision would violate the Equal Protection Clause. That is because the Court of Appeals found that in this case respondent had alleged an extra factor as well — a factor that the Court of Appeals called "vindictive action," "illegitimate animus," or "ill will."

In my view, the presence of that added factor in this case is sufficient to minimize any concern about transforming run-of-the-mill zoning cases into cases of constitutional right. For this reason, along with the others mentioned by the Court, I concur in the result.

NOTES

1. In *Engquist v. Oregon Dep't of Agriculture*, 553 U.S. 591 (2008), the Court limited the scope of the "class of one" equal protection suit, holding that it "has no place in the public employment context." Engquist and another employee had quarreled for some years. When a new supervisor promoted her antagonist and eliminated Engquist's position, she sued on several grounds, including a "class of one" claim that she was fired for "arbitrary, vindictive, and malicious reasons." At trial the jury found in her favor on that claim. On appeal the Ninth Circuit reversed and the Supreme Court affirmed the Ninth Circuit ruling.

Relying on earlier public employment cases, including public employee speech cases, see *infra* section C, the Court said:

> Our precedent in the public-employee context . . . establishes two main principles: First, although government employees do not lose their constitutional rights when they accept their positions, those rights must be balanced against the realities of the employment context. Second, in striking the appropriate balance, we consider whether the asserted employee right implicates the basic concerns of the relevant constitutional provision, or whether the claimed right can more readily give way to the requirements of the government as [employer.]

> Our equal protection jurisprudence has typically been concerned with governmental classifications that affect some groups differently than [others.] Plaintiffs in such cases generally allege that they have been arbitrarily classified as members of an identifiable group. [Recognition] of the class-of-one theory of equal protection on the facts in *Olech* was not so much a departure from the principle that the Equal Protection Clause is concerned with arbitrary government classification, as it was an application of that principle. [When] those who appear similarly situated are nevertheless treated differently, the Equal Protection Clause requires at least a rational reason for the difference, to assure that all persons subject to

legislation or regulation are indeed being treated alike, under like circumstances and [conditions.]

What seems to have been significant in *Olech* [was] the existence of a clear standard against which departures, even for a single plaintiff, could be readily assessed. There was no indication in *Olech* that the zoning board was exercising discretionary authority based on subjective, individualized determination — at least not with regard to easement length, however typical such determinations may be as a general zoning matter. Rather, the complaint alleged that the board consistently require only a 15-foot easement, but subjected Olech to a 33-foot [easement.]

There are some forms of state action, however, which by their nature involve discretionary decisionmaking based on a vast array of subjective, individualized assessments. In such cases the rule that people should be "treated alike, under like circumstances and conditions" is not violated when one person is treated differently from others, because treating like individuals differently is an accepted consequence of the discretion granted. In such situations, allowing a challenge based on the arbitrary singling out of a particular persons would undermine the very discretion that such state officials are entrusted to exercise.

Suppose, for example, that a traffic officer is stationed on a busy freeway where people often drive above the speed limit, and there is no basis upon which to distinguish them. If the office gives only one of those people a ticket, it may be good English to say that the officer has created a class of people that did not get speeding tickets, and a "class of one" that did. But assuming that it is in the nature of the particular government activity that not all speeders can be stopped and ticketed, complaining that one has been singled out for no reason does not invoke the fear of improper government classification. [Allowing] an equal protection claim on the ground that a ticket was given to one person and not others, even if for no discernible or articulable reason, would be incompatible with the discretion inherent in the challenged action. It is no proper challenge to what in its nature is a subjective, individualized decision that it was subjective and individualized.

This principle applies most clearly in the employment context, for employment decisions are quite often subjective and individualized, resting on a wide array of factors that are difficult to articulate and quantify. [Thus,] the class-of-one theory of equal protection — which presupposes that like individuals should be treated alike, and that to treat them differently is to classify them in a way that must survive at least rationality review — is simply a poor fit in the public employment context. To treat employees differently is not to classify them in a way that raises equal protection concerns. Rather, it is simply to exercise the broad discretion that typically characterizes the employer-employee relationship.

[Even] if we accepted Enquist's claim, it would be difficult for a plaintiff to show that an employment decision is arbitrary. [The] practical problem with allowing class-of-one claims to go forward in this context is not that it will be too easy for plaintiffs to prevail, but that governments will be forced to defend a multitude of such claims in the first place, and courts will be obliged to sort through them in a search for the proverbial needle in a haystack. The Equal Protection Clause does not require "this displacement of managerial discretion by judicial supervision." *Garcetti v. Ceballos,* [*infra.*]

JUSTICE STEVENS, joined by JUSTICES SOUTER and GINSBURG, dissented:

The majority asserts that public-employment decisions should be carved out of our equal protection jurisprudence because employment decisions (as opposed to, for example, zoning decisions) are inherently discretionary. I agree that employers must be free to exercise discretionary authority. But there is a clear distinction between an exercise of discretion and an arbitrary decision. A discretionary decision represents a choice of one among two or more rational alternatives. [The] choice may be mistaken or unwise without being irrational. [The] hypothetical traffic officer described in the Court's opinion had a rational basis for giving a ticket to *every* speeder passing him on the highway. His inability to arrest every driver on sight provides an adequate justification for making a random choice from a group of equally guilty and equally accessible violators.

A comparable hypothetical decision in the employment context (e.g., a supervisor who is required to eliminate one position due to an involuntary reduction-in-force and who chooses to terminate one of several equally culpable employees) also differs from the instant case insofar as it assumes the existence of a rational basis for the individual decision. The fact that a supervisor might not be able to explain why he terminated one employee rather than another will not give rise to an equal protection claim so long as there was a rational basis for the termination itself and for the decision to terminate just one, rather than all, of the culpable employees.

2.   The Court in *Engquist* states that "all we decide" is that "the class-of-one theory of equal protection has no application in the public employment context." Is the reasoning of the opinion so limited? *Compare Corey Airport Services v. Clear Channel Outdoor,* 682 F.3d 1293, 1297 n.2 (11th Cir. 2012) (class-of-one theory is not available to challenge the discretionary decisions involved in awarding municipal contracts, citing *Engquist*) *with Analytical Diagnostic Labs, Inc. v. Kusel,* 626 F.3d 135, 142 (2d Cir. 2010) (*Engquist* does not bar all class-of-one claims involving discretionary state action).

3.   The Court does not respond directly to the distinction drawn by the dissent between "an exercise of discretion and an arbitrary decision." Why not? Is the Court's traffic officer hypothetical an apt analogy to Engquist's case? Note that, at the end of the opinion, the Court discussed the "practical problem with allowing class-of-one claims to go forward in this context" (i.e., "that governments will be forced to defend a multitude of such claims in the first place.") Is this just another way of expressing the earlier concern with protecting discretionary authority? Does the Court's holding amount to a judgment that, in order to obtain that protection, it is necessary to shield officials who in fact act for "arbitrary, vindictive, and malicious" reasons?

4. Justice Breyer joined the majority in *Engquist.* Is his vote consistent with his concurring opinion in *Olech?* In any event, the "animus" theme he stressed in his *Olech* opinion may be crucial to the plaintiff's success. *Compare Swanson v. City of Chetek,* 719 F.3d 780 (7th Cir. 2013) (plaintiff's evidence of animus is sufficient to survive summary judgment) *with Loesel v. City of Frankenmuth,* 692 F.3d 452 (6th Cir. 2012) (reversing a jury verdict for plaintiff on account of lack of evidence of animus). On the other hand, some courts explicitly disavow the need for such a showing. *See Gerhart v. Lake County, Montana,* 637 F.3d 1013, 1022 (9th Cir. 2011) ("By looking for evidence of the Commissioners' personal animosity towards Gerhart, the district court incorrectly analyzed Gerhart's 'class of one' claim, which does not require a showing of the government officials' subjective bad feelings towards him.")

C. Public Employee Speech

The most heavily litigated free speech fact pattern in constitutional torts–or in any other context, for that matter — concerns a public employee who is fired or otherwise penalized on account of his speech. The first principle to keep in mind here is that the state may not simply condition public employment on the employee giving up constitutional rights. In *Pickering v. Board of Education,* 391 U.S. 563 (1968), a teacher was fired for writing a letter to the editor of the local paper, in which he criticized school board decisions on school finance. He sued for reinstatement and won. The Supreme Court rejected the view that public employees "may constitutionally be compelled to relinquish the First Amendment rights they would otherwise enjoy as citizens to comment on matters of public interest." On the other hand, the Court also recognized that

> [t]he State has interests as an employer in regulating the speech of its employees that differ significantly from those it possesses in connection with regulation of the speech of the citizenry in general. The problem in any case is to arrive at a balance between the interests of the teacher, as a citizen, in commenting upon matters of public concern and the interest of the State, as an employer, in promoting the efficiency of the public services it performs through its employees.

Applying this balancing test to the facts of Pickering's case, the Court concluded that the statements in the letter would have little if any impact on the efficiency of the workplace, since his "employment relationships with the Board and [the] superintendent are not the kind of close working relationships for which it can persuasively be claimed that personal loyalty and confidence are necessary to their proper functioning." On the other side of the balance, "the question whether a school system requires extra funds is a matter of legitimate public concern." On such a question, "free and open public debate is vital to informed decision-making by the electorate. Teachers are [the] members of the community most likely to have informed and definite opinions as to how funds allotted to the operation of the schools should be spent."

Pickering established that public employees may not be fired just because of their speech. In *Connick v. Myers,* the Supreme Court emphasized that the free speech rights of public employees are more limited than those of "the citizenry in general."

CONNICK v. MYERS
461 U.S. 138 (1983)

JUSTICE WHITE delivered the opinion of the Court.

Sheila Myers was employed as an Assistant District Attorney in New Orleans for five and a half years. She served at the pleasure of petitioner Harry Connick, the District Attorney for Orleans Parish. During this period Myers competently performed her responsibilities of trying criminal cases.

In the early part of October 1980, Myers was informed that she would be transferred to prosecute cases in a different section of the criminal court. Myers was strongly opposed to the proposed transfer and expressed her view to several of her supervisors, including Connick.

[Myers] prepared a questionnaire soliciting the views of her fellow staff members concerning office transfer policy, office morale, the need for a grievance committee, the level of confidence in supervisors, and whether employees felt pressured to work in political campaigns. Myers distributed the questionnaire to 15 Assistant District Attorneys. Shortly after noon, Dennis Waldron learned that Myers was distributing the survey. He immediately phoned Connick and informed him that Myers was creating a "mini-insurrection" within the office. Connick returned to the office and told Myers that she was being terminated because of her refusal to accept the transfer. She was also told that her distribution of the questionnaire was considered an act of insubordination. Connick particularly objected to the question which inquired whether employees "had confidence in and would rely on the word" of various superiors in the office, and to a question concerning pressure to work in political campaigns which he felt would be damaging if discovered by the press.

Myers filed suit under § 1983, contending that her employment was wrongfully terminated because she had exercised her constitutionally protected right of free speech. [The district court and the court of appeals agreed with Myers. The Supreme Court reversed.]

[Connick] contends at the outset that no balancing of interests is required in this case because Myers' questionnaire concerned only internal office matters and that such speech is not upon a matter of "public concern," as the term was used in *Pickering*. Although we do not agree that Myers' communication in this case was wholly without First Amendment protection, there is much force to Connick's submission. The repeated emphasis in *Pickering* on the right of a public employee "as a citizen, in commenting upon matters of public concern," was not accidental. This language reflects both the historical evolvement of the rights of public employees, and the common-sense realization that government offices could not function if every employment decision became a constitutional matter.

When employee expression cannot be fairly considered as relating to any matter of political, social, or other concern to the community, government officials should enjoy wide latitude in managing their offices, without intrusive oversight by the judiciary in the name of the First Amendment. Perhaps the government employer's dismissal of the worker may not be fair, but ordinary dismissals from government service which violate no fixed tenure or applicable statute or regulation are not subject to judicial review even if the reasons for the dismissal are alleged to be mistaken or unreasonable.

We do not suggest, however, that Myers' speech, even if not touching upon a matter of public concern, is totally beyond the protection of the First Amendment. We in no sense suggest that speech on private matters falls into one of the narrow and well-defined classes of expression which carries so little social value, such as obscenity, that the State can prohibit and punish such expression by all persons in its jurisdiction. For example, an employee's false criticism of his employer on grounds not of public concern may be cause for his discharge but would be entitled to the same protection in a libel action accorded an identical statement made by a man on the street. We hold only that when a public employee speaks not as a citizen upon matters of public concern, but instead as an employee upon matters only of personal interest, absent the most unusual circumstances, a federal court is not the appropriate forum in which to review the wisdom of a personnel decision taken by a public agency allegedly in reaction to the employee's behavior. Our responsibility is to ensure that citizens are not deprived of fundamental rights by virtue of working for the government; this does not require a grant of immunity for employee grievances not afforded by the First Amendment to those who do not work for the State.

Whether an employee's speech addresses a matter of public concern must be determined by the content, form, and context of a given statement, as revealed by the whole record. In this case, with but one exception, the questions posed by Myers to her co-workers do not fall under the rubric of matters of "public concern." We view the questions pertaining to the confidence and trust that Myers' co-workers possess in various supervisors, the level of office morale, and the need for a grievance committee as mere extensions of Myers' dispute over her transfer to another section of the criminal court. Unlike the dissent, we do not believe these questions are of public import in evaluating the performance of the District Attorney as an elected official. Myers did not seek to inform the public that the District Attorney's Office was not discharging its governmental responsibilities in the investigation and prosecution of criminal cases. Nor did Myers seek to bring to light actual or potential wrongdoing or breach of public trust on the part of Connick and others. Indeed, the questionnaire, if released to the public, would convey no information at all other than the fact that a single employee is upset with the status quo. While discipline and morale in the workplace are related to an agency's efficient performance of its duties, the focus of Myers' questions is not to evaluate the performance of the office but rather to gather ammunition for another round of controversy with her superiors. These questions reflect one employee's dissatisfaction with a transfer and an attempt to turn that displeasure into a cause celebre.

To presume that all matters which transpire within a government office are of public concern would mean that virtually every remark — and certainly every criticism directed at a public official — would plant the seed of a constitutional case. [The] First Amendment does not require a public office to be run as a roundtable for employee complaints over internal office affairs.

One question in Myers' questionnaire, however, does touch upon a matter of public concern. Question 11 inquires if assistant district attorneys "ever feel pressured to work in political campaigns on behalf of office supported candidates." [Official] pressure upon employees to work for political candidates not of the worker's own choice constitutes a coercion of belief in violation of fundamental constitutional rights. In addition, there is a demonstrated interest in this country that government service should depend upon meritorious performance rather than political service. Given this history, we believe it apparent that the issue of whether assistant district attorneys are pressured to work in political campaigns is a matter of interest to the community upon which it is essential that public employees be able to speak out freely without fear of retaliatory dismissal. Because one of the questions in Myers' survey touched upon a matter of public concern and contributed to her discharge, we must determine whether Connick was justified in discharging Myers. Here the District Court again erred in imposing an unduly onerous burden on the State to justify Myers' discharge. The District Court viewed the issue of whether Myers' speech was upon a matter of "public concern" as a threshold inquiry, after which it became the government's burden to "clearly demonstrate" that the speech involved "substantially interfered" with official responsibilities. Yet *Pickering* unmistakably states that the State's burden in justifying a particular discharge varies depending upon the nature of the employee's expression. Although such particularized balancing is difficult, the courts must reach the most appropriate possible balance of the competing interests.

The *Pickering* balance requires full consideration of the government's interest in the effective and efficient fulfillment of its responsibilities to the public. [Connick's judgment] was that Myers' questionnaire was an act of insubordination which interfered with working relationships. When close working relationships are essential to fulfilling public responsibilities, a wide degree of deference to the employer's judgment is appropriate. Furthermore, we do not see the necessity for an employer to allow events to unfold to the extent that the disruption of the office and the destruction of working relationships is manifest before taking action. We caution that a stronger showing may be necessary if the employee's speech more substantially involved matters of public concern.

[Also] relevant is the manner, time, and place in which the questionnaire was distributed. [Here] the questionnaire was prepared and distributed at the office; the manner of distribution required not only Myers to leave her work but others to do the same in order that the questionnaire be completed. Although some latitude in when official work is performed is to be allowed when professional employees are involved, and Myers did not violate announced office policy, the fact that Myers, unlike Pickering, exercised her rights to speech at the office supports Connick's fears that the functioning of his office was endangered.

[Finally,] the context in which the dispute arose is also significant. This is not a case where an employee, out of purely academic interest, circulated a questionnaire so as to obtain useful research. Myers acknowledges that it is no coincidence that the questionnaire followed upon the heels of the transfer notice. When employee speech concerning office policy arises from an employment dispute concerning the very application of that policy to the speaker, additional weight must be given to the supervisor's view that the employee has threatened the authority of the employer to run the office. Although we accept the District Court's factual finding that Myers' reluctance to accede to the transfer order was not a sufficient cause in itself for her dismissal, [this] does not render irrelevant the fact that the questionnaire emerged after a persistent dispute between Myers and Connick and his deputies over office transfer policy.

Myers' questionnaire touched upon matters of public concern in only a most limited sense; her survey, in our view, is most accurately characterized as an employee grievance concerning internal office policy. The limited First Amendment interest involved here does not require that Connick tolerate action which he reasonably believed would disrupt the office, undermine his authority, and destroy close working relationships. Myers' discharge therefore did not offend the First Amendment. We reiterate, however, the caveat we expressed in *Pickering:* "Because of the enormous variety of fact situations in which critical statements by . . . public employees may be thought by their superiors . . . to furnish grounds for dismissal, we do not deem it either appropriate or feasible to attempt to lay down a general standard against which all such statements may be judged."

Our holding today is grounded in our longstanding recognition that the First Amendment's primary aim is the full protection of speech upon issues of public concern, as well as the practical realities involved in the administration of a government office. Although today the balance is struck for the government, this is no defeat for the First Amendment. For it would indeed be a Pyrrhic victory for the great principles of free expression if the Amendment's safeguarding of a public employee's right, as a citizen, to participate in discussions concerning public affairs were confused with the attempt to constitutionalize the employee grievance that we see presented here.

JUSTICE BRENNAN, with whom JUSTICE BLACKMUN, JUSTICE MARSHALL, and JUSTICE STEVENS join, dissenting.

[The] Court's decision today is flawed in three respects. First, the Court distorts the balancing analysis required under *Pickering* by suggesting that one factor, the context in which a statement is made, is to be weighed *twice* — first in determining whether an employee's speech addresses a matter of public concern and then in deciding whether the statement adversely affected the government's interest as an employer. Second, in concluding that the effect of respondent's personnel policies on employee morale and the work performance of the District Attorney's Office is not a matter of public concern, the Court impermissibly narrows the class of subjects on which public employees may speak out without fear of retaliatory dismissal. Third, the Court misapplies the *Pickering* balancing test in holding that Myers could constitutionally be dismissed for circulating a questionnaire addressed to at least one subject that *was* "a matter of interest to the community," in the absence of evidence that her conduct disrupted the efficient functioning of the District Attorney's [Office.]

NOTES

1. Suppose an employee speaks privately with a supervisor about race discrimination in the workplace. The employee is fired and sues. The employer argues that the free speech rights of public employees extend only to speech that informs the public. The employee maintains that the key issue is not whether the speech is directed at an audience outside the workplace but whether it is on a matter of public concern. Who has the better of this argument? *See Givhan v. Western Line Consolidated School District*, 439 U.S. 410 (1979) (employee wins).

2. Sometimes it is uncertain whether the employee made the statements attributed to her, and for which she is fired. Does the employee win if she can show that she did not really say the things that led to the dismissal? Conversely, does the employer prevail in such a case, on the theory that the dismissal was not on account of speech? *See Waters v. Churchill*, 511 U.S. 661 (1994). In this case supervisors fired Waters, a nurse, because of comments she was thought to have made disparaging a superior. Justice O'Connor's plurality opinion ruled that the employer would win so long as it made a reasonable investigation into what was said before firing Waters, even if the employer believed the wrong account. *See, e.g., Swetlik v. Crawford*, 738 F.3d 818, 828–29 (7th Cir. 2013) (finding after reviewing the facts, that "the undisputed evidence thus shows that the defendants were justified in bringing termination charges against Swetlik on the basis of the investigation report").

Suppose the employee denies having said anything. *Wasson v. Sonoma County Junior College*, 203 F.3d 659 (9th Cir. 2000), held that "there can be no First Amendment claim when an employee is falsely accused of making statements uttered by someone else." A dissenting judge "would find *Waters* fully applicable to this case: to determine what wasn't said by the employee is equally as important as determining what was said. In this case as well as *Waters*, the issue is whether the employee was wrongfully accused and whether the utterance was or was not protected." (B. Fletcher, J., dissenting.) Who has the better of this argument?

3. *Connick* distinguished between the parts of the questionnaire that dealt with "internal office matters," such as morale among the employees and the one question that asked about pressure to work in political campaigns. The former concerned speech on matters of private concern. Only the latter addressed a matter of public concern. The distinction is critical in litigation in this area, because the employee cannot win unless his speech falls into the public concern category. Following *Connick*, lower courts generally distinguish between speech expressing personal grievances and speech directed at broader topics.

In *Graber v. Clarke*, 763 F.3d 888 (7th Cir. 2014), Graber, a deputy sheriff at the time, had spoken with other officers about mandatory overtime work, doing so in his capacity as a union representative. He was "legitimately concerned that deputies were not getting sufficient rest, raising a potential threat to their safety and the safety of the public." On this occasion, the court said, he spoke as a citizen on an issue of public concern. *Id.* at 895. Yet on another occasion Graber "chose to aggressively approach Nyklewicz, a superior" regarding the situation of a particular officer. The district court "found Nyklewicz to be a credible witness and determined that Graber's speech was that of a disgruntled employee, not a citizen." The appellate court affirmed. *Id.* at 897. *Compare Bradshaw v. Pittsburgh Indep. School Dist.*, 207 F.3d 814, 816–18 (5th Cir. 2000) (high school principal's memoranda regarding buy-out of her contract were not on a matter of public concern); *Holbrook v. City of Alpharetta*, 112 F.3d 1522, 1530 (11th Cir. 1997) (holding that complaint of personal discrimination by the agency was not "public concern"); *Roe v. City & County of San Francisco*, 109 F.3d 578, 585 (9th Cir. 1997) (noting that "if the communication is essentially self-interested [then] it is not of public concern"); *Bernheim v. Litt*, 79 F.3d 318, 324–25 (2d Cir. 1996) (employee's speech related to employment conditions is not on a matter of public concern); *with Paradis v. Montrose Memorial Hospital*, 157 F.3d 815, 818 (10th Cir. 1998) (accusing a hospital administrator of unethical and illegal conduct is public concern speech); *Campbell v. Arkansas Department of Correction*, 155 F.3d 950, 958–59 (8th Cir. 1998) (speaking about corruption and lack of security at a prison is public concern speech); *Thomas v. Whalen*, 51 F.3d 1285, 1290 (6th Cir. 1995) (opposing gun control legislation is public concern speech).

Does a school teacher, in choosing what to cover in class, speak on matters of public or private concern? *See Cockrel v. Shelby County School District*, 270 F.3d 1036, 1051 (6th Cir. 2001) (rejecting the view, adopted by some other courts, that "a teacher, regardless of what he decides to include in his curriculum, is speaking as an employee on a private matter").

4. Even if the employee can show that his speech was on a matter of public concern, he may still lose. *Connick* directs the court to balance the value of the speech against its potential for disrupting and otherwise interfering with the efficient operation of the workplace. In *Cockrel, supra,* the "speech" was the decision by the teacher "to bring industrial hemp advocates into her class." Upon finding that this met the "public concern" test, the court balanced its value against "the State's interest as an employer in maintaining a productive work-place." It concluded that "on balance, the defendants' interests in an efficient operation of the school and a harmonious workplace do not outweigh the plaintiff's interests in speaking about the benefits of industrial hemp, an issue of substantial political and economic concern in Kentucky." A significant factor in the balance was that the school authorities had given prior approval for the presentations, thus this was a case in which "the disruptive effects of the speech can be traced back to the government's express decision permitting the employee to engage in that speech."

Compare Melzer v. New York City Board of Education, 336 F.3d 185 (2d Cir. 2003). Here the plaintiff was fired on account of his membership in the North American Man/Boy Love Association. His membership in the group, and his activities in it, which included editing its publication, became public knowledge. As a result, many students and parents demanded that he be fired.

The court recognized that the case diverged from typical *Pickering* cases "in two ways. One is that Melzer's termination stems not from something done in the workplace, but from First Amendment activities occurring outside the workplace and largely unconnected to it. The second is that the activity which prompted the Board to fire Melzer was not a specific instance of speech, or particular disruptive statement, but an associational activity of which speech was an essential component." Yet the Supreme Court had indicated that "the goal of striking an appropriate balance between employee and government interests is activated whenever the government seeks to regulate employees' protected speech, regardless of where it occurs or how closely it is related to work." As for the associational aspect of the case, "NAMBLA's primary purpose was advocacy, and Melzer, by his active participation and his role as editor of the *Bulletin*, furthered this advocacy. Thus interconnecting associational and speech rights are in play."

Turning to the merits, the court "assume[d] *arguendo* that [Melzer's] activity centers on a matter of public concern, and is thus protected." It then applied the balancing test, finding that "in the context of teaching schoolchildren Melzer's activities strike such a sensitive chord that, despite the protection afforded his activities, the disruption they cause is great enough to warrant the school's action against him." What result if Melzer had worked for the city as an architect? A police officer?

Every case will present its own set of circumstances to be balanced. Nonetheless, some general patterns emerge from a review of many decisions. One is that speech about corruption will receive comparatively more weight than speech about incompetence or policy. In addition, disruption is typically found to be a more serious concern in hierarchical government organizations than in less disciplined institutions. Police and firefighters are less likely to win than are university professors. *See* Michael L. Wells, *Section 1983, the First Amendment, and Public Employee Speech*, 35 GA. L. REV. 939, 995, 997 (2001). The speech of a high level official will more readily be found disruptive than that of a low level employee. *See, e.g., Dixon v. University of Toledo*, 702 F.3d 269, 275 (6th Cir. 2012) (associate vice president of human resources at a public university lost a First Amendment suit challenging dismissal on account of a letter to the editor of a newspaper in which she stated views at odds with school policy).

5.   In order to prevail, the plaintiff must show that she suffered an "adverse employment action." When officials fire the plaintiff, there is no issue here. "A decrease in work days and pay is an adverse employment action." *Dye v. Office of the Racing Commission*, 702 F.3d 286 (6th Cir. 2012). But suppose the plaintiff is shifted to another post or denied a promotion. Some courts have focused on the severity of the action taken against the plaintiff. *See, e.g., Lybrook v. Board of Education*, 232 F.3d 1334, 1340 (10th Cir. 2000). Here a teacher was placed on a "Professional Development Plan," which required her to strive to be more cooperative with others, and was required to meet with a superior every Monday morning. The court ruled that "while the Professional Development Plan and the Monday morning meetings may have been unwelcome to Plaintiff Lybrook, we conclude that they are of insufficient gravity to premise a First Amendment violation."

By contrast, *Coszalter v. City of Salem*, 320 F.3d 968 (9th Cir. 2003), takes the view that the point of liability is to stop the state from inhibiting speech by punishing it. Accordingly,

> [t]o constitute an adverse employment action, a government act of retaliation need not be severe and it need not be of a certain kind. Nor does it matter whether an act of retaliation is in the form of the removal of a benefit or the imposition of a burden. [We] adopt the 'reasonably likely to

deter' test as the proper test for First Amendment employer retaliation cases.

6.   Plaintiffs in public employee speech cases often use the verb "retaliate" to describe what the authorities did to them as a consequence of their speech. It is important to recognize that the success or failure of their claims does not necessarily depend on whether the reaction of their bosses is best described as "retaliation" or as an "effort to remove a disruptive person." Some truly disruptive plaintiffs will win the *Pickering/Connick* balance and some will lose. Some authoritarian bosses, who brook no dissent and whose acts are fairly described as retaliation, will win because the speech was not on a matter of public concern or because they prevail in the balancing test.

That said, there are a variety of situations in which people do bring constitutional tort suits on the theory that some action was taken against them as retaliation for exercising their constitutional rights. As one court put it:

> The three elements of a retaliation claim are:
>
> (1) that the plaintiff was engaged in a constitutionally protected activity; (2) that the defendant's adverse action caused the plaintiff to suffer an injury that would likely chill a person of ordinary firmness from continuing to engage in that activity; and (3) that the adverse action was motivated at least in part as a response to the exercise of the plaintiff's constitutional rights. *Mattox v. City of Forest Park*, 183 F.3d 515, 520 (6th Cir. 1999).

In particular, prisoners frequently make such claims. For example, *Mitchell v. Horn*, 318 F.3d 523 (3d Cir. 2003) held that a prisoner stated a good constitutional tort claim when he asserted that, as retaliation for filing complaints against an officer, the officer planted contraband near his locker, resulting in unjustified punishment. A "retaliatory prosecution" theory is available where the plaintiff claims he was prosecuted for a crime on account of, or in order to prevent or hinder, his own litigation against the police. *See, e.g., Poole v. County of Otero*, 271 F.3d 955 (10th Cir. 2001).

An ordinary citizen may have such a claim as well. *See, e.g., Royal Crown Day Care LLC v. Department of Health and Mental Hygiene of the City of New York*, 746 F.3d 538 (2d Cir. 2014) (day care center operator charged that officials closed down the day care center in retaliation for letter of complaint that the operator sent to a state senator; officials assert qualified immunity; district court's denial of their motion for summary judgment is affirmed). In *Greenwich Citizens Committee v. Counties of Warren and Washington Industrial Development Agency*, 77 F.3d 26 (2d Cir. 1996), the Citizens Committee had sued the agency in state court in connection with construction of a solid waste incinerator. The agency had then counterclaimed, alleging tortious interference with contract among other things. Then the plaintiffs filed this federal section 1983 case, in which they charged that the counterclaims were brought in retaliation for the original lawsuit. The court held that the plaintiffs could win only if they could show that "the counterclaims were filed, not as a legitimate response to litigation, but as a form of retaliation, with the purpose of deterring the exercise of First Amendment rights." *Id.* at 31.

Another variation on this theme is illustrated by *Carpenteria Valley Farms v. Santa Barbara County*, 334 F.3d 796 (9th Cir. 2003). A land owner charged that his efforts to develop his property were hindered by local authorities in retaliation for his criticism of their earlier treatment of him. The court allowed his suit to go forward without awaiting final resolution of the regulatory issues, explaining that if "the County's requirements, conditions, delays and fees were imposed in retaliation for his exercise of his First Amendment rights to publicly criticize the County and to access the courts, [the plaintiff] suffered harm thereby and did not have to await further action by the County.

GARCETTI v. CEBALLOS

In *Garcetti v. Ceballos*, 547 U.S. 410 (2006), the Supreme Court ruled that public employees' speech made in the course of official duties is not protected by the first amendment. Ceballos, a deputy district attorney, found fault with an affidavit that had been used to obtain a search warrant in a criminal case. In a memo and a meeting, he recommended to his superiors that the case be dismissed, but his advice was rejected. "The meeting allegedly became heated, with one [police] lieutenant sharply criticizing Ceballos for his handling of the case." Calling Ceballos as a witness, the defense moved to challenge the warrant, but the trial judge rejected the challenge:

Ceballos claims that in the aftermath of these events he was subjected to a series of retaliatory employment actions. The actions included reassignment from his calendar deputy position to a trial deputy position, transfer to another courthouse, and denial of a promotion.

Ceballos brought a § 1983 suit charging retaliation in violation of his first amendment rights. Finding that Ceballos's speech met the "public concern" requirement, and that the value of the speech outweighed disruption concerns, the 9th circuit ruled in his favor. The Supreme Court reversed:

The controlling factor in Ceballos' case is that his expressions were made pursuant to his duties as a calendar deputy. That consideration — the fact that Ceballos spoke as a prosecutor fulfilling a responsibility to advise his supervisor about how best to proceed with a pending case — distinguishes Ceballos' case from those in which the First Amendment provides protection against discipline. We hold that when public employees make statements pursuant to their official duties, the employees are not speaking as citizens for Fi rst Amendment purposes, and the Constitution does not insulate their communications from employer discipline.

Restricting speech that owes its existence to a public employee's professional responsibilities does not infringe any liberties the employee might have enjoyed as a private citizen. It simply reflects the exercise of employer control over what the employer itself has commissioned or created.

This result is consistent with our precedents' attention to the potential societal value of employee speech. Refusing to recognize First Amendment claims based on government employees' work product does not prevent them from participating in public debate. The employees retain the prospect of constitutional protection for their contributions to the civic discourse. This prospect of protection, however, does not invest them with a right to perform their jobs however they see fit.

Our holding likewise is supported by the emphasis of our precedents on affording government employers sufficient discretion to manage their operations. Employers have heightened interests in controlling speech made by an employee in his or her professional capacity. Official communications have official consequences, creating a need for substantive consistency and clarity. Supervisors must ensure that their employees' official communications are accurate, demonstrate sound judgment, and promote the employer's mission. Ceballos' memo is illustrative. It demanded the attention of his supervisors and led to a heated meeting with employees from the sheriff's department. If Ceballos' superiors thought his memo was inflammatory or misguided, they had the authority to take proper corrective action.

Because none of the parties disputed "that Ceballos wrote his disposition memo pursuant to his employment duties," the Court had no occasion to articulate a comprehensive framework for defining the scope of an employee's duties in cases where there is room for serious debate. We reject, however, the suggestion that employers can restrict employees' rights by creating excessively broad job descriptions.

Justice STEVENS, SOUTER, BREYER, and GINSBURG dissented, arguing, for a variety of reasons, that the majority's absolute bar gave too much weight to the government employer's interests and too little to the value of free speech.

NOTES ON *GARCETTI*

1. In *Lane v. Franks*, 134 S. Ct. 2369 (2014), a unanimous Court limited the reach of *Garcetti*, by holding that it did not apply to "a public employee who provided truthful sworn testimony, compelled by subpoena, outside the course of his ordinary job responsibilities." Rather, the *Pickering* test governs such cases. Lane, a public college administrator, was fired because of his testimony at the criminal trial of another former administrator, Suzanne Schmitz. The Eleventh Circuit had ruled that *Garcetti* controlled the case, because his testimony was based on information he had learned on the job. Even so, the Court, ruled this fact pattern belongs on the *Pickering* side of the line:

> Sworn testimony in judicial proceedings is a quintessential example of speech as a citizen for a simple reason: Anyone who testifies in court bears an obligation, to the court and society at large, to tell the truth. When the person testifying is a public employee, he may bear separate obligations to his employer — for example, an obligation not to show up to court dressed in an unprofessional manner. But any such obligations as an employee are distinct and independent from the obligation, as a citizen, to speak the truth. That independent obligation renders sworn testimony speech as a

citizen and sets it apart from speech made purely in the capacity of an employee.

Justice Sotomayor's opinion for the Court contains reasoning that goes beyond the specific issue of sworn testimony and suggests that *Garcetti* may be curbed in other ways. Thus,

> *Garcetti* said nothing about speech that simply relates to public employment or concerns information learned in the scope of public employment. [The] mere fact that a citizen's speech concerns information acquired by virtue of his public employment does not transform that speech into employee — rather than citizen — speech. The critical question under *Garcetti* is whether the speech at issue is itself ordinarily within the scope of an employee's duties, not whether it merely concerns those duties.

> It bears emphasis that our precedents dating back to *Pickering* have recognized that speech by public employees on subject matter related to their employment holds special value precisely because those employees gain knowledge ofmatters of public concern through their employment. [The] importance of public employee speech is especially evident in the context of this case: a public corruption scandal.

On the other hand, there may be occasions when sworn testimony is *not* protected. It was "undisputed that Lane's ordinary job responsibilities did not include testifying in court proceedings. [We] need not address in this case whether truthful sworn testimony would constitute citizen speech under *Garcetti* when given as part of a public employee's ordinary job duties, and express no opinion on the matter today." 134 S. Ct. at n.4.

In the remainder of the opinion, the Court applied the *Pickering/Connick* balance. It found that the speech was of public concern and that "the employer's side of the *Pickering* scale is entirely empty." The Court nonetheless denied the plaintiff an opportunity to obtain damages from the officer who fired him, on account of official immunity, a topic we address in chapters 7 and 8.

   2.   Questions as to the scope of *Garcetti* come up often in the lower courts. In *Williams v. Dallas Independent School District*, 480 F.3d 689 (5th Cir. 2007), the plaintiff had been the athletic director and head football coach at a public high school. He had sent memoranda to the school's office manager and principal questioning the handling of school athletic funds and had, according to his complaint, been fired for doing so. Relying on *Garcetti*, the 5th circuit affirmed the district court's grant of summary judgment for the defendants:

> In *Garcetti*, Ceballos was acting pursuant to his official duties because he was performing activities *required* to fulfill his duties as a prosecutor and calendar deputy that were not protected by the First Amendment. . . . In the instant case, DISD concedes that an Athletic Director is not required to write memoranda to his principal regarding athletic accounts.

Nonetheless, the court found *Garcetti* controlling. Earlier public employee speech cases, "distinguish between speech that is 'the kind of activity engaged in by citizens who do not work for the government,' *Garcetti*, and activities undertaken in the course of performing one's job. Activities undertaken in the course of performing one's job are activities pursuant to official duties. . . ." The court concluded that "Williams's speech was made in the course of performing his employment."

Would the outcome be different if Williams had written identical letters and sent them to the local newspaper instead of to the office manager and the principal? Would *Williams* come out the same way after *Lane v. Franks, supra?*

Do teaching and writing on academic matters by state-employed teachers come within *Garcetti* and thus have no First Amendment protection. *See Demers v. Austin,* 746 F.3d 402, 411 (9th Cir. 2014) ("We conclude that if applied to teaching and academic writing, *Garcetti* would directly conflict with the important First Amendment values previously articulated by the Supreme Court." The opinion goes on to document the Supreme Court's concern with maintaining academic freedom.) Is *Demers* consistent with *Williams?*

Suppose a police detective discloses alleged use of abusive interrogation tactics by other officers, to the police department's Internal Affairs unit, but also, and against orders from his superiors, to others outside the police department. Despite *Garcetti,* these communications were found protected by the First Amendment in *Dahlia v. Rodriguez,* 735 F.3d 1060, 1074 (9th Cir. 2013). The court set forth several "guiding principles relevant to the case before us." Thus, "[w]hen a public employee communicates outside his chain of command, it is unlikely that he is speaking pursuant to his duties." In addition,

> the subject matter of the communication is also of course highly relevant to the ultimate determination whether the speech is protected by the First Amendment. [When] an employee raises within the department broad concerns about corruption or systemic abuse, it is unlikely that such complaints can reasonably be classified as being within the job duties of an average public employee.

Also, "when a public employee speaks in direct contravention to his supervisor's orders, that speech may often fall outside of the speaker's professional duties." Applying these principles to rule on a motion to dismiss, the court upheld the complaint against a *Garcetti* defense.

For a general discussion of *Garcetti,* see Sheldon Nahmod, *Public Employee Speech, Categorical Balancing and Section 1983: A Critique of* Garcetti v. Ceballos, U. RICH. L. REV. 561 (2008).

Chapter 4

"SECURED BY THE CONSTITUTION AND LAWS" AFFIRMATIVE CONSTITUTIONAL DUTIES AND RIGHTS SECURED BY FEDERAL LAWS

A significant portion of the preceding chapter addressed the question of whether government-inflicted injury can be characterized as a denial of substantive or procedural due process. The defendants in those cases actively injured the plaintiffs, and the issue was whether their conduct amounted to a deprivation of life, liberty or property without due process of law. The first part of this chapter considers a variation of this issue. The cases below involve defendants who allow the plaintiff to be injured or fail to prevent some third party from injuring the plaintiff, as when a police officer passively observes a citizen being beaten or robbed. A question common to these cases is whether the Constitution imposes any affirmative obligations on government officials to protect persons from harm. Although the vast majority of section 1983 claims are based on alleged violations of constitutional rights, the statute also provides a remedy for "the deprivation of any rights . . . secured by [federal] laws." What are "rights . . . secured by [federal] laws" in this context? Can the violation of federal statutes give rise to a claim under section 1983? Part II of this chapter addresses special issues presented by non-constitutional based claims of violations of federal "laws."

I. AFFIRMATIVE DUTIES

The common law tort system has long struggled with the scope of affirmative duties for both private and public actors. The first principle of the common law of affirmative duties is that government, like private individuals, owes no general tort obligation to help anyone. *See, e.g., Riss v. City of New York*, 240 N.E.2d 860 (N.Y. 1968). The rationale for the no-duty rule differs sharply depending on whether the defendant is public or private. The no-duty rule as applied to private individuals rests primarily on libertarian values. A state-imposed duty to act would seriously impinge upon individual freedom and autonomy. *See* Richard Epstein, *A Theory of Strict Liability*, 2 J. LEGAL STUD. 151, 199–200 (1973). When the defendant is the government or its officer, individual autonomy is not an issue. The no-duty rule as applied to governments rests primarily on the need to preserve legislative and executive discretion in the allocation of limited public resources. For a more extended discussion of the tort policies implicated in the governmental affirmative duty context, see Wells and Eaton, *Affirmative Duty and Constitutional Tort*, 16 U. MICH. J.L. REF. 1, 3–11 (1982).

What additional considerations are involved when the scope of affirmative duties of government is raised in the context of constitutional tort? What are the practical and theoretical consequences of framing the affirmative duty issue in terms of constitutional (in contrast to common law) tort? To what extent can a state legislature modify a common law rule imposing an affirmative duty on a government or its officials? To what extent can a state legislature modify an affirmative duty recognized under constitutional law?

A. The Supreme Court's Framework

DESHANEY v. WINNEBAGO COUNTY DEPARTMENT OF SOCIAL SERVICES
489 U.S. 189 (1989)

CHIEF JUSTICE REHNQUIST delivered the opinion of the Court.

Petitioner is a boy who was beaten and permanently injured by his father, with whom he lived. Respondents are social workers and other local officials who received complaints that petitioner was being abused by his father and had reason to believe that this was the case, but nonetheless did not act to remove petitioner from his father's custody. Petitioner sued respondents claiming that their failure to act deprived him of his liberty in violation of the Due Process Clause of the Fourteenth Amendment to the United States Constitution. We hold that it did not.

The facts of this case are undeniably tragic. Petitioner Joshua DeShaney was born in 1979. In 1980, a Wyoming court granted his parents a divorce and awarded custody of Joshua to his father, Randy DeShaney. The father shortly thereafter moved to Neenah, a city located in Winnebago County, Wisconsin, taking the infant Joshua with him. There he entered into a second marriage, which also ended in divorce.

The Winnebago County authorities first learned that Joshua DeShaney might be a victim of child abuse in January 1982, when his father's second wife complained to the police, at the time of their divorce, that he had previously "hit the boy causing marks and [was] a prime case for child abuse." The Winnebago County Department of Social Services (DSS) interviewed the father, but he denied the accusations, and DSS did not pursue them further. In January 1983, Joshua was admitted to a local hospital with multiple bruises and abrasions. The examining physician suspected child abuse and notified DSS, which immediately obtained an order from a Wisconsin juvenile court placing Joshua in the temporary custody of the hospital. Three days later, the county convened an ad hoc "Child Protection Team" — consisting of a pediatrician, a psychologist, a police detective, the county's lawyer, several DSS caseworkers, and various hospital personnel — to consider Joshua's situation. At this meeting, the Team decided that there was insufficient evidence of child abuse to retain Joshua in the custody of the court. The Team did, however, decide to recommend several measures to protect Joshua, including enrolling him in a preschool program, providing his father with certain counseling services, and encouraging his father's girlfriend to move out of the home. Randy DeShaney entered into a voluntary agreement with DSS in which he promised to cooperate with them in accomplishing these goals.

Based on the recommendation of the Child Protection Team, the juvenile court dismissed the child protection case and returned Joshua to the custody of his father. A month later, emergency room personnel called the DSS caseworker handling Joshua's case to report that he had once again been treated for suspicious injuries. The caseworker concluded that there was no basis for action. For the next six months, the caseworker made monthly visits to the DeShaney home, during which she observed a number of suspicious injuries on Joshua's head; she also noticed that he had not been enrolled in school, and that the girl-friend had not moved out. The caseworker dutifully recorded these incidents in her files, along with her continuing suspicions that someone in the DeShaney household was physically abusing Joshua, but she did nothing more. In November 1983, the emergency room notified DSS that Joshua had been treated once again for injuries that they believed to be caused by child abuse. On the caseworker's next two visits to the DeShaney home, she was told that Joshua was too ill to see her. Still DSS took no action.

In March 1984, Randy DeShaney beat 4-year-old Joshua so severely that he fell into a life-threatening coma. Emergency brain surgery revealed a series of hemorrhages caused by traumatic injuries to the head inflicted over a long period of time. Joshua did not die, but he suffered brain damage so severe that he is expected to spend the rest of his life confined to an institution for the profoundly retarded. Randy DeShaney was subsequently tried and convicted of child abuse.

Joshua and his mother brought this action under 42 U.S.C. § 1983 in the United States District Court for the Eastern District of Wisconsin against respondents Winnebago County, DSS, and various individual employees of DSS. The complaint alleged that respondents had deprived Joshua of his liberty without due process of law, in violation of his rights under the Fourteenth Amendment, by failing to intervene to protect him against a risk of violence at his father's hands of which they knew or should have known. The District Court granted summary judgment for respondents.

The Court of Appeals for the Seventh Circuit affirmed. . . .

Because of the inconsistent approaches taken by the lower courts in determining when, if ever, the failure of a state or local governmental entity or its agents to provide an individual with adequate protective services constitutes a violation of the individual's due process rights, see *Archie v. Racine* (collecting cases) and the importance of the issue to the administration of state and local governments, we granted certiorari. We now affirm.

II

The Due Process Clause of the Fourteenth Amendment provides that "no State shall . . . deprive any person of life, liberty, or property, without due process of law." Petitioners contend that the State deprived Joshua of his liberty interest in "freedom from . . . unjustified intrusions on personal security," by failing to provide him with adequate protection against his father's violence. The claim is one invoking the substantive rather than the procedural component of the Due Process Clause; petitioners do not claim that the State denied Joshua protection without according him appropriate procedural safeguards but that it was categorically obligated to protect him in these circumstances.[1]

But nothing in the language of the Due Process Clause itself requires the State to protect the life, liberty, and property of its citizens against invasion by private actors. The Clause is phrased as a limitation on the State's power to act, not as a guarantee of certain minimal levels of safety and security. It forbids the State itself to deprive individuals of life, liberty, or property without "due process of law," but its language cannot fairly be extended to impose an affirmative obligation on the State to ensure that those interests do not come to harm through other means. Nor does history support such an expansive reading of the constitutional text. Like its counterpart in the Fifth Amendment, the Due Process Clause of the Fourteenth Amendment was intended to prevent government "from abusing [its] power, or employing it as an instrument of oppression." Its purpose was to protect the people from the State, not to ensure that the State protected them from each other. The Framers were content to leave the extent of governmental obligation in the latter area to the democratic political processes.

Consistent with these principles, our cases have recognized that the Due Process Clauses generally confer no affirmative right to governmental aid, even where such aid may be necessary to secure life, liberty, or property interests of which the government itself may not deprive the individual. See, *e.g.*, *Harris v. McRae* (no obligation to fund abortions or other medical services) (discussing Due Process Clause of Fifth Amendment); *Lindsey v. Normet* (no obligation to provide adequate housing) (discussing Due Process Clause of Fourteenth Amendment); see also *Youngberg v. Romeo*, supra, ("As a general matter, a State is under no constitutional duty to provide substantive services for those within its border"). As we said in *Harris v. McRae*: "Although the liberty protected by the Due Process Clause affords protection against unwarranted government interference . . . , it does not confer an entitlement to such [governmental aid] as may be necessary to realize all the advantages of that freedom."448 U.S., at 317–318 (emphasis added). If the Due Process Clause does not require the State to provide its citizens with particular protective services, it follows that the State cannot be held liable under the Clause for injuries that could have been averted had it chosen to provide them.[2] As a general matter, then, we conclude that a State's failure to protect an individual against private violence simply does not constitute a violation of the Due Process Clause. Petitioners contend, however, that even if the Due Process Clause imposes no affirmative obligation on the State to provide the general public with adequate protective services, such a duty may arise out of certain "special relationships" created or assumed by the State with respect to particular individuals. Petitioners

---

[1] [2] Petitioners also argue that the Wisconsin child protection statutes gave Joshua an "entitlement" to receive protective services in accordance with the terms of the statute, an entitlement which would enjoy due process protection against state deprivation under our decision in *Board of Regents of State Colleges v. Roth*. But this argument is made for the first time in petitioners' brief to this Court: it was not pleaded in the complaint, argued to the Court of Appeals as a ground for reversing the District Court, or raised in the petition for certiorari. We therefore decline to consider it here. . . .

[2] [3] The State may not, of course, selectively deny its protective services to certain disfavored minorities without violating the Equal Protection Clause. *See Yick Wo v. Hopkins*. But no such argument has been made here.

argue that such a "special relationship" existed here because the State knew that Joshua faced a special danger of abuse at his father's hands, and specifically proclaimed, by word and by deed, its intention to protect him against that danger. Having actually undertaken to protect Joshua from this danger — which petitioners concede the State played no part in creating — the State acquired an affirmative "duty," enforceable through the Due Process Clause, to do so in a reasonably competent fashion. Its failure to discharge that duty, so the argument goes, was an abuse of governmental power that so "shocks the conscience," as to constitute a substantive due process violation.

We reject this argument. It is true that in certain limited circumstances the Constitution imposes upon the State affirmative duties of care and protection with respect to particular individuals. In *Estelle v. Gamble* we recognized that the Eighth Amendment's prohibition against cruel and unusual punishment, made applicable to the States through the Fourteenth Amendment's Due Process Clause, requires the State to provide adequate medical care to incarcerated prisoners. We reasoned that because the prisoner is unable "by reason of the deprivation of his liberty [to] care for himself," it is only "just" that the State be required to care for him.

In *Youngberg v. Romeo* we extended this analysis beyond the Eighth Amendment setting, holding that the substantive component of the Fourteenth Amendment's Due Process Clause requires the State to provide involuntarily committed mental patients with such services as are necessary to ensure their "reasonable safety" from themselves and others (dicta indicating that the State is also obligated to provide such individuals with "adequate food, shelter, clothing, and medical care"). As we explained: "If it is cruel and unusual punishment to hold convicted criminals in unsafe conditions, it must be unconstitutional [under the Due Process Clause] to confine the involuntarily committed — who may not be punished at all — in unsafe conditions." See also *Revere v. Massachusetts General Hospital* (holding that the Due Process Clause requires the responsible government or governmental agency to provide medical care to suspects in police custody who have been injured while being apprehended by the police).

But these cases afford petitioners no help. Taken together, they stand only for the proposition that when the State takes a person into its custody and holds him there against his will, the Constitution imposes upon it a corresponding duty to assume some responsibility for his safety and general well-being. The rationale for this principle is simple enough: when the State by the affirmative exercise of its power so restrains an individual's liberty that it renders him unable to care for himself, and at the same time fails to provide for his basic human needs — e. g., food, clothing, shelter, medical care, and reasonable safety — it transgresses the substantive limits on state action set by the Eighth Amendment and the Due Process Clause. The affirmative duty to protect arises not from the State's knowledge of the individual's predicament or from its expressions of intent to help him, but from the limitation which it has imposed on his freedom to act on his own behalf. In the substantive due process analysis, it is the State's affirmative act of restraining the individual's freedom to act on his own behalf — through incarceration, institutionalization, or other similar restraint of personal liberty — which is the "deprivation of liberty" triggering the protections of the Due Process Clause, not its failure to act to protect his liberty interests against harms inflicted by other means.

The *Estelle-Youngberg* analysis simply has no applicability in the present case. Petitioners concede that the harms Joshua suffered did not occur while he was in the State's custody, but while he was in the custody of his natural father, who was in no sense a state actor.[3] While the State may have been aware of the dangers that Joshua faced in the free world, it played no part in their creation, nor did it do anything to render him any more vulnerable to them. That the State once took temporary custody of Joshua does not alter the analysis, for when it returned him to his father's custody, it placed him in no worse position than that in which he would have been had it not acted at all; the State does not become the permanent guarantor of an individual's safety by having once offered him shelter. Under these circumstances, the State had no constitutional duty to protect Joshua.

It may well be that, by voluntarily undertaking to protect Joshua against a danger it concededly played no part in creating, the State acquired a duty under state tort law to provide him with adequate protection against that danger. See Restatement (Second) of Torts § 323 (1965) (one who undertakes to render services to another may in some circumstances be held liable for doing so in a negligent fashion); see generally W. Keeton, D. Dobbs, R. Keeton, & D. Owen, Prosser and Keeton on the Law of Torts § 56 (5th ed. 1984) (discussing "special relationships" which may give rise to affirmative duties to act under the common law of tort). But the claim here is based on the Due Process Clause of the Fourteenth Amendment, which, as we have said many times, does not transform every tort committed by a state actor into a constitutional violation. A State may, through its courts and legislatures, impose such affirmative duties of care and protection upon its agents as it wishes. But not "all common-law duties owed by government actors were . . . constitutionalized by the Fourteenth Amendment." Because, as explained above, the State had no constitutional duty to protect Joshua against his father's violence, its failure to do so — though calamitous in hindsight — simply does not constitute a violation of the Due Process Clause.[4]

Judges and lawyers, like other humans, are moved by natural sympathy in a case

---

[3] [9] Complaint ¶ 16, App. 6 ("At relevant times to and until March 8, 1984, [the date of the final beating,] Joshua DeShaney was in the custody and control of Defendant Randy DeShaney"). Had the State by the affirmative exercise of its power removed Joshua from free society and placed him in a foster home operated by its agents, we might have a situation sufficiently analogous to incarceration or institutionalization to give rise to an affirmative duty to protect. Indeed, several Courts of Appeals have held, by analogy to Estelle and Youngberg, that the State may be held liable under the Due Process Clause for failing to protect children in foster homes from mistreatment at the hands of their foster parents. *See Doe v. New York City Dept. of Social Services. Catholic Home Bureau v. Doe; Taylor ex rel. Walker v. Ledbetter*, cert. pending *Ledbetter v. Taylor*. We express no view on the validity of this analogy, however, as it is not before us in the present case.

[4] [10] Because we conclude that the Due Process Clause did not require the State to protect Joshua from his father, we need not address respondents' alternative argument that the individual state actors lacked the requisite "state of mind" to make out a due process violation. See *Daniels v. Williams*. Similarly, we have no occasion to consider whether the individual respondents might be entitled to a qualified immunity defense, see *Anderson v. Creighton*, or whether the allegations in the complaint are sufficient to support a § 1983 claim against the county and DSS under *Monell v. New York City Dept. of Social Services*, and its progeny.

like this to find a way for Joshua and his mother to receive adequate compensation for the grievous harm inflicted upon them. But before yielding to that impulse, it is well to remember once again that the harm was inflicted not by the State of Wisconsin, but by Joshua's father. The most that can be said of the state functionaries in this case is that they stood by and did nothing when suspicious circumstances dictated a more active role for them. In defense of them it must also be said that had they moved too soon to take custody of the son away from the father, they would likely have been met with charges of improperly intruding into the parent-child relationship, charges based on the same Due Process Clause that forms the basis for the present charge of failure to provide adequate protection.

The people of Wisconsin may well prefer a system of liability which would place upon the State and its officials the responsibility for failure to act in situations such as the present one. They may create such a system, if they do not have it already, by changing the tort law of the State in accordance with the regular lawmaking process. But they should not have it thrust upon them by this Court's expansion of the Due Process Clause of the Fourteenth Amendment.

Affirmed.

JUSTICE BRENNAN, with whom JUSTICE MARSHALL and JUSTICE BLACKMUN join, dissenting.

It may well be, as the Court decides that the Due Process Clause as construed by our prior cases creates no general right to basic governmental services. That, however, is not the question presented here; indeed, that question was not raised in the complaint, urged on appeal, presented in the petition for certiorari, or addressed in the briefs on the merits. No one, in short, has asked the Court to proclaim that, as a general matter, the Constitution safeguards positive as well as negative liberties.

This is more than a quibble over dicta; it is a point about perspective, having substantive ramifications. In a constitutional setting that distinguishes sharply between action and inaction, one's characterization of the misconduct alleged under may effectively decide the case. Thus, by leading off with a discussion (and rejection) of the idea that the Constitution imposes on the States an affirmative duty to take basic care of their citizens, the Court foreshadows — perhaps even preordains — its conclusion that no duty existed even on the specific facts before us. This initial discussion establishes the baseline from which the Court assesses the DeShaneys' claim that, when a State has–"by word and by deed," — announced an intention to protect a certain class of citizens and has before it facts that would trigger that protection under the applicable state law, the Constitution imposes upon the State an affirmative duty of protection.

The Court's baseline is the absence of positive rights in the Constitution and a concomitant suspicion of any claim that seems to depend on such rights. From this perspective, the DeShaneys' claim is first and foremost about inaction (the failure, here, of respondents to take steps to protect Joshua), and only tangentially about action (the establishment of a state program specifically designed to help children like Joshua). And from this perspective, holding these Wisconsin officials liable — where the only difference between this case and one involving a general claim to protective services is Wisconsin's establishment and operation of a program to protect children — would seem to punish an effort that we should seek to promote.

I would begin from the opposite direction. I would focus first on the action that Wisconsin has taken with respect to Joshua and children like him, rather than on the actions that the State failed to take. Such a method is not new to this Court. Both *Estelle v. Gamble* and *Youngberg v. Romeo* began by emphasizing that the States had confined J. W. Gamble to prison and Nicholas Romeo to a psychiatric hospital. This initial action rendered these people helpless to help themselves or to seek help from persons unconnected to the government. . . . Cases from the lower courts also recognize that a State's actions can be decisive in assessing the constitutional significance of subsequent inaction. For these purposes, moreover, actual physical restraint is not the only state action that has been considered relevant. See, e. g., *White v. Rochford* (police officers violated due process when, after arresting the guardian of three young children, they abandoned the children on a busy stretch of highway at night).

Because of the Court's initial fixation on the general principle that the Constitution does not establish positive rights, it is unable to appreciate our recognition in *Estelle* and *Youngberg* that this principle does not hold true in all circumstances. . . . I do not mean to suggest that "the State's affirmative act of restraining the individual's freedom to act on his own behalf," was irrelevant in *Youngberg*; rather, I emphasize that this conduct would have led to no injury, and consequently no cause of action under § 1983, unless the State then had failed to take steps to protect Romeo from himself and from others. In addition, the Court's exclusive attention to state — imposed restraints of "the individual's freedom to act on his own behalf," suggests that it was the State that rendered Romeo unable to care for himself, whereas in fact — with an I. Q. of between 8 and 10, and the mental capacity of an 18-month-old child — he had been quite incapable of taking care of himself long before the State stepped into his life. Thus, the fact of hospitalization was critical in *Youngberg* not because it rendered Romeo helpless to help himself, but because it separated him from other sources of aid that, we held, the State was obligated to replace. Unlike the Court, therefore, I am unable to see in *Youngberg* a neat and decisive divide between action and inaction.

Moreover, to the Court, the only fact that seems to count as an "affirmative act of restraining the individual's freedom to act on his own behalf" is direct physical control, (listing only "incarceration, institutionalization, [and] other similar restraint of personal liberty" in describing relevant "affirmative acts"). I would not, however, give *Youngberg* and *Estelle* such a stingy scope. I would recognize, as the Court apparently cannot, that "the State's knowledge of [an] individual's predicament [and] its expressions of intent to help him" can amount to a "limitation of his freedom to act on his own behalf" or to obtain help from others. Thus, I would read *Youngberg* and *Estelle* to stand for the much more generous proposition that, if a State cuts off private sources of aid and then refuses aid itself, it cannot wash its hands of the harm that results from its inaction.

Youngberg and *Estelle* are not alone in sounding this theme. In striking down a filing fee as applied to divorce cases brought by indigents, see *Boddie v. Connecticut*, and in deciding that a local government could not entirely foreclose the opportunity to speak in a public forum, see, *e.g., Schneider v. State*; *Hague v. Committee for Industrial Organization*; *United States v. Grace*, we have acknowledged that a State's actions — such as the monopolization of a particular path of relief — may impose upon the State certain positive duties. Similarly, *Shelley v. Kraemer* and *Burton v. Wilmington Parking Authority* suggest that a State may be found complicit in an injury even if it did not create the situation that caused the harm.

Wisconsin has established a child-welfare system specifically designed to help children like Joshua. Wisconsin law places upon the local departments of social services such as respondent (DSS or Department) a duty to investigate reported instances of child abuse. While other governmental bodies and private persons are largely responsible for the reporting of possible cases of child abuse, Wisconsin law channels all such reports to the local departments of social services for evaluation and, if necessary, further action. Even when it is the sheriff's office or police department that receives a report of suspected child abuse, that report is referred to local social services departments for action; the only exception to this occurs when the reporter fears for the child's immediate safety. In this way, Wisconsin law invites — indeed, directs — citizens and other governmental entities to depend on local departments of social services such as respondent to protect children from abuse.

The specific facts before us bear out this view of Wisconsin's system of protecting children. Each time someone voiced a suspicion that Joshua was being abused, that information was relayed to the Department for investigation and possible action. When Randy DeShaney's second wife told the police that he had "hit the boy causing marks and [was] a prime case for child abuse," the police referred her complaint to DSS. When, on three separate occasions, emergency room personnel noticed suspicious injuries on Joshua's body, they went to DSS with this information. When neighbors informed the police that they had seen or heard Joshua's father or his father's lover beating or otherwise abusing Joshua, the police brought these reports to the attention of DSS. And when respondent Kemmeter, through these reports and through her own observations in the course of nearly 20 visits to the DeShaney home, compiled growing evidence that Joshua was being abused, that information stayed within the Department — chronicled by the social worker in detail that seems almost eerie in light of her failure to act upon it. (As to the extent of the social worker's involvement in, and knowledge of, Joshua's predicament, her reaction to the news of Joshua's last and most devastating injuries is illuminating: "I just knew the phone would ring some day and Joshua would be dead.")

Even more telling than these examples is the Department's control over the decision whether to take steps to protect a particular child from suspected abuse. While many different people contributed information and advice to this decision, it was up to the people at DSS to make the ultimate decision (subject to the approval of the local government's corporation counsel) whether to disturb the family's current arrangements. When Joshua first appeared at a local hospital with injuries signaling physical abuse, for example, it was DSS that made the decision to take him into temporary custody for the purpose of studying his situation — and it was DSS, acting in conjunction with the corporation counsel, that returned him to his father. Unfortunately for Joshua DeShaney, the buck effectively stopped with the Department.

In these circumstances, a private citizen, or even a person working in a government agency other than DSS, would doubtless feel that her job was done as soon as she had reported her suspicions of child abuse to DSS. Through its child-welfare program, in other words, the State of Wisconsin has relieved ordinary citizens and governmental bodies other than the Department of any sense of obligation to do anything more than report their suspicions of child abuse to DSS. If DSS ignores or dismisses these suspicions, no one will step in to fill the gap. Wisconsin's child-protection program thus effectively confined Joshua DeShaney within the walls of Randy DeShaney's violent home until such time as DSS took action to remove him. Conceivably, then, children like Joshua are made worse off by the existence of this program when the persons and entities charged with carrying it out fail to do their jobs.

It simply belies reality, therefore, to contend that the State "stood by and did nothing" with respect to Joshua. Through its child-protection program, the State actively intervened in Joshua's life and, by virtue of this intervention, acquired ever more certain knowledge that Joshua was in grave danger. These circumstances, in my view, plant this case solidly within the tradition of cases like *Youngberg* and *Estelle*.

I do not suggest that such irrationality was at work in this case; I emphasize only that we do not know whether or not it was. I would allow Joshua and his mother the opportunity to show that respondents' failure to help him arose, not out of the sound exercise of professional judgment that we recognized in *Youngberg* as sufficient to preclude liability, . . . , but from the kind of arbitrariness that we have in the past condemned. . . .

As the Court today reminds us, "the Due Process Clause of the Fourteenth Amendment was intended to prevent government 'from abusing [its] power, or employing it as an instrument of oppression.' " My disagreement with the Court arises from its failure to see that inaction can be every bit as abusive of power as action, that oppression can result when a State undertakes a vital duty and then ignores it. Today's opinion construes the Due Process Clause to permit a State to displace private sources of protection and then, at the critical moment, to shrug its shoulders and turn away from the harm that it has promised to try to prevent. Because I cannot agree that our Constitution is indifferent to such indifference, I respectfully dissent.

JUSTICE **BLACKMUN**, dissenting.

The Court . . . attempts to draw a sharp and rigid line between action and inaction. But such formalistic reasoning has no place in the interpretation of the broad and stirring Clauses of the Fourteenth Amendment. Indeed, I submit that these Clauses were designed, at least in part, to undo the formalistic legal reasoning that infected antebellum jurisprudence . . . .

Like the antebellum judges who denied relief to fugitive slaves, the Court today claims that its decision, however harsh, is compelled by existing legal doctrine. On the contrary, the question presented by this case is an open one, and our Fourteenth Amendment precedents may be read more broadly or narrowly depending upon how one chooses to read them. Faced with the choice, I would adopt a "sympathetic" reading, one which comports with dictates of fundamental justice and recognizes that compassion need not be exiled from the province of judging . . . .

Poor Joshua! Victim of repeated attacks by an irresponsible, bullying, cowardly, and intemperate father, and abandoned by respondents who placed him in a dangerous predicament and who knew or learned what was going on, and yet did essentially nothing except, as the Court revealingly observes, "dutifully recorded these incidents in [their] files." It is a sad commentary upon American life, and constitutional principles — so full of late of patriotic fervor and proud proclamations about "liberty and justice for all," that this child, Joshua DeShaney, now is assigned to live out the remainder of his life profoundly retarded. Joshua and his mother, as petitioners here, deserve — but now are denied by this Court — the opportunity to have the facts of their case considered in the light of the constitutional protection that 42 U.S.C. § 1983 is meant to provide.

NOTES

1. Would the result in *DeShaney* be any different if the social worker did nothing to protect Joshua while actually observing the beatings?

2. The Supreme Court has recognized the constitutional right of a parent to retain custody of a minor child. This "fundamental right" is limited by a "compelling state interest" in protecting a minor child from imminent danger of abuse or neglect. *Troxel v. Granville*, 530 U.S. 57 (2000); *Santosky v. Kramer*, 455 U.S. 745 (1982). Would Randy DeShaney have had a section 1983 claim if the DSS caseworker had taken action to remove Joshua from his custody? Should caseworkers be immune from such claims? Most courts have held that case-workers are protected by qualified immunity for actions taken in the investigation of child abuse cases. *E.g., Roska v. Peterson*, 328 F.3d 1230 (10th Cir. 2003); *Berman v. Young*, 291 F.3d 976 (7th Cir. 2002); *Doe v. Braddy*, 673 F.3d 1313 (11th Cir. 2012); *Tamas v. Dept. of Social and Health Services*, 630 F.3d 833 (9th Cir. 2010); *Estate of B.I.C. v. Gillen*, 761 F. 3d 1099 (10th Cir. 2014). *See infra*, Chapter 8. Local governments, on the other hand, have no immunity when their official policies or customs cause a constitutional violation. *See infra*, Chapter 5. How would these various immunity doctrines affect litigation strategies? What effect would these immunity doctrines likely have on caseworkers' decisions on whether to intervene in a particular case? How does the "no duty" rationale of *DeShaney* affect the incentives for action or inaction in close cases?

3. How useful is the "act/omission" distinction as a principle of adjudication? Some critics maintain that since government plays some role in virtually every aspect of daily life, it is formalistic and naive to accord decisive weight to the difference between active and passive defaults of government officials. Consider Professor Tribe's critique of *DeShaney*:

My trouble is with the majority's quite primitive vision of the state of Wisconsin as some sort of distinct object, a kind of machine that must be understood to act upon a pre-political, natural order of private life. From the majority's perspective, the state of Wisconsin operates as a thing, its arms exerting force from a safe distance upon a sometimes unpleasant natural world, in which the abuse of children is an unfortunate, yet external, ante-legal and pre-political fact of our society. Courts, as passive and detached observers, may reach in to offer a helping hand only when another arm of the state has reached out and shattered this natural, pre-political order by itself directly harming a young child.

. . . [T]here is no hint that the hand of the observing state may itself have played a major role in shaping the world it observes . . . [T]he Supreme Court majority . . . did not inquire whether the hand of the state may have altered an already political landscape in a way that encouraged such child-beating to go uncorrected. The majority's question in *DeShaney* was simply, "did the State of Wisconsin beat up that child?", and not, "did the law of Wisconsin, taken in its entirety, warp the legal landscape so that it in effect deflected the assistance otherwise available to Joshua De-Shaney?"

Laurence H. Tribe, *The Curvature of Constitutional Space: What Lawyers Can Learn from Modern Physics*, 103 HARV. L. REV. 1, 9–10 (1989). If Professor Tribe's point of view were to prevail, what limits would there be on recognizing affirmative constitutional duties under the due process clause?

Professor Barbara E. Armacost, on the other hand, defends *DeShaney*, contending that the opinion is

better explained, not by constitutional text or history, but by judicial reluctance to second-guess legislative decisions about budgetary matters, the same concerns that account for the presumptive rule of nonliability in tort. This rationale for the nonliability rules makes *DeShaney* a much harder case on its facts and goes a long way toward a more satisfying positive account of the Supreme Court's approach to this line of cases. It also provides a plausible counterargument to the moral and constitutional objections to nonliability in cases like *DeShaney*.

Barbara E. Armacost, *Affirmative Duties, Systemic Harms, and the Due Process Clause*, 94 MICH. L. REV. 982, 985 (1996). *See also* Frank B. Cross, *The Error of Positive Rights*, 48 U.C.L.A. L. REV. 857, 923–24 (2001) (arguing that the general adoption of positive rights under the Constitution would be unwise, ineffective, and counterproductive).

4. One problem inherent in the act/omission distinction is that of characterization. Labeling misconduct as active or passive may turn on how one poses the question. Assume, for example, a policeman impounds a car, arrests the driver and leaves the children-passengers stranded on a busy highway. Are the children endangered by the officer's *acts* of impounding the car and arresting the driver, or by the *failure to rescue* the children? *Cf. White v. Rochford*, 592 F.2d 381 (7th Cir. 1979). How difficult is it for courts to ascertain whether a particular claim actually turns on an act or omission? Judge Posner expressed the problem as follows: "The term 'affirmative act' appears in some of the cases, but is unhelpful. All acts are affirmative, including standing still when one could save a person by warning him of some impending danger." *Slade v. Bd. of School Directors of the City of Milwaukee*, 702 F.3d 1027, 1030 (7th Cir. 2012).

Suppose the plaintiff challenged the state's practice of not providing an indigent mother with a free transcript of lower court proceedings necessary to appeal a decision to terminate her parental rights? Would the plaintiff's claim be most fairly characterized as challenging the state's *act* in terminating parental rights or challenging the state's *refusal to provide needed assistance* in pursuing her appeal? *See M.L.B. v. S.L.J.*, 519 U.S. 102, 125 (1996) in which the majority of the court distinguished *DeShaney* stating that the plaintiff "is endeavoring to defend against the State's destruction of her family bonds and to resist the brand associated with a parental unfitness adjudication."

5. The majority in *DeShaney* notes that the due process clause "generally confer[s] no affirmative right to governmental aid" and cites cases in which the government was found to have no obligation to provide housing or to fund abortions or other medical services. The dissenting Justices discuss other cases that they believe could support recognizing a duty to protect Joshua. Professor Currie has identified several lines of cases in which the Court has found the state to have a constitutional obligation to act in some positive way. In addition to cases like *Youngberg* and *Estelle* dealing with the protection of the involuntarily confined, Currie notes the constitutional obligations to provide legal counsel for the indigent charged with crimes, to enforce contracts, and to provide access to certain information and to public forums. *See* David P. Currie, *Positive and Negative Constitutional Rights*, 53 U. Chi. L. Rev. 864, 872–880 (1986). Professor Currie also cites *Truax v. Corrigan*, 257 U.S. 312 (1921) in which the court ruled that a state law restricting the use of injunctions in labor disputes deprived the employer of property without due process of law. Does *Truax* support the proposition that the Due Process Clause may require the state to protect persons from the acts of private parties? While Professor Currie dismisses as "profoundly a historical" the notion that the Constitution offers a positive right to basic welfare services, he warns that "it would be dangerous to read too much, even at the theoretical level, into the generally valid principle that ours . . . is a Constitution of negative rather than positive liberties." 53 U. Chi. L. Rev. at 878 and 887. Given the conflicting strains of cases, what is the proper role of precedent in deciding cases like *DeShaney* presenting novel issues regarding the scope of constitutional protection and obligation?

6. When the person who actively injures the plaintiff is a private party, the affirmative duty issue sometimes becomes confused with the "under color of" state law element of a section 1983 claim. As discussed in Chapter 2, section 1983 grants a remedy only for acts taken "under color of" state law. Where, as in *DeShaney*, the active wrongdoer is a private citizen, some courts have denied liability on the grounds that the injury was not the product of state action. In *Milburn v. Anne Arundel Department of Social Services*, 871 F.2d 474 (4th Cir. 1989), for example, the court reasoned that the abusive acts of the state-approved foster parents of a voluntarily-placed infant were not state action. The Fourth Circuit drew support for this conclusion from Supreme Court decisions finding private action adversely affecting liberty or property is not subject to the demands of procedural due process despite some involvement of the state. *See e.g., Blum v. Yaretsky*, 457 U.S. 991 (1982); *Rendell-Baker v. Kohn*, 457 U.S. 830 (1982); *Jackson v. Metropolitan Edison Co.*, 419 U.S. 345 (1974).

The issue of state action, however, is only marginally relevant to the issue of affirmative duty in the constitutional tort context. On a superficial level, both lines of cases raise the question of whether the state bears any responsibility for the conduct of a nominally private actor. On closer examination, however, the two lines of cases address distinctly different issues. The affirmative duty cases raise the question of whether a state official owes an obligation to protect the plaintiff from some peril — not whether the peril itself can be said to be that of the state. State action is often a key issue in cases where the defendant is a government official, but the relationship between his governmental status and the injury is called into question. Claims arising from the off-duty actions of police officers are commonly analyzed in terms of state action. *See e.g., Gibson v. City of Chicago*, 910 F.2d 1510 (7th Cir. 1990) (shooting by suspended police officer was not under color of law); *Rossignol v. Voorhaar*, 316 F.3d 516 (4th Cir. 2003) (off-duty deputies who purchased all the local newspapers in an attempt to influence the outcome of an election acted under color of state law). *See supra* Chapter 2.

7. *Town of Castle Rock v. Gonzales*, 545 U.S. 748 (2005), resolved an issue explicitly left open in *DeShaney*: Does a state law requiring police to enforce a protective order establish a species of constitutional "property" which would enjoy due process protection against state deprivation? The Supreme Court held that Jessica Gonzales did not have a constitutionally protected property interest in having the police enforce a restraining order despite the mandatory language used in the Colorado statue and despite the police having probable cause to believe the order had been violated. Lacking a constitutional property interest, Ms. Gonzales could not prevail in her § 1983 claim that she was deprived of property without due process when the police failed to respond properly to her repeated reports that her estranged husband was violating the terms of the restraining order. Together, *DeShaney* and *Castle Rock* reject the general theory that the state deprives a person of liberty or property when it fails to protect him from harm at the hands of a third party. As illustrated in section B, however, there are a number of circumstances in which such a claim has been recognized. For a more detailed exposition of *Castle Rock* see the comments to Chapter 3, Part I, section A. *See also, Estate of Smithers v. City of Flint*, 602 F.3d 758 (6th Cir. 2010) (decedent did not have a constitutional "property" right in enforcing a minimum detention provision that was part of Michigan domestic violence law).

8. Despite the broad rhetoric of *DeShaney*, a large number of cases continue to raise issues of affirmative constitutional duties. The explanation for this may be twofold. First, state involvement in the affairs of its citizens is pervasive and may induce reliance on government for protection and other basic services. Thus, demand for affirmative duties remains high. Second, ambiguity within the *De-Shaney* opinion leaves open several doctrinal bases for recognizing such duties. The majority opinion appears to leave open the possibility that "special relationships" giving rise to an affirmative constitutional duty of protection might be recognized under other circumstances. *See generally* Eaton and Wells, *Governmental Inaction as a Constitutional Tort. DeShaney and Its Aftermath*, 66 Wash. L. Rev. 107 (1991). The following case explores the viability of affirmative duty constitutional tort claims after *DeShaney*.

B.   Affirmative Duties, State Created Dangers, and Special Relationships

KNEIPP v. TEDDER
95 F.3d 1199 (3d Cir. 1996)

Mansmann, Circuit Judge.

[Samantha Kneipp and her husband Joseph were stopped by officer Tedder as they were walking home on January 23, 1993. At the time she was stopped, Samantha was] visibly intoxicated — she smelled of urine, staggered when she walked and, at times, was unable to walk without assistance. [An expert witness] projected that Samantha's blood alcohol level at the time . . . would have been .25% . . . [which would have produced] serious incapacitation of muscular coordination, critical judgment, normal perception, and cognitive functions . . . [Joseph explained to officer Tedder that] he had a babysitter watching his son and that he was supposed to be home by now. Joseph then asked the officer if he could go home, to which the officer replied, 'Yeah, sure.' . . . Joseph . . . assumed that because Samantha was drunk, the police officers were going to take her either to the hospital or to the police station . . . Officer Tedder, however, sent Samantha home alone; she never reached her apartment building. . . . At approximately 1:51 a.m., . . . Samantha was found unconscious at the bottom of an embankment . . . across the street from the Kneipp's home . . . . As a result of her exposure to the cold, Samantha suffered hypothermia, which caused a condition known as anoxia . . . [which] resulted in permanent brain damage impairing many basic body functions.

Samantha's legal guardians instituted this civil rights action under 42 U.S.C. § 1983 against the City of Philadelphia and several police officers, alleging that the police officers were aware of Samantha's intoxication and "the potential for her to suffer harm because of her profoundly impaired faculties." By voluntarily assuming responsibility for her protection when they told Joseph he could leave, it was alleged that the officers affirmatively created a danger and increased the risk that Samantha might be injured when they later abandoned her. It is further alleged that the police conduct made Samantha "more vulnerable . . . [by] interfer[ing] with the efforts of Joseph. . . . to assist his wife to safety." Because the police officers acted with "deliberate or reckless indifference, callous disregard, or in such an arbitrary or abusive manner so as to shock the conscience," the legal guardians maintained that Samantha was deprived of her right to substantive due process and her liberty interest in personal security in violation of the Fourteenth Amendment of the United States Constitution. * * *

In granting the defendants' motion for summary judgment, the district court found that the legal guardians had failed to prove a constitutional violation under either the "special relationship" test or the state-created danger theory. The court also denied a motion for reconsideration.

II.

We begin our analysis with a discussion of the requirements for establishing a constitutional claim under 42 U.S.C. § 1983. * * *

Section 1983 does not, by its own terms, create substantive rights; it provides only remedies for deprivations of rights established elsewhere in the Constitution or federal laws. In order to establish a section 1983 claim, a plaintiff "must demonstrate a violation of a right secured by the Constitution and the laws of the United States [and] that the alleged deprivation was committed by a person acting under color of state law." Here, Samantha Kneipp's legal guardians have alleged that the City and police officers violated Samantha's right to substantive due process guaranteed by the Fourteenth Amendment.

In *DeShaney v. Winnebago Co. Dep't of Social Serv.*, the Supreme Court considered whether the due process clause of the Fourteenth Amendment imposed upon the state an affirmative duty to protect an individual against private violence where a special relationship exists between the state and the private individual. The Court found that the special relationship which would impose affirmative duties of care and protection on the state existed only in certain limited circumstances, such as when the state takes a person into its custody and holds him there against his will. The Court explained:

> In the substantive due process analysis, it is the State's affirmative act of restraining the individual's freedom to act on his own behalf — through incarceration, institutionalization, or other similar restraint of personal liberty — which is the "deprivation of liberty" triggering the protections of the Due Process Clause, not its failure to act to protect his liberty interests against harms inflicted by other means.

Applying this principle to the facts in *DeShaney*, the Court did not find a due process violation as the harms suffered by the child occurred while he was in the custody of his father, not in the state's custody.

In the case before us, we agree with the district court that the special relationship required by *DeShaney* did not exist between Samantha and the police officers. We disagree, however, with the holding of the district court insofar as it adds a special relationship requirement to the state-created danger theory. In *DeShaney*, the Supreme Court left open the possibility that a constitutional violation might have occurred despite the absence of a special relationship when it stated: "While the State may have been aware of the dangers that Joshua faced in the free world, it played no part in their creation, nor did it do anything to render him any more vulnerable to them." Several of our sister courts of appeals have cited this comment by the Court as support for utilizing a state-created danger theory to establish a constitutional claim under 42 U.S.C. § 1983. Moreover, two other courts of appeals, in decisions predating *DeShaney*, recognized the state-created danger theory as a basis for establishing a constitutional claim under section 1983.

In previous cases, we have considered the possible viability of the state-created danger theory as a mechanism for establishing a constitutional claim pursuant to 42 U.S.C. § 1983. Until now, we have not, however, been presented with the appropriate factual background to support a finding that state actors created a danger which deprived an individual of her Fourteenth Amendment right to substantive due process. Samantha Kneipp's case presents the right set of facts which, if believed, would trigger the application of the state-created danger theory. We turn first to our previous decisions in this area.

[An extended discussion of prior decisions is omitted.]

In the 1995 case of *Mark v. Borough of Hatboro*, [51 F.3d 1137 (3d Cir. 1995)], we suggested a test for applying the state-created danger theory. We found that cases predicating constitutional liability on a state-created danger theory have four common elements:

> (1) the harm ultimately caused was foreseeable and fairly direct; (2) the state actor acted in willful disregard for the safety of the plaintiff; (3) there existed some relationship between the state and the plaintiff; (4) the state actors used their authority to create an opportunity that otherwise would not have existed for the third party's crime to occur.

We further noted that "[t]he cases where the state-created danger theory was applied were based on discrete, grossly reckless acts committed by the state or state actors using their peculiar positions as state actors, leaving a discrete plaintiff vulnerable to foreseeable injury." Those courts which have recognized the state-created danger theory have employed a deliberate indifference standard.[5]

We . . . declined to adopt the state-created danger theory in *Mark* because its facts were dissimilar to the courts of appeals cases which upheld its use. The alleged constitutional violation in *Mark* arose from the borough's "failure to follow adequate policies to ensure that applicants to the fire department were screened sufficiently for tendencies towards arson." We concluded that when the alleged violation involved a policy directed at the public in general, such as the one at issue in *Mark*, the basis for the state-created danger theory was obviated insofar as the defendant lacked specific knowledge of the plaintiffs' condition, and a relationship between the defendants and plaintiffs did not exist.

We turn now to the unique facts presented in the case before us.

---

[5] [21] In the past, we have declined to distinguish terms such as "deliberate indifference," "reckless indifference," "gross negligence," or "reckless disregard" in the context of a violation of substantive due process under the Fourteenth Amendment. In attempting to reconcile the shocks the conscience standard with the reckless disregard test, we noted . . . that the reckless disregard standard appeared to apply only in those cases where the victim was in custody. We further commented that the reckless disregard threshold was "appropriate in custody cases because the government has restricted an individual's liberty and thereby increased his or her vulnerability to abusive governmental action or to private harm." By way of analogy, the alleged constitutional violation here should also be judged by the reckless disregard standard, as the rationale for employing such a threshold in custody cases is equally pertinent to the facts before us.

III.

We begin by applying the four common elements we set forth in *Mark* for the state-created danger theory. First, the injuries to Samantha were foreseeable — Dr. Saferstein stated in his report that at a blood alcohol level of .25%, Samantha's muscular coordination was seriously impaired. Joseph's testimony as to how he had to help his wife walk, even carry her at times, also tends to show that Samantha's ability to walk was impaired. A reasonable trier of fact could conclude that in Samantha's state of intoxication, she would be more likely to fall and injure herself if left unescorted than someone who was not inebriated. Based on the facts and inferences most favorable to the legal guardians, we hold that a reasonable jury could find that the harm likely to befall Samantha if separated from Joseph while in a highly intoxicated state in cold weather was indeed foreseeable.

Second, we find the plaintiffs have adduced sufficient evidence to raise a material issue as to whether Officer Tedder acted in willful disregard for Samantha's safety. The plaintiffs presented evidence regarding Samantha's level of intoxication and impairment; by Officer Tedder's own testimony, he admitted that he knew Samantha was drunk. Moreover, Tedder's statement that he sent Samantha and Joseph home together is contradicted by the testimony of Joseph, Officer Healy and Tina Leone.

We also believe the legal guardians have proved the third element — a relationship between the state and the person injured (here Officer Tedder and Samantha and Joseph Kneipp) during which the state places the victim in danger of a foreseeable injury.[6] *Mark*, 51 F.3d at 1153. Here it is alleged that Officer Tedder, exercising his powers as a police officer, placed Samantha in danger of foreseeable injury when he sent her home unescorted in a visibly intoxicated state in cold weather. A reasonable jury could find that Officer Tedder exerted sufficient control over Samantha to meet the relationship requirement.

Finally, there is sufficient evidence in the summary judgment record to show that Officer Tedder and the other police officers used their authority as police officers to create a dangerous situation or to make Samantha more vulnerable to danger had they not intervened. The conduct of the police, in allowing Joseph to go home alone and in detaining Samantha, and then sending her home unescorted in a seriously intoxicated state in cold weather, made Samantha more vulnerable to harm. It is conceivable that, but for the intervention of the police, Joseph would have continued to escort his wife back to their apartment where she would have been safe. A jury could find that Samantha was in a worse position after the police intervened than she would have been if they had not done so. As a result of the affirmative acts of the police officers, the danger or risk of injury to Samantha was greatly increased.

---

[6] [22] We view the "state-created danger" relationship to be different than the "special relationship" required by *DeShaney* to impose liability under section 1983. The relationship requirement under the state-created danger theory contemplates some contact such that the plaintiff was a foreseeable victim of a defendant's acts in a tort sense. The special relationship in *DeShaney*, on the other hand, has a custodial element to it — the state must affirmatively act to restrain an individual's freedom to act on his or her own behalf either through incarceration, institutionalization, or some other comparable limit of personal liberty.

Thus, we believe that a reasonable jury could find that the fourth and final requirement of *Mark* was satisfied here.

We find additional support for our position in the courts of appeals' decisions previously cited. *See Reed v. Gardner*, 986 F.2d at 1127 (police officer who removed a sober driver and left behind a passenger whom he knew to be drunk with the keys to the car was subject to liability under 42 U.S.C. § 1983); *Freeman v. Ferguson*, 911 F.2d at 54 (police chief, by interfering with police officers' enforcement of restraining order, created the danger which resulted in the victims' deaths and thus deprived victims of their constitutional rights); *White v. Rochford*, 592 F.2d at 385 (police officers who arrested uncle for drag racing and left minor children alone in abandoned car on the side of a busy, limited-access highway in cold weather had deprived children of their constitutional rights to personal security where the abandonment resulted in physical and emotional injury to the children).

In contrast to the above cited authority stands the en banc decision of the United States Court of Appeals for the Eighth Circuit in *Gregory v. City of Rogers, Arkansas*, 974 F.2d 1006 (8th Cir. 1992), *cert. denied*, 507 U.S. 913 (1993). In that case, the plaintiffs brought a civil rights action against the municipality and one of its police officers on the basis that defendants had a duty to provide for the safety of the passengers of a drinking group after the police arrested their designated driver on an outstanding warrant. After detaining the designated driver along the road for several minutes, the police allowed the designated driver to drive the car to the police station. The intoxicated passengers remained in the car, which was parked in front of the police station, while the designated driver cleared up the outstanding warrant inside the station with the police. After waiting approximately thirty minutes, one of the intoxicated passengers, the owner of the car, drove the car away and subsequently was involved in a one-car accident, killing himself and seriously injuring his passenger. Plaintiffs contended that the police officer actively placed the passengers in danger by permitting them to stay in the car unattended while waiting for the designated driver at the police station " 'in spite of their obviously intoxicated condition.' "

In *Gregory*, the plaintiffs' argument turned on whether the police officer knew or should have known the passengers were intoxicated. The court of appeals found that the plaintiffs failed to submit sufficient evidence which would lead a reasonable trier of fact to conclude that the police officer knew or should have known that the passengers were intoxicated and unfit to drive, and thus, upheld the district court's grant of summary judgment. The court of appeals, however, did not end its analysis there. It went on to say that even if the police officers knew the passengers were intoxicated, a reasonable jury could not find that the police officer affirmatively placed the passengers in danger by leaving them unattended in the car at the station. The court explained that it was the designated driver who placed the passengers in danger by leaving the keys in the car when he went into the police station. To impose a duty on the police to take affirmative action to protect the passengers, the court held, would circumvent the general rule that plaintiffs do not have a constitutional right to be protected by the police against harm inflicted by third persons.

Gregory, however, is distinguishable from this case in two respects. First the court of appeals in *Gregory* found that the police officer did not know that the passengers were intoxicated — neither the testimony of the witnesses, nor the behavior of the two passengers observed during the traffic stop on the roadway indicated they were intoxicated. In contrast here, Officer Tedder admitted that he knew Samantha was drunk at the time he was questioning her, and Samantha was observed staggering, walking and standing with difficulty, requiring that she lean on parked cars or be carried by her husband.

The second distinction is *who* created the danger — in *Gregory*, the court found that the third party created the danger by leaving the keys in the car; in the case before us, the police officers intervened to cut off Samantha's private source of protection by giving Joseph permission to go home alone, thereby increasing the danger that Samantha would suffer harm in her visibly intoxicated state when they abandoned her. The affirmative acts of the police officers here created a dangerous situation, requiring that they take additional measures to ensure Samantha's safety. That they failed to take the appropriate measures, knowing that Samantha was severely intoxicated, shows that the police officers acted with reckless disregard for her safety. On the other hand, the conduct of the police officer in *Gregory* did not rise to a level of recklessness. He did not know the passengers were drunk; nor did he take any affirmative action to create the dangerous situation — leaving the keys in the car. Put another way, the passengers in *Gregory* were never abandoned; all they had to do was remain in the safety of the car and await the return of their driver. Samantha, however, was isolated from her husband and then abandoned by the police. Clearly then, because of these two important distinctions, *Gregory* is not dispositive of the issue before us. * * *

Under the particular circumstances of this case, we hold that the state-created danger theory is a viable mechanism for establishing a constitutional claim under 42 U.S.C. § 1983. When viewed in the light most favorable to the legal guardians, the evidence submitted was sufficient to raise a triable issue of fact as to whether the police officers affirmatively placed Samantha in a position of danger. The district court erred, therefore, in granting summary judgment for the defendant police officers based on its finding that a constitutional violation had not occurred.

[The court's discussion of municipal liability is omitted.]

We will, therefore, reverse the order of the district court granting summary judgment for the defendants and remand for trial on this issue, and for further consideration of the municipal liability claims against the City of Philadelphia in light of our opinion.

NOTES

1. Almost every circuit court has recognized constitutional tort claims based on a "state-created danger" theory. *See e.g., Dwares v. City of New York*, 985 F.2d 94 (2d Cir. 1993) (police assured a group of "skinheads" that they would not interfere with their attack on political protesters who burned an American flag); *Robinson v. Lioi*, 2013 U.S. App. LEXIS 15458, at *9 (4th Cir. July 30, 2013) (police officer who intentionally withheld a warrant for domestic violence, warned the abusive husband about the warrant, and refused to arrest or serve the warrant, "created the dangerous situation that resulted in the victim's injury."); *Butera v. District of Columbia*, 235 F.3d 637 (D.C. Cir. 2001) (police failed to provide adequate protection for undercover operative); *Kallstrom v. City of Columbus*, 136 F.3d 1055 (6th Cir. 1998) (city released the addresses and phone numbers of undercover police officers to the attorney for gang members charged with drug offenses); *Monfils v. Taylor*, 165 F.3d 511 (7th Cir. 1998) (despite assurances to the contrary, police released tape of tip provided by anonymous informant; informant was murdered); *Freeman v. Ferguson*, 911 F.2d 52 (8th Cir. 1990) (police chief directed subordinate officers not to intervene in a domestic dispute); *Wood v. Ostrander*, 879 F.2d 583 (9th Cir. 1989) (police arrested drunk driver and impounded his vehicle, leaving the driver's female passenger stranded in a high crime area at 2:30 a.m.). The philosophy underlying these rulings was expressed in a pre-*DeShaney* case as follows: "If a state puts a man in a position of danger from private persons and then fails to protect him, it will not be heard to say that its role is merely passive; it is as much an active tortfeasor as if it had thrown him into a snake pit." *Bowers v. De Vito*, 686 F.2d 616, 618 (7th Cir. 1982).

The opinions of the Fifth Circuit Court of Appeals reflect a reluctance to embrace the state created danger theory of recovery. One opinion stated that while "[m]any of our sister circuits . . . [have accepted] some version of this 'state-created danger' theory . . . this court . . . [has] not yet determined whether a state official has a . . . [constitutional] duty to protect individuals from state created dangers." *McClendon v. City of Columbia*, 305 F.3d 314, 324 (5th Cir. 2002). Subsequent decisions appear to accept the state created danger theory in principle, but find that it does not apply to the facts of the particular case. *See e.g.*, *Doe v. Covington County School Dist.*, 675 F.3d 849 (5th Cir. 2012) (*en banc*) (absent specific evidence that school officials had actual knowledge of any immediate danger to the plaintiff, the officials could not be said to have created the danger by allowing a child to be signed out of school by a man who molested the child).

2. While courts agree in principle that a duty may arise under the due process clause when state officials create or increase the danger that ultimately results in the plaintiff's harm, the cases do not reflect a uniform approach to such claims. Common threads running throughout the variously articulated standards are (a) an affirmative act by the defendant that creates or increases the risk of danger to the plaintiff; and (b) that the defendant acted with the requisite level of culpability.

Whether the alleged governmental conduct is sufficient to trigger a constitutional duty is often a controversial and fact sensitive issue. In functional terms, the question is whether the conduct created a *sufficiently significant* danger or *sufficiently* increased the plaintiff's exposure to trigger a constitutional duty. Consider *Kovacic v. Villarreal*, 628 F.3d 209 (5th Cir. 2010). Zachary Kovacic (the decedent) was arrested by police for public intoxication and taken from a bar and the company of his friends. Due to overcrowding at the local jail and the non-violent nature of the offense, Kovacic was not taken to jail. At Kovacic's request, he was released at a convenience store so he could call his wife. Within a half-hour of his release, Kovacic was fatally struck by an unknown hit and run driver as he walked along a highway approximately 1/4 mile from where he was released by the police. The court held that these facts could not support a claim under the state created danger theory because the police did not have any reason to think that Kovacic would not call his wife to pick him up. What explains why summary judgment was not proper in *Kneipp*, but was proper in *Kovacic*? Did the police do more to create the danger to Samantha Kneipp than it did to Zacary Kovacic? Is there a significant difference in the level of culpability in the two cases?

Also consider *Kennedy v. City of Richfield*, 439 F.3d 1055 (9th Cir. 2006). Mrs. Kennedy reported to the police that she suspected that her 13-year-old neighbor, Michael Burns, had molested her 9 year old daughter. When meeting with the police, Kennedy informed officer Shields that Burns had a history of violence, including having set a cat on fire and breaking into his girl friend's house and beating her with a baseball bat. Kennedy expressed concern that Burns would retaliate violently if he learned that she had made the report to the police. Kennedy asked that she be given notice prior to any police contact with the Burns family about her allegations. Shields promised to do so. Instead, however, Shields told Burns of the allegations before warning the Kennedy. Shields told Kennedy of his meeting with Burns fifteen minutes after it had occurred. Shields promised to increase police patrols in the area that night. When Mr. Kennedy returned home at 10:00 p.m., he and his wife decided to stay in the house that evening and leave the next morning. Unfortunately, Burns broke into the house during the early morning hours and shot the Kennedys while they slept. Mr. Kennedy was killed and Mrs. Kennedy was seriously wounded.

Was officer Shields' informing Burns of the allegations against him an affirmative act that created or increased the risk of danger to the Kennedys? How is it similar to or different from officer Tedder's conduct in *Kneipp*? Of what relevance, if any, are Shields' promise to notify Kennedy before confronting Burns, or his promise to increase police patrols in the area? Of what relevance, if any, is the fact that Kennedy was told of the confrontation with Burns within 15 minutes of its occurrence?

3. The Third Circuit subsequently reformulated the fourth *Kneipp* factor to require evidence that "a state actor *affirmatively* used his or her authority in a way that created a danger to the citizen that rendered the citizen more vulnerable to danger than had the state not acted at all." *Bright v. Westmoreland County*, 443 F.3d 276 (3d Cir. 2006) (emphasis supplied).

Compare the four-part test articulated in *Kneipp* with the six-part test formulated by the Tenth Circuit:

> To state a prima facie case under the "danger creation" exception [to *DeShaney*] the plaintiff must show that: (1) the charged state actors created the danger or increased the plaintiff's vulnerability to the danger in some way; (2) the plaintiff was a member of a limited and specifically identifiable group; (3) the defendants' conduct put the plaintiff at substantial risk of serious, immediate, and proximate harm; (4) the risk was obvious and known; (5) the defendants acted recklessly in conscious disregard of that risk; and (6) the conduct, when viewed in total, shocks the conscience.

Ruiz v. McDonnell, 299 F.3d 1173, 1182–83 (10th Cir. 2002).

Are there any significant differences between these two standards? What does it mean for *Kneipp* to require "some relationship between the state and the plaintiff?"

What is a "limited and specifically identifiable group" as required in *Ruiz*? Suppose a sheriff gives a jail inmate unsupervised use of a patrol car and the inmate used the car to pull over a motorist who he later kills. *See Nishiyama v. Dickson County*, 814 F.2d 277 (6th Cir. 1987) (upholding the claim). Or suppose that a motorist is struck by a drunk driver after the police had arrested the sober driver and left the keys with the visibly intoxicated passenger? *Reed v. Gardner*, 986 F.2d 1122 (7th Cir. 1993) (upholding the claim). Has the state by affirmative action created or increased the risk of the harms that occurred? Would these claims be actionable under *Kneipp* or *Ruiz*? Did the victims in these cases have a relationship with the state or were they members of a limited and specifically identifiable group? Should these claims be allowed?

Judge Posner believes that such formulas create unnecessary confusion. "Shouldn't it be enough to say that it violates the due process clause for a government employee acting within the scope of his employment to commit a reckless act that by gratuitously endangering a person results in an injury to that person? Are there not virtues in simplicity, even in the law?" *Slade v. Bd. of School Directors of the City of Milwaukee*, 702 F.3d 1027, 1033 (7th Cir. 2012) (7th grader drowned on a school filed trip; upholding summary judgment for the supervising teacher whose conduct was not, as a matter of law, reckless)

4. Can detrimental reliance on an unfulfilled promise of protection support a claim under section 1983? For the most part, such claims have failed. *See e.g., Ye v. United States*, 484 F.3d 634 (3d Cir. 2007) (county physician assuring patient complaining about chest pains that "there is nothing to worry about and that he is fine" is "not an affirmative act sufficient to trigger constitutional obligations"). The *Ye* court cited other cases in which alleged detrimental reliance on governmental assurances of help were not deemed sufficient to trigger a constitutional affirmative duty. *See Rivera v. Rhode Island*, 402 F.3d 27 (1st Cir. 2005) (promise to protect witness testifying in a murder trial); *Wyke v. Polk County Bd. of Edu.*, 129 F.3d 560 (11th Cir. 1997) (mother assured by Dean of Students that "he would take care of" child's suicide attempt); *Gray v. University of Colorado Hosp. Authority*, 672 F.3d 909 (10th Cir. 2012) (assurance that patient would be monitored at all times). Collectively, these cases indicate that detrimental reliance on a governmental promise to intervene is not a sufficient affirmative act to support a constitutional obligation. But cf. *Kennedy v. City of Ridgefield*, 439 F.3d 1055 (9th Cir. 2006) (a complaint adequately alleged state created danger where plaintiff reported to police that her neighbor was a child molester and the police violated promises to patrol the neighborhood and to warn her before they talked to the neighbor; unfulfilled promises by themselves were not the basis of the state created danger; rather they were "additional and aggravating factors").

5. Some state-created danger claims arise in the workplace. In *Collins v. City of Harker Heights*, 503 U.S. 115 (1992) the Court affirmed the dismissal of a complaint that alleged that the city had a policy and custom of deliberate indifference toward the safety of its employees. The complaint focused on the city's alleged "custom and policy of not training its employees about the dangers of working in sewer lines and manhole, not providing safety equipment at job sites, and not providing safety warnings." 503 U.S. at 117. These allegations were not actionable under section 1983 because they could not "properly be characterized as arbitrary or conscience-shocking in a constitutional sense." 503 U.S. at 128.

In *L.W. v. Grubbs*, 974 F.2d 119 (9th Cir. 1992), a prison nurse was raped and beaten by an inmate with a history of sexual violence. She sued prison officials alleging that they led her to believe that she would not be required to work alone with violent sex offenders. The court of appeals reversed the district court's dismissal of her claim emphasizing that elevating the inmate to "cart boy status," prison officials created the opportunity for the inmate to attack the plaintiff. Moreover, the defendants "enhanced L.W.'s vulnerability to attack by misrepresenting to her the risks attending her work." 974 F.2d at 121. The court distinguished *Collins* reasoning that "[u]nlike Collins, L.W. alleges that the Defendants took affirmative steps to place her at significant risk, and that they knew of the risks." 974 F.2d at 122.

In *White v. Lemacks*, 183 F.3d 1253 (11th Cir. 1999) an inmate of a county jail brutally beat two nurses who had been assured that adequate security measures would be in place to protect them from injury. An earlier post-*DeShaney* Eleventh Circuit opinion had upheld an analogous claim under the state-created danger theory. *Corneilius v. Town of Highland Lake*, 880 F.2d 348 (11th Cir. 1989) (defendant assigned prison inmate with known violent propensities to work near city hall; town clerk abducted). The Court of Appeals in *White*, however, held that *Collins* required overruling *Corneilius* and the dismissal of White's suit. According to the court of appeals, *Collins* establishes the proposition that "[w]hile deliberate indifference to the safety of government employees in the workplace may constitute a tort under state law, it does not rise to the level of a substantive due process violation under the federal Constitution." 183 F.3d at 1259.

In *Lombardi v. Whitman*, 485 F.3d 73 (2d Cir. 2007) workers performing search, rescue, and clean-up work at the World Trade Center site in the aftermath of the September 11, 2001 terrorist attacks sued federal officials for allegedly making knowingly false statements about the air quality in lower Manhattan. The plaintiffs alleged that they relied on these statements by working without needed respiratory equipment. The complaint was dismissed because these allegations "did not shock the conscience even if the defendants acted with deliberate indifference: when agency officials decide how to reconcile competing governmental obligations in the face of disaster, only an intent to cause harm arbitrarily can shock the conscience in a way that justifies constitutional liability."

Should the state-created danger theory be evaluated by different standards when the victim is a government employee? Could government indifference to workplace safety ever be "conscience-shocking in a constitutional sense?"

6. Much of the focus of the preceeding notes is on the various ways a state official may create or increase the risk of harm so as to trigger a duty under the due process clause. The level of culpability (or state of mind) is also an important element of a substantive due process claim. Footnote 5[21] in *Kneipp* speaks of "deliberate indifference," "reckless disregard," "gross negligence," and "shocks the conscience." The contours of these different articulations of culpability were addressed in Chapter 3. *Kneipp* adopted a "reckless disregard" standard. In *Butera v. District of Columbia*, 235 F.3d 637 (D.C. Cir. 2001) the court held "[t]o assert a substantive due process violation [under a state-created danger theory] . . . , the plaintiff must also show that the [government's] conduct was 'so egregious, so outrageous, that it may fairly be said to shock the contemporary conscience.'" 235 F.3d at 279, quoting *County of Sacramento v. Lewis*, 523 U.S. 833, 847 n.8 (1998). In *Bukowski v. City of Akron*, 326 F.3d 702, 710 (6th Cir. 2003) the court reasoned that the shocks the conscience standard (as defined in *County of Sacramento v. Lewis*, 523 U.S. 833 (1998)) would apply when there was no time for reflection, but a deliberate indifference standard (as defined in *Farmer v. Brennan*, 511 U.S. 825 (1994)) would govern claims when the defendant had the opportunity to deliberate. What is the appropriate standard to support a substantive due process claim under the state-created danger theory? Does *Kneipp*'s acceptance of "reckless disregard" need to be reevaluated in light of *Farmer v. Brennan*? Should the standard differ depending on the opportunity for deliberation as suggested by *Bukowski*?

Judge Posner, writing for the Seventh Circuit, finds phrases like "shocks the conscience" and "deliberate indifference" to unhelpful and perhaps confusing. He suggests that the more well understood notion of "recklessness" should be the state of mind required to impose liability. Recklessness requires "knowledge of a serious risk to another person, coupled with failure to avert the risk though it could easily have been averted." *Slade v. Bd. of School Directors of the City of Milwaukee*, 702 F.3d 1027, 1029 (7th Cir. 2012).

7.   Courts that have adopted the state-created danger theory will deny claims when (a) the plaintiff fails to present sufficient evidence that affirmative acts by the defendant created or increased the risk of danger; or (b) the defendant's conduct does not meet the requisite level of culpability. *See e.g., Bukowski v. City of Akron*, 326 F.3d 702, 709 (6th Cir. 2003) (returning a 19-year-old mentally impaired woman at her request to her residence where she was subsequently raped by another occupant of the apartment "did nothing to increase [the plaintiff's] vulnerability to danger."); *S.S. v. McMullen*, 225 F.3d 960 (8th Cir. 2000) (defendant's act of returning child to father who allowed child to be left alone with known pedophile did not create greater risk than if the child had not been removed from her father); *Ruiz v. McDonnell*, 299 F.3d 1173, 1183 (10th Cir. 2002) (improper licensing and failure to investigate day care facility was not "the requisite affirmative conduct necessary to state a viable section 1983 claim."). Both *Bukowski* and *Ruiz* further held that the conduct alleged by the plaintiffs did not shock the conscience of the court. See also, *Slade v. Bd. of School Directors of the City of Milwaukee*, 702 F.3d 1027 (7th Cir. 2012) (school officials were not reckless with regard to drowning of 12-year-old child on a school field trip).

8.   Suppose one law enforcement officer passively observes as another officer inflicts excessive force or conducts an illegal search. Does the bystander officer have a constitutional duty to protect the plaintiff? This scenario, commonly referred to as "bystander liability," is well accepted by the lower courts. The general principles were summarized as follows: "To succeed on a theory of bystander liability, a plaintiff must demonstrate that a law-enforcement officer '(1) [knew] that a fellow officer [was] violating an individual's constitutional rights; (2) ha[d] a reasonable opportunity to prevent the harm; and (3) cho[se] not to act.'" *Stevenson v. City of Seat Pleasant*, 743 F.3d 411, 417 (4th Cir. 2014) quoting *Randall v. Prince George's County*, 302 F.3d 188, 203 (4th Cir. 2002) (collecting cases). Curiously, these opinions often do not cite *DeShaney* or identify the source of the bystander officer's

constitutional duty to protect the plaintiff. What is the constitutional basis for a duty of one officer to prevent the constitutional violation being committed by another officer? Some decisions imply that bystander liability can be imposed if the bystander officer "observes or has reason to know" that a constitutional violation is being committed. *E.g., Randall v. Prince George's County, supra.* Other decisions hold that the bystander "liability will not attach where an officer is not present at the scene of the constitutional violation." *Whitley v. Hanna,* 726 F.3d 631, 646 (5th Cir. 2013).

The Supreme Court's opinion in *Ashcroft v. Iqbal,* 556 U.S. 662 (2009) states that a federal supervisor can be held liable under *Bivens* only if that supervisor's conduct violates the constitutional rights of the plaintiff. The impact of this ruling on the theory of supervisory liability is discussed in Chapter 5, *infra.* Does *Iqbal* also call into the theory of bystander liability? Or does the officer who passively observes his partner inflicting excessive force also violate the constitutional rights of the victim? Several post-*Iqbal* opinions affirm the vitality of bystander liability without directly resolving the issue of whether the failure of the bystander to intervene violates the constitutional rights of the victim. *E.g., Stevenson v. City of Seat Pleasant,* 743 F.3d 411 (4th Cir. 2014) (officers who allegedly were present and did not intervene to prevent other officers from inflicting excessive force could be held liable under a bystander theory of liability). *Cf. Wilkerson v. Seymour,* 736 F.3d 974 (11th Cir. 2013) (acknowledging a "long line" of cases imposing a "duty to intervene", but finding that this duty did not arise when the defendant officer arrived on the scene after the alleged illegal arrest); *Whitley v. Hanna,* 726 F.3d 631 (5th Cir. 2013) (acknowledging the wide-spread acceptance of bystander liability, but holding that it did not apply to officers who were not present when another officer sexually abused the plaintiff).

9. The court in *Kneipp* briefly mentions that the due process clause of the Fourteenth Amendment may impose upon a government official an affirmative duty to protect an individual against private violence where a "special relationship" exists between the government and the individual. *Deshaney* expressly acknowledged that there are "certain limited circumstances" in which the Constitution imposes affirmative obligations to care for and protect individuals. The first such context is criminal incarceration. *See e.g., Farmer v. Brennan* (principal case in Chapter 3) (duty to protect an inmate from assaults by other inmates); *Estelle v. Gamble,* 429 U.S. 97 (1976) (duty to provide medical care for state inmate with serious medical need); *City of Revere v. Massachusetts General Hospital,* 463 U.S. 239 (1983) (medical care for pre-trial detainee). The second context in which a special relationship has been deemed to trigger an affirmative duty is the involuntary confinement of the mentally ill. *See Youngberg v. Romeo,* 457 U.S. 307 (1982) (conditions of confinement of persons involuntarily committed to a state hospital for the mentally ill). The involuntary and custodial nature of the relationship renders it "special" and explains why the pre-trial detainee, the incarcerated criminal, and involuntarily confined mentally ill patient are entitled to affirmative constitutional protection. As explained by the Court in *DeShaney,* "[t]he affirmative duty to protect [in such cases] arises not from the State's knowledge of the individual's predicament or from its expressions of intent to help him, but from the limitation which it has imposed on his freedom to act on his own behalf."

Footnote 3[9] in *DeShaney* suggests that there may be other situations "sufficiently analogous to incarceration and institutionalization to give rise to a duty to protect." As foreshadowed by that footnote, lower courts have found that the state's removal of a child from the custody of her parents and placing her in foster care does create a special relationship triggering a duty to protect. *See e.g.*, *Schwartz v. Booker*, 702 F.3d 573 (10th Cir. 2012); *H.A.L. v. Foltz*, 551 F.3d 1227 (11th Cir. 2008); *Berman v. Young*, 291 F.3d 976 (7th Cir. 2001); *Burton v. Richmond*, 276 F.3d 973 (8th Cir. 2002). Of course, even if a special relationship is found to exist, the claim will fail if the defendant's conduct does not reach the required level of culpability. *E.g.*, *McLean v. Gordon*, 548 F.3d 613 (8th Cir. 2008) (social worker's failure to check foster home for unsecured firearms did not shock the conscience of the court).

Is a child's compulsory attendance in public school sufficiently analogous to placing a child in foster care? Almost every court to face this question has ruled that there is no special relationship within the meaning of *DeShaney* between public school students and school officials. Thus, school officials do not have an affirmative duty under the due process clause to protect students from sexual or physical harassment by teachers or fellow students. *See e.g.*, *Morrow v. Balaski*, 719 F.3d 160 (3d Cir. 2012) (cyber-bullying and in school threats by fellow students; court notes that every circuit has concluded that compulsory school attendance laws do not create a special relationship triggering affirmative constitutional duties); *Patel v. Kent School Dist.*, 648 F.3d 965 (9th Cir. 2011) (no constitutional duty to protect developmentally disabled student; noting that all circuit courts have refused to apply the special relationship principle to children attending public schools under state compulsory attendance laws); *Doe v. Covington County School Dist.*, 675 F.3d 849 (5th Cir. 2012) (*en banc*) (no constitutional duty to protect a 9-year-old fourth grade student; explicit rejection of special relationship theory).

These courts reason that compulsory attendance laws are not sufficiently custodial and do not sufficiently restrain a student's ability to protect himself or herself to trigger a constitutional obligation to protect. Should the outcome be different if the child was a resident of the state school for the deaf? *See Walton v. Alexander*, 44 F.3d 1297 (5th Cir. 1995) (*en banc*) (no special relationship because custody was voluntary). *Cf. Vernonia Sch. Dist. 47J v. Acton*, 515 U.S. 646, 655 (1995) (public school's custody of students is cited to justify mandatory drug testing of athletes, but this control is not of a "sufficient degree" to give rise to a constitutional duty to protect).

The absence of a custodial relationship and the lack of state-imposed restraints on self-protection have also been cited to deny constitutional tort claims stemming for a child drowning at a city day camp, *Deanzona v. City and County of Denver*, 222 F.3d 1229 (10th Cir. 2000); a child choking to death on a grape when there was a delay in EMT response to a 911 emergency call, *Brown v. Pa. Dept. of Health Emergency Med. Servs. Training*, 318 F.3d 473 (3d Cir. 2003); and failing to serve a domestic order of protection on plaintiff's abusive ex-husband, *Jones v. Union County*, 296 F.3d 417 (6th Cir. 2002). Do these cases imply that traditional common law tort concepts of undertaking and detrimental reliance are not sufficient to create a special relationship triggering a constitutional duty to protect? If so, what more is needed? Why is it needed?

10. Claims that might be characterized in terms of affirmative duties under the due process clause might also be presented under different statutes or constitutional provisions. Recall from Note 9 that most courts have held that school officials do not have a duty under the due process clause to protect students from sexual harassment by teachers or fellow students. Such claims may be actionable, however, under Title IX of the Education Amendments of 1972, 20 U.S.C.§ 1681. Title IX prohibits recipients of federal funds from engaging in sex discrimination in education programs. In *Franklin v. Gwinnett County Public Schools*, 503 U.S. 60 (1992), the Court recognized an implied private right of action against school districts under Title IX for its alleged failure to prevent the sexual harassment of a student by a teacher. In *Gebser v. Lago Vista Independent School District*, 524 U.S. 274 (1998), the Court held that the school district could not be held liable for such a claim simply because the harassing teacher was an employee of the district. Rather, the plaintiff must show that the school district as an entity did something wrong. To do this, the plaintiff must prove that (a) an official with authority to address the alleged harassment and to institute corrective measures on behalf of the school (b) had actual knowledge of the harassment and (c) responded with deliberate indifference. 524 U.S. at 290. Moreover, the alleged harassment must be sufficiently severe, pervasive and objectively offensive that it denies the victims equal access to education. *Davis v. Monroe County Board of Education*, 526 U.S. 629, 650 (1999). *Davis* also held that the failure to prevent student-on-student sexual harassment could violate Title IX so long as the actual knowledge and deliberate indifference standards were satisfied. While the "actual knowledge" and "deliberate indifference" standards pose significant burdens on potential plaintiffs, a Title IX claim may succeed when a section 1983 affirmative duty claim would probably fail. *E.g.*, *Williams v. Board of Regents*, 441 F.3d 1287 (11th Cir. 2006) (student's section 1983 claims against University President and Athletic Director based on student-on-student sexual harassment were dismissed; claims under Title IX survived a motion to dismiss). How do the elements of a Title IX claim compare with those required to establish governmental liability under section 1983? *See supra* Chapter 5. For an overview of Title IX, see HAROLD S. LEWIS & ELIZABETH J. NORMAN, CIVIL RIGHTS LAW AND PRACTICE §§ 4.15–4.22 (2001).

Jones v. Union County, 296 F.3d 417 (6th Cir. 2002), also discussed in note 9, is typical of cases that deny affirmative duty due process claims based on the failure of the defendant to protect the victim from domestic violence. However, as foreshadowed by footnote 2[3] in *DeShaney*, such claims have been recognized, however, when couched in terms of a denial of equal protection. More specifically, courts have held that victims of domestic violence may have a claim against police officials if they can show: "(1) that a policy or custom was adopted by the defendants to provide less protection to victims of domestic assault than to other assault victims; (2) that discrimination against women was the motivating factor for the defendants; and (3) that the injury was caused by the operation of the policy or custom." *Shipp v. McMahon*, 234 F.3d 907, 913 (5th Cir. 2000) (collecting cases). Proving intent to discriminate may be difficult, however. *See Soto v. Flores*, 103 F.3d 1056, 1067 (1st Cir. 1997) ("Without a smoking gun of an overtly discriminatory statement by a decisionmaker, it may be very difficult to offer sufficient proof of such a purpose."); *Eagleston v. Guido*, 41 F.3d 865, 878 (2d Cir. 1994) (statistics showing that domestic violence complaints were less likely to result in arrest than were stranger assault complaints and evidence of under-enforcement of official domestic violence policy did not constitute evidence of discriminatory intent or purpose); *Ricketts v. City of Columbia*, 36 F.3d 775, 781 (8th Cir. 1994) (although over 90% of victims of domestic abuse are women, police statements that they disfavor getting involved in domestic disputes is not evidence to discriminate against women). Some courts appear to apply a less exacting standard of proof of intent. *See e.g., Balistreri v. Pacifica Police Dept.*, 901 F.2d 696, 701 (9th Cir. 1988) (remark by officer that the husband was entitled to hit his wife because she was "carrying on" suggests an animus against women sufficient to survive a motion to dismiss). An equal protection theory might be available in other contexts as well. *See e.g., Dwares v. City of New York*, 985 F.2d 94 (2d Cir. 1993) (holding that the district court erred in dismissing a suit alleging that police intentionally discriminated against "flag burners" by failing to protect them from an attack by "skinheads" during a political protest).

II. SECTION 1983 AND FEDERAL "LAWS"

Under the terms of section 1983, suit may be brought not only for constitutional wrongs, but also for violations of federal "laws." The Supreme Court so held in *Maine v. Thiboutot*, 448 U.S. 1 (1980). The issue was whether suits to enforce provisions of the Social Security Act could be brought under section 1983. Justice Brennan's opinion for the Court adopted a "plain meaning" approach to interpreting the statute.

> The question before us is whether the phrase 'and laws,' as used in section 1983, means what it says, or whether it should be limited to some subset of laws. Given that Congress attached no modifiers to the phrase, the plain language of the statute undoubtedly embraces respondents' claim that petitioners violated the Social Security Act.

Does the Court always follow the "plain meaning" approach to interpreting section 1983? If not, why does it shift from one interpretive theory to another as it moves from case to case?

Despite the "plain meaning" reasoning of *Thiboutot*, the Court has never allowed plaintiffs to use section 1983 as a vehicle for enforcing all federal "laws." In *Middlesex County Sewerage Authority v. National Sea Clammers Assn*, 453 U.S. 1 (1981), it restricted the availability of section 1983 for enforcement of federal statutes in two ways. Section 1983 would not be available if "the statute at issue was [not] the kind that created enforceable 'rights' under section 1983," or if "Congress had foreclosed private enforcement" of the statute on which the plaintiff sought to base the substance of the lawsuit. Section A addresses the first of these issues and section B the second.

A. Enforceable Rights

GONZAGA UNIVERSITY v. DOE
536 U.S. 273 (2002)

CHIEF JUSTICE REHNQUIST delivered the opinion of the Court.

The question presented is whether a student may sue a private university for damages under § 1983, to enforce provisions of the Family Educational Rights and Privacy Act of 1974 (FERPA or Act), 20 U.S.C. § 1232g, which prohibit the federal funding of educational institutions that have a policy or practice of releasing education records to unauthorized persons. We hold such an action foreclosed because the relevant provisions of FERPA create no personal rights to enforce under § 1983.

[Doe] is a former undergraduate in the School of Education at Gonzaga University, a private university in Spokane, Washington. He planned to graduate and teach at a Washington public elementary school. Washington at the time required all of its new teachers to obtain an affidavit of good moral character from a dean of their graduating college or university. In October 1993, Roberta League, Gonzaga's "teacher certification specialist," overheard one student tell another that respondent engaged in acts of sexual misconduct against Jane Doe, a female undergraduate. League launched an investigation and contacted the state agency responsible for teacher certification, identifying respondent by name and discussing the allegations against him. Respondent did not learn of the investigation, or that information about him had been disclosed, until March 1994, when he was told by League and others that he would not receive the affidavit required for certification as a Washington schoolteacher.

[Doe] then sued Gonzaga and League [alleging state law claims as well as a] violation of § 1983 for the release of personal information to an "unauthorized person" in violation of FERPA. A jury found for [Doe] on all counts, awarding him $1,155,000, including $150,000 in compensatory damages and $300,000 in punitive damages on the FERPA claim.

The Washington Court of Appeals reversed in relevant part, concluding that FERPA does not create individual rights and thus cannot be enforced under § 1983. The Washington Supreme Court reversed that decision, and ordered the FERPA damages reinstated. The court acknowledged that "FERPA itself does not give rise to a private cause of action," but reasoned that FERPA's nondisclosure provision "gives rise to a federal right enforceable under section 1983."

Like the Washington Supreme Court and the state court of appeals below, other state and federal courts have divided on the question of FERPA's enforceability under § 1983. The fact that all of these courts have relied on the same set of opinions from this Court suggests that our opinions in this area may not be models of clarity. We therefore granted certiorari, to resolve the conflict among the lower courts and in the process resolve any ambiguity in our own opinions.

Congress enacted FERPA under its spending power to condition the receipt of federal funds on certain requirements relating to the access and disclosure of student educational records. The Act directs the Secretary of Education to withhold federal funds from any public or private "educational agency or institution" that fails to comply with these conditions. As relevant here, the Act provides:

"No funds shall be made available under any applicable program to any educational agency or institution which has a policy or practice of permitting the release of education records (or personally identifiable information contained therein . . .) of students without the written consent of their parents to any individual, agency, or organization." 20 U.S.C. § 1232g(b)(1).

The Act directs the Secretary of Education to enforce this and other of the Act's spending conditions. The Secretary is required to establish an office and review board within the Department of Education for "investigating, processing, reviewing, and adjudicating violations of [the Act]." Funds may be terminated only if the Secretary determines that a recipient institution "is failing to comply substantially with any requirement of [the Act]" and that such compliance "cannot be secured by voluntary means."

Respondent contends that this statutory regime confers upon any student enrolled at a covered school or institution a federal right, enforceable in suits for damages under § 1983, not to have "education records" disclosed to unauthorized persons without the student's express written consent. But we have never before held, and decline to do so here, that spending legislation drafted in terms resembling those of FERPA can confer enforceable rights.

In *Maine v. Thiboutot*, 448 U.S. 1 (1980), six years after Congress enacted FERPA, we recognized for the first time that § 1983 actions may be brought against state actors to enforce rights created by federal statutes as well as by the Constitution. There we held that plaintiffs could recover payments wrongfully withheld by a state agency in violation of the Social Security Act. A year later, in *Pennhurst State School and Hospital v. Halderman*, 451 U.S. 1 (1981), we rejected a claim that the Developmentally Disabled Assistance and Bill of Rights Act of 1975 conferred enforceable rights, saying:

"In legislation enacted pursuant to the spending power, the typical remedy for state noncompliance with federally imposed conditions is not a private cause of action for noncompliance but rather action by the Federal Government to terminate funds to the State."

We made clear that unless Congress "speaks with a clear voice," and manifests an "unambiguous" intent to confer individual rights, federal funding provisions provide no basis for private enforcement by § 1983.

Since *Pennhurst*, only twice have we found spending legislation to give rise to enforceable rights. In *Wright v. Roanoke Redevelopment and Housing Authority*, 479 U.S. 418 (1987), we allowed a § 1983 suit by tenants to recover past overcharges under a rent-ceiling provision of the Public Housing Act, on the ground that the provision unambiguously conferred "a mandatory [benefit] focusing on the individual family and its income." The key to our inquiry was that Congress spoke in terms that "could not be clearer," and conferred entitlements "sufficiently specific and definite to qualify as enforceable rights under *Pennhurst*." Also significant was that the federal agency charged with administering the Public Housing Act "had never provided a procedure by which tenants could complain to it about the alleged failures [of state welfare agencies] to abide by [the Act's rent-ceiling provision]."

Three years later, in *Wilder v. Virginia Hospital Assn.*, 496 U.S. 498 (1990), we allowed a § 1983 suit brought by health care providers to enforce a reimbursement provision of the Medicaid Act, on the ground that the provision, much like the rent-ceiling provision in *Wright*, explicitly conferred specific monetary entitlements upon the plaintiffs. Congress left no doubt of its intent for private enforcement, we said, because the provision required States to pay an "objective" monetary entitlement to individual health care providers, with no sufficient administrative means of enforcing the requirement against States that failed to comply.

Our more recent decisions, however, have rejected attempts to infer enforceable rights from Spending Clause statutes. In *Suter v. Artist M.*, 503 U.S. 347 (1992), the Adoption Assistance and Child Welfare Act of 1980 required States receiving funds for adoption assistance to have a "plan" to make "reasonable efforts" to keep children out of foster homes. A class of parents and children sought to enforce this requirement against state officials under § 1983, claiming that no such efforts had been made. We [found] no basis for the suit, saying:

> "Careful examination of the language . . . does not unambiguously confer an enforceable right upon the Act's beneficiaries. The term 'reasonable efforts' in this context is at least as plausibly read to impose only a rather generalized duty on the State, to be enforced not by private individuals, but by the Secretary in the manner [of reducing or eliminating payments]."

Since the Act conferred no specific, individually enforceable rights, there was no basis for private enforcement, even by a class of the statute's principal beneficiaries.

Similarly, in *Blessing v. Freestone*, 520 U.S. 329 (1997), Title IV-D of the Social Security Act required States receiving federal child-welfare funds to "substantially comply" with requirements designed to ensure timely payment of child support. Five Arizona mothers invoked § 1983 against state officials on grounds that state child-welfare agencies consistently failed to meet these requirements. We found no basis for the suit, saying,

> "Far from creating an *individual* entitlement to services, the standard is simply a yardstick for the Secretary to measure the *systemwide* performance of a State's Title IV-D program. Thus, the Secretary must look to the aggregate services provided by the State, not to whether the needs of any particular person have been satisfied." (emphases in original).

Because the provision focused on "the aggregate services provided by the State," rather than "the needs of any particular person," it conferred no individual rights and thus could not be enforced by § 1983. We emphasized: "To seek redress through § 1983, . . . a plaintiff must assert the violation of a federal *right*, not merely a violation of federal *law*." (emphases in original).

[Doe] reads this line of cases to establish a relatively loose standard for finding rights enforceable by § 1983. He claims that a federal statute confers such rights so long as Congress intended that the statute "benefit" putative plaintiffs. He further contends that a more "rigorous" inquiry would conflate the standard for inferring a private right of action under § 1983 with the standard for inferring a private right of action directly from the statute itself, which he admits would not exist under FERPA. As authority, respondent points to *Blessing* and *Wilder*, which, he says, used the term "benefit" to define the sort of statutory interest enforceable by § 1983.

[Some] language in our opinions might be read to suggest that something less than an unambiguously conferred right is enforceable by § 1983. *Blessing*, for example, set forth three "factors" to guide judicial inquiry into whether or not a statute confers a right: "Congress must have intended that the provision in question benefit the plaintiff," "the plaintiff must demonstrate that the right assertedly protected by the statute is not so 'vague and amorphous' that its enforcement would strain judicial resources," and "the provision giving rise to the asserted right must be couched in mandatory, rather than precatory, terms." In the same paragraph, however, *Blessing* emphasizes that it is only violations of *rights*, not *laws*, which give rise to § 1983 actions. This confusion has led some courts to interpret *Blessing* as allowing plaintiffs to enforce a statute under § 1983 so long as the plaintiff falls within the general zone of interest that the statute is intended to protect; something less than what is required for a statute to create rights enforceable directly from the statute itself under an implied private right of action. Fueling this uncertainty is the notion that our implied private right of action cases have no bearing on the standards for discerning whether a statute creates rights enforceable by § 1983.

[We] now reject the notion that our cases permit anything short of an unambiguously conferred right to support a cause of action brought under § 1983. Section 1983 provides a remedy only for the deprivation of "rights, privileges, or immunities secured by the Constitution and laws" of the United States. Accordingly, it is *rights*, not the broader or vaguer "benefits" or "interests," that may be enforced under the authority of that section. This being so, we further reject the notion that our implied right of action cases are separate and distinct from our § 1983 cases. To the contrary, our implied right of action cases should guide the determination of whether a statute confers rights enforceable under § 1983.

We have recognized that whether a statutory violation may be enforced through § 1983 "is a different inquiry than that involved in determining whether a private right of action can be implied from a particular statute." But the inquiries overlap in one meaningful respect — in either case we must first determine whether Congress *intended to create a federal right*. Thus we have held that "the question whether Congress . . . intended to create a private right of action [is] definitively answered in the negative" where "a statute by its terms grants no private rights to any identifiable class." For a statute to create such private rights, its text must be "phrased in terms of the persons benefited." We have recognized, for example, that Title VI of the Civil Rights Act of 1964 and Title IX of the Education Amendments of 1972 create individual rights because those statutes are phrased "with an *unmistakable focus* on the benefited class." (emphasis added). But even where a statute is phrased in such explicit rights-creating terms, a plaintiff suing under an implied right of action still must show that the statute manifests an intent "to create not just a private *right* but also a private *remedy*." *Alexander v. Sandoval*, 532 U.S. 275, 286 (2001) (emphases added).

Plaintiffs suing under § 1983 do not have the burden of showing an intent to create a private remedy because § 1983 generally supplies a remedy for the vindication of rights secured by federal statutes. Once a plaintiff demonstrates that a statute confers an individual right, the right is presumptively enforceable by § 1983. But the initial inquiry — determining whether a statute confers any right at all — is no different from the initial inquiry in an implied right of action case, the express purpose of which is to determine whether or not a statute "confers rights on a particular class of persons." This makes obvious sense, since § 1983 merely provides a mechanism for enforcing individual rights "secured" elsewhere, *i.e.*, rights independently "secured by the Constitution and laws" of the United States. "One cannot go into court and claim a 'violation of § 1983' — for § 1983 by itself does not protect anyone against anything."

A court's role in discerning whether personal rights exist in the § 1983 context should therefore not differ from its role in discerning whether personal rights exist in the implied right of action context. [Both] inquiries simply require a determination as to whether or not Congress intended to confer individual rights upon a class of beneficiaries. [Accordingly,] where the text and structure of a statute provide no indication that Congress intends to create new individual rights, there is no basis for a private suit, whether under § 1983 or under an implied right of action.

Justice Stevens disagrees with this conclusion principally because separation-of-powers concerns are, in his view, more pronounced in the implied right of action context as opposed to the § 1983 context. But we fail to see how relations between the branches are served by having courts apply a multi-factor balancing test to pick and choose which federal requirements may be enforced by § 1983 and which may not. Nor are separation-of-powers concerns within the Federal Government the only guideposts in this sort of analysis. See *Will v. Michigan Dept. of State Police*, 491 U.S. 58, 65 (1989) ("If Congress intends to alter the 'usual constitutional balance between the States and the Federal Government,' it must make its intention to do so 'unmistakably clear in the language of the statute.' ")

With this principle in mind, there is no question that FERPA's nondisclosure provisions fail to confer enforceable rights. To begin with, the provisions entirely lack the sort of "rights-creating" language critical to showing the requisite congressional intent to create new rights. Unlike the individually focused terminology of Titles VI and IX ("no person shall be subjected to discrimination"), FERPA's provisions speak only to the Secretary of Education, directing that "no funds shall be made available" to any "educational agency or institution" which has a prohibited "policy or practice." This focus is two steps removed from the interests of individual students and parents and clearly does not confer the sort of "*individual* entitlement" that is enforceable under § 1983.

[FERPA's] nondisclosure provisions further speak only in terms of institutional policy and practice, not individual instances of disclosure. See 1232g(b)(1)–(2) (prohibiting the funding of "any educational agency or institution which has a *policy or practice* of permitting the release of education records" (emphasis added)). Therefore, [they] have an "aggregate" focus, they are not concerned with "whether the needs of any particular person have been satisfied," and they cannot "give rise to individual rights." Recipient institutions can further avoid termination of funding whether a cause of action should be implied from a federal statute. The latter question is similar to one we have already encountered in chapter 1. There we saw that, beginning at least as long ago as *Bivens*, the Supreme Court has sometimes implied a cause of action from constitutional provisions, thereby allowing persons to seek damages for violations of constitutional rights without statutory authorization. We also saw that, over the past twenty five years, the Court has considerably narrowed the circumstances in which that cause of action will be available.

The cases on implying remedies from federal statutes and administrative regulations have followed a similar pattern. In *J. I. Case Co. v. Borak*, 377 U.S. 426 (1964), the Court implied a cause of action to enforce § 14 (a) of the Securities Exchange Act of 1934, a prohibition on fraud in the solicitation of proxy material. It reasoned that "it is the duty of the courts to provide such remedies as are necessary to make effective the congressional purpose." Allowing a suit for damages, though the statute did not provide one, was an effective way to enforce Congress's aims. Between 1964 and 1975 the Court used this rationale to liberally imply causes of action to enforce statutes. It changed direction in *Cort v. Ash*, 422 U.S. 66 (1975). That case introduced the notion that litigants seeking to imply a cause of action to enforce a statute had to show that Congress intended to create one. This test is typically met only when the statute was enacted during the pre-*Cort* years and the legislative history shows that Congress did not bother to insert a cause-of-action provision, simply because it knew the Court would imply one under the case law then in force. *See, e.g., Touche, Ross & Co. v. Redington*, 442 U.S. 560 (1979).

Alexander v. Sandoval, 532 U.S. 275 (2001), is the Court's most recent foray into this area. Refusing to imply a cause of action to enforce "disparate-impact regulations promulgated [by the Department of Justice] under Title VI of the Civil Rights Act of 1964," the Court stressed that "[t]he judicial task is to interpret the statute Congress has passed to determine whether it displays an intent to create not just a private right but also a private remedy." Since Title VI prohibits only *intentional* discrimination, the necessary legislative intent to create a remedy for disparate impact was lacking. By the same token, *Sandoval* did not undermine, and indeed affirmed the existence of, an implied cause of action to enforce administrative regulations that implement Title VI's ban on intentional discrimination. *See Peters v. Jenney*, 327 F.3d 307, 315 (4th Cir. 2003).

The Court in *Gonzaga University* declares that the reasoning of *Sandoval* will henceforth govern the issue of whether to allow a section 1983 "laws" action. *Sandoval* is typical of most of the cases since *Cort* in refusing to imply a cause of action. But some of the reasoning in *Sandoval* seems to make it harder for the plaintiff to establish Congressional intent. The pre-*Sandoval* cases would occasionally find that intent to create a private remedy could be implied from the "contemporary legal context," i.e., the fact that the statute was enacted during the freewheeling era of *Borak* and before *Cort*. But *Sandoval* rejects this reasoning, asserting that "[i]n determining whether statutes create private rights of action, as in interpreting statutes generally, legal context matters only to the extent it clarifies text." *Gonzaga University*'s reliance on *Sandoval* suggests that the Court in "laws" cases may approve section 1983 suits only where Congress's intent to allow a section 1983 remedy for violation of federal law is explicitly stated in the statute. *See* Bradford C. Mank, *Suing Under Section 1983: The Future After* Gonzaga University v. Doe, 39 HOUSTON L. REV. 1417, 1419–20 (2003) (asserting that "the *Gonzaga* decision places a heavy and unnecessary burden of proof on plaintiffs by requiring unambiguous and explicit evidence that Congress intended to create an individual right benefiting a class including the plaintiff").

Dissenting in *Gonzaga University,* Justice Stevens objected to the Court's use of implied cause of action principles in the section 1983 "laws" context, arguing that the separation of powers concerns that underlie the former doctrine are not relevant to the latter. How did the Court meet this contention? Is the Court's answer persuasive?

3. Notice that *Gonzaga University* concerned a statute enacted under Congress's spending power. By its terms the statute tells institutions that receive federal funds that the money may be cut off unless the recipient safeguards student privacy. Part of the Court's reasoning stresses this aspect of the statutory scheme. The Court declares that "unless Congress speaks with a clear voice, and manifests an unambiguous intent to confer individual rights, federal funding provisions provide no basis for private enforcement." Does the Court mean to limit the scope of the ruling to spending cases?

An example of non-spending legislation that raises the "laws" issue is federal law that preempts state regulation of some area. The Court has held that the preemption may create "enforceable rights". *See Golden State Transit Corp. v. City of Los Angeles,* 493 U.S. 103 (1989). At an earlier stage of the *Golden State* litigation the Court had decided that the city violated federal labor law by requiring Golden State to settle a labor dispute with its union as a condition of renewing Golden State's taxicab license. On remand Golden State sought both injunctive relief and damages, relying on section 1983 for its cause of action to recover damages. The district court enjoined the city but refused to allow the section 1983 suit for damages, on the ground that "the supremacy clause does not create enforceable rights that may be vindicated in an action for damages under section 1983." The Supreme Court agreed that the supremacy clause "of its own force, does not create rights enforceable under section 1983." Here, however, Golden State "was the intended beneficiary of a statutory scheme that prevents governmental interference with the collective-bargaining process and . . . the NLRA gives it rights enforceable against governmental interference in an action under section 1983." The Court continued:

> In the NLRA, Congress has not just "occupied the field" with legislation that is passed solely with the interests of the general public in mind. In such circumstances, when congressional pre-emption benefits particular parties only as an incident of the federal scheme of regulation, a private damages remedy under section 1983 may not be available. The NLRA, however, creates rights in labor and management both against one another and against the State. By its terms, the Act confers certain rights "generally on employees and not merely as against the employer." We have thus stated that "[i]f the state law regulates conduct that is actually protected by federal law, . . . preemption follows . . . as a matter of substantive right . . ."

in the [the statute] and Congress' express efforts to place on local and state educational agencies the primary responsibility for developing a plan to accommodate the needs of each individual handicapped child").

In *Rancho Palos Verdes*, we again focused on a statute's remedial scheme in inferring congressional intent for exclusivity. After being denied a permit to build a radio tower on his property, the plaintiff brought claims for injunctive relief under the Telecommunications Act of 1996 (TCA) and for damages and attorney's fees under § 1983. Noting that the TCA provides highly detailed and restrictive administrative and judicial remedies, and explaining that "limitations upon the remedy contained in the statute are deliberate and are not to be evaded through § 1983," we again concluded that Congress must have intended the statutory remedies to be exclusive.

In all three cases, the statutes at issue required plaintiffs to comply with particular procedures and/or to exhaust particular administrative remedies prior to filing suit. Offering plaintiffs a direct route to court via § 1983 would have circumvented these procedures and given plaintiffs access to tangible benefits — such as damages, attorney's fees, and costs — that were unavailable under the statutes. "Allowing a plaintiff to circumvent" the statutes' provisions in this way would have been "inconsistent with Congress' carefully tailored scheme." *Smith, supra*, at 1012.

B

1

Section 901(a) of Title IX provides:

"No person in the United States shall, on the basis of sex, be excluded from participation in, be denied the benefits of, or be subjected to discrimination under any education program or activity receiving Federal financial assistance." 20 U.S.C. § 1681(a).

The statute's only express enforcement mechanism, § 1682, is an administrative procedure resulting in the withdrawal of federal funding from institutions that are not in compliance. In addition, this Court has recognized an implied private right of action. Cannon v. University of Chicago, 441 U.S. 677, 717 (1979). In a suit brought pursuant to this private right, both injunctive relief and damages are available. *Franklin v. Gwinnett County Public Schools*, 503 U.S. 60, 76, (1992).

These remedies — withdrawal of federal funds and an implied cause of action — stand in stark contrast to the "unusually elaborate," "carefully tailored," and "restrictive" enforcement schemes of the statutes at issue in *Sea Clammers, Smith,* and *Rancho Palos Verdes* Unlike those statutes, Title IX has no administrative exhaustion requirement and no notice provisions. Under its implied private right of action, plaintiffs can file directly in court, *Cannon, supra,* at 717, and can obtain the full range of remedies, see *Franklin, supra,* at 72 (concluding that "Congress did not intend to limit the remedies available in a suit brought under Title IX"). As a result, parallel and concurrent § 1983 claims will neither circumvent required procedures, nor allow access to new remedies.

Moreover, this Court explained in *Rancho Palos Verdes* that "[t]he provision of an *express*, private means of redress in the statute itself" is a key consideration in determining congressional intent, and that "the existence of a more restrictive private remedy for statutory violations has been the dividing line between those cases in which we have held that an action would lie under § 1983 and those in which we have held that it would not." 544 U.S., at 121 (emphasis added). As noted, Title IX contains no express private remedy, much less a more restrictive one. This Court has never held that an implied right of action had the effect of precluding suit under § 1983, likely because of the difficulty of discerning congressional intent in such a situation. See *Franklin, supra,* at 76 (Scalia, J., concurring in judgment) ("Quite obviously, the search for what was Congress' *remedial* intent as to a right whose very existence Congress did not expressly acknowledge is unlikely to succeed"). Mindful that we should "not lightly conclude that Congress intended to preclude reliance on § 1983 as a remedy for a substantial equal protection claim," *Smith,* 468 U.S., at 1012, we see no basis for doing so here.

2

A comparison of the substantive rights and protections guaranteed under Title IX and under the Equal Protection Clause lends further support to the conclusion that Congress did not intend Title IX to preclude § 1983 constitutional suits. Title IX's protections are narrower in some respects and broader in others. Because the protections guaranteed by the two sources of law diverge in this way, we cannot agree with the Court of Appeals that "Congress saw Title IX as the sole means of vindicating the constitutional right to be free from gender discrimination perpetrated by educational institutions."

Title IX reaches institutions and programs that receive federal funds, 20 U.S.C. § 1681(a), which may include nonpublic institutions, § 1681(c), but it has consistently been interpreted as not authorizing suit against school officials, teachers, and other individuals, see, e.g., *Hartley v. Parnell,* 193 F.3d 1263, 1270 (CA11 1999). The Equal Protection Clause reaches only state actors, but § 1983 equal protection claims may be brought against individuals as well as municipalities and certain other state entities. *West v. Atkins,* 487 U.S. 42 (1988).

Title IX exempts from its restrictions several activities that may be challenged on constitutional grounds. For example, Title IX exempts elementary and secondary schools from its prohibition against discrimination in admissions, § 1681(a)(1); it exempts military service schools and traditionally single-sex public colleges from all of its provisions, §§ 1681(a)(4)-(5). Some exempted activities may form the basis of equal protection claims. See *United States v. Virginia,* 518 U.S. 515, 534 (1996) (men-only admissions policy at Virginia Military Institute violated the Equal Protection Clause); *Mississippi Univ. for Women v. Hogan,* 458 U.S. 718, 731 (1982) (women-only admission policy at a traditionally single-sex public college violated the Equal Protection Clause).

Even where particular activities and particular defendants are subject to both Title IX and the Equal Protection Clause, the standards for establishing liability may not be wholly congruent. For example, a Title IX plaintiff can establish school district liability by showing that a single school administrator with authority to take corrective action responded to harassment with deliberate indifference. *Gebser v. Lago Vista Independent School Dist.*, 524 U.S. 274, 290 (1998). A plaintiff stating a similar claim via § 1983 for violation of the Equal Protection Clause by a school district or other municipal entity must show that the harassment was the result of municipal custom, policy, or practice. *Monell v. New York City Dept. of Social Servs.*, 436 U.S. 658, 694 (1978).

In light of the divergent coverage of Title IX and the Equal Protection Clause, as well as the absence of a comprehensive remedial scheme comparable to those at issue in *Sea Clammers, Smith,* and *Rancho Palos Verdes,* we conclude that Title IX was not meant to be an exclusive mechanism for addressing gender discrimination in schools, or a substitute for § 1983 suits as a means of enforcing constitutional rights. Accordingly, we hold that § 1983 suits based on the Equal Protection Clause remain available to plaintiffs alleging unconstitutional gender discrimination in schools.

3

This conclusion is consistent with Title IX's context and history. In enacting Title IX, Congress amended 42 U.S.C. § 2000h-2 to authorize the Attorney General to intervene in private suits alleging discrimination on the basis of sex in violation of the Equal Protection [Clause.] Accordingly, it appears that the Congress that enacted Title IX explicitly envisioned that private plaintiffs would bring constitutional claims to challenge gender discrimination; it must have recognized that plaintiffs would do so via 42 U.S.C. § 1983.

Moreover, Congress modeled Title IX after Title VI of the Civil Rights Act of 1964, and passed Title IX with the explicit understanding that it would be interpreted as Title VI was. At the time of Title IX's enactment in 1972, Title VI was routinely interpreted to allow for parallel and concurrent § 1983 claims, and we presume Congress was aware of this when it passed Title IX, see *Franklin,* 503 U.S., at 71 (in assessing Congress' intent, "we evaluate the state of the law when the Legislature passed Title IX"). In the absence of any contrary evidence, it follows that Congress intended Title IX to be interpreted similarly to allow for parallel and concurrent § 1983 claims. At the least, this indicates that Congress did not affirmatively intend Title IX to preclude such claims.

III

[As] the Fitzgeralds note, no court has addressed the merits of their constitutional claims or eve[n the sufficiency of their pleadings. Ordinarily, "we do not decide in the first instance issues not decided below," and we see no reason for doing so here.

Accordingly, we reverse the Court of Appeals' judgment that the District Court's dismissal of the § 1983 claims was proper and remand this case for further proceedings consistent with this opinion.

It is so ordered.

NOTE

Bear in mind that the "enforceable rights" and "Congressional preclusion" principles are distinct. Notwithstanding *Fitzgerald*, a prospective § 1983 plaintiff who has "enforceable rights" under a given statute may be thwarted by the "Congressional preclusion" prong even if, like Title IX, the statute recognizes civil rights. For example, the Individuals With Disabilities Education Act, 20 U.S.C. § 1400 et seq., meets the "enforceable rights" requirement, because it entitles students with disabilities to a free appropriate public education. Yet most circuit courts have applied the "Congressional preclusion" principle to deny access to § 1983, ruling that "IDEA's comprehensive enforcement scheme provides the sole remedy for statutory violations." *K.A. v. Fulton County School District*, 741 F.3d 1195, 1210 (11th Cir. 2013) (joining five other circuits, but noting that the Second and Seventh Circuits have allowed § 1983 suits). Under IDEA's enforcement scheme, an aggrieved parent is entitled to a due process administrative hearing with judicial review, and may obtain injunctive and declaratory relief and private school tuition, among other remedies. *See School Committee of Burlington v. Department of Education*, 471 U.S. 369 (1985) (discussing some of the statutory remedies available under IDEA). A successful plaintiff can obtain attorney's fees. 20 U.S.C. § 1415(i)(2)-(3). Still, "[b]ecause most courts have ruled that compensatory damages are not available for violations of IDEA, many parents have turned to § 1983" in those circuits that allow § 1983 suits. Candace Chun, Comment: *The Use of § 1983 as a Remedy for Violations of the Individuals with Disabilities Education Act*, 72 Albany L. Rev. 461, 476 (2009).

Chapter 5

"EVERY PERSON": GOVERNMENTAL LIABILITY

The preceding chapters deal generally with the elements of every section 1983 prima facie case. This chapter focuses in particular on the important subject of section 1983 governmental liability which requires that the plaintiff allege and prove even more elements in order to make out a prima facie case. Supervisory liability and ethical considerations are also addressed. Specifically, this chapter is organized around the following questions: (1) what governmental bodies are "persons" suable under section 1983? (2) why sue a governmental body under section 1983? (3) how does one sue a governmental body? (4) what are the various theories of governmental liability under section 1983?

The purpose of this chapter is to teach you about the requirements of section 1983 governmental liability at both the theoretical and practical levels so that you understand and are comfortable with this kind of litigation. Throughout the discussion of various obstacles to recovering against governments, bear in mind a general requirement that the plaintiff must meet: He must establish a violation of his constitutional rights. *City of Los Angeles v. Heller*, 475 U.S. 796 (1986) (*per curiam*). The logic of the doctrine would seem to apply in the same way to § 1983 suits for damages for *statutory* violations, which are discussed in the last section of chapter 4. But there is little litigation of such claims for damages against local governments.

I. WHAT GOVERNMENTAL BODIES ARE PERSONS?

The short answer to the question of what governmental bodies are suable persons under section 1983 is that after *Monell v. Department of Social Services*, 436 U.S. 658 (1978), set out later, *all* local governments are. In contrast, *state* governmental bodies are not. However, the long answer is considerably more complex. For example, you will see that, at least in some states and for some purposes, the County Sheriff and the County Health Department may *not* be suable under § 1983.

The long answer begins by breaking the question down into parts. Why is there a difference between state governments and local governments, such that the latter may be sued, but not the former? The short answer to this question is that § 1983 authorizes suits against "[e]very person" who violates the plaintiff's constitutional (and some statutory) rights. *Monell* held that local governments are "persons" covered by the statute. A year later, *Quern v. Jordan*, 440 U.S. 332 (1979) held that state governments are not "persons" as the statute defines that term. Why then is there a difference? Here, the answer begins with a distinction drawn by the Supreme Court in 1890: State governments enjoy sovereign immunity from suit for their violations of federal law, *Hans v. Louisiana*, 134 U.S. 1 (1890), while local governments do not, *Lincoln County v. Luning*, 133 U.S. 529 (1890). Though this distinction may seem arbitrary today, there are historical grounds for it, as local governments originated as quasi-private corporations.

But that is only a partial answer, because state sovereign immunity against suits based on federal law is not absolute. It is possible for Congress to abrogate the state's sovereign immunity when it enacts a statute under its power to enforce the Fourteenth Amendment, granted it in § 5 of that Amendment. *Fitzpatrick v. Bitzer*, 427 U.S. 445 (1976). Since § 1983 was enacted pursuant to that power, it might well be understood as having abrogated state sovereign immunity. In *Quern*, however, the Court said that abrogation will be found only when Congress makes a "clear statement" of its intent to subject states to suit, and the "every person" language of § 1983 is not a clear statement.

After *Quern*, an important issue remained open: The states' sovereign immunity is explicitly protected by the Eleventh Amendment, which limits "[t]he judicial power of the United States" over suits against state governments. Could the bar imposed in *Quern* be avoided by suing in *state* court instead, on the theory that the "clear statement" rule is based on state sovereign immunity and the Eleventh Amendment immunity only applies in federal court? The Court rejected this theory in *Will v. Michigan Dept of State Police*, 491 U.S. 58 (1989):

> That Congress, in passing § 1983, had no intention to disturb the States' Eleventh Amendment immunity and so to alter the federal-state balance in that respect was made clear in our decision in *Quern*. Given that a principal purpose behind the enactment of § 1983 was to provide a federal forum for civil rights claims, and that Congress did not provide such a federal forum for civil rights claims against States, we cannot accept petitioner's argument that Congress intended nevertheless to create a cause of action against States to be brought in state courts, which are precisely the courts Congress sought to allow civil rights claimants to avoid through § 1983.

If the Court's legislative intent reasoning is not wholly convincing, a later case provides a constitutional foundation for the holding. In *Alden v. Maine*, 527 U.S. 706 (1999) the Court ruled that the states' sovereign immunity is located in the original constitution, not only the Eleventh Amendment, and extends to suits in state court as well as suits in federal court

The distinction between local governments and state governments invites other questions: One is how state governments can be held to account for constitutional violations if they cannot be sued under § 1983? At least since *Ex parte Young*, 209 U.S. 123 (1908), litigants suing for *prospective* relief may avoid state sovereign immunity altogether by suing the officials who act for the state, from the governor on down, seeking an injunction or a declaratory judgment. This doctrine, the Court candidly acknowledges, "has existed alongside our sovereign-immunity jurisprudence for more than a century, accepted as necessary to 'permit the federal courts to vindicate federal rights.' " *Virginia Office for Protection and Advocacy v. Stewart*, 131 S. Ct. 1632 (2011). But that route is not an all-purpose solution, as it is of no help to plaintiffs seeking damages from the state.

Given that the plaintiff wants backward-looking relief, a further question arises: How does one determine whether a given entity is part of state government or of local government? The answer lies in the Court's distinction between governmental entities that are "arms of the State" and those that are not. Only the former are shielded by the state's sovereign immunity. For example, in *Northern Insurance Company v. Chatham County, Ga.*, 547 U.S. 189 (2006), a Georgia county claimed "residual" sovereign immunity, but the Court rebuffed the effort and reiterated its longstanding rule that local governments are not arms of the state. Beyond the sharp distinction between political subdivisions and the state itself, the Court has provided little guidance as to which entities fall on one side of the line or the other, so the governing law remains uncertain.

Lower courts do address the issue from time to time and have developed a variety of approaches, reaching results that sometimes seem in tension with *Northern Insurance Co.. See, e.g., Bland v. Roberts*, 730 F.3d 368, 390 (4th Cir. 2013) (City Sheriff's Office is an arm of the state); *Town of Smyrna, Tn. v. Municipal Gas Authority of Georgia*, 723 F.3d 640 (6th Cir. 2013) (Muncipal Gas Authority is not an arm of the state); *Ross v. Jefferson County Dept. of Health*, 695 F.3d 1183 (11th Cir. 2012), *vacated by, substituted opinion at* 701 F.3d 655 (11th Cir. 2012) (county health department is an arm of the state); *Fournerat v. Wisconsin Law Review*, 2011 U.S. App. LEXIS 7576 (10th Cir. Apr. 12, 2011) (Wisconsin Law Review is an arm of the state); *Lewis v. University of Texas Medical Branch*, 665 F.3d 625 (5th Cir. 2011) (University of Texas is an arm of the state); *Betts v. New Castle Youth Development Center*, 621 F.3d 249 (3d Cir. 2010) (juvenile detention center is an arm of the state); *Burrus v. State Lottery Commission of Indiana*, 546 F.3d 417 (7th Cir. 2008) (state lottery commission is not an arm of the state); *Del Campo v. Kennedy*, 517 F.3d 1070 (9th Cir. 2008) (private company contracting with District Attorney for services related to California bad check diversion program was not an arm of the state).

Our focus in this chapter is on suits for damages against local governments, which under the rule of *Northern Insurance* are not arms of the state. We will revisit the "arm of the state" doctrine in Part III, because it is relevant to determining whether local governments are liable under § 1983 in certain situations.

A.   The Prior Law Under *Monroe*

Before the Supreme Court decided *Monell* in 1978, the rule was that governmental bodies were not "persons" within the meaning of section 1983. This rule derived from the Court's decision in *Monroe v. Pape*, 365 U.S. 167 (1961), discussed earlier in Chapter 1, which held that the City of Chicago could not be sued under section 1983. The plaintiff there sued individual police officers as well as the City of Chicago under a respondeat superior theory. Writing for the Court, Justice Douglas purported to rely solely on particular legislative debates for the conclusion that "we are of the opinion that Congress did not undertake to bring municipal corporations within the ambit of [section 1983]." *Id.* at 187.

In *Monroe*, the plaintiff made various policy arguments supporting governmental liability: the compensation of injured plaintiffs, the encouragement of compliance with the Fourteenth Amendment and the provision of a federal forum for section 1983 claims. Interestingly, the Court in *Monroe* simply did not address these arguments, relying instead on its reading of legislative history. For discussion of why the local government liability issue in *Monroe* was dealt with in rather summary fashion, see Nahmod, *Section 1983 Is Born: The Interlocking Supreme Court Stories of Tenney and Monroe*, 17 LEWIS & CLARK L. REV. 1019 (2013).

This holding was much criticized. *See, e.g.*, Levin, *The Section 1983 Municipal Immunity Doctrine*, 65 GEO. L.J. 1483 (1977); Kates & Kouba, *Liability of Public Entities Under Section 1983 of the Civil Rights Act*, 45 S. CAL. L. REV. 131 (1972); *Developments in the Law — Section 1983 and Federalism*, 90 HARV. L. REV. 1133 (1977). Nevertheless, the outcome was not in question. A local (and state) governmental body was not liable in damages for the unconstitutional conduct of its officials or employees. In addition, the Court later ruled that local governments could not be sued in their own names for injunctive relief either. *City of Kenosha v. Bruno*, 412 U.S. 507 (1973). Thus, section 1983 plaintiffs had a remedy only against individual defendants who, unless they were covered by insurance or governmentally provided indemnification, would often be judgment proof.

This all changed dramatically in 1978 when the Court decided *Monell v. Department of Social Services*.

B. The Change in *Monell*

MONELL v. DEPARTMENT OF SOCIAL SERVICES
436 U.S. 658 (1978)

MR. JUSTICE BRENNAN delivered the opinion of the Court.

Petitioners, a class of female employees of the Department of Social Services and of the Board of Education of the city of New York, commenced this action under 42 U.S.C. § 1983 in July 1971. The gravamen of the complaint was that the Board and the Department had as a matter of official policy compelled pregnant employees to take unpaid leaves of absence before such leaves were required for medical reasons. *Cf. Cleveland Board of Education v. LaFleur.* The suit sought injunctive relief and back-pay for periods of unlawful forced leave. Named as defendants in the action were the Department and its Commissioner, the Board and its Chancellor, and the city of New York and its Mayor. In each case, the individual defendants were sued solely in their official capacities.

We granted certiorari in this case to consider "Whether local governmental officials and/or local independent school boards are 'persons' within the meaning of 42 U.S.C. § 1983 when equitable relief in the nature of back pay is sought against them in their official capacities?"

Although, after plenary consideration, we have decided the merits of over a score of cases brought under § 1983 in which the principal defendant was a school board and, indeed, in some of which § 1983 and its jurisdictional counterpart, 28 U.S.C. § 1343, provided the only basis for jurisdiction — we indicated in *Mt. Healthy City*

Board of Education v. Doyle last Term that the question presented here was open and would be decided "another day." That other day has come and we now overrule *Monroe v. Pape, supra,* insofar as it holds that local governments are wholly immune from suit under § 1983.

I

In *Monroe v. Pape,* we held that "Congress did not undertake to bring municipal corporations within the ambit of [§ 1983]." The sole basis for this conclusion was an inference drawn from Congress' rejection of the "Sherman amendment" to the bill which became the Civil Rights Act of 1871, the precursor of § 1983. The amendment would have held a municipal corporation liable for damage done to the person or property of its inhabitants by private persons "riotously and tumultuously assembled." Although the Sherman amendment did not seek to amend § 1 of the Act, which is now § 1983, and although the nature of the obligation created by that amendment was vastly different from that created by § 1, the Court nonetheless concluded in *Monroe* that Congress must have meant to exclude municipal corporations from the coverage of § 1 because " 'the House [in voting against the Sherman amendment] had solemnly decided that in their judgment Congress had no constitutional power to impose any *obligation* upon county and town organizations, the mere instrumentality for the administration of state law.' " This statement, we thought, showed that Congress doubted its "constitutional power . . . to impose civil liability on municipalities," and that such doubt would have extended to any type of civil liability.

A fresh analysis of the debate on the Civil Rights Act of 1871, and particularly of the case law which each side mustered in its support, shows, however, that *Monroe* incorrectly equated the "obligation" of which Representative Poland spoke with "civil liability."

A. An Overview

There are three distinct stages in the legislative consideration of the bill which became the Civil Rights Act of 1871. On March 28, 1871, Representative Shellabarger, acting for a House select committee, reported H. R. 320, a bill "to enforce the provisions of the fourteenth amendment to the Constitution of the United States, and for other purposes." H. R. 320 contained four sections. Section 1, now codified as 42 U.S.C. § 1983, was the subject of only limited debate and was passed without amendment. Sections 2 through 4 dealt primarily with the "other purpose" of suppressing Ku Klux Klan violence in the Southern States. The wisdom and constitutionality of these sections — not § 1, now § 1983 — were the subject of almost all congressional debate and each of these sections was amended. The House finished its initial debates on H. R. 320 on April 7, 1871, and one week later the Senate also voted out a bill. Again, debate on § 1 of the bill was limited and that section was passed as introduced.

Immediately prior to the vote on H.R. 320 in the Senate, Senator Sherman introduced his amendment. This was *not* an amendment to § 1 of the bill, but was to be added as § 7 at the end of the bill. Under the Senate rules, no discussion of the amendment was allowed and, although attempts were made to amend the amendment, it was passed as introduced. In this form, the amendment did *not* place liability on municipal corporations, but made any inhabitant of a municipality liable for damage inflicted by persons "riotously and tumultuously assembled."

The House refused to acquiesce in a number of amendments made by the Senate, including the Sherman amendment, and the respective versions of H. R. 320 were therefore sent to a conference committee. Section 1 of the bill, however, was not a subject of this conference since, as noted, it was passed verbatim as introduced in both Houses of Congress.

On April 18, 1871, the first conference committee completed its work on H. R. 320. The main features of the conference committee draft of the Sherman amendment were these:

First, a cause of action was given to persons injured by

"any persons riotously and tumultuously assembled together . . . with intent to deprive any person of any right conferred upon him by the Constitution and laws of the United States, or to deter him or punish him for exercising such right, or by reason of his race, color, or previous condition of servitude. . . ."

Second, the bill provided that the action would be against the county, city, or parish in which the riot had occurred and that it could be maintained by either the person injured or his legal representative. Third, unlike the amendment as proposed, the conference substitute made the government defendant liable on the judgment if it was not satisfied against individual defendants who had committed the violence. If a municipality were liable, the judgment against it could be collected

"by execution, attachment, mandamus, garnishment, or any other proceeding in aid of execution or applicable to the enforcement of judgments against municipal corporations; and such judgment [would become] a lien as well upon all moneys in the treasury of such county, city, or parish, as upon the other property thereof."

In the ensuing debate on the first conference report, which was the first debate of any kind on the Sherman amendment, Senator Sherman explained that the purpose of his amendment was to enlist the aid of persons of property in the enforcement of the civil rights laws by making their property "responsible" for Ku Klux Klan damage. Statutes drafted on a similar theory, he stated, had long been in force in England and were in force in 1871 in a number of States. Nonetheless there were critical differences between the conference substitute and extant state and English statutes: The conference substitute, unlike most state riot statutes, lacked a short statute of limitations and imposed liability on the government defendant whether or not it had notice of the impending riot, whether or not the municipality was authorized to exercise a police power, whether or not it exerted all reasonable efforts to stop the riot, and whether or not the rioters were caught and punished.

The first conference substitute passed the Senate but was rejected by the House.

House opponents, within whose ranks were some who had supported § 1, thought the Federal Government could not, consistent with the Constitution, obligate municipal corporations to keep the peace if those corporations were neither so obligated nor so authorized by their state charters. And, because of this constitutional objection, opponents of the Sherman amendment were unwilling to impose damages liability for nonperformance of a duty which Congress could not require municipalities to perform. This position is reflected in Representative Poland's statement that is quoted in *Monroe*.

Because the House rejected the first conference report a second conference was called and it duly issued its report. The second conference substitute for the Sherman amendment abandoned municipal liability and, instead, made "any person or persons having knowledge [that a conspiracy to violate civil rights was afoot], and having power to prevent or aid in preventing the same," who did not attempt to stop the same, liable to any person injured by the conspiracy. The amendment in this form was adopted by both Houses of Congress and is now codified as 42 U.S.C. § 1986.

The meaning of the legislative history sketched above can most readily be developed by first considering the debate on the report of the first conference committee. This debate shows conclusively that the constitutional objections raised against the Sherman amendment — on which our holding in *Monroe* was based — would not have prohibited congressional creation of a civil remedy against state municipal corporations that infringed federal rights. Because § 1 of the Civil Rights Act does not state expressly that municipal corporations come within its ambit, it is finally necessary to interpret § 1 to confirm that such corporations were indeed intended to be included within the "persons" to whom that section applies.

C. Debate on § 1 of the Civil Rights Bill

From the foregoing discussion, it is readily apparent that nothing said in debate on the Sherman amendment would have prevented holding a municipality liable under § 1 of the Civil Rights Act for its own violations of the Fourteenth Amendment. The question remains, however, whether the general language describing those to be liable under § 1 — "any person" — covers more than natural persons. An examination of the debate on § 1 and application of appropriate rules of construction show unequivocally that § 1 was intended to cover legal as well as natural persons.

Representative Shellabarger was the first to explain the function of § 1:

> "[Section 1] not only provides a civil remedy for persons whose former condition may have been that of slaves, but also to all people where, under color of State law, they or any of them may be deprived of rights to which they are entitled under the Constitution by reason and virtue of their national citizenship."

By extending a remedy to all people, including whites, § 1 went beyond the mischief to which the remaining sections of the 1871 Act were addressed. Representative Shellabarger also stated without reservation that the constitutionality of § 2 of the Civil Rights Act of 1866 controlled the constitutionality of § 1 of the 1871 Act, and that the former had been approved by "the supreme courts of at least three States of this Union" and by Mr. Justice Swayne, sitting on circuit, who had concluded: "We have no doubt of the constitutionality of every provision of this act." Representative Shellabarger then went on to describe how the courts would and should interpret § 1:

> "This act is remedial, and in aid of the preservation of human liberty and human rights. All statutes and constitutional provisions authorizing such statutes are liberally and beneficently construed. It would be most strange and, in civilized law, monstrous were this not the rule of interpretation. As has been again and again decided by your own Supreme Court of the United States, and everywhere else where there is wise judicial interpretation, the largest latitude consistent with the words employed is uniformly given in construing such statutes and constitutional provisions as are meant to protect and defend and give remedies for their wrongs to all the people. . . . Chief Justice Jay and also Story say: "Where a power is remedial in its nature there is much reason to contend that it ought to be construed liberally, and it is generally adopted in the interpretation of laws."

The sentiments expressed in Representative Shellabarger's opening speech were echoed by Senator Edmunds, the manager of H. R. 320 in the Senate:

> "The first section is one that I believe nobody objects to, as defining the rights secured by the Constitution of the United States when they are assailed by any State law or under color of any State law, and it is merely carrying out the principles of the civil rights bill [of 1866], which have since become a part of the Constitution."

> "[Section 1 is] so very simple and really [reenacts] the Constitution."

And he agreed that the bill "[secured] the rights of white men as much as of colored men."

In both Houses, statements of the supporters of § 1 corroborated that Congress, in enacting § 1, intended to give a broad remedy for violations of federally protected civil rights. Moreover, since municipalities through their official acts could, equally with natural persons, create the harms intended to be remedied by § 1, and, further, since Congress intended § 1 to be broadly construed, there is no reason to suppose that municipal corporations would have been excluded from the sweep of § 1. *Cf.,* *e.g., Ex parte Virginia; Home Tel. & Tel. Co. v. Los Angeles.* One need not rely on this inference alone, however, for the debates show that Members of Congress understood "persons" to include municipal corporations.

Representative Bingham, for example, in discussing § 1 of the bill, explained that he had drafted § 1 of the Fourteenth Amendment with the case of *Barron v. Mayor of Baltimore* especially in mind. "In [that] case the city had taken private property for public use, without compensation . . . , and there was no redress for the wrong. . . ." Bingham's further remarks clearly indicate his view that such takings by cities, as had occurred in Barron, would be redressable under § 1 of the bill. More generally, and as Bingham's remarks confirm, § 1 of the bill would logically be the vehicle by which Congress provided redress for takings, since that section provided the only civil remedy for Fourteenth Amendment violations and that Amendment unequivocally prohibited uncompensated takings. Given this purpose, it beggars reason to suppose that Congress would have exempted municipalities from suit, insisting instead that compensation for a taking come from an officer in his individual capacity rather than from the government unit that had the benefit of the property taken.

In addition, by 1871, it was well understood that corporations should be treated as natural persons for virtually all purposes of constitutional and statutory analysis. This had not always been so. When this Court first considered the question of the status of corporations, Mr. Chief Justice Marshall, writing for the Court, denied that corporations "as such" were persons as that term was used in Art. III and the Judiciary Act of 1789. See *Bank of the United States v. Deveaux.* By 1844, however, the *Deveaux* doctrine was unhesitatingly abandoned:

> "[A] corporation created by and doing business in a particular state, is to be deemed to all intents and purposes as a person, although an artificial person, . . . capable of being treated as a citizen of that state, as much as a natural person." *Louisville R. Co. v. Letson.*

And only two years before the debates on the Civil Rights Act, in *Cowles v. Mercer County*, the *Letson* principle was automatically and without discussion extended to municipal corporations. Under this doctrine, municipal corporations were routinely sued in the federal courts and this fact was well known to Members of Congress.

That the "usual" meaning of the word "person" would extend to municipal corporations is also evidenced by an Act of Congress which had been passed only months before the Civil Rights Act was passed. This Act provided that

> "in all acts hereafter passed . . . the word 'person' may extend and be applied to bodies politic and corporate . . . unless the context shows that such words were intended to be used in a more limited sense."

Municipal corporations in 1871 were included within the phrase "bodies politic and corporate" and, accordingly, the "plain meaning" of § 1 is that local government bodies were to be included within the ambit of the persons who could be sued under § 1 of the Civil Rights Act. Indeed, a Circuit Judge, writing in 1873 in what is apparently the first reported case under § 1, read the Dictionary Act in precisely this way in a case involving a corporate plaintiff and a municipal defendant. *See Northwestern Fertilizing Co. v. Hyde Park.*

II

Our analysis of the legislative history of the Civil Rights Act of 1871 compels the conclusion that Congress did intend municipalities and other local government units to be included among those persons to whom § 1983 applies.[1] Local governing

---

[1] [54] There is certainly no constitutional impediment to municipal liability. "The Tenth Amendment's reservation of non-delegated powers to the States is not implicated by a federal-court judgment enforcing the express prohibitions of unlawful state conduct enacted by the Fourteenth Amendment." *Milliken v. Bradley*; see *Ex parte Virginia.* For this reason, *National League of Cities v. Usery* is

bodies,[2] therefore, can be sued directly under § 1983 for monetary, declaratory, or injunctive relief where, as here, the action that is alleged to be unconstitutional implements or executes a policy statement, ordinance, regulation, or decision officially adopted and promulgated by that body's officers. Moreover, although the touchstone of the § 1983 action against a government body is an allegation that official policy is responsible for a deprivation of rights protected by the Constitution, local governments, like every other § 1983 "person," by the very terms of the statute, may be sued for constitutional deprivations visited pursuant to governmental "custom" even though such a custom has not received formal approval through the body's official decision-making channels. As Mr. Justice Harlan, writing for the Court, said in *Adickes v. S. H. Kress & Co.*: "Congress included customs and usages [in § 1983] because of the persistent and widespread discriminatory practices of state officials . . . , Although not authorized by written law, such practices of state officials could well be so permanent and well settled as to constitute a 'custom or usage' with the force of law."

On the other hand, the language of § 1983, read against the background of the same legislative history, compels the conclusion that Congress did not intend municipalities to be held liable unless action pursuant to official municipal policy of some nature caused a constitutional tort. In particular, we conclude that a municipality cannot be held liable solely because it employs a tortfeasor — or, in other words, a municipality cannot be held liable under § 1983 on a respondeat superior theory.

We begin with the language of § 1983 as originally passed:

> "[A]ny person who, under color of any law, statute, ordinance, regulation, custom, or usage of any State, *shall subject, or cause to be subjected*, any person . . . to the deprivation of any rights, privileges, or immunities secured by the Constitution of the United States, shall, any such law, statute, ordinance, regulation, custom, or usage of the State to the contrary notwithstanding, be liable to the party injured in any action at law, suit in equity, or other proper proceeding for redress. . . ."

The italicized language plainly imposes liability on a government that, under color of some official policy, "causes" an employee to violate another's constitutional rights. At the same time, that language cannot be easily read to impose liability vicariously on governing bodies solely on the basis of the existence of an employer-employee relationship with a tortfeasor. Indeed, the fact that Congress did specifically provide that A's tort became B's liability if B "caused" A to subject another to a tort suggests that Congress did not intend § 1983 liability to attach

---

irrelevant to our consideration of this case. Nor is there any basis for concluding that the Eleventh Amendment is a bar to municipal liability. *See, e.g., Fitzpatrick v. Bitzer; Lincoln County v. Luning.* Our holding today is, of course, limited to local government units which are not considered part of the State for Eleventh Amendment purposes.

[2] [55] Since official-capacity suits generally represent only another way of pleading an action against an entity of which an officer is an agent — at least where Eleventh Amendment considerations do not control analysis — our holding today that local governments can be sued under § 1983 necessarily decides that local government officials sued in their official capacities are "persons" under § 1983 in those cases in which, as here, a local government would be suable in its own name.

where such causation was absent. *See Rizzo v. Goode.*

Equally important, creation of a federal law of respondeat superior would have raised all the constitutional problems associated with the obligation to keep the peace, an obligation Congress chose not to impose because it thought imposition of such an obligation unconstitutional. To this day, there is disagreement about the basis for imposing liability on an employer for the torts of an employee when the sole nexus between the employer and the tort is the fact of the employer-employee relationship. *See* W. Prosser, *Law of Torts* § 69, p. 459 (4th ed. 1971). Nonetheless, two justifications tend to stand out. First is the commonsense notion that no matter how blameless an employer appears to be in an individual case, accidents might nonetheless be reduced if employers had to bear the cost of accidents. *See, e.g.,* ibid.; 2 F. Harper & F. James, *Law of Torts*, § 26.3, pp. 1368–1369 (1956). Second is the argument that the cost of accidents should be spread to the community as a whole on an insurance theory. *See, e.g., id.,* § 26.5; Prosser, *supra,* at 459.[3]

The first justification is of the same sort that was offered for statutes like the Sherman amendment: "The obligation to make compensation for injury resulting from riot is, by arbitrary enactment of statutes, affirmatory law, and the reason of passing the statute is to secure a more perfect police regulation." This justification was obviously insufficient to sustain the amendment against perceived constitutional difficulties and there is no reason to suppose that a more general liability imposed for a similar reason would have been thought less constitutionally objectionable. The second justification was similarly put forward as a justification for the Sherman amendment: "we do not look upon [the Sherman amendment] as a punishment. . . . It is a mutual insurance." Again, this justification was insufficient to sustain the amendment.

We conclude, therefore, that a local government may not be sued under § 1983 for an injury inflicted solely by its employees or agents. Instead, it is when execution of a government's policy or custom, whether made by its lawmakers or by those whose edicts or acts may fairly be said to represent official policy, inflicts the injury that the government as an entity is responsible under § 1983. Since this case unquestionably involves official policy as the moving force of the constitutional violation found by the District Court, we must reverse the judgment below. In so doing, we have no occasion to address, and do not address, what the full contours of municipal liability under § 1983 may be. We have attempted only to sketch so much of the § 1983 cause of action against a local government as is apparent from the history of the 1871 Act and our prior cases, and we expressly leave further development of this action to another day.

---

[3] [58] A third justification, often cited but which on examination is apparently insufficient to justify the doctrine of respondeat superior, see, e.g., 2 F. Harper & F. James, § 26.3, is that liability follows the right to control the actions of a tortfeasor. By our decision in *Rizzo v. Goode* we appear to have decided that the mere right to control without any control or direction having been exercised and without any failure to supervise is not enough to support § 1983 liability.

IV

Since the question whether local government bodies should be afforded some form of official immunity was not presented as a question to be decided on this petition and was not briefed by the parties or addressed by the courts below, we express no views on the scope of any municipal immunity beyond holding that municipal bodies sued under § 1983 cannot be entitled to an absolute immunity, lest our decision that such bodies are subject to suit under § 1983 "be drained of meaning," *Scheuer v. Rhodes.*

V

For the reasons stated above, the judgment of the Court of Appeals is

Reversed.

[The concurring opinions of Justices **Powell** and **Stevens** and the dissenting opinion of Justice **Rehnquist** and Chief Justice **Burger** are omitted.]

NOTES

1. *Monell*'s holding that local governments are "persons" subject to § 1983 suits has won wide acceptance. Its rejection of respondeat superior remains controversial. In order to win, the plaintiff must prove more than that the constitutional violation took place in the course of the official's employment. He must show that the constitutional violation resulted from an official "policy" or "custom," a topic we take up in section III of this chapter. Consider the following critique in a Seventh Circuit case:

> The rejection of *respondeat superior* liability for municipalities in *Monell* has been the subject of extensive analysis and criticism [citing dissenting opinions by Justice Stevens and Breyer as well as several commentators]. These commentators have pointed out many critical problems with *Monell*'s conclusion that *respondeat superior* claims against municipalities are not permitted under § 1983.

> Perhaps the most important criticism to emerge from this literature is that *Monell* failed to grapple with the fact that *respondeat superior* liability for employers was a settled feature of American law that was familiar to Congress in 1871, when § 1983 was enacted. Congress therefore enacted § 1983 against the backdrop of *respondeat superior* liability, and presumably assumed that courts would apply it in claims against corporations under § 1983. Cf. *Smith v. Wade*, 461 U.S. 30, 38–45 (1983) (considering common law in 1871 to decide standard for punitive damages under *§ 1983*); *Carey v. Piphus*, 435 U.S. 247, 257–59 (1978) (considering common law in 1871 to decide that actual injury is needed to recover compensatory damages under § 1983).

> The Court's reliance on the Sherman Amendment is also problematic. The rejection of the proposal to hold municipalities liable for actions of

private citizens it could not control says little about whether a municipality should be held liable for constitutional torts committed by its own employees acting within the scope of their employment. [Finally,] the Court gave only cursory and tentative treatment to the strongest foundation for *respondeat superior* liability: an employer should be held responsible for the torts of employees whose actions it can control and from whose actions it profits.

Given these flaws on the surface of its reasoning, *Monell* is probably best understood as simply having crafted a compromise rule that protected the budgets of local governments from automatic liability for their employees' wrongs, driven by a concern about public budgets and the potential extent of taxpayer liability.

Of course, the critiques of *Monell's* rejection of *respondeat superior* liability for municipalities have not yet persuaded the Supreme Court to reconsider that rule. Given our position in the judicial hierarchy, then, we are bound to follow *Monell* as far as municipal liability is concerned.

Shields v. Illinois Dept. of Corrections, 746 F.3d 782, 791–92 (7th Cir. 2014).

2. Suppose a private corporation is sued for damages under section 1983 for the allegedly unconstitutional conduct of its employees. If color of law — discussed in Chapter 2 — is present, can the corporation be held liable under a respondeat superior theory, or must an official policy or custom be proved? Does the assumption of color of law beg the very question at issue? That is, once there is color of law, does it follow that respondeat superior liability is no longer implicated?

The general rule in the lower courts is that *Monell* applies. *See, e.g., Tsao v. Desert Palace*, 698 F.3d 1128, 1139 (9th Cir. 2012) ("Every one of our sister circuits to have considered the issue has concluded that the requirements of *Monell* do apply to suits against private entities under § 1983. [The court cited cases from a majority of the circuits.] Like those circuits, we see no basis in the reasoning underlying *Monell* to distinguish between municipalities and private entities acting under color of state law.").

The Seventh Circuit is among those that have applied Monell to suits against private corporations. In *Shields v. Illinois Department of Corrections*, 746 F.3d 782, 790–795 (7th Cir. 2014), Judge Hamilton, joined by Judge Posner, called for reconsidering that approach. After criticizing *Monell's* holding as to municipal corporations (see note 1 above) the majority opinion marshals arguments against applying that rule to private corporations. Judge Hamilton points out that respondeat superior is "an old and well-settled feature of American law," which should not be ignored "without powerful reasons to do so," *id.* at 792. He asserts that neither the text of § 1983, nor *Monell's* interpretation of § 1983, nor any other Supreme Court decision requires extending the principle to private corporations. But the court declined to pursue the matter further, as the plaintiff had not asked that the rule be reconsidered. 746 F.3d at 795.

3. After *Monell*, a plaintiff may sue either the local government or official or both. In the (confusing) vocabulary that is sometimes used to distinguish between the two defendants — officer and government — the plaintiff may sue the official in his "individual" capacity or in his "official" capacity. The practical point of the distinction is that if he sues the official in his "individual" capacity, he must contend with the official immunity doctrines discussed in chapters 7 and 8. On the other hand, if he sues the official in his "official" capacity, he is in fact suing the government for whom the official works and must contend with *Monell's* "policy" or "custom" requirement. Thus, a suit against the officer in his "individual" capacity is *not* a suit against the officer as a private individual. And a suit against the officer in his "official" capacity is *not* a suit against the officer at all, but rather a suit against the government. Confusion can be avoided by simply remembering to sue the officer in his individual capacity and, in the event one wants to sue the government, naming it as a defendant. There is, of course, no bar to suing both.

One implication of this set of rules is that the plaintiff should not sue a local government officer solely in his "official capacity" unless the plaintiff is prepared to meet the "policy" or "custom" requirement. That requirement applies even if he only seeks prospective relief. *Los Angeles County v. Humphries*, 562 U.S. 29 (2010). Another implication is that one should never bring a suit for damages against a state government officer in his "official capacity," as the suit would be barred under *Quern* and *Will* above. Distinguish suits for prospective relief, which are brought against state officials under the *Ex parte Young* principle, above. In this type of litigation, the plaintiff may and typically does sue the officer in his official capacity. *See* R. FALLON, ET AL., HART & WECHSLER'S THE FEDERAL COURTS AND THE FEDERAL SYSTEM 958 (6th ed. 2009). Supreme Court opinions discussing this topic include *Hafer v. Melo*, 502 U.S. 21 (1991) and *Kentucky v. Graham*, 473 U.S. 159 (1985).

4. Since the plaintiff may sue both the officer and the government, and a trier of fact may, if it sees fit, rule against the city but in favor of the officer, questions sometimes arise as to whether the judgment against the city can stand. In this regard, recall the threshold requirement of *Los Angeles v. Heller*, 475 U.S. 796 (1986) that the plaintiff must show a constitutional violation. The ruling in favor of the officer may be inconsistent with finding that the city committed a constitutional violation.

Consider *Speer v. City of Wynne*, 276 F.3d 980 (8th Cir. 2002), an Eighth Circuit case involving a claimed violation of procedural due process by a city in failing to provide a pre-termination name-clearing hearing to a discharged police officer where the city's mayor disseminated false and damaging information about him to the public. The district court, after a bench trial, entered judgment for the mayor but against the city. On appeal, the Eighth Circuit ruled that the judgment against the city could *theoretically* stand, despite *Heller*, because it was possible that the district court determined that the procedural due process violation occurred only when the plaintiff was denied a name-clearing hearing by the city through officials who had final employment-policymaking authority. Thus, the mayor's conduct alone could have been insufficient for individual liability. As a result, the Eighth Circuit remanded to the district court to make specific findings of fact and conclusions of law as to the city's liability and the mayor's non-liability.

The Eighth Circuit explained its general approach in such cases as follows, *id.* at 986:

The appropriate question under *Heller* is whether a verdict or decision exonerating the individual governmental actors can be harmonized with a concomitant verdict or decision imposing liability on the municipal entity. The outcome of the inquiry depends on the nature of the constitutional violation alleged, the theory of municipal liability asserted by the plaintiff, and the defenses set forth by the individual actors. . . . [S]ituations may arise where the combined actions of multiple officials or employees may give rise to a constitutional violation, supporting municipal liability, but where no one individual's actions are sufficient to establish personal liability for the violation.

5. Our focus in this chapter is on suits brought under § 1983. Another Reconstruction-era civil rights statute, the Civil Rights Act of 1866, now codified at 42 U.S.C. § 1981, prohibits race discrimination in contracting by both public and private actors. *Runyon v. McCrary*, 427 U.S. 160, 168 (1976). In *Jett v. Dallas Independent School District*, 491 U.S. 701 (1989), the Court closed off a potential escape from *Monell*, holding that the rule barring municipal liability based on respondeat superior applies in § 1981 suits as well. Though there was no majority opinion on the issue, five Justices endorsed the holding. *See* 491 U.S. at 711–31 (plurality opinion of O'Connor, J.), 491 U.S. at 735–36 (opinion of the Court), 491 U.S. at 738–39 (opinion of Scalia, J.)

In another section of Justice O'Connor's opinion (in which she wrote for a majority) the Court rejected attempts to judicially imply a respondeat superior remedy, *see* 491 U.S. at 732, or to borrow respondeat superior from state law, *see* 491 U.S. at 732–33. The Court held that § 1983 "provides the exclusive federal damages remedy for the violation of the rights guaranteed by § 1981 when the claim is pressed against a state actor." 491 U.S. at 735.

The Civil Rights Act of 1991 amended § 1981, mainly in response to the Supreme Court's ruling in *Patterson v. McLean Credit Union*, 491 U.S. 164 (1989), which had disallowed § 1981 claims based on racial harassment in the workplace. Though none of the changes were specifically directed at *Jett*, litigants have argued that the amendments undermined *Jett*'s authority. That argument prevailed in *Federation of African American Contractors v. City of Oakland*, 96 F.3d 1204 (9th Cir. 1996), though the court nonetheless retained the rule against respondeat superior. 96 F. 3d at 1215. The notion that the 1991 statute overrides *Jett* has been rejected elsewhere. *See, e.g., Campbell v. Forest Preserve Dist. of Cook Co.*, 752 F.3d 665, 671 (7th Cir. 2014) (joining six other circuits in ruling "that *Jett* remains good law and consequently, § 1983 remains the exclusive remedy for violations of § 1981 committed by state actors.") Besides reaffirming *Jett*'s limit on municipal liability, the practical importance of this holding is that sometimes, different procedural rules may apply depending on whether the suit is brought under § 1981 or § 1983. In *Campbell*, for example, the relevant statute of limitations depended on whether the case was properly brought under § 1981 or § 1983.

II. MUNICIPAL GOVERNMENTS HAVE NO IMMUNITY FROM SUIT

We will see in chapters 7 and 8 that officers sued under § 1983 often avoid liability for damages on account of "official immunity," a defense that has deep common law roots, and one that the Court has long applied in § 1983 litigation. One question raised by *Monell* was whether local governments would also enjoy such a defense. In *Owen*, the Court held that they do not.

OWEN v. CITY OF INDEPENDENCE, MISSOURI
445 U.S. 622 (1980)

Mr. Justice **Brennan** delivered the opinion of the Court.

Monell v. New York City Dept. of Social Services overruled *Monroe v. Pape* insofar as *Monroe* held that local governments were not among the "persons" to whom 42 U.S.C. § 1983 applies and were therefore wholly immune from suit under the statute. *Monell* reserved decision, however, on the question whether local governments, although not entitled to an absolute immunity, should be afforded some form of official immunity in § 1983 suits. In this action brought by petitioner in the District Court for the Western District of Missouri, the Court of Appeals for the Eighth Circuit held that respondent city of Independence, Mo., "is entitled to qualified immunity from liability" based on the good faith of its officials: "We extend the limited immunity the district court applied to the individual defendants to cover the City as well, because its officials acted in good faith and without malice." We granted certiorari. We reverse.

II

Petitioner named the city of Independence, City Manager Alberg, and the present members of the City Council in their official capacities as defendants in this suit. Alleging that he was discharged without notice of reasons and without a hearing in violation of his constitutional rights to procedural and substantive due process, petitioner sought declaratory and injunctive relief, including a hearing on his discharge, back-pay from the date of discharge, and attorney's fees. The District Court, after a bench trial, entered judgment for respondents.

[T]he Court of Appeals affirmed the judgment of the District Court denying petitioner any relief against the respondent city, stating:

> "The Supreme Court's decisions in *Board of Regents v. Roth*, and *Perry v. Sindermann*, crystallized the rule establishing the right to a name-clearing hearing for a government employee allegedly stigmatized in the course of his discharge. The Court decided those two cases two months after the discharge in the instant case. Thus, officials of the City of Independence could not have been aware of [petitioner's] right to a name-clearing hearing in connection with the discharge. The City of Independence should not be charged with predicting the future course of constitutional law. We extend the limited immunity the district court

applied to the individual defendants to cover the City as well, because its officials acted in good faith and without malice. We hold the City not liable for actions it could not reasonably have known violated [petitioner's] constitutional rights."

We turn now to the reasons for our disagreement with this holding.

III

Because the question of the scope of a municipality's immunity from liability under § 1983 is essentially one of statutory construction, see *Wood v. Strickland; Tenney v. Brandhove,* the starting point in our analysis must be the language of the statute itself. *Andrus v. Allard; Blue Chip Stamps v. Manor Drug Stores.* By its terms, § 1983 "creates a species of tort liability that on its face admits of no immunities." *Imbler v. Pachtman.* Its language is absolute and unqualified; no mention is made of any privileges, immunities, or defenses that may be asserted. Rather, the Act imposes liability upon "every person" who, under color of state law or custom, "subjects, or causes to be subjected, any citizen of the United States . . . to the deprivation of any rights, privileges, or immunities secured by the Constitution and laws." And *Monell* held that these words were intended to encompass municipal corporations as well as natural "persons."

Moreover, the congressional debates surrounding the passage of § 1 of the Civil Rights Act of 1871, 17 Stat. 13 — the forerunner of § 1983 — confirm the expansive sweep of the statutory language. Representative Shellabarger, the author and manager of the bill in the House, explained in his introductory remarks the breadth of construction that the Act was to receive:

"I have a single remark to make in regard to the rule of interpretation of those provisions of the Constitution under which all the sections of the bill are framed. This act is remedial, and in aid of the preservation of human liberty and human rights. All statutes and constitutional provisions authorizing such statutes are liberally and beneficently construed. It would be most strange and, in civilized law, monstrous were this not the rule of interpretation. As has been again and again decided by your own Supreme Court of the United States, and everywhere else where there is wise judicial interpretation, the largest latitude consistent with the words employed is uniformly given in construing such statutes and constitutional provisions as are meant to protect and defend and give remedies for their wrongs to all the people."

Similar views of the Act's broad remedy for violations of federally protected rights were voiced by its supporters in both Houses of Congress. See *Monell v. New York City Dept. of Social Services.*

However, notwithstanding § 1983's expansive language and the absence of any express incorporation of common-law immunities, we have, on several occasions, found that a tradition of immunity was so firmly rooted in the common law and was supported by such strong policy reasons that "Congress would have specifically so provided had it wished to abolish the doctrine." *Pierson v. Ray.* Thus in *Tenney v. Brandhove, supra,* after tracing the development of an absolute legislative privilege from its source in 16th-century England to its inclusion in the Federal and State Constitutions, we concluded that Congress "would [not] impinge on a tradition so well grounded in history and reason by covert inclusion in the general language" of § 1983.

Subsequent cases have required that we consider the personal liability of various other types of government officials. Noting that "[few] doctrines were more solidly established at common law than the immunity of judges from liability for damages for acts committed within their judicial jurisdiction," *Pierson v. Ray, supra*, held that the absolute immunity traditionally accorded judges was preserved under § 1983. In that same case, local police officers were held to enjoy a "good faith and probable cause" defense to § 1983 suits similar to that which existed in false arrest actions at common law. Several more recent decisions have found immunities of varying scope appropriate for different state and local officials sued under § 1983. See *Procunier v. Navarette* (qualified immunity for prison officials and officers); *Imbler v. Pachtman* (absolute immunity for prosecutors in initiating and presenting the State's case); *O'Connor v. Donaldson* (qualified immunity for superintendent of state hospital); *Wood v. Strickland* (qualified immunity for local school board members); *Scheuer v. Rhodes* (qualified "good-faith" immunity for state Governor and other executive officers for discretionary acts performed in the course of official conduct).

In each of these cases, our finding of § 1983 immunity "was predicated upon a considered inquiry into the immunity historically accorded the relevant official at common law and the interests behind it." *Imbler v. Pachtman*. Where the immunity claimed by the defendant was well established at common law at the time § 1983 was enacted, and where its rationale was compatible with the purposes of the Civil Rights Act, we have construed the statute to incorporate that immunity. But there is no tradition of immunity for municipal corporations, and neither history nor policy supports a construction of § 1983 that would justify the qualified immunity accorded the city of Independence by the Court of Appeals. We hold, therefore, that the municipality may not assert the good faith of its officers or agents as a defense to liability under § 1983.

In sum, we can discern no "tradition so well grounded in history and reason" that would warrant the conclusion that in enacting § 1 of the Civil Rights Act, the 42d Congress sub silentio extended to municipalities a qualified immunity based on the good faith of their officers. Absent any clearer indication that Congress intended so to limit the reach of a statute expressly designed to provide a "broad remedy for violations of federally protected civil rights," *Monell v. New York City Dept. of Social Services*, we are unwilling to suppose that injuries occasioned by a municipality's unconstitutional conduct were not also meant to be fully redressable through its sweep.

B

Our rejection of a construction of § 1983 that would accord municipalities a qualified immunity for their good-faith constitutional violations is compelled both by the legislative purpose in enacting the statute and by considerations of public policy. The central aim of the Civil Rights Act was to provide protection to those persons wronged by the "[misuse] of power, possessed by virtue of state law and made possible only because the wrongdoer is clothed with the authority of state law." *Monroe v. Pape* (quoting *United States v. Classic*). By creating an express federal remedy, Congress sought to "enforce provisions of the Fourteenth Amendment against those who carry a badge of authority of a State and represent it in some capacity, whether they act in accordance with their authority or misuse it." *Monroe v. Pape*.

How "uniquely amiss" it would be, therefore, if the government itself — "the social organ to which all in our society look for the promotion of liberty, justice, fair and equal treatment, and the setting of worthy norms and goals for social conduct" — were permitted to disavow liability for the injury it has begotten. See *Adickes v. Kress & Co.* A damages remedy against the offending party is a vital component of any scheme for vindicating cherished constitutional guarantees, and the importance of assuring its efficacy is only accentuated when the wrongdoer is the institution that has been established to protect the very rights it has transgressed. Yet owing to the qualified immunity enjoyed by most government officials, see *Scheuer v. Rhodes*, many victims of municipal malfeasance would be left remediless if the city were also allowed to assert a good-faith defense. Unless countervailing considerations counsel otherwise, the injustice of such a result should not be tolerated.

Moreover, § 1983 was intended not only to provide compensation to the victims of past abuses, but to serve as a deterrent against future constitutional deprivations, as well. The knowledge that a municipality will be liable for all of its injurious conduct, whether committed in good faith or not, should create an incentive for officials who may harbor doubts about the lawfulness of their intended actions to err on the side of protecting citizens' constitutional rights. Furthermore, the threat that damages might be levied against the city may encourage those in a policymaking position to institute internal rules and programs designed to minimize the likelihood of unintentional infringements on constitutional rights. Such procedures are particularly beneficial in preventing those "systemic" injuries that result not so much from the conduct of any single individual, but from the interactive behavior of several government officials, each of whom may be acting in good faith. *Cf.* Note, *Developments in the Law: Section 1983 and Federalism*, 90 Harv. L. Rev. 1133, 1218–1219 (1977).

Our previous decisions conferring qualified immunities on various government officials are not to be read as derogating the significance of the societal interest in compensating the innocent victims of governmental misconduct. Rather, in each case we concluded that overriding considerations of public policy nonetheless demanded that the official be given a measure of protection from personal liability. The concerns that justified those decisions, however, are less compelling, if not wholly inapplicable, when the liability of the municipal entity is at issue.

In *Scheuer v. Rhodes*, The Chief Justice identified the two "mutually dependent rationales" on which the doctrine of official immunity rested:

> "(1) the injustice, particularly in the absence of bad faith, of subjecting to liability an officer who is required, by the legal obligations of his position, to exercise discretion; (2) the danger that the threat of such liability would deter his willingness to execute his office with the decisiveness and the

judgment required by the public good."

The first consideration is simply not implicated when the damages award comes not from the official's pocket, but from the public treasury. It hardly seems unjust to require a municipal defendant which has violated a citizen's constitutional rights to compensate him for the injury suffered thereby. Indeed, Congress enacted § 1983 precisely to provide a remedy for such abuses of official power. Elemental notions of fairness dictate that one who causes a loss should bear the loss.

It has been argued, however, that revenue raised by taxation for public use should not be diverted to the benefit of a single or discrete group of taxpayers, particularly where the municipality has at all times acted in good faith. On the contrary, the accepted view is that stated in *Thayer v. Boston* — "that the city, in its corporate capacity, should be liable to make good the damage sustained by an [unlucky] individual, in consequence of the acts thus done." After all, it is the public at large which enjoys the benefits of the government's activities, and it is the public at large which is ultimately responsible for its administration. Thus, even where some constitutional development could not have been foreseen by municipal officials, it is fairer to allocate any resulting financial loss to the inevitable costs of government borne by all the taxpayers, than to allow its impact to be felt solely by those whose rights, albeit newly recognized, have been violated.

The second rationale mentioned in *Scheuer* also loses its force when it is the municipality, in contrast to the official, whose liability is at issue. At the heart of this justification for a qualified immunity for the individual official is the concern that the threat of personal monetary liability will introduce an unwarranted and unconscionable consideration into the decisionmaking process, thus paralyzing the governing official's decisiveness and distorting his judgment on matters of public policy. The inhibiting effect is significantly reduced, if not eliminated, however, when the threat of personal liability is removed. First, as an empirical matter, it is questionable whether the hazard of municipal loss will deter a public officer from the conscientious exercise of his duties; city officials routinely make decisions that either require a large expenditure of municipal funds or involve a substantial risk of depleting the public fisc.

More important, though, is the realization that consideration of the *municipality's* liability for constitutional violations is quite properly the concern of its elected or appointed officials. Indeed, a decisionmaker would be derelict in his duties if, at some point, he did not consider whether his decision comports with constitutional mandates and did not weigh the risk that a violation might result in an award of damages from the public treasury. As one commentator aptly put it: "Whatever other concerns should shape a particular official's actions, certainly one of them should be the constitutional rights of individuals who will be affected by his actions. To criticize section 1983 liability because it leads decisionmakers to avoid the infringement of constitutional rights is to criticize one of the statute's *raisons d'etre*."

IV

In sum, our decision holding that municipalities have no immunity from damages liability flowing from their constitutional violations harmonizes well with developments in the common law and our own pronouncements on official immunities under § 1983. Doctrines of tort law have changed significantly over the past century, and our notions of governmental responsibility should properly reflect that evolution. No longer is individual "blameworthiness" the acid test of liability; the principle of equitable loss-spreading has joined fault as a factor in distributing the costs of official misconduct.

We believe that today's decision, together with prior precedents in this area, properly allocates these costs among the three principals in the scenario of the § 1983 cause of action: the victim of the constitutional deprivation; the officer whose conduct caused the injury; and the public, as represented by the municipal entity. The innocent individual who is harmed by an abuse of governmental authority is assured that he will be compensated for his injury. The offending official, so long as he conducts himself in good faith, may go about his business secure in the knowledge that a qualified immunity will protect him from personal liability for damages that are more appropriately chargeable to the populace as a whole. And the public will be forced to bear only the costs of injury inflicted by the "execution of a government's policy or custom, whether made by its lawmakers or by those whose edicts or acts may fairly be said to represent official policy." *Monell v. New York City Dept. of Social Services.*

Reversed.

MR. JUSTICE **POWELL**, with whom THE **CHIEF JUSTICE**, MR. JUSTICE **STEWART**, and MR. JUSTICE **REHNQUIST** join, dissenting.

The Court today holds that the City of Independence may be liable in damages for violating a constitutional right that was unknown when the events in this case occurred. It finds a denial of due process in the city's failure to grant petitioner a hearing to clear his name after he was discharged. But his dismissal involved only the proper exercise of discretionary powers according to prevailing constitutional doctrine. The city imposed no stigma on petitioner that would require a "name clearing" hearing under the Due Process Clause.

On the basis of this alleged deprivation of rights, the Court interprets 42 U.S.C. § 1983 to impose strict liability on municipalities for constitutional violations. This strict liability approach inexplicably departs from this Court's prior decisions under § 1983 and runs counter to the concerns of the 42d Congress when it enacted the statute. The Court's ruling also ignores the vast weight of common-law precedent as well as the current state law of municipal immunity. For these reasons, and because this decision will hamper local governments unnecessarily, I dissent.

The Court turns a blind eye to this overwhelming evidence that municipalities have enjoyed a qualified immunity and to the policy considerations that for the life of this Republic have justified its retention. This disregard of precedent and policy is especially unfortunate because suits under § 1983 typically implicate evolving constitutional standards. A good-faith defense is much more important for those actions than in those involving ordinary tort liability. The duty not to run over a pedestrian with a municipal bus is far less likely to change than is the rule as to what process, if any, is due the bus driver if he claims the right to a hearing after discharge.

The right of a discharged government employee to a "name clearing" hearing was not recognized until our decision in *Board of Regents v. Roth*. That ruling was handed down 10 weeks after Owen was discharged and 8 weeks after the city denied his request for a hearing. By stripping the city of any immunity, the Court punishes it for failing to predict our decision in Roth. As a result, local governments and their officials will face the unnerving prospect of crushing damages judgments whenever a policy valid under current law is later found to be unconstitutional. I can see no justice or wisdom in that outcome.

NOTES

1. The practical impact of *Owen* is that a plaintiff who can overcome the "policy" or "custom" hurdle (*see* section III below) does not face an "immunity" hurdle as well. By contrast, in his suit against an officer (a suit that may well be litigated in tandem with the one against the government) he is not required to show policy or custom, but he must deal with immunity. The broader point is that "municipal entities are not entitled to absolute [or any other kind of] immunity even where the entity's officers are entitled to immunity." *Capra v. Cook County Bd. of Review*, 733 F.3d 705, 711 (7th Cir. 2013). Thus, for example, plaintiff may win (having shown policy or custom) against the government, while losing against the officer (due to official immunity). Or he may lose against the government (having failed to show "policy" or "custom") and prevail against the officer (having defeated immunity.) He may prevail against both if he not only meets policy or custom but also overcomes immunity. Of course, all of these potential paths to success depend on meeting the threshold requirement of establishing a constitutional violation. Even if he proves a constitutional violation, he may lose against both if he cannot show "policy" or "custom" nor overcome "official immunity."

2. In *Owen*, the defendants fired the plaintiff without due process, but they did so several months before the Supreme Court held, in *Board of Regents v. Roth*, 408 U.S. 564 (1972) and *Perry v. Sindermann*, 408 U.S. 593 (1972), that a due process hearing was required in the circumstances. The "no immunity" rule of *Owen* does not by itself foreclose all defenses based on surprise. In principle, the city could still maintain (at least in 1980) that *Roth* and *Perry* should be applied prospectively only, and not to conduct that occurred before they were decided. But today that avenue is foreclosed by another case, *Harper v. Virginia Dept. of Taxation*, 509 U.S. 86 (1993), which states a very general rule that Supreme Court decisions apply retroactively on direct review, to conduct that occurred before they were decided so long as the litigation regarding that conduct is not yet final.

The lack of an immunity defense means not only that local governments are liable when officials fail to anticipate new constitutional rules, but also that they are liable when officials mistakenly believe that federal regulations oblige them to act as they did. *See, e.g., Galarza v. Szalczyk*, 745 F.3d 634 (3d Cir. 2014). In this case, local governments were held liable when local officials detained the plaintiff on suspicion of being an illegal alien pursuant to a municipal policy. That policy was based on local authorities' understanding of a federal regulation, namely, that immigration detainers were mandatory. The court ruled that the local government officers had read the federal regulation in the wrong way (despite the fact that a federal agent described it to them as mandatory).

3.   In his history of the common law Holmes defended the proposition that tort liability should be based on fault. In arguing against strict liability he wrote that "[a] choice which entails a concealed consequence is as to that consequence no choice." O. W. Holmes, Jr., The Common Law 76 (Mark DeWolfe Howe ed. 1963). He explained that, absent a fault requirement, an actor is liable even though he cannot foresee that one course of action is more dangerous than another. The actor has no grounds on which to choose between the safe and unsafe alternatives and has therefore made no choice in favor of the unsafe one. It is, he reasoned, unfair to impose liability on such an actor. Does this "fairness" argument for requiring fault apply to cases like *Owen* and *Galarza*? If it does, is it (as the Court seems to hold) outranked by the deterrent and compensatory goals served by denying an immunity defense? Is there a danger that the denial of such a defense will hinder rather than advance the recognition of constitutional rights, because courts will be loathe to impose damages liability on blameless governments? *See* John C. Jeffries, Jr., *Compensation for Constitutional Torts: Reflections on the Significance of Fault*, 88 Mich. L. Rev. 82 (1989); John C. Jeffries, Jr., *In Praise of the Eleventh Amendment and Section 1983*, 84 Va. L. Rev. 47 (1998); John C. Jeffries, Jr., *The Right-Remedy Gap in Constitutional Law*, 109 Yale L.J. 87 (1999); John C. Jeffries, Jr., *The Liability Rule for Constitutional Torts*, 99 Va. L. Rev. 207 (2013). Professor Jeffries argues (among other things) that constitutional tort liability should be based on fault, and, in particular, that *Owen* was wrong for failure to give due regard to the fairness and "constitutional rights development" grounds for a fault requirement.

III.   FOUR ROUTES TO GOVERNMENTAL LIABILITY

In ordinary tort law, the respondeat superior rule effectively imposes liability on businesses for every tort committed by their employees in the course of their employment. *Monell*'s rejection of respondeat superior for § 1983 litigation gives rise to a distinctive set of issues in constitutional tort law: Governments only act through the people who work for them in one capacity or another. Among all of the actions taken in the course of the employment, what ones will trigger governmental liability, and which will not? What are the principles for distinguishing between those two sets of cases? While the Supreme Court has not yet fully worked out the answers to these questions, there are four overlapping fact patterns in which courts will impose liability on local governments. A given case may fit into more than one of the templates we discuss in this section, and in some situations the law is ambiguous as to which is appropriate. Of course, litigants are not required to choose a single theory at the outset of the litigation. They can plead more than one, and often do so.

A. Formal Official Policy

1. *Monell v. Department of Social Services* was an easy case in which to find official policy because there the challenged conduct was an officially promulgated policy regarding pregnancy leaves. Similarly easy are those cases in which a local government formally and as a body makes a decision which, when executed by the body itself or its employees, gives rise to the alleged constitutional violation. Policy statements, ordinances, regulations and similar decisions are good examples. *See, e.g., Bell v. City of Winter Park*, 745 F.3d 1318 (11th Cir. 2014) (ordinance regulating picketing or protesting near dwellings challenged on free speech grounds); *Hayden v. Greensburg Community School Corp.*, 743 F.3d 569 (7th Cir. 2014) (school policy requiring male basketball players to keep their hair cut short challenged on equal protection grounds); *Frudden v. Pilling*, 742 F.3d 1199 (9th Cir. 2014) (school policy requiring students to wear uniforms challenged on free speech grounds); *Gravelet-Blondin v. Shelton*, 728 F.3d 1086, 1096 (9th Cir. 2013) (challenge to "the City's policy . . . defining tasers as a low level of force" that may be used even where the officer is not threatened); *Catron v. City of St. Petersburg*, 658 F.3d 1260 (11th Cir. 2011) (challenge to a local trespass ordinance by homeless residents claiming that it violated their free speech and procedural due process rights); *Saieg v. City of Dearborn*, 641 F.3d 727 (6th Cir. 2011) ("police department's leafleting policy, made with the authority that the City Council delegated to it, fairly represents official City policy"; thus "Saieg may hold the City liable for violating his First Amendment right to free speech").

2. It does not matter whether the policy or decision is general and in the form of an ordinance or regulation, or is specific and particularized, affecting only one or a few individuals. *See, e.g., Bateson v. Geisse*, 857 F.2d 1300 (9th Cir. 1988) (single decision of city council to withhold building permit). It has also been held that a local government resolution adopted by a city council and directed against a named individual constituted an official policy although it was not an enforceable law. *Little v. City of North Miami*, 805 F.2d 962 (11th Cir. 1986). Suppose some but not all members of the city council act for an unconstitutional motive. This issue is illustrated by the facts of *Bogan v. Scott-Harris*, 523 U.S. 44 (1998), a case we discuss in chapter 7 for its holding on legislative immunity. The city council effectively fired the plaintiff by a 6-2 vote. The plaintiff proved that two of the city council members voted against her for unconstitutional motives. The First Circuit found that the city could not be held liable in these circumstances. The Supreme Court noted that holding but did not pursue the matter. Its opinion addresses only the question of whether the city council members may assert absolute legislative immunity. The Court held that they could do so.

3. Distinguish between the city's policy and the officer's execution of the policy. The city can be liable for the former but not the latter, if the officer deviates. For example, in *Campbell v. Miller*, 499 F.3d 711 (7th Cir. 2007), a police officer arrested Campbell on suspicion that he possessed marijuana. A city policy instructed officers to conduct "immediate and thorough body search[es]" of those under arrest. The officer, pursuant to that policy, proceeded "to take Campbell into the open backyard of his friend's house and subject him to a strip search involving a visual inspection of Campbell's anal cavity," in plain sight of the friend and of neighbors. The officer was liable for an unreasonable search, in violation of the Fourth Amendment. But the city escaped liability, as "[t]here [was] no evidence in the record that it was the City's policy that arrestees had to be searched *in public*, and that is the only aspect of this particular search that violates the Constitution." 499 F.3d at 719. Should the city nonetheless be liable on the theory that the city policy evidently did not explicitly forbid this type of search?

The distinction between the policy and its application does not mean that the city is never liable in a suit complaining that the ordinance is unconstitutional "as applied" to plaintiff's conduct. For example, in *Christensen v. Park City Mun. Corp.*, 554 F.3d 1271, 1279 (10th Cir. 2009), the ordinance prohibited selling one's goods on city property without a license. Plaintiff, a "visual artist" who sold his work on city property, was arrested and then sued the city on free speech grounds. He did not challenge the facial validity of the ordinance but asserted that it was unconstitutional as applied to him. He was allowed to sue the city because the officers were not "acting at their own discretion or initiative. They were not freelancing; they were enforcing a city ordinance in accordance with its terms." (The court did not reach the merits of the free speech issue.)

4. Formal policy is just one of four paths to liability. Each of the other three can be illustrated by variations on *Campbell*. One is "custom." Even if the formal policy is valid, the plaintiff may be able to show an unconstitutional practice. Returning to *Campbell*, the court indicated that the plaintiff could have won against the city on a "custom" theory if he had offered evidence of "a practice and custom on the street to perform strip searches more invasive than the City's policy permitted." *See* section III B below.

Another path is to show that the key actor is a "final policymaker." Even if the formal policy is valid, and even if the plaintiff cannot establish a custom, and even if the official's constitutional violation is due to his exercise of discretion, the plaintiff may prevail against the government by showing that the officer is a "final policy maker." *See* section III C below.

The last path is "inadequate" training or hiring. Even if none of the grounds for liability discussed above work for the plaintiff, he can win a "policy" suit by showing that the city's training of police officers was so inadequate as to be "deliberately indifferent" to his constitutional rights, and that this deliberate indifference was the "moving force" behind the officer's violation of his rights. *See* section III D below.

There is, of course, no guarantee that any of these four paths will lead to municipal liability in every instance in which the city should fairly be held responsible for a violation of constitutional rights. Suppose, for example, the violation is produced by a combination of a mediocre but constitutionally valid formal policy, occasional but not sufficiently widespread violations by lower level employees, careless but not sufficiently egregious oversight by their superiors, and superficial but barely adequate training. There is no catch-all liability rule the plaintiff can fall back on when each of these paths is blocked but there is nonetheless a strong case for municipal liability. The problem, to which there is as yet no solution, was recognized early in the development of constitutional tort law.

See Christina B. Whitman, *Government Responsibility for Constitutional Torts*, 85 MICH. L. REV. 226 (1986).

B. Custom

1. *Monell* declares that a local government may be liable not only for its official policy but for its custom as well. What does "custom" mean? There are no post-*Monell* Supreme Court cases addressing this question, but the Court has reiterated the principle, *e.g.*, in *Bd. of County Commissioners v. Brown*, 520 U.S. 397, 404 (1997) (Unwritten customs not "formally approved by an appropriate decisionmaker" can create municipal liability if the "practice is so widespread as to have the force of law.") Though the Supreme Court has not shown much interest in developing the doctrine, "custom" is a viable theory in the lower federal courts. As *Campbell, supra*, suggests, custom is a *de facto* official policy, for which the city is responsible under § 1983 even though there is no *formal* evidence of its establishment.

2. A custom may be a practice by lower level officers, accompanied by high level officials' actual or constructive knowledge of the practice. Or it may be a pattern of behavior for which high level officials are directly responsible, differing from the "formal" policy category in that it is not written down.

An illustrative case in the first category is *Webster v. City of Houston*, 689 F.2d 1220 (5th Cir. 1982), *aff'd*, 739 F.2d 993 (5th Cir. 1984), in which plaintiff proved a widespread practice by police officers of putting a "throw down" gun near a person who had been shot.

The latter category may be illustrated by *Gschwind v. Heiden*, 692 F.3d 844, 848 (7th Cir. 2012). A school superintendent told the plaintiff that

> it was the policy of the school district and the Board of Education to allow principals and assistant principals to make evaluation and employment decisions as they see fit with respect to the teachers they supervise and for the school district and the Board of Education to follow these decisions and recommendations.

The court, in an opinion by Judge Posner, found that this statement "was evidence of a policy of the school district of condoning unconstitutional terminations, since principals and assistant principals might 'see fit' to fire teachers on unconstitutional grounds."

3. Because customs are not written down, the plaintiff must put in evidence to show that officers act unconstitutionally. But proving a few instances of illegality is not enough. The plaintiff needs enough instances to justify a conclusion that the practice is so widespread as to amount to a custom. Consider the following cases:

Jackson v. Barnes, 749 F.3d 755, 763 (9th Cir. 2014) (allegation that one police sergeant "routinely declined to give *Miranda* warnings, and that the [Sheriff's] Department in fact did not supervise the practices of its deputies" would success-fully "plead[] a policy of inaction" by the county);

D'Ambrosio v. Marino, 747 F.3d 378, 388 (6th Cir. 2014) ("allegations regarding the repeated failures of only one prosecutor" in Cuyhoga County, Ohio are insufficient to state a "custom" claim);

Johnson v. Douglas Co. Medical Dept., 725 F.3d 825, 829 (8th Cir. 2013) (purported custom of providing inmates with inadequate medical care; "multiple incidents involving a single plaintiff could establish a 'custom' if some evidence indicates that the incidents occurred over a course of time sufficiently long to permit notice of, and then deliberate indifference to or tacit authorization of, the conduct by policymaking officials," but the single incident proved in this case did not suffice to present a jury question as to custom);

World Wide Street Preachers v. Town of Columbia, 591 F.3d 747, 755 (5th Cir. 2009) (evidence that "generally Columbia officers allowed the preachers to demonstrate without interference," and "[t]here were only a few isolated incidents where officers sought to restrict the preachers' rights," supported the district court's finding "that there was no persistent, widespread practice of applying inappropriate statutes to the preachers to restrict their First Amendment rights");

Matusick v. Erie County Water Authority, 757 F.3d 31, 63 (2d Cir. 2014) (custom of harassing the plaintiff because of his interracial relationship; affirming a jury verdict in favor of plaintiff against a local government for race discrimination, because "the acts of discrimination and harassment alleged by Matusick were frequent and severe. . . . [Many] human resources personnel, including the director of human resources, were aware of his complaints well before he was terminated. They failed to act.").

4. The quoted language from *Johnson* and *Matusick* suggests, and other cases confirm, that the plaintiff is required to show that high level officials ("final policy makers," in the Supreme Court's vocabulary, see section C below) are, or should be, aware of the practice. But it is unclear precisely what level of knowledge will trigger municipal liability. Some opinions suggest that negligence ("should have known") is enough, while others require a showing of "deliberate indifference" to the unconstitutional practice by lower level officers.

Compare Curtis v. Anthony, 710 F.3d 587, 595 (5th Cir. 2013) (purported policy involved deputy's dog-scent lineups; "a plaintiff must [show] that the body governing a municipality, or an official to whom the body has delegated its policy-making authority, had actual or constructive knowledge of the custom or policy at issue") *with Palmer v. Marion County*, 327 F.3d 588, 595–96 (7th Cir. 2003) (custom of jailors letting inmates fight; proof of isolated acts of misconduct will not suffice; a series of violations must be presented to lay the premise of deliberate indifference).

Jackson, Matusick, Curtis, and *Palmer* all involve low level officers whose unconstitutional actions should (with some level of awareness) be known to higher authorities. In *Gschwind, supra*, the custom was actually implemented by high level officers. But the plaintiff is not required to specify the origins of the practice. He can win without identifying any specific higher-up who either instituted it or failed to do anything about it. In *B.S. v. Somerset County*, 704 F.3d 250, 275 (3d Cir. 2013), county officials transferred custody of a child from the mother to the father. The mother claimed that the county violated her procedural and substantive due process rights and the court ruled in her favor on that claim:

> [W]hile the relevant policymaker is not readily apparent, the evidence shows conclusively that, when a non-custodial parent is available to take a child, it is customary for the County to temporarily suspend the other parent's custody rights without a hearing, when abuse is suspected. That custom was used with official approbation in this case.

5. Why should custom give rise to section 1983 local government liability? The Ninth Circuit answered as follows: "The existence of custom as a basis for liability under § 1983 . . . serves a critical role in insuring that local government entities are held responsible for widespread abuses or practices that cannot be affirmatively attributed to the decisions or ratification of an official government policy maker but are so pervasive as to have the force of law." *Thompson v. City of Los Angeles*, 885 F.2d 1439, 1444 (9th Cir. 1989).

6. Some of these "custom" cases refer to the knowledge of "final policymakers." The "final policymaker" ground for local government liability is discussed in detail in the next section, but it should already be apparent that the "custom" theory and the "final policymaker" theory cannot be neatly separated.

C. Final Policy Makers

Recall that *Monell* declared without much explanation that local government liability can be premised on the unconstitutional conduct of those "whose edicts or acts may fairly be said to represent official policy." Many custom cases refer to the inaction of a final policy maker, who failed to act against widespread illegality by lower officers despite his knowledge (or some lesser state of awareness of the practice, such as deliberate indifference.) The acts of a "final policy maker" may trigger municipal liability in other contexts as well. *Pembaur* is the Supreme Court's leading case on this topic.

PEMBAUR v. CITY OF CINCINNATI
475 U.S. 469 (1986)

JUSTICE BRENNAN delivered the opinion of the Court, except as to Part II-B.

In *Monell v. New York City Dept. of Social Services* the Court concluded that municipal liability under 42 U.S.C. § 1983 is limited to deprivations of federally protected rights caused by action taken "pursuant to official municipal policy of some nature. . . ." The question presented is whether, and in what circumstances, a decision by municipal policymakers on a single occasion may satisfy this requirement.

I

[Pembaur, a physician, owned Rockdle Medical Center in Cincinnati. The local prosecutor investigated him for fraud. The case was assigned to Assistant Prosecutor William Whalen and Pembaur was indicted by a grand jury.]

During the investigation, the grand jury issued subpoenas for the appearance of two of Pembaur's employees. When these employees failed to appear as directed, the Prosecutor obtained capias for their arrest and detention from the Court of Common Pleas of Hamilton County.

On May 19, 1977, two Hamilton County Deputy Sheriffs attempted to serve the capiases at Pembaur's clinic. [Pembaur] refused to let them enter, claiming that the police had no legal authority to be there and requesting that they leave. [The Deputy Sheriffs telephoned Whalen and informed him of the situation. Whalen conferred with County Prosecutor Leis, who told Whalen to instruct the Deputy Sheriffs to "go in and get [the witnesses]." Whalen in turn passed these instructions along to the Deputy Sheriffs.

After a final attempt to persuade Pembaur voluntarily to allow them to enter, the Deputy Sheriffs tried unsuccessfully to force the door. City police officers, who had been advised of the County Prosecutor's instructions to "go in and get" the witnesses, obtained an axe and chopped down the door. The Deputy Sheriffs then entered and searched the clinic. Two individuals who fit descriptions of the witnesses sought were detained, but turned out not to be the right persons.

[On] April 20, 1981, Pembaur filed [this lawsuit.] . Pembaur sought damages under 42 U.S.C. § 1983, alleging that the county and city police had violated his rights under the Fourth and Fourteenth Amendments. His theory was that, absent exigent circumstances, the Fourth Amendment prohibits police from searching an individual's home or business without a search warrant even to execute an arrest warrant for a third person. We agreed with that proposition in *Steagald v. United States*, decided the day after Pembaur filed this lawsuit. Pembaur sought $10 million in actual and $10 million in punitive damages, plus costs and attorney's fees.

The Court of Appeals affirmed the District Court's dismissal of Pembaur's claim against Hamilton County. [Pembaur] petitioned for certiorari to review only the dismissal of his claim against Hamilton County. The decision of the Court of Appeals conflicts with holdings in several other Courts of Appeals, and we granted the petition to resolve the conflict. We reverse.

II
A

Our analysis must begin with the proposition that "Congress did not intend municipalities to be held liable unless action pursuant to official municipal policy of some nature caused a constitutional tort." *Monell v. New York City Dept. of Social Services*. As we read its opinion, the Court of Appeals held that a single decision to take particular action, although made by municipal policymakers, cannot establish the kind of "official policy" required by *Monell* as a predicate to municipal liability under § 1983. The Court of Appeals reached this conclusion without referring to *Monell* — indeed, without any explanation at all. However, examination of the opinion in *Monell* clearly demonstrates that the Court of Appeals misinterpreted its holding.

Monell is a case about responsibility. In the first part of the opinion, we held that local government units could be made liable under § 1983 for deprivations of federal rights, overruling a contrary holding in *Monroe v. Pape*. In the second part of the opinion, we recognized a limitation on this liability and concluded that a municipality cannot be made liable by application of the doctrine of respondeat superior. See *Monell*. In part, this conclusion rested upon the language of § 1983, which imposes liability only on a person who "subjects, or causes to be subjected," any individual to a deprivation of federal rights; we noted that this language "cannot easily be read to impose liability vicariously on government bodies solely on the basis of the existence of an employer-employee relationship with a tortfeasor." Primarily, however, our conclusion rested upon the legislative history, which disclosed that, while Congress never questioned its power to impose civil liability on municipalities for their own illegal acts, Congress did doubt its constitutional power to impose such liability in order to oblige municipalities to control the conduct of others. We found that, because of these doubts, Congress chose not to create such obligations in § 1983. Recognizing that this would be the effect of a federal law of respondeat superior, we concluded that § 1983 could not be interpreted to incorporate doctrines of vicarious liability.

The conclusion that tortious conduct, to be the basis for municipal liability under § 1983, must be pursuant to a municipality's "official policy" is contained in this discussion. The "official policy" requirement was intended to distinguish acts of the municipality from acts of employees of the municipality, and thereby make clear that municipal liability is limited to action for which the municipality is actually responsible. *Monell* reasoned that recovery from a municipality is limited to acts that are, properly speaking, acts "of the municipality" — that is, acts which the municipality has officially sanctioned or ordered.

With this understanding, it is plain that municipal liability may be imposed for a single decision by municipal policymakers under appropriate circumstances. No one has ever doubted, for instance, that a municipality may be liable under § 1983 for a single decision by its properly constituted legislative body — whether or not that body had taken similar action in the past or intended to do so in the future — because even a single decision by such a body unquestionably constitutes an act of official government policy. See, e.g., *Owen v. City of Independence* (City Council passed resolution firing plaintiff without a pre-termination hearing); *Newport v. Fact Concerts, Inc.* (City Council canceled license permitting concert because of dispute over content of performance). But the power to establish policy is no more the exclusive province of the legislature at the local level than at the state or national level. *Monell's* language makes clear that it expressly envisioned other officials "whose acts or edicts may fairly be said to represent official policy," *Monell*, and whose decisions therefore may give rise to municipal liability under § 1983.

Indeed, any other conclusion would be inconsistent with the principles underlying § 1983. To be sure, "official policy" often refers to formal rules or understandings — often but not always committed to writing — that are intended to, and do, establish fixed plans of action to be followed under similar circumstances consistently and over time. That was the case in *Monell* itself, which involved a written rule requiring pregnant employees to take unpaid leaves of absence before such leaves were medically necessary. However, as in *Owen* and *Newport*, a government frequently chooses a course of action tailored to a particular situation and not intended to control decisions in later situations. If the decision to adopt that particular course of action is properly made by that government's authorized decisionmakers, it surely represents an act of official government "policy" as that term is commonly understood. More importantly, where action is directed by those who establish governmental policy, the municipality is equally responsible whether that action is to be taken only once or to be taken repeatedly. To deny compensation to the victim would therefore be contrary to the fundamental purpose of § 1983.

B

Having said this much, we hasten to emphasize that not every decision by municipal officers automatically subjects the municipality to § 1983 liability. Municipal liability attaches only where the decisionmaker possesses final authority to establish municipal policy with respect to the action ordered. The fact that a particular official — even a policymaking official — has discretion in the exercise of particular functions does not, without more, give rise to municipal liability based on an exercise of that discretion. See, e.g., *Oklahoma City v. Tuttle.* The official must also be responsible for establishing final government policy respecting such activity before the municipality can be held liable.[4] Authority to make municipal policy may be granted directly by a legislative enactment or may be delegated by an official who possesses such authority, and of course, whether an official had final policymaking authority is a question of state law. However, like other governmental entities, municipalities often spread policymaking authority among various officers and official bodies. As a result, particular officers may have authority to establish binding county policy respecting particular matters and to adjust that policy for the county in changing circumstances. To hold a municipality liable for actions ordered by such officers exercising their policymaking authority is no more an application of the theory of respondeat superior than was holding the municipalities liable for the decisions of the City Councils in *Owen* and *Newport.* In each case municipal liability attached to a single decision to take unlawful action made by municipal policymakers. We hold that municipal liability under § 1983 attaches where — and only where — a deliberate choice to follow a course of action is made from among various alternatives by the official or officials responsible for establishing final policy with respect to the subject matter in question. See *Tuttle* (" 'policy' generally implies a course of action consciously chosen from among various alternatives").

---

[4]　[12] Thus, for example; the County Sheriff may have discretion to hire and fire employees without also being the county official responsible for establishing county employment policy. If this were the case, the Sheriff's decisions respecting employment would not give rise to municipal liability, although similar decisions with respect to law enforcement practices, over which the Sheriff is the official policymaker, would give rise to municipal liability. Instead, if county employment policy was set by the Board of County Commissioners, only that body's decisions would provide a basis for county liability. This would be true even if the Board left the Sheriff discretion to hire and fire employees and the Sheriff exercised that discretion in an unconstitutional manner; the decision to act unlawfully would not be a decision of the Board. However, if the Board delegated its power to establish final employment policy to the Sheriff, the Sheriff's decisions would represent county policy and could give rise to municipal liability.

C

Applying this standard to the case before us, we have little difficulty concluding that the Court of Appeals erred in dismissing petitioner's claim against the county. The Deputy Sheriffs who attempted to serve the capiases at petitioner's clinic found themselves in a difficult situation. Unsure of the proper course of action to follow, they sought instructions from their supervisors. The instructions they received were to follow the orders of the County Prosecutor. The Prosecutor made a considered decision based on his understanding of the law and commanded the officers forcibly to enter petitioner's clinic. That decision directly caused the violation of petitioner's Fourth Amendment rights.

Respondent argues that the County Prosecutor lacked authority to establish municipal policy respecting law enforcement practices because only the County Sheriff may establish policy respecting such practices. Respondent suggests that the County Prosecutor was merely rendering "legal advice" when he ordered the Deputy Sheriffs to "go in and get" the witnesses. Consequently, the argument concludes, the action of the individual Deputy Sheriffs in following this advice and forcibly entering petitioner's clinic was not pursuant to a properly established municipal policy.

We might be inclined to agree with respondent if we thought that the Prosecutor had only rendered "legal advice." However, the Court of Appeals concluded, based upon its examination of Ohio law, that both the County Sheriff and the County Prosecutor could establish county policy under appropriate circumstances, a conclusion that we do not question here. Ohio Rev. Code Ann. § 309.09(A) (1979) provides that county officers may "require . . . instructions from [the County Prosecutor] in matters connected with their official duties." Pursuant to standard office procedure, the Sheriff's Office referred this matter to the Prosecutor and then followed his instructions. The Sheriff testified that his Department followed this practice under appropriate circumstances and that it was "the proper thing to do" in this case. We decline to accept respondent's invitation to overlook this delegation of authority by disingenuously labeling the Prosecutor's clear command mere "legal advice." In ordering the Deputy Sheriffs to enter petitioner's clinic the County Prosecutor was acting as the final decisionmaker for the county, and the county may therefore be held liable under § 1983.

The decision of the Court of Appeals is reversed, and the case is remanded for further proceedings consistent with this opinion.

JUSTICE **WHITE**, concurring.

The forcible entry made in this case was not then illegal under federal, state, or local law. The city of Cincinnati frankly conceded that forcible entry of third-party property to effect otherwise valid arrests was standard operating procedure. There is no reason to believe that respondent county would abjure using lawful means to execute the capiases issued in this case or had limited the authority of its officers to use force in executing capiases. Further, the county officials who had the authority to approve or disapprove such entries opted for the forceful entry, a choice that was later held to be inconsistent with the Fourth Amendment. Vesting discretion in its officers to use force and its use in this case sufficiently manifested county policy to warrant reversal of the judgment [below.]

JUSTICE STEVENS, concurring in part and concurring in the judgment.

This is not a hard case. If there is any difficulty, it arises from the problem of obtaining a consensus on the meaning of the word "policy" — a word that does not appear in the text of 42 U.S.C. § 1983, the statutory provision that we are supposed to be construing. The difficulty is thus a consequence of this Court's lawmaking efforts rather than the work of the Congress of the United States.

JUSTICE POWELL, with whom THE CHIEF JUSTICE and JUSTICE REHNQUIST join, dissenting.

[In] my view, proper resolution of the question whether official policy has been formed should focus on two factors: (i) the nature of the decision reached or the action taken, and (ii) the process by which the decision was reached or the action was taken.

Focusing on the nature of the decision distinguishes between policies and mere ad hoc decisions. Such a focus also reflects the fact that most policies embody a rule of general applicability. That is the tenor of the Court's statement in *Monell* that local government units are liable under § 1983 when the action that is alleged to be unconstitutional "implements or executes a policy statement, ordinance, regulation, or decision officially adopted and promulgated by that body's officers." The clear implication is that policy is created when a rule is formed that applies to all similar situations — a "governing principle [or] plan." *Webster's New Twentieth Century Dictionary* 1392 (2d ed. 1979). When a rule of general applicability has been approved, the government has taken a position for which it can be held responsible.

Another factor indicating that policy has been formed is the process by which the decision at issue was reached. Formal procedures that involve, for example, voting by elected officials, prepared reports, extended deliberation, or official records indicate that the resulting decisions taken "may fairly be said to represent official policy." *Monell, supra. Owen v. City of Independence* provides an example. The City Council met in a regularly scheduled meeting. One member of the Council made a motion to release to the press certain reports that cast an employee in a bad light. After deliberation, the Council passed the motion with no dissents and one abstention. Although this official action did not establish a rule of general applicability, it is clear that policy was formed because of the process by which the decision was reached.

Applying these factors to the instant case demonstrates that no official policy was formulated. Certainly, no rule of general applicability was adopted. The Court correctly notes that the Sheriff "testified that the Department had no written policy respecting the serving of capiases on the property of third persons and that the proper response in any given situation would depend upon the circumstances." Nor could he recall a specific instance in which entrance had been denied and forcibly gained. The Court's result today rests on the implicit conclusion that the Prosecutor's response — "go in and get them" — altered the prior case-by-case approach of the Department and formed a new rule to apply in all similar cases. Nothing about the Prosecutor's response to the inquiry over the phone, nor the circumstances surrounding the response, indicates that such a rule of general applicability was formed.

Similarly, nothing about the way the decision was reached indicates that official policy was formed. The prosecutor, without time for thoughtful consideration or consultation, simply gave an off-the-cuff answer to a single question. There was no process at all. The Court's holding undercuts the basic rationale of *Monell*, and unfairly increases the risk of liability on the level of government least able to bear it. I dissent.

[The concurring opinion of JUSTICE O'CONNOR is omitted.]

NOTE

While there is no majority opinion in *Pembaur* on the key issue of how to identify "officials determining final policy," the case made an important first step in framing the "policy" and "policy maker" issues. A majority of the Justices rejected Justice Powell's view that a policy is "a rule of general applicability" that is "adopted" after "thoughtful consideration or consultation." Rather, a single act by a "persons with final authority to establish municipal policy" would suffice. The ensuing case law has focused on identifying these actors and determining which of their decisions qualify as municipal policy.

Justice Brennan states, in section II B of his opinion, that "whether an official had final policymaking authority is a question of state law." Although Justice Brennan spoke for only a plurality of the Court in this section of the opinion, the focus on state law became the Court's rule. The next step in the development of the doctrine is *Praprotnik*, though again there is no majority opinion.

CITY OF ST. LOUIS v. PRAPROTNIK
485 U.S. 112 (1988)

JUSTICE O'CONNOR announced the judgment of the Court and delivered an opinion, in which THE CHIEF JUSTICE, JUSTICE WHITE, and JUSTICE SCALIA join.

This case calls upon us to define the proper legal standard for determining when isolated decisions by municipal officials or employees may expose the municipality itself to liability under 42 U.S.C. § 1983.

I

The principal facts are not in dispute. Respondent James H. Praprotnik is an architect who began working for petitioner city of St. Louis in 1968. For several years, respondent consistently received favorable evaluations of his job performance, uncommonly quick promotions, and significant increases in salary. By 1980, he was serving in a management-level city planning position at petitioner's Community Development Agency (CDA).

The Director of CDA, Donald Spaid, had instituted a requirement that the agency's professional employees, including architects, obtain advance approval before taking on private clients. Respondent and other CDA employees objected to the requirement. In April 1980, respondent was suspended for 15 days by CDA's Director of Urban Design, Charles Kindleberger, for having accepted outside employment without prior approval. Respondent appealed to the city's Civil Service Commission, a body charged with reviewing employee grievances. Finding the penalty too harsh, the Commission reversed the suspension, awarded respondent back pay, and directed that he be reprimanded for having failed to secure a clear understanding of the rule.

The Commission's decision was not well received by respondent's supervisors at CDA. Kindleberger later testified that he believed respondent had lied to the Commission, and that Spaid was angry with respondent.

Respondent's next two annual job performance evaluations were markedly less favorable than those in previous years. In discussing one of these evaluations with respondent, Kindleberger apparently mentioned his displeasure with respondent's 1980 appeal to the Civil Service Commission. Respondent appealed both evaluations to the Department of Personnel. In each case, the Department ordered partial relief and was upheld by the city's Director of Personnel or the Civil Service Commission.

In April 1981, a new mayor came into office, and Donald Spaid was replaced as Director of CDA by Frank Hamsher. As a result of budget cuts, a number of layoffs and transfers significantly reduced the size of CDA and of the planning section in which respondent worked. Respondent, however was retained.

In the spring of 1982, a second round of layoffs and transfers occurred at CDA. At that time, the city's Heritage and Urban Design Division (Heritage) was seeking approval to hire someone who was qualified in architecture and urban planning. Hamsher arranged with the Director of Heritage, Henry Jackson, for certain functions to be transferred from CDA to Heritage. This arrangement, which made it possible for Heritage to employ a relatively high-level "city planning manager," was approved by Jackson's supervisor, Thomas Nash. Hamsher then transferred respondent to Heritage to fill this position.

Respondent objected to the transfer, and appealed to the Civil Service Commission. The Commission declined to hear the appeal because respondent had not suffered a reduction in his pay or grade. Respondent then filed suit in federal district court, alleging that the transfer was unconstitutional. The city was named as a defendant, along with Kindleberger, Hamsher, Jackson (whom respondent deleted from the list before trial), and Deborah Patterson, who had succeeded Hamsher at CDA.

At Heritage, respondent became embroiled in a series of disputes with Jackson and Jackson's successor, Robert Killen. Respondent was dissatisfied with the work he was assigned, which consisted of unchallenging clerical functions far below the level of responsibilities that he had previously enjoyed. At least one adverse personnel decision was taken against respondent, and he obtained partial relief after appealing that decision.

In December 1983, respondent was laid off from Heritage. The lay off was attributed to a lack of funds, and this apparently meant that respondent's supervisors had concluded that they could create two lower-level positions with the funds that were being used to pay respondent's salary. Respondent then amended the complaint in his lawsuit to include a challenge to the layoff. He also appealed to the Civil Service Commission, but proceedings in that forum were postponed because of the pending lawsuit and have never been completed.

The case went to trial on two theories: (1) that respondent's First Amendment rights had been violated through retaliatory actions taken in response to his appeal of his 1980 suspension; and (2) that respondent's layoff from Heritage was carried out for pre-textual reasons in violation of due process. The jury returned special verdicts exonerating each of the three individual defendants, but finding the city liable under both theories. Judgment was entered on the verdicts, and the city appealed.

III
A

In the years since *Monell* was decided, the Court has considered several cases involving isolated acts by government officials and employees. We have assumed that an unconstitutional governmental policy could be inferred from a single decision taken by the highest officials responsible for setting policy in that area of the government's business. See, e.g., *Owen v. City of Independence; Newport v. Fact Concerts, Inc., Cf. Pembaur.* At the other end of the spectrum, we have held that an unjustified shooting by a police officer cannot, without more, be thought to result from official policy. *Tuttle* (plurality opinion).

Two terms ago, in *Pembaur, supra,* we undertook to define more precisely when a decision on a single occasion may be enough to establish an unconstitutional municipal policy. Although the Court was unable to settle on a general formulation, Justice Brennan's plurality opinion articulated several guiding principles. First, a majority of the Court agreed that municipalities may be held liable under § 1983 only for acts for which the municipality itself is actually responsible, "that is, acts which the municipality has officially sanctioned or ordered." Second, only those municipal officials who have "final policymaking authority" may by their actions subject the government to § 1983 liability. Third, whether a particular official has "final policymaking authority" is a question of state law. Fourth, the challenged action must have been taken pursuant to a policy adopted by the official or officials responsible under state law for making policy in that area of the city's business.

The Courts of Appeals have already diverged in their interpretations of these principles. Today, we set out again to clarify the issue that we last addressed in *Pembaur.*

B

We begin by reiterating that the identification of policymaking officials is a question of state law. "Authority to make municipal policy may be granted directly by a legislative enactment or may be delegated by an official who possesses such authority, and of course, whether an official had final policymaking authority is a question of state law." *Pembaur v. Cincinnati* (plurality opinion).

Thus the identification of policymaking officials is not a question of federal law and it is not a question of fact in the usual sense. The States have extremely wide latitude in determining the form that local government takes, and local preferences have led to a profusion of distinct forms. Among the many kinds of municipal corporations, political subdivisions, and special districts of all sorts, one may expect to find a rich variety of ways in which the power of government is distributed among a host of different officials and official bodies. Without attempting to canvass the numberless factual scenarios that may come to light in litigation, we can be confident that state law (which may include valid local ordinances and regulations) will always direct a court to some official or body that has the responsibility for making law or setting policy in any given area of local government's business.

We are not, of course, predicting that state law will always speak with perfect clarity. We have no reason to suppose, however, that federal courts will face greater difficulties here than those that they routinely address in other contexts. We are also aware that there will be cases in which policymaking responsibility is shared among more than one official or body. In the case before us, for example, it appears that the mayor and aldermen are authorized to adopt such ordinances relating to personnel administration as are compatible with the City Charter. The Civil Service Commission, for its part, is required to "prescribe . . . rules for the administration and enforcement of the provisions of this article, and of any ordinance adopted in pursuance thereof, and not inconsistent therewith." Assuming that applicable law does not make the decisions of the Commission reviewable by the mayor and aldermen, or vice versa, one would have to conclude that policy decisions made either by the mayor and aldermen or by the Commission would be attributable to the city itself. In any event, however, a federal court would not be justified in assuming that municipal policymaking authority lies somewhere other than where the applicable law purports to put it. And certainly there can be no justification for giving a jury the discretion to determine which officials are high enough in the government that their actions can be said to represent a decision of the government itself.

As the plurality in *Pembaur* recognized, special difficulties can arise when it is contended that a municipal policymaker has delegated his policymaking authority to another official. If the mere exercise of discretion by an employee could give rise to a constitutional violation, the result would be indistinguishable from respondeat superior liability. If, however, a city's lawful policymakers could insulate the government from liability simply by delegating their policymaking authority to others, § 1983 could not serve its intended purpose. It may not be possible to draw an elegant line that will resolve this conundrum, but certain principles should provide useful guidance.

First, whatever analysis is used to identify municipal policymakers, egregious attempts by local government to insulate themselves from liability for unconstitutional policies are precluded by a separate doctrine. Relying on the language of § 1983, the Court has long recognized that a plaintiff may be able to prove the existence of a widespread practice that, although not authorized by written law or express municipal policy, is "so permanent and well settled as to constitute a custom or usage' with the force of law." *Adickes v. S. H. Kress & Co.* That principle, which has not been affected by *Monell* or subsequent cases, ensures that most deliberate municipal evasions of the Constitution will be sharply limited.

Second, as the *Pembaur* plurality recognized, the authority to make municipal policy is necessarily the authority to make final policy. When an official's discretionary decisions are constrained by policies not of that official's making, those policies, rather than the subordinate's departures from them, are the act of the municipality. Similarly, when a subordinate's decision is subject to review by the municipality's authorized policymakers, they have retained the authority to measure the official's conduct for conformance with their policies. If the authorized policymakers approve a subordinate's decision and the basis for it, their ratification would be chargeable to the municipality because their decision is final.

C

Whatever refinements of these principles may be suggested in the future, we have little difficulty concluding that the Court of Appeals applied an incorrect legal standard in this case. In reaching this conclusion, we do not decide whether the First Amendment forbade the city from retaliating against respondent for having taken advantage of the grievance mechanism in 1980. Nor do we decide whether there was evidence in this record from which a rational jury could conclude either that such retaliation actually occurred or that respondent suffered any compensable injury from whatever retaliatory action may have been taken. Finally, we do not address petitioner's contention that the jury verdict exonerating the individual defendants cannot be reconciled with the verdict against the city. Even assuming that all these issues were properly resolved in respondent's favor, we would not be able to affirm the decision of the Court of Appeals.

The city cannot be held liable under § 1983 unless respondent proved the existence of an unconstitutional municipal policy. Respondent does not contend that anyone in city government ever promulgated, or even articulated, such a policy. Nor did he attempt to prove that such retaliation was ever directed against anyone other than himself. Respondent contends that the record can be read to establish that his supervisors were angered by his 1980 appeal to the Civil Service Commission; that new supervisors in a new administration chose, for reasons passed on through some informal means, to retaliate against respondent two years later by transferring him to another agency; and that this transfer was part of a scheme that led, another year and a half later, to his lay off. Even if one assumes that all this was true, it says nothing about the actions of those whom the law established as the makers of municipal policy in matters of personnel administration. The mayor and aldermen enacted no ordinance designed to retaliate against respondent or against similarly situated employees. On the contrary, the city established an independent Civil Service Commission and empowered it to review and correct improper personnel actions. Respondent does not deny that his repeated appeals from adverse personnel decisions repeatedly brought him at least partial relief, and the Civil Service Commission never so much as hinted that retaliatory transfers or lay offs were permissible. Respondent points to no evidence indicating that the Commission delegated to anyone its final authority to interpret and enforce the following policy set out in article XVIII of the city's Charter, § 2(a):

> "Merit and fitness. All appointments and promotions to positions in the
> service of the city and all measures for the control and regulation of
> employment in such positions, and separation therefrom, shall be on the
> sole basis of merit and fitness. . . ."

The Court of Appeals concluded that "appointing authorities," like Hamsher and
Killen, who had the authority to initiate transfers and layoffs, were municipal
"policymakers." The court based this conclusion on its findings (1) that the decisions
of these employees were not individually reviewed for "substantive propriety" by
higher supervisory officials; and (2) that the Civil Service Commission decided
appeals from such decisions, if at all, in a circumscribed manner that gave
substantial deference to the original decisionmaker. We find these propositions
insufficient to support the conclusion that Hamsher and Killen were authorized to
establish employment policy for the city with respect to transfers and layoffs. To the
contrary, the City Charter expressly states that the Civil Service Commission has
the power and the duty:

> "To consider and determine any matter involved in the administration and
> enforcement of this [Civil Service] article and the rules and ordinances
> adopted in accordance therewith that may be referred to it for decision by
> the director [or personnel], or on appeal by any appointing authority,
> employee, or taxpayer of the city, from any act of the director or of any
> appointing authority. The decision of the commission in all such matters
> shall be final, subject, however, to any right of action under any law of the
> state or of the United States."

This case therefore resembles the hypothetical example in *Pembaur*: "If [city]
employment policy was set by the [Mayor and Aldermen and by the Civil Service
Commission], only [those] bod[ies'] decisions would provide a basis for [city]
liability. This would be true even if the [mayor and aldermen and the Commission]
left the [appointing authorities] discretion to hire and fire employees and [they]
exercised that discretion in an unconstitutional manner. . . ." A majority of the
Court of Appeals panel determined that the Civil Service Commission's review of
individual employment actions gave too much deference to the decisions of
appointing authorities like Hamsher and Killen. Simply going along with discretionary decisions made by one's subordinates, however, is not a delegation to them
of the authority to make policy. It is equally consistent with a presumption that the
subordinates are faithfully attempting to comply with the policies that are supposed
to guide them. It would be a different matter if a particular decision by a
subordinate was cast in the form of a policy statement and expressly approved by
the supervising policymaker. It would also be a different matter if a series of
decisions by a subordinate official manifested a "custom or usage" of which the
supervisor must have been aware. In both those cases, the supervisor could
realistically be deemed to have adopted a policy that happened to have been
formulated or initiated by a lower-ranking official. But the mere failure to
investigate the basis of a subordinate's discretionary decisions does not amount to
a delegation of policymaking authority, especially where (as here) the wrongfulness
of the subordinate's decision arises from a retaliatory motive or other unstated

rationale. In such circumstances, the purposes of § 1983 would not be served by treating a subordinate employees' decision as if it were a reflection of municipal policy.

Justice Brennan's opinion, concurring in the judgment, finds implications in our discussion that we do not think necessary or correct. We nowhere say or imply, for example, that "a municipal charter's precatory admonition against discrimination or any other employment practice not based on merit and fitness effectively insulates the municipality from any liability based on acts inconsistent with that policy." *Post.* Rather, we would respect the decisions, embodied in state and local law, that allocated policymaking authority among particular individuals and bodies. Refusals to carry out stated policies could obviously help to show that a municipality's actual policies were different from the ones that had been announced. If such a showing were made, we would be confronted with a different case than the one we decide today.

Nor do we believe that we have left a "gaping hole" in § 1983 that needs to be filled with the vague concept of "de facto final policymaking authority." *Post.* Except perhaps as a step towards overruling *Monell* and adopting the doctrine of respondeat superior, ad hoc searches for officials possessing such "de facto" authority would serve primarily to foster needless unpredictability in the application of § 1983.

IV

We cannot accept either the Court of Appeals' broad definition of municipal policy-makers or respondent's suggestion that a jury should be entitled to define for itself which officials' decisions should expose a municipality to liability. Respondent has suggested that the record will support an inference that policymaking authority was in fact delegated to individuals who took retaliatory action against him and who were not exonerated by the jury. Respondent's arguments appear to depend on a legal standard similar to the one suggested in Justice Stevens' dissenting opinion, which we do not accept. Our examination of the record and state law, however, suggests that further review of this case may be warranted in light of the principles we have discussed. That task is best left to the Court of Appeals, which will be free to invite additional briefing and argument if necessary. Accordingly, the decision of the Court of Appeals is reversed, and the case is remanded for further proceedings consistent with this opinion.

JUSTICE BRENNAN, with whom JUSTICE MARSHALL and JUSTICE BLACKMUN join, concurring.

Despite its somewhat confusing procedural background, this case at bottom presents a relatively straightforward question: whether respondent's supervisor at the Community Development Agency, Frank Hamsher, possessed the authority to establish final employment policy for the city of St. Louis such that the city can be held liable under 42 U.S.C. § 1983 for Hamsher's allegedly unlawful decision to transfer respondent to a dead-end job. Applying the test set out two Terms ago by the plurality in *Pembaur v. Cincinnati*, I conclude that Hamsher did not possess such authority and I therefore concur in the Court's judgment reversing the decision below. I write separately, however, because I believe that the commendable desire of today's plurality to "define more precisely when a decision on a single occasion may be enough" to subject a municipality to § 1983 liability has led it to embrace a theory of municipal liability that is both unduly narrow and unrealistic, and one that ultimately would permit municipalities to insulate themselves from liability for the acts of all but a small minority of actual city policymakers.

In concluding that Frank Hamsher was a policymaker, the Court of Appeals relied on the fact that the City had delegated to him "the authority, either directly or indirectly, to act on [its] behalf," and that his decisions within the scope of this delegated authority were effectively final. In *Pembaur*, however, we made clear that a municipality is not liable merely because the official who inflicted the constitutional injury had the final authority to act on its behalf; rather, as four of us explained, the official in question must possess "final authority to establish municipal policy with respect to the [challenged] action." Thus, we noted, "the fact that a particular official — even a policymaking official — has discretion in the exercise of particular functions does not, without more, give rise to municipal liability based on an exercise of that discretion." By way of illustration, we explained that if, in a given county, the Board of County Commissioners established county employment policy and delegated to the County Sheriff alone the discretion to hire and fire employees, the county itself would not be liable if the Sheriff exercised this authority in an unconstitutional manner, because "the decision to act unlawfully would not be a decision of the Board." We pointed out, however, that in that same county the Sheriff could be the final policymaker in other areas, such as law enforcement practices, and that if so, his or her decisions in such matters could give rise to municipal liability. In short, just as in *Owen* and *Fact Concerts* we deemed it fair to hold municipalities liable for the isolated, unconstitutional acts of their legislative bodies, regardless of whether those acts were meant to establish generally applicable "policies," so too in *Pembaur* four of us concluded that it is equally appropriate to hold municipalities accountable for the isolated constitutional injury inflicted by an executive final municipal policymaker, even though the decision giving rise to the injury is not intended to govern future situations. In either case, as long as the contested decision is made in an area over which the official or legislative body could establish a final policy capable of governing future municipal conduct, it is both fair and consistent with the purposes of § 1983 to treat the decision as that of the municipality itself, and to hold it liable for the resulting constitutional deprivation.

In my view, *Pembaur* controls this case. As an "appointing authority," Hamsher was empowered under the City Charter to initiate lateral transfers such as the one challenged here, subject to the approval of both the Director of Personnel and the appointing authority of the transferee agency. The Charter, however, nowhere confers upon agency heads any authority to establish city policy, final or otherwise, with respect to such transfers. Thus, for example, Hamsher was not authorized to promulgate binding guidelines or criteria governing how or when lateral transfers were to be accomplished. Nor does the record reveal that he in fact sought to exercise any such authority in these matters. There is no indication, for example, that Hamsher ever purported to institute or announce a practice of general applicability concerning transfers. Instead, the evidence discloses but one transfer decision — the one involving respondent — which Hamsher ostensibly undertook pursuant to a city-wide program of fiscal restraint and budgetary reductions. At most, then, the record demonstrates that Hamsher had the authority to determine how best to effectuate a policy announced by his superiors, rather than the power to establish that policy. Like the hypothetical Sheriff in *Pembaur's* footnote 12, Hamsher had discretionary authority to transfer CDA employees laterally; that he may have used this authority to punish respondent for the exercise of his First Amendment rights does not, without more, render the city liable for respondent's resulting constitutional injury. The court below did not suggest that either Killen or Nash, who together orchestrated respondent's ultimate layoff, shared Hamsher's constitutionally impermissible animus. [Because the court identified only one unlawfully motivated municipal employee involved in respondent's transfer and layoff, and because that employee did not possess final policymaking authority with respect to the contested decision, the city may not be held accountable for any constitutional wrong respondent may have suffered.]

III

These determinations, it seems to me, are sufficient to dispose of this case, and I therefore think it unnecessary to decide, as the plurality does, who the actual policymakers in St. Louis are. I question more than the mere necessity of these determinations, however, for I believe that in the course of passing on issues not before us, the plurality announces legal principles that are inconsistent with our earlier cases and unduly restrict the reach of § 1983 in cases involving municipalities.

I cannot endorse the plurality's determination, based on nothing more than its own review of the City Charter, that the mayor, the aldermen, and the CSC are the only policymakers for the city of St. Louis. While these officials may well have policymaking authority, that hardly ends the matter; the question before us is whether the officials responsible for respondent's allegedly unlawful transfer were final policymakers. As I have previously indicated, I do not believe that CDA Director Frank Hamsher possessed any policymaking authority with respect to lateral transfers and thus I do not believe that his allegedly improper decision to transfer respondent could, without more, give rise to municipal liability. Although the plurality reaches the same result, it does so by reasoning that because others could have reviewed the decisions of Hamsher and Killen, the latter officials simply could not have been final policymakers.

This analysis, however, turns a blind eye to reality, for it ignores not only the lower court's determination, nowhere disputed, that CSC review was highly circumscribed and deferential, but that in this very case the Commission refused to judge a propriety of Hamsher's transfer decision because a lateral transfer was not an "adverse" employment action falling within its jurisdiction. Nor does the plurality account for the fact that Hamsher's predecessor, Donald Spaid, promulgated what the city readily acknowledges was a binding policy regarding secondary employment; although the CSC ultimately modified the sanctions respondent suffered as a result of his apparent failure to comply with that policy, the record is devoid of any suggestion that the Commission reviewed the substance or validity of the policy itself. Under the plurality's analysis, therefore, even the hollowest promise of review is sufficient to divest all city officials save the mayor and governing legislative body of final policymaking authority. While clarity and ease of application may commend such a rule, we have remained steadfast in our conviction that Congress intended to hold municipalities accountable for those constitutional injuries inflicted not only by their lawmakers, but "by those whose edicts or acts may fairly be said to represent official policy." *Monell.* Because the plurality's mechanical "finality" test is fundamentally at odds with the pragmatic and factual inquiry contemplated by *Monell*, I cannot join what I perceive to be its unwarranted abandonment of the traditional factfinding process in § 1983 actions involving municipalities.

Finally, I think it necessary to emphasize that despite certain language in the plurality opinion suggesting otherwise, the Court today need not and therefore does not decide that a city can only be held liable under § 1983 where the plaintiff "prov[es] the existence of an unconstitutional municipal policy." Just last Term, we left open for the second time the question whether a city can be subjected to liability for a policy that, while not unconstitutional in and of itself, may give rise to constitutional deprivations. See *Springfield v. Kibbe*; see also *Oklahoma City v. Tuttle*. That question is certainly not presented by this case, and nothing we say today forecloses its future consideration.

[The dissenting opinion of JUSTICE STEVENS is omitted; JUSTICE KENNEDY did not participate.]

NOTES

1. In *Jett v. Dallas Independent School District*, 491 U.S. 701 (1989), the plaintiff, a former athletic director and football coach, sued a school district and principal alleging that they had deprived him of his position in violation of equal protection and the First Amendment. One of the issues in the case was whether the school district's superintendent was a policy maker in light of the plurality opinion in *Praprotnik*. In remanding the cast for consideration of this issue, the Court made clear that the approach of the *Praprotnik* plurality, with its reliance on state law and the role of the trial judge, was to govern on remand. The Court declared:

> As with other questions of state law relevant to the application of federal law, the identification of those officials whose decisions represent the official policy of the local governmental unit is itself a legal question to be resolved by the trial judge *before* the case is submitted to the jury. Reviewing the relevant legal materials, including state and local positive law, as well as "custom or usage" having the force of law, the trial judge must identify those officials or governmental bodies who speak with final policymaking authority for the local governmental actor concerning the action alleged to have caused the particular constitutional or statutory violation at issue. Once those officials who have the power to make official policy on a particular issue have been identified, it is for the jury to determine whether *their* decisions have caused the deprivation of rights at issue by policies which affirmatively command that it occur, or by acquiescence in a

longstanding practice or custom which constitutes the "standard operating procedure" of the local governmental entity.

What is significant about *Jett* is that Justice O'Connor's opinion for the Court was joined by four other justices, including Justice Kennedy. There are two take aways. First, a majority of the Court ruled that state law governs the policy maker inquiry. Second, the Court in *Jett* retreated somewhat from the apparent insistence in the *Praprotnik* plurality opinion that state *formal* law alone was determinative of the policy maker issue. This is demonstrated by its reference in *Jett* to a trial court's use of "relevant legal materials, including state and local positive law, as well as 'custom or usage' having the force of law" in deciding the policy maker issue.

2.   After *Jett*, the hard cases are those in which the unconstitutional act is taken by someone other than the officer designated by state law as the policymaker, yet the policymaker may be somehow responsible for the act, either because he delegated the task to the subordinate or because he ratified the act. Thus, by either means the subordinate may be the *de facto* policymaker. Cases involving a policymaker's passive acquiescence in decisions made by lower-level officers raise questions the Court has not yet definitively answered. A threshold issue is how they should be characterized: Do they belong in the "custom" category, or does the acquiescence result in shifting responsibility to a new "policymaker," namely the lower-level officer? Some passages in *Praprotnik* seem to treat this type of case under the heading of "custom," see section III B of Justice O'Connor's plurality opinion, while other passages discuss "delegation" as a "policymaker" issue, see III C of Justice O'Connor's opinion. The passage from *Jett* set out above could be read either way.

As the following notes illustrate, many but not all lower courts characterize these as "policymaker" cases. A notable exception to the general trend in the lower courts is *Milligan-Hitt v. Board of Trustees of Sheridan County School District No. 2*, 523 F.3d 1219, 1225 (10th Cir. 2008). In a forceful opinion, Judge McConnell took *Praprotnik* as his guidepost, read *Praprotnik* as a ruling that "policymaker" status is entirely an issue of state law, and held that the *de facto* cases belong in the "custom" category.

One reason it makes a difference how acquiescence cases are characterized is that the elements of the cause of action differ depending on whether plaintiff must prove a custom (in which case he ordinarily must prove a widespread practice) or the single act of a policymaker (which does not require proving a widespread practice). In addition, the characterization of these cases can make a difference on the question of whether the judge or the jury decides the governmental liability issue. Thus, in *Milligan-Hitt*, the court followed *Pratprotnik's* principle that the "policymaker" issue "is itself a legal question to be resolved by the trial judge *before* the case is submitted to the jury." *Milligan-Hitt* held that evidence of a practice that is contrary to state law cannot support a finding that a given official is a policymaker. Of course, such evidence would be relevant to custom. But the court said that the custom "doctrine is not at issue here," 523 F.3d at 1225, presumably because the plaintiff failed to raise it.

Would *Milligan-Hitt*, which seems to channel more litigation into the "custom" category and less into the "final policymaker" theory of municipal liability, generate as many instances of governmental liability as an approach that holds local governments liable for constitutional violations committed by subordinates to whom final policymakers have delegated decisionmaking? Liability based on delegation is described in note 3 below.

3.   The gap between formal lines of authority and actual practice comes up when the officials authorized by state law to make policy choose to delegate their authority to subordinates, and do not review the decisions their subordinates make. For example, in *Kristofek v. Village of Orland Hills*, 712 F.3d 979, 987 (7th Cir. 2013), a police officer was fired by Scully (the police chief) and sued both Scully and the city, claiming that the chief was the policymaker for firing decisions in the police department. The court upheld his complaint against a motion to dismiss, because "[t]he complaint suggests Scully was fully in charge of the police department and that his firing decisions were not reviewed."

The *de facto* policymaker issue is discussed in more detail in *Lytle v. Carl*, 382 F.3d 978, 982–85 (9th Cir. 2004). A teacher was fired and claimed that it was done in retaliation for protected speech. She sued the school district, charging that the decision to dismiss her was made by the superintendent and assistant superintendent, who were de facto policymakers for firing issues, even though state law designated "the Board of Trustees for a School District as the body responsible for setting all District policies." The court upheld a jury verdict for the plaintiff despite state law. Writing for the panel, Judge William Fletcher said that "[a] municipal employee may act as a *de facto* policymaker under § 1983 without explicit authority under state law." The court recognized that an examination of state law is the main inquiry in determining who is a final policy maker. It then cited *Jett* for the proposition that "[d]epending on the circumstances, however, we may also look to the way a local government entity operates in practice." Here, state law authorized the Board to delegate powers to the superintendent, and the evidence supported the inference that it had delegated firing decisions to him and the assistant superintendent. Although the Board formally retained the authority to review the superintendent's decisions, "[t]he record reflects that the Board did not review discipline of individual employees such as Lytle, and did not retain the authority to review such discipline."

Both *Lytle* and *Kristofek* stress the unreviewability of the officer's decisions as a ground for finding that he is a policymaker. For a different view, *see Bolton v. City of Dallas*, 541 F.3d 545, 549 (5th Cir. 2008), holding that a city manager who fired the plaintiff was not the final policymaker with regard to the firing, even though the decision was not reviewable. Citing the *Pembaur* plurality's footnote 12, the court distinguished between policy making and decision making and ruled that employment policy was set by the City Council, even though the city manager had the authotity to fire the police chief without any review.

Reread *Pembaur*'s footnote 12. Do you think Justice Brennan would agree with the use to which it was put in *Bolton*?

4.   Suppose *Bolton* is wrong to reject the proposition that lack of "reviewability" will justify treating an officer as a final policymaker. What will suffice to show that a decision is reviewable? In *Lytle* the school district argued that the superintendent's decision to fire plaintiff was not final because the plaintiff could obtain review

from an arbitrator under the grievance process established by a collective bargaining agreement. The court rejected the argument:

> The District's argument mistakes the meaning of "final policy maker" and the role of an independent arbitrator. The arbitrator does not work for the District. In determining who was a final policymaker for the District, we focus on whether the official's decisions were subject to review by the *District*'s authorized policymakers. 382 F.3d at 985–86 (emphasis in original)

See also Carter v. City of Melbourne, Fla., 731 F.3d 1161, 1167 (11th Cir. 2013) (endorsing *Lytle* on this point).

5. The delegation theory is not necessarily limited to delegations to subordinates inside the government. For a holding that a local government can be liable for decisions made by a private company to which its policymakers have delegated a task, *see King v. Kramer*, 680 F.3d 1013, 1020–21 (7th Cir. 2012) ("The evidence presented for summary judgment purposes shows that the County's policy was to entrust final decision-making authority to HPL [a private company] over inmates' access to physicians and medications. . . . [The] County's express policies as embodied in the contract show that the County delegated to HPL final authority to make decisions about inmates' medical care.")

6. Distinguish the "delegation" fact pattern discussed in the preceding notes from a situation in which the final policymaker reviews the action of a subordinate and arguably "ratifies" it. These are two distinct paths to municipal liability. *See, e.g., Darchak v. City of Chicago Board of Education*, 580 F.3d 622, 630 (7th Cir. 2009) (To maintain her § 1983 claim, "Darchak must demonstrate that the Board either delegated final policymaking authority to Acevedo [a public school principal] or ratified Acevedo's action.")

Whether a final policymaker has "ratified" a subordinate's decision is a recurring fact pattern in § 1983 litigation. In *Praprotnik* all of the Justices except Justice Stevens agreed that the final policymakers had not "ratified" the unconstitutionally-motivated decision of lower level officials to discipline Pratprotnik, but they nonetheless recognized that ratification is a viable theory. Thus, just before part IIIC, Justice O'Connor states a general rule: "If the authorized policymakers approve a subordinate's decision and the basis for it, their ratification would be chargeable to the municipality because their decision is final." 485 U.S. at 127 (plurality opinion). Although there is no majority opinion, it was quite clear that a majority supported some version of liability based on ratification. Justices Brennan, Marshall, and Blackmun concurred only in the judgment, because they thought the Court's general approach did not go far enough in imposing liability, and Justice Stevens dissented because he favored an even broader municipal liability rule. The case is universally read as endorsing the proposition that, on a proper set of facts, a government may be liable on a ratification theory.

Here is a typical summary of the doctrine:

> To show ratification, a plaintiff must prove that the authorized policymakers approve a subordinate's decision and the basis for it. We have found

municipal liability on the basis of ratification when the officials involved adopted and expressly approved of the acts of others who caused the constitutional violation.

Sheehan v. City and County of San Francisco, 743 F.3d 1211, 1231 (9th Cir. 2014) (citations and internal quotaiton marks omitted).

Sheehan illustrates one of the limits of the theory. Two police officers had used deadly force againt a mentally ill woman. She sued the city as well as the officers.

> Sheehan contends that the city ratified the officers' conduct by not disciplining them. Ratification, however, generally requires more than mere acquiescence. There is no evidence in the record that policymakers made a deliberate choice to endorse the officers' actions. The mere failure to discipline Reynolds and Holder does not amount to ratification of their allegedly unconstitutional actions.

Suppose Al, a low level official, fires Cathy, the plaintiff, subject to review by a final policymaker, Bob. Al undertakes the dismissal process as retaliation for Cathy's protected speech. Bob approves the firing. Is this set of facts sufficient to show ratification? *See Waters v. City of Chicago*, 580 F.3d 575, 584–85 (7th Cir.2009) ("simply going along with discretionary decisions made by one's subordinates [is] not a delegation to them of the authority to make policy; [the] mere failure to investigate the basis of a subordinate's discretionary decisions does not amount to a delegation of policymaking authority, especially where (as here) the wrongfulness of the subordinate's decision arises from a retaliatory motive or other unstated rationale"). What result if Bob knows of Al's unconstitutional motive but can show that he approved of the dismissal for different and wholly legitimate reasons?

Waters uses the term "delegation" to describe the plaintiff's theory. But the fact pattern in which the policymaker "simply go[es] along with discretionary decisions made by one's subordinates" could also (and perhaps with more descriptive accuracy) be framed as a "ratification" issue.

Proper characterization of the plaintiff's claim can make a difference in the elements of proof and in outcome. The proof of delegation involves steps taken by the policymaker before the event giving rise to litigation. Ratification is after-the-fact. It is clear ever since *Praprotnik* that delegation requires more than "simply going along with" subordinate's decisions. A more or less deliberate decision to hand over policymaking is requied. Despite its ubiquity in the case law, the precise content of the "ratification" doctrine remains unsettled. In *Praprotnik*, Justice O'Connor defines ratification as approval of "a subordinate's decision and the basis for it." *Waters* and *Sheehan* seem to follow that approach. But some cases seem to adopt a more expansive approach to ratification, by allowing the plaintiff to recover from the city if he can show "that the policymaking official was aware of the employee's unconstitutional actions and consciously chose to ignore them." *Jones v. Town of East Haven*, 691 F.3d 72 (2d Cir. 2012).

McMILLIAN: POLICYMAKER FOR WHICH ENTITY, THE LOCAL GOVERNMENT OR THE STATE?

The foregoing materials demonstrate that, under state and local law, a highranking local government official can be a policymaker for one purpose and not for another. But matters can be even more complicated than that. As the following important case illustrates, a high-ranking official who appears to be a local government policymaker may turn out instead to be a state policymaker as a matter of state law, with the result that neither the local government nor the state (recall *Quern* and *Will*) can be held liable for the unconstitutional conduct of that official.

McMILLIAN v. MONROE COUNTY, ALABAMA
520 U.S. 781 (1997)

CHIEF JUSTICE **REHNQUIST** delivered the opinion of the Court.

Petitioner sued Monroe County, Alabama under 42 U.S.C. § 1983 for allegedly unconstitutional actions taken by Monroe County Sheriff Tom Tate. If the sheriff's actions constitute county "policy," then the county is liable for them. The parties agree that the sheriff is a "policymaker" for § 1983 purposes, but they disagree about whether he is a policymaker for Monroe County or for the State of Alabama. We hold that, as to the actions at issue here, Sheriff Tate represents the State of Alabama and is therefore not a county policymaker. We thus affirm the Court of Appeals' dismissal of petitioner's § 1983 claims against Monroe County.

I

In November 1986, Ronda Morrison was murdered in Monroe County, a sparsely populated county located in southwest Alabama. Petitioner and one Ralph Myers were indicted for this crime. Myers then pleaded guilty to a lesser offense and testified against petitioner at his trial. A jury convicted petitioner of capital murder, and the trial court sentenced him to death. After two remands, the Alabama Court of Criminal Appeals reversed petitioner's conviction, holding that the State had violated *Brady v. Maryland*, by suppressing statements from Myers that contradicted his trial testimony and other exculpatory evidence. Thus, after spending six years in prison, petitioner was released.

He then brought this § 1983 lawsuit in the District Court for the Middle District of Alabama against respondent Monroe County and numerous officials, including the three men in charge of investigating the Morrison murder — Tom Tate, the Sheriff of Monroe County; Larry Ikner, an investigator with the District Attorney's office in Monroe County; and Simon Benson, an investigator with the Alabama Bureau of Investigation. Only two of the officials were sued in their official capacities — Sheriff Tate and investigator Ikner — and it is only these official-capacity suits that concern us here. Petitioner principally alleged that Tate and Ikner, in their capacities as officials of Monroe County, not as officers of the State of Alabama, intimidated Myers into making false statements and suppressed exculpatory evidence.

The District Court dismissed the claims against Monroe County and the claims against Tate and Ikner in their official capacities. The court held that "any unlawful acts of Defendants Tate and Ikner cannot be said to represent [Monroe] County's policy," because "an Alabama county has [no] authority to make policy in the area of law enforcement." Petitioner appealed the District Court's decision as to Sheriff Tate. The Court of Appeals for the Eleventh Circuit affirmed, agreeing with the District Court that "Sheriff Tate is not a final policymaker for Monroe County in the area of law enforcement, because Monroe County has no law enforcement authority." We granted certiorari, and now affirm.

II

A

We held in *Monell*, that a local government is liable under § 1983 for its policies that cause constitutional torts. These policies may be set by the government's lawmakers, "or by those whose edicts or acts may fairly be said to represent official policy." A court's task is to "identify those officials or governmental bodies who speak with final policymaking authority for the local governmental actor concerning the action alleged to have caused the particular constitutional or statutory violation at issue." *Jett v. Dallas Independent School Dist.* Here, the parties agree that Sheriff Tate has "final policymaking authority" in the area of law enforcement. They sharply disagree, however, about whether Alabama sheriffs are policymakers for the State or for the county when they act in a law enforcement capacity.

In deciding this dispute, our inquiry is guided by two principles. First, the question is not whether Sheriff Tate acts for Alabama or Monroe County in some categorical, "all or nothing" manner. Our cases on the liability of local governments under § 1983 instruct us to ask whether governmental officials are final policymakers for the local government in a particular area, or on a particular issue. Thus, we are not seeking to make a characterization of Alabama sheriffs that will hold true for every type of official action they engage in. We simply ask whether Sheriff Tate represents the State or the county when he acts in a law enforcement capacity.

Second, our inquiry is dependent on an analysis of state law. This is not to say that state law can answer the question for us by, for example, simply labeling as a state official an official who clearly makes county policy. But our understanding of the actual function of a governmental official, in a particular area, will necessarily be dependent on the definition of the official's functions under relevant state law.

B

The Court of Appeals for the Eleventh Circuit determined that under Alabama law, a sheriff acting in his law enforcement capacity is not a policymaker for the county. Since the jurisdiction of the Court of Appeals includes Alabama, we defer considerably to that court's expertise in interpreting Alabama law.

We begin with the Alabama Constitution, "the supreme law of the state." We agree with the Court of Appeals that the constitutional provisions concerning sheriffs, the historical development of those provisions, and the interpretation given them by the Alabama Supreme Court strongly support Monroe County's contention that sheriffs represent the State, at least for some purposes.

Turning from the Alabama Constitution to the Alabama Code, the relevant provisions are less compelling, but still support the conclusion of the Court of Appeals to some extent. Section 36-22-3 of the Code sets out a sheriff's duties. First, a sheriff must "attend upon" the state courts in his county, must "obey the lawful orders and directions" of those courts, and must "execute and return the process and orders" of any state court, even those outside his county. Thus, judges may order the sheriff to take certain actions, even if the judge sits in a distant county. And under Ala. Code § 12-17-24 (1995), the presiding circuit judge "exercises a general supervision" over the county sheriffs in his circuit, just as if the sheriffs are normal "court [i.e., state] employees" (see § 12-17-1).

Second, the sheriff must give to the county treasurer a sworn written statement detailing the funds he has received for the county since his last statement, and must pay these funds to the treasurer. In contrast to the state judges, however, the county treasurer does not appear to have any statutory authority to direct the sheriff to take specific actions. Third and most importantly, "it shall be the duty of sheriffs in their respective counties, by themselves or deputies, to ferret out crime, to apprehend and arrest criminals and, insofar as within their power, to secure evidence of crimes in their counties and to present a report of the evidence so secured to the district attorney or assistant district attorney for the county." By this mandate, sheriffs are given complete authority to enforce the state criminal law in their counties. In contrast, the "powers and duties" of the counties themselves — creatures of the State who have only the powers granted to them by the State, do not include any provision in the area of law enforcement. Ala. Code § 11-3-11 (1989). Thus, the "governing body" of the counties — which in every Alabama county is the county commission, cannot instruct the sheriff how to ferret out crime, how to arrest a criminal, or how to secure evidence of a crime. And when the sheriff does secure such evidence, he has an obligation to share this information not with the county commission, but with the district attorney (a state official).

[T]he county's payment of the sheriff's salary does not translate into control over him, since the county neither has the authority to change his salary nor the discretion to refuse payment completely. The county commissions do appear to have the discretion to deny funds to the sheriffs for their operations beyond what is "reasonably necessary." But at most, this discretion would allow the commission to exert an attenuated and indirect influence over the sheriff's operations. Petitioner's contention that sheriffs are county officials because "state policymakers" typically make policy for the entire State (without limits on their jurisdiction) and are typically elected on a statewide (not local) basis, surely has some force. But district attorneys and state judges are often considered (and in Alabama are considered) state officials, even though they too have limited jurisdictions and are elected locally. These characteristics are therefore consistent with an understanding of the 67 Alabama sheriffs as state officials who have been locally placed throughout the State, with an element of control granted to the officials and residents of the county which receives the sheriff's services.

In sum, although there is some evidence in Alabama law that supports petitioner's argument, we think the weight of the evidence is strongly on the side of the conclusion reached by the Court of Appeals: Alabama sheriffs, when executing their law enforcement duties, represent the State of Alabama, not their counties.

C

Petitioner argues that this conclusion will create a lack of uniformity in Alabama and throughout the country. First, he argues that it is anomalous to have 67 different "state policymakers" in the person of Alabama's 67 county sheriffs, all of whom may have different "state law enforcement policies" in their counties. Second, he points out that most Federal Courts of Appeals have found county sheriffs to be county, not state, officials, and he implies that our affirmence of the Court of Appeals will either call those decisions into question or create an unacceptable patchwork of rulings as to § 1983 liability of counties for the acts of their sheriffs. We reject both arguments: the first ignores the history of sheriffs, and the second ignores our Nation's federal nature.

The final concern of petitioner and his amici is that state and local governments will manipulate the titles of local officials in a blatant effort to shield the local governments from liability. But such efforts are already foreclosed by our decision in Praprotnik. See 485 U.S. at 127 (plurality opinion) ("Egregious attempts by local governments to insulate themselves from liability for unconstitutional policies are precluded" by allowing plaintiffs to prove that "a widespread practice" has been established by " 'custom or usage' with the force of law"). And there is certainly no evidence of such manipulation here; indeed, the Alabama provisions that cut most strongly against petitioner's position predate our decision in Monell by some time. The judgment of the Court of Appeals is therefore Affirmed.

JUSTICE GINSBURG, with whom JUSTICE STEVENS, JUSTICE SOUTER, and JUSTICE BREYER join, dissenting.

Sheriff Tate, it is uncontested, has "final policymaking authority" under Alabama law over matters of law enforcement in Monroe County. Our precedent instructs that, if the Sheriff makes policy for the State, Monroe County would not be accountable, under § 1983, for that policy; if, on the other hand, the Sheriff acts as law enforcement policymaker for Monroe County, then the County would be answerable under § 1983.

Alabama has 67 county sheriffs, each elected, paid, and equipped locally, each with countywide, not statewide, authority. Unlike judges who work within the State's judicial hierarchy, or prosecutors who belong to a prosecutorial corps superintended by the State's Attorney General, sheriffs are not part of a state command and serve under no "State Sheriff General." The Court, nonetheless, holds that the policies set by Sheriff Tate in Monroe County, though discrete from and uncoordinated with, the policies of sheriffs in other counties, "may fairly be said to represent [Alabama] policy." I disagree.

In my view, Alabama law defining the office of sheriff indicates that the sheriff acts within and for the county when setting and implementing law enforcement policy. In explaining why it concludes otherwise and deems the sheriff the State's, not the county's, policymaker, the Court leans heavily on provisions of the State's

Constitution. The Court relies on the Alabama Constitution's designation of "a sheriff for each county" as a member of the State's "executive department." *See* Ala. Const., Art. V, § 112. In addition, the Court points to two 1901 amendments relating to the impeachment of sheriffs. These measures are the strongest supports for the Court's classification of county sheriffs as state actors. They are not sturdy enough, however, to justify the Court's holding that county sheriffs are state officials.

The prime controllers of a sheriff's service are the county residents, the people who select their sheriff at quadrennial elections. Sheriff Tate owes his position as chief law enforcement officer of Monroe County to the county residents who elected him, and who can unseat him. *See* Ala. Const., Art. V, § 138, as amended by Amdt. No. 35 ("A sheriff shall be elected in each county by the qualified electors thereof. . . ."). On the ballot, candidates for the office of sheriff are grouped with candidates for other county offices, and are not listed with state office candidates. *See* Ala. Code § 17-8-5 (1995).

Traditionally, Alabama sheriffs have had autonomy to formulate and execute law enforcement policy within the geographic confines of their counties. Under Alabama law, "it shall be the duty of sheriffs in their respective counties . . . to ferret out crime, to apprehend and arrest criminals and . . . to secure evidence of crimes." Ala. Code § 36-22-3(4) (1991); see also Ala. Code § 15-6-1 (1995) ("The sheriff is the principal conservator of the peace in his county, and it is his duty to suppress riots, unlawful assemblies and affrays. In the execution of such duty, he may summon to his aid as many of the men of his county as he thinks proper."); § 15-10-1 (sheriffs may make arrests "within their respective counties").

Monroe County pays Sheriff Tate's salary, *see* Ala. Code § 36-22-16(a) (1991) (sheriffs shall be paid "out of the county treasury as the salaries of other county employees are paid"), and the sheriff operates out of an office provided, furnished, and equipped by the county, see § 36-22-18. The obligation to fully equip the sheriff is substantial, requiring a county commission to "furnish the sheriff with the necessary quarters, books, stationery, office equipment, supplies, postage and other conveniences and equipment, including automobiles and necessary repairs, maintenance and all expenses incidental thereto." *Ibid.* These obligations are of practical importance, for they mean that purse strings can be pulled at the county level; a county is obliged to provide a sheriff only what is "reasonably needed for the proper and efficient conduct of the affairs of the sheriff's office." How generously the sheriff will be equipped is likely to influence that officer's day to day conduct to a greater extent than the remote prospect of impeachment. *See ibid.; see also Geneva Cty. Comm'n v. Tice*, 578 So. 2d 1070, 1075 (Ala. 1991) (county may reasonably limit budget for overtime pay for sheriff's deputies); Ala. Code § 36-22-16(a) (1991) (sheriff's salary, paid by county, may be increased "by law by general or local act"); § 36-22-3(3) (sheriff must render to county treasurer a periodic written statement of moneys collected by sheriff on behalf of county).

Sheriff Tate, in short, is in vital respects a county official. Indeed, one would be hard-pressed to think of a single official who more completely represents the exercise of significant power within a county.

The Court observes that it is "most important" to its holding that Alabama sheriffs "are given complete authority to enforce the state criminal law in their counties." If the Court means to suggest that Sheriff Tate should be classified as a state actor because he is enforcing state (as opposed to county or municipal) law, the Court proves far too much. Because most criminal laws are of statewide application, relying on whose law the sheriff enforces yields an allstate categorization of sheriffs, despite the Court's recognition that such blanket classification is inappropriate. Sheriffs in Arkansas, Texas, and Washington, just like sheriffs in Alabama, enforce the State's law, but that does not make them policymakers for the State rather than the county.

In emphasizing that the Monroe County Commission cannot instruct Sheriff Tate how to accomplish his law enforcement mission, the Court indirectly endorses the Eleventh Circuit's reasoning: Because under Alabama law a county commission does not possess law enforcement authority, a sheriff's law enforcement activities cannot represent county policy. There is an irony in this approach: If a county commission lacks law enforcement authority, then the sheriff becomes a state official; but if a county commission possesses such authority and directs the sheriff's activities, then the sheriff presumably would not be a final policymaker in the realm of law enforcement, *see St. Louis v. Praprotnik* (plurality).

Moreover, in determining who makes county policy, this Court has never reasoned that all policymaking authority must be vested in a single body that either exercises that power or formally delegates it to another. Few local governments would fit that rigid model. *Cf. id.*, at 124–125 ("The States have extremely wide latitude in determining the form that local government takes. . . . One may expect to find a rich variety of ways in which the power of government is distributed among a host of different officials and official bodies."). Nor does *Monell* support such a constricted view of the exercise of municipal authority; there, we spoke of § 1983 liability for acts by "lawmakers or by those whose edicts or acts may fairly be said to represent official policy." In this case, Sheriff Tate is "the county's final policymaker in the area of law enforcement, not by virtue of delegation by the county's governing body but, rather, by virtue of the office to which the sheriff has been elected." ("The Sheriff, an elected county official [in Texas], had equal authority to the county commissioners in that jurisdiction [so] that his actions constituted those of the county just as much as those of the commissioners."). An Alabama sheriff is a county policymaker because he independently exercises law enforcement authority for the county. In this most crucial respect, the Alabama arrangement resembles the "unique structure of county government" in Texas.

Whatever English history may teach, "throughout U.S. history, the sheriff has remained the principal law enforcement officer in the county." G. Felkenes, The Criminal Justice System: Its Functions and Personnel 53 (1973); *see id.*, at 52–53 (referring specifically to Alabama sheriffs). In the United States, "in order to reserve control over the sheriff's department and its police functions, the people made the sheriff an elective officer." It is this status as the county's law enforcement officer chosen by the county's residents that is at the root of the contemporary understanding of the sheriff as a county officer.

A sheriff locally elected, paid, and equipped, who autonomously sets and implements law enforcement policies operative within the geographic confines of a county, is ordinarily just what he seems to be: a county official. Nothing in Alabama law warrants a different conclusion. It makes scant sense to treat sheriffs' activities differently based on the presence or absence of state constitutional provisions of the limited kind Alabama has adopted.

The Court's Alabama-specific approach, however, assures that today's immediate holding is of limited reach. The Court does not appear to question that an Alabama sheriff may still be a county policymaker for some purposes, such as hiring the county's chief jailor. And, as the Court acknowledges, under its approach sheriffs may be policymakers for certain purposes in some States and not in others. The Court's opinion does not call into question the numerous Court of Appeals decisions, some of them decades old, ranking sheriffs as county, not state, policymakers. Furthermore, the Court's recognition of the historic reasons why Alabama listed sheriffs as members of the State's "executive department," should discourage endeavors to insulate counties and municipalities from *Monell* liability by change-the-label devices. Thus, the Court's opinion, while in my view misguided, does little to alter § 1983 county and municipal liability in most jurisdictions.

NOTES

1.   Bear in mind that the issue in *McMillian* is not whether the sheriff can be sued for damages under § 1983. Nor is it whether prospective relief can be obtained in a properly pleaded suit against an officer acting on behalf of the state. It is whether the local government can be sued, for either damages or prospective relief, for certain acts of certain officers. *McMillian* states a general rule that when a given act of a given officer is performed on behalf of the state rather than the local government, the local government may not be sued for it under § 1983.

Some cases are easier than *McMillian.* Local election officials plainly enforce state law rather than local law when they apply state statutes. For example, in *Snyder v. King*, 745 F.3d 242 (7th Cir. 2014), the court said that a local government could not be sued for local officials' implementation of state election law. By contrast, *McMillian* involved a locally-elected, locally paid, locally-equipped sheriff engaged in law enforcement, and the Court divided 5-4 on whether he acted on behalf of the state or the local government. Does *McMillian* mean that local governments may never be sued for any action taken by a sheriff? As Part II A of the opinion clearly states, the answer is not "never." Rather, one asks "whether governmental officials are final policymakers for the local government in a particular area, or on a particular issue." *See, e.g., Goldstein v. City of Long Beach*, 715 F.3d 750, 759 (9th Cir. 2013) (concluding, after an examination of California law, "that the district attorney acts on behalf of the state when conducting prosecutions, but that the local administrative policies [involving the use of jailhouse informants] challenged by Goldstein are distinct from the prosecutorial act"). In addition, the answer may vary from state to state, because the "inquiry is dependent on an analysis of state law." Thus, the "sheriff" issue may come out differently in California than in Alabama, or in connection with a different function. *See Streit v. County of Los Angeles*, 236 F.3d 552, 555–556 (9th Cir. 2001):

> Does the Los Angeles County Sheriff's Department (the "LASD") in adopting and administering its policy of requiring that a records check, including review of all wants and holds received on a prisoner's release date,

act on behalf of the state of California or on behalf of the County of Los Angeles (the "County")? . . . Because we conclude that the LASD, when implementing its policy of conducting prisoner release records checks, acts for the county in its capacity as the administrator of the Los Angeles County jails, we hold that both the LASD and the County are subject to liability under section 1983. We also reject the LASD's contention that it is an "arm of the state," reiterating our determination that it is subject to liability under section 1983. We also conclude that the LASD is a "public entity" that is separately suable in federal court.

By contrast, Georgia sheriffs act for the state in their management of county jails. *Manders v. Lee*, 338 F.3d 1304 (11th Cir. 2003) (*en banc*).

Does it make a difference whether the sheriff is enforcing a state law or a local ordinance? *See Abusaid v. Hillsborough County [Florida] Bd. of County Commissioners*, 405 F.3d 1298 (11th Cir. 2005) (local policymaker when enforcing a local ordinance).

2. In *McMillian*, the Court states that its "inquiry is dependent on state law." It does not follow that the issue of whether a given officer is a local policymaker or a state policymaker is a state law question. On the contrary, this is a matter of determining the scope of § 1983, a federal statute. It is a question of federal law, albeit one that requires an examination of state law. *Streit, supra,* at 560 ("Although we must consider the state's legal characterization of the [sheriff's department] federal law provides the rule of decision in section 1983 cases.") As *McMillian* explains, the point of examining state law is not that state law controls the outcome. It is that "our understanding of the actual function of a government official, in a particular area, will necessarily be dependent on the definition of the official's functions under relevant state law." Suppose the function at issue is local, and state law nonetheless declares that the officer acts for the state and not the locality. In that event, the state law will not control. That is essentially what happened in *Streit*.

Would the answer be different if the state courts have definitively held that, as a matter of state law, the officer is a state rather than a county actor for the relevant purpose? *See Jackson v. Barnes*, 749 F.3d 755, 765 (9th Cir. 2014) ("State case law does not control our decision; rather, the ultimate decision we make is one of federal law.")

Another way to make this point is to imagine the implications of a rule that state law actually governed the issue. If that were so, states could quite easily circumvent the holdings of *Lincoln County v. Luning* (that local governments do not have state sovereign immunity, see the introduction to this chapter) and *Monell*. They could put a stop to all local government liability under § 1983 simply by enacting statutes stating that all local policymaking officials are, in all of their functions, making state policy and not local policy.

3. Recall from the beginning of this chapter that, under the U.S. Constitution, states may assert sovereign immunity against suits based on federal law in many circumstances, but local governments may not. In some of the cases on whether a local government may be held liable for the acts of a sheriff or a prosecutor or some other officer, courts resolve the issue by applying the "arm of the state" doctrine

discussed in the introductory material to this chapter. They ask whether, in exercising the task at issue, the officer acts as an "arm of the state." If he does, the local government escapes liability for damages for violating federal law, because in that event the appropriate governmental defendant is the state, and the state cannot be sued under § 1983 on account of *Quern v. Jordan*, 440 U.S. 332 (1979) and *Will v. Michigan Department of State Police*, 491 U.S. 58 (1989). *See, e.g., Manders, supra; Bland v. Roberts*, 730 F.3d 368, 389–91 (4th Cir. 2013); *Woods v. Rondout Valley Central School District*, 466 F.3d 232 (2d Cir. 2006) (school district may be sued for firing a teacher).

For example, in *Manders*, the 11th Circuit adopted a four factor test for determining whether the sheriff was an arm of the state. The four Eleventh Amendment factors relied on were: (1) how Georgia law defined the sheriff's office, (2) where Georgia vested control, (3) where the sheriff's office derived its funds, and (4) the source of the funds that would pay any adverse judgment against the sheriff's office. *Woods* looked at the following factors: (1) how the entity is identified in the relevant documents of origin; (2) how the governing members of the entity are appointed; (3) how the entity is funded; (4) whether the entity's function is traditionally a local function; (5) whether the state has veto power over the entity's acts; and (6) whether the entity's financial obligations bind the state. Applying this test to a school district, the court concluded that the first three factors cut against Eleventh Amendment immunity, the fourth and fifth were neutral at most, and the sixth factor also weighed against immunity.

Both *Manders* and *Woods* draw on Supreme Court cases involving the "arm of the state" doctrine. The *Manders* and *Woods* tests differ because the Supreme Court has not yet provided definitive guidance on the question of how to determine whether a given entity is an arm of the state. Nor has the Court indicated whether an Eleventh Amendment approach is the right way to resolve the question of whether someone is a local or state policymaker for purposes of local government liability under § 1983. It is impossible to evaluate the merits of the approaches taken in *Manders* and *Woods* until the Supreme Court addresses these two issues.

D. Failure to Adequately Hire, Train, and Supervise

In ordinary tort law an actor may be held liable for failure to take appropriate care in choosing whom to hire, or in training employees, or in supervising them. This liability exists quite apart from respondeat superior. By the same token, the rule against respondeat superior in constitutional torts is not a bar to recognizing an analogous constitutional tort liability for a local government's shortcomings in connection with hiring, training, and supervision. The Court has issued important rulings in connection with hiring and training. This section examines those theories of recovery. In the context of governmental liability, failure to supervise may be litigated either as an analogue of failure to train, or on a "custom" theory, as discussed above. *See, e.g., Haley v. City of Boston*, 657 F.3d 39, 52–53 (1st Cir. 2011) (plaintiff advanced both custom and inadequate training theories on the same set of facts, which involved police officers' failure to disclose exculpatory evidence); *Craig v. Floyd County*, 643 F.3d 1306, 1310 (11th Cir. 2011) (discusses "custom" and cites *Canton* and *Connick*, below;) *Reynolds v. Guiliani*, 506 F.3d 183, 191–92 (2d Cir.

2007) (using vocabulary associated with both approaches).

A distinct set of issues arise with regard to the individual liability of the supervisor. Because the supervisor's liability is a recurring issue, because it is closely related to the government's liability in many of the cases, and because the Supreme Court has provided little definitive guidance on the issue, we think it is appropriate to briefly address that topic here as well. In order to avoid confusion, bear in mind that our treatment of the supervisor's individual liability is an exception to the organizational principle (governmental liability) that we follow throughout the rest of the chapter

1.   Failure to Train

CITY OF CANTON, OHIO v. HARRIS
489 U.S. 378 (1989)

JUSTICE WHITE delivered the opinion of the Court.

In this case, we are asked to determine if a municipality can ever be liable under 42 U.S.C. § 1983 for constitutional violations resulting from its failure to train municipal employees. We hold that, under certain circumstances, such liability is permitted by the statute.

In April 1978, respondent Geraldine Harris was arrested by officers of the Canton Police Department. Mrs. Harris was brought to the police station in a patrol wagon.

When she arrived at the station, Mrs. Harris was found sitting on the floor of the wagon. She was asked if she needed medical attention, and responded with an incoherent remark. After she was brought inside the station for processing, Mrs. Harris slumped to the floor on two occasions. Eventually, the police officers left Mrs. Harris lying on the floor to prevent her from falling again. No medical attention was ever summoned for Mrs. Harris. After about an hour, Mrs. Harris was released from custody, and taken by an ambulance (provided by her family) to a nearby hospital. There, Mrs. Harris was diagnosed as suffering from several emotional ailments; she was hospitalized for one week and received subsequent outpatient treatment for an additional year.

Some time later, Mrs. Harris commenced this action alleging many state-law and constitutional claims against the city of Canton and its officials. Among these claims was one seeking to hold the city liable under 42 U.S.C. § 1983 for its violation of Mrs. Harris' right, under the Due Process Clause of the Fourteenth Amendment, to receive necessary medical attention while in police custody.

A jury trial was held on Mrs. Harris' claims. Evidence was presented that indicated that, pursuant to a municipal regulation, shift commanders were authorized to determine, in their sole discretion, whether a detainee required medical care. In addition, testimony also suggested that Canton shift commanders were not provided with any special training (beyond first-aid training) to make a determination as to when to summon medical care for an injured detainee.

At the close of the evidence, the District Court submitted the case to the jury, which rejected all of Mrs. Harris' claims except one: her § 1983 claim against the city resulting from its failure to provide her with medical treatment while in custody. In rejecting the city's subsequent motion for judgment notwithstanding the verdict, the District Court explained the theory of liability as follows:

> "The evidence construed in a manner most favorable to Mrs. Harris could be found by a jury to demonstrate that the City of Canton had a custom or policy of vesting complete authority with the police supervisor of when medical treatment would be administered to prisoners. Further, the jury could find from the evidence that the vesting of such carte blanche authority with the police supervisor without adequate training to recognize when medical treatment is needed was grossly negligent or so reckless that future police misconduct was almost inevitable or substantially certain to result."

On appeal, the Sixth Circuit affirmed this aspect of the District Court's analysis, holding that "a municipality is liable for failure to train its police force, [where] the plaintiff . . . prove[s] that the municipality acted recklessly, intentionally, or with gross negligence." The Court of Appeals also stated that an additional prerequisite of this theory of liability was that the plaintiff must prove "that the lack of training was so reckless or grossly negligent that deprivations of persons' constitutional rights were substantially certain to result." Thus, the Court of Appeals found that there had been no error in submitting Mrs. Harris' "failure to train" claim to the jury. However, the Court of Appeals reversed the judgment for respondent, and remanded this case for a new trial, because it found that certain aspects of the District Court's jury instructions might have led the jury to believe that it could find against the city on a mere respondeat superior theory. Because the jury's verdict did not state the basis on which it had ruled for Mrs. Harris on her § 1983 claim, a new trial was ordered.

The city petitioned for certiorari, arguing that the Sixth Circuit's holding represented an impermissible broadening of municipal liability under § 1983. We granted the petition.

III

In *Monell v. New York City Dept. of Social Services*, we decided that a municipality can be found liable under § 1983 only where the municipality itself causes the constitutional violation at issue. Respondeat superior or vicarious liability will not attach under § 1983. "It is only when the 'execution of the government's policy or custom . . . inflicts the injury' that the municipality may be held liable under § 1983." *Springfield v. Kibbe* (quoting *Monell, supra*).

Thus, our first inquiry in any case alleging municipal liability under § 1983 is the question whether there is a direct causal link between a municipal policy or custom and the alleged constitutional deprivation. The inquiry is a difficult one; one that has left this Court deeply divided in a series of cases that have followed *Monell*; one that is the principal focus of our decision again today.

A

Based on the difficulty that this Court has had defining the contours of municipal liability in these circumstances, petitioner urges us to adopt the rule that a municipality can be found liable under § 1983 only where "the policy in question [is] itself unconstitutional." Whether such a rule is a valid construction of § 1983 is a question the Court has left unresolved. Under such an approach, the outcome here would be rather clear: we would have to reverse and remand the case with instructions that judgment be entered for petitioner. There can be little doubt that on its face the city's policy regarding medical treatment for detainees is constitutional. The policy states that the city jailer "shall . . . have [a person needing medical care] taken to a hospital for medical treatment, with permission of his supervisor. . . ." It is difficult to see what constitutional guarantees are violated by such a policy.

Nor, without more, would a city automatically be liable under § 1983 if one of its employees happened to apply the policy in an unconstitutional manner, for liability would then rest on respondeat superior. The claim in this case, however, is that if a concededly valid policy is unconstitutionally applied by a municipal employee, the city is liable if the employee has not been adequately trained and the constitutional wrong has been caused by that failure to train. For reasons explained below, we conclude, as have all the Courts of Appeals that have addressed this issue, that there are limited circumstances in which an allegation of a "failure to train" can be the basis for liability under § 1983. Thus, we reject petitioner's contention that only unconstitutional policies are actionable under the statute.

B

Though we agree with the court below that a city can be liable under § 1983 for inadequate training of its employees, we cannot agree that the District Court's jury instructions on this issue were proper, for we conclude that the Court of Appeals provided an overly broad rule for when a municipality can be held liable under the "failure to train" theory. Unlike the question whether a municipality's failure to train employees can ever be a basis for § 1983 liability — on which the Courts of Appeals have all agreed — there is substantial division among the lower courts as to what degree of fault must be evidenced by the municipality's inaction before liability will be permitted. We hold today that the inadequacy of police training may serve as the basis for § 1983 liability only where the failure to train amounts to deliberate indifference to the rights of persons with whom the police come into contact.[5] This rule is most consistent with our admonition in *Monell* and *Polk*

---

[5] [8] The "deliberate indifference" standard we adopt for section 1983 "failure to train" claims does not turn on the degree of fault (if any) that a plaintiff must show to make out a constitutional violation. For example, this Court has never determined what degree of culpability must be shown before the particular constitutional violation asserted in this case — a denial of the due process right to medical care while in detention — is established. Indeed, in *Revere v. Massachusetts General Hospital*, we reserved decision on the question whether something less than the Eighth Amendment's "deliberate indifference" test may be applicable to claims by detainees asserting violations of the due process right to medical care while in custody.

We need not resolve the question left open in *Revere* for two reasons. First, petitioner has conceded

County v. Dodson, that a municipality can be liable under § 1983 only where its policies are the "moving force [behind] the constitutional violation." Only where a municipality's failure to train its employees in a relevant respect evidences a "deliberate indifference" to the rights of its inhabitants can such a shortcoming be properly thought of as a city "policy or custom" that is actionable under § 1983. As Justice Brennan's opinion in *Pembaur v. Cincinnati* (plurality) put it: "Municipal liability under § 1983 attaches where — and only where — a deliberate choice to follow a course of action is made from among various alternatives" by city policymakers. Only where a failure to train reflects a "deliberate" or "conscious" choice by a municipality — a "policy" as defined by our prior cases — can a city be liable for such a failure under § 1983.

Monell's rule that a city is not liable under § 1983 unless a municipal policy causes a constitutional deprivation will not be satisfied by merely alleging that the existing training program for a class of employees, such as police officers, represents a policy for which the city is responsible. That much may be true. The issue in a case like this one, however, is whether that training program is adequate; and if it is not, the question becomes whether such inadequate training can justifiably be said to represent "city policy." It may seem contrary to common sense to assert that a municipality will actually have a policy of not taking reasonable steps to train its employees. But it may happen that in light of the duties assigned to specific officers or employees the need for more or different training is so obvious, and the inadequacy so likely to result in the violation of constitutional rights, that the policymakers of the city can reasonably be said to have been deliberately indifferent to the need. In that event, the failure to provide proper training may fairly be said to represent a policy for which the city is responsible, and for which the city may be held liable if it actually causes injury.

In resolving the issue of a city's liability, the focus must be on adequacy of the training program in relation to the tasks the particular officers must perform. That a particular officer may be unsatisfactorily trained will not alone suffice to fasten liability on the city, for the officer's shortcomings may have resulted from factors other than a faulty training program. It may be, for example, that an otherwise sound program has occasionally been negligently administered. Neither will it suffice to prove that an injury or accident could have been avoided if an officer had had better or more training, sufficient to equip him to avoid the particular injury-causing conduct. Such a claim could be made about almost any encounter resulting in injury, yet not condemn the adequacy of the program to enable officers to respond properly to the usual and recurring situations with which they must deal. And plainly, adequately trained officers occasionally make mistakes; the fact that they do says little about the training program or the legal basis for holding the city liable.

Moreover, for liability to attach in this circumstance the identified deficiency in

---

that, as the case comes to us, we must assume that respondent's constitutional right to receive medical care was denied by city employees — whatever the nature of that right might be. Second, the proper standard for determining when a municipality will be held liable under section 1983 for constitutional wrongs does not turn on any underlying culpability test that determines when such wrongs have occurred.

a city's training program must be closely related to the ultimate injury. Thus in the case at hand, respondent must still prove that the deficiency in training actually caused the police officers' indifference to her medical needs. Would the injury have been avoided had the employee been trained under a program that was not deficient in the identified respect? Predicting how a hypothetically well-trained officer would have acted under the circumstances may not be an easy task for the factfinder, particularly since matters of judgment may be involved, and since officers who are well trained are not free from error and perhaps might react very much like the untrained officer in similar circumstances. But judge and jury, doing their respective jobs, will be adequate to the task.

To adopt lesser standards of fault and causation would open municipalities to unprecedented liability under § 1983. In virtually every instance where a person has had his or her constitutional rights violated by a city employee, a § 1983 plaintiff will be able to point to something the city "could have done" to prevent the unfortunate incident. See *Oklahoma City v. Tuttle* (opinion of Rehnquist, J.). Thus, permitting cases against cities for their "failure to train" employees to go forward under § 1983 on a lesser standard of fault would result in de facto respondeat superior liability on municipalities — a result we rejected in *Monell*. It would also engage the federal courts in an endless exercise of second-guessing municipal employee-training programs. This is an exercise we believe the federal courts are ill suited to undertake, as well as one that would implicate serious questions of federalism.

Consequently, while claims such as respondent's — alleging that the city's failure to provide training to municipal employees resulted in the constitutional deprivation she suffered — are cognizable under § 1983, they can only yield liability against a municipality where that city's failure to train reflects deliberate indifference to the constitutional rights of its inhabitants.

IV

The final question here is whether this case should be remanded for a new trial, or whether, as petitioner suggests, we should conclude that there are no possible grounds on which respondent can prevail. It is true that the evidence in the record now does not meet the standard of § 1983 liability we have set forth above. But, the standard of proof the District Court ultimately imposed on respondent (which was consistent with Sixth Circuit precedent) was a lesser one than the one we adopt today. Whether respondent should have an opportunity to prove her case under the "deliberate indifference" rule we have adopted is a matter for the Court of Appeals to deal with on remand.

V

Consequently, for the reasons given above, we vacate the judgment of the Court of Appeals and remand this case for further proceedings consistent with this opinion.

[The concurring opinion of JUSTICE BRENNAN and the concurring in part and dissenting in part opinion of JUSTICES O'CONNOR, SCALIA and KENNEDY are omitted.]

NOTES

1. In *Connick v. Thompson*, 131 S. Ct. 1350 (2011), the plaintiff (Thompson) was a man who had been convicted of attempted armed robbery, and later of murder. In habeas corpus litigation, both convictions were vacated, because both were tainted by a constitutional violation. The New Orleans district attorney's office had violated his constitutional rights (under *Brady v. Maryland*, 373 U.S. 83 (1963)) by failing to disclose a crime lab report that supported his innocence in the armed robbery trial, and this violation also affected the murder trial. Thompson then brought a § 1983 suit against the prosecutors and the city. He lost against the prosecutors on account of absolute prosecutorial immunity, see chapter 7. But at trial he won a $14 million verdict against the city, on the theory that District Attorney Connick, a final policymaker, had shown deliberate indifference to his constitutional rights by not adequately training the assistant district attorneys on their constitutional responsibilities under *Brady*.

The Supreme Court reversed. The problem was that the plaintiff had proven only the one *Brady* violation:

> A pattern of similar constitutional violations by untrained employees is ordinarily necessary to demonstrate deliberate indifference for purposes of failure to train. [Without] notice that a course of training is deficient in a particular respect, decisionmakers can hardly be said to have deliberately chosen a training program that will cause violations of constitutional rights. 131 S. Ct. at 1360.

Thompson did show that "during the ten years preceding his armed robbery trial, Louisiana courts had overturned four convictions because of *Brady* violations in Connick's office." But these

> could not have put Connick on notice that the office's *Brady* training was inadequate with respect to the constitutional violation at issue here. None of those cases involved a failure to disclose blood evidence, a crime lab report, or physical or scientific evidence of any kind. Because those incidents are not similar to the violation at issue here, they could not have put Connick on notice that specific training was necessary to avoid this constitutional violation.

The Court acknowledged that *Canton* "left open the possibility that, in a narrow range of circumstances, a pattern of similar violations might not be necessary to show deliberate indifference." The point of leaving that issue open was that "the unconstitutional consequences of failing to train could be so patently obvious that a city could be liable under § 1983 without proof of a pre-existing pattern of violations," as in a scenario where the city does not train officers on constitutional limits on the use of deadly force. By contrast, "[t]he obvious need for specific legal training in the *Canton* scenario is absent here." The Court went on to point out that law students and lawyers have plenty of opportunities, and prosecutors have a professional obligation, to learn about *Brady*. 131 S. Ct. at 1361–62.

Granting the force of the Court's rebuttal to the plaintiff's second argument (the "patently obvious" exception to the need to show a pattern) are you persuaded that plaintiff failed to show a pattern of *Brady* violations? On the premise that there is a sufficient showing of a pattern, could New Orleans nonetheless win on the ground that its failure to train was not the "moving force" behind the violation of Thompson's rights? The point of this last question is that *Brady* is well-known rule. It seems unlikely that even a rookie prosecutor would need further training in order to understand it.

"Single act" inadequate training cases are harder for the plaintiff to win after *Connick v. Thompson*. But on a proper set of facts, the plaintiff may still succeed. In *Thomas v. Cumberland County*, 749 F.3d 217 (3d Cir. 2014), an inmate alleged that he was attacked by other inmates. Guards were present but did not act effectively to stop the assault. He sued the county for inadequately training prison guards and "put forward evidence that fights regularly occurred in the prison." But he could not show a pattern of constitutional violations. Nonetheless, the court reversed summary judgment for the county. In this set of facts, "the potential for conflict was high and there was a complete lack of training on de-escalation and intervention." And

> [i]n contrast to *Connick*, the officers here have no reason to have an independent education, knowledge base, or ethical duty that would prepare them to handle the volatile conflicts that might lead to inmate-on-inmate violence. Also unlike in *Connick*, there is no nuance to the training Thomas seeks to require.

2.   Under *Canton*, the plaintiff must show that the inadequate training was the "moving force" behind the constitutional violation. *Thomas*, *supra*, addressed this requirement as well:

> Thomas put forward evidence from Santiago — the first inmate who struck Thomas — that the officers could have stopped the argument before violence broke out. He also presented an inmate witness's statement that the officers allowed the inmates to fight. There is ample evidence in the record that [Officer] Martinez was present throughout the argument, which lasted for several minutes, before Thomas was struck. Thomas offered expert opinion evidence that the [correctional facility's] lack of de-escalation training, among other things, contributed to the serious injuries that Thomas sustained. Similar expert opinion evidence was offered to preclude summary judgment in [an earlier case.] Presented with this evidence and using their judgment and common sense, a reasonable jury could have concluded that the lack of training in conflict de-escalation and intervention caused Thomas's injuries. 749 F.3d at 226–27.

3.   The plaintiff is not required to show that the government itself committed a constitutional violation in order to win a *City of Canton* failure to train suit. He is only required to show that an employee violated his constitutional right, that the city, by its failure to train, was "deliberately indifferent" to the violation, and that the city's deliberate indifference was the "moving force" behind the violation. What does *City of Canton's* deliberate indifference standard mean? Is it, for example, primarily subjective or objective or some combination thereof?

Consider in this connection the relevance of the Supreme Court's important Eighth Amendment prison conditions decision in *Farmer v. Brennan*, 511 U.S. 825

(1994), also noted in Chapter 3. The Court unanimously held that prison officials could be liable in damages under the Eighth Amendment for their deliberate indifference in failing to protect inmates from harm caused by other inmates. In the case before it the plaintiff federal prisoner, a transsexual with feminine characteristics, was beaten and raped shortly after he was placed in the general population. The Court defined deliberate indifference in a *subjective* manner as meaning the failure to act when prison officials actually knew of a "substantial risk of serious harm," even though an inmate did not warn them of a particular threat and even if they did not believe that harm would occur to a particular inmate. It also went on say that an "inference from circumstantial evidence" could suffice to demonstrate that prison officials had the requisite knowledge. Thus, the plaintiff's failure in *Farmer* to express concern over his own safety did not warrant dismissal of his Eighth Amendment damages action. In general, then, a prison official could be liable for denying humane conditions only if he knew that inmates faced a substantial risk of serious harm and disregarded that risk by failing to take reasonable measures to abate it.

The *Farmer* Court insisted on the essentially *subjective* nature of deliberate indifference in a prison setting with respect to *individual* liability. By contrast, *Farmer* sharply distinguished the subjective nature of this kind of deliberate indifference from what it termed the different *objective* nature of the deliberate indifference inquiry in a local government failure to train context. *City of Canton's* inquiry calls for a focus on obviousness or constructive notice. "It would be hard to describe the *Canton* understanding of deliberate indifference, permitting liability to be premised on obviousness or constructive notice, as anything but objective." 511 U.S. at 841.

See, e.g., Duvall v. Dalls County. Texas, 631 F.3d 203, 210 (5th Cir. 2011) (distinguishing the "subjective" version of deliberate indifference needed for individual liability from the "objective" version needed for municipal liability).

Why not determine municipal liability by a subjective inquiry into the awareness of the final policymakers who may or may not have taken adequate steps to train street level officers?

Note that *both* versions of "deliberate indifference" may be litigated in the same case, as where an inmate claims a constitutional violation based on the deliberate indifference of guards or medical personnel, and also claims municipal liability based on policymakers' deliberate indifference to the constitutional violations committed by the medical personnel or guards. *See, e.g., Thomas v. Cumberland County*, 749 F.3d 217 (3d Cir. 2014); *Ford v. County of Grand Traverse*, 535 F.3d 483 (6th Cir. 2008).

Does *Farmer* change your understanding of *City of Canton* or does it just explain *City of Canton*?

2. *Bryan County* and Single Hiring Decisions by Policymakers

Pembaur held that a single unconstitutional decision by a policymaker can be attributed to a local government body, thereby rendering it liable under section 1983. At the same time section 1983 liability cannot be based on respondeat superior. What happens if a single hiring decision is made by a local government's policymaker and the employee so hired violates a plaintiff's constitutional rights? Under what circumstances, if any, can the local government be held liable under section 1983? Is the *City of Canton* liability standard relevant to this question? Consider the following important case.

BOARD OF COUNTY COMMISSIONERS OF BRYAN COUNTY, OKLAHOMA v. BROWN
520 U.S. 397 (1997)

JUSTICE O'CONNOR delivered the opinion of the Court.

Respondent Jill Brown brought a claim for damages against petitioner Bryan County under Rev. Stat. § 1979, 42 U.S.C. § 1983. She alleged that a county police officer used excessive force in arresting her, and that the county itself was liable for her injuries based on its sheriff's hiring and training decisions. She prevailed on her claims against the county following a jury trial, and the Court of Appeals for the Fifth Circuit affirmed the judgment against the county on the basis of the hiring claim alone. We granted certiorari. We conclude that the Court of Appeals' decision cannot be squared with our recognition that, in enacting § 1983, Congress did not intend to impose liability on a municipality unless deliberate action attributable to the municipality itself is the "moving force" behind the plaintiff's deprivation of federal rights. *Monell v. New York City Dept. of Social Servs.*

I

In the early morning hours of May 12, 1991, respondent Jill Brown and her husband were driving from Grayson County, Texas, to their home in Bryan County, Oklahoma. After crossing into Oklahoma, they approached a police checkpoint. Mr. Brown, who was driving, decided to avoid the checkpoint and return to Texas. After seeing the Browns' truck turn away from the checkpoint, Bryan County Deputy Sheriff Robert Morrison and Reserve Deputy Stacy Burns pursued the vehicle. Although the parties' versions of events differ, at trial both deputies claimed that their patrol car reached speeds in excess of 100 miles per hour. Mr. Brown testified that he was unaware of the deputies' attempts to overtake him. The chase finally ended four miles south of the police checkpoint.

After he got out of the squad car, Deputy Sheriff Morrison pointed his gun toward the Browns' vehicle and ordered the Browns to raise their hands. Reserve Deputy Burns, who was unarmed, rounded the corner of the vehicle on the passenger's side. Burns twice ordered respondent Jill Brown from the vehicle. When she did not exit, he used an "arm bar" technique, grabbing respondent's arm at the wrist and elbow, pulling her from the vehicle, and spinning her to the ground. Respondent's knees were severely injured, and she later underwent corrective surgery. Ultimately, she may need knee replacements.

Respondent sought compensation for her injuries under 42 U.S.C. § 1983 and state law from Burns, Bryan County Sheriff B. J. Moore, and the county itself. Respondent claimed, among other things, that Bryan County was liable for Burns' alleged use of excessive force based on Sheriff Moore's decision to hire Burns, the son of his nephew. Specifically, respondent claimed that Sheriff Moore had failed to adequately review Burns' background. Burns had a record of driving infractions and had pleaded guilty to various driving-related and other misdemeanors, including assault and battery, resisting arrest, and public drunkenness. Oklahoma law does not preclude the hiring of an individual who has committed a misdemeanor to serve as a peace officer. At trial, Sheriff Moore testified that he had obtained Burns' driving record and a report on Burns from the National Crime Information Center, but had not closely reviewed either. Sheriff Moore authorized Burns to make arrests, but not to carry a weapon or to operate a patrol car.

In a ruling not at issue here, the District Court dismissed respondent's § 1983 claim against Sheriff Moore prior to trial. Counsel for Bryan County stipulated that Sheriff Moore "was the policy maker for Bryan County regarding the Sheriff's Department." At the close of respondent's case and again at the close of all of the evidence, Bryan County moved for judgment as a matter of law. As to respondent's claim that Sheriff Moore's decision to hire Burns triggered municipal liability, the county argued that a single hiring decision by a municipal policymaker could not give rise to municipal liability under § 1983. The District Court denied the county's motions. The court also overruled the county's objections to jury instructions on the § 1983 claim against the county.

To resolve respondent's claims, the jury was asked to answer several interrogatories. The jury concluded that Stacy Burns had arrested respondent without probable cause and had used excessive force, and therefore found him liable for respondent's injuries. It also found that the "hiring policy" and the "training policy" of Bryan County "in the case of Stacy Burns as instituted by its policymaker, B. J. Moore," were each "so inadequate as to amount to deliberate indifference to the constitutional needs of the Plaintiff." The District Court entered judgment for respondent on the issue of Bryan County's § 1983 liability. The county appealed on several grounds, and the Court of Appeals for the Fifth Circuit affirmed. The court held, among other things, that Bryan County was properly found liable under § 1983 based on Sheriff Moore's decision to hire Burns. The court addressed only those points that it thought merited review; it did not address the jury's determination of county liability based on inadequate training of Burns, nor do we. We granted certiorari to decide whether the county was properly held liable for respondent's injuries based on Sheriff Moore's single decision to hire Burns. We now reverse.

II

The parties join issue on whether, under Monell and subsequent cases, a single hiring decision by a county sheriff can be a "policy" that triggers municipal liability.

Relying on our decision in Pembaur, respondent claims that a single act by a decisionmaker with final authority in the relevant area constitutes a "policy" attributable to the municipality itself. So long as a § 1983 plaintiff identifies a decision properly attributable to the municipality, respondent argues, there is no risk of imposing respondeat superior liability. Whether that decision was intended to govern only the situation at hand or to serve as a rule to be applied over time is immaterial. Rather, under respondent's theory, identification of an act of a proper municipal decisionmaker is all that is required to ensure that the municipality is held liable only for its own conduct. The Court of Appeals accepted respondent's approach. As our § 1983 municipal liability jurisprudence illustrates, however, it is not enough for a § 1983 plaintiff merely to identify conduct properly attributable to the municipality. The plaintiff must also demonstrate that, through its deliberate conduct, the municipality was the "moving force" behind the injury alleged. That is, a plaintiff must show that the municipal action was taken with the requisite degree of culpability and must demonstrate a direct causal link between the municipal action and the deprivation of federal rights. Where a plaintiff claims that a particular municipal action itself violates federal law, or directs an employee to do so, resolving these issues of fault and causation is straightforward. Section 1983 itself "contains no state-of-mind requirement independent of that necessary to state a violation" of the underlying federal right. In any § 1983 suit, however, the plaintiff must establish the state of mind required to prove the underlying violation. Accordingly, proof that a municipality's legislative body or authorized decision-maker has intentionally deprived a plaintiff of a federally protected right necessarily establishes that the municipality acted culpably. Similarly, the conclusion that the action taken or directed by the municipality or its authorized decisionmaker itself violates federal law will also determine that the municipal action was the moving force behind the injury of which the plaintiff complains. Sheriff Moore's hiring decision was itself legal, and Sheriff Moore did not authorize Burns to use excessive force. Respondent's claim, rather, is that a single facially lawful hiring decision can launch a series of events that ultimately cause a violation of federal rights. Where a plaintiff claims that the municipality has not directly inflicted an injury, but nonetheless has caused an employee to do so, rigorous standards of culpability and causation must be applied to ensure that the municipality is not held liable solely for the actions of its employee. *See Canton, Tuttle* (plurality opinion).

In relying heavily on *Pembaur*, respondent blurs the distinction between § 1983 cases that present no difficult questions of fault and causation and those that do. To the extent that we have recognized a cause of action under § 1983 based on a single decision attributable to a municipality, we have done so only where the evidence that the municipality had acted and that the plaintiff had suffered a deprivation of federal rights also proved fault and causation. For example, *Owen v. Independence*, and *Newport v. Fact Concerts, Inc.*, involved formal decisions of municipal legislative bodies. In *Owen*, the city council allegedly censured and discharged an employee without a hearing. In *Fact Concerts*, the city council canceled a license permitting a concert following a dispute over the performance's content. Neither decision reflected implementation of a generally applicable rule. But we did not question that each decision, duly promulgated by city lawmakers, could trigger municipal liability if the decision itself were found to be unconstitutional. Because fault and causation were obvious in each case, proof that the municipality's decision was unconstitutional would suffice to establish that the municipality itself was liable for the plaintiff's constitutional injury.

Similarly, *Pembaur v. Cincinnati* concerned a decision by a county prosecutor, acting as the county's final decisionmaker, to direct county deputies to forcibly enter petitioner's place of business to serve capiases upon third parties. Relying on *Owen* and *Newport*, we concluded that a final decisionmaker's adoption of a course of action "tailored to a particular situation and not intended to control decisions in later situations" may, in some circumstances, give rise to municipal liability under § 1983. In *Pembaur*, it was not disputed that the prosecutor had specifically directed the action resulting in the deprivation of petitioner's rights. The conclusion that the decision was that of a final municipal decisionmaker and was therefore properly attributable to the municipality established municipal liability. No questions of fault or causation arose. Claims not involving an allegation that the municipal action itself violated federal law, or directed or authorized the deprivation of federal rights, present much more difficult problems of proof. That a plaintiff has suffered a deprivation of federal rights at the hands of a municipal employee will not alone permit an inference of municipal culpability and causation; the plaintiff will simply have shown that the employee acted culpably. We recognized these difficulties in *Canton v. Harris*, where we considered a claim that inadequate training of shift supervisors at a city jail led to a deprivation of a detainee's constitutional rights. We held that, quite apart from the state of mind required to establish the underlying constitutional violation — in that case, a violation of due process — a plaintiff seeking to establish municipal liability on the theory that a facially lawful municipal action has led an employee to violate a plaintiff's rights must demonstrate that the municipal action was taken with "deliberate indifference" as to its known or obvious consequences. A showing of simple or even heightened negligence will not suffice. We concluded in *Canton* that an "inadequate training" claim could be the basis for § 1983 liability in "limited circumstances." We spoke, however, of a deficient training "program," necessarily intended to apply over time to multiple employees. Existence of a "program" makes proof of fault and causation at least possible in an inadequate training case. If a program does not prevent constitutional violations, municipal decisionmakers may eventually be put on notice that a new program is called for. Their continued adherence to an approach that they know or should know has failed to prevent tortious conduct by employees may establish the conscious disregard for the consequences of their action — the "deliberate indifference" — necessary to trigger municipal liability. ("It could . . . be that the police, in exercising their discretion, so often violate constitutional rights that the need for further training must have been plainly obvious to the city policymakers, who, nevertheless, are 'deliberately indifferent' to the need"); (O'Connor, J., concurring in part and dissenting in part) ("Municipal liability for failure to train may be proper where it can be shown that policymakers were aware of, and acquiesced in, a pattern of constitutional violations"). In addition, the existence of a pattern of tortious conduct by inadequately trained employees may tend to show that the lack of proper training, rather than a one-time negligent administration of the program or factors peculiar to the officer involved in a particular incident, is the "moving force" behind the plaintiff's injury.

Before trial, counsel for Bryan County stipulated that Sheriff Moore "was the policy maker for Bryan County regarding the Sheriff's Department." Indeed, the county sought to avoid liability by claiming that its Board of Commissioners participated in no policy decisions regarding the conduct and operation of the office of the Bryan County Sheriff. Accepting the county's representations below, then, this case presents no difficult questions concerning whether Sheriff Moore has final authority to act for the municipality in hiring matters. Respondent does not claim that she can identify any pattern of injuries linked to Sheriff Moore's hiring practices. Indeed, respondent does not contend that Sheriff Moore's hiring practices are generally defective. The only evidence on this point at trial suggested that Sheriff Moore had adequately screened the backgrounds of all prior deputies he hired. Respondent instead seeks to trace liability to what can only be described as a deviation from Sheriff Moore's ordinary hiring practices. Where a claim of municipal liability rests on a single decision, not itself representing a violation of federal law and not directing such a violation, the danger that a municipality will be held liable without fault is high. Because the decision necessarily governs a single case, there can be no notice to the municipal decisionmaker, based on previous violations of federally protected rights, that his approach is inadequate. Nor will it be readily apparent that the municipality's action caused the injury in question, because the plaintiff can point to no other incident tending to make it more likely that the plaintiff's own injury flows from the municipality's action, rather than from some other intervening cause.

In *Canton*, we did not foreclose the possibility that evidence of a single violation of federal rights, accompanied by a showing that a municipality has failed to train its employees to handle recurring situations presenting an obvious potential for such a violation, could trigger municipal liability. 489 U.S. at 390. ("It may happen that in light of the duties assigned to specific officers or employees the need for more or different training is so obvious . . . that the policymakers of the city can reasonably be said to have been deliberately indifferent to the need"). Respondent purports to rely on *Canton*, arguing that Burns' use of excessive force was the plainly obvious consequence of Sheriff Moore's failure to screen Burns' record. In essence, respondent claims that this showing of "obviousness" would demonstrate both that Sheriff Moore acted with conscious disregard for the consequences of his action and that the Sheriff's action directly caused her injuries, and would thus substitute for the pattern of injuries ordinarily necessary to establish municipal culpability and causation.

The proffered analogy between failure-to-train cases and inadequate screening cases is not persuasive. In leaving open in *Canton* the possibility that a plaintiff might succeed in carrying a failure-to-train claim without showing a pattern of constitutional violations, we simply hypothesized that, in a narrow range of circumstances, a violation of federal rights may be a highly predictable consequence of a failure to equip law enforcement officers with specific tools to handle recurring situations. The likelihood that the situation will recur and the predictability that an officer lacking specific tools to handle that situation will violate citizens' rights could justify a finding that policymakers' decision not to train the officer reflected "deliberate indifference" to the obvious consequence of the policymakers' choice — namely, a violation of a specific constitutional or statutory right. The high degree of predictability may also support an inference of causation — that the municipality's indifference led directly to the very consequence that was so predictable. Where a plaintiff presents a § 1983 claim premised upon the inadequacy of an official's review of a prospective applicant's record, however, there is a particular danger that a municipality will be held liable for an injury not directly caused by a deliberate action attributable to the municipality itself. Every injury suffered at the hands of a municipal employee can be traced to a hiring decision in a "but-for" sense: But for the municipality's decision to hire the employee, the plaintiff would not have suffered the injury. To prevent municipal liability for a hiring decision from collapsing into respondeat superior liability, a court must carefully test the link between the policymaker's inadequate decision and the particular injury alleged.

In attempting to import the reasoning of *Canton* into the hiring context, respondent ignores the fact that predicting the consequence of a single hiring decision, even one based on an inadequate assessment of a record, is far more difficult than predicting what might flow from the failure to train a single law enforcement officer as to a specific skill necessary to the discharge of his duties. As our decision in *Canton* makes clear, "deliberate indifference" is a stringent standard of fault, requiring proof that a municipal actor disregarded a known or obvious consequence of his action. Unlike the risk from a particular glaring omission in a training regimen, the risk from a single instance of inadequate screening of an applicant's background is not "obvious" in the abstract; rather, it depends upon the background of the applicant. A lack of scrutiny may increase the likelihood that an unfit officer will be hired, and that the unfit officer will, when placed in a particular position to affect the rights of citizens, act improperly. But that is only a generalized showing of risk. The fact that inadequate scrutiny of an applicant's background would make a violation of rights more likely cannot alone give rise to an inference that a policymaker's failure to scrutinize the record of a particular applicant produced a specific constitutional violation. After all, a full screening of an applicant's background might reveal no cause for concern at all; if so, a hiring official who failed to scrutinize the applicant's background cannot be said to have consciously disregarded an obvious risk that the officer would subsequently inflict a particular constitutional injury. We assume that a jury could properly find in this case that Sheriff Moore's assessment of Burns' background was inadequate. Sheriff Moore's own testimony indicated that he did not inquire into the underlying conduct or the disposition of any of the misdemeanor charges reflected on Burns' record before hiring him. But this showing of an instance of inadequate screening is not enough to establish "deliberate indifference." In layman's terms, inadequate screening of an applicant's record may reflect "indifference" to the applicant's background. For purposes of a legal inquiry into municipal liability under § 1983, however, that is not the relevant "indifference." A plaintiff must demonstrate that a municipal decision reflects deliberate indifference to the risk that a violation of a particular constitutional or statutory right will follow the decision. Only where adequate scrutiny of an applicant's background would lead a reasonable policymaker to conclude that the plainly obvious consequence of the decision to hire the applicant would be the deprivation of a third party's federally protected right can the official's failure to adequately scrutinize the applicant's background constitute "deliberate indifference."

Neither the District Court nor the Court of Appeals directly tested the link between Burns' actual background and the risk that, if hired, he would use excessive force. The District Court instructed the jury on a theory analogous to that reserved in *Canton.* The court required respondent to prove that Sheriff Moore's inadequate screening of Burns' background was "so likely to result in violations of constitutional rights" that the Sheriff could "reasonably [be] said to have been deliberately indifferent to the constitutional needs of the Plaintiff." The court also instructed the jury, without elaboration, that respondent was required to prove that the "inadequate hiring . . . policy directly caused the Plaintiff's injury." As discussed above, a finding of culpability simply cannot depend on the mere probability that any officer inadequately screened will inflict any constitutional injury. Rather, it must depend on a finding that this officer was highly likely to inflict the particular injury suffered by the plaintiff. The connection between the background of the particular applicant and the specific constitutional violation alleged must be strong. What the District Court's instructions on culpability, and therefore the jury's finding of municipal liability, failed to capture is whether Burns' background made his use of excessive force in making an arrest a plainly obvious consequence of the hiring decision. The Court of Appeals' affirmence of the jury's finding of municipal liability depended on its view that the jury could have found that "inadequate screening of a deputy could likely result in the violation of citizens' constitutional rights." Beyond relying on a risk of violations of unspecified constitutional rights, the Court of Appeals also posited that Sheriff Moore's decision reflected indifference to "the public's welfare."

Even assuming without deciding that proof of a single instance of inadequate screening could ever trigger municipal liability, the evidence in this case was insufficient to support a finding that, in hiring Burns, Sheriff Moore disregarded a known or obvious risk of injury. To test the link between Sheriff Moore's hiring decision and respondent's injury, we must ask whether a full review of Burns' record reveals that Sheriff Moore should have concluded that Burns' use of excessive force would be a plainly obvious consequence of the hiring decision. On this point, respondent's showing was inadequate. To be sure, Burns' record reflected various misdemeanor infractions. Respondent claims that the record demonstrated such a strong propensity for violence that Burns' application of excessive force was highly likely. The primary charges on which respondent relies, however, are those arising from a fight on a college campus where Burns was a student. In connection with this single incident, Burns was charged with assault and battery, resisting arrest, and public drunkenness. In January 1990, when he pleaded guilty to those charges, Burns also pleaded guilty to various driving-related offenses, including nine moving violations and a charge of driving with a suspended license. In addition, Burns had previously pleaded guilty to being in actual physical control of a vehicle while intoxicated.

The fact that Burns had pleaded guilty to traffic offenses and other misdemeanors may well have made him an extremely poor candidate for reserve deputy. Had Sheriff Moore fully reviewed Burns' record, he might have come to precisely that conclusion. But unless he would necessarily have reached that decision because Burns' use of excessive force would have been a plainly obvious consequence of the hiring decision, Sheriff Moore's inadequate scrutiny of Burns' record cannot constitute "deliberate indifference" to respondent's federally protected right to be free from a use of excessive force. Justice Souter's reading of the case is that the jury believed that Sheriff Moore in fact read Burns' entire record. That is plausible, but it is also irrelevant. It is not sufficient for respondent to show that Sheriff Moore read Burns' record and therefore hired Burns with knowledge of his background. Such a decision may reflect indifference to Burns' record, but what is required is deliberate indifference to a plaintiff's constitutional right. That is, whether Sheriff Moore failed to examine Burns' record, partially examined it, or fully examined it, Sheriff Moore's hiring decision could not have been "deliberately indifferent" unless in light of that record Burns' use of excessive force would have been a plainly obvious consequence of the hiring decision. Because there was insufficient evidence on which a jury could base a finding that Sheriff Moore's decision to hire Burns reflected conscious disregard of an obvious risk that a use of excessive force would follow, the District Court erred in submitting respondent's inadequate screening claim to the jury.

III

Cases involving constitutional injuries allegedly traceable to an ill-considered hiring decision pose the greatest risk that a municipality will be held liable for an injury that it did not cause. In the broadest sense, every injury is traceable to a hiring decision. Where a court fails to adhere to rigorous requirements of culpability and causation, municipal liability collapses into respondeat superior liability. As we recognized in *Monell* and have repeatedly reaffirmed, Congress did not intend municipalities to be held liable unless deliberate action attributable to the municipality directly caused a deprivation of federal rights. A failure to apply stringent culpability and causation requirements raises serious federalism concerns, in that it risks constitutionalizing particular hiring requirements that States have themselves elected not to impose. *Cf. Canton v. Harris.* Bryan County is not liable for Sheriff Moore's isolated decision to hire Burns without adequate screening, because respondent has not demonstrated that his decision reflected a conscious disregard for a high risk that Burns would use excessive force in violation of respondent's federally protected right. We therefore vacate the judgment of the Court of Appeals and remand this case for further proceedings consistent with this opinion.

It is so ordered.

JUSTICE SOUTER, with whom JUSTICE STEVENS and JUSTICE BREYER join, dissenting.

In *Pembaur v. Cincinnati*, we held a municipality liable under 42 U.S.C. § 1983 for harm caused by the single act of a policymaking officer in a matter within his authority but not covered by a policy previously identified. The central question presented here is whether that rule applies to a single act that itself neither violates nor commands a violation of federal law. The answer is yes if the single act amounts to deliberate indifference to a substantial risk that a violation of federal law will result. With significant qualifications, the Court assumes so, too, in theory, but it raises such skeptical hurdles to reaching any such conclusion in practice that it virtually guarantees its disposition of this case: it holds as a matter of law that the sheriff's act could not be thought to reflect deliberate indifference to the risk that his subordinate would violate the Constitution by using excessive force. I respectfully dissent as much from the level of the Court's skepticism as from its reversal of the judgment.

Under this prior law, Sheriff Moore's failure to screen out his 21-year-old great-nephew Burns on the basis of his criminal record, and the decision instead to authorize Burns to act as a deputy sheriff, constitutes a policy choice attributable to Bryan County under § 1983. There is no serious dispute that Sheriff Moore is the designated policymaker for implementing the sheriff's law enforcement powers and recruiting officers to exercise them, or that he "has final authority to act for the municipality in hiring matters." As the authorized policymaker, Sheriff Moore is the county for purposes of § 1983 municipal liability arising from the sheriff's department's exercise of law enforcement authority. As I explain in greater detail below, it was open to the jury to find that the sheriff knew of the record of his nephew's violent propensity, but hired him in deliberate indifference to the risk that he would use excessive force on the job, as in fact he later did. That the sheriff's act did not itself command or require commission of a constitutional violation (like the order to perform an unlawful entry and search in *Pembaur*) is not dispositive under § 1983, for we have expressly rejected the contention that "only unconstitutional polices are actionable" under § 1983, and have never suggested that liability under the statute is otherwise limited to policies that facially violate other federal law. The sheriff's policy choice creating a substantial risk of a constitutional violation therefore could subject the county to liability under existing precedent.

The Court's formulation that deliberate indifference exists only when the risk of the subsequent, particular constitutional violation is a plainly obvious consequence of the hiring decision, while derived from *Canton*, is thus without doubt a new standard. As to the "particular" violation, the Court alters the understanding of deliberate indifference as set forth in *Canton*, where we spoke of constitutional violations generally. As to "plainly obvious consequence," the Court's standard appears to be somewhat higher, for example, than the standard for "reckless" fault in the criminal law, where the requisite indifference to risk is defined as that which "consciously disregards a substantial and unjustifiable risk that the material element exists or will result . . . [and] involves a gross deviation from the standard of conduct that a law-abiding person would observe in the actor's situation." *See* American Law Institute, Model Penal Code § 2.02(2)(c)(1985).

*   *   *

The Court's skepticism that the modified standard of fault can ever be met in a single-act case of inadequate screening without a patently unconstitutional policy, both reveals the true value of the assumption that in theory there might be municipal liability in such a case, and dictates the result of the Court's review of the record in the case before us. It is skepticism gone too far.

While the Court should rightly be skeptical about predicating municipal or individual liability merely on a failure to adopt a crime-free personnel policy or on a particular decision to hire a guilty trucker, why does it extend that valid skepticism to the quite unsound point of doubting liability for hiring the violent scofflaw? The Court says it fears that the latter sort of case raises a danger of liability without fault. But if the Court means fault generally (as distinct from the blame imputed on classic respondeat superior doctrine), it need only recall that whether a particular violent scofflaw is violent enough or scoffing enough to implicate deliberate indifference will depend on applying the highly demanding standard the Court announces: plainly obvious consequence of particular injury. It is the high threshold of deliberate indifference that will ensure that municipalities be held liable only for considered acts with substantial risks. That standard will distinguish single-act cases with only a mild portent of injury from single-act cases with a plainly obvious portent, and from cases in which the harm is only the latest in a series of injuries known to have followed from the policymaker's action. The Court has fenced off the slippery slope.

A second stated reason of the skeptical majority is that, because municipal liability under *Monell* cannot rest on respondeat superior, "a court must carefully test the link between the policymaker's inadequate decision and the particular injury alleged." But that is simply to say that the tortious act must be proximately caused by the policymaker. The policy requirement is the restriction that bars straightforward respondeat superior liability, and the need to "test the link" is merely the need to apply the law that defines what a cognizable link is. The restriction on imputed fault that saves municipalities from liability has no need of categorical immunization in single-act cases.

In short, the Court's skepticism is excessive in ignoring the fact that some acts of a policymaker present substantial risks of unconstitutional harm even though the acts are not unconstitutional per se. And the Court's purported justifications for its extreme skepticism are washed out by the very standards employed to limit liability.

The county escapes from liability through the Court's untoward application of an enhanced fault standard to a record of inculpatory evidence showing a contempt for constitutional obligations as blatant as the nepotism that apparently occasioned it. The novelty of this escape shows something unsuspected (by me, at least) until today. Despite arguments that *Monell's* policy requirement was an erroneous reading of § 1983, *see Oklahoma City v. Tuttle* (Stevens, J., dissenting), I had not previously thought that there was sufficient reason to unsettle the precedent of *Monell*. Now it turns out, however, that *Monell* is hardly settled. That being so, Justice Breyer's powerful call to reexamine § 1983 municipal liability afresh finds support in the Court's own readiness to rethink the matter.

I respectfully dissent.

JUSTICE **BREYER**, with whom JUSTICE **STEVENS** and JUSTICE **GINSBURG** join, dissenting.

In *Monell v. New York City Dept. of Social Servs.*, this Court said that municipalities cannot be held liable for constitutional torts under 42 U.S.C. § 1983 "on a respondeat superior theory," but they can be held liable "when execution of" a municipality's "policy or custom . . . inflicts the injury." That statement has produced a highly complex body of interpretive law. Today's decision exemplifies the law's complexity, for it distinguishes among a municipal action that "itself violates federal law," an action that "intentionally deprives a plaintiff of a federally protected right," and one that "has caused an employee to do so." It then elaborates this Court's requirement that a consequence be "so likely" to occur that a policymaker could "reasonably be said to have been deliberately indifferent" with respect to it, *Canton v. Harris*, with an admonition that the unconstitutional consequence must be "plainly obvious." The majority fears that a contrary view of prior precedent would undermine *Monell's* basic distinction. That concern, however, rather than leading us to spin ever finer distinctions as we try to apply *Monell's* basic distinction between liability that rests upon policy and liability that is vicarious, suggests that we should reexamine the legal soundness of that basic distinction itself.

First, consider *Monell's* original reasoning. The *Monell* "no vicarious liability" principle rested upon a historical analysis of § 1983 and upon § 1983's literal language — language that imposes liability upon (but only upon) any "person." Justice Stevens has clearly explained why neither of these rationales is sound. Essentially, the history on which *Monell* relied consists almost exclusively of the fact that the Congress that enacted § 1983 rejected an amendment (called the Sherman amendment) that would have made municipalities vicariously liable for the marauding acts of private citizens. That fact, as Justice Stevens and others have pointed out, does not argue against vicarious liability for the act of municipal employees — particularly since municipalities, at the time, were vicariously liable for many of the acts of their employees.

Without supporting history, it is difficult to find § 1983's words "every person" inconsistent with respondeat superior liability. In 1871 "bodies politic and corporate," such as municipalities were "persons." *See* Act of Feb. 25, ch. 71, § 2, 16 Stat. 431 (repealed 1939). Section 1983 requires that the "person" either "subject" or "cause" a different person "to be subjected" to a "deprivation" of a right. As a purely linguistic matter, a municipality, which can act only through its employees, might be said to have "subjected" a person or to have "caused" that person to have been "subjected" to a loss of rights when a municipality's employee acts within the scope of his or her employment. Federal courts on occasion have interpreted the word "person" or the equivalent in other statutes as authorizing forms of vicarious liability.

Second, *Monell's* basic effort to distinguish between vicarious liability and liability derived from "policy or custom" has produced a body of law that is neither readily understandable nor easy to apply. Today's case provides a good example. The District Court in this case told the jury it must find (1) Sheriff Moore's screening "so likely to result in violations of constitutional rights" that he could "reasonably [be] said to have been deliberately indifferent to the constitutional needs of the Plaintiff" and (2) that the "inadequate hiring . . . policy directly caused the Plaintiff's injury." This instruction comes close to repeating this Court's language in *Canton v. Harris*. In *Canton*, the Court said (of the city's failure to train officers in the use of deadly force):

> In light of the duties assigned to specific officers or employees the need for more or different training is so obvious, and the inadequacy so likely to result in the violation of constitutional rights, that the policymakers of the city can reasonably be said to have been deliberately indifferent to the need.

Consider some of the other distinctions that this Court has had to make as it has sought to distinguish liability based upon policymaking from liability that is "vicarious." It has proved necessary, for example, to distinguish further, between an exercise of policymaking authority and an exercise of delegated discretionary policy-implementing authority. Without some such distinction, "municipal liability [might] collapse into respondeat superior," for the law would treat similarly (and hold municipalities responsible for) both a police officer's decision about how much force to use when making a particular arrest and a police chief's decision about how much force to use when making a particular kind of arrest. But the distinction is not a clear one. It requires federal courts to explore state and municipal law that distributes different state powers among different local officials and local entities. That law is highly specialized; it may or may not say just where policymaking authority lies, and it can prove particularly difficult to apply in light of the Court's determination that a decision can be "policymaking" even though it applies only to a single instance. *See also* Schnapper, *A Monell Update: Clarity, Conflict, and Complications*, Practising Law Institute, Litigation and Administrative Practice Series, No. 381, Vol. 2, p. 36 (1989); Schuck, *Municipal Liability Under Section 1983: Some Lessons From Tort Law and Organization Theory*, 77 Geo. L. J. 1753, 1774–1779 (1989).

Nor does the location of "policymaking" authority pose the only conceptually difficult problem. Lower courts must also ask decide whether a failure to make policy was "deliberately indifferent," rather than "grossly negligent." And they must decide, for example, whether it matters that some such failure occurred in the officer-training, rather than the officer-hiring, process.

Given the basic *Monell* principle, these distinctions may be necessary, for without them, the Court cannot easily avoid a "municipal liability" that "collapses into respondeat superior." But a basic legal principle that requires so many such distinctions to maintain its legal life may not deserve such longevity.

Finally, relevant legal and factual circumstances may have changed in a way that affects likely reliance upon *Monell's* liability limitation. The legal complexity just described makes it difficult for municipalities to predict just when they will be held liable based upon "policy or custom." Moreover, their potential liability is, in a sense, greater than that of individuals, for they cannot assert the "qualified immunity" defenses that individuals may raise. Further, many States have statutes that appear to, in effect, mimic respondeat superior by authorizing indemnification of employees found liable under § 1983 for actions within the scope of their employment. These statutes — valuable to government employees as well as to civil rights victims — can provide for payments from the government that are similar to those that would take place in the absence of *Monell's* limitations. To the extent that they do so, municipal reliance upon the continuation of *Monell's* "policy" limitation loses much of its significance.

Any statement about reliance, of course, must be tentative, as we have not heard argument on the matter. We do not know the pattern of indemnification: how often, and to what extent, States now indemnify their employees, and which of their employees they indemnify. I also realize that there may be other reasons, constitutional and otherwise, that I have not discussed that argue strongly for reaffirmation of *Monell's* holding.

Nonetheless, for the reasons I have set forth, I believe the case for reexamination is a strong one. Today's decision underscores this need. Consequently, I would ask for further argument that would focus upon the continued viability of *Monell's* distinction between vicarious municipal liability and municipal liability based upon policy and custom.

NOTES

1. After *Bryan County*, what are the requirements for local government liability for a policymaker's hiring decisions? Are those requirements stringent? If so, should they be? In any event, there are few reported circuit court decisions in which plaintiffs win or even attempt to win based solely on inadequate pre-hiring investigation.

Wilson v. Cook County, 742 F.3d 775 (7th Cir. 2014), illustrates some of the hurdles plaintiffs face. Felice Vanaria was a politically-appointed staffer at a county hospital. "Vanaria used the promise of a phony job to convince [Krystal] Almaguer [now Wilson] to give him erotic massages and engage in sexual conduct." *Id.* at 777. No background check was conducted before hiring Vanaria. Yet in an earlier job as a probation officer, "Vanaria was involved in several incidents in which female probationers alleged he had sought sexual favors in exchange for looser conditions of probation."

In upholding summary judgment for the county, the court said:

> [T]he most troubling conduct Vanaria engaged in [as a probation officer] was the coercion of female probationers who were under his supervision. That occurred during the 1990s, and resulted in his termination in 1998. During the ensuing seven years, Vanaria was employed, apparently without incident, at a casino and with Commissioner Moreno beginning in 2002. [Given] the passage of time without incident and the fact that Vanaria had aged seven years, it is difficult to conclude that Vanaria's misconduct with respect to Almaguer was so obvious that any jury could find causation or deliberate indifference. 742 F.3d at 782.

The court went on to cite *Bryan County* for the proposition that hiring liability depends on a finding that *this* officer was highly likely to inflict the *particular* injury. That requirement was not met here. The court distinguished between Vanaria's past conduct, which it characterized as "abuse of power," and his conduct toward Almaguer.

> [H]e was able to entice Almaguer through a ruse he concocted, but the manner in which he operated was a sharp deviation from his past misconduct. That is, even if the county had known about his probation history, it could hardly have expected that Vanaria would have impersonated a human resources employee and lured a complete stranger into the building. He had no history of such conduct. 742 F.3d at 782.

See also Schneider v. City of Grand Junction Police Department, 717 F.3d 760 (10th Cir. 2013) (plaintiff made both hiring and training claims, but lost on both); *Crete v. City of Lowell*, 418 F.3d 54, 65–66 (1st Cir. 2005) (police officer allegedly used excessive force; applying *Bryan County*, the court affirmed summary judgment for the city even though it hired the officer with knowledge of his earlier conviction for assault and battery). *See also* note 3 below.

2. Does *Bryan County* modify *City of Canton*? That is, do the *Bryan County* requirements now apply to *all* failure to train and supervise cases? Should they? In *Connick v. Thompson, supra,* the Court gives no indication that *Bryan* County effected such a change. Some lower courts have applied *Bryan County* to failure to train cases, *see, e.g., Allen v. Muskogee, Okl.*, 119 F.3d 837 (10th Cir. 1997) (applying *Bryan County* in a single incident failure to train police case but overturning district court's grant of summary judgment to city and remanding) and *Snyder v. Trepagnier*, 142 F.3d 791 (5th Cir. 1998) (applying *Bryan County* in failure to train police case and reversing jury verdict and judgment against city). But most of the cases continue to cite and follow *Canton*, though they may cite *Bryan County* as well. Examples include:

Burgess v. Fischer, 735 F.3d 462, 478 (6th Cir. 2013) (citing circuit court precedent that relied on *Canton*);

Belbachir v. County of McHenry, 726 F.3d 975, 983 (7th Cir. 2013) (citing circuit court precedent decided under Canton);

Schneider v. City of Grand Junction Police Department, 717 F.3d 760, 771–74 (10th Cir. 2013) (applying Brown to a hiring claim and *Canton* to a training claim);

B.A.B. Jr. v. Board of Education of St. Louis, 698 F.3d 1037, 1039–40 (8th Cir. 2012) (citing *Canton*);

Mueller v. Auker, 694 F.3d 989, 1002 (9th Cir. 2012) (citing *Canton* but not *Bryan County*);

Jones v. Town of East Haven, 691 F.3d 72, 81 (2d Cir. 2012) (citing and following *Canton; Brown* is cited, but no change in the *Canton* test is identified or is apparent from the court's reasoning);

Haley v. City of Boston, 657 F.3d 39, 51–52 (1st Cir. 2011) (similar to *Jones*);

Craig v. Floyd County, Ga., 643 F.3d 1306, 1310 (11th Cir. 2011) (citing circuit court precedent decided under *Canton*).

In short, it does not appear that *Bryan County* has brought about, or was intended to bring about, any major shift in failure to train doctrine. The more important limit on *Canton* is *Connick v. Thompson*'s insistence that a pattern of violations usually must be shown. After that case there may be little to be gained by framing the litigation in "failure to train" terms rather than "custom," since a widespread practice must be shown to assure victory in either type of litigation, and the "custom" theory does not require the plaintiff to identify any extra or different training the city should have done.

See generally Nahmod, *The Long and Winding Road from* Monroe *to* Connick, 13 LOYOLA J. PUB. INT. L. 427 (2012).

3. A post-*Bryan County* First Circuit case, *Young v. City of Providence ex rel Napolitano*, 404 F.3d 4 (1st Cir. 2005). involved a Fourth Amendment excessive force claim against a white police officer who fatally shot a black off-duty police officer, as well as a failure to train claim against a city based on this incident. Upholding a jury verdict against the officer, the First Circuit explained:

> [T]here was evidence presented at the phase one trial that Cornel was identifying himself as a police officer, was holding his gun with two hands as a police officer would, and was immediately recognized by bystanders as an off-duty officer. We think that a jury could find that an objectively reasonable officer would have recognized Cornel as an officer, and thus would have recognized that he was not a threat and would not have shot him There was also evidence that Cornel's gun was pointing downwards, and not at [a suspect] or anyone else, and that the officers shot him extraordinarily quickly, almost immediately after he left the restaurant, and without giving him adequate warning.

More important for present purposes, the First Circuit addressed the failure to train claim and reversed the district court's grant of summary judgment to the city. It determined that a jury could find that the police officer made such mistakes because of the police department's lack of training in "on-duty/off-duty interactions, avoiding misidentifications of off-duty officers, and other issues relating to the City's always armed/always on-duty policy . . . [and] that this training deficiency constituted deliberate indifference to Cornel's rights." The First Circuit observed that the plaintiff did not necessarily have to demonstrate a pattern of prior constitutional violations to show deliberate indifference. There was testimony that it was common knowledge within the police community of the substantial risk of "friendly fire" stemming from the always armed/always on-duty policy. Also, there was evidence that the city knew its training program was deficient. Is this holding still good law after *Connick v. Thompson*?

In the same case, the First Circuit addressed the plaintiff's deficient hiring claim against the city and affirmed summary judgment for the city. After noting, in reliance on the Supreme Court's decision in *Bryan County* that hiring claims based on a single incident can seldom if ever serve as the basis for liability because the "plainly obvious consequence" standard was so stringent, the court pointed out that the procedures used in the hiring process for the officer were not so inadequate as to raise a jury question regarding the city's deliberate indifference. There was a background check, the officer's prior supervisors were spoken to and provided good reviews, and a questionable incident came to light and was discussed before the officer was hired. The First Circuit concluded: "The recent trend of Supreme Court cases, which use very particularized notions of causation and fault, make it unlikely that the training claim and the hiring claim could be combined into one mishmash, despite the hiring claim's inability to survive on its own, and given to the jury."

3. Supervisory Liability

Plaintiffs in § 1983 cases typically sue not only the officers who directly violate their rights and the local governments that employ them, but also the officers' supervisors. The distinctive question in suits against supervisors is whether the plaintiff is required to show that the supervisor committed a constitutional violation, or whether some lesser showing, such as "deliberate indifference to plaintiff's constitutional rights" will suffice for liability.

The Supreme Court briefly addressed this type of litigation in *Ashcroft v. Iqbal*, 556 U.S. 662 (2009), a *Bivens* case (*see* chapter 1) brought against the U.S. Attorney General and others, claiming that the plaintiff was treated in an unconstitutionally abusive manner. In the course of an opinion that focused on the inadequacy of the plaintiff's pleading (for lack of specificity), the Court said:

> In the limited settings where *Bivens* does apply, the implied cause of action is the "federal analog to suits brought against state officials under 42 U.S.C. § 1983." Based on the rules our precedents establish, respondent correctly concedes that Government officials may not be held liable for the unconstitutional conduct of their subordinates under a theory of *respondeat superior. See* [*Monell*] (finding no vicarious liability for a municipal "person" under 42 U.S.C. § 1983); *see also Dunlop v. Munroe*, 11 U.S. 242, 3 L. Ed. 329, 7 Cranch 242, 269 (1812) (a federal official's liability "will only result from his own neglect in not properly superintending the discharge" of his subordinates' duties); *Robertson v. Sichel*, 127 U.S. 507, 515–516 (1888) ("A public officer or agent is not responsible for the misfeasances or positive wrongs, or for the nonfeasances, or negligences, or omissions of duty, of the sub-agents or servants or other persons properly employed by or under him, in the discharge of his official duties"). Because vicarious liability is inapplicable to *Bivens* and § 1983 suits, a plaintiff must plead that each Government-official defendant, through the official's own individual actions, has violated the Constitution. 556 U.S. at 676 (some citations omitted).

The last sentence of this passage seems to require, rather unambiguously, that the plaintiff prove a constitutional violation by the supervisor. One might try to distinguish *Iqbal* from § 1983 litigation on the ground that the Court had earlier held that *Bivens* cases must be brought only against the officer and not against his employer, *Correctional Services v. Malesko*, 534 U.S. 61 (2001); *FDIC v. Meyer*, 510 U.S. 471 (1994), and for *Bivens* purposes the supervisor might be analogized to the employer. But the passage set out above, taken as a whole, strongly suggests that the Court means to treat the two contexts alike, not to draw a distinction between them.

Yet it is not at all clear that the lower courts, even post-*Iqbal*, require the plaintiff to show that the supervisor violated the plaintiff's constitutional right. Here is typical statement of the doctrine, from a case in which a prison inmate sued under the Eighth Amendment for failure to protect him from inmate-on-inmate assault:

> [A] plaintiff seeking to hold a supervisor liable for constitutional violations must show that the supervisor either participated directly in the unconstitutional conduct or that a causal connection exists between the supervisor's actions and the alleged constitutional violation.

Harrison v. Culliver, 746 F.3d 1288, 1298 (11th Cir. 2014). The court then went on to quote from an earlier case:

> The necessary causal connection can be established when a history of widespread abuse puts the responsible supervisor on notice of the need to correct the alleged deprivation, and he fails to do so. Alternatively, the causal connection may be established when a supervisor's custom or policy . . . result[s] in deliberate indifference to constitutional rights or when facts support an inference that the supervisor directed the subordinates to act unlawfully or knew that the subordinates would act unlawfully and failed to stop them from doing so.

746 F.3d at 1298, *quoting Cottone v. Jenne*, 326 F.3d 1352, 1360 (11th Cir. 2003).

Granting that this test is a demanding one, is it fully consistent with *Iqbal*? Here are some roughly similar statements of the supervisory liability doctrine in other circuit courts:

Wilkins v. Montgomery, 751 F.3d 214, 226 (4th Cir. 2014) ("that the supervisor had actual or constructive knowledge" of subordinate's "conduct that posed a pervasive and unreasonable risk of constitutional injury to citizens like the plaintiff", "that the supervisor's response to that knowledge was so inadequate as to show deliberate indifference to or tacit authorization of the alleged offensive practices", and "an affirmative causal link between the supervisor's inaction and the particular constitutional injury suffered by the plaintiff");

Crowley v. Bannister, 734 F.3d 967, 977 (9th Cir. 2013) ("the moving force of a constitutional violation");

Wilson v. Montano, 715 F.3d 847, 856 (10th Cir. 2013) (ambiguous language, some of which suggests that plaintiff must show that the supervisor committed a constitutional violation);

Campbell v. City of Springboro, Ohio, 700 F.3d 779, 790 (6th Cir. 2012) ("a plaintiff must show that the official at least implicitly authorized, approved, or knowingly acquiesced in the unconstitutional conduct of the offending officers");

Backes v. Village of Peoria Heights, 662 F.3d 866, 870 (7th Cir. 2011) ("supervisors must know about the conduct and facilitate it, approve it, condone it, or turn a blind eye for fear of what they might see," quoting a pre-*Iqbal* case).

In *Jackson v. Nixon*, 747 F.3d 537 (8th Cir. 2014), the court cited *Iqbal* for the proposition that "[t]o state a claim under § 1983, the plaintiff must plead that a government official has personally violated the plaintiff's constitutional rights." 747 F.3d at 543. It then elaborated, stating that

> Even if a supervisor is not involved in day-to-day operations, his personal involvement may be found if he is involved in creating, applying, or interpreting a policy that gives rise to unconstitutional conditions. In requiring a plaintiff to allege that each defendant was personally involved in the deprivation of his constitutional rights, we assess each defendant relative to his authority over the claimed constitutional violation. *Id.*

In *Jackson*, the plaintiff was an inmate at Western Reception, Diagnostic, and Correctional Center (WRDCC). He "challenged the WRDCC's Offenders Under

Treatment Program (OUTP) as violating his rights under the First Amendment." 747 F.3d at 539–40. Jackson, an atheist, was required to complete this (religion-oriented) program to be eligible for early release on parole. In his complaint he charged that he was "coerced by and through an atmosphere designed and intended to change or alter my thinking and behavior." He withdrew from the program and in his lawsuit claimed that "he was denied an early release for failure to complete OUTP." 747 F.3d at 540. Jackson sued Crawford (Director of the Missouri Department of Corrections), Burgess (WRDCC Warden) and Salisbury ((WRDCC OUTP Director.) The court ruled that Crawford could be held liable for establishing the policy, but that Jackson had not stated good supervisory liability claims against Burgess. The court then turned to Salisbury:

> Jackson's claims regarding Salisbury's involvement are more specific than his statements regarding the other defendants. In particular, he alleged that as director of the treatment program, she could have allowed him to avoid the religious portions of the program but still remain enrolled in order to comply with his parole stipulation. The scope of her authority as to the OUTP curriculum and inmates' participation in it is unclear. Even if she did not determine the OUTP curriculum, however, the claim concerns her ability to help ameliorate the constitutional violation alleged. [Affording] Jackson reasonable inferences from the facts in his complaint, we find that he has plausibly alleged Salsbury's personal involvement.

Is this holding consistent with *Iqbal*?

Note that, even if the court is mistaken on supervisory liability, officers may be sued in their *official* capacities for *prospective* relief, such as a declaratory judgment that the current version of OUTP violates the First Amendment or an injunction directing the defendants to make changes in OUTP. For the distinction between these "official capacity" suits and "individual capacity" suits (the context in which supervisory liability is an important issue) see the introduction to this chapter.

For extensive discussion of *Iqbal* and supervisory liability and for the argument that *Iqbal* got it right, see Nahmod, *Constitutional Tort, Over-Deterrence and Supervisory Liability*, 14 Lewis & Clark L. Rev. 279 (2010).

IV. ETHICAL CONSIDERATIONS

Because of the possibility of local government liability in many cases, potential conflicts of interest may arise for attorneys who represent local governments at the same time they represent individual officials or employees of those governments. Why should this be? Consider in this connection the leading case of *Dunton v. City of Suffolk*, 729 F.2d 903 (2d Cir. 1984).

DUNTON v. COUNTY OF SUFFOLK, STATE OF NEW YORK
729 F.2d 903 (2d Cir. 1984)

MESKILL, CIRCUIT JUDGE:

Robert Pfeiffer appeals from a judgment entered against him after a jury trial in the United States District Court for the Eastern District of New York, Glasser, J., awarding Emerson Dunton, Jr. $10,000 compensatory damages and $10,000 punitive damages on a state law battery claim. Angela Pfeiffer appeals from a judgment entered against her in the same trial, awarding Dunton $5,000 compensatory damages and $20,000 punitive damages for malicious prosecution. We reverse the judgment against Robert Pfeiffer and remand for a new trial and reverse the judgment against Angela Pfeiffer and remand to the district court with instructions to dismiss the complaint.

I

Defendant-appellant Angela Pfeiffer attended a retirement party for a fellow employee on the evening of May 20, 1981. As the party broke up, plaintiffappellee Emerson Dunton Jr., a co-worker and attendee, accompanied Ms. Pfeiffer to her car. The accounts of the subsequent events differ; Ms. Pfeifer claims that Dunton began making improper advances while they were seated in her car, while Dunton asserts that Ms. Pfeiffer willingly participated in the maneuvers. Defendant appellant Robert Pfeiffer, Angela's husband and also a Suffolk County police officer, came upon the scene in his patrol car, threw Dunton out of Ms. Pfeiffer's car, struck him repeatedly and left him lying in the parking lot. Dunton suffered non-disabling and non-permanent injuries from the incident.

Dunton was arrested after Angela Pfeiffer filed a criminal complaint on June 18, alleging third degree sexual abuse in violation of N.Y. Penal Law § 130.55. When the matter did not come to trial by November 16, Dunton moved to dismiss on the ground that the sixty day limit for trial had been exceeded. The motion was denied and Dunton moved for reconsideration. On December 23, the Suffolk County district court concluded that it had erred in computing the sixty day period and that sixty-seven days were actually chargeable to the prosecution. Accordingly, it granted the motion to dismiss. The Appellate Division affirmed.

On August 17, 1981, Dunton filed this action against Suffolk County, the Suffolk County Police Department and the Pfeiffers seeking $50 million compensatory damages, $50 million punitive damages and reasonable attorney's fees. Dunton alleged violations of 42 U.S.C. § 1983 by Officer Pfeiffer and his patrol car partner for the actions in the parking lot, by a desk sergeant for failing to make a report, and by Officer Pfeiffer and other members of the police department for covering up and conspiring to cover up the incident. He also alleged that the Pfeiffers violated 42 U.S.C. §§ 1983 and 1985 by conspiring to cover up the incident with Angela's malicious prosecution complaint of sexual abuse. Finally, he alleged pendent state claims of assault and battery against Robert Pfeiffer and false arrest and malicious prosecution against Angela Pfeiffer.

By local law, Suffolk County provides for the representation of its employees sued under section 1983. Robert Pfeiffer and Suffolk County were represented in this action by the office of the Suffolk County Attorney (County Attorney). An indication that this joint representation might create a conflict came in a form letter from the County Attorney to Robert Pfeiffer dated August 25, 1981 suggesting that because "plaintiff has alleged that [Pfeiffer] acted in [his] personal capacity and/or has demanded punitive damages" and because of possible counterclaims, Pfeiffer should contact private counsel "for such additional advice as may be appropriate." Angela Pfeiffer retained her own attorney.

The County Attorney's answer to Dunton's complaint included an affirmative defense that Robert Pfeiffer was acting in good faith pursuant to his official duties and responsibilities. However, it was the last time that the defense contended that Pfeiffer was acting in good faith as a police officer. The County Attorney told the jury in opening statements that Pfeiffer "acted as a husband, not even as an officer,". Similarly, he told the jury in closing statements that it was obvious Pfeiffer "was acting as an irate husband rather than a police officer," and that he acted "with the human spirit as a husband, not really as an officer," This was clearly the County Attorney's theory of the case, as he made similar statements to the trial judge.

All of Dunton's claims were dismissed by the court as merciless except for the section 1983 claim against Robert Pfeiffer and that state law claims of battery against Robert Pfeiffer and malicious prosecution against Angela Pfeiffer. The jury found Robert Pfeiffer not liable under section 1983, but awarded $10,000 compensatory and $10,000 punitive damages on the battery claim. Angela Pfeiffer was held liable for $5,000 compensatory and $20,000 punitive damages for malicious prosecution.

Robert Pfeiffer then made a series of post-trial motions relating to the County Attorney's conflict of interest. While the district court acknowledged that there was a conflict, it denied the motions on the ground that Pfeiffer was not prejudiced thereby. It stated that even if Pfeiffer had been shown to be acting under color of state law, damages would still have been awarded for the unjustified battery, and that punitive damages would also have been awarded in any event.

II

Robert Pfeiffer appeals on the ground that the Suffolk County Attorney failed to represent his interest adequately because of the attorney's conflicting representation of Suffolk County. Specifically, Officer Pfeiffer claims that it was in his interest to assert his immunity from section 1983 liability based on good faith actions within the scope of his employment. See *Harlow v. Fitzgerald; Pierson v. Ray*. Pfeiffer contends that the attorney undermined the good faith immunity defense by repeatedly stating that Pfeiffer acted not as a police officer but as an "irate husband."

Municipalities commonly provide counsel for their employees and themselves when both municipality and employee are sued. The Suffolk County Attorney's representation of Officer Pfeiffer here was mandated by statute. Prior to 1978, such representation would not have caused a conflict because municipalities were not "persons" subject to section 1983 liability. See *Monroe v. Pape*. Thus, a municipality would have had not reason to give an employee less than full representation.

However, since the Supreme Court's decision in *Monell v. Department of Social Services*, municipalities can be held liable under section 1983 for employees' actions taken pursuant to municipal policy. After *Monell* the interests of a municipality and its employee as defendants in a section 1983 action are in conflict. A municipality may avoid liability by showing that the employee was not acting within the scope of his official duties, because his unofficial actions would not be pursuant to municipal policy. The employee, by contrast, may partially or completely avoid liability by showing that he was acting within the scope of his official duties. If he can show that his actions were pursuant to an official policy, he can at least shift part of his liability to the municipality. If he is successful in asserting a good faith immunity defense, the municipality may be wholly liable because it cannot assert the good faith immunity of its employees as a defense to a section 1983 action. *Owen v. City of Independence.*

Because of the imminent threat of a serious conflict, disqualification would have been appropriate here even before any proceedings began. See *Shadid v. Jackson* (granting motion to disqualify in virtually identical case because of "high potential for conflicting loyalties"). *Cf. Armstrong v. McAlpin* (en banc) (disqualification appropriate when conflict will taint a trial by affecting attorney's presentation of a case). This conflict surfaced when the County Attorney stated that Pfeiffer was not acting under color of state law but rather as an "irate husband." This was a good defense for the county, which eventually was dismissed from the action. However, it was not in the best interest of Pfeiffer, who was ultimately found liable in his individual capacity. Pfeiffer's failure to object to the multiple representation before or during trial did not constitute a waiver. As a layman, he could not be expected to appreciate his need to prove a good faith defense. Furthermore, he was never advised that his counsel would take positions directly contrary to his interest.

The County Attorney's multiple representation in this case was inconsistent with his professional obligation to Officer Pfeiffer. It was also inconsistent with Canons 5 and 9 of the ABA Code of Professional Responsibility. A violation of Canons 5 and 9 of the Code, which call for exercising independent judgment on behalf of a client and avoiding any appearance of impropriety, provides ample grounds for disqualifying an attorney. As soon as the County Attorney began to undermine Officer Pfeiffer's good faith immunity defense by stating that Pfeiffer acted as an "irate husband" and not as a police officer, he was not only failing to act as a conscientious advocate for Pfeiffer, but was acting against Pfeiffer's interest. The seriousness of this conflict made disqualification appropriate.

Where a conflict is serious and disqualification might be warranted, the district court is under a duty to ensure that the client fully appreciates his situation. This Court has stated that [w]hen a potential or actual conflict of interest situation arises, it is the court's duty to ensure that the attorney's client, so involved, is fully aware of the nature of the conflict and understands the potential threat to the protection of his interest." *In re Taylor.*

There are at least two reasons why a court should satisfy itself that no conflict exists or at least provide notice to the affected party if one does. First, a court is under a continuing obligation to supervise the members of its Bar. *E.g., In re Taylor*, see *Musicus v. Westinghouse Electric Corp.* (per curiam) (district court obligated to take measures against unethical conduct occurring in proceedings before it). Second, trial courts have a duty "to exercise that degree of control required by the facts and circumstances of each case to assure the litigants of a fair trial." *Koufakis v. Carvel.* When a litigant's statutorily appointed counsel is acting against the litigant's interests because of a conflict that the litigant has not been informed of and cannot be expected to understand on his own, the litigant is not receiving a fair trial. *Cf. Wood v. Georgia* (divided loyalties of counsel may create due process violation)

In holding that the trial court had a duty to inform Pfeiffer of the conflict, we in no way excuse the conduct of the other attorneys here. Attorneys are officers of the court and are obligated to adhere to all disciplinary rules and to report incidents of which they have unprivileged knowledge involving violations of a disciplinary rule. See *In re Walker* (as officers of court, attorneys required to notify parties and court of error in court order). The County Attorney had to know of the serious conflict his multiple representation created, and knew or should have known that he could not fulfill his ethical obligations to the county without seriously undercutting Pfeiffer's legal position. The plaintiff's attorney should also have been aware of the problem and should have called it to the attention of the court. See *Estates Theatres, Inc. v. Columbia Pictures Industries, Inc.* ("[T]hose attorneys representing other parties to the litigation were obligated to report relevant facts [regarding conflict of interest of opponent's attorney] to the Court. . . .").

Neither do we believe that Pfeiffer waived his objections to multiple representation by failing to object before or during trial. The letter to Pfeiffer only said that there was a possibility of punitive damages, personal liability or counterclaims, and only suggested that Pfeiffer contact outside counsel. It did not say anything about the most serious conflict, that the County Attorney would take a basic position throughout the litigation which was adverse to Pfeiffer's interest. Pfeiffer presumably knew little or nothing about the law of attorney conflicts and could not be expected to discern the nature of the conflict. He would naturally rely on his attorney to protect him. See *Wood v. Georgia* (lawyer on whom conflict-of-interest charge focuses is unlikely to concede that his actions were improper).

The district court acknowledged that there was a conflict in Pfeiffer's representation but denied the motion for a new trial in the mistaken belief that the conflict was not prejudicial. We do not agree. If Pfeiffer's first trial had been fair, he might have escaped liability altogether. The county had agreed to indemnify Pfeiffer for compensatory damages. If the jury found that Pfeiffer was acting in good faith as a police officer, it might not have awarded punitive damages. We believe that because the jury never had a chance to consider Pfeiffer's good faith immunity defense, Pfeiffer did not receive the fair trial to which he was entitled. See *Turner v. Gilbreath* (reversing trial court's failure to grant new trial); see also *Jedwabny v. Philadelphia Transportation Co.* (affirming trial court's decision to grant new trial); *In re Estate of Richard* (violation of Code of Professional Responsibility that prevents a fair trial constitutes reversible error).

The conflict of interest not only prejudiced Pfeiffer, it may also have resulted in an improper benefit to the municipal defendants. The claim that Pfeiffer acted under color of state law was never presented to the jury in the trial below. If Pfeiffer had the opportunity to contend that he did act under color of state law but was immune from liability based on good faith actions within the scope of his duties, Suffolk County or the Police Department may still have been found liable under section 1983. While Dunton did not cross-appeal on this issue, this Court may consider questions of law not raised by the parties in order to prevent injustice. Because the liability of the County and the Police Department were not determined in a fair trial, failure to reinstate those parties in the action would work an injustice on Dunton, who did not create the conflict of interest at issue here.

Accordingly, we vacate the judgment against Robert Pfeiffer and the orders dismissing Suffolk County and the Suffolk County Police Department and remand the entire cause of action against them for a new trial.

NOTES

1. *Dunton* was distinguished in a later § 1983 case, *Patterson v. Balsamico*, 440 F.3d 104, 114 (2d Cir. 2006). Patterson and Balsamico were both police officers working for Oneida County. Patterson claimed that Balsamico and others harassed him on account of his race and sued both Balsamico and Oneida County for race discrimination. He charged that Balsamico and others had, among other things, assaulted him with mace and shaving cream. Gorman represented both defendants throughout the early stages of the litigation. On an earlier appeal, the court affirmed dismissal of the case against Oneida County but remanded the case against Balsamico for trial. Gorman was then replaced by another lawyer (Diodati) and Balsamico lost a jury trial. Here is the court's response to one of his arguments on appeal:

> Balsamico argues that he is entitled to a new trial because Gorman's joint representation of him and the County through the initial appeal in this case prejudiced him because of an inherent conflict of interest between Balsamico's interests and those of the County. He relies principally on *Dunton v. County of Suffolk*, 729 F.2d 903 (2d Cir. 1984), *amended on other grounds*, 748 F.2d 69 (2d Cir. 1984), in which this Court required a new trial due to a conflict of interest arising from an attorney's joint representation of a county and its officers in an action brought under Section 1983. *Dunton* involved a lawsuit against a county and an individual county police officer who had physically assaulted the plaintiff upon finding him sitting in a car with the officer's wife. At trial, the same attorney represented both the county and the individual officer and argued that, at the time of the alleged violation, the officer had acted "as an 'irate husband' " rather than within the scope of his employment as a police officer. We noted that this line of argument served the county's interests, but was a poor defense for the officer, because "[a] municipality may avoid liability by showing that the employee was not acting within the scope of his official duties" while "the employee, by contrast, may partially or completely avoid liability by showing that he was acting within the scope of his official duties." If the employee can show that the employee's actions were pursuant to an official

policy, the employee can shift part of the liability to the municipality, and if the employee can also successfully assert a defense of qualified immunity, the entire liability may rest on the municipality because it cannot assert such a defense. This Court concluded that the attorney's conflict of interest had prejudiced the individual officer while potentially providing "an improper benefit to the municipal defendants," and remanded the case for a new trial.

In so holding, we noted that the potential for such a conflict of interest is inherent in Section 1983 cases. In *Dunton*, however, this court declined to create a per se rule requiring disqualification whenever a municipality and its employees are jointly represented in a Section 1983 case. *Id.* at 908 n.4. Rather, a case-by-case determination is required, and it is clear that the facts of this case do not rise to the level of those in *Dunton*. It is true that Gorman represented all defendants from the time this action was first filed on December 18, 2000 until shortly after this Court remanded the case to the district court. However, Gorman had successfully obtained the dismissal of all claims against all defendants in the district court, and there was no apparent conflict in the interests Gorman represented on appeal. Balsamico's position was that he did not participate in the January 1999 incident. That position was not inconsistent with the County's position. Moreover, on September 17, 2004, approximately five weeks before the commencement of trial on October 25, 2004, a new lawyer, Diodati, was substituted for Gorman to represent Balsamico. At trial, therefore, Balsamico was represented by counsel who had no potential conflict of interest.

This case is materially distinguishable from *Dunton*, where the same attorney represented both the municipality and an individual defendant at trial and where there was an actual conflict of interest in the positions that were of benefit to the two clients. This Court has found a new trial unnecessary even where municipal counsel actually represented individual officers employed by the municipality at trial where there was no actual conflict of interest. *Rodick v. City of Schenectady*, 1 F.3d 1341, 1350 (2d Cir. 1993). The defense attorney in *Rodick*, as here, had jointly represented the municipality and individual police officers prior to trial, and had successfully sought dismissal of the claims against the municipality. Although, unlike this case, the same attorney remained on the case on behalf of the individual defendants throughout the trial, this Court concluded that whatever potential conflict may have existed did not require a new trial because defense counsel advanced and argued all possible defenses available to the officers, including the qualified immunity defense.

This case more closely resembles *Rodick* than *Dunton*. We required a new trial in *Dunton* because the defense attorney had in fact advanced arguments at trial that were directly contrary to the individual officer's interests. A showing was therefore made that "counsel actively represented conflicting interests and that an actual conflict of interest adversely affected [the defense] lawyer's performance" during the trial. *Gordon v. Norman*, 788 F.2d 1194, 1198 (6th Cir. 1986). In contrast, this Court found in *Rodick* that the potential conflict had never materialized, and distinguished

Dunton for precisely that reason. *Rodick*, 1 F.3d at 1350. It is clear that, as was true in *Rodick*, Balsamico cannot make the required showing of a sufficiently serious actual conflict of interest.

The particular conflict cited in *Dunton* as inherent in Section 1983 actions against municipalities, namely that the municipality can escape liability by arguing that its employees were not acting within the scope of official employment while the employee can escape liability by arguing the opposite, is simply not present here. At no time did Gorman assert that Balsamico was acting "outside the scope of his employment" during the January 1999 assault, as the attorney had in *Dunton*. Rather, Balsamico's defense, before and during trial, was that he had not actively participated in the January 1999 assault.

Nor can Balsamico argue that Gorman failed, because of his loyalty to the County, to present a qualified immunity defense on his behalf. Even after Gorman was replaced by Diodati, a wholly independent attorney, Balsamico never attempted to assert a qualified immunity defense. Balsamico would not have been entitled to qualified immunity in any event, because Patterson's equal protection claim arising out of that incident involved "clearly established statutory or constitutional rights of which a reasonable person would have known." *Harlow v. Fitzgerald*, 457 U.S. 800, 818 (1982); *see also Jemmott v. Coughlin*, 85 F.3d 61, 67 (2d Cir. 1996) (rejecting qualified immunity defense where a plaintiff alleged actions sufficient to establish a hostile work environment on the basis of race). Balsamico, moreover, testified at trial that he knew treating people differently on the basis of race was unconstitutional. Gorman therefore neither advanced an argument contrary to Balsamico's interest, such as that Balsamico was acting outside the scope of his employment, nor failed to present a valid defense for reasons of loyalty to his other client.

Balsamico argues that he was prejudiced at trial because Gorman drafted an affidavit when preparing the motion for summary judgment on behalf of all defendants, which Balsamico signed, in which Balsamico denied Patterson's allegations against him. This affidavit, though consistent with Balsamico's contention at trial that he did not participate in the assault on Patterson, did not mention that Balsamico had seen Patterson covered in shaving cream on the night in question, a fact that Balsamico disclosed during his direct testimony at trial. Balsamico argues that he is entitled to a new trial because the omission, which made him more susceptible to impeachment on cross-examination, may have been motivated by Gorman's desire not to implicate the County by presenting evidence tending to establish that the assault actually took place.

There are a number of difficulties with this argument. First, there is no evidence that Balsamico told Gorman that he had seen Patterson covered in shaving cream. To the contrary, Balsamico testified at trial that, at the time he signed the affidavit, he did not think that it was important enough to include. Balsamico's memo to Chief William Chapple, admitted into evidence at the trial, also denied that Balsamico participated in the incident but made no mention of his having seen Patterson covered with shaving cream.

More importantly, as explained above, Balsamico was represented at trial by new counsel unaffected by any conflict of interest Gorman may have had. His trial attorney was fully capable of eliciting testimony to explain the difference between the affidavit and Balsamico's trial testimony and the reasons for such difference, and his trial attorney did elicit such testimony on the redirect examination. Balsamico therefore already had an opportunity, during the first trial, to raise any arguments with respect to the affidavit that would be available to him in a new trial. Furthermore, because the affidavit was a prior statement by a party offered against that party by the party opponent, it is unlikely that it would be excluded in a new trial. *See* Fed. R. Evid. 801(d)(2)(A). We cannot conclude that Balsamico's argument with respect to the affidavit, or any other aspect of Gorman's joint representation of the County and Balsamico prior to trial, provides a basis for a new trial.

Granting that *Patterson* can be distinguished from *Dunton*, a per se rule against joint representation would eliminate the need to draw such distinctions. Why not adopt such a rule? What is the downside of doing so?

2. Is it primarily the plaintiff's attorney's responsibility to raise the conflict of interest issue? The local government's attorney's responsibility? What does *Dunton* indicate?

3. Could there be an ethical problem even where the local government is not sued? The Sixth Circuit in *Gordon v. Norman*, 788 F.2d 1194 (6th Cir. 1986), suggested that the answer is yes, although it did not find one in the case before it. Still, it warned that the bar should be concerned about such ethical issues and possible malpractice liability. Suppose the defendants win in such a case. Does the plaintiff nonetheless have a good case for disqualification? *See Wilson v. Morgan*, 477 F.3d 326, 345–46 (6th Cir. 2007) (no).

4. This kind of ethical issue is (or should be) extensively addressed in professional responsibility courses taught at most law schools. Our purpose here is to alert you to the fact that it arises quite often in the section 1983 setting.

Chapter 6

"[S]UBJECTS OR CAUSES: TO BE SUBJECTED . . .": CAUSATION

The issue of causation is fundamental to every section 1983 claim. Causation provides the bridge between culpable conduct and injury that most observers deem necessary as a matter of fairness to support liability. *E.g.* Weinrib, *Causation and Wrongdoing*, 63 CHI.-KENT L. REV. 407 (1987). Money damages are not recoverable unless the defendant is found to have caused the plaintiff to be deprived of some right secured by the constitution or laws of the United States, and that deprivation is the cause of some legally cognizable harm.

Causation has a long and rich history in the context of common law tort. Hundreds of law review articles and books explore the nuances of causation in tort. Under the traditional approach, causation is divided into two separate inquires: cause in fact and proximate cause. Conduct is viewed as the cause in fact of an injury if it is a necessary condition for its occurrence. RESTATEMENT (THIRD) OF TORTS § 26 (2003). Common law courts generally invoke the familiar "but for" test in determining whether a defendant's conduct is a cause in fact of the plaintiff's injury. DAN B. DOBBS, THE LAW OF TORTS § 168 (2000). Proximate or legal cause addresses limitations on liability for conduct that is the cause in fact of harm. *Id.* at § 180. The problems posed by thin skulls, intervening forces, and unforeseeable consequences are considered under the umbrella of proximate cause.

While the general contour of common law tort rules of causation is long-standing, constitutional tort litigation is of comparatively recent origin. Perhaps it is not surprising that the familiar common law lexicon often appears in court decisions that discuss causation in the constitutional tort context. *See, e.g.*, *Drumgold v. Callahan*, 707 F.3d 28, 48 (1st Cir. 2013) ("As a general rule, we employ common law tort principles when conducting inquiries into causation under [section] 1983.") (internal quotations omitted). Although common law tort doctrine may provide a convenient starting point for discussing constitutional tort causation issues, it is not controlling. Throughout this chapter, the student should consider whether the constitutional foundation of most section 1983 litigation justify the adoption of standards of causation different from those applied in the common law context.

I. CAUSE IN FACT

Most section 1983 opinions employ the familiar "but for" test to determine cause in fact. That is, the defendant's conduct may be considered the cause in fact of the plaintiff's injury if the harm would not have occurred "but for" the defendant's unconstitutional conduct. For example, a jury could find that the defendants' delay in cutting down the body of an inmate found hanging in his cell was the cause in fact of his death when an expert testified that the inmate had a 95% chance of survival had resuscitation efforts been initiated immediately. *Heflin v. Stewart County*, 958 F.2d 709 (6th Cir. 1992). On the other hand, the state's Chief Medical Examiner's protected speech was not the cause in fact of his termination when his employer proved the plaintiff would have been terminated for insubordination and allegations of sexual harassment regardless of his protected speech. *Trant v. State of Oklahoma*, 754 F.3d 1158 (10th Cir. 2014).

The "but for" test is problematic in that it is impossible to know with absolute certainty "what would have happened" if the defendant had acted differently. Courts must determine how much leeway to give juries to decide this inherently speculative question. The rigor with which courts scrutinize evidence of causation necessarily reflects subtle, but significant, policy choices. Plaintiffs benefit from rules that give juries considerable discretion, while rules demanding strict proof favor defendants. *See* Malone, *Ruminations on Cause in Fact*, 9 STAN. L. REV. 60 (1956). The following cases should be examined with this point in mind. Consider how the courts deal with the uncertainty inherent in the but for test.

A.   Mixed Motives

MT. HEALTHY CITY SCHOOL DISTRICT BOARD OF EDUCATION v. DOYLE
429 U.S. 274 (1976)

JUSTICE REHNQUIST delivered the opinion of the Court.

Respondent Doyle sued petitioner Mt. Healthy Board of Education in the United States District Court for the Southern District of Ohio. Doyle claimed that the Board's refusal to renew his contract in 1971 violated his rights under the First and Fourteenth Amendments to the United States Constitution. After a bench trial the District Court held that Doyle was entitled to reinstatement with back pay. The Court of Appeals for the Sixth Circuit affirmed the judgment, and we granted the Board's petition for certiorari to consider an admixture of jurisdictional and constitutional claims.

Doyle was first employed by the Board in 1966. He worked under one-year contracts for the first three years, and under a two-year contract from 1969 to 1971. In 1969 he was elected president of the Teachers' Association, in which position he worked to expand the subjects of direct negotiation between the Association and the Board of Education. During Doyle's one-year term as president of the Association, and during the succeeding year when he served on its executive committee, there was apparently some tension in relations between the Board and the Association.

Beginning early in 1970, Doyle was involved in several incidents not directly connected with his role in the Teachers' Association. In one instance, he engaged in an argument with another teacher which culminated in the other teacher's slapping him. Doyle subsequently refused to accept an apology and insisted upon some punishment for the other teacher. His persistence in the matter resulted in the suspension of both teachers for one day, which was followed by a walkout by a number of other teachers, which in turn resulted in the lifting of the suspensions.

On other occasions, Doyle got into an argument with employees of the school cafeteria over the amount of spaghetti which had been served him; referred to students, in connection with a disciplinary complaint, as "sons of bitches"; and made an obscene gesture to two girls in connection with their failure to obey commands made in his capacity as cafeteria supervisor. Chronologically the last in the series of incidents which respondent was involved in during his employment by the Board was a telephone call by him to a local radio station. It was the Board's consideration of this incident which the court below found to be a violation of the First and Fourteenth Amendments.

In February 1971, the principal circulated to various teachers a memorandum relating to teacher dress and appearance, which was apparently prompted by the view of some in the administration that there was a relationship between teacher appearance and public support for bond issues. Doyle's response to the receipt of the memorandum — on a subject which he apparently understood was to be settled by joint teacher-administration action — was to convey the substance of the memorandum to a disc jockey at WSAI, a Cincinnati radio station, who promptly announced the adoption of the dress code as a news item. Doyle subsequently apologized to the principal, conceding that he should have made some prior communication of his criticism to the school administration.

Approximately one month later the superintendent made his customary annual recommendations to the Board as to the rehiring of non-tenure teachers. He recommended that Doyle not be rehired. The same recommendation was made with respect to nine other teachers in the district, and in all instances, including Doyle's, the recommendation was adopted by the Board. Shortly after being notified of this decision, respondent requested a statement of reasons for the Board's actions. He received a statement citing "a notable lack of tact in handling professional matters which leaves much doubt as to your sincerity in establishing good school relationships." That general statement was followed by references to the radio station incident and to the obscene-gesture incident.

The District Court found that all of these incidents had in fact occurred. It concluded that respondent Doyle's telephone call to the radio station was "clearly protected by the First Amendment," and that because it had played a "substantial part" in the decision of the Board not to renew Doyle's employment, he was entitled to reinstatement with back-pay. The District Court did not expressly state what test it was applying in determining that the incident in question involved conduct protected by the First Amendment, but simply held that the communication to the radio station was such conduct. The Court of Appeals affirmed . . . .

We . . . accept the District Court's finding that [Doyle's] communication [with the radio station] was protected by the First and Fourteenth Amendments. We are not, however, entirely in agreement with that court's manner of reasoning from this finding to the conclusion that Doyle is entitled to reinstatement and back pay.

The District Court made the following "conclusions" on this aspect of the case:

"1) If a non-permissible reason, *e.g.*, exercise of First Amendment rights, played a substantial part in the decision not to renew — even in the face of other permissible grounds — the decision may not stand (citations omitted)."

"2) A non-permissible reason did play a substantial part. That is clear from the letter of the Superintendent immediately following the Board's decision, which stated two reasons — the one, the conversation with the radio station clearly protected by the First Amendment. A court may not engage in any limitation of First Amendment rights based on 'tact' — that is not to say that the 'tactfulness' is irrelevant to other issues in this case."

At the same time, though, it stated that

"[i]n fact, as this Court sees it and finds, both the Board and the Superintendent were faced with a situation in which there did exist in fact reason . . . independent of any First Amendment rights or exercise thereof, to not extend tenure."

Since respondent Doyle had no tenure, and there was therefore not even a state-law requirement of "cause" or "reason" before a decision could be made not to renew his employment, it is not clear what the District Court meant by this latter statement. Clearly the Board legally *could* have dismissed respondent had the radio station incident never come to its attention. One plausible meaning of the court's statement is that the Board and the Superintendent not only could, but in fact *would* have reached that decision had not the constitutionally protected incident of the telephone call to the radio station occurred. We are thus brought to the issue whether, even if that were the case, the fact that the protected conduct played a "substantial part" in the actual decision not to renew would necessarily amount to a constitutional violation justifying remedial action. We think that it would not.

A rule of causation which focuses solely on whether protected conduct played a part, "substantial" or otherwise, in a decision not to rehire, could place an employee in a better position as a result of the exercise of constitutionally protected conduct than he would have occupied had he done nothing. The difficulty with the rule enunciated by the District Court is that it would require reinstatement in cases where a dramatic and perhaps abrasive incident is inevitably on the minds of those responsible for the decision to rehire, and does indeed play a part in that decision — even if the same decision would have been reached had the incident not occurred. The constitutional principle at stake is sufficiently vindicated if such an employee is placed in no worse a position than if he had not engaged in the conduct. A borderline or marginal candidate should not have the employment question resolved against him because of constitutionally protected conduct. But that same candidate ought not to be able, by engaging in such conduct, to prevent his employer from assessing his performance record and reaching a decision not to rehire on the basis of that record, simply because the protected conduct makes the employer more certain of the correctness of its decision.

This is especially true where, as the District Court observed was the case here, the current decision to rehire will accord "tenure." The long-term consequences of an award of tenure are of great moment both to the employee and to the employer. They are too significant for us to hold that the Board in this case would be precluded, because it considered constitutionally protected conduct in deciding not to rehire Doyle, from attempting to prove to a trier of fact that quite apart from such conduct Doyle's record was such that he would not have been rehired in any event.

In other areas of constitutional law, this Court has found it necessary to formulate a test of causation which distinguishes between a result caused by a constitutional violation and one not so caused. We think those are instructive in formulating the test to be applied here.

In *Lyons v. Oklahoma* the Court held that even though the first confession given by a defendant had been involuntary, the Fourteenth Amendment did not prevent the State from using a second confession obtained 12 hours later if the coercion surrounding the first confession had been sufficiently dissipated as to make the second confession voluntary. In *Wong Sun v. United States* the Court was willing to assume that a defendant's arrest had been unlawful, but held that "the connection between the arrest and the statement [given several days later] had 'become so attenuated as to dissipate the taint.' *Nardone v. United States.*" *Parker v. North Carolina* held that even though a confession be assumed to have been involuntary in the constitutional sense of the word, a guilty plea entered over a month later met the test for the voluntariness of such a plea. The Court in *Parker* relied on the same quoted language from *Nardone*, supra, as did the Court in *Wong Sun*, supra. While the type of causation on which the taint cases turn may differ somewhat from that which we apply here, those cases do suggest that the proper test to apply in the present context is one which likewise protects against the invasion of constitutional rights without commanding undesirable consequences not necessary to the assurance of those rights.

Initially, in this case, the burden was properly placed upon respondent to show that his conduct was constitutionally protected, and that this conduct was a "substantial factor" — or, to put it in other words, that it was a "motivating factor" in the Board's decision not to rehire him. Respondent having carried that burden, however, the District Court should have gone on to determine whether the Board had shown by a preponderance of the evidence that it would have reached the same decision as to respondent's re-employment even in the absence of the protected conduct.

We cannot tell from the District Court opinion and conclusions, nor from the opinion of the Court of Appeals affirming the judgment of the District Court, what conclusion those courts would have reached had they applied this test. The judgment of the Court of Appeals is therefore vacated, and the case remanded for further proceedings consistent with this opinion.

So ordered.

NOTES

1.   *Mt. Healthy* establishes a two-part test of causation in so-called mixed motive cases. The plaintiff must first prove by a preponderance of the evidence that the adverse action taken against her was motivated "in substantial part" by constitutionally impermissible factors, such as protected speech or racial discrimination. If the plaintiff fails to discharge this burden, the defendant will prevail. *E.g., Graber v. Clarke*, 763 F.3d 888 (7th Cir. 2014) (deputy sheriff failed to prove that his statements that mandatory overtime violated the union's collective bargaining agreement was a motivating factor in his receiving a seven-day suspension for signing a deficient memo book); *Garrett v. Barnes*, 961 F.2d 629 (7th Cir. 1992); *Erickson v. Pierce County*, 960 F.2d 801 (9th Cir. 1992) (plaintiffs in both cases failed to prove that termination of employment was substantially motivated by political affiliation). *See also Stanley v. City of Dalton*, 219 F.3d 1280, 1291 (11th Cir. 2000) ("the plaintiff's burden in this regard is not a heavy one"). If the plaintiff proves that the adverse action was substantially motivated by unconstitutional factors, the burden shifts to the defendant to prove by a preponderance of the evidence that the same action would have been taken even in the absence of the constitutionally impermissible motive. Thus, even though religious discrimination played a substantial part in the decision to terminate the studies of a doctoral student, the student could not recover damages when the defendant proved that the student would have been dismissed because of his poor research skills regardless of the religious discrimination. *Al-Zubaidi v. Ijaz*, 917 F.2d 1347 (4th Cir. 1990). Similarly, in *Harris v. Shelby County Bd. of Education*, 99 F.3d 1078 (11th Cir. 1996) the plaintiff presented evidence to support his claim that race and protected speech were factors in the decision to not select him to be the principal of a public high school. The defendant prevailed, however, on the strength of "overwhelming evidence" that it selected a "much more qualified candidate," so that the same decision would have been reached even if the plaintiff's race and protected speech had not been considered.

Jury instructions must clearly differentiate the burdens of the plaintiff and defendant in retaliation cases. In *Mays v. Springborn*, 719 F.3d 631 (7th Cir. 2013) an inmate complained that he was subjected to humiliating strip searches in retaliation for his having filed grievances against prison officials. It was plain error for the trial judge to instruct the jury that the inmate had the burden to prove that his protected conduct (filing grievances) was "the sole cause" of the strip searches. The jury should have been instructed that if the plaintiff proved that his protected conduct was a motivating factor, the defendants had the burden of proving that, more likely than not, that the strip searches would have taken place even in the absence of a retaliatory motive.

The Supreme Court has applied the *Mt. Healthy* test in a variety of contexts other than section 1983. *See Price Waterhouse v. Hopkins*, 490 U.S. 228 (1990) (Title VII employment discrimination); *NLRB v. Transportation Management Corp.*, 462 U.S. 393 (1983) (unfair labor practice). However, the *Mt. Healthy* test does not apply in age discrimination cases. In *Gross v. FBL Financial Services, Inc.*, 129 S. Ct. 2393 (2009), the Court held that a plaintiff who alleges that he was demoted because of his age must prove 'but for' causation without the burden-shifting aspect of *Mt. Healthy*. The Court explained that different standards of causation applied in litigation under Title VII and the Age Discrimination in Employment Act is the result of differences in statutory language of the two civil rights laws. *Cf. Carey v. Piphus*, 435 U.S. 247 (1978) (plaintiff cannot recover damages for injuries caused by his suspension from public schools without a hearing if he would have been suspended had a proper hearing been held).

2.   The litigation of mixed-motive cases often focuses on the nature of the plaintiff's and defendant's respective burdens under the *Mt. Healthy* test. As a practical matter, the critical issue is whether the claim can survive the defendant's motion for summary judgment.

What is the plaintiff's burden under the first prong of the *Mt. Healthy* test? That is, what sort of evidence must the plaintiff present to support a jury finding that an adverse decision was substantially motivated by constitutionally impermissible considerations? Consider *Ulrich v. City and County of San Francisco*, 308 F.3d 968 (9th Cir. 2002) in which a doctor contended that adverse actions were taken against him because he had protested a decision by the hospital to lay off a group of doctors. In reviewing the lower court's granting of the defendants' motion for summary judgment, the court stated that proof of impermissible motive can be established by direct or circumstantial evidence. Direct evidence would include statements made by the person alleged to have taken the adverse action. 308 F.3d at 980. Circumstantial evidence showing motive "may fall into three, nonexclusive categories: (1) proximity of time between the protected speech and the alleged retaliation; (2) the employer's expressed opposition to the speech; and (3) other evidence that the reasons proffered by the employer for the adverse action were false and pre-textual." *Id.* Dr. Ulrich presented evidence that the adverse action was initiated the week after he publically criticized the hospital's decision; the hospital's medical director expressed concern about Dr. Ulrich's protest; and the stated reasons for the actions taken against him conflicted with the hospital bylaws. The court of appeals reversed the summary judgment and held that this was sufficient evidence "from which a jury could infer that his protected speech formed a substantial motivation for the adverse treatment of him." 308 F.3d at 980. The Supreme Court has also ruled that a plaintiff may rely on circumstantial evidence to establish that an impermissible consideration was a motivating factor in terminating employment. *Desert Palace Inc., v. Costa*, 539 U.S. 90 (2003).

As noted in *Ulrich*, the time between the defendant becoming award of the protected speech and the adverse action is often an important factor. Many courts have referred to the "temporal proximity" of the protected speech and the adverse action as a circumstance that supports a finding of retaliatory motive. In addition to *Ulrich, see e.g., Surita v. Carrasco*, 665 F.3d 860 (7th Cir. 2011). Some courts caution, however, that "temporal proximity . . . without more" is not sufficient to establish retaliatory motive. *Trant v. State of Oklahoma*, 754 F.3d 1158, 1166 n.3 (10th Cir. 2014). Moreover, remoteness in time may indicate that protected speech was not a substantial motivating factor for the adverse action. *E.g., Leary v. Daeschner*, 228 F.3d 729, 738–39 (6th Cir. 2000). It bears noting, however, that "gaps in time, standing alone, do not preclude [a plaintiff] from producing enough evidence for a reasonable jury to conclude that protected speech was a substantial factor in the decision to terminate him." *Stanley v. City of Dalton*, 219 F.3d 1280, 1291 (11th Cir. 2000) (four-year gap between protected speech and termination) *quoting Beckwith v. City of Daytona Beach*, 58 F.3d 1554, 1567 (11th Cir. 1995) (fourteen-month lapse in time).

3.   What is the defendant's burden under the second prong of the *Mt. Healthy* test? How does a defendant prove that a legitimate reason would have motivated it to make the same employment decision? Can this ever be resolved as a matter of summary judgment? A comparison of two Eleventh Circuit opinions illustrates the fact-sensitive nature of these issues. In *Harris v. Shelby County Board of Education*, 99 F.3d 1078 (11th Cir. 1996) the plaintiff alleged that he had not been selected to become the principal of an Alabama high school because of race and the fact that he had engaged in protected speech. The plaintiff offered evidence that he commented to a newspaper that local schools were troubled by gangs and racial tensions. The woman who played a central role in selecting the principal admitted that she was "mad as hell" about the newspaper article and that the plaintiff was "too controversial" for the position. 99 F.3d at 1081. This evidence was deemed to satisfy the first element of the *Mt. Healthy* test. Despite this, however, the court of appeals held the school district was entitled to summary judgment. The court concluded that the defendant established as a matter of law that the same decision would have been made absent the protected speech. The uncontroverted facts cited by the court in support of this ruling were that the person chosen had nine years experience as a principal (the plaintiff had none), was certified for school administration (which the plaintiff was not), and had been named the Outstanding Secondary School Principal in Alabama and the President of the Alabama Association of Secondary School Principals. 99 F.3d at 1085–86.

In *Stanley v. City of Dalton*, 219 F.3d 1280 (11th Cir. 2000) a police officer sued the chief of police for wrongful termination in violation of his First Amendment rights. In 1993, the plaintiff told Georgia Bureau of Investigation (GBI) officials that he suspected that the defendant (who then was the deputy chief in charge of the evidence room) was the person responsible for the theft of money from the evidence room. The GBI never solved this case and did not identify anyone as responsible for the theft. The defendant later became the chief and, according to the plaintiff, soon began a series of retaliatory actions culminating in the termination of the plaintiff in 1997. The defendant claimed that the plaintiff was fired because of "unprofessional conduct in the presence of a subordinate with the use of profanity, failure to control his temper, and providing false statements in an internal investigation." 219 F.3d at 1284. The court of appeals ruled that the statements given to the GBI in 1993 were protected speech and a jury could find that this protected speech was a substantial motivating factor in the decision to terminate him. 219 F.3d at 1291. As to the second element of *Mt. Healthy*, the court of appeals could not say as a matter of law that the chief would have terminated the plaintiff absent the plaintiff's prior accusation of theft. The court observed that the facts underlying the alleged incidents of using profanity and loss of temper were contested and the alleged false statements concerned "whether he used profanity and lost his temper . . . rather than any form of criminal activity or sexual harassment of other employees." 219 F.3d at 1294 Thus, the evidence offered by the defendant in *Stanley* was deemed to be less persuasive than that presented in *Harris* to support summary judgment. *See also Trant v. State of Oklahoma*, 754 F.3d 1158 (10th Cir. 2014) (employer established that it would have terminated the plaintiff for insubordination and allegations of sexual harassment regardless of his protected speech).

Defendants are often found to have discharged their burden under *Mt. Healthy* when the person who disciplined the plaintiff is someone other than the official with the bad motive or when adverse decision is independently reviewed by someone "free of the taint of a biased subordinate employee." *Pennington v. City of Huntsville*, 261 F.3d 1262, 1270 (11th Cir. 2001). *Accord, Beattie v. Madison County School* Dist., 254 F.3d 595 (5th Cir. 2001); *Willis v. Marion County Auditor's Office*, 118 F.3d 542, 547 (7th Cir. 1997). *See* Michael L. Wells, *Section 1983, The First Amendment, and Public Employee Speech: Shaping the Right to Fit the Remedy (And Vice Versa)*, 35 GA. L. REV. 939, 969–971 (2001).

4. What other approaches might be taken to resolve the issue of causation in mixed motive cases? Consider various models that have developed in common law contexts.

(a) Motive is often a critical issue in the common law torts of intentional interference with contract, defamation, and malicious prosecution. Specifically, whether certain conduct is tortious or privileged may turn on the motive of the defendant. As in *Mt. Healthy*, the motive of the defendant is often disputed. Many courts apply a "dominant purpose" test in such cases. *E.g., Alyeska Pipeline Service Co. v. Aurora Air Service, Inc.*, 604 P.2d 1090 (Alaska 1979) (interference with contract); *Nodar v. Galbreath*, 462 So.2d 803 (Fla. 1984) (defamation); *Nesmith v. Alford*, 318 F.2d 110 (5th Cir. 1963) (malicious prosecution). *See generally* DAN B. DOBBS, THE LAW OF TORTS 1166 (2000) (common law privilege to publish otherwise defamatory statements will be lost if the "chief motivation" is "ill will, hostility, threats, or rivalry"); P. KEETON, D. DOBBS, R. KEETON, AND D. OWEN, PROSSER AND KEETON ON THE LAW OF TORTS 1094 (5th ed. 1984) ("It may be suggested that [with regard to interference with contract], as in the case of mixed motives in the exercise of a privilege in defamation and malicious prosecution, the court may well look to the predominant purpose underlying the defendant's conduct."); *Restatement (Second) of Torts* § 668 (1977) ("To subject a person to liability for malicious prosecution, the proceedings must have been initiated primarily for a purpose other than that of bringing an offender to justice.") How is a "dominant purpose" test similar to or different from that adopted by the Court in *Mt. Healthy*? Does either approach offer a tactical advantage to plaintiffs or defendants? Which approach, *Mt. Healthy* or a dominant purpose text, lends itself more to summary adjudication? *See* Michael Wells, *Three Arguments Against Mt. Healthy: Tort Theory, Constitutional Torts, and Freedom of Speech*, 51 MERCER L. REV. 583, 589 (2000).

(b) Could the mixed motive termination of Doyle be analogized to the concurrent sufficient causation cases in common law tort where two independently sufficient forces combine to produce an injury? The paradigm example of such a case is where two independent fires combine to destroy the plaintiff's property. Under prevailing common law principles, each fire would be considered a cause in fact of the injury. Thus, a railroad which negligently ignites one fire that combines with a second fire of independent origin and burns the plaintiff's property may be held liable for the resulting injury even if the second fire alone would have burned the plaintiff's property. *E.g., Anderson v. Minneapolis, St. Paul & Sault Ste. Marie Ry.*, 146 Minn. 430, 179 N.W. 45 (1920). *See generally Restatement (Third) of Torts* § 27 (2003). This common law rule developed as an exception to the but for test and is predicated on the belief that holding the wrongdoer responsible in such situations provides needed deterrence of future misconduct, vindicates the plaintiff's rights, and compensates the plaintiff for her injuries. *See* Carpenter, *Concurrent Causation*, 83 PA. L. REV. 941, 949–52 (1935). If a railroad can not escape common law tort liability by proving that the plaintiff's property would have burned just the same through other causes, why can the defendants escape constitutional tort liability in cases like *Mt. Healthy* by proving that plaintiff would have been terminated for legitimate reasons? Does *Mt. Healthy* provide less protection against invasions of constitutional rights than the common law provides for invasions of common law rights? If so, what policy considerations might explain this result?

Three of the authors of this casebook have favored the application of this common law approach to causation in the constitutional tort context. Thomas A. Eaton, *Causation in Constitutional Torts*, 67 IOWA L. REV. 443, 455–56 (1982); Michael Wells, *Three Arguments Against Mt. Healthy; Tort Theory, Constitutional Torts, and Freedom of Speech*, 51 MERCER L. REV. 583, 587–88 (2000); Sheldon Nahmod, *Mt. Healthy and Causation-in-Fact: The Court Still Doesn't Get It!*, 50 MERCER L. REV. 603, 614–15 (2000).

Although common law principles governing concurrent sufficient causation have not been adopted in mixed motive cases, they have been invoked in section 1983 cases in which more than one actor is responsible for the plaintiff's injury. In *Northington v. Marin*, 102 F.3d 1564 (10th Cir. 1996), Northington was assaulted by other inmates after Marin and other deputies spread rumors that Northington was a "snitch." Marin argued that causation was not established because "[h]ad Marin not spread the rumor, the statements of other deputies to inmates would have spread rapidly with the probable result that Northington would have been beaten." 102 F.3d at 1568. Thus, Marin's conduct could not be considered a but for cause of the beating. Both the district court and court of appeals rejected this argument drawing explicitly on the merging fire line of cases. "Here, two forces were actively operating to spread the rumor — Marin and the other deputies . . . the conduct of each . . . by itself was sufficient to cause Northington to be beaten . . . [t]herefore. . . . Marin and the other deputies were substantial factors in bringing about the harm to Northington, and thus were concurrent causes of the harm . . . Multiple tortfeasors who concurrently cause an indivisible injury are jointly and severally liable . . . . These [common law] rules apply in section 1983 actions." 102 F.3d at 1569. Why are common law principles of concurrent causation appropriate when the conduct of two actors combine to produce a constitutional injury, but these principles do not apply when a single actor has two motives? *But see Drumgold v. Callahan*, 707 F.3d 28 (1st Cir. 2013) (error to give concurrent causation instruction in section 1983 case based on prosecutor's withholding of material exculpatory evidence during a criminal trial; plaintiff must prove there was a reasonable probability that he would not have been convicted but for the wrongful withholding of the exculpatory evidence).

(c) Many states have embraced principles of proportional recovery through a variety of legal doctrines, including comparative fault, the modification of joint and several liability, market share liability, and allowing recovery for "loss of chance." *See generally*, Makdisi, *Proportional Liability: A Comprehensive Rule to Apportion Tort Damages Based on Probability*, 67 U.N.C. L. REV. 1063 (1989). Could these developments in the traditional tort context be adapted to mixed motive constitutional tort claims? If both constitutionally permissible and impermissible factors motivate a decision, should a claimant be allowed to recover a proportion of the resulting damages? In *Mt. Healthy*, could the fact finder rationally assign percentages to the extent that the protected speech and rude gestures contributed to the decision to not rehire Doyle?

In *Doll v. Brown*, 75 F.3d 1200, 1206 (7th Cir. 1996) Judge Posner suggested that the "lost chance" doctrine adopted by many states would be "peculiarly appropriate" in mixed-motive employment cases. But "[b]ecause of the novelty of the issue and the fact that it has not been briefed, we do not hold that the lost-chance theory is available in employment discrimination cases. We merely commend it to the consideration of bench and bar as a possible method of arriving at more just and equitable results in cases such as this." 75 F.3d at 1207. In what respect might a lost chance approach be seen as more just and equitable than the *Mt. Healthy* approach?

5.   As illustrated by the various common law doctrines described in the preceding note, legal standards for determining whether conduct causes injury are rife with policy choices. For a classic discussion of the role of policy in fashioning cause in fact doctrine in common law tort, *see* Malone, *Ruminations on Cause in Fact*, 9 STAN. L. REV. 60 (1956). To what extent do the *constitutional* underpinnings of most section 1983 claims affect the policy choices regarding causation standards? On the one hand, the fundamental nature of constitutional rights might support causation rules that greatly protect the civil liberties of individuals. On the other hand, constitutional rules are purposefully less susceptible to democratic modification than are common law rules. This characteristic of section 1983 litigation might counsel for principles of causation that better preserve legislative and executive discretion. Does *Mt. Healthy* strike an appropriate balance between the competing interests of the individual and government? *See* Thomas A. Eaton, *Causation in Constitutional Torts*, 67 IOWA L. REV. 443, 454–61 (1982).

6.   Suppose a government is actually motivated by racial discrimination in firing an employee, but later learns of a permissible ground for the decision. Should "after-acquired evidence" affect the defendant's liability under section 1983? *McKennon v. Nashville Banner Publishing Co.*, 513 U.S. 352 (1995). (No. Defendant-employer was improperly granted summary judgment in an age discrimination case when after-acquired evidence of violations of work rules provided a legitimate basis for firing a 62-year-old secretary). Are after-acquired evidence cases different from mixed motive cases? Do the same policy considerations that support the second part of the *Mt. Healthy* test apply with equal force when the legitimate reason was not an actual motivating factor at the time of the decision? For a thorough analysis of these issues, *see* Rebecca White and Robert Brussack, *The Proper Role of After-Acquired Evidence in Employment Discrimination Litigation*, 35 B.C. L. Rev. 49 (1993).

TEXAS v. LESAGE
528 U.S. 18 (1999)

Per Curiam.

Respondent Francois Daniel Lesage, an African immigrant of Caucasian descent, applied for admission to the Ph.D. program in counseling psychology at the University of Texas' Department of Education for the 1996–1997 academic year. In the year Lesage applied, the school received 223 applications for the program and offered admission to roughly 20 candidates. It is undisputed that the school considered the race of its applicants at some stage during the review process. The school rejected Lesage's application and offered admission to at least one minority candidate. Lesage filed suit seeking money damages and injunctive relief. He alleged that, by establishing and maintaining a race-conscious admissions process, the school had violated the Equal Protection Clause of the Fourteenth Amendment and § 1977, 42 U.S.C. § 1981, 42 U.S.C. § 1983 and 42 U.S.C. § 2000d.

Petitioners sought summary judgment, offering evidence that, even if the school's admissions process had been completely colorblind, Lesage would not have been admitted. At least 80 applicants had higher undergraduate grade point averages (GPA's) than Lesage, 152 applicants had higher Graduate Record Examination (GRE) scores, and 73 applicants had both higher GPA's and higher GRE scores. In an affidavit, Professor Ricardo Ainslie, one of two members of the school's admissions committee, stated that Lesage's personal statement indicated that he had " 'a rather superficial interest in the field with a limited capacity to convey his interests and ideas,' "and that his letters of recommendation were "weak." Ainslie stated that Lesage's application was rejected early in the review process, when the committee was winnowing the full application pool to a list of 40. The District Court concluded that "any consideration of race had no effect on this particular individual's rejection," and that there was "uncontested evidence that the students ultimately admitted to the program ha[d] credentials that the committee considered superior to Plaintiff's." It therefore granted summary judgment for petitioners with respect to all of Lesage's claims for relief.

The Court of Appeals for the Fifth Circuit reversed. The court did not review the District Court's conclusion that there was no genuine issue as to whether the school would have rejected Lesage under a colorblind admissions process. Instead, it held that such a determination was "irrelevant to the pertinent issue on summary judgment, namely, whether the state violated Lesage's constitutional rights by rejecting his application in the course of operating a racially discriminatory admissions program." An applicant who was rejected at a stage of the review process that was race conscious, the court reasoned, has "suffered an implied injury" — the inability to compete on an equal footing. Because there remained a factual dispute as to whether the stage of review during which Lesage's application was eliminated was in some way race conscious, the court held that summary judgment was inappropriate and remanded the case for trial.

Insofar as the Court of Appeals held that summary judgment was inappropriate on Lesage's § 1983 action seeking damages for the school's rejection of his application for the 1996–1997 academic year even if petitioners conclusively established that Lesage would have been rejected under a race-neutral policy, its decision is inconsistent with this Court's well-established framework for analyzing such claims. Under *Mt. Healthy City Bd. of Ed. v. Doyle*, even if the government has considered an impermissible criterion in making a decision adverse to the plaintiff, it can nonetheless defeat liability by demonstrating that it would have made the same decision absent the forbidden consideration. Our previous decisions on this point have typically involved alleged retaliation for protected First Amendment activity rather than racial discrimination, but that distinction is immaterial. The underlying principle is the same: The government can avoid liability by proving that it would have made the same decision without the impermissible motive.

Simply put, where a plaintiff challenges a discrete governmental decision as being based on an impermissible criterion and it is undisputed that the government would have made the same decision regardless, there is no cognizable injury warranting relief under § 1983.

Of course, a plaintiff who challenges an ongoing race-conscious program and seeks forward-looking relief need not affirmatively establish that he would receive the benefit in question if race were not considered. The relevant injury in such cases is "the inability to compete on an equal footing." But where there is no allegation of an ongoing or imminent constitutional violation to support a claim for forward-looking relief, the government's conclusive demonstration that it would have made the same decision absent the alleged discrimination precludes any finding of liability.

[The Court stated that it appeared that Lesage had abandoned his claim for injunctive relief.]

Insofar as the Court of Appeals held that petitioners were not entitled to summary judgment on Lesage's § 1983 claim for damages relating to the rejection of his application for the 1996–1997 academic year even if he would have been denied admission under a race-neutral policy, its decision contradicts our holding in *Mt. Healthy*. We therefore grant the petition for writ of certiorari and reverse the judgment of the Court of Appeals in this respect.

Lesage also asserted claims under 42 U.S.C. §§ 1981 and 2000d. Whether these claims remain, and whether Lesage has abandoned his claim for injunctive relief on the ground that petitioners are continuing to operate a discriminatory admissions process, are matters open on remand. The case is remanded for further proceedings consistent with this opinion.

It is so ordered.

NOTES

1. Given the procedural posture of the case, the lower courts and the Supreme Court merely *assumed* that the Texas admissions policy was unconstitutional. The constitutionality of university affirmative action admissions policies would now be evaluated under the cases of *Fisher v. University of Texas*, 133 S. Ct. 2411 (2013); *Gratz v. Bollinger*, 539 U.S. 244 (2003); and *Grutter v. Bollinger*, 539 U.S. 306 (2003).

2. Lesage argued that the race-conscious admissions policy violated his rights under the equal protection clause of the Fourteenth Amendment. The Court states that if his application would have been denied under a race-neutral admissions policy, Lesage suffered no "cognizable injury" to support an award of damages under Section 1983. Yet, it also states that for purposes of securing injunctive relief, the "relevant injury" is "the inability to compete on an equal footing." Why isn't the "the inability to compete on an equal footing" a sufficient injury to support an award of at least nominal damages and perhaps damages for emotional distress?

In *Carey v. Piphus*, 435 U.S. 247 (1978) a high school student was suspended without a hearing in violation of his right to procedural due process. The Court ruled that the plaintiff could not recover damages to compensate him for the injuries *resulting from the suspension* if he would have been suspended even if a proper hearing had been held. The plaintiff could, however, recover nominal damages and damages for any proven emotional distress *caused by the denial of procedural due process itself. See* Chapter 9. *Carey* acknowledged that the denial of procedural due process could produce "strong feelings of mental and emotional distress in the individual who is denied this 'feeling of just treatment' " even if the ultimate decision is justified. 435 U.S. at 261. Would the same rationale apply to plaintiffs like Lesage? Is it plausible that Lesage felt emotional distress by the state-imposed "the inability to compete on an equal footing," even if he would have been denied admission under a color blind policy? Is there any way to reconcile *Carey* with *Lesage*? Why can a student who would have been suspended recover nominal damages and be given the chance to prove emotional distress, but an applicant denied admission under a racially discriminatory process cannot?

For an argument that *Lesage* in inconsistent with *Carey* and favoring the *Carey* approach *see* Sheldon Nahmod, Mt. Healthy *and Causation-in-Fact: The Court Still Doesn't Get It!*, 51 MERCER L. REV. 603, 611–12 (2000). Professor Whitman writes that *Lesage* "suggests that the Court may be rethinking (or ignoring) its promise in *Carey v. Piphus* that section 1983 plaintiffs can recover nominal damages and, when actual injury can be established, damages for mental and emotional distress." Christiana B. Whitman, *An Essay on* Texas v. Lesage, 51 MERCER L. REV. 621 (2000). However, others warn that too much should not be read into a "cryptic opinion" that was reached "without briefing or oral argument." HAROLD S. LEWIS, JR. AND ELIZABETH J. NORMAN, CIVIL RIGHTS LAW AND PRACTICE § 2.26 (2d ed. 2004).

3. Does the "no cognizable injury" language of *Lesage* mean that the plaintiff has no standing to recover damages under Article III? Although the opinion does not specifically mention standing, several lower courts have construed *Lesage* in those terms. *E.g., Cotter v. City of Boston*, 323 F.3d 160, 194–85 (1st Cir. 2003) (white police officers who would not have been promoted if race-neutral criteria had been used do not have standing to recover damages); *Aiken v. Hackett*, 281 F.3d 516, 519 (6th Cir. 2002) (same). *Cf. Wooden v. Bd. of Regents*, 247 F.3d 1262, 1277–81 (11th Cir. 2001) (plaintiff whose application was denied under a racially discriminatory admissions policy has standing to challenge that policy even though race was not a factor at the stage at which he was denied admission). *See also* RONALD D. ROTUNDA AND JOHN E. NOWAK, TREATISE ON CONSTITUTIONAL LAW § 2.13(f) (4th ed. 2007) (*Lesage* characterized as a case dealing with standing under Article III).

If the "no cognizable injury" language of *Lesage* addresses Article III standing to recover damages, does the "the inability to compete on an equal footing" pertain to standing to secure injunctive relief? At least one court has explicitly so held. *See Donahue v. City of Boston*, 304 F.3d 110, 118 (1st Cir. 2002) (*Lesage* is a "clear cue" from the Supreme Court that courts cannot apply identical standing analyses to claims for damages and claims for prospective relief; the "equal footing" analysis of *Lesage* applies only to injunctive relief). For a contrary view *see* Sheldon Nahmod, Mt. Healthy *and Causation-in-Fact: The Court Still Doesn't Get It!*, 51 MERCER L. REV. 603, 617 (2000) (arguing that *Lesage* should not be read as a "standing" case because the "Court never even hinted that *Mt. Healthy*'s burden shift raises standing issues.")

4.   Under what circumstances might claimants who cannot establish a cognizable injury to support a claim for damages nonetheless be entitled to injunctive relief? The leading Supreme Court decision on the use of prospective relief under Section 1983 is *City of Los Angeles v. Lyons*, 461 U.S. 95 (1983) and is considered in detail in Chapter 9. Under *Lyons*, injunctive relief will be denied when the plaintiff fails to prove that the defendants unconstitutional conduct is producing an on-going harm or is likely to cause future harm to the plaintiff. The requirement of probable future injury often leads to a denial of injunctive relief when the plaintiff's encounter with the challenged conduct is random or discrete. *E.g., City of Los Angeles v. Lyons*, 461 U.S. 95 (1983) (plaintiff challenging city policy on use of "chokeholds" by police was not entitled to injunction when it was not proven that plaintiff would encounter police in the future); *Johnson v. Bd. of Regents*, 263 F.3d 1234, 1266–68 (11th Cir. 2001) (plaintiffs challenging university affirmative action admissions policy are not entitled to injunctive relief when they would not reapply to the University and be subject to the challenged policy in the future). *Cf., Smith v. University of Washington*, 233 F.3d 1188 (9th Cir. 2000) (request for injunctive relief is moot when the challenged affirmative action admission policy was discontinued following passage of state initiative). *Morrison v. Garraghty*, 239 F.3d 648 (4th Cir. 2001) illustrates the circumstances when injunctive relief is appropriate. The plaintiff was an African-American inmate who sought Native American religious articles. Prison policy prohibited the receipt of such articles by inmates other than Native Americans. The court found that this policy discriminated on the basis of race. Given the length of the plaintiff's sentence, the racially discriminatory policy constituted an on-going violation of his constitutional rights warranting the issuing of an injunction.

B. Governmental and Supervisory Liability

Chapter Five addressed issues pertaining to the liability of governmental entities and supervisory personnel for the constitutional violations committed by others. A brief review of those materials may help set the stage for considering the issue of causation in that context. In *Monell v. Department of Social Services*, 436 U.S. 658 (1978), the court held that cities were "persons" that could be sued under section 1983, but that liability could not be based on principles of respondeat superior. The latter ruling was grounded in the "subjects, or causes to be subjected" language of the statute. The court viewed principles of vicarious liability as inconsistent with the requirement of causation set forth in section 1983. *Monell*, 436 U.S. at 691. Instead, plaintiffs must prove that governmental policy or custom was "the moving force" behind the unconstitutional conduct of municipal employees. *Monell*, 436 U.S. at 694. A plurality of the court later emphasized that "[a]t the very least, there must be an affirmative link between the policy and the particular constitutional violation alleged." *City of Oklahoma City v. Tuttle*, 471 U.S. 808, 823 (1985).

Phrases like "moving force" and "affirmative link" provide little concrete guidance as to how to evaluate the causal relationship between governmental policy and a violation of constitutional rights. The court elaborated on this issue in *City of Canton v. Harris*, 489 U.S. 378 (1989). The plaintiff alleged that she was denied her rights under the due process clause of the Fourteenth Amendment to medical care while in police custody. The city's liability was based on its alleged failure to train the police force. After ruling that inadequate training could be considered a "policy," the court addressed the issue of causation.

> Moreover, for liability to attach in this circumstance the identified deficiency in a city's training program must be closely related to the ultimate injury. Thus, in the case at hand, respondent must still prove that the deficiency in training actually caused the police officers' indifference to her medical needs. Would the injury have been avoided had the employee been trained under a program that was not deficient in the identified respect? Predicting how a hypothetically well-trained officer would have acted under the circumstances may not be an easy task for the factfinder, particularly since matters of judgment may be involved, and since officers who are well trained are not free from error and perhaps might react very much like the untrained officer in similar circumstances. But judge and jury, doing their respective jobs, will be adequate to the task.

City of Canton, 489 U.S. at 391.

In *Board of the County Commissioners of Bryan County v. Brown*, 520 U.S. 1283 (1997) the Court again addressed the relationship between governmental policy and causation. As you will recall from Chapter 5, the central claim in *Brown* was that the county, through its policymaker, the sheriff, was deliberately indifferent in the hiring of a deputy with a prior arrest record who later inflicted excessive force upon the plaintiff. The Court held the county was not liable, warning that "[c]ases involving constitutional injuries allegedly traceable to an ill-considered hiring decision pose the greatest risk that a municipality will be held liable for an injury that it did not cause. In the broadest sense, every injury is traceable to a hiring decision." 520 U.S. at 1393–94. Courts must apply "rigorous requirements of culpability and causation" to prevent a de facto "collapse into *respondeat superior* liability." 520 U.S. at 1394.

Supervisors also are not vicariously liable for the unconstitutional actions of the police officers, prison guards or others whom they supervise. *E.g., Rizzo v. Goode*, 423 U.S. 362, 376 (1976) (supervisory liability requires a showing of "direct responsibility" for the unconstitutional actions of subordinates). Yet prior to *Ashcroft v. Iqbal*, 556 U.S. 662 (2009), lower courts routinely upheld liability when a supervisor was shown to have been deliberately indifferent to the risk that a subordinate would violate the plaintiff's constitutional rights. *E.g., Larez v. City of Los Angeles*, 946 F.2d 630 (9th Cir. 1991) (police chief held liable for use of excessive force by police officers); *Baynard v. Malone*, 268 F.3d 228 (4th Cir. 2001) (school principal held liable for sexual molestation by teacher). *See generally* Kit Kinports, *The Buck Does Not Stop Here: Supervisory Liability in Section 1983*, 1997 U. Ill. L. Rev. 147 (1997). The continued vitality of supervisory liability has been called into question by *Ashcroft v. Iqbal*, 556 U.S. 662 (2009) ("In a *§ 1983* suit or a *Bivens* action — where masters do not answer for the torts of their servants — the term "supervisory liability" is a misnomer. Absent vicarious liability, each Government official, his or her title notwithstanding, is only liable for his or her own misconduct."). After *Iqbal*, there appears to be confusion, sometimes within the same circuit, about the contours of supervisory liability. *Compare Starr v. Baca*, 652 F.3d 1202, 1207 (9th Cir. 2011) ("We see nothing in *Iqbal* indicating that the Supreme Court intended to overturn longstanding case law on deliberate indifferent claims against supervisors . . .") *with OSU Student Alliance v. Ray*, 699 F.3d 1053, 1073 n. 15 (9th Cir. 2012) ("We understand *Iqbal*'s language eliminating the doctrine of supervisory liability to overrule circuit law that . . . had applied a uniform test of supervisory liability across the spectrum of constitutional claims."). *See generally* Kit Kinports, Iqbal *and Constitutional Torts:* Iqbal *and Supervisory Liability*, 114 Penn St. L. Rev. 1291 (2010). To the extent that a supervisor my be held liable when he knows of and acquiesces in a subordinates' unconstitutional action, there still must be a causal connection between the deliberately indifferent supervision and the conduct of the subordinate.

How is a factfinder to determine whether a city's policy or a supervisor's conduct caused someone to violate another's constitutional rights? The following case illustrates how lower courts address this issue of causation in the context of governmental liability.

ALLEN v. MUSKOGEE
119 F.3d 837 (10th Cir. 1997)

Paul Kelly, Jr. Circuit Judge.

On the morning of February 20, 1994, Terry Allen left his home after an altercation with his wife and children. He took ammunition and several guns with him, and later parked in front of the Muskogee residence of his sister, Rhonda Lee-Oakley. The altercation was reported to the Wagoner County Sheriff's Department, which sent a teletype to the Muskogee Police Department (MPD), describing Mr. Allen and his car and advising that Mr. Allen was armed and had threatened family members. The teletype also advised that there was a 1983 warrant outstanding for Mr. Allen's arrest for impersonating an officer. Lt. Donald Smith of the MPD relayed the information to other officers during a squad meeting at 1:30 p.m.

Some time after the meeting, Lt. Smith was advised that Mr. Allen might be at his sister's house in Muskogee. Before he could meet with other officers, a radio dispatcher advised him that a 911 call had been made from Ms. Oakley's home and that Mr. Allen was threatening suicide. Lt. Smith proceeded to the Oakley home, approached the bystanders who were standing near Mr. Allen's vehicle, and ordered them to step back, which they did. Mr. Allen was sitting in the driver's seat with one foot out of the vehicle. He had a gun in his right hand, which was resting on the console between the seats.

As Lt. Smith repeatedly told Mr. Allen to drop his gun, Officer Bentley McDonald arrived and joined Lt. Smith at the driver's side door. Lt. Smith then reached into the vehicle and attempted to seize Mr. Allen's gun, while Officer Bentley held Mr. Allen's left arm. Officer Bryan Farmer, who arrived with Officer Bentley, approached Mr. Allen's car from the passenger side, and attempted to open a passenger side door. Mr. Allen reacted by pointing the gun toward Officer Farmer, who ducked and moved behind the car. Mr. Allen then swung the gun toward Lt. Smith and Officer McDonald, and shots were exchanged. Lt. Smith and Officer McDonald fired a total of twelve rounds into the vehicle, striking Mr. Allen four times. The entire sequence, from the time Lt. Smith arrived to the time Mr. Allen was killed, lasted approximately ninety seconds.

Plaintiff brought this § 1983 claim against the officers involved and against the City of Muskogee. Defendants subsequently moved for summary judgment, and set forth a statement of facts in their brief supporting the motion. In her response, Plaintiff did not dispute Defendants' statement of facts. The district court granted Defendants' motion, holding that there was no genuine issue of material fact and that Defendants were entitled to judgment as a matter of law.

I. The Individual Officers

We analyze a § 1983 claim of excessive force by determining whether the officers' actions were objectively reasonable in light of the surrounding facts and circumstances. *Graham v. Connor*, 490 U.S. 386, 397. The district court found no genuine issues of material fact, and held that the officers acted in an objectively reasonable way. We conclude, however, that the individual Defendants failed to carry their initial burden of demonstrating the absence of a genuine issue of material fact. . . .

The Defendants have not shown that there is a lack of a genuine issue of material fact with regard to the officers' reasonableness. Indeed, it seems to us that Defendants have pointed out the presence of a genuine issue. Defendants acknowledged before the district court that there are differences among the eyewitness depositions. For example, some deposition testimony indicates that Lt. Smith ran "screaming" up to Mr. Allen's car and immediately began shouting at Mr. Allen to get out of his car; other testimony indicates that Lt. Smith approached cautiously and tried talking Mr. Allen into giving up the gun.

. . . The entire incident, from the time Lt. Smith arrived to the time of the shooting, took only ninety seconds. Clearly, the officers' preceding actions were so "immediately connected" to Mr. Allen's threat of force that they should be included in the reasonableness inquiry. The differences in eyewitness testimony regarding the officers' approach are therefore material factual disputes.

The disputes are not only material, but they are also genuine. . . . While we express no opinion on the merits, a reasonable jury could conclude on the basis of some of the testimony presented that the officers' actions were reckless and precipitated the need to use deadly force.

II. The City of Muskogee

The plaintiff also claimed the City of Muskogee was liable under 42 U.S.C. § 1983 for inadequate training of the individually-sued police officers. After the district court determined the individual officers committed no constitutional violation, the court granted summary judgment to the City, reasoning that municipal liability requires a constitutional violation by the officers. Even assuming the court correctly interpreted that law of municipal liability, a question we need not and do not resolve, the court erred in entering summary judgment on that ground because we have concluded plaintiff presented sufficient evidence that the officers committed a constitutional violation to withstand a summary judgment motion. We review the propriety of summary judgment for the City de novo and find sufficient support for plaintiff's claim against the City to withstand summary judgment. . . .

"[T]he inadequacy of police training may serve as a basis for § 1983 liability only where the failure to train amounts to deliberate indifference to the rights of persons with whom the police come into contact." *City of Canton v. Harris*, 489 U.S. 378, 388, To establish a city's liability under 42 U.S.C. § 1983 for inadequate training of police officers in the use of force, a plaintiff must show (1) the officers exceeded constitutional limitations on the use of force; (2) the use of force arose under circumstances that constitute a usual and recurring situation with which police officers must deal; (3) the inadequate training demonstrates a deliberate indifference on the part of the city toward persons with whom the police officers come into contact, and (4) there is a direct causal link between the constitutional deprivation and the inadequate training. As regards the second and third requirements, a showing of specific incidents which establish a pattern of constitutional violations is not necessary to put the City on notice that its training program is inadequate. Rather, evidence of a single violation of federal rights, accompanied by a showing that a municipality has failed to train its employees to handle recurring situations presenting an obvious potential for such a violation, is sufficient to trigger municipal liability. *See Board of County Com'rs v. Brown*, 520 U.S. 397 (1997).

The first requirement is satisfied here because, as concluded in Section I of this opinion, there was evidence in the record to support the claim that the officers exceeded constitutional limitations on the use of force. As regards the second requirement, exhibits presented to the district court contained evidence that it was common for officers to have to deal with mentally ill or emotionally disturbed people and people under the influence of drugs or alcohol. Nor is it uncommon for officers to have to deal with persons armed with deadly weapons. Thus, there was evidence that the use of force arose under circumstances that constituted a usual and recurring situation with which police officers must deal.

The third requirement is also satisfied. The record supports an inference that the training demonstrates a deliberate indifference on the part of the City toward people with whom the police come into contact. . . .

There was evidence presented to the district court that the officers received inadequate training on how to deal with mentally ill or emotionally upset persons who are armed with firearms. Plaintiff relied principally on her expert witness, Dr. George Kirkham, a former police officer and college professor and now a consultant on police and security matters. The record does not show that defendants challenged Dr. Kirkham's qualifications as an expert on police tactics and procedures.

Dr. Kirkham testified in his deposition that the officers' actions were reckless and totally contrary to proper police practices for dealing with armed mentally ill or emotionally upset persons. According to Dr. Kirkham, all authorities on police tactics and procedures, in both the law enforcement and expert witness communities, agree it is not appropriate to leave cover and approach a suicidal armed person to try to take away a gun. Such action is likely to provoke a violent response, resulting in a high risk of death to officers, the armed person, and other civilians. Dr. Kirkham stated the proper procedure would have been for the officers to take cover behind their police cars, to ask the people standing by Allen's car to come toward them in order to get them out of harm's way and to obtain information, and then to try to communicate with Allen from a safe position without doing anything aggressive that could provoke a violent response.

In Dr. Kirkham's opinion, there were only two possibilities that could give rise to the present incident — either the officers failed to follow their training or they were improperly trained. Lieutenant Brook, the Muskogee Police Department training coordinator from 1984 to 1993, testified the officers acted in accordance with their training in approaching the car and trying to take away the gun. Relying principally on this testimony, Dr. Kirkham concluded the officers' training was inadequate. Dr. Kirkham was also aware that Lieutenant Smith testified he acted in accordance with his police training. Moreover, the affidavit of Glen McIntyre, the state firearms training coordinator, stated the officers followed their training. The evidence supports an inference that the City trained its officers to leave cover and approach armed suicidal persons to try to disarm them.

Dr. Kirkham was highly critical of the officers' training:

> I don't believe you'll find any reputable expert in the United States, no one that I know of, that could possibly take the position in contradiction of virtually every piece of training material that I have ever seen that says you handle it in this way. These are such well established principles. I don't think a reputable specialist could say, "Hey, yeah. You walkup to the

situation, stand in the open, keep trying to grab the gun." It is just reckless behavior.

He stated if the officers were trained to respond to this kind of call by staying in the open, leaving innocent people in the open, and doing provocative things like trying to grab the gun and get into the car, the training was "out of synch with the entire United States in terms of what police are being trained to do."

> To my knowledge, I'm not aware of any significant debate in the law enforcement or expert witness community about the fundamental principles we're talking about here. Cover is better than no cover. Communicating from a safe distance is better than not. Getting innocent people as safely out of the way as possible is desirable. Not engaging in certain actions with mentally disturbed armed people, not getting close to them is preferable.

> I've never heard any knowledgeable debate or argument about any of those subjects in the 25 years I've been doing this type of work.

Referring to the training provided the officers through a state program, Dr. Kirkham stated:

> If the State of Oklahoma through CLEET trains their officers to not be mindful of cover, to be aggressive with mentally ill people, do all these things that are totally off the board, then the State is wrong and out of synch with the rest of the country in the police profession.

When read as a whole and viewed in the light most favorable to the plaintiff as the party opposing summary judgment, the record supports an inference that the City trained its officers to leave cover and approach armed suicidal, emotionally disturbed persons and to try to disarm them, a practice contrary to proper police procedures and tactical principles.

The testimony of Lieutenant Brook and Lieutenant Smith and the affidavit of Glen McIntyre support an inference that the content of the training was inadequate. The City points to evidence that the officers completed many hours of training, including training on use of deadly force and dealing with upset or mentally disturbed people, but that cannot rebut the inference that the training was inadequate because it does not address the content of that training.

Relying on *Evers v. General Motors Corp.*, 770 F.2d 984 (11th Cir.1985), the City argues Kirkham's deposition must be disregarded as insufficient to raise genuine issues of material fact regarding the adequacy of the training. In *Evers*, the court held a four-paragraph affidavit by plaintiff's expert witness was insufficient to create genuine issues of material fact because its conclusory allegations were not based on specific facts. Dr. Kirkham's deposition is not comparable to the brief conclusory affidavit in *Evers*. The deposition is over 300 pages in length and Dr. Kirkham's opinion was based on specific facts in the record. His extensive and detailed testimony shows that although he may not have read all relevant documents, he was very familiar with the circumstances of the incident.

Dr. Kirkham characterized the officers' actions in this case as diametrically opposed to proper police procedures, out of synch with the rest of the police profession, and "plain foolishness." Because there was evidence that the officers acted in accordance with their training, his criticism also applied to their training. When viewed in the light most favorable to the plaintiff, the record contains evidence that the officers were trained to act recklessly in a manner that created a high risk of death. The evidence is sufficient to support an inference that the need for different training was so obvious and the inadequacy so likely to result in violation of constitutional rights that the policymakers of the City could reasonably be said to have been deliberately indifferent to the need.[1]

[As regards the fourth requirement, there was evidence of a direct causal link between the training and the alleged constitutional deprivation.] According to Dr. Kirkham, approaching and trying to grab a gun from an emotionally disturbed, suicidal person created a high risk of death for officers, the armed person, and other civilians, and was reckless. There was evidence the officers were trained to act in such manner and, thus, were trained to do precisely the wrong thing. The causal link between the officers' training and the alleged constitutional deprivation is more direct than in cases in which officers are not given enough training to know the correct response to a dangerous situation. Dr. Kirkham attributed the incident to improper training, stating: "[I]f police trainers in the State of Oklahoma are using this case as an example of how you properly handle a mentally ill individual, then police officers will assuredly die, and other mentally ill people and probably innocent people will die." It was his opinion that if the officers had been properly trained in the fundamental principles of maintaining a covered position and trying to communicate with armed emotionally upset persons rather than approaching and physically attempting to disarm them, the incident would not have happened.

Because there was evidence supporting each of the requirements of *Canton*, as explained in *Zuchel*, the district court erred in entering summary judgment in favor of the City. *City of Oklahoma City v. Tuttle*, 471 U.S. 808, 105 S.Ct. 2427, 85 L.Ed.2d 791 (1985), does not require a different conclusion. In *Tuttle*, the Court held it was error to instruct a jury it could infer from a single incident of unusually excessive force that the constitutional violation was attributable to a city policy of inadequate training or supervision. Here, plaintiff does not rely solely on proof of the single incident to support an inference that the incident was caused by inadequate training and that the inadequate training was city policy. She relies on evidence that the officers followed police training in recklessly rushing Allen's car and trying to disarm him. *Tuttle* and *Canton* do not require evidence of more than one incident to establish a policy of inadequate training and that the training caused the constitutional deprivation. These cases simply require evidence in addition to the occurrence of a single incident. [A plaintiff can properly rely on the single incident if there is other evidence of inadequate training.] By providing direct evidence of inadequate training, as discussed above, plaintiff provided sufficient evidence beyond the occurrence of the single incident to withstand summary judgment.

Nor does *Brown*, 520 U.S. 397, require a different result. The case before us is within the "narrow range of circumstances" recognized by *Canton* and left intact by

---

[1] [1] There is no contention that the training given the officers was anything other than official city policy and Lieutenant Brook's testimony that the officers followed their training in handling the incident tends to show it was official policy. He was the training coordinator from 1984 to 1993.

Brown, under which a single violation of federal rights may be a highly predictable consequence of failure to train officers to handle recurring situations with an obvious potential for such a violation. The likelihood that officers will frequently have to deal with armed emotionally upset persons, and the predictability that officers trained to leave cover, approach, and attempt to disarm such persons will provoke a violent response, could justify a finding that the City's failure to properly train its officers reflected deliberate indifference to the obvious consequence of the City's choice. The likelihood of a violent response to this type of police action also may support an inference of causation — that the City's indifference led directly to the very consequence that was so predictable.

Reversed and Remanded.

KELLY, CIRCUIT JUDGE, dissenting in part.

I respectfully dissent from Section II of the court's opinion. . . .

The court views this case as one in which "evidence of a single violation of federal rights, accompanied by a showing that a municipality has failed to train its employees to handle recurring situations presenting an obvious potential for such a violation . . . trigger[s] municipal liability." Although sufficient evidence of a single violation of federal rights exists, Ms. Allen has not made any showing — much less a sufficient showing — of an inadequate policy, nor is there proof that the allegedly inadequate policy presented such an "obvious potential" for constitutional harm that liability can or should be triggered.

The evidence is insufficient to establish the inadequacy of Muskogee's training because absolutely no evidence exists regarding the content of Muskogee's training. . . . Ms. Allen does not dispute that the Muskogee training exceeds Oklahoma's requirements for law enforcement training. In fact, the only evidence on the content of Muskogee's training at all are affidavits of two law enforcement officials that the individual officers acted in accord with that training. Ms. Allen's expert, Dr. Kirkham, stated that because the officers' actions were, in his opinion, contrary to proper police practices, and because two law enforcement officials stated that the officers acted in accord with their training, then Muskogee's training must have been inadequate. Dr. Kirkham admitted, however, that he had not read either Muskogee's or Oklahoma's training materials. The court emphasizes that this evidence supports an "inference" that the City of Muskogee inadequately trained its police officers. Although we must draw all factual inferences in favor of the nonmovant, those inferences must be reasonable. Dr. Kirkham's testimony, grounded in speculation, may raise an inference that Muskogee inadequately trained its officers, but it is not sufficient to withstand summary judgment. Rather, this inference, if it can be so called, constitutes, at best, a "mere scintilla" of evidence, on which a judgment in favor of the nonmovant cannot be upheld.

Even assuming that Ms. Allen has put forward sufficient evidence of inadequate training, that is still not enough under the circumstances. The evidence is not even close to establishing the kind of inadequate training that is "so obvious, and . . . so likely to result in the violation of constitutional rights, that the policymakers of the city can reasonably be said to have been deliberately indifferent to the need." *Canton*, 489 U.S. at 390. In most cases, plaintiffs meet this standard by demonstrating that a pattern of constitutional violations has put the municipality on notice that its training is inadequate, and that the municipality's continued adherence to its training thus constitutes deliberate indifference. In this case, however, there is no allegation that previous similar incidents had put the City of Muskogee on notice that its training was inadequate.

Given that there was no evidence before the court regarding the content of Muskogee's training, any deliberate indifference exhibited by Muskogee is pure speculation and conjecture. I do not believe there exists any evidence tending to place Plaintiff's case within the "narrow range of circumstances" in which liability may attach without any pattern of past constitutional violations. Ms. Allen has failed to make a showing sufficient to establish an element on which she would bear the burden of proof at trial. Accordingly, I would affirm as to the City of Muskogee.

NOTES

1. The rejection of principles of vicarious liability in *Monell v. Department of Social Services*, 436 U.S. 658 (1978), requires courts to determine whether a governmental policy or custom causes another person to deprive the plaintiff of a constitutional right. The causal relationship between municipal policy and the unconstitutional acts of employees is most easily found where the alleged constitutional violation follows from the implementation of an official policy which itself is unconstitutional. For example, the plaintiff in *Monell* challenged the constitutionality of the city's policy of compelling pregnant employees to take unpaid leaves of absences before such leaves were required for medical reasons. Once the compulsory maternity leave policy is found to be unconstitutional, the causal connection between that policy and the violation of the plaintiff's constitutional rights is apparent. *See also, Christensen v. Park City Municipal Corp.*, 554 P.3d 1271 (10th Cir. 2009) ("If a governmental entity makes and enforces a law that is unconstitutional as applied, it may be subject to liability under § 1983."). As noted by Professor Kritchevsky,

> [w]hen an unconstitutional policy is proved, courts generally assume that the policy alone caused the injury. The courts assume that the violation of the plaintiff's constitutional rights occurred because the state actor was following a municipal policy, and not because of any improper personal motive.

Kritchevsky, *"Or Causes to Be Subjected": The Role of Causation in Section 1983 Municipal Liability Analysis*, 35 U.C.L.A. L. Rev. 1187, 1208 (1988).

2. "Failure to train" cases like *Allen*, present more difficult causation issues. Recall that the Supreme Court in *City of Canton* framed the causation issue in terms of a "but for" test ("Would the injury have been avoided had the employee been trained under a program that was not deficient in the identified respect?", 489 U.S. at 391 (1989)). In the context of common law torts, commentators have long recognized the inherent uncertainty in the hypothetical nature of the but for test. *E.g.*, Leon Green, *The Causal Relation Issue in Negligence Law*, 60 Mich. L. Rev.

543 (1962); Thode, *The Indefensible Use of the Hypothetical Case to Determine Cause in Fact*, 46 TEX. L. REV. 423 (1968); Strassfeld, *If. . . : Counterfactuals in the Law*, 60 GEO. WASH. L. REV. 340 (1992). This uncertainty is heightened when causal question concerns the effect of a hypothetical change in the defendant's policy on the actions or inactions of third parties. How is a jury to determine how a police officer would have acted if trained differently? The Court in *City of Canton* acknowledged that "predicting how a hypothetically well-trained officer would have acted under the circumstances may not be an easy task for the factfinder," but expressed confidence the "judge and jury, doing their respective jobs, will be adequate to the task." *City of Canton*, 489 U.S. at 391. What are the respective jobs of judge and jury?

3.   Some decisions allow juries considerable leeway in assessing the causal connection between municipal training and supervision policies and police misconduct. *See Gentile v. County of Suffolk*, 926 F.2d 142, 152 (2d Cir. 1991) (plaintiff need not prove that individual defendants knew of and acted on county's policy not to discipline police and prosecutors for misconduct; the jury could "reasonably infer" causation from proof of policy and custom); *Bielevicz v. Dubinon*, 915 F.2d 845, 851 (3d Cir. 1990) (jury could find that plaintiffs' arrests were caused by a municipal custom of tolerating arrests for public intoxication without probable cause; "[a]s long as the causal link is not too tenuous, the question whether the municipal policy or custom proximately caused the constitutional infringement should be left to the jury."); *Bordanaro v. McLeod*, 871 F.2d 1151 (1st Cir. 1989) (custom of breaking down doors without a warrant to arrest suspected felons created risk of Fourth Amendment violation; jury could find causal relationship between the policy and the violation).

4.   Other decisions rely on expert testimony. In *Allen*, Dr. Kirkham testified that if the officers had been properly trained, the incident would not have occurred. In *Vineyard v. County of Murray*, 990 F.2d 1207 (11th Cir. 1993), the court upheld a judgment against a county and its Sheriff when two deputies used excessive force against a pretrial detainee. The county's policies of inadequate training, discipline and supervision were found to have caused the constitutional violation. In affirming the judgment, the court stated:

> The testimony of Professor White supports the jury's finding of causation. When asked to assume [the plaintiff's] version of what occurred at the hospital to be true, Professor White offered his opinion that these events would not have occurred if the county policies were such that officers knew they must report any confrontation, that others could call the Sheriff's Department to report complaints to the department, and that the department would investigate the complaints.

Vineyard, 990 F.2d at 1213. What could be the basis for Drs. Kirkham and White's opinions regarding causation?

A more critical assessment of expert testimony appears in *Berry v. City of Detroit*, 25 F.3d 1342 (6th Cir. 1994). In *Berry*, a jury awarded the plaintiff $6 million for the death of her son who was shot by a Detroit police officer. The plaintiff claimed that the city's customary failure to discipline its police officers amounted to deliberate indifference to the rights of its citizens. In support of her claim, the plaintiff offered the testimony of a former sheriff who purported to be an expert in "police policies and practices." In reversing the lower court's judgment, the court of appeals offered the following criticism of the testimony of the expert witness:

> If there is some formal training that would allow one to testify from a scientific standpoint on how failure to discipline officer "A" would impact on the conduct of his peer, officer "B," it is clear that [the plaintiff's expert] does not have such training. Thus, for this kind of testimony to be admissible, a foundation would have to have been laid based upon the witness's firsthand familiarity with disciplining police officers and the effect of lax discipline on the entire force. . . .

> If . . . [plaintiff's expert] had testified that when he became sheriff there were "x" number of incidents involving alleged excessive force, but two years after he instituted a training program, there were "x-y" incidents, we would have a starting point. If he then said that after the training program was in place, he increased the regularity and severity of discipline for infractions and incidents fell to "x-y2," then at least there would be some basis for his opinions . . .

> The danger in doing what the trial judge did here is that there is no such "field" as "police policies and practices." . . . This term . . . is so broad as to be devoid of meaning. It is like declaring an attorney an expert in the "law." . . .

> With all due respect to [the plaintiff's expert], his credentials . . . do not qualify him to know any more about what effect claimed disciplinary shortcomings would have on the future conduct of 5,000 different police officers than does any member of the jury . . .

Berry, 25 F.3d at 1350 and 1352. *See also Snyder v. Trepagnier*, 142 F.3d 791 (5th Cir. 1998) (concluding that expert opinion failed to establish "moving force" causation).

Why were the expert opinions in *Allen* and *Vineyard* sufficient to establish causation, while the testimony of the plaintiff's experts in *Berry* and *Snyder* were not? Is expert testimony essential in these cases? What sort of qualifications should an expert have to offer opinion testimony regarding causation?

See also Robinson v. Hager, 292 F.3d 560, 564 (8th Cir. 2002) ("When an injury is sophisticated proof of causation generally must be established by expert testimony." Expert testimony needed to prove that drug treatment center personnel's failure to give an inmate his medication for hypertension caused his stroke); *Long v. County of Los Angeles*, 442 F.3d 1178 (9th Cir. 2006) (conflicting expert opinions on the adequacy of policies regarding transfer of inmates from jail to medical facilities; plaintiff must prove that his injury would have been avoided had the County had adequate policies in place; jury issue).

5.   *Hartman v. Moore*, 547 U.S. 250 (2006), illustrates the complexity of the cause in fact issue when one defendant is alleged to have caused another person to violate the plaintiff's constitutional rights. In *Hartman*, the defendant postal inspectors presented a prosecutor with evidence that Moore had committed a crime.

Moore was charged and subsequently acquitted of the crime. Moore then filed a constitutional tort claim against the postal inspectors alleging that they initiated the criminal proceedings in retaliation against Moore's exercise of free speech. The issue in *Hartman* was whether the plaintiff had to prove the absence of probable cause in addition to a retaliatory motive in order to recover from the defendants. In the course of the opinion, the Court stated:

> [T]he requisite causation between the defendant's retaliatory animus and the plaintiff's injury is usually more complex than it is in other retaliation cases, and the need to show this more complex connection supports a requirement that no probable cause be alleged and proven. A *Bivens* (or § 1983) action for retaliatory prosecution will not be brought against the prosecutor, who is absolutely immune from liability for the decision to prosecute. Instead, the defendant will be a non-prosecutor, an official, like an inspector here, who may have influenced the prosecutorial decision but did not himself make it, and the cause of action will not be strictly for retaliatory prosecution, but for successful retaliatory inducement to prosecute. The consequence is that a plaintiff like Moore must show that the nonprosecuting official acted in retaliation, and must also show that he induced the prosecutor to bring charges that would not have been initiated without his urging.
>
> Thus, the causal connection required here is not merely between the retaliatory animus of one person and that person's injurious action, but between the retaliatory animus of one person and the action of [another].
>
> Herein lies the distinct problem of causation in cases like this one. Evidence of an inspector's animus does not necessarily show that the inspector induced the action of a prosecutor who would not have pressed charges otherwise. Moreover, to the factual difficulty of divining the influence of an investigator or other law enforcement officer upon the prosecutor's mind, there is an added legal obstacle in the longstanding presumption of regularity accorded to prosecutorial decisionmaking.
>
> [A] retaliatory motive on the part of an official urging prosecution combined with an absence of probable cause supporting the prosecutor's decision to go forward are reasonable grounds to suspend the presumption of regularity behind the charging decision, and enough for a prima facie inference that the unconstitutionally motivated inducement infected the prosecutor's decision to bring the [charge].
>
> In sum, the complexity of causation in a claim that prosecution was induced by an official bent on retaliation should be addressed specifically in defining the elements of the tort. Probable cause or its absence will be at least an evidentiary issue in practically all such cases. Because showing an absence of probable cause will have high probative force, and can be made mandatory with little or no added cost, it makes sense to require such a showing as an element of a plaintiff's case, and we hold that it must be pleaded and proven.

This discourse appears to be consistent with the principles announced in the governmental and supervisory liability cases. Specifically, recall that *Monell* requires that the official policy or custom of a local government must be "the moving force" behind its employee's unconstitutional action. *City of Canton* and *Board of Commissioners of Bryan County* also emphasize that the plaintiff must prove not only that a local government's training and hiring policies are deliberately indifferent to risk of violating the plaintiff's constitutional rights, but also that these deficient policies "actually caused" and were the "moving force" behind the individual officials' unconstitutional conduct. In all these cases the defendant (city/supervisor/person initiating criminal proceedings) is alleged to have done something that *causes* someone else to violate the plaintiff's constitutional rights. The common thread here is that it is not enough for a plaintiff to prove that a defendant engaged in culpable conduct and a constitutional violation occurred; the plaintiff must also prove that the culpable conduct *caused* someone else (an employee/subordinate/prosecutor) to violate the plaintiff's constitutional rights.

6.   Professor Malone once observed that the standard used to determine cause in fact is based as much on "policy" as it is on "estimates of factual likelihood." Malone, *Ruminations on Cause in Fact*, 9 STAN. L. REV. 60, 72 (1956). To what extent are decisions like *Mt. Healthy* and *Allen* the product of "policy" or "estimates of factual likelihood?" What sort of policy considerations might influence the cause in fact standards applied in Section 1983 cases? Are these policies grounded in principles of tort or the constitutional underpinnings of such claims?

7.   Should courts adapt the *Mt. Healthy* test to address governmental liability? If the plaintiff establishes that a governmental policy or custom was a substantial factor in producing the constitutional violation, should the burden shift to the defendant to prove that the same injury would have occurred in any event? As a matter of policy, who should bear the burden of explaining what would have happened if the government's policy had been different?

8.   *Allen* illustrates that in municipal liability cases, the plaintiff must prove the existence of an official policy or custom, the requisite culpability (*i.e.*, deliberate indifference), and a causal connection between the deficient policy and the unconstitutional actions of the employee. In theory, each of these elements are analytically distinct. Notice, however, that the *Allen* court's discussion of policy and culpability is considerably longer and more detailed than its perfunctory treatment of causation. This suggests that the elements of policy, deliberate indifference, and causation may not be completely independent. That is, causation is more likely to be found when the evidence of official policy and culpability is strong. Conversely, causation is more likely to be deemed lacking when the evidence of official policy or culpability is weak. *Compare Piotrowski v. City of Houston*, 237 F.3d 567, 581 (5th Cir. 2001) (customary practice of allowing police to "moonlight" for a private investigator with a criminal history was characterized as "poor judgment," but not necessarily deliberate indifference; even if the policy demonstrated deliberate indifference "the evidence is . . . insufficient to establish that it was the moving force that caused [the plaintiff] to be shot.") *and Ricketts v. City of Columbia*, 36 F.3d 775, 780–81 (6th Cir. 1994) (plaintiffs failed to prove that a pattern of making fewer arrests in cases of domestic violence was motivated by an intent to discriminate against women; causal connection between the failure to arrest husband on a prior incident of harassment and subsequent violent acts was characterized as "pure speculation") *with Gibson v. County of Washoe*, 290 F.3d 1175 (9th Cir. 2002) (undisputed county policy of delaying medical screening of combative inmates was characterized as posing a "substantial risk of serious harm" to detainees with mental illnesses; "a jury easily could conclude that the County caused [the plaintiff's] death") *and Lawson v. Dallas County*, 286 F.3d 257 (5th Cir. 2002) (jail policies limiting the number of times nurses could change the dressings on a paraplegic inmate were characterized as "deliberate indifference;" "[h]ad these policies not been in effect, it is reasonable to expect that [the plaintiff] would have received much more personal assistance from the nurses at the jail. . . . The district court did not err in finding that the County's policies were the 'moving force' behind any constitutional violations.").

9.   As discussed in Chapter 5, supervisors may be held liable in their individual capacities if their deliberate indifference causes another to be deprived a constitutional right. The same conduct may also subject a governmental entity to liability if the supervisor is acting as a "policymaker" for the government. In *Larez v. City of Los Angeles*, 946 F.2d 630 (9th Cir. 1991), for example, a jury found that the plaintiffs' constitutional rights were violated by an unreasonable search executed through the use of excessive force by police officers. The defendants included the Chief of Police and the City of Los Angeles. The Chief of Police was held liable in his individual capacity because he condoned, ratified and encouraged the excessive use of force. The Chief's conduct also subjected the City to liability because the Chief was an "official policymaker" for the City on police matters. *Larez*, 946 F.2d at 646–48. It is important to remember, however, that the supervisor in his individual capacity may enjoy a qualified immunity, but the city does not. *Compare Owen v. City of Independence*, 445 U.S. 622 (1980) discussed in Chapter 5, with the cases discussed in Chapter 8, *infra*.

10.   Principles of supervisory liability have been summarized as follows:

> supervisory liability under section 1983 occurs either when the supervisor personally participates in the alleged unconstitutional conduct or when there is a causal connection between the actions of a supervising official and the alleged constitutional deprivation. The necessary causal connection can be established 'when a history of widespread abuse puts the responsible supervisor on notice of the need to correct the alleged deprivation, and he fails to do so.' Alternatively, the causal connection may be established when a supervisor's 'custom or policy . . . results[s] in deliberate indifference to constitutional rights' or when facts support 'an inference that the supervisor directed the subordinates to act unlawfully or knew that the subordinates would act unlawfully and failed to stop them from doing so.'

Cottone v. Jenne, 326 F.3d 1352 (11th Cir. 2003). *Accord, Starr v. Bacca*, 652 F.3d 1202 (9th Cir. 2011).

11.   During a period of urban unrest, the mayor issues a proclamation instructing the police to "shoot to kill" anyone engaged in unlawful activity. A police officer thereafter shoots a fleeing 12 year old boy suspected of committing a misdemeanor. Assuming that the officer used excessive force, what would be the causation issues presented by claims against the mayor and city? What sort of

evidence would you try to present as counsel for the plaintiff or defendants? *See Palmer v. Hall*, 517 F.2d 705 (5th Cir. 1975).

II. PROXIMATE OR LEGAL CAUSE

A. Remote Consequences

MARTINEZ v. CALIFORNIA
444 U.S. 277 (1980)

Mr. Justice Stevens:

The two federal questions that appellants ask us to decide are (1) whether the Fourteenth Amendment invalidates a California statute granting absolute immunity to public employees who make parole-release determinations, and (2) whether such officials are absolutely immune from liability in an action brought under the federal Civil Rights Act of 1871, 42 U. S. C. § 1983. We agree with the California Court of Appeal that the state statute is valid when applied to claims arising under state law, and we conclude that appellants have not alleged a claim for relief under federal law.

The case arises out of the murder of a 15-year-old girl by a parolee. Her survivors brought this action in a California court claiming that the state officials responsible for the parole-release decision are liable in damages for the harm caused by the parolee.

The complaint alleged that the parolee, one Thomas, was convicted of attempted rape in December 1969. He was first committed to a state mental hospital as a "Mentally Disordered Sex Offender not amenable to treatment" and thereafter sentenced to a term of imprisonment of 1 to 20 years, with a recommendation that he not be paroled. Nevertheless, five years later, appellees decided to parole Thomas to the care of his mother. They were fully informed about his history, his propensities, and the likelihood that he would commit another violent crime. Moreover, in making their release determination they failed to observe certain "requisite formalities." Five months after his release Thomas tortured and killed appellants' decedent. We assume, as the complaint alleges, that appellees knew, or should have known, that the release of Thomas created a clear and present danger that such an incident would occur. Their action is characterized not only as negligent, but also as reckless, willful, wanton and malicious. Appellants prayed for actual and punitive damages of $2 million.

The trial judge sustained a demurrer to the complaint and his order was upheld on appeal. After the California Supreme Court denied appellants' petition for a hearing, we noted probable jurisdiction.

[The Court ruled that a California statute conferring absolute immunity on parole officials was constitutional as applied to claims arising under state law.]

We turn then to appellants' § 1983 claim that appellees, by their action in releasing Thomas, subjected appellants' decedent to a deprivation of her life without due process of law. It is clear that the California immunity statute does not control this claim even though the federal cause of action is being asserted in the state courts. We also conclude that it is not necessary for us to decide any question concerning the immunity of state parole officials as a matter of federal law because, as we recently held in *Baker v. McCollan*, "[the] first inquiry in any § 1983 suit . . . is whether the plaintiff has been deprived of a right 'secured by the Constitution and laws' " of the United States. The answer to that inquiry disposes of this case.

Appellants contend that the decedent's right to life is protected by the Fourteenth Amendment to the Constitution. But the Fourteenth Amendment protected her only from deprivation by the "State . . . of life . . . without due process of law." Although the decision to release Thomas from prison was action by the State, the action of Thomas five months later cannot be fairly characterized as state action. Regardless of whether, as a matter of state tort law, the parole board could be said either to have had a "duty" to avoid harm to his victim or to have proximately caused her death . . . we hold that, taking these particular allegations as true, appellees did not "deprive" appellants' decedent of life within the meaning of the Fourteenth Amendment.

Her life was taken by the parolee five months after his release. He was in no sense an agent of the parole board. Further, the parole board was not aware that appellants' decedent, as distinguished from the public at large, faced any special danger. We need not and do not decide that a parole officer could never be deemed to "deprive" someone of life by action taken in connection with the release of a prisoner on parole. But we do hold that at least under the particular circumstances of this parole decision, appellants' decedent's death is too remote a consequence of the parole officers' action to hold them responsible under the federal civil rights law. Although a § 1983 claim has been described as "a species of tort liability," *Imbler v. Pachtman*, it is perfectly clear that not every injury in which a state official has played some part is actionable under that statute.

The judgment is affirmed.

So ordered.

NOTES

1.   What is the state action alleged to have violated the plaintiffs' constitutional rights? Was the allegedly reckless decision to release Thomas a cause in fact of the death of the plaintiffs' daughter? Was the death of plaintiffs' daughter a foreseeable consequence of the allegedly reckless parole decision? In what sense was the death of the plaintiffs' daughter "too remote a consequence" of the decision to release Thomas on parole? Would the murder be too remote if it occurred two months after release? The same day? *See Rodriquez-Cirilo v. Garcia*, 115 F.3d 50, 52 (1st Cir. 1997) (police officer's failure to enforce temporary detention order against the victim's brother was not the proximate cause of stabbing two weeks later); *Janan v. Trammell*, 785 F.2d 557, 560 (6th Cir. 1986) ("We do not believe that the Supreme Court intended to provide us with a due process timetable such that a five month gap does not deprive one of due process while a two month gap automatically does.

We decline to place such weight on the temporal factor."); *Commonwealth Bank & Trust Co. v. Russell*, 825 F.2d 12 (3d Cir. 1987) (brief interval between escape and murder does not take the case out of the rule in *Martinez*; the same "causal nexus" is missing). *But see Reed v. Gardner*, 986 F.2d 1122, 1127 (7th Cir. 1993) ("Despite the two hour time lapse between and distance between the place [where the police left a car in the custody of an allegedly intoxicated person] and the car accident, the events are not sufficiently attenuated to relieve the defendants of 1983 liability."). Would it have made any difference in *Martinez* if the plaintiff was not just a member of the general public but was an individually identifiable potential victim? *Compare Jones v. Phyfer*, 761 F.2d 642 (11th Cir. 1985) (furloughed prisoner attacked a woman who had previously been victimized by prisoner; *Martinez* controls) *with Hardmon v. County of Lehigh*, 613 F. Supp. 649 (E.D. Pa. 1985) (furloughed prisoner attacked a child whom correctional officials knew had been threatened by the prisoner; *Martinez* distinguished).

2.   The Supreme Court in *Martinez* notes that state courts might address the question of the defendants' liability in terms of duty or proximate cause. The *Martinez* court, however, invokes proximate cause terminology when it speaks of remote consequences. In the subsequent case of *DeShaney v. Winnebago County Department of Social Services*, 489 U.S. 189 (1989) (see Chapter 4) the Court used an affirmative duty analysis to explain why welfare officials could not be held liable under section 1983 for the beating of a child by his father. Are the controlling issues presented by the two cases fundamentally different? Does it matter whether the limitation on liability is phrased in terms of duty or proximate cause? Tort scholars have long recognized that "[i]t is quite possible to state every question which arises in connection with 'proximate cause' in the form of a single question: was the defendant under a duty to protect the plaintiff against the event which did in fact occur." P. Keeton, D. Dobbs, R. Keeton, and D. Owen, Prosser and Keeton on Torts 274 (5th ed. 1984). *See also* Dan B. Dobbs, The Law of Torts § 182 (2000) ("some courts will use the language of proximate cause to resolve some cases that other courts might resolve in the language of duty"). Several noted scholars advocate using a duty analysis because it provides a more open and direct way for judges to resolve the policy choices that underlie the question of the extent of liability. *See* L. Green, *The Rationale of Proximate Cause* 11–43 (1927); Thode, *Tort Analysis: Duty-Risk v. Proximate Cause and the Rational Allocation of Functions Between Judge and Jury*, 1977 Utah L. Rev. 1. Consider the comments of Professor Nahmod,

> The 1983 proximate cause question of the extent of liability could conceivably be dealt with primarily as a question of the scope of the constitutional duty breached, thereby largely eliminating the terminology of proximate cause and the concomitant jury role. Doing so could, however, result in "overloading" the constitutional inquiry by making it determinative not only of the constitutionally required standard of conduct, but also of the ultimate liability, a remedial issue. Thus it is probably better that courts in appropriate section 1983 cases continue to use the language of proximate cause.

S. Nahmod, Civil Rights and Civil Liberties Litigation § 3:105 (4th ed. 2014). How would the constitutional inquiry be "overloaded" by analyzing the extent of government officials' liability in terms of the scope of duty?

3.   In resolving proximate cause issues in section 1983 cases, courts often rely on principles developed in the context of common law torts. *E.g., Herzog v. Village of Winnetka*, 309 F.3d 1041, 1044 (7th Cir. 2002) ("ordinary rules of tort causation apply to constitutional tort suits"); *Drumgold v. Callahan*, 707 F.3d 28 (1st Cir. 2013) ("As a general rule, 'we employ common law tort principles when conducting inquiries into causation under [Section] 1983'.") (internal citations omitted). *Cf., OSU Student Alliance v. Ray*, 699 F.3d 1053 (9th Cir. 2011) ("like common law torts, constitutional torts require proximate cause."). For example, in *Herzog*, the court held that a police officer who arrested the plaintiff for DUI without probable cause could be held liable for the damage to the plaintiff's tooth caused by the forceful insertion of a breath-screening device "because it was a reasonably probable consequence" of the illegal arrest. 309 F.3d at 1044. *See also Sheets v. Salt Lake County*, 45 F.3d 1383, 1389 (10th Cir. 1995) ("A defendant is the proximate cause of a plaintiff's injury if the injury is a natural consequence of the defendant's actions"). Similarly, courts have routinely applied the common law "thin skull" or "eggshell skull" rule in constitutional tort cases to hold a defendant "fully liable for the resulting damage even though the injured plaintiff had a preexisting condition that made the consequences of the wrongful act more severe than they would have been for a normal victim." *Figueroa-Torres v. Toledo-Davila*, 232 F.3d 270, 275–76 (1st Cir. 2000) (collecting cases). In *Figueroa-Torres*, a police officer inflicted excessive force while arresting a criminal suspect. The suspect died after his spleen ruptured. Invoking the common law "eggshell skull" principle, the defendant was held liable for the death notwithstanding the fact that the suspect had a preexisting injury or weakness in the spleen.

4.   While courts frequently refer to common law principles of proximate cause, it is important to remember that the proper proximate cause rule in constitutional tort cases is a matter of federal — not state-law. This is so "because 'cause' is part of the definitional language of section 1983 and has been construed by the Supreme Court without reference to specific state law." *Stokes v. Bullins*, 844 F.2d 269, 276 (5th Cir. 1988). Moreover, the function of proximate cause is to define the extent of the law's protection of the underlying right. In section 1983 litigation, the underlying right is the constitution or a federal law so federal rules should determine the scope of liability for violations of federal rights. *See* Thomas A. Eaton, *Causation in Constitutional Torts*, 67 Iowa L. Rev. 443, 446–52 (1982). *See also*, Sheldon Nahmod, Civil Rights and Civil Liberties Litigation: The Law of Section 1983, section 3:106 (4th ed. 2014) ("tort law purposes and interests are often different from [section] 1983 purposes and interests, and thus tort law concepts should not be blindly applied."). Thus, courts may be guided by common law principles in establishing federal rules of proximate cause governing section 1983 claims, but are not bound by decisions of state courts.

The proximate cause issue that has proven to be most problematic in the constitutional tort context is superseding cause. When will the actions taken by others serve to cut off the liability of the original constitutional tortfeasor? This issue is addressed in the next case.

B. Intervening Acts

TOWNES v. CITY OF NEW YORK
176 F.3d 138 (2d Cir. 1999)

JACOBS, CIRCUIT JUDGE:

Victor Townes, currently incarcerated for matters not the subject of this case, initiated this 42 U.S.C. § 1983 lawsuit *pro se* in the United States District Court for the Southern District of New York, claiming that his constitutional rights were violated by several officers of the New York Police Department — and derivatively by the City of New York ("the City") — during a 1984 police stop of a taxicab in which he was a passenger. After halting the taxicab, the officers ordered Townes out, searched him (finding nothing), searched the taxicab (finding handguns), arrested Townes, and searched him again at the police station (finding cocaine). Townes alleges that he was subjected to an unconstitutional seizure and search that resulted in his spending more than two years in prison on weapons-possession and drug-possession charges.

Background

For purposes of this appeal, we accept as true the factual allegations contained in Townes's complaint. In November 1984, Townes and two other persons were passengers in a livery taxicab en route to Manhattan from the Bronx. The taxicab pulled over after it entered Manhattan, and Townes waited inside while his companions stepped away. Sitting there, Townes noticed several on-duty plain-clothes officers of the New York City Police Department watching him from an unmarked police car. He then removed two fully loaded handguns from his person, and hid them, one under the front seat, the other under the passenger seat. After Townes's companions returned, and the three resumed their trip, the officers stopped the taxicab. We assume (as the Appellate Division of the New York Supreme Court later found, and the parties do not dispute) that the taxicab did not violate any traffic law, that the driver did not signal for help, and that the police lacked probable cause to make the stop.

The officers identified themselves, ordered the three passengers from the taxicab at gunpoint, and frisked them, but found nothing. The officers proceeded to search the taxicab, and found the two handguns that Townes had hidden. The three passengers were taken into custody and driven to the 32nd Precinct, where they were searched again, at which time cocaine was discovered on Townes's person. Townes was arrested and charged with two counts of criminal possession of a weapon in the third degree and one count of criminal possession of a controlled substance in the seventh degree.

Townes's motion to suppress the evidence concerning the handguns and the cocaine was denied (without a hearing), after which he entered a plea of guilty and was jailed. More than two years later, the Appellate Division reversed the conviction on the ground that the police lacked probable cause to stop and search the taxicab. The New York Court of Appeals later remitted the case to the New York Supreme

Court for a hearing on the original motion to suppress. Eventually, the indictment was dismissed.

Townes commenced the present action in 1994, pleading: (1) claims against each of the individual police officers under 42 U.S.C. § 1983 for violating his Fourth Amendment rights; and (2) a § 1983 claim against the City for failing to train or supervise the individual police officers.

Discussion

I

The individual defendants argue that they are immune from suit for their conduct.

A

Judge Wood correctly concluded that Townes enjoyed a clearly established right to be free from an unreasonable seizure while a passenger in a taxicab.

We think that Judge Wood's reasoning justifies the conclusion that the individual police officers lack immunity for their stop of the taxicab and for their seizure and search of Townes at the scene. However, exercising pendent appellate jurisdiction, we proceed to consider the related issue of whether the stop and search were a proximate cause of the damages that the plaintiff is seeking.

The only constitutional right that Townes asserts in this constitutional tort action is his Fourth Amendment right to be free of unreasonable search and seizure. Here, the only actionable violations of that right are the stop of the taxicab and the associated seizure and search of Townes's person, which alone might at most support slight or nominal damages. Townes, however, seeks damages not for those injuries, but only for the ultimate harm he suffered by his conviction and incarceration. Neither of the two theories Townes adduces to connect the defendants' conduct to his claimed injury — the fruit of the poisonous tree doctrine (discussed at oral argument), and traditional common law tort principles of causation (pleaded in Townes's complaint) — is sufficient.

II

The fruit of the poisonous tree doctrine cannot link the unreasonable seizure and search to Townes's conviction and incarceration because this evidentiary doctrine is inapplicable to civil § 1983 actions. *Costello v. United States*, 365 U.S. 265, 2880 (1961) ("[T]he 'fruit of the poisonous tree' doctrine excludes evidence obtained from or as a consequence of lawless official acts. . . ."). The doctrine is an extension of the long-recognized exclusionary rule, and as such has generally been held "to apply only in criminal trials." We find no case in which the doctrine has been successfully invoked to support a § 1983 claim, and we see no reason why it could be.

B

The fruit of the poisonous tree doctrine is calculated "to deter future unlawful police conduct" and protect liberty by creating an incentive — avoidance of the suppression of illegally seized evidence — for state actors to respect the constitutional rights of suspects. Like the exclusionary rule, the fruit of the poisonous tree doctrine "is a judicially created remedy designed to safeguard Fourth Amendment rights generally through its deterrent effect, rather than a personal constitutional right of the party aggrieved." . . .

C

Civil actions brought under § 1983 are analogous to state common law tort actions, serving primarily the tort objective of compensation. ("Deterrence is also an important purpose of this system, but it operates through the mechanism of damages that are *compensatory* — damages grounded in determinations of plaintiffs' actual losses."). A § 1983 action, like its state tort analogs, employs the principle of proximate causation.

The fruit of the poisonous tree doctrine, however, disregards traditional causation analysis to serve different objectives. To extend the doctrine to § 1983 actions would impermissibly recast the relevant proximate cause inquiry to one of taint and attenuation.

In a § 1983 suit, constitutionally invalid police conduct that by itself causes little or no harm is assessed on ordinary principles of tort causation and entails little or nominal damages. The fruit of the poisonous tree doctrine is not available to elongate the chain of causation.

III

The next inquiry is whether Townes's conviction and incarceration were proximately (or legally) caused by the defendants' constitutional torts. It is arguable that such seizures and searches could foreseeably cause the discovery of inculpatory evidence, but as a matter of law, the unconstitutional seizure and search of Townes's person was not a proximate cause of his conviction because of (at least) one critical circumstance: the trial court's refusal to suppress the evidence, which is an intervening and superseding cause of Townes's conviction.

The chain of events in this case is Townes's illegal possession of handguns and cocaine, the stop of the taxicab, the seizure of Townes's person, the search of Townes's person, the search of the taxicab, the discovery of Townes's handguns in the taxicab, Townes's arrest, the search of Townes at the police station, the discovery of cocaine on Townes's person at the police station, the ruling of the trial judge denying suppression of the handguns and cocaine evidence (reversed on appeal some years later on the basis of the fruit of the poisonous tree doctrine), Townes's conviction for offenses he uncontestedly committed, and his imprisonment. Given this chain, it is clear enough that *but for* the defendants' unreasonable seizure and search, Townes's handguns and cocaine would have gone undetected (at least for the time being), and he would not have been convicted of the precise offenses under these precise circumstances.

However, the trial court's failure to suppress the evidence concerning Townes's own criminal acts constituted a superseding cause of Townes's conviction and imprisonment. In the common law, "[a] superseding cause is an act of a third person or other force which by its intervention prevents the actor from being liable for harm to another which his antecedent negligence is a substantial factor in bringing about." *Restatement (Second) of Torts* § 440 (1965).

Townes does not plead conduct tantamount to malicious prosecution or false imprisonment. He alleges only a violation of his Fourth Amendment rights via an unreasonable seizure and search. By the time Townes was arraigned and filed his motion to suppress the handguns and cocaine, the defendants' allegedly tortious conduct had long since ended. The state trial court, which alone had the power to suppress the improperly obtained evidence, had control over the ultimate outcome of Townes's case. That court should have recognized that the defendants violated Townes's clearly established Fourth Amendment rights, and should have suppressed the evidence under the fruit of the poisonous tree doctrine, as the Appellate Division later ruled. The state trial court's exercise of independent judgment in deciding not to suppress the evidence, though later ruled to be erroneous, broke the chain of causation for purposes of § 1983 liability for the plaintiff's conviction and incarceration.

It is well settled that the chain of causation between a police officer's unlawful arrest and a subsequent conviction and incarceration is broken by the intervening exercise of independent judgment. At least that is so in the absence of evidence that the police officer misled or pressured the official who could be expected to exercise independent judgment. There is no claim of such evidence in this case. Therefore, Townes cannot recover damages for his conviction and incarceration from the defendants, and the defendants were entitled to dismissal of Townes's complaint pursuant to Fed.R.Civ.P. 12(b)(6).

IV

Townes is foreclosed from recovery for a second, independent reason: the injury he pleads (a violation of his Fourth Amendment right to be free from unreasonable searches and seizures) does not fit the damages he seeks (compensation for his conviction and incarceration).

A

The goal of the Court's § 1983 jurisprudence has been to tailor liability to fit the interests protected by the particular constitutional right in question. In other words, § 1983 damages should be made available only for risks that are "constitutionally relevant." John C. Jeffries, Jr., *Damages for Constitutional Violations: The Relation of Risk to Injury in Constitutional Torts*, 75 Va. L. Rev. 1461, 1475 (1989). Here, there is a gross disconnect between the constitutional violations (Townes's Fourth Amendment right to be free from unreasonable searches and seizures) and the injury or harm for which Townes seeks a recovery (his subsequent conviction and incarceration). The evil of an unreasonable search or seizure is that it invades privacy, not that it uncovers crime, which is no evil at all.[2]

No Fourth Amendment value would be served if Townes, who illegally possessed firearms and narcotics, reaps the financial benefit he seeks. Townes has already reaped an enormous benefit by reason of the illegal seizure and search to which he was subjected: his freedom, achieved by the suppression of evidence obtained in violation of the Fourth Amendment. That benefit to Townes is merely incidental to the purpose of suppression, which is to compel law enforcement compliance with the Fourth Amendment and thereby prevent the invasions of law-abiding citizens' privacy. Now Townes seeks damages to compensate him for his conviction and time served, on top of the benefit he enjoys as a result of the suppression. That remedy would vastly overdeter police officers and would result in a wealth transfer that "is peculiar, if not perverse." Jeffries, *supra*, at 1475.

We conclude that constitutional tort liability under § 1983 is limited to "the kind of injury that the [constitutional right at issue] was designed to prevent." *Id.* Victims of unreasonable searches or seizures may recover damages directly related to the invasion of their privacy — including (where appropriate) damages for physical injury, property damage, injury to reputation, etc.; but such victims cannot be compensated for injuries that result from the discovery of incriminating evidence and consequent criminal prosecution. *See id.* In this manner, "[t]he penalty for the violation is . . . likely to be at least roughly proportionate to the wrong done by the violator."

B

Townes seeks compensatory damages relating to his conviction and incarceration, including "damage to his reputation, isolation from society, separation from friends and family, and loss of potential earnings." Because he fails to allege that the defendants' conduct effectively amounted to malicious prosecution, however, those damages are not recoverable. . . .

Neither may Townes recover compensatory damages for his arrest and prearraignment detention. As an initial matter, it is unclear from his complaint that he seeks such damages; if he did, he could not recover them. Although the common law tort of false arrest (or false imprisonment) allows plaintiffs to seek damages from "the time of detention up until issuance of process or arraignment, but not more," the existence of probable cause defeats any such claim. The individual defendants here lacked probable cause to stop and search Townes, but they certainly had probable cause to arrest him upon discovery of the handguns in the passenger compartment of the taxicab in which he was riding. The lack of probable cause to stop and search does not vitiate the probable cause to arrest, because (among other reasons) the fruit of the poisonous tree doctrine is not available to assist a § 1983 claimant.

Ultimately, Townes's only possible damage claim would be limited to the brief

---

[2] [5] It is hardly necessary to say that an unreasonable search cannot lead foreseeably to a criminal conviction unless the victim has in fact committed a crime. *See* Jeffries, *supra*, at 1474–75.

invasion of privacy related to the seizure and initial search of his person. Townes's complaint pleads no such damages, and Townes's counsel stated at oral argument that Townes was not seeking damages for this invasion. Therefore, because Townes does not seek the only relief to which he may have been entitled, his complaint should have been dismissed pursuant to Fed.R.Civ.P. 12(b)(6).

Conclusion

We reverse the denial of the motion to dismiss Townes's § 1983 claims and remand this case to the district court with directions to dismiss these federal claims. The interlocutory appeal from the immunity ruling does not confer appellate jurisdiction over the dismissal of Townes's state law claim, and we decline to exercise pendent appellate jurisdiction over that claim. We therefore dismiss the cross-appeal.

NOTES

1.   Why is it inappropriate to apply the "fruit of the poisonous tree" doctrine in the constitutional tort context? The application of this principle in the criminal prosecution led to Townes' ultimate release from custody. Doesn't that indicate there is a causal connection between the unreasonable seizure and his confinement in prison? If the causal connection between the violation of Townes' Fourth Amendment rights and his incarceration is sufficient to justify his release from custody, why is it not sufficient to justify payment of compensation? Is the balance between the competing interests of the criminal suspect and law enforcement officials different when the stakes are freedom as opposed to money damages? Are the public's interests different? For an argument that the fruit of the poisonous tree standard should govern claims for damages, *see* Martin P. Schwartz, Comment, *Compensating Victims of Police-Fabricated Confessions*, 70 U. CHI. L. REV. 1119 (2003).

2.   There are numerous cases in which the intervening acts of government officials are labeled "superceding cause" thereby cutting off the liability of the defendant who initially violated the plaintiff's constitutional rights. Some of these cases involve allegedly unconstitutional employment decisions that were independently reviewed or implemented by superiors untainted by the defendant's impermissible motive. *Dixon v. Burke County*, 303 F.3d 1271 (11th Cir. 2002) (the causal connection between the district attorney's advising a grand jury to fill a vacancy on the school board based on the race and gender of the candidates and the plaintiff not being appointed was severed by the intervening independent acts of the grand jury and the state judge who made the final appointment); *Taylor v. Brentwood Union Free School Dist.*, 143 F.3d 679 (2d Cir. 1998) (the intervening acts of the school board and disciplinary hearing panel severed the casual connection between a principal's racially motivated initiation of disciplinary action and the suspension of a teacher).

There are also many cases like *Townes* in which the independent acts of a grand jury, prosecutor, or judge were deemed to be superceding causes of prosecutions and convictions initiated by the unconstitutional arrests, searches, or questioning by police officers. *E.g., Murray v. Earle*, 405 F.3d 278 (5th Cir. 2005) (officer coerced a confession used to convict plaintiff; conviction was subsequently overturned on the grounds that the confession should not have been admitted into evidence; § 1983 claim against the officer who coerced the confession was dismissed on proximate cause grounds because of the intervening act of the trial judge in erroneously admitting the confession into evidence); *Wray v. City of New York*, 490 F.3d 1889 (2d Cir. 2007) (defendant officers conducted what was later determined to be an "unduly suggestive" identification procedure; the identification was admitted into evidence at the criminal trial in which the plaintiff was convicted; the plaintiff secured a writ of habeas corpus on the grounds that the suggestive identification violated his constitutional right to due process and a fair trial; plaintiff's § 1983 claim against the officers who conducted the "show up" was dismissed on proximate cause grounds reasoning that the decision of the trial judge to admit the evidence was a superceding cause of his conviction); *Barts v. Joyner*, 865 F.2d 1187 (11th Cir. 1989) (sheriff's alleged unconstitutional seizure and detention of the plaintiff was not the proximate cause of her conviction because the intervening acts of the prosecutor, grand jury, judge and jury "each break the chain of causation"); *Hand v. Gary*, 838 F.2d 1420 (5th Cir. 1988) (independent acts of prosecutor and grand jury break the chain of causation between an illegal arrest and subsequent injury); *Smiddy v. Varney*, 803 F.2d 1469 (9th Cir. 1981), 803 F.2d 261 (prosecutor as superceding cause); *Duncan v. Nelson*, 466 F.2d 939 (7th Cir. 1972) (sentencing judge as superceding cause).

3.   On the other hand, there are also numerous cases in which the intervening acts of government officials were not considered to be superceding causes. The plaintiffs in *Malley v. Briggs*, 475 U.S. 335 (1986) brought a section 1983 action against a state trooper who obtained an arrest warrant on the basis of information obtained from a court-authorized wire tap. The warrant itself was issued by a state judge. The plaintiffs alleged that the trooper violated their Fourth Amendment rights by presenting the judge with a complaint and a supporting affidavit which failed to establish probable cause. The district court directed a verdict for the trooper on the grounds that the judge in issuing the arrest warrants "broke the causal chain" between the trooper's filing of a complaint and the plaintiffs' arrest. The district court also held that an officer who believes the facts stated in his affidavit are true and who submits them to a neutral magistrate is entitled to qualified immunity. The court of appeals reversed, holding that qualified immunity does not apply unless the trooper has an objectively reasonable basis for believing the facts alleged in his affidavit are sufficient to establish probable cause. The Supreme Court affirmed the circuit court's decision with regard to immunity. In the course of the opinion the Court noted

> Petitioner has not pressed the argument that in a case like this the officer should not be liable because the judge's decision to issue the warrant breaks the causal chain between the application for the warrant and the improvident arrest. It should be clear, however, that the District Court's "no causation" rationale in this case is inconsistent with our interpretation of section 1983. As we stated in *Monroe v. Pape*, 365 U.S. 167, 187 (1961), section 1983 "should be read against the background of tort liability that makes a man responsible for the natural consequences of his actions." Since

Chapter 7

"EVERY PERSON": ABSOLUTE IMMUNITY

Suppose that a plaintiff properly pleads and proves all of the requisite elements of the section 1983 cause of action for damages against an individual defendant. Does it follow that the defendant will be held liable? Somewhat surprisingly, the answer is "no" despite the broad "person" language of section 1983. Indeed, it turns out that when certain defendants are sued for damages, they are treated, essentially for policy reasons, as if they are not "persons" at all and are protected by absolute immunity.

Absolute immunity is a powerful defense when it is successfully asserted. First, the defendant escapes liability even though he or she may have violated the plaintiff's constitutional rights and caused harm. Second, and equally important, absolute immunity protects the defendant from having to defend against the section 1983 action at all. As a practical matter, the absolutely immune defendant can admit the allegations of the plaintiff's complaint in the course of moving, early in the litigation, either to dismiss the complaint for failure to state a claim or for summary judgment on absolute immunity grounds.

As we shall see, privileged defendants protected by absolute immunity generally fall into four classes: state and local legislators, judges, witnesses and prosecutors. The Supreme Court has protected them by claiming to interpret section 1983 against the background of common law immunity in 1871, the year section 1983 was enacted. Significantly, though, absolute immunity only protects them when they act in particular ways: legislators must act in a legislative capacity, judges must act judicially, witnesses must in fact act in that capacity in judicial proceedings and prosecutors must act in an advocative role. If, for example, legislators, judges or prosecutors act administratively, they lose their absolute immunity (although they are still protected by qualified immunity). This approach to immunity, based not upon status but rather on *function,* is also considered in this chapter.

This chapter addresses the following questions: (1) who is protected by absolute immunity? (2) what are the reasons for absolute immunity? (3) what is the scope of absolute immunity? (4) does the functional approach also protect those who would not ordinarily be protected by absolute immunity? Also briefly considered are the burden of pleading absolute immunity and appeals from denials of absolute immunity summary judgment motions.

I. ABSOLUTE LEGISLATIVE IMMUNITY

A. *Tenney*: The Seminal Case on Absolute Legislative Immunity

Interestingly, *Tenney v. Brandhove*, 341 U.S. 367 (1951), the first Supreme Court decision dealing with immunities was handed down in 1951, ten years before *Monroe v. Pape*. *Tenney* articulated an approach to section 1983 immunities that has dominated the Court's immunities jurisprudence ever since.

TENNEY v. BRANDHOVE
341 U.S. 367 (1951)

MR. JUSTICE **FRANKFURTER** delivered the opinion of the Court.

William Brandhove brought this action in the United States District Court for the Northern District of California, alleging that he had been deprived of rights guaranteed by the Federal Constitution. The defendants are Jack B. Tenney and other members of a committee of the California Legislature, the Senate Fact-Finding Committee on Un-American Activities, colloquially known as the Tenney Committee. Also named as defendants are the Committee and Elmer E. Robinson, Mayor of San Francisco.

The action is based on §§ 43 and 47 (3) of Title 8 of the United States Code. These sections derive from one of the statutes, passed in 1871, aimed at enforcing the Fourteenth Amendment. Section 43 provides:

> "Every person who, under color of any statute, ordinance, regulation, custom, or usage, of any State or Territory, subjects, or causes to be subjected, any citizen of the United States or other person within the jurisdiction thereof to the deprivation of any rights, privileges, or immunities secured by the Constitution and laws, shall be liable to the party injured in an action at law, suit in equity, or other proper proceeding for redress."

Section 47 (3) provides a civil remedy against "two or more persons" who may conspire to deprive another of constitutional rights, as therein defined.

Reduced to its legal essentials, the complaint shows these facts. The Tenney Committee was constituted by a resolution of the California Senate on June 20, 1947. On January 28, 1949, Brandhove circulated a petition among members of the State Legislature. He alleges that it was circulated in order to persuade the Legislature not to appropriate further funds for the Committee. The petition charged that the Committee had used Brandhove as a tool in order "to smear Congressman Franck R. Havenner as a 'Red' when he was a candidate for Mayor of San Francisco in 1947; and that the Republican machine in San Francisco and the campaign management of Elmer E. Robinson, Franck Havenner's opponent, conspired with the Tenney Committee to this end." In view of the conflict between this petition and evidence previously given by Brandhove, the Committee asked local prosecuting officials to institute criminal proceedings against him. The

Committee also summoned Brandhove to appear before them at a hearing held on January 29. Testimony was there taken from the Mayor of San Francisco, allegedly a member of the conspiracy. The plaintiff appeared with counsel, but refused to give testimony. For this, he was prosecuted for contempt in the State courts. Upon the jury's failure to return a verdict this prosecution was dropped. After Brandhove refused to testify, the Chairman quoted testimony given by Brandhove at prior hearings. The Chairman also read into the record a statement concerning an alleged criminal record of Brandhove, a newspaper article denying the truth of his charges, and a denial by the Committee's counsel — who was absent — that Brandhove's charges were true.

Brandhove alleges that the January 29 hearing "was not held for a legislative purpose," but was designed "to intimidate and silence plaintiff and deter and prevent him from effectively exercising his constitutional rights of free speech and to petition the Legislature for redress of grievances, and also to deprive him of the equal protection of the laws, due process of law, and of the enjoyment of equal privileges and immunities as a citizen of the United States under the law, and so did intimidate, silence, deter, and prevent and deprive plaintiff." Damages of $10,000 were asked "for legal counsel, traveling, hotel accommodations, and other matters pertaining and necessary to his defense" in the contempt proceeding arising out of the Committee hearings. The plaintiff also asked for punitive damages.

The action was dismissed without opinion by the District Judge. The Court of Appeals for the Ninth Circuit held, however, that the complaint stated a cause of action against the Committee and its members. We brought the case here because important issues are raised concerning the rights of individuals and the power of State legislatures.

We are again faced with the Reconstruction legislation which caused the Court such concern in *Screws v. United States* and in the *Williams* cases decided this term. But this time we do not have to wrestle with far-reaching questions of constitutionality or even of construction. We think it is clear that the legislation on which this action is founded does not impose liability on the facts before us, once they are related to the presuppositions of our political history.

The privilege of legislators to be free from arrest or civil process for what they do or say in legislative proceedings has taproots in the Parliamentary struggles of the Sixteenth and Seventeenth Centuries. As Parliament achieved increasing independence from the Crown, its statement of the privilege grew stronger. In 1523, Sir Thomas More could make only a tentative claim. In 1668, after a long and bitter struggle, Parliament finally laid the ghost of Charles I, who had prosecuted Sir John Elliot and others for "seditious" speeches in Parliament. In 1689, the Bill of Rights declared in unequivocal language: "That the Freedom of Speech, and Debates or Proceedings in Parliament, ought not to be impeached or questioned in any Court or Place out of Parliament."

Freedom of speech and action in the legislature was taken as a matter of course by those who severed the Colonies from the Crown and founded our Nation. It was deemed so essential for representatives of the people that it was written into the Articles of Confederation and later into the Constitution. Article V of the Articles of Confederation is quite close to the English Bill of Rights: "Freedom of speech and debate in Congress shall not be impeached or questioned in any court or place out of Congress. . . ." Article I, § 6, of the Constitution provides: ". . . for any Speech or Debate in either House, [the Senators and Representatives] shall not be questioned in any other Place."

The reason for the privilege is clear. It was well summarized by James Wilson, an influential member of the Committee of Detail which was responsible for the provision in the Federal Constitution. "In order to enable and encourage a representative of the public to discharge his public trust with firmness and success, it is indispensably necessary, that he should enjoy the fullest liberty of speech, and that he should be protected from the resentment of every one, however powerful, to whom the exercise of that liberty may occasion offence."

The provision in the United States Constitution was a reflection of political principles already firmly established in the States. Three State Constitutions adopted before the Federal Constitution specifically protected the privilege. The Maryland Declaration of Rights, Nov. 3, 1776, provided: "That freedom of speech, and debates or proceedings, in the legislature, ought not to be impeached in any other court or judicature." Art. VIII. The Massachusetts Constitution of 1780 provided: "The freedom of deliberation, speech and debate, in either house of the legislature, is so essential to the rights of the people, that it cannot be the foundation of any accusation or prosecution, action, or complaint, in any other court or place whatsoever." Chief Justice Parsons gave the following gloss to this provision in *Coffin v. Coffin*:

> "These privileges are thus secured, not with the intention of protecting the members against prosecutions for their own benefit, but to support the rights of the people, by enabling their representatives to execute the functions of their office without fear of prosecutions, civil or criminal. I therefore think that the article ought not to be construed strictly, but liberally, that the full design of it may be answered. I will not confine it to delivering an opinion, uttering a speech, or haranguing in debate; but will extend it to the giving of a vote, to the making of a written report, and to every other act resulting from the nature, and in the execution, of the office; and I would define the article as securing to every member exemption from prosecution, for every thing said or done by him, as a representative, in the exercise of the functions of that office, without inquiring whether the exercise was regular according to the rules of the house, or irregular and against their rules."

The New Hampshire Constitution of 1784 provided: "The freedom of deliberation, speech, and debate, in either house of the legislature, is so essential to the rights of the people, that it cannot be the foundation of any action, complaint, or prosecution, in any other court or place whatsoever."

It is significant that legislative freedom was so carefully protected by constitutional framers at a time when even Jefferson expressed fear of legislative excess. For the loyalist executive and judiciary had been deposed, and the legislature was supreme in most States during and after the Revolution. "The legislative department is every where extending the sphere of its activity, and drawing all power into its impetuous vortex." Madison, The Federalist, No. XLVIII.

As other States joined the Union or revised their Constitutions, they took great care to preserve the principle that the legislature must be free to speak and act without fear of criminal and civil liability. Forty-one of the forty-eight States now have specific provisions in their Constitutions protecting the privilege.

Did Congress by the general language of its 1871 statute mean to overturn the tradition of legislative freedom achieved in England by Civil War and carefully preserved in the formation of State and National Governments here? Did it mean to subject legislators to civil liability for acts done within the sphere of legislative activity? Let us assume, merely for the moment, that Congress has constitutional power to limit the freedom of State legislators acting within their traditional sphere. That would be a big assumption. But we would have to make an even rasher assumption to find that Congress thought it had exercised the power. These are difficulties we cannot hurdle. The limits of §§ 1 and 2 of the 1871 statute — now §§ 43 and 47 (3) of Title 8 — were not spelled out in debate. We cannot believe that Congress — itself a staunch advocate of legislative freedom — would impinge on a tradition so well grounded in history and reason by covert inclusion in the general language before us.

We come then to the question whether from the pleadings it appears that the defendants were acting in the sphere of legitimate legislative activity. Legislatures may not of course acquire power by an unwarranted extension of privilege. The House of Commons' claim of power to establish the limits of its privilege has been little more than a pretense since *Ashby v. White*. This Court has not hesitated to sustain the rights of private individuals when it found Congress was acting outside its legislative role.

The claim of an unworthy purpose does not destroy the privilege. Legislators are immune from deterrents to the uninhibited discharge of their legislative duty, not for their private indulgence but for the public good. One must not expect uncommon courage even in legislators. The privilege would be of little value if they could be subjected to the cost and inconvenience and distractions of a trial upon a conclusion of the pleader, or to the hazard of a judgment against them based upon a jury's speculation as to motives. The holding of this Court in *Fletcher v. Peck*, that it was not consonant with our scheme of government for a court to inquire into the motives of legislators, has remained unquestioned.

Investigations, whether by standing or special committees, are an established part of representative government. Legislative committees have been charged with losing sight of their duty of disinterestedness. In times of political passion, dishonest or vindictive motives are readily attributed to legislative conduct and as readily believed. Courts are not the place for such controversies. Self-discipline and the voters must be the ultimate reliance for discouraging or correcting such abuses. The courts should not go beyond the narrow confines of determining that a committee's inquiry may fairly be deemed within its province. To find that a committee's investigation has exceeded the bounds of legislative power it must be obvious that there was a usurpation of functions exclusively vested in the Judiciary or the Executive. The present case does not present such a situation. Brandhove indicated that evidence previously given by him to the committee was false, and he raised serious charges concerning the work of a committee investigating a problem within legislative concern. The Committee was entitled to assert a right to call the plaintiff before it and examine him.

It should be noted that this is a case in which the defendants are members of a legislature. Legislative privilege in such a case deserves greater respect than where an official acting on behalf of the legislature is sued or the legislature seeks the affirmative aid of the courts to assert a privilege. In *Kilbourn v. Thompson* this Court allowed a judgment against the Sergeant-at-Arms, but found that one could not be entered against the defendant members of the House.

We have only considered the scope of the privilege as applied to the facts of the present case. As Mr. Justice Miller said in the *Kilbourn* case: "It is not necessary to decide here that there may not be things done, in the one House or the other, of an extraordinary character, for which the members who take part in the act may be held legally responsible." We conclude only that here the individual defendants and the legislative committee were acting in a field where legislators traditionally have power to act, and that the statute of 1871 does not create civil liability for such conduct.

The judgment of the Court of Appeals is reversed and that of the District Court *affirmed*.

MR. JUSTICE DOUGLAS, dissenting.

I agree with the opinion of the Court as a statement of general principles governing the liability of legislative committees and members of the legislatures. But I do not agree that all abuses of legislative committees are solely for the legislative body to police.

We are dealing here with a right protected by the Constitution — the right of free speech. The charge seems strained and difficult to sustain; but it is that a legislative committee brought the weight of its authority down on respondent for exercising his right of free speech. Reprisal for speaking is as much an abridgment as a prior restraint. If a committee departs so far from its domain to deprive a citizen of a right protected by the Constitution, I can think of no reason why it should be immune. Yet that is the extent of the liability sought to be imposed on petitioners under 8 U.S.C. § 43.

It is speech and debate in the legislative department which our constitutional scheme makes privileged. Included, of course, are the actions of legislative committees that are authorized to conduct hearings or make investigations so as to lay the foundation for legislative action. But we are apparently holding today that the actions of those committees have no limits in the eyes of the law. May they depart with impunity from their legislative functions, sit as kangaroo courts, and try men for their loyalty and their political beliefs? May they substitute trial before committees for trial before juries? May they sit as a board of censors over industry, prepare their blacklists of citizens, and issue pronouncements as devastating as any bill of attainder?

No other public official has complete immunity for his actions. Even a policeman who exacts a confession by force and violence can be held criminally liable under the

Civil Rights Act, as we ruled only the other day in *Williams v. United States*. Yet now we hold that no matter the extremes to which a legislative committee may go it is not answerable to an injured party under the civil rights legislation. That result is the necessary consequence of our ruling since the test of the statute, so far as material here, is whether a constitutional right has been impaired, not whether the domain of the committee was traditional. It is one thing to give great leeway to the legislative right of speech, debate, and investigation. But when a committee perverts its power, brings down on an individual the whole weight of government for an illegal or corrupt purpose, the reason for the immunity ends. It was indeed the purpose of this civil rights legislation to secure federal rights against invasion by officers and agents of the states. I see no reason why any officer of government should be higher than the Constitution from which all rights and privileges of an office obtain.

[The concurring opinion of JUSTICE BLACK is omitted.]

NOTES

1. What is the Court's approach to interpreting section 1983's "person" language?

2. Is the Court's reliance on the Speech or Debate Clause convincing? What of the common law background?

3. According to the Court, if Congress had intended that absolute legislative immunity *not* apply to section 1983, what should Congress have done?

4. What are the policy considerations underlying absolute legislative immunity? Do they play any real role in *Tenney*? If *Tenney* is a statutory interpretation case, *should* such policy considerations play a role?

5. Suppose the plaintiff could in fact prove that the defendants knowingly violated his First Amendment rights by interrogating and prosecuting him? Would the result be any different?

6. If legislators are to be protected by absolute immunity, does the allegedly unconstitutional conduct of the defendants in *Tenney* itself present an easy or hard case for such immunity?

7. For discussion of the Cold War and anti-Communist context in which *Tenney* arose as well as the roles played by Justices Douglas and Frankfurter, see Nahmod, *Section 1983 Is Born: The Interlocking Supreme Court Stories of Tenney and Monroe*, 17 LEWIS & CLARK L. REV. 1019 (2013).

B. The Functional Approach of *Lake Country Estates*: Local and Regional Legislators

After *Tenney*, at least two major questions were left open. First, which legislators are protected by absolute immunity? After all, *Tenney* deals with state legislators. What of local legislators like city council members and aldermen? Second, what kind of conduct is protected by absolute immunity? The Supreme

Court's 1979 decision in *Lake Country Estates, Inc. v. Tahoe Regional Planning Agency*, 440 U.S. 391 (1979), effectively answered both questions.

Lake Country Estates involved a section 1983 action against an interstate-compact planning agency and its officers. The basis of the suit was the agency's adoption of a land use ordinance and general plan that allegedly destroyed the value of the plaintiffs' property. The Court, in an opinion by Justice Stevens, first found that the defendants' conduct had been undertaken *under color of state law* within the meaning of section 1983, even though federal approval was required and had been given for the interstate compact. Thus, a section 1983 cause of action was stated. The Court next concluded that the Eleventh Amendment did not bar suits in federal court against the planning agency and also suggested that the agency was a suable person under its decision in *Monell v. Department of Social Services*.

Finally, the Court held that the individual officers of the interstate planning agency were absolutely immune from section 1983 damages liability for actions taken in their legislative (as distinct from executive) capacities. Repeating *Tenney v. Brandhove's* assertion that "[o]ne must not expect uncommon courage even in legislators," the Court reasoned that it was for the public good that regional legislators, as well as federal and state legislators, be protected by an absolute immunity. It then remanded for determination of whether the defendants acted in a legislative capacity, that is, "in a capacity comparable to that of members of a state legislature."

Justices Brennan, Marshall, and Blackmun dissented on the immunity issue and argued that the individual defendants should not have *Tenney's* absolute immunity protection. Justice Blackmun specifically questioned whether the defendants were even properly characterizable as "regional legislators":

> Their duties are not solely legislative; they possess some executive powers. They are not in equipoise with other branches of government, and the concept of separation of powers has no relevance to them. They are not subject to the responsibility and the brake of the electoral process. And there is no provision for discipline within the body, as the Houses of Congress and the state legislatures possess.

The Court expressly left open the question of the relevance of *Lake Country Estates* for the immunity of local legislators. However, Justice Marshall, in his dissent, asserted that "the majority's reasoning in this case leaves little room to argue that municipal legislators stand on a different footing than their regional counterparts." In his view, the Court applied a functional test for absolute immunity to the defendants in *Lake Country Estates*, a test which, if applied to the legislative acts of local legislators, would in all likelihood lead to the same result.

1. After *Lake Country Estates*, should absolute immunity protect the following acts of local legislators: enacting an ordinance? reducing the number of liquor licenses? budget making? *See Aitchison v. Raffiani*, 708 F.2d 96 (3d Cir. 1983) (enacting ordinance), *Reed v. Village of Shorewood*, 704 F.2d 943 (7th Cir. 1983) (liquor license reduction) and *Rateree v. Rockett*, 852 F.2d 946 (7th Cir. 1988) (budget making), all of which applied absolute immunity.

2. What if a city's high-ranking executive vetoes an ordinance or votes to enter into a contract? *See Hernandez v. City of Lafayette*, 643 F.2d 1188 (5th Cir. 1981) (ordinance veto) and *Healy v. Town of Pembroke*, 831 F.2d 989 (11th Cir. 1987), 831 F.2d 980 (vote to contract), both of which applied absolute immunity. What additional factor is present in these two cases?

3. Because local legislators often perform non-legislative functions, it is sometimes difficult for courts to distinguish acts protected by absolute immunity from those that are not. One bright line, in theory at least, is between legislative and administrative acts, the latter being unprotected by absolute immunity. For example, the discharge of a local legislator's aide was found not protected by absolute immunity because it was administrative in nature. *Gross v. Winter*, 876 F.2d 165 (D.C. Cir. 1989). Similarly, judges who promulgated a personnel rule were found not protected by legislative immunity because their conduct was administrative. *Gutierrez v. Municipal Court*, 838 F.2d 1031 (9th Cir. 1988).

4. What factors do you consider significant in determining whether challenged conduct is legislative in nature? Consider the following, all of which have played some role in the cases:

(a) Was the challenged conduct a general policy or overall plan, or was it administrative in nature because it was not based on legislative facts and its impact was particularized?

(b) Was the challenged conduct the adoption of prospective, legislative-type rules or was it the enforcement of such rules?

(c) Was the challenged conduct the formulation of a policy or did it involve monitoring and administering, thereby being executive in nature?

d. Under state law, was the proper legislative procedure used in connection with the challenged conduct so that it was legislative in nature, or was the challenged conduct not a proper exercise of legislative powers?

See generally S. Nahmod, 2 Civil Rights And Civil Liberties Litigation: The Law of Section 1983 § 7:10 (4th ed. 2014)

5. Evaluate the following Fifth Circuit cases.

In *Hughes v. Tarrant County*, 948 F.2d 918 (5th Cir. 1991), the plaintiff state court clerk sued county commissioners for unconstitutionally refusing to pay for attorney's fees incurred in contempt proceedings brought against him. Ruling against the commissioners, the Fifth Circuit rejected the argument that their refusal to pay was a decision regarding the allocation of county monies and was thus legislative in nature. Instead, after canvassing the case law in the circuits, the court relied on a distinction between legislative facts and administrative facts and determined that the challenged decision "was based on specific facts of an individual situation related to the [plaintiff and] did not purport to establish a general policy; it was particular to [plaintiff]." Thus, it was administrative in nature.

Compare Calhoun v. St Bernard Parish, 937 F.2d 172 (5th Cir. 1991), where the plaintiff developer sued parish police jurors who adopted a series of construction moratoria that delayed his housing project. The Fifth Circuit held that the defendants were protected by absolute legislative immunity even though their challenged conduct was not the initial enforcement of a zoning code but rather spot zoning. The court relied for this determination on *Shelton v. City of College Station*, 780 F.2d 475 (5th Cir. 1986), which "held that the denial of a request for a variance from a zoning ordinance was a legislative decision" because it involved legislative facts. 937 F.2d at 174. According to the Fifth Circuit, the same was true in this case.

Calhoun is one of many examples of a legislative immunity case arising in the land use regulation setting.

C. *Bogan v. Scott-Harris*: The Broad Scope of Local Legislator Immunity

BOGAN v. SCOTT-HARRIS
523 U.S. 44 (1998)

Justice Thomas delivered the opinion of the Court.

It is well established that federal, state, and regional legislators are entitled to absolute immunity from civil liability for their legislative activities. In this case, petitioners argue that they, as local officials performing legislative functions, are entitled to the same protection. They further argue that their acts of introducing, voting for, and signing an ordinance eliminating the government office held by respondent constituted legislative activities. We agree on both counts and therefore reverse the judgment below.

I

Respondent Janet Scott-Harris was administrator of the Department of Health and Human Services (DHHS) for the city of Fall River, Massachusetts, from 1987 to 1991. In 1990, respondent received a complaint that Dorothy Biltcliffe, an employee serving temporarily under her supervision, had made repeated racial and ethnic slurs about her colleagues. After respondent prepared termination charges against Biltcliffe, Biltcliffe used her political connections to press her case with several state and local officials, including petitioner Marilyn Roderick, the vice president of the Fall River City Council. The city council held a hearing on the charges against Biltcliffe and ultimately accepted a settlement proposal under which Biltcliffe would be suspended without pay for 60 days. Petitioner Daniel Bogan, the mayor of Fall River, thereafter substantially reduced the punishment.

While the charges against Biltcliffe were pending, Mayor Bogan prepared his budget proposal for the 1992 fiscal year. Anticipating a 5 to 10 percent reduction in state aid, Bogan proposed freezing the salaries of all municipal employees and eliminating 135 city positions. As part of this package, Bogan called for the elimination of DHHS, of which respondent was the sole employee. The City Council Ordinance Committee, which was chaired by Roderick, approved an ordinance eliminating DHHS. The city council thereafter adopted the ordinance by a vote of 6 to 2, with petitioner Roderick among those voting in favor. Bogan signed the ordinance into law.

Respondent then filed suit under Rev. Stat. § 1979, 42 U.S.C. § 1983, against the city, Bogan, Roderick, and several other city officials. She alleged that the elimination of her position was motivated by racial animus and a desire to retaliate against her for exercising her First Amendment rights in filing the complaint against Biltcliffe. The District Court denied Bogan's and Roderick's motions to dismiss on the ground of legislative immunity, and the case proceeded to trial.

The jury returned a verdict in favor of all defendants on the racial discrimination charge, but found the city, Bogan, and Roderick liable on respondent's First Amendment claim, concluding that respondent's constitutionally protected speech was a substantial or motivating factor in the elimination of her position. On a motion for judgment notwithstanding the verdict, the District Court again denied Bogan's and Roderick's claims of absolute legislative immunity, reasoning that "the ordinance amendment passed by the city council was an individually-targeted administrative act, rather than a neutral, legislative elimination of a position which incidentally resulted in the termination of plaintiff."

The United States Court of Appeals for the First Circuit set aside the verdict against the city but affirmed the judgments against Roderick and Bogan. Although the court concluded that petitioners have "absolute immunity from civil liability for damages arising out of their performance of legitimate legislative activities," it held that their challenged conduct was not "legislative." Relying on the jury's finding that "constitutionally sheltered speech was a substantial or motivating factor" underlying petitioners' conduct, the court reasoned that the conduct was administrative, rather than legislative, because Roderick and Bogan "relied on facts relating to a particular individual [respondent] in the decision-making calculus."

II

The principle that legislators are absolutely immune from liability for their legislative activities has long been recognized in Anglo-American law. This privilege "has taproots in the Parliamentary struggles of the Sixteenth and Seventeenth Centuries" and was "taken as a matter of course by those who severed the Colonies from the Crown and founded our Nation." *Tenney v. Brandhove.* The Federal Constitution, the constitutions of many of the newly independent States, and the common law thus protected legislators from liability for their legislative activities.

Recognizing this venerable tradition, we have held that state and regional legislators are entitled to absolute immunity from liability under § 1983 for their legislative activities. We explained that legislators were entitled to absolute immunity from suit at common law and that Congress did not intend the general language of § 1983 to "impinge on a tradition so well grounded in history and reason." Because the common law accorded local legislators the same absolute immunity it accorded legislators at other levels of government, and because the rationales for such immunity are fully applicable to local legislators, we now hold that local legislators are likewise absolutely immune from suit under § 1983 for their legislative activities.

The common law at the time § 1983 was enacted deemed local legislators to be absolutely immune from suit for their legislative activities. New York's highest court, for example, held that municipal aldermen were immune from suit for their discretionary decisions. The court explained that when a local legislator exercises discretionary powers, he "is exempt from all responsibility by action for the motives which influence him, and the manner in which such duties are performed. If corrupt, he may be impeached or indicted, but the law will not tolerate an action to redress the individual wrong which may have been done." These principles, according to the court, were "too familiar and well settled to require illustration or authority."

Shortly after § 1983 was enacted, the Mississippi Supreme Court reached a similar conclusion, holding that town aldermen could not be held liable under state law for their role in the adoption of an allegedly unlawful ordinance. The court explained that "it certainly cannot be argued that the motives of the individual members of a legislative assembly, in voting for a particular law, can be inquired into, and its supporters be made personally liable, upon an allegation that they acted maliciously towards the person aggrieved by the passage of the law." The court thus concluded that "whenever the officers of a municipal corporation are vested with legislative powers, they hold and exercise them for the public good, and are clothed with all the immunities of government, and are exempt from all liability for their mistaken use."

Treatises of that era confirm that this was the pervasive view. A leading treatise on municipal corporations explained that "where the officers of a municipal corporation are invested with legislative powers, they are exempt from individual liability for the passage of any ordinance within their authority, and their motives in reference thereto will not be inquired into." 1 J. Dillon, Law of Municipal Corporations § 313, pp. 326–327 (3d ed. 1881). Thomas Cooley likewise noted in his influential treatise on the law of torts that the "rightful exemption" of legislators from liability was "very plain" and applied to members of "inferior legislative bodies, such as boards of supervisors, county commissioners, city councils, and the like." [T. COOLEY, LAW OF TORTS 376 (1880)]

Even the authorities cited by respondent are consistent with the view that local legislators were absolutely immune for their legislative, as distinct from ministerial, duties. In the few cases in which liability did attach, the courts emphasized that the defendant officials lacked discretion, and the duties were thus ministerial. The treatises cited by respondent confirm that this distinction between legislative and ministerial duties was dispositive of the right to absolute immunity. See, e.g., Cooley 377 (stating that local legislators may be held liable only for their "ministerial" duties).

Absolute immunity for local legislators under § 1983 finds support not only in history, but also in reason. The rationales for according absolute immunity to federal, state, and regional legislators apply with equal force to local legislators. Regardless of the level of government, the exercise of legislative discretion should not be inhibited by judicial interference or distorted by the fear of personal liability. Furthermore, the time and energy required to defend against a lawsuit are of particular concern at the local level, where the part-time citizen-legislator remains commonplace. And the threat of liability may significantly deter service in local government, where prestige and pecuniary rewards may pale in comparison to the threat of civil liability. *See Harlow v. Fitzgerald.* Moreover, certain deterrents to legislative abuse may be greater at the local level than at other levels of government. Municipalities themselves can be held liable for constitutional violations, whereas States and the Federal Government are often protected by sovereign immunity. *Lake Country Estates.* And, of course, the ultimate check on legislative abuse — the electoral process — applies with equal force at the local level, where legislators are often more closely responsible to the electorate. *Cf. Tenney* (stating that "self-discipline and the voters must be the ultimate reliance for discouraging or correcting such abuses").

Any argument that the rationale for absolute immunity does not extend to local legislators is implicitly foreclosed by our opinion in *Lake Country Estates.* There, we held that members of an interstate regional planning agency were entitled to absolute legislative immunity. Bereft of any historical antecedent to the regional agency, we relied almost exclusively on *Tenney's* description of the purposes of legislative immunity and the importance of such immunity in advancing the "public good." Although we expressly noted that local legislators were not at issue in that case, *see Lake Country Estates,* we considered the regional legislators at issue to be the functional equivalents of local legislators, noting that the regional agency was "comparable to a county or municipality" and that the function of the regional agency, regulation of land use, was "traditionally a function performed by local governments." Thus, we now make explicit what was implicit in our precedents: Local legislators are entitled to absolute immunity from § 1983 liability for their legislative activities.

III

Absolute legislative immunity attaches to all actions taken "in the sphere of legitimate legislative activity." The Court of Appeals held that petitioners' conduct in this case was not legislative because their actions were specifically targeted at respondent. Relying on the jury's finding that respondent's constitutionally protected speech was a substantial or motivating factor behind petitioners' conduct, the court concluded that petitioners necessarily "relied on facts relating to a particular individual" and "devised an ordinance that targeted [respondent] and treated her differently from other managers employed by the City." Although the Court of Appeals did not suggest that intent or motive can overcome an immunity defense for activities that are, in fact, legislative, the court erroneously relied on petitioners' subjective intent in resolving the logically prior question of whether their acts were legislative.

Whether an act is legislative turns on the nature of the act, rather than on the motive or intent of the official performing it. The privilege of absolute immunity "would be of little value if [legislators] could be subjected to the cost and inconvenience and distractions of a trial upon a conclusion of the pleader, or to the hazard of a judgment against them based upon a jury's speculation as to motives." *Tenney.* Furthermore, it simply is "not consonant with our scheme of government for a court to inquire into the motives of legislators." *Ibid.* We therefore held that the defendant in *Tenney* had acted in a legislative capacity even though he allegedly singled out the plaintiff for investigation in order "to intimidate and silence plaintiff and deter and prevent him from effectively exercising his constitutional rights." This leaves us with the question whether, stripped of all considerations of intent and motive, petitioners' actions were legislative. We have little trouble concluding that they were. Most evidently, petitioner Roderick's acts of voting for an ordinance were, in form, quintessentially legislative. Petitioner Bogan's introduction of a budget and signing into law an ordinance also were formally legislative, even though he was an executive official. We have recognized that officials outside the legislative branch are entitled to legislative immunity when they perform legislative functions. Bogan's actions were legislative because they were integral steps in the legislative process.

Respondent, however, asks us to look beyond petitioners' formal actions to consider whether the ordinance was legislative in substance. We need not determine whether the formally legislative character of petitioners' actions is alone sufficient to entitle petitioners to legislative immunity, because here the ordinance, in substance, bore all the hallmarks of traditional legislation. The ordinance reflected a discretionary, policymaking decision implicating the budgetary priorities of the city and the services the city provides to its constituents. Moreover, it involved the termination of a position, which, unlike the hiring or firing of a particular employee, may have prospective implications that reach well beyond the particular occupant of the office. And the city council, in eliminating DHHS, certainly governed "in a field where legislators traditionally have power to act." *Tenney.* Thus, petitioners' activities were undoubtedly legislative.

For the foregoing reasons, the judgment of the Court of Appeals is *reversed*.

NOTES

1. Is *Bogan* an easy or hard case?

2. Is *Bogan* consistent with *Tenney's* approach to section 1983 interpretation? Is it consistent with a functional approach to immunities?

3. After *Bogan*, what is the relevance to the legislative immunity inquiry of formal compliance with legislative procedures? Of legislative reliance on particularized facts?

4. With respect to high-level executives who act legislatively, the First Circuit applied *Bogan* and held that the Governor of Puerto Rico, sued under § 1983 for damages for signing allegedly unconstitutional legislation into law, was protected by absolute legislative immunity because the challenged conduct was clearly legislative in nature. The court rejected the plaintiffs' argument that legislative immunity is abrogated where legislation is motivated by impermissible intent, pointing out that this very argument was rejected by the Supreme Court in *Bogan. Torres Rivera v. Calderon Serra*, 412 F.3d 205 (1st Cir. 2005).

5. Compare *Thornton v. City of St. Helens*, 425 F.3d 1158, 1163 (9th Cir. 2005), where the plaintiffs, owners of an automobile wrecking yard, sued a city and various officials, including the city's manager and planner, for allegedly unlawfully conditioning the approval of their application for renewal of their wrecker's certificate on compliance with certain land use regulations. The Ninth Circuit ruled that the city manager and city planner were not entitled to legislative immunity. For one thing, their jobs were administrative in nature. For another, the challenged conduct — "[p]rocessing an individual application pursuant to an established policy" — was not a legislative function but was rather administrative in nature.

6.	Where the former executive director of a police and fire retirement board, an at-will employee, sued an Arkansas state legislator, co-chair of the legislature's Joint Committee on Public Retirement and Social Security Programs, for violating her First Amendment rights through the defendant' participation in introducing a bill to reduce the number of members of the board (which plaintiff opposed), the Eighth Circuit had little difficulty in concluding that the defendant was protected by legislative immunity. *Hinshaw v. Smith*, 436 F.3d 997 (8th Cir. 2006). All actions taken by the defendant in connection with the bill (which passed) were quintessentially legislative in nature. In addition, the defendant was responsible for submitting names to the governor for filling vacant board positions, so his discussions with the governor about plaintiff's representations about what the board wanted fell within his legislative duties. Finally, defendant's communications with the board about plaintiff's responsiveness also fell within his legislative duties, regardless of his motive to take plaintiff's position as executive director when his legislative term expired.

7.	The plaintiffs who engaged in sand and gravel removal operations on their property sued various defendants, including individual members of a town's city council, for enacting a zoning ordinance that effectively prevented plaintiffs from extending their operations. They alleged violations of substantive due process and equal protection under § 1983, among other things. Ruling against the plaintiffs in this regard, the Third Circuit determined that the council members were protected by legislative immunity. First, the ordinance, even if it turned out to apply only to plaintiffs' land, was legislative in nature, and did not constitute the enforcement of an already existing zoning law. Second, the challenged conduct, enacting the ordinance, followed established legislative procedures. *County Concrete Corporation v. Town of Roxbury*, 442 F.3d 159 (3d Cir. 2006).

## D.	A Note on Prospective Relief

As we shall see, neither judges nor prosecutors are absolutely immune from prospective relief liability, in marked contrast to their absolute immunity from damages liability. *See Pulliam v. Allen*, 466 U.S. 522 (1984) (judges), subsequently modified by the Federal Court Improvements Act of 1996, noted below, and *Supreme Court v. Consumers Union*, 446 U.S. 719 (1980) (prosecutors). However, state legislators are different in that they are protected from both. The Supreme Court so held in *Supreme Court v. Consumers Union*, noted above. *Consumers Union* involved a section 1983 suit against, among others, the Supreme Court of Virginia and its chief justice (in his official capacity) challenging on First Amendment grounds the Virginia Supreme Court's disciplinary rule for lawyer advertising. A three-judge district court held the challenged rule unconstitutional and enjoined the defendants from enforcing it. Defendants' argument that absolute immunity protected them both from declaratory or injunctive relief was rejected.

In an opinion by Justice White, the Supreme Court vacated and remanded. It first found that the Virginia Supreme Court acted in a legislative capacity in promulgating lawyer disciplinary rules. In fact, "the Virginia Court is exercising the State's 'entire legislative power' with respect to regulating the Bar, and its members are the *State's legislators* for the purpose of issuing the Bar Code." The Court then discussed its decision in *Eastland v. United States Servicemen's Fund*, 421 U.S. 491 (1975), which held that the Speech or Debate Clause immunizes members of Congress from suits for both prospective relief and damages. The Court reasoned, citing *Tenney v. Brandhove*, that *Eastland's* concern with interference with the federal legislative function through injunctive relief was equally applicable to state legislators sued under section 1983 for prospective relief. Thus, because the Virginia Supreme Court had acted in a legislative capacity in promulgating the challenged rule, it and its members were absolutely immune from suit.

Nevertheless, the Court, after expressly leaving open the question of whether judicial immunity bars prospective relief, held that the Virginia Supreme Court and its chief justice could be sued for injunctive relief in their *enforcement* capacities (as distinguished from their legislative and judicial capacities) like other enforcement officers and agencies. The Court here referred to the Virginia Supreme Court's "independent authority of its own to initiate proceedings against attorneys," and affirmed that prosecutors, despite their absolute immunity from liability for damages, could be sued for injunctive and declaratory relief.

1. *Consumers Union*, which obviously takes a functional approach, makes clear that state legislators are absolutely immune from prospective relief liability (although prosecutors are not). Does this double-barreled immunity for state legislators make sense? If it does, should it protect *local* legislators as well?

2. Congress, reacting to *Pulliam v. Allen*, noted above, enacted section 309 of the Federal Courts Improvement Act of 1996 and "overruled" *Pulliam* in part by adding the following at the end of the first sentence of section 1983: "except that in any action brought against a judicial officer for an act or omission taken in such judicial officer's judicial capacity, injunctive relief shall not be granted unless a declaratory decree was violated or declaratory relief was unavailable." Does the Act affect the availability of injunctive relief against judges for their non-judicial conduct such as administrative behavior? Is it relevant that *Pulliam* itself dealt only judicial conduct?

3. Do state of mind requirements for particular constitutional violations also serve to protect against injunctive relief? Consider, for example, the Supreme Court's important 1994 decision in *Waters v. Churchill*, 511 U.S. 661 (1994), *rev'g*, 977 F.2d 1114 (7th Cir. 1993), a First Amendment employment case, also noted in Chapter 3.

In *Waters*, the relevant question presented in the petition for certiorari was the following: "May public employer that terminates employee based on credible, substantiated reports of unprotected, insubordinate speech be held liable for retaliatory discharge under First Amendment if it is later shown that reports were inaccurate and that employee actually spoke on protected matters of public concern, when employer's ignorance of protected speech is result of incomplete investigation?" There was no opinion for the Court in *Waters* but the plurality, in an opinion by Justice O'Connor, adopted a reasonableness requirement under which an employee may not be dismissed or otherwise disciplined unless the employer had a reasonable basis for believing that the speech was either disruptive or that it involved a matter of purely private concern outside the scope of the First Amendment. There was thus a First Amendment duty to conduct a reasonable investigation into the nature and content of the speech, although not a full-scale investigation. Subjective good faith, standing alone, was not sufficient to avoid liability. In short, First Amendment protection depended on what the employer reasonably believed the nature and content of the speech to be, and not on what the speech actually was.

Justice Scalia, in an opinion joined by Justices Kennedy and Thomas, concurred in the result. He maintained that reasonableness was not the appropriate standard because it would subject public employers to "intolerable legal uncertainty." Rather, a public employer should be liable under the First Amendment only where it retaliated against the employee for speaking on a matter of public concern; there was no duty to investigate. Justices Stevens and Blackmun dissented, arguing that the plurality did not go far enough in providing First Amendment protection to employee speech. In their view, what was determinative was the *actual* nature and content of the speech, not what the public employer thought, reasonably or otherwise, it was.

The *Waters* plurality standard staked out the middle ground between an intent requirement on the one hand (Justice Scalia's position) and a kind of strict liability approach on the other (Justices Stevens and Blackmun). Does it follow from this kind of negligence standard that section 1983 plaintiffs seeking reinstatement will not get their jobs back if they are unable to prove by a preponderance of the evidence that the defendant public employers acted unreasonably with respect to investigating the nature and content of their speech, even though it turns out that the speech was such that it was in fact nondisruptive speech on a matter of public concern? If so, is that fair?

Is *Waters* a qualified immunity case in disguise? Should the Court have dealt with it on that ground and adopted the First Amendment approach of Justices Stevens and Blackmun so that the reasonableness inquiry would be relevant not to the state of mind requirement for the prima facie First Amendment cause of action but rather to the objective reasonableness inquiry called for by qualified immunity? Wouldn't that have avoided the non-reinstatement harshness inasmuch as qualified immunity is relevant only to damages liability of individuals (although not that of local governments)? Qualified immunity is addressed in Chapter 8, state of mind requirements for particular constitutional violations are considered in Chapter 3, local government liability is addressed in Chapter 5 and remedies in general are dealt with in Chapter 9.

II. ABSOLUTE JUDICIAL IMMUNITY

A. The Common Law Immunity Background in 1871: *Bradley*

Consider *Bradley v. Fisher*, 80 U.S. 335 (1871), on which much absolute judicial immunity doctrine is premised. *Bradley* involved a criminal court judge of the District of Columbia who was sued for damages by a lawyer whom he removed from practice before his court without notice and the opportunity to defend. The Court elaborately set out the general absolute judicial immunity rules, *id.* at 351–52 (emphasis added):

> [J]udges of courts of superior or general jurisdiction are not liable to civil actions for their judicial acts, even when such acts are in excess of their jurisdiction, and are alleged to have been done maliciously or corruptly. A distinction must be here observed between excess of jurisdiction and the clear absence of all jurisdiction over the subject-matter. Where there is clearly no jurisdiction over the subjectmatter any authority exercised is a usurped authority, and for the exercise of such authority, when the want of jurisdiction is known to the judge, no excuse is permissible. But where jurisdiction over the subject-matter is invested by law in the judge, or in the court which he holds, the manner and extent in which the jurisdiction shall be exercised are generally as much questions for his determination as any other questions involved in the case, although upon the correctness of his determination in these particulars the validity of his judgments may depend. Thus, if a probate court, invested only with authority over wills and the settlement of estates of deceased persons, should proceed to try parties for public offences, jurisdiction over the subject of offences being entirely wanting in the court, and this being necessarily known to its judge, his commission would afford no protection to him in the exercise of the usurped authority. But if on the other hand a judge of a criminal court, invested with general criminal jurisdiction over offences committed within a certain district, should hold a particular act to be a public offence, which is not by the law made an offence, and proceed to the arrest and trial of a party charged with such act, or should sentence a party convicted to a greater punishment than that authorized by the law upon its proper construction, no personal liability to civil action for such acts would attach to the judge, although those acts would be in excess of his jurisdiction, or of the jurisdiction of the court held by him, for these are particulars for his judicial consideration, whenever his general jurisdiction over the subject-matter is invoked. Indeed some of the most difficult and embarrassing questions which a judicial officer is called upon to consider and determine relate to his jurisdiction, or that of the court held by him, or the manner in which the jurisdiction shall be exercised. And the same principle of exemption from liability which obtains for errors committed in the ordinary prosecution of a suit where there is jurisdiction of both subject and person, applies in cases of this kind, and for the same reasons.

In applying these principles to the facts before it, the Supreme Court in *Bradley* observed that, while the defendant judge had the power to remove a lawyer from the bar, this should not ordinarily be done without notice and an opportunity to explain and defend. Nevertheless, even though the defendant judge erred in not giving plaintiff such notice, this action constituted at most an excess of jurisdiction but "did not make the act any less a judicial act. . . . It was not as though the court had proceeded without any jurisdiction whatever over its attorneys." Thus, the defendant judge was absolutely immune from liability for damages for the allegedly wrongful disbarment.

1. Why did the case before the Court not involve the "clear absence of all jurisdiction?"

2. What does "jurisdiction" mean"? Is it limited to subject matter jurisdiction? Does it include personal jurisdiction?

3. Is the language of jurisdiction helpful in this setting?

4. How would you describe the margin for judicial error articulated in *Bradley*?

B. *Pierson*: The Seminal Case on Section 1983 Absolute Judicial Immunity

The jurisdiction language of *Bradley* was combined with the common law background approach of *Tenney* in *Pierson v. Ray*, 386 U.S. 547 (1967), the seminal section 1983 absolute judicial immunity case. In *Pierson*, the plaintiffs had been arrested by the defendant police officers in 1961 and then convicted and given the maximum sentence by the defendant municipal police justice for violating a Mississippi breach of the peace statute. This statute was held unconstitutional by the Supreme Court as applied to similar facts four years later but prior to the Court's decision in Pierson. After plaintiffs had been vindicated in a trial de novo, they sued the defendants for damages under section 1983 as well as for false arrest and imprisonment at common law.

In holding that the police justice was absolutely immune from liability for damages under section 1983, the Court compared judicial immunity at common law to legislative immunity. Following *Tenney's* approach, the Court stated:

> The legislative record gives no clear indication that Congress meant to abolish wholesale all common-law immunities. . . . The immunity of judges for acts within the judicial role is equally well established [as absolute legislative immunity], and we presume that Congress would have specifically so provided had it wished to abolish the doctrine.

As to the scope and application of the doctrine, the Court observed that the only act of the police justice was to find plaintiffs guilty. It then went on to hold that judges are absolutely immune from liability for damages for acts committed within their judicial jurisdiction . . . even when the judge is accused of acting maliciously and corruptly. . . . It is a judge's duty to decide all cases within his judicial jurisdiction that are brought before him, including controversial cases that arouse the most intense feelings in the litigants. His errors may be corrected on appeal, but he should not have to fear that unsatisfied litigants may hound him with litigation charging malice or corruption. Imposing such a burden on judges would contribute not to principled and fearless decision making but to intimidation.

1. As a matter of policy, is absolute judicial immunity as defensible as absolute legislative immunity?

2. Is absolute judicial immunity defensible as a matter of legislative history? Justice Douglas argued in dissent in *Pierson* that section 1983's legislative history indicated that it was to apply to judges. He stated: "It was recognized [in 1871] that certain members of the judiciary were instruments of oppression and were partially responsible for the wrongs to be remedied." It has also been argued that absolute judicial immunity was not as well established at common law as absolute legislative immunity. *See Note, Developments in the Law — Section 1983 and Federalism*, 90 HARV. L. REV. 1133, 1201 (1977). *See also* Kates, *Immunity of State Judges Under the Federal Civil Rights Acts*: Pierson v. Ray *Reconsidered*, 65 Nw. U. L. REV. 615 (1970). Should these historical considerations make a difference? For the argument that the Court's historical methodology is seriously flawed, see Matasar, *Personal Immunities Under Section 1983: The Limits of the Court's Historical Analysis*, 40 ARK. L. REV. 741 (1987).

3. Is absolute judicial immunity defensible as a matter of economic analysis? It has been asserted that the answer is yes. *See* Cass, *Damage Suits Against Public Officers*, 129 U. PA. L. REV. 110 (1981). Under this view, although "judges lack any significant incentive, intrinsic to the judicial process, for responding to the parties' (and ultimately the society's) interests in minimizing costs on the one hand and benefits on the other," they nevertheless generally reach appropriate decisions because of the seriousness with which they approach their job. There also are review mechanisms available to correct improper initial decisions. Most significantly, the cost of assessing liability is likely to be extraordinarily high because "the same difficult decisions must be repeated."

4. On its *facts*, is Pierson an easy or hard absolute judicial immunity case? How does it compare with *Stump v. Sparkman*, the next case?

C. The Broad Scope of Absolute Judicial Immunity: *Stump*

STUMP v. SPARKMAN
435 U.S. 349 (1978)

MR. JUSTICE **WHITE** delivered the opinion of the Court.

This case requires us to consider the scope of a judge's immunity from damages liability when sued under 42 U.S.C. § 1983.

I

The relevant facts underlying respondents' suit are not in dispute. On July 9, 1971, Ora Spitler McFarlin, the mother of respondent Linda Kay Spitler Sparkman, presented to Judge Harold D. Stump of the Circuit Court of DeKalb County, Ind., a document captioned "Petition To Have Tubal Ligation Performed On Minor and Indemnity Agreement." The document had been drafted by her attorney, a petitioner here. In this petition Mrs. McFarlin stated under oath that her daughter was 15 years of age and was "somewhat retarded," although she attended public school and had been promoted each year with her class. The petition further stated that Linda had been associating with "older youth or young men" and had stayed out overnight with them on several occasions. As a result of this behavior and Linda's mental capabilities, it was stated that it would be in the daughter's best interest if she underwent a tubal ligation in order "to prevent unfortunate circumstances. . . ." In the same document Mrs. McFarlin also undertook to indemnify and hold harmless Dr. John Hines, who was to perform the operation, and the DeKalb Memorial Hospital, where the operation was to take place, against all causes of action that might arise as a result of the performance of the tubal ligation.

The petition was approved by Judge Stump on the same day. He affixed his signature as "Judge, DeKalb Circuit Court," to the statement that he did "hereby approve the above Petition by affidavit form on behalf of Ora Spitler McFarlin, to have Tubal Ligation performed upon her minor daughter, Linda Spitler, subject to said Ora Spitler McFarlin covenanting and agreeing to indemnify and keep indemnified Dr. John Hines and the DeKalb Memorial Hospital from any matters or causes of action arising therefrom."

On July 15, 1971, Linda Spitler entered the DeKalb Memorial Hospital, having been told that she was to have her appendix removed. The following day a tubal ligation was performed upon her. She was released several days later, unaware of the true nature of her surgery.

Approximately two years after the operation, Linda Spitler was married to respondent Leo Sparkman. Her inability to become pregnant led her to discover that she had been sterilized during the 1971 operation. As a result of this revelation, the Sparkmans filed suit in the United States District Court for the Northern District of Indiana against Mrs. McFarlin, her attorney, Judge Stump, the doctors who had performed and assisted in the tubal ligation, and the DeKalb Memorial Hospital. Respondents sought damages for the alleged violation of Linda Sparkman's constitutional rights; also asserted were pendent state claims for assault and battery, medical malpractice, and loss of potential fatherhood.

[The district court found absolute immunity applicable, but the Seventh Circuit disagreed and reversed. The Supreme Court in turn reversed.]

II

The governing principle of law is well established and is not questioned by the parties. As early as 1872, the Court recognized that it was "a general principle of the highest importance to the proper administration of justice that a judicial officer, in exercising the authority vested in him, [should] be free to act upon his own convictions, without apprehension of personal consequences to himself." *Bradley v. Fisher.* For that reason the Court held that "judges of courts of superior or general jurisdiction are not liable to civil actions for their judicial acts, even when such acts are in excess of their jurisdiction, and are alleged to have been done maliciously or corruptly." Later we held that this doctrine of judicial immunity was applicable in suits under § 1 of the Civil Rights Act of 1871, 42 U.S.C. § 1983, for the legislative record gave no indication that Congress intended to abolish this long-established principle. *Pierson v. Ray.*

The Court of Appeals correctly recognized that the necessary inquiry in determining whether a defendant judge is immune from suit is whether at the time he took the challenged action he had jurisdiction over the subject matter before him. Because "some of the most difficult and embarrassing questions which a judicial officer is called upon to consider and determine relate to his jurisdiction . . . ," *Bradley*, the scope of the judge's jurisdiction must be construed broadly where the issue is the immunity of the judge. A judge will not be deprived of immunity because the action he took was in error, was done maliciously, or was in excess of his authority; rather, he will be subject to liability only when he has acted in the "clear absence of all jurisdiction."

We cannot agree that there was a "clear absence of all jurisdiction" in the DeKalb County Circuit Court to consider the petition presented by Mrs. McFarlin. As an Indiana Circuit Court Judge, Judge Stump had "original exclusive jurisdiction in all cases at law and in equity whatsoever . . . ;" jurisdiction over the settlement of estates and over guardianships, appellate jurisdiction as conferred by law, and jurisdiction over "all other causes, matters and proceedings where exclusive jurisdiction thereof is not conferred by law upon some other court, board or officer." This is indeed a broad jurisdictional grant; yet the Court of Appeals concluded that Judge Stump did not have jurisdiction over the petition authorizing Linda Sparkman's sterilization.

In so doing, the Court of Appeals noted that the Indiana statutes provided for the sterilization of institutionalized persons under certain circumstances, but otherwise contained no express authority for judicial approval of tubal ligations. It is true that the statutory grant of general jurisdiction to the Indiana circuit courts does not itemize types of cases those courts may hear and hence does not expressly mention sterilization petitions presented by the parents of a minor. But in our view, it is more significant that there was no Indiana statute and no case law in 1971 prohibiting a circuit court, a court of general jurisdiction, from considering a petition of the type presented to Judge Stump. The statutory authority for the sterilization of institutionalized persons in the custody of the State does not warrant the inference that a court of general jurisdiction has no power to act on a petition for sterilization of a minor in the custody of her parents, particularly where the parents have authority under the Indiana statutes to "consent to and contract for medical or hospital care or treatment of [the minor] including surgery." The District Court concluded that Judge Stump had jurisdiction under § 33-4-4-3 to entertain and act upon Mrs. McFarlin's petition. We agree with the District Court, it appearing that neither by statute nor by case law has the broad jurisdiction granted to the circuit courts of Indiana been circumscribed to foreclose consideration of a petition for authorization of a minor's sterilization.

We conclude that the Court of Appeals, employing an unduly restrictive view of the scope of Judge Stump's jurisdiction, erred in holding that he was not entitled to judicial immunity. Because the court over which Judge Stump presides is one of general jurisdiction, neither the procedural errors he may have committed nor the lack of a specific statute authorizing his approval of the petition in question rendered him liable in damages for the consequences of his actions.

The respondents argue that even if Judge Stump had jurisdiction to consider the petition presented to him by Mrs. McFarlin, he is still not entitled to judicial immunity because his approval of the petition did not constitute a "judicial" act. It is only for acts performed in his "judicial" capacity that a judge is absolutely immune, they say. We do not disagree with this statement of the law, but we cannot characterize the approval of the petition as a nonjudicial act.

Respondents themselves stated in their pleadings before the District Court that Judge Stump was "clothed with the authority of the state" at the time that he approved the petition and that "he was acting as a county circuit court judge." They nevertheless now argue that Judge Stump's approval of the petition was not a judicial act because the petition was not given a docket number, was not placed on file with the clerk's office, and was approved in an ex parte proceeding without notice to the minor, without a hearing, and without the appointment of a guardian ad litem.

This Court has not had occasion to consider, for purposes of the judicial immunity doctrine, the necessary attributes of a judicial act; but it has previously rejected the argument, somewhat similar to the one raised here, that the lack of formality involved in the Illinois Supreme Court's consideration of a petitioner's application for admission to the state bar prevented it from being a "judicial proceeding" and from presenting a case or controversy that could be reviewed by this Court. *In re Summers*. Of particular significance to the present case, the Court in *Summers* noted the following: "The record does not show that any process issued or that any appearance was made. . . . While no entry was placed by the Clerk in the file, on a docket, or in a judgment roll, the Court took cognizance of the petition and passed an order which is validated by the signature of the presiding officer." Because the Illinois court took cognizance of the petition for admission and acted upon it, the Court held that a case or controversy was presented.

Similarly, the Court of Appeals for the Fifth Circuit has held that a state district judge was entitled to judicial immunity, even though "at the time of the altercation [giving rise to the suit] Judge Brown was not in his judge's robes, he was not in the courtroom itself, and he may well have violated state and/or federal procedural requirements regarding contempt citations." *McAlester v. Brown*. Among the factors relied upon by the Court of Appeals in deciding that the judge was acting within his judicial capacity was the fact that "the confrontation arose directly and immediately out of a visit to the judge in his official capacity."

The relevant cases demonstrate that the factors determining whether an act by a judge is a "judicial" one relate to the nature of the act itself, i.e., whether it is a function normally performed by a judge, and to the expectations of the parties, i.e., whether they dealt with the judge in his judicial capacity. Here, both factors indicate that Judge Stump's approval of the sterilization petition was a judicial act. State judges with general jurisdiction not infrequently are called upon in their official capacity to approve petitions relating to the affairs of minors, as for example, a petition to settle a minor's claim. Furthermore, as even respondents have admitted, at the time he approved the petition presented to him by Mrs. McFarlin, Judge Stump was "acting as a county circuit court judge." We may infer from the record that it was only because Judge Stump served in that position that Mrs. McFarlin, on the advice of counsel, submitted the petition to him for his approval. Because Judge Stump performed the type of act normally performed only by judges and because he did so in his capacity as a Circuit Court Judge, we find no merit to respondents' argument that the informality with which he proceeded rendered his action nonjudicial and deprived him of his absolute immunity.

The Indiana law vested in Judge Stump the power to entertain and act upon the petition for sterilization. He is, therefore, under the controlling cases, immune from damages liability even if his approval of the petition was in error.

Accordingly, the judgment of the Court of Appeals is reversed, and the case is remanded for further proceedings consistent with this opinion.

MR. JUSTICE STEWART, with whom MR. JUSTICE MARSHALL and MR. JUSTICE POWELL join, dissenting.

It is established federal law that judges of general jurisdiction are absolutely immune from monetary liability "for their judicial acts, even when such acts are in excess of their jurisdiction, and are alleged to have been done maliciously or corruptly." *Bradley v. Fisher*. It is also established that this immunity is in no way diminished in a proceeding under 42 U.S.C. § 1983. But the scope of judicial immunity is limited to liability for "judicial acts" and I think that what Judge Stump did on July 9, 1971, was beyond the pale of anything that could sensibly be called a judicial act.

Neither in *Bradley v. Fisher* nor in *Pierson v. Ray* was there any claim that the conduct in question was not a judicial act, and the Court thus had no occasion in either case to discuss the meaning of that term. Yet the proposition that judicial immunity extends only to liability for "judicial acts" was emphasized no less than seven times in Mr. Justice Field's opinion for the Court in the *Bradley* case. *Cf. Imbler v. Pachtman*. And if the limitations inherent in that concept have any realistic meaning at all, then I cannot believe that the action of Judge Stump in approving Mrs. McFarlin's petition is protected by judicial immunity.

The Court finds two reasons for holding that Judge Stump's approval of the sterilization petition was a judicial act. First, the Court says, it was "a function normally performed by a judge." Second, the Court says, the act was performed in Judge Stump's "judicial capacity." With all respect, I think that the first of these grounds is factually untrue and that the second is legally unsound.

In sum, what Judge Stump did on July 9, 1971, was in no way an act "normally performed by a judge." Indeed, there is no reason to believe that such an act has ever been performed by any other Indiana judge, either before or since.

* * *

It seems to me, rather, that the concept of what is a judicial act must take its content from a consideration of the factors that support immunity from liability for the performance of such an act. Those factors were accurately summarized by the Court in *Pierson v. Ray*:

> "[I]t 'is . . . for the benefit of the public, whose interest it is that the judges should be at liberty to exercise their functions with independence and without fear of consequences.' . . . It is a judge's duty to decide all cases within his jurisdiction that are brought before him, including controversial cases that arouse the most intense feelings in the litigants. His errors may be corrected on appeal, but he should not have to fear that unsatisfied litigants may hound him with litigation charging malice or corruption. Imposing such a burden on judges would contribute not to principled and fearless decision-making but to intimidation."

Not one of the considerations thus summarized in the *Pierson* opinion was present here. There was no "case," controversial or otherwise. There were no litigants. There was and could be no appeal. And there was not even the pretext of principled decisionmaking. The total absence of any of these normal attributes of a judicial proceeding convinces me that the conduct complained of in this case was not a judicial act.

[The dissenting opinion of JUSTICE **POWELL** is omitted; JUSTICE **BRENNAN** did not participate.]

NOTES

1.   Is *Stump* an easy or hard case in which to find absolute judicial immunity applicable? Why?

2.   Does *Stump* retain the language of jurisdiction that we saw in *Bradley* and *Pierson*? If so, how is it applied in *Stump*? What does it add?

3.   What of the argument that the judge acted in the clear absence of all *personal* jurisdiction?

4.   What does the Court mean by a "judicial act?" Is the challenged judicial conduct in *Stump* a judicial act? Can there be a *judicial act* in the clear absence of all jurisdiction? Can there be a *nonjudicial act* which is only in excess of jurisdiction? Is *Stump* wrong because what the defendant did was not correctable on appeal? *See* Rosenberg, Stump v. Sparkman: *The Doctrine of Judicial Impunity*, 64 VA. L. REV. 833 (1978).

5.   Is a judicial punch in the mouth protected by absolute judicial immunity? Why not? *See Gregory v. Thompson*, 500 F.2d 59 (9th Cir. 1974) (judge's physical assault on plaintiff not a judicial act).

6.   Suppose a judge is accused of ordering a police officer to use excessive force to bring an attorney to him in his courtroom. In *Mireles v. Waco*, 502 U.S. 9 (1991) (*per curiam*), the Supreme Court summarily found absolute immunity applicable to such a case. It noted that the plaintiff was dealing with the defendant in the latter's judicial capacity because the plaintiff was called into the courtroom in connection with a pending case. While the defendant's alleged direction to use excessive force

was not a normal judicial function, this was to put the inquiry at too particular a level. Under *Stump*, the inquiry was into the nature or function of the act, not the "act itself." The Court explained:"In other words, we look to the particular act's relation to a general function normally performed by a judge, in this case the function of directing police officers to bring counsel in a pending case before the court."

The Court also rejected the argument that the challenged conduct was transformed into an executive act through its implementation by a police officer. It went on to conclude that the defendant did not act in the clear absence of all jurisdiction because his conduct, even if legally erroneous, was in aid of his jurisdiction.

What do all of these cases suggest about the scope of absolute judicial immunity? Do you suppose that there is an impulse toward judicial self-preservation at work here?

7. *Mireles v. Waco*, noted just above, makes clear that a judge who orders a police officer or bailiff to do whatever is necessary to bring an attorney or litigant to the judge's courtroom is protected by absolute judicial immunity. But is the police officer or bailiff who allegedly used excessive force in violation of the Fourth Amendment also protected by absolute immunity on the ground that he or she was following a court order and that it would be unfair to absolutely protect the judge who gave the order but not the police officer or bailiff who carried out the order? *In Martin v. Hendren*, 127 F.3d 720 (8th Cir. 1997), Judge Lay dissenting, the Eighth Circuit found absolute immunity applicable, while the Seventh Circuit, in *Richman v. Sheahan*, 270 F.3d 430 (7th Cir. 2001), Judge Bauer dissenting, expressly disagreed with *Martin* and found only qualified immunity applicable. Which decision is more sound? Is there a possible difference for this purpose between enforcement of a court order that is *presumptively* valid on its face and enforcement of a court order that is *presumptively invalid*? For extensive discussion of these and related issues, including the so-called "Nuremberg defense," see Nahmod, *From the Courtroom to the Street: Court Orders and Section 1983*, 29 HAST. CONST. L.Q. 613 (2002).

8. As yet another example of the broad scope of absolute judicial immunity, see In *Ballard v. Wall*, 413 F.3d 510 (5th Cir. 2005), where the plaintiff sued a judge and private attorneys (and their firm) alleging that they conspired to keep him in jail until he paid his debt to the firm's client, in effect operating a debtor's prison. Reversing the district court's dismissal of the complaint against the attorneys, the Fifth Circuit determined that the plaintiff's allegations that the judge exceeded her jurisdiction and abused her authority by imprisoning him until he paid his debt, that she called the law firm but it would not release a bond, that he would have to pay $10,000 in cash or he would go to jail, that he or his wife would have to pay the money directly to one of the attorneys and that the attorneys were involved in these acts of the judge, were sufficient to allege § 1983 joint participation and a conspiracy. However, as to the judge, the Fifth Circuit, affirming the district court in this respect, found that absolute judicial immunity applied to her challenged acts in ordering officers to arrest the plaintiff and incarcerate him. The judge did not act outside the scope of her judicial authority: the challenged acts were acts normally performed by a judge; the judge had subject matter jurisdiction over the case;

plaintiff's allegations of bad faith and malice were insufficient to overcome judicial immunity; and the order to arrest the plaintiff and incarcerate was prompted by plaintiff's failure to appear as required.

9. In *Sibley v. Lando*, 437 F.3d 1067 (11th Cir. 2005), the plaintiff alleged that the state court judge who ordered his incarceration for failure to pay child support acted in the complete absence of all jurisdiction because he had filed seven affidavits seeking her recusal, with the result that her subsequent incarceration of him should not be protected by judicial immunity. Rejecting the argument, the Eleventh Circuit pointed out that under Florida law, an affidavit of this kind did not automatically oust the judge of jurisdiction. Also, under Florida law, a trial judge was not automatically disqualified even if he or she failed to act on a disqualification motion within 30 days. Further, even after the first affidavit was filed seeking her disqualification, the judge retained the jurisdiction to perform ministerial acts and had some subject matter jurisdiction. Thus, at most she acted only in excess of jurisdiction when she issued the incarceration order, and not in the clear absence of all jurisdiction.

10. A state court judge was protected by judicial immunity even though, after sentencing the plaintiff to a twelve-month term of incarceration for attempted theft and after she began serving it, he unlawfully resentenced her to a term between twelve and thirty-two months. The judge did so because he discovered that his original sentence was based on mistaken assumptions about the plaintiff's criminal record that worked to the plaintiff's detriment. According to the Ninth Circuit, under Nevada law the court could only modify a sentence if the mistaken assumptions worked to the state's detriment, not a criminal defendant's. Still, the judge was protected by judicial immunity because he acted only in excess of jurisdiction, not in the clear absence of it. *Sadoski v. Mosley*, 435 F.3d 1076 (9th Cir. 2006). Judge Gould concurred, discussing at different issue. *Id.* at 1080.

D. The Functional Approach to Judicial Immunity as a Double-Edged Sword: Judges, Court Reporters and Prison Disciplinary Hearing Officers

We saw earlier in connection with absolute legislative immunity that the Supreme Court has adopted a functional approach to immunities. The Court explained it this way in *Forrester v. White*, 484 U.S. 219, 224 (1988), a judicial immunity case:

> Running through our cases, with fair consistency, is a "functional" approach to immunity questions other than those that have been decided by express constitutional or statutory enactment. Under that approach, we examine the nature of the functions with which a particular official or class of officials has been lawfully entrusted, and we seek to evaluate the effect that exposure to liability would likely have on the appropriate exercise of those functions. Officials who seek exemption for personal liability have the burden of showing that such an exemption is justified by overriding considerations of public policy, and the Court has recognized a category of "qualified immunity" that avoids unnecessarily extending the scope of the traditional concept of absolute immunity.

The Court applied this functional approach in *Forrester* itself and held that absolute judicial immunity did *not* protect a state judge accused of violating equal protection by firing a probation officer because of her sex. According to the Court, this conduct was administrative in nature, not judicial. It was true that such administrative conduct was important to the operation of a sound judicial system and also that suits by disgruntled former employees could interfere with judicial decision making. However, these considerations did not warrant absolute judicial immunity for administrative conduct.

1. Will there be many cases in which it will be difficult to distinguish between judicial and non-judicial acts for absolute immunity purposes?

2. Do judges engage in non-judicial acts to the same extent that local legislators engage in non-legislative acts? To the same extent that prosecutors engage in non-advocative acts?

3. What about others whose functions are closely related to the judicial process, such as court reporters? Consider *Antoine v. Byers & Anderson*, 508 U.S. 429 (1993), *rev'g*, 950 F.2d 1471 (9th Cir. 1991), where the Supreme Court ruled unanimously that absolute judicial immunity did not protect a court reporter accused of failing to provide a criminal trial transcript in a timely manner to the plaintiff, which delayed his appeal for over four years. The Ninth Circuit had found absolute immunity applicable, reasoning that preparing a trial transcript was part of the appellate judicial function which was "inextricably intertwined with the adjudication of claims." 950 F.2d at 1476. Reversing in an opinion by Justice Stevens, the Supreme Court first noted that there was no history of common law immunity for professional court reporters because they did not exist when the common law doctrine of judicial immunity developed. It then rejected the defendant's proposed analogy to common law judges who made handwritten notes during trial. For one thing, those notes were not verbatim reports of trials. For another, even if a judge were to make such verbatim notes, under the functional approach it was likely that this conduct would be characterized as administrative in nature and hence protected only by qualified immunity. The Court went on to emphasize that court reporter did not perform quasi-judicial functions because they did not really exercise discretion. And finally, there was no real demonstration that court reporters needed absolute immunity so that they could do their jobs: cases like this one were relatively rare.

Is *Antoine* consistent with the functional approach? What does *Antoine* indicate about the respective roles of the common law of immunity and policy considerations in absolute immunity determinations? Is *Antoine* comparable to the Court's refusal in *Burns v. Reed*, considered later in this chapter, to confer absolute judicial immunity on a prosecutor for rendering legal advice to law enforcement officers?

4. What about those enforcement officers whose acts appear quasi-judicial in nature? Are they protected by absolute judicial immunity under the functional approach? Consider *Cleavinger v. Saxner*, 474 U.S. 193 (1985), where the Court held that members of a federal prison's disciplinary committee who heard cases involving inmate rule infractions were protected by qualified immunity, not absolute immunity. Such persons were not functionally comparable to judges: they were not independent, were not professional hearing officers, and were under pressure to resolve disputes in favor of the institution. In addition, there often were few procedural safeguards available in the prison disciplinary context. Thus, according to the Court, such defendants should be treated the same way as school board members who adjudicate and who, under *Wood v. Strickland*, 420 U.S. 308 (1975), were protected only by qualified immunity.

What is the significance of the Court's reliance in *Cleavinger* on the incentive structure of federal prison disciplinary committees? Why should the objectivity of the decisionmaking process be considered relevant to characterizing that process functionally as judicial in nature?

Compare Cleavinger to *Shelly v. Johnson*, 849 F.2d 228 (6th Cir. 1988) (*per curiam*), where, despite *Cleavinger*, the Sixth Circuit held that Michigan prison hearing officers were absolutely immune from damages liability for acts done in their official capacity. Under Michigan law, prison hearing officers were professionals in the nature of administrative law judges who were required to be attorneys and were not simply prison employees subordinate to prison wardens. Additionally, their adjudicatory functions were specified in the law, their decisions were in writing and supported by findings of fact, and judicial review was available. For these reasons, they were entitled to the protection of absolute judicial immunity consistent with their independence and authority as fulltime judicial officers. The Sixth Circuit distinguished *Cleavinger v. Saxner* on the ground that the prison disciplinary committee members sued there were not similarly exercising independent authority pursuant to quasi-judicial procedures.

The concept of "quasi-judicial" immunity is not limited to the criminal context; it applies to certain disciplinary proceedings as well. For example, the Sixth Circuit relied again on the concept of "quasi-judicial" absolute immunity from suit in *Dixon v. Clem*, 492 F.3d 665, 668, 674 (6th Cir. 2007). There, a state administrative tribunal upheld a high-school teacher's termination after reviewing the evidence that led to the teacher's dismissal. The hearing officers actions, the Sixth Circuit concluded, were "clearly taken in [their] judicial capacity." Similarly, the First, Second, Ninth and Tenth Circuits have all applied the concept of quasi-judicial immunity to certain disciplinary proceedings. *Wang v. N.H. Bd. of Registration in Med.*, 55 F.3d 698, 701 (1st Cir. 1995); *Applewhite v. Briber*, 506 F.3d 181, 182 (2d Cir. 2007); *Olsen v. Idaho State Bd. of Med.*, 363 F.3d 916, 923–26 (9th Cir. 2004); *Guttman v. Khalsa*, 446 F.3d 1027, 1032–34 (10th Cir. 2006).

A comparison of *Applewhite* and *DiBlasio v. Novello*, 344 F.3d 292, 296–302 (2d Cir. 2003), helps establish the parameters of when disciplinary proceedings trigger quasi-judicial immunity. In *Applewhite*, the Second Circuit found that those serving on a board tasked with revoking medical licenses were entitled to quasi-judicial immunity. The court explained that "absolute judicial immunity attaches to a state medical review board's disciplinary proceeding where, as here, the individual charged has the right to be represented by counsel, to present evidence and to cross-examine witnesses, and where the board articulates its findings and conclusions in a binding order-as opposed to a mere recommendation-under a preponderance of the evidence standard." By contrast in *DiBlasio*, the court rejected a claim of absolute immunity where disciplinary proceedings as to whether to suspend a medical license "lacked equivalent hallmarks and safeguards of a judicial proceeding that would render absolute immunity for those officials involved appropriate."

What else, other than disciplinary decisions, implicate the "quasi-judicial" immunity doctrine? The Third Circuit has sometimes applied the doctrine to protect officials who serve on zoning boards. *See, e.g., Omnipoint Corp. v. Zoning Hearing Bd.*, 181 F.3d 403, 409 (3d Cir.1999); *Bass v. Attardi*, 868 F.2d 45 (3d Cir. 1989). That court reasoned in *Dotzel v. Ashbridge*, 438 F.3d 320, 325 (3d Cir. 2006), that "[r]egardless of his job title, if a state official must walk, talk, and act like a judge as part of his job, then he is as absolutely immune from lawsuits arising out of that walking, talking, and acting as are judges who enjoy the title and other formal indicia of office." Are zoning decisions of the type that are generally associated with the judicial role? Note that the *Dotzel* court cited the adversarial nature of the township's zoning proceedings, as well as the fact that decisions were appealable to the Pennsylvania Court of Common Pleas.

See generally S. NAHMOD, 2 CIVIL RIGHTS AND CIVIL LIBERTIES LITIGATION: THE LAW OF SECTION 1983 §§ 7:34–7:39 (4th ed. 2014), which collects cases dealing with officials of various boards, commissions and agencies.

E. *Pulliam* and Prospective Relief

It was observed earlier in the discussion of absolute legislative immunity and *Supreme Court v. Consumers Union* that judges, unlike state legislators, are not protected from prospective relief. This applies even to judicial acts engaged in with unquestioned jurisdiction. However, *Consumers Union* expressly left that question open. It was only in *Pulliam v. Allen*, 466 U.S. 522 (1984) that the Court finally put this matter to rest.

Pulliam involved a section 1983 prospective relief action against a magistrate accused of unconstitutionally imposing bail on persons arrested for nonjailable offenses under Virginia law and of incarcerating those persons if they could not meet the bail. The district court found for the plaintiffs, enjoined the practice, and awarded attorney's fees against the defendant magistrate under 42 U.S.C. section 1988. The Fourth Circuit affirmed, as did the Supreme Court in an opinion by Justice Blackmun.

The Court first addressed the issue of judicial immunity from prospective relief liability. Acknowledging that there were no injunctions against common law judges, the Court nevertheless found a parallel in the collateral relief available against judges through the use of "the King's prerogative writs," especially prohibition and mandamus. It next observed that it had never declared an absolute judicial immunity rule for prospective relief, that the prevailing approach in the circuits was that there was no such immunity, and that the absence of such immunity had not had a "chilling effect" on judicial independence. Further, Article III limitations on injunctive relief against a judge, together with equitable requirements in general, both assured that injunctive relief against judges would be sparingly granted and provided sufficient safeguards of comity and federalism. Finally, there was no indication that Congress in enacting section 1983 intended to provide absolute judicial immunity from prospective relief. Indeed, all indications in the legislative history were to the contrary.

As to attorney's fees under section 1988, the Court simply noted that it was for Congress, not the Court, to provide for judicial immunity from attorney's fees awards. Since section 1988 was intended to provide fees in actions to enforce section 1983, it applied as well to judges successfully sued for prospective relief.

Chief Justice Burger and Justices Rehnquist and O'Connor joined in a dissenting opinion by Justice Powell. They contended that, under the common law, judges were absolutely immune from prospective relief liability as well as from damages liability. Both kinds of immunity were necessary to protect judicial independence from the burdens of litigation. In addition, they rejected the majority's reliance on prerogative writs as misplaced: such writs were used "only to control the proper exercise of jurisdiction, they posed no threat to judicial independence and implicated none of the policies of judicial immunity." Finally, the dissenters argued that the effect on judicial independence of section 1983 prospective relief suits would be aggravated by the possibility of attorney's fees awards under section 1988.

Attorney's fees, a topic of immense practical significance, are addressed in Chapter 12. For present purposes, consider the following questions.

1. Why should judges, but not state legislators, be subject to prospective relief actions?

2. Will it ordinarily be easy for a section 1983 plaintiff to secure prospective relief against a judge? Do Article III requirements pose special problems in this regard?

3. What of institutional and equitable constraints on such relief? *See In re Justices of the Supreme Court*, 695 F.2d 17 (1st Cir. 1982) (pre-*Pulliam* case refusing to grant prospective relief against the justices of the Puerto Rico Supreme Court on institutional grounds) and *Sterling v. Calvin*, 874 F.2d 571 (8th Cir. 1989) (refusing to grant prospective relief against state trial judge on equitable grounds)

4. As noted earlier, Congress, in section 309 of the Federal Courts Improvement Act of 1996, amended section 1983 and legislated absolute judicial immunity from injunctive relief for judicial acts except where a declaratory decree is violated or where declaratory relief is not available.

F.   A Note on Witness Immunity and Its Connection to Judicial Immunity: *Briscoe*

In *Briscoe v. LaHue*, 460 U.S. 325 (1983), a case closely related to the Supreme Court's judicial immunity decisions, the Court ruled that police officer witnesses accused of perjury at criminal trials are absolutely immune from damages liability. *Briscoe* involved consolidated cases in which the plaintiffs sued police officers and a private party for allegedly testifying falsely at their respective criminal trials and thereby violating plaintiffs' rights to due process and to trial by an impartial jury. The Seventh Circuit held that all these defendants were entitled to absolute immunity in connection with their testimony. Upon review, the Supreme Court affirmed in an opinion by Justice Stevens. The Court observed that when section 1983 was enacted, the common law background of absolute lay witness immunity was well established. The underlying policy was the prevention of witness self-censorship. Similarly, judges are absolutely immune under section 1983 for the protection of the judicial process itself. Thus, whether a police officer witness is like a lay witness or like an official playing an important role in the judicial process, the police officer witness is entitled to absolute immunity. The Court also found nothing in section 1983's legislative history to compel a different conclusion.

The Court rejected the contention that there should be an exception for police officer witness immunity on the ground that the policy reasons for lay witness immunity do not apply with the same force to police officers who testify as part of their official duties. The Court took a functional approach to absolute immunity, as opposed to a status approach. Justices Brennan, Marshall, and Blackmun dissented, arguing that police officer witnesses accused of perjury are not entitled to absolute immunity.

1. In light of the Supreme Court's solicitude for the judicial process and its emphasis on the 1871 common law, is *Briscoe* a surprising decision?

2. Should absolute witness immunity protect law enforcement officers for their testimony in pretrial adversarial proceedings?

3. Should absolute witness immunity protect a witness at a grand jury proceeding? In *Rehberg v. Paulk*, 132 S. Ct. 1497 (2012), a unanimous Supreme Court held that they do. Citing *Briscoe*, the Court reasoned that "[t]he factors that justify absolute immunity for trial witnesses apply with equal force to grand jury witnesses." The Court "conclude[d] that grand jury witnesses should enjoy the same immunity as witnesses at trial."

4. Can *Briscoe* be end-run by alleging an *extrajudicial conspiracy* to present false testimony? The Tenth Circuit answered in the negative, explaining that "[i]nstead of suing state witnesses for perjured testimony, a [criminal] defendant could simply transform the perjury complaint into an allegation of a conspiracy to do the same." *Miller v. Glanz*, 948 F.2d 1562, 1571 (10th Cir. 1991).

A majority of the circuits have taken this position. Furthermore, the Eleventh Circuit has held that absolutely immune false testimony may not be used as evidence of conspiratorial conduct that is *not* immune. Thus, in *Rowe v. City of Fort Lauderdale*, 279 F.3d 1271, 1282 (11th Cir. 2002), a prosecutorial immunity case, the Eleventh Circuit stated: "We have previously concluded that a witness's absolute immunity from liability for testifying forecloses any use of that testimony as evidence of the witness's membership in a conspiracy prior to his taking the stand." In this regard, *Rowe* cited *Mastroianni v. Bowers*, 173 F.3d 1363 (11th Cir. 1999), and described *Mastroianni's* reasoning as follows: "If getting on the stand to testify exposed a witness to liability, the absolute immunity extended to a witness would be illusory, and that is true even in the exposure was limited to liability for a conspiracy proven through use of the testimony. Thus a witness must be immune from having her testimony used to show a conspiracy." 279 F.3d at 1282.

III.   ABSOLUTE PROSECUTORIAL IMMUNITY

A.   *Imbler*: The Seminal Absolute Prosecutorial Immunity Case

IMBLER v. PACHTMAN
424 U.S. 409 (1976)

MR. JUSTICE POWELL delivered the opinion of the Court.

The question presented in this case is whether a state prosecuting attorney who acted within the scope of his duties in initiating and pursuing a criminal prosecution is amenable to suit under 42 U.S.C. § 1983 for alleged deprivations of the defendant's constitutional rights. The Court of Appeals for the Ninth Circuit held that he is not. We affirm.

I

. . . In April 1972, Imbler filed a civil rights action, under 42 U.S.C. § 1983 and related statutes, against [prosecutor] Pachtman, [a] police fingerprint expert, and various other officers of the Los Angeles police force. He alleged that a conspiracy among them unlawfully to charge and convict him had caused him loss of liberty and other grievous injury. He demanded $2.7 million in actual and exemplary damages from each defendant, plus $15,000 attorney's fees.

. . . The gravamen of his complaint against Pachtman was that he had "with intent, and on other occasions with negligence" allowed Costello [a witness] to give false testimony as found by the District Court, and that the fingerprint expert's suppression of evidence was "chargeable under federal law" to Pachtman. In addition Imbler claimed that Pachtman had prosecuted him with knowledge of a lie detector test that had "cleared" Imbler, and that Pachtman had used at trial a police artist's sketch of Hasson's killer made shortly after the crime and allegedly altered to resemble Imbler more closely after the investigation had focused upon him.

II

Title 42 U.S.C. § 1983 provides that "[e]very person" who acts under color of state law to deprive another of a constitutional right shall be answerable to that person in a suit for damages. The statute thus creates a species of tort liability that on its face admits of no immunities, and some have argued that it should be applied as stringently as it reads. But that view has not prevailed.

The decision in *Tenney* established that § 1983 is to be read in harmony with general principles of tort immunities and defenses rather than in derogation of them. Before today the Court has had occasion to consider the liability of several types of government officials in addition to legislators. The common-law absolute immunity of judges for "acts committed within their judicial jurisdiction," *see Bradley v. Fisher*, was found to be preserved under § 1983 in *Pierson v. Ray*. In the same case, local police officers sued for a deprivation of liberty resulting from unlawful arrest were held to enjoy under § 1983 a "good faith and probable cause" defense co-extensive with their defense to false arrest actions at common law. We found qualified immunities appropriate in two recent cases.[1] In *Scheuer v. Rhodes*, we concluded that the Governor and other executive officials of a State had a qualified immunity that varied with "the scope of discretion and responsibilities of the office and all the circumstances as they reasonably appeared at the time of the action. . . ." Last Term in *Wood v. Strickland*, we held that school officials, in the context of imposing disciplinary penalties, were not liable so long as they could not reasonably have known that their action violated students' clearly established constitutional rights, and provided they did not act with malicious intention to cause constitutional or other injury. In *Scheuer* and in *Wood*, as in the two earlier cases, the considerations underlying the nature of the immunity of the respective officials in suits at common law led to essentially the same immunity under § 1983.

III

This case marks our first opportunity to address the § 1983 liability of a state prosecuting officer. The Courts of Appeals, however, have confronted the issue many times and under varying circumstances. Although the precise contours of their holdings have been unclear at times, at bottom they are virtually unanimous that a prosecutor enjoys absolute immunity from § 1983 suits for damages when he acts within the scope of his prosecutorial duties. These courts sometimes have described the prosecutor's immunity as a form of "quasi-judicial" immunity and referred to it as derivative of the immunity of judges recognized in *Pierson v. Ray*. Petitioner focuses upon the "quasi-judicial" characterization, and contends that it illustrates a fundamental illogic in according absolute immunity to a prosecutor. He argues that the prosecutor, as a member of the executive branch, cannot claim the immunity reserved for the judiciary, but only a qualified immunity akin to that accorded other executive officials in this Court's previous cases.

Petitioner takes an overly simplistic approach to the issue of prosecutorial liability. As noted above, our earlier decisions on § 1983 immunities were not products of judicial fiat that officials in different branches of government are differently amenable to suit under § 1983. Rather, each was predicated upon a considered inquiry into the immunity historically accorded the relevant official at common law and the interests behind it. The liability of a state prosecutor under § 1983 must be determined in the same manner.

A

The function of a prosecutor that most often invites a common-law tort action is his decision to initiate a prosecution, as this may lead to a suit for malicious

---

[1] [13] The procedural difference between the absolute and the qualified immunities is important. An absolute immunity defeats a suit at the outset, so long as the official's actions were within the scope of the immunity. The fate of an official with qualified immunity depends upon the circumstances and motivations of his actions, as established by the evidence at trial. *See Scheuer v. Rhodes; Wood v. Strickland*.

prosecution if the State's case misfires. The first American case to address the question of a prosecutor's amenability to such an action was *Griffith v. Slinkard*. The complaint charged that a local prosecutor without probable cause added the plaintiff's name to a grand jury true bill after the grand jurors had refused to indict him, with the result that the plaintiff was arrested and forced to appear in court repeatedly before the charge finally was nolle prossed. Despite allegations of malice, the Supreme Court of Indiana dismissed the action on the ground that the prosecutor was absolutely immune.

The *Griffith* view on prosecutorial immunity became the clear majority rule on the issue. The question eventually came to this Court on writ of certiorari to the Court of Appeals for the Second Circuit. In *Yaselli v. Goff*, the claim was that the defendant, a Special Assistant to the Attorney General of the United States, maliciously and without probable cause procured plaintiff's grand jury indictment by the willful introduction of false and misleading evidence. Plaintiff sought some $300,000 in damages for having been subjected to the rigors of a trial in which the court ultimately directed a verdict against the Government. The District Court dismissed the complaint, and the Court of Appeals affirmed. After reviewing the development of the doctrine of prosecutorial immunity, that court stated:

> "In our opinion the law requires us to hold that a special assistant to the Attorney General of the United States, in the performance of the duties imposed upon him by law, is immune from a civil action for malicious prosecution based on an indictment and prosecution, although it results in a verdict of not guilty rendered by a jury. The immunity is absolute, and is grounded on principles of public policy."

After briefing and oral argument, this Court affirmed the Court of Appeals in a per curiam opinion.

The common-law immunity of a prosecutor is based upon the same considerations that underlie the common-law immunities of judges and grand jurors acting within the scope of their duties. These include concern that harassment by unfounded litigation would cause a deflection of the prosecutor's energies from his public duties, and the possibility that he would shade his decisions instead of exercising the independence of judgment required by his public trust. One court expressed both considerations as follows:

> "The office of public prosecutor is one which must be administered with courage and independence. Yet how can this be if the prosecutor is made subject to suit by those whom he accuses and fails to convict? To allow this would open the way for unlimited harassment and embarrassment of the most conscientious officials by those who would profit thereby. There would be involved in every case the possible consequences of a failure to obtain a conviction. There would always be a question of possible civil action in case the prosecutor saw fit to move dismissal of the case. . . . The apprehension of such consequences would tend toward great uneasiness and toward weakening the fearless and impartial policy which should characterize the administration of this office. The work of the prosecutor would thus be impeded and we would have moved away from the desired objective of stricter and fairer law enforcement." *Pearson v. Reed*.

B

The common-law rule of immunity is thus well settled. We now must determine whether the same considerations of public policy that underlie the common-law rule likewise countenance absolute immunity under § 1983. We think they do.

If a prosecutor had only a qualified immunity, the threat of § 1983 suits would undermine performance of his duties no less than would the threat of common-law suits for malicious prosecution. A prosecutor is duty bound to exercise his best judgment both in deciding which suits to bring and in conducting them in court. The public trust of the prosecutor's office would suffer if he were constrained in making every decision by the consequences in terms of his own potential liability in a suit for damages. Such suits could be expected with some frequency, for a defendant often will transform his resentment at being prosecuted into the ascription of improper and malicious actions to the State's advocate. Further, if the prosecutor could be made to answer in court each time such a person charged him with wrongdoing, his energy and attention would be diverted from the pressing duty of enforcing the criminal law.

Moreover, suits that survived the pleadings would pose substantial danger of liability even to the honest prosecutor. The prosecutor's possible knowledge of a witness' falsehoods, the materiality of evidence not revealed to the defense, the propriety of a closing argument, and — ultimately in every case — the likelihood that prosecutorial misconduct so infected a trial as to deny due process, are typical of issues with which judges struggle in actions for post-trial relief, sometimes to differing conclusions. The presentation of such issues in a § 1983 action often would require a virtual retrial of the criminal offense in a new forum, and the resolution of some technical issues by the lay jury. It is fair to say, we think, that the honest prosecutor would face greater difficulty in meeting the standards of qualified immunity than other executive or administrative officials. Frequently acting under serious constraints of time and even information, a prosecutor inevitably makes many decisions that could engender colorable claims of constitutional deprivation. Defending these decisions, often years after they were made, could impose unique and intolerable burdens upon a prosecutor responsible annually for hundreds of indictments and trials.

The affording of only a qualified immunity to the prosecutor also could have an adverse effect upon the functioning of the criminal justice system. Attaining the system's goal of accurately determining guilt or innocence requires that both the prosecution and the defense have wide discretion in the conduct of the trial and the presentation of evidence. The veracity of witnesses in criminal cases frequently is subject to doubt before and after they testify, as is illustrated by the history of this case. If prosecutors were hampered in exercising their judgment as to the use of such witnesses by concern about resulting personal liability, the triers of fact in criminal cases often would be denied relevant evidence.

The ultimate fairness of the operation of the system itself could be weakened by subjecting prosecutors to § 1983 liability. Various post-trial procedures are available to determine whether an accused has received a fair trial. These procedures include the remedial powers of the trial judge, appellate review, and state and federal post-conviction collateral remedies. In all of these the attention of the reviewing judge or tribunal is focused primarily on whether there was a fair trial under law. This focus should not be blurred by even the subconscious knowledge that a post-trial decision in favor of the accused might result in the prosecutor's being called upon to respond in damages for his error or mistaken judgment.

We conclude that the considerations outlined above dictate the same absolute immunity under § 1983 that the prosecutor enjoys at common law. To be sure, this immunity does leave the genuinely wronged defendant without civil redress against a prosecutor whose malicious or dishonest action deprives him of liberty. But the alternative of qualifying a prosecutor's immunity would disserve the broader public interest. It would prevent the vigorous and fearless performance of the prosecutor's duty that is essential to the proper functioning of the criminal justice system. Moreover, it often would prejudice defendants in criminal cases by skewing post-conviction judicial decisions that should be made with the sole purpose of insuring justice. With the issue thus framed, we find ourselves in agreement with Judge Learned Hand, who wrote of the prosecutor's immunity from actions for malicious prosecution:

> "As is so often the case, the answer must be found in a balance between the evils inevitable in either alternative. In this instance it has been thought in the end better to leave unredressed the wrongs done by dishonest officers than to subject those who try to do their duty to the constant dread of retaliation." *Gregoire v. Biddle.*

We emphasize that the immunity of prosecutors from liability in suits under § 1983 does not leave the public powerless to deter misconduct or to punish that which occurs. This Court has never suggested that the policy considerations which compel civil immunity for certain governmental officials also place them beyond the reach of the criminal law. Even judges, cloaked with absolute civil immunity for centuries, could be punished criminally for willful deprivations of constitutional rights on the strength of 18 U.S.C. § 242, the criminal analog of § 1983. The prosecutor would fare no better for his willful acts. Moreover, a prosecutor stands perhaps unique, among officials whose acts could deprive persons of constitutional rights, in his amenability to professional discipline by an association of his peers. These checks undermine the argument that the imposition of civil liability is the only way to insure that prosecutors are mindful of the constitutional rights of persons accused of crime.

IV

It remains to delineate the boundaries of our holding. [T]he Court of Appeals emphasized that each of respondent's challenged activities was an "integral part of the judicial process." The purpose of the Court of Appeals' focus upon the functional nature of the activities rather than respondent's status was to distinguish and leave standing those cases, in its Circuit and in some others, which hold that a prosecutor engaged in certain investigative activities enjoys, not the absolute immunity associated with the judicial process, but only a goodfaith defense comparable to the policeman's. We agree with the Court of Appeals that respondent's activities were intimately associated with the judicial phase of the criminal process, and thus were functions to which the reasons for absolute immunity apply with full force. We have no occasion to consider whether like or similar reasons require immunity for those aspects of the prosecutor's responsibility that cast him in the role of an administrator or investigative officer rather than that of advocate. We hold only that in initiating a prosecution and in presenting the State's case, the prosecutor is immune from a civil suit for damages under § 1983. The judgment of the Court of Appeals for the Ninth Circuit accordingly is

Affirmed.

[The concurring opinion of JUSTICES **WHITE**, **BRENNAN** and **MARSHALL** is omitted; JUSTICE **STEVENS** did not participate.]

NOTES

1. Is *Imbler* consistent with the Court's interpretive approaches in the legislative and judicial immunity cases? Does the result in *Imbler* follow from the 1871 common law background? Does it follow from the policy considerations we have seen?

2. What precisely is the challenged prosecutorial conduct in *Imbler*?

3. What does it mean to describe protected prosecutorial conduct as that of an advocate "intimately associated with the judicial phase of the criminal process?" What else do prosecutors do besides participate as advocates in criminal proceedings?

4. Does the Court draw any bright line between protected advocative conduct and other kinds of prosecutorial conduct that are unprotected? Is it even possible to draw a bright line? Recall the functional approach of *Lake Country Estates* for legislators and of *Forrester v. White* for judges. *See* Note, *Delimiting the Scope of Prosecutorial Immunity from Section 1983 Damage Suits*, 52 N.Y.U. L. REV. 173 (1977).

5. Where is the line between the advocative and investigative conduct of a prosecutor? Is it important to draw that line? Why? Is it relevant that, as Chapter 8 indicates, police officers engaged in law enforcement activities are ordinarily protected only by qualified immunity?

It took the Supreme Court over fifteen years to confront these questions. In *Buckley v. Fitzsimmons*, 509 U.S. 259 (1993), the Court held that prosecutors accused of fabricating evidence for the purpose of creating probable cause to arrest were not protected by absolute immunity. The Court emphasized several factors in addition to the absence at common law of prosecutorial immunity for such conduct. First, the challenged conduct occurred prior to the existence of probable cause to arrest. And second, such conduct was identical to that ordinarily engaged in by police officers.

Note, however, that the Supreme Court has granted certiorari in *Pottawattamie County v. McGhee*, 129 S. Ct. 2002 (2009), granting cert. in *McGhee v. Pottawattamie County*, 547 F.3d 922, 933 (8th Cir. 2008), where the Eighth Circuit was confronted with a substantive due process claim against prosecutors based on allegations that defendants obtained, manufactured, coerced and fabricated evidence before the filing of the information against plaintiffs, all of which resulted in plaintiffs' murder convictions (which were ultimately vacated). Ruling that neither absolute nor qualified immunity protected the defendants with respect to these challenged acts, the Eighth Circuit stated: "We find that immunity does not extend to the actions of a County Attorney who violates a person's substantive due process rights by obtaining, manufacturing, coercing, and fabricating evidence before filing formal charges, because this is not 'a distinctly prosecutorial function.' " However, the court also observed, as the district court had held, that absolute immunity covered defendants' use of this evidence at trial.

The Question Presented is the following: "May prosecutor be subjected to civil trial and potential damages for wrongful conviction and incarceration when prosecutor allegedly (a) violated criminal defendant's 'substantive due process' rights by procuring false testimony during criminal investigation and then (b) introduced that same testimony against criminal defendant at trial?" The case will be argued and decided in the Court's 2009 Term.

Does this case differ from *Buckley* in any significant respect? What is the relevance, if any, of the fact that the prosecutors "introduced that same testimony against criminal defendant at trial?"

6. Once absolute prosecutorial immunity for advocative conduct is accepted, is *Imbler* an easy or hard case?

7. Should absolute prosecutorial immunity protect a prosecutor accused of conspiring to bring false criminal charges? Accused of withholding evidence favorable to the plaintiff and of instructing a witness to testify falsely? Accused of having the plaintiff indicted and, at the criminal trial, suborning perjury and filing false affidavits? Are these easy or hard cases?

8. Should absolute prosecutorial immunity protect communications to the media? In *Buckley v. Fitzsimmons*, 509 U.S. 259 (1993), the Supreme Court said no. In addition to noting that such conduct was not protected by absolute immunity at common law, the Court applied a functional approach, reasoning that such conduct was clearly not advocative in nature.

9. Should absolute prosecutorial immunity protect the giving of legal advice to police officers and others? *See Burns v. Reed*, set out next.

B. *Burns*: The Prosecutor as Legal Advisor

BURNS v. REED
500 U.S. 478 (1991)

JUSTICE **WHITE** delivered the opinion of the Court.

The issue in this case is whether a state prosecuting attorney is absolutely immune from liability for damages under 42 U.S.C. § 1983 for giving legal advice to the police and for participating in a probable cause hearing. The Court of Appeals for the Seventh Circuit held that he is. We reverse in part.

II

The Court in *Imbler* declined to accord prosecutors only qualified immunity because, among other things, suits against prosecutors for initiating and conducting prosecutions "could be expected with some frequency, for a defendant often will transform his resentment at being prosecuted into the ascription of improper and malicious actions to the State's advocate"; lawsuits would divert prosecutors' attention and energy away from their important duty of enforcing the criminal law; prosecutors would have more difficulty than other officials in meeting the standards for qualified immunity; and potential liability "would prevent the vigorous and fearless performance of the prosecutor's duty that is essential to the proper functioning of the criminal justice system." The Court also noted that there are other checks on prosecutorial misconduct, including the criminal law and professional discipline.

The Court therefore held that prosecutors are absolutely immune from liability under § 1983 for their conduct in "initiating a prosecution and in presenting the State's case," insofar as that conduct is "intimately associated with the judicial phase of the criminal process". Each of the charges against the prosecutor in *Imbler* involved conduct having that association, including the alleged knowing use of false testimony at trial and the alleged deliberate suppression of exculpatory evidence. The Court expressly declined to decide whether absolute immunity extends to "those aspects of the prosecutor's responsibility that cast him in the role of an administrator or investigative officer rather than that of an advocate." It was recognized, though, that "the duties of the prosecutor in his role as advocate for the State involve actions preliminary to the initiation of a prosecution and actions apart from the courtroom."

Decisions in later cases are consistent with the functional approach to immunity employed in *Imbler*. These decisions have also emphasized that the official seeking absolute immunity bears the burden of showing that such immunity is justified for the function in question. The presumption is that qualified rather than absolute immunity is sufficient to protect government officials in the exercise of their duties. We have been "quite sparing" in our recognition of absolute immunity, and have refused to extend it any "further than its justification would warrant."

III

We now consider whether the absolute prosecutorial immunity recognized in *Imbler* is applicable to (a) respondent's participation in a probable cause hearing, which led to the issuance of a search warrant, and (b) respondent's legal advice to the police regarding the use of hypnosis and the existence of probable cause to arrest petitioner.

A

We address first respondent's appearance as a lawyer for the State in the probable cause hearing, where he examined a witness and successfully supported the application for a search warrant. The decision in *Imbler* leads to the conclusion that respondent is absolutely immune from liability in a § 1983 suit for that conduct.

Initially, it is important to determine the precise claim that petitioner has made against respondent concerning respondent's role in the search warrant hearing. An examination of petitioner's complaint, the decisions by both the District Court and Seventh Circuit, and the questions presented in the Petition for a Writ of Certiorari in this Court reveals that petitioner has challenged only respondent's participation in the hearing, and not his motivation in seeking the search warrant or his conduct outside of the courtroom relating to the warrant.

Petitioner's challenge to respondent's participation in the search warrant hearing is similar to the claim in *Briscoe v. LaHue*. There, the plaintiff's § 1983 claim was based on the allegation that a police officer had given perjured testimony at the plaintiff's criminal trial. In holding that the officer was entitled to absolute immunity, we noted that witnesses were absolutely immune at common law from subsequent damages liability for their testimony in judicial proceedings "even if the witness knew the statements were false and made them with malice."

Like witnesses, prosecutors and other lawyers were absolutely immune from damages liability at common law for making false or defamatory statements in judicial proceedings (at least so long as the statements were related to the proceeding), and also for eliciting false and defamatory testimony from witnesses. See also *King v. Skinner*, Lofft 55, 56, 98 Eng. Rep. 529, 530 (K. B. 1772), where Lord Mansfield observed that "neither party, witness, counsel, jury, or Judge can be put to answer, civilly or criminally, for words spoken in office."

This immunity extended to "any hearing before a tribunal which performed a judicial function." W. Prosser, Law of Torts § 94, pp. 826–827 (1941). In *Yaselli v. Goff*, for example, this Court affirmed a decision by the Court of Appeals for the Second Circuit in which that court had held that the commonlaw immunity extended to a prosecutor's conduct before a grand jury.

In addition to finding support in the common law, we believe that absolute immunity for a prosecutor's actions in a probable cause hearing is justified by the policy concerns articulated in *Imbler*. There, the Court held that a prosecutor is absolutely immune for initiating a prosecution and for presenting the State's case. The Court also observed that "the duties of the prosecutor in his role as advocate for the State involve actions preliminary to the initiation of a prosecution."

The prosecutor's actions at issue here — appearing before a judge and presenting evidence in support of a motion for a search warrant — clearly involve the prosecutor's "role as advocate for the State," rather than his role as "administrator or investigative officer," the protection for which we reserved judgment in *Imbler*. Moreover, since the issuance of a search warrant is unquestionably a judicial act, appearing at a probable cause hearing is "intimately associated with the judicial phase of the criminal process." It is also connected with the initiation and conduct of a prosecution, particularly where the hearing occurs after arrest, as was the case here.

As this and other cases indicate, pretrial court appearances by the prosecutor in support of taking criminal action against a suspect present a substantial likelihood of vexatious litigation that might have an untoward effect on the independence of the prosecutor. Therefore, absolute immunity for this function serves the policy of protecting the judicial process, which underlies much of the Court's decision in *Imbler*. Furthermore, the judicial process is available as a check on prosecutorial actions at a probable cause hearing. "The safeguards built into the judicial system tend to reduce the need for private damages actions as a means of controlling unconstitutional conduct." *Butz*.

Accordingly, we hold that respondent's appearance in court in support of an application for a search warrant and the presentation of evidence at that hearing are protected by absolute immunity.

B

Turning to respondent's acts of providing legal advice to the police, we note first that neither respondent nor the court below has identified any historical or common-law support for extending absolute immunity to such actions by prosecutors. Indeed, the Court of Appeals stated that its "review of the historical or common law basis for the immunity in question does not yield any direct support for the conclusion that a prosecutor's immunity from suit extends to the act of giving legal advice to police officers."

The Court of Appeals did observe that Indiana common law purported to provide immunity " 'whenever duties of a judicial nature are imposed upon a public officer.' " The court then reasoned that giving legal advice is "of a judicial nature" because the prosecutor is, like a judge, called upon to render opinions concerning the legality of conduct. We do not believe, however, that advising the police in the investigative phase of a criminal case is so "intimately associated with the judicial phase of the criminal process," that it qualifies for absolute immunity. Absent a tradition of immunity comparable to the common-law immunity from malicious prosecution, which formed the basis for the decision in *Imbler*, we have not been inclined to extend absolute immunity from liability under § 1983.

The United States, as amicus curiae, argues that the absence of common-law support here should not be determinative because the office of public prosecutor was largely unknown at English common law, and prosecutors in the 18th and 19th centuries did not have an investigatory role, as they do today. We are not persuaded. First, it is American common law that is determinative, and the office of public prosecutor was known to American common law. Second, although "the precise contours of official immunity" need not mirror the immunity at common law, we look to the common law and other history for guidance because our role is "not to make a freewheeling policy choice," but rather to discern Congress' likely intent in enacting § 1983. "We do not have a license to establish immunities from § 1983 actions in the interests of what we judge to be sound public policy." *Tower v. Glover*. Thus, for example, it was observed that "since the statute [§ 1983] on its face does not provide for any immunities, we would be going far to read into it an absolute immunity for conduct which was only accorded qualified immunity in 1871."

The next factor to be considered — risk of vexatious litigation — also does not support absolute immunity for giving legal advice. The Court of Appeals asserted that absolute immunity was justified because "a prosecutor's risk of becoming entangled in litigation based on his or her role as a legal advisor is as likely as the risks associated with initiating and prosecuting a case." We disagree. In the first place, a suspect or defendant is not likely to be as aware of a prosecutor's role in giving advice as a prosecutor's role in initiating and conducting a prosecution. But even if a prosecutor's role in giving advice to the police does carry with it some risk of burdensome litigation, the concern with litigation in our immunity cases is not merely a generalized concern with interference with an official's duties, but rather is a concern with interference with the conduct closely related to the judicial process. Absolute immunity is designed to free the judicial process from the harassment and intimidation associated with litigation. That concern therefore justifies absolute prosecutorial immunity only for actions that are connected with the prosecutor's role in judicial proceedings, not for every litigation-inducing conduct.

The Court of Appeals speculated that anything short of absolute immunity would discourage prosecutors from performing their "vital obligation" of giving legal advice to the police. But the qualified immunity standard is today more protective of officials than it was at the time that Imbler was decided. "As the qualified immunity defense has evolved, it provides ample support to all but the plainly incompetent or those who knowingly violate the law." *Malley*. Although the absence of absolute immunity for the act of giving legal advice may cause prosecutors to consider their advice more carefully, " 'where an official could be expected to know that his conduct would violate statutory or constitutional rights, he should be made to hesitate.' " Indeed, it is incongruous to allow prosecutors to be absolutely immune from liability for giving advice to the police, but to allow police officers only qualified immunity for following the advice. Ironically, it would mean that the police, who do not ordinarily hold law degrees, would be required to know the clearly established law, but prosecutors would not.

The United States argues that giving legal advice is related to a prosecutor's roles in screening cases for prosecution and in safeguarding the fairness of the criminal judicial process. That argument, however, proves too much. Almost any action by a prosecutor, including his or her direct participation in purely investigative activity, could be said to be in some way related to the ultimate decision whether to prosecute, but we have never indicated that absolute immunity is that expansive. Rather, as in *Imbler*, we inquire whether the prosecutor's actions are closely associated with the judicial process. Indeed, we implicitly rejected the United States' argument in *Mitchell*, where we held that the Attorney General was not absolutely immune from liability for authorizing a warrantless wiretap. Even though the wiretap was arguably related to a potential prosecution, we found that the Attorney General "was not acting in a prosecutorial capacity" and thus was not entitled to the immunity recognized in *Imbler*.

As a final basis for allowing absolute immunity for legal advice, the Court of

Appeals observed that there are several checks other than civil litigation to prevent abuses of authority by prosecutors. Although we agree, we note that one of the most important checks, the judicial process, will not necessarily restrain out-of-court activities by a prosecutor that occur prior to the initiation of a prosecution, such as providing legal advice to the police. This is particularly true if a suspect is not eventually prosecuted. In those circumstances, the prosecutor's action is not subjected to the "crucible of the judicial process."

In sum, we conclude that respondent has not met his burden of showing that the relevant factors justify an extension of absolute immunity to the prosecutorial function of giving legal advice to the police.

IV

For the foregoing reasons, we affirm in part and reverse in part the judgment of the Court of Appeals.

[The opinion by JUSTICES SCALIA and BLACKMUN, joined in part by JUSTICE MARSHALL, which concurs in part and dissents in part, is omitted.]

NOTES

1. What are the specific challenged acts in *Burns*? Which are protected by absolute prosecutorial immunity and which by qualified immunity?

2. After *Imbler*, is it surprising that absolute prosecutorial immunity protects the conduct of a prosecutor at a probable cause hearing?

3. Why should the giving of legal advice *not* be protected by absolute prosecutorial immunity? Isn't that activity closely related to the decision to prosecute and the judicial process?

4. Does *Burns* tell us what the line is between advocative and investigative conduct? If the test is, in *Burns's* words, "whether the prosecutor's actions are closely associated with the judicial process," does that not create such uncertainty and unpredictability that the policies underlying absolute prosecutorial immunity are undermined?

5. Since *Burns* adheres to the now-familiar functional approach, does it necessarily follow that in cases involving many different allegedly unconstitutional acts of prosecutors, each and every one of those acts must be measured for absolute prosecutorial immunity?

6. Under the functional approach, even nonprosecutors who engage in prosecutorial functions may be protected by absolute prosecutorial immunity. *See Millspaugh v. County Department of Public Welfare*, 937 F.2d 1172 (7th Cir. 1991) (applying absolute prosecutorial immunity to certain acts of a social worker in initiating and participating in proceedings to determine whether plaintiffs' children should be removed from their home and placed in foster homes); *Knowlton v. Shaw*, 704 F.3d 1, 6 (1st Cir. 2013) (applying absolute prosecutorial immunity to state officials tasked with imposing civil penalties against insurance companies where

. . . We intend no disrespect to the officer applying for a warrant by observing that his action, while a vital part of the administration of criminal justice, is further removed from the judicial phase of criminal proceedings than the act of a prosecutor in seeking an indictment. Furthermore, petitioner's analogy, while it has some force, does not take account of the fact that the prosecutor's act in seeking an indictment is but the first step in the process of seeking a conviction. Exposing the prosecutor to liability for the initial phase of his prosecutorial work could interfere with his exercise of independent judgment at every phase of his work, since the prosecutor might come to see later decisions in terms of their effect on his potential liability. Thus, we shield the prosecutor seeking an indictment because any lesser immunity could impair the performance of a central actor in the judicial process.

475 U.S. at 341–343.

These cases make it quite clear that petitioner's activities in connection with the preparation and filing of two of the three charging documents — the information and the motion for an arrest warrant — are protected by absolute immunity. Indeed, except for her act in personally attesting to the truth of the averments in the certification, it seems equally clear that the preparation and filing of the third document in the package was part of the advocate's function as well. The critical question, however, is whether she was acting as a complaining witness rather than a lawyer when she executed the certification "under penalty of perjury." We now turn to that question.

IV

The Fourth Amendment requires that arrest warrants be based "upon probable cause, supported by Oath or affirmation" — a requirement that may be satisfied by an indictment returned by a grand jury, but not by the mere filing of criminal charges in an unsworn information signed by the prosecutor. . . . Accordingly, since most prosecutions in Washington are commenced by information, Washington law requires, in compliance with the constitutional command, that an arrest warrant be supported by either an affidavit "or sworn testimony establishing the grounds for issuing the warrant." The "Certification for Determination of Probable Cause" executed by petitioner was designed to satisfy those requirements.

Although the law required that document to be sworn or certified under penalty of perjury, neither federal nor state law made it necessary for the prosecutor to make that certification. In doing so, petitioner performed an act that any competent witness might have performed. Even if she may have been following a practice that was routinely employed by her colleagues and predecessors in King County, Washington, that practice is surely not prevalent in other parts of the country and is not even mandated by law in King County. Neither petitioner nor amici argue that prosecutors routinely follow the King County practice. Indeed, tradition, as well as the ethics of our profession, generally instruct counsel to avoid the risks associated with participating as both advocate and witness in the same proceeding.[3]

Nevertheless, petitioner argues that the execution of the certificate was just one incident in a presentation that, viewed as a whole, was the work of an advocate and was integral to the initiation of the prosecution. That characterization is appropriate for her drafting of the certification, her determination that the evidence was sufficiently strong to justify a probable-cause finding, her decision to file charges, and her presentation of the information and the motion to the court. Each of those matters involved the exercise of professional judgment; indeed, even the selection of the particular facts to include in the certification to provide the evidentiary support for the finding of probable cause required the exercise of the judgment of the advocate. But that judgment could not affect the truth or falsity of the factual statements themselves. Testifying about facts is the function of the witness, not of the lawyer. No matter how brief or succinct it may be, the evidentiary component of an application for an arrest warrant is a distinct and essential predicate for a finding of probable cause. Even when the person who makes the constitutionally required "Oath or affirmation" is a lawyer, the only function that she performs in giving sworn testimony is that of a witness. Finally, petitioner argues that denying her absolute immunity will have a "chilling effect" on prosecutors in the administration of justice. We are not persuaded.

Accordingly, the judgment of the Court of Appeals for the Ninth Circuit is *Affirmed.*

JUSTICE SCALIA, with whom JUSTICE THOMAS joins, concurring.

I agree that Ms. Kalina performed essentially the same "function" in the criminal process as the police officers in *Malley v. Briggs,* 475 U.S. 335, 106 S. Ct. 1092, 89 L. Ed. 2d 271 (1986), and so I join the opinion of the Court. I write separately because it would be a shame if our opinions did not reflect the awareness that our "functional" approach to 42 U.S.C. § 1983 immunity questions has produced some curious inversions of the common law as it existed in 1871, when § 1983 was enacted. A conscientious prosecutor reading our cases should now conclude that there is absolute immunity for the decision to seek an arrest warrant after filing an information, but only qualified immunity for testimony as a witness in support of that warrant. The common-law rule was, in a sense, exactly opposite.

But no analytical approach based upon "functional analysis" can faithfully replicate the common law, as is demonstrated in the Court's opinion today. By describing the subset of actors in the criminal process who are subject to suit as "complaining witnesses," the Court implies that testifying is the critical event. But a "complaining witness" could be sued for malicious prosecution whether or not he ever provided factual testimony, so long as he had a role in initiating or procuring the prosecution; in that sense, the "witness" in "complaining witness" is misleading. As applied to the police officers in *Malley,* that confusion was more or less harmless. Here, however, *Imbler* and *Malley* collide to produce a rule that stands the common

---

[3] [17] *See, e.g.,* Washington Rule of Professional Conduct 3.7 ("A lawyer shall not act as advocate at a trial in which the lawyer . . . is likely to be a necessary witness," unless four narrow exceptions apply); ABA Model Rules of Professional Conduct 3.7 (1992).

complaints, announced in *Elliott v. Perez*, 751 F.2d 1472, 1482 (5th Cir. 1985):

> Once a complaint against a defendant state legislator, judge, or prosecutor (or similar officer) adequately raises the likely issue of [absolute] immunity the district court should on its own require of the plaintiff a detailed complaint alleging with particularity all material facts on which he contends he will establish his right to recovery, which will include detailed facts supporting the contention that the plea of immunity cannot be sustained.

However, recall from Chapter 5 that in *Leatherman v. Tarrant County*, 507 U.S. 163 (1993), the Supreme Court unanimously rejected a heightened pleading requirement in local government liability failure to train cases. While it specifically left the immunity-pleading issue open, probably because of Justice Kennedy's concurring opinion in *Siegert v. Gilley*, 500 U.S. 226 (1991), in which he approved heightened pleading requirements in certain circumstances, the tone and reasoning of *Leatherman* suggested that these requirements were seriously questionable.

Interestingly, in *Burns-Toole v. Byrne*, 11 F.3d 1270 (5th Cir. 1994), a post-*Leatherman* case where the plaintiff sued members of the Texas State Board of Dental Examiners alleging religious discrimination, the Fifth Circuit found no need to reexamine its heightened pleading requirement and affirmed the district court's grant of summary judgment for the defendants. The court "decline[d] this invitation" to revisit *Elliot v. Perez* because in this case, plaintiff had no evidentiary basis for charges even "[u]nder the most generous standard applicable to a motion for summary judgment." *Id.* at 1275. Subsequently, the Fifth Circuit again finessed the question whether *Elliott v. Perez* survives *Leatherman*. *See Schultea v. Wood*, 47 F.3d 1427 (5th Cir. 1995) (*en banc*) and *Anderson v. Pasadena Indep. School Dist.*, 184 F.3d 439 (5th Cir. 1999).

In contrast, as noted in Chapter 5, other circuits have abandoned their heightened pleading requirements in section 1983 actions against individuals as well as local governments. Recall, however, as set out in Chapter 1, that in *Ashcroft v. Iqbal*, 129 S. Ct. 1937 (2009), the Supreme Court declared that the plausibility standard of *Bell Atlantic v. Twombly*, 550 U.S. 544 (2007), applies to Bivens and section 1983 claims, and to complaints in federal court generally.

B.   A Note on Appeal from Denial of an Absolute Immunity Motion to Dismiss or for Summary Judgment

As we will see in more detail in Chapter 8 when we consider qualified immunity, it turns out that the Supreme Court has modified the final judgment rule and the Federal Rules of Appellate Procedure to allow for immediate appeal from a district court's denial of a motion to dismiss or for summary judgment grounded on absolute or qualified immunity. *Mitchell v. Forsyth*, 472 U.S. 511 (1985). The Court reasoned in *Mitchell* that inasmuch as both absolute and qualified immunity are immunities from suit itself (and from having to defend them), immediate appeals must be permitted in order to make these immunities from suit meaningful.

In light of *Mitchell*, should it come as any surprise that some federal courts, like the Fifth Circuit in *Elliott v. Perez*, should have attempted to amend the Federal

Rules of Civil Procedure by requiring fact-specific pleading in certain section 1983 cases?

Chapter 8

"EVERY PERSON": QUALIFIED IMMUNITY

Suppose that a plaintiff properly pleads and proves all of the elements of a section 1983 cause of action against an individual defendant. We saw in Chapter 7 that certain classes of individual defendants are protected by absolute immunity and are thereby treated as if they were not suable "persons" under section 1983. You will recall that these privileged defendants included state and local legislators, judges, witnesses and prosecutors. You will also remember that the Supreme Court has developed a functional approach to absolute immunity.

What happens if the defendant is unprotected by absolute immunity? It turns out that those individual defendants (officials and employees of state and local governments) who are not protected by absolute immunity are protected by qualified immunity.

Qualified immunity, when successfully asserted, is almost as powerful a defense as absolute immunity. Qualified immunity began as a two-part test for immunity from liability but, in a series of important decisions, it has been converted by the Supreme Court into an "objective reasonableness" test which in many respects is the functional equivalent of absolute immunity. Thus, as we shall see, a qualified immunity defense motion to dismiss or for summary judgment effectively stops a plaintiff's discovery on the case in chief. In addition, when a federal district court denies such a motion, an interlocutory appeal is available even though there has obviously been no final judgment.

This chapter is organized as follows: (1) The Evolution of Qualified Immunity; (2) When Is Law "Clearly Established"? (3) The "Order of Battle"; (4) Procedural Aspects of Qualified Immunity; and (5) Who Is Protected by Qualified Immunity?

I. THE EVOLUTION OF QUALIFIED IMMUNITY

PIERSON v. RAY
386 U.S. 547 (1967)

Mr. Chief Justice Warren delivered the opinion of Court.

These cases present issues involving the liability of local police officers and judges under § 1 of the Civil Rights Act of 1871, 17 Stat. 13, now 42 U.S.C. § 1983. Petitioners were members of a group of 15 white and Negro Episcopal clergymen who attempted to use segregated facilities at an interstate bus terminal in Jackson, Mississippi, in 1961. They were arrested by respondents Ray, Griffith, and Nichols, policemen of the City of Jackson, and charged with violating § 2087.5 of the

Mississippi Code, which makes guilty of a misdemeanor anyone who congregates with others in a public place under circumstances such that a breach of the peace may be occasioned thereby, and refuses to move on when ordered to do so by a police officer. Petitioners waived a jury trial and were convicted of the offense by respondent Spencer, a municipal police justice. They were each given the maximum sentence of four months in jail and a fine of $200. On appeal petitioner Jones was accorded a trial de novo in the County Court, and after the city produced its evidence the court granted his motion for a directed verdict. The cases against the other petitioners were then dropped.

Having been vindicated in the County Court, petitioners brought this action for damages in the United States District Court for the Southern District of Mississippi, Jackson Division, alleging that respondents had violated § 1983, and that respondents were liable at common law for false arrest and imprisonment. A jury returned verdicts for respondents on both counts. On appeal, the Court of Appeals for the Fifth Circuit held that respondent Spencer was immune from liability under both § 1983 and the common law of Mississippi for acts committed within his judicial jurisdiction. As to the police officers, the court noted that § 2087.5 of the Mississippi Code was held unconstitutional as applied to similar facts in *Thomas v. Mississippi*. Although Thomas was decided years after the arrest involved in this trial, the court held that the policemen would be liable in a suit under § 1983 for an unconstitutional arrest even if they acted in good faith and with probable cause in making an arrest under a state statute not yet held invalid. The court believed that this stern result was required by *Monroe v. Pape*. Under the count based on the common law of Mississippi, however, it held that the policemen would not be liable if they had probable cause to believe that the statute had been violated, because Mississippi law does not require police officers to predict at their peril which state laws are constitutional and which are not. Apparently dismissing the common-law claim, the Court of Appeals reversed and remanded for a new trial on the § 1983 claim against the police officers because defense counsel had been allowed to cross-examine the ministers on various irrelevant and prejudicial matters, particularly including an alleged convergence of their views on racial justice with those of the Communist Party. At the new trial, however, the court held that the ministers could not recover if it were proved that they went to Mississippi anticipating that they would be illegally arrested because such action would constitute consent to the arrest under the principle of volenti non fit injuria, he who consents to a wrong cannot be injured.

We granted certiorari to consider whether a local judge is liable for damages under § 1983 for an unconstitutional conviction and whether the ministers should be denied recovery against the police officers if they acted with the anticipation that they would be illegally arrested. We also granted the police officers' petition to determine if the Court of Appeals correctly held that they could not assert the defense of good faith and probable cause to an action under § 1983 for unconstitutional arrest.

We find no difficulty in agreeing with the Court of Appeals that Judge Spencer is immune from liability for damages for his role in these convictions. The record is barren of any proof or specific allegation that Judge Spencer played any role in these arrests and convictions other than to adjudge petitioners guilty when their cases came before his court. Few doctrines were more solidly established at common law than the immunity of judges from liability for damages for acts committed within their judicial jurisdiction, as this Court recognized when it adopted the doctrine, in *Bradley v. Fisher*. This immunity applies even when the judge is accused of acting maliciously and corruptly, and it "is not for the protection or benefit of a malicious or corrupt judge, but for the benefit of the public, whose interest it is that the judges should be at liberty to exercise their functions with independence and without fear of consequences." It is a judge's duty to decide all cases within his jurisdiction that are brought before him, including controversial cases that arouse the most intense feelings in the litigants. His errors may be corrected on appeal, but he should not have to fear that unsatisfied litigants may hound him with litigation charging malice or corruption. Imposing such a burden on judges would contribute not to principled and fearless decision-making but to intimidation.

We do not believe that this settled principle of law was abolished by § 1983, which makes liable "every person" who under color of law deprives another person of his civil rights. The legislative record gives no clear indication that Congress meant to abolish wholesale all common-law immunities. Accordingly, this Court held in *Tenney v. Brandhove* that the immunity of legislators for acts within the legislative role was not abolished. The immunity of judges for acts within the judicial role is equally well established, and we presume that Congress would have specifically so provided had it wished to abolish the doctrine.

The common law has never granted police officers an absolute and unqualified immunity, and the officers in this case do not claim that they are entitled to one. Their claim is rather that they should not be liable if they acted in good faith and with probable cause in making an arrest under a statute that they believed to be valid. Under the prevailing view in this country a peace officer who arrests someone with probable cause is not liable for false arrest simply because the innocence of the suspect is later proved. Restatement, Second, Torts § 121 (1965); 1 Harper & James, The Law of Torts § 3.18, at 277–278 (1956). A policeman's lot is not so unhappy that he must choose between being charged with dereliction of duty if he does not arrest when he has probable cause, and being mulcted in damages if he does. Although the matter is not entirely free from doubt, the same consideration would seem to require excusing him from liability for acting under a statute that he reasonably believed to be valid but that was later held unconstitutional, on its face or as applied.

The Court of Appeals held that the officers had such a limited privilege under the common law of Mississippi, and indicated that it would have recognized a similar privilege under § 1983 except that it felt compelled to hold otherwise by our decision in *Monroe v. Pape. Monroe v. Pape* presented no question of immunity, however, and none was decided. . . . As we [said in *Monroe*], § 1983 "should be read against the background of tort liability that makes a man responsible for the natural conse-quences of his actions." Part of the background of tort liability, in the case of police officers making an arrest, is the defense of good faith and probable cause.

We hold that the defense of good faith and probable cause, which the Court of Appeals found available to the officers in the common-law action for false arrest and imprisonment, is also available to them in the action under § 1983. This holding does not, however, mean that the count based thereon should be dismissed. The Court of

Appeals ordered dismissal of the common-law count on the theory that the police officers were not required to predict our decision in *Thomas v. Mississippi*. We agree that a police officer is not charged with predicting the future course of constitutional law. But the petitioners in this case did not simply argue that they were arrested under a statute later held unconstitutional. They claimed and attempted to prove that the police officers arrested them solely for attempting to use the "White Only" waiting room, that no crowd was present, and that no one threatened violence or seemed about to cause a disturbance. The officers did not defend on the theory that they believed in good faith that it was constitutional to arrest the ministers solely for using the waiting room. Rather, they claimed and attempted to prove that they did not arrest the ministers for the purpose of preserving the custom of segregation in Mississippi, but solely for the purpose of preventing violence. They testified, in contradiction to the ministers, that a crowd gathered and that imminent violence was likely. If the jury believed the testimony of the officers and disbelieved that of the ministers, and if the jury found that the officers reasonably believed in good faith that the arrest was constitutional, then a verdict for the officers would follow even though the arrest was in fact unconstitutional. The jury did resolve the factual issues in favor of the officers but, for reasons previously stated, its verdict was influenced by irrelevant and prejudicial evidence. Accordingly, the case must be remanded to the trial court for a new trial.

It is necessary to decide what importance should be given at the new trial to the substantially undisputed fact that the petitioners went to Jackson expecting to be illegally arrested. We do not agree with the Court of Appeals that they somehow consented to the arrest because of their anticipation that they would be illegally arrested, even assuming that they went to the Jackson bus terminal for the sole purpose of testing their rights to unsegregated public accommodations. The case contains no proof or allegation that they in any way tricked or goaded the officers into arresting them. The petitioners had the right to use the waiting room of the Jackson bus terminal, and their deliberate exercise of that right in a peaceful, orderly, and inoffensive manner does not disqualify them from seeking damages under § 1983.

The judgment of the Court of Appeals is affirmed in part and reversed in part, and the cases are remanded for further proceedings consistent with this opinion.

[The dissenting opinion of JUSTICE DOUGLAS on the issue of judicial immunity is omitted.]

NOTES

1. The text of 42 U.S.C. § 1983, reprinted in Chapter 1, does not mention any immunities or other defenses. In the absence of any explicit textual support, how does the Court justify its conclusion that a judge is protected by absolute immunity and police officers are protected by a "limited privilege" if they acted in "good faith and probable cause"? Does textual silence signal acceptance of then-existing common law defenses into a new statutory cause of action? Justice Douglas was not convinced. In dissent in *Pierson*, Justice Douglas wrote, "[t]he position that Congress did not intend to change the common-law rule of judicial immunity ignores the fact that every member of Congress who spoke to the issue assumed that the words of the statute meant what they said and that judges would be liable." *Pierson*, 386 U.S. at 561.

2.   Absolute judicial immunity and its limits were explored in Chapter 7. This Chapter will explore qualified immunity which has its origins in what the *Pierson* Court referred to as the more "limited privilege" afforded police officers. What exactly is the scope of the privilege the Court recognizes for police officers? Does the "limited privilege" given to police officers have both an objective and subjective state of mind component? For an early critique of the subjective part of *Pierson*'s qualified immunity test, see Theis, *"Good Faith" as a Defense to Suits for Police Deprivations of Individual Rights*, 59 MINN. L. REV. 991 (1975).

3.   How does the limited privilege given to police offers differ from the immunity given to judges? What considerations justify treating judges and police officers differently? What role does the common law play in answering these questions?

4.   After *Pierson*, the Court made clear that the two-part qualified immunity test applied to all those state and local government officials and employees not covered by absolute immunity. Thus, qualified immunity governed the conduct of governors, *Scheuer v. Rhodes*, 416 U.S. 232 (1974); mental health officials, *O'Connor v. Donaldson*, 422 U.S. 563 (1975); prison officials, *Procunier v. Navarette*, 434 U.S. 555 (1978); and school officials, *Wood v. Strickland*, 420 U.S. 308 (1975).

5.   *Wood v. Strickland* is especially significant, because it explicated the two-part test in considerable detail. The following extensive quote from *Wood* is set out because it is necessary for understanding the Supreme Court's later decision in *Harlow v. Fitzgerard*, which we consider next.

> The official himself must be acting sincerely and with a belief that he is doing right, but an act violating a student's constitutional rights can be no more justified by ignorance or disregard of settled, indisputable law on the part of one entrusted with supervision of students' daily lives than by the presence of actual malice. To be entitled to a special exemption from the categorical remedial language of section 1983 in a case in which his action violated a student's constitutional rights, a school board member, who has voluntarily undertaken the task of supervising the operation of the school and the activities of the students, must be held to a standard of conduct based not only on permissible intentions, but also on knowledge of the basic, unquestioned constitutional rights of his charges. Such a standard imposes neither an unfair burden upon a person assuming a responsible public office requiring a high degree of intelligence and judgment for the proper fulfillment of its duties, nor an unwarranted burden in light of the value which civil rights have in our legal system. Any lesser standard would deny much of the promise of section 1983. Therefore, in the specific context of school discipline, we hold that a school board member is not immune from liability for damages under section 1983 if he knew or reasonably should have known that the action he took within his sphere of official responsibility would violate the constitutional rights of the student affected, or if he took the action with the malicious intention to cause a deprivation of constitutional rights or other injury to the student. That is not to say that

school board members are "charged with predicting the future course of constitutional law." . . . A compensatory award will be appropriate only if the school board member has acted with such an impermissible motivation or with such disregard of the student's clearly established constitutional rights that his action cannot reasonably be characterized as being in good faith.

Wood v. Strickland, 420 U.S. at 321–22 .

6. Does *Wood* retain the two-part test of *Pierson*? Does *Wood* change it in any way?

What is the objective part of the qualified immunity inquiry after *Wood*? What is the subjective part of the qualified immunity inquiry after *Wood*? What is the role of a defendant's actual knowledge? Of a defendant's "malicious intention?" Who determines this issue in litigation?

HARLOW v. FITZGERALD
457 U.S. 800 (1982)

JUSTICE POWELL delivered the opinion of the Court.

The issue in this case is the scope of the immunity available to the senior aides and advisers of the President of the United States in a suit for damages based upon their official acts.

I

In this suit for civil damages petitioners Bryce Harlow and Alexander Butterfield are alleged to have participated in a conspiracy to violate the constitutional and statutory rights of the respondent A. Ernest Fitzgerald. Respondent avers that petitioners entered the conspiracy in their capacities as senior White House aides to former President Richard M. Nixon. As the alleged conspiracy is the same as that involved in *Nixon v. Fitzgerald*, the facts need not be repeated in detail.

Respondent claims that Harlow joined the conspiracy in his role as the Presidential aide principally responsible for congressional relations. At the conclusion of discovery the supporting evidence remained inferential. As evidence of Harlow's conspiratorial activity respondent relies heavily on a series of conversations in which Harlow discussed Fitzgerald's dismissal with Air Force Secretary Robert Seamans. The other evidence most supportive of Fitzgerald's claims consists of a recorded conversation in which the President later voiced a tentative recollection that Harlow was "all for canning" Fitzgerald.

Disputing Fitzgerald's contentions, Harlow argues" that exhaustive discovery has adduced no direct evidence of his involvement in any wrongful activity. He avers that Secretary Seamans advised him that considerations of efficiency required Fitzgerald's removal by a reduction in force, despite anticipated adverse congressional reaction. Harlow asserts he had no reason to believe that a conspiracy existed. He contends that he took all his actions in good faith.

Together with their co-defendant Richard Nixon, petitioners Harlow and But-terfield moved for summary judgment on February 12, 1980. In denying the motion the District Court upheld the legal sufficiency of Fitzgerald's *Bivens* (*Bivens v. Six Unknown Fed. Narcotics Agents*) claim under the First Amendment and his "inferred" statutory causes of action under 5 U.S.C. § 7211 and 18 U.S.C. § 1505. The court found that genuine issues of disputed fact remained for resolution at trial. It also ruled that petitioners were not entitled to absolute immunity.

Independently of former President Nixon, petitioners invoked the collateral order doctrine and appealed the denial of their immunity defense to the Court of Appeals for the District of Columbia Circuit. The Court of Appeals dismissed the appeal without opinion. Never having determined the immunity available to the senior aides and advisers of the President of the United States, we granted certiorari.

II

As we reiterated today in *Nixon v. Fitzgerald*, our decisions consistently have held that government officials are entitled to some form of immunity from suits for damages. As recognized at common law, public officers require this protection to shield them from undue interference with their duties and from potentially disabling threats of liability.

Our decisions have recognized immunity defenses of two kinds. For officials whose special functions or constitutional status requires complete protection from suit, we have recognized the defense of "absolute immunity." The absolute immunity of legislators, in their legislative functions, and of judges, in their judicial functions, now is well settled. Our decisions also have extended absolute immunity to certain officials of the Executive Branch. These include prosecutors and similar officials, see *Butz v. Economou*, executive officers engaged in adjudicative functions, and the President of the United States, see *Nixon v. Fitzgerald*.

For executive officials in general, however, our cases make plain that qualified immunity represents the norm. In *Scheuer v. Rhodes*, we acknowledged that high officials require greater protection than those with less complex discretionary responsibilities. Nonetheless, we held that a governor and his aides could receive the requisite protection from qualified or good-faith immunity. In *Butz v. Econo-mou*, we extended the approach of *Scheuer* to high federal officials of the Executive Branch. Discussing in detail the considerations that also had underlain our decision in *Scheuer*, we explained that the recognition of a qualified immunity defense for high executives reflected an attempt to balance competing values: not only the importance of a damages remedy to protect the rights of citizens, but also "the need to protect officials who are required to exercise their discretion and the related public interest in encouraging the vigorous exercise of official authority." Without discounting the adverse consequences of denying high officials an absolute immu-nity from private lawsuits alleging constitutional violations — consequences found sufficient in *Spalding v. Vilas*, and *Barr v. Matteo*, to warrant extension to such officials of absolute immunity from suits at common law — we emphasized our expectation that insubstantial suits need not proceed to trial:

"Insubstantial lawsuits can be quickly terminated by federal courts alert to the possibilities of artful pleading. Unless the complaint states a compensable claim for relief . . . , it should not survive a motion to dismiss. Moreover, the Court recognized in *Scheuer* that damages suits concerning constitutional violations need not proceed to trial, but can be terminated on a properly supported motion for summary judgment based on the defense of immunity. . . . In responding to such a motion, plaintiffs may not play dog in the manger; and firm application of the Federal Rules of Civil Procedure will ensure that federal officials are not harassed by frivolous lawsuits."

Butz continued to acknowledge that the special functions of some officials might require absolute immunity. But the Court held that "federal officials who seek absolute exemption from personal liability for unconstitutional conduct must bear the burden of showing that public policy requires an exemption of that scope." This we reaffirmed today in *Nixon v. Fitzgerald*.

III

A

Petitioners argue that they are entitled to a blanket protection of absolute immunity as an incident of their offices as Presidential aides.

In deciding this claim we do not write on an empty page. In *Butz v. Economou*, the Secretary of Agriculture — a Cabinet official directly accountable to the President — asserted a defense of absolute official immunity from suit for civil damages. We rejected his claim. In so doing we did not question the power or the importance of the Secretary's office. Nor did we doubt the importance to the President of loyal and efficient subordinates in executing his duties of office. Yet we found these factors, alone, to be insufficient to justify absolute immunity. "[The] greater power of [high] officials," we reasoned, "affords a greater potential for a regime of lawless conduct." Damages actions against high officials were therefore "an important means of vindicating constitutional guarantees." Moreover, we concluded that it would be "untenable to draw a distinction for purposes of immunity law between suits brought against state officials under [42 U.S.C.] § 1983 and suits brought directly under the Constitution against federal officials."

Having decided in *Butz* that Members of the Cabinet ordinarily enjoy only qualified immunity from suit, we conclude today that it would be equally untenable to hold absolute immunity an incident of the office of every Presidential subordinate based in the White House. Members of the Cabinet are direct subordinates of the President, frequently with greater responsibilities, both to the President and to the Nation, than White House staff. The considerations that supported our decision in *Butz* apply with equal force to this case. It is no disparagement of the offices held by petitioners to hold that Presidential aides, like Members of the Cabinet, generally are entitled only to a qualified immunity.

Even if they cannot establish that their official functions require absolute immunity, petitioners assert that public policy at least mandates an application of the qualified immunity standard that would permit the defeat of insubstantial claims without resort to trial. We agree.

IV

A

The resolution of immunity questions inherently requires a balance between the evils inevitable in any available alternative. In situations of abuse of office, an action for damages may offer the only realistic avenue for vindication of constitutional guarantees. It is this recognition that has required the denial of absolute immunity to most public officers. At the same time, however, it cannot be disputed seriously that claims frequently run against the innocent as well as the guilty — at a cost not only to the defendant officials, but to society as a whole. These social costs include the expenses of litigation, the diversion of official energy from pressing public issues, and the deterrence of able citizens from acceptance of public office. Finally, there is the danger that fear of being sued will "dampen the ardor of all but the most resolute, or the most irresponsible [public officials], in the unflinching discharge of their duties." *Gregoire v. Biddle.*

In identifying qualified immunity as the best attainable accommodation of competing values, in *Butz*, as in *Scheuer*, we relied on the assumption that this standard would permit "[insubstantial] lawsuits [to] be quickly terminated." Yet petitioners advance persuasive arguments that the dismissal of insubstantial lawsuits without trial — a factor presupposed in the balance of competing interests struck by our prior cases — requires an adjustment of the "good faith" standard established by our decisions.

B

Qualified or "good faith" immunity is an affirmative defense that must be pleaded by a defendant official. Decisions of this Court have established that the "good faith" defense has both an "objective" and a "subjective" aspect. The objective element involves a presumptive knowledge of and respect for "basic, unquestioned constitutional rights." *Wood v. Strickland.* The subjective component refers to "permissible intentions." Characteristically, the Court has defined these elements by identifying the circumstances in which qualified immunity would not be available. Referring both to the objective and subjective elements, we have held that qualified immunity would be defeated if an official "knew or reasonably should have known that the action he took within his sphere of official responsibility would violate the constitutional rights of the [plaintiff], or if he took the action with the malicious intention to cause a deprivation of constitutional rights or other injury. . . ."

The subjective element of the good-faith defense frequently has proved incompatible with our admonition in *Butz* that insubstantial claims should not proceed to trial. Rule 56 of the Federal Rules of Civil Procedure provides that disputed questions of fact ordinarily may not be decided on motions for summary judgment. And an official's subjective good faith has been considered to be a question of fact that some courts have regarded as inherently requiring resolution by a jury.

In the context of *Butz*'s attempted balancing of competing values, it now is clear that substantial costs attend the litigation of the subjective good faith of government officials. Not only are there the general costs of subjecting officials to the risks of trial — distraction of officials from their governmental duties, inhibition of discretionary action, and deterrence of able people from public service. There are special costs to "subjective" inquiries of this kind. Immunity generally is available only to officials performing discretionary functions. In contrast with the thought processes accompanying "ministerial" tasks, the judgments surrounding discretionary action almost inevitably are influenced by the decisionmaker's experiences, values, and emotions. These variables explain in part why questions of subjective intent so rarely can be decided by summary judgment. Yet they also frame a background in which there often is no clear end to the relevant evidence. Judicial inquiry into subjective motivation therefore may entail broad-ranging discovery and the deposing of numerous persons, including an official's professional colleagues. Inquiries of this kind can be peculiarly disruptive of effective government.

Consistently with the balance at which we aimed in *Butz*, we conclude today that bare allegations of malice should not suffice to subject government officials either to the costs of trial or to the burdens of broad-reaching discovery. We therefore hold that government officials performing discretionary functions, generally are shielded from liability for civil damages insofar as their conduct does not violate clearly established statutory or constitutional rights of which a reasonable person would have known.[1]

Reliance on the objective reasonableness of an official's conduct, as measured by reference to clearly established law, should avoid excessive disruption of government and permit the resolution of many insubstantial claims on summary judgment. On summary judgment, the judge appropriately may determine, not only the currently applicable law, but whether that law was clearly established at the time an action occurred. If the law at that time was not clearly established, an official could not reasonably be expected to anticipate subsequent legal developments, nor could he fairly be said to "know" that the law forbade conduct not previously identified as unlawful. Until this threshold immunity question is resolved, discovery should not be allowed. If the law was clearly established, the immunity defense ordinarily should fail, since a reasonably competent public official should know the law governing his conduct. Nevertheless, if the official pleading the defense claims extraordinary circumstances and can prove that he neither knew nor should have known of the relevant legal standard, the defense should be sustained. But again, the defense would turn primarily on objective factors.

By defining the limits of qualified immunity essentially in objective terms, we provide no license to lawless conduct. The public interest in deterrence of unlawful conduct and in compensation of victims remains protected by a test that focuses on the objective legal reasonableness of an official's acts. Where an official could be expected to know that certain conduct would violate statutory or constitutional rights, he should be made to hesitate; and a person who suffers injury caused by

---

[1] [30] This case involves no issue concerning the elements of the immunity applicable to state officials sued for constitutional violations under 42 U.S.C. section 1983. We have found previously, however, that it would be "untenable to draw a distinction for purposes of immunity law between suits brought against state officials under section 1983 and suits brought directly under the constitution against federal officials."

such conduct may have a cause of action. But where an official's duties legitimately require action in which clearly established rights are not implicated, the public interest may be better served by action taken "with independence and without fear of consequences." *Pierson v. Ray*.

V

The judgment of the Court of Appeals is vacated, and the case is remanded for further action consistent with this opinion.

JUSTICE **BRENNAN**, with whom JUSTICE **MARSHALL** and JUSTICE **BLACKMUN** join, concurring.

I agree with the substantive standard announced by the Court today, imposing liability when a public-official defendant "knew or should have known" of the constitutionally violative effect of his actions. This standard would not allow the official who actually knows that he was violating the law to escape liability for his actions, even if he could not "reasonably have been expected" to know what he actually did know. Thus the clever and unusually well-informed violator of constitutional rights will not evade just punishment for his crimes. I also agree that this standard applies "across the board," to all "government officials performing discretionary functions." I write separately only to note that given this standard, it seems inescapable to me that some measure of discovery may sometimes be required to determine exactly what a public-official defendant did "know" at the time of his actions. In this respect the issue before us is very similar to that addressed in *Herbert v. Lando*, in which the Court observed that "[to] erect an impenetrable barrier to the plaintiff's use of such evidence on his side of the case is a matter of some substance, particularly when defendants themselves are prone to assert their [good faith] . . .". Of course, as the Court has already noted, summary judgment will be readily available to public-official defendants whenever the state of the law was so ambiguous at the time of the alleged violation that it could not have been "known" then, and thus liability could not ensue. In my view, summary judgment will also be readily available whenever the plaintiff cannot prove, as a threshold matter, that a violation of his constitutional rights actually occurred. I see no reason why discovery of defendants' "knowledge" should not be deferred by the trial judge pending decision of any motion of defendants for summary judgment on grounds such as these.

[The separate concurring statements of JUSTICES **BRENNAN**, **WHITE**, **MARSHALL** and **BLACKMUN** is omitted, as are the concurring opinion of JUSTICE **REHNQUIST** and the dissenting opinion of CHIEF JUSTICE **BURGER**.]

NOTES

1. Is *Harlow* a section 1983 case? What difference does it make whether a claim is brought pursuant to section 1983 or under a *Bivens* theory? Recall that in *Pierson*, the Court reasoned that Congress must have intended to apply well-established common law defenses in section 1983 claims. Is that reasoning relevant

in *Bivens* actions? Does the Court intend *Harlow* to govern section 1983 cases? What does footnote 1 [30] suggest?

2. Why does the Court eliminate the subjective element of the qualified immunity test? Exactly what are the perceived costs of state of mind inquiries?

3. Can state of mind inquires be avoided altogether? What if the alleged substantive constitutional violation requires proof of the defendant's motive, as in retaliation claims? In *Crawford-El v. Britton*, 523 U.S. 574 (1998), the plaintiff was, as the Court described, "a litigious and outspoken prisoner." Due to overcrowding, he was transferred to a number of facilities across the country. Crawford-El had three boxes of personal belongings, including legal materials that were transferred separately. The inmate alleged that the defendant deliberately misdirected the boxes to punish him for exercising his First Amendment rights and to deter similar conduct in the future. The defendant denied having any retaliatory motive and had arranged for Crawford-El's family to ship the boxes. Because the boxes were not shipped by prison officials, there was a delay in delivering them to Crawford-El. The district court initially denied the defendant's motion to dismiss. After an appeal, a remand, a new ruling by the district court and a new appeal, the matter came before the court of appeals en banc. The majority held that *Harlow* dictated that special measures were needed to protect defendants from the costs of litigating "unconstitutional-motive" cases. The special measure the court adopted was elevating the plaintiff's burden of proof to clear and convincing evidence.

The Supreme Court reversed. Justice Stevens, writing for a five Justice majority, stated that neither the holding nor the reasoning of *Harlow* supported the adoption of a heighted burden of proof. The holding in *Harlow* spoke to the elements of the qualified immunity defense and "did not implicate the elements of the plaintiff's initial burden of proving a constitutional violation." The reasoning of *Harlow* did not warrant a judicially imposed heightened burden of proof because of "countervailing concerns [that arose] . . . when evaluating the elements of the plaintiff's cause of action." One countervailing concern the Court identified was the fact that the state of mind necessary to establish a First Amendment violation was not a generalized "personal animus," but a more specific intent to punish or deter protected speech. Moreover, qualified immunity is designed to protect a government official from the unfairness of "imposing liability on a defendant who could not reasonably be expected to anticipate subsequent legal development, nor . . . fairly be said to know that the law forbade conduct not previously identified as unlawful. . . . [N]o such unfairness can be attributed to holding one accountable for actions that she knew or reasonably should have known, violated the plaintiff's constitutional rights."

4. What, if anything, does *Harlow* do to the objective part of the qualified immunity test? What does objective reasonableness mean? When is law "clearly settled"? What is the role of judge and jury in answering these questions?

5. What is the scope of the protection afforded government officials by qualified immunity? Why is it not enough to immunize them from personal liability? Why go beyond that and insulate them from the cost and inconvenience of having to litigate? After *Harlow*, what is the connection between discovery and qualified immunity? If discovery is ordinarily not to be allowed before the qualified immunity motion for summary judgment is disposed of, how is a plaintiff to develop evidence of genuine issues of material fact in dispute within the meaning of Rule 56 of the Federal Rules of Civil Procedure so as to defeat the defendant's motion? Does *Crawford-El*, discussed in note 3 above, have any implications on the availability or scope of discovery?

6. Almost in passing, the Court in *Harlow* states (emphasis added): "Nevertheless, if the official pleading the defense claims *extraordinary circumstances* and he can prove that he neither knew nor should have known of the relevant legal standard, the defense should be sustained. But again, the defense would turn primarily on objective factors." What are "extraordinary circumstances"? Is reliance on advice of counsel an extraordinary circumstance? *See Kelly v. Borough of Carlisle*, 622 F.3d 248 (3d Cir. 2010) (advice of counsel is a "thumb on the scale" supporting a claim of qualified immunity); *Lawrence v. Reed*, 406 F.3d 1224 (10th Cir. 2005) (in some cases advice of counsel can create the extraordinary circumstances that excuse a violation of clearly established law); *Cox v. Hainey*, 391 F.3d 25 (1st Cir. 2004) (advice of counsel is a factor in the "totality of the circumstances" considered in determining an officer's entitlement to qualified immunity).

What about the timing of when a defendant should have known clearly settled law? *See Doby v. Hickerson*, 120 F.3d 111 (8th Cir. 1997) (defendant prison psychiatrist should have known of applicable Supreme Court decision handed down twenty-two days before she administered anti-psychotic medications without prisoner's consent).

7. What do you make of the Court's use of cost-benefit analysis as a justification for changing the qualified immunity test? How much weight does the Court give to society's interest in constitutional compliance? To the individual's interest in being compensated for constitutional harm? For the argument that *Harlow* overstates the costs of liability for constitutional violations, see NAHMOD, 2 CIVIL RIGHTS AND CIVIL LIBERTIES LITIGATION: THE LAW OF SECTION 1983 § 8:5 (4th ed. 2014).

In general, does qualified immunity make sense from an economic perspective, or might enterprise liability be preferable? Is the typical government official likely to capture the benefits of exposing others to risks like the hypothetical reasonable private person in the usual common law torts situation? What effect does your answer have on the appropriate function of qualified immunity and its relation to over-deterrence? *See* Cass, *Damage Suits Against Public Officers*, 129 U. PA. L REV. 1110 (1981).

8. *Harlow* asserts that qualified immunity is needed because the risk of personal liability will "dampen the ardor of all but the most resolute, or the most irresponsible [public officials], in the unflinching discharge of their duties." (Quoting *Gregoire v. Biddle*.) There is increasing evidence, however, that police officers and correctional officials do not, in fact, face the risk of personal liability. In a major empirical study, Professor Joanna Schwartz examined the indemnification practices of law enforcement agencies across the country. She found that police officers are almost always indemnified for any civil rights liabilities; that 99.98% of dollars paid in settlement or judgment of civil rights claims are paid by governments (not individual defendants); no officer in her study ever had to pay a punitive damage award; and individual officers almost never contributed anything to settlements or judgments even in jurisdictions that prohibited indemnification. Joanna C.

Schwartz, *Police Indemnifications*, 89 N.Y.U. L. REV. 885 (June 2014). Professor Schwartz concluded that evidence that police officers almost never contribute to settlements or judgments undermines the Court's rationale for qualified immunity. *Id.* at 943. In a similar vein, Professor Slanger reports that individual correctional officers do not pay for the cost of defense or any resulting settlement or judgment in civil rights cases. Margo Schlanger, *Inmate Litigation*, 116 HARV. L. REV. 1555 (2003). Professor Jeffries has informally polled police officers trained at the FBI Academy over a twenty year period and reports that none of the officers know anyone who has been denied indemnification for a civil rights violation. John C. Jeffries, *In Praise of the Eleventh Amendment and Section 1983*, 84 U. VA. L. REV. 47, 50 n.16 (1998). How seriously do these studies undermine the rationale for qualified immunity? Is the defense justifiable on other grounds?

ANDERSON v. CREIGHTON
483 U.S. 635 (1987)

JUSTICE SCALIA delivered the opinion of the Court.

The question presented is whether a federal law enforcement officer who participates in a search that violates the Fourth Amendment may be held personally liable for money damages if a reasonable officer could have believed that the search comported with the Fourth Amendment.

I

Petitioner Russell Anderson is an agent of the Federal Bureau of Investigation. On November 11, 1983, Anderson and other state and federal law enforcement officers conducted a warrant less search of the home of respondents, the Creighton family. The search was conducted because Anderson believed that Vadaain Dixon, a man suspected of a bank robbery committed earlier that day, might be found there. He was not.

The Creightons later filed suit against Anderson in a Minnesota state court, asserting among other things a claim for money damages under the Fourth Amendment, see *Bivens v. Six Unknown Fed. Narcotics Agents*. After removing the suit to Federal District Court, Anderson filed a motion to dismiss or for summary judgment, arguing that the *Bivens* claim was barred by Anderson's qualified immunity from civil damages liability. See *Harlow v. Fitzgerald*. Before any discovery took place, the District Court granted summary judgment on the ground that the search was lawful, holding that the undisputed facts revealed that Anderson had had probable cause to search the Creighton's home and that his failure to obtain a warrant was justified by the presence of exigent circumstances. [On appeal, the Eighth Circuit reversed.]

II

When government officials abuse their offices, "action[s] for damages may offer the only realistic avenue for vindication of constitutional guarantees." *Harlow v.*

Fitzgerald. On the other hand, permitting damages suits against government officials can entail substantial social costs, including the risk that fear of personal monetary liability and harassing litigation will unduly inhibit officials in the discharge of their duties. Our cases have accommodated these conflicting concerns by generally providing government officials performing discretionary functions with a qualified immunity, shielding them from civil damages liability as long as their actions could reasonably have been thought consistent with the rights they are alleged to have violated. See, e. g., *Malley v. Briggs* (qualified immunity protects "all but the plainly incompetent or those who knowingly violate the law") (police officers applying for warrants are immune if a reasonable officer could have believed that there was probable cause to support the application); *Mitchell v. Forsyth* (officials are immune unless "the law clearly proscribed the actions" they took). Somewhat more concretely, whether an official protected by qualified immunity may be held personally liable for an allegedly unlawful official action generally turns on the "objective legal reasonableness" of the action, *Harlow*, assessed in light of the legal rules that were "clearly established" at the time it was taken.

The operation of this standard, however, depends substantially upon the level of generality at which the relevant "legal rule" is to be identified. For example, the right to due process of law is quite clearly established by the Due Process Clause, and thus there is a sense in which any action that violates that Clause (no matter how unclear it may be that the particular action is a violation) violates a clearly established right. Much the same could be said of any other constitutional or statutory violation. But if the test of "clearly established law" were to be applied at this level of generality, it would bear no relationship to the "objective legal reasonableness" that is the touchstone of *Harlow*. Plaintiffs would be able to convert the rule of qualified immunity that our cases plainly establish into a rule of virtually unqualified liability simply by alleging violation of extremely abstract rights. *Harlow* would be transformed from a guarantee of immunity into a rule of pleading. Such an approach, in sum, would destroy "the balance that our cases strike between the interests in vindication of citizens' constitutional rights and in public officials' effective performance of their duties," by making it impossible for officials "reasonably [to] anticipate when their conduct may give rise to liability for damages." *Davis v. Scherer.* It should not be surprising, therefore, that our cases establish that the right the official is alleged to have violated must have been "clearly established" in a more particularized, and hence more relevant, sense: The contours of the right must be sufficiently clear that a reasonable official would understand that what he is doing violates that right. This is not to say that an official action is protected by qualified immunity unless the very action in question has previously been held unlawful; but it is to say that in the light of pre-existing law the unlawfulness must be apparent.

Anderson contends that the Court of Appeals misapplied these principles. We agree. The Court of Appeals' brief discussion of qualified immunity consisted of little more than an assertion that a general right Anderson was alleged to have violated — the right to be free from warrant less searches of one's home unless the searching officers have probable cause and there are exigent circumstances — was clearly established. The Court of Appeals specifically refused to consider the argument that it was not clearly established that the circumstances with which

Anderson was confronted did not constitute probable cause and exigent circumstances. The previous discussion should make clear that this refusal was erroneous. It simply does not follow immediately from the conclusion that it was firmly established that warrant less searches not supported by probable cause and exigent circumstances violate the Fourth Amendment that Anderson's search was objectively legally unreasonable. We have recognized that it is inevitable that law enforcement officials will in some cases reasonably but mistakenly conclude that probable cause is present, and we have indicated that in such cases those officials — like other officials who act in ways they reasonably believe to be lawful — should not be held personally liable. The same is true of their conclusions regarding exigent circumstances.

It follows from what we have said that the determination whether it was objectively legally reasonable to conclude that a given search was supported by probable cause or exigent circumstances will often require examination of the information possessed by the searching officials. But contrary to the Creightons' assertion, this does not reintroduce into qualified immunity analysis the inquiry into officials' subjective intent that *Harlow* sought to minimize. The relevant question in this case, for example, is the objective (albeit fact-specific) question whether a reasonable officer could have believed Anderson's warrant less search to be lawful, in light of clearly established law and the information the searching officers possessed. Anderson's subjective beliefs about the search are irrelevant.

The principles of qualified immunity that we reaffirm today require that Anderson be permitted to argue that he is entitled to summary judgment on the ground that, in light of the clearly established principles governing warrant less searches, he could, as a matter of law, reasonably have believed that the search of the Creightons' home was lawful.

The general rule of qualified immunity is intended to provide government officials with the ability "reasonably [to] anticipate when their conduct may give rise to liability for damages." *Davis v. Scherer.* Where that rule is applicable, officials can know that they will not be held personally liable as long as their actions are reasonable in light of current American law. That security would be utterly defeated if officials were unable to determine whether they were protected by the rule without entangling themselves in the vagaries of the English and American common law. We are unwilling to Balkanize the rule of qualified immunity by carving exceptions at the level of detail the Creightons propose. We therefore decline to make an exception to the general rule of qualified immunity for cases involving allegedly unlawful warrant less searches of innocent third parties' homes in search of fugitives.

For the reasons stated, we vacate the judgment of the Court of Appeals and remand the case for further proceedings consistent with this opinion.[2]

---

[2] [6] Noting that no discovery has yet taken place, the Creightons renew their argument that, whatever the appropriate qualified immunity standard, some discovery would be required before Anderson's summary judgment motion could be granted. We think the matter somewhat more complicated. One of the purposes of the *Harlow* qualified immunity standard is to protect public officials from the "broad-ranging discovery" that can be "peculiarly disruptive of effective government." For this reason, we have emphasized that qualified immunity questions should be resolved at the earliest possible

JUSTICE STEVENS, with whom JUSTICE BRENNAN and JUSTICE MARSHALL join, dissenting.

This case is beguiling in its apparent simplicity. The Court accordingly represents its task as the clarification of the settled principles of qualified immunity that apply in damages suits brought against federal officials. Its opinion, however, announces a new rule of law that protects federal agents who make forcible nighttime entries into the homes of innocent citizens without probable cause, without a warrant, and without any valid emergency justification for their warrantless search. The Court stunningly restricts the constitutional accountability of the police by creating a false dichotomy between police entitlement to summary judgment on immunity grounds and damages liability for every police misstep, by responding to this dichotomy with an uncritical application of the precedents of qualified immunity that we have developed for a quite different group of high public office holders, and by displaying remarkably little fidelity to the countervailing principles of individual liberty and privacy that infuse the Fourth Amendment. Before I turn to the Court's opinion, it is appropriate to identify the issue confronted by the Court of Appeals. It is now apparent that it was correct in vacating the District Court's award of summary judgment to petitioner in advance of discovery.

I

The Court of Appeals understood the principle of qualified immunity as implemented in *Harlow v. Fitzgerald*, to shield government officials performing discretionary functions from exposure to damages liability unless their conduct violated clearly established statutory or constitutional rights of which a reasonable person would have known. Applying this principle, the Court of Appeals held that respondents' Fourth Amendment rights and the "exigent circumstances" doctrine were "clearly established" at the time of the search. Moreover, apparently referring to the "extraordinary circumstances" defense left open in *Harlow* for a defendant who "can prove that he neither knew nor should have known of the relevant legal standard," the Court determined that petitioner could not reasonably have been unaware of these clearly established principles of law. Thus, in reviewing the Court of Appeals' judgment rejecting petitioner Anderson's claim to immunity, the first question to be decided is whether *Harlow v. Fitzgerald* requires immunity for a federal law enforcement agent who advances the fact-specific claim that a reasonable person in his position could have believed that his particular conduct would not violate rights that he concedes are clearly established. A negative answer to that question is required, both because *Harlow* provides an inappropriate measure of immunity when police acts that violate the Fourth Amendment are challenged, and also because petitioner cannot make the showing required for *Harlow* immunity.

---

stage of a litigation. Thus, on remand, it should first be determined whether the actions the Creightons allege Anderson to have taken are actions that a reasonable officer could have believed lawful. If they are, then Anderson is entitled to dismissal prior to discovery. If they are not, and if the actions Anderson claims he took are different from those the Creightons allege (and are actions that a reasonable officer could have believed lawful), then discovery may be necessary before Anderson's motion for summary judgment on qualified immunity grounds can be resolved. Of course, any such discovery should be tailored specifically to the question of Anderson's qualified immunity.

Second, apart from the particular requirements of the *Harlow* doctrine, a full review of the Court of Appeals' judgment raises the question whether this Court should approve a double standard of reasonableness — the constitutional standard already embodied in the Fourth Amendment and an even more generous standard that protects any officer who reasonably could have believed that his conduct was constitutionally reasonable.

NOTES

1. What does *Anderson* add to our understanding of the test for qualified immunity? What are the practical effects of framing the clearly settled law inquiry at a more fact specific level? Does *Anderson* make it more or less likely that a defendant can prevail on a motion for summary judgment? Do *Harlow* and *Anderson* combined create a qualified immunity standard that unduly favors the defendant? *See* Rudovsky, *The Qualified Immunity Doctrine in the Supreme Court: Judicial Activism and the Restriction of Constitutional Rights*, 138 U. PA. L. REV. 23 (1989).

2. If the clearly settled law inquiry is to be analyzed in a "more particularized . . . sense," will some discovery be necessary? What guidance does *Anderson* give lower courts regarding discovery when a defendant raises the defense of qualified immunity?

3. What does Justice Stevens mean when he questions whether the Court should approve a "double standard of reasonableness"? On the merits of the qualified immunity defense, *Anderson* holds that an officer is immune if, under the facts, he reasonably believed his conduct was lawful, even if a court later concluded that it was not. In the context of an alleged unreasonable search under the Fourth Amendment (as in *Anderson*), that would mean that a defendant would prevail if the search was found to be reasonable (and hence not a substantive constitutional violation) or if the officer reasonably believed the search was reasonable (and hence qualified immunity applies). Thus, the officer gets two bites at the objective reasonableness apple. *See also Saucier v. Katz*, 533 U.S. 194 (2001) (qualified immunity can apply if an officer makes a reasonable mistake that the amount of force used in making an arrest was reasonable). What, if anything, is wrong with giving a defendant "two bites"? Doesn't every defendant have the possibility of prevailing on the merits as well as prevailing on qualified immunity? Professor Jeffries characterizes as "irreducibly murky" the concept that a reasonable officer could believe that objectively unreasonable force was reasonable. "[I]f the conduct is objectively unreasonable, how could an officer reasonably believe it legal?" John C. Jeffries, Jr., *What's Wrong with Qualified Immunity?*, 62 U. FLA. L. REV. 851, 862 (2010). Jeffries concludes that the message *Anderson* and *Sacucier* send lower courts is that "borderline excessive force claims should be resolved in favor of defendants before trial . . ." *Id.* at 863.

4. *Anderson* involved an alleged violation of the Fourth Amendment which is framed in terms of "reasonable" searches and seizures. Suppose the claim involves an alleged violation of substantive due process, cruel and unusual punishment or equal protection. The state of mind necessary to establish a constitutional violation in such cases is not objective reasonableness, but deliberate indifference, shocks the conscience, intent or some other type of heightened culpability. Could a person reasonably believe his conduct was lawful if it met these states of mind? *Compare Estate of Ford v. Ramierz-Palmer*, 301 F.3d 1043 (9th Cir. 2002) (a correctional official whose deliberate indifference to an inmate's safety violated the Eighth Amendment was protected by qualified immunity), *with Johnson v. Breeden*, 280 F.3d 1308 (11th Cir. 2002) (prison guard who violated an inmate's rights under the Eighth Amendment by employing excessive force that was sadistically and maliciously applied could not claim qualified immunity). *See also* Alan K. Chen, *The Burdens of Qualified Immunity: Summary Judgment and the Role of Facts in Constitutional Tort Law*, 47 Am. U. L. Rev. 1, 62 (1997) (arguing that there can be no qualified immunity for constitutional violations of equal protection for which intent is required; "If the defendant acted with the intent to harm the plaintiff because of her race, no court would find that a reasonable official could believe that there might be some circumstance that made such an act permissible under established law.").

5. In light of *Anderson*, should a plaintiff ever argue that a case raises an important issue of first impression when suing a state or local governmental official? Would your answer be different if the claim was brought against a local government? See Chapter 5 on local government liability.

6. Notice that the *Anderson* approach requires a court to put itself in the defendant's position at the time of the challenged conduct. Professor Nahmod asserts that the Court's substantive and procedural changes in qualified immunity doctrine, including those in *Harlow* and *Anderson*, have promoted a pro-defendant posture of empathy. Nahmod, *The Restructuring of Narrative and Empathy in Section 1983 Cases*, 72 Chi-Kent L. Rev. 819 (1997).

II.   WHEN IS LAW "CLEARLY ESTABLISHED"?

After *Harlow*, qualified immunity shields a government official from money damages unless (1) the official violated a statutory or constitutional right, and (2) that right was "clearly established" at the time of the challenged conduct. *Anderson* informs us that the clearly settled law inquiry must be framed at a level of factually specificity. The material in this section address the issue of when is law clearly settled in a factually specific way. How closely must the facts of the present case track those from previously decided cases? What are the relevant sources of law that determine whether a right has been clearly established?

HOPE v. PELZER
536 U.S. 730 (2002)

Stevens, J., delivered the opinion of the Court.

The Court of Appeals for the Eleventh Circuit concluded that petitioner Larry Hope, a former prison inmate at the Limestone Prison in Alabama, was subjected to cruel and unusual punishment when prison guards twice handcuffed him to a hitching post to sanction him for disruptive conduct. Because that conclusion was not supported by earlier cases with "materially similar" facts, the court held that the respondents were entitled to qualified immunity, and therefore affirmed summary judgment in their favor. We granted certiorari to determine whether the Court of Appeals' qualified immunity holding comports with our decision in *United States v. Lanier*, 520 U.S. 259 (1997).

I

In 1995, Alabama was the only State that followed the practice of chaining inmates to one another in work squads. It was also the only State that handcuffed prisoners to "hitching posts" if they either refused to work or otherwise disrupted work squads.[3] Hope was handcuffed to a hitching post on two occasions. On May 11, 1995, while Hope was working in a chain gang near an interstate highway, he got into an argument with another inmate. Both men were taken back to the Limestone prison and handcuffed to a hitching post. Hope was released two hours later, after the guard captain determined that the altercation had been caused by the other inmate. During his two hours on the post, Hope was offered drinking water and a bathroom break every 15 minutes, and his responses to these offers were recorded on an activity log. Because he was only slightly taller than the hitching post, his arms were above shoulder height and grew tired from being handcuffed so high. Whenever he tried moving his arms to improve his circulation, the handcuffs cut into his wrists, causing pain and discomfort.

On June 7, 1995, Hope was punished more severely. He took a nap during the morning bus ride to the chain gang's worksite, and when it arrived he was less than prompt in responding to an order to get off the bus. An exchange of vulgar remarks led to a wrestling match with a guard. Four other guards intervened, subdued Hope, handcuffed him, placed him in leg irons and transported him back to the prison where he was put on the hitching post. The guards made him take off his shirt, and he remained shirtless all day while the sun burned his skin.[4] He remained attached to the post for approximately seven hours. During this 7-hour period, he was given water only once or twice and was given no bathroom breaks. At one point, a guard taunted Hope about his thirst. According to Hope's affidavit: "[The guard] first gave water to some dogs, then brought the water cooler closer to me, removed its lid, and kicked the cooler over, spilling the water onto the ground."

Hope filed suit under 42 U.S.C. § 1983, in the United States District Court for the Northern District of Alabama against three guards involved in the May incident, one of whom also handcuffed him to the hitching post in June. The case was referred to a Magistrate Judge who treated the responsive affidavits filed by the defendants

---

[3] [1] * * * [T] the hitching post is a horizontal bar "made of sturdy, nonflexible material," placed between 45 and 57 inches from the ground. Inmates are handcuffed to the hitching post in a standing position and remain standing the entire time they are placed on the post. Most inmates are shackled to the hitching post with their two hands relatively close together and at face level.

[4] [2] The most repeated complaint of the hitching post, however, was the strain it produced on inmates' muscles by forcing them to remain in a standing position with their arms raised in a stationary position for a long period of time. In addition to their exposure to sunburn, dehydration, and muscle aches, the inmates are also placed in substantial pain when the sun heats the handcuffs that shackle them to the hitching post, or heats the hitching post itself. Several of the inmates described the way in which the handcuffs burned and chafed their skin during their placement on the post.

as a motion for summary judgment. Without deciding whether "the very act of placing him on a restraining bar for a period of hours as a form of punishment" had violated the Eighth Amendment, the Magistrate concluded that the guards were entitled to qualified immunity. The District Court agreed, and entered judgment for respondents.

The United States Court of Appeals for the Eleventh Circuit affirmed. Before reaching the qualified immunity issue, however, it answered the constitutional question that the District Court had bypassed. The court found that the use of the hitching post for punitive purposes violated the Eighth Amendment. Nevertheless, applying Circuit precedent concerning qualified immunity, the court stated that "'the federal law by which the government official's conduct should be evaluated must be preexisting, obvious and mandatory,'" and established, not by "'abstractions,'" but by cases that are "'materially similar' to the facts in the case in front of us." The court then concluded that the facts in the two precedents on which Hope primarily relied — *Ort v. White*, 813 F.2d 318 (CA11 1987), and *Gates v. Collier*, 501 F.2d 1291 (CA5 1974) — "though analogous," were not "'materially similar' to Hope's situation.'" We granted certiorari to review the Eleventh Circuit's qualified immunity holding.

II

The threshold inquiry a court must undertake in a qualified immunity analysis is whether plaintiff's allegations, if true, establish a constitutional violation. The Court of Appeals held that "the policy and practice of cuffing an inmate to a hitching post or similar stationary object for a period of time that surpasses that necessary to quell a threat or restore order is a violation of the Eighth Amendment." The court rejected respondents' submission that Hope could have ended his shackling by offering to return to work, finding instead that the purpose of the practice was punitive, and that the circumstances of his confinement created a substantial risk of harm of which the officers were aware. Moreover, the court relied on Circuit precedent condemning similar practices and the results of a United States Department of Justice (DOJ) report that found Alabama's systematic use of the hitching post to be improper corporal punishment. We agree with the Court of Appeals that the attachment of Hope to the hitching post under the circumstances alleged in this case violated the Eighth Amendment.

As the facts are alleged by Hope, the Eighth Amendment violation is obvious. Any safety concerns had long since abated by the time petitioner was handcuffed to the hitching post because Hope had already been subdued, handcuffed, placed in leg irons, and transported back to the prison. He was separated from his work squad and not given the opportunity to return to work. Despite the clear lack of an emergency situation, the respondents knowingly subjected him to a substantial risk of physical harm, to unnecessary pain caused by the handcuffs and the restricted position of confinement for a 7-hour period, to unnecessary exposure to the heat of the sun, to prolonged thirst and taunting, and to a deprivation of bathroom breaks that created a risk of particular discomfort and humiliation.[5] The use of the hitching

---

[5] [3] The awareness of the risk of harm attributable to any individual respondent may be evaluated

post under these circumstances violated the "basic concept underlying the Eighth Amendment [which] is nothing less than the dignity of man." This punitive treatment amounts to gratuitous infliction of "wanton and unnecessary" pain that our precedent clearly prohibits.

Despite their participation in this constitutionally impermissible conduct, the respondents may nevertheless be shielded from liability for civil damages if their actions did not violate "clearly established statutory or constitutional rights of which a reasonable person would have known." In assessing whether the Eighth Amendment violation here met the *Harlow* test, the Court of Appeals required that the facts of previous cases be "'materially similar' to Hope's situation." This rigid gloss on the qualified immunity standard, though supported by Circuit precedent, is not consistent with our cases.

As we have explained, qualified immunity operates "to ensure that before they are subjected to suit, officers are on notice their conduct is unlawful." For a constitutional right to be clearly established, its contours "must be sufficiently clear that a reasonable official would understand that what he is doing violates that right. This is not to say that an official action is protected by qualified immunity unless the very action in question has previously been held unlawful, but it is to say that in the light of pre-existing law the unlawfulness must be apparent." *Anderson v. Creighton.*

Officers sued in a civil action for damages under 42 U.S.C. § 1983 have the same right to fair notice as do defendants charged with the criminal offense defined in 18 U.S.C. § 242. Section 242 makes it a crime for a state official to act "willfully" and under color of law to deprive a person of rights protected by the Constitution. In *United States v. Lanier*, we held that the defendant was entitled to "fair warning" that his conduct deprived his victim of a constitutional right, and that the standard for determining the adequacy of that warning was the same as the standard for determining whether a constitutional right was "clearly established" in civil litigation under § 1983.[6]

We explained:

> "This is not to say, of course, that the single warning standard points to a single level of specificity sufficient in every instance. In some circumstances, as when an earlier case expressly leaves open whether a general rule applies to the particular type of conduct at issue, a very high degree of

---

in part by considering the pattern of treatment that inmates generally received when attached to the hitching post. In *Austin v. Hopper*, the District Court cited examples of humiliating incidents resulting from the denial of bathroom breaks. One inmate "was not permitted to use the restroom or to change his clothing for four and one-half hours after he had defecated on himself." "Moreover, certain corrections officers not only ignored or denied inmates' requests for water or access to toilet facilities, but taunted them while they were clearly suffering from dehydration . . ."

[6] [4] "The object of the 'clearly established' immunity standard is not different from that of 'fair warning' as it relates to law 'made specific' for the purpose of validly applying § 242. The fact that one has a civil and the other a criminal law role is of no significance; both serve the same objective, and in effect the qualified immunity test is simply the adaptation of the fair warning standard to give officials (and, ultimately, governments) the same protection from civil liability and its consequences that individuals have traditionally possessed in the face of vague criminal statutes. To require something clearer than 'clearly established' would, then, call for something beyond 'fair warning.'"

prior factual particularity may be necessary. But general statements of the law are not inherently incapable of giving fair and clear warning, and in other instances a general constitutional rule already identified in the decisional law may apply with obvious clarity to the specific conduct in question, even though 'the very action in question has [not] previously been held unlawful.'"

Our opinion in *Lanier* thus makes clear that officials can still be on notice that their conduct violates established law even in novel factual circumstances. Indeed, in *Lanier*, we expressly rejected a requirement that previous cases be "fundamentally similar." Although earlier cases involving "fundamentally similar" facts can provide especially strong support for a conclusion that the law is clearly established, they are not necessary to such a finding. The same is true of cases with "materially similar" facts. Accordingly, pursuant to *Lanier*, the salient question that the Court of Appeals ought to have asked is whether the state of the law in 1995 gave respondents fair warning that their alleged treatment of Hope was unconstitutional. It is to this question that we now turn.

IV

The use of the hitching post as alleged by Hope "unnecessarily and wantonly inflicted pain," and thus was a clear violation of the Eighth Amendment. Arguably, the violation was so obvious that our own Eighth Amendment cases gave the respondents fair warning that their conduct violated the Constitution. Regardless, in light of binding Eleventh Circuit precedent, an Alabama Department of Corrections (ADOC) regulation, and a DOJ report informing the ADOC of the constitutional infirmity in its use of the hitching post, we readily conclude that the respondents' conduct violated "clearly established statutory or constitutional rights of which a reasonable person would have known." *Harlow*.

Cases decided by the Court of Appeals for the Fifth Circuit before 1981 are binding precedent in the Eleventh Circuit today. In one of those cases, decided in 1974, the Court of Appeals reviewed a District Court decision finding a number of constitutional violations in the administration of Mississippi's prisons. *Gates v. Collier*. That opinion squarely held that several of those "forms of corporal punishment run afoul of the Eighth Amendment [and] offend contemporary concepts of decency, human dignity, and precepts of civilization which we profess to possess." Among those forms of punishment were "handcuffing inmates to the fence and to cells for long periods of time, . . . and forcing inmates to stand, sit or lie on crates, stumps, or otherwise maintain awkward positions for prolonged periods." The fact that *Gates* found several forms of punishment impermissible does not, as respondents suggest, lessen the force of its holding with respect to handcuffing inmates to cells or fences for long periods of time. Nor, for the purpose of providing fair notice to reasonable officers administering punishment for past misconduct, is there any reason to draw a constitutional distinction between a practice of handcuffing an inmate to a fence for prolonged periods and handcuffing him to a hitching post for seven hours. The Court of Appeals' conclusion to the contrary exposes the danger of a rigid, overreliance on factual similarity. As the Government submits in its brief *amicus curiae*: "No reasonable officer could have concluded that the constitutional holding of *Gates* turned on the fact that inmates were handcuffed to fences or the bars of cells, rather than a specially designed metal bar designated for shackling. If anything, the use of a designated hitching post highlights the constitutional problem." In light of *Gates*, the unlawfulness of the alleged conduct should have been apparent to the respondents.

The reasoning, though not the holding, in a case decided by the Eleventh Circuit in 1987 sent the same message to reasonable officers in that Circuit. In *Ort v. White*, 813 F.2d 318, the Court of Appeals held that an officer's temporary denials of drinking water to an inmate who repeatedly refused to do his share of the work assigned to a farm squad "should not be viewed as punishment in the strict sense, but instead as necessary coercive measures undertaken to obtain compliance with a reasonable prison rule, *i.e.*, the requirement that all inmates perform their assigned farm squad duties." "The officer's clear motive was to encourage Ort to comply with the rules and to do the work required of him, after which he would receive the water like everyone else." The court cautioned, however, that a constitutional violation might have been present "if later, once back at the prison, officials had decided to deny [*Ort*] water as punishment for his refusal to work." So too would a violation have occurred if the method of coercion reached a point of severity such that the recalcitrant prisoner's health was at risk. Although the facts of the case are not identical, *Ort*'s premise is that "physical abuse directed at [a] prisoner after he terminates his resistance to authority would constitute an actionable eighth amendment violation." This premise has clear applicability in this case. Hope was not restrained at the worksite until he was willing to return to work. Rather, he was removed back to the prison and placed under conditions that threatened his health. *Ort* therefore gave fair warning to the respondents that their conduct crossed the line of what is constitutionally permissible.

Relevant to the question whether *Ort* provided fair warning to respondents that their conduct violated the Constitution is a regulation promulgated by ADOC in 1993. The regulation authorizes the use of the hitching post when an inmate refuses to work or is otherwise disruptive to a work squad. It provides that an activity log should be completed for each such inmate, detailing his responses to offers of water and bathroom breaks every 15 minutes. Such a log was completed and maintained for petitioner's shackling in May, but the record contains no such log for the 7-hour shackling in June and the record indicates that the periodic offers contemplated by the regulation were not made. The regulation also states that an inmate "will be allowed to join his assigned squad" whenever he tells an officer "that he is ready to go to work." [T]he record in this case, indicate[s] that this important provision of the regulation was frequently ignored by corrections officers. If regularly observed, a requirement that would effectively give the inmate the keys to the handcuffs that attached him to the hitching post would have made this case more analogous to the practice upheld in *Ort*, rather than the kind of punishment *Ort* described as impermissible. A course of conduct that tends to prove that the requirement was merely a sham, or that respondents could ignore it with impunity, provides equally strong support for the conclusion that they were fully aware of the wrongful character of their conduct.

The respondents violated clearly established law. Our conclusion that "a reasonable person would have known" of the violation is buttressed by the fact that the

DOJ specifically advised the ADOC of the unconstitutionality of its practices before the incidents in this case took place. The DOJ had conducted a study in 1994 of Alabama's use of the hitching post. Among other findings, the DOJ report noted that ADOC's officers consistently failed to comply with the policy of immediately releasing any inmate from the hitching post who agrees to return to work. The DOJ concluded that the systematic use of the restraining bar in Alabama constituted improper corporal punishment. Accordingly, the DOJ advised the ADOC to cease use of the hitching post in order to meet constitutional standards. The ADOC replied that it thought the post could permissibly be used "'to preserve prison security and discipline.'" In response, the DOJ informed the ADOC that, "'although an emergency situation may warrant drastic action by corrections staff, our experts found that the "rail" is being used systematically as an improper punishment for relatively trivial offenses. Therefore, we have concluded that the use of the "rail" is without penological justification.'" Although there is nothing in the record indicating that the DOJ's views were communicated to respondents, this exchange lends support to the view that reasonable officials in the ADOC should have realized that the use of the hitching post under the circumstances alleged by Hope violated the Eighth Amendment prohibition against cruel and unusual punishment.

The obvious cruelty inherent in this practice should have provided respondents with some notice that their alleged conduct violated Hope's constitutional protection against cruel and unusual punishment. Hope was treated in a way antithetical to human dignity — he was hitched to a post for an extended period of time in a position that was painful, and under circumstances that were both degrading and dangerous. This wanton treatment was not done of necessity, but as punishment for prior conduct. Even if there might once have been a question regarding the constitutionality of this practice, the Eleventh Circuit precedent of *Gates* and *Ort*, as well as the DOJ report condemning the practice, put a reasonable officer on notice that the use of the hitching post under the circumstances alleged by Hope was unlawful. The "fair and clear warning," that these cases provided was sufficient to preclude the defense of qualified immunity at the summary judgment stage.

V

In applying the objective immunity test of what a reasonable officer would understand, the significance of federal judicial precedent is a function in part of the Judiciary's structure. The unreported District Court opinions cited by the officers are distinguishable on their own terms. But regardless, they would be no match for the Circuit precedents in *Gates v. Collier*, which held that "handcuffing inmates to the fence and to cells for long periods of time," was unconstitutional, and *Ort v. White*, which suggested that it would be unconstitutional to inflict gratuitous pain on an inmate (by refusing him water), when punishment was unnecessary to enforce on-the-spot discipline. The vitality of *Gates* and *Ort* could not seriously be questioned in light of our own decisions holding that gratuitous infliction of punishment is unconstitutional, even in the prison context.

JUSTICE THOMAS, with whom THE CHIEF JUSTICE and JUSTICE SCALIA join, dissenting.

The Court today subjects three prison guards to suit based on facts not alleged, law not clearly established, and its own subjective views on appropriate methods of prison discipline. Qualified immunity jurisprudence has been turned on its head.

B

Turning to the merits of respondents' assertion that they are entitled to qualified immunity, the relevant question is whether it should have been clear to McClaran, Pelzer, and Gates in 1995 that attaching petitioner to a restraining bar violated the Eighth Amendment. As the Court notes, at that time Alabama was the only State that used this particular disciplinary method when prisoners refused to work or disrupted work squads. Previous litigation over Alabama's use of the restraining bar, however, did nothing to warn reasonable Alabama prison guards that attaching a prisoner to a restraining bar was unlawful, let alone that the illegality of such conduct was clearly established. In fact, the outcome of those cases effectively forecloses petitioner's claim that it should have been clear to respondents in 1995 that handcuffing petitioner to a restraining bar violated the Eighth Amendment.

For example, a year before the conduct at issue in this case took place, the United States District Court for the Northern District of Alabama rejected the Eighth Amendment claim of an Alabama prisoner who was attached to a restraining bar for five hours after he refused to work and scuffled with guards. See *Lane v. Findley*, No. CV-93-C-1741-S (Aug. 4, 1994). The District Court reasoned that attaching the prisoner to a restraining bar "was a measured response to a potentially volatile situation and a clear warning to other inmates that refusal to work would result in immediate discipline subjecting the offending inmate to similar conditions experienced by work detail inmates rather than a return to inside the institution." The District Court therefore concluded that there was a "substantial penological justification" for attaching the plaintiff to the restraining bar.

The same year that it decided *Lane*, the United States District Court for the Northern District of Alabama dismissed another complaint filed by an Alabama prisoner who was handcuffed to a restraining bar. In that case, the prisoner, after refusing to leave prison grounds with his work squad, was handcuffed to a restraining bar for eight hours. Temperatures allegedly reached 95 degrees while the prisoner was attached to the bar, and he was allegedly denied food, water, and any opportunities to use bathroom facilities. See *Whitson v. Gillikin*, No. CV-93-H-1517-NE (Jan. 24, 1994). As a result of being handcuffed to the bar, the prisoner "suffered lacerations, pain, and swelling in his arms." The District Court, without deciding whether the defendants' conduct violated the Eighth Amendment, held that "there was no clearly established law identifying [their behavior] as unconstitutional."

Federal District Courts in five other Alabama cases decided before 1995 similarly rejected claims that handcuffing a prisoner to a restraining bar or other stationary object violated the Eighth Amendment. By contrast, petitioner is unable to point to any Alabama decision issued before respondents affixed him to the restraining bar holding that a prison guard engaging in such conduct violated the Eighth Amendment.

In the face of these decisions, and the absence of contrary authority, I find it impossible to conclude that respondents either were "plainly incompetent" or "knowingly violating the law" when they affixed petitioner to the restraining bar. A reasonably competent prison guard attempting to obey the law is not only entitled to look at how courts have recently evaluated his colleagues' prior conduct, such judicial decisions are often the only place that a guard can look for guidance, especially in a situation where a State stands alone in adopting a particular policy.

C

In concluding that respondents are not entitled to qualified immunity, the Court is understandably unwilling to hold that our Eighth Amendment jurisprudence clearly established in 1995 that attaching petitioner to a restraining bar violated the Eighth Amendment. It is far from "obvious," that respondents, by attaching petitioner to a restraining bar, acted with "deliberate indifference" to his health and safety.

Moreover, if the application of this Court's general Eighth Amendment jurisprudence to the use of a restraining bar was as "obvious" as the Court claims, one wonders how Federal District Courts in Alabama could have repeatedly arrived at the opposite conclusion, and how respondents, in turn, were to realize that these courts had failed to grasp the "obvious."

D

Unable to base its holding that respondents' conduct violated "'clearly established . . . rights of which a reasonable person would have known,'" on this Court's precedents, the Court instead relies upon "binding Eleventh Circuit precedent, an Alabama Department of Corrections (ADOC) regulation, and a [Department of Justice] report informing the ADOC of the constitutional infirmity in its use of the hitching post." I will address these sources in reverse order.

The Department of Justice report referenced by the Court does nothing to demonstrate that it should have been clear to respondents that attaching petitioner to a restraining bar violated his Eighth Amendment rights. To begin with, the Court concedes that there is no indication the Justice Department's recommendation that the ADOC stop using the restraining bar was ever communicated to respondents, prison guards in the small town of Capshaw, Alabama. In any event, an extraordinarily well-informed prison guard in 1995, who had read both the Justice Department's report and Federal District Court decisions addressing the use of the restraining bar, could have concluded only that there was a dispute as to whether handcuffing a prisoner to a restraining bar constituted an Eighth Amendment violation, not that such a practice was clearly unconstitutional.

The Alabama Department of Corrections regulation relied upon by the Court not only fails to provide support for its holding today, the regulation weighs in respondents' favor because it expressly authorized prison guards to affix prisoners to a restraining bar when they were "disruptive to the work squad." Alabama prison guards were entitled to rely on the validity of a duly promulgated state regulation instructing them to attach prisoners to a restraining bar under specified circumstances. And, as the Court recounts, petitioner was placed on the restraining bar after entering into an argument with another inmate while on work duty (May 11) and a wrestling match with a guard when arriving at his work site (June 7).

Finally, the "binding Eleventh Circuit precedent" relied upon by the Court, was plainly insufficient to give respondents fair warning that their alleged conduct ran afoul of petitioner's Eighth Amendment rights. The Court of Appeals held in *Ort v. White*, that a prison guard did not violate an inmate's Eighth Amendment rights by denying him water when he refused to work, and the Court admits that this holding provides no support for petitioner. Instead, it claims that the "reasoning" in *Ort* "gave fair warning to the respondents that their conduct crossed the line of what is constitutionally permissible." But *Ort* provides at least as much support to respondents as it does to petitioner. For instance, *Ort* makes it abundantly clear that prison guards "ave the authority to use that amount of force or those coercive measures reasonably necessary to enforce an inmate's compliance with valid prison rules" so long as such measures are not undertaken "maliciously or sadistically."

To be sure, the Court correctly notes that the Court of Appeals in *Ort* suggested that it "might have reached a different decision" had the prison officer denied the inmate water after he had returned to the prison instead of while he was out with the work squad. But the suggestion in dicta that a guard might have violated a prisoner's Eighth Amendment rights by denying him water once he returned from work duty does not come close to clearly establishing the unconstitutionality of attaching a disruptive inmate to a restraining bar after he is removed from his work squad and back within prison walls.

Admittedly, the other case upon which the Court relies, *Gates v. Collier*, is more on point. Nevertheless, *Gates* is also inadequate to establish clearly the unlawfulness of respondents' alleged conduct. In *Gates*, the Court of Appeals listed "handcuffing inmates to [a] fence and to cells for long periods of time" as one of many unacceptable forms of "physical brutality and abuse" present at a Mississippi prison. Others included administering milk of magnesia as a form of punishment, depriving inmates of mattresses, hygienic materials, and adequate food, and shooting at and around inmates to keep them standing or moving. The Court of Appeals had "no difficulty in reaching the conclusion that these forms of corporal punishment run afoul the Eighth Amendment."

It is not reasonable, however, to read *Gates* as establishing a bright-line rule forbidding the attachment of prisoners to a restraining bar. For example, in referring to the fact that prisoners were handcuffed to a fence and cells "for long periods of time," the Court of Appeals did not indicate whether it considered a "long period of time" to be 1 hour, 5 hours, or 25 hours. The Court of Appeals also provided no explanation of the circumstances surrounding these incidents. The opinion does not indicate whether the handcuffed prisoners were given water and suitable restroom breaks or whether they were handcuffed in a bid to induce them to comply with prison rules. In the intervening 21 years between *Gates* and the time respondents affixed petitioner to the restraining bar, there were no further decisions clarifying the contours of the law in this area. Therefore, as another court interpreting *Gates* has noted: "There is no blanket prohibition against the use of punishment such as the hitching post in *Gates* which would signal to the Commissioner of Corrections [let alone ordinary corrections officers] that the mere use of the hitching post would be a constitutional violation."

Moreover, Eighth Amendment law has not stood still since *Gates* was decided. In *Farmer v. Brennan*, this Court elucidated the proper test for measuring whether a prison official's state of mind is one of "deliberate indifference," holding that "a prison official cannot be found liable under the Eighth Amendment for denying an inmate humane conditions of confinement unless the official knows of and disregards an excessive risk to inmate health or safety; the official must both be aware of facts from which the inference could be drawn that a substantial risk of serious harm exists, and he must also draw the inference." Because the Court of Appeals in *Gates* did not consider this subjective element, *Gates* alone could not have clearly established that affixing prisoners to a restraining bar was clearly unconstitutional in 1995. Also, in the face of recent Federal District Court decisions specifically rejecting prisoners' claims that Alabama prison guards violated their Eighth Amendment rights by attaching them to a restraining bar as well as a state regulation authorizing such conduct, it seems contrary to the purpose of qualified immunity to hold that one vague sentence plucked out of a 21-year-old Court of Appeals opinion provided clear notice to respondents in 1995 that their conduct was unlawful.

It is most unfortunate that the Court holds that Officer McClaran, Sergeant Pelzer, and Lieutenant Gates are not entitled to qualified immunity. It was not at all clear in 1995 that respondents' conduct violated the Eighth Amendment, and they certainly could not have anticipated that this Court or any other would rule against them on the basis of nonexistent allegations or allegations involving the behavior of other prison guards. For the foregoing reasons, I would affirm the judgment of the Court of Appeals. I respectfully dissent.

NOTES

1.   What is the message that *Hope* sends to lower courts? How closely must the facts of the present case track those from previously decided cases in order for the law to be clearly settled? *See generally* Amanda K. Eaton, Note, *Optical Illusions: The Hazy Contours of "Clearly Established Law" and the Effects of* Hope v. Pelzer *on the Qualified Immunity Doctrine*, 38 GA. L. REV. 661 (2004).

2.   *United States v. Lanier*, 520 U.S. 259 (1997), cited by the Court, involved the federal criminal prosecution of a state judge who sexually assaulted several women in his chambers. Lanier argued that he could not be prosecuted under the federal statute because there had not been a prior Supreme Court decision declaring that a judge who sexually assaulted women in his chambers has deprived them of any constitutional right. The Court held that defendant could have constitutionally required "fair warning" that his conduct was criminal even if there had been no prior court decision involving the identical set of facts. Quoting from a dissent in a lower court opinion, *Lanier* notes that "the easiest cases don't even arise. There has never been a section 1983 case accusing welfare officials of selling foster children into slavery; it does not follow that if such a case arose" the official would be protected by qualified immunity. *See also McDonald v. Haskins*, 966 F.2d 292 (7th Cir. 1992) ("It would create perverse incentives indeed if a qualified immunity defense could succeed against those types of claims that have not previously arisen because the behavior alleged is so egregious that no like case is on the books."). The Court in *Hope* states at various places that the Eighth Amendment violation is "obvious." Is the constitutional violation in *Hope* as obvious as the one set forth in *Lanier* or the hypothetical sale of foster children into slavery?

3. The majority cites *Gates v. Collier* and *Ort v. White* as authorities that gave fair notice to the defendants that their conduct violated Hope's eighth amendment rights. How similar are the facts of *Gates* to the facts of *Hope*? Recall that *Gates* was a class action that challenged a number of prison conditions. Does the inclusion of "handcuffing inmates to a fence" in a list of unconstitutional conditions of confinement place a prison guard on notice that handcuffing an inmate to the hitching post as a form of punishment violated the inmates rights under the Eighth Amendment? The Court also deems the "reasoning, though not the holding" of *Ort* as providing fair notice to prison guards that their conduct crossed the line of what is constitutionally permissible. Do you agree that the reasoning of a decision that ruled in favor of the defendants provides fair notice what conduct is and is not constitutionally permissible?

4. Of what relevance are the 1993 state regulations promulgated by the Alabama Department of Corrections and the Department of Justice report?

5. In dissent, Justice Thomas poses the question: if the law was clearly settled, why did several Alabama district court opinions hold that the use of the hitching post was not unconstitutional? Did the judges (and their law clerks) overlook the relevant case law? Did they not understand the significance of *Gates* and *Ort*? How does the majority opinion respond to these questions?

6. The question of just how factually and legally similar precedent must be in order to clearly settle law remains a challenge for the lower courts. *Compare Kitchen v. Dallas County*, 759 F.3d 468 (5th Cir. 2014) (prior decisions imposing bystander liability on officers who fail to intervene to protect an arrestee from another officer inflicting excessive force in violation of the Fourth Amendment clearly establish that correctional officials who fail to intervene to protect a pretrial detainee from another correctional official's infliction of excessive force violate rights secured by the Eighth Amendment), *with Gilmore v. Hodges*, 738 F.3d 266 (11th Cir. 2013) (prior circuit precedents finding Eighth Amendment violations when inmates were denied dentures, eye glasses and prosthesis did not clearly establish that failing to supply a severely hearing impaired inmate with hearing aids would violate the Eighth Amendment).

7. Supreme Court opinions also are not always easy to reconcile. In *Lane v. Franks*, 134 S. Ct. 2369 (2014), Lane alleged that he was fired in retaliation for having testified truthfully under oath in a criminal trial. The defendant asserted the defense of qualified immunity arguing that it was not clearly settled that the speech (public employee testimony at trial) was protected. Justice Sotomayor, writing for a unanimous Court, concluded that "it is clear" that Lane's sworn testimony was speech as a citizen; that "the content of Lane's testimony — corruption in a public program and misuse of state funds — obviously involves a matter of significant public concern;" and "the employer's side of the *Pickering* scale is entirely empty." Justices Thomas, Scalia and Alito concurred, finding that the analysis of the substantive constitutional violation "requires little more than a straight forward application" of existing Supreme Court precedent. Given the ruling in *Hope*, and the statements the various Justices made in *Lane* about what was "clear," "obvious," and "straightforward," what would be your prediction regarding the Court's assessment of whether nor not the law was clearly settled for purposes of qualified immunity? The Court held that because it was "not beyond debate . . . at the time Franks acted . . . that Lane's testimony was . . . protected by the First Amendment, Franks is entitled to qualified immunity."

8.   For other Supreme Court opinions addressing when law is clearly settled, see *Carroll v. Carman*, 135 S. Ct. 348 (2014) (a statement in a prior opinion that "entry into the curtilage after not receiving an answer at the front door might be reasonable" does not clearly establish that a "knock and talk" must begin at the front door); *Reichle v. Howards*, 132 S. Ct. 2088 (2012) (it was not clearly settled that the First Amendment rights of an arrestee are violated when an is arrest made in retaliation for having engaged in protected speech if there was probable cause to support the charges); *Ashcroft v. al-Kidd*, 131 S. Ct. 2074 (2011) (it was not clearly settled that pretext could render an objectively reasonable arrest pursuant to a material-witness warrant unconstitutional).

Apart from what constitutes clearly settled law, whose decisions are relevant to this determination?

WILSON v. LAYNE
526 U.S. 603 (1999)

Chief Justice **Rehnquist** delivered the opinion of the Court.

While executing an arrest warrant in a private home, police officers invited representatives of the media to accompany them. We hold that such a "media ride along" does violate the Fourth Amendment, but that because the state of the law was not clearly established at the time the search in this case took place, the officers are entitled to the defense of qualified immunity.

In early 1992, the Attorney General of the United States approved "Operation Gunsmoke," a special national fugitive apprehension program in which United States Marshals worked with state and local police to apprehend dangerous criminals. The "Operation Gunsmoke" policy statement explained that the operation was to concentrate on "armed individuals wanted on federal and/or state and local warrants for serious drug and other violent felonies." This effective program ultimately resulted in over 3,000 arrests in 40 metropolitan areas.

One of the dangerous fugitives identified as a target of "Operation Gunsmoke" was Dominic Wilson, the son of petitioners Charles and Geraldine Wilson. Dominic Wilson had violated his probation on previous felony charges of robbery, theft, and assault with intent to rob, and the police computer listed "caution indicators" that he was likely to be armed, to resist arrest, and to "assault police." The computer also listed his address as 909 North Stone Street Avenue in Rockville, Maryland. Unknown to the police, this was actually the home of petitioners, Dominic Wilson's parents. Thus, in April 1992, the Circuit Court for Montgomery County issued three arrest warrants for Dominic Wilson, one for each of his probation violations. The warrants were each addressed to "any duly authorized peace officer," and commanded such officers to arrest him and bring him "immediately" before the Circuit Court to answer an indictment as to his probation violation. The warrants made no mention of media presence or assistance.

In the early morning hours of April 16, 1992, a Gunsmoke team of Deputy United States Marshals and Montgomery County Police officers assembled to execute the Dominic Wilson warrants. The team was accompanied by a reporter and a photographer from the Washington Post, who had been invited by the Marshals to accompany them on their mission as part of a Marshal's Service ride-along policy.

At around 6:45 a.m., the officers, with media representatives in tow, entered the dwelling at 909 North Stone Street Avenue in the Lincoln Park neighborhood of Rockville. Petitioners Charles and Geraldine Wilson were still in bed when they heard the officers enter the home. Petitioner Charles Wilson, dressed only in a pair of briefs, ran into the living room to investigate. Discovering at least five men in street clothes with guns in his living room, he angrily demanded that they state their business, and repeatedly cursed the officers. Believing him to be an angry Dominic Wilson, the officers quickly subdued him on the floor. Geraldine Wilson next entered the living room to investigate, wearing only a nightgown. She observed her husband being restrained by the armed officers.

When their protective sweep was completed, the officers learned that Dominic Wilson was not in the house, and they departed. During the time that the officers were in the home, the Washington Post photographer took numerous pictures. The print reporter was also apparently in the living room observing the confrontation between the police and Charles Wilson. At no time, however, were the reporters involved in the execution of the arrest warrant. The Washington Post never published its photographs of the incident.

Petitioners sued the law enforcement officials in their personal capacities for money damages under *Bivens v. Six Unknown Fed. Narcotics Agents* (the U.S. Marshals Service respondents) and 42 U.S.C. § 1983 (the Montgomery County Sheriff's Department respondents). They contended that the officers' actions in bringing members of the media to observe and record the attempted execution of the arrest warrant violated their Fourth Amendment rights. The District Court denied respondents' motion for summary judgment on the basis of qualified immunity.

On interlocutory appeal to the Court of Appeals, a divided panel reversed and held that respondents were entitled to qualified immunity. The case was twice reheard en banc, where a divided Court of Appeals again upheld the defense of qualified immunity. . . .

Recognizing a split among the Circuits on this issue, we granted certiorari in this case and another raising the same question, *Hanlon v. Berger*, and now affirm the Court of Appeals, although by different reasoning.

II

[The Court's discussion of the history and purposes of the Fourth Amendment is omitted. The Court acknowledged that third parties who "directly aided in the execution of the warrant" could enter the premises without being named in the search warrant, but concluded that the media under Operation Gunsmoke did not provide such direct aid.]

. . . We hold that it is a violation of the Fourth Amendment for police to bring members of the media or other third parties into a home during the execution of a warrant when the presence of the third parties in the home was not in aid of the execution of the warrant.

III

Since the police action in this case violated the petitioners' Fourth Amendment right, we now must decide whether this right was clearly established at the time of the search. As noted above, government officials performing discretionary functions generally are granted a qualified immunity and are "shielded from liability for civil damages insofar as their conduct does not violate clearly established statutory or constitutional rights of which a reasonable person would have known." What this means in practice is that "whether an official protected by qualified immunity may be held personally liable for an allegedly unlawful official action generally turns on the 'objective legal reasonableness' of the action, assessed in light of the legal rules that were 'clearly established' at the time it was taken." *Anderson v. Creighton.*

In *Anderson*, we explained that what "clearly established" means in this context depends largely "upon the level of generality at which the relevant 'legal rule' is to be established." "Clearly established" for purposes of qualified immunity means that "the contours of the right must be sufficiently clear that a reasonable official would understand that what he is doing violates that right. This is not to say that an official action is protected by qualified immunity unless the very action in question has previously been held unlawful, but it is to say that in the light of pre-existing law the unlawfulness must be apparent."

It could plausibly be asserted that any violation of the Fourth Amendment is "clearly established," since it is clearly established that the protections of the Fourth Amendment apply to the actions of police. Some variation of this theory of qualified immunity is urged upon us by the petitioners, and seems to have been at the core of the dissenting opinion in the Court of Appeals. However, as we explained in *Anderson*, the right allegedly violated must be defined at the appropriate level of specificity before a court can determine if it was clearly established. In this case, the appropriate question is the objective inquiry of whether a reasonable officer could have believed that bringing members of the media into a home during the execution of an arrest warrant was lawful, in light of clearly established law and the information the officers possessed.

We hold that it was not unreasonable for a police officer in April 1992 to have believed that bringing media observers along during the execution of an arrest warrant (even in a home) was lawful. First, the constitutional question presented by this case is by no means open and shut. The Fourth Amendment protects the rights of homeowners from entry without a warrant, but there was a warrant here. The question is whether the invitation to the media exceeded the scope of the search authorized by the warrant. Accurate media coverage of police activities serves an important public purpose, and it is not obvious from the general principles of the Fourth Amendment that the conduct of the officers in this case violated the Amendment.

Second, although media ride-alongs of one sort or another had apparently become a common police practice, in 1992 there were no judicial opinions holding that this practice became unlawful when it entered a home. The only published decision directly on point was a state intermediate court decision which, though it did not engage in an extensive Fourth Amendment analysis, nonetheless held that such conduct was not unreasonable. From the federal courts, the parties have only identified two unpublished District Court decisions dealing with media entry into homes, each of which upheld the search on unorthodox non-Fourth Amendment right to privacy theories. These cases, of course, can not "clearly establish" that media entry into homes during a police ride-along violates the Fourth Amendment.

At a slightly higher level of generality, petitioners point to *Bills v. Aseltine*, in which the Court of Appeals for the Sixth Circuit held that there were material issues of fact precluding summary judgment on the question of whether police exceeded the scope of a search warrant by allowing a private security guard to participate in the search to identify stolen property other than that described in the warrant. *Bills*, which was decided a mere five weeks before the events of this case, did anticipate today's holding that police may not bring along third parties during an entry into a private home pursuant to a warrant for purposes unrelated to those justifying the warrant. However, we cannot say that even in light of *Bills*, the law on third-party entry into homes was clearly established in April 1992. Petitioners have not brought to our attention any cases of controlling authority in their jurisdiction at the time of the incident which clearly established the rule on which they seek to rely, nor have they identified a consensus of cases of persuasive authority such that a reasonable officer could not have believed that his actions were lawful.

Finally, important to our conclusion was the reliance by the United States marshals in this case on a Marshal's Service ride-along policy which explicitly contemplated that media who engaged in ride-alongs might enter private homes with their cameras as part of fugitive apprehension arrests. The Montgomery County Sheriff's Department also at this time had a ride-along program that did not expressly prohibit media entry into private homes. Such a policy, of course, could not make reasonable a belief that was contrary to a decided body of case law. But here the state of the law as to third parties accompanying police on home entries was at best undeveloped, and it was not unreasonable for law enforcement officers to look and rely on their formal ride-along policies.

Given such an undeveloped state of the law, the officers in this case cannot have been "expected to predict the future course of constitutional law." Between the time of the events of this case and today's decision, a split among the Federal Circuits in fact developed on the question whether media ride-alongs that enter homes subject the police to money damages. If judges thus disagree on a constitutional question, it is unfair to subject police to money damages for picking the losing side of the controversy.

For the foregoing reasons, the judgment of the Court of Appeals is *affirmed.*

JUSTICE STEVENS, concurring in part and dissenting in part.

Like every other federal appellate judge who has addressed the question, I share the Court's opinion that it violates the Fourth Amendment for police to bring members of the media or other third parties into a private dwelling during the execution of a warrant unless the homeowner has consented or the presence of the third parties is in aid of the execution of the warrant. I therefore join Parts I and II of the Court's opinion.

In my view, however, the homeowner's right to protection against this type of trespass was clearly established long before April 16, 1992. My sincere respect for the competence of the typical member of the law enforcement profession precludes my assent to the suggestion that "a reasonable officer could have believed that bringing members of the media into a home during the execution of an arrest warrant was lawful." I therefore disagree with the Court's resolution of the conflict in the Circuits on the qualified immunity issue. The clarity of the constitutional rule, a federal statute (18 U.S.C. § 3105), common-law decisions, and the testimony of the senior law enforcement officer all support my position that it has long been clearly established that officers may not bring third parties into private homes to witness the execution of a warrant. By contrast, the Court's opposing view finds support in the following sources: its bare assertion that the constitutional question "is by no means open and shut," three judicial opinions that did not directly address the constitutional question, and a public relations booklet prepared by someone in the United States Marshals Service that never mentions allowing representatives of the media to enter private property without the owner's consent.

I

In its decision today the Court has not announced a new rule of constitutional law. Rather, it has refused to recognize an entirely unprecedented request for an exception to a well-established principle. Police action in the execution of a warrant must be strictly limited to the objectives of the authorized intrusion. That principle, like the broader protection provided by the Fourth Amendment itself, represents the confluence of two important sources: our English forefathers' traditional respect for the sanctity of the private home and the American colonists' hatred of the general warrant.

The contours of the rule are fairly described by the Court, and in the cases that it cites on those pages. All of those cases were decided before 1992. None of those cases — nor, indeed, any other of which I am aware — identified any exception to the rule of law that the Court repeats today. In fact, the Court's opinion fails to identify a colorable rationale for any such exception. Respondents' position on the merits consisted entirely of their unpersuasive factual submission that the presence of representatives of the news media served various legitimate — albeit nebulous — law enforcement purposes. The Court's cogent rejection of those post hoc rationalizations cannot be characterized as the announcement of a new rule of law.

During my service on the Court, I have heard lawyers argue scores of cases raising Fourth Amendment issues. Generally speaking, the Members of the Court have been sensitive to the needs of the law enforcement community. In virtually all of them at least one Justice thought that the police conduct was reasonable. In fact, in only a handful did the Court unanimously find a Fourth Amendment violation. That the Court today speaks with a single voice on the merits of the constitutional question is unusual and certainly lends support to the notion that the question is indeed "open and shut."

But the more important basis for my opinion is that it should have been perfectly obvious to the officers that their "invitation to the media exceeded the scope of the search authorized by the warrant." Despite reaffirming that clear rule, the Court nonetheless finds that the mere presence of a warrant rendered the officers' conduct reasonable. The Court fails to cite a single case that even arguably supports the proposition that using official power to enable news photographers and reporters to enter a private home for purposes unrelated to the execution of a warrant could be regarded as a "reasonable" invasion of either property or privacy.

II

The absence of judicial opinions expressly holding that police violate the Fourth Amendment if they bring media representatives into private homes provides scant support for the conclusion that in 1992 a competent officer could reasonably believe that it would be lawful to do so. Prior to our decision in *United States v. Lanier*, 520 U.S. 259, 117 S. Ct. 1219, 137 L. Ed. 2d 432 (1997), no judicial opinion specifically held that it was unconstitutional for a state judge to use his official power to extort sexual favors from a potential litigant. Yet, we unanimously concluded that the defendant had fair warning that he was violating his victim's constitutional rights. *Id.*, at 271 ("The easiest cases don't even arise" (citations and internal quotation marks omitted)).

Nor am I persuaded that the absence of rulings on the precise Fourth Amendment issue presented in this case can plausibly be explained by the assumption that the police practice was common. I assume that the practice of allowing media personnel to "ride along" with police officers was common, but that does not mean that the officers routinely allowed the media to enter homes without the consent of the owners.

In addition to this case, the Court points to three lower court opinions — none of which addresses the Fourth Amendment — as the ostensible basis for a reasonable officer's belief that the rule in *Semayne's Case* was ripe for reevaluation. Two of the cases were decided in 1980 and the third in 1984. In view of the clear restatement of the rule in the later opinions of this Court, those three earlier decisions could not possibly provide a basis for a claim by the police that they reasonably relied on judicial recognition of an exception to the basic rule that the purposes of the police intrusion strictly limit its scope.

That the two federal decisions were not officially reported makes such theoretical reliance especially anomalous. Moreover, as the Court acknowledges, the claim rejected in each of those cases was predicated on the media's alleged violation of the plaintiffs' "unorthodox non-Fourth Amendment right to privacy theories," rather than a claim that the officers violated the Fourth Amendment by allowing the press to observe the execution of the warrant. *Moncrief v. Hanton*, 10 Media L. Rep. 1620 (N.D. Ohio 1984); *Higbee v. Times-Advocate*, 5 Media L. Rep. 2372 (S.D. Cal. 1980). As for the other case, *Prahl v. Brosamle*, 98 Wis. 2d 130, 295 N.W.2d 768 (App. 1980) — cited by the Court, for the proposition that the officer's conduct was "not unreasonable" — it actually held that the defendants' motion to dismiss should have been denied because the allegations supported the conclusion that the officer committed a trespass when he allowed a third party to enter the plaintiff's property. Since that conclusion was fully consistent with a number of common-law cases holding that similar conduct constituted a trespass, it surely does not provide any support for an officer's assumption that a similar trespass would be lawful.

Far better evidence of an officer's reasonable understanding of the relevant law is provided by the testimony of the Sheriff of Montgomery County, the commanding officer of three of the respondents: " 'We would never let a civilian into a home. . . . That's just not allowed.' "

III

The most disturbing aspect of the Court's ruling on the qualified immunity issue is its reliance on a document discussing "ride-alongs" apparently prepared by an employee in the public relations office of the United States Marshals Service. The text of the document makes it quite clear that its author was not a lawyer, but rather a person concerned with developing the proper public image of the Service, with a special interest in creating a favorable impression with the Congress. Although the document occupies 14 pages and suggests handing out free Marshals Service T-Shirts and caps to "grease the skids," it contains no discussion of the conditions which must be satisfied before a newsperson may be authorized to enter private property during the execution of a warrant. There are guidelines about how officers should act and speak in front of the camera, and the document does indicate that "the camera" should not enter a private home until a "signal" is given. It does not, however, purport to give any guidance to the marshals regarding when such a signal should be given, whether it should ever be given without the consent of the homeowner, or indeed on how to carry out any part of their law enforcement mission. The notion that any member of that well-trained cadre of professionals would rely on such a document for guidance in the performance of dangerous law enforcement assignments is too farfetched to merit serious consideration.

The defense of qualified immunity exists to protect reasonable officers from personal liability for official actions later found to be in violation of constitutional rights that were not clearly established. The conduct in this case, as the Court itself reminds us, contravened the Fourth Amendment's core protection of the home. In shielding this conduct as if it implicated only the unsettled margins of our jurisprudence, the Court today authorizes one free violation of the well-established rule it reaffirms.

I respectfully dissent.

NOTES

1. Under *Wilson*, does the officer need to point to relevant authority to support the proposition that a reasonable officer would believe his conduct was constitutional? Or does the plaintiff need to point to relevant authority that demonstrates that a reasonable officer should have known his conduct was unlawful?

2. What are the relevant authorities of law? To what law did the majority turn? The dissent?

3. In some cases, the constitutional text may settle the law. *See, e.g., Groh v. Ramirez*, 540 U.S. 551 (2004) (the language of the Fourth Amendment makes it clear that a search warrant is "constitutionally fatal" if it fails to identify "the person or thing to be seized".)

4. In most instances, the text of the Constitution does not speak with specificity towards the challenged conduct. In such cases, courts must look to judicial decisions for guidance. The Tenth Circuit Court of Appeals has stated: "for a right to be clearly established [in the tenth circuit], there must be a [U.S.] Supreme Court or Tenth Circuit decision on point, or the clearly established weight of authority from other courts must have found the law as the plaintiff maintains." *Panagoulakos v. Yazzie*, 741 F.3d 1126, 1129 (10th Cir. 2013). The Eleventh Circuit has said law can be clearly established for purposes of qualified immunity only by "decisions of the U.S. Supreme Court, Eleventh Circuit Court of Appeals, or the highest court of the state where the case arose." *Jenkins by Hall v. Talladega City Board of Education*, 115 F.3d 821, 827 n.4 (11th Cir. 1988) (en banc). Is there any difference in which decisions these circuits consider in deciding whether law is settled? Suppose a federal official operates in several different states located in multiple circuits. If there is a circuit split on a given issue, must the federal official act differently in the states located in the different circuits? *Cf., Sutterfield v. City of Milwaukee*, 751 F.3d 542 (7th Cir. 2014) (noting that in the Seventh Circuit, the "community caretaking" exception to securing a warrant is limited to searching automobiles, but other circuits apply it to allow warrantless searches of houses).

5. It bears reminding that even though circuit precedent can clearly settle law, whether or not it does so will depend on how factually and legally similar the precedent is to the case at hand. *See Hope v. Pelzer*, above. *See also Caroll v. Carman*, 135 S. Ct. 348 (2014) (a statement in a prior Third Circuit opinion that "entry into the curtilage after not receiving an answer at the front door might be reasonable" does not clearly establish in the Third Circuit that a "knock and talk" must begin at the front door; reversing a Third Circuit Court of Appeals decision denying qualified immunity).

6. When is the "weight of authority from other courts" sufficient to clear settle law? In *Owens v. Baltimore City State's Attorneys Office*, 767 F.3d 379, 400 n.8 (4th Cir. 2014), the court cited Court of Appeals decisions from the Second, Seventh, Fifth, and Eleventh Circuits in support of its conclusion that it was clearly settled that a police officer's bad faith suppression of exculpatory evidence violated the constitutional rights of an accused. In *Jacobson v. McCormick*, 763 F.3d 914, 918 (8th Cir. 2014), the court found that "two decisions from other circuits did not place the issue beyond debate, and a reasonable correctional officer in Minnesota could have believed " that [an arrestee's] admission that he recently smoked a bowl of marijuana gave reasonable suspicion to believe that he could be secreting contraband in the private areas of his body" and thus justify a body-cavity search. In *Panagoulakos v. Yazzie*, 741 F.3d 1126, 1131 (10th Cir. 2013), the court held that a "handful" of decisions from other circuits "do not represent the weight of authority of other courts."

   7.   Of what relevance are district court opinions? One court explained: "[District Court opinions] are evidence of the state of the law. Taken together with other evidence, they might show that the law had been clearly established. But by themselves they cannot clearly establish the law because, while they bind the parties by virtue of the doctrine of res judicata, they are not authoritative as precedent and therefore do not establish the duties of nonparties." *Anderson v. Romero*, 72 F.3d 518, 525 (7th Cir. 1995). *See Kitchen v. Dallas County*, 759 F.3d 468, 479–80 (5th Cir. 2014) (in discussing whether one correctional officer can be held liable for not preventing another correctional officer from inflicting excessive force on a pretrial detainee, the court noted "[this] rule had already been applied consistently by district courts throughout the Fifth Circuit in cases involving both pretrial detainees and prison inmates.").

   8.   Of what relevance are unpublished opinions? *Compare Panagoulakos v. Yazzie*, 741 F.3d 1126, 1129–30 (10th Cir. 2013) ("Notably, an unpublished opinion provides little support for the notion that the law is clearly established.") (internal quotations omitted), *and Owens v. Baltimore City State's Attorneys Office*, 767 F.3d 379, 401 n.10 (4th Cir. 2014) ("unpublished opinions cannot alter the clear rule set forth in the published opinions"), *with Kitchen v. Dallas County*, 759 F.3d 468 (5th Cir. 2014), *and Jasinski v. Tyler*, 729 F.3d 531 (6th Cir. 2013) (both citing unpublished opinions in the course of discussing whether law was clearly settled).

   9.   What about non-case law authorities? Recall that Justice Stevens when writing for the majority in *Hope*, cited a 1993 state regulation promulgated by the Alabama Department of Corrections and the Department of Justice report in support of the proposition that it was clearly settled that handcuffing an inmate to a hitching post violated the inmate's Eighth Amendment rights. Yet Justice Stevens dissenting in *Wilson* is highly critical of the majority's reliance on a U.S. Marshal Services ride-along policy as evidence that it was not clearly settled that such a practice contravened the Fourth Amendment. What is the proper role of such reports, regulations, and policies in deciding whether law is or is not clearly established?

   10.   There may be a temporal dimension to the clearly settled law inquiry. What is settled one day may be changed the next. Suppose that at the time of her arrest for underage drinking in 2009, a 1989 circuit court opinion clearly established that the Fourth Amendment prohibited suspicionless strip-searches of persons arrested for minor offenses. The plaintiff was nonetheless subjected to such a strip search. In 2012, during the pendency of the litigation, the Supreme Court ruled that suspicionless strip searches conducted as part of the intake procedure at the jail do not violate the Fourth Amendment, regardless of the seriousness of the offense giving rise to the arrest. Does the defendant's defense of qualified immunity fail because "a ruling after the fact has no bearing on the official's integrity at the time

of the conduct"? Or does the defense of qualified immunity succeed because under the current clearly settled law, the strip search would not be unlawful? *Cf.*, *T.S. v. Doe*, 742 F.3d 632 (6th Cir. 2014) (defendants are entitled to qualified immunity; the court noted that (1) the prior circuit opinion addressed the arrest of adults, not juveniles and therefore did not clearly settle whether juveniles could be subjected to a strip search; and (2) between the time of the 1989 circuit court opinion and the 2012 Supreme Court decision, a circuit split had developed, undermining the claim that law was clearly settled).

III. THE "ORDER OF BATTLE"[7]

Notice that in both *Hope* and *Wilson*, the Court first determined that the defendants' conduct violated the plaintiff's constitutional rights before addressing the issue of whether those rights were clearly settled at the time. The Court had long suggested that the qualified immunity issues be taken up in that order. *See, e.g.*, *Siegert v. Gilley*, 500 U.S. 226 (1991). In *County of Sacramento v. Lewis*, 523 U.S. 833 (1998), the Court cited *Siegert* for the proposition that when the defense of qualified immunity is raised, the "better approach" is to first determine whether the plaintiff has alleged any constitutional deprivation. If so, then address whether the rights were clearly established. The Court went further in *Saucier v. Katz*, 533 U.S. 194 (2001), to mandate, rather than recommend, this decisional methodology. The Court revisited the issue in *Pearson v. Callahan*, below.

PEARSON v. CALLAHAN
555. U.S. 223 (2009)

JUSTICE ALITO delivered the opinion of the Court.

This is an action brought by respondent under 42 U.S.C. § 1983, against state law enforcement officers who conducted a warrantless search of his house incident to his arrest for the sale of methamphetamine to an undercover informant whom he had voluntarily admitted to the premises. The Court of Appeals held that petitioners were not entitled to summary judgment on qualified immunity grounds. Following the procedure we mandated in *Saucier v. Katz*, 533 U.S. 194 (2001), the Court of Appeals held, first, that respondent adduced facts sufficient to make out a violation of the Fourth Amendment and, second, that the unconstitutionality of the officers' conduct was clearly established. In granting review, we required the parties to address the additional question whether the mandatory procedure set out in *Saucier* should be retained.

We now hold that the *Saucier* procedure should not be regarded as an inflexible requirement and that petitioners are entitled to qualified immunity on the ground that it was not clearly established at the time of the search that their conduct was unconstitutional. We therefore reverse.

---

[7] *Brosseau v. Haugen*, 543 U.S. 194, 201–02 (2004) (Breyer, J. concurring).

I

A

[Based on the consent that Callahan gave an undercover informant, the police entered Pearson's trailer without a warrant and found evidence of drug dealing. The police argued that their entry of the premises was permissible under the 'consent-once-removed' doctrine, which, they argued, "permits a warrantless entry by police officers into a home when consent to enter has already been granted to an undercover officer or informant who has observed contraband in plain view." Pearson maintained that the consent-once-removed doctrine was limited to under-cover officers, not undercover informants. Pearson was initially convicted of unlawful possession and distribution of methamphetamine.]

B

The trial court held that the warrantless arrest and search were supported by exigent circumstances. On respondent's appeal from his conviction, the Utah attorney general conceded the absence of exigent circumstances, but urged that the inevitable discovery doctrine justified introduction of the fruits of the warrantless search. The Utah Court of Appeals disagreed and vacated respondent's conviction. Respondent then brought this damages action under 42 U.S.C. § 1983 in the United States District Court for the District of Utah, alleging that the officers had violated the Fourth Amendment by entering his home without a warrant.

In granting the officers' motion for summary judgment, the District Court noted that other courts had adopted the "consent-once-removed" doctrine, which permits a warrantless entry by police officers into a home when consent to enter has already been granted to an undercover officer or informant who has observed contraband in plain view. Believing that this doctrine was in tension with our intervening decision in *Georgia v. Randolph*, 547 U.S. 103 (2006), the District Court concluded that "the simplest approach is to assume that the Supreme Court will ultimately reject the [consent-once-removed] doctrine and find that searches such as the one in this case are not reasonable under the Fourth Amendment." The court then held that the officers were entitled to qualified immunity because they could reasonably have believed that the consent-once-removed doctrine authorized their conduct.

On appeal, a divided panel of the Tenth Circuit held that petitioners' conduct violated respondent's Fourth Amendment rights. The panel majority stated that "[t]he 'consent-once-removed' doctrine applies when an undercover officer enters a house at the express invitation of someone with authority to consent, establishes probable cause to arrest or search, and then immediately summons other officers for assistance." The majority took no issue with application of the doctrine when the initial consent was granted to an undercover law enforcement officer, but the majority disagreed with decisions that "broade[n] this doctrine to grant informants the same capabilities as undercover officers."

The Tenth Circuit panel further held that the Fourth Amendment right that it recognized was clearly established at the time of respondent's arrest. "In this case," the majority stated, "the relevant right is the right to be free in one's home from unreasonable searches and arrests." The Court determined that, under the clearly established precedents of this Court and the Tenth Circuit, "warrantless entries into a home are per se unreasonable unless they satisfy the established exceptions." In the panel's words, "the Supreme Court and the Tenth Circuit have clearly established that to allow police entry into a home, the only two exceptions to the warrant requirement are consent and exigent circumstances." Against that backdrop, the panel concluded, petitioners could not reasonably have believed that their conduct was lawful because petitioners "knew (1) they had no warrant; (2) [respondent] had not consented to their entry; and (3) [respondent's] consent to the entry of an informant could not reasonably be interpreted to extend to them."

In dissent, Judge Kelly argued that "no constitutional violation occurred in this case" because, by inviting Bartholomew into his house and participating in a narcotics transaction there, respondent had compromised the privacy of the residence and had assumed the risk that Bartholomew would reveal their dealings to the police. Judge Kelly further concluded that, even if petitioners' conduct had been unlawful, they were nevertheless entitled to qualified immunity because the constitutional right at issue — "the right to be free from the warrantless entry of police officers into one's home to effectuate an arrest after one has granted voluntary, consensual entry to a confidential informant and undertaken criminal activity giving rise to probable cause" — was not "clearly established" at the time of the events in question.

As noted, the Court of Appeals followed the *Saucier* procedure. The *Saucier* procedure has been criticized by Members of this Court and by lower court judges, who have been required to apply the procedure in a great variety of cases and thus have much firsthand experience bearing on its advantages and disadvantages. Accordingly, in granting certiorari, we directed the parties to address the question whether *Saucier* should be overruled.

II

A

In *Saucier*, this Court mandated a two-step sequence for resolving government officials' qualified immunity claims. First, a court must decide whether the facts that a plaintiff has alleged or shown make out a violation of a constitutional right. Second, if the plaintiff has satisfied this first step, the court must decide whether the right at issue was "clearly established" at the time of defendant's alleged misconduct. Qualified immunity is applicable unless the official's conduct violated a clearly established constitutional right.

Our decisions prior to *Saucier* had held that "the better approach to resolving cases in which the defense of qualified immunity is raised is to determine first whether the plaintiff has alleged a deprivation of a constitutional right at all." *Saucier* made that suggestion a mandate. For the first time, we held that whether "the facts alleged show the officer's conduct violated a constitutional right . . . must be the initial inquiry" in every qualified immunity case. Only after completing this first step, we said, may a court turn to "the next, sequential step," namely, "whether the right was clearly established."

This two-step procedure, the *Saucier* Court reasoned, is necessary to support the Constitution's "elaboration from case to case" and to prevent constitutional stagnation. "The law might be deprived of this explanation were a court simply to skip ahead to the question whether the law clearly established that the officer's conduct was unlawful in the circumstances of the case."

Lower court judges, who have had the task of applying the *Saucier* rule on a regular basis for the past eight years, have not been reticent in their criticism of *Saucier's* "rigid order of battle." And application of the rule has not always been enthusiastic.

Members of this Court have also voiced criticism of the *Saucier* rule.

Where a decision has "been questioned by Members of the Court in later decisions and [has] defied consistent application by the lower courts," these factors weigh in favor of reconsideration. Collectively, the factors we have noted make our present reevaluation of the *Saucier* two-step protocol appropriate.

III

On reconsidering the procedure required in *Saucier*, we conclude that, while the sequence set forth there is often appropriate, it should no longer be regarded as mandatory. The judges of the district courts and the courts of appeals should be permitted to exercise their sound discretion in deciding which of the two prongs of the qualified immunity analysis should be addressed first in light of the circumstances in the particular case at hand.

A

Although we now hold that the *Saucier* protocol should not be regarded as mandatory in all cases, we continue to recognize that it is often beneficial. For one thing, there are cases in which there would be little if any conservation of judicial resources to be had by beginning and ending with a discussion of the "clearly established" prong. "[I]t often may be difficult to decide whether a right is clearly established without deciding precisely what the existing constitutional right happens to be." In some cases, a discussion of why the relevant facts do not violate clearly established law may make it apparent that in fact the relevant facts do not make out a constitutional violation at all. In addition, the *Saucier* Court was certainly correct in noting that the two-step procedure promotes the development of constitutional precedent and is especially valuable with respect to questions that do not frequently arise in cases in which a qualified immunity defense is unavailable.

B

At the same time, however, the rigid *Saucier* procedure comes with a price. The procedure sometimes results in a substantial expenditure of scarce judicial resources on difficult questions that have no effect on the outcome of the case. There are cases in which it is plain that a constitutional right is not clearly established but far from obvious whether in fact there is such a right. District courts and courts of appeals with heavy caseloads are often understandably unenthusiastic about what may seem to be an essentially academic exercise.

Unnecessary litigation of constitutional issues also wastes the parties' resources. Qualified immunity is "an immunity from suit rather than a mere defense to liability." *Saucier's* two-step protocol "disserve[s] the purpose of qualified immunity" when it "forces the parties to endure additional burdens of suit — such as the costs of litigating constitutional questions and delays attributable to resolving them — when the suit otherwise could be disposed of more readily."

Although the first prong of the *Saucier* procedure is intended to further the development of constitutional precedent, opinions following that procedure often fail to make a meaningful contribution to such development. For one thing, there are cases in which the constitutional question is so factbound that the decision provides little guidance for future cases.

A decision on the underlying constitutional question in a § 1983 damages action or a *Bivens* action may have scant value when it appears that the question will soon be decided by a higher court. When presented with a constitutional question on which this Court had just granted certiorari, the Ninth Circuit elected to "bypass *Saucier's* first step and decide only whether [the alleged right] was clearly established." *Motley v. Parks*, 432 F.3d 1072, 1078, and n 5 (2005) (en banc). Similar considerations may come into play when a court of appeals panel confronts a constitutional question that is pending before the court en banc or when a district court encounters a constitutional question that is before the court of appeals.

A constitutional decision resting on an uncertain interpretation of state law is also of doubtful precedential importance. As a result, several courts have identified an "exception" to the *Saucier* rule for cases in which resolution of the constitutional question requires clarification of an ambiguous state statute. Justifying the decision to grant qualified immunity to the defendant without first resolving, under *Saucier's* first prong, whether the defendant's conduct violated the Constitution, these courts have observed that *Saucier's* "underlying principle" of encouraging federal courts to decide unclear legal questions in order to clarify the law for the future "is not meaningfully advanced . . . when the definition of constitutional rights depends on a federal court's uncertain assumptions about state law."

When qualified immunity is asserted at the pleading stage, the precise factual basis for the plaintiff's claim or claims may be hard to identify. Accordingly, several courts have recognized that the two-step inquiry "is an uncomfortable exercise where . . . the answer [to] whether there was a violation may depend on a kaleidoscope of facts not yet fully developed" and have suggested that "[i]t may be that *Saucier* was not strictly intended to cover" this situation.

There are circumstances in which the first step of the *Saucier* procedure may create a risk of bad decision-making. The lower courts sometimes encounter cases in which the briefing of constitutional questions is woefully inadequate.

Although the *Saucier* rule prescribes the sequence in which the issues must be discussed by a court in its opinion, the rule does not — and obviously cannot — specify the sequence in which judges reach their conclusions in their own internal thought processes. Thus, there will be cases in which a court will rather quickly and easily decide that there was no violation of clearly established law before turning to the more difficult question whether the relevant facts make out a constitutional question at all. In such situations, there is a risk that a court may not devote as much care as it would in other circumstances to the decision of the constitutional issue.

Rigid adherence to the *Saucier* rule may make it hard for affected parties to obtain appellate review of constitutional decisions that may have a serious prospective effect on their operations. Where a court holds that a defendant committed a constitutional violation but that the violation was not clearly established, the defendant may face a difficult situation. As the winning party, the defendant's right to appeal the adverse holding on the constitutional question may be contested. See *Bunting*, 541 U.S., at 1025 (SCALIA, J., dissenting from denial of certiorari) ("The perception of unreviewability undermines adherence to the sequencing rule we . . . created" in *Saucier*);[8] see also *Kalka v. Hawk*, 342 U.S. App. D.C. 90, 215 F.3d 90, 96, n 9 (CADC 2000) (noting that "[n]ormally, a party may not appeal from a favorable judgment" and that the Supreme Court "has apparently never granted the *certiorari* petition of a party who prevailed in the appellate court"). In cases like *Bunting*, the "prevailing" defendant faces an unenviable choice: "compl[y] with the lower court's advisory dictum without opportunity to seek appellate [or *certiorari*] review" or "def[y] the views of the lower court, adher[e] to practices that have been declared illegal, and thus invit[e] new suits" and potential "punitive damages."

Adherence to *Saucier*'s two-step protocol departs from the general rule of constitutional avoidance and runs counter to the "older, wiser judicial counsel 'not to pass on questions of constitutionality . . . unless such adjudication is unavoidable.'"

Because the two-step *Saucier* procedure is often, but not always, advantageous, the judges of the district courts and the courts of appeals are in the best position to determine the order of decisionmaking that will best facilitate the fair and efficient disposition of each case.

C

Any misgivings concerning our decision to withdraw from the mandate set forth in *Saucier* are unwarranted. Our decision does not prevent the lower courts from following the *Saucier* procedure; it simply recognizes that those courts should have the discretion to decide whether that procedure is worthwhile in particular cases. Moreover, the development of constitutional law is by no means entirely dependent on cases in which the defendant may seek qualified immunity. Most of the constitutional issues that are presented in § 1983 damages actions and *Bivens* cases also arise in cases in which that defense is not available, such as criminal cases and

---

[8] [2] In *Bunting*, the Court of Appeals followed the *Saucier* two-step protocol and first held that the Virginia Military Institute's use of the word "God" in a "supper roll call" ceremony violated the Establishment Clause, but then granted the defendants qualified immunity because the law was not clearly established at the relevant time. Although they had a judgment in their favor below, the defendants asked this Court to review the adverse constitutional ruling. Dissenting from the denial of *certiorari*, JUSTICE SCALIA, joined by CHIEF JUSTICE REHNQUIST, criticized "a perceived procedural tangle of the Court's own making." The "tangle" arose from the Court's "'settled refusal' to entertain an appeal by a party on an issue as to which he prevailed" below, a practice that insulates from review adverse merits decisions that are "locked inside" favorable qualified immunity rulings.

§ 1983 cases against a municipality, as well as § 1983 cases against individuals where injunctive relief is sought instead of or in addition to damages.

We also do not think that relaxation of *Saucier*'s mandate is likely to result in a proliferation of damages claims against local governments. It is hard to see how the *Saucier* procedure could have a significant effect on a civil rights plaintiff's decision whether to seek damages only from a municipal employee or also from the municipality. Whether the *Saucier* procedure is mandatory or discretionary, the plaintiff will presumably take into account the possibility that the individual defendant will be held to have qualified immunity, and presumably the plaintiff will seek damages from the municipality as well as the individual employee if the benefits of doing so (any increase in the likelihood of recovery or collection of damages) outweigh the litigation costs.

Nor do we think that allowing the lower courts to exercise their discretion with respect to the *Saucier* procedure will spawn "a new cottage industry of litigation . . . over the standards for deciding whether to reach the merits in a given case." It does not appear that such a "cottage industry" developed prior to *Saucier*, and we see no reason why our decision today should produce such a result.

IV

Turning to the conduct of the officers here, we hold that petitioners are entitled to qualified immunity because the entry did not violate clearly established law. An officer conducting a search is entitled to qualified immunity where clearly established law does not show that the search violated the Fourth Amendment. This inquiry turns on the "objective legal reasonableness of the action, assessed in light of the legal rules that were clearly established at the time it was taken."

When the entry at issue here occurred in 2002, the "consent-once-removed" doctrine had gained acceptance in the lower courts. This doctrine had been considered by three Federal Courts of Appeals and two State Supreme Courts starting in the early 1980's. It had been accepted by every one of those courts. Moreover, the Seventh Circuit had approved the doctrine's application to cases involving consensual entries by private citizens acting as confidential informants. The Sixth Circuit reached the same conclusion after the events that gave rise to respondent's suit, and prior to the Tenth Circuit's decision in the present case, no court of appeals had issued a contrary decision.

The officers here were entitled to rely on these cases, even though their own Federal Circuit had not yet ruled on "consent-once-removed" entries. The principles of qualified immunity shield an officer from personal liability when an officer reasonably believes that his or her conduct complies with the law. Police officers are entitled to rely on existing lower court cases without facing personal liability for their actions. In *Wilson*, we explained that a Circuit split on the relevant issue had developed after the events that gave rise to suit and concluded that "[i]f judges thus disagree on a constitutional question, it is unfair to subject police to money damages for picking the losing side of the controversy." Likewise, here, where the divergence of views on the consent-once-removed doctrine was created by the decision of the

Court of Appeals in this case, it is improper to subject petitioners to money damages for their conduct.

Because the unlawfulness of the officers' conduct in this case was not clearly established, petitioners are entitled to qualified immunity. We therefore reverse the judgment of the Court of Appeals.

It is so ordered.

NOTES

1.   What are the cost and benefits of the rigid "order of battle" mandated by *Saucier*? What are the costs and benefits of the more flexible approach of *Pearson*? When is it appropriate for a court to address the merits of the constitutional claim in the first instance? When is it appropriate for a court to address the "clearly established" issue in the first instance? *See* John C. Jeffries, Jr., *Reversing the Order of Battle in Constitutional Torts*, 2009 S. Ct. Rev. 115 (2009) (courts should decide the "merits" question first in cases where suits for money damages are the primary vehicle for vindicating constitutional rights; courts should decide the "clearly settled" question first when there are alternative remedies for the constitutional violation, such as the exclusionary rule); Michael L. Wells, *The "Order of Battle" in Constitutional Torts*, 60 S.M.U. L. Rev. 1539 (2007) (a pre-*Pearson* article arguing in favor of the mandatory "order of battle" specified in *Saucier*).

2.   The Supreme Court has embraced the flexible approach of *Pearson*, sometimes addressing the merits of the constitutional claim first. *See, e.g., Lane v. Franks*, 134 S. Ct. 2369 (2014) (a public employee's sworn testimony outside the scope of his ordinary job duties is speech protected by the First Amendment; law was not clearly established at the time he was fired in retaliation for the testimony). Other times, the Court addresses the "clearly established" issue without deciding whether the facts alleged or shown would support the claim of a constitutional violation. *E.g., Carroll v. Carman*, 2014 U.S. LEXIS 7430 (Nov. 14, 2014) (*per curiam*) ("We do not decide today whether . . . a police officer may conduct a 'knock and talk' at any entrance that is open to visitors rather than only the front door." Even if such a warrantless entry violates the fourth amendment, that principal "was not 'beyond debate'" at the time of entry. Therefore the officers were entitled to qualified immunity).

3.   Lower courts also have accepted *Pearson*'s invitation to address the "clearly established" prong of a qualified immunity analysis without having to reach the merits of difficult or fact sensitive constitutional issues. *E.g., Jacobson v. McCormick*, 763 F.3d 914 (8th Cir. 2014) ("Without deciding potentially difficult questions about whether the search was reasonable . . . we conclude the strip search of Jacobson did not violate clearly established law in 2009); *Panagoulakos v. Yazzie*, 741 F.3d 1126 (10th Cir. 2013) (alleged unconstitutional arrest; "we have discretion to address either prong [of qualified immunity] first. As the 'clearly established' prong resolves this case, we begin with it."); *Acosta v. City of Costa Mesa*, 694 F.3d 960 (9th Cir. 2012) ("Assuming Acosta's contention accurately reflects [that he was arrested in retaliation for having engaged in protected speech], Acosta's claim still fails under [the clearly established] prong . . . of [qualified immunity].").

4. When the court takes the "merits first" approach, it may decide that the defendant has committed a constitutional violation, yet go on to rule that the right was not clearly established at the time. Thus, the official avoids liability for damages on account of qualified immunity. The plaintiff may, of course, appeal the adverse official immunity ruling. May the defendant also appeal, challenging the ruling against him on the constitutional merits? *See Camreta v. Greene*, 131 S. Ct. 2020 (2011). The Court held that "this Court generally may review a lower court's constitutional ruling at the behest of a government official granted immunity," *id.* at 2027. "This is not because a court has made a retrospective judgment about the lawfulness of the officials' behavior, for that judgment is unaccompanied by any personal liability. Rather, it is because the judgment may have prospective effect on the parties." *Id.* at 2029. Thus, "[s]o long as the [adverse constitutional ruling continues in effect, the official] must either change the way he performs his duties or risk a meritorious damages action. [And] conversely, if the person who initially brought the suit may again be subject to the challenged conduct, she has a stake in preserving the court's holding." *Id.*

Does the same principle apply to circuit court review of district court decisions that find a constitutional violation yet grant official immunity? The Court left this issue open, noting that "the considerations persuading us to permit review of petitions in this posture may not have the same force as applied to a district court decision." *Id.* at 2033 n.7. Quoting a treatise, the Court pointed out that district court decisions do not have binding force in later litigation. The issue raised by this type of case is whether the official has standing to appeal the district court's ruling, which in turn depends on whether he can show that the district court's ruling "injures" him. Granting that the district court's ruling does not necessarily govern future conduct, does the official, nonetheless, suffer an injury when a district court declares that he has violated the plaintiff's constitutional rights?

5. What guidance does Part IV of the opinion provide in how to determine whether law is clearly established?

IV. PROCEDURAL ASPECTS OF QUALIFIED IMMUNITY

Defendants in *Bivens* and section 1983 actions may raise the defense of qualified immunity by a motion to dismiss or a motion for summary judgment. The materials below explore some of the theoretical and practical issues presented by such motions as well as special problems involving interlocutory appeals. This section concludes with a consideration of how the issue of qualified immunity should be addressed at trial.

A. Motions to Dismiss

Ashcroft v. Iqbal, 556 U.S. 662 (2009), is, perhaps, the leading case on motions to dismiss and one most students first encounter in their civil procedure classes. The plaintiff, Javid Iqbal, was a Pakistani citizen and a Muslim. In the aftermath of the terrorist attacks of September 11, Iqbal and thousands of other Muslim men were arrested and detained. Iqbal pled guilty to the charge of fraud pertaining to his identification documents and was incarcerated. Iqbal brought a *Bivens* action against a number of federal officials including John Ashcroft, the former Attorney General of the United States, and Robert Mueller, the Director of the FBI. Iqbal claimed that Ashcroft and Mueller developed and implemented an unconstitutional policy of imposing harsh conditions of confinement based on the plaintiff's race, religion, or national origin. The defendants' motion to dismiss was denied by the district court and the denial was affirmed by the court of appeals. The Supreme Court, in a 5-4 decision, reversed.

The majority acknowledged that under F.R.C.P, Rule 8, a plaintiff need not provide "detailed factual allegations" in the complaint. However, the complaint needs to contain more than "an unadorned the-defendant-unlawfully-harmed me accusation." In ruling on a motion to dismiss, the court should accept the factual allegations of the plaintiff to be true. But, this "assumption of truth" does not apply to "labels and conclusions" or to "formulaic recitations of the elements of a cause of action." The majority deemed to be "conclusory" and "formulaic" the allegations that Ashcroft and Mueller "knew and condoned" a policy of unlawful discrimination, that Ashcroft was "the principal architect of this invidious policy," and that Mueller was "instrumental in adopting and executing it." Stripped of these "labels and conclusions" that were "formulaic" in nature and not entitled to the "assumption of truth," the complaint failed to state a claim that was "plausible" on its face. Consequently, Ashcroft's and Mueller's motions to dismiss should have been granted.

After *Iqbal*, the general standards to be applied when ruling on a motion to dismiss are relatively straight forward. *Jasinski v. Tyler*, 729 F.3d 531, 538 (6th Cir. 2012), summarizes the general standard as follows:

> This Court reviews de novo a district court's decision on a motion for judgment on the pleadings as well as a motion to dismiss under Rule 12(b)(6). To survive a motion to dismiss, a plaintiff must allege facts that, if accepted as true, are sufficient to state a claim for relief that is plausible on its face. A claim has facial plausibility when the plaintiff pleads factual content that allows the court to draw the reasonable inference that the defendant is liable for the misconduct alleged. In reviewing a motion to dismiss, we construe the complaint in the light most favorable to the plaintiff, accept its allegations as true, and allow all reasonable inferences in favor of the plaintiff. Dismissal based on qualified immunity is appropriate if the complaint fails to allege the violation of a constitutional right that is clearly established. (Internal citations and quotations omitted).

Accord, Whitley v. Hanna, 726 F.3d 631, 638 (5th Cir. 2013).

While the general principals are fairly easy to state, their application often proves to be more difficult. When is a claim "facially plausible"? When is an "inference" of the defendant's responsibility "reasonable"? Consider the following two cases. In *Franklin v. Curry*, 738 F.3d 1246 (11th Cir. 2013), a pre-trial detainee was sexually assaulted by Gay, a correctional officer. After a formal investigation, Gay resigned. The plaintiff then filed suit against officials who held various supervisory positions alleging that she had been harmed by the supervisory defendants' deliberate indifference to a substantial risk of serious harm. The defendants filed a motion to dismiss on the basis of qualified immunity which was denied by the district court. The court of appeals reversed, holding that the district court applied an incorrect legal standard and applied it with conclusory allegations. With regard to the latter point, the court of appeals commented that allegations that supervisory defendants were deliberately indifferent "carry no weight," and an assertion that the defendants "knew or should have known" of the risk of sexual assault is simply a "conclusory legal allegation." The court then concluded:

> Striping away [the plaintiff's] conclusory allegations leaves only a handful of properly pleaded facts — specifically, (1) that Gay verbally harassed [the plaintiff] and told her "there is nothing you can do," (2) Gay sexually assaulted [the plaintiff], (3) Gay had previously sexually assaulted another female detainee, and (4) Gay had previously had sexual relations with a third female detainee. Given only these facts, [the] complaint is insufficient to state a plausible claim that each of the Supervisory Defendants should have known of a substantial risk that Gay would sexually assault [the plaintiff], much less that each defendant was subjectively aware of the risk and knowingly disregarded it.

738 F.3d at 1251. Note that the plaintiff had uncovered at least two previous instances of sexual misconduct by the offending officer prior to filing suit. Just how is a plaintiff to obtain more detailed information regarding what supervisors knew of a risk before suit is filed? Is it "plausible" that there was deliberately indifferent supervision when a correctional official commits multiple independent acts of sexual misconduct upon or with inmates? Are there any reasonable inferences regarding supervision one might draw from the statement "there is nothing you can do"?

In *Owens v. Baltimore City State's Attorneys Office*, 767 F.3d 379 (4th Cir. 2014), the plaintiff alleged that prosecuting attorneys and police officers intentionally withheld exculpatory evidence during his trial for rape and murder. Owens was convicted of burglary and felony murder. After having spent more than twenty years in prison, Owens was released from incarceration when post-conviction DNA testing indicated that Owens' DNA did not match the blood and semen evidence found at the scene of the crime. Owens alleged that the prosecutor and three police officers "subjected . . . the state's star witness to a lengthy mid-trial interrogation, in which they threatened and cajoled him to change his testimony repeatedly so as to strengthen [the state's case against Owens]. . . . Moreover, Owens alleged that [the state's star witness] repeatedly changed his story only because the Officers provided additional details about the crime, which they pressured [the witness] to incorporate so as to incriminate Owens." 767 F.3d at 397. The district court dismissed the complaint, in part, for failing to state a claim for which relief could be granted. The court of appeals reversed that portion of the district court's judgment, noting "[w]e have little difficulty concluding that Owens's [sic] allegations state a plausible § 1983 claim." *Id.*

Why are the allegations in *Owens* deemed to be "plausible" while those made in *Franklin* were not?

B. Motions for Summary Judgment

Just as *Iqbal* is central to understanding motions to dismiss, *Celotex Corp. v. Catrett*, 477 U.S. 317 (1986), is key to motions for summary judgment. In *Celotex*, the Court held that in cases where the nonmoving party will bear the burden of proof at trial on a dispositive issue, "a summary judgment motion may properly be made in reliance solely on the 'pleadings, depositions, answers to interrogatories, and admissions on file.'" 477 U.S. at 324. The party moving for summary judgment "bears the initial responsibility of informing the district court of the basis of its motion . . .," but is not required to produce evidence showing the absence of a disputed issue of material fact regarding an issue as to which the nonmoving party will bear the burden of proof at trial. "Instead . . . the burden on the moving party may be discharged by 'showing' — that is, by pointing out to the District Court — that there is an absence of evidence to support the nonmoving party's case." 477 U.S. at 323. Once this is done, the burden shifts to the nonmoving party to designate "specific facts showing that there is a genuine issue for trial." 477 U.S. at 325. In other words, summary judgment is appropriate if (a) there is an absence of a dispute about; (b) a material fact such that; (c) the moving party is entitled to a judgment as a matter of law.

What does *Celotex* means for section 1983 and *Bivens* cases? Recall that *Harlow* recast qualified immunity to eliminate the element of subjective good faith so that the defense rests on the standard of objective legal reasonableness. *Anderson* requires that the objective reasonableness inquiry be framed at a high level of factual specificity. Both *Harlow* and *Anderson* expressly encourage a resolution of a qualified immunity claim at the earliest stage of the litigation, especially before trial. The consequence of all this is that once an individual defendant raises the defense of qualified immunity in a motion for summary judgment, the plaintiff must point to specific evidence that the defendant's conduct violated the plaintiff's constitutional rights and those rights were clearly established at the time of the incident.

Of course, the general rule that the evidence should be viewed in the light most favorable to the non-moving party (usually the plaintiff) applies in section 1983 and *Bivens* actions. The Supreme Court recently sent a reminder to the lower courts to take this principle seriously.

TOLAN v. COTTON
134 S. Ct. 1861 (2014)

Per Curiam.

During the early morning hours of New Year's Eve, 2008, police sergeant Jeffrey Cotton fired three bullets at Robert Tolan; one of those bullets hit its target and punctured Tolan's right lung. At the time of the shooting, Tolan was unarmed on his parents' front porch about 15 to 20 feet away from Cotton. Tolan sued, alleging that Cotton had exercised excessive force in violation of the Fourth Amendment. The District Court granted summary judgment to Cotton, and the Fifth Circuit affirmed, reasoning that regardless of whether Cotton used excessive force, he was entitled to qualified immunity because he did not violate any clearly established right. 713 F.3d 299 (2013). In articulating the factual context of the case, the Fifth Circuit failed to adhere to the axiom that in ruling on a motion for summary judgment, "[t]he evidence of the nonmovant is to be believed, and all justifiable inferences are to be drawn in his favor." *Anderson v. Liberty Lobby, Inc.*, 477 U.S. 242, 255 (1986). For that reason, we vacate its decision and remand the case for further proceedings consistent with this opinion.

I

A

The following facts, which we view in the light most favorable to Tolan, are taken from the record evidence and the opinions below. At around 2:00 on the morning of December 31, 2008, John Edwards, a police officer, was on patrol in Bellaire, Texas, when he noticed a black Nissan sport utility vehicle turning quickly onto a residential street. The officer watched the vehicle park on the side of the street in front of a house. Two men exited: Tolan and his cousin, Anthony Cooper.

Edwards attempted to enter the license plate number of the vehicle into a computer in his squad car. But he keyed an incorrect character; instead of entering plate number 696BGK, he entered 695BGK. That incorrect number matched a stolen vehicle of the same color and make. This match caused the squad car's computer to send an automatic message to other police units, informing them that Edwards had found a stolen vehicle.

Edwards exited his cruiser, drew his service pistol and ordered Tolan and Cooper to the ground. He accused Tolan and Cooper of having stolen the car. Cooper responded, "That's not true." And Tolan explained, "That's my car." Tolan then complied with the officer's demand to lie face-down on the home's front porch.

As it turned out, Tolan and Cooper were at the home where Tolan lived with his parents. Hearing the commotion, Tolan's parents exited the front door in their pajamas. In an attempt to keep the misunderstanding from escalating into something more, Tolan's father instructed Cooper to lie down, and instructed Tolan and Cooper to say nothing. Tolan and Cooper then remained facedown.

Edwards told Tolan's parents that he believed Tolan and Cooper had stolen the vehicle. In response, Tolan's father identified Tolan as his son, and Tolan's mother explained that the vehicle belonged to the family and that no crime had been committed. Tolan's father explained, with his hands in the air, "[T]his is my nephew. This is my son. We live here. This is my house." Tolan's mother similarly offered, "[S]ir this is a big mistake. This car is not stolen. . . . That's our car."

While Tolan and Cooper continued to lie on the ground in silence, Edwards radioed for assistance. Shortly thereafter, Sergeant Jeffrey Cotton arrived on the scene and drew his pistol. Edwards told Cotton that Cooper and Tolan had exited a stolen vehicle. Tolan's mother reiterated that she and her husband owned both the car Tolan had been driving and the home where these events were unfolding. Cotton then ordered her to stand against the family's garage door. In response to Cotton's order, Tolan's mother asked, "[A]re you kidding me? We've lived her[e] 15 years. We've never had anything like this happen before."

The parties disagree as to what happened next. Tolan's mother and Cooper testified during Cotton's criminal trial[9] that Cotton grabbed her arm and slammed her against the garage door with such force that she fell to the ground. Tolan similarly testified that Cotton pushed his mother against the garage door. In addition, Tolan offered testimony from his mother and photographic evidence to demonstrate that Cotton used enough force to leave bruises on her arms and back that lasted for days. By contrast, Cotton testified in his deposition that when he was escorting the mother to the garage, she flipped her arm up and told him to get his hands off. He also testified that he did not know whether he left bruises but believed that he had not.

The parties also dispute the manner in which Tolan responded. Tolan testified in his deposition and during the criminal trial that upon seeing his mother being pushed, he rose to his knees. Edwards and Cotton testified that Tolan rose to his feet.

Both parties agree that Tolan then exclaimed, from roughly 15 to 20 feet away, "[G]et your fucking hands off my mom." The parties also agree that Cotton then drew his pistol and fired three shots at Tolan. Tolan and his mother testified that these shots came with no verbal warning. One of the bullets entered Tolan's chest, collapsing his right lung and piercing his liver. While Tolan survived, he suffered a life-altering injury that disrupted his budding professional baseball career and causes him to experience pain on a daily basis.

B

In May 2009, Cooper, Tolan, and Tolan's parents filed this suit in the Southern District of Texas, alleging claims under Rev. Stat. § 1979, 42 U.S.C. § 1983. Tolan claimed, among other things, that Cotton had used excessive force against him in violation of the Fourth Amendment. After discovery, Cotton moved for summary judgment, arguing that the doctrine of qualified immunity barred the suit. That doctrine immunizes government officials from damages suits unless their conduct has violated a clearly established right.

The District Court granted summary judgment to Cotton. It reasoned that Cotton's use of force was not unreasonable and therefore did not violate the Fourth Amendment. The Fifth Circuit affirmed, but on a different basis. It declined to decide whether Cotton's actions violated the Fourth Amendment. Instead, it held that even if Cotton's conduct did violate the Fourth Amendment, Cotton was entitled to qualified immunity because he did not violate a clearly established right.

In reaching this conclusion, the Fifth Circuit began by noting that at the time Cotton shot Tolan, "it was . . . clearly established that an officer had the right to use deadly force if that officer harbored an objective and reasonable belief that a suspect presented an 'immediate threat to [his] safety.'" Court of Appeals reasoned that Tolan failed to overcome the qualified-immunity bar because "an objectively-

---

[9] [7] The events described here led to Cotton's criminal indictment in Harris County, Texas, for aggravated assault by a public servant. He was acquitted. The testimony of Tolan's mother during Cotton's trial is a part of the record in this civil action.

reasonable officer in Sergeant Cotton's position could have . . . believed" that Tolan "presented an 'immediate threat to the safety of the officers.'" In support of this conclusion, the court relied on the following facts: the front porch had been "dimly-lit"; Tolan's mother had "refus[ed] orders to remain quiet and calm"; and Tolan's words had amounted to a "verba[l] threa[t]." Most critically, the court also relied on the purported fact that Tolan was "moving to intervene in" Cotton's handling of his mother, and that Cotton therefore could reasonably have feared for his life. Accordingly, the court held, Cotton did not violate clearly established law in shooting Tolan.

The Fifth Circuit denied rehearing en banc. Three judges voted to grant rehearing. Judge Dennis filed a dissent, contending that the panel opinion "fail[ed] to address evidence that, when viewed in the light most favorable to the plaintiff, creates genuine issues of material fact as to whether an objective officer in Cotton's position could have reasonably and objectively believed that [Tolan] posed an immediate, significant threat of substantial injury to him."

II

A

In resolving questions of qualified immunity at summary judgment, courts engage in a two-pronged inquiry. The first asks whether the facts, "[t]aken in the light most favorable to the party asserting the injury, . . . show the officer's conduct violated a [federal] right[.]" When a plaintiff alleges excessive force during an investigation or arrest, the federal right at issue is the Fourth Amendment right against unreasonable seizures. The inquiry into whether this right was violated requires a balancing of "'the nature and quality of the intrusion on the individual's Fourth Amendment interests against the importance of the governmental interests alleged to justify the intrusion.'"

The second prong of the qualified-immunity analysis asks whether the right in question was "clearly established" at the time of the violation. Governmental actors are "shielded from liability for civil damages if their actions did not violate 'clearly established statutory or constitutional rights of which a reasonable person would have known.'" "[T]he salient question . . . is whether the state of the law" at the time of an incident provided "fair warning" to the defendants "that their alleged [conduct] was unconstitutional."

Courts have discretion to decide the order in which to engage these two prongs. But under either prong, courts may not resolve genuine disputes of fact in favor of the party seeking summary judgment. This is not a rule specific to qualified immunity; it is simply an application of the more general rule that a "judge's function" at summary judgment is not "to weigh the evidence and determine the truth of the matter but to determine whether there is a genuine issue for trial." Summary judgment is appropriate only if "the movant shows that there is no genuine issue as to any material fact and the movant is entitled to judgment as a matter of law." In making that determination, a court must view the evidence "in the light most favorable to the opposing party."

Our qualified-immunity cases illustrate the importance of drawing inferences in favor of the nonmovant, even when, as here, a court decides only the clearly-established prong of the standard. In cases alleging unreasonable searches or seizures, we have instructed that courts should define the "clearly established" right at issue on the basis of the "specific context of the case." Accordingly, courts must take care not to define a case's "context" in a manner that imports genuinely disputed factual propositions

B

In holding that Cotton's actions did not violate clearly established law, the Fifth Circuit failed to view the evidence at summary judgment in the light most favorable to Tolan with respect to the central facts of this case. By failing to credit evidence that contradicted some of its key factual conclusions, the court improperly "weigh[ed] the evidence" and resolved disputed issues in favor of the moving party.

First, the court relied on its view that at the time of the shooting, the Tolans' front porch was "dimly-lit." The court appears to have drawn this assessment from Cotton's statements in a deposition that when he fired at Tolan, the porch was "'fairly dark,'" and lit by a gas lamp that was "'decorative.'" In his own deposition, however, Tolan's father was asked whether the gas lamp was in fact "more decorative than illuminating." He said that it was not. Moreover, Tolan stated in his deposition that two floodlights shone on the driveway during the incident, and Cotton acknowledged that there were two motion-activated lights in front of the house. And Tolan confirmed that at the time of the shooting, he was "not in darkness."

Second, the Fifth Circuit stated that Tolan's mother "refus[ed] orders to remain quiet and calm," thereby "compound[ing]" Cotton's belief that Tolan "presented an immediate threat to the safety of the officers." But here, too, the court did not credit directly contradictory evidence. Although the parties agree that Tolan's mother repeatedly informed officers that Tolan was her son, that she lived in the home in front of which he had parked, and that the vehicle he had been driving belonged to her and her husband, there is a dispute as to how calmly she provided this information. Cotton stated during his deposition that Tolan's mother was "very agitated" when she spoke to the officers. By contrast, Tolan's mother testified at Cotton's criminal trial that she was neither "aggravated" nor "agitated."

Third, the Court concluded that Tolan was "shouting," and "verbally threatening" the officer, in the moments before the shooting. The court noted, and the parties agree, that while Cotton was grabbing the arm of his mother, Tolan told Cotton, "[G]et your fucking hands off my mom." But Tolan testified that he "was not screaming." And a jury could reasonably infer that his words, in context, did not amount to a statement of intent to inflict harm. Cf. *United States v. White*, 258 F.3d 374, 383 (CA5 2001) ("A threat imports '[a] communicated intent to inflict physical or other harm'" (quoting Black's Law Dictionary 1480 (6th ed. 1990))); *Morris v. Noe*, 672 F.3d 1185, 1196 (CA10 2012) (inferring that the words "Why was you talking to Mama that way" did not constitute an "overt threa[t]"). Tolan's mother testified in Cotton's criminal trial that he slammed her against a garage door with enough force to cause bruising that lasted for days. A jury could well have concluded that a reasonable officer would have heard Tolan's words not as a threat, but as a son's plea not to continue any assault of his mother.

Fourth, the Fifth Circuit inferred that at the time of the shooting, Tolan was "moving to intervene in Sergeant Cotton's" interaction with his mother (characterizing Tolan's behavior as "abruptly attempting to approach Sergeant Cotton," thereby "inflam[ing] an already tense situation"). The court appears to have credited Edwards' account that at the time of the shooting, Tolan was on both feet "[i]n a crouch" or a "charging position" looking as if he was going to move forward. Tolan testified at trial, however, that he was on his knees when Cotton shot him, a fact corroborated by his mother. Tolan also testified in his deposition that he "wasn't going anywhere," and emphasized that he did not "jump up."

Considered together, these facts lead to the inescapable conclusion that the court below credited the evidence of the party seeking summary judgment and failed properly to acknowledge key evidence offered by the party opposing that motion. And while "this Court is not equipped to correct every perceived error coming from the lower federal courts," we intervene here because the opinion below reflects a clear misapprehension of summary judgment standards in light of our precedents.

The witnesses on both sides come to this case with their own perceptions, recollections, and even potential biases. It is in part for that reason that genuine disputes are generally resolved by juries in our adversarial system. By weighing the evidence and reaching factual inferences contrary to Tolan's competent evidence, the court below neglected to adhere to the fundamental principle that at the summary judgment stage, reasonable inferences should be drawn in favor of the nonmoving party.

Applying that principle here, the court should have acknowledged and credited Tolan's evidence with regard to the lighting, his mother's demeanor, whether he shouted words that were an overt threat, and his positioning during the shooting. This is not to say, of course, that these are the only facts that the Fifth Circuit should consider, or that no other facts might contribute to the reasonableness of the officer's actions as a matter of law. Nor do we express a view as to whether Cotton's actions violated clearly established law. We instead vacate the Fifth Circuit's judgment so that the court can determine whether, when Tolan's evidence is properly credited and factual inferences are reasonably drawn in his favor, Cotton's actions violated clearly established law.

The petition for certiorari and the NAACP Legal Defense and Educational Fund's motion to file an *amicus curiae* brief are granted. The judgment of the United States Court of Appeals for the Fifth Circuit is vacated, and the case is remanded for further proceedings consistent with this opinion.

It is so ordered.

JUSTICE **ALITO**, with whom JUSTICE **SCALIA** joins, concurring in the judgment.

The Court takes two actions. It grants the petition for a writ of certiorari, and it summarily vacates the judgment of the Court of Appeals.

The granting of a petition for plenary review is not a decision from which Members of this Court have customarily registered dissents, and I do not do so here. I note, however, that the granting of review in this case sets a precedent that, if followed in other cases, will very substantially alter the Court's practice. See, e.g., this Court's Rule 10 ("A petition for a writ of certiorari is rarely granted when the asserted error consists of erroneous factual findings or the misapplication of a properly stated rule of law"); S. Shapiro, K. Geller, T. Bishop, E. Hartnett, & D. Himmelfarb, Supreme Court Practice § 5.12(c)(3), p. 352 (10th ed. 2013) ("[E]rror correction . . . is outside the mainstream of the Court's functions and . . . not among the 'compelling reasons' . . . that govern the grant of certiorari").

In my experience, a substantial percentage of the civil appeals heard each year by the courts of appeals present the question whether the evidence in the summary judgment record is just enough or not quite enough to support a grant of summary judgment. The present case falls into that very large category. There is no confusion in the courts of appeals about the standard to be applied in ruling on a summary judgment motion, and the Court of Appeals invoked the correct standard here. Thus, the only issue is whether the relevant evidence, viewed in the light most favorable to the nonmoving party, is sufficient to support a judgment for that party. In the courts of appeals, cases presenting this question are utterly routine. There is no question that this case is important for the parties, but the same is true for a great many other cases that fall into the same category.

On the merits of the case, while I do not necessarily agree in all respects with the Court's characterization of the evidence, I agree that there are genuine issues of material fact and that this is a case in which summary judgment should not have been granted.

I therefore concur in the judgment.

NOTES

1. What are the facts asserted by Tolan that could support a conclusion that Cotton employed excessive force in violation of Tolan's rights under the Fourth Amendment? What are the facts asserted by Tolan that could support a conclusion that Cotton's conduct violated clearly established law?

2. Note the subtle distinctions that the plaintiff and defendant draw from the events. The mother says she was calm. Cotton says she was agitated. Could they both be testifying truthfully? Does a suspect's statement "get your fucking hands off my mom" constitute a "threat" to the officer or a "plea" for his mother's safety? Why does it matter whether Tolan was on his knees or crouching?

3. The summary judgment motion can be directed at either prong of the qualified immunity test. Thus, a defendant may prevail on summary judgment if the evidence viewed in the light most favorable to the plaintiff fails to establish the violation of a federal rights. *E.g.*, *Riehm v. Engelking*, 538 F.3d 952 (8th Cir. 2008) ("true threats" of violence by high school student are not protected speech under the First Amendment; no constitutional violation in seizure and detention of student for psychiatric evaluation); *Gladden v. Richbourg*, 759 F.3d 960 (8th Cir. 2014) (mildly intoxicated patron of a restaurant who voluntarily accepted a ride from police officers to the county line and later died from hypothermia had no substantive due process claim based on a state created danger theory; not in custody and no coercion). Summary judgment may also be appropriate if the facts viewed in the light most favorable to the plaintiff show that the alleged constitutional violation was not clearly established at the time of the incident. *E.g., Gilmore v. Hodges*, 738 F.3d 266 (11th Cir. 2013) (hearing impaired inmate has a constitutional right to a hearing aid, but this right was not clearly established at the time of the incident; summary judgment affirmed); *Kelly v. Borough of Carlisle*, 622 F.3d 248 (3d Cir. 2010) (passenger did not have a clearly established First Amendment right to videotape a police officer during a traffic stop; summary judgment for officer affirmed); *Bishop v. Glazier*, 723 F.3d 957 (8th Cir. 2013) (it was not clearly established that force producing de minimus injury could be deemed to be excessive under the Fourth Amendment; summary judgment for officer affirmed).

4. As in *Tolan*, however, summary judgment should be denied if the facts viewed in the light most favorable to the plaintiff could support the conclusion that the defendant's conduct violated the clearly settled constitutional rights of the plaintiff. *E.g., Felders v. Malcom*, 755 F.3d 870 (10th Cir. 2014) (disputed issue whether county deputy facilitated drug dog's entry into vehicle or whether dog alerted prior to entering vehicle precluded summary judgment on qualified immunity); *George v. Morris*, 736 F.3d 829 (9th Cir. 2013) (disputed issues of fact regarding shooting victim's conduct at time of the shooting precludes summary judgment on qualified immunity); *Smego v. Mitchell*, 723 F.3d 752 (7th Cir. 2013) (disputed evidence viewed in the light most favorable to the inmate could establish that the defendant was actually aware of the inmate's serious medical condition and failed to provide needed care; district court's granting of summary judgment, reversed).

5. Justice Alito makes two observations of immense practical importance. First, Justice Alito notes that the issue presented in *Tolan* is "utterly routine" for the courts of appeals, and the Supreme Court rarely reviews cases in which the alleged error is the misapplication of a properly stated rule of law. Second, he comments that a substantial number of appeals present the question of "whether the evidence in the summary judgment record is just enough or not quite enough to support the grant of summary judgment." The "just enough" or "not quite enough" language highlights just how close the issue may be. In those cases in which summary judgment turns on subtle nuances of facts and inferences, the court of appeals decision will likely provide the final resolution.

C. Interlocutory Appeals

Recall from *Harlow* and *Anderson* that one purpose of both absolute and qualified immunity is to protect government officials from having to undergo the rigors of trial. Suppose a district court denies the defendant's motion to dismiss or motion for summary judgment. Must the defendant face trial?

MITCHELL v. FORSYTH
472 U.S. 511 (1985)

JUSTICE WHITE delivered the opinion of the Court.

This is a suit for damages stemming from a warrant less wiretap authorized by petitioner, a former Attorney General of the United States. The case presents three issues: whether the Attorney General is absolutely immune from suit for actions undertaken in the interest of national security; if not, whether the District Court's finding that petitioner is not immune from suit for his actions under the qualified immunity standard of *Harlow v. Fitzgerald* is appealable; and, if so, whether the District Court's ruling on qualified immunity was correct.

[As to the first issue, the Court found qualified immunity, not absolute immunity, applicable.]

III

Although 28 U.S.C. § 1291 vests the courts of appeals with jurisdiction over appeals only from "final decisions" of the district courts, "a decision 'final' within the meaning of § 1291 does not necessarily mean the last order possible to be made in a case." *Gillespie v. United States Steel Corp.* Thus, a decision of a district court is appealable if it falls within "that small class which finally determine claims of right separable from, and collateral to, rights asserted in the action, too important to be denied review and too independent of the cause itself to require that appellate consideration be deferred until the whole case is adjudicated." *Cohen v. Beneficial Industrial Loan Corp.*

A major characteristic of the denial or granting of a claim appealable under *Cohen's* "collateral order" doctrine is that "unless it can be reviewed before [the proceedings terminate], it never can be reviewed at all." *Stack v. Boyle.* When a district court has denied a defendant's claim of right not to stand trial, on double jeopardy grounds, for example, we have consistently held the court's decision appealable, for such a right cannot be effectively vindicated after the trial has occurred. Thus, the denial of a substantial claim of absolute immunity is an order appealable before final judgment, for the essence of absolute immunity is its possessor's entitlement not to have to answer for his conduct in a civil damages action.

At the heart of the issue before us is the question whether qualified immunity shares this essential attribute of absolute immunity — whether qualified immunity is in fact an entitlement not to stand trial under certain circumstances. The conception animating the qualified immunity doctrine as set forth in *Harlow v. Fitzgerald*, is that "where an official's duties legitimately require action in which clearly established rights are not implicated, the public interest may be better served by action taken 'with independence and without fear of consequences.'" As the citation to *Pierson v. Ray* makes clear, the "consequences" with which we were concerned in *Harlow* are not limited to liability for money damages; they also include "the general costs of subjecting officials to the risks of trial — distraction of officials from their governmental duties, inhibition of discretionary action, and deterrence of able people from public service." *Harlow.* Indeed, *Harlow* emphasizes that even such pretrial matters as discovery are to be avoided if possible, as "[inquiries] of this kind can be peculiarly disruptive of effective government."

With these concerns in mind, the *Harlow* Court refashioned the qualified immunity doctrine in such a way as to "permit the resolution of many insubstantial claims on summary judgment" and to avoid "[subjecting] government officials either to the costs of trial or to the burdens of broad-reaching discovery" in cases where the legal norms the officials are alleged to have violated were not clearly established at the time. Unless the plaintiff's allegations state a claim of violation of clearly established law, a defendant pleading qualified immunity is entitled to dismissal before the commencement of discovery. Even if the plaintiff's complaint adequately alleges the commission of acts that violated clearly established law, the defendant is entitled to summary judgment if discovery fails to uncover evidence sufficient to create a genuine issue as to whether the defendant in fact committed those acts. *Harlow* thus recognized an entitlement not to stand trial or face the other burdens of litigation, conditioned on the resolution of the essentially legal question whether the conduct of which the plaintiff complains violated clearly established law. The entitlement is an immunity from suit rather than a mere defense to liability; and like an absolute immunity, it is effectively lost if a case is erroneously permitted to go to trial. Accordingly, the reasoning that underlies the immediate appealability of an order denying absolute immunity indicates to us that the denial of qualified immunity should be similarly appealable: in each case, the district court's decision is effectively unreviewable on appeal from a final judgment.

An appealable interlocutory decision must satisfy two additional criteria: it must "conclusively determine the disputed question," *Coopers & Lybrand v. Livesay*, and that question must involve a "[claim] of right separable from, and collateral to, rights asserted in the action," *Cohen*. The denial of a defendant's motion for dismissal or summary judgment on the ground of qualified immunity easily meets these requirements. Such a decision is "conclusive" in either of two respects. In some cases, it may represent the trial court's conclusion that even if the facts are as asserted by the defendant, the defendant's actions violated clearly established law and are therefore not within the scope of the qualified immunity. In such a case, there will be nothing in the subsequent course of the proceedings in the district court that can alter the court's conclusion that the defendant is not immune. Alternatively, the trial judge may rule only that if the facts are as asserted by the plaintiff, the defendant is not immune. At trial, the plaintiff may not succeed in proving his version of the facts, and the defendant may thus escape liability. Even so, the court's denial of summary judgment finally and conclusively determines the defendant's claim of right not to stand trial on the plaintiff's allegations, and because "[there] are simply no further steps that can be taken in the District Court to avoid the trial the defendant maintains is barred," it is apparent that "*Cohen's* threshold requirement of a fully consummated decision is satisfied" in such a case. *Abney v. United States.*

Similarly, it follows from the recognition that qualified immunity is in part an entitlement not to be forced to litigate the consequences of official conduct that a claim of immunity is conceptually distinct from the merits of the plaintiff's claim that his rights have been violated. An appellate court reviewing the denial of the defendant's claim of immunity need not consider the correctness of the plaintiff's version of the facts, nor even determine whether the plaintiff's allegations actually state a claim. All it need determine is a question of law: whether the legal norms allegedly violated by the defendant were clearly established at the time of the challenged actions or, in cases where the district court has denied summary judgment for the defendant on the ground that even under the defendant's version of the facts the defendant's conduct violated clearly established law, whether the law clearly proscribed the actions the defendant claims he took. To be sure, the resolution of these legal issues will entail consideration of the factual allegations that make up the plaintiff's claim for relief; the same is true, however, when a court must consider whether a prosecution is barred by a claim of former jeopardy or whether a Congressman is absolutely immune from suit because the complained of conduct falls within the protections of the Speech and Debate Clause. In the case of a double jeopardy claim, the court must compare the facts alleged in the second indictment with those in the first to determine whether the prosecutions are for the same offense, while in evaluating a claim of immunity under the Speech and Debate Clause, a court must analyze the plaintiff's complaint to determine whether the plaintiff seeks to hold a Congressman liable for protected legislative actions or for other, unprotected conduct. In holding these and similar issues of absolute immunity to be appealable under the collateral order doctrine, the Court has recognized that a question of immunity is separate from the merits of the underlying action for purposes of the *Cohen* test even though a reviewing court must consider the plaintiff's factual allegations in resolving the immunity issue.

Accordingly, we hold that a district court's denial of a claim of qualified immunity, to the extent that it turns on an issue of law, is an appealable "final decision" within the meaning of 28 U.S.C. § 1291 notwithstanding the absence of a final judgment.

IV

The Court of Appeals thus had jurisdiction over Mitchell's claim of qualified immunity, and that question was one of the questions presented in the petition for certiorari which we granted without limitation. Moreover, the purely legal question on which Mitchell's claim of immunity turns is "appropriate for our immediate resolution" notwithstanding that it was not addressed by the Court of Appeals. We therefore turn our attention to the merits of Mitchell's claim of immunity.

Under *Harlow v. Fitzgerald*, Mitchell is immune unless his actions violated clearly established law. Forsyth complains that in November 1970, Mitchell authorized a warrant less wiretap aimed at gathering intelligence regarding a domestic threat to national security — the kind of wiretap that the Court subsequently declared to be illegal. The question of Mitchell's immunity turns on whether it was clearly established in November 1970, well over a year before *Keith* was decided, that such wiretaps were unconstitutional. We conclude that it was not.

V

We affirm the Court of Appeals' denial of Mitchell's claim to absolute immunity. The court erred, however, in declining to accept jurisdiction over the question of qualified immunity; and to the extent that the effect of the judgment of the Court of Appeals is to leave standing the District Court's erroneous decision that Mitchell is not entitled to summary judgment on the ground of qualified immunity, the judgment of the Court of Appeals is reversed.

[The various concurring and dissenting opinions of CHIEF JUSTICE BURGER, JUSTICES O'CONNOR, STEVENS, BRENNAN and MARSHALL are omitted; JUSTICES POWELL and REHNQUIST did not participate.]

NOTES

1. As a general rule, a party cannot appeal a ruling of the district court until the entire case has been finally adjudicated. The collateral order doctrine stands as an exception to this general rule. How is qualified immunity a "right separable from and collateral to the rights asserted in the action"? Why is qualified immunity a right "too important" and "too independent" of the plaintiff's claim to defer appellate review until the whole case is adjudicated?

2. Does *Mitchell* envision interlocutory appeals from the denial of a motion to dismiss grounded in qualified immunity? If so, and if the appellate court affirms the denial of a motion to dismiss, can the defendant take a second interlocutory appeal if his subsequent motion for summary judgment is also denied? In *Behrens v. Pelletier*, 516 U.S. 299 (1996), the Court held that the unsuccessful interlocutory appeal of the denial of a motion to dismiss did not preclude a second interlocutory appeal if a motion for summary judgment was denied. "[A]n unsuccessful appeal from a denial of a dismissal cannot possibly render the later denial of a motion for summary judgment any less final. . ." 526 U.S. at 307. The Court expressed confidence that courts of appeals could establish procedures to weed out frivolous appeals designed only to delay the proceedings.

3. What are the practical implications of allowing interlocutory appeals? Will section 1983 plaintiffs routinely have to survive motions to dismiss, motions for summary judgment, and one or, perhaps, two interlocutory appeals before going to trial? What will interlocutory appeals do to the cost and delay of litigation?

4. What happens to the district court's jurisdiction over the section 1983 claim against the defendant who files an interlocutory appeal from the denial of a motion for summary judgment based on qualified immunity? *Apostol v. Gallion*, 870 F.2d 1335 (7th Cir. 1989) (district court is ousted of jurisdiction). *See also Stewart v. Donges*, 979 F.2d 179 (10th Cir. 1992) (district court could not award attorney's fees awarded for a trial conducted while the case was on interlocutory appeal; district court was ousted of jurisdiction once the notice of appeal was filed).

5. Recall from *Owen v. City of Independence* in Chapter 5 that cities and other local governments are not protected by qualified immunity. Suppose a plaintiff sues an individual official and the city for an alleged constitutional violation. Further assume that the individual official takes an interlocutory appeal from the denial of a motion for summary judgment based on qualified immunity. Can the case proceed against the city? *Cf., Swint v. Chambers County Comm'n.*, 514 U.S. 35, 51 (1995) ("The Eleventh Circuit's authority immediately to review the District Court's denial of the individual police officer defendants' summary judgment motions did not include authority to review at once the unrelated question of the county commission's liability. The District Court's preliminary ruling regarding the county did not qualify as a 'collateral order,' and there is no 'pendent party' appellate jurisdiction of the kind the Eleventh Circuit purported to exercise.").

6.   Is the availability of an interlocutory appeal under *Mitchell* a substantive federal right that must be made available in section 1983 claims filed in state courts? *See Johnson v. Jones*, 515 U.S. 304 (1995) (no; states may, but do not have to, provide for interlocutory appeals from the denial of motions to dismiss or summary judgment grounded in qualified immunity in section 1983 actions filed in state courts).

7.   Suppose defendant does not take an interlocutory appeal from the denial of a motion to dismiss or summary judgment. Does the failure to take an interlocutory appeal waive the defendant's right to challenge the denial of the qualified immunity defense after the trial? There is no waiver, so long as the defendant preserves the issue by making timely motions for judgment as a matter of law at trial. *E.g., Walden v. City of Providence*, 596 F.3d 38 (1st Cir. 2010) (no waiver when defendant made appropriate motions under Fed. R. Civ. P., Rule 50). But, if the defendant does not renew his motion for a judgment as a matter of law after the jury returns a verdict for the plaintiff, the issue is considered waived and cannot be considered by the appellate court. *Ortiz v. Jordan*, 131 S. Ct. 884 (2011).

JOHNSON v. JONES
515 U.S. 304 (1995)

Justice **Breyer** delivered the opinion of the Court.

This case concerns government officials — entitled to assert a qualified immunity defense in a "constitutional tort" action — who seek an immediate appeal of a district court order denying their motions for summary judgment. The order in question resolved a fact-related dispute about the pretrial record, namely, whether or not the evidence in the pretrial record was sufficient to show a genuine issue of fact for trial. We hold that the defendants cannot immediately appeal this kind of fact-related district court determination. And, we affirm the similar holding of the Court of Appeals for the Seventh Circuit.

I

The plaintiff in this case, Houston Jones, is a diabetic. Police officers found him on the street while he was having an insulin seizure. The officers thought he was drunk, they arrested him, and they took him to the police station. Jones later found himself in a hospital, with several broken ribs. Subsequently, Jones brought this "constitutional tort" action against five named policemen. Jones claimed that these policemen used excessive force when they arrested him and that they beat him at the station.

Three of the officers (the petitioners here) moved for summary judgment arguing that, whatever evidence Jones might have about the other two officers, he could point to no evidence that these three had beaten him or had been present while others did so. Jones responded by pointing to his deposition, in which he swore that officers (though he did not name them) had used excessive force when arresting him and later, in the booking room at the station house. He also pointed to the three officers' own depositions, in which they admitted they were present at the arrest and in or near the booking room when Jones was there.

The District Court denied the officers' summary judgment motion. The court wrote that Seventh Circuit precedent indicated potential liability if the three officers "stood by and allowed others to beat the plaintiff." And, the court held that there was "sufficient circumstantial evidence supporting [Jones'] theory of the case."

The three officers immediately appealed the District Court's denial of their summary judgment motion. They argued, in relevant part, that the denial was wrong because the record contained "not a scintilla of evidence . . . that one or more" of them had "ever struck, punched or kicked the plaintiff, or ever observed anyone doing so." But, the Seventh Circuit refused to consider this argument — namely, that the District Court had improperly rejected their contention that the record lacked sufficient evidence even to raise a "genuine" (i.e., triable) issue of fact. The Seventh Circuit held that it "lack[ed] appellate jurisdiction over this contention," i.e., of the "evidence insufficiency" contention that "we didn't do it." It consequently dismissed their appeal.

Courts of Appeals hold different views about the immediate appealability of such pretrial "evidence insufficiency" claims made by public official defendants who assert qualified immunity defenses. We therefore granted certiorari.

II

A

Three background principles guide our effort to decide this issue. First, the relevant statute grants appellate courts jurisdiction to hear appeals only from "final decisions" of district courts. 28 U.S.C. § 1291. Given this statute, interlocutory appeals — appeals before the end of district court proceedings — are the exception, not the rule. The statute recognizes that rules that permit too many interlocutory appeals can cause harm. An interlocutory appeal can make it more difficult for trial judges to do their basic job — supervising trial proceedings. It can threaten those proceedings with delay, adding costs and diminishing coherence. It also risks additional, and unnecessary, appellate court work either when it presents appellate courts with less developed records or when it brings them appeals that, had the trial simply proceeded, would have turned out to be unnecessary.

Of course, sometimes interlocutory appellate review has important countervailing benefits. In certain cases, it may avoid injustice by quickly correcting a trial court's error. It can simplify, or more appropriately direct, the future course of litigation. And, it can thereby reduce the burdens of future proceedings, perhaps freeing a party from those burdens entirely. Congress consequently has authorized, through other statutory provisions, immediate appeals (or has empowered courts to authorize immediate appeals) in certain classes of cases — classes in which these countervailing benefits may well predominate. None of these special "immediate appeal" statutes, however, is applicable here.

Second, in *Cohen v. Beneficial Industrial Loan Corp.*, this Court held that certain so-called collateral orders amount to "final decisions," immediately appealable under the here-relevant statute, 28 U.S.C. § 1291, even though the district court may have entered those orders before (perhaps long before) the case has ended. These special "collateral orders" were those that fell within that small class which finally determine claims of right separable from, and collateral to, rights asserted in the action, too important to be denied review and too independent of the cause itself to require that appellate consideration be deferred until the whole case is adjudicated.

In determining which "collateral orders" amount to "final decisions," these requirements help qualify for immediate appeal classes of orders in which the considerations that favor immediate appeals seem comparatively strong and those that disfavor such appeals seem comparatively weak. The requirement that the issue underlying the order be " 'effectively unreviewable' " later on, for example, means that failure to review immediately may well cause significant harm. The requirement that the district court's order "conclusively determine" the question means that appellate review is likely needed to avoid that harm. The requirement that the matter be separate from the merits of the action itself means that review now is less likely to force the appellate court to consider approximately the same (or a very similar) matter more than once, and also seems less likely to delay trial court proceedings (for, if the matter is truly collateral, those proceedings might continue while the appeal is pending).

Third, in *Mitchell v. Forsyth*, this Court held that a district court's order denying a defendant's motion for summary judgment was an immediately appealable "collateral order" (i.e., a "final decision") under *Cohen*, where (1) the defendant was a public official asserting a defense of "qualified immunity," and (2) the issue appealed concerned, not which facts the parties might be able to prove, but, rather, whether or not certain given facts showed a violation of "clearly established" law. Applying *Cohen*'s criteria, the *Mitchell* Court held that this kind of summary judgment order was, in a sense, "effectively unreviewable," for review after trial would come too late to vindicate one important purpose of "qualified immunity" — namely, protecting public officials, not simply from liability, but also from standing trial. For related reasons, the Court found that the order was conclusive, i.e., it "conclusively" settled the question of the defendant's immunity from suit.

The Court in *Mitchell* found more difficult the "separability" question, i.e., whether or not the "qualified immunity" issue was "completely separate from the merits of the action." The Court concluded that:

> it follows from the recognition that qualified immunity is in part an
> entitlement not to be forced to litigate the consequences of official conduct

that a claim of immunity is conceptually distinct from the merits of the plaintiff's claim that his rights have been violated.

And, the Court said that this "conceptual distinctness" made the immediately appealable issue "separate" from the merits of the plaintiff's claim, in part because an appellate court reviewing the denial of the defendant's claim of immunity need not consider the correctness of the plaintiff's version of the facts, nor even determine whether the plaintiff's allegations actually state a claim. All it need determine is a question of law: whether the legal norms allegedly violated by the defendant were clearly established at the time of the challenged actions or, in cases where the district court has denied summary judgment for the defendant on the ground that even under the defendant's version of the facts the defendant's conduct violated clearly established law, whether the law clearly proscribed the actions the defendant claims he took.

B

We now consider the appealability of a portion of a district court's summary judgment order that, though entered in a "qualified immunity" case, determines only a question of "evidence sufficiency," i.e., which facts a party may, or may not, be able to prove at trial. This kind of order, we conclude, is not appealable. That is, the District Court's determination that the summary judgment record in this case raised a genuine issue of fact concerning petitioners' involvement in the alleged beating of respondent was not a "final decision" within the meaning of the relevant statute. We so decide essentially for three reasons.

First, consider *Mitchell* itself, purely as precedent. The dispute underlying the *Mitchell* appeal involved the application of "clearly established" law to a given (for appellate purposes undisputed) set of facts. And, the Court, in its opinion, explicitly limited its holding to appeals challenging, not a district court's determination about what factual issues are "genuine," Fed. Rule Civ. Proc. 56(c), but the purely legal issue what law was "clearly established." The opinion, for example, referred specifically to a district court's "denial of a claim of qualified immunity, to the extent that it turns on an issue of law." It "emphasized . . . that the appealable issue is a purely legal one: whether the facts alleged (by the plaintiff, or, in some cases, the defendant) support a claim of violation of clearly established law." It distinguished precedent not permitting interlocutory appeals on the ground that "a qualified immunity ruling . . . is . . . a legal issue that can be decided with reference only to undisputed facts and in isolation from the remaining issues of the case." And, it explained its separability holding by saying that "an appellate court reviewing the denial of the defendant's claim of immunity need not consider the correctness of the plaintiff's version of the facts." Although there is some language in the opinion that sounds as if it might imply the contrary, it does not do so when read in context.

Second, consider, in the context of an "evidence sufficiency" claim, *Cohen*'s conceptual theory of appealability — the theory that brings immediate appealability within the scope of the jurisdictional statute's "final decision" requirement. That theory finds a "final" district court decision in part because the immediately appealable decision involves issues significantly different from those that underlie the plaintiff's basic case. As we have just pointed out, *Mitchell* rested upon the view that "a claim of immunity is conceptually distinct from the merits of the plaintiff's claim." It held that this was so because, although sometimes practically intertwined with the merits, a claim of immunity nonetheless raises a question that is significantly different from the questions underlying plaintiff's claim on the merits (i.e., in the absence of qualified immunity).

Where, however, a defendant simply wants to appeal a district court's determination that the evidence is sufficient to permit a particular finding of fact after trial, it will often prove difficult to find any such "separate" question — one that is significantly different from the fact-related legal issues that likely underlie the plaintiff's claim on the merits.

. . . For one thing, the issue here at stake — the existence, or nonexistence, of a triable issue of fact — is the kind of issue that trial judges, not appellate judges, confront almost daily. Institutionally speaking, appellate judges enjoy no comparative expertise in such matters. . . . And, to that extent, interlocutory appeals are less likely to bring important error-correcting benefits here than where purely legal matters are at issue, as in *Mitchell*.

For another thing, questions about whether or not a record demonstrates a "genuine" issue of fact for trial, if appealable, can consume inordinate amounts of appellate time. Many constitutional tort cases, unlike the simple "we didn't do it" case before us, involve factual controversies about, for example, intent — controversies that, before trial, may seem nebulous. To resolve those controversies — to determine whether there is or is not a triable issue of fact about such a matter — may require reading a vast pretrial record, with numerous conflicting affidavits, depositions, and other discovery materials. This fact means, compared with *Mitchell*, greater delay.

For a third thing, the close connection between this kind of issue and the factual matter that will likely surface at trial means that the appellate court, in the many instances in which it upholds a district court's decision denying summary judgment, may well be faced with approximately the same factual issue again, after trial, with just enough change (brought about by the trial testimony) to require it, once again, to canvass the record. That is to say, an interlocutory appeal concerning this kind of issue in a sense makes unwise use of appellate courts' time, by forcing them to decide in the context of a less developed record, an issue very similar to one they may well decide anyway later, on a record that will permit a better decision.

The upshot is that, compared with *Mitchell*, considerations of delay, comparative expertise of trial and appellate courts, and wise use of appellate resources argue in favor of limiting interlocutory appeals of "qualified immunity" matters to cases presenting more abstract issues of law. Considering these "competing considerations," we are persuaded that "immunity appeals . . . interfere less with the final judgment rule if they [are] limited to cases presenting neat abstract issues of law."

We recognize that, whether a district court's denial of summary judgment amounts to (a) a determination about preexisting "clearly established" law, or (b) a determination about "genuine" issues of fact for trial, it still forces public officials to trial. And, to that extent, it threatens to undercut the very policy (protecting public officials from lawsuits) that (the *Mitchell* Court held) militates in favor of immediate appeals. Nonetheless, the countervailing considerations that we have mentioned (precedent, fidelity to statute, and underlying policies) are too strong to permit the extension of *Mitchell* to encompass appeals from orders of the sort before us.

C

We mention one final point. Petitioners argue that our effort to separate reviewable from unreviewable summary judgment determinations will prove unworkable. First, they say that the parties can easily manipulate our holding. A defendant seeking to create a reviewable summary judgment order might do so simply by adding a reviewable claim to a motion that otherwise would create an unreviewable order. "Here, for example," they say, "petitioners could have contended that the law was unclear on how much force may be exerted against suspects who resist arrest." We do not think this is a serious problem. We concede that, if the District Court in this case had determined that beating respondent violated clearly established law, petitioners could have sought review of that determination. But, it does not automatically follow that the Court of Appeals would also have reviewed the here more important determination that there was a genuine issue of fact as to whether petitioners participated in (or were present at) a beating. Even assuming, for the sake of argument, that it may sometimes be appropriate to exercise "pendent appellate jurisdiction" over such a matter.

Second, petitioners add, if appellate courts try to separate an appealed order's reviewable determination (that a given set of facts violates clearly established law) from its unreviewable determination (that an issue of fact is "genuine"), they will have great difficulty doing so. District judges may simply deny summary judgment motions without indicating their reasons for doing so. How, in such a case, will the court of appeals know what set of facts to assume when it answers the purely legal question about "clearly established" law? This problem is more serious, but not serious enough to lead us to a different conclusion. When faced with an argument that the district court mistakenly identified clearly established law, the court of appeals can simply take, as given, the facts that the district court assumed when it denied summary judgment for that (purely legal) reason. Knowing that this is "extremely helpful to a reviewing court," district courts presumably will often state those facts. But, if they do not, we concede that a court of appeals may have to undertake a cumbersome review of the record to determine what facts the district court, in the light most favorable to the nonmoving party, likely assumed. Regardless, this circumstance does not make a critical difference to our result, for a rule that occasionally requires a detailed evidence-based review of the record is still, from a practical point of view, more manageable than the rule that petitioners urge us to adopt. Petitioners' approach would make that task, not the exception, but the rule. We note, too, that our holding here has been the law in several Circuits for some time. Yet, petitioners have not pointed to concrete examples of the unmanageability they fear.

III

For these reasons, we hold that a defendant, entitled to invoke a qualified immunity defense, may not appeal a district court's summary judgment order insofar as that order determines whether or not the pretrial record sets forth a "genuine" issue of fact for trial. The judgment of the Court of Appeals for the Seventh Circuit is therefore

Affirmed.

NOTES

1.   How was the qualified immunity issue presented in *Johnson* different from that presented in *Mitchell*? How are courts of appeals to determine when they have and when they do not have jurisdiction to immediately review denials of motions to dismiss or for summary judgment based on qualified immunity? How does the Court respond to petitioner's argument that any effort to make such a distinction is unworkable?

2.   In *Fancher v. Barrientos*, 723 F.3d 1191 (10th Cir. 2013), the court articulated the general guidelines regarding the sort of issues that can and cannot be raised on interlocutory appeal. The Court said: "A determination that the law allegedly violated by the defendant was clearly established at the time of the challenged actions is an abstract issue of law that is immediately appealable. A determination that under either party's version of facts the defendant violated clearly established law is also immediately appealable. . . . This court, however, lacks jurisdiction at this stage to review a district court's factual conclusions, such as the existence of a genuine issue of material fact for a jury to decide, or that a plaintiff's evidence is sufficient to support a particular factual inference." 723 F.3d at 1198–99 (internal quotations and citations omitted). Applying these guidelines, the court held it lacked jurisdiction to consider the interlocutory appeal of an officer accused of inflicting excessive force from the district court's denial of a motion for summary judgment. The district court's ruling was based on its conclusion that a reasonable jury could infer from the evidence that there was sufficient time between the first shot and the following shots for the defendant to determine that the decedent was not a continuing danger to himself or the public.

See also Felders v. Malcom, 755 F.3d 870, 878 (10th Cir. 2014) ("Our jurisdiction is . . . limited to a review of abstract legal conclusions, in particular, whether the district court's factual determinations, taken as true, suffice to show a violation of law, and, further, whether that law was clearly established at the time of the alleged violation.") (court of appeals has jurisdiction to review district court's ruling that it was clearly established that an unreasonable search occurs if an officer facilitates a drug dog's entry into a vehicle before probable cause has been established; it does not have jurisdiction to review the district court's determination that a genuine issue of material fact existed regarding whether the defendant did facilitate the dog's entry into the vehicle before probable cause had been established).

3.   In another excessive force case, *George v. Morris*, 736 F.3d 829 (9th Cir. 2013), the court ruled that it did not have authority to review the district court's denial of the defendant's motion for summary judgment. The denial was based on the district court's conclusion that the evidence could support a jury finding that the decedent was physically incapable of holding a gun as the deputies described. "Any

decision by the district court that the parties' evidence presents genuine issues of material fact is categorically unreviewable on interlocutory appeal." 736 F.3d at 834 (internal quotations omitted).

D. Qualified Immunity at Trial

In *Hunter v. Bryant*, 502 U.S. 224 (1991), the Court in a per curium decision stated that qualified immunity presents a question of law rather than fact. Immunity, the Court said, should not routinely be placed "in the hands of the jury. Immunity ordinarily should be decided by the court long before trial." 502 U.S. at 28. But, as *Johnson* and the cases discussed in the notes following *Johnson* indicate, disputed fact issues sometimes make it impossible to resolve the qualified immunity issues prior to trial. Just what are the respective roles of the judge and jury in such instances?

Several courts employ special interrogatories to allow the jury to resolve the disputed issues of fact. "If there are unresolved factual issues which prevent an early disposition of the defense [of qualified immunity], the jury should decide these issues on special interrogatories." *Lore v. City of Syracuse*, 670 F.3d 127, 162 (2d Cir. 2010), *quoting Warrren v. Dwyer*, 906 F.2d 70, 76 (2d Cir. 1990). It then becomes the task of the judge to determine whether or not the defendant is entitled to qualified immunity under the facts as found by the jury. *E.g.*, *Willingham v. Crooke*, 412 F.3d 553, 560 (4th Cir. 2005) (if "a dispute of material fact precludes a conclusive ruling on qualified immunity at the summary judgment stage, the district court should submit factual questions to the jury and reserve for itself the legal question of whether the defendant is entitled to qualified immunity on the facts found by the jury."). *See also Johnson v. Breeden*, 280 F.3d 1308, 1318 (11th Cir. 2002) (approving of a procedure whereby the jury resolves the disputed fact issues by special interrogatories followed by the judge determining whether or not qualified immunity applies given those facts).

Other courts envision a more active role for the jury. For example, the Ninth Crcuit in a post-*Hunter* opinion, ruled that when the case goes to trial, juries should determine whether the officer's conduct was reasonable under the circumstances.

> Special jury verdicts would unnecessarily complicate easy cases, and might be unworkable in complicated ones. . . . [T]here is no reason to think that allowing the jury rather than the judge to determine whether the officer's conduct was reasonable under the circumstances would be inimicable to the policies that animate immunity. On the contrary, evaluating the reasonableness of human conduct is undeniably within the core area of jury competence. Just as the judge can most effectively determine whether a given constitutional right was "clearly established" at a particular point in time, the jury is best suited to determine the reasonableness of an officer's conduct in light of the factual context in which it takes place.

Sloman v. Tadlock, 21 F.3d 1462, 1468 (9th Cir. 1994). *See also Meadours v. Ermel*, 409 Fed. Appx. 784, 786 (5th Cir. 2011) (no error to instruct the jury that if "you find that the Defendants had a reasonable belief that their actions did not violate the constitutional rights of [the plaintiff], then you cannot find them liable even if [the plaintiff's] rights were in fact violated . . ."; instruction came from the Fifth Circuit Pattern Jury Charge).

If a jury returns a verdict for the plaintiff, the defendant can raise the qualified immunity defense through a motion for a judgment as a matter of law under Fed. R. Civ. P., Rule 50(b), and if that motion is denied, he can raise the qualified immunity issue again on appeal. *E.g.*, *Hill v. Crum*, 727 F.3d 312 (4th Cir. 2013) (jury returned a verdict for the plaintiff-inmate in an Eighth Amendment excessive force case; district court denied defendant's post-verdict motion for judgment as a matter of law; reviewing the qualified immunity issue de novo, the court of appeals reversed, holding that it was not clearly settled at the time of the incident that force producing a de minimus injury could be constitutionally excessive).

In very rare cases, a plaintiff may prevail on a post-verdict motion for judgment as a matter of law. In *Sawyer v. Asbury*, 537 Fed. Appx. 283 (4th Cir. 2013), a pre-trial detainee brought a section 1983 excessive force claim against a deputy sheriff. The jury returned a verdict for the defendant. The district judge granted the inmate's post-verdict motion for judgment as a matter of law. The key was videotape evidence of the incident. In the words of the district judge, "I find that no reasonable jury was at liberty to disregard the video evidence showing Deputy Asbury choking and punching Mr. Sawyer for no apparent purpose other than inflicting unnecessary and wanton pain and suffering." The court of appeals affirmed, concluding that the deputy's conduct violated the clearly established constitutional rights of the plaintiff.

V. WHO IS PROTECTED BY QUALIFIED IMMUNITY?

We saw in *Owen v. City of Independence* in Chapter 5 that local governments are not protected by qualified immunity. The potential exposure to liability for this class of section 1983 defendants is limited, however, by the ruling in *Monell* that principles of vicarious liability do not apply to local governments. Rather, a plaintiff must prove that some official policy or custom was the moving force behind the constitutional violation.

A second class of section 1983 defendants for whom qualified immunity may be problematic are private persons. We saw in Chapter 2 that there are situations in which private persons may be deemed to engage in "state action" and act "under color of" state law. These situations include private actors who secure significant assistance from state officials when invoking certain self-help remedies (*e.g.*, *Lugar v. Edmondson Oil Co.*, 457 U.S. 922 (1982)), those who conspire with state actors to deprive the plaintiff of a constitutional right (*e.g.*, *Dennis v. Sparks*, 449 U.S. 24 (1980)), and private actors who perform services the state is obligated to provide (*e.g.*, *West v. Atkins*, 487 U.S. 42 (1988) (private physician providing medical care to prisoners)). Do the same considerations that gave rise to the defense of qualified immunity apply when the defendant is not a government official but is, instead, a private person?

WYATT v. COLE
504 U.S. 158 (1992)

Justice O'Connor delivered the opinion of the Court.

In *Lugar v. Edmondson Oil Co.* we left open the question whether private defendants charged with 42 U.S.C. § 1983 liability for invoking state replevin, garnishment, and attachment statutes later declared unconstitutional are entitled to qualified immunity from suit. We now hold that they are not.

I

This dispute arises out of a soured cattle partnership. In July 1986, respondent Bill Cole sought to dissolve his partnership with petitioner Howard Wyatt. When no agreement could be reached, Cole, with the assistance of an attorney, respondent John Robbins II, filed a state court complaint in replevin against Wyatt, accompanied by a replevin bond of $18,000.

At that time, Mississippi law provided that an individual could obtain a court order for seizure of property possessed by another by posting a bond and swearing to a state court that the applicant was entitled to that property, and that the adversary wrongfully took and detained or wrongfully detained" the property. The statute gave the judge no discretion to deny a writ of replevin.

After Cole presented a complaint and bond, the court ordered the County Sheriff to seize 24 head of cattle, a tractor, and certain other personal property from Wyatt. Several months later, after a post-seizure hearing, the court dismissed Cole's complaint in replevin and ordered the property returned to Wyatt. When Cole refused to comply, Wyatt brought suit in Federal District Court, challenging the constitutionality of the statute and seeking injunctive relief and damages from respondents, the County Sheriff, and the deputies involved in the seizure.

II

Title 42 U.S.C. § 1983 provides a cause of action against every person who, under color of any statute . . . of any State . . . subjects, or causes to be subjected, any citizen . . . to the deprivation of any rights, privileges, or immunities secured by the Constitution and laws. . . ." The purpose of § 1983 is to deter state actors from using the badge of their authority to deprive individuals of their federally guaranteed rights and to provide relief to victims if such deterrence fails.

In *Lugar v. Edmondson Oil Co.*, the Court considered the scope of § 1983 liability in the context of garnishment, prejudgment attachment, and replevin statutes. In that case, the Court held that private parties who attached a debtor's assets pursuant to a state attachment statute were subject to § 1983 liability if the statute was constitutionally infirm. Noting that our garnishment, prejudgment attachment, and replevin cases established that private use of state laws to secure property could constitute "state action" for purposes of the Fourteenth Amendment, the Court held that private defendants invoking a state-created attachment statute act "under color of state law" within the meaning of § 1983 if their actions are fairly attributable to the State.". This requirement is satisfied, the Court held, if two conditions are met. First, the "deprivation must be caused by the exercise of some right or privilege created by the State or by a rule of conduct imposed by the State or by a person for whom the State is responsible." Second, the private party must have "acted together with or . . . obtained significant aid from state officials" or engaged in conduct otherwise chargeable to the State." The Court found potential § 1983 liability in *Lugar* because the attachment scheme was created by the State and because the private defendants, in invoking the aid of state officials to attach the disputed property, were "willful participants in joint activity with the State or its agents."

Citing *Lugar*, the District Court assumed that Cole, by invoking the state statute, had acted under color of state law within the meaning of § 1983, and was therefore liable for damages for the deprivation of Wyatt's due process rights. With respect to Robbins, the court noted that while an action taken by an attorney in representing a client "does not normally constitute an act under color of state law . . . an attorney is still a person who may conspire to act under color of state law in depriving another of secured rights." The court did not determine whether Robbins was liable, however, because it held that both Cole and Robbins were entitled to qualified immunity from suit at least for conduct prior to the statute's invalidation.

Although the Court of Appeals did not review whether, in the first instance, Cole and Robbins had acted under color of state law within the meaning of § 1983, it affirmed the District Court's grant of qualified immunity to respondents. In so doing, the Court of Appeals followed one of its prior cases, *Folsom Investment Co. v. Moore*, in which it held that a § 1983 defendant who has invoked an attachment statute is entitled to an immunity from monetary liability so long as he neither knew nor reasonably should have known that the statute was unconstitutional." The court in Folsom based its holding on two grounds. First, it viewed the existence of a common law probable cause defense to the torts of malicious prosecution and wrongful attachment as evidence that Congress in enacting § 1983 could not have intended to subject to liability those who in good faith resorted to legal process." Although it acknowledged that a defense is not the same as an immunity, the court maintained that it could transform a common law defense extant at the time of § 1983's passage into an immunity." Second, the court held that while immunity for private parties is not derived from official immunity, it is based on the important public interest in permitting ordinary citizens to rely on presumptively valid state laws, in shielding citizens from monetary damages when they reasonably resort to a legal process later held to be unconstitutional, and in protecting a private citizen from liability when his role in any unconstitutional action is marginal." In defending the decision below, respondents advance both arguments put forward by the Court of Appeals in *Folsom*. Neither is availing.

III

Section 1983 "creates a species of tort liability that on its face admits of no immunities." *Imbler v. Pachtman.* Nonetheless, we have accorded certain government officials either absolute or qualified immunity from suit if the "tradition of immunity was so firmly rooted in the common law and was supported by such strong policy reasons that 'Congress would have specifically so provided had it wished to abolish the doctrine.'" *Owen v. City of Independence* (quoting *Pierson v. Ray*). If parties seeking immunity were shielded from tort liability when Congress enacted the Civil Rights Act of 1871 — § 1 of which is codified at 42 U.S.C. § 1983 — we infer from legislative silence that Congress did not intend to abrogate such immunities when it imposed liability for actions taken under color of state law. Additionally, irrespective of the common law support, we will not recognize an immunity available at common law if § 1983's history or purpose counsel against applying it in § 1983 actions.

In determining whether there was an immunity at common law that Congress intended to incorporate in the Civil Rights Act, we look to the most closely analogous torts — in this case, malicious prosecution and abuse of process. At common law, these torts provided causes of action against private defendants for unjustified harm arising out of the misuse of governmental processes.

Respondents do not contend that private parties who instituted attachment proceedings and who were subsequently sued for malicious prosecution or abuse of process were entitled to absolute immunity. And with good reason; although public prosecutors and judges were accorded absolute immunity at common law, such protection did not extend to complaining witnesses who, like respondents, set the wheels of government in motion by instigating a legal action. *Malley v. Briggs* (In 1871, the generally accepted rule was that one who procured the issuance of an arrest warrant by submitting a complaint could be held liable if "the complaint was made maliciously and without probable cause").

Nonetheless, respondents argue that at common law, private defendants could defeat a malicious prosecution or abuse of process action if they acted without malice and with probable cause, and that we should therefore infer that Congress did not intend to abrogate such defenses when it enacted the Civil Rights Act of 1871. We adopted similar reasoning in *Pierson v. Ray*. There, we held that police officers sued for false arrest under § 1983 were entitled to the defense that they acted with probable cause and in good faith when making an arrest under a statute they reasonably believed was valid. We recognized this defense because peace officers were accorded protection from liability at common law if they arrested an individual in good faith, even if the innocence of such person were later established.

The rationale we adopted in *Pierson* is of no avail to respondents here. Even if there were sufficient common law support to conclude that respondents, like the police officers in *Pierson*, should be entitled to a good-faith defense, that would still not entitle them to what they sought and obtained in the courts below: the qualified immunity from suit accorded government officials under *Harlow v. Fitzgerald*.

In *Harlow*, we altered the standard of qualified immunity adopted in our prior § 1983 cases because we recognized that "[t]he subjective element of the good-faith defense frequently [had] prove[n] incompatible with our admonition . . . that insubstantial claims should not proceed to trial." Because of the attendant harms to government effectiveness caused by lengthy judicial inquiry into subjective motivation, we concluded that "bare allegations of malice should not suffice to subject government officials either to the costs of trial or to the burdens of broad-reaching discovery." Accordingly, we held that government officials performing discretionary functions are shielded from "liability for civil damages insofar as their conduct [did] not violate clearly established statutory or constitutional rights of which a reasonable person would have known." This wholly objective standard, we concluded, would "avoid excessive disruption of government and permit the resolution of many insubstantial claims on summary judgment."

That *Harlow* "completely reformulated qualified immunity along principles not at all embodied in the common law," *Anderson v. Creighton*, was reinforced by our decision in *Mitchell v. Forsyth*. *Mitchell* held that *Harlow* established an "*immunity from suit* rather than a mere defense to liability," which, like an absolute immunity, "is effectively lost if a case is erroneously permitted to go to trial." Thus, we held in *Mitchell* that the denial of qualified immunity should be immediately appealable.

It is this type of objectively determined, immediately appealable immunity that respondents asserted below. But, as our precedents make clear, the reasons for recognizing such an immunity were based not simply on the existence of a good-faith defense at common law, but on the special policy concerns involved in suing government officials. Reviewing these concerns, we conclude that the rationales mandating qualified immunity for public officials are not applicable to private parties.

Qualified immunity strikes a balance between compensating those who have been injured by official conduct and protecting government's ability to perform its traditional functions. Accordingly, we have recognized qualified immunity for government officials where it was necessary to preserve their ability to serve the public good or to ensure that talented candidates were not deterred by the threat of damage suits from entering public service. See, e. g., *Wood v. Strickland* (denial of qualified immunity to school board officials would contribute not to principled and fearless decision-making but to intimidation' ") (quoting *Pierson*); *Butz v. Economou* (immunity for Presidential aides warranted partly to protect officials who are required to exercise their discretion and the related public interest in encouraging the vigorous exercise of official authority"); *Mitchell* (immunity designed to prevent the distraction of officials from their governmental duties, inhibition of discretionary action, and deterrence of able people from public service' ") (quoting *Harlow*). In short, the qualified immunity recognized in *Harlow* acts to safeguard government, and thereby to protect the public at large, not to benefit its agents.

These rationales are not transferable to private parties. Although principles of equality and fairness may suggest, as respondents argue, that private citizens who rely unsuspectingly on state laws they did not create and may have no reason to believe are invalid should have some protection from liability, as do their government counterparts, such interests are not sufficiently similar to the traditional purposes of qualified immunity to justify such an expansion. Unlike school board members, or police officers, or Presidential aides, private parties hold no office requiring them to exercise discretion; nor are they principally concerned with enhancing the public good. Accordingly, extending *Harlow* qualified immunity to private parties would have no bearing on whether public officials are able to act forcefully and decisively in their jobs or on whether qualified applicants enter public service. Moreover, unlike with government officials performing discretionary functions, the public interest will not be unduly impaired if private individuals are required to proceed to trial to resolve their legal disputes. In short, the nexus between private parties and the historic purposes of qualified immunity is simply too attenuated to justify such an extension of our doctrine of immunity.

For these reasons, we can offer no relief today. The question on which we granted certiorari is a very narrow one: "Whether private persons, who conspire with state officials to violate constitutional rights, have available the good faith immunity applicable to public officials." The precise issue encompassed in this question, and the only issue decided by the lower courts, is whether qualified immunity, as enunciated in *Harlow*, is available for private defendants faced with § 1983 liability for invoking a state replevin, garnishment or attachment statute. That answer is no. In so holding, however, we do not foreclose the possibility that private defendants faced with § 1983 liability under *Lugar v. Edmondson Oil Co.*, could be entitled to an affirmative defense based on good faith and/or probable cause or that § 1983 suits against private, rather than governmental, parties could require plaintiffs to carry additional burdens. Because those issues are not fairly before us, however, we leave them for another day.

IV

As indicated above, the District Court assumed that under *Lugar v. Edmondson Oil Co.*, Cole was liable under § 1983 for invoking the state replevin under bond statute, and intimated that, but did not decide whether, Robbins also was subject to § 1983 liability. The Court of Appeals never revisited this question, but instead concluded only that respondents were entitled to qualified immunity at least for conduct prior to the statute's invalidation. Because we overturn this judgment, we must remand since there remains to be determined, at least, whether Cole and Robbins, in invoking the replevin statute, acted under color of state law within the meaning of *Lugar*. The decision of the Court of Appeals is reversed and the case is remanded for proceedings consistent with this opinion.

THE CHIEF JUSTICE, with whom JUSTICE SOUTER and JUSTICE THOMAS join, dissenting.

The Court notes that we have recognized an immunity in the § 1983 context in two circumstances. The first is when a similarly situated defendant would have enjoyed an immunity at common law at the time § 1983 was adopted. The second is when important public policy concerns suggest the need for an immunity. Because I believe that both requirements, as explained in our prior decisions, are satisfied here, I dissent.

First, I think it is clear that at the time § 1983 was adopted, there generally was available to private parties a good-faith defense to the torts of malicious prosecution and abuse of process. See *Malley v. Briggs* (noting that the generally accepted rule at common law was that a person would be held liable if the complaint was made maliciously and without probable cause"); *Pierson v. Ray* (noting that at common law a police officer sued for false arrest can rely on his own good faith in making the arrest). And while the Court is willing to assume as much, it thinks this insufficient to sustain respondents' claim to an immunity because the "qualified immunity" respondents' seek is not equivalent to such a "defense".

But I think the Court errs in suggesting that the availability of a good-faith common law defense at the time of § 1983's adoption is not sufficient to support their claim to immunity. The case on which respondents principally rely, *Pierson*, considered whether a police officer sued under § 1983 for false arrest could rely on a showing of good-faith in order to escape liability. And while this Court concluded that the officer could rely on his own good faith, based in large part on the fact that a good-faith defense had been available at common law, the Court was at best ambiguous as to whether it was recognizing a "defense" or an "immunity." Any initial ambiguity, however, has certainly been eliminated by subsequent cases; there can be no doubt that it is a qualified immunity to which the officer is entitled. Similarly, in *Wood v. Strickland*, we recognized that, "although there have been differing emphases and formulations of the common-law immunity," the general recognition under state law that public officers are entitled to a good-faith defense was sufficient to support the recognition of a § 1983 immunity.

Thus, unlike the Court, I think our prior precedent establishes that a demonstration that a good-faith defense was available at the time § 1983 was adopted does, in fact, provide substantial support for a contemporary defendant claiming that he is entitled to qualified immunity in the analogous § 1983 context. While we refuse to recognize a common law immunity if § 1983's history or purpose counsel against applying it, I see no such history or purpose that would so counsel here.

Indeed, I am at a loss to understand what is accomplished by today's decision — other than a needlessly fastidious adherence to nomenclature — given that the Court acknowledges that a good-faith defense will be available for respondents to assert on remand. Respondents presumably will be required to show the traditional elements of a good-faith defense — either that they acted without malice or that they acted with probable cause. The first element, "maliciousness," encompasses an inquiry into subjective intent for bringing the suit. This quite often includes an inquiry into the defendant's subjective belief as to whether he believed success was likely. But the second element, probable cause," focuses principally on objective reasonableness. Thus, respondents can successfully defend this suit simply by establishing that their reliance on the attachment statute was objectively reasonable for someone with their knowledge of the circumstances. But this is precisely the showing that entitles a public official to immunity. *Harlow v. Fitzgerald* (official must show his action did not "violate clearly established statutory or constitutional rights of which a reasonable person would have known").

Nor do I see any reason that this "defense" may not be asserted early in the proceedings on a motion for summary judgment, just as a claim to qualified immunity may be. Provided that the historical facts are not in dispute, the presence or absence of "probable cause" has long been acknowledged to be a question of law. And so I see no reason that the trial judge may not resolve a summary judgment motion premised on such a good-faith defense, just as we have encouraged trial judges to do with respect to qualified immunity claims. Thus, private defendants who have invoked a state attachment law are put in the same position whether we recognize that they are entitled to qualified immunity or if we instead recognize a good-faith defense. Perhaps the Court believes that the defense" will be less amenable to summary disposition than will the "immunity;" perhaps it believes the defense will be an issue that must be submitted to the jury. While I can see no reason why this would be so (given that probable cause is a legal question), if it is true, today's decision will only manage to increase litigation costs needlessly for hapless defendants.

This, in turn, leads to the second basis on which we have previously recognized a qualified immunity — reasons of public policy. Assuming that some practical difference will result from recognizing a defense but not an immunity, I think such a step is neither dictated by our prior decisions nor desirable. It is true, as the Court points out, that in abandoning a strictly historical approach to § 1983 immunities we have often explained our decision to recognize an immunity in terms of the special needs of public officials. But those cases simply do not answer — because the question was not at issue — whether similar (or even completely unrelated) reasons of public policy would warrant immunity for private parties as well.

I believe there are such reasons. The normal presumption that attaches to any law is that society will be benefitted if private parties rely on that law to provide them a remedy, rather than turning to some form of private, and perhaps lawless, relief. In denying immunity to those who reasonably rely on presumptively valid state law, and thereby discouraging such reliance, the Court expresses confidence that today's decision will not "unduly impair," the public interest. I do not share that confidence. I would have thought it beyond peradventure that there is strong public interest in encouraging private citizens to rely on valid state laws of which they have no reason to doubt the validity.

Second, as with the police officer making an arrest, I believe the private plaintiff's lot is "not so unhappy" that he must forgo recovery of property he believes to be properly recoverable through available legal processes or to be "mulcted in damages" *Pierson*, if his belief turns out to be mistaken. For as one Court of Appeals has pointed out, it is at least passing strange to conclude that private individuals are acting "under color of law" because they invoke a state garnishment statute and the aid of state officers, but yet deny them the immunity to which those same state officers are entitled, simply because the private parties are not state employees. *Buller*. While some of the strangeness may be laid at the doorstep of our decision in *Lugar*, there is no reason to proceed still further down this path. Our § 1983 jurisprudence has gone very far afield indeed, when it subjects private parties to greater risk than their public counterparts, despite the fact that § 1983's historic purpose was "to prevent state officials from using the cloak of their authority under state law to violate rights protected against state infringement."

Because I find today's decision dictated neither by our own precedent nor by any sound considerations of public policy, I dissent.

[The concurring opinion of JUSTICE KENNEDY is omitted.]

NOTES

1.   In deciding whether or not Cole should be protected by qualified immunity, should the court be guided more by whether such a defense was recognized at common law in 1871 or by the purposes underlying qualified immunity? Is the current law of qualified immunity driven more by the historic common law rules or contemporary judicial policy?

2.   Who should know more about the potential unconstitutionality of a law, the private citizen who invokes the law or the state official called upon to implement it? Is this what the dissent is referring to when it comments that "it is at least passing strange" that the state officials have greater protection from liability resulting from the enforcement of unconstitutional laws than do private citizens? What might explain this disparity? Are there any reasons to believe that private actors invoking self-help remedies, but denied qualified immunity, will be less susceptible to the risk of over-deterrence than would state officials?

3.   The majority hints that the private actor may have a defense of good faith. The dissent assumes that such a defense will be available. On remand from the Supreme Court, the Fifth Circuit found that the private defendants in this case were protected from monetary liability because the plaintiff did not prove that they knew or should have known that the state attachment statute was unconstitutional. *Wyatt v. Cole*, 994 F.2d 1113 (5th Cir. 1993). What are the practical differences, if any, between qualified immunity and a good faith defense? Of what relevance is the defendant's state of mind? How amenable is the good faith defense to summary adjudication? Would interlocutory appeals be available to the private actor whose motion for summary judgment is denied?

4.   In *Gregg v. Ham*, 678 F.3d 333 (4th Cir. 2012), the court considered the question of whether a bail bondsman who participated with law enforcement officials in an illegal search of the plaintiff's premises was protected by qualified immunity. The bail bondsman argued that he was an adjunct of the court with regard to the apprehension of fugitives. The court rejected that argument and held that the bail bondsman was not entitled to qualified immunity. First, the court noted that bondsmen were not granted any immunity at common law. In fact, they were subject to liability for wrongs committed in the course of their activities. Moreover, the court did not believe the absence of qualified immunity would lead to over-deterrence of bail bondsmen in the performance of their duties. The bail bondsmen, unlike the law enforcement officials, had a strong profit motive in capturing the fugitive.

RICHARDSON v. MCKNIGHT
521 U.S. 399 (1997)

JUSTICE **BREYER** delivered the opinion of the Court.

The issue before us is whether prison guards who are employees of a private prison management firm are entitled to a qualified immunity from suit by prisoners charging a violation of 42 U.S.C. § 1983. We hold that they are not.

I

Ronnie Lee McKnight, a prisoner at Tennessee's South Central Correctional Center (SCCC), brought this federal constitutional tort action against two prison guards, Darryl Richardson and John Walker. He says the guards injured him by placing upon him extremely tight physical restraints, thereby unlawfully "subjecting" him "to the deprivation of" a right "secured by the Constitution" of the United States. Rev. Stat. § 1979, 42 U.S.C. § 1983. Richardson and Walker asserted a qualified immunity from § 1983 lawsuits . . . , and moved to dismiss the action. The District Court noted that Tennessee had "privatized" the management of a number of its correctional facilities, and that consequently a private firm, not the state government, employed the guards. . . . The court held that, because they worked for a private company rather than the government, the law did not grant the guards immunity from suit. It therefore denied the guards' motion to dismiss. The guards appealed to the Sixth Circuit. . . . That court also ruled against them. . . . The Court of Appeals conceded that other courts had reached varying conclusions about whether, or the extent to which, private sector defendants are entitled to immunities of the sort the law provides governmental defendants. . . . But the court concluded, primarily for reasons of "public policy," that the privately employed prison guards were not entitled to the immunity provided their governmental counterparts. We granted certiorari to review this holding. We now affirm.

II

[The Court summarized its ruling in *Wyatt v. Cole*, 504 U.S. 158 (1992), in which it held that a private person conspiring with a state official is not entitled to the defense of qualified immunity. The *Wyatt* majority found that the application of qualified immunity under such circumstances was not supported by history or the "special policy concerns involved in suing government officials." 521 U.S. at 167.]

. . . *Wyatt*, then, did not answer the legal question before us, whether respondents — two employees of a private prison management firm — enjoy a qualified immunity from suit under § 1983. It does tell us, however, to look both to history and to the purposes that underlie government employee immunity in order to find the answer.

B

History does not reveal a "firmly rooted" tradition of immunity applicable to privately employed prison guards. [The Court noted that in the past, private contractors ran jails and prisons in both the United States and England. The admittedly sparse case law appeared to recognize common law claims by prisoners against private contractors who mistreated them.]

C

Whether the immunity doctrine's purposes warrant immunity for private prison guards presents a closer question. *Wyatt*, consistent with earlier precedent, described the doctrine's purposes as protecting "government's ability to perform its traditional functions" by providing immunity where "necessary to preserve" the ability of government officials "to serve the public good or to ensure that talented candidates were not deterred by the threat of damages suits from entering public service." 504 U.S. at 167. Earlier precedent described immunity as protecting the public from unwarranted timidity on the part of public officials by, for example, "encouraging the vigorous exercise of official authority," . . . and by responding to the concern that threatened liability would, in Judge Hand's words, " 'dampen the ardour of all but the most resolute, or the most irresponsible' " public officials. . . .

The guards argue that those purposes support immunity whether their employer is private or public. . . . Since private prison guards perform the same work as state prison guards, they say, they must require immunity to a similar degree. To say this, however, is to misread this Court's precedents. The Court has sometimes applied a functional approach in immunity cases, but only to decide which type of immunity — absolute or qualified — a public officer should receive. . . . And it never has held that the mere performance of a governmental function could make the difference between unlimited § 1983 liability and qualified immunity, . . . especially for a private person who performs a job without government supervision or direction. Indeed a purely functional approach bristles with difficulty, particularly since, in many areas, government and private industry may engage in fundamentally similar activities, ranging from electricity production, to waste disposal, to even mail delivery.

Petitioners' argument also overlooks certain important differences that, from an immunity perspective, are critical. First, the most important special government immunity-producing concern — unwarranted timidity — is less likely present, or at least is not special, when a private company subject to competitive market pressures operates a prison. Competitive pressures mean not only that a firm whose guards are too aggressive will face damages that raise costs, thereby threatening its replacement, but also that a firm whose guards are too timid will face threats of replacement by other firms with records that demonstrate their ability to do both a safer and a more effective job.

These ordinary marketplace pressures are present here. The private prison guards before us work for a large, multi-state private prison management firm. . . . The firm is systematically organized to perform a major administrative task for profit. . . . It performs that task independently, with relatively less ongoing direct state supervision. . . . It must buy insurance sufficient to compensate victims of civil rights torts. . . . And, since the firm's first contract expires after three years, . . . its performance is disciplined, not only by state review, . . . but also by pressure from potentially competing firms who can try to take its place. . . .

In other words, marketplace pressures provide the private firm with strong incentives to avoid overly timid, insufficiently vigorous, unduly fearful, or "nonarduous" employee job performance. And the contract's provisions — including those that might permit employee indemnification and avoid many civil-service restrictions — grant this private firm freedom to respond to those market pressures through rewards and penalties that operate directly upon its employees. . . . To this extent, the employees before us resemble those of other private firms and differ from government employees.

This is not to say that government employees, in their efforts to act within constitutional limits, will always, or often, sacrifice the otherwise effective performance of their duties. Rather, it is to say that government employees typically act within a different system. They work within a system that is responsible through elected officials to voters who, when they vote, rarely consider the performance of individual subdepartments or civil servants specifically and in detail. And that system is often characterized by multi-department civil service rules that, while providing employee security, may limit the incentives or the ability of individual departments or supervisors flexibly to reward, or to punish, individual employees. Hence a judicial determination that "effectiveness" concerns warrant special immunity-type protection in respect to this latter (governmental) system does not prove its need in respect to the former. Consequently, we can find no special immunity-related need to encourage vigorous performance.

Second, "privatization" helps to meet the immunity-related need "to ensure that talented candidates" are "not deterred by the threat of damages suits from entering public service." . . . It does so in part because of the comprehensive insurance-coverage requirements just mentioned. The insurance increases the likelihood of employee indemnification and to that extent reduces the employment discouraging fear of unwarranted liability potential applicants face. Because privatization law also frees the private prison-management firm from many civil service law restraints, . . . it permits the private firm, unlike a government department, to offset any increased employee liability risk with higher pay or extra benefits. In respect to this second government-immunity-related purpose then, it is difficult to find a special need for immunity, for the guards' employer can operate like other private firms; it need not operate like a typical government department. Third, lawsuits may well " 'distract' " these employees " 'from their . . . duties' " . . . , but the risk of "distraction" alone cannot be sufficient grounds for an immunity. Our qualified immunity cases do not contemplate the complete elimination of lawsuit-based distractions. . . . And it is significant that, here, Tennessee law reserves certain important discretionary tasks — those related to prison discipline, to parole, and to good time — for state officials. . . . Given a continual and conceded need for deterring constitutional violations and our sense that the firm's tasks are not enormously different in respect to their importance from various other publicly important tasks carried out by private firms, we are not persuaded that the threat of distracting workers from their duties is enough virtually by itself to justify providing an immunity. Moreover, Tennessee, which has itself decided not to extend sovereign immunity to private prison operators (and arguably appreciated that this decision would increase contract prices to some degree), . . . can be understood to have anticipated a certain amount of distraction.

D

Our examination of history and purpose thus reveals nothing special enough about the job or about its organizational structure that would warrant providing these private prison guards with a governmental immunity. . . . The job is one that private industry might, or might not, perform; and which history shows private firms did sometimes perform without relevant immunities. The organizational structure is one subject to the ordinary competitive pressures that normally help of private animal-welfare organization that contracted with the city to provide animal-welfare services may not assert qualified immunity); *Harrison v. Ash*, 539 F.3d 510 (6th Cir. 2008) (prison nurses employed by a private medical provider cannot assert qualified immunity); *McCullum v. Tepe*, 693 F.3d 696 (6th Cir. 2012) (a prison psychiatrist employed by a non-profit entity may not assert qualified immunity).

6. Note that Justice Breyer commented that the case "does not involve a private party briefly associated with a government body serving as an adjunct to government in an essential governmental capacity, or acting under close official supervision." Does this suggest that such private defendants should be protected by qualified immunity? If so, why? In *Filarsky v. Delia*, 132 S. Ct. 1657 (2012), the defendant was a private attorney who worked together with government employees in connection with an internal affairs investigation of a firefighter under suspicion because of his lengthy absence from work. The private attorney was sued under section 1983 for an alleged violation of the Fourth Amendment. The Supreme Court held that the defendant was entitled to qualified immunity. It first noted that when section 1983 was enacted, local governments commonly relied on professionals and occasional workers to perform governmental functions. The availability of immunity should not vary depending on whether an individual working for the government did so on a full-time or part-time basis. Moreover, the Court concluded that the policies underlying qualified immunity — avoiding undue chilling of independent decision-making and the need to attract capable persons to public employment — applied equally to those working part time for the government. The Court distinguished *Richardson* as a "self-consciously" narrow decision. Unlike the private attorney conducting a limited investigation, the prison management company in *Richardson* was "a private firm, systematically organized to assume a major administrative task (managing an institution) with limited direct supervision by the government, under[taking] that task for profit and potentially in competition with other firms." 132 S.Ct. at 1667. How convincing are those distinctions? Is the private attorney conducting a limited investigation a "for profit" actor in potential competition with other attorneys? Does *Filarsky* signal a retreat from *Richardson*? If there is a tension between *Richardson* and *Filarsky*, which is the better result? Why? *See also Cullinan v. Abramson*, 128 F.3d 301 (6th Cir. 1997) (private attorneys serving as outside counsel to city may asset qualified immunity).

7. For a pre-*Filarsky* analysis of private parties immunities, see Nahmod, *The Emerging Section 1983 Private Party Defense*, 26 Cardozo L. Rev. 81 (2004).

Even if respondents' suspensions were justified, and even if they did not suffer any other actual injury, the fact remains that they were deprived of their right to procedural due process. "It is enough to invoke the procedural safeguards of the Fourteenth Amendment that a significant property interest is at stake, whatever the ultimate outcome of a hearing."

Common-law courts traditionally have vindicated deprivations of certain "absolute" rights that are not shown to have caused actual injury through the award of a nominal sum of money. By making the deprivation of such rights actionable for nominal damages without proof of actual injury, the law recognizes the importance to organized society that those rights be scrupulously observed; but at the same time, it remains true to the principle that substantial damages should be awarded only to compensate actual injury or, in the case of exemplary or punitive damages, to deter or punish malicious deprivations of rights.

Because the right to procedural due process is "absolute" in the sense that it does not depend upon the merits of a claimant's substantive assertions, and because of the importance to organized society that procedural due process be observed, we believe that the denial of procedural due process should be actionable for nominal damages without proof of actual injury. We therefore hold that if, upon remand, the District Court determines that respondents' suspensions were justified, respondents nevertheless will be entitled to recover nominal damages not to exceed one dollar from petitioners.

The judgment of the Court of Appeals is reversed, and the case is remanded for further proceedings consistent with this opinion.

NOTES

1. *Carey* sets forth the basic principle governing damages in section 1983 cases. By stressing that section 1983 creates "a species of tort liability" and holding that "the basic purpose of a section 1983 damages award should be to compensate persons for injuries caused by the deprivation of constitutional rights", the Court sets up a tort framework for adjudicating damages issues. *See* Jean Love, *Damages: A Remedy for the Violation of Constitutional Rights*, 67 CAL. L. REV. 1242 (1979); Note, *Damage Awards for Constitutional Torts: A Reconsideration After* Carey v. Piphus, 93 HARV. L. REV. 966 (1980). According to one court, the "analysis of whether [plaintiff] suffered an actual injury warranting compensatory damages . . . appears to be the same under both section 1983 and [state law]." *Randall v. Prince George's County*, 302 F.3d 188, 208 (4th Cir. 2002). Is this what the Court meant to say in *Carey*?

The compensation principle sometimes results in large awards, if a sufficiently serious harm can be traced to the constitutional violation. For example, in *Thomas v. Cook County Sheriff's Dep't*, 604 F.3d 293 (7th Cir. 2009), a pretrial detainee died of pneumococcal meningitis. His mother won a "deliberate indifference" suit and was (after a remittitur) awarded $4,150,000. In *Florida Transportation Services, Inc. v. Miami-Dade County*, 703 F.3d 1230 (11th Cir. 2012), a stevedore company won $3.55 million for lost profits caused by the defendants' violations of the commerce clause in awarding permits to stevedores. In some cases the litigation results in a settlement for a large amount. *See, e.g.,* "*New York Agrees to Pay $2.75 Million in Death of Rikers Island Prisoner,*" N.Y. TIMES, July 21, 2014 at A14 (national edition).

Does the compensation principle imply that plaintiffs who cannot prove damages go away empty handed? The last paragraph of *Carey* stresses that some relief is still available. Plaintiffs who establish constitutional violations, like plaintiffs who prove common law battery or assault, are entitled to nominal damages even if they have no actual damages. *See, e.g., Gray ex rel. Alexander v. Bostic,* 720 F.3d 887 (11th Cir. 2013).

In *Hazle v. Crofoot,* 727 F.3d 983 (9th Cir. 2013), the plaintiff was a parolee whose parole was revoked (and who therefore spent an additional 100 days in prison) when he refused to participate in a drug treatment program that would have obliged him to recognize the existence of a higher power. He sued for a First Amendment violation and won on the merits. But the jury awarded no damages. The court said "that Hazle was entitled to at least an award of nominal damages as a result of the district judge's finding that the state defendants violated his constitutional rights." 727 F.3d at 991 n.6. But then it went further:

> The district judge's finding of liability establishes that Hazle suffered actual injury when he was unconstitutionally incarcerated. Given this undisputed finding that Hazle's constitutional rights were violated, and applying the rule that the award of compensatory damages is mandatory when the existence of actual injury is beyond dispute, we hold that the district judge erred in refusing to hold that Hazle was, as a matter of law, entitled to compensatory damages.

Is this passage — which seems to equate "actual injury" with violation of constitutional rights — consistent with the distinction drawn in *Carey* between situations in which compensatory damages are available and those in which only nominal damages may be awarded? Does the Ninth Circuit panel confuse "injury" with "damages?" Another way to get to the same result is to focus on the facts of the case at hand (100 days more in prison as a direct result of the constitutional violation) and rule that on these facts a reasonable jury could not find that the compensable harm is zero.

2. Why did the Court choose tort as the model for remedying constitutional violations by monetary awards? As an alternative, consider the pros and cons of supplementing the tort model with a system of bounties, under which plaintiffs who prove that their constitutional rights have been violated are awarded payments reflecting the jury's view of the value of those rights, quite apart from whether the plaintiffs can show any injury. In *Carey* and elsewhere the Court says that deterring constitutional violations and vindicating constitutional rights are the central aims of section 1983. Would the availability of such payments help to deter constitutional violations, by making it more costly for officials and governments to commit them? Would it help to vindicate constitutional rights, in situations where the right is violated but no provable harm results? *See* Michael Wells, *Constitutional Remedies, Section 1983 and the Common Law,* 68 MISS. L.J. 157, 214–22 (1998).

If the answer to these questions is yes, then why does the Court reject this scheme? Is it inconsistent with the language and history of the statute? Section 1983 states that a constitutional violation may be vindicated by "an action at law." But it also authorizes "other proper proceeding for redress", and it does not specify that tort principles must govern the relief available. The *qui tam* action, under which the plaintiff receives a bounty for bringing suit to enforce the law, is (and was in 1871) a well-established institution in American law. Specific statutory authorization is typically required, however. *See* Evan Caminker, *The Constitutionality of* Qui Tam *Actions*, 99 YALE L.J. 341, 345–46 (1989). In evaluating the comparative merits of a bounty scheme and the "compensation principle" adopted in *Carey*, keep in mind a central lesson of the preceding chapters in this book on municipal liability and official immunity: There are many situations in which no damages remedy is available for the violation of a constitutional right. Later in this chapter we will see that forward-looking relief, via an injunction or a declaratory judgment, may be foreclosed as well. Consider, too, the view that the right-remedy gap "has constitutional benefits as well as costs," because it "facilitates constitutional change by reducing the costs of innovation." John C. Jeffries, Jr., *The Right-Remedy Gap in Constitutional Law*, 109 YALE L.J. 87, 90 (1999).

Notice that the tort model and the alternative suggested in the preceding paragraphs both assume that governments and officials will respond to liability in the same way as rational private actors, by changing their behavior if the costs imposed upon them are sufficiently high. For skepticism about whether governments will behave in this way, *see* Daryl J. Levinson, *Making Government Pay: Markets, Politics, and the Allocation of Constitutional Costs*, 67 U. CHI. L. REV. 345 (2000). Levinson's view is challenged in Myriam E. Gilles, *In Defense of Making Government Pay: The Deterrent Effect of Constitutional Tort Remedies*, 35 GA. L. REV. 845 (2001). The force of Levinson's argument is stronger to the extent governments indemnify their employees for constitutional tort liability. *See* John C. Jeffries, Jr., *In Praise of the Eleventh Amendment and Section 1983*, 84 VA. L. REV. 47, 50 (1998) (asserting that this is generally the case). Assuming that governments do generally pay, and assuming that they do not respond to the disincentives provided by liability rules, does it follow that constitutional tort is useless? For one view, *see* Bernard P. Dauenhauer & Michael L. Wells, *Corrective Justice and Constitutional Torts*, 35 GA. L. REV. 903 (2001) (arguing that considerations of justice would nonetheless justify the imposition of liability).

3.   In practice, federal courts begin from the premise that federal common law governs damages issues in section 1983 cases, see, e.g., *Graham v. Satkoski*, 51 F.3d 710 (7th Cir. 1995), except for certain matters ordinarily regulated by statute. *See* section C, *infra*. They apply modern tort damages principles, including controversial ones, in section 1983 cases. *See, e.g., Cooper v. Casey*, 97 F.3d 914, 919 (7th Cir. 1996) (applying the principle that defendants are jointly liable, and damages will not be apportioned among them, in a case where "the kicking and punching and macing and refusal to provide prompt medical assistance coalesced to produce a quantity of pain in which the contributions of the individual defendants could not be distinguished"); *Clark v. Taylor*, 710 F.2d 4 (1st Cir. 1983) (allowing recovery for plaintiff's fear of developing cancer as a result of defendants' wrongful administration of a drug); *Bell v. City of Milwaukee*, 746 F.2d 1205, 1250 (7th Cir. 1984)

(extending consortium recovery beyond spouses to include a parent's recovery for death of his child).

In *Green v. Johnson*, 977 F.2d 1383 (10th Cir. 1992) a prisoner successfully sued for mistreatment by guards, recovering $15,000 in compensatory damages. On appeal, he argued that the award was too low. In turning him down, the court said, among other things: "Given that plaintiff is a ward of the state, provided with room, board, and medical care, his need for financial restitution based on his injuries is substantially less than that of persons responsible for their own economic support." *Id. at* 1389. Is this sentence consistent with the common law collateral source rule, under which the existence of collateral sources of compensation for the plaintiff's injuries is irrelevant to the calculation of damages owed by the tortfeasor? After *Carey*, are lower courts free to replace the general common law rule with a rule of their own choosing?

4. Is it relevant that many states have enacted statutes that modify the common law rule by permitting or requiring juries to take account of collateral sources? This issue was addressed in Gill v. Maciejewski, 546 F.3d 557 (8th Cir. 2008), a case from Minnesota in which Gill sued Maciejewski, a police officer, for excessive force in arrest and won a jury verdict for $10,000 in compensatory damages. His insurer paid him $9,906.98 to cover the cost of medical treatment. The district court, following the common law collateral source rule, refused to deduct this amount from the jury's award. On appeal, Maciejewski argued that "the district court erroneously applied the common law collateral source rule instead of Minnesota's rule found at Minn. Stat. Ann. § 548.36(3)." The 8th Circuit rejected this contention and affirmed the award, explaining that "Maciejewski offers no explanation for why the federal common law applied by the district court fails to provide a suitable remedy." *Id.* at 565.

Suppose a state abolishes joint and several liability, in favor of a rule that tort liability is several only, as many have done. *See, e.g., McReynolds v. Krebs*, 725 S.E.2d 584 (Ga. 2012) (discussing Georgia law). Should the Georgia rule be applied in § 1983 litigation in Georgia?

Certain cases present a distinct "role of state law" issue. In some circumstances, a federal statute, 42 U.S.C. § 1988, directs the federal courts to apply state law, unless it is contrary to federal policy. For example, state statutes providing for the survival of tort actions after the death of the victim are ordinarily applied in § 1983 cases. *See Robertson v. Wegmann*, below. Suppose a state survival statute prohibits recovery for pre-death pain and suffering. Should that provision apply to § 1983 cases in which the death was caused by the constitutional violation? *See Chaudhry v. City of Los Angeles*, 751 F.3d 1096, 1105 (9th Cir. 2014) (no, because this particular application of state law would conflict with the aims of § 1983).

5. State and local governments are not constitutionally obligated to indemnify their employees for constitutional tort liability and litigation costs. *See Allen v. City of Los Angeles*, 92 F.3d 842 (9th Cir. 1996). Of course, state law may require or permit indemnity. Should the jury be instructed that, in the event an officer is found liable, his municipal employer may indemnify him? *See Larez v. Holcomb*, 16 F.3d 1513, 1519 (9th Cir. 1994) (no, applying the common law rule).

6. While the basic principles of tort damages are well-settled in the common law, there are areas of dispute. For example, some common law courts allow parents and children to sue for consortium, while others restrict it to spouses. Some allow recovery for the fear of some future catastrophe (like developing cancer) made more likely by the defendant's breach of duty, while others require current injury. Some authorize a separate instruction to the jury on lost enjoyment of life, while others insist that this be made a part of the pain and suffering instruction.

Granted that common law damages principles apply to constitutional tort cases, how should courts in section 1983 cases address controverted issues like these? Should the federal court treat section 1983 cases as indistinguishable from other tort cases, or does the constitutional context matter, perhaps justifying a different result than the same court would reach in a common law tort case? If the constitutional context does matter, which way does it cut? Does it justify more liberal damages awards, because constitutional rights are more vital than common law rights and hence require broader remedies for their effective enforcement? Or does the anti-democratic nature of constitutional rights mean that courts should erect a more restrictive set of remedial principles, so as to limit the intrusion of constitutional tort on majoritarian rule? Are there other arguments for or against one or the other of these approaches to constitutional remedies? Can you think of a better alternative than either of them?

7. As in common law torts, damage awards in constitutional cases are reviewable by the trial judge and appellate courts for excessiveness. *See, e.g., Lesende v. Borrero*, 752 F.3d 324 (3d Cir. 2014) (reviewing the district court's handling of remittitur issues in a case in which a jury awarded $2.7 million and then, after remittitur, a second jury awarded $4 million); *Knussman v. Maryland*, 272 F.3d 625, 641–42 (4th Cir. 2001) ($375,000 emotional distress damages were excessive where the relationship between the unconstitutional conduct and the emotional distress was "attenuated," in that much of the emotional distress was a product of the litigation itself and not a direct result of the constitutional violation that gave rise to it). They may also (though much more rarely) be overturned for inadequacy. *See, e.g., Parish v. City of Elkhart, Ind.*, 702 F.3d 997 (7th Cir. 2012) (ordering a new trial on damages when the plaintiff succeeded on the merits, showing that his eight years of imprisonment were caused by an unfair trial, but received only $73,125 in compensatory damages and $5000 in punitive damages); *Preyer v. Slavic*, 251 F.3d 448, 453–54 (3d Cir. 2001) (upholding new trial order where plaintiff introduced evidence of significant injuries from a beating by prison guards and the jury awarded $1 in nominal damages).

One approach to this task is to measure the amount of the award against the evidence and make an intuitive judgment as to whether the evidence reasonably supports it. Other courts apply a "comparability" approach, under which they look to awards made in other cases in evaluating the one at hand. For example, in *Parish, supra*, the plaintiff "presented the court with evidence indicating that the average jury award was nearly $950,000 per year of wrongful imprisonment . . . . The award here of approximately $9,000 per year is an extreme outlier.") In *Disorbo v. Hoy*, 343 F.3d 172, 183 (2d Cir. 2003), DiSorbo sued police offices and the city of Schenectady for police brutality. The jury awarded $1.675 million in compensatory and punitive damages. The court said that its "determination of whether a compensatory damages award is excessive should not be conducted 'in a vacuum,' but should instead should include consideration of the amounts awarded in other, comparable cases." Finding that similar injuries had resulted in smaller awards in earlier cases, the court ordered a new trial on damages unless the plaintiff would accept a reduction in the compensatory award from $400,000 to $250,000.

Which method is better? Does the case-by-case approach result in unfairness, since different juries may accord disparate treatment to similar cases? Is there a parallel danger that the comparability approach will treat different cases similarly, by giving too much weight to superficial similarities between cases and ignoring subtle differences? Does comparability amount to an unwillingness on the part of appellate judges to take responsibility for their actions? Does the comparability approach rest on the premise that the first few cases to consider the proper award for a certain injury more than likely reach the right results? If not, why require later cases to toe the line established in earlier ones? If so, why should earlier judges and juries be presumed more capable of reaching correct results than later ones? In any event, it is clear that the results in early cases will heavily influence appellate review of later awards, is it not? Does comparability intrude on the jury's role, in violation of the Seventh Amendment? For discussion of these issues, see J. Patrick Elsevier, Note, *Out-of-Line: Federal Courts Using Comparability to Review Damage Awards*, 33 Ga. L. Rev. 243 (1998).

8. The universal common law principle is that the plaintiff is entitled to one full recovery, no matter how many defendants he successfully sues. Does *Carey*, with its stress on the compensation principle, adopt this as the federal rule? Whether it necessarily follows from *Carey* or not, it is the rule in the lower federal courts. *See, e.g., Watts v. Laurent*, 774 F.2d 168, 179 (7th Cir. 1985) ("[T]he very nature of damages as compensation for injury suffered requires that once the plaintiff has been fully compensated for his injuries by one or more tortfeasors, he may not thereafter recover any additional compensation from any of the remaining tortfeasors.") Plaintiffs in § 1983 suits often assert more than one constitutional basis for recovery, or bring state tort claims as well as constitutional ones. When both claims are aimed at recovery for the same harm, they are entitled to just one award. For example, in *Bogan v. City of Boston*, 489 F.3d 417 (1st Cir. 2007) plaintiffs raised (among other claims) 4th and 14th amendment objections to the city's inspection of their property. Some of the claims were litigated and others were deferred. After winning a jury verdict, they argued that the verdict only covered the Fourth Amendment theory, and sought to continue on with the Fourteenth Amendment theory. That effort failed. They were entitled to only one award because "[t]he magistrate judge concluded that the Bogans' trial presentation of their Fourth and Fourteenth Amendment theories was identical — encompassing both the City's inspection and post-inspection conduct and seeking all damages incurred as a result. [This] view is consistent with the Bogans' statement at the pretrial conference that *all* of their claims were based on the same underlying facts. And it is also consistent with the Bogans' acceptance of a verdict form on the § 1983 claim that did not require the jury to distinguish between the Fourth Amendment and Fourteenth Amendment theories of liability."

Sometimes plaintiffs have more success. In *Berry v. Oswalt*, 143 F.3d 1127 (8th Cir. 1998), for example, a female prisoner was raped by a guard and sued him for both an Eighth Amendment violation as well as the common law "outrage" tort. The jury awarded compensatory and punitive damages on both theories, but the district judge eliminated the outrage awards, "finding them to be duplicative of the section 1983 awards." A panel of the Eighth Circuit reversed that ruling, noting that "[t]he tort of outrage and the violation of constitutional rights are legally distinct claims," with different elements of proof required for each. (For example, an Eighth Amendment violation does not require showing *severe* emotional distress, *see* Chapter 3, *supra*.) In this case, the district judge had "carefully warned against confusion of the two claims," and the verdict form reminded the jurors of the distinction between them. "The Court's emphasis that the claims were to be considered separately, as well as the different amounts that the jury awarded for each, support[ed the appellate court's] conclusion that the jury apportioned Berry's total damages between the two theories and did not allow a double recovery."

After grappling with similar problems, in a case involving two plaintiffs, multiple theories, and multiple defendants, a Seventh Circuit panel made some suggestions to trial judges:

> Most of the issues surrounding the damages award in this case could have been avoided with a better verdict form, and we take this opportunity to offer some general guidance on what the proper sequence of inquiries on a civil verdict form should be. A verdict form should not ask a jury to assess damages before liability. In cases involving joint and several liability for a single indivisible injury, a verdict form should ask the jury first, to indicate which, if any, of the defendants are liable. Second, if at least one defendant is found liable, the form should instruct the jury to determine the total amount of damages for the plaintiff's injury, an inquiry that is wholly separate from the liability decisions made in the first step. The form should not be structured in a way that would invite the jury to divide the damages for a single injury among defendants or theories of recovery. A verdict form that takes a jury through these steps in this sequence — reinforced by clear instructions from the court not to duplicate damages or divide the amount among defendants — will go far to help future litigants avoid the problems that arose in this case. Tort concepts of single indivisible injuries and joint and several liability are potentially confusing for a jury, and verdict forms should help remedy potential confusion, not add to it.

Thomas v. Cook County Sheriff's Dept., 604 F.3d 293, 312–13 (7th Cir. 2010).

9.   Granting that monetary awards in section 1983 cases should be governed by the "principle of compensation," does the Court correctly apply that principle to the procedural due process violation at issue in *Carey*? The Court held that the plaintiffs cannot recover damages due to their suspension from school unless they show that, had a due process hearing been held, they would have escaped that punishment. Is this ruling consistent with the common law tort principle that one may recover damages only if, but for the defendant's tortious conduct, the injury would not have occurred?

Carey's requirement of a causal link between the constitutional violation and the plaintiff's harm is not limited to procedural due process. Lack of causation can be an obstacle to the recovery of substantial damages for other constitutional violations as well. In *Amato v. City of Saratoga Springs*, 170 F.3d 311 (2d Cir. 1999), the plaintiff sued for the city and police officers for using excessive force in arresting him. The jury found in his favor on the merits, awarded nominal damages of $1, and punitive damages of $20,000 (reduced by the trial judge to $15,000), but no compensatory damages. Despite videotaped evidence that the police had beaten Amato, the court upheld the jury's decision. Among other things, the court noted that though the officer's behavior, "yelling, grabbing, possibly shoving Amato into the wall," was "clearly aggressive," five minutes later Amato could "be seen standing at the booking counter, with a casual demeanor, appearing fairly alert, and not showing signs of experiencing pain." *See also Gibeau v. Nellis*, 18 F.3d 107 (2d Cir. 1994) (although guard used excessive force in striking plaintiff three times, substantial damages would be inappropriate if the jury found that the first blow was not excessive and that the plaintiff's contusion was caused by the first blow); *Butler v. Dowd*, 979 F.2d 661 (8th Cir. 1992) (upholding award of nominal damages to prisoners who could show that they were raped and that prison officials were deliberately indifferent to their safety, where the jury could also find that the rapes were not caused by the defendants' deliberate indifference but by the plaintiff's own conduct). In *Olsen v. Correiro*, 189 F.3d 52 (1st Cir. 1999), the plaintiff was, in an earlier criminal proceeding, convicted of murder. He succeeded in having the conviction overturned on account of police officers' failure to disclose an audiotaped interview with the prosecution's chief witness. He then pleaded nolo contendere to manslaughter and was sentenced to time served. In his section 1983 suit, he sought damages for his incarceration. The court ruled against him, reasoning that "as to the validity of the sentence rendered, a nolo plea is the equivalent of a guilty plea."

Conversely, the plaintiff can recover for all the foreseeable consequences of the constitutional violation. In *Herzog v. Village of Winnetka*, 309 F.3d 1041, 1044 (7th Cir. 2002), the defendant police officer, according to the plaintiff's account, arrested the plaintiff without probable cause, in violation of her Fourth Amendment rights. He then put a breath-screening device into her mouth, cracking a tooth. Reversing a summary judgment for the defendants, the court said:

> [E]ven though cracking Herzog's tooth by inserting the personal breath-screening device into her mouth too forcefully may have been accidental, she can obtain damages for that injury also, because it was a reasonably probable consequence of an arrest made by a police officer who, if the plaintiff's facts are believed, was totally incompetent.

See also Malloy v. Monahan, 73 F.3d 1012 (10th Cir. 1996). There the plaintiff was allowed to recover over $150,000, almost entirely for lost profits. Malloy "had been involved in the purchase, rehabilitation, and sale of distressed residential properties." The case arose out of police response to a dispute between Malloy and his estranged wife, in which police officers used excessive force in arresting Malloy, *see* Chapter 3, *supra*. The evidence of lost profits was that "the beating left [plaintiff] unable to pursue his real estate ventures and thus robbed him of anticipated profits." Causation is addressed in greater detail in Chapter 6.

Suppose plaintiff Piphus loses on the causation issue, because the principal has conclusive proof that he was smoking marijuana. Can he still recover damages for the violation of his right to due process? Is it sufficient that he can prove emotional distress resulting from this episode? If not, can he obtain damages by showing that the emotional distress was caused by the failure to give him the process that was due, and not by other events, like the suspension itself? *See Harden v. Pataki*, 320 F.3d 1289, 1300 (11th Cir. 2003) (allowing recovery in the latter situation).

10. Juries sometimes award substantial amounts for emotional distress. In *Bogle v. McClure*, 332 F.3d 1347, 1358–59 (11th Cir. 2003), seven librarians employed by Fulton County, Georgia, were transferred to menial jobs (but at no loss of pay) on account of race. The librarians "testified to the emotional and mental pain they suffered as a result of being transferred from meaningful, supervisory positions to dead-end, nonmanagerial jobs." They "testified that the race-based transfers effectively destroyed their careers, and some testified the transfers caused them to resign or go on workers' compensation. [Some] librarians testified the transfers caused them to become depressed and one even became suicidal. Other than their own testimony, the librarians presented no independent medical evidence of mental or physical harm." After declaring that "general compensatory damages, as opposed to special damages, need not be proved with a high degree of specificity and may be inferred from the circumstances," the Eleventh circuit upheld an award of $500,000 each for emotional harm.

Courts are divided on whether the plaintiff's testimony, standing alone, can support such an award for emotional distress, pain, and suffering. *Bogle* clearly gives an affirmative answer to that question. *See also Hendrickson v. Cooper*, 589 F.3d 887 (7th Cir. 2009) (objective medical evidence not required to sustain award for back pain, "given the uniquely subjective nature of pain"); *Mendez-Matos v. Municipality of Guaynabo*, 557 F.3d 36, 47 (1st Cir. 2009) ("A plaintiff does not need to present expert testimony to recover damages for emotional distress caused by the violation of his civil rights"); *Forsyth v. City of Dallas*, 91 F.3d 769 (5th Cir. 1996) (upholding jury verdict awarding two plaintiffs $100,000 and $75,000 respectively in emotional anguish damages based on their testimony that they suffered weight loss, depression, intestinal troubles, marital problems, and sleeplessness after they were demoted within the police force for making allegations of illegal wiretapping within the police department). Other cases set a higher bar for the plaintiff. *See, e.g., Patrolmen's Benevolent Ass'n v. City of New York*, 310 F.3d 43, 55–56 (2d Cir. 2002) ("A plaintiff's subjective testimony, standing alone, is generally insufficient to sustain an award of emotional distress damages"). The court elaborated:

> [T]he plaintiff's testimony of emotional injury must be substantiated by other evidence that such an injury occurred, such as the testimony of witnesses to the plaintiff's distress or the objective circumstances of the violation itself. Evidence that a plaintiff has sought medical treatment for the emotional injury, while helpful, is not required. [An earlier case] should not be read to require physical symptoms of emotional distress in [section 1983] cases.

In this case, the plaintiffs were police officers who successfully challenged their transfers from one precinct to another on the ground that the transfers were based on race in violation of the equal protection clause. The court upheld awards for emotional distress of $50,000 per plaintiff. *See also Price v. City of Charlotte*, 93 F.3d 1241, 1255 (4th Cir. 1996) (finding the plaintiffs' testimony insufficient to support an award of emotional distress damages, where they "never offered evidence of any need for medicine, physical symptoms, psychological disturbance or counseling, loss of income or pecuniary expense, a description of their emotional distress, or how their conduct changed or if others observed their conduct change. Also conspicuously absent from their evidence is any corroboration of their emotional distress or any manifestation it may have assumed"). Is *Price* consistent with *Bogle*?

There is a special rule for prisoners. Under the Prison Litigation Reform Act, 42 U.S.C. § 1997e(e), "[n]o federal civil action may be brought by a prisoner . . . for mental or emotional injury suffered while in custody without a prior showing of physical injury." *Herman v. Holiday*, 238 F.3d 660, 665–66 (5th Cir. 2001) (holding that a prisoner who proves no physical injury is "not entitled to money damages for the mental and emotional stress, which knowledge of an increased risk of possible future asbestos-related illnesses may have caused").

11. *Malloy, supra,* illustrates recovery for economic loss in constitutional tort cases. Another example is *Florida Transportation Services, Inc. v. Miami-Dade County*, 703 F.3d 1230 (11th Cir. 2012), in which a stevedore company won $3.55 million for lost profits caused by the defendants' violations of the commerce clause in awarding permits to stevedores.

Evidentiary rulings can figure significantly in calculating economic loss. In *Tri County Industries, Inc. v. District of Columbia*, 200 F.3d 836 (D.C. Cir. 2000), a business successfully sued the District of Columbia on the theory that its suspension of a building permit deprived it of property without procedural due process. The jury awarded $5 million, mainly for lost profits, but the trial judge overturned the award. At the retrial, the District was allowed to introduce evidence that Tri County may have ultimately been forbidden to build in any event on account of health and safety concerns that "may have led to community resistance and, perhaps, regulatory barriers to Tri County's project." The jury awarded $100 at the second trial. Affirming the original verdict, the appellate court said the evidence of health and safety concerns was properly excluded the first time, because "the District never met the trial court's repeated injunction to show how the health and safety issue would have triggered additional regulatory procedures or otherwise allowed the District to rescind its earlier approval."

12. Damages are usually "retrospective;" in other words, they are aimed at making up for the past. A worker fired illegally is normally entitled to reinstatement. But reinstatement may not be appropriate, as where the post has been eliminated or where the return of the worker would be unduly disruptive to the organization. *See, e.g., Dirrane v. Brookline Police Department*, 315 F.3d 65, 72 (1st Cir. 2002). In that event, the court may award "frontpay" instead. In *Hill v. City of Pontotoc*, 993 F.2d 422, 426 (5th Cir. 1993) the court affirmed an award of $30,000 compensatory damages and $103,704 frontpay to a firefighter discharged without proper procedural safeguards, based on a jury finding that "had Hill's procedural due process rights been observed, that is, had Hill been given a fair opportunity to answer [the] charges [brought against him], the City would not have fired Hill." May a court decline to award both reinstatement and frontpay? *See Stanley v. Chilhowee R-IV School District*, 5 F.3d 319, 321–22 (8th Cir. 1993) (yes). The court said:

Reinstatement and front pay are equitable remedies. . . . Ordinarily, reinstatement would follow a finding of section 1983 liability for non-renewal of a teaching contract. [But here there are special circumstances.] The Chilhowee R-IV School District is extremely small; the district has only one school building, which houses all of the approximately 150–155 students in kindergarten through twelfth grade. . . . The trial record bristles with extensive testimony about the tense and hostile atmosphere that existed at the school [that] would make future cooperation impossible. [With regard to front pay] after a jury finds section 1983 liability in a loss-of-employment case, the court must attempt to make the plaintiff whole, yet the court must avoid granting the plaintiff a windfall. . . . Here, [plaintiffs] were all probationary teachers with one-year contracts. [The] jury's award of damages compensated [them] for their lost salary and benefits for [three years]. We cannot conclude that the District Court abused its discretion in declining to award front pay, thereby limiting [their] recovery to the three school years immediately following [their] final year in the employ of the district.

Because frontpay is an "equitable" remedy, whether to award it is (as *Stanley* illustrates) a matter of discretion, and the decision is made by the judge, not the jury. *See, e.g., Ballard v. Muckogee Regional Medical Center*, 238 F.3d 1250 (10th Cir. 2001). If the benefits are speculative, such as pension benefits that would vest far in the future, the district judge may choose to deny any recovery. Thus, in *Bourdais v. New Orleans*, 485 F.3d 294, 301 (5th Cir. 2007), the court upheld a district judge's ruling against frontpay. "The dollar amount of damages attributable to the delayed pension benefits is extremely speculative, and given the uncertainty of whether the pensions will ever vest, the district court was within its discretion to find that awarding such damages would go beyond making the plaintiffs whole." When the defendant is a state government, or a state official sued in his "official capacity," the state's sovereign immunity precludes an award of frontpay, according to *Campbell v. Arkansas Department of Corrections*, 155 F.3d 950, 962 (8th Cir. 1998). Is *Campbell* a sound application of the principles of sovereign immunity?

Suppose Piphus cannot prove any emotional distress, but seeks to recover compensation for the inherent value of his right to due process. How much will he be permitted to recover after *Carey*? Why does the Court reject "presumed damages"? Are its reasons peculiar to the procedural context, or does the Court mean to foreclose all awards of presumed damages in constitutional tort cases? These issues are addressed in the following case.

MEMPHIS COMMUNITY SCHOOL
DISTRICT v. STACHURA
477 U.S. 299 (1986)

JUSTICE POWELL delivered the opinion of the Court.

This case requires us to decide whether 42 U.S.C. § 1983 authorizes an award of compensatory damages based on the factfinder's assessment of the value or importance of a substantive constitutional right.

> "[Stachura, a tenured public school teacher, showed students pictures of his wife during her pregnancy, as well as films on human growth and sexuality provided by the local health department, in a segment of a 7th grade science class devoted to human reproduction.] After the showing of the pictures and the films, a number of parents complained to school officials about respondent's teaching methods. These complaints, which appear to have been based largely on inaccurate rumors about the allegedly sexually explicit nature of the pictures and films, were discussed at an open School Board meeting held on April 23,1979. . . . The day after the meeting, [Stachura] was suspended with pay. [Stachura] sued the School District, the Board of Education, various Board members and school administrators, and two parents who had participated in the April 23 School Board meeting. The complaint alleged that respondent's suspension deprived him of both liberty and property without due process of law and violated his First Amendment right to academic freedom. [Stachura] sought compensatory and punitive damages [for] these constitutional violations."

At the close of trial on these claims, the District Court instructed the jury as to the law governing the asserted bases for liability. Turning to damages, the court instructed the jury that on finding liability it should award a sufficient amount to compensate respondent for the injury caused by petitioners' unlawful actions:

> "You should consider in this regard any lost earnings; loss of earning capacity; out-of-pocket expenses; and any mental anguish or emotional distress that you find the Plaintiff to have suffered as a result of conduct by the Defendants depriving him of his civil rights."

In addition to this instruction on the standard elements of compensatory damages, the court explained that punitive damages could be awarded, and described the standards governing punitive awards. Finally, at respondent's request and over petitioners' objection, the court charged that damages also could be awarded based on the value or importance of the constitutional rights that were violated:

> "If you find that the Plaintiff has been deprived of a Constitutional right, you may award damages to compensate him for the deprivation. Damages for this type of injury are more difficult to measure than damages for a physical injury or injury to one's property. There are no medical bills or other expenses by which you can judge how much compensation is

appropriate. In one sense, no monetary value we place upon Constitutional rights can measure their importance in our society or compensate a citizen adequately for their deprivation. However, just because these rights are not capable of precise evaluation does not mean that an appropriate monetary amount should not be awarded.

"The precise value you place upon any Constitutional right which you find was denied to Plaintiff is within your discretion. You may wish to consider the importance of the right in our system of government, the role which this right has played in the history of our republic, [and] the significance of the right in the context of the activities which the Plaintiff was engaged in at the time of the violation of the right."

The jury found petitioners liable, and awarded a total of $275,000 in compensatory damages and $46,000 in punitive damages. The District Court entered judgment notwithstanding the verdict as to one of the defendants, reducing the total award to $266,750 in compensatory damages and $36,000 in punitive damages.

[The Court of Appeals affirmed the award.] We granted certiorari limited to the question whether the Court of Appeals erred in affirming the damages award in the light of the District Court's instructions that authorized not only compensatory and punitive damages, but also damages for the deprivation of "any constitutional right." We reverse, and remand for a new trial limited to the issue of compensatory damages. . . .

The damages instructions were divided into three distinct segments: (i) compensatory damages for harm to respondent, (ii) punitive damages, and (iii) additional "compensat[ory]" damages for violations of constitutional rights. No sensible juror could read the third of these segments to modify the first. On the contrary, the damages instructions plainly authorized — in addition to punitive damages — two distinct types of "compensatory" damages: one based on respondent's actual injury according to ordinary tort law standards, and another based on the "value" of certain rights. We therefore consider whether the latter category of damages was properly before the jury. . . .

Punitive damages aside, damages in tort cases are designed to provide "compensation for the injury caused to plaintiff by defendant's breach of duty." To that end, compensatory damages may include not only out-of-pocket loss and other monetary harms, but also such injuries as "impairment of reputation, personal humiliation, and mental anguish and suffering." *Gertz v. Robert Welch, Inc.* See also *Carey v. Piphus.* Deterrence is also an important purpose of this system, but it operates through the mechanism of damages that are *compensatory* — damages grounded in determinations of plaintiffs' actual losses. *e.g.*, 4 F. Harper, F. James, & O. Gray, *Law of Torts* § 25.3 (2d ed. 1986) (discussing need for certainty in damages determinations); D. Dobbs, *Law of Remedies* § 3.1, pp. 135–136 (1973). Congress adopted this common-law system of recovery when it established liability for "constitutional torts." Consequently, "the basic purpose" of § 1983 damages is "to *compensate persons for injuries* that are caused by the deprivation of constitutional rights. . . ."

The instructions at issue here cannot be squared with *Carey*, or with the principles of tort damages on which *Carey* and § 1983 are grounded. The jurors in this case were told that, in determining how much was necessary to "compensate [respondent] for the deprivation" of his constitutional rights, they should place a money value on the "rights" themselves by considering such factors as the particular right's "importance . . . in our system of government," its role in American history, and its "significance . . . in the context of the activities" in which respondent was engaged. These factors focus, not on compensation for provable injury, but on the jury's subjective perception of the importance of constitutional rights as an abstract matter. *Carey* establishes that such an approach is impermissible. The constitutional right transgressed in *Carey* — the right to due process of law — is central to our system of ordered liberty. We nevertheless held that *no* compensatory damages could be awarded for violation of that right absent proof of actual injury. *Carey* thus makes clear that the abstract value of a constitutional right may not form the basis for § 1983 damages.

[Stachura] nevertheless argues that *Carey* does not control here, because in this case a *substantive* constitutional right — respondent's First Amendment right to academic freedom — was infringed. The argument misperceives our analysis in *Carey*. That case does not establish a two-tiered system of constitutional rights, with substantive rights afforded greater protection than "mere" procedural safeguards. We did acknowledge in *Carey* that "the elements and prerequisites for recovery of damages" might vary depending on the interests protected by the constitutional right at issue. But we emphasized that, whatever the constitutional basis for § 1983 liability, such damages must always be designed "to *compensate injuries* caused by the [constitutional] deprivation." That conclusion simply leaves no room for noncompensatory damages measured by the jury's perception of the abstract "importance" of a constitutional right.

Nor do we find such damages necessary to vindicate the constitutional rights that § 1983 protects. Section 1983 presupposes that damages that compensate for actual harm ordinarily suffice to deter constitutional violations. Moreover, damages based on the "value" of constitutional rights are an unwieldy tool for ensuring compliance with the Constitution. History and tradition do not afford any sound guidance concerning the precise value that juries should place on constitutional protections. Accordingly, were such damages available, juries would be free to award arbitrary amounts without any evidentiary basis, or to use their unbounded discretion to punish unpopular defendants. Such damages would be too uncertain to be of any great value to plaintiffs, and would inject caprice into determinations of damages in § 1983 cases. We therefore hold that damages based on the abstract "value" or "importance" of constitutional rights are not a permissible element of compensatory damages in such cases.

Respondent further argues that the challenged instructions authorized a form of "presumed" damages — a remedy that is both compensatory in nature and traditionally part of the range of tort law remedies. Alternatively, respondent argues that the erroneous instructions were at worst harmless error.

Neither argument has merit. Presumed damages are a *substitute* for ordinary compensatory damages, not a *supplement* for an award that fully compensates the alleged injury. When a plaintiff seeks compensation for an injury that is likely to have occurred but difficult to establish, some form of presumed damages may possibly be appropriate. In those circumstances, presumed damages may roughly approximate the harm that the plaintiff suffered and thereby compensate for harms that may be impossible to measure. As we earlier explained, the instructions at issue in this case did not serve this purpose, but instead called on the jury to measure damages based on a subjective evaluation of the importance of particular constitutional values. Since such damages are wholly divorced from any compensatory purpose, they cannot be justified as presumed damages.[1] Moreover, no rough substitute for compensatory damages was required in this case, since the jury was fully authorized to compensate [Stachura] for both monetary and nonmonetary harms caused by petitioners' conduct.

Nor can we find that the erroneous instructions were harmless. When damages instructions are faulty and the verdict does not reveal the means by which the jury calculated damages, "[the] error in the charge is difficult, if not impossible, to correct without retrial, in light of the jury's general verdict." The jury was authorized to award three categories of damages: (i) compensatory damages for injury to respondent, (ii) punitive damages, and (iii) damages based on the jury's perception of the "importance" of two provisions of the Constitution. The submission of the third of these categories was error. Although the verdict specified an amount for punitive damages, it did not specify how much of the remaining damages was designed to compensate respondent for his injury and how much reflected the jury's estimation of the value of the constitutional rights that were infringed. The effect of the erroneous instruction is therefore unknowable, although probably significant: the jury awarded respondent a very substantial amount of damages, none of which could have derived from any monetary loss. It is likely, although not certain, that a major part of these damages was intended to "compensate"

---

[1] [14] For the same reason, *Nixon v. Herndon* and similar cases do not support the challenged instructions. In *Nixon*, the Court held that a plaintiff who was illegally prevented from voting in a state primary election suffered compensable injury. This holding did not rest on the "value" of the right to vote as an abstract matter; rather, the Court recognized that the plaintiff had suffered a particular injury — his inability to vote in a particular election — that might be compensated through substantial money damages. See [*Nixon*] ("the petition . . . seeks to recover for private damage").

Nixon followed a long line of cases, going back to Lord Holt's decision in *Ashby v. White*, authorizing substantial money damages as compensation for persons deprived of their right to vote in particular elections. Although these decisions sometimes speak of damages for the value of the right to vote, their analysis shows that they involve nothing more than an award of presumed damages for a nonmonetary harm that cannot easily be quantified:

> "In the eyes of the law th[e] right [to vote] is so valuable that damages are presumed from the wrongful deprivation of it without evidence of actual loss of money, property, or any other valuable thing, and the amount of the damages is a question peculiarly appropriate for the determination of the jury, because each member of the jury has personal knowledge of the value of the right."

See also Ashby v. White ("As in an action for slanderous words, though a man does not lose a penny by reason of the speaking [of] them, yet he shall have an action"). The "value of the right" in the context of these decisions is the money value of the particular loss that the plaintiff suffered — a loss of which "each member of the jury has personal knowledge." It is *not* the value of the right to vote as a general, abstract matter, based on its role in our history or system of government. Thus, whatever the wisdom of these decisions in the context of the changing scope of compensatory damages over the course of this century, they do not support awards of noncompensatory damages such as those authorized in this case.

respondent for the abstract "value" of his due process and First Amendment rights. For these reasons, the case must be remanded for a new trial on compensatory damages. . . .

JUSTICE MARSHALL, with whom JUSTICE BRENNAN, JUSTICE BLACKMUN, and JUSTICE STEVENS join, concurring in the judgment.

[Certain] portions of the Court's opinion . . . can be read to suggest that damages in § 1983 cases are necessarily limited to "out-of-pocket loss," "other monetary harms," and "such injuries as 'impairment of reputation, personal humiliation, and mental anguish and suffering.' " I do not understand the Court so to hold, and I write separately to emphasize that the violation of a constitutional right, in proper cases, may itself constitute a compensable injury. . . .

Following *Carey*, the Courts of Appeals have recognized that invasions of constitutional rights sometimes cause injuries that cannot be redressed by a wooden application of common-law damages rules. In *Hobson v. Wilson*, plaintiffs claimed that defendant Federal Bureau of Investigation agents had invaded their First Amendment rights to assemble for peaceable political protest, to associate with others to engage in political expression, and to speak on public issues free of unreasonable government interference. The District Court found that the defendants had succeeded in diverting plaintiffs from, and impeding them in, their protest activities. The Court of Appeals for the District of Columbia Circuit held that injury to a First Amendment–protected interest could itself constitute compensable injury wholly apart from any "emotional distress, humiliation and personal indignity, emotional pain, embarrassment, fear, anxiety and anguish" suffered by plaintiffs. The court warned, however, that injury could be compensated with substantial damages only to the extent that it was "reasonably quantifiable"; damages should not be based on "the so-called inherent value of the rights violated."

I believe that the *Hobson* court correctly stated the law. When a plaintiff is deprived, for example, of the opportunity to engage in a demonstration to express his political views, it is facile to suggest that no damage is done. Loss of such an opportunity constitutes loss of First Amendment rights in their most pristine and classic form. There is no reason why such an injury should not be compensable in damages. At the same time, however, the award must be proportional to the actual loss sustained.

The instructions given the jury in this case were improper because they did not require the jury to focus on the loss actually sustained by respondent. Rather, they invited the jury to base its award on speculation about "the importance of the right in our system of government" and "the role which this right has played in the history of our republic," guided only by the admonition that "[i]n one sense, no monetary value we place on Constitutional rights can measure their importance in our society or compensate a citizen adequately for their deprivation." These instructions invited the jury to speculate on matters wholly detached from the real injury occasioned respondent by the deprivation of the right. Further, the instructions might have led the jury to grant respondent damages based on the "abstract value" of the right to procedural due process — a course directly barred by our decision in *Carey*.

The Court therefore properly remands for a new trial on damages. I do not understand the Court, however, to hold that deprivations of constitutional rights can never themselves constitute compensable injuries. Such a rule would be inconsistent with the logic of *Carey*, and would defeat the purpose of § 1983 by denying compensation for genuine injuries caused by the deprivation of constitutional rights.

NOTES

1. Does the Court hold that presumed damages are unavailable in section 1983 suits brought to recover for First Amendment violations? Based on the reasoning set forth in the opinion, what arguments might be advanced on either side of that question? Did the Court accurately characterize the instruction that it found faulty? Did it endorse the old cases, cited in footnote 14, allowing damages for loss of the right to vote? Are those cases properly viewed as presumed damages cases? Courts do continue to award substantial damages for voting rights violations. *See Taylor v. Howe*, 280 F.3d 1210 (8th Cir. 2002) (affirming awards of $500 to $2000 to each of seven plaintiffs).

For one view, see Jean Love, *Presumed General Damages in Constitutional Tort Litigation*, 49 WASH. & LEE L. REV. 67, 80 (1992) (arguing that "although the court will not recognize presumed general damages for *abstract deprivations* of constitutional rights, the Court might be willing to allow the recovery of presumed general damages for certain *intangible injuries* caused by violations of constitutional rights" such as the right to vote) (emphasis in original).

After *Stachura* some courts remain receptive to presumed damages. *See, e.g., Siebert v. Severino*, 256 F.3d 648, 655 (7th Cir. 2001) ("The law recognizes that law-abiding citizens can sue and recover general (or presumed) damages for a Fourth Amendment violation, even without proof of injury."); *Trevino v. Gates*, 99 F.3d 911, 921 (9th Cir. 1996) (approving district judge's refusal of a presumed damages instruction, but citing *Carey* for the proposition that "[p]resumed damages are appropriate when there is a great likelihood of injury coupled with great difficulty of proving damages"); *Walje v. City of Winchester*, 827 F.2d 10 (6th Cir. 1987) (upholding a $5,000 presumed damages award to a plaintiff government employee who was suspended in violation of his First Amendment rights).

By contrast, some cases hold that under *Stachura* the plaintiff has the burden of proving actual harm, and cannot recover substantial damages merely because his constitutional rights were violated. In *Norwood v. Bain*, 143 F.3d 843, 855 (4th Cir. 1998), the district court declined to award any damages for a Fourth Amendment violation arising from warrantless searches of motorcyclists' clothing, saddlebags and motorcycles, at a police checkpoint at the entrance to a motorcycle rally. The appellate court affirmed. After citing *Carey* and *Stachura* for the proposition that one can recover damages "only for any actual harms caused by the violation and not for the violation standing alone," the court reasoned:

> The only evidence of emotional distress came in the form of testimony by Norwood and four other class members that they felt annoyance, humiliation, and indignity at being subjected to the searches. None testified that their emotional upset was caused by oppressive or threatening conduct by

the checkpoint officers; instead, from all that appears, that conduct was civil and non-threatening throughout the process. Under the circumstances, we agree with the district court that this testimony failed to prove emotional distress other than any that may have been experienced as a sense of indignity from the very violation of a constitutional right. And that, as indicated, is not a compensable harm in § 1983 litigation.

Siebert and *Norwood* seem irreconcilable. Which of these cases better reflects the principles laid down in *Carey* and *Stachura*?

2. Putting aside the problem of interpreting the ambiguous opinion in *Stachura*, another interesting question regarding presumed damages and constitutional violations is the normative one: *Should* presumed damages be available in section 1983 cases?

Granting the correctness of the Court's holding in *Carey*, that a violation of procedural due process is a different sort of injury for which presumed damages are not appropriate, how should courts deal with substantive rights like freedom of speech and religion, the right against unreasonable searches and seizures, the right not to be subjected to cruel and unusual punishments, and the substantive due process right against arbitrary acts by government officers? Sometimes these violations produce physical injuries, loss of a job, emotional distress, and other more or less quantifiable injuries. Should these quantifiable losses exhaust the recovery available to someone injured by substantive constitutional violations? Should persons who suffer violations that produce no such consequences go without a substantial award?

Common law courts have long allowed presumed damages for "dignitary" torts, such as assault, battery, malicious prosecution, defamation, and invasion of privacy. *See* D. Dobbs, Law of Remedies § 7.3 at 635 (2d ed. 1993). Can a person who has suffered no provable emotional distress as a result of unlawfully being forbidden to demonstrate, for example, credibly argue that he has suffered any injury? *Compare Doe v. Santa Fe Independent School District*, 168 F.3d 806, 824 (5th Cir. 1999) (plaintiff, who offered no proof of emotional distress, suffered no compensable injury as a result of teacher's establishment clause violation in handing out religious literature in class).

3. Defamation is a lively area of contemporary tort law. Because recovery for defamation may threaten freedom of speech, presumed damages is one area that has received attention from the Supreme Court. Perhaps some useful comparisons and contrasts can be drawn between defamation and constitutional tort with respect to the role of presumed damages. The rationale for presumed damages in defamation law is that the harm done to one's reputation by a defamatory publication, especially a writing that is defamatory on its face, will likely be hard to trace. No one can tell who might read the libel and be deterred from dealing with the plaintiff. Consequently, effective compensation for the injury would be thwarted if the plaintiff were required to offer proof of actual harm. *See Dun & Bradstreet, Inc. v. Greenmoss Builders, Inc.*, 472 U.S. 749, 760–61 (1985). Does this rationale apply to denials of freedom of speech?

If violations of substantive constitutional rights do not produce harm by their insidious effects on unknown persons, it may be misleading to compare them to defamation. Does it follow that presumed damages are inappropriate? Given that the harm constitutional violations produce does not entail any impact on others, are there other grounds for favoring presumed damages in constitutional tort cases? Isn't the harm resulting from a constitutional violation even more inchoate, even harder to prove, and consequently more deserving of presumed damages, than the harm to reputation produced by libel per se?

In the defamation context the Supreme Court has restricted the availability of presumed damages. If the subject matter of the defamation is of public concern, or the plaintiff is a public figure or public official, they may be awarded only upon a showing that the defendant knew the statement was false or acted with reckless disregard of its truth or falsity. *See* Douglas Laycock, Modern American Remedies 187 (4th ed. 2010). What is the relevance of this development to the role of presumed damages for constitutional torts? Do constitutional values bear on the two contexts in the same way, thereby suggesting similar limits on presumed damages in section 1983 cases?

One reason for restrictions on presumed damages in the defamation context, adverted to by *Stachura*, is that juries are "free to award arbitrary amounts without any evidentiary basis, or to use their unbounded discretion to punish unpopular defendants." 477 U.S. at 310 (citing *Gertz v. Robert E. Welch*, 418 U.S. 323 (1974), a defamation case in which the Court held that private plaintiffs may not recover punitive damages without showing reckless disregard of truth or falsity). Is the danger that presumed damages would be used to punish unpopular defendants as great in the section 1983 context as it is in libel?

B. Punitive Damages

SMITH v. WADE
461 U.S. 30 (1983)

Justice Brennan delivered the opinion of the Court.

We granted certiorari in this case to decide whether the District Court for the Western District of Missouri applied the correct legal standard in instructing the jury that it might award punitive damages under 42 U.S.C. § 1983. The Court of Appeals for the Eighth Circuit sustained the award of punitive damages. We affirm.

The petitioner, William H. Smith, is a guard at Algoa Reformatory, a unit of the Missouri Division of Corrections for youthful first offenders. The respondent, Daniel R. Wade, was assigned to Algoa as an inmate in 1976. In the summer of 1976 Wade voluntarily checked into Algoa's protective custody unit. Because of disciplinary violations during his stay in protective custody, Wade was given a short term in punitive segregation and then transferred to administrative segregation. On the evening of Wade's first day in administrative segregation, he was placed in a cell with another inmate. Later, when Smith came on duty in Wade's dormitory, he placed a third inmate in Wade's cell. According to Wade's testimony, his cellmates harassed, beat, and sexually assaulted him.

Wade brought suit under 42 U.S.C. § 1983 against Smith and four other guards and correctional officials, alleging that his Eighth Amendment rights had been violated. At trial his evidence showed that he had placed himself in protective custody because of prior incidents of violence against him by other inmates. The third prisoner whom Smith added to the cell had been placed in administrative segregation for fighting. Smith had made no effort to find out whether another cell was available; in fact there was another cell in the same dormitory with only one occupant. Further, only a few weeks earlier, another inmate had been beaten to death in the same dormitory during the same shift, while Smith had been on duty. Wade asserted that Smith and the other defendants knew or should have known that an assault against him was likely under the circumstances.

[T]he District Judge . . . instructed the jury that Wade could make out an Eighth Amendment violation only by showing "physical abuse of such base, inhumane and barbaric proportions as to shock the sensibilities." Further, because of Smith's qualified immunity as a prison guard, the judge instructed the jury that Wade could recover only if the defendants were guilty of "gross negligence" (defined as "a callous indifference or a thoughtless disregard for the consequences of one's act or failure to act") or "[e]gregious failure to protect" (defined as "a flagrant or remarkably bad failure to protect") Wade. He reiterated that Wade could not recover on a showing of simple negligence.

The District Judge also charged the jury that it could award punitive damages on a proper showing:

> "In addition to actual damages, the law permits the jury, under certain circumstances, to award the injured person punitive and exemplary damages, in order to punish the wrongdoer for some extraordinary misconduct, and to serve as an example or warning to others not to engage in such conduct.

> "If you find the issues in favor of the plaintiff, and if the conduct of one or more of the defendants is shown to be *a reckless or callous disregard of, or indifference to, the rights or safety of others*, then you may assess punitive or exemplary damages in addition to any award of actual damages. . . .

> "The amount of punitive or exemplary damages assessed against any defendant may be such sum as you believe will serve to punish that defendant and to deter him and others from like conduct."

[The jury] found Smith liable and awarded $25,000 in compensatory damages and $5,000 in punitive damages. The District Court entered judgment on the verdict, and the Court of Appeals affirmed.

In this Court, Smith attacks only the award of punitive damages. He does not challenge the correctness of the instructions on liability or qualified immunity, nor does he question the adequacy of the evidence to support the verdict of liability for compensatory damages.

Section 1983 [was] intended to create "a species of tort liability" in favor of persons deprived of federally secured rights. We noted in *Carey* that there was little in the section's legislative history concerning the damages recoverable for this tort liability.

In the absence of more specific guidance, we looked first to the common law of torts (both modern and as of 1871), with such modification or adaptation as might be necessary to carry out the purpose and policy of the statute. We have done the same in other contexts arising under § 1983, especially the recurring problem of common-law immunities.

Smith correctly concedes that "punitive damages are available in a 'proper' § 1983 action." Although there was debate about the theoretical correctness of the punitive damages doctrine in the latter part of the last century, the doctrine was accepted as settled law by nearly all state and federal courts, including this Court. It was likewise generally established that individual public officers were liable for punitive damages for their misconduct on the same basis as other individual defendants. Further, although the precise issue of the availability of punitive damages under § 1983 has never come squarely before us, we have had occasion more than once to make clear our view that they are available; indeed, we have rested decisions on related questions on the premise of such availability.

Smith argues, nonetheless, that this was not a "proper" case in which to award punitive damages. More particularly, he attacks the instruction that punitive damages could be awarded on a finding of reckless or callous disregard of or indifference to Wade's rights or safety. Instead, he contends that the proper test is one of actual malicious intent — "ill will, spite, or intent to injure." He offers two arguments for this position: first, that actual intent is the proper standard for punitive damages in all cases under § 1983; and second, that even if intent is not always required, it should be required here because the threshold for punitive damages should always be higher than that for liability in the first instance. We address these in turn.

Smith does not argue that the common law, either in 1871 or now, required or requires a showing of actual malicious intent for recovery of punitive damages.

Perhaps not surprisingly, there was significant variation (both terminological and substantive) among American jurisdictions in the latter 19th century on the precise standard to be applied in awarding punitive damages-variation that was exacerbated by the ambiguity and slipperiness of such common terms as "malice" and "gross negligence." Most of the confusion, however, seems to have been over the degree of negligence, recklessness, carelessness, or culpable indifference that should be required — not over whether actual intent was essential. On the contrary, the rule in a large majority of jurisdictions was that punitive damages (also called exemplary damages, vindictive damages, or smart money) could be awarded without a showing of actual ill will, spite, or intent to injure.

This Court so stated on several occasions, before and shortly after 1871. [Here the Court reviewed some of its nineteenth century punitive damages cases.]

The large majority of state and lower federal courts were in agreement that punitive damages awards did not require a showing of actual malicious intent; they permitted punitive awards on variously stated standards of negligence, recklessness, or other culpable conduct short of actual malicious intent.[2]

The same rule applies today. *The Restatement (Second) of Torts* (1979), for example, states: "Punitive damages may be awarded for conduct that is outrageous, because of the defendant's evil motive *or his reckless indifference to the rights of others*." § 908(2) (emphasis added). Most cases under state common law, although varying in their precise terminology, have adopted more or less the same rule, recognizing that punitive damages in tort cases may be awarded not only for actual intent to injure or evil motive, but also for recklessness, serious indifference to or disregard for the rights of others, or even gross negligence.

The remaining question is whether the policies and purposes of § 1983 itself require a departure from the rules of tort common law. As a general matter, we discern no reason why a person whose federally guaranteed rights have been violated should be granted a more restrictive remedy than a person asserting an ordinary tort cause of action. Smith offers us no persuasive reason to the contrary.

Smith's argument, which he offers in several forms, is that an actual-intent standard is preferable to a recklessness standard because it is less vague. He points out that punitive damages, by their very nature, are not awarded to compensate the injured party. He concedes, of course, that deterrence of future egregious conduct is a primary purpose of both § 1983, and of punitive damages. But deterrence, he contends, cannot be achieved unless the standard of conduct sought to be deterred is stated with sufficient clarity to enable potential defendants to conform to the law and to avoid the proposed sanction. Recklessness or callous indifference, he argues, is too uncertain a standard to achieve deterrence rationally and fairly. A prison guard, for example, can be expected to know whether he is acting with actual ill will or intent to injure, but not whether he is being reckless or callously indifferent.

Smith's argument, if valid, would apply to ordinary tort cases as easily as to § 1983 suits; hence, it hardly presents an argument for adopting a different rule under § 1983. In any event, the argument is unpersuasive. While, arguendo, an intent standard may be easier to understand and apply to particular situations than a recklessness standard, we are not persuaded that a recklessness standard is too vague to be fair or useful. In the *Milwaukee* case, 91 U.S. 489 (1876), we adopted a recklessness standard rather than a gross negligence standard precisely because recklessness would better serve the need for adequate clarity and fair application.

---

[2] [12] In the often-cited case of *Welch v. Durand*, for example, the court held that punitive damages were proper where the defendant's pistol bullet, fired at a target, ricocheted and hit the plaintiff:

> "In what cases then may smart money be awarded in addition to the damages? The proper answer to this question . . . seems to be, in actions of tort founded on the malicious or wanton misconduct or culpable neglect of the defendant . . .

> "In this case the defendant was guilty of wanton misconduct and culpable neglect . . . It is an immaterial fact that the injury was unintentional, and that the ball glanced from the intended direction . . . [If] the act is done where there are objects from which the balls may glance and endanger others, the act is wanton, reckless, without due care, and grossly negligent." *Id.* . . .

[The remainder of the footnote discusses other nineteenth century cases and maintains that "Justice Rehnquist's assertion that a "solid majority of jurisdictions' required actual malicious standard is simply untrue."]

Almost a century later, in the First Amendment context, we held that punitive damages cannot be assessed for defamation in the absence of proof of "knowledge of falsity or reckless disregard for the truth." Our concern [was] that the threat of punitive damages, if not limited to especially egregious cases, might "inhibit the vigorous exercise of First Amendment freedoms," — a concern at least as pressing as any urged by Smith in this case. Yet we did not find it necessary to impose an actual-intent standard there. Just as Smith has not shown why § 1983 should give higher protection from punitive damages than ordinary tort law, he has not explained why it gives higher protection than we have demanded under the First Amendment.

More fundamentally, Smith's argument for certainty in the interest of deterrence overlooks the distinction between a standard for punitive damages and a standard of liability in the first instance. Smith seems to assume that prison guards and other state officials look mainly to the standard for punitive damages in shaping their conduct. We question the premise; we assume, and hope, that most officials are guided primarily by the underlying standards of federal substantive law — both out of devotion to duty, and in the interest of avoiding liability for compensatory damages. At any rate, the conscientious officer who desires clear guidance on how to do his job and avoid lawsuits can and should look to the standard for actionability in the first instance. The need for exceptional clarity in the standard for punitive damages arises only if one assumes that there are substantial numbers of officers who will not be deterred by compensatory damages; only such officers will seek to guide their conduct by the punitive damages standard. The presence of such officers constitutes a powerful argument *against* raising the threshold for punitive damages. . . .

[I]n the absence of any persuasive argument to the contrary based on the policies of § 1983, we are content to adopt the policy judgment of the common law-that reckless or callous disregard for the plaintiff's rights, as well as intentional violations of federal law, should be sufficient to trigger a jury's consideration of the appropriateness of punitive damages.

Smith contends that even if § 1983 does not ordinarily require a showing of actual malicious intent for an award of punitive damages, such a showing should be required in this case. He argues that the deterrent and punitive purposes of punitive damages are served only if the threshold for punitive damages is higher in every case than the underlying standard for liability in the first instance. In this case, while the District Judge did not use the same precise terms to explain the standards of liability for compensatory and punitive damages, the parties agree that there is no substantial difference between the showings required by the two instructions; both apply a standard of reckless or callous indifference to Wade's rights. Hence, Smith argues, the District Judge erred in not requiring a higher standard for punitive damages, namely, actual malicious intent.

This argument incorrectly assumes that, simply because the instructions specified the same threshold of liability for punitive and compensatory damages, the two forms of damages were equally available to the plaintiff. The argument overlooks a key feature of punitive damages-that they are never awarded as of right, no matter how egregious the defendant's conduct. "If the plaintiff proves sufficiently serious misconduct on the defendant's part, the question whether to award punitive damages is left to the jury, which may or may not make such an award." D. Dobbs, *Law of Remedies* 204 (1973) (footnote omitted). Compensatory damages, by contrast, are mandatory; once liability is found, the jury is required to award compensatory damages in an amount appropriate to compensate the plaintiff for his loss. Hence, it is not entirely accurate to say that punitive and compensatory damages were awarded in this case on the same standard. To make its punitive award, the jury was required to find not only that Smith's conduct met the recklessness threshold (a question of ultimate fact), but *also* that his conduct merited a punitive award of $5,000 in addition to the compensatory award (a discretionary moral judgment).

Moreover, the rules of ordinary tort law are once more against Smith's argument. There has never been any general common-law rule that the threshold for punitive damages must always be higher than that for compensatory liability. On the contrary, both the *First* and *Second Restatements of Torts* have pointed out that "in torts like malicious prosecution that require a particular antisocial state of mind, the improper motive of the tortfeasor is both a necessary element in the cause of action and a reason for awarding punitive damages." Accordingly, in situations where the standard for compensatory liability is as high as or higher than the usual threshold for punitive damages, most courts will permit awards of punitive damages without requiring any extra showing. . . .

This common-law rule makes sense in terms of the purposes of punitive damages. . . . The focus is on the character of the tortfeasor's conduct — whether it is of the sort that calls for deterrence and punishment over and above that provided by compensatory awards. If it is of such a character, then it is appropriate to allow a jury to assess punitive damages; and that assessment does not become less appropriate simply because the plaintiff in the case faces a more demanding standard of actionability. . . . As with his first argument, Smith gives us no good reason to depart from the common-law rule in the context of § 1983.

We hold that a jury may be permitted to assess punitive damages in an action under § 1983 when the defendant's conduct is shown to be motivated by evil motive or intent, or when it involves reckless or callous indifference to the federally protected rights of others. We further hold that this threshold applies even when the underlying standard of liability for compensatory damages is one of reckless-ness. Because the jury instructions in this case are in accord with this rule, the judgment of the Court of Appeals is *affirmed.*

JUSTICE REHNQUIST, with whom THE CHIEF JUSTICE and JUSTICE POWELL join, dissenting.

[In] my view, a forthright inquiry into the intent of the 42d Congress and a balanced consideration of the public policies at issue compel the conclusion that the proper standard for an award of punitive damages under § 1983 requires at least some degree of bad faith or improper motive on the part of the defendant. . . .

[I]t is useful to consider briefly the purposes of punitive damages. A fundamental premise of our legal system is the notion that damages are awarded to *compensate* the victim — to redress the injuries that he or she *actually* has suffered. In sharp contrast to this principle, the doctrine of punitive damages permits the award of "damages" beyond even the most generous and expansive conception of actual injury to the plaintiff. This anomaly is rationalized principally on three grounds. First, punitive damages "are assessed for the avowed purpose of visiting a *punishment* upon the defendant." Second, the doctrine is rationalized on the ground that it deters persons from violating the rights of others. Third, punitive damages are justified as a "bounty" that encourages private lawsuits seeking to assert legal rights.

Despite these attempted justifications, the doctrine of punitive damages has been vigorously criticized throughout the Nation's history. Countless cases remark that such damages have never been "a favorite of the law. . . ."

Punitive damages are generally seen as a windfall to plaintiffs, who are entitled to receive full compensation for their injuries — but no more. Even assuming that a punitive "fine" should be imposed after a civil trial, the penalty should go to the State, not to the plaintiff-who by hypothesis is fully compensated. Moreover, although punitive damages are "quasi-criminal," their imposition is unaccompanied by the types of safeguards present in criminal proceedings. This absence of safeguards is exacerbated by the fact that punitive damages are frequently based upon the caprice and prejudice of jurors. . . . Finally, the alleged deterrence achieved by punitive damages awards is likely outweighed by the costs — such as the encouragement of unnecessary litigation and the chilling of desirable conduct — flowing from the rule, at least when the standards on which the awards are based are ill-defined.

[Justice Rehnquist argued that, since the issue was one of statutory interpretation, the intent of the 42nd Congress was the key to resolving it. Accordingly, recourse to common law decisions should be limited to doctrine with which the members of that Congress would have been familiar. The availability of punitive damages should depend on the state of the law in 1871. After examining a number of cases, he concluded that at that time the Supreme Court and most state courts "took the view that the standard for an award of punitive damages included a requirement of ill will."]

Finally, even if the evidence of congressional intent were less clearcut, I would be persuaded to resolve any ambiguity in favor of an actual-malice standard. It scarcely needs repeating that punitive damages are not a "favorite of the law," owing to the numerous persuasive criticisms that have been leveled against the doctrine. The majority reasons that these arguments apply to all awards of punitive damages, not just to those under § 1983; while this is of course correct, it does little to reduce the strength of the arguments, and, if they are persuasive, we should not blindly follow the mistakes other courts have made.

Much of what has been said above regarding the failings of a punitive damages remedy is equally appropriate here. It is anomalous, and counter to deep-rooted legal principles and common-sense notions, to punish persons who meant no harm, and to award a windfall, in the form of punitive damages, to someone who already has been fully compensated. These peculiarities ought to be carefully limited — not expanded to every case where a jury may think a defendant was too careless, particularly where a vaguely defined, elastic standard like "reckless indifference" gives free reign to the biases and prejudices of juries. In short, there are persuasive reasons not to create a new punitive damages remedy unless it is clear that Congress so intended.

This argument is particularly powerful in a case like this, where the uncertainty resulting from largely random awards of punitive damages will have serious effects upon the performance by state and local officers of their official duties. One of the principal themes of our immunity decisions is that the threat of liability must not deter an official's "willingness to execute his office with the decisiveness and the judgment required by the public good." To avoid stifling the types of initiative and decisiveness necessary for the "government to govern," we have held that officials will be liable for compensatory damages only for certain types of conduct. Precisely the same reasoning applies to liability for punitive damages. Because punitive damages generally are not subject to any relation to actual harm suffered, and because the recklessness standard is so imprecise, the remedy poses an even greater threat to the ability of officials to take decisive, efficient action. After the Court's decision, governmental officials will be subjected to the possibility of damages awards unlimited by any harm they may have caused or the fact they acted with unquestioned good faith: when swift action is demanded, their thoughts likely will be on personal financial consequences that may result from their conduct — but whose limits they cannot predict — and not upon their official duties. It would have been difficult for the Court to have fashioned a more effective Damoclean sword than the open-ended, standardless, and unpredictable liability it creates today.

Moreover, notwithstanding the Court's inability to discern them, there are important distinctions between a right to damages under § 1983 and a similar right under state tort law. A leading rationale seized upon by proponents of punitive damages to justify the doctrine is that "the award is . . . a covert response to the legal system's overt refusal to provide financing for litigation."

Yet, 42 U.S.C. § 1988 provides not just a "covert response" to plaintiffs' litigation expenses but an explicit provision for an award to the prevailing party in a § 1983 action of "a reasonable attorney's fee as part of the costs." By permitting punitive damages *as well* as attorney's fees, § 1983 plaintiffs, unlike state tort law plaintiffs, get not just one windfall but two — one for them, and one for their lawyer. This difference between the incentives that are present in state tort actions, and those in § 1983 actions, makes the Court's reliance upon the standard for punitive damages in the former entirely inapposite: in fashioning a new financial lure to litigate under § 1983 the Court does not act in a vacuum, but, by adding to existing incentives, creates an imbalance of inducements to litigate that may have serious consequences.

The staggering effect of § 1983 claims upon the work load of the federal courts has been decried time and again. The torrent of frivolous claims under that section threatens to incapacitate the judicial system's resolution of claims where true injustice is involved; those claims which truly warrant redress are in a very real danger of being lost in a sea of meritless suits. Yet, apparently oblivious to this, the Court today reads into the silent, inhospitable terms of § 1983 a remedy that is designed to serve as a "bounty" to encourage private litigation. In a time when the courts are flooded with suits that do not raise colorable claims, in large part because of the existing incentives for litigation under § 1983, it is regrettable that the Court should take upon itself, in apparent disregard for the likely intent of the 42nd Congress, the legislative task of encouraging yet more litigation. There is a limit to what the federal judicial system can bear.

Finally, by unquestioningly transferring the standard of punitive damages in *state* tort actions to *federal* § 1983 actions, the Court utterly fails to recognize the fundamental difference that exists between an award of punitive damages by a federal court, acting under § 1983, and a similar award by a state court acting under prevailing local laws. While state courts may choose to adopt such measures as they deem appropriate to punish offices of the jurisdiction in which they sit, the standards they choose to adopt can scarcely be taken as evidence of what it is appropriate for a federal court to do. When federal courts enforce punitive damages awards against local officials they intrude into sensitive areas of sovereignty of coordinate branches of our Nation, thus implicating the most basic values of our system of federalism. Moreover, by yet further distorting the incentives that exist for litigating claims against local officials in federal court, as opposed to state courts, the Court's decision makes it even more difficult for state courts to attempt to conform the conduct of state officials to the Constitution.

JUSTICE **O'CONNOR**, dissenting.

Although I agree with the result reached in Justice Rehnquist's dissent, I write separately because I cannot agree with the approach taken by either the Court or Justice Rehnquist. Both opinions engage in exhaustive, but ultimately unilluminating, exegesis of the common law of the availability of punitive damages in 1871. Although both the Court and Justice Rehnquist display admirable skills in legal research and analysis of great numbers of musty cases, the results do not significantly further the goal of the inquiry: to establish the intent of the 42d Congress. In interpreting § 1983, we have often looked to the common law as it existed in 1871, in the belief that, when Congress was silent on a point, it intended to adopt the principles of the common law with which it was familiar. This approach makes sense when there was a generally prevailing rule of common law, for then it is reasonable to assume that Congressmen were familiar with that rule and imagined that it would cover the cause of action that they were creating. But when a significant split in authority existed, it strains credulity to argue that Congress simply assumed that one view rather than the other would govern. Particularly in a case like this one, in which those interpreting the common law of 1871 must resort to dictionaries in an attempt to translate the language of the late 19th century into terms that judges of the late 20th century can understand, and in an area in which the courts of the earlier period frequently used inexact and contradictory language, we cannot safely infer anything about congressional intent from the divided contemporaneous judicial opinions. The battle of the string citations can have no winner.

Once it is established that the common law of 1871 provides us with no real guidance on this question, we should turn to the policies underlying § 1983 to determine which rule best accords with those policies. [We have] identified the purposes of § 1983 as pre-eminently to compensate victims of constitutional violations and to deter further violations. The conceded availability of compensatory damages, particularly when coupled with the availability of attorney's fees under § 1988, completely fulfills the goal of compensation, leaving only deterrence to be served by awards of punitive damages. We must then confront the close question whether a standard permitting an award of unlimited punitive damages on the basis of recklessness will chill public officials in the performance of their duties more than it will deter violations of the Constitution, and whether the availability of punitive damages for reckless violations of the Constitution in addition to attorney's fees will create an incentive to bring an ever-increasing flood of § 1983 claims, threatening the ability of the federal courts to handle those that are meritorious. Although I cannot concur in Justice Rehnquist's wholesale condemnation of awards of punitive damages in any context or with the suggestion that punitive damages should not be available even for intentional or malicious violations of constitutional rights, I do agree with the discussion in Part V of his opinion of the special problems of permitting awards of punitive damages for the recklessness of public officials. Since awards of compensatory damages and attorney's fees already provide significant deterrence, I am persuaded that the policies counseling against awarding punitive damages for the recklessness of public officials outweigh the desirability of any incremental deterrent effect that such awards may have. Consequently, I dissent.

NOTES

1. *City of Newport v. Fact Concerts, Inc.*, 453 U.S. 247 (1981), decided two years before *Smith*, held that municipal governments are immune from liability for punitive damages. It relied upon both "the common-law background and policy considerations."

First, the Court examined nineteenth century tort law and concluded that "[b]y the time Congress enacted what is now section 1983, the immunity of a municipal corporation from punitive damages at common law was not open to serious question." Turning to policy, the Court noted that punitive damages "are not intended to compensate the injured party, but rather to punish the tortfeasor whose wrongful action was intentional or malicious, and to deter him and others from similar extreme conduct." It declared that "punitive damages imposed on a municipality are in effect a windfall to a fully compensated plaintiff, and are likely accompanied by an increase in taxes or a reduction of public services for the citizens footing the bill. Neither reason nor justice suggests that such retribution should be visited upon the shoulders of blameless or unknowing taxpayers."

Insofar as the aim of punitive damages is deterrence of wrongdoing rather than retribution, the court noted:

> [I]t is far from clear that municipal officials . . . would be deterred from wrongdoing by the knowledge that large punitive awards could be assessed based on the wealth of their municipality . . . .

> Moreover, there is available a more effective means of deterrence. By allowing juries and courts to assess punitive damages in appropriate circumstances against the offending official . . . the statute directly

advances the public's interest in preventing repeated constitutional deprivations . . . .

Finally, although the benefits associated with awarding punitive damages against municipalities under section 1983 are of doubtful character,
the costs may be very real [especially since statutory as well as constitutional violations may be redressed under the statute.] Under this expanded
liability, municipalities and other units of state and local government face
the possibility of having to assure compensation for persons harmed by
abuses of governmental authority covering a large range of activity in
everyday life. To add the burden of exposure for the malicious conduct of
individual government employees may create a serious risk to the financial
integrity of these governmental entities.

To what extent is the holding in *Smith v. Wade* based on the reasoning behind
City of Newport?

Given the reasoning of *City of Newport*, should municipal governments be
permitted to indemnify their employees against liability for punitive damages? In
Cornwell v. City of Riverside, 896 F.2d 398, 399 (9th Cir. 1990), the plaintiff sought
to compel the individual defendants to pay the damages but the court held that
"there is no federal prohibition against the city paying the punitive damages."

In *Cornwell*, a local government exercised its option under state law to pay
punitive damages awards against police officers because it determined that they
acted within the scope of their employment, in good faith, and in its best interests.
The Ninth Circuit observed that this result was not in conflict with federal policy.
It said that if the result were otherwise, there would be cases where punitive
damages awards in favor of section 1983 plaintiffs would go unsatisfied because
individual defendants could be judgment proof. Furthermore, giving the option to
plaintiffs to accept or reject such payments from local governments would provide
plaintiffs with an "extraordinary weapon" for negotiation purposes.

Despite the Ninth Circuit's opinion, doesn't *Cornwell* in fact undercut the
punitive function of section 1983 punitive damages awards? Does it undercut their
deterrent function? How would federal courts administer a contrary rule? Could
they stop wealthy individuals from reimbursing police officers for punitive damages?

Assuming that indemnification is permissible, how, if at all, should the indemnification be taken into account in calculating the amount to be awarded?

See Bell v. Clackamas County, 341 F.3d 858, 868 (9th Cir. 2003) (ruling that "to
the degree that defendants seek reduction of punitive damages because of their
inability to pay, any indemnification by the County for the payment of such damages
may be taken into account"). In *Mathie v. Fries*, 121 F.3d 808, 816 (2d Cir. 1997), the
court did "not decide the question of whether a fact-finder can rely upon the
existence of an indemnity agreement in order to *increase* the award of punitive
damages," but it did "rule that a fact-finder can properly consider the existence of
such an agreement as obviating the need to determine whether a defendant's
limited financial resources justifies some *reduction* in the amount that would
otherwise be awarded." What is the difference between the question the court

decided and the one it deferred? A later Second Circuit case seems to treat the availability of indemnification as a ground for reducing the punitive award, as "it is the taxpaying public that bears the brunt of an excessive award, which compounds the injury done by the tortfeasor." *Payne v. Jones*, 711 F.3d 85, 95 (2d Cir. 2013).

Suppose a municipality's governing body (for example, a county board of supervisors) decides to indemnify employees for punitive damages awards. Do the board members thereby risk being held liable for having facilitated constitutional violations on the part of the officers they have protected? *See Navarro v. Block*, 250 F.3d 729 (9th Cir. 2001) (upholding, against a motion to dismiss, a complaint that alleged that the county supervisors could be liable if they acted in bad faith in indemnifying police officers for punitive damages).

Does *City of Newport* give due weight to the deterrence rationale for punitive damages? *See Ciraolo v. City of New York*, 216 F.3d 236, 243 (2d Cir. 2000) (Calabresi, J., concurring). Judge Calabresi argued that "[t]he Court's analysis . . . neglected at least one aspect of the deterrence function of punitive damages." He explained:

> Punitive damages can ensure that a wrongdoer bears all the costs of its actions, and is thus appropriately deterred from causing harm, in those categories of cases in which compensatory damages alone result in systematic underassessment of costs, and hence in systematic underdeterrence." In *Ciraolo*, for example, the constitutional violation was a strip-search policy for all persons arrested for misdemeanors. "Counsel for the City estimated at trial that about 65,000 people arrested for misdemeanors had been subjected to strip searches under the policy. Under ordinary circumstances, very few of those 65,000 victims would have been likely to sue, both because the compensatory damages they would have received would have been relatively low and because they were, no doubt, in the main, relatively poor and unsophisticated."

In a footnote, *City of Newport* held out the possibility that a municipality might yet be held liable for punitive damages: "It is perhaps possible to imagine an extreme situation where the taxpayers are directly responsible for perpetrating an outrageous abuse of constitutional rights. Nothing of that kind is presented by this case. Moreover, such an occurrence is sufficiently unlikely that we need not anticipate it here." 453 U.S. at 267 n.29. Can you think of circumstances that would justify an exception to the rule? Suppose the voters enacted laws mandating racial discrimination. Could the municipality defend (against punitive damages) on the ground that its taxpayers cannot fairly be held responsible for the actions of the voters?

Besides the possible footnote 29 exception, the municipality may be deemed to have waived the immunity. *See Saldana-Sanchez v. Lopez-Gerena*, 256 F.3d 1 (1st Cir. 2001), where plaintiffs "articulated plausible grounds supporting a possible waiver of immunity," by asserting that the municipal council had passed resolutions "indicting a consent to pay the full judgment, including punitive damages."

Though *City of Newport* will ordinarily place no obstacles in the way of the recovery of punitive damages against city *officials*, such as the mayor or the police chief, one special case should be noted. When a plaintiff sues officials solely in their "official capacity" (as opposed to their "individual capacity"), the suit is treated as a suit against the municipality. It follows that the plaintiff may not obtain punitive damages against the officials. *See, e.g., Mitchell v. Dupnik*, 75 F.3d 517, 527 (9th Cir. 1995). One may avoid falling into this trap by taking care always to sue an official in his "individual capacity" and, in the event one wishes to sue the municipality, accomplish that goal simply by naming it as a defendant.

See Chapter 5 for a treatment of local government liability.

2. Under the reasoning of *Smith*, is it necessary that compensatory damages be recovered in order to receive punitive damages? *See Caban-Wheeler v. Elsea*, 71 F.3d 837 (11th Cir. 1996) (affirming award of $1 in nominal damages and $100,000 in punitive damages for a procedural due process violation in connection with her termination where the plaintiff "presented evidence from which a reasonable jury could conclude, first, that the defendants maliciously, wantonly, or oppressively quashed subpoenas at the review hearing, and second, that portions of the tape recording from the hearing were maliciously, wantonly, or oppressively erased").

What is the bearing of *BMW v. Gore*, 517 U.S. 559 (1996), on this issue? In that case, the plaintiff sued for deceptive trade practices when he was sold a BMW that, unknown to him, had been scratched in transit and repainted before he took delivery. The lower courts had awarded $2 million in punitive damages for a $4000 harm. The Supreme Court ruled that the due process clause places limits on the amount of punitive damages that may be awarded. It instructed lower courts that in determining whether an award was "grossly excessive" in violation of the due process clause they should consider the reprehensibility of the tortious conduct, the ratio of punitive to compensatory damages, and the difference between the award and other civil penalties available in similar cases. Later, in *State Farm Mutual Auto Insurance Co. v. Campbell*, 538 U.S. 408 (2003), the Court reaffirmed this ruling, striking down a $145 million punitive award in a case where compensatory damages were $1 million.

Caban-Wheeler was decided shortly before *BMW*. A later case suggests that very large punitive awards, coupled with nominal damages, may be vulnerable after *BMW* and *State Farm*. In *Provost v. City of Newburgh*, 262 F.3d 146 (2d Cir. 2001), Provost had been arrested on account of comments the police found offensive. He sued for violation of his First and Fourth Amendment rights, won on the merits, and was awarded $1 nominal damages and $10,000 punitive damages against each of two defendants. On appeal, he challenged the punitive damages instruction for allowing the jury to take account of the officers' limited financial resources, even though the officers had not presented evidence of their financial circumstances. The court agreed with Provost that, in the circumstances, the instruction should not have been given, for it "not only relieved the defendants of their burden in this regard, but also left the jurors to speculate about the depth of the pockets from which the punitive damages would come."

Even so, the court ruled that the error was harmless:

> Because the defendants have not raised the issue, we of course do not decide whether the jury's award is "grossly excessive" in violation of the

Due Process Clause of the Fourteenth Amendment." *BMW v. Gore*. But we note that on the particular facts of this case and under the criteria set forth in *Gore*, the $10,000 punitive damages sum approaches the limits of what we would deem consistent with constitutional constraints. It follows that Provost could not have been harmed by the disputed instruction.

Does the court in *Provost* give due weight to the distinctive features of section 1983 litigation, notably the frequent difficulty of showing substantial compensatory damages and the utility of exposure to significant liability as a means of deterring constitutional violations?

On the other hand, by the time the case gets to the trial judge or (in *Provost*) an appellate court for review, a jury has seen the evidence firsthand and has made a judgment that large punitive damages are warranted. For an argument that, whatever the rule may be with regard to ordinary torts, courts should approve large punitive awards in constitutional tort cases even where the plaintiff is entitled to only nominal damages, *see* Michael Wells, *Punitive Damages for Constitutional Torts*, 56 La. L. Rev. 841, 871–72 (1996). *See also Cooper v. Casey*, 97 F.3d 914, 919–20 (7th Cir. 1996) (approving a punitive award of $60,000 for each of two plaintiffs, where the compensatory award was $5,000 per plaintiff.) The court noted that "[t]he smaller the compensatory damages, the higher the ratio of punitive to compensatory damages has to be in order to fulfill the objectives of awarding punitive damages"). For a post-*BMW* case talking this view, *see Williams v. Kaufman County*, 343 F.3d 689, 711 (5th Cir. 2003) (approving punitive awards of $15,000 per plaintiff though nominal damages of $100 were awarded).The court in *Mendez v. County of San Bernardino*, 540 F.3d 1109, 1122 (9th Cir. 2008) accepted this logic, but nonetheless ruled that the punitive award should be limited in light of *Gore*. The plaintiff had obtained nominal damages and the jury awarded $250,000 in punitive damages. The appellate court upheld the district court's reduction of this award to $5000.

Even if an award of punitive damages can withstand due process objections under the *BMW* criteria, it is reviewable for excessiveness on the ground that the evidence of malice, recklessness, or callous disregard for constitutional rights is too weak to support the amount awarded. In *Payne v. Jones*, 711 F.3d 85 (2d Cir. 2013), the plaintiff won an excessive force suit against a police officer. The jury awarded $60,000 in compensatory damages and $300,000 in punitive damages. Despite the single-digit ratio of punitive to compensatory damages the panel ordered a remittitur of $200,000 of the punitive damages, because the award was "excessive." 711 F.3d at 97. The point was not that the amount was so excessive as to violate the Due Process Clause. Rather, the district court's approval of the jury's award was an "abuse of discretion" given the appellate court's assessment of the degree of reprehensibility of the officer's conduct, comparisons with punitive awards in similar cases, and the civil and criminal penalties for similar acts.

Patterson v. Balsamico, 440 F.3d 104 (2d Cir. 2006), identified the defendant's lack of wealth as another factor that would justify reducing the punitive damages award. Balsamico, a corrections officer, had been found liable for assaulting another officer by spraying him with mace, covering him with shaving cream, and taunting him with racial slurs. The jury had awarded $20,000 punitive damages, along with

$100,000 damages for emotional distress. The appellate court upheld the compensatory award, but remanded for a new trial unless the plaintiff accepted a reduction in the punitive award to $10,000. It explained that "Balsamico was earning an annual salary of approximately $37,632 at the time of the verdict. [Balsamico] owned a home he purchased form approximately $51,000 and refinanced in 2003 for $87,000. He identified several bank accounts totaling about $470, and debt in excess of $5,000. He was married and had two children aged 14 and 11. [In] light of the evidence of Balsamico's financial condition in this case, we conclude that an award of no more than $10,000 will provide a sufficient punishment and deter future conduct of this sort." *Compare Gregory v. Shelby County*, 220 F.3d 433 (6th Cir. 2000), where the court upheld a jury verdict of $778,000 in compensatory damages and $2.2 million in punitive damages to the estate of an inmate against a guard who had unlocked cell doors in order to allow another inmate to attack him, and had provided no medical assistance afterward. There was also evidence that the guard had sexually assaulted the plaintiff.

Sometimes juries award, and courts uphold, large punitive damage awards in cases that do not involve physical injury. In *Bogle v. McClure*, 332 F.3d 1347, 1359–62 (11th Cir. 2003), the victorious plaintiffs were seven Fulton County, Georgia, librarians who had been transferred to menial jobs on account of their race. Besides approving a compensatory award of over $3 million, the 11th circuit rejected a *BMW/State Farm* challenge to a punitive award totaling over $13 million against three defendants. The court began by noting that the Supreme Court considers "the degree of reprehensibility of the defendant's conduct" to be "the most important indicium of the reasonableness of a punitive damages award."

> [Here the] wrongdoing was more than mere accident. There was evidence that, in the face of repeated warnings, [defendants] intentionally discriminated against the Librarians on the basis of race and used trickery and deceit to cover it up under the guise of a 'reorganization.'
>
> Furthermore, [defendants] intentionally discriminated against the Librarians with full knowledge of recent cases of employment discrimination brought by Caucasian employees against other Fulton County officials which resulted in jury verdicts for the plaintiffs or settlements. . . . Repeatedly, courts have found intentional discrimination to be reprehensible conduct under *Gore*'s first guidepost. . . .
>
> Turning to *Gore*'s second guidepost [i.e., the ratio between compensatory and punitive damages], the ratio in this case is in the neighborhood of 4:1, a range which the Supreme Court found to be 'instructive. . . .'
>
> Under the third *Gore* guidepost [i.e., a comparison of the award with analogous criminal or civil penalties, defendants] ask us to compare the punitive damages award to the statutory cap of $300,000 per plaintiff for compensatory and punitive damages under Title VII. . . . [W]e will not apply the Title VII cap by analogy to employment discrimination cases under section 1983 [because] Congress has not seen fit to impose any recovery caps in case under [section 1983]. Furthermore, although the punitive damages awarded here are more than the damages available under Title VII for analogous conduct, the difference is not enough, by itself, to

suggest that the punitive damages award violates due process.

3. *Smith* identifies deterrence of unconstitutional conduct as a primary aim of punitive damages in section 1983 litigation. If this is so, then why not allow juries to grant them any time compensatory damages may be awarded? The same question arises in common law torts. According to some common law tort theorists, the reason is that the decision on liability may be wrong, however much we strive to get it right. The threat of a mistaken imposition of punitive damages, on top of a potentially mistaken compensatory award, would unduly deter persons from engaging in the activity that gave rise to the injury. *See, e.g.,* Dorsey D. Ellis, Jr., *Fairness and Efficiency in the Law of Punitive Damages,* 56 S. CAL. L. REV. 1 (1982). By contrast, when the activity is itself without social value, as where someone recklessly (*i.e.,* with a subjective appreciation of the high risk that he is violating the plaintiff's rights), or willfully and wantonly, or intentionally violates someone's rights, no such danger is present and punitive damages are appropriate. *Compare Naucke v. City of Park Hills,* 284 F.3d 923, 929 (8th Cir. 2002) (punitive damages were appropriate where the defendant repeatedly punished subordinates for exercising First Amendment rights) *with Iacobucci v. Boulter,* 193 F.3d 14, 26–27 (1st Cir. 1999) (denying punitive damages in a case where a police officer arrested a reporter who refused to stop filming a meeting, the court said that "the evidence shows no more than that an exasperated police officer, acting in the heat of the moment, made an objectively unreasonable mistake.")

C. Survival, Wrongful Death, and Other Damages Issues Ordinarily Addressed by Statutes

Some state law tort damages issues are typically dealt with by statutes rather than common law rules. Early on, common law courts adopted a rule that the death of the victim extinguished the lawsuit. Legislatures in all states have enacted "wrongful death" statutes and "survival" statutes, both of which permit the case to go forward. Typically, wrongful death statutes allow certain close relatives to maintain a tort suit to recover for their losses due to the tort and the death that resulted from it. By the same token, survival statutes allow the estate of the deceased victim to recover for damages suffered by the victim before his death.

While statutes vary, the cause of death is generally irrelevant to the viability of a survival action, while a wrongful death action may be pursued only if the tort caused the death. For example, in *Phillips ex rel. Phillips v. Monroe County,* 311 F.3d 369 (5th Cir. 2002), the deceased died of cancer while in state custody. His mother sued under section 1983, claiming that the prison officials were "deliberately indifferent" to his medical needs in violation of his Eighth Amendment rights, see Chapter 3, *supra.* The suit was brought under the wrongful death statute and failed because the evidence showed that his cancer was far advanced by the time he entered the prison system and could not have been successfully treated in any event. The court pointed out that "[i]f Phillips had brought this suit as a survival action, the causation analysis would be different because that type of claim redresses any constitutional injuries suffered by the Decedent *before* his death." 311 F.3d at 373 n.1. *See generally* R. EPSTEIN, CASES AND MATERIALS ON TORTS 789–96 (1990).

Robertson is the Supreme Court's leading case on survival.

ROBERTSON v. WEGMANN
436 U.S. 584 (1978)

MR. JUSTICE MARSHALL delivered the opinion of the Court.

In early 1970, Clay L. Shaw filed a civil rights action under 42 U.S.C. § 1983 in the United States District Court for the Eastern District of Louisiana. Four years later, before trial had commenced, Shaw died. The question presented is whether the District Court was required to adopt as federal law a Louisiana survivorship statute, which would have caused this action to abate, or was free instead to create a federal common-law rule allowing the action to survive. Resolution of this question turns on whether the state statute is "inconsistent with the Constitution and laws of the United States." 42 U.S.C. § 1988.[3]

In 1969, Shaw was tried in a Louisiana state court on charges of having participated in a conspiracy to assassinate President John F. Kennedy. He was acquitted by a jury but within days was arrested on charges of having committed perjury in his testimony at the conspiracy trial. Alleging that these prosecutions were undertaken in bad faith, [Shaw filed a section 1983 action against the district attorney and others.] Trial was set for November 1974, but in August 1974 Shaw died. The executor of his estate, respondent Edward F. Wegmann (hereafter respondent), moved to be substituted as plaintiff, and the District Court granted the motion. Petitioner and other defendants then moved to dismiss the action on the ground that it had abated on Shaw's death. . . .

[T]he applicable survivorship rule is governed by 42 U.S.C. § 1988. This statute recognizes that in certain areas "federal law is unsuited or insufficient 'to furnish suitable remedies'"; federal law simply does not "cover every issue that may arise in the context of a federal civil rights action." When federal law is thus "deficient," § 1988 instructs us to turn to "the common law, as modified and changed by the constitution and statutes of the [forum] State," as long as these are "not inconsistent with the Constitution and laws of the United States." Regardless of the source of the law applied in a particular case, however, it is clear that the ultimate rule adopted under § 1988 " 'is a federal rule responsive to the need whenever a federal right is impaired. . . .' "

---

[3] [1] Title 42 U.S.C. § 1988 provides in pertinent part:

"The jurisdiction in civil and criminal matters conferred on the district courts by the provisions of this chapter and Title 18, for the protection of all persons in the United States in their civil rights, and for their vindication, shall be exercised and enforced in conformity with the laws of the United States, so far as such laws are suitable to carry the same into effect; but in all cases where they are not adapted to the object, or are deficient in the provisions necessary to furnish suitable remedies and punish offenses against law, the common law, as modified and changed by the constitution and statutes of the State wherein the court having jurisdiction of such civil or criminal cause is held, so far as the same is not inconsistent with the Constitution and laws of the United States, shall be extended to and govern the said courts in the trial and disposition of the cause, and, if it is of a criminal nature, in the infliction of punishment on the party found guilty."

One specific area not covered by federal law is that relating to "the survival of civil rights actions under § 1983 upon the death of either the plaintiff or defendant." State statutes governing the survival of state actions do exist, however. These statutes, which vary widely with regard to both the types of claims that survive and the parties as to whom survivorship is allowed, were intended to modify the simple, if harsh, 19th-century common-law rule: "[An] injured party's personal claim was [always] extinguished . . . upon the death of either the injured party himself or the alleged wrongdoer." Under § 1988, this state statutory law, modifying the common law, provides the principal reference point in determining survival of civil rights actions, subject to the important proviso that state law may not be applied when it is "inconsistent with the Constitution and laws of the United States." Because of this proviso, the courts below refused to adopt as federal law the Louisiana survivorship statute and in its place created a federal common-law rule.

In resolving questions of inconsistency between state and federal law raised under § 1988, courts must look not only at particular federal statutes and constitutional provisions, but also at "the policies expressed in [them]." Of particular importance is whether application of state law "would be inconsistent with the federal policy underlying the cause of action under consideration." The instant cause of action arises under 42 U.S.C. § 1983, one of the "Reconstruction civil rights statutes" that this Court has accorded " 'a sweep as broad as [their] language.' "

Despite the broad sweep of § 1983, we can find nothing in the statute or its underlying policies to indicate that a state law causing abatement of a particular action should invariably be ignored in favor of a rule of absolute survivorship. The policies underlying § 1983 include compensation of persons injured by deprivation of federal rights and prevention of abuses of power by those acting under color of state law. No claim is made here that Louisiana's survivorship laws are in general inconsistent with these policies, and indeed most Louisiana actions survive the plaintiff's death. Moreover, certain types of actions that would abate automatically on the plaintiff's death in many States — for example, actions for defamation and malicious prosecution — would apparently survive in Louisiana. In actions other than those for damage to property, however, Louisiana does not allow the deceased's personal representative to be substituted as plaintiff; rather, the action survives only in favor of a spouse, children, parents, or siblings. But surely few persons are not survived by one of these close relatives, and in any event no contention is made here that Louisiana's decision to restrict certain survivorship rights in this manner is an unreasonable one.

It is therefore difficult to see how any of § 1983's policies would be undermined if Shaw's action were to abate. The goal of compensating those injured by a deprivation of rights provides no basis for requiring compensation of one who is merely suing as the executor of the deceased's estate. And, given that most Louisiana actions survive the plaintiff's death, the fact that a particular action might abate surely would not adversely affect § 1983's role in preventing official illegality, at least in situations in which there is no claim that the illegality caused the plaintiff's death. A state official contemplating illegal activity must always be prepared to face the prospect of a § 1983 action being filed against him. In light of this prospect, even an official aware of the intricacies of Louisiana survivorship law would hardly be influenced in his behavior by its provisions.

It is true that § 1983 provides "a uniquely federal remedy against incursions under the claimed authority of state law upon rights secured by the Constitution and laws of the Nation." That a federal remedy should be available, however, does not mean that a § 1983 plaintiff (or his representative) must be allowed to continue an action in disregard of the state law to which § 1988 refers us. A state statute cannot be considered "inconsistent" with federal law merely because the statute causes the plaintiff to lose the litigation. If success of the § 1983 action were the only benchmark, there would be no reason at all to look to state law, for the appropriate rule would then always be the one favoring the plaintiff, and its source would be essentially irrelevant. But § 1988 quite clearly instructs us to refer to state statutes; it does not say that state law is to be accepted or rejected based solely on which side is advantaged thereby. Under the circumstances presented here, the fact that Shaw was not survived by one of several close relatives should not itself be sufficient to cause the Louisiana survivorship provisions to be deemed "inconsistent with the Constitution and laws of the United States." 42 U.S.C. § 1988.

Our holding today is a narrow one, limited to situations in which no claim is made that state law generally is inhospitable to survival of § 1983 actions and in iwhich the particular application of state survivorship law, while it may cause abatement of the action, has no independent adverse effect on the policies underlying § 1983. A different situation might well be presented, as the District Court noted, if state law "did not provide for survival of any tort actions," or if it significantly restricted the types of actions that survive. Cf. *Carey v. Piphus* (failure of common law to "recognize an analogous cause of action" is not sufficient reason to deny compensation to § 1983 plaintiff). We intimate no view, moreover, about whether abatement based on state law could be allowed in a situation in which deprivation of federal rights caused death.

Here it is agreed that Shaw's death was not caused by the deprivation of rights for which he sued under § 1983, and Louisiana law provides for the survival of most tort actions. Respondent's only complaint about Louisiana law is that it would cause Shaw's action to abate. We conclude that the mere fact of abatement of a particular lawsuit is not sufficient ground to declare state law "inconsistent" with federal law.

Mr. Justice **Blackmun**, with whom Mr. Justice **Brennan** and Mr. Justice **White** join, dissenting.

It is disturbing to see the Court, in this decision, although almost apologetically self-described as "a narrow one," cut back on what is acknowledged, to be the "broad sweep" of 42 U.S.C. § 1983. Accordingly, I dissent.

I do not read the emphasis of § 1988, as the Court does, to the effect that the Federal District Court "was required to adopt" the Louisiana statute, and was free to look to federal common law only as a secondary matter. It seems to me that this places the cart before the horse. Section 1988 requires the utilization of federal law ("shall be exercised and enforced in conformity with the laws of the United States"). It authorizes resort to the state statute only if the federal laws "are not adapted to the object" of "protection of all persons in the United States in their civil rights, and for their vindication" or are "deficient in the provisions necessary to furnish suitable remedies and punish offenses against law." Even then, state statutes are an alternative source of law only if "not inconsistent with the Constitution and laws of the United States." Surely, federal law is the rule and not the exception.

Accepting this as the proper starting point, it necessarily follows, it seems to me, that the judgment of the Court of Appeals must be affirmed, not reversed. To be sure, survivorship of a civil rights action under § 1983 upon the death of either party is not specifically covered by the federal statute. But that does not mean that "the laws of the United States" are not "suitable" or are "not adapted to the object" or are "deficient in the provisions necessary." The federal law and the underlying federal policy stand bright and clear. And in the light of that brightness and of that clarity, I see no need to resort to the myriad of state rules governing the survival of state actions.

First. . . . The statute was intended to give courts flexibility to shape their procedures and remedies in accord with the underlying policies of the Civil Rights Acts, choosing whichever rule *"better* serves" those policies. I do not understand the Court to deny a federal court's authority under § 1988 to reject state law when to apply it seriously undermines substantial federal concerns. But I do not accept the Court's apparent conclusion that, absent such an extreme inconsistency, § 1988 restricts courts to state law on matters of procedure and remedy. That conclusion too often would interfere with the efficient redress of constitutional rights.

Second. The Court's reading of § 1988 cannot easily be squared with its treatment of the problems of immunity and damages under the Civil Rights Acts. Only this Term, in *Carey v. Piphus,* the Court set a rule for the award of damages under § 1983 for deprivation of procedural due process by resort to "federal common law." Though the case arose from Illinois, the Court did not feel compelled to inquire into Illinois' statutory or decisional law of damages, nor to test that law for possible "inconsistency" with the federal scheme, before embracing a federal common-law rule. Instead, the Court fashioned a federal damages rule, from common-law sources and its view of the type of injury, to govern such cases uniformly State to State.

Similarly, in constructing immunities under § 1983, the Court has consistently relied on federal common-law rules. As *Carey v. Piphus* recognizes, in attributing immunity to prosecutors, to judges, and to other officials, matters on which the language of § 1983 is silent, we have not felt bound by the tort immunities recognized in the particular forum State and, only after finding an "inconsistency" with federal standards, then considered a uniform federal rule. Instead, the immunities have been fashioned in light of historic common-law concerns and the policies of the Civil Rights Acts.

Third. A flexible reading of § 1988, permitting resort to a federal rule of survival because it "better serves" the policies of the Civil Rights Acts, would be consistent with the methodology employed in the other major choice-of-law provision in the federal structure, namely, the Rules of Decision Act. 28 U.S.C. § 1652.[4] That Act provides that state law is to govern a civil trial in a federal court "except where the

---

4 [2] "The laws of the several states, except where the Constitution or treaties of the United States or Acts of Congress otherwise require or provide, shall be regarded as rules of decision in civil actions in the courts of the United States, in cases where they apply."

Constitution or treaties of the United States or Acts of Congress otherwise require or provide." The exception has not been interpreted in a crabbed or wooden fashion, but, instead, has been used to give expression to important federal interests. Thus, for example, the exception has been used to apply a federal common law of labor contracts in suits under § 301 (a) of the Labor Management Relations Act, 1947, to apply federal common law to transactions in commercial paper issued by the United States where the United States is a party, and to avoid application of governing state law to the reservation of mineral rights in a land acquisition agreement to which the United States was a party and that bore heavily upon a federal wildlife regulatory program.

Just as the Rules of Decision Act cases disregard state law where there is conflict with federal *policy*, even though no explicit conflict with the terms of a federal statute, so, too, state remedial and procedural law must be disregarded under § 1988 where that law fails to give adequate expression to important federal concerns. The opponents of the 1866 Act were distinctly aware that the legislation that became § 1988 would give the federal courts power to shape federal common-law rules.

Fourth. Section 1983's critical concerns are compensation of the victims of unconstitutional action, and deterrence of like misconduct in the future. Any crabbed rule of survivorship obviously interferes directly with the second critical interest and may well interfere with the first.

The unsuitability of Louisiana's law is shown by the very case at hand. It will happen not infrequently that a decedent's only survivor or survivors are non-relatives or collateral relatives who do not fit within the four named classes of Louisiana statutory survivors. Though the Court surmises that "surely few persons are not survived" by a spouse, children, parents, or siblings, any lawyer who has had experience in estate planning or in probating estates knows that situation is frequently encountered. The Louisiana survivorship rule applies no matter how malicious or ill-intentioned a defendant's action was . . . The federal interest in specific deterrence, when there was malicious intention to deprive a person of his constitutional rights, is particularly strong. Insuring a specific deterrent under federal law gains importance from the very premise of the Civil Rights Act that state tort policy often is inadequate to deter violations of the constitutional rights of disfavored groups.

The Louisiana rule requiring abatement appears to apply even where the death was intentional and caused, say, by a beating delivered by a defendant. The Court does not deny this result, merely declaiming that in such a case it might reconsider the applicability of the Louisiana survivorship statute. But the Court does not explain how either certainty or federalism is served by such a variegated application of the Louisiana statute, nor how an abatement rule would be workable when made to depend on a fact of causation often requiring an entire trial to prove.

It makes no sense to me to make even a passing reference to behavioral influence. The Court opines that no official aware of the intricacies of Louisiana survivorship law would "be influenced in his behavior by its provisions." But the defendants in Shaw's litigation obviously have been "sweating it out" through the several years of proceedings and litigation in this case. One can imagine the relief occasioned when the realization dawned that Shaw's death might — just might — abate the action. To that extent, the deterrent against behavior such as that attributed to the defendants in this case surely has been lessened.

As to compensation, it is no answer to intimate, as the Court does that Shaw's particular survivors were not personally injured, for obviously had Shaw been survived by parents or siblings, the cause of action would exist despite the absence in them of so deep and personal an affront, or any at all, as Shaw himself was alleged to have sustained. The Court propounds the unreasoned conclusion that the "goal of compensating those injured by a deprivation of rights provides no basis for requiring compensation of one who is merely suing as the executor of the deceased's estate." But the Court does not purport to explain why it is consistent with the purposes of § 1983 to recognize a derivative or independent interest in a brother or parent, while denying similar interest to a nephew, grandparent, or legatee.

Fifth. The Court regards the Louisiana system's structuring of survivorship rights as not unreasonable. The observation, of course, is a gratuitous one, for as the Court immediately observes it does not resolve the issue that confronts us here. We are not concerned with the reasonableness of the Louisiana survivorship statute in allocating tort recoveries. We are concerned with its application in the face of a claim of civil rights guaranteed the decedent by federal law. . . .

Sixth. A federal rule of survivorship allows uniformity, and counsel immediately know the answer. Litigants identically aggrieved in their federal civil rights, residing in geographically adjacent States, will not have differing results due to the vagaries of state law. Litigants need not engage in uncertain characterization of a § 1983 action in terms of its nearest tort cousin, a questionable procedure to begin with, since the interests protected by tort law and constitutional law may be quite different. Nor will federal rights depend on the arcane intricacies of state survival law — which differs in Louisiana according to whether the right is "strictly personal," whether the action concerns property damage, or whether it concerns "other damages."

The policies favoring so-called "absolute" survivorship, *viz.*, survivorship in favor of a decedent's nonrelated legatees in the absence of familial legatees, are the simple goals of uniformity, deterrence, and perhaps compensation. A defendant who has violated someone's constitutional rights has no legitimate interest in a windfall release upon the death of the victim. A plaintiff's interest in certainty, in an equal remedy, and in deterrence supports such an absolute rule. . . .

Seventh. Rejecting Louisiana's survivorship limitations does not mean that state procedure and state remedies will cease to serve as important sources of civil rights law. State law, for instance, may well be a suitable source of statutes of limitation, since that is a rule for which litigants prudently can plan. Rejecting Louisiana's survivorship limitations means only that state rules are subject to some scrutiny for suitability. Here the deterrent purpose of § 1983 is disserved by Louisiana's rule of abatement.

It is unfortunate that the Court restricts the reach of § 1983 by today's decision construing § 1988. Congress now must act again if the gap in remedy is to be filled.

NOTES

1. *Carlson v. Green*, 446 U.S. 14 (1980), was a *Bivens* case, brought under a cause of action implied from the Eighth Amendment against federal prison officials on behalf of the estate of a prisoner who died, allegedly because of unconstitutionally inadequate medical care. Under state law the claim would not survive his death. The Court distinguished *Robertson* as follows:

> There the plaintiff's death was not caused by the acts of the defendants upon which the suit was based. Moreover, *Robertson* expressly recognized that to prevent frustration of the deterrence goals of section 1983 (which in part also underlie *Bivens* actions . . .) "[a] state official contemplating illegal activity must always be prepared to face the prospect of a section 1983 action being filed against him." A federal official contemplating unconstitutional conduct similarly must be prepared to face the prospect of a *Bivens* action. A uniform rule that claims such as respondent's survive the decedent's death is essential if we are not to "frustrate in [an] important way the achievement" of the goals of *Bivens* actions.

Does it follow that state law limitations on survival will not apply to section 1983 cases where the victim died as a result of the unconstitutional act? Or do federalism considerations require different treatment for section 1983 cases, where the defendants are typically state rather than federal officers? Is uniformity less important in section 1983 cases than in *Bivens* cases?

2. The Supreme Court invokes section 1988 in situations where the point at issue is typically governed by statute, but section 1983 does not speak to it. Hence, state statutes govern not only survivorship but also time-based limitations on bringing suit, *Wilson v. Garcia*, 471 U.S. 261 (1985), and notice of claim issues, *Felder v. Casey*, 487 U.S. 131 (1988). These latter topics are addressed in Chapter 10, on procedural defenses to section 1983 suits. In *Felder* you will see that, as with survivorship, the borrowing of state law may be overridden if the Court deems the state rule to be inconsistent with the aims of section 1983.

3. Suppose a state's statute provides that once the plaintiff has died, no punitive damages will be available. Is this provision inconsistent with section 1983? *See McFadden v. Sanchez*, 710 F.2d 907 (2d Cir. 1983) (refusing to apply the provision in a case where the death resulted from the constitutional violation). How should the case come out if the victim fortuitously dies of other causes?

In *County of Los Angeles v. Superior Court*, 981 P.2d 68 (Cal. 1999), the plaintiff brought a section 1983 case for sex discrimination but died before judgment of other causes. The issue in the case was whether California's survival statute, which does not permit recovery of pain and suffering, should be applied in section 1983 suits. The California Supreme Court applied the statutory bar, noting, among other things, that "psychic injury does not reduce the value of the plaintiff's estate compared to what it would have been in the absence of the injury, and the legislature's decision not to allow the estate to recover damages for such damages was reasonable." Does this reasoning take due account of the compensatory and deterrent purposes of section 1983? The Court left open whether the exclusion would apply in cases in which the constitutional violation caused the death.

Suppose a policeman unconstitutionally shoots the plaintiff's decedent, who dies immediately. The state's survival statute denies recovery when the victim of a tort dies instantly, feeling no pain and suffering between the commission of the tort and his death. Should the case be dismissed, or is this provision of the statute inconsistent with section 1983, and hence not applicable under section 1988? *See Jaco v. Bloeche*, 739 F.2d 239, 244 (6th Cir. 1984) (refusing to apply the statutory barrier on the ground that "to suggest that the Congress had intended that a civil rights infringement be cognizable only when the victim encounters pain and suffering before his demise, is absurd"). Is the court's ruling compatible with *Robertson*?

4. Why did the *Jaco* court not simply allow suit under the wrongful death statute? It said:

> Ohio's wrongful death statute creates an action in tort in favor of the decedent's heirs for damages resulting from losses of prospective advantages which have been pretermitted by the death of the victim. Certainly, in a sense, the heirs are injured parties as a result of decedent's premature demise however, [sic] to arbitrarily conclude that their injuries resulted from an infringement of their civil rights would be sheer obfuscation of the issue. Simply stated, the wrongful death of the decedent resulting from a tort, which gives rise to the cause of action for the benefit of his heirs, is not equivalent to decedent's personal section 1983 claim, and decedent's administratrix is therefore without standing in the federal forum to commence an action, pursuant to section 1983 and 1988, under either the Ohio survivor or wrongful death statute.

Some courts have allowed recovery for wrongful death in a section 1983 suit without addressing the conceptual problem identified in *Jaco*. *See, e.g., Williams v. Kelley*, 624 F.2d 695 (5th Cir. 1980).

5. Is there a good answer to the objection to a wrongful death action raised in *Jaco*? Suppose the administrator of the estate of a person unconstitutionally killed by the police brings a section 1983 suit and, as part of the same lawsuit, the dependents seek to raise a claim under the state's wrongful death statute. May the wrongful death cause of action be litigated in federal court under the doctrine of pendent jurisdiction? Under *United Mine Workers of America v. Gibbs*, 383 U.S. 715 (1966), pendent jurisdiction may be appropriate if the federal and state claims "derive from a common nucleus of operative fact," and if "considerations of judicial economy, convenience, and fairness to litigants" would be served by litigating the two claims at the same time. Is it likely that these conditions would be met in cases where the estate sought to join a wrongful death claim to the decedent's case against the police? Does it matter that the estate is the plaintiff in the decedent's case, while the plaintiffs in the wrongful death case are his dependents? *See* 28 U.S.C. § 1367 (authorizing pendent party jurisdiction).

If the wrongful death statute places ceilings on the recovery available to the dependents, may they successfully argue that those limits should not apply where the death was caused by a federal constitutional violation?

6. *Robertson* and the preceding notes begin from the premise that courts should look to state statutes as the measures of recovery once the victim has died. Should the Court have adopted Justice Blackmun's view that the focus should be on effective remedies for constitutional violations rather than state survival and wrongful death statutes? Why should the development of section 1983 be bound by the modern implications of ancient (and rather dubious) common law decisions? Note that the approach taken in *Robertson* requires in each case an evaluation of whether a particular state rule is consistent with the purposes of section 1983. Would it not be more straightforward to consider how to achieve an effective remedy and then implement that judgment by an appropriate set of rules, regardless of state law?

There is a more fundamental problem with reference to state law. Even liberal rules on survivorship and wrongful death leave a significant gap in coverage. They allow recovery of damages up to the death, and they allow dependents to recover for their loss of support. Even taken together, however, they do not permit recovery for the death itself, or for the full value of the life that was lost. For example, in *Bell v. City of Milwaukee*, 746 F.2d 1205, 1236 (7th Cir. 1984), the court pointed out that "the Wisconsin statutory scheme creates a survival action in favor of the estate for pre-death injuries and a wrongful death action in favor of the victim's survivors, and neither type of action traditionally allows recovery of damages for loss of life itself." It went on to hold that "the application and policy of this point of Wisconsin law are inconsistent with those of section 1983 and the Fourteenth Amendment protection of life. Therefore, Wisconsin law cannot be applied to preclude the estate's recovery for loss of life . . ." By contrast, the Colorado Supreme Court held in *Jones v. Hildebrant*, 550 P.2d 339 (Colo. 1976), that state law limitations on the kind and amount of damages were applicable to section 1983 actions. This issue was revisited by the Colorado Supreme Court in *Espinoza v. O'Dell*, 633 P.2d 455, 465 (Colo. 1981), which overruled *Jones v. Hildebrant* "to the extent it implied that state wrongful death limitations must be applied to a federal section 1983 claim brought by children of the deceased who allege the deprivation of a constitutional liberty in their continuing relationship with the one whose life has been unlawfully taken under color of state law."

One recent application of Alabama's abatement statute makes evident how state law can sometimes lead to a liability gap in constitutional litigation. In *Estate of Gilliam ex rel. Waldroup v. City of Prattville*, 639 F.3d 1041, 1050 (11th Cir. 2011), officers used tasers to fire dozens of rounds of electrodes into a 22-year-old man, striking him 27 times over the course of three-and-a half minutes. The man died seven hours later. His family then sued, alleging that the officers engaged in excessive force in violation of the Fourth Amendment's command against unreasonable seizures. While a jury agreed, entering a verdict in favor of the family, the Eleventh Circuit reversed. That court found that under Alabama law, the deceased could not sue on behalf of the deceased because the claims did not survive his death. The court emphasized that there had been no judicial finding that the officer's force proximately caused the death of the decedent. To the contrary, the district court granted summary judgment to the defendants on the family's wrongful death claims. Judge Beverly Martin dissented: "I would conclude that the Alabama survivorship statute, to the extent that it permits the abatement of tort actions for wrongful conduct that immediately contributes to a person's death, is inconsistent with both the abuse prevention and compensation goals underlying and embodied in 42 U.S.C. § 1983."

Which view should the Supreme Court adopt? Should courts in section 1983 cases respond to the lacunae in state statutory regimes by making a federal common law of wrongful death damages?

7. Wrongful death statutes allow the dependents to recover sums they would have received but for the tortiously caused death. May family members sue under section 1983 for loss of the decedent's society and companionship, despite state rules limiting consortium to the spouse? *See Moreland v. Las Vegas Metropolitan Police Dept.*, 159 F.3d 365, 371 (9th Cir. 1998) (mother and children of decedent Douglas "each may assert a Fourteenth Amendment claim based on the [deprivation] of their liberty interest arising out of their relationship with Douglas"). By contrast, *Shepherd v. Wellman*, 313 F.3d 963 (6th Cir. 2002), dismissed a "loss of parental consortium" claim on the ground that "Kentucky law did not recognize the loss of parental consortium as a cause of action at the time that this complaint was filed." Which is the better approach? In making a choice between *Moreland* and *Shepherd*, be sure to distinguish between two distinct questions: (a) whether federal or state law should govern the issue; and (b) assuming federal law should govern, what should be the substantive content of the rule. In principle, *Moreland* may be right on the first question but wrong on the second, while *Shepherd* could be wrong on the first question but right on the second. For a survey of the circuit court case law, see *Carringer v. Rodgers*, 331 F.3d 844, 850 n.9 (11th Cir. 2003) (finding that "there are at least four different theories used by circuit courts to determine what claims after death may proceed under section 1983").

8. Some states have enacted "tort reform" statutes that modify some of the common law principles governing damages for tort cases in general, not just for survival and wrongful death cases. *See, e.g.*, Joseph Sanders & Craig Joyce, *"Off to the Races": The 1980s Tort Crisis and the Law Reform Process*, 27 HOUSTON L. REV. 207 (1990). For example, these statutes may abolish joint and several liability, or modify the collateral source rule, or limit the amount of non-pecuniary (e.g., pain and suffering) and punitive damages that may be recovered in a tort case. Does *Robertson* require federal courts to follow these state rules? Or is such a statute inconsistent with the purposes of section 1983, and hence not applicable under section 1988? Assuming that such a statute would not limit recovery in a section 1983 case, consider a further issue: The common law rule is that there is no right of "contribution" among joint tortfeasors. Many states have adopted statutes that change that rule, giving tort feasors who pay more than their share of the damages a right to pursue other tortfeasors. Should federal law govern contribution issues, or can they be distinguished from the question of what damages are available to the victorious plaintiff? *See Rockford Board of Education v. Illinois State Board of Education*, 150 F.3d 686 (7th Cir. 1998) (rejecting a claim for contribution brought by the local board against "an alleged joint tortfeasor, the state board of education," noting that "the federal civil rights laws do not confer a right to sue on the violators of those laws," and that "the violators are not intended beneficiaries of the laws and have no right to invoke them"). *See also* 1 SHELDON H. NAHMOD, CIVIL RIGHTS AND CIVIL LIBERTIES LITIGATION — THE LAW OF SECTION 1983 at § 4:8 (4th ed. 2003).

II. PROSPECTIVE RELIEF

Throughout this book, you have seen that it is often important to distinguish between damages, on the one hand, and injunctive and declaratory relief on the other. Damages are aimed at redressing an injury that occurred in the past, and they influence future conduct only indirectly, by signaling to officials that courts may impose liability on them if they violate federal law. When the plaintiff's case arises from an isolated incident that will not likely recur, he may recover only damages, and may recover nothing at all on account of such doctrines as official immunity and the difficulty of proving harm from many constitutional violations. Prospective relief may be appropriate when the illegality is ongoing or the plaintiff shows that the challenged conduct will recur unless the defendant is ordered to stop it. An injunction specifically directs officials to do or to refrain from particular acts, or else face not only actions for damages but fines or imprisonment for contempt of court. Declaratory relief nudges them in that direction by letting them know that an injunction will likely be forthcoming if they act contrary to the rules the court sets forth in the declaratory judgment.

In some respects, prospective relief is easier to obtain than are damages. On account of the Eleventh Amendment, damages and other forms of retrospective relief are not available against state governments unless Congress explicitly abrogates state immunity, and section 1983 does not do so. On the other hand, the principle of *Ex Parte Young* in effect permits prospective relief against them. Immunity doctrines often bar recovery of damages; only legislators are immune from prospective relief. At the same time, requests for prospective relief raise issues of their own. Some of these issues arise from efforts by Congress and the Supreme Court to channel certain kinds of litigation to the state courts. Such barriers to federal court include the Tax Injunction Act, which prohibits federal injunctions against state tax collection, the Johnson Act, which prohibits federal injunctions against state utility rate making, and the *Pullman, Younger*, and *Burford* abstention doctrines, which postpone or forbid federal injunctions against state action in a variety of circumstances. These doctrines are discussed in detail in courses on federal jurisdiction, and are summarized in Chapter 10.

Once these procedural barriers are overcome, questions arise as to the circumstances in which prospective relief may be appropriate and what form it should take. *City of Los Angeles v. Lyons* illustrates some of the obstacles plaintiffs face in obtaining prospective relief, even in cases where the abstention doctrines do not exclude them from federal court altogether.

CITY OF LOS ANGELES v. LYONS
461 U.S. 95 (1983)

JUSTICE **WHITE** delivered the opinion of the Court.

The issue here is whether respondent Lyons satisfied the prerequisites for seeking injunctive relief in the Federal District Court.

This case began on February 7, 1977, when respondent, Adolph Lyons, filed a complaint for damages, injunction, and declaratory relief in the United States

District Court for the Central District of California. The defendants were the City of Los Angeles and four of its police officers. The complaint alleged that on October 6, 1976, at 2 a.m., Lyons was stopped by the defendant officers for a traffic or vehicle code violation and that although Lyons offered no resistance or threat whatsoever, the officers, without provocation or justification, seized Lyons and applied a "chokehold"[5] — either the "bar arm control" hold or the "carotidartery control" hold or both-rendering him unconscious and causing damage to his larynx. Counts I through IV of the complaint sought damages against the officers and the City. Count V, with which we are principally concerned here, sought a preliminary and permanent injunction against the City barring the use of the control holds. That count alleged that the City's police officers, "pursuant to the authorization, instruction and encouragement of Defendant City of Los Angeles, regularly and routinely apply these choke holds in innumerable situations where they are not threatened by the use of any deadly force whatsoever," that numerous persons have been injured as the result of the application of the chokeholds, that Lyons and others similarly situated are threatened with irreparable injury in the form of bodily injury and loss of life, and that Lyons "justifiably fears that any contact he has with Los Angeles Police officers may result in his being choked and strangled to death without provocation, justification or other legal excuse." Lyons alleged the threatened impairment of rights protected by the First, Fourth, Eighth, and Fourteenth Amendments. Injunctive relief was sought against the use of the control holds "except in situations where the proposed victim of said control reasonably appears to be threatening the immediate use of deadly force." Count VI sought declaratory relief against the City, i.e., a judgment that use of the chokeholds absent the threat of immediate use of deadly force is a per se violation of various constitutional rights.

[After proceedings in the district court and the Ninth Circuit, the district court granted Lyons a preliminary injunction against the use of chokeholds on persons who did not pose a threat to the police. The Ninth Circuit affirmed, but the injunction had not yet gone into effect, on account of stays issued by the ninth circuit and the Supreme Court.]

Since our grant of certiorari, circumstances pertinent to the case have changed. Originally, Lyons' complaint alleged that at least two deaths had occurred as a result of the application of chokeholds by the police. His first amended complaint alleged that 10 chokehold-related deaths had occurred. By May 1982, there had been five more such deaths. On May 6, 1982, the Chief of Police in Los Angeles prohibited the use of the bar-arm chokehold in any circumstances. A few days later, on May 12, 1982, the Board of Police Commissioners imposed a 6-month morato-

---

[5] [1] The police control procedures at issue in this case are referred to as "control holds," "choke-holds," "strangleholds," and "neck restraints." All these terms refer to two basic control procedures: the "carotid" hold and the "bar arm" hold. In the "carotid" hold, an officer positioned behind a subject places one arm around the subject's neck and holds the wrist of that arm with his other hand. The officer, by using his lower forearm and bicep muscle, applies pressure concentrating on the carotid arteries located on the sides of the subject's neck. The "carotid" hold is capable of rendering the subject unconscious by diminishing the flow of oxygenated blood to the brain. The "bar arm" hold, which is administered similarly, applies pressure at the front of the subject's neck. "Bar arm" pressure causes pain, reduces the flow of oxygen to the lungs, and may render the subject unconscious.

rium on the use of the carotid artery chokehold except under circumstances where deadly force is authorized.

Based on these events, on June 3, 1982, the City filed in this Court a memorandum suggesting a question of mootness, reciting the facts but arguing that the case was not moot. Lyons in turn filed a motion to dismiss the writ of certiorari as improvidently granted. We denied that motion but reserved the question of mootness for later consideration.

In his brief and at oral argument, Lyons has reasserted his position that in light of changed conditions, an injunctive decree is now unnecessary because he is no longer subject to a threat of injury. He urges that the preliminary injunction should be vacated. The City, on the other hand, while acknowledging that subsequent events have significantly changed the posture of this case, again asserts that the case is not moot because the moratorium is not permanent and may be lifted at any time.

We agree with the City that the case is not moot, since the moratorium by its terms is not permanent. Intervening events have not "irrevocably eradicated the effects of the alleged violation." We nevertheless hold, for another reason, that the federal courts are without jurisdiction to entertain Lyons' claim for injunctive relief.

It goes without saying that those who seek to invoke the jurisdiction of the federal courts must satisfy the threshold requirement imposed by Art. III of the Constitution by alleging an actual case or controversy. Plaintiffs must demonstrate a "personal stake in the outcome" in order to "assure that concrete adverseness which sharpens the presentation of issues" necessary for the proper resolution of constitutional questions. Abstract injury is not enough. The plaintiff must show that he "has sustained or is immediately in danger of sustaining some direct injury" as the result of the challenged official conduct and the injury or threat of injury must be both "real and immediate," not "conjectural" or "hypothetical."

In *O'Shea v. Littleton* we dealt with a case brought by a class of plaintiffs claiming that they had been subjected to discriminatory enforcement of the criminal law. Among other things, a county magistrate and judge were accused of discriminatory conduct in various respects, such as sentencing members of plaintiff's class more harshly than other defendants. The Court of Appeals reversed the dismissal of the suit by the District Court, ruling that if the allegations were proved, an appropriate injunction could be entered.

We reversed for failure of the complaint to allege a case or controversy. Although it was claimed in that case that particular members of the plaintiff class had actually suffered from the alleged unconstitutional practices, we observed that "[p]ast exposure to illegal conduct does not in itself show a present case or controversy regarding injunctive relief . . . if unaccompanied by any continuing, present adverse effects." Past wrongs were evidence bearing on "whether there is a real and immediate threat of repeated injury." But the prospect of future injury rested "on the likelihood that [plaintiffs] will again be arrested for and charged with violations of the criminal law and will again be subjected to bond proceedings, trial, or sentencing before petitioners." The most that could be said for plaintiffs' standing was "that *if* [plaintiffs] proceed to violate an unchallenged law and *if* they are charged, held to answer, and tried in any proceedings before petitioners, they will be subjected to the discriminatory practices that petitioners are alleged to have followed." We could not find a case or controversy in those circumstances: the threat to the plaintiffs was not "sufficiently real and immediate to show an existing controversy simply because they anticipate violating lawful criminal statutes and being tried for their offenses. . . ." It was to be assumed that "[plaintiffs] will conduct their activities within the law and so avoid prosecution and conviction as well as exposure to the challenged course of conduct said to be followed by petitioners."

We further observed that case-or-controversy considerations "obviously shade into those determining whether the complaint states a sound basis for equitable relief," and went on to hold that even if the complaint presented an existing case or controversy, an adequate basis for equitable relief against petitioners had not been demonstrated:

> "[Plaintiffs] have failed, moreover, to establish the basic requisites of the issuance of equitable relief in these circumstances — the likelihood of substantial and immediate irreparable injury, and the inadequacy of remedies at law. We have already canvassed the necessarily conjectural nature of the threatened injury to which [plaintiffs] are allegedly subjected. And if any of the [plaintiffs] are ever prosecuted and face trial, or if they are illegally sentenced, there are available state and federal procedures which could provide relief from the wrongful conduct alleged."

Another relevant decision for present purposes is *Rizzo v. Goode*, a case in which plaintiffs alleged widespread illegal and unconstitutional police conduct aimed at minority citizens and against city residents in general. The Court reiterated the holding in *O'Shea* that past wrongs do not in themselves amount to that real and immediate threat of injury necessary to make out a case or controversy. The claim of injury rested upon "what one of a small, unnamed minority of policemen might do to them in the future because of that unknown policeman's perception" of departmental procedures. This hypothesis was "even more attenuated than those allegations of future injury found insufficient in *O'Shea* to warrant [the] invocation of federal jurisdiction." The Court also held that plaintiffs' showing at trial of a relatively few instances of violations by individual police officers, without any showing of a deliberate policy on behalf of the named defendants, did not provide a basis for equitable relief. . . .

No extension of *O'Shea* and *Rizzo* is necessary to hold that respondent Lyons has failed to demonstrate a case or controversy with the City that would justify the equitable relief sought. Lyons' standing to seek the injunction requested depended on whether he was likely to suffer future injury from the use of the chokeholds by police officers. Count V of the complaint alleged the traffic stop and choking incident five months before. That Lyons may have been illegally choked by the police on October 6, 1976, while presumably affording Lyons standing to claim damages against the individual officers and perhaps against the City, does nothing to establish a real and immediate threat that he would again be stopped for a traffic violation, or for any other offense, by an officer or officers who would illegally choke him into unconsciousness without any provocation or resistance on his part. The additional allegation in the complaint that the police in Los Angeles routinely apply chokeholds in situations where they are not threatened by the use of deadly force falls far short of the allegations that would be necessary to establish a case or controversy between these parties.

In order to establish an actual controversy in this case, Lyons would have had not only to allege that he would have another encounter with the police but also to make the incredible assertion either (1) that *all* police officers in Los Angeles *always* choke any citizen with whom they happen to have an encounter, whether for the purpose of arrest, issuing a citation, or for questioning, or (2) that the City ordered or authorized police officers to act in such manner. Although Count V alleged that the City authorized the use of the control holds in situations where deadly force was not threatened, it did not indicate why Lyons might be realistically threatened by police officers who acted within the strictures of the City's policy. If, for example, chokeholds were authorized to be used only to counter resistance to an arrest by a suspect, or to thwart an effort to escape, any future threat to Lyons from the City's policy or from the conduct of police officers would be no more real than the possibility that he would again have an encounter with the police and that either he would illegally resist arrest or detention or the officers would disobey their instructions and again render him unconscious without any provocation.

Under *O'Shea* and *Rizzo*, these allegations were an insufficient basis to provide a federal court with jurisdiction to entertain Count V of the complaint. . . . The Court of Appeals . . . asserted that Lyons "had a live and active claim" against the City "if only for a period of a few seconds" while the stranglehold was being applied to him and that for two reasons the claim had not become moot so as to disentitle Lyons to injunctive relief: First, because under normal rules of equity, a case does not become moot merely because the complained of conduct has ceased; and second, because Lyons' claim is "capable of repetition but evading review" and therefore should be heard. We agree that Lyons had a live controversy with the City. Indeed, he still has a claim for damages against the City that appears to meet all Art. III requirements. Nevertheless, the issue here is not whether that claim has become moot but whether Lyons meets the preconditions for asserting an injunctive claim in a federal forum. The equitable doctrine that cessation of the challenged conduct does not bar an injunction is of little help in this respect, for Lyons' lack of standing does not rest on the termination of the police practice but on the speculative nature of his claim that he will again experience injury as the result of that practice even if continued.

The rule that a claim does not become moot where it is capable of repetition, yet evades review, is likewise inapposite. Lyons' claim that he was illegally strangled remains to be litigated in his suit for damages; in no sense does that claim "evade" review. Furthermore, the capable-of-repetition doctrine applies only in exceptional situations, and generally only where the named plaintiff can make a reasonable showing that he will again be subjected to the alleged illegality. As we have indicated, Lyons has not made this demonstration. . . .

Lyons fares no better if it be assumed that his pending damages suit affords him Art. III standing to seek an injunction as a remedy for the claim arising out of the October 1976 events. The equitable remedy is unavailable absent a showing of irreparable injury, a requirement that cannot be met where there is no showing of any real or immediate threat that the plaintiff will be wronged again — a "likelihood of substantial and immediate irreparable injury." *O'Shea v. Littleton*. The speculative nature of Lyons' claim of future injury requires a finding that this prerequisite of equitable relief has not been fulfilled.

Nor will the injury that Lyons allegedly suffered in 1976 go unrecompensed; for that injury, he has an adequate remedy at law. Contrary to the view of the Court of Appeals, it is not at all "difficult" under our holding "to see how anyone can ever challenge police or similar administrative practices." The legality of the violence to which Lyons claims he was once subjected is at issue in his suit for damages and can be determined there.

Absent a sufficient likelihood that he will again be wronged in a similar way, Lyons is no more entitled to an injunction than any other citizen of Los Angeles; and a federal court may not entertain a claim by any or all citizens who no more than assert that certain practices of law enforcement officers are unconstitutional. . . .

We decline the invitation to slight the preconditions for equitable relief; for as we have held, recognition of the need for a proper balance between state and federal authority counsels restraint in the issuance of injunctions against state officers engaged in the administration of the States' criminal laws in the absence of irreparable injury which is both great and immediate. . . . In exercising their equitable powers federal courts must recognize "[t]he special delicacy of the adjustment to be preserved between federal equitable power and State administration of its own law." The Court of Appeals failed to apply these factors properly and therefore erred in finding that the District Court had not abused its discretion in entering an injunction in this case.

As we noted in *O'Shea*, withholding injunctive relief does not mean that the "federal law will exercise no deterrent effect in these circumstances." If Lyons has suffered an injury barred by the Federal Constitution, he has a remedy for damages under § 1983. Furthermore, those who deliberately deprive a citizen of his constitutional rights risk conviction under the federal criminal laws.

Beyond these considerations the state courts need not impose the same standing or remedial requirements that govern federal-court proceedings. The individual States may permit their courts to use injunctions to oversee the conduct of law enforcement authorities on a continuing basis. But this is not the role of a federal court, absent far more justification than Lyons has proffered in this case.

JUSTICE **MARSHALL**, with whom JUSTICE **BRENNAN**, JUSTICE **BLACKMUN**, and JUSTICE **STEVENS** join, dissenting.

There is plainly a "case or controversy" concerning the constitutionality of the city's chokehold policy. The constitutionality of that policy is directly implicated by Lyons' claim for damages against the city. The complaint clearly alleges that the officer who choked Lyons was carrying out an official policy, and a municipality is liable under [§ 1983] for the conduct of its employees only if they acted pursuant to such a policy. Lyons therefore has standing to challenge the city's chokehold policy and to obtain whatever relief a court may ultimately deem appropriate. None of our prior decisions suggests that his requests for particular forms of relief raise any additional issues concerning his standing. Standing has always depended on whether a plaintiff has a "personal stake in the outcome of the controversy," not on the "precise nature of the relief sought. . . ."

At the outset it is important to emphasize that Lyons' entitlement to injunctive relief and his entitlement to an award of damages both depend upon whether he can show that the city's chokehold policy violates the Constitution. An indispensable prerequisite of municipal liability under [§ 1983] is proof that the conduct complained of is attributable to an unconstitutional official policy or custom . . . for a municipality will not be held liable solely on a theory of respondeat superior.

The Court errs in suggesting that Lyons' prayer for injunctive relief in Count V of his first amended complaint concerns a policy that was not responsible for his injuries and that therefore could not support an award of damages. Paragraph 8 of the complaint alleges that Lyons was choked "without provocation, legal justification or excuse." Paragraph 13 expressly alleges that "[the] Defendant Officers were carrying out *the official policies, customs and practices* of the Los Angeles Police Department and the City of Los Angeles," and that "*by virtue thereof,* defendant City is liable for the actions" of the officers. These allegations are incorporated in each of the Counts against the city, including Count V. . . .

Since Lyons' claim for damages plainly gives him standing, and since the success of that claim depends upon a demonstration that the city's chokehold policy is unconstitutional, it is beyond dispute that Lyons has properly invoked the District Court's authority to adjudicate the constitutionality of the city's chokehold policy. The dispute concerning the constitutionality of that policy plainly presents a "case or controversy" under Art. III. The Court nevertheless holds that a federal court has no power under Art. III to adjudicate Lyons' request, in the same lawsuit, for injunctive relief with respect to that very policy. This anomalous result is not supported either by precedent or by the fundamental concern underlying the standing requirement. Moreover, by fragmenting a single claim into multiple claims for particular types of relief and requiring a separate showing of standing for each form of relief, the decision today departs from this Court's traditional conception of standing and of the remedial powers of the federal courts.

It is simply disingenuous for the Court to assert that its decision requires "[no] extension" of *O'Shea v. Littleton* and *Rizzo v. Goode*. In contrast to this case *O'Shea* and *Rizzo* involved disputes focusing solely on the threat of future injury which the plaintiffs in those cases alleged they faced. In *O'Shea* the plaintiffs did not allege past injury and did not seek compensatory relief.[6] In *Rizzo*, the plaintiffs sought only declaratory and injunctive relief and alleged past instances of police misconduct only in an attempt to establish the substantiality of the threat of future injury. . . .

Because Lyons has a claim for damages against the city, and because he cannot

---

[6] [13] Although counsel for the plaintiffs in *O'Shea* suggested at oral argument that certain plaintiffs had been exposed to illegal conduct in the past, in fact "[no] damages were sought against the petitioners . . . nor were any specific instances involving the individually named respondents set forth in the claim against these judicial officers." The Court referred to the absence of past injury repeatedly.

prevail on that claim unless he demonstrates that the city's chokehold policy violates the Constitution, his personal stake in the outcome of the controversy adequately assures an adversary presentation of his challenge to the constitutionality of the policy. Moreover, the resolution of this challenge will be largely dispositive of his requests for declaratory and injunctive relief. No doubt the requests for injunctive relief may raise additional questions. But these questions involve familiar issues relating to the appropriateness of particular forms of relief, and [7] have never been thought to implicate a litigant's standing to sue. The denial of standing separately to seek injunctive relief therefore cannot be justified by the basic concern underlying the Art. III standing requirement. . . .

Apparently because it is unwilling to rely solely on its unprecedented rule of standing, the Court goes on to conclude that, even if Lyons has standing, "[the] equitable remedy is unavailable. . . ." With the single exception of *Rizzo v. Goode*, supra,[8] all of the cases relied on by the Court concerned injunctions against state criminal proceedings. The rule of *Younger v. Harris*, that such injunctions can be issued only in extraordinary circumstances in which the threat of injury is "great and immediate," reflects the venerable rule that equity will not enjoin a criminal prosecution, the fact that constitutional defenses can be raised in such a state prosecution, and an appreciation of the friction that injunctions against state judicial proceedings may produce.

Our prior decisions have repeatedly emphasized that where an injunction is not directed against a state criminal or quasi-criminal proceeding, "the relevant principles of equity, comity, and federalism" that underlie the *Younger* doctrine "have little force." Outside the special context in which the *Younger* doctrine applies, we have held that the appropriateness of injunctive relief is governed by traditional equitable considerations. Whatever the precise scope of the *Younger* doctrine may be, the concerns of comity and federalism that counsel restraint when a federal court is asked to enjoin a state criminal proceeding simply do not apply to an injunction directed solely at a police department.

If the preliminary injunction granted by the District Court is analyzed under general equitable principles, rather than the more stringent standards of *Younger v. Harris*, it becomes apparent that there is no rule of law that precludes equitable relief and requires that the preliminary injunction be set aside. "In reviewing such interlocutory relief, this Court may only consider whether issuance of the injunction constituted an abuse of discretion."

---

[7] [16] In *O'Shea* itself the Court suggested that the absence of a damages claim was highly pertinent to its conclusion that the plaintiff had no standing. The Court noted that plaintiffs' "claim for relief against the State's Attorney[,] where specific instances of misconduct with respect to particular individuals *are* alleged," stood in "sharp contrast" to their claim for relief against the magistrate and judge, which did not contain similar allegations. The plaintiffs did seek damages against the State's Attorney. See *Spomer v. Littleton*. Like the claims against the State's Attorney in *O'Shea*, Lyons' claims against the city allege both past injury and the risk of future injury. Whereas in *O'Shea* the Court acknowledged the significance for standing purposes of past injury, the Court today inexplicably treats Lyons' past injury for which he is seeking redress as wholly irrelevant to the standing inquiry before us.

[8] [24] . . . *Rizzo v. Goode* does not support a decision barring Lyons from obtaining any injunctive relief, for that case involved an injunction which entailed judicial supervision of the workings of a municipal police department, not simply the sort of preventive injunction that Lyons seeks.

The District Court concluded, on the basis of the facts before it, that Lyons was choked without provocation pursuant to an unconstitutional city policy. Given the necessarily preliminary nature of its inquiry, there was no way for the District Court to know the precise contours of the city's policy or to ascertain the risk that Lyons, who had alleged that the policy was being applied in a discriminatory manner, might again be subjected to a chokehold. But in view of the Court's conclusion that the unprovoked choking of Lyons was pursuant to a city policy, Lyons has satisfied "the usual basis for injunctive relief, 'that there exists some cognizable danger of recurrent violation.'" The risk of serious injuries and deaths to other citizens also supported the decision to grant a preliminary injunction. Courts of equity have much greater latitude in granting injunctive relief "in furtherance of the public interest than . . . when only private interests are involved." In this case we know that the District Court would have been amply justified in considering the risk to the public, for after the preliminary injunction was stayed, five additional deaths occurred prior to the adoption of a moratorium. Under these circumstances, I do not believe that the District Court abused its discretion. . . .

Under the view expressed by the majority today, if the police adopt a policy of "shoot to kill," or a policy of shooting 1 out of 10 suspects, the federal courts will be powerless to enjoin its continuation. The federal judicial power is now limited to levying a toll for such a systematic constitutional violation.

NOTES

1.   Why did the city file a memorandum suggesting a question of mootness and then oppose a finding of mootness?

Does the plaintiff have standing to seek damages? Why does he not have standing to seek injunctive relief? Do the policies behind the standing requirement support the Court's premise that the plaintiff must *independently* establish standing as to his request for injunctive relief? Do *O'Shea* and *Rizzo* support that premise?

Is there anyone for whom the claim for injunctive relief is any more appropriate for adjudication than Lyons' own claim? *Compare Kolender v. Lawson*, 461 U.S. 352, 355 n.3 (1983) (a person who had been stopped 15 times under a state law has standing to seek prospective relief); *City of Houston v. Hill*, 482 U.S. 451, 459 n.7 (1987) (similar). When a pattern of official conduct can be established, it is not necessary that all of the instances of it be directed at a single person. In *Easyriders Freedom F.I.G.H.T. v. Hannigan*, 92 F.3d 1486 (9th Cir. 1996), a group of motorcyclists challenged the enforcement of helmet laws by the state police. The court found that prospective relief was appropriate: "While we are dealing with a relatively small number of citations of fourteen individual plaintiffs in this case, the citations have been the result of a clear CHP citation policy in violation of the Fourth Amendment." *Id. at* 1501. *See generally* Daniel J. Meltzer, *Deterring Constitutional Violations by Law Enforcement Officials: Plaintiffs and Defendants as Private Attorneys General*, 88 COLUM. L. REV. 247 (1988).

Lyons was distinguished in a case closer to it on the facts in *Melendres v. Arpaio*, 695 F.3d 990 (9th Cir. 2012). Latino motorists sued a county sheriff's office, charging that the sheriff, under the auspices of enforcing immigration laws, had "a custom, policy, and practice of racial profiling toward Latino persons in Maricopa County and an unconstitutional policy and practice of stopping Latino drivers and passengers pretextually and without individualized suspicion or cause, and of subjecting them to different, burdensome, stigmatizing and injurious treatment once stopped." The case was brought with the aim of having it certified as a class action, but the court did not rule on whether a class was properly certified. *See* notes 9 and 10 below. It did not rule ultimately on the merits, either, confining its holding to approval of the district court's grant of interim relief.

Although the five named plaintiffs asserted that they were among those motorists mistreated by the sheriff's office, the defendants challenged their standing, asserting that none of them could "demonstrate a credible and genuine threat of future traffic stop interaction with the defendants." 695 F.3d at 997. The court distinguished *Lyons* (in which the plaintiff did not claim that any particular group was targeted) and upheld the district court's grant of interim relief. On the standing issue, it noted that here the defendants claimed authority "based only upon a reasonable suspicion" to detain persons they believed to be illegally in the country, and the plaintiffs presented evidence that the sheriff's office targeted Latinos in conducting traffic stops.

2. In *Lyons* the Court wrestled with issues of standing, mootness, and ripeness in connection with a request for injunctive relief by a plaintiff who could show that he was injured in the past but could not show that he would likely be injured again in the future. As *Lyons* illustrates, these principles rarely stand in the way of plaintiffs seeking damages. The case typically is "ripe" as soon as the injury occurs. It is not "moot" so long as the defendant refuses to redress the harm. And the injury for which the plaintiff sues is sufficient to give him "standing." These doctrines come to the fore when the plaintiff asks for prospective relief, in the form of an injunction that will forbid or direct the state to act in a certain way, or a declaratory judgment that will state the plaintiff's rights and warn the defendant against violating them.

See 28 U.S.C. §§ 2201–2202 for the federal declaratory judgment act. The statute provides that federal courts may issue judgments declaring the rights and duties of the parties so long as the constitutional requirements (such as standing) of an article III "case" are present, even if no other relief is appropriate. There are, for example, a variety of more or less important obstacles to obtaining injunctive relief. Some of these are historical relics that can be neatly bypassed by seeking a declaratory judgment, with the idea that in the event the plaintiff obtains declaratory relief and the defendant then violates the decree, the plaintiff can go back to obtain an injunction to force compliance. Failure to comply with the injunction will then lead to a contempt citation, accompanied by a fine or incarceration for the recalcitrant official. For the historical background of the statute, see RICHARD H. FALLON ET AL., HART & WECHSLER'S THE FEDERAL COURTS AND THE FEDERAL SYSTEM 800 (6th ed. 2009).

The declaratory judgment act has especial importance in litigation seeking relief against judges, as a recent amendment to section 1983 forbids injunctive relief against a judicial officer "unless a declaratory decree was violated or declaratory relief was unavailable." *See Tesmer v. Granholm*, 333 F.3d 683, 703 (6th Cir. 2003).

Michigan state courts followed a general practice of denying state funds for appellate counsel for indigents who pleaded guilty, and a statute codified the practice. The plaintiffs in this case were indigent criminal defendants and attorneys who represented indigents in criminal cases. Plaintiffs sued certain state judges under section 1983 in federal court and obtained a declaratory judgment that the practice violated the indigents' right to due process. When some state judges (including judges who were not defendants in the litigation) refused to abide by the judgment, they sought an injunction against those judges. The Sixth Circuit declined to order injunctive relief against judges who were not parties to the original litigation. Stressing that "[e]njoining a judge is a serious matter," the court ruled that "[f]ailure of a judge unnamed in a declaratory decree to abide by such declaration does not allow a district court to throw caution to the winds and summarily bind all judges. . . . We hold that with respect to Judge Kolenda, a non-party to the original suit, and to the unnamed and uncertified class of Michigan judges, the injunction cannot issue."

Though some cases assert that the declaratory judgment is a "milder" remedy than the injunction, the actual practice of courts indicates that "[w]hen used prospectively, these remedies are rough substitutes." Samuel L. Bray, *The Myth of the Mild Delaratory Judgment*, 63 DUKE L. J. 1091 (2014). According to Professor Bray, the real difference between the two is that the injunction "has features that make it easier for courts to manage the parties" in cases in which the remedy involves ongoing supervision of the defendant's activities, such as school desegregation or prison reform. In this regard, notable features of the injunctive remedy include "specificity, the information generated by the contempt process, the prospect of modification and dissolution, the permissibility of prophylaxis, and the use of monitors and receivers." By contrast, the advantage of declaratory relief is that "the declaratory judgment is sometimes available at an earlier point in the lifecycle of a dispute than an injunction is."

3. In some respects, the plaintiffs in the typical "prospective relief" case may appear to be in a weaker position than Lyons, because they often cannot show that they have suffered an injury in the past. Yet they may obtain relief that will constrain the actions of officials in the future. For example, in *Donahue v. City of Boston*, 304 F.3d 110 (1st Cir. 2002), a white applicant for a city job challenged an affirmative action policy and was denied damages because he could not show he would have been hired absent the policy. Even so, he had standing to sue for prospective relief under the principle of *Texas v. Lesage*, 528 U.S. 18 (1999) (discussed in Chapter 6, *supra*), because he had a cognizable interest in competing for future jobs on an equal footing.

Lyons holds that prospective relief is unavailable because Lyons cannot show that he is likely to be the victim of a chokehold in the future. The general principle underlying that holding is that the plaintiff can establish his standing to sue only by showing that he suffers, or will suffer, an "injury" in the event the court allows the defendant to do as he pleases. In some cases, this requirement will be met by a showing that the defendants will likely violate the plaintiff's personal constitutional rights in the future. *See Kolender, supra; Donahue, supra.* Sometimes, and especially in cases that raise issues regarding the first amendment prohibition on establishments of religion, the constitutional violation affects everyone in the same way and is not directed at the plaintiff in particular. Courts generally hold that anyone exposed to state-sponsored religion has standing to challenge it. *See, e.g., Glassroth v. Moore*, 335 F.3d 1282 (11th Cir. 2003) (attorneys whose professional duties require them regularly to enter a courthouse have standing to challenge a display of the ten commandments in the courthouse); *Doe v. School Board of Ouachita Parish*, 274 F.3d 289, 292 (5th Cir. 2001) (public school students and parents have standing to challenge "the practice of verbal prayer in their schools").

On occasion, people who object to government policy on constitutional grounds, but who suffer no particularized injury, will claim that they are injured as taxpayers. With one exception, these litigants virtually always lose. For a recent example, see *Higgenbotham v. Oklahoma ex rel. Oklahoma Transportation Commission*, 328 F.3d 638 (10th Cir. 2003) (rejecting taxpayer standing to challenge federal statute authorizing federal government to reimburse states for costs associated with issuance of bonds for state transportation projects). Again, establishment clause cases are treated differently. *See, e.g., Plans, Inc. v. Sacramento City Unified School District*, 319 F.3d 504 (9th Cir. 2003) (upholding taxpayer standing to challenge, on establishment clause grounds, the use of public money to support the curriculums of certain private schools). But the Supreme Court has narrowed the scope of this exception in recent years. *E.g., Arizona Christian School Tuition Org. v Winn*, 131 S. Ct. 1436 (2011) (no taxpayer standing to challenge tax credits for contributions to school tuition organizations on Establishment Clause grounds); *Hein v. Freedom from Religion Foundation, Inc.*, 551 U.S. 587 (2007) (no taxpayer standing to challenge executive branch expenditures on Establishment Clause grounds).

4. A plaintiff seeking prospective relief, and who has established an injury, may be thwarted by the mootness doctrine if the objectionable conduct has now ceased and is unlikely to resume. In *Reyes v. City of Lynchburg*, 300 F.3d 449 (4th Cir. 2002), the plaintiffs' free speech challenge to the city's parade ordinance was ruled moot after the ordinance was repealed and there was "no reasonable expectation that Lynchburg [would] reenact the ordinance." If, however, the issue is "capable of repetition, yet evading review," courts make an exception to the mootness principle. This rule applies when "(1) the challenged action was too short in duration to be fully litigated prior to its cessation or expiration; and (2) there is a reasonable expectation that the same complaining party will be subjected to the same action again." *First National Bank of Boston v. Bellotti*, 435 U.S. 765, 774 (1978). In *Porter v. Jones*, 319 F.3d 483 (9th Cir. 2003), the plaintiffs had operated a vote swapping internet site in the 2000 presidential election. They sued to challenge on free speech grounds state laws that prohibited brokering the exchange of votes. Though the election was over by the time their case reached the court, the court ruled that the request for prospective relief was not moot. This case, like many election cases, met the first prong of the exception "because the inherently brief duration of an election is almost invariably too short to enable full litigation on the merits." The second prong was met because "Porter has expressed his intent to create a similar website in future presidential elections, the other plaintiffs are likely to use such a website, and there is no indication that [the California secretary of state] will not enforce the election laws against Plaintiffs in the future." Why was this exception not applicable to Lyons' request for injunctive relief? Keep in mind that the mootness of a request for prospective relief does not preclude the plaintiff from seeking damages for past injury. For example, in *Donovan ex rel. Donovan v. Punxsutawney School Board*, 336 F.3d 211 (3d Cir. 2003), a high school student, through her parents, brought a section 1983 suit challenging a school policy that excluded religious clubs from the school. When the student graduated, the court ruled that her request for injunctive and declaratory relief was moot, but that she could continue to pursue her claims for damages and attorney's fees.

5. A somewhat different problem arises when the plaintiff has not yet suffered an injury, but fears that the defendant will harm him in the future in the absence of judicial intervention. By bifurcating Lyons's claims for damages and prospective relief, the Court could rule that the claim for prospective relief was on shaky ground, as the "injury" for which prospective relief was sought was too speculative. Other litigants seeking anticipatory relief sometimes have more success. A typical section 1983 fact pattern features a plaintiff who wishes to challenge a state criminal or civil sanction, on the ground that he wishes to engage in the prohibited conduct and the statute is unconstitutional. The requested remedy in such suits is usually either a declaration that the statute is unconstitutional, or an injunction against its enforcement. If he violates the law and is prosecuted, his federal suit will be precluded by the doctrine of *Younger v. Harris*, 401 U.S. 37 (1971). See Chapter 10 for a discussion of the *Younger* doctrine. But if he tries to challenge the law without violating it, he must deal with the objection that his anticipatory challenge is not "ripe." In *PeTA v. Rasmussen*, 298 F.3d 1198 (10th Cir. 2002), demonstrators staged a protest at a junior high school and had been arrested under a law that applied to demonstrations at colleges. Their effort to enjoin future enforcement of the law was denied because "PeTA [had] not indicated an intention to stage protests at institutions of higher education." Since the demonstrators were unlikely to be charged under the law again, they suffered no continuing injury.

In *Ward v. Utah*, 321 F.3d 1263, 1269 (10th Cir. 2003), the Tenth Circuit distinguished *PeTA*. An animal rights activist was tried for disorderly conduct, and the charge was elevated to a felony under a hate crimes law. The criminal case was dismissed and he brought a section 1983 case challenging the hate crimes law. His claim of injury was "the threat of future prosecution under the hate-crimes statute." The court allowed the suit to go forward, explaining that, in contrast to *PeTA*, "Ward has been given no assurances that he will not be charged under the hate-crimes statute if he engages in future animal-rights protests similar to the one that was the basis for his felony charge. . . . Utah has not indicated either that the underlying primary offense statutes do not apply to Ward's protesting activities or that the felony enhancement under the hate-crimes statute does not apply to Ward's activities." Notice that under this reasoning, the federal plaintiff is not necessarily obliged to show a *threat* of prosecution. Rather, it may be sufficient that he show the absence of an assurance that he will *not* be prosecuted. *See also Hays v. City of Urbana*, 104 F.3d 102, 103 (7th Cir. 1997) ("What is necessary for standing is a concrete injury, redressable by success in the litigation. Costs of compliance necessary to avoid prosecution can constitute that injury."); *California Pro-Life Council, Inc. v. Getman*, 328 F.3d 1088, 1095 (9th Cir. 2003) (self-censorship due to reasonable fear of prosecution is sufficient "injury"). *See also* DOUGLAS LAYCOCK, MODERN AMERICAN REMEDIES 596 (4th ed. 2010) ("Most of the [Supreme] Court's cases hold or assume that a suit to enjoin enforcement is ripe when the statute is on the books and the plaintiff wants to violate it.").

6. Reread the last two sentences of Justice Marshall's dissent. Is Justice Marshall engaging in rhetorical hyperbole? As a plaintiff's lawyer, and taking the court's opinion as controlling law, could you distinguish a case in which the police routinely violated the rights of arrestees, but no individual plaintiff could show that he would likely be arrested in the future? Didn't Lyons claim that this was itself such a case? Could the problem with injunctive relief raised by the Court in *Lyons* be solved by bringing a class action? *See* notes 9 and 10 below.

Other than injunctive relief, with its threat of contempt if the injunction is not obeyed, is there any other way to deter such unconstitutional conduct on the part of a municipality that is undeterred by the prospect of paying compensatory damages? Would such a case be appropriate for an exception to *City of Newport*? Would criminal penalties against the officers be appropriate? In this regard, recall that the officers who beat Rodney King were tried in federal court under 18 U.S.C. § 242, the criminal counterpart of section 1983.

7. In its discussion of the equitable grounds for denying injunctive relief, the Court in *Lyons* states that "principles of equity, comity, and federalism [should] inform the judgment of federal courts when asked to oversee state law enforcement authorities." Granting that federal courts should not issue intrusive injunctions without a compelling reason for doing so, is it appropriate to reject injunctive relief before a trial on the merits, as the Court does in *Lyons*? Consider the following observations:

> Once standing is established and a constitutional violation identified, the availability of an injunction, as well as the form of injunctive relief, should depend on a calculus more complex than that employed by *Lyons*. The Court should weigh attentively the relevant statutory policy. In balancing statutory policy against competing interests, the Court should also attend more closely to particular facts to identify how deeply the various asserted interests are implicated. . . . [Plaintiffs are] entitled to a balancing of the public and private interests unique to the circumstances of their situations.

Richard H. Fallon, Jr., *Of Justiciability, Remedies, and Public Law Litigation: Notes on the Jurisprudence of* Lyons, 59 N.Y.U. L. REV. 1, 72–73 (1984). Fallon contrasts such a system of case-by-case weighing of interests to the "door-closing prescriptions of *Lyons*." *Id. at* 74. Why might the Court prefer rules like the one in *Lyons* over more particularized decision making? All things considered, which approach is better, Fallon's or the Court's?

8. Does the *Lyons* barrier apply only to constitutional claims arising out of random police encounters or does it extend to other constitutional cases? In *Henschen v. City of Houston*, 959 F.2d 584 (5th Cir. 1992), plaintiffs sought a parade permit for a march on the opening day of the 1990 Economic Summit. The request was refused and the plaintiffs sued, asserting that their First Amendment rights were violated and seeking damages and injunctive relief. The court began its analysis by noting that, under *Lyons*, "[j]usticiability must be analyzed separately on the issues of money damages and the propriety of injunctive relief." The court held that the plaintiffs' damages suit could go forward, but the request for prospective injunctive relief could not. In spite of the alleged wrong done them, they could not

> show that they are imperiled by a present threat of unlawful speech restrictions. . . . [Appellants] formed a loose confederation of community activists who coalesced to demonstrate at the 1990 Economic Summit. Upon the conclusion of the Summit, their *raison d'etre* withered. [After the summit] the group wholly dissolved, except for the purpose of pursuing this action. Thus, they suffer no continuing threat of harm from the City's enforcement of the parade permit scheme.

If a group such as these plaintiffs asked you for advice on maintaining the request for prospective relief, what would you tell them to do?

9. *County of Riverside v. McLaughlin*, 500 U.S. 44 (1991) was a class action brought on behalf of a class of persons arrested without a warrant, challenging the county's practice of combining probable cause determinations with its arraignment procedures. The substantive issue was whether probable cause determinations were made soon enough to satisfy the constitution. Before reaching the merits the Court addressed the plaintiffs' standing. The County argued that

> the main thrust of plaintiffs' suit is that they are entitled to "prompt" probable cause determinations and insists that this is, by definition, a time-limited violation. Once enough time has passed, the County argues, the constitutional violation is complete because a probable cause determination made after that point would no longer be "prompt." Thus, at least as to the named plaintiffs, there is no standing because it is too late for them to receive a prompt hearing and, under *Lyons*, they cannot show that they are likely to be subjected again to the unconstitutional conduct.

The Court responded:

> We reject the County's argument. [At] the time the [complaint] was filed, [some named] plaintiffs [had] been arrested without warrants and were being held in custody without having received a probable cause determination, prompt or otherwise. Plaintiffs alleged in their complaint that they were suffering a direct and current injury as a result of this detention, and would continue to suffer that injury until they received the probable cause determination to which they were entitled. Plainly, plaintiffs' injury was at that moment capable of being redressed through injunctive relief. The County's argument that the constitutional violation had already been "completed" relies on a crabbed reading of the complaint. This case is easily distinguishable from Lyons, in which the constitutionally objectionable practice ceased altogether before the plaintiff filed his complaint.

Does this case represent a retreat from *Lyons*, or merely a refusal to extend its reach? Does it suggest that, compared to suits brought by individuals solely on their own behalf, class actions are less vulnerable to objections based on *Lyons*, simply because the likelihood that a member of the class will be subjected to the challenged practice in the future is greater than the likelihood that an individual plaintiff will be subjected to it?

Melendres v. Arpaio, supra, was brought as a class action, but the court did not rule on whether the case was appropriately certified as a class action. 695 F.3d at 999 (concluding that "complete review of the class certification order is best had once a final judgment has been entered").

10.   Class actions in the federal courts are governed by F. R. Civ. P. 23, which provides, in part:

Rule 23.   Class Actions

(a)   Prerequisites. One or more members of a class may sue or be sued as representative parties on behalf of all members only if:

(1) the class is so numerous that joinder of all members is impracticable;

(2) there are questions of law or fact common to the class;

(3) the claims or defenses of the representative parties are typical of the claims or defenses of the class; and

(4) the representative parties will fairly and adequately protect the interests of the class.

(b)   Types of Class Actions. A class action may be maintained if Rule 23(a) is satisfied and if:

(1) prosecuting separate actions by or against individual class members would create a risk of:

(A) inconsistent or varying adjudications with respect to individual class members that would establish incompatible standards of conduct for the party opposing the class; or

(B) adjudications with respect to individual class members that, as a practical matter, would be dispositive of the interests of the other members not parties to the individual adjudications or would substantially impair or impede their ability to protect their interests;

(2) the party opposing the class has acted or refused to act on grounds that apply generally to the class, so that final injunctive relief or corresponding declaratory relief is appropriate respecting the class as a whole; or

(3) the court finds that the questions of law or fact common to class members predominate over any questions affecting only individual members, and that a class action is superior to other available methods for fairly and efficiently adjudicating the controversy. The matters pertinent to these findings include:

(A) the class members' interests in individually controlling the prosecution or defense of separate actions;

(B) the extent and nature of any litigation concerning the controversy already begun by or against class members;

(C) the desirability or undesirability of concentrating the litigation of the claims in the particular forum; and (D) the likely difficulties in managing a class action.

In some § 1983 cases, the class action may be appropriate for some but not all of the relief sought. For example, in *Pierce v. County of Orange*, 526 F.3d 1190 (9th Cir. 2008), pretrial detainees in Orange County jails brought a class action asserting among other things that the jails were "operated in an unconstitutional manner, depriving them of opportunities for exercise, unduly limiting their access to common areas, and impermissibly restricting their ability to practice religion." They sought both damages and injunctive relief, but the district judge declined to allow the class action for damages to go forward, reasoning that "Rule 23(b)(3) would not offer a superior method for fair and efficient adjudication in light of expected difficulties identifying class members and determining appropriate damages." In affirming that ruling, the 9th circuit noted "the size of the class and the array of variables related to causation and damages." *Id.* at 1200.

If the circumstances of members of the class vary too much, even a class action limited to injunctive relief may be inappropriate. *See, e.g.*, *Vallario v. Vandehey*, 554 F.3d 1259, 1268 (10th Cir. 2009) ("Under Rule 23(b)(2), the injuries sustained by the class must be sufficiently similar that they can be addressed in a single injunction that need not differentiate between class members."). In *Vallario*, a class of county jail inmates challenged such practices as the use of restraint chairs and pepper spray, imposition of especially harsh conditions of confinement, and denial of access to psychiatric care for indigent inmates. The court remanded with directions that the district judge determine whether the plaintiffs had met this requirement.

11. Plaintiffs seeking a prospective remedy often request interim relief, in the form of a preliminary injunction that would halt the practice they challenge while the litigation goes forward. The standard is discussed in *Bronx Household of Faith v. New York Board of Education*, 331 F.3d 342, 348–49 (2d Cir. 2003). This case was a challenge brought by an evangelical Christian church seeking to compel the Board of Education to rent space to it in a public school for Sunday morning meetings. The Board resisted on account of a long-standing policy against allowing the use of its space for religious purposes. On the interim relief issue, the court said:

> To obtain a preliminary injunction a party must demonstrate: (1) that it will be irreparably harmed if an injunction is not granted; and (2) either (a) a likelihood of success on the merits or (b) sufficiently serious questions going to the merits to make them a fair ground for litigation, and a balance of the hardships tipping decidedly in its favor. Where the requested preliminary injunction would stay government action taken in the public interest pursuant to a statutory or regulatory scheme — as it does here — the less rigorous burden of proof standard envisioned by the phrase "fair ground for litigation" does not apply, and instead the party seeking injunctive relief must satisfy the more rigorous "likelihood of success. . . ." Moreover, an even higher standard of proof comes into play when the

injunction sought will alter rather than maintain the status quo. In such case, the movant must show a "clear" or "substantial" likelihood of success.

Finding that the plaintiffs' allegation of a first amendment violation entitled them "to a presumption of irreparable harm," and that they were substantially likely to prevail on the merits, the court affirmed the district court's grant of a preliminary injunction.

The court's reference to "irreparable harm" requires some elaboration. Traditionally, injunctive relief was disfavored, and plaintiffs seeking it were obliged to show that they would suffer "irreparable harm" if they were limited to obtaining damages. Since freedom of speech serves a critical role in self government, the harm suffered by suppressing protected speech is often found to be "irreparable" by the recovery of damages, as the opinion in *Bronx Household of Faith* illustrates. It is unclear just how big a role should be played by the concept of "irreparable injury" in determining whether injunctive relief (interim or permanent) should be granted. A leading scholar in the law of remedies minimizes its importance. *See* DOUGLAS LAYCOCK, THE DEATH OF THE IRREPARABLE INJURY RULE (1991). For a more recent treatment, suggesting that irreparable injury may be regaining some of its importance, *see* Doug Rendleman, *Irreparability Resurrected?: Does a Recalibrated Irreparable Injury Rule Threaten the Warren Court's Establishment Clause Legacy?*, 59 WASH. & LEE L. REV. 1343 (2002).

Chapter 10

PROCEDURAL DEFENSES

This chapter explores a number of defenses to a section 1983 action that do not directly pertain to the merits of the underlying claim. A common thread running throughout these materials is the tension inherent in the dual sovereignty aspects of a federal system of government. Should state or federal law govern a particular issue? When is it appropriate for federal courts to adjudicate claims against state and local officials? Should states be given the first opportunity to redress wrongs committed by its officials against its citizens? Many of the doctrines explored in this chapter are driven by a desire to maintain an appropriate balance between federal authority to protect federal constitutional rights and a respect for state sovereignty.

Keep in mind that these doctrines are not only of theoretical importance but are of immense practical significance for litigation as well.

I. STATUTES OF LIMITATIONS

There are important procedural issues affecting section 1983 litigation that are not governed by a specific uniform federal rule. For example, section 1983 does not contain a specific statute of limitations. Should federal courts fashion a federal common law limitations period, or should they look to analogous state law? If the latter, which state limitations period would be most appropriate? The interplay of state and federal law is especially important in statute of limitations issues. Before turning to the cases, consider the following statute.

42 U.S.C. § 1988 provides in relevant part:

> The jurisdiction in civil and criminal matters conferred on the district courts by the provisions of this Title, and of Title "CIVIL RIGHTS," and of Title "CRIMES," for the protection of all persons in the United States in their civil rights, and for their vindication, shall be exercised and enforced in conformity with the laws of the United States, so far as such laws are suitable to carry the same into effect; but in all cases where they are not adapted to the object, or are deficient in the provisions necessary to furnish suitable remedies and punish offenses against law, the common law, as modified and changed by the constitution and statutes of the State wherein the court having jurisdiction of such civil or criminal cause is held, so far as the same is not inconsistent with the Constitution and laws of the United States, shall be extended to and govern the said courts in the trial and disposition of the cause. . . .

Of what relevance is this statute in determining the proper limitations period for section 1983 claims?

WILSON v. GARCIA
471 U.S. 261 (1985)

JUSTICE STEVENS delivered the opinion of the Court.

In this case we must determine the most appropriate state statute of limitations to apply to claims enforceable under . . . 42 U.S.C. § 1983.

On January 28, 1982, respondent brought this § 1983 action in the United States District Court for the District of New Mexico seeking "money damages to compensate him for the deprivation of his civil rights guaranteed by the Fourth, Fifth and Fourteenth Amendments to the United States Constitution and for the personal injuries he suffered which were caused by the acts and omissions of the [petitioners] acting under color of law." The complaint alleged that on April 27, 1979, petitioner Wilson, a New Mexico State Police officer, unlawfully arrested the respondent, "brutally and viciously" beat him, and sprayed his face with tear gas; that petitioner Vigil, the Chief of the New Mexico State Police, had notice of Officer Wilson's allegedly "violent propensities," and had failed to reprimand him for committing other unprovoked attacks on citizens; and that Vigil's training and supervision of Wilson was seriously deficient.

The respondent's complaint was filed two years and nine months after the claim purportedly arose. Petitioners moved to dismiss on the ground that the action was barred by the 2-year statute of limitations contained in § 41-4-15(A) of the New Mexico Tort Claims Act. The petitioners' motion was supported by a decision of the New Mexico Supreme Court which squarely held that the Tort Claims Act provides "the most closely analogous state cause of action" to § 1983, and that its 2-year statute of limitations is therefore applicable to actions commenced under § 1983 in the state courts. *DeVargas v. New Mexico*. In addition to the 2-year statute of limitations in the Tort Claims Act, two other New Mexico statutes conceivably could apply to § 1983 claims: § 37-1-8, which provides a 3-year limitation period for actions "for an injury to the person or reputation of any person"; and § 37-1-4, which provides a 4-year limitation period for "all other actions not herein otherwise provided for." If either of these longer statutes applies to the respondent's § 1983 claim, the complaint was timely filed.

[The district court denied the motion to dismiss. It ruled that *DeVargas* was not controlling because "the characterization of the nature of the right being vindicated under § 1983 is a matter of federal, rather than state law." The court then concluded that the residual 4-year limitation period should apply. The court of appeals affirmed the district court on different grounds. The court of appeals agreed that *DeVargas* was not controlling, but held that § 1983 actions were best analogized to "an action for injury to personal rights," subject to a 3-year limitation period.]

[T]he conflict, confusion, and uncertainty concerning the appropriate statute of limitations to apply to this most important, and ubiquitous, civil rights statute provided compelling reasons for granting certiorari. 469 U.S. 815 (1984). We find the reasoning in the Court of Appeals' opinion persuasive, and affirm.

I

The Reconstruction Civil Rights Acts do not contain a specific statute of limitations governing § 1983 actions — "a void which is commonplace in federal statutory law." *Board of Regents v. Tomanio*. When Congress has not established a time limitation for a federal cause of action, the settled practice has been to adopt a local time limitation as federal law if it is not inconsistent with federal law or policy to do so. In 42 U.S.C. § 1988, Congress has implicitly endorsed this approach with respect to claims enforceable under the Reconstruction Civil Rights Acts.

The language of § 1988, directs the courts to follow "a three-step process" in determining the rules of decision applicable to civil rights claims:

> "First, courts are to look to the laws of the United States 'so far as such laws are suitable to carry [the civil and criminal civil rights statutes] into effect.' [42 U.S.C. § 1988.] If no suitable federal rule exists, courts undertake the second step by considering application of state 'common law, as modified and changed by the constitution and statutes' of the forum state. Ibid. A third step asserts the predominance of the federal interest: courts are to apply state law only if it is not 'inconsistent with the Constitution and laws of the United States.' Ibid." *Burnett v. Grattan*

This case principally involves the second step in the process: the selection of "the most appropriate," or "the most analogous" state statute of limitations to apply to this § 1983 claim.

In order to determine the most "most appropriate" or "most analogous" New Mexico statute to apply to the respondent's claim, we must answer three questions. We must first consider whether state law or federal law governs the characterization of a § 1983 claim for statute of limitations purposes. If federal law applies, we must next decide whether all § 1983 claims should be characterized in the same way, or whether they should be evaluated differently depending upon the varying factual circumstances and legal theories presented in each individual case. Finally, we must characterize the essence of the claim in the pending case, and decide which state statute provides the most appropriate limiting principle. Although the text of neither § 1983 nor § 1988 provides a pellucid answer to any of these questions, all three parts of the inquiry are, in final analysis, questions of statutory construction.

II

Our identification of the correct source of law properly begins with the text of § 1988. Congress' first instruction in the statute is that the law to be applied in adjudicating civil rights claims shall be in "conformity with the laws of the United States, so far as such laws are suitable." This mandate implies that resort to state law — the second step in the process — should not be undertaken before principles of federal law are exhausted. The characterization of § 1983 for statute of limitations purposes is derived from the elements of the cause of action, and Congress' purpose in providing it. These, of course, are matters of federal law. Since federal law is available to decide the question, the language of § 1988 directs that the matter of characterization should be treated as a federal question. Only the length of the limitations period, and closely related questions of tolling and application, are to be governed by state law.

This interpretation is also supported by Congress' third instruction in § 1988: state law shall only apply "so far as the same is not inconsistent with" federal law. This requirement emphasizes "the predominance of the federal interest" in the borrowing process, taken as a whole. Even when principles of state law are borrowed to assist in the enforcement of this federal remedy, the state rule is adopted as "a federal rule responsive to the need whenever a federal right is impaired." *Sullivan v. Little Hunting Park, Inc.* The importation of the policies and purposes of the States on matters of civil rights is not the primary office of the borrowing provision in § 1988; rather, the statute is designed to assure that neutral rules of decision will be available to enforce the civil rights actions, among them § 1983. Congress surely did not intend to assign to state courts and legislatures a conclusive role in the formative function of defining and characterizing the essential elements of a federal cause of action.

[T]he federal interest in uniformity and the interest in having "firmly defined, easily applied rules," support the conclusion that Congress intended the characterization of § 1983 to be measured by federal rather than state standards. The Court of Appeals was therefore correct in concluding that it was not bound by the New Mexico Supreme Court's holding in *DeVargas*.

III

A federal cause of action "brought at any distance of time" would be "utterly repugnant to the genius of our laws." *Adams v. Woods*. Just determinations of fact cannot be made when, because of the passage of time, the memories of witnesses have faded or evidence is lost. In compelling circumstances, even wrongdoers are entitled to assume that their sins may be forgotten.

The borrowing of statutes of limitations for § 1983 claims serves these policies of repose. Of course, the application of any statute of limitations would promote repose. By adopting the statute governing an analogous cause of action under state law, federal law incorporates the State's judgment on the proper balance between the policies of repose and the substantive policies of enforcement embodied in the state cause of action. However, when the federal claim differs from the state cause of action in fundamental respects, the State's choice of a specific period of limitation is, at best, only a rough approximation of "the point at which the interests in favor of protecting valid claims are outweighed by the interests in prohibiting the prosecution of stale ones." *Johnson v. Railway Express Agency, Inc.*

[P]ractical considerations help to explain why a simple, broad characterization of all § 1983 claims best fits the statute's remedial purpose. The experience of the courts that have predicated their choice of the correct statute of limitations on an analysis of the particular facts of each claim demonstrates that their approach inevitably breeds uncertainty and time-consuming litigation that is foreign to the central purposes of § 1983. Almost every § 1983 claim can be favorably analogized to more than one of the ancient common-law forms of action, each of which may be governed by a different statute of limitations. In the case before us, for example, the respondent alleges that he was injured by a New Mexico State Police officer who used excessive force to carry out an unlawful arrest. This § 1983 claim is arguably analogous to distinct state tort claims for false arrest, assault and battery, or personal injuries. Moreover, the claim could also be characterized as one arising under a statute, or as governed by the special New Mexico statute authorizing recovery against the State for the torts of its agents.

A catalog of other constitutional claims that have been alleged under § 1983 would encompass numerous and diverse topics and subtopics: discrimination in public employment on the basis of race or the exercise of First Amendment rights, discharge or demotion without procedural due process, mistreatment of schoolchildren, deliberate indifference to the medical needs of prison inmates, the seizure of chattels without advance notice or sufficient opportunity to be heard — to identify only a few. If the choice of the statute of limitations were to depend upon the particular facts or the precise legal theory of each claim, counsel could almost always argue, with considerable force, that two or more periods of limitations should apply to each § 1983 claim. Moreover, under such an approach different statutes of limitations would be applied to the various § 1983 claims arising in the same State,[1] and multiple periods of limitations would often apply to the same case.[2] There is no reason to believe that Congress would have sanctioned this interpretation of its statute.

When § 1983 was enacted, it is unlikely that Congress actually foresaw the wide diversity of claims that the new remedy would ultimately embrace. The simplicity of the admonition in § 1988 is consistent with the assumption that Congress intended the identification of the appropriate statute of limitations to be an uncomplicated task for judges, lawyers, and litigants, rather than a source of uncertainty, and unproductive and ever-increasing litigation. Moreover, the legislative purpose to create an effective remedy for the enforcement of federal civil rights is obstructed by uncertainty in the applicable statute of limitations, for scarce resources must be dissipated by useless litigation on collateral matters.

Although the need for national uniformity "has not been held to warrant the displacement of state statutes of limitations for civil rights actions," *Board of Regents v. Tomanio*, uniformity within each State is entirely consistent with the borrowing principle contained in § 1988. We conclude that the statute is fairly construed as a directive to select, in each State, the one most appropriate statute of limitations for all § 1983 claims. The federal interests in uniformity, certainty, and the minimization of unnecessary litigation all support the conclusion that Congress favored this simple approach.

---

[1] [32] For example, compare *McGhee v. Ogburn* (2-year Florida statute), with *Williams v. Rhoden* (4-year Florida statute); *Hines v. Board of Education of Covington, Ky.* (1-year Kentucky statute), with *Garner v. Stephens* (5-year Kentucky statute); and *Whatley v. Department of Education* (20-year Georgia statute), with *Wooten v. Sanders* (2-year Georgia statute).

[2] [33] For example, in *Polite v. Diehl* the plaintiff alleged that police officers unlawfully arrested him, beat him and sprayed him with mace, coerced him into pleading guilty to various offenses, and had his automobile towed away. The court held that a 1-year false arrest statute of limitations applied to the arrest claim, a 2-year personal injuries statute applied to the beating and coerced-plea claims, and a 6-year statute for actions seeking the recovery of goods applied to the towing claim. . . .

IV

After exhaustively reviewing the different ways that § 1983 claims have been characterized in every Federal Circuit, the Court of Appeals concluded that the tort action for the recovery of damages for personal injuries is the best alternative available. We agree that this choice is supported by the nature of the § 1983 remedy, and by the federal interest in ensuring that the borrowed period of limitations not discriminate against the federal civil rights remedy.

The atrocities that concerned Congress in 1871 plainly sounded in tort. Relying on this premise we have found tort analogies compelling in establishing the elements of a cause of action under § 1983, and in identifying the immunities available to defendants. As we have noted, however, the § 1983 remedy encompasses a broad range of potential tort analogies, from injuries to property to infringements of individual liberty.

Among the potential analogies, Congress unquestionably would have considered the remedies established in the Civil Rights Act to be more analogous to tort claims for personal injury than, for example, to claims for damages to property or breach of contract. The unifying theme of the Civil Rights Act of 1871 is reflected in the language of the Fourteenth Amendment that unequivocally recognizes the equal status of every "person" subject to the jurisdiction of any of the several States. The Constitution's command is that all "persons" shall be accorded the full privileges of citizenship; no person shall be deprived of life, liberty, or property without due process of law or be denied the equal protection of the laws. A violation of that command is an injury to the individual rights of the person.

Had the 42d Congress expressly focused on the issue decided today, we believe it would have characterized § 1983 as conferring a general remedy for injuries to personal rights.

The relative scarcity of statutory claims when § 1983 was enacted makes it unlikely that Congress would have intended to apply the catchall periods of limitations for statutory claims that were later enacted by many States. Section 1983, of course, is a statute, but it only provides a remedy and does not itself create any substantive rights. Although a few § 1983 claims are based on statutory rights most involve much more. The rights enforceable under § 1983 include those guaranteed by the Federal Government in the Fourteenth Amendment: that every person within the United States is entitled to equal protection of the laws and to those "fundamental principles of liberty and justice" that are contained in the Bill of Rights and "lie at the base of all our civil and political institutions." These guarantees of liberty are among the rights possessed by every individual in a civilized society, and not privileges extended to the people by the legislature.

Finally, we are satisfied that Congress would not have characterized § 1983 as providing a cause of action analogous to state remedies for wrongs committed by public officials. It was the very ineffectiveness of state remedies that led Congress to enact the Civil Rights Acts in the first place. Congress therefore intended that the remedy provided in § 1983 be independently enforceable whether or not it duplicates a parallel state remedy. *Monroe v. Pape.* The characterization of all § 1983 actions as involving claims for personal injuries minimizes the risk that the choice of a state statute of limitations would not fairly serve the federal interests vindicated by § 1983. General personal injury actions, sounding in tort, constitute a major part of the total volume of civil litigation in the state courts today, and probably did so in 1871 when § 1983 was enacted. It is most unlikely that the period of limitations applicable to such claims ever was, or ever would be, fixed in a way that would discriminate against federal claims, or be inconsistent with federal law in any respect.

V

In view of our holding that § 1983 claims are best characterized as personal injury actions, the Court of Appeals correctly applied the 3-year statute of limitations governing actions "for an injury to the person or reputation of any person." N.M. Stat. Ann. § 37-1-8 (1978). The judgment of the Court of Appeals is affirmed.

It is so ordered.

JUSTICE **POWELL** took no part in the consideration or decision of this case. [The dissenting opinion of JUSTICE **O'CONNOR** is omitted.]

NOTES

1. When and to what extent should federal courts look to state law under section 1988? When would state law be considered "inconsistent with the Constitution and laws of the United States"? Why are federal courts free to ignore state supreme court determinations as to which state statute of limitations is most appropriate? The majority characterizes the issue as one of statutory construction. Is the Court's conclusion that a single state statute of limitations should govern all section 1983 cases most strongly supported by the language of section 1988, its legislative history, or contemporary policy?

2. Unlike New Mexico, many states do not provide a single limitations period for "the tort action for the recovery of damages for personal injuries." It is common for states to have one or more limitations period for certain intentional torts, and a residual or general limitations period for all other personal injury actions. In such instances, which limitations period controls the section 1983 claim? In *Owens v. Okure*, 488 U.S. 235 (1989), the Court held that residual or general limitations period for personal injury actions should govern section1983 claims. Thus, New York's three-year general personal injury statute of limitations governed the plaintiff's excessive force section 1983 claim, rather than the one-year period for intentional torts. Would it matter if the general personal injury limitations period is shorter than the period for intentional torts? Should it matter that many section 1983 claims require evidence of "deliberate indifference," a standard more closely analogous to intentional torts than to negligence? The *Owens* Court emphasized that choosing a state's residual limitations period was appropriate only where "state law provides multiple statutes of limitations for personal injury actions and the residual one embraces either explicitly or by judicial construction, unspecified personal injury actions." *Owens*, 488 U.S. at 250 n.12.

3. Are states free to enact special statutes of limitations exclusively for section 1983 claims? In 1987, Utah enacted a statute imposing a 2-year limitations period for section 1983 claims (Utah Code Ann. § 78-12-28(3)), the same as provided for claims under state law against state officials for violations of official duties. The residual statute of limitations for personal injuries in Utah is 4 years. Utah Code Ann. § 78-12-25(3). Is the specific statute of limitations for section 1983 claims the "most analogous" limitations period under *Wilson* and *Owens*? Is a specific statute of limitations of two years for section 1983 claims "consistent" with federal law and policy? Is it relevant that the special limitations period for section 1983 claims is the same as applicable to similar claims against state officials under state law? The Tenth Circuit Court of Appeals struck down the Utah statute. *Arnold v. Duchesne County*, 26 F.3d 982 (10th Cir. 1994). The court held that the statute was inconsistent with federal law and policy. Among the reasons cited by the court was that the special limitations period was "at least partially motivated by . . . [a desire] to reduce the number of [prisoner section 1983] suits." *Arnold*, 26 F.3d 988. Would the outcome in *Arnold* be different if the special statute of limitations for section 1983 claims was longer than the residual personal injury statute of limitations?

4. Under *Wilson*, the governing limitations period for section 1983 claims necessarily will vary from state to state. In most jurisdictions, the limitations period is two or three years. *E.g.*, Behavorial Institute of *Indiana v. Hobart City of Common Council*, 406 F.3d 926 (7th Cir. 2005) (Indiana 2-year statute of limitations); *McIntosh v. Antonio*, 71 F.3d 29 (1st Cir. 1995) (Massachusetts 3-year limitations period); *Leon v. Murphy*, 988 F.2d 303 (2d Cir. 1993) (New York 3-year limitations period); *Genty v. Resolution Trust Corp.*, 937 F.2d 899 (3d Cir. 1991) (New Jersey 2 year limitations period). In California, Louisiana, and Tennessee, however, the limitations period is only one year. *Kines v. Stone* 84 F.3d 1121 (9th Cir. 1996); *Mapes v. Bishop*, 541 F.3d 582 (5th Cir. 2008); *Merriweather v. Memphis*, 107 F.3d 396 (6th Cir. 1997). Is there a principled reason why a civil rights claimant should have three years in which to file her suit in New York, but only one year in California. For a compilation of applicable limitation periods by state, see Martin A. Schwartz, 1B Section 1983 Claims and Defenses § 12.02 (4th ed 2009 Supp.).

5. The issue of when a cause of action "accrues" for purposes of the statute of limitations is determined by federal law. *Delaware State College v. Ricks*, 449 U.S. 250 (1980). In *Ricks*, a college professor complained that he was denied tenure because of his national origin. The Court ruled that his claim accrued (and the limitations period began to run) on the date was notified of the tenure decision, not when his contract expired. *Ricks* held that as a matter of federal law, the section 1983 claim accrued on the date of the challenged conduct. Suppose that on the date of the challenged conduct, the plaintiff did not have reason to know that the defendants' decision was unconstitutionally discriminatory. Should the cause of action accrue when the plaintiff discovers the impermissible discriminatory motive? The Supreme Court applied such a discovery rule in a medical malpractice claim brought under the Federal Tort Claims Act. In *United States v. Kubrick*, 444 U.S. 111 (1979), the Court held that a cause of action accrues when the patient is, or reasonably should be, aware of an injury and its probable cause, but not necessarily the possibility of negligence. Suppose an African-American is denied a liquor license by the defendant in 1979 and a white couple is granted a license for the same location in 1981. Would the African-American's section 1983 claim of alleged racial discrimination accrue on the date his application was denied, or on the date the white application was granted? *See Calhoun v. Alabama Alcoholic Beverage Control Board*, 705 F.2d 422, 425 (11th Cir. 1983) ("the statute does not begin to run until the facts which would support a cause of action are apparent or should be apparent to a person with a reasonably prudent regard for his rights."). *See also Orniston v. Nelson*, 117 F.3d 69 (2d Cir. 1997); *Collyer v. Darling*, 98 F.3d 211 (6th Cir. 1996) (both adopting a discovery rule).

Accrual issues may be particularly complex in cases involving abstention, exhaustion of remedies, or similar doctrines. Some examples of such complexity are discussed in the notes following *Heck v. Humphrey* in Part IV, *infra*. For an interesting discussion of when the statute of limitations begins to run in a section 1983 challenge to the method of execution in a death penalty case, see *McNair v. Allen*, 515 F.3d 1168 (11th Cir. 2008) (holding that "a method of execution claim accrues on the later of the date on which state review is complete, or the date on which the capital litigant becomes subject to a new or substantially changed execution protocol"); *see also* Ty Alper, *Blind Dates: When Should the Statute of Limitations Begin to Run on a Method-of-Execution Challenge?*, 60 Duke L.J. 865 (2011) (assessing lower courts' approaches to determining when a claim challenging a method of execution).

6.   Several courts have applied the "continuing violation" doctrine under which the plaintiff can recover damages for a course of conduct that began outside but continued within the limitation period. *See, e.g. Kuhnle Bros. v. County of Georgia*, 103 F.3d 513 (6th Cir. 1997); *Gutowsky v. County of Placer*, 108 F.3d 256 (9th Cir. 1997). The doctrine will not permit recovery, however, for discreet acts of discrimination that occurred outside the statutory period. *E.g. Bell v. Ohio State University*, 351 F.3d 240 (6th Cir. 2003). *Cf. AMTRAK v. Morgan*, 536 U.S. 101 (2002) (Title VII clam). "The courts have experienced difficulties defining what a continuing violation is, resulting in case law that is inconsistent and confusing. It is not a always easy to determine whether a claimant alleges a single wrong, a series of separate acts for which the limitation begins anew for each violation, or a violation resulting from . . . a continuing illegal practice or policy." Martin A. Schwartz, 1B Section 1983 Claims And Defenses § 12.03 (4th ed. 2009 Supp.)

7.   Though accrual is governed by federal law, the tolling of the limitations period is controlled by state law. *Board of Regents v. Tomanio*, 446 U.S. 478 (1980) (rejecting the application of a federal tolling rule). Historically, many states have tolled the running of the statute of limitations for minors, the insane and the imprisoned. Such state tolling rules have enabled inmates to bring actions against prison officials many years after the challenged conduct occurred. *See Hardin v. Straub*, 490 U.S. 536 (1989) (applying the Michigan tolling statute). Perhaps in response to decisions like *Hardin*, some states modified their tolling statutes for claims by inmates against prison officials. Suppose a state eliminates its tolling provisions for claims by inmates against prison officials, but retains it for claims by inmates against all other defendants. Would such a statute be considered "inconsistent" with the purposes of section 1983, and hence not controlling? *See Dixon v. Chrans*, 986 F.2d 201 (7th Cir. 1993) (Illinois law is "inconsistent" with the purposes of section 1983 and will not be applied to section 1983 claims; subsequently, Illinois

completely abolished the tolling rule for prison inmates).

8. Suppose police officers fraudulently conceal the identity of the officers who used excessive force in arresting the plaintiff. Should state or federal law control whether the limitation period is tolled? It is widely recognized that federal courts will apply state equitable tolling provisions. *E.g., Estate of Blue v. Los Angeles*, 120 F.3d 982 (9th Cir. 1997); *Singletary v. Continental National Bank*, 9 F.3d 1236 (7th Cir. 1993). Courts have, on occasion, fashioned a federal rule of equitable tolling. *See e.g., Smith v. City of Chicago Heights*, 951 F.2d 834 (7th Cir. 1992) (applying a federal rule of "equitable tolling" when the state fraudulent concealment statute did not apply). *Cf. Ashafa v. Chicago*, 146 F.3d 459 (7th Cir. 1998) (observing that the Supreme Court has not resolved whether tolling provisions operate exclusive of or are in conjunction with the federal doctrine of equitable tolling). Is the application of a federal rule of equitable tolling consistent with *Tomanio* cited in the preceding note? Could any apparent inconsistency be avoided by characterizing equitable tolling as an aspect of accrual which, as discussed in note 5, is governed by federal law?

9. Many states have laws that require that notice be given within a short time of injury in order to bring tort claims against local governments or their officials. Should such notice of claim statutes apply to section 1983 claims brought in federal or state court? In *Felder v. Casey*, 487 U.S. 131, 138 (1988), the Supreme Court concluded that Wisconsin's four-month notice-of-claim statute "conflicts both in its purpose and effects with the remedial objectives of section 1983" and therefore could not be applied to section 1983 claims brought in state court. *See* Chapter 11 *infra*.

II. RELEASE-DISMISSAL AGREEMENTS

The statute of limitations materials illustrate one type of federal-state conflict in section 1983 litigation: whether federal or state law should control a particular issue. The absence of a uniform federal statute of limitations creates the need for federal courts to borrow from and apply state law. The procedural defenses addressed in the remainder of this chapter implicate an additional type of federal-state conflict: to what extent should state proceedings affect a subsequent section 1983 claim? For example, many section 1983 claims arise from alleged infringements of constitutional rights occurring in the course of a state criminal investigation or prosecution. Challenges to the constitutionality of a search or arrest often are raised first in state court as a defense to the criminal prosecution. The case below considers whether the terms of an agreement dismissing state criminal charges can effectively bar a section 1983 suit pertaining to the legality of the arrest and prosecution.

TOWN OF NEWTON v. RUMERY
480 U.S. 386 (1987)

JUSTICE POWELL announced the judgment of the Court and delivered the opinion of the Court with respect to Parts I, II, III-A, IV, and V, and an opinion with respect to Part III-B, in which THE CHIEF JUSTICE, JUSTICE WHITE, and JUSTICE SCALIA join.

The question in this case is whether a court properly may enforce an agreement in which a criminal defendant releases his right to file an action under 42 U.S.C. § 1983 in return for a prosecutor's dismissal of pending criminal charges.

I

In 1983, a grand jury in Rockingham County, New Hampshire, indicted David Champy for aggravated felonious sexual assault. Respondent Bernard Rumery, a friend of Champy's, read about the charges in a local newspaper. Seeking information about the charges, he telephoned Mary Deary, who was acquainted with both Rumery and Champy. Coincidentally, Deary had been the victim of the assault in question and was expected to be the principal witness against Champy. The record does not reveal directly the date or substance of this conversation between Rumery and Deary, but Deary apparently was disturbed by the call. On March 12, according to police records, she called David Barrett, the Chief of Police for the town of Newton. She told him that Rumery was trying to force her to drop the charges against Champy. Rumery talked to Deary again on May 11. The substance of this conversation also is disputed. Rumery claims that Deary called him and that she raised the subject of Champy's difficulties. According to the police records, however, Deary told Chief Barrett that Rumery had threatened that, if Deary went forward on the Champy case, she would "end up like" two women who recently had been murdered in Lowell, Massachusetts. Barrett arrested Rumery and accused him of tampering with a witness. . . .

Rumery promptly retained Stephen Woods, an experienced criminal defense attorney. Woods contacted Brian Graf, the Deputy County Attorney for Rockingham County. He warned Graf that he "had better [dismiss] these charges, because we're going to win them and after that we're going to sue." After further discussions, Graf and Woods reached an agreement, under which Graf would dismiss the charges against Rumery if Rumery would agree not to sue the town, its officials, or Deary for any harm caused by the arrest. All parties agreed that one factor in Graf's decision not to prosecute Rumery was Graf's desire to protect Deary from the trauma she would suffer if she were forced to testify. . . .

Woods drafted an agreement in which Rumery agreed to release any claims he might have against the town, its officials, or Deary if Graf agreed to dismiss the criminal charges (the release-dismissal agreement). After Graf approved the form of the agreement, Woods presented it to Rumery. Although Rumery's recollection of the events was quite different, the District Court found that Woods discussed the agreement with Rumery in his office for about an hour and explained to Rumery that he would forgo all civil actions if he signed the agreement. Three days later, on

June 6, 1983, Rumery returned to Woods' office and signed the agreement. The criminal charges were dropped.

Ten months later, on April 13, 1984, Rumery filed an action under § 1983 in the Federal District Court for the District of New Hampshire. He alleged that the town and its officers had violated his constitutional rights by arresting him, defaming him, and imprisoning him falsely. The defendants filed a motion to dismiss, relying on the release-dismissal agreement as an affirmative defense. Rumery argued that the agreement was unenforceable because it violated public policy. . . .

[The District Court rejected Rumery's argument and dismissed the § 1983 action on the basis of the release-dismissal agreement. The Court of Appeals reversed, holding that all such agreements are per se invalid.]

Because the case raises a question important to the administration of criminal justice, we granted the town's petition for a writ of certiorari. We reverse.

II

We begin by noting the source of the law that governs this case. The agreement purported to waive a right to sue conferred by a federal statute. The question whether the policies underlying that statute may in some circumstances render that waiver unenforceable is a question of federal law. We resolve this question by reference to traditional common-law principles, as we have resolved other questions about the principles governing § 1983 actions. The relevant principle is well established: a promise is unenforceable if the interest in its enforcement is outweighed in the circumstances by a public policy harmed by enforcement of the agreement.

III

The Court of Appeals concluded that the public interests related to release-dismissal agreements justified a per se rule of invalidity. We think the court overstated the perceived problems and also failed to credit the significant public interests that such agreements can further. Most importantly, the Court of Appeals did not consider the wide variety of factual situations that can result in release-dismissal agreements. Thus, although we agree that in some cases these agreements may infringe important interests of the criminal defendant and of society as a whole, we do not believe that the mere possibility of harm to these interests calls for a per se rule.

A

Rumery's first objection to release-dismissal agreements is that they are inherently coercive. He argues that it is unfair to present a criminal defendant with a choice between facing criminal charges and waiving his right to sue under § 1983. We agree that some release-dismissal agreements may not be the product of an informed and voluntary decision. The risk, publicity, and expense of a criminal trial may intimidate a defendant, even if he believes his defense is meritorious. But this possibility does not justify invalidating all such agreements. In other contexts criminal defendants are required to make difficult choices that effectively waive constitutional rights. For example, it is well settled that plea bargaining does not violate the Constitution even though a guilty plea waives important constitutional rights . . . .[3]

In many cases a defendant's choice to enter into a release-dismissal agreement will reflect a highly rational judgment that the certain benefits of escaping criminal prosecution exceed the speculative benefits of prevailing in a civil action. Rumery's voluntary decision to enter this agreement exemplifies such a judgment. Rumery is a sophisticated businessman. He was not in jail and was represented by an experienced criminal lawyer, who drafted the agreement. Rumery considered the agreement for three days before signing it. The benefits of the agreement to Rumery are obvious: he gained immunity from criminal prosecution in consideration of abandoning a civil suit that he may well have lost.

Because Rumery voluntarily waived his right to sue under 1983, the public interest opposing involuntary waiver of constitutional rights is no reason to hold this agreement invalid. Moreover, we find that the possibility of coercion in the making of similar agreements insufficient by itself to justify a per se rule against release-dismissal bargains. If there is such a reason, it must lie in some external public interest necessarily injured by release-dismissal agreements.

B

. . . [T]he Court of Appeals held that all release-dismissal agreements offend public policy because it believed that these agreements "temp prosecutors to trump up charges in reaction to a defendant's civil rights claim, suppress evidence of police misconduct, and leave unremedied deprivations of constitutional rights." We can agree that in some cases there may be a substantial basis for this concern. It is true, of course, that § 1983 actions to vindicate civil rights may further significant public interests. But it is important to remember that Rumery had no public duty to institute a § 1983 action merely to further the public's interest in revealing police misconduct. Congress has confined the decision to bring such actions to the injured individuals, not to the public at large. Thus, we hesitate to elevate more diffused public interests above Rumery's considered decision that he would benefit personally from the agreement.

We also believe the Court of Appeals misapprehended the range of public interests arguably affected by a release-dismissal agreement. The availability of such agreements may threaten important public interests. They may tempt prosecutors to bring frivolous charges, or to dismiss meritorious charges, to protect

---

[3] [3] We recognize that the analogy between plea bargains and release-dismissal agreements is not complete. The former are subject to judicial oversight. Moreover, when the State enters a plea bargain with a criminal defendant, it receives immediate and tangible benefits, such as promptly imposed punishment without the expenditure of prosecutorial resources. Also, the defendant's agreement to plead to some crime tends to ensure some satisfaction of the public's interest in the prosecution of crime and confirms that the prosecutor's charges have a basis in fact. The benefits the State may realize in particular cases from release-dismissal agreements may not be as tangible, but they are not insignificant.

the interests of other.[4] But a per se rule of invalidity fails to credit other relevant public interests and improperly assumes prosecutorial misconduct.[5]

The vindication of constitutional rights and the exposure of official misconduct are not the only concerns implicated by § 1983 suits. No one suggests that all such suits are meritorious. Many are marginal and some are frivolous. Yet even when the risk of ultimate liability is negligible, the burden of defending such lawsuits is substantial. Counsel may be retained by the official, as well as the governmental entity. Preparation for trial, and the trial itself, will require the time and attention of the defendant officials, to the detriment of their public duties. In some cases litigation will extend over a period of years. This diversion of officials from their normal duties and the inevitable expense of defending even unjust claims is distinctly not in the public interest. To the extent release-dismissal agreements protect public officials from the burdens of defending such unjust claims, they further this important public interest.

A per se rule invalidating release-dismissal agreements also assumes that prosecutors will seize the opportunity for wrongdoing. . . . Our decisions . . . uniformly have recognized that courts normally must defer to prosecutorial decisions as to whom to prosecute. The reasons for judicial deference are well known. Prosecutorial charging decisions are rarely simple. In addition to assessing the strength and importance of a case, prosecutors also must consider other tangible and intangible factors, such as government enforcement priorities. Finally, they also must decide how best to allocate the scarce resources of a criminal justice system that simply cannot accommodate the litigation of every serious criminal charge.[6] Because these decisions "are not readily susceptible to the kind of analysis the courts are competent to undertake," we have been "properly hesitant to examine the decision whether to prosecute."

Against this background of discretion, the mere opportunity to act improperly does not compel an assumption that all — or even a significant number of — release-dismissal agreements stem from prosecutors abandoning "the independence of judgment required by [their] public trust," *Imbler v. Pachtman*.[7] Rather,

---

[4] Actions taken for these reasons properly have been recognized as unethical. See ABA Model Code of Professional Responsibility, Disciplinary Rule 7-105 (1980).

[5] Prosecutors themselves rarely are held liable in section 1983 actions. See *Imbler v. Pachtman* (discussing prosecutorial immunity). Also, in many States and municipalities-perhaps in most — prosecutors are elected officials and are entirely independent of the civil authorities likely to be defendants in section 1983 suits. There may be situations, of course, when a prosecutor is motivated to protect the interests of such officials or of police. But the constituency of an elected prosecutor is the public, and such a prosecutor is likely to be influenced primarily by the general public interest.

[6] In 1985, the federal district courts disposed of 47,360 criminal cases. Of these, only 6,053, or about 12.8%, ended after a trial. Annual Report of the Director of the Administrative Office of the U.S. Courts 374 (1985). As we have recognized, if every serious criminal charge were evaluated through a full-scale criminal trial, "the States and the Federal Government would need to multiply by many times the number of judges and court facilities," *Santobello v. New York*.

[7] Of course, the Court has found that certain actions are so likely to result from prosecutorial misconduct that it has "'[p]resumed' an improper vindictive motive," *United States v. Goodwin*. E. g., *Blackledge v. Perry* (holding that it violates the Due Process Clause for a prosecutor to increase charges in response to a defendant's exercise of his right to appeal). But the complexity of pretrial decisions by

tradition and experience justify our belief that the great majority of prosecutors will be faithful to their duty. . . .

Because release-dismissal agreements may further legitimate prosecutorial and public interests, we reject the Court of Appeals' holding that all such agreements are invalid per se.

IV

Turning to the agreement presented by this case, we conclude that the District Court's decision to enforce the agreement was correct. . . . [I]t is clear that Rumery voluntarily entered the agreement. Moreover, in this case the prosecutor had an independent, legitimate reason to make this agreement directly related to his prosecutorial responsibilities. The agreement foreclosed both the civil and criminal trials concerning Rumery, in which Deary would have been a key witness. She therefore was spared the public scrutiny and embarrassment she would have endured if she had had to testify in either of those cases. Both the prosecutor and the defense attorney testified in the District Court that this was a significant consideration in the prosecutor's decision.

In sum, we conclude that this agreement was voluntary, that there is no evidence of prosecutorial misconduct, and that enforcement of this agreement would not adversely affect the relevant public interests.[8]

V

We reverse the judgment of the Court of Appeals and remand the case to the District Court for dismissal of the complaint.

It is so ordered.

JUSTICE O'CONNOR, concurring in part and concurring in the judgment.

I join in Parts I, II, III-A, IV, and V of the Court's opinion. . . .

[T]he dangers of the release-dismissal agreement do not preclude its enforcement in all cases. The defendants in a § 1983 suit may establish that a particular release executed in exchange for the dismissal of criminal charges was voluntarily made, not the product of prosecutorial overreaching, and in the public interest. But

---

prosecutors suggests that judicial evaluation of those decisions should be especially deferential. Thus, the Court has never accepted such a blanket claim with respect to pretrial decisions.

[8] [10] We note that two Courts of Appeals have applied a voluntariness standard to determine the enforceability of agreements entered into after trial, in which the defendants released possible § 1983 claims in return for sentencing considerations. See *Bushnell v. Rossetti; Jones v. Taber.* We have no occasion in this case to determine whether an inquiry into voluntariness alone is sufficient to determine the enforceability of release-dismissal agreements. We also note that it would be helpful to conclude release-dismissal agreements under judicial supervision. Although such supervision is not essential to the validity of an otherwise-proper agreement, it would help ensure that the agreements did not result from prosecutorial misconduct.

they must prove that this is so; the courts should not presume it as I fear portions of Part III-B of the plurality opinion may imply.

Against the convincing evidence that Rumery voluntarily entered into the agreement and that it served the public interest, there is only Rumery's blanket claim that agreements such as this one are inherently coercive. While it would have been preferable, and made this an easier case, had the release-dismissal agreement been concluded under some form of judicial supervision, I concur in the Court's judgment, and all but Part III-B of its opinion, that Rumery's § 1983 suit is barred by his valid, voluntary release.

JUSTICE STEVENS, with whom JUSTICE BRENNAN, JUSTICE MARSHALL, and JUSTICE BLACKMUN join, dissenting.

The question whether the release-dismissal agreement signed by respondent is unenforceable is much more complex than the Court's opinion indicates. A complete analysis of the question presented by this case cannot end with the observation that respondent made a knowing and voluntary choice to sign a settlement agreement. Even an intelligent and informed, but completely innocent, person accused of crime should not be required to choose between a threatened indictment and trial, with their attendant publicity and the omnipresent possibility of wrongful conviction, and surrendering the right to a civil remedy against individuals who have violated his or her constitutional rights. Moreover, the prosecutor's representation of competing and possibly conflicting interests compounds the dangerous potential of release-dismissal agreements. . . .

I

Respondent is an innocent man. As a matter of law, he must be presumed to be innocent.

From respondent's point of view, it is unquestionably true that the decision to sign the release-dismissal agreement was, as the Court emphasizes, "voluntary, deliberate, and informed." It reflected "a highly rational judgment that the certain benefits of escaping criminal prosecution exceed the speculative benefits of prevailing in a civil action." As the plurality iterates and reiterates, respondent made a "considered decision that he would benefit personally from the agreement." I submit, however, that the deliberate and rational character of respondent's decision is not a sufficient reason for concluding that the agreement is enforceable. Otherwise, a promise to pay a state trooper $20 for not issuing a ticket for a traffic violation, or a promise to contribute to the police department's retirement fund in exchange for the dismissal of a felony charge, would be enforceable. . . .

Thus, even though respondent's decision in this case was deliberate, informed, and voluntary, this observation does not address two distinct objections to enforcement of the release-dismissal agreement. The prosecutor's offer to drop charges if the defendant accedes to the agreement is inherently coercive; moreover, the agreement exacts a price unrelated to the character of the defendant's own conduct.

II

When the prosecutor negotiated the agreement with respondent, he represented three potentially conflicting interests. His primary duty, of course, was to represent the sovereign's interest in the evenhanded and effective enforcement of its criminal laws. In addition, as the covenant demonstrates, he sought to represent the interests of the town of Newton and its Police Department in connection with their possible civil liability to respondent. Finally, as the inclusion of Mary Deary as a covenantee indicates, the prosecutor also represented the interest of a potential witness who allegedly accused both respondent and a mutual friend of separate instances of wrongdoing.

If we view the problem from the standpoint of the prosecutor's principal client, the State of New Hampshire, it is perfectly clear that the release-dismissal agreement was both unnecessary and unjustified. For both the prosecutor and the State of New Hampshire enjoy absolute immunity from common-law and § 1983 liability arising out of a prosecutor's decision to initiate criminal proceedings. . . .

The record in this case indicates that an important reason for obtaining the covenant was "[t]o protect the police department." There is, however, an obvious potential conflict between the prosecutor's duty to enforce the law and his objective of protecting members of the Police Department who are accused of unlawful conduct. The public is entitled to have the prosecutor's decision to go forward with a criminal case, or to dismiss it, made independently of his concerns about the potential damages liability of the Police Department. It is equally clear that this separation of functions cannot be achieved if the prosecutor may use the threat of criminal prosecution as a weapon to obtain a favorable termination of a civil claim against the police.

. . . When release agreements are enforceable, consideration of the police interest in avoiding damages liability severely hampers the prosecutor's ability to conform to the strictures of professional responsibility in deciding whether to prosecute. In particular, the possibility that the suspect will execute a covenant not to sue in exchange for a decision not to prosecute may well encourage a prosecutor to bring or to continue prosecutions in violation of his or her duty to "refrain from prosecuting a charge that the prosecutor knows is not supported by probable cause." ABA Model Rules of Professional Conduct, Rule 3.8(a) (1984).[9]

The prosecutor's potential conflict of interest increases in magnitude in direct proportion to the seriousness of the charges of police wrongdoing. . . .

. . . [T]here is a potential conflict between the public interest represented by the prosecutor and the private interests of a recalcitrant witness. As a general matter

---

[9] [16] See also ABA Model Code of Professional Responsibility, Disciplinary Rule 7-103 (1980) ("A public prosecutor or other government lawyer shall not institute or cause to be instituted criminal charges when he knows or it is obvious that the charges are not supported by probable cause"), and Ethical Consideration 7–14 ("A government lawyer who has discretionary power relative to litigation should refrain from instituting or continuing litigation that is obviously unfair"); ABA Standards for Criminal Justice 3-3.9(a) (2d ed. 1980) ("It is unprofessional conduct for a prosecutor to institute, or cause to be instituted, or to permit the continued pendency of criminal charges when it is known that the charges are not supported by probable cause").

there is no reason to fashion a rule that either requires or permits a prosecutor always to defer to the interests of a witness. The prosecutor's law enforcement responsibilities will sometimes diverge from those interests; there will be cases in which the prosecutor has a plain duty to obtain critical testimony despite the desire of the witness to remain anonymous or to avoid a courtroom confrontation with an offender. There may be other cases in which a witness has given false or exaggerated testimony for malicious reasons. It would plainly be unwise for the Court to hold that a release-dismissal agreement is enforceable simply because it affords protection to a potential witness.

It may well be true that a full development of all the relevant facts would provide a legitimate justification for enforcing the release-dismissal agreement. In my opinion, however, the burden of developing those facts rested on the defendants in the § 1983 litigation, and that burden has not been met by mere conjecture and speculation concerning the emotional distress of one reluctant witness.

III

Because this is the first case of this kind that the Court has reviewed, I am hesitant to adopt an absolute rule invalidating all such agreements.[10] I am, however, persuaded that the federal policies reflected in the enactment and enforcement of § 1983 mandate a strong presumption against the enforceability of such agreements and that the presumption is not overcome in this case by the facts or by any of the policy concerns discussed by the plurality. . . . [T]he plurality's decision seems to rest on the unstated premise that § 1983 litigation imposes a net burden on society. If that were a correct assessment of the statute, it should be repealed. Unless that is done, however, we should respect the congressional decision to attach greater importance to the benefits associated with access to a federal remedy than to the burdens of defending these cases.

Accordingly, although I am not prepared to endorse all of the reasoning of the Court of Appeals, I would affirm its judgment.

---

[10] [22] It seems likely, however, that the costs of having courts determine the validity of release-dismissal agreements will outweigh the benefits that most agreements can be expected to provide. A court may enforce such an agreement only after a careful inquiry into the circumstances under which the plaintiff signed the agreement and into the legitimacy of the prosecutor's objective in entering into the agreement. This inquiry will occupy a significant amount of the court's and the parties' time, and will subject prosecutorial decisionmaking to judicial review. But the only benefit most of these agreements will provide is another line of defense for prosecutors and police in section 1983 actions. This extra protection is unnecessary because prosecutors already enjoy absolute immunity and because police have been afforded qualified immunity. Thus, the vast majority of "marginal or frivolous" section 1983 suits can be dismissed under existing standards with little more burden on the defendants than is entailed in defending a release-dismissal agreement. Moreover, there is an oddly suspect quality to this extra protection; the agreement is one that a public official signs, presumably in good faith, but that a court must conclude is invalid unless that official proves otherwise. In most cases, if social and judicial resources are to be expended at all, they would seem better spent on an evaluation of the merits of the section 1983 claim rather than on a detour into the enforceability of a release-dismissal agreement.

NOTES

1. Given the division of the Court, what is the precise holding of *Rumery*? Does the section 1983 plaintiff have the burden of proving that the release-dismissal agreement is invalid, or does the section 1983 defendant bear the burden of establishing its validity? What are the relevant factors to consider? Which facts most strongly support enforcement of the release-dismissal agreement in *Rumery*?

2. *Rumery* envisions a case-by-case determination of the enforceability of release-dismissal agreements. The outcome in any particular case will depend on its specific facts. Thus, generalizations are of limited value. Nonetheless, most post-*Rumery* lower court opinions have focused on the same three factors: (1) voluntariness; (2) indications of prosecutorial overreaching: and (3) public policy. *e.g.*, *MacBoyle v. City of Parma*, 383 F.3d 456 (6th Cir. 2004); *Gonnalez v. Kokot*, 314 F.3d 311 (7th Cir. 2002); *Hill v. City of Cleveland*, 12 F.3d 575 (6th Cir. 1993); *Vallone v. Lee*, 7 F.3d 196 (11th Cir. 1993); *Cain v. Darby Borough*, 7 F.3d 377 (3d Cir. 1993) (*en banc*). Does the vague term "public policy" have any independent content?

3. A determination of voluntariness may be influenced by a number of factors. One court summarized these factors as follows

> the sophistication of the signer, cost/benefit considerations by the signer, and the circumstances of the signing, i.e, whether the signer is in custody at the time of the signing. . . .

> Additional factors in determining voluntariness are: whether the signer was represented by counsel, the time with which the signer considered the document, and whether the signer's attorney drafted the document. Courts also consider whether the signer expressed any unwillingness, and whether the release is clear on its face.

Woods v. Rhodes, 994 F.2d 494, 499–500 (8th Cir. 1993) (citations omitted). *See also Rodriguez v. Smithfield Packing Co.*, 338 F.3d 348 (4th Cir. 2003) (release-dismissal agreement deemed voluntary when initiated by arrestee who was facing only misdemeanor charges, was knowledgeable about the criminal justice system, and was represented by counsel).

Several courts have emphasized the coercive aspects of incarceration in finding that particular release agreements were not voluntary. *E.g.*, *Vallone v. Lee*, 7 F.3d 196 (11th Cir. 1993) (affirming a verdict for the plaintiff; the jury found that a release agreement was not voluntary because the inmate's release from jail on bail was improperly conditioned on signing the release); *Hall v. Ochs*, 817 F.2d 920 (1st Cir. 1987) (forcing plaintiff to sign release to get out of jail was not voluntary and therefore not enforceable). However, the fact that the signer is in custody does not render the release agreement involuntary *per se*, if other factors suggest otherwise. *Berry v. Peterson*, 887 F.2d 635 (5th Cir. 1989) (emphasizing that the plaintiff was represented by competent counsel).

4. A few post-*Rumery* decisions have refused to enforce release agreements that were found (or assumed) to be voluntary, when there was evidence of prosecutorial overreaching or other public policy concerns. In *Cain v. Darby*

Borough, 7 F.3d 377 (3d Cir. 1993) (en banc), the plaintiff signed a release-dismissal agreement in exchange for a recommendation by prosecutors that she be enrolled in an alternative sentencing program known as ARD. The local district attorney's office had a "blanket policy" of requiring the execution of a release from every ARD petitioner who might have a civil rights claim against government officials. The court held that the release agreement violated public policy so that she could proceed with her section 1983 claim. The court reasoned that the "blanket policy" was "wholly and patently unrelated to the goals of ARD. . . . [I]t may allow unqualified criminal defendants to be admitted into ARD if they sign releases and at the same time exclude the otherwise qualified because they did not. . . . The policy does not distinguish between frivolous and meritorious litigation; it indiscriminately curtails both." *Cain*, 7 F.3d at 383. *See also, Salkil v. Mount Sterling Township Police Department*, 458 F.3d 520 (6th Cir. 2006) (plaintiff's challenge to city's "blanket policy" of requiring the execution of a release-dismissal agreement in all cases was not "frivolous;" district court's award of sanctions against plaintiff was reversed).

In *Lynch v. City of Alhambra*, 880 F.2d 1122 (9th Cir. 1989), an off-duty deputy marshall alleged that he was roughed up by city police officers investigating a crime. The police officers claimed that Lynch was injured in the course of resisting arrest. Lynch was not threatened with prosecution for resisting arrest until after he initiated his civil claims against the city. Lynch released his section 1983 claims in exchange for non-prosecution of the criminal charges. Despite finding that Lynch voluntarily entered into the release-dismissal agreement, the court of appeals held the agreement may violate public policy. Police records indicated that Lynch's arrest was "questionable", and perhaps "invalid". Under these circumstances, the court of appeals directed the district court to determine whether the defendants used the threat of criminal prosecution for the impermissible purpose of suppressing civil rights claims.

5. Courts of appeals are in general agreement that *Rumery* places the burden on the section 1983 defendant to prove that the release-dismissal agreement is enforceable. *E.g., Gonzalez v. Kokot*, 314 F.3d 311 (7th Cir. 2002); *Coughlen v. Coots*, 5 F.3d 970 (6th Cir. 1993); *Lynch v. City of Alhambra*, 880 F.2d 1122 (9th Cir. 1989); *Cain v. Darby Borough*, 7 F.3d 377 (3d Cir. 1993) (en banc). There is a split among the circuit courts regarding the extent of that burden. *Compare Livingstone v. North Belle Vernon Borough*, 91 F.3d 515 (3d Cir. 1996) (burden is clear and convincing evidence) *with Gonzalez v. Kokot*, 314 F.3d 311 (7th Cir. 2002) and *Burke v. Johnson*, 167 F.3d 276 (6th Cir. 1999) (both holding that the burden is a preponderance of evidence).

Is the validity of the release agreement susceptible to summary adjudication? Are voluntariness, prosecutorial overreaching, and public policy questions of fact or law? Are they issues to be decided by the district court or a jury? In two cases, courts of appeals reversed jury verdicts for the plaintiffs, holding that the release-dismissal agreements in question were enforceable as a matter of law. In each case, a dissenting judge would have left the determination of voluntariness to the jury. *Woods v. Rhodes*, 994 F.2d 494 (8th Cir. 1993); *Berry v. Peterson*, 887 F.2d 635 (5th Cir. 1989). *See also Coughlen v. Coots*, 5 F.3d 970 (6th Cir. 1993) (district court must make "specific determinations" regarding voluntariness, prosecutorial overreaching, and public policy); *Vallone v. Lee*, 7 F.3d 196 (11th Cir. 1993) (upholding a jury finding that the release agreement was not voluntary). *See also, Dye v. Wargo*, 253 F.3d 296 (7th Cir. 2001) *MacBoyle v. City of Parma*, 383 F.3d 456 (6th Cir. 2009) (affirming summary judgment for the defendant).

Suppose that a release-dismissal agreement is negotiated during the course of a criminal trial at the suggestion of the presiding judge. In addition to the entry of a judgment of acquittal of the criminal charges, the oral agreement called for the government to pay for the medical expenses and property damage occasioned by the arrest. The agreement was never reduced to writing and the criminal defendants section 1983 plaintiffs never submitted any bills for payment. Although they were represented by defense counsel at the time the oral agreement was negotiated, the criminal defendants section 1983 plaintiffs claim they did not understand the nature and terms of the purported agreement. Are the section 1983 defendants entitled to summary judgment on the basis of the oral release-dismissal agreement? *See Livingstone v. North Belle Vernon Borough*, 12 F.3d 1205 (3d Cir. 1993) (en banc) (disputed issue of voluntariness precluded summary judgment). A jury subsequently ruled that the agreement had been entered into voluntarily and the district court entered a verdict for the defendants. The court of appeals again reversed holding that there were several unresolved issues of material fact, including whether the agreement was in the public's interest. 91 F.3d 515 (3d Cir. 1996).

Are there any steps that a prosecutor could take to reduce the vulnerability of a release-dismissal agreement to a subsequent challenge?

6. Is the merit of the section section 1983 claim relevant to the determination of the enforceability of the release-dismissal agreement? In *Coughlen v. Coots*, 5 F.3d 970, at 974 (6th Cir. 1993), the court commented that "the existence of substantial evidence of police misconduct . . . could be probative of the motives of the prosecutor for seeking such an agreement, as well as the degree to which enforcing the agreement would serve the public interest."

7. Quite often, a person is represented by counsel in the criminal matter at the time he executes the release-dismissal agreement. In *Lynch, Vallone,* and *Cain,* attorneys for the criminal defendants recommended that their clients sign release agreements that were later found to have been involuntary, involve prosecutorial misconduct, or violate public policy. Why would a criminal defense attorney advise a client to sign such a document? Consider the observations of Professor Kreimer:

> Defense lawyers also have an economic interest in encouraging the execution of release-dismissal agreements, which risks coloring the advice tendered to a client. Many private defense lawyers are paid a flat rate in advance, a system that provides an incentive to avoid protracted litigation whenever possible. . . . Moreover, relatively few defense lawyers handle plaintiff's civil rights litigation. They thus have little economic incentive to preserve civil rights claims for they would not handle claims if they are brought. Public defenders suffer from their own incentives to dispose of cases rapidly and are often entirely barred from private litigation.

Kreimer, *Releases, Redress, and Police Misconduct: Reflections on Agreements to Waive Civil Rights Actions in Exchange for Dismissal of Criminal Charges*, 136 U. PA. L. REV. 851, 874–75 (1988) (footnotes omitted). What are the ethical obligations of the criminal defense attorney vis-á-vis the civil section 1983 claim?

8. Consider the following Ethics Opinion issued by the Colorado Bar Association:

> It is improper for a public prosecutor to require that a defendant, as a condition of charging or sentencing concessions, release governmental agencies or their agents from actual or potential civil claims which arise from the same transactions as the criminal episode. It is also improper for a city attorney to make such a request of a public prosecutor.

Colorado Bar Association, Ethics Opinion No. 62 (November 20, 1982), reprinted at 12 COLORADO LAW. 455 (1983). The Colorado Bar Association substantially based its opinion on the American Bar Association Ethical Consideration 7–21, which states that "[t]hreatening to use, or using, the criminal process to coerce adjustment of private claims or controversies is a subversion of [the civil adjudicative] process." *See also*, Bartholomy, *An Ethical Analysis of the Release-Dismissal Agreement*, N.D. J. OF L. ETHICS & PUB. POL. 331 (1993).

After having considered the arguments in *Rumery* and the post-*Rumery* lower court opinions, is such an across-the-board prohibition preferable to a case-by-case assessment of the validity of release-dismissal agreements?

III. ISSUE AND CLAIM PRECLUSION

Many section 1983 actions concern claims or issues that were or might have been first raised in state judicial or administrative proceedings. Mr. Rumery, for example, could have challenged the constitutionality of his arrest in the trial of the state criminal charges brought against him. Instead, Rumery signed a release-dismissal agreement that disposed of both the state criminal charges and the federal section 1983 claim. Many other section 1983 claimants, however, have participated in some state judicial or administrative proceeding before filing their section 1983 suit. For example, a section 1983 plaintiff who claims to be the victim of an illegal search may have raised this issue in a motion to suppress evidence in his state court criminal trial; or a state worker who believes she was fired from her job for a constitutionally impermissible reason may have raised this issue in a state administrative forum before filing the section 1983 action. This section explores the effect of prior state judicial or administrative proceedings on subsequent section 1983 actions in federal court.

The preclusive effect of prior proceedings on subsequent litigation often is referred to in terms of res judicata and collateral estoppel. The Supreme Court first addressed the preclusive effect of state court proceedings on subsequent section 1983 suits in *Allen v. McCurry*, 449 U.S. 90 (1980). There the Court explained the policies underlying res judicata and collateral estoppel as follows:

> The federal courts have traditionally adhered to the related doctrines of res judicata and collateral estoppel. Under res judicata, a final judgment on

the merits of an action precludes the parties or their privies from relitigating issues that were or could have been raised in that action. Under collateral estoppel, once a court has decided an issue of fact or law necessary to its judgment, that decision may preclude relitigation of the issue in a suit on a different cause of action involving a party to the first case. As this Court and other courts have often recognized, res judicata and collateral estoppel relieve parties of the cost and vexation of multiple lawsuits, conserve judicial resources, and, by preventing inconsistent decisions, encourage reliance on adjudication.

In recent years, this Court has reaffirmed the benefits of collateral estoppel in particular, finding the policies underlying it to apply in contexts not formerly recognized at common law. Thus, the Court has eliminated the requirement of mutuality in applying collateral estoppel to bar relitigation of issues decided earlier in federal-court suits and has allowed a litigant who was not a party to a federal case to use collateral estoppel "offensively" in a new federal suit against the party who lost on the decided issue in the first case. But one general limitation the Court has repeatedly recognized is that the concept of collateral estoppel cannot apply when the party against whom the earlier decision is asserted did not have a "full and fair opportunity" to litigate that issue in the earlier case.

The federal courts generally have also consistently accorded preclusive effect to issues decided by state courts. Thus, res judicata and collateral estoppel not only reduce unnecessary litigation and foster reliance on adjudication, but also promote the comity between state and federal courts that has been recognized as a bulwark of the federal system. . . .

Allen v. McCurry, 449 U.S. at 94–96 (citations and footnotes omitted).

With this background in mind, consider whether a federal court in a section 1983 case should be bound by the actual or potential resolution of a particular claim or issue in some prior state proceeding. Should the preclusive effect of a prior state proceeding be determined by state or federal law? Should it make any difference whether the prior proceeding was judicial or administrative in nature? Should it make any difference whether the section 1983 claimant had any choice in participating in the prior state proceeding?

MIGRA v. WARREN CITY SCHOOL DISTRICT
BOARD OF EDUCATION
465 U.S. 75 (1984)

JUSTICE BLACKMUN delivered the opinion of the Court.

This case raises issues concerning the claim preclusive effect[11] of a state-court judgment in the context of a subsequent suit, under 42 U.S.C. §§ 1983 and 1985

---

[11] [1] The preclusive effects of former adjudication are discussed in varying and, at times, seemingly conflicting terminology, attributable to the evolution of preclusion concepts over the years. These effects are referred to collectively by most commentators as the doctrine of "res judicata" See Restatement

(1976 ed., Supp. V), in federal court.

I

[Dr. Ethel D. Migra was employed by the defendants to serve as the supervisor of elementary education. The Board initially voted to renew Dr. Migra's contract, but then later voted not to renew it. Dr. Migra filed suit in state court alleging breach of contract by the Board and wrongful interference by individual members with her contract of employment. The state trial court ruled in favor of Dr. Migra on the breach of contract claim and "reserved and continued" the "issue of conspiracy". On Dr. Migra's motion, the trial court dismissed without prejudice "the issue of conspiracy and individual board member liability." The lower court's ruling on the breach of contract issue was affirmed by the Ohio Court of Appeals.]

[Dr. Migra then filed an action in federal court alleging that] the Board's actions were intended to punish her for the exercise of her First Amendment rights. She also claimed that the actions deprived her of property without due process and denied her equal protection. Her federal claim thus arose under the First, Fifth, and Fourteenth Amendments and 42 U.S.C. §§ 1983 and 1985 (1976 ed., Supp. V). She requested injunctive relief and compensatory and punitive damages. Answers were filed in due course and shortly thereafter the defendants moved for summary judgment on the basis of res judicata and the bar of the statute of limitations.

The District Court granted summary judgment for the defendants and dismissed the complaint. The United States Court of Appeals for the Sixth Circuit, by a short unreported order, affirmed. Because of the importance of the issue, and because of differences among the Courts of Appeals, we granted certiorari.

II

The Constitution's Full Faith and Credit Clause[12] is implemented by the federal full faith and credit statute, 28 U.S.C. § 1738. That statute reads in pertinent part:

(Second) of Judgments, Introductory Note before ch. 3 (1982); 18 C. Wright, A. Miller,& E. Cooper, Federal Practice and Procedure § 4402 (1981). Res judicata is often analyzed further to consist of two preclusion concepts: "issue preclusion" and "claim preclusion." Issue preclusion refers to the effect of a judgment in foreclosing relitigation of a matter that has been litigated and decided. See Restatement, *supra*, § 27. This effect also is referred to as direct or collateral estoppel. Claim preclusion refers to the effect of a judgment in foreclosing litigation of a matter that never has been litigated, because of a determination that it should have been advanced in an earlier suit. Claim preclusion therefore encompasses the law of merger and bar. See *id.*, Introductory Note before § 24.

This Court on more than one occasion has used the term "res judicata" in a narrow sense, so as to exclude issue preclusion or collateral estoppel. See, e.g., *Allen v. McCurry; Brown v. Felsen*. When using that formulation, "res judicata" becomes virtually synonymous with "claim preclusion." In order to avoid confusion resulting from the two uses of "res judicata," this opinion utilizes the term "claim preclusion" to refer to the preclusive effect of a judgment in foreclosing litigation of matters that should have been raised in an earlier suit. For a helpful explanation of preclusion vocabulary, see *Wright et al., supra*, § 4402."

[12] [4] "Full Faith and Credit shall be given in each State to the public Acts, Records, and judicial Proceedings of every other State. And the Congress may by general Laws prescribe the Manner in which such Acts, Records and Proceedings shall be proved, and the Effect thereof." U.S. Const., Art. IV, § 1.

"Such Acts, records and judicial proceedings or copies thereof, so authenticated, shall have the same full faith and credit in every court within the United States and its Territories and Possessions as they have by law or usage in the courts of such State, Territory or Possession from which they are taken."

It is now settled that a federal court must give to a state-court judgment the same preclusive effect as would be given that judgment under the law of the State in which the judgment was rendered. In *Allen v. McCurry* this Court said:

"Indeed, though the federal courts may look to the common law or to the policies supporting res judicata and collateral estoppel in assessing the preclusive effect of decisions of other federal courts, Congress has specifically required all federal courts to give preclusive effect to state-court judgments whenever the courts of the State from which the judgments emerged would do so. . . ." Id., at 96.

. . . Accordingly, in the absence of federal law modifying the operation of § 1738, the preclusive effect in federal court of petitioner's state-court judgment is determined by Ohio law.

In *Allen*, the Court considered whether 42 U.S.C. § 1983 modified the operation of § 1738 so that a state-court judgment was to receive less than normal preclusive effect in a suit brought in federal court under § 1983. In that case, the respondent had been convicted in a state-court criminal proceeding. In that proceeding, the respondent sought to suppress certain evidence against him on the ground that it had been obtained in violation of the Fourth Amendment. The trial court denied the motion to suppress. The respondent then brought a § 1983 suit in federal court against the officers who had seized the evidence. The District Court held the suit barred by collateral estoppel (issue preclusion) because the issue of a Fourth Amendment violation had been resolved against the respondent by the denial of his suppression motion in the criminal trial. The Court of Appeals reversed. That court concluded that, because a § 1983 suit was the respondent's only route to a federal forum for his constitutional claim,[13] and because one of § 1983's underlying purposes was to provide a federal cause of action in situations where state courts were not adequately protecting individual rights, the respondent should be allowed to proceed to trial in federal court unencumbered by collateral estoppel. This Court, however, reversed the Court of Appeals, explaining:

"[N]othing in the language of § 1983 remotely expresses any congressional intent to contravene the common-law rules of preclusion or to repeal the express statutory requirements of the predecessor of 28 U.S.C. § 1738. . . . Section 1983 creates a new federal cause of action. It says nothing about the preclusive effect of state-court judgments.

"Moreover, the legislative history of § 1983 does not in any clear way suggest that Congress intended to repeal or restrict the traditional

---

[13] [5] The respondent had not asserted that the state courts had denied him a "full and fair opportunity" to litigate his search and seizure claim; he therefore was barred by *Stone v. Powell* from seeking a writ of habeas corpus in federal district court.

doctrines of preclusion. . . . [T]he legislative history as a whole . . . lends only the most equivocal support to any argument that, in cases where the state courts have recognized the constitutional claims asserted and provided fair procedures for determining them, Congress intended to override § 1738 or the common-law rules of collateral estoppel and res judicata. Since repeals by implication are disfavored . . . much clearer support than this would be required to hold that § 1738 and the traditional rules of preclusion are not applicable to § 1983 suits."

Allen therefore made clear that issues actually litigated in a state-court proceeding are entitled to the same preclusive effect in a subsequent federal § 1983 suit as they enjoy in the courts of the State where the judgment was rendered.

The Court in *Allen* left open the possibility, however, that the preclusive effect of a state-court judgment might be different as to a federal issue that a § 1983 litigant could have raised but did not raise in the earlier state-court proceeding. 449 U.S., at 97, n.10. That is the central issue to be resolved in the present case. Petitioner did not litigate her § 1983 claim in state court, and she asserts that the state-court judgment should not preclude her suit in federal court simply because her federal claim could have been litigated in the state-court proceeding. Thus, petitioner urges this Court to interpret the interplay of § 1738 and § 1983 in such a way as to accord state-court judgments preclusive effect in § 1983 suits only as to issues actually litigated in state court.

It is difficult to see how the policy concerns underlying § 1983 would justify a distinction between the issue preclusive and claim preclusive effects of state-court judgments. The argument that state-court judgments should have less preclusive effect in § 1983 suits than in other federal suits is based on Congress' expressed concern over the adequacy of state courts as protectors of federal rights. *Allen* recognized that the enactment of § 1983 was motivated partially out of such concern, but *Allen* nevertheless held that § 1983 did not open the way to relitigation of an issue that had been determined in a state criminal proceeding. Any distrust of state courts that would justify a limitation on the preclusive effect of state judgments in § 1983 suits would presumably apply equally to issues that actually were decided in a state court as well as to those that could have been. If § 1983 created an exception to the general preclusive effect accorded to state-court judgments, such an exception would seem to require similar treatment of both issue preclusion and claim preclusion. Having rejected in *Allen* the view that state-court judgments have no issue preclusive effect in § 1983 suits, we must reject the view that § 1983 prevents the judgment in petitioner's state-court proceeding from creating a claim preclusion bar in this case.

Petitioner suggests that to give state-court judgments full issue preclusive effect but not claim preclusive effect would enable litigants to bring their state claims in state court and their federal claims in federal court, thereby taking advantage of the relative expertise of both forums. Although such a division may seem attractive from a plaintiff's perspective, it is not the system established by § 1738. That statute embodies the view that it is more important to give full faith and credit to state-court judgments than to ensure separate forums for federal and state claims. This reflects a variety of concerns, including notions of comity, the need to prevent its merits in the prior litigation. If the ruling in the prior suit did not actually decide the issue or claim in question, it may be litigated in the subsequent section 1983 action. *E.g., Davenport v. North Carolina Department of Transportation*, 3 F.3d 89, 97 (4th Cir. 1993) ("we believe these procedural and substantive differences between the state administrative claim [for wrongful discharge without just cause] and the section 1983 claims [for politically motivated discharge in violation of the First Amendment] would cause them to be treated as different claims for res judicata purposes by the North Carolina courts."); *Wade v. City of Pittsburgh*, 765 F.2d 405 (3d Cir. 1985) (under Pennsylvania law, prior summary judgment for the defendant on state law immunity did not preclude section 1983 claim as immunity does not address the merits).

5. As reflected in the immediately preceding note, in some states the preclusive effect of a prior state proceeding may turn on determining precisely what was actually decided in that proceeding. What is decided when a person pleads guilty to a criminal charge? Should a guilty plea to a criminal charge bar a subsequent section 1983 claim alleging the police conducted an illegal search of his apartment? In *Haring v. Prosise*, 462 U.S. 306 (1983) a unanimous court ruled that such a section 1983 claim was not barred on the grounds of collateral estoppel. The Court began its analysis by noting that the preclusive effect of the state court judgment is governed by state law. It then offered three reasons why the doctrine of collateral estoppel would not be invoked in this case under Virginia law.

> First, the legality of the search of Prosise's apartment was not actually litigated in the criminal proceedings. . . . Second, the criminal proceedings did not actually decide against Prosise any issue on which he must prevail in order to establish his section 1983 claim. . . . [The] question [of guilt] is simply irrelevant to the legality of the search under the Fourth Amendment or to Prosise's right to compensation from state officials under section 1983.

> Finally, . . . a determination that the county police officers engaged in no illegal police conduct would not have been essential to the trial court's acceptance of Prosise's guilty plea. . . . Neither state nor federal law requires that a guilty plea in state court be supported by legally admissible evidence where the accused's valid waiver of his right to stand trial is accompanied by a confession of guilt.

Haring v. Prosise, 462 U.S. at 316. The Court further rejected the argument that the guilty plea constituted a waiver of any claim involving a Fourth Amendment violation under federal law. *Prosise*, 462 U.S. at 319.

Why did the prior state court ruling in the suppression hearing preclude the section 1983 claim in *Allen v. McCurry*, 449 U.S. 90 (1980), while the guilty plea in *Prosise* did not have such a preclusive effect? As a matter of policy, should a guilty plea preclude a section 1983 claim arising from events pertaining to the investigation and arrest of the plaintiff? Why or why not? *See generally* Shapiro, *Should a Guilty Plea Have Preclusive Effect?*, 70 Iowa L. Rev. 27 (1984).

Can the prosecuting attorney handling the criminal case take any steps to insulate police officers and local governments from subsequent section 1983 claims? *See Town of Newton v. Rumery*, 480 U.S. 386 (1987) discussed *supra*.

UNIVERSITY OF TENNESSEE v. ELLIOT
478 U.S. 788 (1986)

JUSTICE WHITE delivered the opinion of the Court.

A state Administrative Law Judge determined that petitioner University of Tennessee (hereafter petitioner or University) was not motivated by racial prejudice in seeking to discharge respondent. The question presented is whether this finding is entitled to preclusive effect in federal court, where respondent has raised discrimination claims under various civil rights laws, including Title VII of the Civil Rights Act of 1964, 78 Stat. 253, as amended, 42 U.S.C. § 2000e et seq., and 42 U.S.C. § 1983.

I

In 1981, petitioner informed respondent, a black employee of the University's Agricultural Extension Service, that he would be discharged for inadequate work performance and misconduct on the job. Respondent requested a hearing under the Tennessee Uniform Administrative Procedures Act, Tenn. Code Ann. § 4-5-101 et seq. (1985), to contest his proposed termination. Prior to the start of the hearing, respondent also filed suit in the United States District Court for the Western District of Tennessee, alleging that his proposed discharge was racially motivated and seeking relief under Title VII and other civil rights statutes, including 42 U.S.C. § 1983. The relief sought included damages, an injunction prohibiting respondent's discharge, and classwide relief from alleged patterns of discrimination by petitioner.

[Pursuant to state law, a hearing was conducted over a five month period involving more than 100 witnesses and 150 exhibits.] The focus of the hearing was on 10 particular charges that the University gave as grounds for respondent's discharge. Respondent denied these charges, which he contended were motivated by racial prejudice, and also argued that the University's subjecting him to the charges violated his rights under the Constitution, Title VII, and other federal statutes. The ALJ held that he lacked jurisdiction to adjudicate respondent's federal civil rights claims, but did allow respondent to present, as an affirmative defense, evidence that the charges against him were actually motivated by racial prejudice and hence not a proper basis for his proposed discharge.

After hearing extensive evidence, the ALJ found that the University had proved some but not all of the charges against respondent, and that the charges were not racially motivated. Concluding that the proposed discharge of respondent was too severe a penalty, the ALJ ordered him transferred to a new assignment with supervisors other than those with whom he had experienced conflicts. Respondent appealed to the University's Vice President for Agriculture, who affirmed the ALJ's ruling. The Vice President stated that his review of the record persuaded him that the proposed discharge of respondent had not been racially motivated.

Respondent did not seek review of these administrative proceedings in the Tennessee courts; instead, he returned to federal court to pursue his civil rights claims. There, petitioner moved for summary judgment on the ground that

It is so ordered.

Justice Marshall took no part in the consideration or decision of this case.

Justice Stevens, with whom Justice Brennan and Justice Blackmun join, concurring in part and dissenting in part.

[Justice Stevens concurred with the majority that 28 U.S.C. § 1738 does not require that state administrative rulings be given full faith and credit in subsequent federal litigation. He further agreed that petitioner's claims under Title VII were not precluded by the unreviewed state administrative rulings. He then addressed whether the unreviewed state administrative rulings should have a preclusive effect on claims and issues brought under section 1983.]

Preclusion of claims brought under the post-Civil War Acts does not advance the objectives typically associated with finality or federalism. In the employment setting which concerns us here, precluding civil rights claims based on the Reconstruction-era statutes fails to conserve the resources of either the litigants or the courts, because the complainant's companion Title VII claim will still go to federal court under today's decision.[16] Nor does preclusion show respect for state administrative determinations, because litigants apprized of this decision will presumably forgo state administrative determinations for the same reason they currently forgo state judicial review of those determinations — to protect their entitlement to a federal forum.

Due respect for the intent of the Congress that enacted the Civil Rights Act of 1871, as revealed in the voluminous legislative history of that Act, should preclude the Court from creating a judge-made rule that bars access to the express legislative remedy enacted by Congress.

Accordingly, I respectfully dissent from Part IV of the Court's opinion.

---

[16] [1] "The difficulties that will be encountered with this schizophrenic approach [ruling that state administrative findings may establish preclusion as to the claims under these Civil Rights Acts, at the same time as the same issues are relitigated as to the Title VII claim] are obvious. A way out of these difficulties remains to be found. As to any issues that must be retried, with perhaps inconsistent results, it may prove better simply to retry the issues as to all statutory claims. Application of preclusion as to part of the case saves no effort, does not prevent the risk of inconsistent findings, and may distort the process of finding the issues. The opportunity for repose is substantially weakened by the remaining exposure to liability. Insistence on preclusion in these circumstances has little value, and more risk than it may be worth." 18 C. Wright, A. Miller, & E. Cooper, Federal Practice and Procedure § 4471, p. 169 (Supp. 1985).

Moreover, in this case, and presumably in many other cases as well, even the section 1983 claim may be litigated in federal court, at least to the extent of determining whether the complainant was afforded a full and fair opportunity to litigate before the state administrative tribunal.

NOTES

1. In *Kremer v. Chemical Construction*, 456 U.S. 461 (1982), the Court, applying 28 U.S.C. § 1738, gave full faith and credit to a New York court decision upholding a state administrative agency's decision rejecting the plaintiff's claim of employment discrimination. Under New York law, a judicially reviewed administrative ruling precluded relitigation of the same question. The Court relied on this state rule of preclusion in holding that the plaintiff was barred from bringing his Title VII claim in federal court in the face of his unsuccessful appeal of an adverse agency ruling. Under *Kremer*, a Title VII claim may be precluded by a prior judicially reviewed state administrative proceeding, while under *Elliot* the Title VII claim is subject to a trial *de novo* in federal court if the prior state administrative proceeding was not reviewed by a court. The different preclusive potential of judicially reviewed and unreviewed agency rulings is justified in terms of the language and legislative history of Title VII. *Elliot*, 478 U.S. at 795–96. Given the often limited scope of judicial review of agency action, does this different treatment make sense as a matter of policy?

2. As discussed in *Migra*, 28 U.S.C. § 1738 directs federal courts to determine the preclusive effect of a prior state court proceeding according to state law. *Elliot*, on the other hand, applies federal common law rules of preclusion to a prior unreviewed state administrative proceeding. The preclusive effect of prior federal proceedings is also determined by federal common law. *E.g., Nagle v. Lee*, 807 F.2d 435 (5th Cir. 1987). Federal and state rules of preclusion may differ from one another. For example, some states limit the application of collateral estoppel to prior proceedings involving the same parties, while mutuality of parties is not required under federal common law rules of preclusion. *Compare B.C.R. Transportation Co., v. Fontaine*, 727 F.2d 7 (1st Cir. 1984) (mutuality of parties required under Massachusetts law) *with Parklane Hosiery Co. v. Shore*, 439 U.S. 322 (1979) (mutuality of parties not required under federal common law rules of preclusion). Is the potential for differences among the states and between federal and state rules of preclusion a healthy aspect of federalism? Would uniform rules of preclusion better serve the purposes of federal civil rights legislation?

3. Suppose a woman filed a complaint with a state agency claiming that she was terminated from her employment because of her race, color, and gender. The state agency issued an order concluding that there was "no probable cause to believe that the employer engaged in the unlawful discriminatory practice complained of." The plaintiff did not appeal the adverse agency ruling until after the 60-day period allowed by statute had expired. Her appeal was dismissed by the state court on statute of limitations grounds. She then filed a civil rights suit in federal court. For res judicata purposes under state law, a dismissal on statute of limitations grounds is considered a final judgment on the merits. How would you frame the defendant's motion for summary judgment based on claim or issue preclusion? How would you frame the plaintiff's response? Is the preclusive effect of the prior state proceeding determined by state or federal law? Does it matter whether the federal claim is based on Title VII or section 1983? *Cf. Bray v. New York Life Insurance*, 851 F.2d 60 (2d Cir. 1988) (Title VII claim is barred by prior state proceedings). *See also Durgins v. City of East St. Louis*, 272 F.3d 841 (7th Cir. 2001) (failure to raise First Amendment issue in state administrative proceeding precludes section 1983 claim).

4. Should the preclusive effect of the prior state proceeding depend on who initiated the proceeding? In both *Migra* and *Elliot*, the plaintiffs chose to challenge their respective adverse employment decisions in state forums. Suppose that the collateral estoppel argument was made against a party who was a defendant in the prior state proceeding. Should the party who did not select the state forum be precluded from having a federal court pass on the fact issues crucial to the resolution of the federal claim? Justice Blackmun, who authored the majority opinion in *Migra*, made the following argument in his dissent in *Allen v. McCurry*:

> A state criminal defendant cannot be held to have chosen "voluntarily" to litigate his Fourth Amendment Claim in the state court. The risk of conviction puts pressure upon him to raise all possible defenses. . . . To hold that a criminal defendant who raises a Fourth Amendment claim at his criminal trial "freely and without reservation submits his federal claims for decision by the state courts," . . . is to deny reality. The criminal defendant is an involuntary litigant in the state tribunal . . . To force him to a choice between forgoing either a potential defense or a federal forum for his constitutional civil claim is fundamentally unfair.

449 U.S. at 115–16 (1980). *See also* footnote 14 [7] in *Migra, supra*. Does this argument apply with equal force to a defendant in a state civil proceeding? Does the judicial or administrative nature of the state forum bear on the question? The special problems posed by litigating section 1983 claims in state court are considered in the next chapter.

5. Should a determination in an arbitration proceeding that there was "just cause" to terminate the plaintiff's employment preclude a subsequent section 1983 action alleging he was discharged for exercising his First Amendment rights? In *McDonald v. City of West Branch*, 466 U.S. 284 (1984), a unanimous Court held that a federal court should not afford res judicata or collateral estoppel effect to arbitration rulings. Since arbitration is not a "judicial proceeding", 28 U.S.C. § 1738 does not require that it be given full faith and credit. Moreover, the Court declined to fashion a federal rule of preclusion because

> First, an . . . arbitrator may not . . . have the expertise required to resolve the complex legal questions that arise in section 1983 actions. . . .

> Second, because an arbitrator's authority derives solely from the contract . . . an arbitrator may not have the authority to enforce section 1983. . . .

> Third, [a union may have control over how the grievance is presented, and] may present the employee's grievance less vigorously, or make different strategic choices, than would the employee. . . .

> Finally, arbitral fact-finding is generally not equivalent to judicial fact-finding.

McDonald, 466 U.S. at 290–91. However, the arbitration award can be used as evidence in the subsequent federal proceedings.

IV. EXHAUSTION OF REMEDIES

As is evident from the preceding section, plaintiffs sometimes choose to pursue state judicial or administrative remedies prior to instigating a section 1983 suit. Should they be required to do so? Requiring exhaustion of state remedies would reduce federal intrusions upon state sovereignty by allowing states to redress wrongs committed by its officials without federal court intervention. Moreover, providing compensation under state tort law could avoid the unnecessary adjudication of federal constitutional issues.

As will be recalled from Chapter 1, the Court in the seminal case of *Monroe v. Pape*, 365 U.S. 167 (1961), emphatically rejected this proposition. The Court reviewed the legislative history of section 1983 and concluded that Congress intended to provide a federal remedy in federal court even where a state remedy was theoretically adequate. "It is no answer that the State has a law which if enforced would give relief. The federal remedy is supplementary to the state remedy, and the latter need not first be sought and refused before the federal one is invoked." *Monroe*, 365 U.S. at 183.

This aspect of *Monroe* was reaffirmed in *Patsy v. Board of Regents*, 457 U.S. 496 (1982), where the court held that the plaintiff did not have to exhaust her state administrative remedies before filing a section 1983 action. Together, *Monroe* and *Patsy* clearly establish that there is no general principle of exhaustion of judicial or administrative remedies as a prerequisite to bringing a section 1983 action. There are, however, a limited number of situations, many of which involve criminal matters or prison inmates, where exhaustion of state remedies may be required, or where other legal doctrine produce exhaustion-like consequences. The following materials briefly explore these situations.

PORTER v. NUSSLE
534 U.S. 516 (2002)

JUSTICE GINSBURG delivered the opinion of the Court.

This case concerns the obligation of prisoners who claim denial of their federal rights while incarcerated to exhaust prison grievance procedures before seeking judicial relief. Plaintiff-respondent Ronald Nussle, an inmate in a Connecticut prison, brought directly to court, without filing an inmate grievance, a complaint charging that corrections officers singled him out for a severe beating, in violation of the Eighth Amendment's ban on "cruel and unusual punishments." Nussle bypassed the grievance procedure despite a provision of the Prison Litigation Reform Act of 1995 (PLRA), 42 U.S.C. § 1997e(a), that directs: "No action shall be brought with respect to prison conditions under § 1983 of this title, or any other Federal law, by a prisoner confined in any jail, prison, or other correctional facility until such administrative remedies as are available are exhausted."

The Court of Appeals for the Second Circuit held that § 1997e(a) governs only conditions affecting prisoners generally, not single incidents, such as corrections officers' use of excessive force, actions that immediately affect only particular prisoners. Nussle defends the Second Circuit's judgment, but urges that the relevant distinction is between excessive force claims, which, he says, need not be pursued administratively, and all other claims, which, he recognizes, must proceed first through the prison grievance process. We reject both readings and hold, in line with the text and purpose of the PLRA, our precedent in point, and the weight of lower court authority, that § 1997e(a)'s exhaustion requirement applies to all prisoners seeking redress for prison circumstances or occurrences.

I

Respondent Ronald Nussle is an inmate at the Cheshire Correctional Institution in Connecticut. According to his complaint, corrections officers at the prison subjected him to "a prolonged and sustained pattern of harassment and intimidation" from the time of his arrival there in May 1996. Nussle alleged that he was singled out because he was "perceived" to be a friend of the Governor of Connecticut, with whom corrections officers were feuding over labor issues.

Concerning the episode in suit, Nussle asserted that, on or about June 15,1996, several officers, including defendant-petitioner Porter, ordered Nussle to leave his cell, "placed him against a wall and struck him with their hands, kneed him in the back, [and] pulled his hair." Nussle alleged that the attack was unprovoked and unjustified, and that the officers told him they would kill him if he reported the beating.

Then, as now, the Connecticut Department of Correction provided a grievance system for prisoners. Under that system, grievances must be filed within 30 days of the "occurrence." Rules governing the grievance process include provisions on confidentiality and against reprisals.

Without filing a grievance, on June 10, 1999, Nussle commenced an action in Federal District Court under 42 U.S.C. § 1983; he filed suit days before the three-year statute of limitations ran out on the § 1983 claim. Nussle charged, principally, that the corrections officers' assault violated his right to be free from cruel and unusual punishment under the Eighth Amendment, as made applicable to the States by the Fourteenth Amendment. The District Court, relying on § 1997e(a), dismissed Nussle's complaint for failure to exhaust administrative remedies.

Construing § 1997e(a) narrowly because it is an exception "to the general rule of non-exhaustion in § 1983 cases," the Court of Appeals for the Second Circuit reversed the District Court's judgment; the appeals court held that "exhaustion of administrative remedies is not required for [prisoner] claims of assault or excessive force brought under § 1983." Section 1997e(a) requires administrative exhaustion of inmates' claims "with respect to prison conditions," but contains no definition of the words "prison conditions." The appeals court found the term "scarcely free of ambiguity."[17] For purposes of the PLRA's exhaustion requirement, the court

---

[17] [2] Another provision of the PLRA, 18 U.S.C. § 3626(g)(2) the court observed, does define "prison conditions." That provision, which concerns prospective relief, defines "prison conditions" to mean "the conditions of confinement or the effects of actions by government officials on the lives of persons confined in prison." The Second Circuit found the § 3626(g)(2) definition "no less ambiguous" than the bare text

concluded, the term was most appropriately read to mean " 'circumstances affecting everyone in the area,' "rather than " 'single or momentary matter[s],' such as beatings . . . directed at particular individuals."

The Court of Appeals found support for its position in the PLRA's legislative history. Floor statements "overwhelmingly suggest[ed]" that Congress sought to curtail suits qualifying as "frivolous" because of their "subject matter," *e.g.*, suits over "insufficient storage locker space," "a defective haircut," or "being served chunky peanut butter instead of the creamy variety." 224 F.3d, at 105 (internal quotation marks omitted). Actions seeking relief from corrections officer brutality, the Second Circuit stressed, are not of that genre. Further, the Court of Appeals referred to pre-PLRA decisions in which this Court had "disaggregate[d] the broad category of Eighth Amendment claims so as to distinguish [for proof of injury and *mens rea* purposes] between 'excessive force' claims, on the one hand, and 'conditions of confinement' claims, on the other." *Id.*, at 106 (citing *Hudson v. McMillian*, 503 U.S. 1, 112 S.Ct. 995, 117 L.Ed.2d 156 (1992), and *Farmer v. Brennan*, 511 U.S. 825, 114 S.Ct. 1970, 128 L.Ed.2d 811 (1994)).

In conflict with the Second Circuit, other Federal Courts of Appeals have determined that prisoners alleging assaults by prison guards must meet § 1997e(a)'s exhaustion requirement before commencing a civil rights action. We granted certiorari to resolve the intercircuit conflict, and now reverse the Second Circuit's judgment.

II

Ordinarily, plaintiffs pursuing civil rights claims under 42 U.S.C. § 1983 need not exhaust administrative remedies before filing suit in court. See *Patsy v. Board of Regents of Fla.*, 457 U.S. 496, 516, (1982). Prisoner suits alleging constitutional deprivations while incarcerated once fell within this general rule.

In 1980, however, Congress introduced an exhaustion prescription for suits initiated by state prisoners. See Civil Rights of Institutionalized Persons Act, 42 U.S.C. § 1997e. This measure authorized district courts to stay a state prisoner's § 1983 action "for a period of not to exceed 180 days" while the prisoner exhausted available "plain, speedy, and effective administrative remedies." § 1997e(a)(1). Exhaustion under the 1980 prescription was in large part discretionary; it could be ordered only if the State's prison grievance system met specified federal standards, and even then, only if, in the particular case, the court believed the requirement "appropriate and in the interests of justice." §§ 1997e(a) and (b). We described this provision as a "limited exhaustion requirement" in *McCarthy v. Madigan*, 503 U.S. 140, 150–151 (1992), and thought it inapplicable to prisoner suits for damages when monetary relief was unavailable through the prison grievance system.

In 1996, as part of the PLRA, Congress invigorated the exhaustion prescription.

---

of § 1997e(a). Neither of the alternative § 3626(g)(2) formulations, the court said, would be used in "everyday" speech to describe "particular instances of assault or excessive force." The Second Circuit ultimately concluded that it would be improper, in any event, automatically to import § 3626(g)(2)'s "definition of 'civil actions brought with respect to prison conditions' into 42 U.S.C. § 1997e(a)" because the two provisions had "distinct statutory purposes."

The revised exhaustion provision, titled "Suits by prisoners," states: "No action shall be brought with respect to prison conditions under section 1983 of this title, or any other Federal law, by a prisoner confined in any jail, prison, or other correctional facility until such administrative remedies as are available are exhausted." 42 U.S.C. § 1997e(a).

The current exhaustion provision differs markedly from its predecessor. Once within the discretion of the district court, exhaustion in cases covered by § 1997e(a) is now mandatory. See *Booth v. Churner*, 532 U.S. 731 (2001). All "available" remedies must now be exhausted; those remedies need not meet federal standards, nor must they be "plain, speedy, and effective." Even when the prisoner seeks relief not available in grievance proceedings, notably money damages, exhaustion is a prerequisite to suit. And unlike the previous provision, which encompassed only § 1983 suits, exhaustion is now required for all "action [s] . . . brought with respect to prison conditions," whether under § 1983 or "any other Federal law." Thus federal prisoners suing under *Bivens v. Six Unknown Fed. Narcotics Agents*, 403 U.S. 388 (1971), must first exhaust inmate grievance procedures just as state prisoners must exhaust administrative processes prior to instituting a § 1983 suit.

Beyond doubt, Congress enacted § 1997e(a) to reduce the quantity and improve the quality of prisoner suits; to this purpose, Congress afforded corrections officials time and opportunity to address complaints internally before allowing the initiation of a federal case. In some instances, corrective action taken in response to an inmate's grievance might improve prison administration and satisfy the inmate, thereby obviating the need for litigation. *Booth*, 532 U.S. at 737. In other instances, the internal review might "filter out some frivolous claims." And for cases ultimately brought to court, adjudication could be facilitated by an administrative record that clarifies the contours of the controversy.

Congress described the cases covered by § 1997e(a)'s exhaustion requirement as "action[s] . . . brought with respect to prison conditions." Nussle's case requires us to determine what the § 1997e(a) term "prison conditions" means, given Congress' failure to define the term in the text of the exhaustion provision. We are guided in this endeavor by the PLRA's text and context, and by our prior decisions relating to "[s]uits by prisoners," § 1997e.[18]

As to precedent, the pathmarking opinion is *McCarthy v. Bronson*, 500 U.S. 136, (1991), which construed 28 U.S.C. § 636(b)(1)(B), a Judicial Code provision authorizing district judges to refer to magistrate judges, *inter alia*, "prisoner petitions challenging conditions of confinement." The petitioning prisoner in *McCarthy* argued that § 636(b)(1)(B) allowed nonconsensual referrals "only when a prisoner

---

[18] [4] In reaching its decision, the Second Circuit referred to its "obligation to construe statutory exceptions narrowly, in order to give full effect to the general rule of non-exhaustion in § 1983." 224 F.3d, at 106. The Second Circuit did not then have available to it our subsequently rendered decision in *Booth v. Churner*, 532 U.S. 731 (2001). *Booth* held that § 1997e(a) mandates initial recourse to the prison grievance process even when a prisoner seeks only money damages, a remedy not available in that process. In so ruling, we observed that "Congress . . . may well have thought we were shortsighted" in failing adequately to recognize the utility of the administrative process to satisfy, reduce, or clarify prisoner grievances. While the canon on which the Second Circuit relied may be dependable in other contexts, the PLRA establishes a different regime. For litigation within § 1997e(a)'s compass, Congress has replaced the "general rule of non-exhaustion" with a general rule of exhaustion.

challenges ongoing prison conditions." The complaint in *McCarthy* targeted no "ongoing prison conditions;" it homed in on "an isolated incident" of excessive force. For that reason, according to the *McCarthy* petitioner, nonconsensual referral of his case was impermissible.

. . . .

We did not "quarrel with" the prisoner's assertion in *McCarthy* that "the most natural reading of the phrase 'challenging conditions of confinement,' when viewed in isolation, would not include suits seeking relief from isolated episodes of unconstitutional conduct." We nonetheless concluded that the petitioner's argument failed upon reading the phrase "in its proper context." We found no suggestion in § 636(b)(1)(B) that Congress meant to divide prisoner petitions "into subcategories." "On the contrary," we observed, "when the relevant section is read in its entirety, it suggests that Congress intended to authorize the nonconsensual reference of *all* prisoner petitions to a magistrate." The Federal Magistrates Act, we noted, covers actions of two kinds: challenges to "conditions of confinement"; and "applications for habeas corpus relief." Congress, we concluded, "intended to include in their entirety th[ose] two primary categories of suits brought by prisoners."

"Just three years before [§ 636(b)(1)(B)] was drafted," we explained in *McCarthy*, "our opinion in *Preiser v. Rodriguez*, 411 U.S. 475, (1973), had described [the] two broad categories of prisoner petitions: (1) those challenging the fact or duration of confinement itself; and (2) those challenging the conditions of confinement." *Preiser v. Rodriguez*, 411 U.S. 475, (1973), left no doubt, that "the latter category unambiguously embraced the kind of single episode cases that petitioner's construction would exclude." We found it telling that Congress, in composing the Magistrates Act, chose language "that so clearly parallel[ed] our *Preiser* opinion." We considered it significant as well that the purpose of the Magistrates Act — to lighten the caseload of overworked district judges — would be thwarted by opening the door to satellite litigation over "the precise contours of [the] suggested exception for single episode cases."

As in *McCarthy*, we here read the term "prison conditions" not in isolation, but "in its proper context." The PLRA exhaustion provision is captioned "Suits by prisoners," see § 1997e; this unqualified heading scarcely aids the argument that Congress meant to bi-sect the universe of prisoner suits.

This Court generally "presume[s] that Congress expects its statutes to be read in conformity with th[e] Court's precedents." That presumption, and the PLRA's dominant concern to promote administrative redress, filter out groundless claims, and foster better prepared litigation of claims aired in court, see *Booth*, 532 U.S. at 737, persuade us that § 1997e(a)'s key words "prison conditions" are properly read through the lens of *McCarthy* and *Preiser*. Those decisions tug strongly away from classifying suits about prison guards' use of excessive force, one or many times, as anything other than actions "with respect to prison conditions."

Nussle places principal reliance on *Hudson v. McMillian*, 503 U.S. 1 (1992), and *Farmer v. Brennan*, 511 U.S. 825, 835–836 (1994), and the Second Circuit found support for its position in those cases as well. *Hudson* held that to sustain a claim of excessive force, a prisoner need not show significant injury. In so ruling, the Court did indeed distinguish excessive force claims from "conditions of confinement" claims; to sustain a claim of the latter kind "significant injury" must be shown. *Hudson* also observed that a "conditions of confinement" claim may succeed if a prisoner demonstrates that prison officials acted with "deliberate indifference," while a prisoner alleging excessive force must demonstrate that the defendant acted "maliciously and sadistically to cause harm," *Farmer* similarly distinguished the mental state that must be shown to prevail on an excessive force claim, *i.e.*, "purposeful or knowing conduct," from the lesser *mens rea* requirement governing "conditions of confinement" claims, *i.e.*, "deliberate indifference." We do not question those decisions and attendant distinctions in the context in which they were made. But the question presented here is of a different order.

Hudson and *Farmer* trained solely and precisely on proof requirements: what injury must a plaintiff allege and show; what mental state must a plaintiff plead and prove. Proof requirements once a case is in court, however, do not touch or concern the threshold inquiry before us: whether resort to a prison grievance process must precede resort to a court. We have no reason to believe that Congress meant to release the evidentiary distinctions drawn in *Hudson* and *Farmer* from their moorings and extend their application to the otherwise invigorated exhaustion requirement of § 1997e(a). Such an extension would be highly anomalous given Congress' elimination of judicial discretion to dispense with exhaustion and its deletion of the former constraint that administrative remedies must be "plain, speedy, and effective" before exhaustion could be required.

Nussle contends that Congress added the words "prison conditions" to the text of § 1997e(a) specifically to exempt excessive force claims from the now mandatory exhaustion requirement; he sees that requirement as applicable mainly to " 'prison conditions' claims that may be frivolous as to subject matter," It is at least equally plausible, however, that Congress inserted "prison conditions" into the exhaustion provision simply to make it clear that preincarceration claims fall outside § 1997e(a), for example, a Title VII claim against the prisoner's preincarceration employer, or, for that matter, a § 1983 claim against his arresting officer.

Other infirmities inhere in the Second Circuit's disposition. [I]n the prison environment a specific incident may be symptomatic rather than aberrational. An unwarranted assault by a corrections officer may be reflective of a systemic problem traceable to poor hiring practices, inadequate training, or insufficient supervision. Nussle himself alleged in this very case not only the beating he suffered on June 15, 1996; he also alleged, extending before and after that date, "a prolonged and sustained pattern of harassment and intimidation by corrections officers." Nussle urges that his case could be placed in the isolated episode category, but he might equally urge that his complaint describes a pattern or practice of harassment climaxing in the alleged beating. It seems unlikely that Congress, when it included in the PLRA a firm exhaustion requirement, meant to leave the need to exhaust to the pleader's option.

Under Nussle's view and that of the Second Circuit, moreover, bifurcation would be normal when a prisoner sues both a corrections officer alleged to have used excessive force and the supervisor who allegedly failed adequately to monitor those in his charge. The officer alone could be taken directly to court; the charge against the supervisor would proceed first through the internal grievance process. Similarly split proceedings apparently would be in order, under the Second Circuit's decision, when the prisoner elects to pursue against the same officers both discrete instance and ongoing conduct charges.

Finally, we emphasize a concern over and above the complexity augured by the Second Circuit's disposition: Scant sense supports the single occurrence, prevailing circumstance dichotomy. Why should a prisoner have immediate access to court when a guard assaults him on one occasion, but not when beatings are widespread or routine? Nussle's distinction between excessive force claims and all other prisoner suits, presents a similar anomaly. Do prison authorities have an interest in receiving prompt notice of, and opportunity to take action against, guard brutality that is somehow less compelling than their interest in receiving notice and an opportunity to stop other types of staff wrongdoing?

For the reasons stated, we hold that the PLRA's exhaustion requirement applies to all inmate suits about prison life, whether they involve general circumstances or particular episodes, and whether they allege excessive force or some other wrong. Accordingly, the judgment of the Court of Appeals is reversed, and the case is remanded for further proceedings consistent with this opinion.

It is so ordered.

NOTES

1. The Supreme Court has addressed other aspects of the exhaustion requirement of the PLRA. In the earlier case of *Booth v. Churner*, 532 U.S. 731 (2001) the Court held that prisoners must exhaust administrative remedies even when such remedies do not provide for money damages.

2. Lower courts have also grappled with various exhaustion issues under the PLRA. Is an inmate who has been released from prison required to file an administrative grievance for an incident that occurred while he was incarcerated? *E.g., Greig v. Goord*, 169 F.3d 165 (2d Cir. 1999) (exhaustion of administrative remedies is not required when the section 1983 suit is filed after the inmate has been released from prison). Prison officials often contend that administrative remedies have not been properly exhausted (and hence the section 1983 claim must be dismissed) because the inmate did not file his grievance in a timely fashion or did not provide sufficient factual detail. Whether an administrative grievance filed by an inmate is timely or sufficiently detailed may depend on the requirements of state procedure. *See e.g., Marella v. Terhune*, 562 F.3d 983 (9th Cir. 2009) (inmate's section 1983 claim should not be dismissed for failing to exhaust administrative remedies when state prison regulations provide for an exception to the timely filing requirement if the prisoner does not have the opportunity to file within the prescribed time constraints); *Espinal v. Goord*, 554 F.3d 216 (2d Cir. 2009) (state grievance procedures did not require an inmate to specifically identify parties allegedly responsible for violating constitutional rights; inmate did not fail to exhaust his administrative remedies under the PLRA by omitting the names of individual officers in his grievance); *Griffin v. Arpaio*, 557 F.3d 1117 (9th Cir. 2009) (administrative remedies were not properly exhausted under the PLRA when inmate's grievance did not allege a denial of adequate medical care; section 1983 suit properly dismissed); *Days v. Johnson*, 322 F.3d 863 (5th Cir. 2003) (inmate claimed he could not fill out prison grievance procedure forms in a timely fashion because he had a broken hand; section 1983 claim is properly dismissed for failing to exhaust administrative remedies under the PLRA). Suppose there are disputed issues of material fact regarding whether an inmate had a valid excuse for not submitting his grievance in a timely fashion. Is the inmate entitled to a jury trial on the issue of excuse? *See Pavey v. Conley*, 544 F.3d 739 (7th Cir. 2008) (no).

For a critique of the exhaustion requirement of the PLRA and suggested improvements, see Lynn S. Branham, *The Prison Litigation Reform Act's Enigmatic Exhaustion Requirement: What It Means and What Congress, Courts, and Correctional Officials Can Learn from It*, 86 CORNELL L. REV. 483 (2001).

3.   Considering the materials on issue and claim preclusion included in Part III of this chapter, what is the practical effect of the mandatory exhaustion requirements of the PLRA?

4.   Congress enacted the Prison Litigation Reform Act (PLRA) in an effort to reduce the amount and scope of section 1983 litigation brought by prison inmates. This legislation was driven by two overriding concerns. First, proponents of the PLRA believed that federal courts were playing too active a role in overseeing the day to day operations of state prisons through injunctions and consent decrees issued in institutional reform litigation. The PLRA was designed to restrict federal court remedial discretion and intervention in state prisons. Second, proponents of the PLRA wanted to stem the rising number of frivolous or meritless prisoner suits and appeals. The number of inmate suits alleging constitutional violations at the hands of prison officials had grown from 218 cases in 1966 to more than 56,000 in 1994. Julie M. Riewe, Note, *The Least Among Us: Unconstitutional Changes in Prisoner Litigation Under the Prison Litigation Reform Act* of 1995, 47 DUKE L.J. 117, 118 (1997).

The PLRA restricts federal court remedial discretion in several respects. First, it promulgates narrow standards for granting prospective relief in civil actions concerning prison conditions. Specifically, a court "shall not grant or approve any prospective relief unless the court finds that such relief is narrowly drawn, extends no further than necessary to correct the violation of the Federal right, and is the least intrusive means necessary to correct the violation of the Federal right." 18 U.S.C. § 3626(a)(1)(A). Second, the PLRA cabins a court's authority to order the release of prisoners to remedy unconstitutional over-crowding. A court may not order the release of prisoners unless the court already has ordered "less intrusive relief that has failed to remedy the deprivation of the Federal right" and the defendant has had a reasonable period of time in which to comply with the earlier, less intrusive order. 18 U.S.C. § 3626(a)(3)(A)(i). Furthermore, a release order can only be issued by a three judge panel that finds by clear and convincing evidence that crowding is the primary cause of the constitutional violation and that no other relief will remedy the violation. 18 U.S.C. § 3626(a)(3)(B), (E). Third, the PLRA provides for the immediate termination and automatic stay of injunctive relief.

Prospective relief is terminable upon the motion of any party or intervenor two years after the date the court granted or approved the prospective relief or one year after the date the court entered an order denying termination of prospective relief. 18 U.S.C. § 3626(b)(1). Prospective relief is subject to "immediate termination" if the relief was approved or granted without express findings that the relief is narrowly drawn, extends not further than necessary to correct the constitutional violation, and is the least restrictive means to correct the violation. 18 U.S.C. § 3626(b)(2). Moreover, prospective relief is automatically stayed on the thirtieth day after a motion to terminate is filed. 18 U.S.C. § 3626(e)(2). For a more detailed description of these provisions, *see* Kristin L. Burns, Note, *Return to Hard Time: The Prison Litigation Reform Act of 1995*, 31 GA. L. REV. 879, 891–894 (1997).

The PLRA purports to deter frivolous or meritless litigation in a number of ways. First, the PLRA modifies an inmate's ability to file a complaint or appeal in forma pauperis. Under the PLRA, inmates must file a statement identifying funds held in their prison accounts when seeking permission to file a complaint or appeal in forma pauper-is. Prisoners alleging indigent status must now use a portion of whatever funds they have in their prison account to satisfy filing fees. 28 U.S.C. § 1915(a)(2), (b)(1). Thus, filing a complaint or appeal is no longer free. Second, under what is widely known as the "three strikes" provision, in forma pauperis status may be revoked entirely if an inmate has "on three or more prior occasions . . . brought an action or appeal in a court . . . that was dismissed on the grounds that it is frivolous, malicious, or fails to state a claim upon which relief may be granted, unless the prisoner is under imminent danger of serious physical injury." 28 U.S.C. § 1915(g). Third, as discussed in *Nussle*, prisoners are required to exhaust all administrative remedies before filing suit in federal court. 42 U.S.C. § 1997e(a). Fourth, the PLRA limits the substantive grounds for recovery by providing that "federal no civil action may be brought by a prisoner . . . for mental or emotional injury suffered while in custody without a prior showing of physical injury." 42 U.S.C. § 1997e(e). Finally, the statute confers on courts expanded power to dismiss a prisoner's case sua sponte for failure to state a claim upon which relief may be granted or if the complaint seeks monetary relief against a defendant who is immune from such liability. 28 U.S.C. § 1915(e)(2)(B).

5. The PLRA has spawned considerable litigation.

(a) In *Miller v. French*, 530 U.S. 327 (2000), the Court considered an attack on the provisions of the PLRA that limit federal courts' power to issue injunctive relief. In 1975 the correctional facility in question was found to be in violation of Eighth Amendment regarding conditions of confinement, and had been operating under an injunction issued by the district court. Prison officials argued that the automatic stay provisions of the PLRA operated to lift the injunction. The plaintiffs argued that (1) as a matter of statutory construction, the PLRA did not preclude federal courts from exercising their equitable power to enjoin the PLRA's automatic stay provision; and (2) if the PLRA purported to limit the federal court's equitable power, it violated constitutional principles of separation of powers. A majority of the Court held that the Congress clearly intended to make the operation of the PLRA's automatic stay provision mandatory, thus precluding courts from exercising equitable power to enjoin the stay, and that this provision does not violate separation of powers principles. Justices Breyer and Stevens dissented on the grounds that a reasonable construction of the statute would allow for federal courts to exercise equitable powers to enjoin the automatic stay under certain circumstances. Justices Souter and Ginsburg believed that the plaintiffs' complaint raised "a serious separation-of-powers issue" that required additional factual development.

(b) *Carey v. Piphus*, 435 U.S. 247 (1978) established the general rule that mental and emotional distress can constitute a compensable injury in suits for damages under section 1983. Again, the PLRA creates a separate and more restrictive rule for constitutional tort suits brought by prison inmates. This provision of the PLRA allows courts to dismiss claims without having to reach the underlying substantive constitutional issue. In *Davis v. District of Columbia*, 158 F.3d 1342 (D.C. Cir. 1998), for example, the court affirmed the sua sponte dismissal of a complaint in which an inmate alleged to have suffered emotional distress as a result of an unconstitutional invasion of medical privacy. *See also, Zehner v. Trigg*, 133 F.3d 459 (7th Cir. 1997) (affirming dismissal of section 1983 claims brought by inmates allegedly exposed to asbestos while working in a prison kitchen). Both *Davis* and *Zehner* upheld over equal protection challenges the PLRA's restriction on inmates' recovery for emotional distress absent physical injury.

(c) As discussed in Chapter 12, *infra*, the PLRA requires a prevailing inmate to contribute a portion of any monetary award he may receive to attorney's fees and places limits on the overall amount of fees award. These limitations have been upheld over equal protection challenges. *E.g., Johnson v. Daley*, 339 F.3d 582 (7th Cir. 2003); *Jackson v. State Bd. of Pardon and Parole*, 331 F.3d 790 (11th Cir. 2003); *Boivin v. Black*, 225 F.3d 36 (1st Cir. 2000).

(d) The "three strikes" provisions and other limitations on in forma pauperis filings have proven to be a fruitful mechanism for dismissing inmate litigation. *E.g., Dubuc v. Johnson*, 314 F.3d 1205 (10th Cir. 2003) (prisoner who filed three prior frivolous actions could not proceed in forma pauperis; failure to pay filing fee would result in dismissal); *In re Alea*, 286 F.3d 378 (6th Cir. 2002) (prison officials can collect filing fee for action filed by inmate but dismissed under the three strike rule); *Malik v. McGinnis*, 293 F.3d 559 (2d Cir. 2002) (affirming district court's dismissal of inmate's action under the three strikes rule). *But see Troville v. Venz*, 303 F.3d 1256 (11th Cir. 2002) (PLRA applies only to persons incarcerated as punishment for a criminal conviction; restrictions on in forma pauperis filings did not apply to a civil detainee).

6. Habeas corpus is the traditional remedy for a person who is illegally confined. By statute, a state inmate must exhaust his state remedies before seeking a writ of habeas corpus in federal court. 28 U.S.C. § 2254(b). A recurring and trouble-some issue concerns the proper characterization of a prisoner's complaint. Suppose a prisoner alleges that he has been deprived of good behavior time credits without due process. Should this suit be characterized as one seeking a writ of habeas corpus or a section 1983 challenge to prison procedures? The Supreme Court in *Preiser v. Rodriguez*, 411 U.S. 475, 500 (1973) ruled that this claim fell under the heading of habeas corpus and set down the following guiding principle:

> when a state prisoner is challenging the very fact or duration of his physical imprisonment, and the relief he seeks is a determination that he is entitled

to immediate release or a speedier release from that imprisonment, his sole federal remedy is a writ of habeas corpus.

Suppose an inmate alleges that the defendants violated his constitutional rights by destroying exculpatory evidence and fabricating incriminating evidence, but seeks only money damages as relief. Is this suit properly cast as a section 1983 action or in terms of corpus? Consider the following case.

HECK v. HUMPHREY
512 U.S. 477 (1994)

JUSTICE SCALIA delivered the opinion of the Court.

This case presents the question whether a state prisoner may challenge the constitutionality of his conviction in a suit for damages under 42 U.S.C. § 1983.

I

Petitioner Roy Heck was convicted in Indiana state court of voluntary manslaughter for the killing of Rickie Heck, his wife, and is serving a 15-year sentence in an Indiana prison. While the appeal from his conviction was pending, petitioner, proceeding *pro se*, filed this suit in Federal District Court under 42 U.S.C. § 1983, naming as defendants respondents James Humphrey and Robert Ewbank, Dearborn County prosecutors, and Michael Krinoph, an investigator with the Indiana State Police. The complaint alleged that respondents, acting under color of state law, had engaged in an "unlawful, unreasonable, and arbitrary investigation" leading to petitioner's arrest; "knowingly destroyed" evidence "which was exculpatory in nature and could have proved [petitioner's] innocence"; and caused "an illegal and unlawful voice identification procedure" to be used at petitioner's trial. The complaint sought, among other things, compensatory and punitive monetary damages. It did not ask for injunctive relief, and petitioner has not sought release from custody in this action. Heck's conviction was upheld on appeal and the lower federal courts denied his petitions for writ of habeas corpus. Heck did not contest that his section 1983 suit effectively challenged the legality of his conviction.

II

This case lies at the intersection of the two most fertile sources of federal-court prisoner litigation — § 1983 and the federal habeas corpus statute. Both of these provide access to a federal forum for claims of unconstitutional treatment at the hands of state officials, but they differ in their scope and operation. In general, exhaustion of state remedies "is *not* a prerequisite to an action under § 1983," *Patsy v. Board of Regents of Fla.*, 457 U.S. 496, 501, (1982), even an action by a state prisoner. The federal habeas corpus statute, by contrast, requires that state prisoners first seek redress in a state forum.[19]

---

[19] [3] 28 U.S.C. § 2254(b) provides: "An application for a writ of habeas corpus in behalf of a person in custody pursuant to the judgment of a State court shall not be granted unless it appears that the

prosecution alone provides the answer. Common-law tort rules can provide a "starting point for the inquiry under § 1983," but we have relied on the common law in § 1983 cases only when doing so was thought to be consistent with ordinary rules of statutory construction, as when common-law principles have textual support in other provisions of [§ 1983] or when those principles were so fundamental and widely understood at the time § 1983 was enacted that the 42d Congress could not be presumed to have abrogated them silently. At the same time, we have consistently refused to allow common-law analogies to displace statutory analysis, declining to import even well-settled common-law rules into § 1983 "if [the statute's] history or purpose counsel against applying [such rules] in § 1983 actions."

[Justice Souter explains that the technical elements of a nineteenth century common law tort claim for malicious prosecution are not well suited to resolve a modern section 1983 claim.]

We are not, however, in any such strait, for our enquiry in this case may follow the interpretive methodology employed in *Preiser v. Rodriguez*, 411 U.S. 475, (1973). In *Preiser*, we read the "general" § 1983 statute in light of the "specific federal habeas corpus statute," which applies only to "person[s] in custody," and the habeas statute's policy, embodied in its exhaustion requirement, § 2254(b), that state courts be given the first opportunity to review constitutional claims bearing upon a state prisoner's release from custody. Though in contrast to *Preiser* the state prisoner here seeks damages, not release from custody, the distinction makes no difference when the damages sought are for unconstitutional conviction or confinement. As the Court explains, nothing in *Preiser* nor in *Wolff v. McDonnell*, is properly read as holding that the relief sought in a § 1983 action dictates whether a state prisoner can proceed immediately to federal court. Whether or not a federal-court § 1983 damages judgment against state officials in such an action would have preclusive effect in later litigation against the State, mounting damages against the defendant-officials for unlawful confinement (damages almost certainly to be paid by state indemnification) would, practically, compel the State to release the prisoner. Because allowing a state prisoner to proceed directly with a federal-court § 1983 attack on his conviction or sentence "would wholly frustrate explicit congressional intent" as declared in the habeas exhaustion requirement, the statutory scheme must be read as precluding such attacks. This conclusion flows not from a preference about how the habeas and § 1983 statutes ought to have been written, but from a recognition that "Congress has determined that habeas corpus is the appropriate remedy for state prisoners attacking the validity of the fact or length of their confinement, [a] specific determination [that] must override the general terms of § 1983."

That leaves the question of how to implement what statutory analysis requires. It is at this point that the malicious-prosecution tort's favorable-termination requirement becomes helpful, not in dictating the elements of a § 1983 cause of action, but in suggesting a relatively simple way to avoid collisions at the intersection of habeas and § 1983. A state prisoner may seek federal-court § 1983 damages for unconstitutional conviction or confinement, but only if he has previously established the unlawfulness of his conviction or confinement, as on appeal or on habeas. This has the effect of requiring a state prisoner challenging the lawfulness of his confinement to follow habeas's rules before seeking § 1983 damages for unlawful confinement in federal court, and it is ultimately the Court's holding today. It neatly resolves a problem that has bedeviled lower courts, legal commentators, and law students. The favorable-termination requirement avoids the knotty statute-of-limitations problem that arises if federal courts dismiss § 1983 suits filed before an inmate pursues federal habeas, and (because the statute-of-limitations clock does not start ticking until an inmate's conviction is set aside) it does so without requiring federal courts to stay, and therefore to retain on their dockets, prematurely filed § 1983 suits.[26]

That would be a sensible way to read the opinion, in part because the alternative would needlessly place at risk the rights of those outside the intersection of § 1983 and the habeas statute, individuals not "in custody" for habeas purposes. If these individuals (people who were merely fined, for example, or who have completed short terms of imprisonment, probation, or parole, or who discover (through no fault of their own) a constitutional violation after full expiration of their sentences), like state prisoners, were required to show the prior invalidation of their convictions or sentences in order to obtain § 1983 damages for unconstitutional conviction or imprisonment, the result would be to deny any federal forum for claiming a deprivation of federal rights to those who cannot first obtain a favorable state ruling. The reason, of course, is that individuals not "in custody" cannot invoke federal habeas jurisdiction, the only statutory mechanism besides § 1983 by which individuals may sue state officials in federal court for violating federal rights. That would be an untoward result.

It is one thing to adopt a rule that forces prison inmates to follow the federal habeas route with claims that fall within the plain language of § 1983 when that is necessary to prevent a requirement of the habeas statute from being undermined. . . .

It would be an entirely different matter, however, to shut off federal courts altogether to claims that fall within the plain language of § 1983. "[I]rrespective of the common law support" for a general rule disfavoring collateral attacks, the Court lacks the authority to do any such thing absent unambiguous congressional direction where, as here, reading § 1983 to exclude claims from federal court would run counter to "§ 1983's history" and defeat the statute's "purpose." Consider the

---

[26] [4] The requirement that a state prisoner seeking section 1983 damages for unlawful conviction or confinement be successful in state court or on federal habeas strikes me as soundly rooted in the statutory scheme. Because "Congress has determined that habeas corpus is the appropriate remedy for state prisoners attacking the validity of the fact or length of their confinement, [a] specific determination [that] override[s] the general terms of section 1983," a state prisoner whose constitutional attacks on his confinement have been rejected by state courts cannot be said to be unlawfully confined unless a federal habeas court declares his "custody [to be] in violation of the Constitution or laws or treaties of the United States". An unsuccessful federal habeas petitioner cannot, therefore, consistently with the habeas statute, receive section 1983 damages for unlawful confinement. That is not to say, however, that a state prisoner whose request for release has been (or would be) rejected by state courts or by a federal habeas court is necessarily barred from seeking any section 1983 damages for violations of his constitutional rights. If a section 1983 judgment in his favor would not demonstrate the invalidity of his confinement he is outside the habeas statute and may seek damages for a constitutional violation even without showing "favorable termination." A state prisoner may, for example, seek damages for an unreasonable search that produced evidence lawfully or harmlessly admitted at trial, or even nominal damages for, say, a violation of his right to procedural due process.

case of a former slave framed by Ku Klux Klan-controlled law-enforcement officers and convicted by a Klan-controlled state court of, for example, raping a white woman; and suppose that the unjustly convicted defendant did not (and could not) discover the proof of unconstitutionality until after his release from state custody. If it were correct to say that § 1983 independently requires a person not in custody to establish the prior invalidation of his conviction, it would have been equally right to tell the former slave that he could not seek federal relief even against the law-enforcement officers who framed him unless he first managed to convince the state courts that his conviction was unlawful. That would be a result hard indeed to reconcile either with the purpose of § 1983 or with the origins of what was "popularly known as the Ku Klux Act, the statute having been enacted in part out of concern that many state courts were "in league with those who were bent upon abrogation of federally protected rights," It would also be a result unjustified by the habeas statute or any other post-§ 1983 enactment.

Nor do I see any policy reflected in a congressional enactment that would justify denying to an individual today federal damages (a significantly less disruptive remedy than an order compelling release from custody) merely because he was unconstitutionally fined by a State, or to a person who discovers after his release from prison that, for example, state officials deliberately withheld exculpatory material. And absent such a statutory policy, surely the common law can give us no authority to narrow the "broad language" of § 1983, which speaks of deprivations of "any" constitutional rights, privileges, or immunities, by "[e]very" person acting under color of state law, and to which "we have given full effect [by] recognizing that § 1983 'provide[s] a remedy, to be broadly construed, against all forms of official violation of federally protected rights.' "

In sum, while the malicious-prosecution analogy provides a useful mechanism for implementing what statutory analysis requires, congressional policy as reflected in enacted statutes must ultimately be the guide. I would thus be clear that the proper resolution of this case (involving, of course, a state prisoner) is to construe § 1983 in light of the habeas statute and its explicit policy of exhaustion. I would not cast doubt on the ability of an individual unaffected by the habeas statute to take advantage of the broad reach of § 1983.

NOTES

1. *Heck* was decided before the enactment of the Prison Litigation Reform Act (PLRA) discussed in the notes following *Porter v. Nussle*. At the time of the decision, a prisoner's section 1983 claim would not be subject to any exhaustion of remedies requirement while a petition for a writ of habeas corpus would be subject to the exhaustion rules governing that action. If filed today, would Heck's claim be subject to the exhaustion requirements of PLRA? When might the PLRA exhaustion requirement come into play? What are the differences between the exhaustion requirements of the PLRA and the habeas corpus statute? What is the relationship between the exhaustion of remedies requirements of the PLRA and habeas corpus and the preclusion principles discussed in the previous section?

2. After *Heck v. Humphrey*, the line separating § 1983 and habeas corpus remains an issue of some importance. In *Hill v. McDonough*, 547 U.S. 573 (2006), a death row inmate filed an action under § 1983 alleging that Florida's lethal injection protocol constituted cruel and unusual punishment under the Eighth Amendment. Hill sought injunctive relief. The defendant argued that Hill's claim was the functional equivalent of a habeas corpus petition which was barred because he had raised the issue in a prior habeas petition. A unanimous Court held that Hill's claim could proceed under 42 U.S.C. § 1983. The protocol for lethal injection in Florida called for the administration of an anesthetic (sodium pentothal) followed by the administration of two drugs (pancuronium bromide and potassium chloride) that would bring about the death of the inmate. Hill alleged that the anesthetic would not be sufficient to render painless the administration of the second and third drugs. He alleged that "he could remain conscious and suffer severe pain as the pancuronium paralyzed his lungs and body and the potassium chloride caused muscle cramping and a fatal heart attack." The Court held that this challenge should not be characterized as the functional equivalent of a habeas petition because "the injunction Hill seeks would not necessarily foreclose the State from implementing the lethal injection sentence under present law. . . . Any incidental delay cause by allowing Hill to file suit does not cast on his sentence the kind of negative legal implication that would require him to proceed in a habeas action." *Hill v. McDonough* relies upon another recent decision, *Nelson v. Campbell*, 541 U.S. 637 (2004) which allowed an Alabama inmate to challenge Alabama's lethal injection procedure under § 1983.

The precise circumstances in which a section 1983 claim is barred by the rule in *Heck* continue to be worked out by the lower courts. Would a section 1983 claim alleging the use of excessive force by a deputy sheriff be barred by the rule in *Heck* when the plaintiff was convicted of resisting arrest and defending one's self from the infliction of excessive force could be an affirmative defense to the charge of resisting arrest? See *Dyer v. Lee*, 488 F.3d 876 (11th Cir. 2007) (*Heck* did not bar the section 1983 claim since the court could not say with absolute certainty that every act of violence with which the claimant was charged was committed as act of self-defense in response to the officer's use of excessive force); *Tracy v. Freshwater*, 623 F.3d 90 (2d Cir. 2010) (same). In many instances, a complaint may contain claims that are barred by the rule in *Heck* and claims that are not barred. *See e.g., Moore v. Sims*, 200 F.3d 1170 (8th Cir. 2000) (claim based on allegation that defendants planted inculpatory evidence is barred by the rule in *Heck*; claim based on alleged unlawful seizure of person is not barred); *Figueroa v. Rivera*, 147 F.3d 77 (1st Cir. 1998) (claim alleging a conspiracy to frame the plaintiff is barred by the rule in *Heck*; 8th Amendment claim for denial of medical care while in custody is not barred); *Channer v. Mitchell*, 43 F.3d 786 (2d Cir. 1994) (claim alleging unconstitutional use of perjured testimony is barred by the rule in *Heck*; claim alleging cruel and unusual punishment is not barred). Of course, *Heck* will not bar a section 1983 claim if the criminal conviction has been reversed on direct appeal. *E.g., Clay v. Allen*, 242 F.3d 679 (5th Cir. 2001).

Suppose an inmate sues a state attorney under section 1983 seeking an injunction ordering the defendant to give him access to biological evidence so he could conduct DNA tests. The inmate is not seeking money damages. Nor is he seeking release from custody or directly attacking the validity of his conviction. He is seeking the means by which he might *later* challenge his conviction. Would this

criminal defendant had an adequate remedy at law and would not suffer an irreparable injury if denied equitable relief. *Younger*, 401 U.S. at 45. Moreover, principles of "comity" and "Our Federalism," require a "proper respect for state functions" and a commitment to protect federal rights "in ways that will not unduly interfere with legitimate activities of the States." *Younger*, 401 U.S. at 44.

The *Younger* rule has been applied when the federal suit was filed before the state criminal proceeding. *Hicks v. Miranda*, 422 U.S. 332 (1975). It has been extended to administrative and private civil proceedings implicating important state interests. *Ohio Civil Rights Comm'n v. Dayton Christian Schools, Inc.*, 477 U.S. 619 (1986) (*Younger* barred suit to enjoin pending state administrative proceedings); *Pennzoil Co. v. Texaco, Inc.*, 481 U.S. 1 (1987) (*Younger* barred suit to enjoin the execution of state judgment pending appeal to state appellate courts).

Should the *Younger* rule apply when the section 1983 plaintiff seeks damages and not injunctive or declaratory relief? Does a damage remedy interfere with state functions in a qualitatively different way than an injunction? In *Deakins v. Monaghan*, 484 U.S. 193 (1988), the Court considered whether the *Younger* doctrine required dismissal of a section 1983 claims for damages brought by plaintiffs who were the subjects of an ongoing state grand jury investigation. While not resolving the issue completely, the Court stated:

> We need not decide the extent to which the *Younger* doctrine applies to a federal action seeking only monetary relief, however, because even if the *Younger* doctrine requires abstention here, the District Court has no discretion to dismiss rather than to stay claims for monetary relief that cannot be redressed in the state proceeding.

Deakins, 484 U.S. at 202. *Deakins* suggests that while *Younger* does not require outright dismissal, it permits (but does not compel) district courts to stay federal section 1983 damages actions where those damages claims cannot be redressed in the state proceedings.

3. In *Railroad Commission v. Pullman*, 312 U.S. 496 (1941), the plaintiff filed a suit in federal court alleging that a state agency's order violated state law and various federal constitutional provisions. The state law claim turned on an unresolved issue of state law whose resolution might avoid the need to deal with the federal constitutional claims. The Supreme Court fashioned a rule of "abstention," under which lower federal courts abstain from deciding the federal issues while the parties seek a decision in state court on the unresolved issue of state law. The federal court retains jurisdiction pending such a state court determination. In a subsequent opinion, the Supreme Court protected the interest of the plaintiff in having a federal forum for his federal claims. Under *England v. Louisiana State Board of Medical Examiners*, 375 U.S. 411 (1964), a plaintiff who is forced to state court under *Pullman*-abstention can preserve his right to a federal forum by informing the state court of his intention to return to the federal court on his federal claims.

Many states have "certification procedures" whereby state supreme courts can entertain questions from federal courts about issues of state law. The Supreme Court has commented that the certified question procedures serves much the same purpose as *Pullman* abstention, but with many advantages. *See Arizonans for Official English v. Arizona*, 520 U.S. 43 (1997).

4. A category of section 1983 cases producing exhaustion-like consequences involves challenges to the enforcement of allegedly unconstitutional land use regulations. The typical complaint alleges that the regulation in question so greatly restricts what an owner can do with her property as to constitute a "taking" under the Fifth and Fourteenth Amendments. The Supreme Court has held that under certain conditions land use regulations can amount to a taking, thereby triggering a constitutional obligation to provide just compensation. *E.g., Dolan v. City of Tigard*, 512 U.S. 374 (1994) (a city's conditioning of its approval of petitioner's request for a zoning variance on dedication of a flood plain and bicycle/pedestrian easement was a taking requiring just compensation). *Lucas v. South Carolina Coastal Council*, 505 U.S. 1003 (1992) (South Carolina Beachfront Management Act that denied all economically beneficial or productive use of land may constitute a taking). *Cf. Nollan v. California Coastal Commission*, 483 U.S. 825 (1987) (California law conditioning the issuance of a building permit on the granting of a public access easement constituted a taking).

A section 1983 claim of this nature is not "ripe," however, until the governmental entity charged with implementing the regulation has reached a "final decision". Thus, a constitutional challenge to a zoning ordinance was dismissed on ripeness grounds when the plaintiff had not applied for a variance. *Williamson County Regional Planning Commission v. Hamilton Bank*, 473 U.S.172 (1985). Justice Brennan explained that until the plaintiff applies for and receives a final ruling on a request for a variance, a court cannot determine whether the plaintiff has been denied all reasonable beneficial use of the property. *Williamson*, 473 U.S. at 194. Moreover, a taking is unconstitutional only if "just compensation" is not provided. A plaintiff must pursue available state procedures to determine whether the government will provide just compensation.

Thus, a court cannot pass on either the "taking" or "just compensation" issue until the plaintiff has pursued available state procedures. Although conceptually different from exhaustion, the ripeness doctrine applied in this context produces exhaustion-like consequences.

See also MacDonald, Sommer & Frates v. Yolo County, 477 U.S. 340 (1986) (without a final and authoritative determination by the planning commission as to how the land use regulation at issue will be applied to the plaintiff's property, the court cannot determine whether a taking has occurred or whether the county failed to provide just compensation).

5. A somewhat analogous situation arises in the procedural due process context. Recall that *Parratt v. Taylor*, 451 U.S. 527 (1981) and its progeny hold that the availability of post-deprivation remedies under state law may satisfy the demands of "due process" under some circumstances. *See* Chapter 3. Where this principle applies, a deprivation of life, liberty or property in not unconstitutional because adequate post-deprivation state remedies provide due process. The Supreme Court has acknowledged the similarity between *Parratt* and the ripeness requirement in takings cases. *See Williamson Planning Comm'n v. Hamilton Bank*, 473 U.S. 172, 195 (1985) ("The recognition that a property owner has not

suffered a violation of the Just Compensation Clause until the owner has unsuccessfully attempted to obtain just compensation through the procedures provided
by the State for obtaining such compensation is analogous to the Court's holding in
Parratt v. Taylor, 451 U.S. 527 (1981).").

Chapter 11

LITIGATING SECTION 1983 CLAIMS IN STATE COURTS

Monroe v. Pape establishes the principle that persons complaining of unconstitutional treatment by state officers have access to federal court. Although most section 1983 cases go to federal courts, state courts have concurrent jurisdiction over these cases, and some plaintiffs prefer to litigate in state court. The complexities of our federal system generate some interesting issues for state court adjudication of section 1983 cases: May state courts refuse to hear section 1983 cases? Why might a plaintiff prefer state (or federal) court? How do the terms upon which the litigation is conducted differ depending on the choice of a state or federal forum? To what extent are state courts required to forego their normal practices for the sake of the federal rights at stake in section 1983 litigation?

An important point to keep in mind throughout these materials is that the case will remain in state court only if both sides want to keep it there. The defendant may thwart the plaintiff's preference for state court by shifting the litigation to federal court under 28 U.S.C. § 1441(a), which provides, in relevant part, that "any civil action brought in a State court of which the district courts [have] original jurisdiction, may be removed by the defendant [to] the district court." If there are two or more defendants, the case maybe removed only if they all agree. *See* RICHARD FALLON ET AL., HART & WECHSLER'S THE FEDERAL COURTS AND THE FEDERAL SYSTEM 1431 (6th ed. 2009).

I. MUST STATE COURTS HEAR SECTION 1983 CLAIMS?

HAYWOOD v. DROWN
556 U.S. 729 (2009)

JUSTICE STEVENS delivered the opinion of the Court.

In our federal system of government, state as well as federal courts have jurisdiction over suits brought pursuant to 42 U.S.C. § 1983, the statute that creates a remedy for violations of federal rights committed by persons acting under color of state law. While that rule is generally applicable to New York's supreme courts — the State's trial courts of general jurisdiction — New York's Correction Law § 24 divests those courts of jurisdiction over § 1983 suits that seek money damages from correction officers. New York thus prohibits the trial courts that generally exercise jurisdiction over § 1983 suits brought against other state officials from hearing virtually all such suits brought against state correction officers. The question presented is whether that exceptional treatment of a limited category of § 1983 claims is consistent with the Supremacy Clause of the United States Constitution.

I

Petitioner, an inmate in New York's Attica Correctional Facility, commenced two § 1983 actions against several correction employees alleging that they violated his civil rights in connection with three prisoner disciplinary proceedings and an altercation. Proceeding *pro se*, petitioner filed his claims in State Supreme Court and sought punitive damages and attorney's fees. The trial court dismissed the actions on the ground that, under N. Y. Correct. Law Ann. § 24 (West 1987) (hereinafter Correction Law § 24), it lacked jurisdiction to entertain any suit arising under state or federal law seeking money damages from correction officers for actions taken in the scope of their employment. The intermediate appellate court summarily affirmed the trial court.

The New York Court of Appeals, by a 4-to-3 vote, also affirmed the dismissal of petitioner's damages action. The Court of Appeals rejected petitioner's argument that Correction Law § 24's jurisdictional limitation interfered with § 1983 and therefore ran afoul of the Supremacy Clause of the United States Constitution. The majority reasoned that, because Correction Law § 24 treats state and federal damages actions against correction officers equally (that is, neither can be brought in New York courts), the statute should be properly characterized as a "neutral state rule regarding the administration of the courts" and therefore a "valid excuse" for the State's refusal to entertain the federal cause of action. The majority understood our Supremacy Clause precedents to set forth the general rule that so long as a State does not refuse to hear a federal claim for the "sole reason that the cause of action arises under federal law," its withdrawal of jurisdiction will be deemed constitutional. So read, discrimination *vel non* is the focal point of Supremacy Clause [analysis.]

Recognizing the importance of the question decided by the New York Court of Appeals, we granted certiorari. We now reverse.

II

Motivated by the belief that damages suits filed by prisoners against state correction officers were by and large frivolous and vexatious, New York passed Correction Law § 24. The statute employs a two-step process to strip its courts of jurisdiction over such damages claims and to replace those claims with the State's preferred alternative. The provision states in full:

> "1. No civil action shall be brought in any court of the state, except by the attorney general on behalf of the state, against any officer or employee of the department, in his personal capacity, for damages arising out of any act done or the failure to perform any act within the scope of employment and in the discharge of the duties by such officer or employee.

> "2. Any claim for damages arising out of any act done or the failure to perform any act within the scope of employment and in the discharge of the duties of any officer or employee of the department shall be brought and

a state law that granted state courts discretion to decline jurisdiction over state and federal claims alike when neither party was a resident of the State. Later, in *Herb v. Pitcairn*, 324 U.S. 117 (1945), a city court dismissed an action brought under the Federal Employers' Liability Act (FELA), for want of jurisdiction because the cause of action arose outside the court's territorial jurisdiction. We upheld the dismissal on the ground that the State's venue laws were not being applied in a way that discriminated against the federal claim. In a third case, *Missouri ex rel. Southern R. Co. v. Mayfield*, 340 U.S. 1 (1950), we held that a State's application of the *forum non conveniens* doctrine to bar adjudication of a FELA case brought by nonresidents was constitutionally sound as long as the policy was enforced impartially. And our most recent decision finding a valid excuse, *Johnson v. Fankell*, 520 U.S. 911 (1997), rested largely on the fact that Idaho's rule limiting interlocutory jurisdiction did not discriminate against § 1983 actions.

Although the absence of discrimination is necessary to our finding a state law neutral, it is not sufficient. A jurisdictional rule cannot be used as a device to undermine federal law, no matter how evenhanded it may appear. As we made clear in [*Howlett v. Rose*], "[t]he fact that a rule is denominated jurisdictional does not provide a court an excuse to avoid the obligation to enforce federal law if the rule does not reflect the concerns of power over the person and competence over the subject matter that jurisdictional rules are designed to protect." Ensuring equality of treatment is thus the beginning, not the end, of the Supremacy Clause analysis.

In addition to giving too much weight to equality of treatment, respondents mistakenly treat this case as implicating the "great latitude [States enjoy] to establish the structure and jurisdiction of their own courts." [*Howlett*]. Although Correction Law § 24 denies state courts authority to entertain damages actions against correction officers, this case does not require us to decide whether Congress may compel a State to offer a forum, otherwise unavailable under state law, to hear suits brought pursuant to § 1983. The State of New York has made this inquiry unnecessary by creating courts of general jurisdiction that routinely sit to hear analogous § 1983 actions. New York's constitution vests the state supreme courts with general original jurisdiction, and the "inviolate authority to hear and resolve all causes in law and equity." *Pollicina v. Misericordia Hospital Medical Center*, 624 N.E.2d 974, 977 (1993). For instance, if petitioner had attempted to sue a police officer for damages under § 1983, the suit would be properly adjudicated by a state supreme court. Similarly, if petitioner had sought declaratory or injunctive relief against a correction officer, that suit would be heard in a state supreme court. It is only a particular species of suits — those seeking damages relief against correction officers — that the State deems inappropriate for its trial courts.

We therefore hold that, having made the decision to create courts of general jurisdiction that regularly sit to entertain analogous suits, New York is not at liberty to shut the courthouse door to federal claims that it considers at odds with its local policy. A State's authority to organize its courts, while considerable, remains subject to the strictures of the Constitution. We have never treated a State's invocation of "jurisdiction" as a trump that ends the *Supremacy Clause* inquiry, and we decline to do so in this case. Because New York's supreme courts generally have personal jurisdiction over the parties in § 1983 suits brought by prisoners against correction officers and because they hear the lion's share of all other *§ 1983* actions, we find little concerning "power over the person and competence over the subject matter" in Correction Law § 24. [*Howlett v. Rose*] (conducting a similar analysis and concluding that the Florida courts of general jurisdiction were "fully competent to provide the remedies [§ 1983] requires").

Accordingly, the dissent's fear that "no state jurisdictional rule will be upheld as constitutional" is entirely unfounded. Our holding addresses only the unique scheme adopted by the State of New York — a law designed to shield a particular class of defendants (correction officers) from a particular type of liability (damages) brought by a particular class of plaintiffs (prisoners). Based on the belief that damages suits against correction officers are frivolous and vexatious, Correction Law § 24 is effectively an immunity statute cloaked in jurisdictional garb. Finding this scheme unconstitutional merely confirms that the Supremacy Clause cannot be evaded by formalism.

V

The judgment of the New York Court of Appeals is reversed, and the case is remanded to that court for further proceedings not inconsistent with this opinion.

It is so ordered.

JUSTICE **Thomas**, with whom the **Chief Justice**, JUSTICE **Scalia**, and JUSTICE **Alito** join as to Part III, dissenting.

[In Parts I and II of his dissenting opinion, Justice Thomas takes issue with the Court's earlier rulings in connection with the state courts' obligation to enforce federal law.]

I

Even accepting the entirety of the Court's precedent in this area of the law, however, I still could not join the majority's resolution of this case as it mischaracterizes and broadens this Court's [decisions.]

A

The majority mischaracterizes this Court's precedent when it asserts that jurisdictional neutrality is "the beginning, not the end, of the *Supremacy Clause* [analysis.]" Here, it is conceded that New York has deprived its courts of subject-matter jurisdiction over a particular class of claims on terms that treat federal and state actions equally. That is all this Court's precedent requires.

The majority's assertion that jurisdictional neutrality is not the touchstone because "[a] jurisdictional rule cannot be used as a device to undermine federal law, no matter how even-handed it may appear," reflects a misunderstanding of the law. A jurisdictional statute simply deprives the relevant court of the power to decide the case [altogether.]

Such a statute necessarily operates without prejudice to the adjudication of the matter in a competent forum. Jurisdictional statutes therefore by definition are incapable of undermining federal law. NYCLA § 24 no more undermines § 1983 than the amount-in-controversy requirement for federal diversity jurisdiction undermines state law. See 28 U.S.C. § 1332. The relevant law (state or federal) remains fully operative in both circumstances. The sole consequence of the jurisdictional barrier is that the law cannot be enforced in one particular judicial forum.

As a result, the majority's focus on New York's reasons for enacting this jurisdictional statute is entirely misplaced. The States "remain independent and autonomous within their proper sphere of authority." *Printz v. United States*, 521 U.S. 898, 928 (1997). New York has the organic authority, therefore, to tailor the jurisdiction of state courts to meet its policy [goals.]

It may be true that it was "Congress' judgment that *all* persons who violate federal rights while acting under color of state law shall be held liable for damages." But Congress has not enforced that judgment by statutorily requiring the States to open their courts to *all* § 1983 claims. And this Court has "never held that state courts must entertain § 1983 suits." *National Private Truck Council, Inc. v. Oklahoma Tax Comm'n*, 515 U.S. 582, 587, n. 4 (1995). Our decisions have held only that the States cannot use jurisdictional statutes to discriminate against federal claims. Because NYCLA § 24 does not violate this command, any policy-driven reasons for depriving jurisdiction over a "federal claim in addition to an identical state claim," are irrelevant for purposes of the Supremacy Clause.

This Court's decision in *Howlett* is not to the contrary. Despite the majority's assertion, *Howlett* does not stand for the proposition "that a State cannot employ a jurisdictional rule 'to dissociate itself from federal law because of disagreement with its content or a refusal to recognize the superior authority of its source.' " As an initial matter, the majority lifts the above quotation — which was merely part of a passage explaining that a "State may not discriminate against federal causes of action," — entirely out of context. *Howlett's* reiteration of *McKnett's* neutrality command, which is all the selected quotation reflects, offers no refuge to the majority in light of its concession that NYCLA § 24 affords "equal treatment" to "federal and state claims."

Howlett instead stands for the unremarkable proposition that States may not add immunity defenses to § 1983. A state law is not jurisdictional just because the legislature has "denominated" it as such. As the majority observes, the State's "invocation of 'jurisdiction' " cannot "trump" the "Supremacy Clause inquiry." The majority, therefore, is correct that a state court's decision "to nullify a federal right or cause of action [that it] believe[s] is inconsistent with [its] local policies" cannot evade the Supremacy Clause by hiding behind a jurisdictional label, because "the Supremacy Clause cannot be evaded by formalism." Rather, a state statute must in fact *operate* jurisdictionally: It must deprive the court of the power to hear the claim and it must not preclude relitigation of the action in a proper forum. *Howlett* proved the point by striking down a state-law immunity rule that bore the jurisdictional label but operated as a defense on the merits and provided for the dismissal of the state court action with prejudice.

But the majority's axiomatic refrain about jurisdictional labels is entirely unresponsive to the issue before the Court — *i.e.*, whether NYCLA § 24 operates jurisdictionally. Unlike the Florida immunity rule in *Howlett*, NYCLA § 24 is not a defense to a federal claim and the dismissal it authorizes is without [prejudice.] For this reason, NYCLA § 24 is not merely "denominated" as jurisdictional — it actually is jurisdictional. The New York courts, therefore, have not declared a "category" of § 1983 claims to be " 'frivolous' " or to have " 'no merit' " in order to " 'relieve congestion' " in the state-court system [as Florida had done in *Howlett*.] These courts have simply recognized that they lack the power to adjudicate this category of claims regardless of their [merit.]

The majority's principal response is that NYCLA § 24 "is effectively an immunity statute cloaked in jurisdictional garb." But this curious rejoinder resurrects an argument that the majority abandons earlier in its own opinion. The majority needs to choose. Either it should definitively commit to making the impossible case that a statute denying state courts the power to entertain a claim without prejudice to its reassertion in federal court is an immunity defense in disguise, or it should clearly explain why some other aspect of *Howlett* controls the outcome of this case. This Court has required Congress to speak clearly when it intends to "upset the usual constitutional balance of federal and state powers." It should require no less of itself.

At bottom, the majority's warning that upholding New York's law "would permit a State to withhold a forum for the adjudication of any federal cause of action with which it disagreed as long as the policy took the form of a jurisdictional rule" is without any basis in fact. This Court's jurisdictional neutrality command already guards against antifederal discrimination. A decision upholding NYCLA § 24, which fully adheres to that rule, would not "circumvent our prior decisions." It simply would adhere to them.

B

The majority also incorrectly concludes that NYCLA § 24 is not a neutral jurisdictional statute because it applies to a "narrow class of defendants," and because New York courts "hear the lion's share of all other § 1983 actions." A statute's jurisdictional status does not turn on its narrowness or on its breadth. [Rather,] a statute's jurisdictional status turns on the grounds on which the state-law dismissal rests and the consequences that follow from such rulings. No matter how narrow the majority perceives NYCLA § 24 to be, it easily qualifies as jurisdictional under this established standard. Accordingly, it is immaterial that New York has chosen to allow its courts of general jurisdiction to entertain § 1983 actions against certain categories of defendants but not others (such as correction officers), or to entertain § 1983 actions against particular defendants for only certain types of relief.

Building on its assumption that a statute's jurisdictional status turns on its scope, the majority further holds that "having made the decision to create courts of general jurisdiction that regularly sit to entertain analogous suits, New York is not at liberty to shut the courthouse door to federal claims that it considers at odds with its local policy." But whether two claims are "analogous" is relevant only for

state law grounds, on account of the Eleventh Amendment prohibition on federal suits against state governments. *Pennhurst* overturned seventy five years of the contrary practice, under which federal courts faced with a request to enjoin state action would first look to state law and only if no state ground were available turn to the constitution. *See Siler v. Louisville & Nashville R. Co.*, 213 U.S. 175, 191–93 (1909) (authorizing that practice). After *Pennhurst*, plaintiffs seeking injunctive relief on both state and federal grounds must either bifurcate the case between state and federal court or bring the whole case in state court. *See* Erwin Chemerinsky, *State Sovereignty and Federal Court Power: The Eleventh Amendment after* Pennhurst v. Halderman, 12 HASTINGS CONST. L.Q. 643 (1985); David Shapiro, Comment, *Wrong Turns: The Eleventh Amendment and the* Pennhurst *Case*, 98 HARV. L. REV. 61 (1984).

9.   Defendants may remove section 1983 suits filed in state court. 28 U.S.C. § 1441(a). Do the considerations bearing on the decision whether to remove parallel those that may influence the plaintiff's initial decision where to file? Are there additional considerations defendants may take into account? When the plaintiff files in state court on account of the convenience of trying the whole case in one place and the defendant removes the federal part of it to federal court, the plaintiff may then seek pendent (or "supplemental") jurisdiction over the state claims. Should the federal court simply apply the *Gibbs* criteria in determining whether to hear the state claim, or should it consider also the defendant's action in removing to federal court as a factor weighing in favor of pendent jurisdiction?

Recall that there are two potential obstacles to pendent jurisdiction. First, the state claims may not arise out of the same nucleus of operative fact as the federal claims. If this is so, then there is a constitutional barrier to hearing the state claims. But other reasons for not hearing the state claims are within the district court's discretion. The recent statute codifying pendent jurisdiction states that the district court "may" decline to exercise supplemental jurisdiction if, for example, the court has dismissed the federal claims. 28 U.S.C. § 1367(c). The statute does not mention the situation envisioned in this note. Does that omission doom the plaintiff's effort to obtain pendent jurisdiction where a discretionary factor might otherwise preclude it?

There is ordinarily no federal constraint whatsoever on the power of state governments to assert sovereign immunity as a shield against *state* law claims. In *Lapides v. Board of Regents*, 535 U.S. 613 (2002), the plaintiffs sued the University of Georgia Board of Regents in state court, on both state and federal grounds. The Board of Regents is an "arm of the state," i.e., an entity that enjoys the state's sovereign immunity from suit. Under applicable state law, however, the state had waived its immunity against state court suits in the matter at hand. The Board of Regents, wishing nonetheless to benefit from immunity, removed the case to federal court and asserted Eleventh Amendment immunity there, on the theory that the waiver of immunity did not extend to federal court suits. The Regents may have thought they were on solid ground because, as a general proposition, states may limit their waivers of immunity to state court suits. Here, however, the state's decision to remove the case made a decisive difference. A unanimous Supreme Court ruled that the state waived its sovereign immunity on the state law claims when it removed the case from state to federal court. Is *Lapides* relevant to the pendent jurisdiction issue raised in the preceding paragraphs of this note?

Suppose a litigant brings a section 1983 suit in federal court, and seeks supplemental jurisdiction over state claims. At some point the federal court decides that supplemental jurisdiction is inappropriate and dismisses the state claims. Suppose further that, in the meantime the state statute of limitations has (evidently) expired on the state claims. A provision of the supplemental jurisdiction statute, 28 U.S.C. § 1367 (d), preserves the plaintiff's state law rights by requiring that a state statute of limitations be tolled "while the claim is pending [in federal court] and for a period of 30 days after it si dismissed unless State law provides for a longer tolling period." In *Jinks v. Richland County*, 538 U.S. 456 (2003), a section 1983 case, a unanimous Supreme Court upheld the constitutionality of this tolling rule against a variety of objections. In particular, Richland County maintained that the tolling provision should not be applied against a state's political subdivisions. In support of this position, it cited *Raynor v. Regents of University of Minnesota*, 534 U.S. 533 (2002), where the Court had ruled that section 1367(d) does not apply to suits filed against state governments but subsequently dismissed on sovereign immunity grounds. The Court explained that it had limited the scope of the tolling rule in *Raynor* "to avoid interpreting the statute in a manner that would raise 'serious constitutional doubt' in light of [its] decisions protecting a *State's* sovereign immunity from congressional abrogation." (emphasis in original). Because Richland County does not share the state's sovereign immunity, "no such doubt arises" as to Congress's power to impose liability on it.

II. THE CHOICE BETWEEN STATE AND FEDERAL LAW

FELDER v. CASEY
487 U.S. 131 (1988)

JUSTICE **BRENNAN** delivered the opinion of the Court.

A Wisconsin statute provides that before suit may be brought in state court against a state or local governmental entity or officer, the plaintiff must notify the governmental defendant of the circumstances giving rise to the claim, the amount of the claim, and his or her intent to hold the named defendant liable. The statute further requires that, in order to afford the defendant an opportunity to consider the requested relief, the claimant must refrain from filing suit for 120 days after providing such notice. Failure to comply with these requirements constitutes grounds for dismissal of the action. In the present case, the Supreme Court of Wisconsin held that this notice-of-claim statute applies to federal civil rights actions brought in state court under 42 U.S.C. § 1983. Because we conclude that these requirements are preempted as inconsistent with federal law, we reverse.

[The case arose out of an altercation between Felder and some Milwaukee police officers on July 4, 1981.] Nine months after the incident, petitioner filed this [§ 1983] action in the Milwaukee County Circuit Court against the city of Milwaukee and certain of its police officers, alleging that the beating and arrest were unprovoked and racially motivated, and violated his rights under the Fourth and Fourteenth

Amendments to the United States Constitution. [The] officers moved to dismiss the suit based on petitioner's failure to comply with the State's notice-of-claim statute. That statute provides that no action may be brought or maintained against any state governmental subdivision, agency, or officer unless the claimant either provides written notice of the claim within 120 days of the alleged injury, or demonstrates that the relevant subdivision, agency, or officer had actual notice of the claim and was not prejudiced by the lack of written notice. The statute further provides that the party seeking redress must also submit an itemized statement of the relief sought to the governmental subdivision or agency, which then has 120 days to grant or disallow the requested relief. Finally, claimants must bring suit within six months of receiving notice that their claim has been disallowed.

[The Wisconsin Supreme Court upheld application of the notice-of-claim statute, reasoning that] while Congress may establish the procedural framework under which claims are heard in federal courts, States retain the authority under the Constitution to prescribe the rules and procedures that govern actions in their own tribunals. Accordingly, a party who chooses to vindicate a congressionally created right in state court must abide by the State's procedures.

We granted certiorari and now reverse.

No one disputes the general and unassailable proposition relied upon by the Wisconsin Supreme Court below that States may establish the rules of procedure governing litigation in their own courts. By the same token, however, where state courts entertain a federally created cause of action, the "federal right cannot be defeated by the forms of local practice." The question before us today, therefore, is essentially one of premptiom : is the application of the State's notice-of-claim provision to § 1983 actions brought in state courts consistent with the goals of the federal civil rights laws, or does the enforcement of such a requirement instead "stand as an obstacle to the accomplishment and execution of the full purposes and objectives of Congress"? Under the Supremacy Clause of the Federal Constitution, "the relative importance to the State of its own law is not material when there is a conflict with a valid federal law," for "any state law, however clearly within a State's acknowledged power, which interferes with or is contrary to federal law, must yield." Because the notice-of-claim statute at issue here conflicts in both its purpose and effects with the remedial objectives of § 1983, and because its enforcement in such actions will frequently and predictably produce different outcomes in § 1983 litigation based solely on whether the claim is asserted in state or federal court, we conclude that the state law is pre-empted when the § 1983 action is brought in a state court.

Section 1983 creates a species of liability in favor of persons deprived of their federal civil rights by those wielding state authority. As we have repeatedly emphasized, "the central objective of the Reconstruction-Era civil rights statutes [is] to ensure that individuals whose federal constitutional or statutory rights are abridged may recover damages or secure injunctive relief." Thus, § 1983 provides "a uniquely federal remedy against incursions [upon] rights secured by the Constitution and laws of the Nation," and is to be accorded "a sweep as broad as its language."

Any assessment of the applicability of a state law to federal civil rights litigation, therefore, must be made in light of the purpose and nature of the federal right. This is so whether the question of state-law applicability arises in section 1983 litigation brought in state courts, which possess concurrent jurisdiction over such actions, or in federal-court litigation, where, because the federal civil rights laws fail to provide certain rules of decision thought essential to the orderly adjudication of rights, courts are occasionally called upon to borrow state law. Accordingly, we have held that a state law that immunizes government conduct otherwise subject to suit under section 1983 is preempted, even where the federal civil rights litigation takes place in state court, because the application of the state immunity law would thwart the congressional remedy, *see Martinez v. California*, 444 U.S. 277 [(1980).]

[Wisconsin's] notice-of-claim statute is part of a broader legislative scheme governing the rights of citizens to sue the State's subdivisions. The statute, both in its earliest and current forms, provides a circumscribed waiver of local governmental immunity that limits the amount recoverable in suits against local governments and imposes the notice requirements at issue here . . . The purposes of these conditions, however, mirror those of the judicial immunity the statute replaced. Such statutes "are enacted primarily for the benefit of governmental defendants," and enable those defendants to "investigate early, prepare a stronger case, and perhaps reach an early settlement." Moreover, where the defendant is unable to obtain a satisfactory settlement, the Wisconsin statute forces claimants to bring suit within a relatively short period after the local governing body disallows the claim, in order to "assure prompt initiation of litigation."

[In] sum, as respondents explain, the State has chosen to expose its subdivisions to large liability and defense costs, and, in light of that choice, has made the concomitant decision to impose conditions that "assist municipalities in controlling those costs." The decision to subject state subdivisions to liability for violations of federal rights, however, was a choice that Congress, not the Wisconsin Legislature, made, and it is a decision that the State has no authority to override. Thus, however understandable or laudable the State's interest in controlling liability expenses might otherwise be, it is patently incompatible with the compensatory goals of the federal legislation, as are the means the State has chosen to effectuate it.

[This] burdening of a federal right, moreover, is not the natural or permissible consequence of an otherwise neutral, uniformly applicable state rule. Although it is true that the notice-of-claim statute does not discriminate between state and federal causes of action against local governments, the fact remains that the law's protection extends only to governmental defendants and thus conditions the right to bring suit against the very persons and entities Congress intended to subject to liability. We therefore cannot accept the suggestion that this requirement is simply part of "the vast body of procedural rules, rooted in policies unrelated to the definition of any particular substantive cause of action, that forms no essential part of 'the cause of action' as applied to any given plaintiff." On the contrary, the notice-of-claim provision is imposed only upon a specific class of plaintiffs-those who sue governmental defendants and, as we have seen, is firmly rooted in policies very much related to, and to a large extent directly contrary to, the substantive cause of action provided those plaintiffs. This defendant-specific focus of the notice requirement serves to distinguish it, rather starkly, from rules uniformly applicable to all suits, such as rules governing service of process or substitution of parties, which

Professor Neuborne complains that arcane state pleading requirements discourage plaintiffs' lawyers unfamiliar with state procedure from filing section 1983 cases in state courts. Is that a good reason for requiring state courts to change their ways? Professor Steinglass recognizes the differences between federal and state pleading rules but thinks that "few cases actually turn on issues of pleading," because "when issues are actually tried on theories actionable under section 1983, plaintiffs can usually amend their complaints to conform to the evidence." STEINGLASS, *supra*, at § 12:5.

(b) *Class Actions.* Many state procedural systems place significant restrictions on the use of class actions. *See* STEINGLASS, *supra*, § 8:13. Should plaintiffs with section 1983 claims be bound by those limits, or should Federal Rule 23(b) and federal principles governing class actions apply to state court section 1983 claims? In answering this question, the analytical framework of *Felder*, with its emphasis on whether the state rule will frequently and predictably affect outcomes, may be inapposite. Perhaps the focus should be on whether the broad availability of class actions in state courts is necessary to achieve the purposes of section 1983? Consider Professor Neuborne's analysis:

> Traditional cross-forum collateral rule analysis has required the forum jurisdiction to apply the collateral rules of the generative jurisdiction in defining the class of eligible plaintiffs. [He then qualifies this generalization, citing *Robertson v. Wegmann*, 436 U.S. 584 (1978) (discussed in Chapter 9) as an exception to it. In *Robertson*,] the plaintiff's death was unrelated to the defendants' acts, [so that] the survivorship rule was wholly unconnected to the policies underlying section 1983. The issue, therefore, in the context of section 1983 litigation in state court is whether the collateral rules governing the ability of a class of plaintiffs to enforce section 1983 is linked to the policies underlying section 1983 . . . or is wholly divorced from them as in *Robertson.*

Neuborne, *supra*, at 783. In Neuborne's view,

> the potential for class action relief should exercise substantial deterrent effect on persons contemplating activity at the margins of constitutional protection. . . . Since the availability of a class action will not merely affect, but will actually control, much preincident behavior by placing direct restraints on an official's freedom of action, and since members of the typical section 1983 class are unlikely to be in a position to assert their rights individually, the availability of class relief is no less integral to the policies underlying section 1983 than the power to award attorney's fees and the ability to define immunity from suit. Accordingly, its availability should similarly be governed by uniformly applicable federal rules.

Id. at 783–84. Do you agree? What arguments might be advanced against Neuborne's view? Is it relevant that Congress has nowhere expressed any intent to require state courts to undertake the arduous tasks associated with managing class actions?

(c) *Discovery.* State courts often follow less liberal discovery policies than federal courts do. *See* R. FIGG, R. MCCULLOUGH & J. UNDERWOOD, CIVIL TRIAL MANUAL 76–78

(1977). Professor Steinglass reports that, with some exceptions, "[s]tate courts [have] assumed that issues involving the scope of discovery, including the applicable privileges, are matters of state law, even when state courts are entertaining section 1983 or other federal causes of action." STEINGLASS, *supra*, at § 8:9. In *Denari v. Superior Court*, 215 Cal. App. 3d 1488 (1989) for example, the California Court of Appeal applied an evidentiary privilege under state law to deny a discovery request for the names of persons arrested and booked at a county jail, made by a section 1983 plaintiff seeking potential witnesses. The plaintiff had proposed testing the claim of privilege under a federal balancing test.

This case, the court held, was not like *Felder*:

> The recognition of the right to privacy of all citizens of the state, along with the concomitant protection of such right in the context of civil discovery, is certainly not antagonistic to the remedial objectives of section 1983; the effect of such right does not necessarily conflict with the objectives of the civil rights tort. [Unlike] the [notice of claim statute at issue in *Felder*] our qualified protection of a privacy right does not play a conclusive role in defining the outcome of the cause of action. [This] is not to say that in a particular case the results might not differ depending upon the forum, only that the rule itself is not outcome determinative with respect to the litigation in general. [Finally,] the *Felder* Court considered whether the rule was "a neutral and uniformly applicable rule of procedure." Here, of course, the limits on discovery pursuant to the right of privacy apply in both civil and criminal cases and are equally applicable to all parties.

215 Cal. App. 3d at 1499, 1501–02.

Does the court successfully distinguish *Felder*? Is it relevant that the evidentiary privilege it relies on is aimed at protecting the privacy of arrestees rather than, as in *Felder*, shielding the government from onerous liability? Would a state discovery rule absolutely privileging official documents pass muster? *Felder* concerned a state rule that put an extra obstacle in the way of the constitutional tort plaintiff. Should federal law govern when the state rule diverges from the federal one by *favoring* the plaintiff? That is the issue in the following case.

JOHNSON v. FANKELL
520 U.S. 911 (1997)

JUSTICE STEVENS delivered the opinion of the Court.

The question presented is whether defendants in an action brought under 42 U.S.C. § 1983 in state court have a federal right to an interlocutory appeal from a denial of qualified immunity. We hold that they do not.

Petitioners are officials of the Idaho Liquor Dispensary. Respondent, a former liquor store clerk, brought this action for damages under § 1983 in the District Court for the County of Bonner, Idaho. She alleged that petitioners deprived her of property without due process of law in violation of the Fourteenth Amendment to the Federal Constitution when they terminated her employment. Petitioners moved to dismiss the complaint on the ground that they were entitled to qualified immunity. They contended that, at the time of respondent's dismissal, they reasonably believed that she was a probationary employee who had no property interest in her job. Accordingly, petitioners argued, her termination did not violate clearly established law. The trial court denied the motion, and petitioners filed a timely notice of appeal to the Supreme Court of the State of Idaho.

The State Supreme Court entered an order dismissing the appeal. The Court explained that an order denying a motion for summary judgment is not appealable under Idaho Appellate Rule 11(a)(1) "for the reason it is not from a final order or Judgment." It also rejected petitioners' arguments that the order was appealable under 42 U.S.C. § 1983. [Petitioners sought Supreme Court review, pointing] out that some state courts, unlike the Idaho Supreme Court, allow interlocutory appeals of orders denying qualified immunity on the theory that such review is necessary to protect a substantial federal right. We granted certiorari to resolve the conflict, and now affirm.

We have recognized a qualified immunity defense for both federal officials sued under the implied cause of action asserted in *Bivens v. Six Unknown Fed. Narcotics Agents*, and state officials sued under 42 U.S.C. § 1983. In both situations, "officials performing discretionary functions, generally are shielded from liability for civil damages insofar as their conduct does not violate clearly established statutory or constitutional rights of which a reasonable person would have known." *Harlow v. Fitzgerald.* This "qualified immunity" defense is valuable to officials asserting it for two reasons. First, if it is found applicable at any stage of the proceedings, it determines the outcome of the litigation by shielding the official from damages liability. Second, when the complaint fails to allege a violation of clearly established law or when discovery fails to uncover evidence sufficient to create a genuine issue whether the defendant committed such a violation, it provides the defendant with an immunity from the burdens of trial as well as a defense to liability. Indeed, one reason for adopting the objective test announced in Harlow was to "permit the resolution of many insubstantial claims on summary judgment."

Consistent with that purpose, we held in *Mitchell v. Forsyth* [Ch. 8, *supra*] that a Federal District Court order rejecting a qualified immunity defense on the ground that the defendant's actions — if proven — would have violated clearly established law may be appealed immediately as a "final decision" within the meaning of the general federal appellate jurisdiction statute, 28 U.S.C. § 1291. If this action had been brought in a federal court, therefore, petitioners would have had a right to take an appeal from the trial court's order denying their motion for summary judgment.

Relying on the facts (a) that respondent has asserted a federal claim under a federal statute, and (b) that they are asserting a defense provided by federal law, petitioners submit that the Idaho courts must protect their right to avoid the burdens of trial by allowing the same interlocutory appeal that would be available in a federal court. They support this submission with two different arguments: First, that when the Idaho courts construe their own rules allowing appeals from final judgments, they must accept the federal definition of finality in cases brought under § 1983; and second, that if those rules do not authorize the appeal, they are pre-empted by federal law. We find neither argument persuasive.

We can easily dispense with petitioners' first contention that Idaho must follow the federal construction of a "final decision." Even if the Idaho and federal statutes contained identical language — and they do not — the interpretation of the Idaho statute by the Idaho Supreme Court would be binding on federal courts. Neither this Court nor any other federal tribunal has any authority to place a construction on a state statute different from the one rendered by the highest court of the state. This proposition, fundamental to our system of federalism, is applicable to procedural as well as substantive rules.

The definition of the term "final decision" that we adopted in *Mitchell* was an application of the "collateral order" doctrine first recognized in *Cohen v. Beneficial Industrial Loan Corp.* In that case, as in all of our cases following it, we were construing the federal statutory language of 28 U.S.C. § 1291. While some States have adopted a similar "collateral order" exception when construing their jurisdictional statutes, we have never suggested that federal law compelled them to do so. Indeed, a number of States employ collateral order doctrines that reject the limitations this Court has placed on § 1291. Idaho could, of course, place the same construction on its Appellate Rule 11(a)(1) as we have placed on § 1291. But that is clearly a choice for that Court to make, not one that we have any authority to command. Petitioners also contend that, to the extent that Idaho Appellate Rule 11(a)(1) does not allow an interlocutory appeal, it is pre-empted by § 1983. Relying heavily on *Felder v. Casey*, petitioners first assert that pre-emption is necessary to avoid "different outcomes in § 1983 litigation based solely on whether the claim is asserted in state or federal court." Second, they argue that the state procedure "impermissibly burdens" the federal immunity from suit because it does not adequately protect their right to prevail on the immunity question in advance of trial. For two reasons, petitioners have a heavy burden of persuasion in making this argument. First, our normal presumption against pre-emption is buttressed by the fact that the Idaho Supreme Court's dismissal of the appeal rested squarely on a neutral state rule regarding the administration of the state [courts.] A second barrier to petitioners' argument arises from the nature of the interest protected by the defense of qualified immunity. Petitioners' argument for pre-emption is bottomed on their claims that the Idaho rules are interfering with their federal rights. While it is true that the defense has its source in a federal statute (§ 1983), the ultimate purpose of qualified immunity is to protect the state and its officials from overenforcement of federal rights. The Idaho Supreme Court's application of the State's procedural rules in this context is thus less an interference with federal interests than a judgment about how best to balance the competing state interests of limiting interlocutory appeals and providing state officials with immediate review of the merits of their defense.

Petitioner's arguments for pre-emption are not strong enough to overcome these considerable hurdles. Contrary to petitioners' assertions, Idaho's decision not to provide appellate review for the vast majority of interlocutory orders — including denials of qualified immunity in § 1983 cases — is not "outcome determinative" in the sense that we used that term when we held that Wisconsin's notice-of-claim statute could not be applied to defeat a federal civil rights action brought in state courts under § 1983. *Felder.* The failure to comply with the Wisconsin statute in Felder resulted in a judgment dismissing a complaint that would not have been dismissed — at least not without a judicial determination of the merits of the claim — if the case had been filed in a federal court. One of the primary grounds for our decision was that, because the notice-of-claim requirement would "frequently and predictably produce different outcomes" depending on whether § 1983 claims were brought in state or federal court, it was inconsistent with the federal interest in uniformity.

Petitioners' reliance on Felder is misplaced because "outcome," as we used the term there, referred to the ultimate disposition of the case. If petitioners' claim to qualified immunity is meritorious, there is no suggestion that the application of the Idaho rules of procedure will produce a final result different from what a federal ruling would produce. Petitioners were able to argue their immunity from suit claim to the trial court, just as they would to a federal court. And the claim will be reviewable by the Idaho Supreme Court after the trial court enters a final judgment, thus providing the petitioners with a further chance to urge their immunity. Consequently, the postponement of the appeal until after final judgment will not affect the ultimate outcome of the case.

Petitioners' second argument for pre-emption of the state procedural rule is that the rule does not adequately protect their right to prevail in advance of trial. In evaluating this contention, it is important to focus on the precise source and scope of the federal right at issue. The right to have the trial court rule on the merits of the qualified immunity defense presumably has its source in § 1983, but the right to immediate appellate review of that ruling in a federal case has its source in § 1291. The former right is fully protected by Idaho. The latter right, however, is a federal procedural right that simply does not apply in a nonfederal forum.

The locus of the right to interlocutory appeal in § 1291, rather than in § 1983 itself, is demonstrated by our holding in *Johnson v. Jones.* In that case, government officials asserting qualified immunity claimed entitlement to an interlocutory appeal of a District Court order denying their motion for summary judgment on the ground that the record showed a genuine issue of material fact whether the officials actually engaged in the conduct that constituted a clear violation of constitutional law. We concluded that this circumstance was different from that presented in *Mitchell,* in which the subject of the interlocutory appeal was whether a given set of facts showed a violation of clearly established law, and held that although § 1291 did allow an interlocutory appeal in the latter circumstance, such an appeal was not allowed in the former. In so holding, we acknowledged that "whether a district court's denial of summary judgment amounts to (a) a determination about pre-existing 'clearly established' law, or (b) a determination about 'genuine' issues of fact for trial, it still forces public officials to trial." But we concluded that the strong "countervailing considerations" surrounding appropriate interpretation of § 1291 were of sufficient importance to outweigh the officials' interest in avoiding the burdens of litigation. The "countervailing considerations" at issue here are even stronger than those presented in Johnson. When pre-emption of state law is at issue, we must respect the "principles [that] are fundamental to a system of federalism in which the state courts share responsibility for the application and enforcement of federal law." *Howlett.* This respect is at its apex when we confront a claim that federal law requires a State to undertake something as fundamental as restructuring the operation of its courts. We therefore cannot agree with petitioners that 1983's recognition of the defense of qualified immunity pre-empts a State's consistent application of its neutral procedural rules, even when those rules deny an interlocutory appeal in this context.

The judgment of the Supreme Court of the State of Idaho dismissing petitioners' appeal is therefore affirmed.

NOTE

In *Felder* the Court foreshadowed its holding in *Johnson*, by declaring that "[s]tates may make the litigation of federal claims as congenial as they see fit [because] such congeniality does not stand as an obstacle to the accomplishment of Congress' goals." Nonetheless, there may be some tension between *Johnson* and *Mitchell v. Forsyth*, Chapter 8, *supra*, where the Court characterized official immunity as "an entitlement not to stand trial or face the other burdens of litigation," not merely a defense to liability. If immunity is an "entitlement not to stand trial," that is granted defendants by section 1983, then a state policy that effectively deprives the defendant of the entitlement seems as much at odds with federal law as was the notice-of-claim statute in *Felder*. Is it a satisfactory answer to this argument to point out that the defendant in a state court section 1983 case may remove the litigation to the federal courts under 28 U.S.C. § 1441(a)? Thanks to this option, the defendant retains access to an interlocutory appeal despite *Johnson*. Is this rejoinder compatible with the principle that federal law entitles both parties to litigate in the state courts? In any event, *Johnson* surely diminishes defendants' willingness to allow section 1983 cases to remain in the state courts. Would values of federalism have been better served by forcing state courts to follow the federal rule on interlocutory appeals, so as to encourage defendants to litigate in state court? Keep in mind that the premise of these questions is that state and federal law diverge on the availability of an interlocutory appeal. Some states may allow interlocutory appeals of denials of official immunity.

See generally Scott T. Schultz, Note, *How Far Is Too Far: Analyzing the Collateral Law Applicable in State Court Section 1983 Litigation*, 72 CHI.-KENT L. REV. 875 (1997).

Chapter 12

ATTORNEY'S FEES

The award of attorney's fees in section 1983 litigation is a recent development of extraordinary importance. Under what is known as the "American Rule," attorney's fees generally are not awarded to the prevailing party in civil litigation in the absence of a specific authorizing statute. In *Alyeska Pipeline Service Co. v. Wilderness Society*, 421 U.S. 240 (1975), the Supreme Court reaffirmed the "American Rule" and disapproved lower court awards of attorney's fees to successful civil rights plaintiffs under principles of equity. Congress responded to *Alyeska Pipeline Service* with the enactment of The Civil Rights Attorney's Fees Award Act of 1976, 42 U.S.C. § 1988(b), which provides in pertinent part:

> In any action or proceeding to enforce a provision of sections 1981, 1982, 1983, 1985, and 1986 of this title, title IX of Public Law 92-318 [20 U.S.C. §§ 1681–1688], or title VI of the Civil Rights Act of 1964 [42 U.S.C. §§ 2000d–2000d-4], the court, in its discretion, may allow the prevailing party, other than the United States, a reasonable attorney's fee as part of the costs.

This chapter explores the contours of this relatively brief statute. It addresses three basic questions: When is a party entitled to attorney's fees? How does a court determine what is a "reasonable" fee? And what are the strategic and ethical implications of a potential fee award?

Two points should be made at the outset. First, there are dozens of federal fee shifting statutes that resemble section 1988(b). As a result, judicial constructions of other attorney's fee legislation often provides guidance in interpreting section 1988. *E.g., City of Burlington v. Dague*, 505 U.S. 557 (1992) (method of calculating a "reasonable fee" under the fee shifting provisions of the Solid Waste Disposal Act, 42 U.S.C. § 7002(e) and the Clean Water Act, 33 U.S.C. § 1365(d) also applies to section 1988). Second, because of the statutory foundation of attorney's fee awards in constitutional tort litigation, court decisions often refer to legislative history and Congressional intent in addressing issues concerning the availability and computation of fees. Before turning to specific cases, consider the Senate Report that accompanied the Civil Rights Attorney's Fees Awards Act of 1976.

I. LEGISLATIVE HISTORY

THE CIVIL RIGHTS ATTORNEY'S FEES AWARD ACT OF 1976
Senate Report No. 94-1011

Statement

The purpose and effect of S. 2278 are simple — it is designed to allow courts to provide the familiar remedy of reasonable counsel fees to prevailing parties in suits to enforce the civil rights acts which Congress has passed since 1866. S. 2278 follows the language of Titles II and VII of the Civil Rights Act of 1964, 42 U.S.C. § 2000a-3(b) and 2000e-5(k), and § 402 of the Voting Rights Act Amendments of 1975, 42 U.S.C. § 1973(e). All of these civil rights laws depend heavily upon private enforcement, and fee awards have proved an essential remedy if private citizens are to have a meaningful opportunity to vindicate the important Congressional policies which these laws contain.

In many cases arising under our civil rights laws, the citizen who must sue to enforce the law has little or no money with which to hire a lawyer. If private citizens are to be able to assert their civil rights, and if those who violate the Nation's fundamental laws are not to proceed with impunity, then citizens must have the opportunity to recover what it costs them to vindicate these rights in court.

Congress recognized this need when it made specific provision for such fee shifting in Titles II and VII of the Civil Rights Act of 1964:

> "When a plaintiff brings an action under [Title II] he cannot recover damages. If he obtains an injunction, he does so not for himself alone but also as a "private attorney general," vindicating a policy that Congress considered of the highest priority. If successful plaintiffs were routinely forced to bear their own attorneys' fees, few aggrieved parties would be in a position to advance the public interest by invoking the injunctive powers of the Federal courts. Congress therefore enacted the provision for counsel fees — * * * to encourage individuals injured by racial discrimination to seek judicial relief under Title II." *Newman v. Piggie Park Enterprises, Inc.*, 390 U.S. 400, 402 (1968).

The idea of the "private attorney general" is not a new one, nor are attorneys' fees a new remedy. Congress has commonly authorized attorneys' fees in laws under which "private attorneys general" play a significant role in enforcing our policies. We have, since 1870, authorized fee shifting under more than 50 laws. . . .

The remedy of attorneys' fees has always been recognized as particularly appropriate in the civil rights area, and civil rights and attorneys' fees have always been closely interwoven. In the civil rights area, Congress has instructed the courts to use the broadest and most effective remedies available to achieve the goals of our civil rights laws. The very first attorneys' fee statute was a civil rights law, . . . which provided for attorneys' fees in three separate provisions protecting voting rights.

Modern civil rights legislation reflects a heavy reliance on attorneys' fees as well. In 1964, seeking to assure full compliance with the Civil Rights Act of that year, we authorized fee shifting for private suits establishing violations of the public accommodations and equal employment provisions. 42 U. S. C. § 2000a-3(b) and 2000e-5(k). Since 1964, every major civil rights law passed by the Congress has included, or has been amended to include, one or more fee provisions. . . .

These fee shifting provisions have been successful in enabling vigorous enforcement of modern civil rights legislation, while at the same time limiting the growth of the enforcement bureaucracy. Before May 12, 1975, when the Supreme Court handed down its decision in *Alyeska Pipeline Service Co. v. Wilderness Society*, 421 U.S. 240 (1975), many lower Federal courts throughout the Nation had drawn the obvious analogy between the Reconstruction Civil Rights Acts and these modern civil rights acts, and, following Congressional recognition in the newer statutes of the "private attorney general" concept, were exercising their traditional equity powers to award attorneys' fees under early civil rights laws as well.

These pre-*Alyeska* decisions remedied a gap in the specific statutory provisions and restored an important historic remedy for civil rights violations. However, in *Alyeska*, the United States Supreme Court, while referring to the desirability of fees in a variety of circumstances, ruled that only Congress, and not the courts, could specify which laws were important enough to merit fee shifting under the "private attorney general" theory. The Court expressed the view, in dictum, that the Reconstruction Acts did not contain the necessary congressional authorization. This decision and dictum created anomalous gaps in our civil rights laws whereby awards of fees are, according to *Alyeska*, suddenly unavailable in the most fundamental civil rights cases. For instance, fees are authorized in an employment discrimination suit under Title VII of the 1964 Civil Rights Act, but not in the same suit brought under 42 U.S.C. § 1981, which protects similar rights but involves fewer technical prerequisites to the filing of an action. Fees are allowed in a housing discrimination suit brought under Title VIII of the Civil Rights Act of 1968, but not in the same suit brought under 42 U.S.C. § 1982, a Reconstruction Act protecting the same rights. Like-wise, fees are allowed in a suit under Title II of the 1964 Civil Rights Act challenging discrimination in a private restaurant, but not in suits under 42 U.S.C. § 1983 redressing violations of the Federal Constitution or laws by officials sworn to uphold the laws.

This bill, S. 2278, is an appropriate response to the *Alyeska* decision. It is limited to cases arising under our civil rights laws, a category of cases in which attorneys fees have been traditionally regarded as appropriate. It remedies gaps in the language of these civil rights laws by providing the specific authorization required by the Court in *Alyeska*, and makes our civil rights laws consistent.

It is intended that the standards for awarding fees be generally the same as under the fee provisions of the 1964 Civil Rights Act. A party seeking to enforce the rights protected by the statutes covered by S. 2278, if successful, "should ordinarily recover an attorney's fee unless special circumstances would render such an award unjust." *Newman v. Piggie Park Enterprises, Inc.*, 390 U.S. 400, 402 (1968). Such "private attorneys general" should not be deterred from bringing good faith actions to vindicate the fundamental rights here involved by the prospect of having to pay their opponent's counsel fees should they lose. . . . This bill thus deters frivolous suits by authorizing an award of attorneys' fees against a party shown to have litigated in "bad faith" under the guise of attempting to enforce the Federal rights created by the statutes listed in S. 2278. Similar standards have been followed not only in the Civil Rights Act of 1964, but in other statutes providing for attorneys' fees. . . .

In appropriate circumstances, counsel fees under S. 2278 may be awarded pendente lite. Such awards are especially appropriate where a party has prevailed on an important matter in the course of litigation, even when he ultimately does not prevail on all issues. . . . Moreover, for purposes of the award of counsel fees, parties may be considered to have prevailed when they vindicate rights through a consent judgment or without formally obtaining relief.

. . . It is intended that the amount of fees awarded under S. 2278 be governed by the same standards which prevail in other types of equally complex Federal litigation, such as antitrust cases and not be reduced because the rights involved may be nonpecuniary in nature. The appropriate standards, see *Johnson v. Georgia Highway Express*, 488 F.2d 714 (5th Cir. 1974),[1] are correctly applied in [district court] cases . . . [that] have resulted in fees which are adequate to attract competent counsel, but which do not produce windfalls to attorneys. In computing the fee, counsel for prevailing parties should be paid, as is traditional with attorneys compensated by a fee-paying client, "for all time reasonably expended on a matter."

This bill creates no startling new remedy — it only meets the technical requirements that the Supreme Court has laid down if the Federal Courts are to continue the practice of awarding attorneys' fees which had been going on for years prior to the Court's May decision. It does not change the statutory provisions regarding the protection of civil rights except as it provides the fee awards which are necessary if citizens are to be able to effectively secure compliance with these existing statutes. There are very few provisions in our Federal laws which are self-executing. Enforcement of the laws depends on governmental action and, in some cases, on private action through the courts. If the cost of private enforcement actions becomes too great, there will be no private enforcement. If our civil rights laws are not to become mere hollow pronouncements which the average citizen cannot enforce, we must maintain the traditionally effective remedy of fee shifting in these cases.

---

[1] [editors' note]. Johnson listed 12 factors relevant in determining a fee award: (1) the time and labor required; (2) the novelty and difficulty of the questions; (3) the skill requisite to perform the legal service properly; (4) the preclusion of employment by the attorney due to acceptance of the case; (5) the customary fee; (6) whether the fee is fixed or contingent; (7) time limitations imposed by the client or the circumstances; (8) the amount involved and the results obtained; (9) the experience, reputation, and ability of the attorneys; (10) the "undesirability" of the case; (11) the nature and length of the professional relationship with the client; and (12) awards in similar cases.

NOTES

1. Suppose a jury finds that a government official deprived the plaintiff of liberty and property without due process, but that this constitutional violation was not the proximate cause of any pecuniary harm. Can the plaintiff be considered a "prevailing party" under section 1988? Should the trial court award the plaintiff attorney's fees in such a case? If so, what is a "reasonable" fee? How much guidance does Senate Report No. 94-1011 provide in resolving these questions?

2. Suppose the plaintiff seeks to enjoin an allegedly unconstitutional practice and because of the suit the defendant ceases the challenged conduct prior to a judicial ruling. Can the plaintiff be said to have prevailed? How much guidance does Senate Report 94-10011 provide in resolving this question?

3. What standards did Congress intend to govern the determination of the amount of a "reasonable" fee? Would the amount of a fee calculated by a contingency formula be relevant to the determination of a "reasonable" fee under section 1988? Can plaintiff's attorneys enter into contingency fee contracts with their clients in civil rights cases? How much guidance does Senate Report No. 94-1011 provide in resolving these questions?

II.   WHEN IS A PARTY ENTITLED TO ATTORNEY'S FEES UNDER 42 U.S.C. § 1988?

FARRAR v. HOBBY
506 U.S. 103 (1992)

JUSTICE **THOMAS** delivered the opinion of the Court.

We decide today whether a civil rights plaintiff who receives a nominal damages award is a "prevailing party" eligible to receive attorney's fees under 42 U.S.C. § 1988. The Court of Appeals for the Fifth Circuit reversed an award of attorney's fees on the ground that a plaintiff receiving only nominal damages is not a prevailing party. Although we hold that such a plaintiff is a prevailing party, we affirm the denial of fees in this case.

I

[Joseph Farrar filed suit under § 1983 against the then-Lieutenant Governor of Texas, William Hobby, and others alleging that they deprived him of his liberty and property without due process through malicious prosecution aimed at closing a school he owned and operated. Prior to trial, Farrar dropped his claim for injunctive relief and increased the request for damages to $17 million.]

The case was tried before a jury in the Southern District of Texas on August 15, 1983. Through special interrogatories, the jury found that all of the defendants except Hobby had conspired against the plaintiffs but that this conspiracy was not a proximate cause of any injury suffered by the plaintiffs. The jury also found that Hobby had "committed an act or acts under color of state law that deprived Plaintiff

Joseph Davis Farrar of a civil right," but it found that Hobby's conduct was not "a proximate cause of any damages" suffered by Joseph Farrar. . . . In accordance with the jury's answers to the special interrogatories, the District Court ordered that "Plaintiffs take nothing, that the action be dismissed on the merits, and that the parties bear their own costs."

The Court of Appeals . . . affirmed the failure to award compensatory or nominal damages against the conspirators because the plaintiffs had not proved an actual deprivation of a constitutional right. Because the jury found that Hobby had deprived Joseph Farrar of a civil right, however, the Fifth Circuit remanded for entry of judgment against Hobby for nominal damages.

The plaintiffs then sought attorney's fees under 42 U.S.C. § 1988. On January 30, 1987, the District Court entered an order awarding the plaintiffs $280,000 in fees, $27,932 in expenses, and $9,730 in prejudgment interest against Hobby. The court denied Hobby's motion to reconsider the fee award on August 31, 1990.

A divided Fifth Circuit panel reversed the fee award. . . . [T]he majority held that the plaintiffs were not prevailing parties and were therefore ineligible for fees under § 1988. . . .

II

[In enacting the Civil Rights Attorney's Fees Award Act of 1976, 42 U.S.C. § 1988(b)], "Congress intended to permit the . . . award of counsel fees only when a party has prevailed on the merits." Therefore, in order to qualify for attorney's fees under § 1988, a plaintiff must be a "prevailing party." Under our "generous formulation" of the term, "plaintiffs may be considered "prevailing parties" for attorney's fees purposes if they succeed on any significant issue in litigation which achieves some of the benefit the parties sought in bringing suit." "[L]iability on the merits and responsibility for fees go hand in hand; where a defendant has not been prevailed against, either because of legal immunity or on the merits, § 1988 does not authorize a fee award against that defendant." *Kentucky v. Graham.*

We have elaborated on the definition of prevailing party in three recent cases. In *Hewitt v. Helms* we addressed "the peculiar-sounding question whether a party who litigates to judgment and loses on all of his claims can nonetheless be a 'prevailing party.' " *Id.* In his § 1983 action against state prison officials for alleged due process violations, respondent Helms obtained no relief. "The most that he obtained was an interlocutory ruling that his complaint should not have been dismissed for failure to state a constitutional claim." *Id.* Observing that "respect for ordinary language requires that a plaintiff receive at least some relief on the merits of his claim before he can be said to prevail," we held that Helms was not a prevailing party. *Id.* We required the plaintiff to prove "the settling of some dispute which affects the behavior of the defendant towards the plaintiff." *Id.*

In *Rhodes v. Stewart* (per curiam), we reversed an award of attorney's fees premised solely on a declaratory judgment that prison officials had violated the plaintiffs' First and Fourteenth Amendment rights. By the time the District Court entered judgment, "one of the plaintiffs had died and the other was no longer in custody." *Id.* Under these circumstances, we held, neither plaintiff was a prevailing party. We explained that "nothing in [*Hewitt*] suggested that the entry of [a declaratory] judgment in a party's favor automatically renders that party prevailing under § 1988." *Id.* We reaffirmed that a judgment — declaratory or otherwise — "will constitute relief, for purposes of § 1988, if, and only if, it affects the behavior of the defendant toward the plaintiff." *Id.* Whatever "modification of prison policies" the declaratory judgment might have effected" could not in any way have benefitted either plaintiff, one of whom was dead and the other released." *Ibid.*

Finally, in *Texas State Teachers Assn. v. Garland Independent School Dist.*, we synthesized the teachings of *Hewitt* and *Rhodes.* "To be considered a prevailing party within the meaning of § 1988," we held, "the plaintiff must be able to point to a resolution of the dispute which changes the legal relationship between itself and the defendant." We reemphasized that "the touchstone of the prevailing party inquiry must be the material alteration of the legal relationship of the parties." *Id.* Under this test, the plaintiffs in *Garland* were prevailing parties because they "obtained a judgment vindicating [their] First Amendment rights [as] public employees" and "materially altered the [defendant] school district's policy limiting the rights of teachers to communicate with each other concerning employee organizations and union activities." *Id.*

Therefore, to qualify as a prevailing party, a civil rights plaintiff must obtain at least some relief on the merits of his claim. The plaintiff must obtain an enforceable judgment against the defendant from whom fees are sought, or comparable relief through a consent decree or settlement. Whatever relief the plaintiff secures must directly benefit him at the time of the judgment or settlement. Otherwise the judgment or settlement cannot be said to "affec[t] the behavior of the defendant toward the plaintiff." *Rhodes.* Only under these circumstances can civil rights litigation effect "the material alteration of the legal relationship of the parties and thereby transform the plaintiff into a prevailing party. *Garland.* In short, a plaintiff "prevails" when actual relief on the merits of his claim materially alters the legal relationship between the parties by modifying the defendant's behavior in a way that directly benefits the plaintiff.

III

A

Doubtless "the basic purpose of a § 1983 damages award should be to compensate persons for injuries caused by the deprivation of constitutional rights." *Carey v. Piphus.* For this reason, no compensatory damages may be awarded in a § 1983 suit absent proof of actual injury. We have also held, however, that "the denial of procedural due process should be actionable for nominal damages without proof of actual injury." *Carey.* The awarding of nominal damages for the "absolute" right to procedural due process "recognizes the importance to organized society that [this] righ[t] be scrupulously observed" while "remain[ing] true to the principle that substantial damages should be awarded only to compensate actual injury." Thus, *Carey* obligates a court to award nominal damages when a plaintiff establishes the violation of his right to procedural due process but cannot prove actual injury.

We therefore hold that a plaintiff who wins nominal damages is a prevailing party under § 1988. When a court awards nominal damages, it neither enters judgment for defendant on the merits nor declares the defendant's legal immunity to suit. To be sure, a judicial pronouncement that the defendant has violated the Constitution, unaccompanied by an enforceable judgment on the merits, does not render the plaintiff a prevailing party. Of itself, "the moral satisfaction [that] results from any favorable statement of law" cannot bestow prevailing party status. *Hewitt*. No material alteration of the legal relationship between the parties occurs until the plaintiff becomes entitled to enforce a judgment, consent decree, or settlement against the defendant. A plaintiff may demand payment for nominal damages no less than he may demand payment for millions of dollars in compensatory damages. A judgment for damages in any amount, whether compensatory or nominal, modifies the defendant's behavior for the plaintiff's benefit by forcing the defendant to pay an amount of money he otherwise would not pay. As a result, the Court of Appeals for the Fifth Circuit erred in holding that petitioners' nominal damages award failed to render them prevailing parties.

[W]e hold that the prevailing party inquiry does not turn on the magnitude of the relief obtained. We recognized as much in *Garland* when we noted that "the *degree* of the plaintiff's success" does not affect "eligibility for a fee award."

Although the "technical" nature of a nominal damages award or any other judgment does not affect the prevailing party inquiry, it does bear on the propriety of fees awarded under § 1988. Once civil rights litigation materially alters the legal relationship between the parties, "the degree of the plaintiff's overall success goes to the reasonableness" of a fee award under *Hensley v. Eckerhart*. Indeed, "the most critical factor" in determining the reasonableness of a fee award "is the degree of success obtained." In this case, petitioners received nominal damages instead of the $17 million in compensatory damages that they sought. This litigation accomplished little beyond giving petitioners "the moral satisfaction of knowing that a federal court concluded that [their] rights had been violated" in some unspecified way. We have already observed that if "a plaintiff has achieved only partial or limited success, the product of hours reasonably expended on the litigation as a whole times a reasonable hourly rate may be an excessive amount." Yet the District Court calculated petitioners' fee award in precisely this fashion, without engaging in any measured exercise of discretion. . . .

In some circumstances, even a plaintiff who formally "prevails" under § 1988 should receive no attorney's fees at all. A plaintiff who seeks compensatory damages but receives no more than nominal damages is often such a prevailing party. As we have held, a nominal damages award does render a plaintiff a prevailing party by allowing him to vindicate his "absolute" right to procedural due process through enforcement of a judgment against the defendant. In a civil rights suit for damages, however, the awarding of nominal damages also highlights the plaintiff's failure to prove actual, compensable injury. Whatever the constitutional basis for substantive liability, damages awarded in a § 1983 action "must always be designed 'to compensate injuries caused by the [constitutional] deprivation.'" *Memphis Community School Dist. v. Stachura* (quoting *Carey*) (emphasis and brackets in original). When a plaintiff recovers only nominal damages because of his failure to prove an essential element of his claim for monetary relief, the only reasonable fee is usually no fee at all. In an apparent failure to heed our admonition that fee awards under § 1988 were never intended to "'produce windfalls to attorneys,'" the District

Court awarded $280,000 in attorney's fees without "consider[ing] the relationship between the extent of success and the amount of the fee award."

Although the Court of Appeals erred in failing to recognize that petitioners were prevailing parties, it correctly reversed the District Court's fee award. We accordingly affirm the judgment of the Court of Appeals.

So ordered.

JUSTICE O'CONNOR, concurring.

If ever there was a plaintiff who deserved no attorney's fees at all, that plaintiff is Joseph Farrar. He filed a lawsuit demanding 17 million dollars from six defendants. After 10 years of litigation and two trips to the Court of Appeals, he got one dollar from one defendant. As the Court holds today, that is simply not the type of victory that merits an award of attorney's fees.

I

Congress has authorized the federal courts to award "a reasonable attorney's fee" in certain civil rights cases, but only to "the prevailing party." 42 U.S.C. § 1988. To become a prevailing party, a plaintiff must obtain, at an absolute minimum, "actual relief on the merits of [the] claim," which "affects the behavior of the defendant towards the plaintiff," . . . Joseph Farrar met that minimum condition for prevailing party status. Through this lawsuit, he obtained an enforceable judgment for one dollar in nominal damages. One dollar is not exactly a bonanza, but it constitutes relief on the merits. And it affects the defendant's behavior toward the plaintiff, if only by forcing him to pay one dollar — something he would not otherwise have done.

Nonetheless, *Garland* explicitly states that an enforceable judgment alone is not always enough: "Beyond th[e] absolute limitation [of some relief on the merits], a technical victory may be so insignificant . . . as to be insufficient" to support an award of attorney's fees. While *Garland* may be read as indicating that this de minimis or technical victory exclusion is a second barrier to prevailing party status, the Court makes clear today that, in fact, it is part of the determination of what constitutes a reasonable fee. . . . And even if the exclusion's location is debatable, its effect is not: When the plaintiff's success is purely technical or de minimis, no fees can be awarded. Such a plaintiff either has failed to achieve victory at all, or has obtained only a pyrrhic victory for which the reasonable fee is zero. The Court's opinion today and its unanimous opinion in *Garland* are thus in accord. . . .

Consequently, the Court properly holds that, when a plaintiff's victory is purely technical or de minimis, a district court need not go through the usual complexities involved in calculating attorney's fees. . . . As a matter of common sense and sound judicial administration, it would be wasteful indeed to require that courts laboriously and mechanically go through those steps when the de minimis nature of the victory makes the proper fee immediately obvious. Instead, it is enough for a court to explain why the victory is de minimis and announce a sensible decision to "award low fees or no fees" at all.

[In enacting § 1988(b), Congress intended] to restore the former equitable practice of awarding attorney's fees to the prevailing party in certain civil rights cases, a practice this Court had disapproved in *Alyeska Pipeline Services Co. v. Wilderness Society*. . . . That practice included the denial of fees to plaintiffs who, although technically prevailing parties, had achieved only de minimis success. . . .

Indeed, § 1988 contemplates the denial of fees to de minimis victors through yet another mechanism. The statute only authorizes courts to award fees "as part of the costs." 42 U.S.C. § 1988. As a result, when a court denies costs, it must deny fees as well; if there are no costs, there is nothing for the fees to be awarded "as part of." And when Congress enacted § 1988, the courts would deny even a prevailing party costs under Federal Rule of Civil Procedure 54(d) where the victory was purely technical. . . . Just as a pyrrhic victor would be denied costs under Rule 54(d), so too should it be denied fees under § 1988.

II

In the context of this litigation, the technical or de minimis nature of Joseph Farrar's victory is readily apparent: He asked for a bundle and got a pittance. While we hold today that this pittance is enough to render him a prevailing party, it does not by itself prevent his victory from being purely technical. . . . That is not to say that all nominal damages awards are de minimis. Nominal relief does not necessarily a nominal victory make. But, as in pre-Alyeska and Rule 54(d) practice, a substantial difference between the judgment recovered and the recovery sought suggests that the victory is in fact purely technical. . . . Here that suggestion is quite strong. Joseph Farrar asked for 17 million dollars; he got one. It is hard to envision a more dramatic difference.

The difference between the amount recovered and the damages sought is not the only consideration, however. *Carey v. Piphus* makes clear that an award of nominal damages can represent a victory in the sense of vindicating rights even though no actual damages are proved. Accordingly, the courts also must look to other factors. One is the significance of the legal issue on which the plaintiff claims to have prevailed. Petitioners correctly point out that Joseph Farrar in a sense succeeded on a significant issue — liability. But even on that issue he cannot be said to have achieved a true victory. Respondent was just one of six defendants and the only one not found to have engaged in a conspiracy. If recovering one dollar from the least culpable defendant and nothing from the rest legitimately can be labeled a victory — and I doubt that it can — surely it is a hollow one. Joseph Farrar may have won a point, but the game, set, and match all went to the defendants.

Given that Joseph Farrar got some of what he wanted — one seventeen millionth, to be precise — his success might be considered material if it also accomplished some public goal other than occupying the time and energy of counsel, court, and client. . . . Yet one searches these facts in vain for the public purpose this litigation might have served. The District Court speculated that the judgment, if accompanied by a large fee award, might deter future lawless conduct, but did not identify the kind of lawless conduct that might be prevented. Nor is the conduct to be deterred apparent from the verdict, which even petitioners acknowledge is "regrettably obtuse." Such a judgment cannot deter misconduct any more than a bolt of lightning can; its results might be devastating, but it teaches no valuable lesson because it carries no discernable meaning. . . .

III

In this case, the relevant indicia of success — the extent of relief, the significance of the legal issue on which the plaintiff prevailed, and the public purpose served — all point to a single conclusion: Joseph Farrar achieved only a de minimis victory. As the Court correctly holds today, the appropriate fee in such a case is no fee at all. Because the Court of Appeals gave Joseph Farrar every thing he deserved — nothing — I join the Court's opinion affirming the judgment below.

JUSTICE WHITE, with whom JUSTICE BLACKMUN, JUSTICE STEVENS, and JUSTICE SOUTER join, concurring in part and dissenting in part.

We granted certiorari in this case to decide whether 42 U.S.C. § 1988 entitles a civil rights plaintiff who recovers nominal damages to reasonable attorney's fees. Following our [prior] decisions . . . the Court holds that it does. With that aspect of today's decision, I agree. Because Farrar won an enforceable judgment against respondent, he has achieved a "material alteration" of their legal relationship, and thus he is a "prevailing party" under the statute.

However, I see no reason for the Court to reach out and decide what amount of attorney's fees constitutes a reasonable amount in this instance. That issue was neither presented in the petition for certiorari nor briefed by petitioners. The opinion of the Court of Appeals was grounded exclusively in its determination that Farrar had not met the threshold requirement under § 1988. At no point did it purport to decide what a reasonable award should be if Farrar was a prevailing party.

It may be that the District Court abused its discretion and misapplied our precedents by belittling the significance of the amount of damages awarded in ascertaining petitioners' fees. But it is one thing to say that the court erred as a matter of law in awarding $280,000; quite another to decree, especially without the benefit of petitioners' views or consideration by the Court of Appeals, that the only fair fee was no fee whatsoever.[2]

Litigation in this case lasted for more than a decade, has entailed a 6-week trial and given rise to two appeals. Civil rights cases often are complex, and we therefore have committed the task of calculating attorney's fees to the trial court's discretion for good reason. . . . Estimating what specific amount would be reasonable in this particular situation is not a matter of general importance on which our guidance is

---

[2] [*] In his brief to the Fifth Circuit, respondent did not argue that petitioners should be denied all fees even if they were found to be prevailing parties. Rather, he asserted that the District Court misapplied the law by awarding "excessive" fees and requested that they be reduced. *See* Brief for Defendant-Appellant in No. 90-2830, pp. 38–42.

needed. Short of holding that recovery of nominal damages never can support the award of attorney's fees — which, clearly, the majority does not — the Court should follow its sensible practice and remand the case for reconsideration of the fee amount. Indeed, respondent's counsel all but conceded at oral argument that, assuming the Court found Farrar to be a prevailing party, the question of reasonableness should be addressed on remand.

I would vacate the judgment of the Court of Appeals and remand the case for further proceedings. Accordingly, I dissent.

NOTES

1. Given the division of the Court, what is the precise holding of the case? In what sense did Farrar prevail? What difference does it make to base a decision to deny attorney's fees on the rationale applied by the court of appeals (Farrar did not prevail), or that applied by a majority of the Supreme Court (Farrar did prevail, but no fee is the only reasonable fee)? Is the Court's ruling consistent with Senate Report No. 94-1011?

2. The Court in *Farrar* relies heavily on three prior cases, *Hewitt v. Helms*, 482 U.S. 755 (1987); *Rhodes v. Stewart*, 488 U.S. 1 (1988); and *Texas State Teachers Association v. Garland Independent School District*, 489 U.S. 782 (1989). In *Hewitt*, an inmate sued prison officials seeking damages and injunctive relief to redress his allegedly unconstitutional disciplinary confinement. Although the Court agreed that the plaintiff's due process rights had been violated, his claim for damages was defeated by the defendants' immunity. State correctional officials subsequently revised their disciplinary procedures. The inmate had abandoned his claim for injunctive relief because he had been released from prison on parole prior to the conclusion of the litigation. In this context, the Court concluded that the plaintiff was not a prevailing party.

In *Rhodes*, two inmates claimed that their First Amendment rights were violated by prison officials who denied them access to certain magazines. The district court agreed and entered a declaratory judgment in favor of the inmates. Prior to the entry of the declaratory judgment, however, one of the plaintiffs had died and the other had been released from custody. The Court held that the inmates could not be considered prevailing parties under these circumstances. The declaratory judgment entered by the district court was not sufficient relief to support an award of attorney's fees because it did not affect the behavior of the defendants towards the plaintiffs.

In *Garland*, individual teachers and a teachers' union sued a school district claiming that a variety of district policies violated the teachers' First Amendment rights. Some of the policies were upheld while others were found to be unconstitutional. The court of appeals held that the plaintiffs were not entitled to attorney's fees because they did not prevail on the "central issue" in the litigation. The Supreme Court reversed, holding that a fee award was appropriate when plaintiffs' prevailed on a "significant issue" and the litigation resolved a dispute which changed the legal relationship between the parties.

Collectively, how strongly do *Hewitt, Rhodes,* and *Garland* support the holding that although Farrar prevailed, as a matter of law the only reasonable fee is no fee?

3. Section 1988 makes clear that "prevailing party" status is a threshold requirement for an award of attorney's fees, and all nine justices in *Farrar* agree that a plaintiff who secures a judgment for nominal damages is a prevailing party. May a party who recovers damages under a pendent state claim be considered a prevailing party under section 1988 for purposes of attorney's fees? *Compare Carreras v. City of Anaheim* 768 F.2d 1039 (9th Cir. 1985) (court ruled for the plaintiff on state constitutional grounds without reaching the federal constitutional issues; attorney's fees awarded) *with D.C., Inc. v. Missouri,* 627 F.3d 698 (8th Cir. 2010) (attorney's fees not awarded to plaintiff who prevailed on state law claims; district court ruled against the plaintiff on some federal constitutional claims, but did not reach others); *Duran v. City and County of Denver,* 2014 U.S. Dist. LEXIS 117851 (D. Colo. Aug. 25, 2014) (attorneys' fees awarded plaintiff who recovered nominal damages on his section 1983 excessive force claim, but recovered substantial damages on his related pendent state claim for wrongful death). Fee awards may be authorized under state law to plaintiffs who prevail under state civil rights laws. *See e.g., Joyce v. Town of Dennis,* 720 F.3d 12 (1st Cir. 2013) (female golfer who successfully challenged city decision to not allow her to play in a men's golf tournament was awarded fees under a Massachusetts antidiscrimination statute).

4. A plaintiff who secures a permanent injunction is a prevailing party for purposes of a fee award. *E.g., Lefemine v. Wideman,* 133 S. Ct. 9 (2012) (anti-abortion protestors who secured injunctive relief, but no damages, are prevailing parties). This conclusion is not surprising given the history of the fee statute. The Senate Report accompanying the Civil Rights Attorney's Fees Award Act of 1976 cited with approval *Newman v. Piggie Park Enterprises, Inc.,* 390 U.S. 400 (1968) in which attorney's fees were awarded to civil rights plaintiffs who secured an injunction prohibiting racial discrimination in public accommodations under Title II of the 1964 Civil Rights Act. Damages were not authorized under Title II. We will return to problems associated with fee awards an injunctive relief in the notes following *Buckhannon Board and Care Home, Inc. v. West Virginia Dep't of Health and Human Resources* which follows these notes.

5. After *Farrar,* can a district court ever award attorney's fees when a plaintiff seeks substantial compensatory and punitive damages, but recovers only low or nominal damages? Recall that Justice O'Connor, who provided the decisive fifth vote needed to reach a majority, indicated that sometimes a plaintiff who was awarded nominal damages could be considered a prevailing party for purposes of a fee award. She stated that "the difference between the amount recovered and the damages sought is not the only consideration . . . . [A]n award of nominal damages can represent a victory in the sense of vindicating rights even though no actual damages are proved. . . . Accordingly, the Courts must look to other factors[,] . . . [such as] the significance of the legal issue on which the plaintiff claims to have prevailed . . . [and whether the litigation] accomplish some public goal. . . ."

Lower courts have struggled with determining whether a fee award is appropriate when the plaintiff prevails, but secures only nominal damages or significantly lower compensatory damages than originally sought. Several cases appear to take the position that attorney's fees should not be awarded when the plaintiff recovers nominal or low compensatory damages. *E.g., Gray v. Bostic*, 720 F.3d 887 (11th Cir. 2013) (deputy violated clearly settled law by handcuffing a 9-year-old girl without probable cause; jury awarded the plaintiff $1 in nominal damages; award of approximately $70,000 in fees and costs was an abuse of discretion); *Aponte v. City of Chicago*, 728 F.3d 724 (7th Cir. 2013) (denial of attorney's fees affirmed when plaintiff recovered $100 in compensatory damages for an illegal search; plaintiff sought $25,000). *Cf., Richardson v. City of Chicago*, 740 F.3d 1099 (7th Cir. 2014) (dicta indicating that any fee award "would be unwarranted" if the only relief granted the plaintiff was nominal damages); *McAfee v. Boczar*, 738 F.3d 81 (4th Cir. 2013) (abuse of discretion to award almost $350,000 in attorney's fees and costs to plaintiff who recovered $2,943.60 in compensatory damages stemming from an arrest without probable cause despite an explicit finding by the district court that the judgment vindicated the plaintiff's constitutional rights and deterred future violations).

Other courts, however, have approved substantial fee awards based on nominal or low damages. *E.g., Hescott v. City of Saginaw*, 757 F.3d 518 (6th Cir. 2014) (plaintiffs prevailed in their claim that the city unconstitutionally seized and destroyed their property; plaintiffs had sought more than $40,000 in compensatory and $250,000 in punitive damages; they were awarded $5,000 in compensatory damages; district court's denial of fee award was reversed as an abuse of discretion; "a rule that eliminates attorneys' fees in civil rights cases due to the size of the damages awarded would seriously undermine Congress' purpose in enacting [the fee statute]"); *Murray v. City of Onawa*, 323 F.3d 616 (8th Cir. 2003) (attorney's fees awarded to plaintiff who recovered nominal damages from City that failed to protect her from sexual harassment; a "clear public policy is served by this case. Specifically, police departments and cities should be on notice that they cannot ignore allegations of sexual harassment and other abuses."); *Depee v. Mahcah-Watkins*, 593 F.3d 1054 (9th Cir. 2010) (more than $136,000 in attorney's fees and costs awarded to plaintiff awarded nominal damages following fatal shooting).

Recovery of punitive damages can support an award of attorney's fees even if the compensatory damages are nominal. *E.g., Richardson v. City of Chicago*, 740 F.3d 1099 (7th Cir. 2013) ("If the jury had stopped with the $1 in nominal damages, then under *Farrar* an award of attorney's fees would be unwarranted. But the $3,000 in punitive damages was enough, in the judge's view, to justify some attorney's fees."); *Nazario v. Rodriguez*, 554 F.3d 196 (1st Cir. 2009) (plaintiff who was awarded punitive damages but no compensatory or nominal damages is a prevailing party entitled to attorney's fees.)

6. Should attorney's fees be awarded in a case where the prevailing plaintiff was represented by a nonprofit legal service organization? Are statutory attorney's fees needed to induce representation in such a case? Does section 1988 purport to distinguish between public interest attorneys and private counsel? If attorney's fees are awarded for work performed by a nonprofit legal service organization, should the fee be based on market rates, the cost to the organization, or some other criteria? *See Blum v. Stenson*, 465 U.S. 886 (1984) (awarding attorney's fees to the Legal Aid Society based on market rates). In *Kay v. Ehrler*, 499 U.S. 432 (1991), the Court held that an award of attorney's fees under section 1988 should not be made to a lawyer who successfully represented himself in the litigation. Why award attorney's fees for work performed by the Legal Aid Society but not the *pro se* attorney? *See also Rickley v. County of Los Angeles*, 654 F.3d 950, (9th Cir. 2011) (attorney's fees awarded for legal services provided by the spouse of the plaintiff).

7. Should prevailing defendants, like prevailing plaintiffs, enjoy a strong presumption of entitlement to an attorney's fee award? The Supreme Court has construed section 1988 to authorize an award of attorney's fees to a prevailing defendant "only where the suit was vexatious, frivolous, or brought to harass or embarrass the defendant." *Hensley v. Eckerhart*, 461 U.S. 424, 429 n.2 (1983). This standard was drawn from cases involving Title VII employment discrimination claims. *Christiansburg Garment Co. v. EEOC*, 434 U.S. 412–421 (1978). Why would Congress impose such a double standard? What does Senate Report No. 94-1011 suggest? *See Karam v. City of Burbank*, 340 F.3d 884 (9th Cir. 2003) (awarding attorneys' fees to defendants; plaintiff's Fourth Amendment claim deemed frivolous); *N.E. v. Hedges*, 391 F.3d 832 (6th Cir. 2004) (biological father's substantive due process challenge to state child support law deemed frivolous; defendant awarded attorney's fees).

What fees, if any, should be awarded to a defendant when some of the plaintiff's claims are frivolous and others are not? *Fox v. Vice*, 131 S. Ct. 2205 (2011) involved a mix of state tort claims, including defamation, and federal civil rights claims brought pursuant to Section 1983 for alleged dirty tricks undertaken during a contested election. The federal claims ultimately were found to be frivolous and the state law claims were deemed to have some merit. Discovery taken in connection with the frivolous Section 1983 claims could be of some use in defending the non-frivolous state tort claims. Because the plaintiff's federal claims were deemed to be frivolous, the district court awarded fees to the defendant. This fee award did not differentiate between time defending the Section 1983 claims and time spent defending the state tort claims. The district court reasoned that the federal and state law claims were interrelated as they arose from the same transaction, *i.e.*, the alleged dirty tricks. The court of appeals affirmed.

A unanimous Supreme Court reversed as to the amount of the fee award. The Court held that a defendant should not be awarded fees for time that would have been incurred defending the non-frivolous state law claims.

> Section 1988 allows a defendant to recover reasonable attorney's fees incurred because of, but only because of a frivolous claim . . . In a suit of this kind involving both frivolous and non-frivolous claims, a defendant may recover the reasonable attorney's fees expended solely because of the frivolous allegations. And that is all.

By way of example, the Court mentioned that if a deposition of a particular witness would be necessary to defend against the non-frivolous state tort claims as well as the frivolous federal claims, that time should not be factored into the defendant's fee award.

As we will see later in *Hensley v. Eckerhart*, *infra*, the standards for computing a fee award to a prevailing plaintiff are more generous. A prevailing plaintiff may receive a fee award based on time spent prosecuting successful and unsuccessful claims provided they involve a "common core of facts or [are] based on related legal theories." *See* Note 2 following *Hensley, infra.* As illustrated by *Fox v. Vice*, however, a defendant can only recover fees if the plaintiff's federal claim is deemed to be frivolous and, if so, only for time spent exclusively defending the frivolous claim. This disparity in treatment of plaintiffs and defendants regarding fee awards is justified in terms of legislative intent. Congress intended to be more generous to prevailing plaintiffs regarding fee awards in order encourage the vindication of civil rights laws; however, Congress only sought to protect defendants from the burdens of defending against frivolous or vexatious claims.

After *Fox v. Vice*, lower court have ruled that the defendant bears the burden of proving which fees are attributable to defending the frivolous claims. *See, e.g., Efron v. Mora Development Corp.*, 675 F.3d 45 (1st Cir. 2012) (opinion by Justice Souter sitting by designation); *Harris v. Maricopa County Superior Court*, 631 F.3d 963 (9th Cir. 2011).

8.   Can a prevailing party recover attorney's fees against federal officials who violate the plaintiff's constitutional rights? Section 1988 does not expressly permit the recovery of attorney's fees against the United States or federal officials. Instead, it authorizes an award of attorney's fees to parties who prevail in claims brought under specific civil rights statutes, the most significant of which section 1983. Section 1983 claims are limited to actions taken under color of *state* — not federal — law. For this reason, section 1988 typically does not authorize a fee award against federal defendants who violate the plaintiff's constitutional rights.

Other statutes, however, may support such an award. The most important statute is the Equal Access to Justice Act (EAJA), 28 U.S.C. § 2412. The EAJA authorizes an award of attorney's fees against the "United States or any agency and any official . . . acting in his or her official capacity . . . to the same extent that any other party would be liable under the common law or under the terms of any statute which specifically provides for such award." 28 U.S.C. § 2412(b). The EAJF goes on to specify that attorney's fees are recoverable from the federal government if its prelitigation or litigation position was "not substantially justified." 28 U.S.C. § 2412(d)(1)(A). This provision can support fee awards in constitutional litigation, *e.g., United States v. $12,248 U.S. Currency*, 957 F.2d 1513 (9th Cir. 1991), although the "not substantially justified" requirement puts a heavier burden on the prevailing plaintiff than is imposed in cases brought against state officials under section 1983.

Does the EAJA's reference to "any statute" serve to incorporate section 1988 so as to allow the routine award of attorney's fees against federal officials who are found to have deprived plaintiffs of constitutional rights? Courts agree that the incorporation language of the EAJA authorizes an award of attorney's fees against federal defendants who violate the specific civil rights statutes listed in section 1988. *See generally Unification Church v. I.N.S.*, 762 F.2d 1077, 1080–81 (D.C. Cir. 1985); *Premachandra v. Mitts*, 753 F.2d 635, 637 n.7 (8th Cir. 1985) (*en banc*). Thus, attorney's fees may be awarded against federal defendants who violate 42 U.S.C. § 1981 or § 1982 for racial discrimination in transactions involving contracts or real or personal property, or who violate 42 U.S.C. § 1985 by conspiring with state actors to violate a person's civil rights. However, most courts have concluded that the EAJA does not authorize an award of attorney's fees against the United States or its officers in a pure *Bivens* type action. Some opinions explain that *Bivens* actions are brought against the federal officers in their individual — not official — capacity, and hence are not suits against the United States for which fees are authorized by the EAJA. *E.g., Saxner v. Benson*, 727 F.2d 669, 673 (7th Cir. 1984), aff'd on other grds. sub. nom, *Cleavinger v. Saxner*, 474 U.S. 193 (1985); *Lauritzen v. Lehman*, 736 F.2d 550 (9th Cir. 1984); *Kreines v. United States*, 812 F. Supp. 164 (N.D. Cal. 1992). Other decisions interpret the "to the same extent" language of the EAJA to mean that

> the federal government is not liable for fees under section 1988 unless it actually violates one of the statutes giving rise to fees under that section, regardless of whether a state might be liable for such fees had the state taken the same actions under color of state law as the federal government took under color of federal law.

Unification Church v. I.N.S. 762 F.2d 1077, 1080 (D.C. Cir. 1985). *See also Martin v. Heckler*, 773 F.2d 1145, 1154 (11th Cir. 1985) (*en banc*). Thus, although subsection b of the EAJA incorporates section 1988, it also incorporates the "under color of" state law limitation of section 1983. *See* Chapter 2 *supra*.

BUCKHANNON BOARD AND CARE HOME, INC.
v. WEST VIRGINIA DEPARTMENT OF HEALTH AND
HUMAN RESOURCES
532 U.S. 598 (2001)

CHIEF JUSTICE REHNQUIST delivered the opinion of the Court.

Numerous federal statutes allow courts to award attorney's fees and costs to the "prevailing party." The question presented here is whether this term includes a party that has failed to secure a judgment on the merits or a court-ordered consent decree, but has nonetheless achieved the desired result because the lawsuit brought about a voluntary change in the defendant's conduct. We hold that it does not.

Buckhannon Board and Care Home, Inc., which operates care homes that provide assisted living to their residents, failed an inspection by the West Virginia Office of the State Fire Marshal because some of the residents were incapable of "self-preservation" as defined under state law. *See* W. Va.Code §§ 16-5H-1, 16-5H-2 (1998) (requiring that all residents of residential board and care homes be capable of "self-preservation," or capable of moving themselves "from situations involving imminent danger, such as fire"); On October 28, 1997, after receiving cease and desist orders requiring the closure of its residential care facilities within 30 days, Buckhannon Board and Care Home, Inc., on behalf of itself and other similarly situated homes and residents (hereinafter petitioners), brought suit in the United States District Court for the Northern District of West Virginia against the State of West Virginia, two of its agencies, and 18 individuals (hereinafter respondents), seeking declaratory and injunctive relief that the "self-preservation" requirement violated the Fair Housing Amendments Act of 1988 (FHAA), 42 U.S.C. § 3601 *et seq.*, and the Americans with Disabilities Act of 1990 (ADA) 42 U.S.C. § 12101 *et seq.*

Respondents agreed to stay enforcement of the cease-and-desist orders pending resolution of the case and the parties began discovery. In 1998, the West Virginia Legislature enacted two bills eliminating the "self-preservation" requirement, and respondents moved to dismiss the case as moot. The District Court granted the motion, finding that the 1998 legislation had eliminated the allegedly offensive provisions and that there was no indication that the West Virginia Legislature would repeal the amendments.

Petitioners requested attorney's fees as the "prevailing party" under the FHAA, Petitioners argued that they were entitled to attorney's fees under the "catalyst theory," which posits that a plaintiff is a "prevailing party" if it achieves the desired result because the lawsuit brought about a voluntary change in the defendant's conduct. Although most Courts of Appeals recognize the "catalyst theory," the Court of Appeals for the Fourth Circuit rejected it in *S-1 and S-2 v. State Bd. of Ed. of N. C.*, 21 F.3d 49, 51 (C.A.4 1994) (en banc) ("A person may not be a 'prevailing party' . . . except by virtue of having obtained an enforceable judgment, consent decree, or settlement giving some of the legal relief sought"). The District Court accordingly denied the motion and, for the same reason, the Court of Appeals affirmed in an unpublished, *per curiam* opinion.

To resolve the disagreement amongst the Courts of Appeals, we granted certiorari, and now affirm.

In the United States, parties are ordinarily required to bear their own attorney's fees — the prevailing party is not entitled to collect from the loser. Under this "American Rule," we follow "a general practice of not awarding fees to a prevailing party absent explicit statutory authority." Congress, however, has authorized the award of attorney's fees to the "prevailing party" in numerous statutes in addition to those at issue here, such as the Civil Rights Attorney's Fees Awards Act of 1976. 42 U.S.C. § 1988.

In designating those parties eligible for an award of litigation costs, Congress employed the term "prevailing party," a legal term of art. Black's Law Dictionary 1145 (7th ed. 1999) defines "prevailing party" as "[a] party in whose favor a judgment is rendered, regardless of the amount of damages awarded [in certain cases, the court will award attorney's fees to the prevailing party]. — Also termed *successful party.*" This view that a "prevailing party" is one who has been awarded some relief by the court can be distilled from our prior cases.[3]

In *Hanrahan v. Hampton*, we reviewed the legislative history of § 1988 and found that "Congress intended to permit the interim award of counsel fees only when a party has prevailed on the merits of at least some of his claims." Our "[r]espect for ordinary language requires that a plaintiff receive at least some relief on the merits of his claim before he can be said to prevail." We have held that even

---

[3] [5] We have never had occasion to decide whether the term "prevailing party" allows an award of fees under the "catalyst theory" described above. Dictum in *Hewitt v. Helms*, 482 U.S. 755, 760, alluded to the possibility of attorney's fees where "voluntary action by the defendant . . . affords the plaintiff all or some of the relief . . . sought," but we expressly reserved the question, ("We need not decide the circumstances, if any, under which this 'catalyst' theory could justify a fee award"). And though the Court of Appeals for the Fourth Circuit relied upon our decision in *Farrar v. Hobby*, in rejecting the "catalyst theory," *Farrar* "involved no catalytic effect." Thus, there is language in our cases supporting both petitioners and respondents, and last Term we observed that it was an open question here.

plaintiff may have "prevailed" as Webster's defines that term — "gain[ed] victory by virtue of strength or superiority." But I doubt it was greater strength in financial resources, or superiority in media manipulation, rather than *superiority in legal merit*, that Congress intended to reward.

It could be argued, perhaps, that insofar as abstract justice is concerned, there is little to choose between the dissent's outcome and the Court's: If the former sometimes rewards the plaintiff with a phony claim (there is no way of knowing), the latter sometimes denies fees to the plaintiff with a solid case whose adversary slinks away on the eve of judgment. But it seems to me the evil of the former far outweighs the evil of the latter. There is all the difference in the world between a rule that denies the extraordinary boon of attorney's fees to some plaintiffs who are no less "deserving" of them than others who receive them, and a rule that causes the law to be the very instrument of wrong — exacting the payment of attorney's fees to the extortionist.

The dissent's ultimate worry is that today's opinion will "impede access to court for the less well-heeled". But, of course, the catalyst theory also harms the "less well-heeled," putting pressure on them to avoid the risk of massive fees by abandoning a solidly defensible case early in litigation. Since the fee-shifting statutes at issue here allow defendants as well as plaintiffs to receive a fee award, we know that Congress did not intend to *maximize* the quantity of "the enforcement of federal law by private attorneys general". Rather, Congress desired an *appropriate* level of enforcement — which is more likely to be produced by limiting fee awards to plaintiffs who prevail "on the merits," or at least to those who achieve an enforceable "alteration of the legal relationship of the parties," than by permitting the open-ended inquiry approved by the dissent.

JUSTICE GINSBURG, with whom JUSTICE STEVENS, JUSTICE SOUTER, and JUSTICE BREYER join, dissenting.

The Court today holds that a plaintiff whose suit prompts the precise relief she seeks does not "prevail," and hence cannot obtain an award of attorney's fees, unless she also secures a court entry memorializing her victory. The entry need not be a judgment on the merits. Nor need there be any finding of wrongdoing. A court-approved settlement will do.

The Court's insistence that there be a document filed in court — a litigated judgment or court-endorsed settlement — upsets long-prevailing Circuit precedent applicable to scores of federal fee-shifting statutes. The decision allows a defendant to escape a statutory obligation to pay a plaintiff's counsel fees, even though the suit's merit led the defendant to abandon the fray, to switch rather than fight on, to accord plaintiff sooner rather than later the principal redress sought in the complaint. Concomitantly, the Court's constricted definition of "prevailing party," and consequent rejection of the "catalyst theory," impede access to court for the less well heeled, and shrink the incentive Congress created for the enforcement of federal law by private attorneys general.

In my view, the "catalyst rule," as applied by the clear majority of Federal Circuits, is a key component of the fee-shifting statutes Congress adopted to advance enforcement of civil rights. Nothing in history, precedent, or plain English warrants the anemic construction of the term "prevailing party" the Court today imposes.

Prior to 1994, every Federal Court of Appeals (except the Federal Circuit, which had not addressed the issue) concluded that plaintiffs in situations like Buckhannon's and Pierce's could obtain a fee award if their suit acted as a "catalyst" for the change they sought, even if they did not obtain a judgment or consent decree. The Courts of Appeals found it "clear that a party may be considered to have prevailed even when the legal action stops short of final . . . judgment due to . . . intervening mootness." Interpreting the term "prevailing party" in "a practical sense," federal courts across the country held that a party "prevails" for fee-shifting purposes when "its ends are accomplished as a result of the litigation,"

The array of federal-court decisions applying the catalyst rule suggested three conditions necessary to a party's qualification as "prevailing" short of a favorable final judgment or consent decree. A plaintiff first had to show that the defendant provided "some of the benefit sought" by the lawsuit. Under most Circuits' precedents, a plaintiff had to demonstrate as well that the suit stated a genuine claim, *i.e.*, one that was at least "colorable," not "frivolous, unreasonable, or groundless." Plaintiff finally had to establish that her suit was a "substantial" or "significant" cause of defendant's action providing relief. In some Circuits, to make this causation showing, plaintiff had to satisfy the trial court that the suit achieved results "by threat of victory," not "by dint of nuisance and threat of expense." One who crossed these three thresholds would be recognized as a "prevailing party" to whom the district court, "in its discretion," could award attorney's fees.

Developed over decades and in legions of federal-court decisions, the catalyst rule and these implementing standards deserve this Court's respect and approbation.

The Court today detects a "clear meaning" of the term prevailing party,, that has heretofore eluded the large majority of courts construing those words. "Prevailing party," today's opinion announces, means "one who has been awarded some relief by the court," *ante*, at 1839. The Court derives this "clear meaning" principally from Black's Law Dictionary, which defines a "prevailing party," in critical part, as one "in whose favor a judgment is rendered," *ibid.* (quoting Black's Law Dictionary 1145 (7th ed.1999)).

One can entirely agree with Black's Law Dictionary that a party "in whose favor a judgment is rendered" prevails, and at the same time resist, as most Courts of Appeals have, any implication that *only* such a party may prevail. In prior cases, we have not treated Black's Law Dictionary as preclusively definitive; instead, we have accorded statutory terms, including legal "term [s] of art," a contextual reading.

The spare "prevailing party" language of the fee-shifting provisions now before the Court, contrast with prescriptions that so tightly bind fees to judgments as to exclude the application of a catalyst concept. The Prison Litigation Reform Act of 1995, for example, directs that fee awards to prisoners under § 1988 be "proportionately related to the *court ordered relief* for the violation." 42 U.S.C. § 1997e(d)(1)(B)(i) (1994 ed., Supp. V) (emphasis added). That statute, by its express agreement, but retained jurisdiction for purposes of enforcement. The district court held that the plaintiffs were not prevailing parties reasoning that the continuing jurisdiction for purposes of enforcement did not amount to "judicial sanctioning" of the agreement. The Court of Appeals reversed, concluding "that judicial action other than a judgment on the merits or a consent decree can support an award of attorneys' fees, so long as it carries with it sufficient judicial imprimatur." The explicit retention of jurisdiction for enforcement made the settlement agreement "not significantly different" from a consent decree and therefore the plaintiffs could be considered prevailing parties for purposes of an attorneys' fee award. *See also Smyth v. Rivero*, 282 F.3d 268 (4th Cir. 2002) (some settlement agreements may confer prevailing party status on the plaintiff if they are sufficiently analogous to a consent decree); *John T. v. Del. County Intermediate Unit*, 318 F.3d 545 (3d Cir. 2003) (a stipulated settlement can confer prevailing party status where is was entitled an "order," signed by the district judge, and provided for judicial enforcement).

Suppose the plaintiff sued the City seeking return of papers and other items seized during a traffic stop of a vehicle. During a hearing, "at the district court's nudging," the City agreed to return some of the seized materials to the plaintiff. The City returned photocopies of some of the seized papers, but continued to use the originals in its investigation. Is the plaintiff a prevailing party? *See Richardson v. Miller*, 279 F.3d 1 (1st Cir. 2002) (plaintiff is not a prevailing party; the "nudging" by the district court was not an enforceable order and, hence, not "akin" to a consent decree).

After surveying a host of lower court rulings, one court commented

> Although an enforceable judgment on the merits and a court-ordered consent decree have sufficient judicial *imprimatur*, these examples are not exclusive. . . . As a result, lower courts have had difficulties in ascertaining what other forms of judicial action have the "necessary judicial *imprimatur* to create prevailing party status . . . . Without a Supreme Court decision on point, circuit courts considering the issue have announced fact-specific standards that are anything but uniform.

Dearmore v. City of Garland, 519 F.3d 517, 521 (5th Cir. 2008).

4. *Lefemine v. Wideman*, 133 S. Ct. 9 (2012) makes clear that a plaintiff who secures a permanent injunction is a prevailing party who is presumptively entitled to a fee award. But what if the plaintiff obtains a preliminary, but not permanent, injunction? Can this plaintiff be said to have prevailed? Does it matter what the reason was for issuing the preliminary injunction? Or what the reason was why permanent injunctive relief was not granted?

The Court addressed some of these issues in *Sole v. Wyner*, 551 U.S. 74 (2007). The plaintiff wanted to conduct an anti-war protest on a beach located in a Florida state park. The protest consisted of assembling a group of nude protesters into the shape of peace symbol. A Florida administrative regulation, however, prohibited nudity on public beaches. The plaintiff filed suit alleging that the Florida "bathing suit rule" violated the First Amendment rights of the protesters. The plaintiff offered to erect a large curtain around the protest event shielding beachgoers from viewing the naked bodies. Based on this representation, the district court entered a preliminary injunction prohibiting the enforcement of the bathing suit rule to the protest. Contrary to the agreement, however, the protest took place outside the curtain and once disassembled from the peace symbol formation, the protestors went running into the water in the nude.

Contemplating a second protest, both sides moved for summary judgment on the constitutionality of the bathing suit rule. The district court ruled for the defendants on the merits and denied the plaintiff's request for a permanent injunction. The plaintiff was awarded attorney's fees, however, based on having secured the preliminary injunction. The court of appeals affirmed the fee award.

The Supreme Court reversed the award of attorney's fees. Writing for a unanimous Court, Justice Ginsburg stated:

> Wyner is not a prevailing party, we conclude, for her initial victory was ephemeral. A plaintiff who "secur[es] a preliminary injunction, then loses on the merits as the case plays out and judgment is entered against [her]," has "[won] a battle but los[t] the war". . . . .

> We express no view on whether in the absence of a final decision on the merits of a claim for permanent injunctive relief, success in gaining a preliminary injunction may sometimes warrant an award of counsel fees.

5. Consider the last paragraph from *Wyner* quoted in the preceding note. Suppose the plaintiff dismissed her complaint (thereby abandoning the claim for a permanent injunction) after securing the preliminary injunction and conducting the protest. Would she then have been a prevailing party? Suppose the defendants repealed the bathing suit rule after the preliminary injunction had been issued but before there had been a ruling on request for a permanent injunction? Under *Buckhannon* and *Wyner*, could the plaintiff be considered a prevailing party?

Lower courts have held that a plaintiff who secures preliminary injunctive relief can be a prevailing party for purposes of a fee award under certain circumstances. The key circumstances are whether the preliminary relief was based on an assessment of the probability of success and the reason why there was no final resolution on the merits of the case. *E.g., Higher Taste v. City of Tacoma,* 717 F.3d 712 (9th Cir. 2013) (error to deny fees to plaintiff who secured a preliminary injunction enjoining an ordinance restricting tee shirt sales in public park; final relief was not granted because the case settled on terms that permitted the plaintiff to continue selling the tee shirts); *Common Cause v. Billups,* 554 F.3d 1340 (11th Cir. 2009) (fees awarded to plaintiff who secured a preliminary injunction enjoining the enforcement of a voter ID law; law was repealed before a final ruling on the merits); *People Against Police Violence v. City of Pittsburgh,* 520 F.3d 226 (3d Cir. 2008) (plaintiff secured a preliminary injunction enjoining the enforcement of a city ordinance regulating expressive activities in public forums; court-encouraged "meet and confer" sessions resulted in the enactment of a new ordinance that addressed most of the plaintiffs' concerns; case was then dismissed without any final ruling on the merits; fees in excess of $100,000 awarded to the plaintiff).

After commenting on the lack of uniform standards in the lower courts, the Fifth Circuit Court of Appeals adopted the following: "to qualify as a prevailing party product of hours reasonably expended on the litigation as a whole times a reasonable hourly rate may be an excessive amount. This will be true even where the plaintiff's claims were interrelated, nonfrivolous, and raised in good faith. Congress has not authorized an award of fees whenever it was reasonable for a plaintiff to bring a lawsuit or whenever conscientious counsel tried the case with devotion and skill. Again, the most critical factor is the degree of success obtained.

Application of this principle is particularly important in complex civil rights litigation involving numerous challenges to institutional practices or conditions. . . . In this case, for example, the District Court's award of fees based on 2,557 hours worked may have been reasonable in light of the substantial relief obtained. But had respondents prevailed on only one of their six general claims, for example the claim that petitioners' visitation, mail, and telephone policies were overly restrictive, a fee award based on the claimed hours clearly would have been excessive.

There is no precise rule or formula for making these determinations. The district court may attempt to identify specific hours that should be eliminated, or it may simply reduce the award to account for the limited success. The court necessarily has discretion in making this equitable judgment. This discretion, however, must be exercised in light of the considerations we have identified.

C

A request for attorney's fees should not result in a second major litigation. Ideally, of course, litigants will settle the amount of a fee. Where settlement is not possible, the fee applicant bears the burden of establishing entitlement to an award and documenting the appropriate hours expended and hourly rates. The applicant should exercise "billing judgment" with respect to hours worked, and should maintain billing time records in a manner that will enable a reviewing court to identify distinct claims.[11]

We reemphasize that the district court has discretion in determining the amount of a fee award. This is appropriate in view of the district court's superior understanding of the litigation and the desirability of avoiding frequent appellate review of what essentially are factual matters. It remains important, however, for the district court to provide a concise but clear explanation of its reasons for the fee award. When an adjustment is requested on the basis of either the exceptional or limited nature of the relief obtained by the plaintiff, the district court should make clear that it has considered the relationship between the amount of the fee awarded and the results obtained.

IV

[The District Court made] a commendable effort to explain the fee award. Given the interrelated nature of the facts and legal theories in this case, the District Court

---

[11] [12] We recognize that there is no certain method of determining when claims are "related" or "unrelated." Plaintiff's counsel, of course, is not required to record in great detail how each minute of his time was expended. But at least counsel should identify the general subject matter of his time expenditures. . . .

did not err in refusing to apportion the fee award mechanically on the basis of respondents' success or failure on particular issues. And given the findings with respect to the level of respondents' success, the District Court's award may be consistent with our holding today.

We are unable to affirm the decisions below, however, because the District Court's opinion did not properly consider the relationship between the extent of success and the amount of the fee award. The court's finding that "the [significant] extent of the relief clearly justifies the award of a reasonable attorney's fee" does not answer the question of what is "reasonable" in light of that level of success. We emphasize that the inquiry does not end with a finding that the plaintiff obtained significant relief. A reduced fee award is appropriate if the relief, however significant, is limited in comparison to the scope of the litigation as a whole.

V

We hold that the extent of a plaintiff's success is a crucial factor in determining the proper amount of an award of attorney's fees under 42 U.S.C. § 1988. Where the plaintiff has failed to prevail on a claim that is distinct in all respects from his successful claims, the hours spent on the unsuccessful claim should be excluded in considering the amount of a reasonable fee. Where a lawsuit consists of related claims, a plaintiff who has won substantial relief should not have his attorney's fee reduced simply because the district court did not adopt each contention raised. But where the plaintiff achieved only limited success, the district court should award only that amount of fees that is reasonable in relation to the results obtained. On remand the District Court should determine the proper amount of the attorney's fee award in light of these standards.

The judgment of the Court of Appeals is vacated, and the case is remanded for further proceedings consistent with this opinion.

It is so ordered.

CHIEF JUSTICE **BURGER**, concurring.

I read the Court's opinion as requiring that when a lawyer seeks to have his adversary pay the fees of the prevailing party, the lawyer must provide detailed records of the time and services for which fees are sought. It would be inconceivable that the prevailing party should not be required to establish at least as much to support a claim under 42 U.S.C. § 1988 as a lawyer would be required to show if his own client challenged the fees. A district judge may not, in my view, authorize the payment of attorney's fees unless the attorney involved has established by clear and convincing evidence the time and effort claimed and shown that the time expended was necessary to achieve the results obtained.

. . . [T]he party who seeks payment must keep records in sufficient detail that a neutral judge can make a fair evaluation of the time expended, the nature and need for the service, and the reasonable fees to be allowed.

[The opinion of JUSTICE BRENNAN, concurring in part and dissenting in part, is omitted.]

NOTES

1. *Hensley* sets out the basic approach for calculating a reasonable attorney's fee. The starting point is the product of reasonable time expended times a reasonable hourly rate. This approach is commonly referred to as the "lodestar." MARTIN A. SCHWARTZ & JOHN E. KIRKLIN, SECTION 1983 LITIGATION: ATTORNEY'S FEES 1.03 (Wolters Klewer 2014). Of course, the parties may disagree as to the reasonableness of time expended or the proposed hourly rate. Those points are further developed in *Jane L. v. Bangerter*, 828 F. Supp. 1544 (D. Utah 1993), *infra*. The lodestar calculation "is presumed to be the reasonable fee contemplated by section 1988." *Blum v. Stenson*, 465 U.S. 886, 897 (1984). After determining the lodestar the court may consider whether the fee should be adjusted upward or downward to account for factors which are not included in a time times rate formula.

2. In many constitutional tort suits, the plaintiff may sue several defendants and rely on several different legal theories. What guidelines does *Hensley* provide to determine what is a reasonable fee when the plaintiff prevails only against some defendants or only as to some claims? How is a district court to determine whether a lawsuit involves "distinctly different claims" or whether it concerns "a common core of facts or . . . related legal theories," so that it "cannot be viewed as a series of discrete claims."? *Hensley*, 461 U.S. at 434–35. Suppose a plaintiff does not prevail on his claim that he was subjected to excessive force in the course of an arrest, but does prevail on his claim that the arrest was racially motivated. Are the equal protection and excessive force claims sufficiently related that an attorney's fee award can be based on the time spent on both issues? Suppose the plaintiff is also unsuccessful on his additional claim that he was maliciously prosecuted. Is the malicious prosecution claim sufficiently related to the equal protection claim that an attorney's fee award can be based on the time spent on both issues? *See Lenard v. Argento*, 808 F.2d 1242, 1246–47 (7th Cir. 1987) (equal protection and excessive force claims were sufficiently related because they both involved the arrest itself; the equal protection claim was not related to the malicious prosecution claim because the prosecution took place at a later time). Suppose a plaintiff proves that a school district's decision not to rehire her was made in retaliation for her exercise of first amendment rights, but is unsuccessful on her claim that she was denied procedural due process. Should a full award of attorney's fees be made? *See Durant v. Independent School District No. 16*, 990 F.2d 560, 566 (10th Cir. 1993) (remanded to district court for consideration). Should fees be awarded for the time spent litigating an unsuccessful failure to train claim against the city and county when the plaintiff prevailed on an excessive force claims against the individual officer? *See Duran v. City and County of Denver*, 2014 U.S. Dist. Lexis 117851 (D. Colo. Aug. 25, 2014) (fees awarded; claims based on common core of facts and related legal theories).

Suppose the plaintiff sues multiple defendants, but prevails only against some of them. Does *Hensley* address the multiple defendant situation? Should an award of attorney's fees be reduced to reflect the lack of success as to some of the defendants? In *Cobb v. Miller*, 818 F.2d 1227 (5th Cir. 1987) the plaintiff sued three defendants for an alleged use of excessive force, but prevailed only against one. The magistrate reduced the attorney's fee award by 2/3, but the court of appeals reversed, characterizing the claims as interrelated. *Accord., Lunday v. City of Albany*, 42 F.3d 131 (2d Cir. 1994).

In *Buffington v. Baltimore County*, 913 F.2d 113 (4th Cir. 1990) the plaintiffs sued the mayor of Baltimore, Baltimore County, and several individual police officers in connection with the suicide of an inmate. The court of appeals reversed the jury verdict against the mayor and county, but upheld it as to some of the officers. Can the attorney's fees awarded against the officers include time spent litigating the unsuccessful claims against the county and mayor? The court of appeals remanded the attorney's fees issue to the district court to determine whether the claims against the mayor and county were "distinct" or "inextricably intermingled." *Buffington*, 913 F.2d at 128. The court of appeals intimated that even if the claims were interrelated, a reduction in fees might be appropriate because the claims against the county and mayor were considered to be more significant than those against the individual officers. *Id.* at 127–29. *Compare Duran v. City and County of Denver*, 2014 U.S. Dist. Lexis 117851 (D. Colo. Aug. 25, 2014) (plaintiff did not prevail on a failure to train claim against the city and county, but did prevail on the excessive force claim against the individual officer; fees awarded for time spent on failure to train claim; claims based on common core of facts and related legal theories).

3. Suppose that the lodestar fee greatly exceeds the amount of damages awarded the plaintiff. Does *Hensley* indicate that the fee must be proportional to the amount of damages recovered? In *City of Riverside v. Rivera*, 477 U.S. 561 (1986), the district court awarded the plaintiffs $245,456.25 in attorney's fees in a case in which the compensatory and punitive damages were $33,350. The Court affirmed the award calculated under the lodestar. Justice Brennan, writing for a plurality of four justices, explained:

> A rule of proportionality would make it difficult, if not impossible, for individuals with meritorious civil rights claims but relatively small potential damages to obtain redress from the courts. This is totally inconsistent with Congress' purpose in enacting section 1988. Congress recognized that private-sector fee arrangements were inadequate to ensure sufficiently vigorous enforcement of civil rights. In order to ensure that lawyers would be willing to represent persons with legitimate civil rights grievances, Congress determined that it would be necessary to compensate lawyers for all time reasonably expended on a case.

> [H]ad respondents had to rely on private-sector fee arrangements, they might well have been unable to obtain redress for their grievances. It is precisely for this reason that Congress enacted section 1988.

City of Riverside, 477 U.S. at 578–80 (footnote omitted). Four justices argued that the size of the fee award should be proportional to the damage award. Justice Rehnquist wrote that the District Court failed at almost every turn to apply any kind of "billing judgment"or to seriously consider the "results obtained," which we described in *Hensley* as "the important factor" in determining a "reasonable" fee award. . . .

The very "reasonableness" of the hours expended on a case by a plaintiff's attorney necessarily will depend, to a large extent, on the amount that may be expected to be recovered if the plaintiff prevails.

Nearly 2,000 attorney-hours spent on a case in which the total recovery was on $33,000 . . . and in which the District Court expressed the view that . . . juries typically were reluctant to award substantial damages against police officers, is simply not a "reasonable" expenditure of time.

City of Riverside, 477 U.S. at 590, 593, 595 (Rehnquist, J., dissenting).

Justice Powell based his decisive vote affirming the award on the "District Court's detailed findings of fact, which were approved by the Court of Appeals." *City of Riverside*, 477 U.S. at 581 (Powell, J., concurring in the judgment).

Which approach is most consistent with *Hensley*? Does *Farrar* resurrect the proportionality issue supposedly laid to rest in *City of Riverside*? *See Hescott v. City of Saginaw*, 757 F.3d 518 (6th Cir. 2014) ("A rule that eliminates attorneys' fees in civil rights cases due to the size of the damages awarded 'would seriously undermine Congress' purpose in enacting [section] 1988.'"). *See also* Note 5 following *Farrar, supra.*

4. As reflected in S. Rep. No. 94-1011, many civil rights plaintiffs lack the resources to hire counsel on a fee for time basis. Section 1988(b) offers the prospect of attorney's fees to the prevailing plaintiff. *Farrar* illustrates, however, that civil rights litigation may be protracted and result in no fee award. Thus, attorneys who represent civil rights plaintiffs run the risk that they will receive no fee in some cases. When plaintiffs do prevail with a level of success that justifies some fee award, should the lodestar be enhanced to reflect the contingent nature of the practice? Consider the comments of Professor Leubsdorf:

A lawyer who both bears the risk of not being paid and provides legal services is not receiving the fair market value of his work if he is paid only for the second of these functions. If he is paid no more, competent counsel will be reluctant to accept fee award cases.

Leubsdorf, *The Contingency Factor in Attorney Fee Awards*, 90 Yale L.J. 473, 480 (1981).

The Supreme Court in City of *Burlington v. Dague*, 505 U.S. 557 (1992), however, held that an enhancement of the lodestar for contingency is not permitted under federal fee-shifting statutes. The majority believed that a contingency enhancement was not needed to attract competent counsel and posed a danger of encouraging the filing of nonmeritorious claims.

5. The Court in *Hensley* indicated that "in some cases of exceptional success an enhanced [fee] award may be justified." The Court revisited that issue in *Perdue v. Kenny A.*, 559 U.S. 542 (2010). This class action litigation involved wide ranging challenges to various aspects of the Georgia foster care program. The litigation took more than three years and was resolved by a consent decree that obligated the state to make significant reforms of the system. The plaintiffs requested a fee award of more than $14 million, roughly half of which was for an enhancement for exceptional success. The district court made an award of $10.5 million which was comprised of approximately $6 million under the lodestar (which included a reduction in the number of hours) and $4.5 million in enhancement. The district judge based the 75% fee enhancement on several factors: (1) plaintiffs' counsel advanced expenses of $1.7 million over a three year period; (2) plaintiffs' counsel worked three years without any compensation for their time; (3) the contingent nature of the fee; and (4) the exceptional skill exhibited by the attorneys and the exceptional results produced by the litigation. With regard to the last point, the district judge stated that in his 27 years on the bench, he had not seen lawyers who exhibited a "higher degree of skill, commitment, dedication and professionalism." He also commented that in his 58 years as a practicing attorney and judge, he had not seen a plaintiff achieve "such a favorable result on such a comprehensive scale."

The Supreme Court, in a 5-4 decision, reversed the fee award. The majority reiterated that a fee enhancement is sometimes permissible, but only in the rarest of cases. Exceptional results, the majority noted, may be due to factors other than the skill of the plaintiffs' lawyers, such as inferior performance by defense counsel, unexpectedly favorable rulings, or "simple luck." The novelty and complexity of the litigation are not grounds for an enhancement because those factors should already have been taken into account in determining the reasonable hourly rate under the lodestar. The Court also rejected the argument that the trend towards performance-based billing in the private sector supported fee enhancements for exceptional results in civil rights cases. Performance-based billing usually includes a reduction in the base hourly rate, something not done in calculating the lodestar. The majority indicated that a fee enhancement would be permissible only when the reasonable hourly rate used in the lodestar calculation did not adequately measure the attorney's true market value; when there has been an extraordinary outlay of expenses and the litigation is exceptionally protracted; or when there is an exceptional delay in the payment of fees.

The dissenting justices would have affirmed the fee enhancement. They emphasized the specific findings of the district judge and noted that he, rather than the twice removed Supreme Court, is in a much better position to determine whether the skill of the attorneys and the outcome of the litigation were truly exceptional.

As a general proposition, do you think fee enhancements are ever needed to achieve the Congressional goals set forth in the legislative history? Consider the following argument:

> The lodestar award, without the possibility of enhancement does not provide [sufficient incentives for attorneys to represent plaintiffs in civil rights cases]. This is partly because the "trend in the marketplace is toward great use of performance-or result based fee structures." The basic lodestar calculation . . . cannot account for this trend. Therefore, without the possibility of enhancements, "the potential remuneration [attorneys]

billing their time) are present at meetings, hearings, and depositions: "The more lawyers representing a side of the litigation, the greater the likelihood will be for duplication of services." . . .

In this case, among the attorneys of record for plaintiffs were three local attorneys, several attorneys from the Center for Reproductive Law and Policy, attorneys in a private non-local law firm, and an attorney from Planned Parenthood Federation of America. In all, 17 lawyers and one paralegal submitted affidavits in connection with plaintiffs' request for attorneys' fees. Few of these lawyers participated in oral argument. Plaintiffs' time records indicate that an enormous amount of time, much of it duplicative, was spent discussing the case with each other on the telephone or in meetings.

As to time spent in hearings, this court determines that plaintiffs' have made excessive claims for compensation with respect to at least two occasions. Four of plaintiffs' attorneys submitted compensation requests for attending the March 13, 1992 hearing concerning the Motion to Dismiss and Motion for Summary Judgment. Seven attorneys submitted compensation requests for attending the April 10, 1992 hearing.

. . . "[T]he presence of more than two lawyers during trial or the presence of more than one lawyer at depositions and hearings must be justified to the court." [*Ramos v. Lamm*]. The court further declared that "[if] three attorneys are present at a hearing when one would suffice, compensation should be denied for the excess time." *Id.* (citation omitted).

Plaintiffs were obligated to eliminate this excess and duplicative time from their time records before submitting them to the court. Because plaintiffs have failed to do this, the court is compelled to make appropriate reductions itself.

4. Public Relations, Press Lobbying Etc.

In this case, plaintiffs' attorneys spent a great deal of time in public relations efforts, including press conferences, interviews, and lobbying efforts at the legislative level.

Time spent by attorneys in public relations is noncompensable. . . . Moreover, time spent on advertisements submitted or created in connection with litigation is not compensable.[12] Plaintiffs time entries are replete with references to media and public relations matters.

5. Post Judgment Time

Plaintiffs' attorneys spent a significant block of time after this court's December 17, 1992 final decision posturing for and planning an appeal. There was also

---

[12] [8] On March 14, 1991, Janet Benshoof claims 2.75 hours for an entry which includes "ad work." This "ad work"apparently relates to her creation of an advertisement run in New York City newspapers that "In Utah, They Know How To Punish A Woman Who Has An Abortion. Shoot Her." See Lance Gurwell, Utah Congressman Blasts ACLU Over Abortion Ad, U.P.I., March 26, 1991. (available on LEXIS/NEXIS).

substantial time spent lobbying members of the Utah Legislature to change Utah's abortion statutes. However, it is evident that most of the hours devoted to these two activities pertained to issues upon which plaintiffs did not prevail.

This time does not fit under the rubric of "fees for a prevailing party." To the contrary, compensation for all such hours is inappropriate.

6. Preparation of Fee Application

Reasonable hours expended in preparation of a fee application are at least partially compensable, "although hours not spent representing the client are at best on the borderline of what Congress intended to be compensable." *Mares v. Credit Bureau of Raton.* Plaintiffs' attorneys spent over 130 hours on their fee application and in opposing defendants' application. In the opinion of this court, these hours are excessive, and should be reduced.

7. Clerical or Overhead Time

Plaintiffs' records also refer to time spent filing and retrieving documents, time devoted to reading background cases, and other miscellaneous matters. These hours should be eliminated or reduced. This is the sort of time that is generally absorbed by a private firm as overhead, and is therefore not properly billable to defendants.

Pursuant to the principles enunciated above, and after extensive review of plaintiffs' time records, this court determines that plaintiffs' requested hours far exceed the hours that reasonably would be required by reasonably competent attorneys in handling this litigation . . . .

Because Julie Mertus failed to provide the court with any time records supporting her hours request, the court reduces her request by 90%. The court reduces by 1/3 the hours requested by the other four attorneys who failed to submit adequate time documentation. [The specific reductions in the number of compensable hours are reflected in Appendix A]

B. Reasonable Hourly Rates

Appropriate hourly rates for counsel are calculated according to the "prevailing market rates in the relevant community." *Blum v. Stenson.* In determining those rates, the fee applicant should produce evidence that "the requested rates are in line with those prevailing in the community for similar services by lawyers of reasonably comparable skill, experience, and reputation." *Id.* . . .

Defendants have not objected to the rates requested by plaintiffs' local counsel, but take serious issue with the rates requested by the New York attorneys.[13] These

---

[13] [12] Plaintiffs' lead counsel, Janet Benshoof and Rachael Pine, are currently president and director of domestic legal projects, respectively, of the Center for Reproductive Law & Policy. From the beginning of this litigation until June, 1992, they were employed as director and senior staff attorney, respectively, of the American Civil Liberties Union's Reproductive Freedom Project ("RFP"). Similarly,

rates range from a high of $355.00 per hour for Janet Benshoof[14] and $310.00 per hour for Rachel Pine,[15] to an average of around $200.00 for the other New York attorneys. The prevailing rates locally for excellent trial counsel experienced in civil rights litigation range from $135.00 to $185.00 per hour. Local rates for attorneys with less experience range from $70.00 to $125.00 per hour. Rates claimed by seasoned and highly competent counsel representing the State of Utah range from $155 per hour to $50 per hour. This court has looked to years of experience as one important factor in fixing rates. Out-of-state counsel are not entitled to premium rates based on rate structures in other communities when similar expertise — with significantly lower rates — is available locally.

The overall experience of Ms. Benshoof and Ms. Pine in litigation is not equal to that of local seasoned front-line litigators, with more years of experience. However, their specialized backgrounds in abortion matters is a factor of importance. Accordingly, the court fixes the rate of Ms. Benshoof and Roger K. Evans, Director of Planned Parenthood, at $155.00 per hour, and that of Ms. Pine at $125.00 per hour. The court has correspondingly adjusted the rates of other plaintiffs' attorneys to reflect the rates of the relevant community. [The specific reductions in hourly rates are reflected in Appendix A.]

C. Adjustments to the Lodestar

The Supreme Court stated in *Hensley* that "the product of reasonable hours times a reasonable rate does not end the inquiry." Where a plaintiff has prevailed on only some claims, there remain two questions to address:

> First, did the plaintiff fail to prevail on claims that were unrelated to the claims on which he succeeded? Second, did the plaintiff achieve a level of success that makes the hours reasonably expended a satisfactory basis for making a fee award?

Id.

With regard to the first question, this court dismissed 17 of the 28 plaintiffs in its May 22, 1992 decision because their claims were found to be without merit. *Jane L. v. Bangerter* 794 F. Supp. 1537, 1551 (D. Utah 1992) [*Jane L. II*]. Plaintiffs claim that the dismissed claims were so "inextricably intertwined" with their success on the "core issues" of this case that it is inappropriate not to compensate them for all work done on the case. The issue here is whether the unsuccessfully prosecuted claims were related or unrelated to the successfully prosecuted claims. . . .

In the opinion of this court, this case falls within the category of several separate lawsuits brought in one action. For example, challenges to the serious medical emergency statute, the spousal notification statute, and the statute banning fetal experimentation all involve completely different sets of facts. Further, the legal

---

for much of the time for which fees are requested, Dominique Bravo, Simon Heller, Andrew Dwyer, Ellen Goetz, Julie Mertus and Margaret Martin, were employees of the RFP.

[14] [13] Janet Benshoof has 20 years of experience in the practice of law and is experienced in abortion litigation.

[15] [14] Rachel Pine has practiced law for 9 years and is experienced in abortion litigation.

theories of involuntary servitude, equal protection, separation of church and state, free exercise of religion, freedom of speech, and the corresponding state constitutional claims are not interrelated with the theories behind the successfully prosecuted claims. In this case, it appears that at least in some instances, separate law firms and counsel were engaged to develop separate claims and theories. In all events, this court concludes that the various claims brought by plaintiffs stand independent of one another. Hence, "work on an unsuccessful claim cannot be deemed to have been 'expended in pursuit of the ultimate result achieved'" and, therefore, "no fee may be awarded for services on the unsuccessful claim." [*Hensley*] (citations omitted).

Due to the lack of specificity in plaintiffs' time records, it is impossible to determine exactly how many hours were spent on unsuccessful claims. It is apparent to the court, however, that a very substantial portion of requested time was spent on claims essentially unrelated to the successfully prosecuted claims.

With regard to the second issue identified in Hensley, the Supreme Court stated that in determining a reasonable fee, "the most critical factor is the degree of success obtained." *Hensley*. Plaintiffs achieved success on significant issues in this case by maintaining women's right to abortions before 21 weeks without undue interference by the state, and by obtaining a ruling striking down the spousal notification statute. However, in terms of what was presented and argued to the court, plaintiffs' losses were even more significant. Plaintiffs failed to persuade the court that the 21 weeks abortion cut-off date set out in § 76-7-302(3) was impermissible. This court's ruling that § 76-7-307 and 308 (post-viability abortion requirements for doctors) are constitutional also went against plaintiffs. Other unsuccessful statutory challenges were those brought against § 76-7-314 (criminal liability) and § 76-7-315 (serious medical emergency). Plaintiffs not only did not prevail on their state constitutional claims, but attempted to abandon them. Finally, plaintiffs prevailed on a very small percentage of their legal theories for relief on the claims in which they were successful.

In acknowledgment of the limited success of their claims, plaintiffs have voluntarily reduced their lodestar claim by 20%, from $827,484.30 to $661,987.44. Based upon reasonable compensable hours and hourly rates, the court has calculated plaintiffs' lodestar figure to be $293,741.55. The court finds that in order to reflect plaintiffs' limited success in this action, this lodestar figure should be reduced by 85% for the firm of Berle, Kass & Case, and 75% for the other plaintiffs' counsel, yielding an adjusted fee award of $69,656.37.

II. DEFENDANTS' ATTORNEYS' FEES

Defendants have submitted a request for attorneys' fees and expenses totaling $300,000.77. Prevailing defendants are granted attorneys' fees under § 1988 only in limited circumstances:

A prevailing defendant may recover an attorney's fee only where the suit was vexatious, frivolous, or brought to harass or embarrass the defendant. See HR Rep. No. 94-1558, p. 7 (1976); *Christiansburg Garment Co. v. E.E.O.C.* ("[A] district court may in its discretion award attorney's fees to a prevailing defendant in a Title VII case upon a finding that the plaintiff's action was frivolous, unreasonable, or without foundation, even though not brought in subjective bad faith.")

Hensley v. Eckerhart. This court has determined that plaintiffs' case involved "unrelated claims," which should be treated as if they had been raised in separate lawsuits. To the extent these claims are frivolous, or meritless, defendants may receive attorneys' fees involved in responding to them under 42 U.S.C. § 1988. An additional basis for such an award is found in the inherent powers of the court. *Chambers v. NASCO, Inc.* To the extent that such claims were unreasonable and prosecuted in bad faith, defendants also may be entitled to an award under 28 U.S.C. § 1927 and Federal Rule of Civil procedure 11.

A. Defendants' Time Records and Fees

Defendants' time records are clear, concise, and specific. It is also apparent that defendants' counsel exercised appropriate billing judgment before submitting their records to the court. They did not bill for excessive travel or public relations time, and, with few exceptions, time entries for hearings, meetings, and conference calls were billed to only one attorney to avoid excessive duplicative time. Those instances where an attorney listed multiple activities under one time entry usually involved fully compensable activities. This court further finds, with one exception, that defendants' requested hourly rates are reasonable.[16]

B. Claims For Which Defendants Are Awarded Attorneys' Fees

Defendants have alleged that most of plaintiffs' lawsuit is frivolous, groundless, and/or brought in bad faith. After review of these arguments, the court concurs as to the following four claims:

1. Involuntary Servitude

In their Sixth Cause of Action, plaintiffs allege that prohibiting abortion forces women into slavery or involuntary servitude in violation of the Thirteenth Amendment of the United States Constitution. In May 1992, this court held that "it strains credulity to equate the carrying of a child to term with 'compulsory labor,' and concluded that "the argument borders on the frivolous." *Jane L. v. Bangerter* 794 F. Supp. 1528 (D. Utah 1992) [*Jane L. II*].

The frivolity or groundlessness of the Involuntary Servitude claim was not before the court at the time the May 22, 1992 Memorandum Decision and Order was issued. However, upon analysis of the historical background of the Thirteenth Amendment, along with consideration of more recent Supreme Court interpretation of the Amendment's scope, this court found at that time that the "contention

---

[16] [20] Stuart Jones requests a rate of $70 per hour for work done as a law clerk. The court reduces this rate to $55 per hour. The rates asserted by several of defendants' counsel appear to be significantly understated. For example, Professor Richard Wilkins requests a rate of $50 per hour, doubtless meant to reflect a purposeful reduction in the nature of public service. Plaintiffs have not challenged the reasonableness of any of defendants' claimed hourly rates.

that one of the purposes of the Thirteenth Amendment was to secure the right of elective abortion totally lacks merit." *Id.* Because plaintiffs' Thirteenth Amendment claim was frivolous and groundless, the court awards defendants attorneys' fees incurred in opposing this argument in the amount of $8,071.46.

2. Equal Protection

Plaintiffs' Fourth Cause of Action alleges that because the Utah Abortion Act primarily impinges upon women's procreative choices, the Act discriminates on the basis of gender in violation of the Fourteenth Amendment of the United States Constitution. This court summarily disposed of the equal protection claim because plaintiffs were unable to establish that the Utah Act did anything more than " 'realistically reflect the fact that the sexes are not similarly situated in certain circumstances.' " *Id.* (quoting *Michael M. v. Sonoma County Superior Court*). In addition, plaintiffs did not allege facts sufficient to support an allegation of "invidious discrimination." Accordingly, this Court finds their claim to have been without foundation. Defendants are therefore granted attorneys' fees of $5,880.37.

3. Establishment Clause

In their Fifth Cause of Action, plaintiffs alleged that the Utah Act violated the Establishment Clause of the First Amendment. Plaintiffs argued that the Act failed the three-part test set forth in *Lemon v. Kurtzman* in that (1) its preamble embodied a prohibited "religious viewpoint" concerning rights of unborn children; and (2) the Act mirrored and therefore unconstitutionally endorsed the position of the Church of Jesus Christ of Latter-Day Saints.

Similar arguments have been soundly rejected in previous Supreme Court cases. In *Harris v. McRae* the Court held that a statute does not violate the "secular purpose" prong of the Lemon test simply "because it 'happens to coincide or harmonize with the tenets of some or all religions.' " *Id.* (citation omitted). Subsequent cases have reaffirmed this rule. . . . Moreover, the *Harris* Court explicitly held that provisions similar to those set forth in the Act are "as much a reflection of 'traditionalist' values towards abortion, as it is an embodiment of the views of any particular religion." *Harris.* Furthermore, it is manifest that the evidence supporting the plaintiffs' argument in Harris was much more substantial than the evidence supporting plaintiffs' claim here.

Plaintiffs' allegations that the Utah Act violated the "primary effect" prong of the Lemon test were likewise frivolous and without foundation. This is even more apparent in light of the Supreme Court's ruling in *Bowen v. Kendrick* which involved legislation posing a significantly greater danger of having an unconstitutional "effect" on religion than does the Utah Act. The "entanglement" prong of the Lemon test was inapplicable to this case.

Based on the evidence before it, and given the clear holdings of *Harris, Wallace,* and *Bowe,* this court finds that plaintiffs knew, or should have known, that their Establishment Clause claims were frivolous, and without legal or factual foundation at the time they filed their Complaint. . . . Litigating these claims wasted valuable time and resources and unnecessarily delayed the final resolution of this case. For this reason, the court awards defendants attorneys' fees of $29,879.63.

4. State Constitutional Claims

Plaintiffs brought eight causes of action based on the Federal Constitution, and eight analogous causes of action based on the Utah Constitution. Plaintiffs did not prevail on any of these state constitutional claims. For the most part, state law in this case mirrors federal law. The court has already found that several of plaintiffs' federal claims were frivolous and without foundation. It follows that the corresponding state claims were frivolous as well.

5. Fee Application

Prevailing defendants, like prevailing plaintiffs are entitled to at least partial compensation for the time spent preparing their fee application. The court awards defendants 50% of the amount requested, or $7,719.50.

III. COSTS AND EXPENSES

Both parties request reimbursement for costs and out-of-pocket expenses incurred in the course of litigation. . . .

A. Costs

Rule 54(d) of the Federal Rules of Civil Procedure states that "costs shall be allowed as of course to the prevailing party unless the court otherwise directs." (emphasis added). The word "costs" in rule 54(d) is a term of art, defined by 28 U.S.C. § 1920. . . . While this court is given broad discretion in awarding costs, "it has no discretion to award items as costs that are not set out in § 1920." *Bee v. Greaves.* Only the following items may be taxed as costs:

(1) Fees of the clerk and marshal;

(2) Fees of the court reporter for all or any part of the stenographic transcript necessarily obtained for use in the case;

(3) Fees and disbursements for printing and witnesses;

(4) Fees for exemplification and copies of papers necessarily obtained for use in the case;

(5) Docket fees under § 1923 of [Title 28];

(6) Compensation of court appointed experts, compensation of interpreters, and salaries, fees, expenses, and costs of special interpretation services under § 1828 of [Title 28].

28 U.S.C. § 1920.

1. Plaintiffs' Costs

In their memorandum in support of their application for attorneys' fees, plaintiffs requested reimbursement for the following "costs" and "expenses":

* CRLP
  (a) airfare : $22,709.57
  (b) overnight courier service $2,510.31
  (c) copies, postage, phone, faxes, LEXIS research $13,546.49
  (d) deposition transcripts $9,223.59
  (e) court transcript costs $795.50
  (f) filing fee for complaint $120.00
* Planned Parenthood
  (a) deposition transcript costs $2,765.10
* Jeffrey Oritt
  (a) notice of appeal fee $105.00
* TOTAL $51,775.56

Plaintiffs have lumped together their "costs," with "expenses" which are more appropriately sought as part of an attorney's fee under § 1988. The parties' "categorization of items is not dispositive of their recoverability," so the court will separate the claimed amounts into "costs" and "expenses."

Of the items listed above, the following are properly categorized as "costs" under Rule 54(d):

* deposition transcripts $11,988.69
* court transcript costs $795.50
* filing fee for complaint $120.00
* notice of appeal fee $105.00
                                                        _____
                                                        $13,009.19

Some of plaintiffs' identified costs are not recoverable. For instance, the Notice of Appeal filing fee pertains to claims on which plaintiffs lost, and should not be included in the taxation of costs.

2. Defendants' Costs

Defendants have filed a bill of costs amounting to $12,754.69. The items sought include court reporter fees ($1,326.50), exemplification of copies fees ($3,571.98), and deposition transcript fees ($7,856.21).

A prevailing party under Rule 54(d) is usually the one for whom judgment is entered. In this case, however, both parties were successful on some claims, and both parties have requested costs in approximately equal amounts. For these reasons, the court exercises its discretion and orders the parties to bear their own costs.

B. Expenses

Section 1988 provides that, in civil rights actions, "the court, in its discretion, may allow the prevailing party . . . a reasonable attorney's fee as part of the costs. "42 U.S.C. 1988(b). While only those items listed under § 1920 may be awarded as "costs," other out-of-pocket expenses incurred during litigation may be awarded as "attorney's fees" under § 1988 if (1) the expenses are not absorbed as part of law firm overhead but are normally billed to a private client, and (2) the expenses are reasonable. *Bee v. Greaves* (citing *Ramos v. Lamm*).

1. Plaintiffs' Expenses

Plaintiffs request the following "expenses" under § 1988:

* airfare	$22,709.57
* overnight courier service	$2,510.31
* copies, postage, phone, faxes, LEXIS research	$13,546.49
	$38,766.37

Attorney travel expenses are normally billed to a private client and are therefore appropriately reimbursed as "attorney's fees" under § 1988. However, as has already been discussed, this case could have been handled adequately by local attorneys. The Tenth Circuit has explained that it is generally improper to award travel expenses incurred by out-of-state attorneys in traveling to the place of litigation . . . Plaintiffs' request for travel expenses is therefore denied.

As to the other out-of-pocket expenses amounting to $16,056.80, the court finds that many of these expenses are generally billed to the client. The court further finds that one-half of these expenses were reasonably incurred.

This amount is included with plaintiffs' lodestar figure and adjusted to reflect plaintiffs' limited success on the merits. Accordingly, the court adds $2,007.10 in expenses to plaintiffs' attorneys' fee award.

2. Defendants' Expenses

Defendants seek reimbursement for $3,120.75 of travel expenses incurred in relation to fighting plaintiffs' Establishment Clause and Free Exercise Clause claims. These travel expenses are normally billed to the client, and, to the extent they relate to the Establishment Clause claims, should be included in defendants' attorneys' fees award. Accordingly, the court awards defendants 50% of these travel expenses, or $1,560.37, as representing the expenses defendants incurred fighting plaintiffs' Establishment Clause claims.

Based upon the foregoing, plaintiffs' application for attorneys' fees in the amount of $700,753.813 is reduced by $629,090.34. Defendants' application for attorneys' fees of $300,000.77 is reduced by $231,135.97.

Accordingly, it is hereby

ORDERED, that plaintiffs whose claims were successfully prosecuted are entitled to an award of $71,663.47 for attorneys' fees in this action; it is

FURTHER ORDERED, that defendants are entitled to an award of $68,957.80 for attorneys' fees in this action, to be paid $53,110.33 by plaintiffs whose claims are declared to be frivolous, and $15,847.47 by plaintiffs' counsel; it is

FURTHER ORDERED, that the parties shall bear their own costs.

IT IS SO ORDERED.

NOTES

1. A district court's award of attorney's fees is reviewable under an abuse of discretion standard. *Hensley v. Eckerhart*, 461 U.S. 424, 437 (1983). Findings on underlying questions of fact are subject to the clearly erroneous standard. *ACLU of Georgia v. Barnes*, 168 F.3d 423, 427 (11th Cir. 1999); *Mares v. Credit Bureau of Raton*, 801 F.2d 1197, 1201 (10th Cir. 1986). A district court's statutory interpretation or legal analysis providing the basis for the fee award is reviewable de novo. *Homeward Bound, Inc. v. Hissom Memorial Center*, 963 F.2d 1352, 1355 (10th Cir. 1992). Given these principles, which portions of the District Court's rulings in *Jane L.*, if any, are most vulnerable to attack?

While the abuse of discretion and clearly erroneous standards of review give great deference to the district court, appellate courts will reverse, vacate, or remand on occasion. For instance, it is error to deny fees to a prevailing plaintiff without issuing findings of fact and conclusions of law that identify specific special circumstances that justify that result. *American Broadcasting Co., Inc. v. Miller*, 550 F.3d 786 (9th Cir. 2008). A fee award also may be vacated and remanded when the district court first reduced the number of hours in the lodestar calculation by engaging in an hour-by-hour analysis of the attorney's time records and then further reduced these hours by an across-the-board percentage. *Bivins v. Wrap It Up, Inc.*, 548 F.3d 1348 (11th Cir. 2008). *See also Gonzalez v. City of Maywood*, 729 F.3d 1196 (9th Cir. 2013) (error to limit fee award to an amount less than the damages awarded to plaintiffs if lodestar justifies a greater fee); *Barnard v. Theobald*, 721 F.3d 1069 (9th Cir. 2013) (abuse of discretion to reduce fee award by 40% without a complete explanation of why that reduction was appropriate; district court admonished to "show your work" in explaining reduction).

2. *Subsequent Developments in Jane L.* The district court's ruling on attorney's fees set the stage for three more years of litigation. The plaintiffs first secured additional relief on the merits on appeal. The court of appeals held that provisions limiting the availability of abortions after twenty weeks were not severable from the pre-twenty week restrictions which had been declared unconstitutional. Consequently, the post-twenty week restrictions were also declared to be invalid. *Jane L. v. Bangerter*, 61 F.3d 1493, 1499 (10th Cir. 1995). The court of appeals also held that the ban on fetal experimentation was unconstitutionally vague, 61 F.3d at 1502, and that the choice of method provisions imposed an undue burden on a woman's constitutional right to choose to terminate a pregnancy. 61 F.3d at 1505.

The court of appeals then addressed the attorney's fees issues in a separate opinion. The court affirmed the district court's calculation of the basic lodestar. It found no abuse of discretion in reducing the number of compensable hours for "sloppy and imprecise time records" or in using Salt Lake City hourly rates. *Jane L. v. Bangerter*, 61 F.3d 1505, 1509–10 (10th Cir. 1995). The court then addressed the district court's reduction of the lodestar by approximately 75% to account for "limited success". In light of the additional success obtained by the plaintiffs on appeal, the case was remanded to the district court "to reassess the wins and losses." 61 F.3d at 1513. The appellate court offered some guidance to the lower court in making this reassessment. The tenth circuit commented that "[g]iven the coincidental correlation between the ratio of successful to unsuccessful claims and the percentage by which the district court reduced the lodestar, it appears that the court did not assess the relative importance of plaintiffs' successes and failures." 61 F.3d at 1511. The district court was specifically advised to "demonstrate on the record its assessment of the losses in light of the time necessarily devoted to the litigation as a whole and the general overall success of plaintiffs." 61 F.3d at 1511. The appellate court also made it clear that the attorney's fees should not be reduced because alternative legal theories were asserted to attack provisions ultimately invalidated on other grounds. 61 F.3d at 1512. Thus, no reduction should be made for the equal protection, establishment clause, and involuntary servitude challenges to the pre-twenty week restrictions. The fee award could be reduced, however, for ultimately unsuccessful attacks on distinct provisions of the Act, such as that dealing with serious medical emergencies. 61 F.3d at 1512–13.

The appellate court went on to consider the award of attorney's fees to the defendants. The district court had awarded the defendants attorney's fees on two grounds. The first portion of the award was based on the district court's determination that certain legal theories advanced by the plaintiffs were frivolous. The second portion of the fee award was based on the finding that plaintiffs' counsel had acted in bad faith in attempting to dismiss without prejudice certain state constitutional claims. The court of appeals reversed the first portion of the fee award. It held that the district court erred in ruling that the equal protection, involuntary servitude, and establishment clause claims were frivolous. 61 F.3d at 1517. Significantly, however, the appellate court did not address the more than $15,000 in fees awarded the defendants against plaintiffs' counsel for bad faith conduct relative to attempts to dismiss without prejudice the state constitutional claims. The tenth circuit concluded that it lacked jurisdiction to review this ruling because plaintiffs counsel — against whom the award was made — were not named as parties to the appeal. 61 F.3d at 1513 n. 3. Finally, the appellate court upheld the district court's exclusion of the cost of travel from recoverable expenses and remanded the case to the district court for a reconsideration of costs in light of the additional success obtained by the plaintiffs on appeal. 61 F.3d at 1517.

On remand, the district court began its recalculation of the fee award with the original lodestar calculation of $293,741. It then revisited the question of limited success and concluded that the lodestar should be reduced by 25%, as opposed to the 75% reduction ordered in its original decision. *Jane L. v. Bangerter*, 914 F. Supp. 484, 486 (D. Utah 1996). The district court also vacated its previous award of attorney's fees to the defendants and revised its previous ruling on costs and expenses. 914 F. Supp. at 486–87.

Then the district judge took the most unusual step of dissenting from his own opinion. The district judge opined that invalidating the post-twenty week restrictions on abortion on the grounds of severability should not count as a "full win" for the plaintiffs, since the appellate court did not reach the substantive constitutional challenge. 914 F. Supp. at 488. The judge felt constrained by the circuit court opinion, however, to give the plaintiffs full credit for prevailing on their challenge to this portion of the Act. The district judge also dissented from his ruling vacating the award of attorney's fees to the defendants. Again, he felt obligated to do so by the appellate court's decision. 914 F. Supp. at 488.

Both sides moved for reconsideration. The district court reinstated the portion of attorney's fees awarded to the defendants based on plaintiffs' counsel's bad faith in seeking a dismissal without prejudice of the state constitutional claims. Since the court of appeals determined it lacked jurisdiction to review that portion of the original fee award, it was not affected by the appellate decision. *Jane L. v. Bangerter*, 920 F. Supp. 1202, 1205 (D. Utah *1996)*. The district court also increased the plaintiffs' award of expenses to account for the increase in the plaintiffs overall level of success.

The original complaint in *Jane L.* was filed in April of 1991. The final ruling on attorney's fees was filed in March of 1996. Litigation over the attorney's fees spanned a three year period. At the end of the litigation and excluding post judgment interest, the plaintiffs were awarded $239,536 in fees and expenses and plaintiffs' counsel were ordered to pay attorney's fees in the amount of $15,847 to the defendants. While *Jane L.* undoubtedly is not a typical Section 1983 fee dispute, it does offer a detailed illustration of the range of legal issues that may arise and the role of judicial discretion in their resolution.

3. What are the lessons to be learned from the District Court's rulings on attorney's fees in *Jane L.*? What message does the opinion send regarding record keeping, the advocacy of innovative legal theories, or the type of activities that an attorney should engage in when representing a client? Does the result in *Jane L.* comport with the purposes of section 1988 as elucidated in Senate Report No. 94-1011?

4. The first factor in computing the lodestar is the reasonable number of hours expended by counsel. The plaintiffs in *Jane L.* requested compensation for 4,431.52 hours of work. The District Court awarded compensation for 2,887.66 hours, a reduction of approximately 35%. Some of that reduction was attributable to inadequately documented time records. The importance of detailed contemporaneous records to support a fee request was summarized by one commentator as follows: "Although noting that "[c]ontemporaneously recorded time sheets are the preferred practice," the Supreme Court has not condemned the after-the-fact reconstruction of time records as the basis for obtaining a fee award. However, some circuit court decisions have announced the rule that contemporaneous time records are a prerequisite for the recovery of fees for the services rendered, and that the reconstruction of time records, no matter how carefully done, cannot serve as the basis for fee compensation. Even in those circuits in which fee applicants are not penalized for the failure to maintain contemporaneous time records, the maintenance of such records is strongly recommended as a "prudent" practice for the practitioner who seeks to sustain the burden of establishing the reasonableness of the hours claimed in a fee petition." MARTIN A. SCHWARTZ & JOHN E. KIRKLIN, SECTION 1983 LITIGATION: ATTORNEY'S FEES 4.14 (Wolters Klewer 2014) (citations omitted).

The District Court in *Jane L.* also reduced the time component of the lodestar because certain listed activities were vague, unnecessary or otherwise not compensable. The court specifically disallowed compensation for time spent by counsel on public relations and lobbying to change the statutes under constitutional attack. These rulings invite an examination of the variety of things lawyers do in the course of representing a client. Should lobbying and public relations be considered a compensable part of representing the client in litigation? Consider the comments of another court:

> Where the giving of press conferences and performance of other lobbying and public relations work is directly and intimately related to the successful representation of a client, private attorneys do such work and bill their clients. Prevailing civil rights plaintiffs may do the same.

Davis v. City and County of San Francisco, 976 F.2d 1536, 1545 (9th Cir. 1992), vacated in part on other grounds, 984 F.2d 345 (9th Cir. 1993) (employment discrimination). *But see Watkins v. Fordice*, 7 F.3d 453, 458 (5th Cir. 1993) ("Because pre-litigation lobbying is not a necessary precursor to the filing of a lawsuit, the district court did not abuse its discretion when it deducted these hours during its lodestar analysis. . . . we find no abuse of discretion in the district court's exclusion of the press-conference hours . . .").

Has public relations become an accepted part of a litigation practice? *See* JAMES F. HAGGERTY, IN THE COURT OF PUBLIC OPINION: WINNING YOUR CASE WITH PUBLIC RELATIONS (2003); Jonathan M. Moses, Note, *Legal Spin Control: Ethics and Advocacy in the Court of Public Opinion*, 95 COLUM. L. REV. 1811 (1995). If private litigants pay attorneys for these activities, should they be included in a fee award? Does the legislative history of the statute shed any light on these questions?

Should the time spent by a public interest groups to find a suitable plaintiff to challenge the constitutionality of a state statute be a compensable part of a fee award? *See ACLU of Georgia v. Barnes*, 68 F.3d 423, 435 (11th Cir. 1999) ("We conclude that hours spent looking for and soliciting potential plaintiffs should not have been included" [in the fee award]). On the other hand, fees may awarded for time spent monitoring and enforcing a consent decree. *E.g., Johnson v. City of Tulsa*, 489 F.3d 1089 (10th Cir. 2007).

Does the legislative history of the attorney's fee statute provide insight as to the scope of activities Congress intended to be included and excluded from the calculation an attorney's fee award?

5. *Hensley* emphasizes that "billing judgment" is an important factor in determining how many "reasonable" hours to include in the lodestar calculation. It was on this basis that the district court in *Jane L* reduced the number of hours for "duplicative time" — having too many attorneys perform a given task. *ACLU of Georgia v. Barnes*, 168 F.3d 1423 (1999) is an instructive case that goes into great detail in analyzing the billing judgment aspect of a fee award. The plaintiffs

prevailed in challenging the constitutionality of a Georgia statute that attempted to criminalize certain internet transmissions. The plaintiffs' application requested a fee based on 1,072.95 hours or attorney and paralegal work. The district court awarded the plaintiffs the full amount of attorneys fees requested ($233,075) plus expenses ($5,791.24). The court of appeals found that this award was an abuse of discretion. Instead of remanding the case to the district court for a recalculation of the award, the appellate court took the unusual step of determining what was the proper lodestar. The appellate court found that the number of hours spent drafting the complaint, motion for preliminary injunction, and supporting affidavits was excessive. 168 F.3d at 430–31. The court noted that 20% of the complaint's 179 paragraphs were derived from a complaint filed in another case and were readily available to counsel. Furthermore, the bulk of the complaint was simply an edited version of the affidavits filed to support the motion for preliminary injunction. 168 F.3d at 430. *See also, Maldonado v. Houstoun*, 256 F.3d 181 (3d Cir. 2001) (169.5 hours claimed to prepare for a one hour oral argument is excessive). The court in *Barnes* also determined that the presence of four attorneys at a "status conference that did not address the merits of the case was patently excessive." 168 F.3d at 433. Similarly, it concluded that it was "patently excessive" for four lawyers to attend an in court demonstration of internet technology for the district judge and that having four lawyers meet with an expert witness before the demonstration constituted "duplicative effort." 168 F.3d at 434. As describe in note 4, the court of appeals also found that the time spent locating potential plaintiffs should not be included in the fee award. After exercising its own billing judgment, the court of appeals reduced the number of hours to be included in the lodestar calculation by 316.10 hours.

6.   The second component of the lodestar is the reasonable hourly rate. *Blum v. Stenson*, 465 U.S. 886, 895 (1984) held that a reasonable fee reflects compensation at "the prevailing market rates in the relevant community. . . . " Should the "relevant community" always, or at least presumptively, be that of the forum? The general rule is that the relevant market is the place where the case is filed. *ACLU of Georgia v. Barnes*, 168 F.3d 423, 437 (11th Cir. 1999). Under what circumstances, if any, would it be appropriate to award attorney's fees calculated on rates other than those prevailing in the forum community? *See ACLU of Georgia v. Barnes*, 168 F.3d 423, 437 (11th Cir. 1999) (a fee applicant seeking to recover at the non-local rate bears the burden of establishing "a lack of attorney practicing in that place who are willing and able to handle his claims."); *Chrapliwy v. Uniroyal, Inc.*, 670 F.2d 760, 769 (7th Cir. 1982) ("If . . . a party does not find counsel readily available in [the forum] locality with whatever degree of skill may reasonably be required, it is reasonable that the party go elsewhere to find an attorney, and the court should make the allowance on the basis of the chosen attorney's billing rate . . ."); *Palmigiano v. Garrahy*, 707 F.2d 636, 637 (1st Cir. 1983) (attorney's fees paid to out-of-state specialist with unique competence in prison civil rights case should be based on out-of-state rates) (dicta). *Cf. Arbor Hills Concerned Citizens Neighborhood Ass'n. v. County of Albany*, 484 F.3d 162, 170 (2d Cir. 2007) ("a district court may use an out-of-district hourly rate — or some rate in between the out-of-district rate sought and the rates charged by local attorneys — in calculating the presumptive reasonable fee if it is clear that a reasonable, paying client would have paid those higher rates.") (voting rights case).

Even when the relevant forum is clear, there may be significant disputes about what is the appropriate hourly rate. *Heller v. District of Columbia*, 670 F.3d 1244 (D.C. 2011) addressed the attorneys' fee award in the litigation that established that municipal bans on handgun possession in one's home violated the Second Amendment. *See District of Columbia v. Heller*, 554 U.S. 570 (2008). Both sides agreed that the plaintiff was a prevailing party entitled to an award of fees. Both sides agreed that the relevant legal market was the District of Columbia. There was also no dispute regarding the experience of plaintiff's counsel. The parties disagreed sharply, however, on how to determine the appropriate hourly rate to apply in this case. The district court could not base the fee award on the lawyers' customary billing practices because the attorneys were engaged in public interest work for which they did not have a "usual billing rate." The court did note that the "plaintiff was represented by a team of skilled litigators with significant experience in the for-profit, non-profit, and government sectors at both trial and appellate level." The court then turned to what is commonly referred to as the "Laffey Matrix" to determine the precise hourly rate. The Laffey Matrix was prepared by the Civil Division of the Office of the United States Attorney and provides the billing rates for attorneys in the Washington, D.C. market with various degrees of legal experience. The initial Laffey Matrix was based upon the prevailing market rates from 1981–82. It is updated using one of two adjustments. One version of the matrix adjusts the 1981–82 figures using the change in the overall cost of living reflected in the consumer price index. The other version adjusts the figures based only on the legal services component of the consumer price index. The plaintiff urged the court to apply a different methodology, one based on the *National Law Journal's* 2009 law firm rate survey buttressed by an affidavit of a legal recruiter familiar with standard billing practices in the D.C. market, the standard billing rates charged by defense counsel in this case, and citations to fee awards in other complex cases. The difference produced by the two approaches was striking. Under the methodology advocated by the defendants, the appropriate hourly rate for one of the more experienced attorneys would be $420 per hour. Under the plaintiff's proposed methodology, the same lawyer would be compensated at $589 per hour. The district court ultimately applied the Laffey Matrix suggested by the defendants. Citing "special caution" that must be exercised when reviewing fee applications to be paid by the government and finding methodological flaws in the plaintiff's approach (*e.g.*, not factoring in billing rates of boutique and smaller firms), the court adopted the lower rates. Instead of the $3,126,397.25 fee award sought by the plaintiff, the court awarded fees and costs of $1,132,182.

7.   The Prison Litigation Reform Act of 1995, discussed in more detail in Chapter 10, provides a more stringent framework for awarding attorney's fees in prison-based constitutional tort suits. Up to 25% of a monetary award of damages secured by a prisoner shall be applied to any attorney's fee award. The balance of the fee award is paid by the defendant, provided the entire award does not exceed 150% of the money damages. Hence, unlike the plaintiff in a traditional section 1983 case, a prevailing prison inmate's fee award must met a statutory proportionality test. Furthermore, the hourly rate used to calculate the fee award is limited to no more than 150% of the hourly rate provided under federal law for court-appointed counsel in criminal cases. *See generally* MARTIN A. SCHWARTZ & JOHN E. KIRKIN, SECTION 1983 LITIGATION: ATTORNEY'S FEES 1.04 (Wolters Klewer 2014).

The limitations on the amount of attorneys' fees under the PLRA can be significant. In *Shepherd v. Goord*, 662 F.3d 603 (2d Cir. 2011), counsel representing an inmate established that prison guards violated the plaintiff's First Amendment rights by touching and "slightly" tearing the inmate's "sacred" dreadlocks. A jury awarded the plaintiff $1 in compensatory damages. Under the PLRA, the fee award was limited to $1.50. Compare Note 5 following *Farrar* for examples of substantial fee awards made when the plaintiff recovered nominal damages in non-PLRA civil rights litigation.

8. Once a court has fixed both the reasonable hours and reasonable rate, it should consider whether any adjustments to the lodestar are appropriate. *Hensley* makes clear that the most important consideration in adjusting the lodestar is the degree of success. How should a court measure the degree of success of litigation?

The district court in *Jane L.* initially reduced the fee award by 75% due to limited success. As explained in note 2, it modified this reduction to 25% in light of the subsequent court of appeals decisions. Measuring the degree of success is complicated by the fact that plaintiffs may sue multiple defendants and assert multiple legal theories, but may only prevail against some of the defendants under some of the theories. *See* note 2 following *Hensley*. Most courts will not automatically reduce the fee award under such circumstances if the claims are grounded in a "common core of facts." *E.g.*, *Lundy v. City of Albany*, 42 F.3d 131 (2d Cir. 1994) (plaintiff sued 5 defendants and received a verdict against one; fee not reduced for limited success); *Brodziak v. Runyon*, 145 F.3d 194 (4th Cir. 1998) (abuse of discretion to reduce fee award by 40% based on plaintiff prevailing on 40% of claims asserted; fee award should be based on whether the claims on which the plaintiff prevailed were "related" to those on which the plaintiff did not prevail); *Schneider v. Colegio de Abogados de Puerto Rico*, 187 F.3d 30 (1st Cir. 1999) (district court did not abuse its discretion in not reducing fee award when plaintiff prevailed on one claim but not on others; lower court properly found that all the claims were sufficiently related to justify full award).

If the plaintiff only recovers a fraction of damages sought in the complaint, should the fee award be downwardly adjusted due to limited success? It appears that the district court has considerable discretion. In addition to the discussion in Note 5 following *Farrar*, supra, compare *Cole v. Wodziak*, 169 F.3d 486 (7th Cir. 1999) (no abuse of discretion in reducing fee award when plaintiff sought $50,000 in compensatory damages but was awarded $4,500) *with Cruz v. City of Cicero*, 275 F.3d 579 (7th Cir. 2001) (no abuse of discretion in not reducing fee award when plaintiffs sought more than $1 million in compensatory damages but were awarded $402,000) and *Lundy v. City of Albany*, 42 F.2d 131 (2d Cir. 1994) (no abuse of discretion in not reducing fee award when plaintiff sought more than $7 million in damages but was awarded $35,000). At least one court has held that "attorney's fees awarded under 42 U.S.C. § 1988 must be adjusted downward where the plaintiff has obtained limited success on his pleaded claims, and does not confer a meaningful public benefit." *McCown v. City of Fontana*, 565 F.3d 1097, 1103 (9th Cir. 2009). McCown sued city and various police officers for injuries stemming from use of tasar during his arrest. His claims against the individual officers were dismissed. McCown sought "damages in excess of $75,000" in his complaint and demanded $251,000 in settlement. However, he eventually settled with the city for $20,000. The district court awarded McCown attorney's fees of $200,000. The award was reversed and the case remanded for reconsideration.

Note that the court in *McCown* leaves open the possibility that the 'level of success' might include intangible benefits to the community at large. *See City of Riverside v. Rivera*, 477 U.S. 561, 574–77 (1986) (vindication of constitutional rights "cannot be valued solely in monetary terms"). How does a plaintiff demonstrate a 'meaningful public benefit'? In *Robinson v. City of Harvey*, 489 F.3d 864 (7th Cir. 2007) the appellate court affirmed a full lodestar fee award of $507,183 when the plaintiff was awarded $25,000 in compensatory and $275,000 in punitive damages. In rejecting the defendants' argument that the fee award should be reduced for 'limited success,' the court noted that damages were not minimal and had produced significant public benefit.

> He [the plaintiff] effectively persuaded a jury that a significant number of City of Harvey officials conspired to plant a gun at the crime scene — a victory that serves the public interest by exposing to light disturbing police malfeasance and grave municipal institutional failures, and one that will presumably help to deter future constitutional violations by the City's officers. These achievements are anything by minimal.

Robinson, 489 F.3d at 872.

9. Defendants may be awarded attorney's fees in civil rights cases only when the plaintiff's action was "vexatious, frivolous, or brought to harass or embarrass." *Hensley v. Eckerhart*, 461 U.S. 424, 429 n.2 (1983) *citing Christiansburg Garment Co. v. EEOC*, 434 U.S. 412, 421 (1978). How can courts apply this standard so as to protect governments and officials from the costs of defending patently meritless litigation without unduly chilling the advocacy of civil rights? Should a legal theory be labeled "frivolous" when it finds some support among individual jurists and legal scholars, but has not been accepted by a court? The equal protection, involuntary servitude, and establishment clause claims found to be frivolous by the district court in *Jane L.* each have such support. *See* Ruth Bader Ginsburg, *Speaking in a Judicial Voice*, 67 N.Y.U. L. Rev. 1185, 1199–1200 (1992) (supporting an equal protection approach to abortion law); *Webster v. Reproductive Health Services*, 492 U.S. 490, 566 (1989) (Stevens, J., concurring in part, dissenting in part) (embracing an establishment clause attack on the preamble to a Missouri abortion statute); *Roe v. Rampton*, 394 F. Supp. 677, 689 (D. Utah 1975) (Ritter, C.J., dissenting on other grounds) (characterizing compelled pregnancy as "a form of involuntary servitude"), *aff'd*, 535 F.2d 1219 (10th Cir. 1976). On the other hand, defendants have a legitimate interest in avoiding the expense incurred in defending suits that attempt to establish new constitutional theories. At what point should the plaintiff bear the financial risk of experimenting with constitutional law? *See Karam v. City of Burbank*, 340 F.3d 884 (9th Cir. 2003) (attorneys' fee awarded against activist whose Fourth Amendment claim was deemed frivolous); *Vakas v. Rodriquez*, 728 F.2d 1293, 1297 (10th Cir. 1984) (unsuccessful theories having "some slight legal support" could be deemed frivolous).

Recall from Chapter 2 that under certain circumstances the employment of state self-help remedies with the assistance of public officials may be actionable under section 1983. In *Revis v. Meldrum*, 489 F.3d 273 (6th Cir. 2007), the plaintiff sued private judgment creditors and public law enforcement officials who assisted them in enforcing a writ of execution against the plaintiff's property. Revis asserted there was a racially motivated conspiracy to deprive him of his property without procedural due process. The court ultimately held that the state law denied the plaintiff procedural due process, the state actor defendants were entitled to qualified immunity, there was no evidence to support the allegation of a racially motivated conspiracy, and that the private-party defendants were not state actors. The trial court awarded the private-party defendants $65,000 in attorney's fees. The court of appeals held that in the absence of any supporting evidence, it was not an abuse of discretion to characterize the racial discrimination claim as frivolous. However, the notorious confusion surrounding the state action doctrine "casts significant doubt on whether this determination [*i.e.*, that the private-party defendants were not state actors] was so obvious as to render the [due process] claim frivolous." *Revis*, 489 F.3d at 293. The fee award was vacated and the matter remanded to the district court for reconsideration.

10. An attorney's fee award under section 1988 may include compensation for paralegals, law clerks, and other support personnel. In *Missouri v. Jenkins*, 491 U.S. 274 (1989), the Court stated that the increasingly widespread custom of separately billing for the services of paralegals and law clerks must be taken into account so that "an attorney's fee awarded under section 1988 . . . yield[s] the same level of compensation that would be available from the market. . . ." *Jenkins*, 491 U.S. at 286.

Should expert witness fees also be awarded? In *West Virginia University Hospitals, Inc. v. Casey*, 499 U.S. 83 (1991), the Court held that expert witness expenses could not be included in an award of attorney's fees under section 1988. Limited compensation ($40 per day) for the testimonial services of expert witnesses could be assessed as "costs" under 28 U.S.C. § 1821(b). This limitation on recovery for expert witness fees was seen by many civil rights advocates as a major barrier to effective representation. In 1991, Congress amended section 1988 to authorize the court, "in its discretion," to included expert witness fees as part of the attorney's fee award. This amendment, however, only applies to claims brought pursuant to 42 U.S.C. § 1981, and not section 1983 actions.

11. Should an award of attorney's fees under section 1988 include time spent representing the claimant in forums other than the one in which the section 1983 claim was filed? Recall from Chapter 10 that *Patsy v. Board of Regents*, 457 U.S. 496 (1982), held that a civil rights plaintiff does not have to exhaust her state administrative remedies before filing a section 1983 claim. Nonetheless, suppose a plaintiff first unsuccessfully seeks redress in a state administrative forum and later prevails in her section 1983 claim. Should the time spent in the state administrative proceeding be included in calculating the attorney's fee award under section 1988? In *Webb v. County Board of Education*, 471 U.S. 234, 241–43 (1985) the Court held that such hours were not "automatically" compensable; however, a "discrete portion" of the time spent in the state administrative proceeding could be included in the section 1988 award of attorney's fees if it was "both useful and of a type ordinarily necessary to advance the [subsequent] civil rights litigation . . . ." May a plaintiff who prevails in the state administrative proceeding recover attorney's fees under section 1988? *See North Carolina Department of Transportation v. Crest*

Street Community Council, 479 U.S. 6 (1986) (No; "section 1988 does not authorize a court to award attorney's fees except in an action to enforce the listed civil rights laws."). Do these cases encourage claimants' counsel to file a section 1983 claim in federal court before attempting to resolve the dispute on nonconstitutional grounds in a state administrative forum? Are there countervailing strategic or ethical considerations that might lead an attorney to pursue state agency remedies anyway? If so, does the result in *Crest Street* square with the purposes of section 1988?

Recall also that there are various abstention doctrines that may force a civil rights plaintiff to pursue remedies in state court before a federal court will consider her section 1983 claim. *See* Chapter 10. Several courts have included in their award of attorney's fees to an ultimately successful section 1983 claimant, time spent unsuccessfully representing the plaintiff in state court pursuant to an abstention doctrine. *See Bartholomew v. Watson*, 665 F.2d 910 (9th Cir. 1982); *Lampher v. Zagel*, 755 F.2d 99 (7th Cir. 1985); *Stathos v. Bowden*, 728 F.2d 15 (1st Cir. 1984). One abstaining federal court awarded fees when the case was resolved in the state court on state law grounds, thus rendering moot the section 1983 claim. *Exeter-West Greenwich Regional School v. Pontarelli*, 788 F.2d 47 (1st Cir. 1986). Are these cases consistent with *Webb* and *Crest Street Community Council*? Are they consistent with the lower court cases cited in note 3 following *Farrar*, concerning fee awards for work on pendent state claims in federal court?

12.   In cases involving multiple defendants, should responsibility for a fee award run jointly and severally or should it be apportioned between the defendants. If it is to be apportioned, what would be the basis for the division of responsibility? In *Torres-Rivera v. O'Neill-Cancel*, 524 F.3d 331 (1st Cir. 2008), two teenage boys were beaten by a Puerto Rican police officer (Espada-Cruz) while an agent of the Puerto Rico Treasury Department (O'Neill-Cancel) stood by without intervening and trained his gun on the mother of one of the boys as she witnessed the beating. A default judgment was entered against Espada-Cruz. O'Neill-Cancel mounted what was described by the court as a "ferocious defense." 524 F.3d at 335. The jury ultimately found O'Neill-Cancel liable to both plaintiffs for failing to intervene. The jury also awarded the plaintiffs a total of $220,000 in damages against Espada-Cruz and $120,000 in damages against O'Neill-Cancel. The district court ruled that the responsibility for attorneys' fees should not run jointly and severally, but should be apportioned between the defendants. This aspect of the lower court's ruling was not challenged and was characterized by the court of appeals as "eminently reasonable." 524 F.3d at 338. What was disputed was the method of apportionment. O'Neill-Cancel urged the court to adopt a "relative liability" method of apportionment whereby responsibility for attorneys' fees would approximate the percentage liability for damages. Under this approach, 65% of the fee award would be apportioned to Espada-Cruz and 35% to O'Neill-Cancel. The plaintiffs argued that fees should be apportioned according to the "time expended" method whereby responsibility for fees would be based on the amount of time spent litigating against each defendant. Since a default judgment was entered against Espada-Cruz and he did not participate in the trial, the "time expended" method would result in apportioning responsibility for almost all the fees to O'Neill-Cancel. The district court adopted the "relative liability" method of apportionment. The court of appeals held that this ruling was an abuse of discretion. "Where apportionment is indicated, the choice among available options generally lies within the district court's sound discretion. But when the time required to litigate against one defendant is grossly disproportionate to the time required to litigate another defendant and the two defendants are not in privity, then the time expended method of apportionment should be used." 524 F.3d at 339.

As a matter of policy, should responsibility for attorneys' fees run jointly and severally or be apportioned? If some sort of apportionment is desirable, when, if ever, would the relative liability method be appropriate?

IV. STRATEGIC AND ETHICAL ASPECTS OF ATTORNEY'S FEE AWARDS

The previous sections considered when attorney's fees are recoverable and how such an award is calculated. We turn now to the strategic and ethical implications of attorney's fee awards on litigation. How might the potential availability of attorney's fees affect litigation strategy? Is the potential for an attorney's fees award likely to promote or inhibit the settlement of cases? Can the defendant structure a settlement proposal in such a way as to drive a wedge between the plaintiff and her attorney? If so, would such a proposal be ethical?

EVANS v. JEFF D.
475 U.S. 717 (1986)

JUSTICE STEVENS delivered the opinion of the Court.

The Civil Rights Attorney's Fees Awards Act of 1976 (Fees Act) provides that "the court, in its discretion, may allow the prevailing party . . . a reasonable attorney's fee" in enumerated civil rights actions. 90 Stat. 2641, 42 U.S.C. § 1988. In *Maher v. Gagne* we held that fees may be assessed against state officials after a case has been settled by the entry of a consent decree. In this case, we consider the question whether attorney's fees must be assessed when the case has been settled by a consent decree granting prospective relief to the plaintiff class but providing that the defendants shall not pay any part of the prevailing party's fees or costs. We hold that the District Court has the power, in its sound discretion, to refuse to award fees.

I

The petitioners are the Governor and other public officials of the State of Idaho responsible for the education and treatment of children who suffer from emotional and mental handicaps. Respondents are a class of such children who have been or will be placed in petitioners' care.

On August 4, 1980, respondents commenced this action by filing a complaint against petitioners in the United States District Court for the District of Idaho. The factual allegations in the complaint described deficiencies in both the educational programs and the health care services provided respondents. These deficiencies allegedly violated the United States Constitution, the Idaho Constitution, four federal statutes, and certain provisions of the Idaho Code. The complaint prayed for injunctive relief and for an award of costs and attorney's fees, but it did not seek damages.

. . . [The District Court appointed a lawyer, Johnson, from the Idaho Legal Aid Society to represent the plaintiff. Because the Legal Aid Society was prohibited from representing persons capable of paying attorney's fees, an award of fees under section 1988 was the only potential source of payment in this case. The parties quickly settled the claims relating to educational services. This settlement, which included a waiver of attorney's fees, was approved by the District Court. The parties were unable to reach a settlement on the treatment issues. The District Court certified the class and the parties prepared for trial.]

In March 1983, one week before trial, petitioners presented respondents with a new settlement proposal. As respondents themselves characterize it, the proposal "offered virtually all of the injunctive relief [they] had sought in their complaint." Brief for Respondents 5. See App. 89. The Court of Appeals agreed with this characterization, and further noted that the proposed relief was "more than the district court in earlier hearings had indicated it was willing to grant." As was true of the earlier partial settlement, however, petitioners' offer included a provision for a waiver by respondents of any claim to fees or costs. Originally, this waiver was unacceptable to the Idaho Legal Aid Society, which had instructed Johnson to reject any settlement offer conditioned upon a waiver of fees, but Johnson ultimately determined that his ethical obligation to his clients mandated acceptance of the proposal. The parties conditioned the waiver on approval by the District Court.

After the stipulation was signed, Johnson filed a written motion requesting the District Court to approve the settlement "except for the provision on costs and attorney's fees," and to allow respondents to present a bill of costs and fees for consideration by the court. At the oral argument on that motion, Johnson contended that petitioners' offer had exploited his ethical duty to his clients — that he was "forced," by an offer giving his clients "the best result [they] could have gotten in this court or any other court," to waive his attorney's fees.

. . . [The District Court rejected the plaintiff's argument and approved the settlement, including the waiver of attorney's fees. The Court of Appeals, however,] invalidated the fee waiver and left standing the remainder of the settlement; it then instructed the District Court to "make its own determination of the fees that are reasonable" and remanded for that limited purpose.

The importance of the question decided by the Court of Appeals, together with the conflict between its decision and the decisions of other Courts of Appeals, led us to grant certiorari. We now reverse.

II

To begin with, the Court of Appeals' decision rested on an erroneous view of the District Court's power to approve settlements in class actions. Rule 23(e) wisely requires court approval of the terms of any settlement of a class action, but the power to approve or reject a settlement negotiated by the parties before trial does not authorize the court to require the parties to accept a settlement to which they have not agreed . . . The District Court could not enforce the settlement on the merits and award attorney's fees any more than it could, in a situation in which the attorney had negotiated a large fee at the expense of the plaintiff class, preserve the fee award and order greater relief on the merits. . . .

. . . Although respondents contend that Johnson, as counsel for the class, was faced with an "ethical dilemma" when petitioners offered him relief greater than that which he could reasonably have expected to obtain for his clients at trial (if only he would stipulate to a waiver of the statutory fee award), and although we recognize Johnson's conflicting interests between pursuing relief for the class and a fee for the Idaho Legal Aid Society, we do not believe that the "dilemma" was an "ethical" one in the sense that Johnson had to choose between conflicting duties under the prevailing norms of professional conduct. Plainly, Johnson had no ethical obligation to seek a statutory fee award. His ethical duty was to serve his clients loyally and competently. Since the proposal to settle the merits was more favorable than the probable outcome of the trial, Johnson's decision to recommend acceptance was consistent with the highest standards of our profession . . .

The defect, if any, in the negotiated fee waiver must be traced not to the rules of ethics but to the Fees Act[17]. . . . [R]espondents argue that the statute must be construed to forbid a fee waiver that is the product of "coercion." They submit that a "coercive waiver" results when the defendant in a civil rights action (1) offers a settlement on the merits of equal or greater value than that which plaintiffs could reasonably expect to achieve at trial but (2) conditions the offer on a waiver of plaintiffs' statutory eligibility for attorney's fees. Such an offer, they claim, exploits the ethical obligation of plaintiffs' counsel to recommend settlement in order to avoid defendant's statutory liability for its opponents' fees and costs.[18]

. . . [W]e are not persuaded that Congress has commanded that all such

---

[17] [15] Even state bar opinions holding it unethical for defendants to request fee waivers in exchange for relief on the merits of plaintiffs' claims are bottomed ultimately on section 1988. See District of Columbia Bar Legal Ethics Committee, Op. No. 147, reprinted in 113 Daily Wash. L. Rep. 389, 394–395 (1985); Committee on Professional and Judicial Ethics of the New York City Bar Association, Op. No. 82-80, p. 1 (1985); id., at 4–5 (dissenting opinion); Committee on Professional and Judicial Ethics of the New York City Bar Association, Op. No. 80-94, reprinted in 36 Record of N. Y. C. B. A. 507, 508–511 (1981); Grievance Commission of Board of Overseers of the Bar of Maine, Op. No. 17, reprinted in Advisory Opinions of the Grievance Commission of the Board of Overseers of the Bar 69–70 (1983). For the sake of completeness, it should be mentioned that the bar is not of one mind on this ethical judgment. See Final Subcommittee Report of the Committee on Attorney's Fees of the Judicial Conference of the United State Court of Appeals for the District of Columbia Circuit, reprinted in 13 Bar Rep. 4, 6 (1984) (declining to adopt flat rule forbidding waivers of statutory fees). Cf. State Bar of Georgia, Op. No. 39, reprinted in 10 Ga. St. Bar News No. 2, p. 5 (1984) (rejecting the reasoning of the Committee on Professional and Judicial Ethics of the New York City Bar Association in the context of lump-sum settlement offers for the reason, among others, that "[to] force a defendant into proposing a settlement offer wherein plaintiffs['] statutory attorney fees are not negotiated . . . [means that] meaningful settlement proposals might never be made. Such a situation undeniably . . . is inimical to the resolution of disputes between parties").

[18] [16] See Committee on Professional and Judicial Ethics of the New York City Bar Association, Op. No. 80-94, reprinted in 36 Record of N. Y. C. B. A., at 508 ("Defense counsel thus are in a uniquely favorable position when they condition settlement on the waiver of the statutory fee: they make a demand for a benefit which the plaintiff's lawyer cannot resist as a matter of ethics and which the plaintiff will

settlements must be rejected by the District Court. Moreover, on the facts of record in this case, we are satisfied that the District Court did not abuse its discretion by approving the fee waiver.

III

The text of the Fees Act . . . and its legislative history nowhere suggest that Congress intended to forbid all waivers of attorney's fees — even those insisted upon by a civil rights plaintiff in exchange for some other relief to which he is indisputably not entitled[19] — anymore than it intended to bar a concession on damages to secure broader injunctive relief. Thus, while it is undoubtedly true that Congress expected fee shifting to attract competent counsel to represent citizens deprived of their civil rights, it neither bestowed fee awards upon attorneys nor rendered them nonwaivable or nonnegotiable; instead, it added them to the arsenal of remedies available to combat violations of civil rights, a goal not invariably inconsistent with conditioning settlement on the merits on a waiver of statutory attorney's fees.

In fact, we believe that a general proscription against negotiated waiver of attorney's fees in exchange for a settlement on the merits would itself impede vindication of civil rights, at least in some cases, by reducing the attractiveness of settlement . . .

Most defendants are unlikely to settle unless the cost of the predicted judgment, discounted by its probability, plus the transaction costs of further litigation, are greater than the cost of the settlement package. If fee waivers cannot be negotiated, the settlement package must either contain an attorney's fee component of potentially large and typically uncertain magnitude, or else the parties must agree to have the fee fixed by the court. Although either of these alternatives may well be acceptable in many cases, there surely is a significant number in which neither alternative will be as satisfactory as a decision to try the entire case.

. . . We conclude, therefore, that it is not necessary to construe the Fees Act as embodying a general rule prohibiting settlements conditioned on the waiver of fees in order to be faithful to the purposes of that Act.

---

not resist due to lack of interest"). Accord, District of Columbia Bar Legal Ethics Committee, Op. No. 147, reprinted in 113 Daily Wash. L. Rep., at 394.

[19]   [20] Judge Wald has described the use of attorney's fees as a "bargaining chip" useful to plaintiffs as well as defendants. In her opinion concurring in the judgment in *Moore v. National Assn. of Security Dealers, Inc.*, she wrote:

"On the other hand, the *Jeff D.* approach probably means that a defendant who is willing to grant immediate prospective relief to a plaintiff case, but would rather gamble on the outcome at trial than pay attorneys' fees and costs up front, will never settle. In short, removing attorneys' fees as a 'bargaining chip' cuts both ways. It prevents defendants, who in Title VII cases are likely to have greater economic power than plaintiffs, from exploiting that power in a particularly objectionable way; but it also deprives plaintiffs of the use of that chip, even when without it settlement may be impossible and the prospect of winning at trial may be very doubtful."

IV

The question remains whether the District Court abused its discretion in this case by approving a settlement which included a complete fee waiver. As noted earlier, Rule 23(e) wisely requires court approval of the terms of any settlement of a class action. The potential conflict among members of the class — in this case, for example, the possible conflict between children primarily interested in better educational programs and those primarily interested in improved health care — fully justifies the requirement of court approval.

. . . Petitioners and the amici who support them never suggest that the district court is obligated to place its stamp of approval on every settlement in which the plaintiffs' attorneys have agreed to a fee waiver. The Solicitor General, for example, has suggested that a fee waiver need not be approved when the defendant had "no realistic defense on the merits," . . . or if the waiver was part of a "vindictive effort . . . to teach counsel that they had better not bring such cases, . . ."

We find it unnecessary to evaluate this argument, however, because the record in this case does not indicate that Idaho has adopted such a statute, policy, or practice. . . .

. . . [T]he District Court . . . [found] that the extensive structural relief they obtained constituted an adequate quid pro quo for their waiver of attorney's fees. The Court of Appeals did not overturn this finding. Indeed, even that court did not suggest that the option of rejecting the entire settlement and requiring the parties either to try the case or to attempt to negotiate a different settlement would have served the interests of justice. Only by making the unsupported assumption that the respondent class was entitled to retain the favorable portions of the settlement while rejecting the fee waiver could the Court of Appeals conclude that the District Court had acted unwisely.

What the outcome of this settlement illustrates is that the Fees Act has given the victims of civil rights violations a powerful weapon that improves their ability to employ counsel, to obtain access to the courts, and thereafter to vindicate their rights by means of settlement or trial. For aught that appears, it was the "coercive" effect of respondents' statutory right to seek a fee award that motivated petitioners' exceptionally generous offer. Whether this weapon might be even more powerful if fee waivers were prohibited in cases like this is another question,[20] but it is in any event a question that Congress is best equipped to answer. . . . In this case, the District Court did not abuse its discretion in upholding a fee waiver which secured broad injunctive relief, relief greater than that which plaintiffs could reasonably have expected to achieve at trial.

---

[20] [34] We are cognizant of the possibility that decisions by individual clients to bargain away fee awards may, in the aggregate and in the long run, diminish lawyers' expectations of statutory fees in civil rights cases. If this occurred, the pool of lawyers willing to represent plaintiffs in such cases might shrink, constricting the "effective access to the judicial process" for persons with civil rights grievances which the Fees Act was intended to provide. H. R. Rep. No. 94-1558, p. 1 (1976). That the "tyranny of small decisions" may operate in this fashion is not to say that there is any reason or documentation to support such a concern at the present time. Comment on this issue is therefore premature at this juncture. We believe, however, that as a practical matter the likelihood of this circumstance arising is remote. See *Moore v. National Assn. of Securities Dealers, Inc.* (Wald, J., concurring in judgment).

The judgment of the Court of Appeals is reversed.

It is so ordered.

Justice **Brennan**, with whom Justice **Marshall** and Justice **Blackmun** join, dissenting.

Ultimately, enforcement of the laws is what really counts. It was with this in mind that Congress enacted the Civil Rights Attorney's Fees Awards Act of 1976, 42 U.S.C. § 1988 (Act or Fees Act). . . .

[T]he first and most important question to be asked is what Congress' purpose was in enacting the Fees Act. We must then determine whether conditional fee waivers are consistent with this purpose.

III

. . . [B]y awarding attorney's fees Congress sought to attract competent counsel to represent victims of civil rights violations. Congress' primary purpose was to enable "private attorneys general" to protect the public interest by creating economic incentives for lawyers to represent them. The Court's assertion that the Fees Act was intended to do nothing more than give individual victims of civil rights violations another remedy is thus at odds with the whole thrust of the legislation. Congress determined that the public as a whole has an interest in the vindication of the rights conferred by the civil rights statutes over and above the value of a civil rights remedy to a particular plaintiff.

I have gone to great lengths to show how the Court mischaracterizes the purpose of the Fees Act because the Court's error leads it to ask the wrong question. Having concluded that the Fees Act merely creates another remedy to vindicate the rights of individual plaintiffs, the Court asks whether negotiated waivers of statutory attorney's fees are "invariably inconsistent" with the availability of such fees as a remedy for individual plaintiffs. Not surprisingly, the Court has little difficulty knocking down this frail straw man. But the proper question is whether permitting negotiated fee waivers is consistent with Congress' goal of attracting competent counsel. It is therefore necessary to consider the effect on this goal of allowing individual plaintiffs to negotiate fee waivers.

A

. . . [S]ince simultaneous negotiation and waiver may have different effects on the congressional policy of encouraging counsel to accept civil rights cases, each practice must be analyzed independently to determine whether or not it is consistent with the Fees Act. . . . An independent examination leads me to conclude: (1) that plaintiffs should not be permitted to waive the "reasonable fee" provided by the Fees Act; but (2) that parties may undertake to negotiate their fee claims simultaneously with the merits so long as whatever fee the parties agree to is found by the court to be a "reasonable" one under the Fees Act.

B

1

It seems obvious that allowing defendants in civil rights cases to condition settlement of the merits on a waiver of statutory attorney's fees will diminish lawyers' expectations of receiving fees and decrease the willingness of lawyers to accept civil rights cases . . . .

. . . [I]t does not require a sociological study to see that permitting fee waivers will make it more difficult for civil rights plaintiffs to obtain legal assistance. It requires only common sense. Assume that a civil rights defendant makes a settlement offer that includes a demand for waiver of statutory attorney's fees. The decision whether to accept or reject the offer is the plaintiff's alone, and the lawyer must abide by the plaintiff's decision. See, e. g., ABA, Model Rules of Professional Conduct 1.2(a) (1984); ABA, Model Code of Professional Responsibility EC 7-7 to EC 7-9 (1982). As a formal matter, of course, the statutory fee belongs to the plaintiff, . . . and thus technically the decision to waive entails a sacrifice only by the plaintiff. As a practical matter, however, waiver affects only the lawyer. Because "a vast majority of the victims of civil rights violations" have no resources to pay attorney's fees, H. R. Rep. 1, lawyers cannot hope to recover fees from the plaintiff and must depend entirely on the Fees Act for compensation.[21] The plaintiff thus has no real stake in the statutory fee and is unaffected by its waiver . . . . Consequently, plaintiffs will readily agree to waive fees if this will help them to obtain other relief they desire.[22]

. . . We have on numerous prior occasions held that "a statutory right conferred on a private party, but affecting the public interest, may not be waived or released if such waiver or release contravenes the statutory policy." . . .

2

[The fear that restricting fee waiver agreements will impede settlements] is a wholly inadequate justification for the Court's result. First, . . . I agree with the Court that encouraging settlements is desirable policy. But it is judicially created

---

[21] [10] Nor can attorneys protect themselves by requiring plaintiffs to sign contingency agreements or retainers at the outset of the representation. Amici legal aid societies inform us that they are prohibited by statute, court rule, or Internal Revenue Service regulation from entering into fee agreements with their clients . . . Moreover, even if such agreements could be negotiated, the possibility of obtaining protection through contingency fee arrangements is unavailable in the very large proportion of civil rights cases which, like this case, seek only injunctive relief. In addition, the Court's misconceived doctrine of state sovereign immunity, . . . precludes damages suits against governmental bodies, the most frequent civil rights defendants. Finally, even when a suit is for damages, many civil rights actions concern amounts that are too small to provide real compensation through a contingency fee arrangement. Of course, none of the parties has seriously suggested that civil rights attorneys can protect themselves through private arrangements. After all, Congress enacted the Fees Act because, after Alyeska, it found such arrangements wholly inadequate.

[22] [11] This result is virtually inevitable in class actions where, even if the class representative feels sympathy for the lawyer's plight, the obligation to represent the interests of absent class members precludes altruistic sacrifice. In class actions on behalf of incompetents, like this one, it is the lawyer himself who must agree to sacrifice his own interests for those of the class he represents. See, e.g., ABA, Model Code of Professional Responsibility EC 7-12 (1982).

policy, applicable to litigation of any kind and having no special force in the context of civil rights cases. The congressional policy underlying the Fees Act is . . . to create incentives for lawyers to devote time to civil rights cases by making it economically feasible for them to do so. . . . [P]ermitting fee waivers significantly undercuts this policy. Thus, even if prohibiting fee waivers does discourage some settlements, a judicial policy favoring settlement cannot possibly take precedence over this express congressional policy. We must implement Congress' agenda, not our own.

. . . The fact that fee waivers may produce some settlement offers that are beneficial to a few individual plaintiffs is hardly "consistent with the purposes of the Fees Act," . . . if permitting fee waivers fundamentally undermines what Congress sought to achieve. Each individual plaintiff who waives his right to statutory fees in order to obtain additional relief for himself makes it that much more difficult for the next victim of a civil rights violation to find a lawyer willing or able to bring his case. As obtaining legal assistance becomes more difficult, the "benefit" the Court so magnanimously preserves for civil rights plaintiffs becomes available to fewer and fewer individuals, exactly the opposite result from that intended by Congress.

. . . .

Second, . . . the Court greatly exaggerates the effect that prohibiting fee waivers will have on defendants' willingness to make settlement offers. This is largely due to the Court's failure to distinguish the fee waiver issue from the issue of simultaneous negotiation of fees and merits claims. . . . [I]t is a prohibition on simultaneous negotiation, not a prohibition on fee waivers, that makes it difficult for the defendant to ascertain his total liability at the time he agrees to settle the merits. Thus, while prohibiting fee waivers may deter settlement offers simply because requiring the defendant to pay a "reasonable attorney's fee" increases the total cost of settlement, this is a separate issue altogether, and the Court's numerous arguments about why defendants will not settle unless they can determine their total liability at the time of settlement . . . are simply beside the point. . . .

. . . Because the parties can negotiate a fee (or a range of fees) that is not unduly high and condition their settlement on the court's approval of this fee, the magnitude of a defendant's liability for fees in the settlement context need be neither uncertain nor particularly great . . . .

C

I would, on the other hand, permit simultaneous negotiation of fees and merits claims, since this would not contravene the purposes of the Fees Act. Congress determined that awarding prevailing parties a "reasonable" fee would create necessary — and sufficient — incentives for attorneys to work on civil rights cases. Prohibiting plaintiffs from waiving statutory fees ensures that lawyers will receive this "reasonable" statutory fee. Thus, if fee waivers are prohibited, permitting simultaneous fees and merits negotiations will not interfere with the Act; the lawyer will still be entitled to and will still receive a reasonable attorney's fee. Indeed, permitting simultaneous negotiations in such circumstances may even enhance the effectiveness of the Fees Act by making it easier for a lawyer to dispose of his cases more quickly. This frees up the lawyer's time to take other cases and may enhance his reputation as an effective advocate who quickly obtains relief for clients.

IV

. . . The Court's decision in no way limits the power of state and local bar associations to regulate the ethical conduct of lawyers. Indeed, several Bar Associations have already declared it unethical for defense counsel to seek fee waivers. See Committee on Professional Ethics of the Association of the Bar of the City of New York, Op. No. 82-80 (1985); District of Columbia Legal Ethics Committee, Op. No. 147, supra n. 8, 113 Daily Washington Law Reporter, at 389. Such efforts are to be commended and, it is to be hoped, will be followed by other state and local organizations concerned with respecting the intent of Congress and with protecting civil rights.

In addition, it may be that civil rights attorneys can obtain agreements from their clients not to waive attorney's fees. Such agreements simply replicate the private market for legal services (in which attorneys are not ordinarily required to contribute to their client's recovery), and thus will enable civil rights practitioners to make it economically feasible — as Congress hoped — to expend time and effort litigating civil rights claims. . . .

NOTES

1. What are the lessons for defense counsel in *Jeff D.*? What are the lessons for plaintiff's counsel? What type of section 1983 cases are most likely to be affected by the Court's ruling? Does the availability of contingent fee agreements reduce the practical impact of *Jeff D.*? Does the common fund approach to attorney's fees (see note 7 following *Hensley*) reduce the practical impact of *Jeff D.* in class action cases?

2. Suppose a county has a policy of settling civil rights cases only for lump sum, including all attorney's fees. Would such a blanket policy violate a plaintiff's implied federal right under 42 U.S.C. § 1988 to contract with an attorney for representation in exchange for an assignment to the attorney of the right to seek statutory attorney's fees? Does *Jeff D.* foreclose such an argument? In *Bernhardt v. Los Angeles County*, 339 F.3d 920 (9th Cir. 2003), the plaintiff alleged that the county had such a policy and that it "made it impossible for her to retain counsel to represent her" in her excessive force claim. 339 F.3d at 921. The court of appeals held that the district court erred in denying plaintiff's request for a preliminary injunction, in part, because her allegations raised "serious questions" whether the county policy had the practical effect of precluding the payment of statutory attorney fees — an effect the court said would violate the plaintiff's implied rights under 42 U.S.C. § 1988. A subsequent Ninth Circuit opinion speaks more equivocally about a policy of lump sum settlements. In *Poney v. County of Los Angeles*, 433 F.3d 1138, 1145 n.4 (9th Cir. 2006) the court stated "we have never held that a policy of only settling Section 1983 actions on a lump sum basis, including all attorney's fees, would violate the Supremacy Clause, although we have previously alluded to this possibility. *See* Bernhardt v. Los Angeles County, 339 F.3d 920, 926 (9th Cir.

2002) ("Although at this stage of the remand proceedings Bernhardt's case still remains sketchy, she has shown enough to establish that her [challenge based on the Supremacy Clause] presents serious questions about the nature and effect of the County's settlement policy."); *id.* at 926 n.5 ("As in our earlier opinion, we do not now resolve the question of whether Bernhardt properly states a claim pursuant to § 1983 or otherwise states a claim upon which relief can be granted.") (internal quotations omitted); *see also* Evans, 475 U.S. at 737–40. Bernhardt's analysis of the merits of such a claim remains dicta — as would any analysis we might make here."

3.   Defense counsel must be sure that the waiver of attorney's fees is clearly stated in the settlement agreement. In *Muckleshoot Tribe v. Puget Sound Power & Light Co.*, 875 F.2d 695 (9th Cir. 1989), the parties settled a water rights dispute by a consent decree that did not expressly mention costs or attorney's fees. The district court ruled that the plaintiff had waived any claim for attorney's fees. The court of appeals reversed, stating that an intent to waive attorney's fees would not be presumed and such a waiver must be clearly expressed in the settlement agreement. *See also Ashley v. Atlantic Richfield Co.*, 794 F.2d 128 (3d Cir. 1986) (a settlement that released the defendant from "costs" did not release a claim for attorney's fees). *Cf. Wakefield v. Mathews*, 852 F.2d 482 (9th Cir. 1988) (a settlement agreement that released the defendant from "costs or expenses of any nature whatsoever, known or unknown, fixed or contingent," was sufficiently broad to reflect an intent to include a waiver of attorney's fees).

4.   Justice Brennan's dissenting opinion suggests that states may prohibit the practice of conditioning a settlement on a waiver of attorney's fees as a matter of professional ethics. Would such a state rule be preempted by federal law in light of Justice Stevens' reasoning in *Jeff D.*? As reflected in footnotes 17[15] and 18[16] of the majority opinion in *Jeff D.*, several state and local bar associations had prohibited fee waiver agreements prior to the Supreme Court's decision. The Committee on Professional and Judicial Ethics of the New York City Bar Association subsequently withdrew its opinion in light of *Jeff D.*'s ruling that such offers were not inconsistent with the Attorney's Fees Award Act and its purposes. N.Y. Opinion No. 87-4. The California Supreme Court considered, but rejected, a proposed rule (Rule 2–400) that would have prohibited the making of settlement offers that contained fee waiver provisions in civil rights cases. *See* California State Bar Standing Committee on Professional Responsibility and Conduct, Formal Opinion No. 1989-114 (1989). The proposed rule would have permitted the making of a lump sum settlement offer that covered all claims including attorney's fees. For an argument that in light of *Jeff D.*, state ethics committees should not ban fee waiver agreements, *see* Comment, Evans v. Jeff D. *and the Proper Scope of State Ethics Decisions*, 73 Va. L. Rev. 783 (1987). For an argument that such agreements could be prohibited by ethical considerations unrelated to the policies underlying the Attorney's Fee Award Act, *see* Wolfram, *The Second Set of Players: Lawyers, Fee Shifting, and the Limits of Professional Discipline*, 47 Law & Contemp. Prob. 293 (1984).

5.   Justice Brennan also suggests that plaintiffs' counsel might secure agreements from their clients not to waive attorney's fees. Can an attorney ethically do so? Rule 1.2(a) of the American Bar Association, Model Rules of Professional Conduct, makes it clear that the ultimate authority to settle a case rests with the

clients. ("a lawyer shall abide by a client's decision whether to settle a matter.") *Compare Lewis v. S.S. Baune*, 534 F.2d 1115 (5th Cir. 1976) (provision in a retainer agreement between an attorney and client that prohibits a settlement without the attorney's consent is void as against public policy) *with* La. Rev. Stat. Ann. § 37-218 (permitting an attorney by contract to prohibit her client from settling a case without the lawyer's written consent). For further discussion of this question, *see* Paul R. Tremblay, *Acting "A Very Moral Type of God": Triage Among Poor Clients*, 67 Fordham L. Rev. 2475, 2533 n.195 (1999); Calhoun, *Attorney-Client Conflicts of Interest and the Concept of Non-Negotiable Fee Awards under 42 U.S.C. § 1988*, 55 Colo. L. Rev. 341 (1984).

Can a plaintiff's attorney avoid the risks of lump sum (i.e., fee waiver) settlements by having his client assign to the attorney the right to statutory attorneys' fees in the retainer agreement? The theory here would be that once the right to statutory attorneys' fees has been assigned to the lawyer, the client would not have the authority to waive recovery of attorney's fees. The Ninth Circuit has rejected this creative effort to circumvent lump sum settlements. In *Poney v. County of Los Angeles*, 433 F.3d 1138 (9th Cir. 2006), the § 1983 plaintiff case signed a retainer agreement with her lawyer that purported to "irrevocably assign and transfer" to the lawyer all "rights and powers . . . to waive apply for, obtain judgment upon, collect and/or receive any statutory attorney's fee award. . . ." The County offered to settle the plaintiff's claim for a "lump sum, including all attorney's fees." The settlement was acceptable to the plaintiff. Plaintiff's counsel (Mitchell) advised the County that under California law, he was "legally and ethically powerless to resist" the settlement. He also advised the County that despite the lump sum offer, he intended to seek statutory attorney's fees pursuant to his rights under the retainer agreement. The case settled and Mitchell sought to recover fees under the assignment contained in the retainer agreement. The Ninth Circuit held that "[j]ust as plaintiff cannot assign her § 1983 action, she cannot assign an action, such as *Section 1988*, that is derivative of it." Consequently, "the "assignments to Mitchell under the retainer agreement are invalid as a matter of law."

Professor Davies writes that plaintiff's attorneys are able to educate their clients on the importance of attorneys fees and explain to them why they should not always accept a settlement offer continent on a waiver of statutory attorneys fees. She reports that plaintiffs' lawyers find that fee waivers were not much of a problem with their practice. Julie Davies, *Federal Civil Rights Practice in the 1990's: The Dichotomy Between Reality and Theory*, 48 Hastings L.J. 197, 214 (1997).

6. Suppose the plaintiff's counsel has reason to believe the case could be settled on terms favorable to her client, if she waives any claim for attorney's fees, but that no such offer has been made by the defendant. Must or should the plaintiff's attorney raise the possibility of pursuing settlement on those terms with her client? Consider the following comments:

> Even absent such an offer [from the defendant] the attorney may be
> obligated to discuss such a settlement [that includes a fee waiver agree-
> ment] with the client if, for example, there is reason to believe that the
> defense would agree to such a disposition. Failure to recognize such a

situation, or use it to the client's advantage, could well be seen as a violation of the attorney's duty to act competently . . . .

California State Bar Standing Committee on Professional Responsibility and Conduct, Formal Opinion No. 1989-114 (1989).

7. Rule 68 of the Federal Rules of Civil Procedure provides that an adverse party may offer to allow judgment to be taken against him or her "with costs accrued." If the offer is refused and the final judgment is less favorable than the offer, "the offeree must pay the costs incurred after the making of the offer." If the offer of judgment is accepted, the offer or must pay the "costs" accrued as of the date of the offer. The Supreme Court addressed the relationship between Rule 68 and statutory attorney's fees under section 1988 in a case styled *Marek v. Chesny*, 473 U.S. 1 (1985).

In *Marek*, three police officers, responding to a domestic disturbance, shot and killed the plaintiff's decedent. Prior to trial, the defendants offered to settle the case "for a sum, including costs now accrued and attorney's fees" of $100,000. At the time the offer was made, the plaintiff had incurred costs, including attorney's fees of $32,000. The plaintiff rejected the offer and proceeded to trial at which a jury awarded $60,000 in compensatory and punitive damages. The plaintiff's costs, including attorney's fees, after the rejection of the offer were approximately $140,000. Pursuant to section 1988, the plaintiff sought attorney's fees and costs of approximately $172,000. The district court, relying on Rule 68, refused to award the plaintiff the $140,000 in costs incurred after the rejection of the offer of settlement.

The Supreme Court first considered whether an offer of judgment that did not separate damages from costs was valid under Rule 68. The Court held that Rule 68 allowed such lump sum offers. Nothing in the text of Rule 68 requires a bifurcation of an offer between the an amount to settle the substantive claim and an amount to cover accrued costs. Since the combined pre-offer costs, including attorney's fees ($32,000) and the damage award ($60,000), were less than the $100,000 lump sum offer, the plaintiff obtained a less favorable judgment than the offer. *Marek*, 473 U.S. at 7. Consequently, under Rule 68, the defendants were not liable for the prevailing plaintiff's post-offer "costs."

The second major issue in *Marek* was whether the post-offer "costs" for which the defendants were not liable included attorney's fees. The Court held that the term "costs" in Rule 68 included attorney's fees under section 1988. *Marek*, 473 U.S. at 9. Accordingly, the defendants were not liable for the $140,000 in costs, including attorney's fees, incurred after the plaintiff's rejection of the $100,000 settlement offer.

The majority reasoned that this result was consistent with the plain meaning of Rule 68 and the policy of encouraging settlements. Defendants typically are more concerned with the bottom line amount of payment than with the how the payment is divided between the plaintiff and her counsel. Lump sum offers allow defendants to fix their bottom line payment. Moreover, the prospect of forfeiting entitlement to post-offer attorney's fees will force plaintiffs to "think very hard" about continuing litigation after a Rule 68 offer is made. *Marek*, 473 U.S. at 11. Finally, the Court rejected the proposition that special rules should insulate civil rights plaintiffs from such tough choices. "[W]e are convinced that applying Rule 68 in the context of a section 1983 action is consistent with the policies and objectives of section 1988. Section 1988 encourages plaintiffs to bring meritorious civil rights suits; Rule 68 simply encourages settlements. There is nothing incompatible in these two objectives." *Marek*, 473 U.S. at 11.

Defense counsel must be careful to make sure the Rule 68 offer states explicitly that it includes costs and attorneys' fees. If the offer does not state so explicitly, the plaintiff may accept the offer and then seek fees. *See, e.g.*, *Lima v. Newark Police Dept.*, 658 F.3d 324 (3d Cir. 2011); *Bosley v. Mineral County Commission*, 650 F.3d 408 (4th Cir. 2011).

Defendants have argued that an award of "costs" to a defendant who makes a successful Rule 68 offer includes the defendant's post-offer attorney's fees. The argument has largely failed. Appellate courts have uniformly held that the post-offer "costs" awarded to a defendant under Rule 68 do not include attorney's fees. *See, e.g.*, *Hescott v. City of Saginaw*, 757 F.3d 518 (6th Cir. 2014) (collecting cases).

8. What are the strategic considerations in deciding whether to make a Rule 68 offer, the size of the offer (if made), and whether or not to accept it? Suppose defense counsel estimates that a jury would likely award damages in the range of $50,000 to the victim of excessive force by police officers. Defense counsel also estimates that if the case went to trial, the plaintiff's costs, including attorney's fees, would be approximately $150,000 and his own fees would be $100,000. Should the defendant make a Rule 68 offer of judgment? If so, how much should the defendant offer? Suppose the defendant offers $30,000 (including accrued costs and attorney's fees) and the plaintiff's attorney has performed 30 hours of work compensable under section 1988 at a rate of $100 per hour. Should the offer be accepted? Does it matter whether or not the plaintiff has a contingent fee contract with his lawyer? For a detailed analysis of this hypothetical, see Simon, *Rule 68 At The Crossroads: The Relationship Between Offers of Judgment and Statutory Attorney's Fees*, 53 U. CIN. L. REV. 889, 916–929 (1984).

Professor Davies found that "[d]espite Rule 68 's potential to reduce attorneys' fees and induce settlements, in reality, it does not appear to be a major factor in the practices of the civil rights lawyers I interviewed." Julie Davies, *Federal Civil Rights Practice in the 1990's: The Dictotomy Between Reality and Theory*, 48 HASTINGS L.J. 197, 223 (1999). Why wouldn't section 1983 defendants routinely make Rule 68 offers?

One empirical study confirms observations of Professor Davies that Rule 68 offers of judgment do not appear to be a major factor in § 1983 litigation. Professors Lewis and Eaton interviewed 64 experienced lawyers who practice in the areas of employment discrimination and civil rights. (four lawyers in sixteen cities; each cohort of four contained plaintiff and defense lawyers; the sixteen cities were selected to include at least one city in each of the federal circuits and more than one city in those circuits which have the greatest volume of employment discrimination and civil rights litigation). While there were a few places where Rule 68 offers are routinely considered and made in § 1983 cases (New York, Minneapolis, Seattle, Oakland), the prevailing pattern was one of non-use. Some § 1983 defense lawyers reported never having made a Rule 68 offer in decades of practice. A variety of reasons were suggested to explain why Rule 68 is not more frequently invoked. Among the more frequent suggestions were: some defendants do not want a formal "judgment" entered against them; some defendants adopt a "millions for defense, not a penny for tribute" litigation strategy; some attorneys believed they were ultimately going to win the case on the merits (citing the breadth of qualified immunity and the difficulty of proving official policy or custom), so there was not much point in offering the plaintiff any money; and a suspicion that defense lawyers paid on an hourly fee basis were not especially interested in early disposition of cases. For a discussion of this project, see Harold S. Lewis, Jr. & Thomas A. Eaton, *Foreword: Of Offers Not (Frequently) Made and (Rarely) Accepted: The Mystery of Federal Rule 68*, 57 MERCER L. REV. 723 (2006) (the Symposium proceedings, including comments of practicing lawyers, judges, and other academics, are included in this issue of the law review); Harold S. Lewis, Jr. & Thomas A. Eaton, *Rule 68 Offers of Judgment: The Practices and Opinions of Experienced Civil Rights and Employment Discrimination Attorneys*, 241 F.R.D. 332 (2007). For a discussion of how Rule 68 might be amended to better achieve its objectives in fee shifting cases see Harold S. Lewis, Jr. & Thomas A. Eaton, *The Contours of a New Rule 68.1: A Proposed Two-Way Offer of Settlement Provision for Federal Fee-Shifting Cases*, 252 F.R.D. 551 (2008).

9.   The majority in *Marek* states that "at the time an offer is made, the plaintiff knows the amount in damages caused by the challenged conduct." *Marek*, 473 U.S. at 7. How likely is it that plaintiff will *know* what a jury will award in damages? Pain and suffering and emotional distress are notoriously difficult to value. Even in cases where economic loss is the major component of damages, valuing the claim may be difficult. In *Herrington v. County of Sonoma*, 12 F.3d 901 (9th Cir. 1993) the county violated the plaintiffs' constitutional rights by rejecting the plaintiffs' proposed housing development. Prior to trial, the county made a Rule 68 offer of judgment for $501,000. The plaintiffs rejected the offer and proceeded to trial at which the jury awarded them $2.5 million in damages. The court of appeals vacated the damages award as excessive. On remand, the district court found that the plaintiffs' were entitled to damages of $52,123.50 and interest in the amount of $69,348.56 for a total judgment of $121,472.06. Pursuant to Rule 68, the plaintiffs' were denied an award of attorney' fees related to work performed after the date of the county's offer of judgment.

10.   Consider the cumulative effect of the major decisions reprinted in this chapter on counsel's incentives to represent plaintiffs in civil rights actions. Have the Supreme Court's rulings, when viewed in this light, paid adequate heed to Senate Report No. 94-1011 and its explication of the purposes of section 1988?

TABLE OF CASES

[References are to pages]

A

A. D. v. California Highway Patrol 147
Abney v. Coe. 199
Abusaid v. Hillsborough County [Florida] Bd. of
    County Commissioners 321
ACLU of Georgia v. Barnes 754; 757; 758
ACLU of Georgia v. Barnes. 757
Acosta v. City of Costa Mesa 503
Adams v. City of Auburn Hills 184
Adams v. Speers. 199
Adamson v. California 4
Adickes v. Kress 3
Aiken v. Hackett 371
Aitchison v. Raffiani 408
Albright v. Oliver 187, 188
Alden v. Maine 268
Alexander v. Sandoval 35; 251; 257
Alexander, Gray ex rel. v. Bostic 552; 714
Ali v. Rumsfeld 42
Allen v. City of Los Angeles 554
Allen v. McCurry 634; 635; 640, 641
Allen v. Muskogee, Okl. 344; 373
Alyeska Pipeline Service Co. v. Aurora Air Service,
    Inc. 365
Alyeska Pipeline Service Co. v. Wilderness
    Society 701; 703
Al-Zubaidi v. Ijaz 362
Amato v. City of Saratoga Springs 558
American Broadcasting Co., Inc. v. Miller 754
AMTRAK v. Morgan 621
Analytical Diagnostic Labs, Inc. v. Kusel 204
Anderson v. Creighton 39; 470
Anderson v. Liberty Lobby, Inc. 508
Anderson v. Minneapolis, St. Paul & Sault Ste. Marie
    Ry. .366
Anderson v. Pasadena Indep. School Dist. 455
Anderson v. Romero 495
Antoine v. Byers & Anderson 428
Aponte v. City of Chicago 714
Apostol v. Gallion 518
Applewhite v. Briber 429
Arar v. Ashcroft 41
Arbor Hill Concerned Citizens Neighborhood Ass'n v.
    County of Albany 758
Arizona Christian School Tuition Org. v. Winn. .606
Arizonans for Official English v. Arizona. 672
Armstrong v. Squadrito 163

Arnold v. Duchesne County 620
Ashafa v. Chicago 622
Ashcroft v. al-Kidd 487
Ashcroft v. Iqbal 34; 244; 346; 373; 455; 504
Ashley v. Atlantic Richfield Co. 773
Askew v. Bloemker 55

B

B.A.B. v. Bd. of Educ. of St. Louis 344
B.C.R. Transport Co. v. Fontaine 640; 646
B.I.C., Estate of v. Gillen 229
B.S. v. Somerset County 293
Bach, Golden ex rel. v. Anders 148, 149
Backes v. Village of Peoria Heights 347
Bailey v. Pataki 122; 164
Baker v. McCollan 121; 163; 166
Balistreri v. Pacifica Police Dep't 247
Ballard v. Muckogee Regional Medical Center. .561
Ballard v. Wall 426
Bank of Columbia v. Okely 140
Barnard v. Theobald 754
Barnes v. Zaccari 112
Bartholomew v. Watson 763
Barts v. Joyner 396
Bass v. Attardi 430
Bastien v. Goddard 186
Bateson v. Geisse 290
Baynard v. Malone 373
Beattie v. Madison County School Dist. 365
Beckwith v. City of Daytona Beach 364
Beechwood Restorative Care Ctr. v. Leeds. 53
Behrens v. Pelletier 518
Belbachir v. County of McHenry 158; 344
Bell v. Burson 108
Bell v. City of Milwaukee 553; 593
Bell v. City of Winter Park 290
Bell v. Clackamas County 579
Bell v. Ohio State University 621
Bell v. Wolfish 115
Bell Atlantic v. Twombly 39; 455
Bender v. Brumley 149
Benjamin v. Fraser 162
Berman v. Young 229; 245
Bernhardt v. Los Angeles County 772
Bernheim v. Litt 211
Berry v. City of Detroit 381, 382

[References are to pages]

Berry v. Oswalt. 556

Berry v. Peterson. 631, 632

Betts v. New Castle Youth Development Center . 269

Betts v. Shearman. 91

Bielevicz v. Dubinon. 381

Bingham v. New Berlin School Dist. 728

Biodiversity Conservation Alliance v. Stem. . . .731

Bishop v. Glazier. 514

Bishop v. Wood. 110

Bistrian v. Levi. 158

Bivens v. Six Unknown Named Agents . . 1; 22; 31,
                                      32; 35; 651

Bivins v. Wrap It Up, Inc. 754

Black v. Indiana Area School District 78

Blackmon v. Sutton 163

Blanchard v. Bergeron 741

Bland v. Roberts 269; 322

Blessing v. Freestone. 250; 256

Blue, Estate of v. Los Angeles. 622

Blum v. Stenson. 714; 737; 742; 758

Blum v. Yaretsky. 232

BMW v. Gore 581

Board of County Commissioners v. Brown. . . .292

Board of Regents v. Tomanio 621

Board of Regents of State Colleges v. Roth . . .100;
                              106; 108; 110; 119; 288

Board of the County Comm'rs v. Brown. .331; 375;
                                             378

Board of the County Commissioners of Bryan County
   v. Brown. 372, 373

Bodine v. Warwick. 186

Boeing Co. v. Van Gemert. 741

Bogan v. City of Boston. 556

Bogan v. Scott-Harris. 290; 410

Bogle v. McClure. 559; 583

Boivin v. Black. 657

Bolton v. City of Dallas 311

Booth v. Churner 651, 652; 654

Bordanaro v. McLeod 381

Borough of (see name of borough)

Bosley v. Mineral County Commission. 776

Botello v. Gammick 453

Bourdais v. New Orleans 561

Bowers v. De Vito 239

Bradley v. Fisher. 418

Bradshaw v. Pittsburg Indep. Sch. Dist.. 211

Brady v. Maryland 189; 328

Bray v. New York Life Insurance 646

Breard v. Greene. 260

Brentwood Academy v. Tennessee Secondary Sch.
   Ath. Ass'n 80

Bright v. Westmoreland County. 240

Briscoe v. LaHue. 431

Brock v. Wright 159

Brodziak v. Runyon 760

Brokers' Choice of America v. NBC Universal,
   Inc 91

Bronx Household of Faith v. New York Board of
   Education 611

Brosseau v. Haugen 496

Brower v. Inyo County. 183

Brown v. Eppler 112

Brown v. Muhlenberg 174

Brown v. Or. Dep't of Corr.. 125

Brown v. Pa. Dep't of Health Emergency Med. Servs.
   Training Inst. 245

Brown v. Western Ry. of Alabama 694

Buckeye Community Hope v. City of Cuyahoga
   Falls. .151

Buckhannon Bd. & Care Home, Inc. v. W. Va. Dep't of
   Health & Human Res. 717

Buckley v. Fitzsimmons. 438, 439; 448; 452

Buffington v. Baltimore County 738

Bukowski v. City of Akron 243

Bunting v. Mellen 501

Burella v. City of Philadelphia 109

Burgess v. Fischer 188; 344

Burlington, City of v. Dague. 701; 739

Burnett v. Grattan 692

Burns v. Reed. 439; 448

Burns-Toole v. Byrne 455

Burrus v. State Lottery Commission of Indiana. .269

Burton v. Richmond 245

Burton v. Wilmington Parking Authority. 64

Bush v. Lucas. 30; 32

Butera v. District of Columbia. 239; 242, 243

Butler v. Dowd. 558

Butler v. Rio Rancho Public Schools Bd. of
   Educ. .151

Butler v. Sheriff of Palm Beach County 46

Butz v. Economou. 39

C

Caban-Wheeler v. Elsea 581

Cabrera v. Martin 53

Cain v. Darby Borough. 631, 632

Caine v. Hardy. 176

[References are to pages]

Calhoun v. Alabama Alcoholic Beverage Control Board .621

Calhoun v. St Bernard Parish 409

California v. Hodari D.. 184

California Pro-Life Council, Inc. v. Getman . . . 607

Calvert v. Sharp. 77

Camden I Condominium Ass'n, Inc. v. Dunkle. .742

Campbell v. Arkansas Department of Correction.211; 561

Campbell v. City of Springboro, Ohio 347

Campbell v. Forest Preserve Dist. of Cook Co. . 281; 292

Campbell v. Miller. 290

Camreta v. Greene. 504

Cannon v. University of Chicago 263

Canton, City of v. Harris . . 323; 372; 375; 380, 381

Capra v. Cook County Bd. of Review. 288

Carey v. Piphus . . . 3; 278; 363; 370; 545; 657; 667

Carl v. Muskegon County. 76

Carlson v. Green 30; 32, 33; 35; 591

Carmody v. Bd. of Trustees of University of Illinois. 130

Carnes v. Parker. 79

Carpinteria Valley Farms, Ltd. v. County of Santa Barbara. 214

Carreras v. City of Anaheim. 713

Carringer v. Rodgers. 594

Carroll v. Carman. 487; 494; 503

Carter v. City of Melbourne, Fla. 312

Cassady v. Tackett. 45

Castle Rock, Town of v. Gonzales 98; 232

Catron v. City of St. Petersburg 122; 290

Celotex Corp. v. Catrett. 507

Central RR. & Banking Co. v. Pettus. 741

Chalfant v. Wilmington Inst. 79

Channer v. Mitchell 666

Chapman v. Higbee Co.. 46

Chappell v. Wallace. 30; 33

Charleston v. Bd. of Trs. of the Univ. of Ill. at Chi. 112

Chaudhry v. City of Los Angeles 121; 554

Chavez v. Martinez. 190

Chicago v. Morales. 102

Chrapliwy v. Uniroyal, Inc. 758

Christensen v. Park City Mun. Corp. 291; 380

Christiansburg Garment Co. v. EEOC. 715; 761

Churchill v. Waters. 416

Ciraolo v. City of New York. 580

City and County of (see name of city and county)

City of (see name of city)

Claflin v. Houseman. 677

Clark v. Taylor. 553

Classic; United States v.. 43

Clay v. Allen. 666

Cleavinger v. Saxner. 428; 717

Cleveland Bd. of Ed. v. Loudermill. .108; 111; 127; 133

Clukey v. Town of Camden 131

Cobb v. Miller. 738

Cockrel v. Shelby County School District. 211

Codd v. Velger. 122

Cole v. Wodziak. 760

Coleman v. Sweetin 158

Collins v. City of Harker Heights 145; 241

Collyer v. Darling 621

Colon v. Schneider. 120

Combs v. Wilkinson. 161

Common Cause v. Billups. 730

Commonwealth Bank & Trust Co. v. Russell. . .388

Connick v. Myers 206

Connick v. Thompson 328; 344

Cooper v. Casey 553; 582

Corey Airport Services v. Clear Channel Outdoor. 204

Cornelius v. Highland Lake 242

Cornwell v. City of Riverside. 579

Correctional Services Corp. v. Malesko . 33; 38; 346

Cort v. Ash. 257

Costello v. Mitchell Public School District 79 . . 149

Costello v. United States. 391

Coszalter v. City of Salem. 212

Cotter v. City of Boston. 371

Cottone v. Jenne 347; 385

Coughlen v. Coots 632, 633

County Concrete Corporation v. Town of Roxbury. 415

County of (see name of county)

Cox v. Hainey 469

Cox v. Treadway. 186

Craig v. Floyd County, Ga. 77; 322; 344

Crawford-El v. Britton. 468

Crowley v. Bannister. 347

Cruz v. City of Cicero. 760

Cruz v. Kauai County 453

Cullinan v. Abramson 543

Cunefare; People v. 103

Curtis v. Anthony. 293

Cushing v. City of Chicago 175

Cypress Insurance Co. v. Clark 123

D

D'Ambrosio v. Marino. 293

D.C., Inc. v. Missouri 713

Dahlia v. Rodriguez 217

Daily Servs., LLC v. Valentino 173

Daniels v. Williams. 17; 135; 165; 187

Darchak v. City of Chicago Board of Education .312

Darrah v. City of Oak Park 121

Davenport v. North Carolina Department of
    Transportation. 641

Davidson v. Cannon 137

Davis v. City and County of San Francisco. . . .757

Davis v. City of Chicago. 149

Davis v. District of Columbia. 657

Davis v. Monroe County Board of Education. . .246

Davis v. Passman 30; 32

Davis v. Rennie 162

Davis v. Township of Hillside. 145

Days v. Johnson 655

Deakins v. Monaghan 671

Deanzona v. City & County of Denver 245

Dearmore v. City of Garland. 729; 731

DeCamp v. Douglas County Franklin Grand
    Jury 451

DeKalb Stone, Inc. v. DeKalb County 151

Del Campo v. Kennedy 269

Delaware State College v. Ricks. 620

Demers v. Austin. 217

Denari v. Superior Court. 696

Dennis v. Higgins. 97

Dennis v. Sparks. 90; 527

Deorle v. Rutherford. 185

Desert Palace Inc. v. Costa 363

DeShaney v. Winnebago Co. Dep't of Social
    Services. 95; 100; 105; 220; 222; 388

DiBlasio v. Novello 429

Dirrane v. Brookline Police Department 560

Disorbo v. Hoy. 555

District Attorney's Office for Third Judicial Dist. v.
    Osborne. 667

District of Columbia v. Heller. 759

Dixon v. Burke County 395

Dixon v. Chrans 621

Dixon v. Clem. 429

Dixon v. University of Toledo. 212

Doby v. Hickerson. 469

Doe v. Braddy 229

Doe v. Covington County School Dist. . . .239; 245

Doe v. Dep't of Pub. Safety ex rel. Lee. 123

Doe v. Florida Bar 112; 123

Doe v. Hawaii Department of Education 149

Doe v. Nixon. 731

Doe v. Rumsfeld. 42

Doe v. Santa Fe Independent School District. . .568

Doe v. School Board of Ouachita Parish 606

Doe v. Smith 45; 48; 50, 51

Dolan v. City of Tigard 672

Doll v. Brown 367

Donahue v. City of Boston. 371; 605

Donovan v. City of Milwaukee 183

Donovan, Donovan ex rel. v. Punxsutawney School
    Board 607

Dotzel v. Ashbridge 430

Douglas v. New York, N. H. & H. R. Co. 678

Drollinger v. Milligan 669

Drumgold v. Callahan. 357; 366; 389

Dubuc v. Johnson 657

Dun & Bradstreet, Inc. v. Greenmoss Builders,
    Inc. 568

Duncan v. Nelson 396

Dunlop v. Munroe 346

Dunton v. City of Suffolk. 348, 349; 353

Dunton v. County of Suffolk. 353

Duran v. Koehler 713; 737, 738

Durant v. Independent Sch. Dist. No. 16 737

Durgins v. City of East St. Louis 646

Duvall v. Dallas County Tex. 330

Dwares v. City of New York. 94; 238; 247

Dye v. Office of the Racing Commission. 212

Dye v. Wargo. 633

Dyer v. Lee. 666

E

E. F. W. v. St. Stephen's Indian High School . . . 55

Eagleston v. Guido. 246

Easter House v. Felder. 175

Eastland v. United States Servicemen's Fund. . .416

Easyriders Freedom F.I.G.H.T. v. Hannigan. . . .603

Ebonie S. v. Pueblo School Dist. 60 122

Eddings v. City of Hot Springs 111

Edwards v. Balisok. 667

Edwards v. Byrd 163

Efron v. Mora Development Corp. 716

Eisenhour v. Weber County 111

EJS Properties v. City of Toledo 147

El Fundi v. Deroche. 90

Eldredge v. Town of Falmouth 183

Elliott v. Perez. 455

Ellis v. Blum. 55

[References are to pages]

Elwell v. Byers. 121

Engel v. Buchan. 36

England v. Louisiana State Board of Medical
Examiners. 671

Engquist v. Oregon Dep't of Agriculture 202

Erickson v. Pierce County. 362

Espinal v. Goord. 654

Espinoza v. O'Dell. 593

Estate of (see name of party)

Estelle v. Gamble 17; 32; 35; 159; 244

Evans v. Jeff D.. . . . . .719; 764; 773

Evers v. General Motors Corp. 377

Ex parte (see name of relator)

Ex rel. (see name of relator)

Exeter-West Greenwich Regional School v.
Pontarelli 763

F

Fabrikant v. French 80

Fair Assessment in Real Estate Ass'n, Inc. v.
McNary 670

Fancher v. Barrientos. 525

Farmer v. Brennan.34; 152; 155; 243; 329; 650; 652

Farrar v. Hobby 705

Faruq v. Vickers 159

Federal Deposit Ins. Corp. v. Mallen 128

FDIC v. Meyer. 33; 38; 346

Federation of African Americn Contractors v. City of
Oakland 281

Fee v. Herndon. 148

Felder v. Casey 591; 622; 688

Felders v. Malcom 514; 525

Ferencz v. Hairston. 123

Figueroa v. Rivera 666

Figueroa-Torres v. Toledo-Davila 389

Filarsky v. Delia 543

First National Bank of Boston v. Bellotti 606

Fisher v. University of Texas 370

Fitzgerald v. Barnstable Sch. Comm. 37; 260

Fitzpatrick v. Bitzer 268

Flagg Bros., Inc. v. Brooks 57

Flatford v. City of Monroe. 173

Florer v. Congregation Pidyon Shevuyim 76

Florida Transportation Services, Inc.v. Miami-Dade
County. 97; 551; 560

Focus on the Family v. Pinellas Suncoast Transit
Authority 89

Folkerts v. City of Waverly 147

Fontana v. Haskin 145

Ford v. County of Grand Traverse. 330

Ford v. Ramirez-Palmer (Estate of Ford) 475

Forrester v. White 427

Forsyth v. City of Dallas. 559

Fournerat v. Wis. Law Review 269

Fox v. DeSoto 669

Fox v. Vice. 715

Franklin v. Curry 505, 506

Franklin v. Fox 92

Franklin v. Gwinnett County Public Schools. . .246;
263–265

Freeman v. Ferguson. 239

Frey Corp. v. City of Peoria. 112

Frudden v. Pilling 290

Furlong v. Shalala 112

G

Galarza v. Szalczyk 288

Garcetti v. Ceballos 214

Garcia v. City of Albuquerque. 123

Garrett v. Barnes. 362

Gates v. Collier. 477

Gebser v. Lago Vista Indep. Sch. Dist. . . . 246; 265

Geneva Cty. Comm'n v. Tice 318

Gentile v. County of Suffolk. 381

Genty v. Resolution Trust Corp.. 620

George v. Morris 514; 525

Georgia v. Randolph. 497

Gerhart v. Lake County, Montana. 205

Gertz v. Robert E. Welch 569

Getz v. Johnston 722

Ghandi v. Police Department of the City of
Detroit 90

Gibeau v. Nellis 558

Gibson v. City of Chicago. 45; 232

Gibson v. County of Washoe 385

Gilbert v. Homar 111; 126

Gill v. Maciejewski 554

Gilmore v. Hodges 486; 514

Givhan v. Western Line Consolidated School
District. 210

Gladden v. Richbourg 513

Glassroth v. Moore. 606

Glenn v. City of Tyler 186

Goff v. Bise. 186

Goldberg v. Kelly 108

Golden State Transit Corp. v. City of Los
Angeles 258

Goldstein v. Chestnut Ridge Volunteer Fire Co.. .80

Goldstein v. City of Long Beach 320

Gonzaga Univ. v. Doe 248
Gonzalez v. City of Maywood. 754
Gonzalez v. Holland 632
Gonzalez v. Kokot 631, 632
Gonzalez-Droz v. Gonzalez-Colon. 111
Gordon v. Norman 354; 356
Goss v. Lopez 108; 111; 545
Graber v. Clarke 210; 362
Graham v. Connor. 177; 193, 194; 374
Graham v. Satkoski 553
Grapentine v. Pawtucket Credit Union 64
Gratz v. Bollinger 370
Gravelet-Blondin v. Shelton 290
Gray v. University of Colorado Hosp. Authority . 241
Green v. Johnson. 554
Greenwich Citizens Committee v. Counties of Warren
    and Washington Industrial Development
    Agency 213
Gregg v. Ham 535
Gregory v. City of Rogers, Arkansas 237
Gregory v. Shelby County. 583
Gregory v. Thompson 425
Greig v. Goord. 654
Griffin v. Arpaio 655
Griffin v. Maryland 46
Griswold v. Connecticut. 138
Groh v. Ramirez 494
Gross v. FBL Financial Services, Inc.. 362
Gross v. Winter. 409
Grutter v. Bollinger 370
Gschwind v. Heiden 292, 293
Guaranty Trust Co. v. York 694
Gutierrez v. Municipal Court 409
Gutowsky v. County of Placer. 621
Guttman v. Khalsa 429

H

H.A.L. v. Foltz. 245
Hafer v. Melo. 280
Hague v. CIO 4
Hall v. Ochs 631
Hampton v. Hanrahan 54
Hand v. Gary. 396
Hanna v. Plumer. 694
Hans v. Louisiana 268
Harden v. Pataki 559
Hardin v. Straub 621
Hardmon v. County of Lehigh. 388
Harhay v. Town of Ellington Board of
    Education 111

Haring v. Prosise. 641
Harlow v. Fitzgerald 39; 355; 462
Harper v. Virginia Dep't of Taxation 288
Harris v. Maricopa County Superior Court 716
Harris v. Shelby County Bd. of Education . 362; 364
Harrison v. Ash 77; 543
Harrison v. Culliver. 158; 346
Hartley v. Parnell. 264
Hartman v. Moore 382
Harvey v. Plains Township Police Department. . .63
Hawkins v. City of Farmington 183
Hawkins v. Holloway. 146; 149
Hayden v. Greensburg Community School Corp..290
Hays v. City of Urbana 607
Haywood v. Drown 675
Hazle v. Crofoot 552
Healy v. Pembroke Park 409
Heck v. Humphrey. 19; 658
Hector v. Watt 397
Hedrich v. Board of Regents. 123
Heflin v. Stewart County. 358
Hein v. Freedom from Religion Foundation, Inc..606
Heller v. District of Columbia. 759
Hendrickson v. Cooper. 559
Henschen v. City of Houston 608
Hensley v. Eckerhart. 715; 731; 737; 754; 761
Herb v. Pitcairn. 679
Herman v. Holiday. 560
Hernandez v. City of Lafayette 409
Hernandez v. Ridley 147
Hernandez v. Sheahan 164
Herrington v. County of Sonoma 777
Herzog v. Village of Winnetka. 389; 558
Hescott v. City of Saginaw. 714; 739; 776
Hewitt v. Helms. 123; 712; 718, 719
Heyne v. Metropolitan Nashville Public Schools . 131
Hicks v. Miranda. 671
Higbee v. Times-Advocate. 493
Higgenbotham v. Oklahoma ex rel. Oklahoma
    Transportation Commission. 606
Higgs v. Carver. 122
Higher Taste v. City of Tacoma 730
Hill v. City of Cleveland. 631
Hill v. City of Pontotoc 560
Hill v. Crum 527
Hill v. McDonough. 665
Hinshaw v. Smith 415
Hobbs v. Hawkins. 56
Holbrook v. City of Alpharetta 211
Holloway v. Delaware County Sheriff. 164

[References are to pages]

Home Telephone & Telegraph Co. v. City of Los Angeles 165

Homeward Bound, Inc. v. Hissom Memorial Center 754

Honaker v. Smith 45

Hope v. Pelzer 475

Hopson v. Fredericksen 149

Horta v. Sullivan 183

Houston v. Partee 452

Houston, City of v. Hill 603

Howlett v. Rose 678

Hudson v. Hudson 109

Hudson v. McMillian 161; 650; 652

Hudson v. Palmer 19

Huffman v. County of Los Angeles 45

Hughes v. City of Garland 123

Hughes v. Meyer 46

Hughes v. Region VII Area Agency on Aging . . .89

Hughes v. Tarrant County 409

Hui v. Castaneda 36

Hulen v. Yates 112

Hunter v. Bryant 526

Huntington v. Attrill 103

Hydrick v. Hunter 164

I

Iacobucci v. Boulter 584

Imbler v. Pachtman 433; 448

In re (see name of party)

Indiana v. Hobart City of Common Council . . . 620

Ingraham v. Wright . . .19; 115; 122; 134; 146; 166; 172

Int'l. Soc'y for Krishna Consciousness v. City of Evanston 694, 695

J

J. I. Case Co. v. Borak 257

J.R. v. Hansen 131

Jackson v. Barnes 292; 321

Jackson v. Indian Prairie School Dist. 204 147

Jackson v. Metropolitan Edison Co. . .64; 68; 72; 78; 232

Jackson v. Nixon 347

Jackson v. State Bd. of Pardons & Paroles 657

Jaco v. Bloechle 592

Jacobson v. McCormick 494; 503

James Daniel Good Real Property; United States v. 131

Janan v. Trammell 387

Jane L. v. Bangerter . .737; 742; 747; 749; 754; 755; 756

Jannsen v. Condo 112

Jasinski v. Tyler 495; 505

Jeffers v. Gomez 161

Jemmott v. Coughlin 355

Jenkins v. Haubert 668

Jenkins by Hall v. Talladega City Bd. of Educ.. .494

Jett v. Dallas Independent School District. .281; 309

Jinks v. Richland County 688

Jogi v. Voges 260

John T. v. Del. County Intermediate Unit 729

Johnson v. Bd. of Regents 371

Johnson v. Breeden 475; 526

Johnson v. City of Tulsa 757

Johnson v. Daley 657

Johnson v. Douglas County Med. Dep't 293

Johnson v. Fankell 679; 696

Johnson v. Georgia Highway Express 704

Johnson v. Government of the District of Columbia 54

Johnson v. Jones 519

Johnson v. Orr 55

Johnson v. Phillips 44

Joint Anti-Fascist Refugee Comm. v. McGrath. .109

Jones v. Bock 22

Jones v. Hildebrant 593

Jones v. McNeese 122

Jones v. Phyfer 388

Jones v. Town of East Haven 313; 344

Jones v. Union County 245, 246

Joyce v. Town of Dennis 713

Justices of the Supreme Court, In re 431

K

K.A. v. Fulton County Sch. Dist 266

Kalina v. Fletcher 446

Kalka v. Hawk 501

Kallstrom v. City of Columbus 239

Kansas v. Crane 164

Kansas v. Hendricks 164

Karam v. City of Burbank 715; 761

Kay v. Ehrler 714

Kelly v. Borough of Carlisle 469; 514

Kennedy v. Ridgefield City 240, 241

Kenosha, City of v. Bruno 270

Kentner v. City of Sanibel 151

Kentucky v. Graham 280

Kimes v. Stone 620

King v. Fletcher 173
King v. Kramer. 312
King v. Olmsted County. 149
Kingsley v. Hendrickson. 162
Kitchen v. Dallas County. 486; 495
Kneipp by Cusack v. Tedder. 233
Knowlton v. Shaw 444
Knussman v. Maryland. 555
Knutson v. Wisconsin Air National Guard 55
Koessel v. Sublette County Sheriff's Department.147
Kolender v. Lawson 603; 605
Kost v. Kozakiewicz. 77
Kovacic v. Villarreal. 239
Kowalski v. Berkeley County Schools 131
Kreines v. United States. 717
Kremer v. Chemical Construction. 646
Kristofek v. Village of Orland Hills. 311
Kubrick; United States v. 620
Kuhnle Bros. v. County of Geauga 621
Kulwicki v. Dawson 452
Kvapil v. Chippewa County 111

L

L.W. v. Grubbs. 242
Lake Country Estates, Inc. v. Tahoe Regional Planning
  Agency. 55; 408
Lake Nacimiento Ranch Co. v. San Luis Obispo
  County 29
Lampher v. Zagel. 763
Lane v. Franks. 215; 217; 486; 503
Lane v. Williams. 164
Lanier; United States v. 476; 485; 492
Lapides v. Board of Regents. 687
Larez v. City of Los Angeles 373; 385
Larez v. Holcomb 554
Lauritzen v. Lehman. 717
Lawrence v. Reed 469
Lawrence v. Texas. 138
Lawson v. Dallas County 385
Layne v. Sampley. 44
Leary v. Daeschner. 363
Leatherman v. Tarrant County 455; 694
Lebron v. National Railroad Passenger
  Corporation. 83
Lebron v. Rumsfeld. 42
Ledbetter v. City of Topeka 162
Lefemine v. Wideman 713; 729
LeMarbe v. Wisneski. 159
Lenard v. Argento 737
Leon v. Murphy 620

Lesende v. Borrero. 555
Lewis v. S.S. Baune 774
Lewis v. University of Texas Medical Branch . . 269
Lighton v. University of Utah. 112
Lillard v. Shelby County Bd. of Educ.. 37
Lima v. Newark Police Dep't 776
Lincoln County v. Luning. 268
Lindsey v. Detroit Entertainment, LLC. 90
Little v. City of North Miami 290
Livadas v. Bradshaw. 259
Livingstone v. North Belle Vernon Borough. . . .632,
                                                633
Livingstone v. North Belle Vernon Borough . . . 633
Loch v. City of Litchfield 185
Loesel v. City of Frankenmuth 205
Logan v. Zimmerman Brush Co.. . . . . . .108; 172
Lombardi v. Whitman 146; 242
Long v. County of Los Angeles. 382
Long v. Slaton 199
Lore v. City of Syracuse. 526
Los Angeles, City of v. Heller 267; 280
Los Angeles, City of v. Lyons 371; 595; 602
Los Angeles County v. Humphries 280
Los Angeles, County of v. Superior Court 591
Lucas v. South Carolina Coastal Council. 672
Lugar v. Edmondson Oil Co. 47; 79; 527; 539
Lunday v. City of Albany 738; 760
Lusby v. TG&Y Stores, Inc. 46
Lybrook v. Board of Education 212
Lynch v. City of Alhambra 632
Lynch v. Household Finance Corp. 3
Lytle v. Carl 311

M

M.L.B. v. S.L.J. 231
MacBoyle v. City of Parma 631; 633
MacDonald, Sommer & Frates v. Yolo County. .672
Macri v. King County 176
Maddox v. Stephens 121
Mahach-Watkins v. Depee. 714
Maher v. Gagne 720
Maine v. Thiboutot. 247; 249
Maldonado v. Houstoun. 758
Malik v. McGinnis. 657
Malley v. Briggs. 396, 397; 446; 448; 450
Malloy v. Monahan 558
Manders v. Lee. 321, 322
Mangiafico v. Blumenthal 453
Mann v. Vogel. 123

[References are to pages]

Mapes v. Bishop 620; 669

Marek v. Chesny 775–777

Marella v. Terhune 654

Mares v. Credit Bureau of Raton 754

Mark v. Borough of Hatboro 235–237

Marsh v. County of San Diego 147

Martin v. Heckler 717

Martin v. Hendren 426

Martinez v. California 386; 690; 692

Massey v. Ojaniit 398

Mastroianni v. Bowers 432

Mathews v. Eldridge 108, 109; 128; 172

Mathie v. Fries 579

Mattox v. City of Forest Park 213

Matusick v. Erie County Water Authority 293

Mays v. Springborn 362

McAfee v. Boczar 714

McCarthy v. Bronson 651

McCarthy v. Madigan 650

McClendon v. City of Columbia 239

McCown v. City of Fontana 760

McCoy v. Harrison 184

McCullum v. Tepe 543

McDonald v. City of West Branch 640; 647

McDonald v. Haskins 486

McDowell v. Jones 149

McFadden v. Sanchez 591

McGhee v. Pottawattamie County 438

McGugan v. Aldana-Bernier 77

McIntosh v. Antonino 620

McKennon v. Nashville Banner Publishing Co. . 367

McKinley v. City of Mansfield 397

McKinney v. Pate 151

McKnight v. Rees 541

McLean v. Gordon 245

McMillian v. Monroe County 314

McNair v. Allen 621

McNeese v. Board of Education 20

McReynolds v. Krebs 554

Meadours v. Ermel 526

Medellin v. Texas 260

Melendres v. Arpaio 603; 610

Melzer v. New York City Board of Education . . 211

Memphis Community School Dist. v. Stachura . .562

Memphis Light, Gas & Water Div. v. Craft . . . 101;
104; 108; 172

Mendez v. County of San Bernardino 582

Mendez-Matos v. Municipality of Guaynabo . . .559

Merriweather v. City of Memphis 620

Mershon v. Beasley 93; 95

Metzger v. Osbeck 148

Middlesex County Sewerage Auth. v. National Sea
Clammers Ass'n 247; 261; 262

Migra v. Warren City School Dist. Bd. of
Education 635; 637

Milburn v. Anne Arundel Department of Social
Services .231

Miller v. French 656

Miller v. Gammie 453

Miller v. Glanz 432

Milligan-Hitt v. Board of Trustees of Sheridan County
School District No. 2 310

Millspaugh v. County Department of Public
Welfare 444

Milstein v. Cooley 452

Milwaukee & S. P. R. Co. v. Arms 572

Minneapolis & St. Louis R. Co. v. Bombolis . . 677;
684, 685; 695, 696

Minneci v. Pollard 31

Miranda v. Arizona 190

Miranda v. Clark County 76

Mireles v. Waco 425

Mississippi Univ. for Women v. Hogan 264

Missouri v. Jenkins 762

Mitchell v. Dupnik 581

Mitchell v. Forsyth 39; 455; 515

Mitchell v. Horn 213

Mitchell v. W.T. Grant Co. 172

Mitchum v. Foster 3; 677

Moncrief v. Hanton 493

Monell v. Dep't of Soc. Servs. 18; 29; 265; 267;
270; 372; 380

Monell v. Department of Social Services . . 324; 372

Monfils v. Taylor 239

Monroe v. Pape . . 3, 4; 43; 269; 271; 277; 396; 648

Moore v. Sims 666

Moore v. Willis Independent School District . . . 176

Mora v. New York 260

Moreland v. Las Vegas Metro. Police Dep't . . . 594

Morris v. Noe 511

Morrison v. Board of Trustees of Green
Township 186

Morrison v. Garraghty 371

Morrow v. Balaski 245

Motley v. Parks 500

Mt. Healthy City Sch. Dist. Bd. of Educ. v.
Doyle 358; 361

Muckleshoot Tribe v. Puget Sound Power & Light
Co. 773

Mueller v. Auker 344

Muhammad v. Oliver 640

[References are to pages]

Mullins v. Oregon 150
Mulvenon v. Greenwood. 112
Murray v. City of Onawa 714
Murray v. Earle. 396
Muskrat v. Deer Creek Public Schools 149
Myers v. Bowman. 46

N

N.E. v. Hedges. 715
Nadar v. Democratic National Committee 640
Nagle v. Lee. 646
National Cellegiate Athletic Association v. Tarkanian. 83
National Private Truck Council v. Oklahoma Tax Commissioner. 670; 681
National Rifle Association v. City of Chicago . . 728
Naucke v. City of Park Hills. 584
Navarro v. Block. 580
Nazario v. Rodriguez. 714
Neal, Neal ex rel. v. Fulton County Board of Education 149
Nelson v. Campbell 666
Nesmith v. Alford 365
Newman v. Piggie Park Enterprises, Inc.. . 702; 703; 713
Newport, City of v. Fact Concerts, Inc.. 578
Newton v. Rumery 623; 641; 644
Nishiyama v. Dickson County. 241
Nixon v. Fitzgerald 39
NLRB v. Transportation Management Corp.. . . 362
Nnebe v. Daus 111; 173
Nodar v. Galbreath. 365
Nolan v. Memphis City Schools. 148
Nollan v. California Coastal Commission. 672
Nonnette v. Small 668
Norris v. Premier Integrity Solutions, Inc.. 77
North Carolina DOT v. Crest Street Community Council, Inc. 762
Northern Insurance Company v. Chatham County, Ga.. 269
Northington v. Marin. 366
Norwood v. Bain. 567
Nunez v. Simms 112

O

O'Bannon v. Town Court Nursing Center. 104
O'Connor v. Donaldson. 122; 162; 163; 461
Ohio Civil Rights Commission v. Dayton Christian Schools 20; 671

Oklahoma City, City of v. Tuttle. 372; 378
Olsen v. Correiro. 558
Olsen v. Idaho State Bd. of Med.. 429
Omni Behavioral Health v. Miller. 111
Omnipoint Corp. v. Zoning Hearing Bd. 430
$12,248 U.S. Currency; United States v.. 716
Onossian v. Block 145
Ormiston v. Nelson. 621
Ort v. White. 477; 480
Ortiz v. Jordan. 519
Osborn v. Haley. 33
OSU Student Alliance v. Ray 373; 389
Owen v. Independence 282–284; 385
Owens v. Balt. City State's Attys. Office. .494, 495; 506
Owens v. Okure 619

P

Palmer v. City of Monticello 149
Palmer v. Hall. 386
Palmer v. Marion County 293
Palmigiano v. Garrahy. 758
Panagoulakos v. Yazzie. 494, 495; 503
Paradis v. Montrose Memorial Hospital. 211
Parham v. Southwestern Bell Telephone Co.. . . .720; 722
Parish v. City of Elkhart, Ind.. 555
Parklane Hosiery Co. v. Shore. 646
Parratt v. Taylor. 17; 164; 165; 172; 672, 673
Parrilla-Burgos v. Hernandez-Rivera 45
Patel v. Kent School Dist.. 245
Patrolmen's Benevolent Ass'n v. City of New York. 559
Patsy v. Florida Board of Regents . . . 20; 648; 650; 658; 677; 762
Patterson v. Balsamico. 353; 582
Patterson v. McLean Credit Union 281
Paul v. Davis 19; 122; 149; 164; 166
Pavey v. Conley 655
Payne v. Jones 580; 582
Payton v. Rush-Presbyterian-St. Luke's Medical Center. 90
Pearson v. Callahan 496
Pembaur v. City of Cincinnati. 294
Pennhurst State School and Hospital v. Halderman. 249; 686
Pennington v. City of Huntsville 365
Pennzoil Co. v. Texaco, Inc.. . . . . .20; 671
People v. (see name of defendant)

[References are to pages]

People Against Police Violence v. City of
  Pittsburgh 730
Peralta v. Dillard 159
Perdue v. Kenny A. 739
Perkins v. Grimes 162
Perry v. Sindermann 108; 110; 288
PeTA v. Rasmussen 607
Peters v. Jenney 257
Peterson Novelties, Inc. v. City of Berkley 640
Petta v. Rivera 145
Pfeiffer v. School Board for Marion Center Area . 37
Phillips, Phillips ex rel. v. Monroe County 584
Pickering v. Board of Education 205
Pierce v. County of Orange 611
Pierson v. Ray 419; 457; 461
Piotrowski v. City of Houston 384
Pitchell v. Callan 44
Pittman v. County of Madison 162
Plans, Inc. v. Sacramento City Unified School
  District 606
Plumhoff v. Rickard 198
Polk County v. Dodson 76; 87
Pollicina v. Misericordia Hospital Medical
  Center 679
Poney v. County of Los Angeles 772; 774
Poole v. County of Otero 213
Porter v. Jones 606
Porter v. Nussle 648; 650
Pottawattamie County v. McGhee 438
Poventud v. City of New York 189
Prahl v. Brosamle 493
Preiser v. Rodriguez 19; 652; 657; 659; 663
Premachandra v. Mitts 716
Price v. Bd. of Education of the City of Chicago . 113
Price v. City of Charlotte 559
Price Waterhouse v. Hopkins 362
Printz v. United States 681
Procunier v. Navarette 461; 539
Provost v. City of Newburgh 581
Pryer v. C.O. 3 Slavic 555
Pulliam v. Allen 415; 430

Q

Quackenbush v. Allstate Ins. Co. 669
Quern v. Jordan 267; 322
Quinn v. Shirey 134

R

Railroad Commission v. Pullman 671

Ralls Corp. v. Committee on Foreign Investment in the
  United States 131
Rancho Palos Verdes v. Abrams 261, 262
Randall v. Prince George's County . . 243, 244; 551
Range v. Douglas 147
Rasanen v. Doe 186
Rateree v. Rockett 408
Raynor v. Regents of University of Minnesota . . 688
Reed v. Gardner 241; 388
Reed v. Shorewood 408
Rehberg v. Paulk 432
Reichle v. Howards 487
Remer v. Burlington Area School Dist 640
Rendell-Baker v. Kohn 69; 86; 232
Retz v. Seaton 186
Revere, City of v. Massachusetts General
  Hospital 162; 182; 244
Revis v. Meldrum 761, 762
Reyes v. City of Lynchburg 606
Rezaq v. Nalley 125
Rhodes v. Stewart 712
Richardson v. City of Chicago 714
Richardson v. McKnight 535
Richardson v. Miller 729
Richman v. Sheahan 426
Ricketts v. City of Columbia 247; 384
Rickley v. County of Los Angeles 715
Riehm v. Engelking 513
Riley v. Dorton 188
Riss v. City of New York 219
Rivera v. Rhode Island 241
Riverside, City of v. Rivera 738, 739; 761
Riverside, County of v. McLaughlin 609
Rizzo v. Goode 373
Roberson v. Giuliani 728
Roberts v. United States 134
Robertson v. Lucas 189
Robertson v. Plano City 149
Robertson v. Sichel 346
Robertson v. Wegmann 585; 695
Robinson v. City of Harvey 761
Robinson v. Davis 46
Robinson v. Hager 382
Rockford Board of Education v. Illinois State Board of
  Education 594
Rodick v. City of Schenectady 354, 355
Rodriguez v. Passinault 183
Rodriguez v. Smithfield Packing Co 631
Rodriguez-Cirilo v. Garcia 387

Roe v. City & County of San Francisco 211
Roe v. Rampton 761
Roe v. Wade 138
Rogers v. Vicuna. 53
Rolland v. Romney. 256
Rosas v. Brock. 55
Roska v. Peterson 229
Ross v. Jefferson County Dep't of Health. 269
Rossignol v. Voorhaar. 44; 232
Rosu v. City of New York. 112
Rowe v. City of Fort Lauderdale 92; 432
Royal Crown Day Care LLC v. Department of Health
    and Mental Hygiene of the City of New York.213
Ruiz v. McDonnell. 240; 243
Runyon v. McCrary 56; 281

S

S-2 v. State Bd. of Ed. of N. C.. 718
S. P. v. City of Takoma Park 77
S.S. v. McMullen. 243
Sacramento, County of v. Lewis. .17; 139; 243; 496
Sadoski v. Mosley 427
Saieg v. City of Dearborn 290
Saldana-Sanchez v. Lopez-Gerena. 580
Salkil   v.   Mount   Sterling   Township   Police
    Department 632
San Gerónimo Caribe Project, Inc. v. Acevedo-
    Vilá 173
Sandin v. Conner. 103; 114
Santosky v. Kramer 229
Saucier v. Katz. 474; 496
Sawyer v. Asbury. 527
Saxner v. Benson. 717
Saylor v. Board of Education 148
Schaub v. VonWald. 160
Scheuer v. Rhodes. 39; 461
Schmidt v. Creedon 130
Schnabel v. Abramson. 76
Schneider v. City of Grand Junction Police
    Department 344
Schneider v. Colegio de Abogados de Puerto
    Rico. 760
School Committee of Burlington v. Department of
    Education 266
Schultea v. Wood. 455
Schwartz v. Booker 245
Schweiker v. Chilicky. 30; 33
Scott v. Benson. 162
Scott v. Harris 190
Seiner v. Drenon 184

Sheehan v. City and County of San Francisco . . 313
Sheets v. Salt Lake County 389
Shelly v. Johnson. 429
Shelton v. City of College Station. 410
Shepherd v. Goord. 760
Shepherd v. Wellman. 594
Sherlock v. Montefiore Medical Center 77; 79
Shields v. Ill. Dep't of Corr.. 279
Shields v. Ill. Dep't of Corr.. 279
Shipp v. McMahon. 246
Shreve v. Franklin County. 162
Sibley v. Lando. 427
Siebert v. Severino. 567
Siegert v. Gilley. 122, 123; 150; 455; 496
Siglar v. Hightower 149
Siler v. Louisville & Nashville R. Co. 687
Simmons v. O'Brien. 640
Singletary v. Continental National Bank 622
Skinner v. Switzer. 667
Slade v. Bd. of School Directors of the City of
    Milwaukee. 231; 241; 243
Slaughter   v.   Mayor   and   City   Council   of
    Baltimore. 147
Slaughter-House Cases. 4
Sloman v. Tadlock. 526
Smego v. Mitchell. 514
Smiddy v. Varney 396
Smith v. City of Chicago Heights. 622
Smith v. Half Hollow Hills Central School
    District. 148
Smith v. Insley's, Inc.. 78
Smith v. Robinson 37; 261–264
Smith v. Siegelman. 123
Smith v. Univ. of Wash. Law School 371
Smith v. Wade 569
Smithers, Estate of v. City of Flint 232
Smyrna, Tn, Town of v. Municipal Gas Authority of
    Georgia 269
Smyth v. Rivero 729
Snider International Corp. v. Town of Forest
    Heights 131
Snyder v. King. 320
Snyder v. Trepagnier. 344; 382
Sole v. Wyner 729
Soto v. Flores. 246
Southerland v. City of New York 147
Southern R. Co., Missouri ex rel. v. Mayfield . . 679
Speer v. City of Wynne 280
Spencer v. Kemna 668
Sprague v. Ticonic National Bank. 741

St. Louis v. Praprotnik 300; 302

Standley v. Chilhowee R-IV Sch. Dist. 560

Stanley v. City of Dalton 362–364

Stanley; United States v. 3; 53

Starr v. Baca 373; 385

State Farm Mutual Auto Insurance Co. v. Campbell 581

State of (see name of state)

Stathos v. Bowden 763

Steen v. Myers 199

Stengel v. Belcher 45

Sterling v. Calvin 431

Stevenson v. City of Seat Pleasant 243, 244

Stewart v. Donges 518

Stokes v. Bullins 389

Stone v. Powell 669

Street v. Corrections Corporation of America . . . 78

Streit v. County of Los Angeles 320, 321

Strickland v. Shalala 53

Stump v. Sparkman 420

Supreme Court v. Consumers Union 415; 454

Surita v. Hyde 363

Suter v. Artist M. 250

Sutterfield v. City of Milwaukee 494

Swanson v. City of Chetek 205

Swedish Hospital Corp. v. Shalala 741, 742

Swetlik v. Crawford 210

Swierkiewicz v. Sorema N.A. 109

Swint v. Chambers County Comm'n 519

Swoboda v. Dubach 149

Sybalski v. Independent Group Home Living Program .78

T

T.D. v. LaGrange School Dist. 728

T. S. v. Doe 496

Tafflin v. Levitt 678

Tamas v. Dept. of Social and Health Services . . 229

Tarpley; United States v. 45

Taylor v. Brentwood Union Free School Dist. . . . 395

Taylor v. Howe 567

Tennessee v. Garner 179; 184

Tennessee Secondary School Athletic Association v. Brentwood Academy 90

Tenney v. Brandhove 18; 402

Tesmer v. Granholm 604

Texas v. Lesage 368; 605

Texas State Teachers Association v. Garland Independent School District 712

Thomas v. Cook County Sheriff's Dep't. . . .551; 557

Thomas v. Cumberland County 329, 330

Thomas v. Shipka 29

Thomas v. Whalen 211

Thompson v. City of Los Angeles 294

Thornton v. Brown 669

Thornton v. City of St. Helens 414

Tolan v. Cotton 507; 508

Torres Rivera v. Calderon Serra 414

Torres-Rivera v. O'Neill-Cancel 763; 764

Touche, Ross & Co. v. Redington 257

Tower v. Glover 91

Town of (see name of town)

Townes v. City of New York 390

Township of (see name of township)

Tracy v. Freshwater 666

Trant v. State of Oklahoma 358; 363, 364

Traver v. Meshriy 46

Trevino v. Gates 567

Tri County Industries, Inc. v. District of Columbia 560

Troupe v. Sarasota City, Fla. 184

Troville v. Venz 657

Troxel v. Granville 229

Truax v. Corrigan 231

Tsao v. Desert Palace 279

U

Ulichny v. Merton Community School District . .112

Ulrich v. City and County of San Francisco . . . 363

Unification Church v. I.N.S. 716, 717

United Mine Workers of America v. Gibbs . 592; 685

United Pet Supply, Inc. v. City of Chattanooga . .542

United States v. (see name of defendant)

University of Tennessee v. Elliott 642

Upsher v. Grosse Pointe Public School System . .145

V

Vakas v. Rodriquez 761

Vallario v. Vandehey 611

Vallone v. Lee 631; 633

Valmonte v. Bane 123

Van De Kamp v. Goldstein 445

Vance v. Rumsfeld 42

Vaughan v. Cox 146

Venegas v. Mitchell 741

Vernonia Sch. Dist. 47J v. Acton 245

Village of (see name of village)

Vineyard v. County of Murray. 381

Virginia Office for Protection and Advocacy v. Stewart 268

Virginia; United States v. 264

Vitek v. Jones. 164

W

Wade v. Byles. 90

Wade v. City of Pittsburgh. 641

Wagenmann v. Adams 397

Wakefield v. Mathews 773

Walden v. City of Providence 519

Waldroup, Estate of Gilliam ex rel. v. City of Prattville. 593

Walje v. City of Winchester 567

Wallace v. Kato. 668

Walton v. Alexander. 245

Wang v. N.H. Bd. of Registration in Med. 429

Ward v. Utah. 607

Warren v. Dwyer. 526

Washington v. Davis. 17

Washington v. Harper 131

Wasson v. Sonoma County Junior College 210

Waters v. Churchill. 210; 416

Waters v. City of Chicago. 313

Watkins v. Fordice. 757

Watkins v. Oaklawn Jockey Club. 46

Watts v. Laurent 556

Webb v. County Board of Education 762

Webb v. Lawrence County. 158

Webster v. City of Houston 292

Webster v. Houston. 292

Webster v. Reproductive Health Services. 761

West v. Atkins 76; 86; 264; 527

West Virginia University Hospitals, Inc. v. Casey .762

White v. Frank. 397

White v. Lemacks 242

White v. McKinley 94

White v. Rochford 230; 237

White v. Scrivner Corp.. 90

White; United States v.. 511

Whitley v. Hanna. 244; 505

Whitlock v. Brueggemann. 397

Wilder v. Virginia Hosp. Ass'n 250

Wilhelm v. County of Milwaukee. 640

Wilkerson v. Seymour 244

Wilkie v. Robbins. 31; 38

Wilkins v. Montgomery 347

Wilkinson v. Austin 124

Wilkinson v. Dotson 667

Will v. Michigan Dep't of State Police. . . .252; 268; 322

Williams v. Bennett. 29

Williams v. Board of Regents 246

Williams v. Dallas Independent School District. .216

Williams v. Kaufman County 582

Williams v. Kelley. 592

Williams v. Nebraska State Penitentiary. 158

Williams v. Wisconsin. 669

Williamson County Regional Planning Commission v. Hamilton Bank. 133; 176; 672

Willingham v. Crooke 526

Willingham v. Loughnan. 640

Willis v. Marion County Auditor's Office. 365

Willowbrook, Village of v. Olech 201

Wilson v. Cook County 343

Wilson v. Garcia 591; 614

Wilson v. Layne 487

Wilson v. Montano. 347

Wilson v. Morgan 356

Winicki v. Mallard. 670

Winslow v. Smith 147

Wittner v. Banner Health 80

Wojcik v. City of Romulus 113

Wood v. Ostrander. 239

Wood v. Strickland 429; 461, 462

Wooden v. Bd. of Regents. 371

Woods v. Rhodes. 631, 632

Woods v. Rondout Valley Central School District. 322

Woodward & Lothrop v. Hillary 90

World Wide Street Preachers v. Town of Columbia 293

Wray v. City of New York. 396

Wright v. Roanoke Redevelopment and Housing Authority 249

Wudtke v. Davel. 122

Wyatt v. Cole 528; 535; 536

Wyatt v. Fletcher 148, 149

Wyke v. Polk County Bd. of Edu.. 241

X

Xiong v. Wagner. 121

Y

Yarris v. County of Delaware 454

Yates v. District of Columbia 150

Ye v. United States. 241

[References are to pages]

Yeager v. City of MacGregor 80
Young v. City of Providence ex rel Napolitano. .345
Young, Ex parte 160; 268
Youngberg v. Romeo 162; 244
Younger v. Harris 20; 607; 670, 671

Z

Zahrey v. Coffey 397
Zehner v. Trigg 657
Zinermon v. Burch 167; 170

INDEX

[References are to sections.]

A

ADMINISTRATIVE REMEDIES, EXHAUSTION OF
Generally . . . 1[V]

AFFIRMATIVE CONSTITUTIONAL DUTIES
Generally . . . 4[I]
State created dangers and special relationships . . . 4[I][B]
Supreme Court's framework . . . 4[I][A]

ATTORNEY'S FEES
Legislative history . . . 12[I]
Party entitled to attorney's fees under 42 U.S.C. Section 1988 . . . 12[III]
Reasonable fees . . . 12[III]
Strategic and ethical aspects of attorney's fee awards . . . 12[IV]

B

BIVENS ACTIONS
Generally . . . 1[VI]
Current status of . . . 1[VII]

C

CAUSATION
Cause in fact
    Generally . . . 6[I]
    Governmental and supervisory liability . . . 6[I][B]
    Mixed motives . . . 6[I][A]
Proximate/legal cause
    Intervening acts . . . 6[II][B]
    Remote consequences . . . 6[II][A]

CHOICE OF LAW
Section 1983 actions . . . 11[II]

COMPENSATORY DAMAGES
Generally . . . 9[I][A]

CUSTOMS
Governmental liability based on . . . 5[III][B]

D

DAMAGES
Generally . . . 9[I]
Compensatory damages . . . 9[I][A]
Prospective relief . . . 9[II]
Punitive damages . . . 9[I][B]
Survival, wrongful death, and other damages issues ordinarily addressed by statutes . . . 9[I][C]

DEATH, WRONGFUL
Damages recoverable . . . 9[I][C]

DEFENSES
Exhaustion of remedies . . . 10[IV]
Issue and claim preclusion . . . 10[III]
Release-dismissal agreements . . . 10[II]
Statute of limitations . . . 10[I]

DUE PROCESS CLAUSE
Generally . . . 3[I]
Constitutional claims, other
    Generally . . . 3[II]
    Equal protection . . . 3[II][B]
    Fourth Amendment rights . . . 3[II][A]
    Public employee speech . . . 3[II][C]
Constitutional rights of persons in custody . . . 3[I][E]
Equal protection . . . 3[II][B]
Fourth Amendment rights . . . 3[II][A]
Liberty . . . 3[I][B]
Procedural due process . . . 3[I][C]
Property . . . 3[I][A]
Public employee speech . . . 3[II][C]
State remedies to due process litigation, relevance of . . . 3[I][F]
Substantive due process . . . 3[I][D]

E

"ENTWINEMENT"
Private persons, Section 1983 actions against public officers and . . . 2[III][C]

EQUAL PROTECTION
Due Process Clause . . . 3[II][B]

ETHICAL CONSIDERATIONS
Governmental liability . . . 5[IV]

EXHAUSTION OF REMEDIES
Generally . . . 10[IV]
Administrative remedies, exhaustion of . . . 1[V]
Judicial remedies, exhaustion of . . . 1[IV]

F

FAILURE TO TRAIN, LIABILITY FOR
Generally . . . 5[III][D]; 5[III][D][1]

42 U.S.C. 1983 (See SECTION 1983)

FOURTH AMENDMENT RIGHTS
Due Process Clause . . . 3[II][A]

FREE SPEECH
Public employee speech . . . 3[II][C]

G

GOVERNMENTAL LIABILITY
Bryan County and single hiring decisions by policymakers . . . 5[III][D]; 5[III][D][2]
Custom . . . 5[III][B]
Ethical considerations . . . 5[IV]

[References are to sections.]

GOVERNMENTAL LIABILITY—Cont.
"Every person" element
  Generally . . . 5[I]
  Change in *Monell* . . . 5[I][B]
  Prior law under *Monroe* . . . 5[I][A]
Failure to train . . . 5[III][D]; 5[III][D][1]
Final policy makers . . . 5[III][C]
Formal official policy . . . 5[III][A]
Municipal governments have no immunity from suit
  . . . 5[II]
Routes to
  Generally . . . 5[III]
  Bryan County and single hiring decisions by poli-
    cymakers . . . 5[III][D]; 5[III][D][2]
  Custom . . . 5[III][B]
  Failure to train . . . 5[III][D]; 5[III][D][1]
  Final policy makers . . . 5[III][C]
  Formal official policy . . . 5[III][A]
  Single hiring decisions by policymakers, *Bryan
    County* and . . . 5[III][D]; 5[III][D][2]
  Supervisory liability . . . 5[III][D]; 5[III][D][3]
Supervisory liability
  Cause in fact . . . 6[I][B]
  Failure to train, liability for . . . 5[III][D];
    5[III][D][3]

I

IMMUNITY
Absolute judicial immunity
  Bradley and common law immunity background
    in 1871 . . . 7[II][A]
  Briscoe and witness immunity . . . 7[II][F]
  Functional approach to judicial immunity as
    double-edged sword . . . 7[II][D]
  Pierson as seminal case on Section 1983 absolute
    judicial immunity . . . 7[II][B]
  Pulliam and prospective relief . . . 7[II][E]
  Stump and broad scope of absolute judicial im-
    munity . . . 7[II][C]
Absolute legislative immunity
  Bogan v. Scott-Harris and broad scope of local
    legislator immunity . . . 7[I][C]
  Lake County Estates and functional approach to
    local and regional legislators . . . 7[I][B]
  Prospective relief . . . 7[I][D]
  Tenney as seminal case . . . 7[I][A]
Absolute prosecutorial immunity
  Burns and prosecutor as legal advisor
    . . . 7[III][B]
  Circuit court cases . . . 7[III][D]
  Imbler as seminal case . . . 7[III][A]
  Kalina and prosecutor as applicant for arrest war-
    rant . . . 7[III][C]
  Prospective relief . . . 7[III][E]
Procedural aspects of absolute immunity
  Appeal from denial of absolute immunity motion
    to dismiss/for summary judgment
    . . . 7[IV][B]
  Burden of pleading . . . 7[IV][A]
Qualified immunity (See QUALIFIED IMMUNITY)

INTERVENING ACTS
Generally . . . 6[II][B]

ISSUE AND CLAIM PRECLUSION
Generally . . . 10[III]

J

JUDICIAL REMEDIES, EXHAUSTION OF
Generally . . . 1[IV]

L

LIABILITY, GOVERNMENTAL (See GOVERN-
  MENTAL LIABILITY)

LIBERTY
Due Process Clause and . . . 3[I][B]

P

POLICYMAKERS
Bryan County and single hiring decisions by
  . . . 5[III][D]

PRIVATE PERSONS (See SECTION 1983, sub-
  head: Private persons, suits against)

PROCEDURAL DUE PROCESS
Due Process Clause and . . . 3[I][C]

PROPERTY
Due Process Clause and . . . 3[I][A]

PROXIMATE/LEGAL CAUSE
Intervening acts . . . 6[II][B]
Remote consequences . . . 6[II][A]

PUBLIC EMPLOYEE SPEECH
Due Process Clause . . . 3[II][C]

PUNITIVE DAMAGES
Generally . . . 9[I][B]

Q

QUALIFIED IMMUNITY
Dismiss, motions to . . . 8[IV][A]
Evolution of . . . 8[I]
Interlocutory appeals . . . 8[IV][C]
Motions for summary judgment . . . 8[IV][B]
Motions to dismiss . . . 8[IV][A]
Order of battle . . . 8[III]
Period of time when law is clearly established
  . . . 8[II]
Persons protected by qualified immunity . . . 8[V]
Procedural aspects of
  Generally . . . 8[IV]
  Dismiss, motions to . . . 8[IV][A]
  Interlocutory appeals . . . 8[IV][C]
  Motions for summary judgment . . . 8[IV][B]
  Motions to dismiss . . . 8[IV][A]
  Summary judgment, motions for . . . 8[IV][B]
  Trial, qualified immunity at . . . 8[IV][D]
Summary judgment, motions for . . . 8[IV][B]
Trial, at . . . 8[IV][D]

[References are to sections.]

R

RELEASE-DISMISSAL AGREEMENTS
Generally . . . 10[II]

S

SECTION 1983
Administrative remedies, exhaustion of . . . 1[V]
Bivens actions
    Generally . . . 1[VI]
    Current status of . . . 1[VII]
Choice between state and federal law . . . 11[II]
Federal laws and, rights secured by
    Generally . . . 4[II]
    Congressional preclusion . . . 4[II][B]
    Enforceable rights . . . 4[II][A]
History and purposes of . . . 1[II]
Judicial remedies, exhaustion of . . . 1[IV]
Monroe v. Pape . . . 1[III]
Private persons, suits against
    Generally . . . 2[III]
    Contracting out and other symbiotic relationships
      . . . 2[III][B]
    "Entwinement" between public officers and private actors . . . 2[III][C]
    Self-help remedies . . . 2[III][A]
State courts, claims to . . . 11[I]
Text of . . . 1[I]

STATE ACTION
"Under color of law," relationship to . . . 2[II]

STATE COURTS
Choice between state and federal law . . . 11[II]

STATE COURTS—Cont.
Section 1983 claims . . . 11[I]

STATE REMEDIES
Due process litigation, effect of state remedies on
    . . . 3[I][F]

STATUTE OF LIMITATIONS
Defenses . . . 10[I]

SUBSTANTIVE DUE PROCESS
Due Process Clause and . . . 3[I][D]

SURVIVAL STATUTES
Damages recoverable . . . 9[I][C]

U

UNDER COLOR OF LAW
Boundaries of . . . 2[I][B]
Meaning of
    Boundaries of . . . 2[I][B]
    Monroe and . . . 2[I][A]
Private persons under Section 1983, suits against
    (See SECTION 1983, subhead: Private persons, suits against)
Section 1983, suits against private persons under
    (See SECTION 1983, subhead: Private persons, suits against)
State action, relationship to . . . 2[II]

W

WRONGFUL DEATH
Damages recoverable . . . 9[I][C]